OPERA ON RECORD

Opera on Record

Edited by Alan Blyth

Discographies compiled by Malcolm Walker

HUTCHINSON OF LONDON

To my hard-working authors

Hutchinson & Co. (Publishers) Ltd
3 Fitzroy Square, London W1P 6JD

London Melbourne Sydney Auckland
Wellington Johannesburg and agencies
throughout the world

First published 1979

Set in Linotype Times by Input Typesetting Ltd

Printed in Great Britain by The Anchor Press Ltd
and bound by Wm Brendan & Son Ltd
both of Tiptree, Essex

British Library Cataloguing in Publication Data
Opera on record.
1. Opera – History and criticism
2. Phonorecords – History and criticism
I. Blyth, Alan
789.9'136'21   ML1700

ISBN 0 09 139980 7 cased
       0 09 139981 5 paper

Contents

Introduction   9

The Operas of Monteverdi   ROBERT HENDERSON   15

Gluck
Orfeo ed Euridice   MAX LOPPERT   25

Mozart
Idomeneo and *La clemenza di Tito*   WILLIAM MANN   42
Le nozze di Figaro   WILLIAM MANN   55
Don Giovanni   LIONEL SALTER   71
Così fan tutte   GRAHAM SHEFFIELD   86
Die Zauberflöte   PETER BRANSCOMBE   106

Beethoven
Fidelio   LORD HAREWOOD   119

Weber
Der Freischütz   ALAN BLYTH   131

Rossini
Il barbiere di Siviglia   RICHARD OSBORNE   142

Bellini
Norma   ANDREW PORTER   154

Donizetti
L'elisir d'amore   HAROLD ROSENTHAL   173
Lucia di Lammermoor   CHARLES OSBORNE   184
Don Pasquale   HAROLD ROSENTHAL   192

Verdi
Macbeth   HAROLD ROSENTHAL   201

Rigoletto   RICHARD OSBORNE   208
Il trovatore   JOHN HIGGINS AND ALAN BLYTH   225
La traviata   ALAN JEFFERSON   240
Simon Boccanegra   LORD HAREWOOD   250
Un ballo in maschera   LORD HAREWOOD   258
La forza del destino   LORD HAREWOOD   277
Don Carlos   LORD HAREWOOD   292
Aida   JOHN STEANE   304
Otello   ALAN BLYTH   319
Falstaff   HAROLD ROSENTHAL   331

Wagner
Der fliegende Holländer   WILLIAM MANN   338
Tannhäuser   JOHN STEANE   346
Lohengrin   CHARLES OSBORNE   354
Tristan und Isolde   ROBIN HOLLOWAY   363
Der Meistersinger von Nürnberg   RICHARD LAW   376
Der Ring des Nibelungen   ALAN BLYTH   393
Parsifal   ROBIN HOLLOWAY   440

Gounod
Faust   KENNETH FURIE   452

Bizet
Carmen   RODNEY MILNES   461

Massenet
Manon   ALAN BLYTH   481
Werther   LORD HAREWOOD   495

Mussorgsky
Boris Godunov   DAVID HAMILTON   508

Tchaikovsky
Eugene Onegin   ALAN BLYTH   520

Johann Strauss
Die Fledermaus   ALAN BLYTH   532

Mascagni
Cavalleria rusticana
and
Leoncavallo
Pagliacci   CHARLES OSBORNE   542

Richard Strauss
Salome and *Elektra* ALAN JEFFERSON 557
Der Rosenkavalier ALAN JEFFERSON 567

Puccini
La Bohème EDWARD GREENFIELD 577
Tosca EDWARD GREENFIELD 591
Madama Butterfly EDWARD GREENFIELD 605
Turandot EDWARD GREENFIELD 618

Debussy
Pelléas et Mélisande FELIX APRAHAMIAN 629

Britten
Peter Grimes ALAN BLYTH 637

Index 643

Introduction

ALAN BLYTH

This book is inspired by the continuing series of articles entitled 'Opera on the Gramophone' which have appeared in *Opera* magazine over the past twenty years. At first they were selective in their discussion of records; latterly they have become much more comprehensive. The main contributors to the series have been Harold Rosenthal (*Opera*'s editor), Lord Harewood (the magazine's founder), Edward Greenfield, William Mann, and myself. About half this book consists of chapters by these writers, most of which originally appeared in *Opera*. In all cases, they have been substantially revised or completely rewritten. For the remaining chapters I have chosen largely, if you will excuse the cliché, horses for courses – specialists in one or more works.

The series in *Opera* had avoided until now several of the most popular pieces because of the amount of work involved in listening to so many recordings (I vividly recall board meetings at which *Don Giovanni*, for instance, had been suggested and the reluctance of any writer to undertake that task). For this book, I considered it essential to choose the fifty most popular works in the repertory, making allowances for a certain amount of editorial bias; thus *Werther* is included, *Entführung aus dem Serail* is excluded. The most modern opera discussed at length is *Turandot*, because it is the last to have been recorded several times. However, it seemed right and proper that Britten's operas, all of which have been committed to disc except *Gloriana* (may that follow soon), should be added as a postscript in discography form at least, particularly as *Peter Grimes* has just attained the distinction of a second recording. In any case, the total of fifty operas discussed is not strictly correct, as we have cheated to include the three Monteverdi works. *Idomeneo* and *La clemenza di Tito*, *Salome* and *Elektra* in a chapter apiece.

I have deliberately wielded a tolerant and amenable editorial hand. The general objective has been to deal with most commercially recorded complete versions of each opera, and then to relate them to versions of individual arias and ensembles since recording began, on a selective rather than exhaustive basis. It will be noted at once by anyone with knowledge of the subject that what may be appropriate for, say, *Rigoletto* would not be so for Monteverdi. Many of the greatest interpreters of the Verdi operas were active in the era of 78 rpm records; Monteverdi has been recorded for the most part only in the age of LPs. More controversially (although the relevant chapters confirm my view), the interpretation of Mozart, by both singers and conductors, has matured in our own times while that of Wagner and to a lesser extent Verdi (especially where singing is concerned) has declined. There is little difficulty today in casting a Mozart opera several times over, but for Wagner the number of interpreters for the central roles are few, and truly Verdian sopranos are almost as hard to come by. That was not the case in the first fifty years of the century, that is, in the pre-LP period.

Two other points about singing clearly emerge. There can be no doubt that artists in the early part of the century took a more liberal view of the score in hand and justified such liberties by giving a more personal view of the music, enhanced by a greater care over, and love for, words. Their techniques in most cases being more secure, they could devote themselves more fully to thoughts about vocal interpretation. Today, singers are more musically respectable but, as a result, often more dull. Secondly, several contributors, quite separately, have reassessed the reputations of certain singers. Thus Meta Seinemeyer, who died far too young, here assumes her rightful place as one of the century's great sopranos. Similar good work has been done on behalf of the Dutch tenor Jacques Urlus, the French tenor Charles Friant and the Austrian baritone Joseph Schwarz – until now names only for specialist collectors. Other reputations, not only among singers but also among conductors, seem to have suffered under close scrutiny and comparison. I have attempted, as far as possible, to include all first names of artists except, for obvious reasons, in such cases as Toscanini and Caruso.

By and large, contributors have ignored versions of overtures and orchestral extracts except to indicate readings of exceptional merit. In discussing complete sets, contributors have been given a free hand in deciding whether to consider so-called 'private' or 'pirated' issues, most of them emanating from unauthorized tapings of broadcasts. Many of these, although poorly recorded, are of surpassing interest from a historical viewpoint and have demanded attention: to hear how Toscanini directed *Falstaff* and *Die Zauberflöte* in the theatre is a matter of prime importance. In fact, the *Falstaff* is among the large number of live performances recently made available by the Italian Cetra company, and so now given a more general circulation. Their details and numbers are included in Malcolm Walker's discographies at the end of each chapter: I thought it inadvisable to include the numbers of the 'pirated' versions, as these have been available on such a limited and haphazard basis.

In practically every other case, numbers have been sought out and included. Those for complete sets and for highlights are to be found in the detailed discographies, with the most recent numbers given and cassette details where applicable. It would have been impossible to indicate here, or in the numberings in the text, what is currently available, what deleted. Reference to the easily consulted *Gramophone* catalogue will indicate what is attainable in this country; it will also give details of the companies' prefixes and numbers. Many other discs are available as imports from specialist shops. One of the most comprehensive listings is to be found in the German *Bielefelder Katalog*.

Within the text of each chapter will be found numbers of individual items, ordered according to the following principles. The first number given is that of the original 78 disc, where applicable. This is divided by a semi-colon from that of any LP reissue. To avoid repetition and save space, company names have not usually been given. All those 78 numbers without prefixes are those of the pre-1914 Gramophone and Typewriter (G&T), Gramophone Company, Monarch and Grammophon labels. Where titles of the more popular artists were reissued on double-sided DB (twelve-inch) or DA (ten-inch) series, these numbers have been preferred. Other early labels have been foreshortened thus: Fono. for Fonotipia (an invaluable and forwardly recorded series); Od. for Odeon. In the later 78 era, I have preferred Poly. (Polydor) to Gram. (Grammophon). Parlo. refers to Parlophone, Col. to Columbia issues without prefixes. HMV prefixes are as follows: DB, DA, D, E, C, B; Columbia prefixes are L, LX, DX. Columbia ten-inch DBs have 'Col.' before them to indicate they are not HMV DBs. Continental numberings not immediately identifiable can be clarified by reference to Clough and Cumming, *World Encyclopaedia of Recorded Music*. Discs originally issued by Victor in the USA but later issued in Britain are given their British numbering; otherwise they have the word 'Victor' before them. 'H & D' refers to Pathé 'hill-and-dale' date discs, made by the lateral-cut method.

The reissue question is more complex. Throughout the LP era, EMI (which has the largest and most treasurable archives), its German affiliate Electrola, and Deutsche Grammophon (DG) have reissued material from their vaults. Sadly most of these reissues have had all too short a life in the catalogue. In more recent times two smaller companies have brought out important series of reissues. The Austrian firm Preiser has a series called Lebendige Vergangenheit (LV) supplemented by a Court Opera (CO) series by pre-1914 singers. Rubini Records has its Great Voice (GV) series, prepared by the indefatigable Syd Gray at his Lowestoft headquarters and calling on the original records of several distinguished collectors. There is the Pearl list (GEMM) enthusiastically masterminded by Charles Haynes. A fourth, more restricted, source is Olympus (ORL), notable chiefly for its complete Caruso reissue; a fifth company concerned solely with reissues is Ember (GVC prefix). These records should be readily obtainable, particularly since EMI has undertaken the distribution of Preiser discs in Britain.

Wherever possible I have given the reissue numbers of these four companies, or those of EMI (including World Records), Electrola or DG. EMI's affiliates on the Continent now have a complicated numbering system, which begins with a number to indicate the country of origin ('1' for Germany appears most frequently in these pages) followed by a 'C' and then a long number. This series includes the large Bayreuth Centenary Album (ten records) and several two-disc issues devoted to single singers. With the many boxes recently issued by EMI in Britain, the set number rather than that on individual records has been given (e.g. RLS 724 for the first volume of 'The Record of Singing', now unfortunately unobtainable). Where no current reissue is available, I have thought it worthwhile to give the numbers of deleted discs such as HMV's much-missed COLH series, prepared by Desmond Shawe-Taylor in a scrupulous manner, HMV's 'Golden Voice' (HQM, HQS) issues and RCA's Camden (CDN) and Victor (VIC) series. Reissues that have been intermittently available are those of Rococo, a Canadian firm, of Club 99 and of OASI. I have had recourse to these in the text only where more readily available reissues do not exist. In the 1970s, BASF released a great deal of material originating from German broadcasts. Its whole catalogue has since been taken over by the Bellaphon company, using the Acanta label.

A word of warning is needed as regards both 78s and reissues. The speed 78 seems to have been regarded in a haphazard manner, especially in the acoustic era (i.e. before 1926) and often afterwards. That has not always been appreciated in transferring the old discs to LP. Nothing distorts a singer's timbre more than to play his or her performances at the wrong speed. An added complication is that in the old days, and even today (see Lionel Salter's comments on *Don Giovanni* on page 71), singers have not hesitated to transpose arias to suit their convenience, so that not even the score is always the right guide as to how a singer ought to sound. Happily, Rubini, Pearl, and Preiser are, though not blameless in this respect, at least aware of the problem – more than can be said of those in the larger companies who should know better.

Even the LP era now has its historic importance. After all, it is thirty years since the advent of microgroove recording. EMI has understood this to an extent, and has reissued many of the recordings with Callas or those conducted by Karajan and Giulini, but you will look in vain for some of the sets commended in these pages. The book will have done some service if it shames the major companies into again making generally available these interpretations. The *raison d'être* of records is, to my mind, the storing for future generations of a literal record of how music was interpreted at a particular time and to allow those generations to hear the individuality of a voice or of a conductor's reading which otherwise would be lost. Singers such as Martinelli or Seinemeyer or Melchior or Amato or Vallin or Schipa or Flagstad or Callas – to take some famous names at random – ought to be models and spurs for singers today, not to be slavishly aped but to be learnt from in truthful interpretation. In that respect, as I hope the chapters on *Manon*, *Werther* and *Faust* will indicate, a whole school of French singing has been lost and needs to be regained. Its style, in which music and text matter as much as each other, is of the essence in interpreting late nineteenth-century French opera.

It remains to thank my contributors for the many hundreds of hours of listening and for the knowledge and results distilled therefrom, which will, I, hope enlighten those who read their words; Malcolm Walker for his Herculean work on the discographies; and my wife for her patience. I should also like to thank the collectors of records, old and new, without whose help this book could not have been written, among them John Hughes, Edward and Peter Lack, Vivian Liff, George Stuart, Arthur Carton, Christopher Norton Welsh and Bryan Gould who has also been an informed proofreader. The advice given by Derek Lewis of the BBC Gramophone Library has been invaluable. Of course, there has been a great deal of cross-lending between contributors and help from the recording companies. Even with all this assistance, there will undoubtedly be important records which have been ignored or not been heard – indeed in some cases a writer has acknowledged the fact that a vital disc has eluded him. We have no claim to being comprehensive; any such attempt not only would have been impossible but also would have reduced some chapters to a mere list of names. However, I hope readers will find sufficient information and informed criticism to help them widen their knowledge and appreciation of opera, and therefore perhaps to demand higher standards in some of the performances they hear today. Nobody would suggest that any age had all the answers to the interpretation of opera; by the same token it would be foolish to pretend that in every respect time has brought an inevitable or inexorable advance in standards. There seems to be little doubt that in the days before air travel, when a singer remained in one opera house for a long period working within a repertory system, he was able to imbue his roles with a more personal style. In that respect the developments in our time in the operatic field reflect the same trend to uniformity to be found elsewhere. The overall standard may be higher, but the peaks of achievement are fewer. Finally, for the help and encouragement I have had at Hutchinson from Charles Clark, Kevin McDermott and, in the earlier stages, Frances Cormac, my thanks.

Key to discography symbols:
ⓜ mono recording
ⓔ electronically reprocessed for stereo reproduction
ⓒ cassette

The Operas of Monteverdi

ROBERT HENDERSON

Of the seven operas that Monteverdi is known to have composed, only three have survived: *Orfeo*, first performed in Mantua in 1607, and *Il ritorno d'Ulisse in patria* and *L'incoronazione di Poppea*, both of which were produced in Venice in the early 1640s. Dates and places are here of crucial importance and must be constantly borne in mind if we are ever to reach any proper appreciation of the differing needs and character of *Orfeo* on the one hand, and of the two Venetian operas on the other. Whereas *Orfeo* was conceived as a lavish entertainment for the ducal court of the Gonzagas an amalgamation of elements derived from the traditional genres of the Renaissance pastoral and intermezzo, and the newer, more simplified concern with musical continuity explored in the fledgling art of opera by composers associated with the Florentine Camarata, its two successors were designed specifically for the very different environment and resources of the public theatres of Venice when the operatic mode had already become firmly established.

In one sense at least *Orfeo* offers a less teasing problem to its modern interpreters than the two later operas. For the published score that appeared shortly after its initial performance is unusual for its time in giving a quite comprehensive list of the instrumental forces required. Among the instruments mentioned are ten violins and two small violins (playing an octave above the normal violin), two double basses and three bass viols, a double harp, two harpsichords, two archlutes (three are actually called for within the score itself), two chamber organs, a regal (a small portative organ with a nasal, reedy tone), a small flute (probably sopranino recorder), two cornetts (short wooden horns of narrow conical bore), several trumpets (three with mutes) and four or five trombones. Also scattered throughout the score are numerous passages in which the exact nature of the instrumental background is even more precisely defined. The pastoral chorus 'Lasciate i monti' in the first act calls for an accompaniment of strings, three archlutes, double harp, two harpsichords and sopranino recorder, and considerable detail is provided for the subtly variegated scoring of the entire third act, set on the banks of the River Styx, from Charon's first entry to the sound of the regal, to the penultimate chorus of Spirits supported by regal, chamber organ, five trombones, two viola da gambas and double-bass viol. Such information may seem scanty by modern standards, but offers a firm foundation for a plausible reconstruction of the opera as a whole.

The first of Monteverdi's operas to be revived in modern times (by Vincent D'Indy at the Schola Cantorum in 1904), *Orfeo* was also the first to appear on record, in a version issued in 1942 based on the Benvenuti edition of the score published a few years earlier. Though predating the rapid growth of scholarly activity in the reproduction of old instruments, and the now generally accepted need to recreate as accurately as is humanly possible the authentic sound and stylistic conditions of early baroque opera, it is a performance of considerable interest, more scrupulous in its fidelity to Monteverdi's intentions than one might well have expected. Ritornellos are discreetly scored, mostly for strings with the addition of harpsichord and lute, and there is a certain identification of individual characters with particular instruments: Orfeo (the baritone Enrico de Franceschi) with the harpsichord, the Messenger, who in the second act announces Eurydice's death, with the organ and so on. There is some doubling of parts – Charon and Pluto (Albino Marone), La Speranza and Proserpina (Vittoria Palombini) – the singing in general being more conscientious than either imaginative or noticeably refined, and with an especially disappointing Eurydice (Ginevra Vivante), unpleasantly sweet in tone and with an irritatingly obtrusive vibrato. Nor does the conductor, Ferruccio Calusio, secure from his ensemble of singers and players sufficient variety of pace to do any more than modest justice to the opera's fluctuations of light and shade and its closely integrated dramatic structure.

As far as the casting is concerned *Orfeo* requires one outstanding tenor or baritone for the title role, a decent soprano for Eurydice and a relatively small group of male and female singers experienced enough in the baroque idiom to fill in convincingly the parts of shepherds, gods and goddesses. If the 1942 version is still worthy of notice as the first attempt to bring the opera to life on record, the 1951 performance conducted by Helmut Koch, with the Berlin Radio Chorus and Orchestra, is mainly of interest for the casting as Orpheus of the veteran tenor Max Meili. A noted exponent of baroque music, a certain eloquence and style can still be fleetingly discerned through the sometimes tired singing of a fine artist considerably past his prime. Again there is extensive doubling of roles, Gerda Lammers (once a noted Covent Garden Elektra) taking those of Nymph, Messenger, La Speranza and Proserpina, Friedrich Härtel those of Charon and Pluto. Whatever incidental virtues there may be, however, in at least some of the singing and playing, are consistently undermined by the dullness and sluggish pace of the conducting. Rhythms are sometimes unclear, principal and subsidiary melodic lines in the instrumental writing frequently confused. And it is typical of the performance's generally shallow and undramatic character that the unnaturally slack tempo for the opening of the second act, through to Orpheus's aria 'Vi ricorda', should turn it more into a dirge than a joyful celebration of his love for Eurydice, seriously weakening the poignant effect of the sudden twist into tragedy with the Messenger's announcement of Eurydice's death from the bite of a poisonous snake while gathering woodland flowers.

It is just such a dramatic point as this which is so tellingly made by August Wenzinger in the recording that he contributed in the mid 1950s to Deutsche Grammophon's Archiv series. The instrumental sound is rich and sonorous, the colours discreetly varied within each act while remaining true to the spirit of the original. Nor are the few minor cuts of any particular significance in a performance that is not only based on a fine blend of scholarship and imagination but also maintains a much firmer grip than either of its predecessors on those very qualities that have earned *Orfeo* its reputation as the first real opera. With few exceptions, it is also admirably sung, Helmut Krebs (the Apollo in the earlier Koch recording) making an especially vivid and stylish Orpheus, ecstatic in 'Vi ricorda', movingly expressive in the second-act lament 'Tu sei morta', clean, flexible and precise in the great third-act aria 'Possente spirto', the symbolic core of the drama. The brilliant cornett obbligato to its second verse is not very securely managed and elsewhere the choral singing sounds at times a little thin and tentative. But it is from its dramatic cogency, its structural unity and its firm sense of focus that it derives its ultimate strength.

Whereas Wenzinger takes an appropriately long view not only of each closely knit act but also of the opera as a whole, Michel Corboz in his Lausanne performance, in an edition prepared by the baroque trumpet specialist Edward H. Tarr, tends to be much more diffuse and episodic. He also has in Eric Tappy an eloquently accomplished Orpheus, the emotions fluctuating from elation through tenderness and despair to renewed hope, portrayed with a fluid, yet carefully controlled elegance and flexibility of line. There is little in the singing of the sopranos Magali Schwartz and Wally Staempfli as Eurydice and Musica, of the basses François Loup and Jakob Staempfli as Charon and Pluto, of the Proserpina of Juliette Bise or Apollo of Theo Altmeyer, among numerous others, that is not perfectly acceptable. With an orchestra of period instruments, the instrumental background has been thoughtfully reconstructed, the threefold repetition of the opening Toccata strictly observed (Wenzinger gives just one strain), and with drums added to the ensemble, as would have been customary in Monteverdi's own time. Yet in spite of this scholarly responsibility the resultant sound is often disturbingly opaque and unrefined; the abrupt shifts of emphasis, some exaggeratedly slow speeds, and the tendency to treat each brief section as an isolated event disrupting both the musical flow and the dramatic continuity.

That the use of period instruments, as in the Corboz version, in itself cannot ensure a faithful recreation of the kind of subtly nuanced sound that Monteverdi may well have envisaged, was decisively proved with the appearance in 1970 of the complete recording edited and conducted by Nikolaus Harnoncourt. For it is not so much the quality of the singing as the sensitivity, the effortless poise and flawlessly tempered virtuosity of the playing of the Concentus Musicus of Vienna, probably the world's finest ensemble of authentic baroque instruments, that gives to the performance its peculiar distinction. This is obvious at once in the exciting effect produced in the introductory Toccata by the use of seventeenth-century mutes (as the score directs) to raise by a tone the pitch of the small choir of baroque trumpets; it is further distinguished by the assured dexterity of the two cornettists in the brilliant obbligato to 'Possente spirto', by the exemplary clarity of the harp later in the same aria, and indeed throughout the opera by the clear differentiation of the often simple, but ingeniously blended, timbres. Some of the ritornellos ideally require a more dance-like spring in the rhythm, and the chorus is particularly weak. Rotraud Hannsmann is an appealing, freshly toned Eurydice and Musica, Eiko Katanosaka is rich in voice as Proserpina, and Cathy Berberian makes more than most of the Messenger's short, but crucial second-act narration. The disappointment is the unattractive Orpheus of Lajos Kozma, apparently unmoved by the news of Eurydice's death, and unconvincing in his evocation of the power of music in 'Possente spirto'.

If there is one major aspect of *Orfeo* that Harnoncourt underestimates in his otherwise revelatory and always absorbingly musical performance, it is its theatricality and dramatic flair. And, curiously, it is precisely this facet of the work that is so vividly underlined in the many ways equally impressive recording conducted by Jürgen Jürgens, which replaces the earlier Wenzinger version in the Deutsche Grammophon Archiv series. His instrumental realization of the score is not as varied in colour as Harnoncourt's, the ritornellos being mostly restricted to a substantial body of strings with the occasional addition of a few wind, but his judgement of tempi and instinctive feeling for dramatic pace rarely falter. The singing of the Monteverdi Choir of Hamburg is also the most idiomatic and assured of all six versions, superbly responsive to the close relationship between the various choral sections and the Italian madrigal tradition. Nigel Rogers, the Second Shepherd, First Spirit and Echo on the Harnoncourt recording, here moves up to the title role, his singing limited in tone and variety of nuance, but much more secure in style and committed in character than Kozma, and more intrepid than any of his rivals in the taxing vocal decorations of 'Possente spirto'. The controversial choice of a counter-tenor for La Speranza is amply justified by the fine singing of James Bowman in a predominantly English cast.

In the three decades that intervened between the composition of *Orfeo* and that of *Ulisse* and *Poppea*, the very concept of opera had undergone a radical change, shedding the remnants of past traditions and evolving with an astonishing rapidity. Whereas the clues to the instrumentation, scanty as they may be, contained in the published score of *Orfeo* at least provide a reliable starting point, the prospective modern editor and performer of the two later operas have no comparably direct evidence to draw upon; only the bare bones of the vocal lines, continuo bass and the various instrumental interludes set out in the few manuscripts that have survived, with no indication as to which instruments might possibly have been used. Inevitably, the result has been a certain amount of disagreement between those who favour an orchestra similar in its essentials to that employed in *Orfeo*, and those who refuse to admit into their performances much more than the handful of strings and continuo instruments known to have been in general use in Venetian theatres in the 1640s. These conflicting attitudes are neatly exemplified in the only two recordings of *Ulisse* that have so far been attempted.

Rudolf Ewerhart in his 1964 Turnabout recording takes a severely puritan line, mainly reserving his strings for the linking sinfonias and ritornellos, and discreetly accompanying the voices with a small group of continuo instruments – harpsichord and organ, regal, lute, archlute and harp – each identified with a particular character in the drama. Minor cuts in the longer dialogue scenes have been skilfully managed to preserve the natural flow of the action and both the work's musical and dramatic contours. More serious losses are the entire mythological prologue, all the music for Penelope's maid Melanto and Melanto's lover Eurimachus, and the comic lament of Irus which follows Ulysses' slaying of Penelope's suitors. Though some of the singing in the smaller roles is of questionable quality, Margarethe Bence makes a striking personality of the nurse Ericlea, and Eduard Wollitz is a worthy-sounding Neptune. The outstanding performance, however, is Maureen Lehane's Penelope, memorably humane and full of carefully observed expressive character. The Ulysses is Gerald English, who is, as always meticulously attentive to the precise meaning of word and musical phrase.

Harnoncourt's 1971 performance on Telefunken sounds in comparison almost self-indulgently lavish in its variety of instrumental colour. It not only has the obvious advantage of being absolutely complete but it is also clear that every detail of score and text has been rigorously studied and thought afresh. But whereas Ewerhart's economy concentrates the whole of one's attention on the supple beauty of Monteverdi's recitative and the subtle manner in which it mirrors every inflection of the words, with Harnoncourt it is invariably the vivid instrumental playing of the Concentus Musicus which first captures the imagination, often at the expense of the voices. His elaborate realization of the continuo far exceeds anything that could be plausibly improvized, and there seems to be little evidence for the decorative counterpoints for wind, trumpets and so on that he adds as an often distracting accompaniment to the voice. The suspicion that his concern is more for instruments than voices is confirmed by Norma Lerer's characterless Penelope and the stylistic incongruities of Sven Olof Eliasson's awkwardly sung tenor Ulysses. Murray Dickie, on the other hand, makes a splendidly comic set-piece of Irus's parody lament, and there is some equally agreeable singing in several of the other smaller roles. One slight surprise, in view of Harnoncourt's insistence that everything should be sung at the original pitch, is his octave transposition for the personification of Human Frailty in the opening scene of the opera.

Three years later Harnoncourt completed his Monteverdi trilogy with *Poppea*. Like the earlier *Orfeo* and *Ulisse*, it is a performance permeated with a fresh, stimulating, and unmistakable character of its own, mainly derived again from the brilliant and often ravishing sounds that he draws from the virtuoso players and authentic seventeenth-century instruments of his Concentus Musicus. Like the earlier recordings too, this is as complete and inclusive a *Poppea* as there probably ever will be, based on a new and thorough examination of the two extant manuscript sources (which are not at all identical in detail), supplemented by Busenello's manuscript libretto. An additional, and almost insoluble, problem peculiar to *Poppea* is the role of Nero, originally conceived for a heroic castrato, its tessitura lying much too high for the normal counter-tenor or, indeed, mezzo voice. In his performances in the theatre – in the controversial production mounted by Jean-Pierre Ponnelle for the Zurich Opera – Harnoncourt adopts the generally accepted but not altogether satisfactory practice of transposing the role down for tenor. Here, however, he remains faithful to the original pitch; whether the casting for soprano presents a wholly convincing solution, in spite of the fervently dedicated singing of Elisabeth Söderström, remains open to debate. Helen Donath is a seductive Poppaea, ruthless ambition cunningly suggested beneath the teasing sensuality; Paul Esswood an impressive Otho, Cathy Berberian a reasonable Octavia, the singing sustaining a much higher level of achievement than in his recording of *Ulisse*. The casting of Poppaea's nurse Arnalta for tenor is strange, but effective, and it is typical of Harnoncourt's individual approach to the opera that he should introduce a touch of cynicism into the closing love duet. As previously in *Ulisse*, the most serious issue raised by the performance is the highly ornamental realization of the instrumental music, and the filling out of the accompaniments with decorative melodic lines which endlessly compete for attention with the voices. There is no argument about the creative character of Harnoncourt's musicianship and perspicacity, nor about the rigorous nature of his scholarship, but rather about the conclusions that he draws from that scholarship.

The ability of Monteverdi's vocal writing to hold the listener's attention without the diversion of kaleidoscopic changes of instrumental colour was strikingly demonstrated by Alan Curtis in 1966 in the only other recording that comes anywhere near rivalling Harnoncourt's completeness. Through hundreds of pages of recitative and arioso in his impeccably researched edition, Curtis employs only the most basic of continuo instruments – mainly two harpsichords, with an occasional switch to the lute – to underscore contrasts of emotion, character or mood. Except for a few brief passages, his tiny string ensemble is reserved for the ritornellos, with here and there a sparing touch of recorder. Especially telling is the association of Seneca with the individual timbre of the bassoon, two trumpets bringing a note of pomp to the final coronation scene. Rarely relaxing its grip, the whole weight of the performance is thrown on to the singing. And surprisingly good much of it is, too, from a predominantly young cast. Like every other version, apart from Harnoncourt's, it has a tenor Nero, whose self-confidence in the scenes with the attractively voluptuous-sounding Poppaea of Carole Bogard, and whose rashness and scathing impetuosity in those with the imposing Seneca of Herbert Beattie, is conveyed by Charles Bressler in aptly strong, impassioned style. The Otho of the the then-student counter-tenor John Thomas sounds a trifle undernourished, but another young singer, Sharon Hayes, also still a student at the time, does exceptionally well with the demanding role of Octavia, giving a splendid sense of nervous desperation to the scene in which she urges Otho to murder Poppaea.

The three remaining recordings of *Poppea* are all substantially abridged, resulting inevitably in a somewhat distorted impression of the true breadth and stature of Monteverdi's dramatic instinct. The earliest, dating from 1952, is edited and conducted, with the Zurich Tonhalle Orchestra and Chorus, by Walter Goehr, whose distinguished contribution to the Monteverdi revival ought not to be underestimated. Omitted are the prologue, the roles of Mercury and Octavia's nurse, two scenes for Seneca at the beginning of Act 2 – the first in which Mercury warns him of his impending death, the other in which the Captain confirms Nero's actual orders for his death – and Arnalta's comic solo in Act 3. Other scenes are radically shortened, and there are many smaller and, in some ways, even more unacceptable cuts: in the conversational interchanges between the two soldiers near the beginning of the opera, for instance, in several of Otho's solos, and in Seneca's poignant farewell to his family and friends. There is a good deal of overscoring for strings, wind and brass, not only in ritornellos, arias, ariosos and duets, but even in recitatives, its style more appropriate to a much later period and reaching almost late nineteenth-century dimensions in the opulently orchestrated finale. But there is, on the other hand, some responsible and observant singing from Friedrich Brückner-Rüggeberg as an impulsive Nero, Sylvia Gähwiller as a sensuous Poppaea, the alto Mabella Ott-Penetto as a virile-sounding Otho, and from Maria Helbling, whose passionate Octavia suggests something of the grand manner.

Rudolf Ewerhart's 1963 recording, with the Santini Chamber Orchestra, has many of the virtues, and the disadvantages, of his *Ulisse*. On the credit side are its stylistic purity and restrained instrumental palette, an enticingly feminine, gracefully sung Poppaea, an astute, sensitively phrased Otho, and a Nero that is sung with elegance and poise though apparently immune to anything as vulgar as dramatic characterization. But even more than in *Ulisse*, considerable damage is done, not only to the overall dramatic shape, but also to those rapid transitions from emotional weight to lightly etched comedy in which Monteverdi clearly delighted, by extensive and not always judicious cuts which reduce the opera to three records whereas Harnoncourt requires five and Curtis four. Several roles are eliminated, others pared down; as well as Arnalta's final scene, Ewerhart also deletes the riotous duet for Nero and Lucan that follows immediately on from the scene of Seneca's death, and which is wisely retained in the Goehr version.

Even more drastically abbreviated is the two-record set, directed by Raymond Leppard and based on the famous Glyndebourne production of the early 1960s. In its time it fulfilled a laudable function in proving to more than just a handful of specialists the absorbing theatricality and continuing relevance of Monteverdi's operatic masterpiece. Imaginative as it is, Leppard's rich scoring – the glittering cascades of notes produced by the large ensemble of continuo instruments and the swooning strings which both prettify and romanticize the music – was severely criticized even then and now has been superseded entirely. Nor is his reallocation for baritone of the original counter-tenor role of Otho any longer acceptable. What does survive is some worthy singing by Richard Lewis as a vivid, wilfully imperious Nero, Magda Laszlo as a provocative Poppaea, and Hugues Cuenod, unmistakably idiosyncratic in the small part of Lucan.

Though enough has been preserved to give the broad outlines of the action, with this Glyndebourne set of *Poppea* we have already crossed the borderline from anything that can be legitimately identified as a complete recording into the more shady area of highlights and miscellaneous excerpts. The very nature of Monteverdi's dramatic writing, its continuous evolution from heightened declamation through aria and arioso to contemplative monologue, does not lend itself easily to the extraction of isolated episodes, or to distillations such as the single-disc compilation, *La pui'belle pagine dell'Orfeo* conducted by Carlo Felice Cillario (Disco Angelicum STA 8998), which seem to serve little useful purpose. There are a few notable exceptions. Janet Baker, using the Leppard edition, brings a much greater intensity and nobility of spirit to Octavia's two great solos from *Poppea*, 'Disprezzata regina' and 'Addio Roma', than is achieved by any of the singers in the complete versions (SXLP 30280), and Harnoncourt's male casting of Poppaea's nurse Arnalta was anticipated many years before in Ezio Pinza's tenderly inflected singing (with piano accompaniment) of her soothing lullaby 'Oblivion soave' (Victor 17915;

CDN 1021). The deeply felt emotional commitment of Gérard Souzay's moving performance of the lament 'Tu se' morta' from *Orfeo* amply compensates for the cloying string accompaniment provided by the Lamoureux Orchestra (Philips 6580 174) and, within its very brief span, Tito Gobbi manages to make incisively dramatic another of Orpheus's solos, 'Rosa del ciel', included in the two-record set *The Art of Tito Gobbi* (ASD 606-7).

Of particular interest from an earlier age are three short pieces from *Orfeo* – 'Tu se' morta', 'Ahi, sventurata amante' and 'Quale onor' – sung with a typically French refinement and clear, open tone by Yvon le Marc'Hadour (Pathé PAT 76); they have a discreet accompaniment of strings, harpsichord and organ, and a stylish account, in spite of an obviously ageing voice, by Max Meili and the Schola Cantorum Basiliensis, directed by August Wenzinger, of Irus's lament 'O dolor, o martir' from the third act of *Ulisse*, contained in an anthology of early baroque music (Nixa CLP 1085).

The fragment allegedly from Monteverdi's *Orfeo* in the Giuseppe de Luca memorial album is in fact from the *Euridice* of Jacopo Peri.

ORFEO

O Orpheus; *E* Eurydice; *LM* La Musica; *A* Apollo; *LS* La Speranza; *P* Prosperina; *Pl* Pluto; *C* Charon

1951 Meili *O*; Trötschel *E*; Fleischer *LM*; Krebs *A*; Lammers *LS*; *P*; Härtel *Pl*; *C*/Berlin Radio Chorus and Orch./Koch Discophiles Français ⓜ DF 4244; Vox (US) ⓜ PL 6443

1955 Krebs *O*; Mack-Cosack *E*; Guillaume *LM*; *P*; Wunderlich *A*; Deroubaix *LS*; Günther *Pl*; Roth-Ehrang *C*/Hamburg Music College; Hitzacker Festival Orch./Wenzinger DG ⓜ 2708 001

1968 Tappy *O*; Schwartz *E*; W. Staempli *LM*; Altmeyer *A*; Conrad *LS*; J. Staempfli *Pl*; Bise *P*; Loup *C*/Lausanne Complesso Strumentale/Corboz Erato STU 70440-2; RCA (US) ARL 32536

1969 Kozma *O*; Hannsmann *E*; *LM*; Berberian *LS*; van Egmond *A*; Katanosaka *P*; Villisech *Pl*; Simkowsky *C*/Vienna Concentus Musicus/Harnoncourt Telefunken FK6 35020; JY6 35376

1974 Rogers *O*; Petruscu *E*; *LM*; Bowman *LS*; Partridge *A*; Reynolds *P*; Dean *Pl*; Malta *C*/Hamburg Monteverdi Chorus, Hamburg Camerata Accademica/Jürgens DG 2728 018

Excerpts

1942 De Franceschi *O*; Vivante *E*; Lombardi *LM*; Manacchini *A*; Nicolai *LS*; Palombini *P*; Marone *Pl*; *C*/chorus and orch./Calusio EMI ⓜ QALP 10364-5

IL RITORNO D'ULISSE IN PATRIA

U Ulysses; *P* Penelope; *G* Jove; *I* Irus; *N* Neptune; *A* Antino; *J* Juno; *T* Telemachus; *Pi* Pisandro; *An* Anfinomo; *E* Eumente; *Er* Ericlea .

1964 English *U*; Lehane *P*; Michaelis *J*; *I*; Wollitz *N*; *A*; Fahberg *M*; Savridi *Gi*; Whitesides *I*; Bartel *Pi*; Peysang *An*; Kretschmar *E*; Bence *Er*/ Santini CO/Ewerhart Turnabout TV 37016-8S

1971 Eliasson *U*; Lerer *P*; Anderko *J*; Dickie *I*; Simkowsky *N*; Wyatt *A*; Hannsmann *M*; Baker-Genovesi *Gi*; Hansen *T*; Equiluz *Pi*; Esswood *An*; van Egmond *E*; Muhle *Er*/Darmstadt Youth Choir, Vienna Concentus Musicus/ Harnoncourt Telefunken GK6 35024; JY6 35376

L' INCORONAZIONE DI POPPEA

N Nero; *P* Poppaea; *O* Octavia; *Ot* Otho; *S* Seneca; *D* Drusilla; *A* Arnalta; *L* Lucan

1952 Brückner-Rüggeberg *N*; Gähwiller *P*; Juon *O*; Ott-Penetto *Ot*; Kelch *S*; Gamper *D*; Helbling *A*; Witte-Waldbauer *L*/chorus, Zurich Tonhalle Orch./ Goehr Concert Hall (US) ⓜ CHS 1184

1963 Mielsche *N*; Bückel *P*; Zareska *O*; Burgess *Ot*; Wollitz *S*; Wilhelmi *D*; Karamanian *S*/Santini CO/Ewerhart Vox SVBX 5212

1963 (abridged; ed. Leppard) R. Lewis *N*; László *P*; Bible *O*; Alberti *Ot*; Cava *S*; Marimpietri *D*; Dominguez *A*; Cuénod *L*/ Glyndebourne Festival Chorus, RPO/Pritchard EMI SAN 127-8; Seraphim SIB 6063

1966 Bressler *N*; Bogard *P*; Arges *O*; Thomas *Ot*; Beattie *S*; Nelson *D*; Parker *A*; Fankhauser *L*/Oakland SO/Curtis Cambridge CRS-B1901

1974 Söderström *N*; Donath *P*; Berberian *O*; Esswood *Ot*; Luccardi *S*; Hannsmann *D*; Gaifa *A*; Langridge *L*/Vienna Concentus Musicus/Harnoncourt Telefunken HD6 35247; JY6 35376

Orfeo ed Euridice

MAX LOPPERT

The tale of the transformations of *Orfeo ed Euridice*, the *azione teatrale per musica* by Gluck to a libretto by Calzabigi, first given at Vienna in 1762, is a complicated one. It must be told here, albeit in much-abridged form, by way of explanation, for any survey of *Orfeo* recordings has to cope with the fact that in no two sets of the opera is the music exactly the same, or presented in exactly the same order.

The Vienna *Orfeo* had as its hero the alto castrato, Guadagni. When seven years later the work was given at Parma, the role was lifted for a male soprano, Millico. (This version does not appear to have been given in modern times, and has not been recorded.) More significant was the major revision of the work undertaken by Gluck for its production at the Paris Opéra in 1774. *Orphée et Eurydice*, to words by Moline (translator and adaptor of Calzabigi, and author of the new numbers), is a much longer opera than *Orfeo*. To explain in detail all the minor differences between the two – the alterations to the vocal line, reworking of orchestration, expansion or compression of recitative – demands more space than is available here. The important differences are the provision of new music – arias, many new ballet numbers (notably in the Elysian Fields scene), a new Act 3 trio for the principals – and the fact that the hero's role was given to a high tenor, Joseph Legros (strictly speaking an *haute-contre*; there is disagreement over the exact significance of the term, but its range seems to fall between those of tenor and counter-tenor as generally understood today).

In 1859, a version of the opera prepared by Berlioz was given at the Théâtre Lyrique, Paris. For the great mezzo-soprano, Pauline Viardot, the role of Orpheus was returned to alto pitch. It is a commonly held misconception that the Berlioz version is simply the 1774 score with an alto hero (see chart for differences between the two). The most frequently performed and recorded versions of the opera are those later adaptations and 'back-translations' of Berlioz into Italian to which have been restored (not necessarily in the Paris order) the Paris music that Berlioz dropped from his edition. The most common of these composite Italian versions was published by Ricordi after the La Scala revival of 1889. In major part, it corresponds to other 'Berlioz–Paris–Italian' compendia with contralto hero from the later nineteenth century – but not entirely! Tracing and enumerating the various differences between all the *Orfeo* and *Orphée* scores in existence could prove a life's work.

Thus it will soon be appreciated how readily an opera offering so many possibilities for conflation and re-ordering of its various versions to suit the performers in hand can present itself in so many guises on record. The original, revolutionary *Orfeo* (Version A in the table on the chart), is, of the four versions of the score in general currency, still the most powerful and most direct in its impact – and this despite the absence of the beautiful and famous later numbers, and despite the fact that the Plea to the Furies and Orpheus's great lament are more dramatic in their later, extended versions. Of the 1762 *Orfeo* there exist two recordings in more or less pure form. Unfortunately, neither is a worthy or apt rendition of it. In whatever form or language, Gluck is not an easy composer to perform. He demands in his conductors that rare combination of steadiness and dramatic power, in which classical restraint is never confused with massiveness nor emotional urgency with stringency; and from his singers smooth emission and passionate expression, which gives life to the words (in whatever language) with all the immediacy Gluck exacted from his own interpreters, without ever deforming the line.

The recording of the 1762 *Orfeo* made in Leipzig and conducted by Vaclav Neumann offers some of the dullest Gluck on record. The conducting, mostly plodding, slow-for-its-own-sake sluggish, is the opposite of what the music requires – this is emphasized by the boomy recording; it is no help that orchestra and chorus sound conscientious and well-prepared. Grace Bumbry's Orpheus is similarly conscientious – and, for the most part, similarly lifeless. There is an inherent natural vitality in her vibrant tone-quality (not always in crispest focus) which one soon recognizes as somehow separate from her dutiful, superficial response to the music. The verses of 'Chiamo il mio ben' are intoned with all the sentience of a speech-day recitation; the richer and more radiant orchestration and lengthier span of the 1762 'Che puro ciel' seem only to sum up the blankness of singer and conductor in conjunction. Anneliese Rothenberger is a cold Eurydice, tone buttoned-up and prim, in the manner of a schoolteacher scolding a naughty child. Ruth-Margaret Pütz's Cupid is a livelier impersonation that either of these, but plummily or shrilly voiced. The ungainly Teutonic Italian of both sopranos is no help to convincing declamation. As a nod in the direction of 'authenticity', a harpsichord continuo distantly tinkles, and some (not all) obvious appoggiaturas are observed; there is no gracing of the lines.

The principal disadvantages of the set under Karl Richter (1762, apart from the addition of the Dance of the Furies to Act 2) are his conducting – too often nervously or choppily phrased, edgy in style without being dramatic and with none of the long-breathed serenity the music should evoke – and the casting of a baritone Orpheus. All Fischer-Dieskau's interpretative mastery (immediately evident at the start in the threefold cries of 'Euridice!', each one a different kind of emotional outburst), subtle and various handling of recitative, and grave beauty of tone (no barking, no over-sophisticated nuancing or shading) cannot disguise that the voice lies in the wrong octave for the music, and that too often it muddies and contradicts the instrumentation. Eurydice presents a contrast: the weight and colour, the liquid lyricism of Gundula Janowitz's voice are ideal for the role, yet the life seems to have been drained from her dramatic accents. Edda Moser entirely fails to suggest Cupid's plucky, lively personality, and, again, her Italian is uningratiatingly Germanic. Also again, the continuo is more a gesture than a functional part of the orchestra. There eighteenth-century observance ends: the vocal line is kept puritan-plain, and even the most obvious appoggiaturas are ignored. The Munich Bach Choir sings neatly, oratorio-style; their cries, as Furies, of 'No!' make hardly any impact.

Charles Mackerras both conducted and provided the edition of the Vanguard recording. In his sleeve notes, and on record, he makes a good case for the practice (to my mind dubious) of stirring the most famous Paris numbers into an otherwise pure 1762 score, and for treating the work with an awareness of period conventions. The line is liberally graced, the continuo plays an important part, instrumental articulation owes nothing to romantic notions of Gluck, and tempi tend to be ruggedly forward-moving. (I dislike the almost sauntering effect of some vigorous double-dotting in the Hades choruses.) It is spirited conducting, not ideally spacious, yet always dramatic in its purpose, and vivid in character. Alas, the conductor is undermined by a mediocre orchestra and chorus, and by miscasting. The motherly Orpheus of Maureen Forrester coos or hoots the line in tones that are fluffy except when they curdle, and with persistently occluded vowels to hamper clean, forceful declamation. Eurydice is Teresa Stich-Randall at her most mannered – how, I wonder, did she arrive at such a bizarre, quasi-instrumental method of phrasing her 'pure', disembodied tones, and what conceivable relation did she imagine it bore to the character? Hanny Steffek, arch and vocally uneven, swells the ranks of German Cupids mangling the Italian language.

The Covent Garden set conducted by Georg Solti is placed alongside these three, because its edition makes liberal use of 1762 numbers in their original form; but, in general, it is a most peculiar text that the conductor has arrived at, one that swings back and forth between editions to no clearly comprehensible end. Objection to this practice is not purist; there are distinct differences in style and in the tessitura of Orpheus's music between the editions, whereas Solti's magpie edition lacks any clear style. This apart, it is a performance of great conviction and a greatly exciting dramatic impetus. Some may find the conductor too hard-driving at times, and the expansive warmth he brings to the Elysian music may seem, by

contrast, soft-edged. I admire him for being roused to fire, impulsively, by the deep emotions at play under the serene surface of the music.

In Marilyn Horne he has an Orpheus to support and serve his view of the opera. Perhaps the 'Euridice!' cries do not ring out above the chorus in a voice that is quite settled and firm; soon after that, the splendour and fullness of her instrument, its amplitude and evenness of registration over a wide range, draw from the music a line of powerful expressive force. Horne is a commanding singer, decisive in almost every utterance; encouraged by the conductor she rises in the final reprise of 'Che farò?' to thrilling outburst, at once passionate and controlled. She is also capable of true tenderness and beautifully sustained soft singing; the substantial low notes are never boomed for trick effect. Altogether, she is, to my ears, one of the finest exponents of the role on record – I make the affirmation only because she, and the set as a whole, were accorded a distinctly mixed welcome when the recording was first issued. Helen Donath's Cupid is almost on this level. Indeed, her brightly pointed singing and nimble, dashing personality contrive to make something definite of the character. The same cannot be said for Pilar Lorengar, a fluttery, infirm Eurydice, though not entirely lacking in sympathetic moments. A weakness of lesser importance is that the reverberant Decca recording sets up a slight fuzz around the choral singing.

The 1774 version (*B* on the chart) has been recorded three times. This is surprising if one considers that with its high tessitura (B flats dot a line that rises to C and D above the stave) it is deemed unsingable by most tenors today. A more concrete objection to a tenor Orpheus is the unsatisfactory key-relationships caused by transposition to tenor tessitura (this is made even more uncomfortable when the role has to be transposed down still further to ease the incumbent Orpheus's high notes). A more general objection has often been made: that a male Orpheus – especially if fitted out in typical tenor shape and demeanour – somehow robs the character of its symbolic, universal significances. This is a line of argument Gluck himself would hever have understood; to demand from any singer, whether male or female, that the portrayal be at once characterization and universal symbol is to seek an embalming of the role.

The earliest of the tenor sets, sung in Russian translation, lends itself to the confirmation of anti-tenor sentiments, for its Orpheus is 'tenorish' to a point where all sense of the role's classical chastity and candour disappears. One way of dividing the world seems to be into admirers and detractors of Ivan Kozlovsky. For the former, the succulent, dripping sweetness of the Russian tenor provides a paragon of *bel canto*; for the latter, the same qualities clog and devitalize much of the music he sings. His Orpheus boasts all the most notable features of his art – exquisite, long-held soft head notes, phrases caressed and pressed out of familiar shape – and some of the attendant quirks, the most remarkable of which is his echoing of the offstage instrumental echoes in the recitative of

'Chiamo il mio ben'. To my mind, the result is the portrait of an extraordinary singer, not the portrayal of an extraordinary role. All of Kozlovsky's excesses are tolerated by the conductor, Samosud, who indulges in a few of his own: tempi vary from the almost motionless to bursts of speed; in the D minor flute air, the string accompaniment is *pizzicato*, a vile effect. The soprano soloists are thin and squally in the Russian manner; the chorus is broad and bleary in tone.

It is a pleasure to turn to the recordings of the tenor *Orphée* conducted by Louis de Froment and Hans Rosbaud; for in each, the protagonist is not just a curiosity, or just an unsatisfactory alternative to the alto voice. Froment's Orpheus, Nicolai Gedda, was in his prime at the time of recording. The tone is youthfully appealing, often limpid, always securely placed, and all the notes are there at their original pitch, with no need for downward transposition (he omits the bravura ariette, 'L'espoir renaît'). It must be said that he offers a generalized account of the role. While nothing is superficially undertaken and taste is impeccable, there are few phrases that seize the attention and remain to haunt the memory. All the same, it is a most attractive portrayal. So is Janine Micheau's Eurydice. The voice, typically forward and clear, will not please all ears equally, and its high notes take on a Gallic edge; yet there is real distinction in her exact weighting of verbal stress and colour, and unlike most Eurydices on record, she succumbs neither to the lachrymose nor to the over-emphatic manner of conveying grief and suffering. If Lillian Berton's Cupid possessed more vocal substance, it would approach the ideal; as it is, thinness is counteracted by great charm and freshness of manner. The conducting merits the epithets Andrew Porter chose when Froment conducted the opera at Covent Garden, in 1961 – 'unimpassioned, well-judged, dignified, but not heavy'. Only the larger mastery of the music eludes the reading. The conductor makes some inexplicable alterations of sequence – what is the point, for example, of his closing Act 2 with the B flat ballet?

That larger mastery I find in Hans Rosbaud's conducting. If I wished to explain what I meant by a spacious, serene moulding of the music, in which steadiness of tempo is the dominant feature and in which emotional weight is never lacking nor allowed to become mere heaviness of statement, I would base my demonstration on long stretches of his Philips recording. Steadiness of tempo is, indeed, its most remarkable quality. Number after number, whether it be the cumulative dark energy of the Dance of the Furies or the luminous poignancy of 'Objet de mon amour', is unfolded with an unwavering, never rigid hand. There is air and light in the orchestral playing, and breath for the length of the singers' phrases. As Solti's Orpheus suits his purpose, so Rosbaud's: Léopold Simoneau, whose poetic beauty of tone irradiates the whole performance. He is not a fiery hero; feeling does not burst from the depths of his soul. Yet such is the dignity of his utterance, so gracious his shaping of the phrases, that the music takes on an Apollonian nobility. Simoneau's voice does not command the heights of the role, and downward transposition in Act 2 leads to some horrid clashes of tonality. Suzanne Danco is keenly alive to words; for Eurydice, however, the tremulousness characteristic of her tone acts to greater disadvantage than in most of this admirable soprano's other recorded roles. Pierrette Alarie's Cupid swoops and flutters, not always in tune; in common with many Francophone singers of the role, the manner is never wholly soubrettish, always vivid.

I come now to the Berlioz and post-Berlioz scores (*C* and *D*, on the chart). Of the former, proper, there exists only a set of excerpts. It is a famous set, made in 1936, and for many people it defines the art of Gluck singing. Unlike for many of the legends of the gramophone, no ear of faith is needed to appreciate the beauty of Alice Raveau's Orpheus; the impact is immediate. No voice ever poured itself into the music with greater purity or passion. The sensation of a voice being poured is one that recurs. The line seems to be flooded with an intense, burnished tone, yet at the same time the flood is disciplined and directed by the placing of every syllable. Raveau's is an exalted art, difficult to pin down in words; an element soon noted is a fondness for slow tempi. For 'Quel nouveau ciel' the slowness of pace is marvellously apt, like a new world opening out. In certain moods I must confess to finding the famous 'J'ai perdu mon Eurydice' simply *too* slow, though in others it affects me as no other performance on record. (In the original set of 78s, only part of the aria could be fitted on to one twelve-inch side; on the LP transfer of the 78s, the incomplete performance is replaced with the full version, taking two twelve-inch sides, that Raveau recorded at the same time.) The other singers are disappointing, Germaine Féraldy as Eurydice particularly so considering the charm of her other records, and not all the playing or choral singing is of the standard now common in eighteenth-century opera; but Tomasi is an affectionate conductor, supportive of fine singing, and it is for the fine singing of the protagonist that the records continue to be of inestimable value.

An Orpheus of comparable emotional force was Kathleen Ferrier. She never attained to Raveau's noble smoothness. Her singing was always warmer, richer, simpler in its inspiration, and wider, perhaps, in its appeal. The gramophone traces a useful chart of her experience as a Gluck singer. Early versions of 'Che farò?' are discussed later; but they, and the 1947 *Orfeo* excerpts based on Ferrier's Glyndebourne appearances in the role, show that her Orpheus was not always the full-bloodedly dramatic performance it was to become. The 1947 account of the recitative at the close of Act 1, 'Che disse? che ascoltai?' suggests an incomplete grasp of dramatic declamation – the Italian is politely Anglicized, and there is something ladylike in the way the imperatives and affirmatives of Orpheus's resolve are allowed to trip off the tongue. Feeling is strong, but generalized in its expression. In this she is shown up by the Eurydice

of Ann Ayars, whose voice is not beautiful, but whose use of it is
sensitive, and from whose Italian one infers a nice ear for verbal stress
and accent. This set still forms a potent souvenir of Ferrier's strong
natural powers of communication; but it is flawed by her interpretative
immaturity, and by the pedantic, laboured conducting of Fritz Stiedry.

And with such a souvenir of one of the singer's only two operatic roles
(the other was Britten's Lucretia) Ferrier admirers would still have to
content themselves had not EMI recently published a Dutch radio tape
of a live Netherlands Opera performance from January 1951. This
demonstrates just how markedly the singer was to develop in the role.
The performance as a whole hardly claims serious attention: despite the
conductor Charles Bruck's encouragement of clean articulation, and his
firm, purposeful sense of pace, orchestral and choral weaknesses are
everywhere in evidence, and the mournful, limply unrhythmic Eurydice
and tweety Cupid are a sore test of patience. For Ferrier's Orpheus, none
the less, the set remains indispensable. There is new wonderment in 'Che
puro ciel', a new depth of dark tone to the lamenting phrases of 'Che
farò?', a new rapt, transfigured quality for the A flat major expression
of determination to return to Hades. Her Italian has hardened its sinews.
In all this, and in much else, we sense the stage affecting the singer's
artistry, urging her into utterance that carries dramatic weight, that is
sentient as well as beautiful.

Another admired Orpheus, across the complete span of a long career,
was Margarete Klose. By the time she came to record a complete set in
Italian, and a set of excerpts in German, the voice had loosened and
thickened in texture, had begun to lose, in its movement from note to
note and across the registers, the controlled smoothness for which the
singer seemed to be aiming. In her native language one gains a stronger
impression of the majestic Orpheus she must have been in her prime,
for the voice flows more along the words of 'Welch reiner Himmel',
whereas it gums up the phrases of 'Che puro ciel'. In both sets, Arthur
Rother conducts like the archetype of a *Kapellmeister* – securely, with
everything neatly in place, and with a woeful lack of imagination that lets
the music plod, lumber and go grey. Also in both sets, Rita Streich is
one of the prettiest, most delightful Cupids on record, more natural-
sounding in German. I like Erna Berger's clear, fresh tones; but how
Rother makes her labour in Eurydice's F major aria! Anny Schlemm,
Eurydice in the set of excerpts, appears only in the F major aria, which
discloses not much more than her pure command of the top As, and her
similar struggles with the conductor's stodgy tempo.

Also from the early 1950s is Toscanini's complete second act of the
opera, in a recording taken during a Carnegie Hall concert. Pleasure in
the set is diminished only by the typically airless acoustics, and by regret
that so devoted a Gluck champion (*Orfeo* figured regularly in his Scala
seasons) should not have left a complete version of the opera. Toscanini's

genius for keeping music in motion by bringing alive every strand of the orchestral texture is wonderfully in evidence; in the Elysian music, especially, a radiant sensation of fluency and fluidity without haste, of lightness not lacking in body, derives from the muscular firmness of the inner parts. As inhabitants of the underworld, Robert Shaw's chorus seems statuesque, heavy even. Nan Merriman's Orpheus is a little too womanly – the appealing vibrancy of the tone lends a pretty but inappropriate pout to her phrases. Barbara Gibson is a clean, colourless Eurydice. The conductor's added gong-strokes in the music of Hades are a curiosity, given his reputation for fidelity to the printed page.

I pass with relative abruptness over the next two *D* sets, in more or less complete form, of the later 1950s, finding little to encourage lingering. In German, Fischer-Dieskau sounds less soberly eloquent, more given to familiar faults, than in the later Richter set, and so the presence of a baritone hero is even less convincingly defended. Fricsay pulls the music about; seeming to aim at a romantic impulsiveness (and obtaining big-boned orchestral playing in doing so), he ends up by often sentimentalizing the music. Maria Stader is a metallic Eurydice with little character, Streich, once again, a charmer as Cupid, in her truest, most appealing voice here. The RCA Rome Opera set is a sadly lacklustre affair, interesting only for its hints of what might have been if Monteux had been able to impose a more rigorous discipline upon a mediocre chorus and orchestra (one or two glaring mistakes are left uncorrected); and if Risë Stevens had been invited to record the hero's part twenty or even ten years earlier. Lisa Della Casa's Eurydice is an impossibly polite portrayal – the searching interrogatives in the recitative emerge as bland as tea-time conversation. Roberta Peters has the spunk and the spirit for a lively Cupid, but not enough warmth or variety of timbre. I pass even more speedily over the set of highlights from Berlin (in German), with Hermann Prey a bumpily emphatic, lugubrious baritone Orpheus, Lorengar in cleaner and more exact voice than for her later Decca Eurydice, Erika Köth a soubrettish Cupid, and Horst Stein the equable but hardly inspiring conductor.

The second RCA *Orfeo* of the LP era provides a valuable representation of the Ricordi edition, complete in every note apart from the bravura aria that closes Act 1. This allows one to hear all the Paris ballet music (though not in the orginal Paris order). All the instrumental music is beautifully done; indeed, the playing seems to me the most consistently beautiful of any on record, just as the choral singing of the Rome Polyphonic Choir (an apparently short-lived institution) is the most consistently grateful and Italian in warmth of tone – what a pleasure to hear the language delivered by natives after the mealy mouths of alien choirs! – yet lucid, youthful-sounding, and disciplined in a manner not often associated with Italian choirs (assuredly not with the Rome Opera chorus).

I first got to know the opera from this set, and must record a continuing personal affection for it. Fasano's unhurried, gently authoritative conducting inspires affection. Nothing is rushed, nothing drags. In this, it is not unlike an Italian equivalent of Froment's conducting; and for the same reasons, I find that it begins after a while to seem lacking in passion and dramatic impetus. Shirley Verrett's Orpheus merits admiration, for the fine, pure sound of the voice at its best, and for its suggestion of underlying dignity and strength of purpose. The music does not always lie well for her: F to B in the middle range is an area of comparative weakness, and the line requires little hooks and pushes to ease it through. She is at her most affecting in Hades, and when the top of the voice is allowed to ring out in the higher-lying 'Berlioz' line of the third act. Anna Moffo's Eurydice is skilfully voiced without persuading the listener that she came to the recording studio with a fully fledged grasp of the character. Judith Raskin, a gracious Cupid (though with weak Italian consonants), sounds as though she might have made a more decisive Eurydice. Very few appoggiaturas: even the most obvious ones are avoided.

Of Orpheus's first great solo, 'Chiamo il mio ben'/'Object de mon amour', there are surprisingly few examples, none of them from the modern era. Margarete Klose (D: 5, 7, in German – DB 4531) sings the preceding recitative and first verse only; the recording was made in 1937, when the voice moved with splendid evenness throughout its compass – a noble Orpheus caught here in prime form. By comparison, the secure Emmi Leisner (D: 7, 8, 9, in German – Poly. 66735; LV 40) is colourless and uninvolving. Joseph Rogatchewsky (B: 5, 6, 7a, 7b, 7d, 7e, 8 – Col. D 15223) takes two sides, adds preceding and succeeding recitatives, transposes the order of recitative and aria as in C, and lowers it a tone – a vibrant, passionate tenor of memorable utterance, highly emotional yet not unclassical. Cupid's air has one performance, also pre-LP: Yvonne Brothier (B: 12 – Disque K 7342), an Opéra-Comique Cupid of the 1920s, presents the soubrettish view of the character, thin and forward in tone, pert (to my ears, appealingly and prettily so) in manner.

The bravura ariette that Gluck borrowed from his earlier *Aristeo* to close the Paris first act has not been recorded in its original tenor version. In his 1859 score, Berlioz changed the words for Pauline Viardot, whose own high-and-low-flying alteration of the vocal line and whose decorations and tremendous final cadenza (complete with back-reference to 'Objet de mon amour' and two-octave chromatic scale) are preserved in the Saint-Säens–Tiersot–Pelletan edition of the Paris scores. Shirley Verrett (C: 6 – SB 6790) sings the full Viardot version, jibbing only at the recall of 'Objet de mon amour' in the final cadenza; she lavishes upon it a bright, brilliant timbre and manner, though some of the virtuosity is a trifle sketchy, and not every note is tuned in its centre. Louise Homer's 1904 account (D: 17, in English – Victor 85015) is much plainer, delivered with a fair-and-square lack of *élan* typical of this singer. Neither can compare with Marilyn Horne on the Solti set, the only one to include the ariette in a complete performance; her astonishing mastery of vocal bravura transforms an essentially empty number.

Samples from Act 2 are more numerous. Ottilie Metzger's 1910 Plea to the Furies (*A*: 16, in German – Parlo. 1213; CO 310) is in the 1762 version, with orchestra but without chorus – not as commanding as one might expect, though a communicative artist can be sensed. Giuseppina Zinetti, piano-accompanied in the Plea and, on the second side, in 'Mille pene' and 'Men tiranne' (*D*: 22, 24, 26 – Col. D 12318), communicates little beyond gusty forcefulness and crude, at times breast-beating emoting, aspirating every semiquaver, rough and unpoetic with the words. Moving to the Elysian Fields, we encounter a single performance of Eurydice's aria with chorus, 'Cet asile' (*B*: 28). It emanates from a Czech single-LP collection of Gluck operatic excerpts, conducted with refined sensibility, if sometimes an excess of romantic yielding, by Peter Maag, but sung, for the most part, without distinction. The Eurydice is Helena Tattermuschová (Supra. SUA ST 50789), clean, hard-voiced, unidiomatic in French.

From the same disc comes one of the two performances, in ungainly French, of Orpheus's 'Quel nouveau ciel' by East European mezzo-sopranos. What the music needs is a quiet radiance in the tone, and in the succession of descriptive phrases an ability to awaken in the listener a sense of the character's wonderment while marvels unfold before him. It receives from Vera Soukupová (*C*: 10) a baldly matter-of-fact statement and a thready, cloudy tone; and from the Bulgarian, Alexandrina Milcheva-Nonova (*C*: 10), a combination of nice intentions, firm voice, and little imaginative spark. In German, Lorna Sydney (*C*: 10) is duller still, careful and characterless – the piece could easily be taken for a letter dictated to an attendant stenographer.

Among the five accounts of 'Che puro ciel' (all *D*: 33) there is evidence of greater interpretative insight. Not, however, from two more East Europeans – the reliable, here plodding Ruža Pospiš and the dignified, heavyweight Elena Nikolai. Teresa Berganza (SDD 193) voices it with all the dark glow of her youth, though one guesses that today's artist would dig deeper below the surface of the words. After a disappointing orchestral introduction (the ECO, unexpectedly sluggish under Raymond Leppard), Janet Baker (Philips 9500 023) begins the piece, and builds it as one always hopes a singer will – raptly, gently, with all senses heightened; a wonderful account, if perhaps a little less magical than the one she gave at the 1978 Proms. (Was there no one in the studio capable of protecting Dame Janet from an error of Italian pronunciation that flecks 'Che puro ciel' and seriously spoils her 'Che farò?' – that of referring to the heroine as 'Oyrideechay'?) In some ways, the most imaginative singer of all is Gérard Souzay (Philips 6580 174), whose visionary eloquence penetrates through some puffy, infirm tone – and, of course, through the inappropriately ponderous sound of a baritone an octave below proper pitch.

The third act opens with a long sequence of recitatives interspersing two duets (the second number is a duet, that is, in all editions except for the 1762 original; there Eurydice's 'Che fiero momento' is a *da capo* aria uninterrupted by Orpheus's utterances of anguish in the middle section). Throughout this sequence it is essential for both singers to convey and preserve an atmosphere of urgency if the dramatic impulse is not to become bogged down (and if Eurydice is not to seem, as she too often does, no more than a tedious nag). Tiana Lemnitz and Margarete Klose (*C*: 12, in German – DB 6801; WR SHB 47), a partnership of long standing, were recorded in 1948, when both voices were beginning to bear the marks of age. The manner is stately, the spanning and interweaving of the lines magisterial; but the soprano's dainty phrasing does not suggest a serious emotional predicament, and the number becomes a trifle long-winded. For the opening recitative as well as the duet, Mady Mesplé joined Nicolai Gedda (*B*: 35, 36 – 2C 069-14010) some two decades after his complete recording; even though the tenor's highest notes are all still in place – no mean achievement – most of the bloom has been rubbed off them, and what remains is not well paired with the soprano's thin tones, simply too insubstantial for the role and the situation. The Lemnitz-Klose 'Fortune ennemie' (*C*: 13, 14, in German – DB 6801; WR SHB 47), originally the second side of the earlier duet, elicits a response similar to the first. From the Czech LP compilation of Gluck excerpts, Tattermuschová and Soukupová in the same number (*C*: 13, 14 – Supra. SUA ST 50789) sound like oratorio duettists, prosaic in French utterance; the blend of the voices is not very alluring.

And so to Orpheus's great lament, of which I have heard some fifty-two versions. The largest number of these are in Italian. I pass over, as historical curiosities, performers whose high reputation in the role is little explained by their records of the aria: the comically lachrymose Maria Gay (who sings the 1762 version, with its less dramatic coda; *A*: 33 – 053140), the lumpy Fanny Anitua (*D*: 43 – Col. D 4674), the *grande dame* Kirkby-Lunn (*D*: 43 – DB 505), and the niminy-piminy Olszewska (*D*: 43 – D 1490; LV 25). Massenet once described Marie Delna as 'la Musique même'; could it really be the selfsame singer who here (*D*: 43 – Pathé 4878; Rubini SJG 204) trips off the Italian phrases in so cavalier a fashion, and who rushes so inartistically towards the final climax of an egregious top G? Even less admirable are Cyrena van Gordon (*D*: 43 – Am. Col. A 6221) and the ill-focused Enid Szantho (*D*: 43 – Victor 14229). Essie Ackland (*D*: 43 – C 2788) moves the voice cleanly, with power in reserve, but finds no dramatic life in the phrases; Jean Watson (*D*: 43 – DX 1721) intones in a genteel Anglo-Italian; Risë Stevens (*D*:

43 – Am. Col. 71365D; Odyssey Y31738), in much fuller, fresher voice than on her RCA complete recording, leaves with her warm, plummy timbre, a pleasant but unmemorable impression. On LP, a vocally statuesque account (with an ugly climax) by Marianna Radev (*D*: 43 – Jugoton LPY-V-645) carries greater expressive weight than that of Pospiš (*D*: 43), with her unreliable legato; Bumbry (DG 2538 104), perhaps less blank than on the Neumann set, still mouths a well-schooled recitation. These singers all desperately needed to be instructed, as Gluck is supposed to have instructed Guadagni, to 'shout Eurydice's name as if you had suffered a real loss'.

A want of passionate grief can likewise be complained of in the smooth, 'marmoreal' (a Shawe-Taylor adjective) Sigrid Onegin (*D*: 43 – DB 1190), and in the young Berganza (*D*: 43 – SDD 193): beautiful tone, dark, fine-pointed, lacking dramatic direction. The quick vibrato of Nan Merriman, another lovely singer here in her prime (*D*: 42, 43 – RCA 12-0067-A), confers on the aria (preceded by recitative) an inappropriate womanliness, as it did for Toscanini, underlined by pouting portamenti and little gulps. While Ebe Stignani, who recorded the aria twice (*D*: 43 – Parlo. R 30002 and GQX 11377; LV 237 and QALP 10144), was never a passionate singer in the manner demanded by Gluck of Guadagni, the Italianate breadth and spaciousness of her style manifest their own kind of emotional force; in the first-listed, earlier recording, the voice flows more evenly. A sovereign mistress of the large vocal manner was Kirsten Flagstad (*D*: 43 – DB 6913; 1C 147-01 492M), whose voice pours out in grandeur; if the interpretation is unspecific, and not all the corners are precisely turned, the impression is one of heroic splendour. Her pronunciation of the heroine's name is the same as Janet Baker's (*D*: 43 – Philips 9500 023). The fault is less forgivable in the younger singer, who otherwise gives a radiant performance, transposed up a tone, which misses only the last degree of candour and intensity of which she is capable. In Italian it is to two men, entirely dissimilar, that we must turn for the most imaginative handling of the aria. Gérard Souzay (*D*: 42, 43 – Philips 6580 174), with the same breathiness of tone noted in his earlier aria, and also the same impassioned style of delivery, precedes the aria with an electric stretch of recitative. And Tito Schipa (*B*: 40, in Italian – DB 1723; COLH 117), not an archetypal Orpheus, but, with his limpid, sunlit tone, his way of stamping individuality on every syllable, a tenor among the elect. He takes the aria down a semitone.

Is it personal prejudice, though, that finds the classical qualities of the aria, and indeed of the opera, most cogently expressed in French? By no stretch of the imagination is every French-language performance of the aria a model. Those by the East Europeans Erszebet Komlóssy (*C*: 15), Zenaida Palij (*C*: 15), Vera Soukupová (*C*: 15) and the baritone György Melis (*C*: 15) are unsatisfactory in various ways, while those by natives – the hooty, static Jeanne Gerville-Réache (*C*: 15 – Victor 88198;

Rococo R 14), and, in modern times, the powerful, unsubtle Lyne Dourian (*C*: 15) and Kleuza de Pennefort (C: 15), one of the slackest, dullest singers on record – are correct only in matters of enunciation. From her two-record Viardot-Malibran tribute, Marilyn Horne's French-language account of the aria (*C*: 15 – SET 309-10), taken at an unsuitably jaunty lick by Henry Lewis, is straightforward, strong-voiced, clumsily pronounced – there is little of the tragic fervour so notably inspired by Solti on his complete set.

On another level is the Romanian Elena Cernei (*C*: 15 – Electrecord ST-ECEO 378), a voice of attractive, individual timbre moulded into long legato phrases, touching even the final climaxes with a note of gentle pleading. But the truly French manner, as exemplified by three mezzos who sang the role at the Opéra-Comique in the 1950s, depends on forward tone, precise utterance of words, and unfussy directness of statement. All three begin with the recitative immediately after Eurydice's death, 'Malheureux, qu'ai-jet fai'. The most famous of the three was Rita Gorr (*C*: 14, 15 – ALP 1887), ringing, vibrant, the metal in her tone grateful to some ears (including mine), a touching tenderness mitigating her natural forcefulness in the first reprise. Clearly this is an artist of stature. Solange Michel (*C*: 14, 15 – Pathé 33DTX 137) makes a dramatic start, and then maintains throughout the vigour of an impressive, if not, moving, reading. Simone Coudèrc (*C*: 14, 15 – Véga 30 LT 13.008), with a voice less even and less reliably well-tuned, does beautiful, simple things with the words, focusing the unfolding of her performance on characterful utterance. And then there is Callas (aria only, *C*: 15 – 33 CX 1771): at this stage in her career the tone was raw or thin even in middle or low register, but how searingly meaningful, how cogent and passionate her union of words and music! With two words, 'Eurydice, Eurydice!' she distils the whole tragedy. Sharing her pinnacle is a tenor, Fernand Ansseau (*B*: 40 – DB 487) – a brilliant, resolute performer of the rarest kind, who makes us realize the special eloquence of the French language in classical opera, and the variety of emotional expression that can be held within a cleanly sustained line. Joseph Rogatchewsky (*B*: 39, 40 L 2063; LV 239) is almost his equal, except for a moist, slightly tearful quality that comes near to disturbing the flow of the line.

The list of German-language performances of the aria is almost a short-list of honourable Wagnerians of the century – discounting, that is, the mousy Lorna Sydney (*C*: 15, in German – Telef. E 1017), and Emmi Leisner (*C*: 15, in German – Poly. 66735 LV 40); too unvaried in colour. Kerstin Thorborg (*C*: 15, in German, cut – Od. 11971; LV 209) and Martha Mödl (*C*: 15, in German – Telef. BLE 14504) are both animated and unsteady, in Mödl's case tending towards gustiness. Eva Liebenberg, who sings the 1762 version (*A*: 33, in German – Telef. HT 31) is warm-toned, placid. These are three appreciable singers here on the slopes rather than on the heights. Approaching the peak we find Karin Branzell (also 1762, *A*: 33, in German – Poly. 66690; LV 182), who joins Liebenberg's warmth and steadiness to a greater manifestation of dramatic urgency; and Schumann-Heink's 1907 account (*C*: 15, in German – Victor 88091; VIC 1409), swoopy and too obviously emotional, perhaps, but with sincerity and sumptuous vocal resources shining through. The top is reached with Margarete Klose (*C*: 15, in German, cut – DB 4531), a 1937 recording that finds her in superb voice, and fully justifies her great and long reputation in the part.

Three English exponents of Orpheus help to round off the survey. Though praised early in her career by Shaw in this, her only operatic role, Clara Butt (*D*: 42, 43, cut – Col. 6767; GEMM 164), singing in a hearty oratorio Italian, booms and trivializes the music, adding at one point an out-of-place low G. Two Kathleen Ferrier accounts of the aria in English show the early stages of her association with the role, when the response was instinctive rather than poised or deeply thoughtful. An early, piano-accompanied (Gerald Moore) account of the 1762 version (*A*: 33, in English – HLM 7145) reveals the voice in pristine, youthful lustre. The famous 'Housewives' Choice' favourite, 'What is life?' (*C*: 15, in English – K 1466; ACL 308), is by comparison a trifle less glowing, and by later standards interpretatively immature; the generosity of tone and personality still leaps out of the speakers. Edna Thornton was not blessed with Ferrier's soul-stirring timbre; but on the evidence of her recitative and aria (1762 version, *A*: 32, 33, in English – D 691), complete with appoggiaturas, she was a noble Orpheus, dignified but never embalmed in manner, the tone beautifully controlled and spacious – there is almost something of an English Raveau in the unhurried fullness of her utterance. Like Butt, she goes down to a G below the stave; unlike Dame Clara, she makes the sound not a curiosity but a musical gesture that pays off. Bringing up the rear are two other native-language performers: Marta Krásová (*C*: 15, in Czech – Supra. 012-0455G), an important singer caught some way beyond her prime, and the unique Kozlovsky (*B*: 40, in Russian – B9162-3; GV 9), in more youthful voice than on his complete set, easier to take in small doses than in full.

ORFEO ED EURIDICE

O Orpheus; *A* Amor-Amour; *E* Eurydice
The letters **A, B, C, D** and numbers refer to the editions of the opera listed in the chart. Letters and numbers thus given in connection with each recording explain what music (and from which version of the opera) is played therein, in what order.

1936 (excerpts, in French) **C**: 1, 2 (not ch. and ritournelle), 3 (romance and *A*'s recit only), 4, 5, 6 (not air). **A**: 9. **B**: 26 (cut). **C**: 7 (parts 4, 5, 8 and 9 only), 8 (*b*, *c*), 10 (*O*'s recit only – cut), 13, 14 (not recit), 15 (not recit). **D**: 50 (cut). **C**: 16

Raveau *O*; Delille *A*; Féraldy
E/Vlassof Choir, SO/Tomasi Vox
ⓜ OPX 200

1947 (excerpts in Italian) **D**: 1, 2, 6,
10-13, 14 (cut), 15 (cut), 16, 18,
21, 22, 23 (cut), 24-7, 33 (2nd
half = **A**: 23), 37. **C**: 11. **D**: 39-
41, 42 (cut), 43-4, 51 (cut), 45
(cut)
Ferrier *O*; Vlachopoulos *A*;
Ayars *E*/Glyndebourne Festival
Chorus, Southern PO/Stiedry
Decca ⓜ ACL 293

1951 (live performance, in Italian) **D**:
Overture, 1-16. **A**: 10. **D**: 28
(cut), 18-37. **C**: 11. **D**: 39-44,
50, 51 (cut), 45 (cut)
Ferrier *O*; Duval *A*; Koeman *E*/
Netherlands Opera Chorus and
Orch./Bruck HMV ⓜ RLS 725

1951 (live performance, in Italian)
Barbieri *O*; Gabory *A*; Gueden
E/La Scala Chorus and
Orch./Furtwängler
Cetra ⓜ LO 19/2; Turnabout
ⓜ THS 65112-3

1952 (Act 2, live performance in
Italian) **D**: 18-37 Merriman *O*;
Gibson *E*/Robert Shaw Chorale,
NBC SO/Toscanini
RCA ⓜ AT 127

1953 (excerpts, in Italian) Stevens *O*;
Berger *E*/RCA Victor SO/Reiner
RCA (US) ⓜ LM 9010

1953 (in Italian) **D**: Overture, 1-16.
A: 10. **D**: 18-30, 32-7. **C**: 11. **D**:
39-44, 45 (cut), 47, 50, 52, 53
Klose *O*; Streich *A*; Berger
E/Berlin State Opera Chorus
and Orch./Rother
Urania ⓒ US 5223-3; Acanta
ⓜ FA 22140

1954 (excerpts, in German) **D**:
Overture, 7, 10, 11, 15, 28-34,
43
Klose *O*; Streich *A*; Schlemm
E/Bavarian Radio Chorus, Berlin
RIAS SO, Munich PO/Rother
Heliodor ⓜ 478128

1954 (in Russian) **B**: Overture, 1-13.
A: 10. **B**: 15-35, 36 (cut), 37-42,
45 (*a, b, c*)
Kozlovsky *O*; Sakharova *A*;
Shumskaya *E*/USSR Radio

Chorus and Orch./Samosud
MK ⓜ DO 933-40

1955 (in French) **B**: Overture, 1-6. 7
(*a, b, c, d*), 8-13, 26, 15-25, 27-
31, 33, 34, 32, 35-43, 45 (*a, b,
d* – cut, *f, g* – cut), 44
Gedda *O*; Berton *A*; Micheau
E/Paris Conservatoire Chorus
and Orch.-Froment
EMI ⓜ 2C 153 12059-60

1956 (in French) **B**: Overture, 1-13.
A: 10. **B**: 15-43, 45 (*a, b, d*), 44
Simoneau *O*; Alarie *A*; Danco
E/Blanchard Vocal Ensemble,
Lamoureux Orch./Rosbaud
Philips ⓜ PHC 2-014

1956 (in German) **D**: Overture, 1-16.
A: 10. **D**: 18-30, 32-4, 36-7.
C: 11. **D**: 39-45.
Fischer-Dieskau *O*; Streich *A*;
Stader *E*/Berlin Chamber Choir,
Berlin Motet Choir, Berlin
RIAS SO/Fricsay
DG ⓜ LPM 18345-6

1957 (in Italian) **D**: Overture, 1-16,
A: 10. **D**: 18-37. **C**: 11. **D**: 39-
44, 50, 46-49, 51-2, 53 (cut), 45
Stevens *O*; Peters *A*; Della Casa
E/Rome Opera Chorus and
Orch./Monteux
RCA (UK) ⓜ RB 16058-60

1960 (excerpts, in German) **D**: 1, 7-
15, 21, 22 (cut), 27-9, 32, 36. **C**:
11. **D**: 39, 41 (cut), 42 (cut), 43,
44 (cut), 45 (cut)
Prey *O*; Köth *A*; Lorengar
E/Berlin Chamber Choir, Berlin
SO/Stein
HMV ASD 550; EMI 1C 063
28505

1965 (in Italian) **D**: Overture, 1-16.
A: 10. **D**: 18-53
Verrett *O*; Raskin *A*; Moffo
E/Rome Polyphonic Choir,
Virtuosi di Roma and
Instrumental Ensemble of
Collegium Musicum
Italicum/Fasano
RCA (UK) SER 5539-41; (US)
LSC 6169

1966 (in Italian) **A**: Overture, 1-15.
D: 22. **A**: 17-21. **B**: 26, 27 (*a,
b, c*), 28-9. **A**: 23-32. **D**: 37.
A: 34-8

Forrester *O*; Steffek *A*; Stich-Randall *E*/Vienna Academy Choir, Vienna State Opera Orch./Mackerras
Vanguard VSD 70686-7; EMI 1C 147 98121-2

1966 (in Italian) **A**: Overture, 1-14, 16-36, 37 (*a, b, c, d* – cut), 38
Bumbry *O*; Pütz *A*;
Rothenberger *E*/Leipzig Radio Chorus, Leipzig Gewandhaus Orch./Neumann
EMI SMA 91602-3; Angel SBL 3717

1967 (in Italian) **A**: Overture, 1-14. **B**: 26. **A**: 15-36, 37 (*a, b, d*), 38
Fischer-Dieskau *O*; Moser *A*; Janowitz *E*/Munich Bach Choir and Orch./Richter
DG 2726 043

1969 (in Italian) **A**: Overture, 1.**D**: 2. **B**: 3. **A**: 4, 5 (*a, c, e*; recits = **D**: 8,10). **A**: 6. **D**: 12-17. **A**: 11-15. **D**: 22. **A**: 17. **D**: 24. **A**: 19-21. **B**: 16, 27 (*a, b, c*). **D**: 32, 33. **A**: 24, 26-30, 31 (first part; middle part = **D**: 39; da capo = **A**: 31). **A**: 32 (first part; second half = **D**: 42). **D**: 43 (plus orch. coda of **A**: 33). **A**: 34-5. **D**: 50. **B**: 45*e*. **A**: 37d (introduction only), 38.
Horne *O*; Donath *A*; Lorengar *E*/Royal Opera Chorus and Orch./Solti
Decca SET 443-4; London OSA 1285

Idomeneo and
La clemenza di Tito

WILLIAM MANN

Devotees today of Mozart's *Idomeneo* are tempted to assume that it was totally forgotten between 1791, when Mozart died, and 1951, when Fritz Busch and Carl Ebert brought it to Glyndebourne. A glance at Alfred Loewenberg's *Annals of Opera* will show how many times it was produced in the years between (and those *Annals* were deliberately selective). Gramophone records also testify that *Idomeneo* was known about and sung during the first half of this century.

Mozart composed *Idomeneo* for the 1781 carnival season in Munich. The cast for which the opera had to be written included a young and unmusical male soprano as Idamantes, an elderly, reactionary, but still accomplished tenor as Idomeneus, and another veteran tenor as Arbaces. Mozart encountered difficulties with all three singers, and had to revise, cut or add to their music during rehearsals. For practical reasons he made other numerous cuts shortly before the first performance. *Idomeneo* was not staged elsewhere during Mozart's lifetime, to his regret, for he would have liked to revise it 'more in the French style' (that of Gluck's reform operas) and with a bass in the title role. He did conduct a concert performance in Vienna in March 1786, given by noble amateurs at Prince Auersperg's palace. For this he had a tenor Idamantes, and accordingly he rewrote the part where essential (in the ensembles); he replaced the original Ilia–Idamantes duet in Act 3, 'S'io non moro', by a new duet for soprano and tenor, 'Spiegarti non poss' io'. Act 2 began not with Arbaces but Ilia and Idamantes in conversation followed by Idamantes's 'Non temer, amato bene' with violin obbligato. Since he notated it in the soprano clef (though the singer was billed as a tenor), sopranos have often claimed the aria. Mozart set the same text as a concert aria for soprano with piano obbligato, 'Ch'io mi scordi di te'; but that delectable piece has no place in a discussion of *Idomeneo*.

The above may explain why the sets discussed here have such varied contents.

The first of these versions, called 'complete' rather than actually being complete, is the Bavarian Radio one, in Ermanno Wolf-Ferrari's edition (made for the Bavarian State Opera in 1931, the same year as Richard Strauss's more famous version, both to celebrate the work's 150th anniversary). It is sung in E.L. Stahl's German text, based on that printed in the old Mozart Complete Edition, and was recorded, I guess from internal evidence, in about 1949. The extent of the cuts involved must be appreciated, given that the set takes four sides rather than six or eight. Some orchestral recitatives are shortened and transcribed for harpsichord accompaniment; Nos 7 and 8, 12, 22 and 23, 27, 29 and 30*a* (GA 31) are omitted. In the last act particularly Wolf-Ferrari replaced Mozart by orchestral recitatives of his own composition, thematically allusive (as Strauss's version was) but often soupy in style. He rewrote Neptune's 28 with drum-roll accompaniment. Most remarkable of all, he scrupulously wrote graces into the vocal parts so that one hears 1940s German singers singing Mozart more musically than most of their colleagues twenty-five years later. I cannot love Maud Cunitz's edgy, wobbly Ilia, do enjoy much of Marianne Schech's clean, forceful Electra (she struggles in 13), greatly admire Franz Klarwein's Idomeneus, strong and moving in declamation and sinewy, pleasing cantabile (he was the first Flamand in *Capriccio*, and a splendid Tamino in a Munich *Zauberflöte* which I saw in 1950), whose big arias are omitted. Gottfried Riedner is a decent tenor Idamantes, if effortful in runs and trill-less. Chorus and orchestra sound well. The errors, omissions, and blatant rewriting will horrify most listeners, but I liked the set a lot, as I do not the Nixa Haydn Society version of slightly later, much more complete though it is. Perhaps its only advantage is the casting of Idamantes as a soprano, at Mozart's pitch: not a male castrato, but a thick, acid, faintly tremulous girly soprano (Greta Menzel) who ruins her arias and only recommends her presence in the duet 20*a* which sounds hopeless with a tenor Idamantes. This set is less 'complete' than is claimed (there are several internal cuts, merciful given the standard of singing and playing) but it does represent most of the complete opera as printed in the old *Gesamtausgabe*. Gertrude Hopf's Ilia is a noble performance, rich of voice and stylish, not always technically matched to the music (the runs in 'Zeffiretti' are distinctly questionable). Gertrud Grob-Prandl, once a formidable Turandot at Covent Garden, conveys the wounded pride of Electra, but fails in the gentler music of Act 2 and in the hectic staccato runs of her last aria. The Idomeneus, Horst Taubmann, has a nasal delivery, a grainy tone, neat but breathy, by no means fluent. The quartet, 'Andrò ramingo e solo', and the trio, 'Pria di partir', are both disappointing. If you want the longest pronouncement by Neptune (28*c*), it is here, tolerably delivered. The set is poorly conducted, mostly too fast or too slow, with a dozy orchestra and appalling Italian pronunciation (for instance, 'zono' for 'sono').

Fritz Busch did not live to record his *Idomeneo* for Glyndebourne, only some highlights. The set fell to his protégé, John Pritchard, who inherited the strengths and failings of Busch. The Glyndebourne set, memento of many unforgotten delights, does have its drawbacks: brutal small cuts in arias, weak casting of Electra (neither Lucille Udovick nor Dorothy McNeil is apt, and one regrets that Birgit Nilsson was not in the cast as Electra for either recording), Léopold Simoneau's cultivated but unforthcoming tenor Idamantes, the baritone Arbaces instead of a tenor (Nixa had Herbert Handt, a bright, ebullient tenor who was allowed both his arias, most attractively sung). It did have Richard Lewis's handsome, forthcoming Idomeneus, tender, silvery, touching, also cogent (more so in the Busch highlights), and the exquisite Ilia of Sena Jurinac, smoky in timbre, easy of manipulation and irresistibly expressive in word and phrasing (better still in the Fritz Busch excerpts). Pritchard conducts sometimes too lightly for the music's emotion, though he cares for his singers. There is not enough of *Idomeneo*, though what was vouchsafed sounds well. Busch's 78 selections, later issued in the USA as a twelve-inch LP disc, have more character. Alexander Young, the Idamantes, is heard only in the quartet (21).

Next came a 'complete' *Idomeneo* conducted by Hans Schmidt-Isserstedt. The cast included the finest of all recorded Electras, Edda Moser, who sang a proud, passionate, anguished 4, grandly accompanied; a nervous, sharply pitched 13, slightly less tense in the central section of 14; and a dazzling 'D'Oreste, d'Ajace'. The Idomeneus was Nicolai Gedda, a clever piece of casting, not always as ideally sung as we expect: he is explosive in expression, which disrupts his line; the runs are sometimes careless; 'Fuor del mar' is decently sung though the demanding first version, 12a, would have suited Gedda even better. Again there is a tenor Idamantes, Adolf Dallapozza, pleasant but unmemorable (here, as at Glyndebourne, the later soprano–tenor duet, 20b, is preferred). Anneliese Rothenberger is a cold but fluent Ilia. The opera is too reverentially conducted, accepting but not projecting the mood of many numbers. There are cuts, few graces and much Teutonic Italian. Arbaces is given both his arias, which Peter Schreier sings with real distinction; both show the Dresden orchestra in top form. The choruses are all strongly done and they bring out the best in Schmidt-Isserstedt who was, on a good day, a sterling exponent of Viennese classicism.

The Philips set conducted by Colin Davis reveals, from its overture onwards, just what was missing from these other sets – a fervent faith in the splendour of Mozart's music and the knowledge to communicate it without fail. In number after musical number he finds a tempo and orchestral palette that fit the dramatic situation as other conductors on record just fail to do. 'Padre, germani' grows out of the overture and helps Margherita Rinaldi, an expressive, ringing, tender yet noble voice, to bring Ilia instantly and cogently to life (even Hopf, even Jurinac sound somewhat stiff by comparison). Out of it grows 'No, la morte', and

Ryland Davies, as later, convinces one by his vital musicianship and vocal art (and by Davis's sensible tempi) that a tenor Idamantes, if not ideal, is at least a pleasure to listen to, and a musical pleasure (wherever possible he sings his part in ensembles an octave higher to accord with Mozart's vocal textures). Out of that comes the first chorus, strongly and jubilantly sung, and then the arrival of Robert Tear's admirable Arbaces (alas, he is denied his arias) and Pauline Tinsley's splended Electra, almost the equal of Edda Moser, and a formidable character at every turn ('Tutti nel cor' naturally angry, where Moser herself applied the anger without help from the conductor), and so to the appearance of George Shirley's Idomeneus. Here at last is the voice we have been wanting – dark and full, vibrant, a certain prey for the vultures of doom; in 'Vedrommi intorno' the tempi sound perfectly apt, the Andantino for once not too laboured, the Allegro really upset (it does test Shirley's florid technique). One realizes how much of this first act Mozart designed as if in one breath, how few pauses there have been and how intensely the emotions are deployed at once.

Recitatives are given thoroughly dramatic treatment (harpsichord contribution just right) and they are sometimes shortened. Shirley sings the longer version of 'Fuor del mar' not perfectly but in grand style: some may find it too heavy, but Idomeneus is a heavy role by Mozartian tenor standards (more bowed down by responsibility than Mithridates or Sulla or Alexander the Great, let alone Titus) and Davis makes sure that Shirley does not lose sight of Mozart's authorship. 'Torna la pace' is included, but not Idamantes's 'No, la morte' (a fine aria, dramatically redundant as Mozart realized, but surely essential in a complete gramophone performance). With a tenor Idamantes it was perverse to include the two-soprano 'S'io non moro' rather than the equally authentic soprano–tenor 'Spiegarti non poss' io' (more authentic with this casting). Of Mozart's four pronouncements for Neptune, Stafford Dean sings 28d, the second version 1a and b, one minuscule, the other without divine trombones, were later resorts in desperation). 'D'Oreste, d'Ajace' could hardly have been omitted (pace Mozart's misgivings) and powerfully it is done by Tinsley; but there are some other minor cuts in this temple scene.

Before Colin Davis had brought Idomeneo to Covent Garden (but after he recorded it), Karl Böhm, that grand and senior Mozartian, had restored it to the repertory of the Salzburg Summer Festivals. In 1977 he conducted the work for DG, moving for the recording sessions to Dresden (as did Schmidt-Isserstedt for EMI) where once he was musical director. As in Salzburg the Idamantes is a tenor, which means that the duet in Act 3 is 'Spiegarti non poss'io', and that the other ensembles are adjusted as in Mozart's 1786 performance; at the start of Act 2 Idamantes sings the aria with violin obbligato specially composed for that performance, 'Non temer, amato bene'. Since he is Peter Schreier, the music is affectingly, stylishly, and most cleanly sung, not always in fluent Italian (the set as a whole would have benefited from an Italian language coach, normal practice in many countries).

This sterling tenor voice is admirably contrasted with the darker, more mature and vibrant tenor sound of Wieslaw Ochman's Idomeneus, an authoritative but also troubled portrait of the fated king, less perhaps than sovereign in 'Fuor del mar' (though he sings the shorter, less taxing version), not ideally neat in the trio by the ship (16), but often and again poignantly illuminating (for example in the third-act quartet). Edith Mathis is a lovely Ilia, cool and collected in elaborate passages, expressive in her glorious arias and even more, often times, in isolated phrases elsewhere, for example her last, deeply felt admonition before Idamantes's 2, or in her loving confession to him at the start of the third act. These three interpretations are as cogent as any in rival sets, and Julia Varady's Electra, richly pungent, even piquant, in tone, is worthy of their company, though her voice lets her down, in point of accuracy, in 'Idol mio' and the central section of 'Placido è il mar'. Both angry arias are powerfully projected, as indeed are Electra's venomous asides in the third act. The smaller parts are too modestly cast for their music, and the Leipzig chorus betrays weaknesses.

The Dresden orchestra is a joy to hear when Böhm does not force it *ultra vires*. The DG acoustic tends to favour it above voices which sometimes sound backward and muffled. The impress of the performance relies chiefly on Böhm, vital and searching at his best, sometimes unable to make an unconvential tempo sound right, as his Mozartian performances usually do; there are several surprises, some thrilling, some leaden. The performance is said to adopt the New Mozart Edition score, but it includes recitatives omitted in that edition, ignores much of the advice on standard ornamentation, and indulges in copious cuts – not only on numbers which Mozart was constrained to suppress in the premiere, to avoid *longueur*, and in the lengthy recitatives, but even within closed musical numbers – thereby distorting the composer's carefully calculated design. When we describe art as classical, we refer to its perfection of structure; to alter that perfection can only be regarded as vandalism, however honourable the vandal may otherwise seem to be. It is a thousand pities that so splendid a Mozartian as Böhm should not have recorded a perfectly complete *Idomeneo*, ballet music and all. The requirements of theatrical performance are not at all those of the gramophone, which looks chiefly for completeness and durable exegesis.

After listening intently to all these sets, I would add that we need recordings of Mozart's operas which treat the musical grammar of the period (appoggiaturas, decorated reprises, cadenzas, and so on) consistently, as well as intelligently, as an essential article of musical faith. Some Mozart conductors, such as Busch, rejected entirely, like spiritual fundamentalists, any alteration of the printed score. Far too many conductors of eighteenth-century music nowadays allow singers to grace music *ad libitum*, so that one part may be sung with style, answered by another wholly out of style. It happens in Böhm's *Idomeneo* set, and in too many other performances by musicians who should maintain complete stylistic responsibility, rather than meekly put up with elegance and vulgarity cheek by jowl (I exaggerate, but not far from the truth of slapdash present-day performing practice). We still need a complete, truly idiomatic, and really musical recording of *Idomeneo*.

Now for the vocal excerpts on record; the overture is well represented; there is one by the Berlin Philharmonic under Erich Kleiber (DG 2548 739), which may be interesting. Ilia's opening aria, 'Padre, germani, addio' (1), with its preceding orchestral recitative, has been recorded by the Dutch soprano, Erna Spoorenberg with the Academy of St-Martin-in-the-Fields (SDD 335) (see also 11). The voice is girlish, charming and zestful, the words Germanically pronounced, the recitative shorn of twenty-two important bars, the aria complete and decently graced – an attractive account. Rinaldi's glorious reading has been abstracted (SAL 3747). Idamantes's first aria, 'Non ho colpa' (2), is included in a Mozart recital (Telef. 6.35063) where Schreier also sings Idomeneus's 12. His 2 is uncut, short on graces, with trills on the main note, a cadenza at the end; it is ideal of voice, tender yet heroic, vitally rhythmical, aware of the emotions expressed, almost up to Ryland Davies in the Philips set.

Apart from the March (8) in an attractive disc of dances led by Willi Boskovsky, (SDDH 351), and a single from the Schmidt-Isserstedt set, used for Kubrick's film 'Barry Lyndon', the next item separately recorded is 11, Ilia's aria, 'Se il padre perdei', with its rich obbligatos for the Munich woodwind principals. Teresa Stich-Randall takes it slowly (DTL 93075), negotiating the rising and falling sevenths attractively but creating an atmosphere, with her disembodied tonal meticulousness, of a zombie party–hostess, exquisitely mannered but never truly communicative, a sort of *Hoffmann* Olympia. Hilde Gueden (LXT 5242) is given a more cheerful, not to say chirpy, pace for the same aria – reasonable since Ilia is telling Idomeneus how enjoyable her stay in Crete has been, how kind her host. Gueden's voice sounds full and intense, appreciative of those sevenths, the high B flats, and all the other distinctive features of a superb solo, including a delicious accompaniment. Her vocal line does bump under the impress of zeal. Maria Stader's reading (LPEM 19369), is tidily negotiated, pleasing in its refinement of voice, but not memorable by her best standards. Spoorenberg, on the record listed above, is fired by sensitive woodwind colleagues, nicely balanced with her fresh, youthful soprano, to a forthcoming performance which includes the preceding recitative; her vowels are German-orientated. Leontyne Price skilfully fines her tone down for the aria (SB 6813), manipulating the runs evenly and touching the top A flat attractively; but the phrasing is short-breathed, the staccato effortful, the leaps awkward, the rhythm distorted, the expression stilted; given a boxy acoustic, it is not a success, though the woodwind's artistry is appreciable. There is an interesting early version on disc by Ria Ginster (DB 1870; LV 190), sung, unusually for its time, in Italian: it is nicely paced (doubtless to get it on to one 78 side!), has lovely pure soprano tone, judiciously appreciable portamenti and good trills; the runs are questionably tuned. Sabine Meyer recorded it in German (Poly. 65612).

Close on that aria's heels comes Idomeneus's big display piece, 'Fuor del mar' (12), which exists in two versions, since the elderly Anton Raaff persuaded Mozart to respect his waning powers. Most modern tenors gladly accept the less demanding version, not much shorter but kinder to a singer's lungs and florid technique. Shirley, we have seen, dares the long version as, surprisingly and gloriously, did Hermann Jadlowker in 1911 (042527). This account commands admiration. Sung as 'Noch tönt mir ein Meer im Busen', it is abbreviated, chiefly orchestrally (no loss). Sometimes the singer seems short of breath for a tenor of 34, and there are inaccuracies. The timbre is pushed, lacking vibrato (pre-Caruso), but the effect in runs and trills, and general musical intensity, is breathtaking, a lesson to all. A comparable modern rival is Stuart Burrows (DSLO 13), who declaims strongly, cultivates a long breath and a broad dynamic range, includes a cadenza, and negotiates runs (they are fiendish in 12a) carefully but effectively; we sense the importance and potential tragedy of the moment, all the more through the fine orchestral accompaniment by the LSO, John Pritchard's appreciative conducting (after years of thinking about his early 'complete' recording), and the bright Decca acoustic. Schreier (TK 11559) also sings the long version, brilliantly in the difficult runs, his voice neatly contained, expressive of manner though thin in quality (Burrows and Shirley sound more like the doomed king). He understands about appoggiaturas but not about Italian pronunciation, alas, nor gap-filling. He sings an exciting final cadenza, and is excellently accompanied, with plenty of orchestral detail.

Discussing the Schmidt-Isserstedt *Idomeneo* I hazarded that the more taxing version of 'Fuor del mar' would have suited Gedda well. He had already recorded it (33CX 1528) in the Strauss version, which is unaltered, though it has blunt phrase-ends and no cadenza. Gedda's performance then was brave but unready, the runs slithery. A confusing version is recorded by Werner Hollweg, in a DG compilation called 'From the Heart' (2563 555, issued in aid of Cancer Research). He sings the more elaborate 12a, but makes a cut in each half of the aria, musically ill-advised and structurally misleading since a striking passage is removed from the exposition but included in the reprise. Hollweg's tenor is hard in quality and light for the role, recorded less frankly than LPO/Dutoit. His runs are sketchy at first, clean later; he leaves phrase-ends blunt, but has a keen sense of rhythm, and does provide a brief, proud cadenza. Simoneau recorded the simpler version of 12, also Idamantes's 'Non temer' (see below) on ABR 4053; and a pleasantly suave account of the king's final 'Torna la pace' (Ducretet-Thompson DTL 93091).

Electra's central aria, 'Idol mio', shows her in gentler mood, if that is possible in so mixed-up a woman. It has twice been recorded by itself. Margaret Price (SER 5675) deploys her pearly voice and deliciously floated top notes to admiration, sings all the grace-notes in the New Mozart Edition (but not the grammatical ones which the editor forgot), and is charmingly accompanied with a favourable studio acoustic. Out of the opera's context she does not sound an Electra to me, rather an Ilia – chalk not cheese (or vice versa). There is also Elsa Gardelli (Qualiton LPX 1108), gentle, unmemorable except for the inaccuracy of her florid singing.

Nothing also in Act 2 has been recorded separately; but Ilia's 'Zeffiretti lusinghieri' certainly has, many times, understandably since it is a tender, lightsome, delectable soprano aria, preceded by an exquisite orchestral recitative, not always included. Vera Schwarz (Parlo. RO 20391), a much-loved soprano, sang a two-sided version in German with a darkly golden voice which glinted delectably; her runs were heavy, her style uncertain, but there is some lovely singing, and no cuts. Erna Berger (DB 6617) also took two sides and sang in German, including the previous recitative. Here is a more extrovert account, apt to a less sophisticated, indeed girlish soprano (Schwarz has really too metropolitan a voice for a classical Trojan princess, on reflection), and fluently executed, with a delightful orchestral accompaniment. Ria Ginster (DB 1870; LV 190) sang it abbreviated, in German, her soprano lightly vibrant, much given to self-conscious sudden *molto pianissimo* effects, her florid delivery imperfect, the brakes too readily applied. The other side represents her more favourably. Lea Piltti (DB 5668; LV 199) also sang it on one side in German, greatly telescoped, with a leaden orchestra; the resinous quality of the voice and the charming elegance of the singing are worth investigating. Stich-Randall included the orchestral recitative, as LP versions should do, though her orchestra is slow and hard in timbre where she is soft, the runs almost marked rather than sung, the white notes fallible on attack, in fact technically not up to the music.

Elisabeth Schwarzkopf in her vocal prime recorded 'Zeffiretti' on a Mozart operatic recital (33CX 1069). The runs are curiously uneven, there is one wrong note, the delivery might be considered too nasal for pleasure; but the warm, vibrant soprano is a joy, like the sensibility towards words and musical pleasures. Her trill is unnatural, forced, no credit to an Ivogün pupil! (The recital as a whole is full of vocal plums.) Rita Streich (DGM 19137) brings a bright, wooing, tender soprano and a clean style with a decent trill, to the aria, characteristic of her art. Janine Micheau (33FCX 904) makes heavy weather of the number, her timbre unsuitably metallic, but she negotiates the music tidily. Stader's version (LPEM 19369) is sensitively and affectionately accompanied; her pretty, slightly fluttery soprano projects well, she phrases naturally and is decently accompanied. Pilar Lorengar, too, has recorded the aria in German, projecting it strongly, in spite of some aspirated runs, with a keen legato, sense of nuance, and appropriate intensity in the central section. There are two versions by Eleanor Steber, taken from live recitals with piano accompaniment, at Carnegie Hall (Stand SLP 101) and the Continental Baths in New York (RCA ARL 1-D436). Electra's 'D'Oreste', has been done by two Hungarian ladies. Sylvia Sass (SLPX 11812) sounds demure, not electrifying, sorrowful rather than angry: her last staccato scales are impeccable but inexpressive, her top register brilliant. The performance, including the foregoing recitative, means almost nothing, though more than that of Elsa Gardelli, transposed down a tone, and delivered in the stately tones of a mayoress welcoming a deputation of foreign visitors.

The duet, 'Spiegarti non poss' io', has been recorded separately by Simoneau with his wife Pierette Alarie (Concert Hall CM 2183), nicely voiced and fluent though heavily accompanied. Idamantes's third act aria, as revised for Vienna, was recorded by Simoneau (Philips ABR 4053) with pleasing tone and personality. But it is more suitable for a soprano voice – this is the aria, 'Non temer', with violin obbligato. Mozart wrote the vocal part in the old soprano clef, and it sounds better that way, especially with Gueden (ECS 557) partnered by Boskovsky, or Seefried with her husband Schneiderhan (EPL 30045), even richer sung by Margaret Price with Dennis Simons (LRLI 5077). Gueden approaches tears too easily, Seefried offers no trill, Price sings breathily, but all three versions have significant distinctions to offer.

I have not heard 'Tutto nel cor' by Hilde Zadek (Philips A 00207L), nor 'Zeffiretti' sung on Am. Col. ML 4640 by, astonishingly a mezzo-soprano, Jennie Tourel; nor yet Walther Ludwig in Idamantes's 'No, la morte' (sung in German: Top Classic Historia H 712-3) but Karl Erb in the last-named aria, sung in German, recorded in 1939 from a broadcast, displays real fire and keen articulation (Acanta DE 23-106/7).

LA CLEMENZA DI TITO

The last of Mozart's contributions to *opera seria* took some time, even when the Mozart revival of this century gathered momentum, to assert its place in the canon of his great operas. It was not unknown to singers of the acoustic and early electric recording ages. With the advent of the LP and a much more adventurous recorded repertory, *La clemenza di Tito* was soon given the benefit of a 'complete' recording, typically through the enterprise of the Stuttgart Ton-Studio, responsible for so many interesting records of the early 1950s.

That first set, put out in America by Period, in Britain by Nixa, was complete in including all the set numbers but none of the *secco* recitatives which meant that, without a libretto to hand, one could not follow the drama as a complete or coherent experience. Gustav Lund conducts a small but expert and stylish orchestra, a chorus decidedly short on numbers, the then Stuttgart 'house-cast', well known on record, variable in quality, always willing. Hetty Plümacher's Sextus is outstanding on all musical counts, even to adding the appoggiaturas much missed elsewhere (it is not true that Mahler chased them from German opera houses; records show that they were standard until the mid 1920s, with few exceptions). Käthe Nentwig, an accurate and musicianly soprano, was overparted as the evil Vitellia (a difficult role to cast, requiring soprano top D and a substantial alto register, as well as vivid declamation and a fine legato technique): her villainy is not communicated. Albert Weikenmaier brings a flinty tenor and heavy style to Titus's demanding solos. Annius and Servilia are prettily sung at a doll-like level. Even then the recorded sound appeared unduly abrasive. At least record collectors could become familiar with the set numbers (the recitatives are thought to be the work of Mozart's pupil Süssmayr), and imagine how the music might be communicated more eloquently.

For the next *Tito* on records we had to wait until 1967, by which time the Cologne Opera had taken *La clemenza di Tito* into its repertory under the musical directorship of Istvan Kertesz, with success. For Decca he conducted a version recorded in Vienna, the recitatives shortened but substantial, the set numbers complete, the cast international and interesting. The recorded ambience is lean, spacious yet instant, cogently balanced in such dramatic moments as the finale of the first act, with soloists on stage, chorus at a distance. Again the Sextus stands out, in the delectable voice of Teresa Berganza, attentive to situation, touching in expression. Maria Casula successfully masters the comprehensive tessitura of Vitellia's part, from the smooth, melancholy final rondo, 'Non più di fiori', through her vituperative demands and threats, delivered with alarming vocal asperity, to the agile runs and the flaming top D in the trio, 'Vengo, aspettate'. The impersonation is the more remarkable when one remembers that, at about the same time, she also contributed an admired Sextus in the same opera to a Wexford Festival production in Ireland.

Brigitte Fassbaender sings an impressive Annius, to complete the trio of principal mezzo-sopranos suggested by Mozart's writing; the real soprano, Servilia, is attractively taken by Lucia Popp. Werner Krenn has the legato line, ardent manner, and gentle lyrical tenor for the various moods of Titus (a character whose titular clemency is only the regular outcome of many diverse emotions, vividly exploited by Mozart). Publius, a sort of glorified civil servant, is not a major role, but requires a steadier voice than that of Tugomir Franc. Kertesz was an enthusiastic rather than searching Mozart conductor. His set wears well, even with its lack of graces and special felicities: he never races, never allows the music to sound run-of-the mill, always cares for euphony and vitality.

The missing quality in Kertesz's reading is the mature late-Mozartian dark translucency of texture, still eighteenth-century yet looking forward to Beethoven and beyond. That is the extra ingredient of the set conducted by Colin Davis for Philips in 1976, based (with some important changes of cast) on the Covent Garden production, conducted by him, which firmly convinced London, then Milan, audiences of the opera's supreme worth. Here again there are deplorable cuts in the recitatives and essential graces are bluntly ignored (the former regrettable on record even if advisable in the theatre, the latter always reprehensible). Davis's reading blends the formality of *serio* style with the concision and intensity of Mozart's adaptation in *Tito* so as to bring out the human characteristics of the action, more purposefully than Kertesz or Lund. He has the advantage of a responsive and highly expert orchestra ('his' orchestra as the VPO could not be Kertesz's), a splendid chorus, and in the principal parts, Stuart Burrows and Janet Baker, who comfortably surpass all contenders by superior vocalism, artistry and intelligence (though she has to duck the top D in the first trio). Burrows makes Titus more handsome, vigorous and credible than before, Baker communicates a Vitellia not a whit less spoiled and horrible, but more brilliant, radiant, alluring and sympathetic (almost a predecessor of Lulu), long before her melting 'Non più di fiori'. Against strong competition, Yvonne Minton just wins the Sextus stakes by character as well as artistry (though Berganza had the more beguiling voice). With Frederica von Stade's exceptionally positive Annius and Robert Lloyd's eloquently phrased, dependable Publius, this set has very much in its favour, although we still await a really complete and handsomely graced recording of *La clemenza di Tito*. A recording directed by Böhm is in preparation.

The individual items on record are led by two famous interpretations of an earlier age. Louise Kirkby Lunn's 'Non più di fiori' (DB 517; CO 374) is notable for brilliant runs and trills, and a cavernous alto register reached by a noisy gear change (rather to the taste of her audiences, I suspect); musically it is not among her most expressive records. In 1909 Ernestine Schumann-Heink recorded Sextus's 'Parto, parto' (Victor 88196; GV 514), unexpectedly bright and energetic, exemplary in smooth line and at least the idea of gracing as a norm. The solo clarinet (perhaps plural) is adept and well balanced with the singer. There are heavy cuts and some curious Italian.

Of Titus's 'Ah, se fosse intorno' there is a euphonious, fairly virile account by Peter Schreier (Telef. 6.35063), another, honeyed but less compelling, by Léopold Simoneau (ABR 4053). Sextus's 'Parto, parto' was also recorded by Lois Marshall (ALP 1642) in heroic style, with golden tone, artistic nuances and a good trill, but no concern for gracing and not much sensibility towards the special nature of the music. There is a noble version by Margaret Price (SER 5675), a less compelling one from Marilyn Horne below her best (SXL 6149), as well as one by Berganza (SDD 176), who sings it in the Kertesz set. Frederica von Stade (Philips 9500 098) sings both Sextus's and Vitellia's famous arias; her 'Parto' is most sensitive and brilliant, too, the 'Non più di fiori' touching in expression yet unsatisfactory just because it is out of context. Janet Baker (likewise poaching on another role!) has recorded both of Sextus's solos, 'Parto, parto' and 'Deh, per questo instante solo' (Philips 6500 660): admirable versions, with excellent triplet runs and an outstanding clarinet obbligato (from Thea King) in the former and, in the latter, exquisite pathos and some degree of elementary gracing, missed in all versions of 'Parto' except Schumann-Heink's. Titus's aria 'Se all' impero', his most testing solo, was recorded by Gedda (33CX 1528) lightly but not without apparent effort; by Alexander Young (HMS 72; HLP 17) in heroic manner, vocally expert, though the performance is not ideal in style; and by Simoneau (DTL 93091), suave but not really authoritative.

IDOMENEO

I Ilia; *E* Electra; *Id* Idomeneus; *Ida* Idamantes; *A* Arbaces; *H* High Priest; *N* Voice of Neptune

1949 Cunitz *I*; Schech *E*; Klarwein *Id*; Riedner *Ida*; Linz *A*; Messerschmidt *H*; Eibel *N* /Bavarian Radio Choir and Orch./Altmann Mercury ⓜ MG 10052-3

1950 Hopf *I*; Grob-Prandl *E*; Taubmann *Id*; Menzel *Ida;* Handt *A*; Majkut *H*; Heiller *N*/Vienna State Opera Chorus, Vienna SO/Von Zallinger Nixa ⓜ HLP 2020

1956 Jurinac *I*; Udovick *E*; Lewis *Id*; Simoneau *Ida*; Milligan *A*; McAlpine *H*; Alan *N*/Glyndebourne Festival Chorus and Orch./Pritchard World Records SOC 201-3; Seraphim SIC 6070

1969 Rinaldi *I*; Tinsley *E*; Shirley *Id*; Davies *Ida*; Tear *A*; Pilley *H*;

Dean *N*/BBC Chorus and SO/C. Davis Philips 6703 024

1973 Rothenberger *I*; Moser *E*; Gedda *Id*; Dallapozza *Ida*; Schreier *A*; Buchner *H*; Adam *N*/Leipzig Radio Chorus, Dresden State Opera/Schmidt-Isserstedt HMV SLS 965

1977 Mathis *I*; Varady *E*; Ochman *Id*; Schreier *Ida*; Winkler *A*; Büchner *H*/Leipzig Radio Choir, Dresden State Orch./Böhm DG 2740 195

Excerpts

1951 Jurinac *I*; MacNeil *E*; Lewis *Id*; Young *Ida*/Glyndebourne Festival Chorus and Orch./Busch HMV DB 21525-9; RCA ⓜ LHMV 1021

LA CLEMENZA DI TITO

T Titus; *V* Vitellia; *Sex* Sextus; *A* Annius; *Ser* Servilia; *P* Publius

1951 Weikenmeier *T*; Nentwig *V*; Plümacher *Sex*; Mangold *A*; Sailer *Ser*; Müller *P*/Swabian Choral Society, Stuttgart Ton-Studio Orch./Lund Period ⓜ PLP 550/1-3

1967 Krenn *T*; Casula *V*; Berganza *Sex*; Fassbaender *A*; Popp *Ser*; Franc *P*/Vienna State Opera Chorus and Orch./Kertesz Decca SET 357-9; London OSA 1387

1976 Burrows *T*; Baker *V*; Minton
    Sex; von Stade *A*; Popp *Ser*;
    Lloyd *P*/Royal Opera Chorus

and Orch./C. Davis
Philips 6703 079 ④ 7699 038

Le nozze di Figaro

WILLIAM MANN

Figaro, the ex-barber of Seville, has been married a good many times on record since 1934, when HMV's Mozart Opera Society took the first steps towards a complete recording, with the cast of Carl Ebert's famous Glyndebourne production of that year. The records were issued in three volumes: six discs devoted to the concerted ensembles, then two more albums, each of five discs, containing the overture, solo arias and duets. This piecemeal assembly left the *secco* recitatives unrecorded; some musical numbers were also omitted. When the 78 set was transferred to LPs, Act 4 was found to begin at Figaro's recitative, 'Tutto è disposto'; without recitatives to connect the set numbers, the LP transfer seriously lacked operatic continuity. In its day the cast was vastly admired; two decades and a bit later, disappointment extended beyond the omissions to the actual singing, most of it dry or inexpert or downright unstylish, Heddle Nash's Basilio an oasis of musicality, even without his aria.

With the arrival of LPs, complete opera recordings (by no means absent from pre-war catalogues) became more practicable and highly desirable. The first LP *Figaro* (1950) was recorded by Columbia in Vienna, then considered the Mecca of Mozartian operatic expertise. Again, by now perversely, all *secco* recitatives were omitted, with an inevitable lack of dramatic effect, compounded by Herbert von Karajan's predominantly hell-for-leather tempi which sacrificed verbal clarity and musicianly phrasing for all-too-false sparkle. Elisabeth Schwarzkopf sings the Countess's two arias to admiration, even 'Dove sono' which goes too fast for comfort. Something of Sena Jurinac's vocal appeal can be caught in Cherubino's arias, again rushed; the set gives a welcome if incomplete memento of Erich Kunz's endearing Figaro. Otherwise it does not bear careful listening today.

The appearance of the Cetra 'Live Opera' set, made at La Scala in 1954, gave hope that Karajan's earlier reading might be justified, together with some members of the cast. The recitatives are here, of course, included and delivered with infectious energy and spontaneity, so that a sense of drama is fully conveyed. Schwarzkopf's Countess, in gloriously full voice, makes a strong impression, particularly in 'Dove sono', and in the letter duet with Seefried, whose Susanna, the best of her three on record, is often sung with the sustained artistry missing in other sets. Jurinac sounds glorious in Cherubino's arias, and Rolando Panerai's Figaro gives pleasure. Mario Petri offers a strong, ripe-voiced Count, handsome in all his music. The Italian supporting cast is acceptable, especially Mariella Adani's Barbarina and Silvio Maionica's Bartolo; the Antonio is the admirable Franco Calabrese. Karajan again rushes his fences, handicapping his singers. The recorded sound is poor.

The 1951 Cetra set derived from an Italian radio broadcast, and compels attention for the number of singers then making their names in Mozart performances at Glyndebourne. It is not a stylish performance, nor comfortably balanced, and there are many cuts including Almaviva's only aria (the more regrettable since Sesto Bruscantini makes a good impression elsewhere, and this rather than Figaro is his proper role); some recitatives are included, by no means enough for dramatic sense. Alda Noni's strong, engaging Susanna (a delight in 'Venite, inginocchiatevi') and Italo Tajo's dark, vivid Figaro repay attention, as does the promise of the Barbarina, Graziella Sciutti, soon to emerge as a starry Mozartian. Fernando Previtali's tempi and orchestral balancing do not suggest much instinct for Mozart.

With the Mozart bicentenary in the offing, 1955 found several record companies at work on *Le nozze di Figaro*. The most valuable, and durable, was the Decca version recorded in Vienna under Erich Kleiber, an early but convincing essay in stereo recording. The distinguished cast, though based on Vienna performances of the time, was not a regular ensemble; yet Kleiber obtained a performance hallmarked with the insignia of integrity and dramatic interplay. Perhaps its greatest virtues are the cantabile Vienna strings and their impeccably phrased, euphonious woodwind, since the Vienna Philharmonic's qualities spill as if automatically into the work of the cast. One may find Lisa Della Casa a dozy, doughy Contessa (she was later to record the part more distinctively), but her 'Dove sono', angelically accompanied, is a delight. Alfred Poell (like Bartolo, a *doctor medicus* as well as a singer, the company's resident ENT specialist) makes a starchy, Teutonic Almaviva, but how dramatically vivid and personable. Suzanne Danco does not at all suggest the impetuous pageboy, but sings neatly and sweetly. Hilde Gueden is a delicious and energetic Susanna, adept in recitative, a central focus in ensemble, completely involved in the intrigue; so strong a vocal personality should not have been given Marcellina's aria (25) which belongs to another age-group and type of voice. Cesare Siepi has the ideal quality of bass voice, and the vocal artistry for a lively, dangerous Figaro; as early as 3, 'Se vuol ballare', we infer as much amusement as rage behind his strategy. His guttural Italian pronunciation is, as always, a musical liability redeemed here by his musicianship and intelligence. This Decca set (still in the catalogues in 1979, newly and impressively transferred to cassette) includes every musical number and all the recitative (skilfully diversified in pace), but accepts two of the customary cuts in 'Aprite presto' (15). It remains Kleiber's set, spacious but not laggard, lively yet loving, musical and dramatic at once.

The HMV set of 1955, conducted by Vittorio Gui, derived from the Glyndebourne performances of that year and subsequently (since the mischievous, vocally expert Susanna, Graziella Sciutti, did not join the production on stage until 1958). Gui had imported other compatriots for the cast: a noble, fiery Almaviva, imperfectly sung by Calabrese; Bruscantini's jolly, too baritonal Figaro. Bruscantini's then wife, Sena Jurinac, sang her first Countess, lovely in poise and darkling vocal quality, still searching for complete identification. Hugues Cuénod's unparalleled Basilio is splendidly represented, complete with a brilliant characterization of his aria 26. Risë Stevens sounds chesty and careless as Cherubino (she had sung the part at Glyndebourne as early as 1939). The set has piquancy and the allure of warm, romantic lighting, but lacks a consistent approach, and the emotive force which can only follow such a steady vision. The voices are too forwardly recorded for conviction, though the acoustic has the appropriate Glyndebourne intimacy.

Figaro was also recorded live at the Aix-en-Provence festival that year. The Vox sound is hard, acid, insubstantial, Hans Rosbaud's interpretation unyielding and scarcely felt, as if tight-lipped, like the piano accompaniment of the recitatives. The cast is idiosyncratic: best are Pilar Lorengar's delicious young Cherubino, Cuénod's forthcoming Basilio, and Rolando Panerai's vibrant, active Figaro, though in ensembles his baritonal quality matches ill with Heinz Rehfuss's grainy, sable-voiced Count (the music tells us that Figaro must be an assertive bass, Almaviva an elegant baritone). Teresa Stich-Randall, the Countess, had a soprano of vulnerable beauty and flexibility, but neither aria is successfully sung, though there is tenderness in 'Porgi amor'; she is preferable in ensemble. Rita Streich is a pretty Susanna, superficial and sugary, not the dynamic force of the action (this performance does not have one).

Philips's *Figaro* had great merits: the cast was typical of Vienna at its best, moulded together by Karl Böhm who was just then beginning to emerge as a Mozart conductor of exceptional perspicacity. The musical text is Teutonically accented for the most part. But the tempi are sagely judged, never rushed (sometimes the drama is allowed to slacken inadvisedly). Walter Berry's Figaro is a true *basso cantante* with an easy upper extension; Streich's Susanna is far more alert than in the Vox set; Jurinac's Countess has found full bloom within a few months – cool, peachlike femininity with a hinted tear in 'Porgi amor', superb *sostenuto* in 'Dove sono'; the Cherubino of young Christa Ludwig is already memorable. Paul Schöffler makes an elderly Almaviva, still sinister and proud, though Figaro must have suited him better. The recording has a nicely theatrical acoustic.

In 1959 RCA undertook a new recording, also made in Vienna, conducted by Erich Leinsdorf with a fundamentally Metropolitan cast. It was as complete as the Kleiber (all recitatives and arias, but 'Aprite presto', abbreviated, a few bars more so than Kleiber's). Leinsdorf's reading is scrupulous and attentive, smartly paced for gaiety, uneventful in reflective or radiant music. He takes 'Dove sono' faster than Böhm, but makes it sound almost somnolent; the second-act finale, well-paced, appears less than its brilliant self, not more than bright and busy. The shorter finale to Act 4, on the other hand, goes well. Recitatives are apt to drag perhaps because, in the absence of real musical insight, the cast felt obliged to underline eventfulness and comedy by exaggeration. Hence Susanna's mimicry of the Count as she locks herself into the cupboard, and the Countess's mimicry of Susanna when they are disguised (worthwhile and welcome touches), but also Marcellina's deliberately ugly vocalism for comic effect (like the duettists in 'Amanti costanti'), and Bartolo's assumption of the final, ridiculous 'Io' after the sextet, or Figaro's heavy, quasi-myopic enunciation of words. Both Giorgio Tozzi (Figaro) and George London (Almaviva) overload their roles in this way. Della Casa (Countess), sometimes over-effortful likewise, does contribute much lovely singing (for example, in 'Porgi amor'). Roberta Peters offers a spirited, truly sung Susanna, Rosalind Elias a dark-toned, vivid Cherubino, Gabor Carelli's reptilian Basilio is a positive success. The stereo illusion of spectacle is skilfully used in this recording.

By 1959 it was high time for EMI to replace its fragmentary *Figaro* under Karajan with something more complete and modern in sound. As with the *Don Giovanni* recording of a few months earlier, Carlo Maria Giulini was the conductor, and the cast was led by Schwarzkopf (Countess), Eberhard Wächter (Almaviva) and Giuseppe Taddei (Figaro), with an Italian supporting cast, and an Italo-American Susanna, Anna Moffo: Walter Legge (the producer of both sets) was evidently determined that in his new *Figaro*, at least, da Ponte's text would be correctly enunciated and relished – Teutonic Italian had been a drawback of too many previous *Figaro* recordings. It was not the cast of a particular stage production, but part of an attempt by Legge to build a 'house ensemble' of international singers who worked regularly together in the recording studio.

The performance has an individual and consistent sound quality, smooth, darkly translucent, precise and refined: tempo and balance are attuned to this approach, and while Giulini attends lovingly to orchestral detail it is not allowed to distract prime attention from the vocal music, including the words. Dramatic continuity is carefully served by lively recitatives, which are seldom too fast for comfortable intelligibility, and flowing tempi in set numbers, which arise naturally from the context and suggest a mean of quick-witted consideration between the extremes of empty farce and sober reverence. The comedy is happily served by Moffo and Taddei who excel in their recitatives, yet have beautiful voices and natural artistry to bring to solos and duets. Schwarzkopf is here at once the noblest and the most vivacious of the Countesses under consideration in this chapter; 'Dove sono', taken fast, contrives to sound perfectly expressive and in character. Wächter's firm, strong, high baritone suits Almaviva well until moments of rage when the voice blusters unmusically and a German accent creeps into the Italian. Fiorenza Cossotto's Cherubino smoulders impulsively to great purpose in 'Non so più'. Among the smaller parts, each skilfully taken, Piero Cappuccilli's Antonio gives special pleasure. In the fourth act we miss the arias for Marcellina and Basilio, but may particularly enjoy the stereo reflection of the drama's comings and goings.

Deutsche Grammophon first entered the *Figaro* stakes in 1960 with a West Berlin Radio interpretation (though if the cast had any local bias it was to Munich rather than Berlin). Many of Ferenc Fricsay's records testify to his exceptional musicianship; this *Figaro* is not one of them. The ensembles cohere well, there are sensitive orchestral touches (for instance, the prominent flutes in the Count-Susanna duet), but for a comic opera it moves unfluently, even in quick music as in the second-act *terzetto*). As with the Leinsdorf set the cast exaggerates every comic touch (this time doubtless for non-Italian-speaking Germans, as well as their transatlantic counterparts); even the characterizations of Susanna, Figaro and Almaviva suffer from near-caricature. Fischer-Dieskau's first Almaviva has few of the virtues associated with his later interpretations of the role, and far more of the faults (shouting, quasi-parlando, over-emphasis) that typified his early operatic work. Seefried here nudges Susanna's every phrase and sentiment unmercifully, and when her chance comes to sing really beautifully, in the Letter Duet and 'Deh vieni', she misses the boat. She is at her best in the exit from the cupboard and in the sextet. Renato Capecchi was a fine Figaro, as his dark, resilient bass quality here suggests, though his burlesque treatment of his fourth-act aria, and self-indulgent comic inflexion of recitatives, do his artistry less than justice. Maria Stader is miscast as the Countess, who here appears frigid and doll-like. Herta Töpper's Cherubino, by contrast, sounds all too warm and womanly.

Electrola, the German branch of HMV, is so far the only company to have recorded a complete *Figaro* in the vernacular, thus gratifying the many families in German-speaking countries who have known *Figaros Hochzeit* since childhood and would find *Le nozze di Figaro* unfamiliar, perhaps unattractive, if it were so performed in their local opera house (opera in the original language is a recent development in even the largest German cities). Dresden was the venue, and the recording has the reverberant acoustic, reminiscent of an indoor public swimming-bath, so often heard on records from the other side of the Iron Curtain. The cast is of international standing, as is Otmar Suitner who conducts the magnificent Dresden State Orchestra in a spruce, appreciative reading, occasionally too fast for comfort, as in the duet 'Aprite presto' and Antonio's interruption of the second-act finale. Several of the singers have taken part in other *Figaro* recordings, not always in the same role. Gueden is as lovely a Countess as, formerly, a Susanna – the edge of her creamy voice by no means disturbing, though a trace of unsteadiness appears here when she presses her tone. Hermann Prey (see below) is nowadays usually cast as Figaro, but his baritone voice with its honeyed elegance and range of colour seems more completely suited to the part of Almaviva (see also Electrola 60627 below). Anneliese Rothenberger's Susanna is welcome on disc; she and Berry make a cosy, uncontroversial pair of sweethearts, closer to romantic *Singspiel* or operette than to Mozart – and this remains the ultimate impression left by the set, with the sweet, light-on-the-breath Cherubino of Edith Mathis, Fritz Ollendorf's jolly, grainy Bartolo, and Peter Schreier's thornless, charming Basilio. The standard German text overburdens Mozart's vocal lines with dipthongs; does it also remove the sting from the opera, or did Suitner, or is that East German policy? This *Figaro* entertains without challenging the intelligence. There is no aria for Anneliese Burmeister's Marcellina nor one for Schreier. There is an infelicitous side-break (three-four) in the middle of the second-act finale.

Böhm recorded the opera for the third time (including Preiser's transcript of a 1938 Stockholm broadcast, which I have not heard) in 1967 with forces from the Deutsche Oper in West Berlin. As so often nowadays, one could find the same principals at a *Figaro* in San Francisco, London, Paris or Salzburg, so that only the Barbarina and other small parts declare the performance's origin, though here one might guess Germany from the slack Italian pronunciation of the leading singers – even Fischer-Dieskau, who usually cares about language. This time Böhm conducted the opera in full, including the fourth-act arias (but making the standard cuts in 'Aprite presto'). His reading is characteristic, excellent in attack and light, well-detailed texture, less insistent on the singers' accuracy about note-values or consistent attitude to vocal gracing. His judgement of tempi has the soundness of great experience; seldom (except, for example, in the last section of 'Dove sono' and in Susanna's exit from the cupboard) does he let a tempo run without giving positive musical proof to back that judgement.

The cast may suggest type-casting at top level – Prey's jocular, honeyed Figaro, Mathis's silvery, vivacious Susanna, Fischer-Dieskau's wheedling, ranting Count (here in freshest vocal condition, the singer's foibles least in evidence), Tatiana Troyanos as an impassioned Cherubino, let down by too heavy a vibrato (but steady in pitch). The surprise is Gundula Janowitz's Countess who, after a typically exquisite 'Porgi amor' without an intelligible consonant to its name, provides a characterization of extraordinary spirit and acumen, such as only Schwarzkopf has shown on records – and Janowitz's voice has the greater intrinsic beauty of sound.

It is Janowitz as much as Böhm who keeps the two grand finales at their necessary levels of high tension. Patricia Johnson's bright-voiced, spirited Marcellina properly finds its reward in 'Il capro e la capretta', rather than in tardy marriage to the clumsy though ripe Bartolo of Peter Lagger. This *Le nozze di Figaro* is perhaps for casual listening to glorious music superbly performed, with vivid stereo recording suggestive of action on stage, rather than for those much concerned with what happens on that stage.

The next *Figaro* set, conducted by Colin Davis for Philips in 1970, took a far more challenging attitude to the work, nowhere near so beautiful except incidentally, but closely concerned with drama and the ability of music to delve into human emotions, and to express several truths simultaneously. Davis had not yet assumed musical directorship at Covent Garden, and his cast was internationally picked (down to the smallest roles given to British singers of unusual accomplishment) for, one may deduce, a particular dramatic ambience, a conflict of temperaments. Erik Smith's recorded production makes much use of stereo to distance and separate the actors or to pull them forward with claustrophobic effect. The result is sometimes unnerving, and one may not wish to listen often to the whole; but other interpretations of *Le nozze di Figaro* do often send the listener back to Davis for confirmation of some reaction, or for a complete contrast of approach. Davis's recording adopts the sensible Raeburn–Moberly reordering of Act 3 where 'Dove sono', preceded by the dialogue for Barbarina and Cherubino, follows the Count's aria and precedes the sextet. There are convincing grounds for belief that this was the order intended by the authors, who were obliged to change it because the same singer doubled the roles of Bartolo and Antonio. This recording also includes the fourth-act arias, 25 and 26, and, alone among existing sets, performs the duet, 15, absolutely complete as in the New Mozart Edition (whose numbering is here followed throughout).

Some productions of *Le nozze di Figaro* so emphasize the grandeur of Count and Countess Almaviva as to mask the dramatically prime importance of Figaro and, especially, Susanna. The sets discussed here do not make that mistake, the Davis least of all. There remains never a doubt that the protagonist is the Susanna of Mirella Freni, enchanting, wholly natural, anxious, determined, sociable, sometimes near to despair but never at a loss. Her arias are sung beautifully, always with particular attention to situation and content, the ambivalent 'Deh vieni' most illuminating of all; in the fourth-act finale she always remembers to alter her tone when impersonating the Countess, until the one time when Figaro has to recognize the deception. In ensemble she is a neat but positive match for her partners: Wladimiro Ganzarolli's burly, edgy-to-dangerous Figaro is no twinkle-toed Harlequin and perhaps less *soigné* than Beaumarchais's Barber of Seville, but a man capable of smiles and sociability, who enjoys 'Non più andrai' as much as 'Aprite un po' and does not exaggerate either; then her mistress, Jessye Norman, whose spacious soprano conveys dignity, youth and social tension (Rosina was not born to aristocracy), and who refuses to suggest self-pity in either of her arias, indeed makes a point of the Countess's sense of humour as her salvation at all times.

Freni plays up, vocally and in character, to Ingvar Wixell's strong, sardonic Almaviva (the vibrato too broad, the basic vocal quality too thick for my taste), and to Maria Casula's nicely unexaggerated Marcellina. The Cherubino is Yvonne Minton, accomplished in her solos, her characterization somewhat flat. Robert Tear's Basilio radiates the unseen stage whenever he is there. Clifford Grant is the splendid Bartolo, Lillian Watson (nowadays a spry Susanna) a positive and musical Barbarina. Behind them all is the unifying power of Davis's fanatical devotion to the spirit and, if possible, the letter of Mozart's score. The performance is not perfect, but those who listen attentively in a right frame of mind, will have little more time for 'delightful' Mozart.

A year later came HMV's recording under Otto Klemperer, a living legend among great conductors, disciple of Mahler (who renovated the performance of Mozart in his day), and later in the 1920s an evangelist of new music and provocative thought. By 1970 he was an old man, relic of a more leisurely age, and as a Mozartian he was out of fashion, too German, too heavy for our age of express trains, jumbo-jet aircraft and satellite communication. Mozart also belonged to that age, not ours: there may, accordingly, be virtue in Klemperer's approach to *Le nozze di Figaro*.

HMV gave him a vividly separated and distanced stereo production; always we are in a theatre. Klemperer's tempi are measured, deliberate. At first they sound deplorably heavy, dragging the music into the ground. After repeated listening, one recognizes the real humour and human sensibility conveyed by Klemperer's approach. As with Giulini's, it allows words and musical phrases and changes of situation to be savoured. The vivacity of Figaro and Susanna is not sacrificed. Klemperer's approach even enhances the qualities of Geraint Evans's Figaro, a classic portrayal of the third quarter of this century: it gives him time to mould phrases, make particular points, air a beautiful note somewhere in his capacious voice (the ideal *basso cantante* whose upper extension Evans sometimes used for baritone parts, not always judiciously) and sustain tone firmly. His performance is exemplary, nicely matched with the volatile Susanna of Reri Grist, a lovely performance, tender yet tirelessly active, ideal in response to the great demands of 'Deh vieni', realistic as well as charming in 'Venite, inginocchiatevi', and in 17, her duet with the Count, diversely expressive in the sextet – of all Susannas the one who best suggests the heroine trying always to find the other end of a dark and dangerous tunnel.

Elisabeth Söderström is the Countess, stirring to hear, vulnerable as

'Dove sono' shows, sometimes dubious about the outcome, almost overwhelmed in the second-act finale: a true and human, musically uncompromising response. Almaviva is Gabriel Bacquier, fearsome in rage, honeyed in pursuit of womankind, uncertainly responsive to emotions in between, always as attentive to Da Ponte as to Mozart. Teresa Berganza's Cherubino is charming, less pointful than in the Barenboim set discussed below. Anneliese Burmeister makes much of Marcellina with her vicious, coy, solicitous portrayal, but is too alto in voice to manage the aria in Act 4, we suppose. Werner Hollweg, a honeyed and dozy Basilio, is given his aria but makes little of it. The Antonio, shaky in note-values, alluring in tone, is Clifford Grant (as for Davis), the compelling, gorgeous-voiced Barbarina Margaret Price (soon to be Klemperer's Fiordiligi, nowadays an admired Countess Almaviva). Michael Langdon is as distinctive a Bartolo as any on record, euphonious and full of character.

In 1976 came HMV's recording of the Edinburgh Festival's *ad hoc* production conducted with unexpected skill and sensibility by Daniel Barenboim. It has immense spirit, much style (short on the necessary graces expected by Mozart, forgotten mostly in our day), and a real feeling of theatrical performance which reflects its origin in regular performances during two festivals. Evans and Fischer-Dieskau are vocally less cogent than in their previous recordings, but have new subtleties to convey in their parts. Berganza has refined and enlivened her Cherubino to near-perfection. Heather Harper (see below) contributes an immaculate, poignantly human Countess, Judith Blegen a pleasantly shallow Susanna. Birgit Finnilä's Marcellina is hammed, sounding almost like a male drag artist, though less offensively so in the sextet. There is a charming Barbarina, a delightful Bartolo, and a comic, sarcastic Basilio (John Fryatt) who makes much of 'In quegli anni'. It is a worthwhile, sometimes memorable set, very musical.

Decca's most recent *Figaro* was recorded in Vienna with a cast assembled from those who have appeared in Ponnelle's Salzburg Festival production under Karajan in recent years. There are some handsome individual performances here, notably and predictably Ileana Cotrubas's Susanna, Frederica von Stade's Cherubino, Jane Berbié's spirited Marcellina, Heinz Zednik's gorgeously cynical Basilio (these last two are deservedly given their Act 4 arias), and José van Dam's virile, mercurial Figaro, a grand piece of singing. Anna Tomova-Sintov should have been an ideal Countess, with her golden tone and range of mood (gaiety, regret, resentment), but the voice is seldom perfectly steady and sometimes distinctly flat; nevertheless, the Letter Duet goes delightfully, and there are admirable things in her account of 'Dove sono'. Likewise Tom Krause's Almaviva, aptly menacing and libidinous, is ill-focused in pitch. Both Almavivas, sometimes others in the cast, lose grip of the music's note-values and pulse, so that ensemble goes awry.

Karajan may be to blame. His approach to *Figaro* has significantly mellowed since the two hectic recordings discussed above. Tempi are sedate now, kinder to words and vocal articulation, and to the mastery of the VPO (whose bass-line often sounds excessively heavy). One may however notice Karajan in several numbers smoothing the pulse so that the ear is uncertain which beat of the bar has been reached. Another feature of his reading is a predilection for light-breathed, *sotto voce* delivery, not only in intimate conversation, but in public dialogue such as the formal recitative exchanges between Figaro and Almaviva after No. 8, in the sextet No. 17 (much of whose heavenly detail is evened into seamless euphony) and in the choruses whose melodic line wilts: we are not far from the bad old Viennese style of crooning Mozart instead of singing out properly. Mercifully this cast is willing to sing up, though some roles are marred by ugly comic voices (Jules Bastin, Zoltan Kelemen, and Kurt Equiluz, all estimable artists, suffer thereby), and it must be insisted that much of Karajan's contribution is apt and masterly, notably the Wedding March and subsequent Fandango and, vitally, most of the big finales to the second and fourth acts.

He adopts the Raeburn-Moberly order for Act 3 (Christopher Raeburn produced the records), but prefers the shorter, traditional, No. 15 duet, and cuts a few bars from the recitative after No. 25. Raeburn's recorded production includes much significant stage movement and relevant sound effects; the intrigue of the final garden scene benefits here from careful placing and distancing of the several characters on stage.

Since the advent of LPs various record companies have issued single records of highlights from the opera. Some are taken from the more or less complete sets discussed above. Others were made expressly. The Electrola ten-inch disc of highlights, a mish-mash if ever there was one, commemorates Elisabeth Grümmer's creamy-toned, sensuous Countess, Erna Berger's sweetly girlish Susanna, Karl Kohn's grainy, adept Figaro, Gottlob Frick fully relishing Bartolo's Vengeance Aria, and Erika Köth, gentle, breathy, snared by consonants, as Cherubino – all in German, variously conducted. As part of a Decca 'Mozart Opera Festival' (SET 548-9), Istvan Kertesz conducted the Vienna Haydn Orchestra, an expert and stylish body, in five numbers from *Le nozze di Figaro*, recorded with a bright, lively sound. The selection is curious: first comes the trio, 'Cosa sento', a fiery account with Lucia Popp, Werner Krenn, and Tom Krause, vocally well-matched; Krause then changes role from Almaviva to Figaro for 'Non più andrai', lively again, the singer's voice not in perfect focus. Now Brigitte Fassbaender sings Cherubino's first aria sensitively, with a dark, alto-orientated timbre, to a bass-heavy accompaniment. Popp and Krause then give a decent account of 'Crudel, perche finora', and Lucia Popp concludes with 'Deh vieni', sensitively phrased at a leisurely pace, with lovely orchestral partnership. She must be a likely candidate for Susanna in a future *Figaro* set.

An Acanta album devoted to the long career of Paul Schöffler (DE 22694) includes mementos of his German Figaro in 1938 as well as his 1943 Almaviva. With Maria Cebotari as Susanna (in 1947 Londoners heard them as the Almavivas) he sings the first two duets – she a touch wobbly, he young and spirited – including the intervening recitative (with pianoforte accompaniment), then the link into his 'Se vuòl ballare' which shows off Schöffler's radiant upper register and command of verbal inflexion. There is also his fourth-act aria, with preceding recitative, an even more compelling demonstration of Schöffler's masterly phrasing and vocal colouration, which makes one long to hear the Historia recording mentioned above. His 1943 rendering of Almaviva's aria, with the Dresden orchestra under Kurt Striegler, shows a suaver vocal quality and a less tidy technique (for its other contents too this is an album worth having).

A Concert Hall record of highlights, sung in Italian, played by the Vienna Opera Orchestra under Heinz Wallberg, is of interest for an early account by Heather Harper of the Countess's two arias and the Letter Duet, slightly edgy at the top but already well in character. As Figaro, Heinz Holecek deals heartily with 'Se a caso madama' and his three arias, a firm and agreeably dark bass. The Susanna, Oliviera Miljakovic sounds unready for the part, though she has a brave try at 'Deh vieni'. She has not the smooth line for the duet, where her Almaviva is Rudolf Jedlicka, coarse but, in the Count's aria, decidedly promising. Rohangiz Yachmi sings Cherubino's two arias on this disc; too heavily, with a nasty edge in the upper register.

Other LP records of highlights are listed in the discography but are not worth dwelling on, especially since the 78 discography is so rich, and must here be discussed very selectively. No. 2, 'Se a caso Madama', was recorded by Elisabeth Rethberg and Ezio Pinza, together with 17 (in which Pinza switches to Almaviva), a promising partnership (DA 1950), but disappointing since she sounds too matronly for Susanna's music, he too saturnine for Figaro's. Pinza twice recorded Figaro's 'Se vuol ballare' (3), softly and confidentially, with great relish; the neater of the two is the CBS (S 30088). Giuseppe Campanari's 1909 version of both arias on Columbia Tricolour is vivid and steady, a fine voice. Wilhelm Hesch in 1905 (3-42396; CO 300) sang it in German with piano, stiffly but with a strong bass register and smooth, resinous tone. Richard Mayr, also in German (Poly. 62390; LV 1), uses a comic, unfamiliar translation which he inflects ripely, with true comedy. Giuseppe de Luca recorded Figaro's arias twice: the 1907 version of 3 with piano (Fono. 39942; Saga XIG 8006) reveals the grainy yet well-oiled baritone timbre, strongly resonant, the tempo brisk though *meno mosso* at 'L'arte schermendo', which is supposed to go faster, indeed *presto*; de Luca even sings in the orchestral coda! In 1950, aged 73, again with piano, his low register and breath were beginning to show weakness, but otherwise the control and spirit are amazing (Cont. CLP 1003). Gerhard Hüsch recorded warm, elegant versions of this and 10 (Parlo. R 1122). There is a good modern version by Fernando Corena (Decca LX 3095).

Bartolo's Vengeance Aria (4) was recorded by Salvatore Baccaloni (Am. Col. 71193D; Odyssey Y 31736) ripely, less vividly than expected. A famous version is by Alexander Kipnis in German, with its preceding recitative involving Elsa Ruziczkova, dating from 1931, he dark and honeyed in tone, lively in word-painting and patter, most attractive (DB 1551; WR SH 280, LV 5). Cherubino's 'Non so più' (6) receives an exceptionally marvellous performance from Söderström (4E 061 34788), fast, the words tripping easily off the tongue, but smooth and in perfect character, with appreciative graces and flourishes such as one seldom hears nowadays. Galli-Curci's even more rapid performance (DA 214; GVC 22) brims over with effervescence, almost like a popular song, with a solid oompah accompaniment, plenty of appoggiaturas and gratuitous top B flat at the end. Lola Artôt de Padilla, in both Cherubino's arias, is a good representative of the old school, secure yet lively (2–43461-2; CO 372). Elisabeth Schumann's reading (DA 844; COLH 104) remains a classic, deliciously modulated. Frederica von Stade, on stage a lovely Cherubino, has twice recorded 6: on CBS 9500 098 the music is exquisitely nuanced, the mood urgent; CBS 76476 gives Mozart's own transcription for voice and piano with obbligato violin, an engaging curiosity (the manuscript is in the Library of Congress).

Figaro's 'Non più andrai' (10): Sir Charles Santley's 1903 version with piano accompaniment (052000; Rococo 5204) is among the rarest of all records in its original form. It begins with the preceding recitative and is sung with vibrant quality and many appoggiaturas and graces, including a dashing cadenza before the last reprise. Mario Battistini (DB 736) sings it carelessly, but the radiance of voice and supreme cheerfulness of the interpretation are hard to resist. Mario Sammarco (2-052042) displays his light, handsome baritone to admiration but is let down by slovenly intonation; like others mentioned here, he would have been more aptly cast as Almaviva, but the Count has only one solo to Figaro's three! Mayr was a real bass, but his version (Poly. 62390; LV 1) is less distinctive than that of 3. Mariano Stabile (L 2185) sings with the vibrant vivacity and lightness of touch that endeared him to opera-goers well into the 1950s; he slows the pace, at each reprise, for 'delle belle turbando il riposo'. More modern versions include Tito Gobbi, amusing, incisive, fluent and youthful (DA 1946; HLM 7018); Erich Kunz, all charm and *brio* (LX 1123); Pinza (RCA RB 16040), ripe in voice, vivacious in lilt, relishing the text. De Luca's 1950 performance is a charming curiosity; this was his only recording of the aria. Dennis Noble does his bit for the English School (C 3304).

In 'Porgi amor' (11) it must once have been a recognized tradition that the second half, from bar 36 after the rise to A flat above the stave, should be sung *meno mosso*: Melba, Destinn, Rethberg and Lotte

Lehmann all do this, but not Lilli Lehmann, whose 1907 recording in German is the most celebrated of all (Parlo. PO 63; CO 384-5), though she does take her last two lines more slowly. At 59 her vocal quality was astonishingly pure and free, the interpretation dignified, touching, exquisitely graced. Destinn, also in German (Od. 50153), is more substantial in tone, musically almost as beautiful. Melba recorded a short-breathed but tonally admirable account (VB 40; HLM 7084). Rethberg recorded it twice: the 1930 version (Parlo. RO 20115; LV 29) in German has a magical diminuendo in the ascent to that A flat, and a lovely portamento in the last phrase; as in all the above, the introduction is shortened. The later version in Italian (HMV EC 103) is also notable for fine vocal quality with the characteristic Rethberg flutter at the top. Lotte Lehmann's recording in German (Parlo. R 20054; LV 22) is superbly phrased and inflected, that individual timbre at its most appealing, though some appoggiaturas are missed. There is also an earlier, acoustic version by her (Poly. 76414; LV 180). Interesting but less persuasive are the versions by Tiana Lemnitz (DB 3462; LV 101), the young Victoria de los Angeles (DB 6994), and Maria Callas (SAX 2540).

There was also a conventional way of singing Cherubino's 'Voi che sapete' (12) with a gear-change into chest register at 'l'alma avvampar', then an *accelerando* for 'sospiro e gemo' and a heavy *ritenuto* at 'ma pur mi piace' and a pronounced portamento into the reprise of the first verse. Adelina Patti's version with piano accompaniment is particularly famous (03051; HLM 7034) but is unconventional in the many alterations of note-values and even notes – the last line varied to touch a top G – and in its phrase-chopping to permit extra breaths. Melba (DB 367; CSLP 516), in somewhat nasal voice, also adds the high G. Emma Calvé, singing in French when she was 61 (Pathé 0288; GV 57), altered the last line, took the arietta particularly slowly and lingered often, making the slowest portamento of all into the last verse. For beauty of line and phrasing, and intensity of expression, Schumann is unbeatable (DB 946; COLH 154), or in her earlier acoustic versions of this and 6 (Poly. 65654; LV 186) in German, though there are admirable modern recordings by Margaret Price (SER 5675) and von Stade (Philips 9500 098). Schumann also made a delectable record of Susanna's 'Venite, inginocchiatevi' (DA 844; COLH 154).

In the Susanna–Almaviva duet 'Crudel, perche finora' (17), Geraldine Farrar sounds coarsely matched to Antonio Scotti, in superb form (DK 118; Saga XIG 8006); Lotte Lehmann and Heinrich Schlusnus portray the situation perfectly (Poly. 72933), though she draws surprisingly little humour from the 'Ja–Nein' episode (they sing in German).

Almaviva's aria (18) exists in a later, more high-lying version (perhaps made by Mozart for his second Vienna count, Albertarelli) which Fischer-Dieskau has recorded magnificently (SXL 6490). In the Countess's 'Dove sono' (20), Destinn (043096; CO 307) may seem shrill but her flexible, expressive interpretation commands admiration. Claire Dux (043292; LV 84) is both spirited and touching. There is a poised, sympathetic and glowing performance by Lemnitz (DB 3462; LV 101), a golden-voiced, slightly romantic one by Cebotari (DA 1875; 1C 147-29 118) and one in English by Joan Cross. (C 3187), which deserves modern currency for its exemplary nuance and inflection and the stunning brilliance of the faster concluding section. In the early years of this century Emma Eames and Marcella Sembrich were famous for their singing of the Letter Duet, and they recorded it (DK 121; Rococo R 29); the vocal matching and diversification are most expert and artistic, but not finer than Lilli Lehmann and Hedwig Helbig achieved in German on their record (Od. 50357; CO 384-5), which includes some desirable graces omitted by the American ladies even in 1909 when that convention was still normally observed. Perhaps Mahler had talked them out of appoggiaturas.

'Aprite un po quegli occhi' (27) again reminds us that Mozart's Figaro was only recently regarded as a dangerous upstart, then merely a wily, jovial fellow. So the most disturbed aria is interpreted by de Luca twice, in 1905 (Fono. 39941) and in 1950, and by Stabile, charming and far from irate (DQ 701). Young Gobbi makes more of the situation, while remaining debonair of voice (DA 1946; RLS 738). Finally, of Susanna's 'Deh vieni' (28) mention must be made of versions by Selma Kurz in German (DB 909; LV 10), light and flirtatious in tone, yet perfectly smooth, with all desirable graces including trills at 'qui ridono i fioretti'; by Lotte Lehmann (Parlo. PO 158) in German, smooth and graceful, vinous in timbre as is her acoustic version (Poly. 674773; LV 180); by Schumann, radiant and demure in both her Italian (DB 1011; COLH 154) and German (Poly. 65811; LV 186) versions; by the young Seefried, her loveliest record (LX 1145); and more recently by Ileana Cotrubas, secure, sensuously confidential, irresistible (CBS 76521).

LE NOZZE DI FIGARO

A Count Almaviva; *C* Countess Almaviva; *S* Susanna; *F* Figaro; *Ch* Cherubino; *M* Marcellina; *Bas* Basilio; *Bar* Bartolo; *Barb* Barbarina

1934 (omits recitatives) Henderson *A*; Rautawaara *C*; Mildmay *S*; Domgraf-Fassbaender *F*; Helletsgrüber *Ch*; Willis *M*; Nash *Bas*; Tajo, Allin *Bar*; Radford *Barb*/1934 Glyndebourne Festival Chorus and Orch./Busch CfP ⓜ CFP117-8; Turnabout ⓜ THS 65081-3

1938 (Radio Stuttgart broadcast, in German) Ahlersmayer *A*; Teschemacher *C*; Cebotari *S*; Schöffler *F*; Kolniak *Ch*; Waldenau *M*; Vessely *Bas*; Böhme *Bar*; Frank *Barb*/Stuttgart Radio Chorus and Orch./Böhm Preiser ⓜ HF 1-3

1950 (omits recitatives) London *A*; Schwarzkopf *C*; Seefried *S*; Kunz *F*; Jurinac *Ch*; Höngen *M*; Majkut *Bas*; Rus *Bar*; Schwaiger *Barb*/Vienna State Opera Chorus, VPO-Karajan EMI ⓜ 1C147 01751-3M; CBS (US) ⓜ SL 114

1951 Bruscantini *A*; Gatti *C*; Noni *S*;
Tajo *F*; Gardino *Ch*; Truccato-
Pace *M*; Mercuriali *Bas*; Corena
Bar; Sciutti *Barb*/Milan Radio
Chorus and Orch./Previtali
Cetra © LPS 3219
1952 (in German) Anonymous artists,
Leipzig State Opera Chorus and
Orch./von Herten
Royale ⓜ 1502-4
1953 (live performance, Salzburg
Festival) Schöffler *A*;
Schwarzkopf *C*; Seefried *S*;
Kunz *F*; Gueden *Ch*; S. Wagner
M; Klein *Bas*; Koréh *Bar*; Maikl
Barb/Vienna State Opera
Chorus, VPO/Furtwängler
Cetra ⓜ L08/3
1954 (live performance, La Scala,
Milan) Petri *A*; Schwarzkopf *C*;
Seefried *S*; Panerai *F*; Jurinac
Ch; Villa *M*; Pirino *Bas*;
Maionica *Bar*; Adani *Barb*/La
Scala Chorus and Orch./Karajan
Cetra ⓜ LO70-3
1955 Poell *A*; Della Casa *C*; Gueden
S; Siepi *F*; Danco *Ch*; Rössl-
Majdan *M*; M. Dickie *Bas*;
Corena *Bar*; Felbermayer
Barb/Vienna State Opera
Chorus, VPO/E. Kleiber
Decca GOS 585-7 ④K79K32;
London OSA 1402
1955 Calabrese *A*; Jurinac *C*; Sciutti
S; Bruscantini *F*; Stevens *Ch*;
M. Sinclair *M*; Cuénod *Bas*;
Wallace *Bar*; J. Sinclair
Barb/1955 Glyndebourne Festival
Chorus and Orch./Gui
World Records SOX 168-71;
Victor ⓜ LM 6401
1955 Rehfuss *A*; Stich-Randall *C*;
Streich *S*; Panerai *F*; Lorengar
Ch; Gayraud *M*; Cuénod *Bas*;
Cortis *Bar*; Ignal *Barb*/1955 Aix-
en-Provence Festival Chorus,
Paris Conservatoire
Orch./Rosbaud
Vox ⓜ OPBX 1653
1956 Schöffler *A*; Jurinac *C*; Streich
S; Berry *F*; Ludwig *Ch*;
Malaniuk *M*; Majkut *Bas*;
Czerwenka *Bar*/Vienna State
Opera Chorus, Vienna SO/Böhm

Philips 6707 006
1959 London *A*; Della Casa *C*; Peters
S; Tozzi *F*; Elias *Ch*; Warfield
M; Carelli *Bas*; Corena *Bar*;
Felbermayer *Barb*/Vienna State
Opera Chorus, VPO/Leinsdorf
Decca ECS 743-5; RCA (US)
LSC 6408
1959 Wächter *A*; Schwarzkopf *C*;
Moffo *S*; Taddei *F*; Cossotto
Ch; Gatta *M*; Ercolani *Bas*;
Vinco *Bar*; Fusco
Barb/Philharmonia Chorus and
Orch./Giulini
HMV SLS 5152 ④ TC-SLS
5152; Angel SDL 3608
1960 Fischer-Dieskau *A*; Stader *C*;
Seefried *S*; Capecchi *F*; Töpper
Ch; Benningsen *M*; Kuen *Bas*;
Sardi *Bar*; Schwaiger
Barb/Berlin RIAS Chorus, Berlin
Radio SO/Fricsay
DG 2728 004
1964 (in German) Prey *A*; Gueden *C*;
Rothenberger *S*; Berry *F*;
Mathis *Ch*; Burmeister *M*;
Schreier *Bas*; Ollendorf *Bar*;
Rönisch *Barb*/Dresden State
Opera Chorus, Dresden State
Orch./Suitner
Seraphim SIC 6002; EMI 1C 183
30159-61
1967 Fischer-Dieskau *A*; Janowitz *C*;
Mathis *S*; Prey *F*; Troyanos *Ch*;
Johnson *M*; Wohlfahrt *Bas*;
Lagger *Bar*; Vogel *Barb*/German
Opera Chorus and Orch.,
Berlin/Böhm
DG 2740 108 ④ 3371 005
1970 Wixell *A*; Norman *C*; Freni *S*;
Ganzarolli *F*; Minton *Ch*; Casula
M; Tear *Bas*; Grant *Bar*; L.
Watson *Barb*/BBC Chorus, BBC
SO/C. Davis
Philips 6707 014 ④ 7699 055
1970 Bacquier *A*; Söderström *C*; Grist
S; Evans *F*; Berganza *Ch*;
Burmeister *M*; Hollweg *Bas*;
Langdon *Bar*; M. Price
Barb/Alldis Choir, New
Philharmonia Orch./Klemperer
HMV SLS 955; EMI 1C 157
02134-7
1976 Fischer-Dieskau *A*; Harper *C*;

Blegen *S*; Evans *F*; Berganza
Ch; Finnilä *M*; Fryatt *Bas*;
McCue *Bar*; Gale *Barb*/Alldis
Choir, ECO/Barenboim
HMV SLS 995

1979 Krause *A*; Tomova-Sintov *C*;
Cotrubas *S*; van Dam *F*; von
Stade *Ch*; Berbie *M*; Zednik
Bas; Bastin *Bar*; Barbaux
Barb/Vienna State Opera
Chorus, VPO/Karajan
Decca D132D4

Excerpts

1940 Cehanovsky *A*; Della Chiesa *C*;
Dickey *S*; Cordon *F*; Browning
Ch/Publishers Service
SO/Steinberg
RCA (US) ⓜ CAL 227

1951c (abridged) Tomei *A*; Gatti *C*;
Zabia *S*; Neroni *F*; Elmo *Ch*;
Brasini *Bar* La Scala Chorus and
Orch./Questa
Royale ⓜ 1210

1954c Pease *A*; Troxell *C*; Hunt *S*;
Sgarro *F*/orch/Walther

Royale ⓜ 1636

1954c (in German) Metternich *A*;
Kupper *C*; Trötschel *S*; Stader
Ch; Greindl *F*/orchs.
DG ⓜ LPEM 19066

1955 Driessen *A*; Opawsky *C*; van
der Graaf *S*; Jongsma *F*; Meyer
Ch/chorus, Netherlands
PO/Goehr
MMS ⓜ 2020

1959–61 Kohn *A*; Grümmer *C*; Prey
F; Berger *S*; Köth *Ch*; Frick
Bar/Berlin PO, Berlin SO,
North-West German
PO/Schüchter, Klobucar
EMI 1C 047 28574

1960 (in German) Fischer-Dieskau *A*;
Stader *C*; Streich *S*; Berry *F*;
Steffek *Ch*/Berlin PO/Leitner
DG 2535 279 ④ 3335 279

1965 (in German) Muszely *C*; Roth-
Ehrang *F*; Wenglor *S*; Exner
Ch/German Opera Chorus and
Orch./Lange
Ariola-Eurodisc Z75875R

Don Giovanni

LIONEL SALTER

Mozart's own classification of *Don Giovanni* as an *opera buffa* troubled many nineteenth-century conductors and producers, who felt that its suddenly cheerful *envoi*, proclaiming that 'every evildoer meets with his deserts', and its general tone were too frivolous for so cautionary a tale of divine retribution on a profligate: they preferred to regard it, in accordance with its official description of *dramma giocoso,* as a serious drama tinged, like Shakespeare, with comedy. The truth is that this 'opera of all operas', as E.T.A. Hoffmann called it, defies easy categorization; and without a proper appreciation of its combination of sparkle, recklessness, passion and high dramatic tension it can emerge as too earnestly moralistic and Teutonic. Conductors need a sure instinct for tempi and for the almost symphonic relationship of one section to another, a keen ear for Mozart's ever-fresh orchestral texture (including his miraculous wind scoring), and the ability to strike a mean between cramping rigidity and flabby shapelessness.

In any circumstances, production is a matter for the greatest pains in casting singers of the right vocal weight, timbre and temperament to portray the characters and in ensuring that they have a clear idea of their subtle interrelationships – no opera is less amenable to an imperfectly considered 'stand-up-and-sing' approach; but over and above this, when producing for a 'blind' medium like records or radio it is necessary to take special care that to the unaided ear the voices are sufficiently distinctive one from another. It is incidentally worth recalling, since Mozart tailored the work exactly to the cast available for the Prague première in 1787, that the title role was taken by a talented twenty-two-year-old *buffo* actor (who had previously sung the Count in *Figaro*), and later in Vienna was sung by the baritone for whom he wrote the aria 'Un bacio di mano' (K.541). The original orchestra had a string strength of only thirteen.

In some early recordings of isolated arias, niceties of style and characterization counted for little with certain stars, the emphasis being on *vox et praeterea nihil*. There is, for example, a preposterous 1903 recording (52663; Perennial 3001) of Battistini in 'Fin ch'ha del vino' with no sense of rhythm and an ending of his own, and repeating it after enthusiastic applause and cries of 'Bis!' The same LP includes three shots by him at the Serenade – one with piano in 1903 and another with orchestra ten years later, both showing a similar cavalier attitude to rhythm, the last in 1924 being rather steadier but (like the first) sitting on an arbitrary high F sharp at the end; and his singing of 'La ci darem' with its preceding recitative (1907: 05104) exhibits the beauty of tone for which he was famous, but completely obliterates the unfortunate Emilia Corsi in the Allegro. The immense freedom of early recorded singers is confirmed by versions of the Serenade by three famous interpreters: Maurice Renaud (032097; GV 52), in French – who sings two verses in French, a third in Italian! – Victor Maurel (Fono. 39041) and Emilio de Gogorza (DB 184; RLS 724), although all display velvety, seductive tone. We have to take the word of Jean de Reszke's wife that Patti 'did not sing Zerlina, she *was* Zerlina'; but the recording of 1905 (03055; HLM 7034) of her singing 'Batti, batti' a tone down, in E flat – admittedly when she was over 60 – gives out in mid phrase in one place and is approximate in the six-eight.

Much more desirable in every sense is the warm-voiced, confident Zerlina of Lola Artôt de Padilla (043280/1; CO 340) singing unfortunately in German but with the right style – perhaps the Mozartian tradition in these years of primitive recording was preserved more surely in German-speaking theatres.

On the other hand, Lilli Lehmann's splendid performance only a year or so later of 'Or sai chi l'onore' (52577/8; RLS 724), with piano and without any tenor interventions, is remarkable not only for its clean tonal focus and stylish appoggiaturas but for its nobility and sense of outrage. In this aria nothing comparable appeared until Frida Leider's 1928 recording, with a truncated introductory recitative (D 1547; 1C 147-30 785), where the intensity, is however, slightly diluted by unnecessary *ritardandi*. The role of Zerlina was specially attractive to many star singers. Tetrazzini's 'Batti, batti', sung in E (DB 537), shows great purity of intonation, even in the absurdly rushed Allegro, but is wooden and mechanical. Of 'Verdrai carino' there is a lovable performance by Lucrezia Bori (DA 130) which is the quintessence of charm and style, preferable even to Elisabeth Schumann's (DA 845; COLH 154), whose slower speed lends it a certain over-seriousness: Schumann's gentle 'Batti, batti' (DB 946; COLH 154), pronounced 'ideal' by one distinguished vocal pundit, is not impeccable in intonation in the second half. The diminutive Irene Eisinger's pretty but miniature performance (in German) of Zerlina's two arias (Ultraphon A 139; LV 197) is marred by slight sharpening, though in 'La ci darem', with a throaty Hans Reinmar (A 401), she is appealing. Among early Elviras, Gadski (Victor 88253; RLS 724) is appreciable – firm of voice and confident in technique.

Among the men, pride of place goes to John McCormack's 'Il mio tesoro' (DB 324; GEMM 158) for its easy flexibility, purity and exemplary control (taking the notorious seven-bar florid phrase leading back to the reprise in a single breath); one can only agree with the old *Record Guide* that it is 'one of the finest pieces of Mozart singing ever recorded'. Pinza, much invoked for his Giovanni, I find disappointing: his 1930 Champagne aria – to use, for convenience's sake, the term taken from the German translation of the text (DA 1134; GEMM 162) is hard and rhythmically untidy – as it was almost bound to be at so breakneck a speed – and his Serenade, which reveals a tight flutter, slightly flat. An intimate and lilting Serenade (in German) by a youthful-sounding Willi Domgraf-Fassbaender (EG 2906) is altogether delightful.

The advent of the first complete recording of the opera – the 1936 Glyndebourne production conducted by Fritz Busch – at last allowed home listeners to view it as more than a succession of individual party-pieces and to appreciate Mozart's masterly construction: even today, the unity and vitality of this performance come across despite the sound quality, which inevitably seems dated (as does the use of a piano for recitatives). Busch tends at times to push his singers on, but the whole does have drama (and the rushing wind accompanying the entrance of the stone guest is an imaginative production touch that does not jar). The compression of the work on to three discs on the LP transfer, however, results in some unhappy change-overs, disturbing 'Madamina', the Act 2 sextet and 'Non mi dir'. John Brownlee's Giovanni is aristocratic but stolid, thrown into relief by Salvatore Baccaloni's expansively engaging Leporello; Audrey Mildmay is a beguiling Zerlina, Ina Souez an intense Anna (with a good 'Or sai'); Luise Helletsgrüber makes an unimpressive Elvira, with a quick flutter in the voice.

The recording taken from the opening night of the 1950 Salzburg Festival is a collector's piece for technical ineptitude. Besides stage and audience noises and a distractingly obtrusive prompter throughout, the machines are not properly aligned, so that pitch is inconstant (and there are two sickening downward lurches during the music), the orchestra is excruciatingly distorted in the overture, levels and balance fluctuate chaotically, a microphone goes dead in 'Ah fuggi', and the clumsily played harpsichord sounds like something from a science-fiction film. Nevertheless, it gives Furtwängler admirers the opportunity to study his reading: he introduces big *ritardandi*, and some of his tempi are so deliberate as to land his singers in difficulties – Irmgard Seefried clearly wants 'Batti, batti' faster, and Ljuba Welitsch is in such straits in 'Non mi dir' that she snatches breaths in the middle of words. The three outstanding members of the cast are Seefried (in her best form, vividly suggesting an ingenuous girl swept off her feet, roguish in 'Batti, batti', gently teasing in 'Vedrai carino'), Erich Kunz as a lively and well-rounded Leporello, and Schwarzkopf, not as dominating as for Giulini nine years later, but firm-voiced and with an excellent 'Mi tradi' (though she adds a high B flat at the end).

Gobbi makes Giovanni a wholly unsympathetic character, a harsh and cruel hunter; he makes two false entries (one a bad blunder), and in the Serenade is very out of tune (as is Anton Dermota in 'Dalla sua pace'). Welitsch, sharp in the Maskers' trio, is at her best in the accompanied recitative leading up to 'Or sai', though in the aria itself she is nowhere near as good as in her tremendous solo disc (LB 124; CBS 61088), made at about the same time with Reiner conducting, where she is an avenging Fury incarnate. Her pungent tone, however, renders 'Non mi dir' (LB 121; CBS 61088) far from consolatory, brilliantly as she sings it. I have not heard the 1954 Furtwängler/Salzburg performance, nor the 1942 Walter from the Metropolitan, both restricted in circulation.

Two more recordings from the early 1950s are for the most part unsatisfactory. Swarowsky (who gives the work as at the Prague première but with the Vienna additions, 'Dalla sua pace' and 'In quali eccessi', on side 8) conducts insensitively, with often unconvincing tempi and little consideration for his singers, so that the ensemble is frequently untidy. The orchestral sound is edgy and badly balanced, with over-loud wind, and levels generally are variable: the harpsichord sounds horrible, and there is a heavy hum on sides 3 and 4. The Anna is disastrous, the Elvira ill-at-ease, the Ottavio adequate but prosaic. Alfred Poell is effective as a blunt rustic, and Heusser makes a sparrow-like Zerlina (not always very well in tune). The saving graces are Stabile's mercurial Giovanni – well described as a 'dangerous charmer' – and Alois Pernerstorfer's Leporello, weighty on his own but partnering Stabile well.

The Giovanni and Leporello are also the best points in the rough-and-ready three-disc set under Max Rudolf. The orchestral sound here is tight and unlovely, with too prominent oboes, and no attempt has been made to 'place' the stage bands in the Act 1 finale. The singers mostly belt out the ensembles (the Maskers' trio is a case in point); but curiously enough the recitatives – albeit with piano – are well done, with meaningful nuances. That good singing actor, Giuseppe Taddei, makes a haughty and erotic Giovanni, singing the Champagne aria cleanly and the Serenade in a seductive *mezza voce*. Though Italo Tajo's high Ds and Es are not altogether happy, he is a credible Leporello who does not exaggerate the comedy. Apart from an authoritative Commandatore, the rest of the cast need not detain us: an inadequate Anna with conspicuously poor phrasing, a shrill, virago-ish Elvira, a hard-bitten Zerlina, a wooden Masetto and a generally unreliable Ottavio who, despite good breath control, does not give thought to the phrasing of his words.

The 1955 Rudolf Moralt version (another three-disc set with unfortunate change-over points) is unremarkable as a whole but has riveting contributions by three singers, chief among them Sena Jurinac, captivating as an expressive and lovable Elvira, as she was at Glyndebourne; her

'In quali eccessi' and all her recitatives are most intelligently done. Ludwig Weber is the very voice of doom: Simoneau is one of the most dulcet Ottavios, tender in 'Dalla sua pace' and elegant in 'Il mio tesoro' – his solo recording of these arias shortly afterwards with Paumgartner (Philips ABR 4053) is also most rewarding for his fine sense of line. Hilde Zadek, the dark-voiced and far from stable (especially in the sextet) Anna, nevertheless manages to sound softly feminine in 'Non mi dir'; Graziella Sciutti, bright but not altogether at ease, conveys little alarm in her scream in the palace (perhaps, following Mozart's example with his Zerlina, someone should have pinched her bottom?). The master-and-man relationship here is distinctly odd, with a thick and plummy bass-baritone Giovanni (who is short on charm in 'La ci darem' and gabbles the Champagne aria) and too light and mildly characterized a Leporello (whose 'Madamina' suffers from being too far from the microphone). Recitatives are well done, though the harpsichordist's tremolos are out of style; the recording of the overture lacks presence.

In Josef Krips's excellent version there is his feeling for drama (the hellfire scene remains quite spine-chilling), the first-class teamwork he obtains from a less than ideal cast (notice the carefully judged dynamics in the sextet, for example), and his admirable pacing of the accompanied recitatives. (The *secco* recitatives are lively, but the harpsichord support is too faint.) The casting of Giovanni as a bass, upsetting Mozart's distribution of parts, would be a matter for criticism were it not that Cesare Siepi is in such magnificent form. By good vocal acting he suggests a dashing personality, suave and alluring. Fernando Corena makes a good foil although his voice had already lost its first bloom: he takes 'Madamina' at a sensibly restrained speed, and his comedy is not too broad (but why did he fail to have his mouth full during the supper scene?). Walter Berry switches effectively from his usual Leporello (which he has recorded five times) to Masetto, though 'Ho capito' is put up a tone for him; Dermota, good in the sextet, is uncomfortably stretched elsewhere. Lisa Della Casa is the best of the ladies, singing limpidly and musically, but she is temperamentally too cool ('Fuggi il traditor' needs much more bite); Hilde Gueden sounds hard and insufficiently *ingénue*: and Suzanne Danco, for all her excellent diction and phrasing, is miscast, her lightweight voice lacking enough body for Anna.

Danco was better suited to Elvira, as can be heard in the set based on the followng year's Aix-en-Provence Festival production, though even in that role she is unimpassioned (save in 'In quali eccessi'); but her singing is notable, as always, for its intelligence and precision, and her purity of tone is apt enough for a character who, it should be recalled, had originally been a nun. There is a vivacious and lucid overture by an orchestra with a small number of strings (pinched in sound), but thereafter the standard is disappointing. Teresa Stich-Randall is a soft-focus, mannered Anna, Nicolai Gedda a technically assured but inexpressive

Ottavio, Anna Moffo too pert and self-possessed a Zerlina – though the lack of pliancy in her 'Batti, batti' (the cello obbligato only just audible) may be due to Hans Rosbaud's unyielding direction. But the performance founders on a weak, quavery, elderly-sounding Giovanni (worn out with dissipation?), who is paired with a coarse Leporello so boorish as to titter at the end of 'Madamina' – hardly in keeping with that character's expostulations at his master's behaviour!

Leporello is an unpleasant, insensitive ruffian in the Fricsay recording, too, where he serves an oily, very obvious lecher. In his first assumption of the title role on disc, Fischer-Dieskau is strong in the Champagne aria (and has an excellent mandolin for his Serenade), but there is little suggestion of nobility in his portrayal. Ottavio is depicted as a weakling, with a gutless 'Dalla sua pace'. In fact the only likeable male character is Ivan Sardi's Masetto, who wins our sympathy. Jurinac's transfer from Elvira (for Moralt) to Anna is not entirely successful: she is outstanding in her grief-stricken first scene and gives a vivid account of her near-rape, but she forces her tone somewhat in 'Or sai' itself, and finds the second half of 'Non mi dir' a strain (as do most sopranos!). Had she and Maria Stader changed places, at least we should not have had so steely an Elvira (good only in 'Mi tradi') – though this would not have improved Stader's indifferent Italian: besides some actual mistakes she, Karl Kohn and Ernst Haefliger constantly give us, for example, 'kvi' and 'kvel' for 'qui' and 'quel'. There are signs of careful production in this set – ensembles are well balanced, liberal use is made in recitatives of asides, the stone guest scene has great tension (and his knocking at the door has an awesome, sepulchral, resonance) – but Fricsay's conducting is heavy-handed and his overture surprisingly superficial.

At this point we may pause to catch up with some recordings of isolated numbers by artists who do not figure in complete versions of the opera. Boris Christoff is an impudently ingratiating Leporello in his 'Madamina' (DA 2080; RLS 735), with first-class articulation and with specially good verbal nuance in the second half; Kipnis in that aria (sung in German on E 599) is incisively sardonic. Three German 'La ci darem's are worth noting: a masterful but un-wooing Schlusnus with a youthfully charming Berger (Decca-Poly. DE 7070); a smarmy Gerhard Hüsch (anticipating beats with lip-licking consonants) with a sentimental Emmy Bettendorf (Parlo. R 1320), where it is not immediately apparent who is seducing whom; and (after a surprising buckshee bar-for-nothing) a determinedly predatory Hüsch with a sweetly hesitant Margherita Perras (DA 4408).

Ottavio is not a rewarding role in the opera, but his two arias (that in Act 1 added by Mozart for the Vienna tenor who found 'Il mio tesoro' beyond him) have tempted many singers – though objective investigation reveals that not all live up to the reputations surrounding their names. Let us hastily pass by Gigli's 'Il mio tesoro' (DB 3809), the perfect object-lesson in how not to sing Mozart, in favour of Heddle Nash's 'Dalla sua pace' (Col. 9880), elegantly lyrical but with less than idiomatic Italian vowels and rather weak low notes. Tauber gives that aria great polish and beauty of tone (Parlo. R 20444; Od. 0-80959) but is disappointing in 'Il mio tesoro' (0-83391, from the same original), often hardening and sharpening, hurrying in that exacting link, and just sitting stolidly on long notes. There is a fine virile 'Dalla sua pace' in German from Patzak (Poly. 15080; Top Classic TC 9041), clean in tone and even throughout the vocal range; but for really distinguished singing of both arias, showing finesse, beautiful legato line, meaningful words and poised *fioriture* (in 'Il mio tesoro'), it would be hard to better Aksel Schiötz (DB 5264), a treasurable disc.

The compelling overture of Giulini's 1959 set immediately raises high hopes for his version, which indeed turns out to be one of the most deeply satisfying ever available. He secures a reading full of vital energy, crisp in rhythm, in which superb orchestral playing, revealing the utmost care over detail, is matched by polished vocal ensembles – the Maskers' trio has never sounded more beautiful. The production makes full use of stereo in the ballroom scene, where for the first time the three background orchestras and the stage action can be clearly followed; and there is gripping tension in the after-supper·drama.

The casting of two baritones for the main male roles is debatable, but both are strongly characterized: Eberhard Wächter young, violent, hot-blooded, almost manic in the Champagne aria and seductive in 'La ci darem' and the Serenade (where the imperfectly tuned mandolin even suggests the impatience with which he has snatched it up); Taddei vivid, funny and sarcastic to his master (a performance as praiseworthy as his Giovanni for Rudolf). Schwarzkopf makes Elvira the centre of attention at her every appearance – she had, after all, been abducted and seduced ('Mi tradi' here is uncommonly well integrated) whereas Anna had escaped violation; here is a powerful reading, overshadowing the less strongly individualized Sutherland (then just gaining international fame). At the same time Sutherland's lovely tone and technical accomplishment (all her coloratura exactly placed and executed up to tempo) rouse enthusiasm, and her enunciation is clearer than it was to become later. Of the remainder of the cast, Gottlob Frick is imposing, and his interventions in the cemetery are blood-curdling; Sciutti, though light and flexible, again does not do all she could do for the part; and the one really weak spot is Alva, rhythmically stiff and – like so many tenors – flat at the start of his first aria.

There are, sadly, far fewer pros than cons about the Erich Leinsdorf performance, whose chief claim on our interest is that, for the first time, it gave the score absolutely complete, even to the rarely played Leporello –Zerlina comedy scene Mozart added for his Vienna production. Almost the best thing about it is the exceptionally stylish and sympathetic singing of Cesare Valletti as Ottavio; the Siepi–Corena combination of the Krips version (Siepi again turning in a smooth Serenade) sounds less fresh and spirited under Leinsdorf's unimaginative, routine direction (with an over-large orchestra in which he allows the trumpets to blare, and an absurdly over-size chorus). Ensemble is sometimes ragged, especially in the last scene, and on questions of style the cast is all at sixes and sevens. Leontyne Price makes a gorgeous sound, but her *fioriture* in the first-act quartet are unreliable, and she sounds positively cheerful in a light-toned, fast 'Mi tradi'; Nilsson is hopelessly miscast, harshly metallic, slithering about in the sextet and 'Non mi dir', and approximate in intonation; Eugenia Ratti also is poor at accurately placing her 'little-girl' voice. To add to this chapter of woes, the recorded sound is lacklustre, with little presence on the voices, and to judge from the profusion of crude sound effects the producer might have been borrowed from the 'Goon Show'.

Singing *Don Giovanni* other than in Italian inevitably changes its nature to some extent, and despite some interesting casts, most performances in German have only local appeal. Typical is the workmanlike disc of extracts with Fischer-Dieskau and Claire Watson. The former gives a more persuasive reading as Giovanni than his earlier one for Fricsay, sounding young and headstrong, sinister in 'Metà di voi' and supremely self-confident in the Serenade; and the highly experienced Berry backs him well with cleanly focused tone and verbal alertness. Watson plays her part very straight and cautiously (backing off self-consciously at high notes) and seems unwilling to let herself go, even in 'Or sai'; and an un-fresh-sounding Haefliger, under strain in the upper register, also picks his way gingerly through 'Dalla sua pace'. Rita Streich is mostly charming, but there are too many intrusive 'h's in 'La ci darem'. The set is fatally flawed, unfortunately, by a strident, hard-as-nails Elvira with a wide vibrato and poor coloratura.

Even though sung in Italian, Klemperer's performance is ponderously Germanic in conception. His fans may call it 'magisterial' or 'spacious', but for many listeners his humourless, laboured reading achieves the almost impossible in making this masterpiece tedious beyond endurance. The heaviness of the orchestra extends also to the lumpy harpsichord continuo; and the Adagio start of the overture (marked Andante) and the Allegretto opening of the first number (Allegro molto) are only too prophetic of what is to come: the supper party is funereal, and in accompanied recitatives Klemperer's slowness in picking up cues robs them of impetus. The uneven cast includes Franz Crass's far from fearsome stone guest who goes wildly off the rails at 'Rispondi!', Gedda's uneasy Ottavio (out of tune in his first aria), Freni's unsmiling Zerlina (she attacks too many notes from below in 'Batti, batti' and is approximate in its second half), and Paolo Montarsolo's undistinguished Masetto. Watson, as in the previously mentioned recording, is scrupulous but lacking in assurance, especially in 'Non mi dir'; she is outshone by Christa Ludwig as a temperamental Elvira (stronger on revenge than pathos) – for whom, incidentally, a modulatory swerve is made for her to take 'Mi tradi' a tone down. Without question the chief honours go to the two male principals: Berry at his best as a likeable Leporello, making all his verbal points well, and Nicolai Ghiaurov as an authoritative and fascinating Giovanni. The dark timbre of his agile bass voice – beguiling in the Serenade (where he has a good mandolin) and exultant in the Champagne aria, for once gaining by a more restrained speed – makes him a convincing nobleman.

The contrast offered by the next recording, made in the city of the opera's première, could hardly be more striking. The Prague orchestra is by no means in the top flight (the overture is far from tidy) but it is of a size appropriate to the work, and Böhm's perceptive, idiomatic conducting ensures strong dramatic continuity. (The harpsichord treatment too is more varied and stylish.) Quite the most striking members of the cast are Martti Talvela, whose voice is tremendous even without the echo chamber he is given in the final scene (his knocks on the door too are terrifying), and Reri Grist, among the most enchanting of all Zerlinas, with a sense of fun – irresistibly wheedling in 'Batti, batti', tender in 'Vedrai carino' (taken slower than usual). Fischer-Dieskau sounds a bit rough and less than ideally steady (particularly in the Champagne aria), but his 'La ci darem' is persuasive and his Serenade (in which the mandolin plays a slight variant in the first verse) excellent. Ezio Flagello is a splendidly firm Leporello, with good articulation, but makes little attempt to act with his voice; and the same charge can be levelled at Martina Arroyo, although her actual tone is thrilling and her every note in place. Peter Schreier, the Ottavio, sounds uninvolved, and Nilsson once more demonstrates that pre-eminence in Wagnerian roles is no qualification for singing Mozart: neither her intonation nor her rhythm can stand scrutiny, her tone is edgy, and the coloratura of 'Non mi dir' defeats her completely.

The most controversial of all *Don Giovanni* recordings is that conducted by Richard Bonynge, who like Leinsdorf includes everything from both the Prague and the Vienna scores. His very opening, stopping the menacing bass on the first beat of bars 2 and 4 and then double-dotting the rhythmic pattern (though not consistently), gives warning of earnest attempts at musicological authenticity. In principle the use of a chamber orchestra (including harpsichord), of abundant appoggiaturas and of embellished cadential pauses is commendable; but along with this go serious stylistic faults – orchestral trills (in 'Vedrai carino') altered to accord with much earlier baroque practice; Handelian elaboration of vocal reprises (most extreme in 'Dalla sua pace'); an obtrusive and fussy continuo, misconceived, in manner and registration, to accompany the recitatives, which are slow paced as if for the comprehension of a first-year Italian class; and against all 'authenticity' Zerlina is cast as a mezzo, necessitating transposing 'Batti, batti' down a tone. Much more fundamental drawbacks are the conductor's limp rhythmic sense, which constantly undermines the structure, his unconvincing transitions from one section to another, and his tempi, which are not so much eccentric as wilful – accompanied recitatives too free and sentimentalized, 'In quali eccessi' taken *adagissimo* (and then 'Mi tradi' too fast), a metronomic Serenade, too slow an 'Ah taci, ingiusto core' and Maskers' trio (which becomes ragged). All this is the more regrettable in that his cast deserved better – a predatory, sinister Giovanni, a pungent Leporello (showing most character in Act 2), a flexible if small-scale Ottavio, a first-rate Commendatore. Sutherland is assured, though with obscure words, Lorengar warm and charming, properly urgent in 'Ah fuggi', while Horne gives a well-thought-out individual interpretation emphasizing that Zerlina has a genuine affection for her sorely tried bridegroom.

With the Colin Davis issue we come to what is widely agreed to be the most generally compulsive recording. Davis is less interested in appoggiaturas (sometimes added, sometimes not) and authenticity (John Constable's inventive harpsichord twiddles – entertaining on a first hearing, less so on repetition – are anachronistic) and concentrates on more basic matters: his concern is with the right mix of passion, tension and comedy, the creation of atmosphere, clarity of ensemble, and the pointing of orchestral detail: the beautiful singing tone he draws from the Covent Garden orchestra would have won Toscanini's approbation. He is extremely well supported by his technicians, who produce excellent acoustic placing of the three stage orchestras and whose decision to confine the first (offstage) minuet to a single channel is most effective.

It would be difficult to assemble a finer male team than here, the three minor roles in particular each being at the very top of their respective classes: Stuart Burrows presents some of the most distinguished Mozart tenor singing to be found at the present day, with vital words, glorious tone and exemplary control (taking the 'Il mio tesoro' seven bars comfortably in one breath); Richard Van Allan's Masetto is one of the best characterized I have ever heard (though why did he need to have 'Ho capito' put up a tone?); and Luigi Roni's Commendatore, amplified in the last scene, is chillingly overpowering. Ingvar Wixell's keen-witted hedonist of a Giovanni is a memorable interpretation, his evident enjoyment of the Serenade and his cajoling of a deliciously hesitant Zerlina quickly making one forget his pronounced vibrato; and although Ganzarolli is vocally a bit rough at the top (his 'Madamina' is his least successful moment), his is also a brilliant piece of acting, at its best in his recitative exchanges with his master. Of the ladies, Mirella Freni, singing with fewer portamentos than for Klemperer, is most at ease, bringing a delightful lilt to the six-eight section of 'Batti, batti'. Arroyo's opulent, dark voice is perhaps better suited to Anna than to the Elvira she undertook for Böhm, though after a lovely start to 'Non mi dir' it becomes unwieldy. Although her singing is intelligent and mostly very exact (save in the sextet), her 'Or sai' lacks spontaneity and depth. The less experienced Kiri Te Kanawa's silky sound and her admirable 'Ah chi mi dice mai', 'Non ti fidar' and 'In quali eccessi' help to offset some immaturity elsewhere.

A soprano who successfully made the transition from Elvira to Anna can be heard on a highly recommendable disc (SER 5675) of miscellaneous arias. Margaret Price's Anna has dignity and warmth, velvety tone, musicianship and marvellously precise coloratura in 'Non mi dir'. 'Mi tradi', interestingly on the same disc, finds her a little less exact but still very stylish.

It was with *Don Giovanni* that Barenboim made his operatic debut at the 1973 Edinburgh Festival, and that production provided the basis for his recording, which is of the Prague version with the various Vienna additions tacked on as appendices – apparently without much enthusiasm, judging from a leaden 'In quali eccessi' and a wobbly, out-of-tune 'Dalla sua pace' at a dirge-like tempo, both better forgotten. There is in fact a general lack of buoyancy, and Barenboim's speeds tend not merely to lumber but to flag as they go on (as witness the Act 1 finale, the Act 2 trio and 'Vedrai carino') simply because he stops to caress every coloristic detail and is not yet at home in pacing drama. The chief sufferer is Heather Harper, who can make no headway with either 'Ah chi mi dice mai' or 'Ah fuggi'; in addition, an unsettled Alva only just makes it in 'Il mio tesoro'; and even Helen Donath, a disarmingly delightful Zerlina, is slightly unsteady in a trudging 'Batti, batti'. Antigone Sgourda has a big cumbersome voice, conspicously lacking in control. Roger Soyer (a bass-baritone) makes a haughty, self-assured Giovanni, suave in 'La ci darem' and sentimental in the Serenade, but as a personality he takes second place to Geraint Evans's ripe rascally Leporello, relishing his every word. There is a good perspective for the offstage minuet, but arias and recitatives do not always match in either acoustics or level.

Scottish Opera was not lucky with its recording of extracts, the orchestra sounding woolly in the overture and lacking string weight throughout: but among its good points are a well-shaped sextet, a more red-blooded Ottavio (Robert Tear) than usual (abrasive rather than mellifluous) and John Shirley-Quirk's insidious Giovanni, who sings a melting Serenade (the second verse *mezza voce*) but whose words in the Champagne aria could be more distinct. His Leporello is the most gentlemanly on record, and though on the stage Stafford Dean is not without humour, not much of it comes across in his voice alone. There is a powerful Anna who in the ferocity of her 'Or sai' unfortunately sharpens as she lets fly, a sympathetic but lightweight Elvira (the end of 'Mi tradi' wanting greater security), and a colourless Zerlina.

The well-engineered set taken at the 1977 Salzburg Festival was

conducted by the almost 83-year-old Böhm with a maturity and sense of
flow that speak of a lifetime's experience. His dramatic climax is shattering,
but almost more remarkable is the finesse from both orchestra – the
Vienna Philharmonic at its most ravishing – and a totally committed cast.
Thought has evidently been given to the production: Leporello does not
recognize his master's voice in the cemetery because Giovanni disguises
it in order to scare him; this is the only recording in which Leporello
remains audibly shaken after seeing his master dragged down to hell and
does not just shrug it off and join in a happy ending; and Masetto really
suffers from his drubbing instead of playing for sympathy. The flexible
recitatives, varied in pace and with well-timed pauses, give an effect of
spontaneity. The unusual viewpoint adopted here (previously suggested
only in the Giulini reading) is that Elvira, who tries to foil Giovanni's
escapades and make him mend his ways, is a stronger character than
Anna, whose dormant sexuality has just been aroused and who never
directly confronts her would-be seducer.

Accordingly it is Teresa Zylis-Gara who becomes the feminine focal
point, and for this the firmness of her line and timbre, softening for 'Mi
tradi', fits her admirably; Anna Tomova-Sintov, whose lighter-coloured
voice suggests the less experienced girl, gives one of the best performances
of 'Non mi dir' anywhere. Edith Mathis contributes a vivacious study of
Zerlina, irresistible in 'Batti, batti' (aided by a heart-warming cello
obbligato) and sincerely solicitous in 'Vedrai carino', who is helpless
before Sherrill Milnes's violent, heartless Giovanni, a roisterer who will
brook no delay in the satisfaction of his desires and will only fleetingly
assume a honeyed tone in order to inveigle his prey. He takes the
Champagne aria at a speed that allows notes and words to register
properly; but for some reason the Serenade loses momentum. Berry is
vivid as a cynically objective Leporello; Schreier, the only survivor from
Böhm's earlier cast, has mellowed enormously in the interim and now
makes a very positive Ottavio, alive to the responsibility Anna has laid
upon him: in Dale Düsing's hands Masetto becomes a believable wronged
underdog seething with rage; and John Macurdy's rock-steady, rich-voiced
Commendatore is quite superb. The set's one big drawback is that it is
recorded at a high pitch that makes the opera's basic tonality E flat minor
instead of D minor.

The 1978 recording of the opera, from CBS, is hopelessly handicapped
by being performed neither in a studio nor in a theatre, but in the totally
unsuitable acoustics of a large church. The overhang of sound caused by
its lengthy reverberation period results in muddied phrasing and loss of
dynamic finesse, and reduces much of Mozart's exquisite orchestral detail
to mush. The effect is compounded by Maazel's consistently over-fast
tempi and his use of too large a body of strings, whose variations of
microphone placing, now advancing, now receding, bear witness to the
balance engineer's indecision as to how to cope with the problem. The

harpsichordist in the recitatives indulges in fussy arpeggios (mostly with a heavy 16-foot stop coupled) that also produce a jumble of sound.

Giovanni has frequently been sung by a bass before, and individually both Ruggero Raimondi and José van Dam are admirable – the former arrogant and masterful (even in 'La ci darem' and the honeyed insincerity of his Serenade), the latter a ripe Leporello who invests his part with character throughout – but to the ear they are too alike. This may be an advantage when it comes to deceiving Elvira, but in their exchanges at the start of Act 2, for example, the two are all but indistinguishable. the other basses are creditable (John Macurdy appropriately sepulchral in the churchyard scene, though it is a pity he gets one of his few words wrong). Kenneth Riegel makes an uneven Ottavio, eager in personality but distinctly immature in 'Dalla sua pace': 'Il mio tesoro' goes better, if too gustily.

It is the ladies who steal the honours in this performance, particularly Kiri Te Kanawa, whose fresh voice, with its clear tone and pure intonation, creates an endearing image of Elvira as a sentimental young girl. Both 'Ah fuggi il traditor' and 'Mi tradi' are excellently sung, and in the Maskers' Trio the two soprano lines have rarely been so impeccable. For the most part (as there) Edda Moser is an assured and aristocratic Anna, tender in 'Non mi dir' and intensely dramatic in her recognition of Giovanni as the man who killed her father after attempting to violate her. Unfortunately in her very first appearance she is below form, juddering in the quavers of the trio. The unusual casting of Zerlina as a mezzo (as in the Bonynge set) finds justification in the tonal contrast Teresa Berganza offers to the others and the ease with which she manages the higher tessitura. The nuances by which she conveys Zerlina's dazzled hesitation in 'La ci darem' immediately bring the character to life.

DON GIOVANNI

G Giovanni; A Donna Anna; E Donna Elvira; O Don Ottavio; L Leporello; M Masetto; Z Zerlina; C Commendatore

1936 Brownlee G; Souez A; Helletsgrüber E; von Pataky O; Baccaloni L; Henderson M; Mildmay Z; Franklin C/1936 Glyndebourne Festival Chorus and Orch./Busch Turnabout ⓜ THS 65084-6

1942 (live performance, Metropolitan, New York) Pinza G; Bampton A; Novotna E; Kullmann O; Cordon L; Harrell M; Sayão Z; Kipnis C/Metropolitan Opera Chorus and Orch./Walter Cetra ⓜ LO 27/3

1943 (in German) Ahlersmayer G; Schech A; Teschemacher E; Hopf O; Böhme L; Frick M; Wiedlich Z; Pflanzl C/Dresden State Opera Chorus, Saxon State Orch./Elmendorff DG ⓜ LPEM 19250-2

1950 (live performance, Salzburg Festival) Gobbi G; Welitsch A; Schwarzkopf E; Dermota O; Kunz L; Poell M; Seefried Z; Greindl C/Vienna State Opera Chorus, VPO/Furtwängler Olympic ⓜ 9109/4

1951 Stabile *G*; Grob-Prandl *A*; H.
Konetzni *E*; Handt *O*;
Pernerstorfer *L*; Poell *M*;
Heusser *M*; Czerwenka *C*/Vienna
State Opera Chorus, Vienna
SO/Swarowsky
Nixa ⓜ HLP 2030/1-4; Haydn
Society ⓜ 2030/1-4

1953 Taddei *G*; Curtis-Verna *A*;
Gavazzi *E*; Valletti *O*; Tajo *L*;
Susca *M*; Ribetti *Z*; Zerbini
C/Turin Radio Chorus and
Orch./Rudolf
Cetra ⓔ LPS 3253; Everest-
Cetra ⓔ 403/3

1954 (live performance, Salzburg
Festival) Siepi *G*; Grümmer *A*;
Schwarzkopf *E*; Dermota *O*;
Edelmann *L*; Berry *M*; Berger
Z; Ernster *C*/Vienna State
Opera Chorus, VPO/Furtwängler
Cetra ⓜ LO7/4

1955 London *G*; Zadek *A*; Jurinac *E*;
Simoneau *O*; Berry *L*; Wächter
M; Sciutti *Z*; Weber *C*/Vienna
State Opera Chorus, Vienna
SO/Moralt
Philips ⓜ GL 5753-5;
Philips/Mercury ⓔ PHC 3-009

1955 Siepi *G*; Danco *A*; Della Casa
E; Dermota *O*; Corena *L*; Berry
M; Gueden *Z*; Böhme *C*/Vienna
State Opera Chorus, VPO/Krips
Decca GOS 604-6; London OSA
1401

1956 Campo *G*; Stich-Randall *A*;
Danco *E*; Gedda *O*; Cortis *L*;
Vessières *M*; Moffo *Z*; Arié
C/Aix-en-Provence Festival
Chorus, Paris Conservatoire
Orch./Rosbaud
Pathé ⓜ DTX218-21; Vox
ⓜ OPBX 1623

1958 Fischer-Dieskau *G*; Jurinac *A*;
Stader *E*; Haefliger *O*; Köhn *L*;
Sardi *M*; Seefried *Z*; Kreppel
C/Berlin Radio Chorus and
SO/Fricsay
DG 2728 003

1958 Colombo *G*; Kingdon *A*; Graf
E; Giraudeau *O*; Ollendorf *L*
Gorin *M*; Dobbs *Z*; Hafman
C/Netherlands State Opera
Chorus and Orch./Krannhals

Concert Hall SMS 2121

1959 Siepi *G*; Nilsson *A*; L. Price *E*;
Valletti *O*; Corena *L*;
Blankenburg *M*; Ratti *Z*; van
Mill *C*/Vienna State Opera
Chorus, VPO/Leinsdorf
Decca D10 D4; RCA (US) LSC
6410

1959 Wächter *G*; Sutherland *A*;
Schwarzkopf *E*; Alva *O*; Taddei
L; Cappuccilli *M*; Sciutti *Z*;
Frick *C*/Philharmonia Chorus and
Orch./Giulini
HMV SLS 5083 ④ TC-SLS
5083; Angel SDL 3605

1965 Ghiaurov *G*; Watson *A*; Ludwig
E; Gedda *P*; Berry *L*;
Montarsolo *M*; Freni *Z*; Crass
C/New Philharmonia Chorus and
Orch./Klemperer
HMV SLS 923; Angel SDL 3700

1966 Fischer-Dieskau *G*; Nilsson *A*;
Arroyo *E*; Schreier *O*; Flagello
L; Mariotti *M*; Grist *Z*; Talvela
C/Prague National Theatre
Chorus and Orch./Böhm
DG 2711 006 ④ 3371 014

1969 Bacquier *G*; Sutherland *A*;
Lorengar *E*; Krenn *O*; Gramm
L; Monreale *M*; Horne *Z*;
Grant *C*/Ambrosian Opera
Chorus, ECO/Bonynge
Decca SET 412-5; London OSA
1434

1973 Wixell *G*; Arroyo *A*; Kanawa *E*;
Burrows *O*; Ganzarolli *L*; Van
Allan *M*; Freni *Z*; Roni *C*/Royal
Opera Chorus and Orch./C.
Davis
Philips 6707 022 ④ 7699 054

1973 Soyer *G*; Sgourda *A*; Harper *E*;
Alva *O*; Evans *L*; Rinaldi *M*;
Donath *Z*; Lagger *C*/Scottish
Opera Chorus, ECO/Barenboim
HMV SLS 978; Angel SDL 3811

1977 (live performance, Salzburg
Festival) Milnes *G*; Tomova-
Sintov *A*; Zylis-Gara *E*; Schreier
O; Berry *L*; Düsing *M*; Mathis
Z; Macurdy *C*/Vienna State
Opera Chorus, Salzburg
Mozarteum Orch. VPO/Böhm
DG 2790 194 ④ 3371 042

1978 Raimondi *G*; Moser *A*; Te

Kanawa *E*; Riegel *O*; van Dam *L*;
King *M*; Berganza *Z*; Macurdy *C*/
Paris Opéra chorus and Orch./
Maazel
CBS (awaiting release)

1978 Weikl *G*; M. Price *A*; Sass *E*;
Burrows *O*; Bacquier *L*; Sramek
M; Popp *Z*; Moll *C*/London
Opera Chorus, LPO/Solti
Decca D162D4

Excerpts

1950/2 (in German) Schlusnus, Günter
G; Kupper *A*; W. Ludwig *O*;
Greindl *L*/Trötschel *Z*; Berlin
PO/Lehmann
DG ⓜ LPE 17014

1953 Pease *G*; Hunt *A*; Troxell *Z*;
Baccaloni *L*/orch/Walther
Royal ⓜ 1588

1959 (in German) Prey *G*; Grümmer
A; Hillebrecht *E*; Wunderlich *O*;
Köhn *L*; Stewart *M*; Köth *Z*;
Wiemann *C*/Berlin Municipal
Opera Chorus, Berlin
SO/Zanotelli
EMI 1C 063 28418

1960 Pease *G*; Ebers *A*; Lani *E*;
Franco *O*; Lehmann *L*; Leigh
Z/Berlin SO/Ludwig
Hallmark SHM558

1961 (in German) Fischer-Dieskau *G*;
Watson *A*; Salemka *E*; Haefliger
O; Berry *L*; Streich *Z*/
Berlin Radio SO/Löwlein
DG 2535 278

1963 Giongo *G*; Bjöner *A*;
Schwarzenberg *E*; Traxel *O*;
Symonette *L*; Esparza *M*; Paller
Z/Rhine Opera Chorus and
Orch./Zaun
Ariola-Eurodisc 277033R

1963 Pease *G*; Ebers *A*; Leigh *E*;
Dermota *O*; Berry *L*; Rizzoli
Z/Hamburg Radio
Orch./Brückner-Rüggeberg
Saga STFID 2140

1966 Melis *G*; Mátyás *A*; Moldován
E; Bartha *O*; Dene *L*; László
Z; Body *C*/Hungarian State
Opera Orch./Koródy
Qualiton ⓜ LPX 1189

1975 Shirley-Quirk *G*; Mathes *A*;
Armstrong *E*; Tear *O*; Dean *L*;
Jackson *M*; Murray *Z*; Garrard
C/Scottish CO/Gibson
CfP CFP 40246

Così fan tutte

GRAHAM SHEFFIELD

Act 1

1. Trio,	La mia Dorabella capace non è
2. Trio,	E la fede delle femmine
3. Trio,	Una bella serenata
4. Duet,	Ah guarda sorella
5. Aria,	Vorrei dir
6. Quintet,	Sento, o Dio, che questo piede
7. Duet,	Al fato da legge quegli occhi
8. Chorus,	Bella vita militar
9. Quintet with chorus,	Di scrivermi ogni giorno
10. Trio,	Soave si il vento
11. Aria,	Smanie implacabile
12. Aria,	In uomini, in soldati
13. Sextet,	Alla bella Despinetta
14. Aria,	Come scoglio immoto resta
15. Aria,	Non siate ritrosi
15a. Aria,	Rivolgete a lui lo sguardo
16. Trio,	E voi ridete
17. Aria,	Un'aura amorosa
18. Finale,	Ah che tutta in un momento

Act 2

19. Aria,	Una donna a quindici anni
20. Duet,	Prenderò quel brunettino
21. Duet with chorus,	Secondate aurette amiche
22. Quartet,	La mano a me date
23. Duet,	Il core vi dono, bell' idolo mio
24. Aria,	Ah lo veggio quell' anima bella
25. Rondo,	Per pietà, ben mio
26. Aria,	Donne mie la fate a tanti
27. Cavatina,	Tradito, schernito

28. Aria,	E amore un ladroncello
29. Duet,	Fra gli amplessi
30. Andante,	Tutti accusan le donne
31. Finale,	Fate presto o cari amici

If I had to choose one word to describe *Così fan tutte,* without doubt it would be 'elusive', elusive, that is, for audiences and performers alike. The complex, fluctuating web of emotional entanglement should always be insoluble, the inner truth always just out of reach. Each character must play his part straight, but not so straight as to be unable to keep half an eye (and half a vocal chord) directed at the audience, to keep it guessing. The audience must be made to believe one minute that of course it has the answer, only to be bemused and confounded the next with a totally conflicting emotion. Overacting or indeed oversinging at any moment is disastrous, since this immediately hands out the solution on a plate. He or she overacts and therefore *is* merely acting a part and is *not* sincere in feeling. A balance – a very delicate balance – must be struck. The nuances, the innuendoes, the uncertainties are all present in the music and in da Ponte's libretto; every singer must be alive to all of them, no small task when they all have so many technical difficulties to surmount at the same time.

Which brings me back to the word 'elusive', this time as far as performers are concerned. With all the hurdles mentioned above, it is not perhaps surprising that ideal musical and dramatic performances have not been thick on the ground, particularly on record where a singer can only direct half a vocal chord at his audience and not half an eye, where the tantalization must come from the voice alone, from subtle variations of tone colour and subtle inflexions of words.

After all the emotional problems have been scrutinized, analysed, rescrutinized and discarded, *Così fan tutte* is a comedy. Consequently there should be no argument about who ends up with whom at the end, no twentieth-century pseudo-psychoanalytical solution imposed on an eighteenth-century work with eighteenth-century characters, mores, composer and librettist whose only misfortune was to be a cynic – like Don Alfonso.

Ironically for an opera that contains so little action, successful performances on record are hard to find. *Così fan tutte* can so easily slip into being a smooth concert performance, well sung but without dramatic credibility. Therefore, the importance of the role of producers cannot be underlined too heavily. Even a suspect interpretation is preferable to no interpretation at all, and the recordings which are either based on stage performances or which boast a strong producer seem, with one notable exception, to fare better.

Fritz Busch's recording from the 1935 Glyndebourne production is the earliest. The sound and general atmosphere have lasted the forty-odd years since remarkably well. For one who was not familiar with Busch's records and too young to have seen or heard him live, his conducting came as something of a revelation; it is so natural, freely flowing yet sensitive and considered, always taking a firm line and yet at the same time always appearing to let the music speak for itself. These qualities, too, are perhaps even more apparent in the excerpts recorded after the 1950 Glyndebourne production, which unfortunately have never been reissued.

Busch's cast in 1935 is a little variable. The principal assets are Heddle Nash and Willi Domgraf-Fassbaender as Ferrando and Guglielmo; Nash is elegant and stylish as always while Domgraf-Fassbaender brings a wonderful lightness of tone to his role, a lightness, however, that is not above emphasizing the bitter, slightly cynical side of Guglielmo's character, particularly in 'Donne mie la fate a tanti'. The sense of ensemble is also exceptional in this performance, the recitatives (with piano) sprightly and intelligent (despite the absence of Italians in the cast), yielding nothing to later performances in style (despite the absence of appoggiaturas). Quaint sound effects abound, with plenty of glasses clinking and doors being knocked on.

The ladies – Ina Souez (Fiordiligi) and Luise Helletsgruber (Dorabella) – do have their positive qualities but Souez sounds too matronly for the fragile, tender Fiordiligi, while a certain lack of control mars Helletsgruber's attempt to capture Dorabella's mercurial character. The Despina of Irene Eisinger is perfectly acceptable (Busch, incidentally, takes her first aria at a very quick tempo indeed) but John Brownlee's Alfonso, though richly sung, seems a little too straightforward, too British, to suggest the wily schemer. (There are cuts in recitative, both finales and in 29, and 7, 24, 27 and 38 disappear completely.)

If Busch in 1935 brought qualified delight, in 1950 the delight is undiluted. In short, the performance is a sheer joy. Sadly, however, we only have excerpts: 1, 2, 3, 4, 6, 9, 10, 14, 20, 23, 25 and 29 plus a sprinkling of recitative. Once again Busch brings an air of relaxed, fluid control to the music. This is conducting of the highest order; there is all the attention to detail one could ask for, accompaniments are etched in with supreme delicacy, yet never does the interpretation draw attention to itself. Above all, we can feel Busch enjoying himself, with this enjoyment being communicated to his singers. The ensembles, notably the quintets, are excellent, with rhythmic textures drawn from everyone without an ounce of the comedy being lost.

Richard Lewis (Ferrando) is virtually unsurpassed in the ease and elegance with which he sings and characterizes his music (listen, if you can, to the opening phrases of the first trio). Would that he had recorded 'Un' aura amorosa'! Erich Kunz is a winning Guglielmo and Mario Borriello a convincing Don Alfonso. Blanche Thebom sings Dorabella and one immediately senses the susceptibility, the suppressed excitement in her personality from her first phrases in the ladies' first duet. However, it is Sena Jurinac who steals the show with her portrayal of Fiordiligi. Here we have the complete character, the youthfulness in the voice, the fragility, the concealed vulnerability, the subtle variations in colour, the control and the technique – all of which in 'Come scoglo' and 'Per pietà' give us Mozart singing of the highest quality, and in 'Fra gli amplessi' miraculously combine to encompass the breadth of emotion as Fiordiligi wavers and finally surrenders to Ferrando. My immediate reaction to these 78s was to play them again and again, something that did not often happen in the course of my listening.

The less said about the next set (chronologically) the better. It is a performance conducted by Joseph Dünnwald, with the Stuttgart Tonstudio Chorus and Orchestra and a collection of soloists best forgotten with the exception of an amusing Despina from Käthe Nentwig and an adequate Guglielmo in Karl Hoppe. The whole affair (not aided by an unpleasant, 'boxy' acoustic) is an orgy of misjudged tempi and otherwise insensitive conducting, added to a substandard orchestra whose strings persistently fudge difficult phrases and whose woodwind persistently play out of tune. If the ladies in the Busch 1935 version were a little matronly, Erna Hassler and Hetty Plümacher in Dünnwald are positively stentorian. Well-shaped phrases and any feeling of character are virtually absent. Recitatives are heavily shortened, there are cuts within some arias and ensembles, and 7, 24 and 28 thankfully disappear completely. To add insult to injury, the librettist is described on the sleeve as Lorenzo da Ponze and the opera itself as 'Cosi fan tutti', which somewhat alters the nature of the work!

Although almost anything would be an improvement on Dünnwald, Fritz Stiedry's performance (from a Metropolitan production in the early 1950s) has positive attractions of its own, not least among them being the Fiordiligi of Eleanor Steber, altogether a touching portrayal, intelligent and musically satisfying, lacking only a shade of tenderness to complete a fully rounded interpretation. The rest of the cast is less happy: Thebom, a success as Dorabella in what we heard of her in Busch's 1951 excerpts, here shows considerable rhythmical insecurity (particularly in 11) and generally seems less at home in her character. Richard Tucker is certainly ardent and heroic as Ferrando, but hardly a natural Mozart singer with anything like the necessary style or subtlety of approach. The Guglielmo of Frank Guarrera is acceptable in ensemble, but his limitations are harshly exposed in 'Donne mie la fate a tanti'; likewise to a lesser extent the Don Alfonso of Lorenzo Alvary. Roberta Peters's Despina, on the other hand, is a sympathetic portrayal, earthy rather than prim in style, light but not irritating in voice as so many Despinas tend to be.

Stiedry occasionally achieves a fine effect – momentarily; on the other hand he is far too prone to change his tempo in mid-stream, I suspect (charitably) in attempts to bring out particular details in the score. The effect of this approach is usually to disrupt the flow of the music entirely and to lose the singers. The quintet (6) provides a good example of this eccentric approach. Stiedry is also weak in the finales, uncertain in tempo transitions and not nearly attentive enough to marked dynamics.

My enjoyment derives almost wholly from the fact that the recording emanates from a stage performance, so that the characters are actually produced. We can feel the singers thinking about what they are doing, and that in turn involves the listener, however little we may agree with the directional approach. In addition, this is the only set in English, a fact adding to the immediacy of the drama. A caveat, though: the translation is one which tends to be laughed 'at' rather than 'with', and you have to put up with such old chestnuts as 'the proof of the pudding', 'upsetting the applecart', 'bread being buttered on both sides' and 'making hay while the sun shines'. Cuts here are similar to those in Dünnwald's performance, with the additional omission of 27.

One performance at which no Stiedry-like criticisms can be levelled is that conducted by Herbert von Karajan dating from 1954. From the opening bars of the overture we are able to single this out as a performance in the top class. Tempi, as one would expect, are perfectly judged, and Karajan is alive to every musical nuance in the score. It is all imposing and commanding, and there lies the one major criticism of this set. In his quest for musical perfection Karajan fails to realize that this is a comedy; he takes himself too seriously. This reading looks at the opera retrospectively, that is to say, through the eyes of the nineteenth century (this does stand Karajan in good stead in the finales), whereas Busch, Jochum, Böhm and Davis approach it from the eighteenth century, an attitude with which I am more sympathetic. That said, there are marvellous things here, not least among them being the hushed, atmospheric quality that suddenly descends on an ensemble, transporting it almost on to a higher plane of human experience. The entire 'farewell scene' bears witness to this, and although the famous trio itself is just a shade reverential, it is polished to perfection. Moreover, Karajan is one of the first conductors to appreciate the importance of Mozart's viola lines. As far as cuts are concerned, they are heavier than I had expected to the recitatives. Otherwise only 7 and 24 are missing.

Elisabeth Schwarzkopf is Fiordiligi, a superlative musical and theatrical performance, inclined only perhaps to over-interpret in her highly coloured response to the words, a fault (though I hesitate to call it that) less apparent in her recording for Böhm. Superlative again is the only word to describe Sesto Bruscantini's Don Alfonso, marvellously alert, light and intelligent in both recitative and ensemble, a manipulator of great cunning. The third superlative falls to Léopold Simoneau as Ferrando. As with Lewis, here is a singer with the authentic Mozart style, barely a chink in his vocal armour. The cast is completed by Nan Merriman as Dorabella

– a real contrast in timbre with Schwarzkopf, a dark, hooded and sometimes mysterious tone, but a little too poised and deliberate for a flirtatious girl. Rolando Panerai as Guglielmo is better in his *buffo* numbers (26) than in the more lyrical passages (23), and finally Lisa Otto as Despina – convincing but better undisguised! Her 'dottore' and 'notaio' are unpleasant and often horribly sharp, but she is not by any means the only one to fall into that trap.

Apropos of ponderous performances of Mozart's G minor symphony a musician once pleaded 'Save Mozart from the Germans!' Without wishing to take this plea to its logical conclusion, there is perhaps much to be said for injecting 'più d'Italia' into Mozart's Italian music than it is accustomed to receive from German interpreters. A recording conducted by Guido Cantelli encourages support for this view. The performance was recorded live in 1956 at La Scala with a cast in many respects similar to Karajan's, discussed above. Although the sound is far from satisfactory, it is superior to other similar offerings from Cetra. The balance as one might expect, gives the orchestra more prominence than usual. While this has the disadvantage of distancing the singers, there is an advantage in that orchestral lines, totally submerged in other recordings, are here thrown into surprising and often welcome relief (second violins in 3, violas in Alfonso's arioso, solo cello in 10, bassoons in the sextet).

As far as the cast is concerned there is little to say that is not said elsewhere in this chapter. Elisabeth Schwarzkopf and Nan Merriman repeat their excellent partnership from Karajan's recording – Schwarzkopf here less mannered, Merriman more characterful. And how well they listen to one another's singing; the climbing arpeggio phrases at the end of 5 are virtually without equal. As Ferrando, Luigi Alva is fresh and youthful in his approach, much happier under Cantelli than he was to be fifteen years later under Klemperer. Graziella Sciutti (Despina), as under Rudolf Moralt (see below), excels in the role, but Rolando Panerai (Guglielmo) proves once again more successful in his *buffo* numbers.

The only singer not present in other recordings is the Don Alfonso, Franco Calabrese. Too much of a bass for a part that demands a secure high register, he omits the top E at the end of 30, and finds other high passages stressful. In other respects, though expressive enough in a conventional manner, he is inclined to woolliness of tone. The chorus is no more than adequate, the orchestra *just* more than adequate.

Despite its drawbacks (cuts incidentally are small – only 7 and 24 omitted entirely) there is much to enjoy in this set. As I hinted above, it is a very Italian performance; all the men are Italians (unique on record), the conductor likewise (again unique on record), and so is Despina. This fact does make for excellent recitative, crisply and idiomatically performed, and for effective, enunciation, for example the final Presto in the quartet, 22.

Cantelli's contribution is also a positive feature of the set. His is a thoroughly individual approach, always alert to the changing moods and always gently and sympathetically controlled. Tempi are, on the whole, brisk, but there are surprises: the march is very slow (leading to some discrepancy with the chorus) and the quintet (9) is the quickest on record. The accompanied recitative to 27, marked Allegro, is no more than Andante.

The same year as Cantelli, in 1956 (coinciding with the Mozart bicentenary) came a performance conducted by Rudolf Moralt. It is disappointing, though not unrelievedly so. Moralt chooses generally slow tempi but without the necessary authority or single-mindedness to carry them through. Rhythmically unsteady at times too (in 17, for example), he finds himself in serious discord with his singers. Not Moralt's fault perhaps, but the recitative is much too *secco* (an unusual complaint as far as performances of this opera go) and tends to be unimaginative. In short, there is a distinct lack of sparkle. There are also several disturbing and illogical jumps in the acoustic. Cuts are idiosyncratic: apart from the usual tailoring of the recitative, 28 is cut and there are trimmings in both finales, though 7 and 24 are included. Waldemar Kmentt (Ferrando) does not really make a good case for including the latter ('Ah! lo veggio'). It is not the most gracious of Mozart's arias for the tenor voice, but Kmentt is too emphatic; elsewhere I found his singing stiff. After initial reservations, I warmed to Walter Berry's Guglielmo, a little heavy and inaccurate in places, but in all a warm-hearted and attractive suitor. A disastrous Don Alfonso (Deszö Ernster) should certainly have remained a philosopher pure and simple. Teresa Stich-Randall (Fiordiligi) interprets the music less than Schwarzkopf but captures the fragile, girlish quality at least as well. Where she does compare less favourably with Schwarzkopf is in music that needs more voice, but her soft singing is exquisite. Ira Malaniuk is an adequate Dorabella. The Despina is Graziella Sciutti, and one of the best. Crisp and witty in the recitative, she never lapses into shrillness, and in her arias she achieves a depth of emotion not usually associated with the character. The shaping and shading of her phrases is particularly attractive; incidentally, her two arias were the only occasions when Moralt's slow-paced approach paid dividends.

Another conductor who favoured slow tempi, not unexpectedly, was Otto Klemperer, whose performance appeared in 1971. As with Karajan, Klemperer provides another instance of a man seeing *Cosi fan tutte* through the eyes of the nineteenth-century symphonic tradition, only in this case the feeling is more pronounced. Klemperer's account of the overture, while not the sprightliest, is considered and spacious. Thereafter tempi become so ponderous that the fabric of the music falls apart, and the singers find themselves physically unable to bear the strain. Vocal phrases have to be broken up to accommodate these tempi, which only furthers the disintegration. One can sense Klemperer's head disappearing into his score to admire some felicitous detail. The speed immediately slows (listen to the winding down of the tension at 'Giusti numi' in 13, just when it should, if anything, be wound up) and it is as though he has forgotten he has any singers with him at all. Meanwhile one or other of his cast is more than likely left high on a sustained note gasping for survival.

It is remarkable how well most of Klemperer's cast bear up under the strain. Margaret Price and Yvonne Minton make a finely matched pair of ladies. Price's horror at her word, 'divertirci', when Despina suggests that the sisters 'divert' themselves with their menfolk away at the war, gives us just a glimpse of the character she might portray under a more sympathetic baton and, indeed, has done on stage. So, later on, does her touching account of 'Prenderò quel brunettino' along with Minton. Sadly, Dorabella's two lively arias are ruined by Klemperer's elephantine approach, with the vocal line in 11 having to be broken up in the most extraordinary places just for Dorabella to stay alive. 'Downstairs', the Despina here (Lucia Popp) makes a delightful *agente provocateuse,* but her more aristocratic other half, Don Alfonso (Hans Sotin), is dull and uninspired. Of the lovers, poor Luigi Alva with his lightweight tenor finds life hard under Klemperer, but Geraint Evans gives us a fine, *buffo* Guglielmo, a crisp, good-humoured performance despite the handicaps, and suavely lyrical too when required. His seduction of Dorabella (both in recitative and duet) is one of the highlights of the set.

Nos. 7 and 24 are cut, as well as some of the recitative. Strangely and perversely the whole opening recitative to Act 2 disappears, and it begins with Despina's aria.

The man who gives us a performance as near perfection as we are likely to get is Karl Böhm and he has had three attempts at it, though the third was unnecessary. His first (and the first recording in stereo) appeared in 1955, a year after Karajan's version: Böhm is in a brisk mood – almost brusque in places. Granted, the control is there, the authentic eighteenth-century atmosphere, the sense of theatre, too; but in one or two places Böhm seems to be feeling his way, inclined, if in doubt, to take matters a little on the fast side. An odd feature is the host of disfiguring cuts in the music. Nos. 7, 24 and 28 are omitted completely, and elsewhere there are many small snips in arias and ensembles which go far beyond the bounds of that detestable phrase, 'standard theatre cuts'. These, astonishingly, include Don Alfonso's recitative and arioso after the 'Soave il vento'. The cast is variable. Christa Ludwig as Dorabella (in sharp contrast to her 1962 performance discussed below) is curiously muted and detached; likewise the Despina of Emmy Loose is non-committal when compared with the interpretations of Sciutti and Popp. Paul Schöffler makes a disappointing Don Alfonso, too unsophisticated and matter-of-fact in approach, and vocally there are sad lapses in control and intonation. Anton Dermota is the Ferrando, ardent enough but with a slight throatiness to his voice. The Fiordiligi is Lisa della Casa, an acceptable though cool portrayal; she does not possess the notes in her lower register to encompass the line with total ease. Kunz completes the cast, repeating his vivid Guglielmo from Busch's 1950 excerpts.

Böhm's second recording (1962) is in practically every respect an improvement on the first. As with Karajan, Böhm here conducts the excellent Philharmonia Orchestra, and in his direction of it he shows himself less headstrong and altogether more poised and perceptive than in 1955, but without any noticeable loss in wit or spontaneity. Like Busch, Böhm has the quality of being able to control the music and yet, at the same time, allow it to speak for itself, to express the emotions fully. Added to this, in 1962 Böhm had the services of Walter Legge as producer who not only achieved a fine sound balance, allowing great clarity in ensemble and orchestral textures, but also managed to create what few others have done, the authentic atmosphere and excitement of a stage performance within the confines of the recording studio. Every effect is ideally calculated, even the silences between scenes and the spacing of recitative and aria. The magical, watery distancing of the serenade (21) seems exactly right. The text is here discreetly tailored; 7 and 24 omitted, the recitative sensibly cut and only a small cut in the finale to Act 1.

Böhm's cast has no fatal flaws: Alfredo Kraus as Ferrando is the elegant stylist we have come to expect (a marvellous performance of 'Tradito, schernito', for example), and Giuseppe Taddei is a confident, smiling Guglielmo drawing out in his two arias all the character that is needed. Berry seems much happer as Don Alfonso than he did as Guglielmo under Moralt. His is a wonderfully teasing, provocative philosopher, master of the situation and with just the right amount and quality of tone. Hanny Steffek provides an equally provocative foil as Despina – innocence is not one of her qualities! As Dorabella, Ludwig is transformed from her earlier performance. Here she evinces pent-up, girlish excitement, involved and tantalizing from the first phrases in 4, dramatic without overdoing it in 'Smanie implacabile', and exhibiting splendid control and variety of colour in 'E amore e un ladroncello'. Almost the same compliments can be paid to Schwarzkopf's Fiordiligi, admittedly not in such fine voice as on the Karajan set but making up for it in her approach to the text, alive to every nuance, suggestive at almost every turn (marvellously concealed vulnerability in 'Come scoglio') and yet paradoxically less mannered than in 1954. Schwarzkopf and Ludwig together create an unrivalled partnership, superbly *distraites* in the passage after the Albanians have taken poison ('che figure interessanti' and 'possiam, farci un poco avanti' are irresistible) and brilliantly capturing the naughty-schoolgirl atmosphere of 'Prenderò quel brunettino'. Altogether a splended team performance, without sacrificing anything in the quest for the highest musical standards.

Böhm's third recording, to celebrate his eightieth birthday in 1974, was taken live from the stage of the Salzburg Festival with a starry cast and with the Vienna Philharmonic Orchestra (as in Böhm's first version). Disfigured by trimmings in arias and finales, heavy cuts in the recitatives and omissions of 7, 24, 27 and 28, stage noises (infernal tea-cup rattling, even during Despina's first aria) and painfully slow recitative – presumably this speed to accommodate all the stage business. Unjustifiable even on stage, for a recording it is unforgivable. Moreover, though this *is* a stage production, the humour is of the ponderous, thigh-slapping Teutonic variety that is singularly repellent. The drama is here heavily superimposed on the music rather than growing from it as it does in Böhm's 1962 performance – an example of how not to record an opera, just as the earlier version was a perfect example of the right way!

The singing is uniformly less satisfactory than in 1962. Gundula Janowitz occasionally strikes form (in 'Per pietà') but is inclined to swoop. Brigitte Fassbaender is too heavy-handed vocally and dramatically to present a convincing Dorabella. In 20 she sounds more like a middle-aged lady choosing a cream cake than a young lady choosing a lover. Rolando Panerai conjures up visions of a knowing Don Alfonso – he is better heard as Guglielmo under Karajan. Reri Grist (Despina) is too pert; surely the sisters would not turn to such as her for advice. Hermann Prey and Peter Schreier are never less than competent, though Schreier makes an unattractive noise when he gets angry, and he insists on distorting speeds. In 'Un' aura amorosa', every time he has the bar with six semiquavers in it the music almost grinds to a halt.

In 1962, the year of Böhm's great recording, a Deutsche Grammophon set was conducted by Eugen Jochum. The performance promises much. Jochum's approach is marvellously lithe and dramatic, at the same time drawing beautifully detailed and shaped playing from the Berlin Philharmonic. He also shows a truly theatrical instinct in his pacing of the transitions from aria to recitative and vice versa. The poignancy of the viola lines in the whole farewell scene is fully exploited; in the trio itself I had never before heard the 'venti' quite so 'soave'. The recitative is complete here, the only cuts being of 7 and 24. Dietrich Fischer-Dieskau is an exceptional Don Alfonso, a highly individual performance, youthful in tone and greatly responsive to the text – as only Schwarzkopf has been of all the singers discussed so far. Of the others we have Nan Merriman again as Dorabella, a little fuller in voice than she was under Karajan or Cantelli, and Prey once again as Guglielmo, better in this earlier version than he was under Karl Böhm in 1974. With less stage business to distract him he produces a more concentrated reading, less affected and truer in style. Style is the chief asset of Ernst Haefliger, the Ferrando of the set; although he could hardly be said to produce a beautiful sound, he does mould his lines well, is sensitive to phrasing and inner meaning. Throughout, he seems almost retiring dramatically and vocally, in contrast to the more extrovert Prey. With all this enthusiasm, you may be asking what the drawbacks are in this recording. The answers are Erika Köth, an unpleasantly shrill, unsteady Despina and, more crucially, Irmgard Seefried, a wholly inadequate Fiordiligi, unable at that stage in her career (sadly) to cope with any of the technical demands Mozart makes on her.

The first recording complete in both recitative and musical numbers arrived in 1967, conducted by Erich Leinsdorf, with a cast composed entirely of Metropolitan regulars. There is much in common here with the earlier Stiedry set, also Metropolitan-orientated, though the quality of Leinsdorf's performance is far better. It is the atmosphere that is similar: the big sound, the grand approach, almost, though I hesitate to say it, an American approach – not too much subtlety but rich in vitality and above all fully characterized. If the drama is overdone at times, there are compensations in the excitement of the music-making. Moreover, the humour is infinitely preferable to that in Böhm's 1974 performance. At all times the voices respond to Leinsdorf's big-hearted conducting. Leontyne Price and Tatiana Troyanos create a volatile, committed pair of sisters; their singing is perhaps more in the style of Verdi than Mozart but they get away with it. Of course when they do go too far, as in the Act 1 finale, their performance only highlights what I stressed earlier; it makes an audience believe nothing it hears.

The other main criticism (and it goes for most of the cast) concerns ornamentation, which is lavishly added to fermatas in the arias. That is in order if it is done with a consistent and sensitive feeling for style, but unfortunately that is not the case here. George Shirley and Sherrill Milnes both fit in with Leinsdorf's grand concept of the piece. Milnes is particularly successful, portraying a suave, dashing Guglielmo brimming over with self-confidence and meticulous in his reading of Mozart's lines. Shirley's stressful method of tone production is uncomfortable (the closeness of the recording does not help) but he overcomes most of the difficulties and even manages 'Ah! lo veggio' with a degree of accomplishment. Judith Raskin as Despina and Ezio Flagello as Don Alfonso complete the cast. Flagello is in the Bruscantini mould as the philosopher. Though without the others' polish, his is a strong portrayal, and he does keep a subtle smile in the corner of his voice, nicely suggesting the elderly cynic. The harpsichord is recorded close in the recitative, which I found intrusive, and the recitatives themselves are generally oversung and are consequently too ponderous.

Two disappointing sets now, the first one conducted by Otmar Suitner from 1969. In general this is a dull performance, spoiled not only by some routine conducting and a dry acoustic, but also by some uninspired singing, leaving much to be desired in terms of expression and contrast.

The recitatives, however, do go at a brisk pace and, surprisingly, appoggiaturas are more consistently employed than in most performances. To judge from the pictures in the libretto, this East German recording must have stemmed from a stage production, though much of the character seems to have evaporated in the transition from stage to studio. Neither Celestina Casapietra (Fiordiligi) nor Annelies Burmeister (Dorabella) gives very compelling portrayals; indeed, Burmeister's contralto tone does not suit the part of Dorabella. Theo Adam (Don Alfonso) is convincing in the recitative, dull elsewhere. Sylvia Geszty is an energetic Despina, though with an incipient wobble in the voice. Günther Leib presents a lightweight Guglielmo and Peter Schreier a wooden Ferrando, who pulls the tempo about in 'Un' aura amorosa' as he does in Böhm's 1974 performance. A footnote about cuts here: Act 1 is complete (except for the recitative before the finale) but in Act 2 there are recitative cuts and one in the finale, while 24 and (astonishingly) 25 ('Per pietà') are omitted.

The other disappointing performance is also the most recent one, conducted by Alain Lombard. Following on from Suitner's recording we find here another conductor who, by failing to impose any personality on the music, ends up by producing a faceless performance, which sounds like a slightly off-peak final dress rehearsal at just under true voltage (the recitative is pedestrian). Where Lombard strives for breadth and atmosphere he only succeeds in being leaden-footed. His orchestra, the Strasbourg Philharmonic, does not help matters by exhibiting a lack of precision and polish throughout, but fundamentally the criticism must rest with the conductors.

This state of affairs is all the more sad since at least three of the singers (von Stade, Te Kanawa and Rendall) would be a definite attraction on any Mozart cast list. Indeed, the singing of all three, as far as singing itself goes, is fine. It suffers from Lombard's lack of involvement, particularly in the case of Dorabella, where there seems so much more that Frederica von Stade could squeeze from the music; it is just too poised and uninvolved. Of the others in the cast Philippe Huttenlocher is a colourless Guglielmo and Jules Bastin a similarly dull Don Alfonso. Teresa Stratas sings with disturbing unevenness of tone in both her arias, and is singularly irritating and singularly sharp in both her disguises. Nos. 7 and 24 are omitted, there is a cut in the Act 2 finale, and recitative is slightly trimmed.

High intensity marks the complete performance conducted by Sir Georg Solti, which Decca released in 1974, as does a lack of magic and poetry. This is an exciting performance and one which compels attention rather than invites it. Solti is at his best in the two finales, where his innate dramatic insight carries him through with some distinction. Elsewhere I wished he would relax a little – step off the rostrum and even take an objective view of himself conducting Mozart! Solti's high-powered approach, though, does have its advantages in other respects, the main one being that the recitative is taken at something approaching a proper pace – a rare enough feature of the recordings already discussed.

In the cast, Gabriel Bacquier (Don Alfonso), Teresa Berganza (Dorabella) and Tom Krause (Guglielmo) are the successes. Bacquier is irresistible, different from any of the role's other interpreters. He is hardly the richest in tone, but more than makes up for that with the subtle Gallic air he brings to the part and the almost Machiavellian way in which he seems to control the entire opera. Both Krause and Berganza give intelligent, perceptive, lively interpretations, and in their Act 2 scene and duet, 'Il cor vi dono', the one is persuasive, the other susceptible! Pilar Lorengar is the Fiordiligi, a little hard-edged in tone and outshone by her sister; Ryland Davies makes an ungraceful Ferrando. Jane Berbié creates an unusual but not unsuccessful Despina – almost peasant-like in her approach, down-to-earth, experienced and always knowing exactly what she is talking about.

Montserrat Caballé, the Fiordiligi in the complete recording under Colin Davis, would hardly be on everyone's list of ideal Mozart singers, but here she turns in a performance of exquisite beauty, singing with rare insight. Her honeyed tone is not merely liberally spread over the score but used with intelligence and discernment. One particularly memorable phrase is in the quintet (9) but there are many others. What makes the interpretation more surprising is that Caballé is nowhere near as subtle in her reading of the words as many other Fiordiligis, but she compensates for this by characterizing purely with her voice. However, she does tend to sing all her recitative as if it were by Bellini, which slows down proceedings. Elsewhere, recitative is crisp and the harpsichord continuo sympathetic, apart from one or two irritating effects.

Davis's own contribution must count as one of his most successful on record; he rates with the finest conductors of this opera in his constant involvement, his ability to show discreet but firm control and in his attention to tempo indications and orchestral nuances. Happily, his cast generally supports him well: Janet Baker (Dorabella) makes an excellent foil for Caballé (the girl's vacillations are wonderfully captured in the duet, 20), there is a musical Don Alfonso from Richard van Allan and, as Despina, Ileana Cotrubas is cajoling, comic, but never arch. Her disguises too are more subtly done than usual. The disappointments in this set come from the men's department: Wladimiro Ganzarolli a coarse, unstylish Guglielmo, and that fine artist Nicolai Gedda regrettably sounding tired and stressful. However, he brings off a most convincing 'Fra gli amplessi', producing a delicate, hushed tone at the moment of Fiordiligi's capitulation that few others have matched.

For some reason, the arias and ensembles have never been popular material for LP recital records or, more understandably in earlier days for 78s, when the opera was seldom performed. 'Un' aura amorosa' has fared the best, at any rate in terms of numbers, followed closely by

Fiordiligi's two arias and then by those for Despina and Guglielmo (including 'Rivolgete a lui lo sguardo', discarded by Mozart).

The excerpts conducted by Fritz Busch from the 1951 Glyndebourne production have already been discussed. These included the 'farewell trio', but apart from that excellent performance there are surprisingly only two others on disc (the specially recorded version with Pilar Lorengar, Barry McDaniel and Yvonne Minton for the film 'Sunday Bloody Sunday' has never been issued). One of the two (AU 4879 B/MRF7) is appropriately from a Metropolitan Farewell evening and the participants, conducted by Erich Leinsdorf, are Teresa Stratas, Mildred Miller and Frank Guarrera. The performance, in English (only apparent after some minutes), is dominated by the Fiordiligi of Teresa Stratas and not especially distinguished. In addition, the orchestral contribution is barely audible. There is much more satisfaction to be derived from the other version from Decca's so-called 'Mozart Opera Festival' (SET 549), conducted by Istvan Kertesz, with Krause and Fassbaender blending most agreeably with the clear, pure tones of Lucia Popp's Fiordiligi.

Passing hurriedly over the only 'Smanie implacabili' (a family affair sung by Elsa Gardelli and conducted by Lamberto – Qualiton LPX 1108), we arrive at Despina's first homily to the two ladies 'In uomini'. The earliest version I have heard comes from Lucrezia Bori, an acoustic recording (DA 132), but one in which her slender, almost boyish voice and her suggestive interpretation come across with great clarity. From a few years later (1922) there is a performance in German by Vera Schwarz (Od. Rxx 80084; LV 24). She portrays a more mature character than Bori, adding plenty of laughter, occasionally at the expense of rhythmic exactness. Also from the 78 era there is Alda Noni (DA 1986), who sang the role at Glyndebourne in 1950; she is hard-edged, but very spirited.

More recently there have been Anna Moffo in 1959 (Col. SEL 1667), not perhaps everyone's ideal Mozart singer but adequate here despite occasional lapses in intonation, and Graziella Sciutti (SXL 2271), whose considerable merits in this role have been noted in connection with the Moralt performance. Sciutti's fresh-voiced, tantalizing accounts here of both Despina's arias more than confirm those earlier impressions. There are, of course, others who have recorded both arias: Noni, lacking in dynamic range in 'Una donna a quindici anni' but with a most cheeky ritardando at the end; Schwarz, a little pompous, and Moffo (Col. SEL 1690) more characterful on this occasion, clearly relishing her immoral suggestions! Two other German performances of 19 are those of Erna Berger, dictatorial and colourless in approach (1C 047-28 556), and of Lotte Schöne (EJ 262; LV 6), one of the crispest Despinas rhythmically – there is a wonderful dotted quaver in bar 5 – and one who brings to the music a zest matched only by Sciutti. Finally there is Rita Streich (DG EPL 30484), tender and pleasantly shaded, but without much contrast between Andante and Allegretto.

Fiordiligi's two arias are fundamental to her personality, 'rocks' from which her vacillation and vulnerability develop, and from that springs the emotion (inherent in her temperament) that leads to her downfall. The arias are also, as far as her singing is concerned, full of horrifying obstacles. Undoubtedly the oddest rendering of 'Come scoglio' comes from Eleanor Steber on a record bizarrely titled 'Live at the Continental Baths' – well, it makes a change from the Carnegie Hall (ARLI 0436)! The venue was New York, the date 1974, and Steber was apparently giving an entertainment (with piano accompaniment) for the delectation of the baths' patrons. They are much in evidence throughout. As far as Mozart is concerned, I was left wishing that someone had pulled out the plug early in the proceedings. Devotees of her art should turn to her performance on Stiedry's set or to her singing of 'Per pietà' under Bruno Walter (Odyssey 32 160363) – a taut, controlled interpretation of great intensity.

Stich-Randall recorded 'Come scoglio' three times (London DTL 93075, HMV 7ER 5140 and World Records ST 425); in spite of the firmness and directness of her approach, her Fiordiligi is not a compelling character. Of the three recordings, the third (1963) is to be preferred, mellower in tone, lighter in touch and generally more flexible. This is also true of her three performances of 'Per pietà' (DTL 93075, 7ER 5125 and ST 425). From an earlier generation we have a recording of 14 by Gabrielle Ritter-Ciampi (Pathé 0401; Eterna 758), a characterful reading, liberally sprinkled with appoggiaturas as was the custom in the century's early years, but without the precision or cleanness we have come to expect in today's Mozart singing. There is greater cleanness and precision in Berta Kiurina's intelligent, capable account of 'Per pietà' from 1920 (Poly. 50240: LV 91), although the tone is not of the purest. Astonishingly clear, agile coloratura is the principal asset of Lina Pagliughi's performance of 'Come scoglio' (Parlo. E 11317). The sound is inclined at times to be brittle, but it has a bright, girlish quality of great individuality – so girlish that Pagliughi has to transpose up an octave all but one of the phrases that descend below middle C.

Much more recently, Teresa Berganza, with John Pritchard and the London Symphony Orchestra, recorded a whole disc (SDD 176) of Mozart arias. Throughout, technical difficulties seem to dissolve amid her overwhelming musicality. Her 'Come scoglio' is vibrant, forthright and captivating, though temperamentally her character may be more in sympathy with Dorabella – witness either the Solti set or her relaxed and youthful interpretation of 'E amore un ladroncello' (SDD 176), a marginally fresher approach than under Solti. To return to Berganza's Fiordiligi, if her 'Come scoglio' was vibrant then her 'Per pietà' is positively radiant, perfectly capturing the essence of a character still faithful to her ideal, but now just tinged with susceptibility. In the same mould as Berganza, technically fluent in both arias, and by turn exciting and limpid in tone, is Suzanne Danco (Decca K 1732 and K 1815). Unfortunately Elly Ameling (Philips 6500 544) has recorded only 'Come scoglio', but what a fine performance it is, more serious than Berganza's but just as clean and as beautifully contrasted. There is a real sense of horror in her singing, horror at the idea that those Albanians should have dared to enter the house and try to seduce her and her sister. Something of that horror can also be heard from Ina Souez (DX 672), expressive and suitably firm, although Clarence Raybould does seem to make the aria a race against the end of the 78! Other less distinguished interpretations of 14 come from Hjördis Schymberg (DB 6294) and Daniza Ilitsch (Supra. LPM 132) – the latter is excruciating – and of 25 from Elsa Gardelli (Qualiton LPX 1108). By contrast, there is a beautifully phrased, moving account of 'Per pietà' from Joan Cross (DX 1353); her singing is alive and alert and she is well accompanied by the Philharmonia Orchestra under Laurance Collingwood. Finally from 1927 – again in 25 – there is Felicie Hüni-Mihacsek (Poly. 66613; LV 93) pure in tone on the notes, but inclined to over-manner the line and indulge in portamenti that spoil the cleanness of the performance.

Surprisingly, there appears to be only one recording of the duet, 'Prenderò', from 1907, with Lilli Lehmann and her niece Hedwig Helbig (Od. 50397; GV 66). Lehmann sounds incredibly youthful for a woman then approaching the age of 60; Helbig is, by contrast, motherly. The coda here is amusing, both singers taking off at an incredible speed unrelated to the earlier bars.

As far as tenors are concerned the competition is strong. One who would certainly win a prize for originality if nothing else is the composer Reynaldo Hahn (really a baritone!), who croons his way through a cut version of 'Un' aura amorosa' far from unpleasantly to his own piano accompaniment. The key he chooses is G major, an example one or two supposedly more distinguished tenors might care to follow. The earliest truly professional performers of this aria, as one might expect, treat Mozart with flexibility, as music belonging to the nineteenth-century grand tradition. In Leo Slezak's (in German), from 1907 (3-42842; CO 332), the tone is generous, but so also is the rubato; moreover, he finishes his account half-way through the aria on the dominant. Hermann Jadlowker (042536, also in German) sings in his usual spacious, incisive manner with that peculiarly metallic tone of his. He adds appoggiaturas and even a couple of decorations – all very nineteenth-century.

In 1908 Felix Senius recorded the aria (Anker 04978; HLM 7128): heady in tone and bellowy on the top notes, he too is liberal with rhythm, particularly in Schreier's favourite bar. From the 1920s come Koloman von Pataky (Poly. 95374; LV 194), attractively light-voiced but lacking body in the tone, and Helge Roswaenge in German (Od. O 6923; 1C 147-29 240/1). This is undoubtedly musical singing, but it is also unwieldy, and it hints strongly at greater comfort in the nineteenth-century repertory.

Two of the best recordings of 'Un' aura amorosa' appeared in the 1930s: Julius Patzak's moving performance, in German, (CA 8196; LV 191), has virtually everything needed – a beautifully formed line, control and delicacy, character without mannerisms. Walther Ludwig, also in German (EH 957; LV 232), matches Patzak in warmth and clear enunciation, though he blots his copybook slightly at the end.

Closer to our day there is a coarse, throaty effort from Josef Traxel (1C 147-30 774). Werner Krenn (SET 549) is also disappointing, nasal in quality and lacking in contrast. On a more exalted plane lies Aksel Schiotz (DB 5265), light and delicate as was Pataky, although the quick tempo adopted does rob the aria of its atmosphere. Even higher on my list is Anton Dermota (Telef. E 3781; LGX 66048), in much better voice than in his complete performance for Böhm. Excellent diction (German), smooth, relaxed perceptive singing; all these qualities are present here, as they are in Léopold Simoneau's account (Philips ABR 4053), the equal of his fine reading for Karajan, and with just the edge over Dermota in sheer elegance. The most gratifying performance is by Nicolai Gedda (Col. 33CX 1528), gratifying in that it redeems his shortcomings on the Davis set. He is also elegant, and the contrasts are particularly well handled, Gedda achieving at times a magical, almost whispered tone.

Two singers have recorded 'Un' aura amorosa' and 'Tradito, schernito'. Jozsef Reti's fine, full voice has more than a touch of the baritone about it. He is certainly acceptable in both arias, but he does miss the subtler points of interpretation and his approach to the words tends towards the colourless (Hungaroton SLPX 11679). In 27, Schreier (Telef. 6. 235 063), too, is laboured in his diction, syllabic almost, and he also suffers from an over-resonant acoustic. Generally his smooth line and breath control are much to be admired but his note-stretching in 17 is irritatingly self-conscious; interpretatively, moreover, his singing strikes me as bland. The latter criticism can also be levelled at Stuart Burrows throughout his Mozart recital (Oiseau-Lyre DSLO 13). He is alone in having recorded all three tenor arias (17, 24 and 27), with only the singers from the complete sets for comparison in 'Ah! lo veggio'. It is here that Burrows is most successful, encompassing the treacherous lines with a painless ease, control and style not achieved by any of his rivals. In 17 and 27, however, although suavity, purity and beauty of tone are strongly in evidence, emotional involvement is not. In 'Tradito', for example, he does not sound the least bit 'betrayed' or indeed disturbed by his predicament.

The other number in which Ferrando has an important role to play is 29, the duet, 'Fra gli amplessi'. Surprisingly there appear to be only two recordings, one good, the other outstanding. The good one comes from Ina Souez and Heddle Nash (DX 671), with Raybould again conducting the music like a race against time. Souez achieves greater delicacy here than in her recording under Busch, while Nash is as ardent as ever; but, more important, both artists do capture the magic atmosphere of this duet, without which it is nothing. For the other recording (Concert Hall CM 2183) by Léopold Simoneau and his wife Pierrette Alarie with Walter Goehr conducting, there is nothing but praise. Their singing has been described elsewhere as 'delicious'. It is also lively, spontaneous and expressive. Simoneau's qualities have been discussed above, but Alarie's clear, bright-toned singing here is quite as captivating.

Of the equivalent duet for Guglielmo and Dorabella, 'Il core vi dono', there is just one recital performance by Brigitte Fassbaender and Tom Krause (SET 549). This is never less than competent, but it would have benefited from a more imaginative approach. Whereas Simoneau and Alarie made a compelling case for removing their duet from its context, the same cannot be said here.

Recordings of Guglielmo's arias 'Donne mie la fate a tanti' and 'Rivolgete a lui lo sguardo' (15a) are by no means as numerous as those of Ferrando's arias. Einstein confidently states that the latter (discarded only because Mozart felt it held up the action for too long) is 'the most remarkable buffo aria ever written'. He may well be right, but an aria with such variety of effect, both vocal and orchestral, naturally demands a performance of equal stature. This it does not receive from Marco Bakker (5C 065-24 584), in pedestrian mood, nor from Fernando Corena (SXL 2247), blunt in approach. Nor does Prey succeed here, at any rate in the second of his two performances of the aria (SAX 5293); he does have a smile in his voice, but the total effect is too beefy and boorish. For greater subtlety (and for superb support from Jochum) we must turn to his earlier recording (DG LPEM 19278). This is on the highlights disc from Jochum's performance of the opera, but it does not appear in the complete set.

The three finest accounts of this aria, however, come from elsewhere: Italo Tajo (Cetra OLPC 50019), who captures to perfection the buffo spirit of the music in his smiling voice, adopting also at times a convincing hushed, confidential tone; George London (Am. Col. ML 4699), who with his fruitier voice does not convey the youth of the character, but makes up for this with his urgent, committed singing – a stirring performance; finally Håkan Hagegård (my favourite), using his rich, buoyant baritone to stunning effect, as he did in 1978 at Glyndebourne. There is a real spring in his rhythms, all the words are made to tell ('io ardo, io gelo!') and he is tantalizingly confident as he enumerates his and Ferrando's varied talents and pleads with the sisters in turn to submit to their amorous overtures (Caprice CAP 1062).

Unfortunately Hagegård has not yet recorded 'Donne mi le fate'. Five others have done so, however, the most noteworthy being Karl Schmitt-Walter (Telef. KT 11023/1) in German. His velvety tones and intimate, flexible way with the music make this a most convincing account. More strident and more bitter, after the manner of Domgraf-Fassbaender, is

Fernando Corena (LX 3095), and once again there is Prey (SAX 5293) sounding too rushed here. As with 'Rivolgete', Marco Bakker (5C 065-24 584) does not generate much excitement, nor does Marko Rothmuller (C 4054).

Finally, to choose an ideal cast has proved almost as elusive a task as is performing the opera itself. For Fiordiligi I turn to Jurinac and Schwarzkopf; for Dorabella – Berganza or Ludwig; for Ferrando – Lewis, Nash, Simoneau or Kraus; for Guglielmo – Kunz, Domgraf-Fassbaender, Evans or Taddei; for Despina – Sciutti or Popp; and for Alfonso – Bruscantini, Fischer-Dieskau, Bacquier or Berry. To conduct the opera I would be happiest with Busch, Böhm, Jochum or Davis.

COSI FAN TUTTE

F Fiordiligi; *D* Dorabella; *Des* Despina; *Ferr* Ferrando; *G* Guglielmo; *DA* Don Alfonso

1935 Souez *F*; Helletsgrüber *D*;
Eisinger *Des*; Nash *Ferr*;
Domgraf-Fassbaender *G*;
Brownlee *DA*/1935 Glyndebourne
Festival Chorus and Orch./Busch
Turnabout ⓜ THS 65126-8

1952 Hassler *F*; Plümacher *D*;
Nentwig *Des*; Weikenmeier *Ferr*;
K. Hoppe *G*; Kelch
DA/Stuttgart TonStudio Chorus
and Orch./Dünnwald
Nixa ⓜ PLP 555/3; Remington
ⓜ 199-177

1952 (in English) Steber *F*; Thebom
D; Peters *Des*; Tucker *Ferr*;
Guarrera *G*; Alvary
DA/Metropolitan Opera Chorus
and Orch./Stiedry
CBS (US) ⓜ Y 3-32670

1954 Schwarzkopf *F*; Merriman *D*;
Otto *Des*; Simoneau *Ferr*;
Panerai *G*; Bruscantini
DA/Chorus,
Philharmonia/Karajan
World Records ⓜ SOC 195-7;
Angel ⓜ 3522CL

1955 (heavily cut) Della Casa *F*;
Ludwig *D*; Loose *Des*; Dermota
Ferr; Kunz *G*; Schöffler
DA/Vienna State Opera Chorus,
VPO/Böhm
Decca GOS 543-5; London
Richmond SRS 63508

1956 (live performance) Schwarzkopf
F; Merriman *D*; Sciutti *Des*;
Alva *Ferr*; Panerai *G*; Calabrese
DA/La Scala Chorus and
Orch./Cantelli
Cetra ⓜ LO 13/3

1956 Stich-Randall *F*; Malaniuk *D*;
Sciutti *Des*; Kmentt *Ferr*; Berry
G; Ernster *DA*/Vienna State
Opera Chorus, Vienna
SO/Moralt
Philips ⓜ GL 5703-5; Mercury
Phillips PHC 3005

1962 Schwarzkopf *F*; Ludwig *D*;
Steffek *Des*; Kraus *Ferr*; Taddei
G; Berry *DA*/Philharmonia
Chorus and Orch./Böhm
HMV SLS 5028 ④ TC-SLS
5028; Angel SDL 3631

1962 Seefried *F*; Merriman *D*; Köth
Des; Haefliger *Ferr*; Prey *G*;
Fischer-Dieskau *DA*/Berlin RIAS
Chorus, Berlin PO/Jochum
DG 2709 012

1967 L. Price *F*; Troyanos *D*; Raskin
Des; Shirley *Ferr*; Milnes *G*;
Flagello *DA*/Ambrosian Opera
Chorus, New
Philharmonia/Leinsdorf
RCA (UK) SER 5575-8; (US)
LSC 6416

1969 Casapietra *F*; Burmeister *D*;
Geszty *Des*; Schreier *Ferr*; Leib
G; Adam *DA*/Berlin State
Opera Chorus and Orch./Suitner

Ariola-Eurodisc XG 80408R
1971 M. Price *F*; Minton *D*; Popp
Des; Alva *Ferr*; Evans *G*; Sotin
DA/Alldis Choir, New
Philharmonia/Klemperer
HMV SLS 961; EMI 1C 191
02249-52
1973 Lorengar *F*; Berganza *D*; Berbié
Des; Davies *Ferr*; Krause *G*;
Bacquier *DA*/Royal Opera
Chorus and Orch./Solti
Decca D 56D4; London OSA
1442
1974 Caballé *F*; Baker *D*; Cotrubas
Des; Gedda *Ferr;* Ganzarolli *G*;
van Allan *DA*/Royal Opera
Chorus and Orch./C. Davis
Philips 6707 025 ④ 7699 055
1974 Tarrès *F*; Lövaas *D*; Hannsmann
Des; Geisen *Ferr*; Huttenlocher
G; Hirte *DA*/Paris Opéra
Chorus, Monte Carlo Opera
Orch./Colombo
Concert Hall SMS 2933-5
1974 (live performance, Salzburg
Festival) Janowitz *F*;

Fassbaender *D*; Grist *Des*;
Schreier *Ferr*; Prey *G*; Panerai
DA/Vienna State Opera Chorus,
VPO/Böhm
DG 2740 118 ④ 3371 019
1977 Te Kanawa *F*; von Stade *D*;
Stratas *Des*; Rendall *Ferr*;
Huttenlocher *G*; Bastin
DA/Rhine Opera Chorus,
Strasbourg PO/Lombard
RCA Erato STU 71110; RCA
(US) FRL 3 2629 ④ FRK 3
2629

Excerpts

1950 Jurinac *F*; Thebom *D*; Lewis
Ferr; Kunz *G*; Borriello
DA/Glyndebourne Festival
Orch./Busch
HMV DB21115-20; RCA Ⓜ LM
1126
1953c (in German) Camphausen *F*;
Wilhelm *Ferr*; Ramms *G*/Leipzig
Opera Chorus and Orch./Rubahn
Allegro Ⓜ ALL 3058

Die Zauberflöte

PETER BRANSCOMBE

The first complete recording of *Die Zauberflöte* was made as late as 1937, but the gramophone companies could be said to have made up for lost time since then, as the discography at the end of the chapter indicates. Apart from the complete recordings, there have naturally enough been a considerable number of recordings of arias and duets, and also of some of the larger concerted numbers; the most interesting of those that I have been able to hear are discussed at the end.

Although I have referred to complete recordings, some words of explanation are required. *Die Zauberflöte*, subtitled by Mozart 'a German Opera', and by its librettist, Schikaneder, 'Grand Opera', is in fact a *Singspiel*, with lengthy stretches of dialogue. Both in staged performances and on disc it has become customary to abridge the dialogue extensively. Although the music could be (and at least once has been) accommodated on five LP sides, the convention of the three-disc set can readily permit large enough passages of dialogue to convey the essentials of the story, and also to suggest the atmosphere of a stage performance. It is easy to dismiss the text – but this was not Mozart's view, nor was it Goethe's. A recording that omits dialogue is only a concert performance; however strong the dramatic impulse of conductor and cast, there is within the score more often than not no dramatic link between one number and the next.

For this reason it is important to recognize from the outset that the performances conducted by Beecham, Karajan, Klemperer, and by Böhm in his earlier (Decca) recording, cannot, for all their musical virtues, realize the integrity of the work. Of the two private recordings from Salzburg Festival performances, the one under Toscanini contains just the odd spoken phrase that was left in when the poorly engineered LPs were cut, whereas the one conducted by Furtwängler includes a generous proportion of the dialogue without seriously overloading six LP sides. Of the recordings with dialogue, Fricsay's preserves the modicum required if the listener is to follow the story, though here the spoken voices are in some cases obviously not those of the singers. Böhm's later (DG) recording is particularly successful in its use of dialogue, apart from a few hoary and unauthentic jokes. In this respect the Solti and Sawallisch sets are also well served, though again with the inclusion of comments that have no place in the original libretto. The Suitner performance often departs from Schikaneder, but the dialogue is glossed in such a way as to help the ill-informed listener. The Ericson set – the soundtrack of the Bergman film for Swedish television – provides a lot of chat in Swedish which often seems remote from the original; the talk is mainly uttered in loud stage whispers, brilliantly characterized (we could have done without the noises of machinery and stage business).

The earliest recording of *Die Zauberflöte* was made in Berlin for HMV's Mozart Opera Society by a distinguished cast under Sir Thomas Beecham. It has been reissued at least twice – on the World Records and the Turnabout labels, the latter on only five sides; and it remains one of the most exciting and attractive of the dozen or more versions that have been made. Right from the beginning Beecham leaves us in no doubt as to the vivid theatrical qualities of the score – the overture provides the happiest contrast between the weighty (yet paradoxically ethereal) opening Adagio, and the crisp, witty sparkle of the Allegro, with textures clearer than in some stereo versions. Sir Thomas favours fast tempi, yet so winningly does he persuade the Berlin Philharmonic to play, so buoyant are the rhythms, that the listener scarcely ever feels a sense of undue haste (on the contrary, the one feature that justifies reproach is the mannered slowing of the pulse at cadences).

The introduction is taken at a cracking pace, full of excitement and, in the Allegretto middle section, of delicate fun. Helge Roswaenge, one of the few operatic tenors who continued to sing as freshly and stylishly for many years after the war as he had done before it, is on the rough side in his cries for help, but he gets better and better as the opera proceeds. His aria is less relaxed and radiant than one could wish, and for a tenor with so virile a high D he makes surprisingly heavy weather of the Gs. But his solo with flute in the first finale is just right, and he is at his very best in the exchanges with the Orator, exquisitely paced, and rich in subtle contrast (and more naturally and grammatically graced than by most Taminos). The Papageno is that splendid artist Gerhard Hüsch – warm, lovable but unsentimental, his 'r's characteristically rolled, his phrasing and diction full of poise and expressiveness. Erna Berger's Queen of Night is admirably fiery in 'Der Hölle Rache'; but there is something of the hard little girl about her timbre, rather than the imperious monarch. Wilhelm Strienz is quite an impressive Sarastro, though not ideally clean in arioso and recitative, or nimble in the semiquavers of the second aria (which Beecham does not hurry). For me the most disappointing assumption in the set – and in saying so I shall doubtless enrage many who were keen opera-goers before I was born – is Tiana Lemnitz's Pamina. She is rather bumpy in the duet with Papageno, matronly in the Act 1 finale (she is a Pamina who sounds older than her mother); her aria, taken more slowly than usual, is sung with fine control though also with a 'classy' sound quality; she is at her best in the second finale. Heinrich Tessmer's Monostatos is one of the best on record. Not the least virtues of this set are features that by more than thirty years presage recommendations of the New Mozart Edition score, including awareness of appoggiaturas, and of the fact that the Orator should sing the First Priest's music (did Sir Thomas slip into the old Prussian State Library before sessions to check points in Mozart's autograph?!).

Devotees of *Die Zauberflöte* and *aficionados* of two of the greatest conductors of an earlier generation may have come across semi-private recordings made at the Salzburg Festival a couple of years either side of the war. One gives an idea, acoustically and musically distorted, of Toscanini's performance on 30 July 1937. The microphone seems to have been placed dangerously close to the glockenspiel (Papageno in Nibelheim!), and the cutting and montage are amateurish. But the cast was a fine one – Roswaenge as Tamino, Willi Domgraf-Fassbaender as Papageno (he was evidently prepared to concede the conductor a rushed 'Der Vogelfänger bin ich ja' in return for a comparatively relaxed 'Ein Mädchen oder Weibchen'), Alexander Kipnis as Sarastro (casual over note-values in arioso, but rounded and even-toned in 'O Isis und Osiris', taken unusually slowly), Hilde Konetzni as First Lady and Alfred Jerger as the Orator. Julie Osvath fails to live up to the promise she shows in the slow introduction to the Queen's first aria, and Jarmila Novotna is not permitted by Toscanini's rapid tempo to capitalize in Pamina's aria on her natural taste and beauty of tone. William Wernigk is a very good Monostatos. Time after time Toscanini gives the impression that he was in a great hurry (his Allegro in the overture is an absurdly unmusical scramble), yet of course every now and again his positive qualities show through – for instance in an impressive presentation of the chorale of the Men in Armour, at once beautiful and menacing, and in Papageno's final scene, for which a measure of relaxation and charm are allowed.

The other 'unofficial' reminder of a Salzburg *Zauberflöte* is the performance of 27 July 1949 conducted by Wilhelm Furtwängler. This is a proper stage performance, rich in atmosphere; unusually long-playing sides allow a much fuller account of Schikaneder's dialogue than usual. Although the actual quality of the records is variable and never high, there is much to enjoy, especially from the women in the cast: Wilma Lipp crisp though occasionally clumsy as the Queen, Irmgard Seefried alternately arch, then radiant and poignant, as Pamina (her diction is poor), and an uncommonly strong trio of Ladies: Gertrude Grob-Prandl, Sieglinde Wagner and Elisabeth Höngen. Apart from Josef Greindl's sonorous and firm Sarastro, Peter Klein's Monostatos and Ernst Haefliger and Hermann Uhde as the Men in Armour, the male contribution is less distinguished: Walter Ludwig is forthright rather than noble and elegant as Tamino, and Karl Schmitt-Walter is gruff, and at times careless, as Papageno. There are quirks in Furtwängler's reading – a remarkably slow account of the 'Hm, hm, hm' quintet and of 'In diesen heil'gen Hallen'; yet I was never left in any doubt about the stature of the conductor (as I was with the set previously discussed).

Herbert von Karajan's recording of *Die Zauberflöte* is a concert performance by a more or less typical Vienna State Opera cast of early 1950s with the VPO and Singverein der Gesellschaft der Musikfreunde. There is some constriction of tone and an occasional edginess to recall the age of the recording, but the quality is good for its period, and there is a wide dynamic range. Although women are used for the Three Boys in place of the Sängerknaben normally favoured in the theatre, they suggest the ethereal quality required. No one who heard a typical performance in the Theater an der Wien in the years after the war will fail to be delighted at the chance of renewing acquaintance with old friends and happy memories, but for me the recording does not quite come up to expectations. Erich Kunz, incomparable as Papageno on the stage, sounds confidential rather than entirely confident (the dotted *gruppetti* in 'Ein Mädchen oder Weibchen' are distinctly clumsy), and Anton Dermota, apart from treating grace-notes curiously, sounds querulous and over-emphatic in 'Dies Bildnis' (taken very slowly) – though the solo with flute is more even and ingratiating. Ludwig Weber is rough in Sarastro's music in the first finale, but he sings his arias well – if not with the radiant assurance that memory insists he had in the theatre even at this late stage in his career. Sena Jurinac, a marvellous First Lady, is not strongly supported by her companions. Lipp is below her best form as the Queen – she makes heavy weather of her opening recitative and the Andante, though the fluency and incisiveness of her coloratura commands respect. Irmgard Seefried as Pamina tends to swoop to a note, and her line lacks easeful simplicity. George London's imposing Orator, and Emmy Loose's fresh, charming Papagena, join Klein's spirited and individual Monostatos on the credit side. Karajan paces the performance curiously here and there, hustling a few numbers (the Queen's and Monostatos's arias) and dragging Sarastro's second aria; but the playing and the choral singing are very fine. The recording is uncluttered, the performance never less than impressive – but overall I find it short of magic.

The Berlin recording made by Ferenc Fricsay is a worthwhile early attempt to convey the sense of a live performance through sensibly produced dialogue – the exchanges are kept short, which is reasonable, but they are far from the original Schikaneder text. The recording, cut at a low level, certainly shows its age, but the set has some attractive features, not least the authoritative and eloquent Orator of Kim Borg. Ernst Haefliger is a lyrical Tamino, a shade too mild, perhaps, but alert to the importance of his contribution to the concerted numbers. Dietrich

Fischer-Dieskau varies Papageno's strophes skilfully, but he does not sound entirely at home in the Birdcatcher's world – a tourist in *Lederhosen*. Josef Greindl is drab in Sarastro's first phrases, but he sings the first aria well, if not evenly. Neither the trio of Ladies nor that of Boys is particularly good, and the Pamina of Maria Stader is decent rather than exciting. Rita Streich sings the Queen's music well, but without much depth of characterization. Fricsay, one feels, has no special insight into the opera, but gives a performance to which I have often returned over the years for some fine vocal assumptions – and for its very lack of idiosyncrasy or perversity.

The earlier of Karl Böhm's sets is similar to Karajan's in several respects: both are based on Viennese forces, both entirely lack dialogue, and they are often surprisingly similar in respect of tempo and general approach. The cast is not outstanding, but the opera as a whole is persuasively shaped and its stature is properly appreciated. The trios of Ladies and Boys (taken here by women) are good and reliable, and the minor roles are nicely done. Léopold Simoneau is hampered by poor German, but he is an eloquent Tamino, especially in the quiet, introspective passages; and Hilde Gueden, though steely toned and sometimes unfeeling, sings Pamina's aria with real distinction. Like many another Queen of Night, Lipp is happier in the starry heights than in lower register legato. Kurt Böhme is unsteady in Sarastro's music, neither giving much pleasure nor suggesting that he himself felt any. The outstanding assumption is Walter Berry's Papageno – merry, affectionate, busy but not restless. Some attempt has been made to suggest stage action, with characters now close at hand, now some distance away. The orchestra for the most part plays as we all think the Vienna Philharmonic should, though there are one or two patches of poor ensemble.

Otto Klemperer's recording is another to omit the dialogue. It is a spacious reading, clearly recorded, yet with little sense of theatre. Right from the beginning of the overture Klemperer enables us to hear felicities of orchestration, though there is none of the mannered highlighting (for instance, of the bassoon line in 'Soll ich dich, Teurer, nicht mehr sehn') that for me marred his conducting of the work at Covent Garden in 1962. The cast assembled for these sessions is arguably the finest of all, its strength in depth indicated by the inclusion of Karl Liebl and Franz Crass as the Men in Armour, Elisabeth Schwarzkopf, Christa Ludwig and Marga Höffgen as a marvellous trio of Ladies, and Agnes Giebel, Anna Reynolds and Josephine Veasey strong, even if unboyish, as the Three Boys. Lucia Popp is an agile and exciting Queen, though she leans hard on held notes. Gundula Janowitz is a ravishingly eloquent, pure-toned Pamina, but impersonal in the aria. Berry repeats his jolly, though here intermittently almost ponderous, Papageno. Gottlob Frick is inclined to roughness, like most Sarastros; he is more impressive in his first aria than in his second. Nicolai Gedda makes a committed but not entirely smooth-toned Tamino – the solo with flute in the Act 1 finale is strident, and here as elsewhere he lacks true dynamic contrast. But the exchanges with Franz Crass's very impressive Orator are handled with unusual awareness of nuances of pulse and line – time and again in the ensembles there is a lucidity and at the same time a firmness which one realizes one has missed in other performances. All the same, there are passages where Klemperer does not secure absolute unanimity of chording, which have to be set against the life and spirit of which the performance is full. Just occasionally the tempi are too slow ('Bei Männern', the March, 'Ein Mädchen oder Weibchen'), but even here one can see a reason. The Philharmonia Orchestra and Chorus are in their finest, most mellow form.

Böhm's second *Zauberflöte* is in most respects finer than his earlier one; indeed, it is one of the most consistently enjoyable of all. It includes dialogue (close to, sensibly shortened from, Schikaneder's original), and it is strongly cast and affectionately played – the Berlin Philharmonic in top form. Böhm takes a sane, unhurried view of this marvellous music, securing precise ensemble and clear detail. The cast is dominated by Fritz Wunderlich as Tamino – an assumption of such beauty and depth of discernment as to make us feel yet again what we lost through his untimely death. He may have been inconsistent in gracing blunt phrase-ends, but the lyrical ardour and youthful nobility he brings to the part are compelling, and enable him to sustain an unusually slow tempo for 'Dies Bildnis'. Evelyn Lear's Pamina is almost inevitably not of this standard; her phrasing is gusty, she sounds distinctly tentative at times, and only rarely (for instance in the duet with Papageno) does she convey the directness and emotional content of her music. Roberta Peters's Queen is uneven – at her best very good indeed, but rather limp in her slow music. Fischer-Dieskau makes a calmer Papageno than on the Fricsay set – he is not a 'natural' for the part, but he sings ingratiatingly and with wit. A finer pair of Men in Armour than James King and Martti Talvela could not be wished for. Hans Hotter is not in good voice as the Orator; Friedrich Lenz is a Monostatos who makes the most of his chances in the ensembles, but in the aria he sounds timorous rather than evil. Franz Crass is arguably the best Sarastro on record: sonorous, easy of delivery, entirely credible. The RIAS Chamber Choir is especially good in the chorus (18).

Georg Solti recorded his *Zauberflöte* in Vienna. Although he too uses the Vienna Philharmonic and State Opera Chorus, the cast is not Viennese but international. In view of the prevalence of singers whose native language is not German, it is perhaps surprising that the dialogue (close to Schikaneder, though sensibly reduced) was not entrusted to German actors – the collection of accents is motley in the extreme. The recording staff have worked too hard, producing needlessly loud and prolonged thunder, genuine lions roaring away at Papageno in the vaults, fetters rattling and so on. But if the voices are sometimes disconcertingly close, in most respects the balance is good, the acoustic spacious and theatrical. Solti creates a restless impression in the overture, with detail clamouring for attention at the expense of linear development. Thereafter he is less inclined to fuss, but I do not find in this performance enough relaxation to counterbalance the proper urgency he brings to the more overtly dramatic scenes.

Stuart Burrows's first phrases nicely suggest a hero in disarray, and the Three Ladies are very good in their various important functions. Burrows sings his aria ardently, though with insufficient dynamic contrast; in the first finale he outscores Fischer-Dieskau's Orator in respect of graces, and is quite his equal in pointful declamation. Hermann Prey is a fine Papageno: neat, with plenty of wit and vocal presence and – apart from a few silly jokes he is allowed or persuaded to utter in the dialogue – he gives as much pleasure as almost any Papageno on record. Talvela, rare among Sarastros, is equally warm-voiced and at ease at the top and at the bottom of his vocal range, and equally persuasive in the two arias. Pilar Lorengar is an appealing, though sometimes rough (and quite un-German) Pamina. Cristina Deutekom brings many virtues to the part of the Queen: crisp, focused falling intervals are given their full value, and she creates a sense of excitement and awe; but her coloratura has a curiously disembodied quality which is disturbing in the wrong sense (it is almost as though she were gargling with marbles in her throat). The choral singing and the trio of Sängerknaben are of high standard; and a welcome extra, outstanding even among a rich bunch of libretto-booklets accompanying the sets, is the inclusion of the designs that Oskar Kokoschka made for the projected Covent Garden production of 1964, which were later used elsewhere (Geneva, Chicago and Rome). In the last resort, and despite the indisputable excellence of the VPO's playing and of most of the singing, the extent to which this is the version one would choose to live with will depend on personal preference; for me it is rather over-insistent.

Wolfgang Sawallisch conducts the Bavarian State Opera in what is presumably the first quadrophonic recording; hearing it only in stereo I missed the effect of the Queen's first aria being sung from overhead – and I was sorely troubled by what I hope was merely a bad set of pressings. The producer uses space and changes of acoustic well, and the feel of a theatre performance is strong, albeit with cheapened dialogue. Musically the most interesting feature is the inclusion, between the duet 'Bewahret euch vor Weibertücken' and the quintet 'Wie? Wie? Wie?', of the duet for Tamino and Papageno, 'Pamina, wo bist du?' This number, which can be found in the Peters vocal score but is as yet apparently unpublished in full score, is presumed to be by Mozart himself – one of the two numbers (the other said to be a variant of 'Bei Männern, welche Liebe fühlen') that Schikaneder advertised on the playbill for the première of the work in his new Theater an der Wien on 5 January 1802 as having been given him by his friend Mozart. My first impression is that it could be by Mozart, though if it is, he was well below his best when he wrote it. I am suspicious, however, as to whether (and why) Schikaneder would have waited ten years before using two numbers given him by Mozart. In style the duet is close to music familiar from elsewhere in the opera.

The strong cast includes Peter Schreier as Tamino ('Dies Bildnis' exciting, distinctly fast, rather bumpy), Anneliese Rothenberger as Pamina (she tends to go for drama at the expense of line), Edda Moser as an extremely good and neat Queen, Berry as Papageno (trying too hard to be individual), and Kurt Moll as a full, round-toned Sarastro.

Another German version – this time from the east – is conducted by Otmar Suitner on the Eurodisc label. He has the Dresden Staatskapelle, Leipzig Radio Chorus and a good cast which includes a fine trio of Boys from the Kreuzchor. The set is not easy to listen to because of the exceptionally wide dynamic levels and the restlessness of dialogue and production, but it is well worth looking out for in respect of several strong qualities. Suitner's approach is leisurely – several times his turns out to be the slowest account of a number in all the available versions. The modicum of dialogue that is retained (simplified in the interests of clarity and sure identification) allows the feel of a proper performance without any danger to the primacy of the music. The cast is uneven – Theo Adam is among the weakest of recorded Sarastros, and one or two of the minor roles are not impressively filled. But Schreier is both princely and manly in Tamino's music, Sylvia Geszty sings the Queen's arias excitingly and cleanly, Siegfried Vogel makes a fine Orator – and in Helen Donath this set has just about the loveliest of all Paminas, her aria in particular taken exceptionally slowly, but sung with beautiful tonal quality and with finely sustained line. Günther Leib is an un-Viennese Papageno, which is no bad thing – he sings the music very well, with spirit and discernment.

The Rhine Opera set under Alain Lombard, is strongly cast, and the quality of the recorded sound is high; this is a version that for many people will come near the top of the list. Kiri Te Kanawa's name alone will sell it to many opera-lovers, though I find myself cautious in my recommendation of her Pamina, the general beauty of which is marred by unidiomatic German and some gustiness in the phrasing. Edita Gruberova is an impressive Queen, with neat coloratura and trill, though less even in the lower reaches than one could wish. The Three Ladies offer variable German and varying degrees of vibrato, but are otherwise good. Peter Hofmann's Tamino is strong and personable, but a shade unwieldy. The temple is unusually well staffed: Kurt Moll repeats his splendid assumption of Sarastro, José van Dam is a firm, expressive Orator; and the other priest, the Men in Armour, the Three Boys and Monostatos are all notably good. Philippe Huttenlocher is a forthright, slightly over-emphatic Papageno, well supported by Kathleen Battle's Papagena. The chorus and orchestra are reliable if hardly memorable. Lombard's tempi are sometimes faster, sometimes slower than usual, though I take exception only to the *ritardandi* that he introduces late in a number. The dialogue is for the most part nicely characterized. This is a thoroughly competitive version.

The final set is the sound-track of Ingmar Bergman's television production of *Trollflöjten*. I enjoyed the television showing much less than did friends whose judgement I respect, and the recording, with all its noises of machinery and stage business, does nothing to alter my opinion. For each visual touch that cast valid fresh light on the action, there were at least two that wilfully distracted attention – or so it seemed to me. Anyone not minding the opera sung in Swedish will certainly enjoy Ulrik Cold's light but finely sung Sarastro, and Josef Köstlinger's Tamino (not a beautiful voice, but well used apart from the absence of appoggiaturas; and he has an expressive *mezza voce*). Håkan Hagegård's Papageno has many admirers (he loses one strophe of each of the songs). I do not find that he characterizes the music as nicely as he acted the part. Birgit Nordin sings the Queen's arias with admirable venom, though gustily and effortfully; Irma Urrila's Pamina is also uneven, over-emphatic, inclined to shrillness. Ragnar Ulfung, a fine artist, is hustled uncomfortably in Monostatos's aria, though he contributes positively to the concerted numbers.

Eric Ericson conducts such a neat, unexceptionable performance of the overture as to arouse expectations of distinction, but his tempi are often uncomfortably fast (even faster than Toscanini's), and once or twice disconcertingly slow (for instance the Orator's 'Sobald dich führt . . .'). The feature which for me rules this set out of court is the liberty taken with the score – 11, 16 and 19 are removed completely, and the second finale – certainly the longest, and arguably the finest, of all Mozart's operatic numbers – is wickedly tampered with (by comparison with this boorish bravado, the decision to let the Three Boys introduce themselves in the quintet [5] is trifling). The finale opens, as it should, with the scene in which the Three Boys prevent Pamina from killing herself (bars 1–189); we then jump to Papageno's attempted suicide (bars 413–743); the 'Threefold trombone chords' that we missed at the beginning of Act 2 and later are then heard, followed by dialogue, the Priests' chorus (18 – here taken flippantly fast), more dialogue, then back to Mozart's finale for bars 190–412 (the trials by flood and fire); and finally we hear the fourth and last section of Mozart's finale, bars 744 to the end. This version is a permanent memento for admirers of the Bergman film, but its main value otherwise lies in its determined avoidance of portentousness.

There has been a large number of records of excerpts from *Die Zauberflöte*, but I have been able to hear only a proportion of the single numbers recorded on 78s. Many of these were made by singers famous in their generation, and indeed still venerated today. Of around forty numbers that I have been able to listen to, surprisingly few would seem to merit special mention here. To some extent tastes and standards have changed; to some extent it may be claimed that performances of isolated numbers reflect not so much the singer's penetration into a role as his or her ability to sing the music as beautifully as he or she know how (often, in the early days, with an eye to the length of a record side); the result is often bland, characterless.

Of a dozen versions of Tamino's 'Dies Bildnis', four or five struck me as outstanding – Tudor Davies (E 401) sings the aria in English with tender, delicate control, but no lack of ardour; Julius Patzak (Gram. 95437; LV 191) reveals his incomparable clarity of diction and deep insight, if not quite his finest vocal quality; Richard Tauber, in his middle version of three (PXO 1024), is strong yet honeyed in tone, ardently lyrical in phrasing; and Hermann Jadlowker (2-042007; GV 62) is full of feeling, princely in style, if a shade rough once or twice. Jacques Urlus offers smooth, accomplished singing both here (Edison 82260; GV 70) and in 'Wie stark ist nicht dein Zauberton' (Edison; Club 99 reissue), though his German diction is less than entirely assured. There are also appreciable souvenirs of Aksel Schiotz, Heddle Nash, David Lloyd and Marcel Wittrisch.

Easily my favourite version of Papageno's 'Der Vogelfänger bin ich ja' is the warm, beautifully sung account by Gerhard Hüsch (Parlo. R 979). In English, Dennis Noble sings both of Papageno's songs pleasingly, if palely and with one or two liberties over note-values ('Der Vogelfänger' on B 9325, 'Ein Mädchen oder Weibchen' on C 3520). I have not heard a really satisfactory separate recording of Papageno's and Pamina's duet, 'Bei Männern welche Liebe fühlen'; if the Pamina has the radiance and neatness required, she is either cautious-sounding, or let down by her partner; even the famous Perras-Hüsch version (DA 4408) is a bit joyless, definitely on the slow side for Mozart's marking of Andantino.

The versions of the Queen of Night's arias that have come my way are less numerous and memorable than I had expected. Selma Kurz (43739; TQD 3020) tosses off the first with excellent coloratura technique and very neat additional trills, though also with annoying cuts; Frieda Hempel (VB 21; HQM 7026), singing in Italian, is slack in the Andante but brilliant and strong in the Allegro. Neshdanova's 'Der Hölle Rache' in Russian (VB 37; HML 7026) is exciting, though she is naughty to toss in an octave rise at the end; Gwen Catley, singing the same aria in English (B 9674; CLP 3719), fires off the coloratura with firmness and clarity, though some of her note-values are casual. Maria Ivogün (Poly. 85310; LV 67) is even better, firm, positive, accurate.

The more often and more carefully I listened to the versions available to me of Sarastro's arias – including old 78 versions, and those on the complete sets – the more aware I grew of the supreme difficulty for any singer of performing both arias perfectly. 'O Isis und Osiris' at its Adagio tempo requires firmness and evenly sustained legato singing of the highest order (there are only seven pairs of quavers to vary the solemn progress of minims and crotchets); its range from the F below the bass stave to the C above it is less of a problem than is the production of even, steadily focused solemnity of tone. 'In diesen heil'gen Hallen', marked Larghetto, requires a less deliberate tempo, though virtually the same vocal range. Its frequent semiquavers and occasional demisemiquavers demand a flexibility the absence of which would not be remarked in a singer who could sing the other aria superbly. Rare indeed is the artist who can rise equally well to the demands of both of Sarastro's arias. Wilhelm Hesch (3-42616; CO 300), in his slightly cut and chorusless recording of 'O Isis' of 1906, has exactly the tonal and interpretative qualities of the ideal Sarastro; however, in 'In diesen heil'gen Hallen' (3-42625; CO 300), recorded in the same year, he is less happy – despite beautiful touches, there is some uncertainty over tempo which adversely affects the poise of the whole (incidentally, like Alfred Jerger and one or two other singers, he gives us only the first strophe). Of the singers whose recordings I know, Kipnis comes closest to perfection in the two arias. His 'O Isis', recorded in 1930 under Schmalstich (DA 1218; WR SH 280) is ideally even-toned, warm, authoritative; in the 'Hallenarie' (DB 1551; SH 280) he is again very impressive, though in the second strophe his line spreads as he rises to and drops back from the high C sharps; and he cannot resist an octave drop at the end. Of other versions of 'O Isis', Plançon's of 1905 (Victor 85042) has admirable features, but he breaks up the line. That this is not necessarily due to the different syllabification of the Italian text is suggested by Ezio Pinza (DB 1088; Victor 1217), who shows that it is possible to sing the aria in Italian without distorting the phrasing.

Pamina's aria has been frequently recorded, but again few of the versions I have heard have that special quality that demands notice here. Ileana Cotrubas in her 1977 recital (CBS 76521) sings it very well and evenly, though without ultimate distinction. Eide Noréna (DB 4852; Rococo 5259), singing in French, is free with the coloratura in bar 15, and plummy in bars 34-5, but she offers a vital, well-sustained and fresh piece of singing. Lotte Schöne comes very close to the ideal. Her 1928 recording (German HMV EJ 262; LV 6) has just the right blend of pathos and anguish; her clean, noble, beautifully poised singing has an appropriately valedictory note with which to end this short account of some of the most interesting records of single numbers from *Die Zauberflöte*.

DIE ZAUBERFLÖTE

P Pamina; *T* Tamino; *Pap* Papageno; *Papa* Papagena; *Q* Queen of Night; *S* Sarastro; *O* Orator; *M* Monostatos

1937 (live performance, Salzburg Festival) Novotna P; Roswaenge T; Domgraf-Fassbaender Pap; Komarek Papa; Osvath Q; Kipnis S; Jerger O; Wernick M/Vienna State Opera Chorus, VPO/Toscanini
Cetra ⓜ LO 44/3

1937 Lemnitz P; Roswaenge T; Hüsch Pap; Beilke Papa; Berger Q; Strienz S; Grossmann O; Tessmer M/Berlin Favres Choir, Berlin PO/Beecham
World Records ⓜ SH 158-60; Turnabout ⓜ THS 65078-80

1950 Seefried P; Dermota T; Kunz Pap; Loose Papa; Lipp Q; Weber S; London O; Klein M/Vienna State Opera Chorus, VPO/Karajan
HMV ⓔ SLS 5052

1951 (live performance, Salzburg Festival) Seefried P; Dermota T; Kunz Pap; Oravez Papa; Lipp Q; Greindl S; Schöffler O; Klein M/Vienna State Opera Chorus, VPO/Furtwängler
Cetra ⓜ LO9/3

1955 Stader P; Haefliger T; Fischer-Dieskau Pap; Otto Papa; Streich Q; Greindl S; Borg O; Vantin M/Berlin RIAS Choir, Berlin Radio SO/Fricsay
DG ⓜ 2701 015

1955 Gueden P; Simoneau T; Berry Pap; Loose Papa; Lipp Q; Böhme S; Schöffler O; Jaresch M/Vienna State Opera Chorus, VPO/Böhm
Decca GOS 501-3; Richmond SRS 63507

1955 Bijster P; Garen T; Gschwend Pap; Duval Papa; Tyler Q; Hoekman S; Gorin O; Taverne M/Chorus, Netherlands PO/Krannhals
MMS ⓜ 2033

1964 Janowitz P; Gedda T; Berry Pap; Pütz Papa; Popp Q; Frick S; Crass O; Unger M/Philharmonia Chorus and Orch./Klemperer
HMV SLS 912; Angel SCL 3651

1965 Lear P; Wunderlich T; Fischer-Dieskau Pap; Otto Papa; Peters Q; Crass S; Hotter O; Lenz M/Berlin RIAS Choir, Berlin PO/Böhm
DG 2740 108 ④ 3371 002

1968 Donath P; Schreier T; Leib Pap; Hoff Papa; Geszty Q; Adam S; Vogel O; Neukirch M/Leipzig Radio Chorus, Dresden State Orch./Suitner Ariola-Eurodisc XG 80584R

1969 Lorengar P; Burrows T; Prey Pap; Holm Papa; Deutekom Q; Talvela S; Fischer-Dieskau O; Stolze M/Vienna State Opera Chorus, VPO/Solti
Decca SET 479-81 ④ K2A4; London OSA 1397

1972 Rothenberger P; Schreier T; Berry Pap; Miljakovic Papa; Moser Q; Moll S; Adam O; Brokmeier M/Bavarian State Opera Chorus and Orch./Sawallisch
EMI 1C 195 39154-6Q Angel SCL 3807 (Q)

1974 (TV sound track, in Swedish) Urrila P; Köstlinger T; Hagegård Pap; Eriksson Papa; Nordin Q; Cold S; Saedén O; Ulfung M/Swedish Radio Chorus and Orch./Ericson
BBC REK 223; A&M (US) 4577 ④ CS-4577

1978 Te Kanawa P; Hofmann T; Huttenlocher Pap; Battle Papa; Gruberova Q; Moll S; van Dam O; Orth M/Rhine Opera Chorus, Strasbourg PO/Lombard
Barclay 960 012-4 ④ 4-960 012-4

Excerpts

1950s Grümmer P; Traxel T; Prey Pap; Berger Papa; Köth Q; Frick S; Köhn O/Berlin PO, Berlin SO; Regensburger Domspatzen, German Opera Chorus/Schüchter, Schmidt-Boelcke, Stein
EMI 1C 047 28575; Vox STPL 518220

1960 (in French) Micheau P; Giraudeau T; Dens Pap; Berbié

Papa; Robin *Q*; Depraz
S/Froment EMI 2C 061 12144

1964 Lipp *P*; Schock *T*; Kunz *Pap*;
Hallstein *Q*; Frick *S*/orchestras-
Hollreiser, Schüchter, Stein
Ariola-Eurodisc K73739R; World
Records SOH 186

1965 Muszely *P*; Grobe *T*; Bautz
Pap; Geszty *Q*; van Mill *S*/

Hamburg State Opera Chorus and
Orch./Ludwig
Europa 114034.5 ④ 514.034.0

1968 (in Hungarian) László *P*; Réti *T*;
Melis *Pap*; Csengery *Papa*; Agay
Q; Gregor *S*/Hungarian People's
Army Chorus, Hungarian State
Opera Orch./Erdélyi
Qualiton SLPX 11539

Fidelio

LORD HAREWOOD

The story of *Fidelio* for Beethoven was in essence contemporary, based, it is said, on an incident in the 1790s witnessed by the original French librettist, Jean Nicolas Bouilly, and its significance was underlined when the first performance took place in Vienna in November 1805 before an audience consisting mostly of soldiers of the occupying French army.

The inherent problem is quickly stated: Beethoven's aspirations led him to lofty themes, his chosen convention was close to *Singspiel*, and his operatic inexperience prevented a complete reconciliation of the opposing pulls. If the prison scene of Act 2, as we now have it, is pure musico-dramatic gold, this is testimony to Beethoven's instinctive feeling for drama rather than to unerring dramatic shape; Act 1, apart from the quartet and Leonore's aria, is governed mostly by *Singspiel* convention. The conductor, then, who can demonstrate the greatness of Beethoven's musical and dramatic thought, and not falsify the *Singspiel* form (and, occasionally, style) in which much of it is cast, is the one who would come nearest to a complete realization.

Three differing versions of the score of *Fidelio* survive – the first (with a text by Sonnleithner) of 1805; the second of 1806, reduced from three to two acts by Breuning; and the final version of 1814, with Treitschke's textual revision and dramaturgical advice. Nothing is more fascinating than to compare Beethoven's by no means negligible first thoughts, known as *Leonore*, with his last. By 1814, a duet and a trio had been dropped altogether and everything except the march had, by the final version, undergone smaller or more often very extensive changes, most of them obvious improvements (I cannot agree with Ernest Newman when, in *More Opera Nights*, he claims that the hallucinated quick ending to Florestan's aria is less appropriate than the resigned Andante of the original). Of the 1805 score, there exist one commercial and one private recording. The latter has Hans Altmann conducting and a most convincing cast headed by Paula Baumann and Julius Patzak. The commercial recording, with a cast full of reliable singers, provides a low-powered performance, which suffers moreover from a Leonore taxed beyond her comfortable means and a stentorian and clumsy Florestan; yet it is good enough to give the listener a fair impression of a fascinating score and should on no account be missed for the sheer quixotic pleasure of hearing (as opposed to reading about) Beethoven's first thoughts.

Complete recordings of *Fidelio* were first issued only in the LP period, though some have their origins a little earlier. One of the most fascinating, an 'off-the-air' set, comes from a Metropolitan Opera House broadcast of December 1938, with Kirsten Flagstad, René Maison, Friedrich Schorr and Emanuel List in the cast. Main points of interest: the conducting of Bodanzky, who made no commercial operatic records but dominated the German wing of the Metropolitan from 1915 to 1939 and, on this evidence, was clearly a commanding performer; the inclusion of recitatives, composed by Bodanzky; the fine singing of the young Flagstad, and the poised vocalism and musical attack of Schorr, which make him the Pizarro of one's dreams (the grandest start to the dungeon quartet I have ever heard). Another Metropolitan performance in the same series was recorded on 22 February 1941 and conducted by Bruno Walter. Dialogue has replaced recitatives; present (according to Kolodin) are new standards in the orchestra and (witness these discs) splendid choral singing. The performance is nobly conceived, dramatically taut, and seems to me to justify the glowing notices it received at the time, backed up as the eminent conductor was by such as Flagstad, Maison and Herbert Janssen (Don Fernando), to say nothing of the great Alexander Kipnis, whose voice rings out gloriously as Rocco. If the recording is dim by present-day standards, the performance has a rare musical splendour and immediacy, qualities somehow less apparent in another Bruno Walter 'off-the-air' performance recorded in 1951, which includes *Leonore 3*, also played in 1941 but absent from the disc. Flagstad at the end of her career still commands the means to negotiate the music with autumnal glow, Set Svanholm's heroic Florestan remains obstinately earth-bound and Paul Schöffler's tendency to deal with all but the most sustained of Pizarro's music as if it were heightened speech is here heard to have gone uncomfortably far. Compensations for the poor quality of the sound are somehow too few.

Bruno Walter never conducted *Fidelio* in Salzburg, where some of the opera's most famous revivals took place after 1920, but Toscanini did, at the festivals of 1935, 1936 and 1937 (a fascinating first half of Act 1 with Lotte Lehmann survives from 1935, unfortunately in excruciating sound). His radio performance of December 1944 is preserved on RCA, but it belies the great reputation of the 1930s – not surprising seven years later, with no dialogue (even a concert performance should have included Jacquino's interruption of the prison scene), and a less than splendid cast. Toscanini's approach is brisk and forthright, but much of the music comes within an inch of sounding rushed and points are missed – in, for instance, the Act 1 trio – because the singers simply lack the time in which to put them over. None of the singers impresses more than Janssen, one of nature's ministers cast as Don Pizarro and compensating with intelligent enunciation for lack of appropriate vocal weight. Jan Peerce makes a firm, clear if matter-of-fact Florestan; Rose Bampton's intelligent Leonore is reduced in impact by shortness of breath and some raw notes. A splendid *Leonore 3* (interpolated from a later broadcast) might have seemed less relevant were it not that only here was I moved in what is normally the most emotional of operas.

One of the first operatic performances of whose greatness I was (and remain) persuaded was the *Fidelio* under Furtwängler, which dominated post-war Salzburg up to and including 1950. Here was the noble, heart-searching structure revealed at a time when the struggle for freedom was very real in the minds of performers and audience. The casts were: Schlüter/Flagstad, Della Casa/Schwarzkopf/Seefried, Patzak, Schock/Holm/Dermota, Frantz/Schöffler, Alsen/Greindl, Edelmann/Hans Braun. The pity is that the HMV recording made in 1953 (no dialogue, except in Act 2's melodrama and quartet) was with the admirable Vienna cast of that year rather than the inspired Salzburg group of three and four years earlier (though an irreplaceable souvenir of the superb 1950 performance has been issued privately). Even so, it is hard to imagine a finer conception than Furtwängler's – dedicated, beautifully balanced, full of revealing detail. (Where did his reputation for slow tempi come from? A romantic view of Mozart, I should imagine. Here, only Marzelline's aria sounds slow.) Listen in the Act 1 trio to the exquisite chording of two sopranos and bass, in Act 2's introduction to the articulation of the grinding figure in the low-string register, to the weighting of accents in the succeeding passage, to a fine *Leonore 3*. Furtwängler has the benefit of a cast whose every member is at a vocal prime – Martha Mödl, in spite of her difficulty with high-lying passages, so purposeful and heroic as to give a lesson in intensity to many a greater vocalist; Sena Jurinac (immediately post-Fiordiligi) at the top of her lyrical career; Otto Edelmann singing gloriously if without the bite a Schöffler could bring to Pizarro; Gottlob Frick fine; only Wolfgang Windgassen perhaps disappoints, with singing that has clarity but too little intensity.

Technically much better than most radio-originated sets, and important because there are too few complete operatic recordings by conductors established before 1939, Erich Kleiber's Cologne Radio *Fidelio* must, if the label is to be believed, have been made (or perhaps only transmitted) within days of his death at the end of January 1956. No other conductor so easily reconciles the *Singspiel* convention (spritely tempi here) with the later probings of the spirit (a brisk tempo even in the prisoners' chorus) and somehow this performance is quite unlike any other, whether taken from studio or stage: perhaps slighter, certainly less pretentious, less of an artistic testament than others, but, as one would expect from such a master of proportion and detail, at the same time clear, very much alive, as if he had set out to delight his radio audience rather than impress them with the music's profundity (no *Leonore 3*). Kleiber as always gets the best from his singers, and the cast is led by Birgit Nilsson, less monumental and better suited to the role than eight years later with Maazel, the always impressive Frick, and Schöffler, as intense as ever but on radio less stressful than in theatre and singing with better line. Hans Hopf makes a clumsy Florestan, but Ingeborg Wenglor and Gerhard Unger are a nimble pair of lovers. The dialogue is done, not very satisfactorily, by actors, and an unwished-for curiosity is the loss of a line of music at the start of the dungeon quartet. In the end you may conclude (as I did) that there is more to Beethoven's masterpiece than this, but the conductor's admirers will want the set.

An excellently recorded set conducted by Ferenc Fricsay is that made for Deutsche Grammophon in 1958. This is conceived as a studio performance, with whispered *pianissimi* and actors speaking the dialogue. I like Fricsay's pointed, dramatically urgent performance, and his cast is fine by any standards. Fischer-Dieskau is the recorded Pizarro who most fully conveys the hatred and blood-lust of the character, through intensity of diction and tonal colouring; his entrance in the finale of Act 1 is a tremendous thing. Ernst Haefliger makes a fine Florestan, and Irmgard Seefried is the best and subtlest of recorded Marzellines. But Leonie Rysanek's Leonore is the glory of this set, the voice full, flexible, rapturous, ringing out gloriously at climaxes, so as to convince the listener of the importance (and remind him of the rarity) of a confident top register in this role.

Some sets have been superseded, others worth no more than passing mention. Nixa's (1950) was the first available in Europe; the Leipzigers sang the prisoners' chorus as if they meant it, but Margarete Bäumer's authoritative Leonore is well past its vocal prime. Acanta's of a Viennese concert performance under Böhm (1943) is marred by untidy orchestral playing. Schöffler's chill, tortured, utterly credible Pizarro dominates, but Hilde Konetzni's blonde voice – the first I heard in this music – is unkindly recorded. Knappertsbusch succeeded Toscanini at Salzburg in 1938, but in his Westminster recording (1961), tempi are sluggish, and only magnificent performances of the prisoners' chorus and the dungeon scene show this masterly conductor at his best. Jurinac makes a touching, musical Leonore, and Peerce has time to sound more involved as Florestan than seventeen years earlier under Toscanini.

A two-disc recording from Nonesuch in America is notable mainly because it captures much of the extraordinary quality of Julius Patzak's Florestan – the uncannily evocative diction, the sensitive, even serene vocal line, the constant intensity. Otherwise, in spite of a competent Leonore from Gladys Kuchta, disappointing. Decca's set (1964) is headed by Nilsson and James McCracken, a vocally weighty pair and not invariably, at least as far as the tenor is concerned, able to meet the score's considerable demands. Though I yield to none in admiration for Nilsson, I cannot feel that this is one of her most committed performances. Tom Krause is a good Pizarro, but the performance, for all Lorin Maazel's admirable musical qualities, sounds inexperienced and lacking in balance compared with the best of its rivals.

The excellent Russian recording of about 1960 provides evidence to substantiate Melik-Peshayev's reputation as a 'singers' conductor'. Outstanding in a good cast is Galina Vishnevskaya, exhibiting not only the vocal brilliance which makes her one of the outstanding singers of our day, but also the title role's intensity and tragic stature. The dialogue is oddly inflated at times, and Jacquino's interruption in the dungeon becomes nothing less than a harangue. I am sorry not to have been able to hear the earlier Russian set with Kozlovsky as Florestan.

Klemperer's, with extensive dialogue and no *Leonore 3*, is, as you would expect, a monumental performance, each section beautifully balanced with the next and within itself. Accents are strong, rhythms crisp – for instance in the march – and no one else to my mind catches so perfectly that feeling of constant and inexorable advance which is Beethoven's, and nobody conveys it with so consistently buoyant a quality. Christa Ludwig is exultantly immersed in the drama and sings splendidly; Walter Berry good as Pizarro; Frick makes a senior but still excellent Rocco; Ingeborg Hallstein (it is now known that her dialogue was spoken by Elisabeth Schwarzkopf) and Gerhard Unger a good pair of lovers. I have fine memories of Jon Vickers's Florestan in the opera house at the time of this recording (1961), and it was a surprise to find it taking less well to disc, where the sheer size and weight of the voice militate against verisimilitude as Beethoven's symbol of oppressed innocence.

In 1969 Karl Böhm returned to old pastures in Dresden to record *Fidelio* with strong local backing and an international cast. Voices and orchestra are well related but the performance, ideal of balance to begin with, seems somehow gradually to lose this quality, so that the prisoners' chorus is short at the start of that important sense of wonder, and tempi in the dungeon scene and even in *Leonore 3* (allotted a complete side so that the set can be played easily without it!) verge on the hectic. Reservations about the cast are few but important. Theo Adam, wholly appropriately voiced for Pizarro, shows more menace in dialogue than in singing, Franz Crass in fine voice makes a touching Rocco, and James King, not perhaps ideally committed, supplies the best-supported singing of Florestan in any set. Edith Mathis and, even more, Peter Schreier are ideal as Marzelline and Jacquino, and Martti Talvela is incomparably sonorous as Don Fernando. Had Gwyneth Jones recorded the title role at a period when she could have brought greater vocal control to florid and high-lying passages, her natural beauty of voice and already fine projection of this most womanly of heroines would have put hers in the highest category, along perhaps with Leonie Rysanek, among recorded

Leonores. As it is, her performance is something less than it could have been.

Hard on the heels of Böhm came Karajan (1970), with his powerful Berlin Philharmonic basis and a strong Salzburg Easter-type cast. The balance favours orchestra rather than voice and this is awkward when going from a purely orchestral passage such as the overture to one with voices; pauses between number and dialogue are often uncomfortably long. Beautiful orchestral detail, overpowering moments like the re-entry of Pizarro in Act 1, much polish as in the perfectly poised start of the prisoners' chorus – these positive factors somehow add up to a little less than the great whole which *Fidelio* must be. With Helga Dernesch you must attempt to reconcile the constant strain at the top of the voice with its intrinsic beauty lower down, whereas with Vickers it is the fine intentions of the artist which must be weighed against the singer's more limited vocal possibilities. Zoltan Kelemen does with Pizarro what a high-class Alberich can and no more, Helen Donath and Horst Laubenthal make a lightweight pair, and Karl Ridderbusch only emphasizes that singers sometimes sound at less than their best on Karajan's recordings.

Bernstein's 1978 recording lives up to the legend created by his 1970 Vienna performances and reveals a serious, deeply considered view of the score, full of strongly contrasted tempi (the Allegro molto in the first-act trio, for instance, is much faster than the initial Allegro ma non troppo). No other group has more natural authority in this music than the Vienna Philharmonic and the State Opera Chorus (though there is a tiny false entry in the prisoners' chorus), and the cast is strong without being outstanding. Gundula Janowitz, slimmer – slighter? – of voice than one is used to, brings accuracy but little heroism or pathos to Leonore, René Kollo attacks his great recitative softly, but unsteadiness already intrudes as he swells the first note, and Manfred Jungwirth as Rocco is no more than reliable. Sympathetic are Lucia Popp (Marzelline) and Adolf Dallapozza (Jacquino), and Fischer-Dieskau, however personal his approach, brings immense authority to Don Fernando. It is left to Hans Sotin, a Wotan voice in full flood, to provide genuine vocal distinction as Pizarro. A curiosity is that in *Leonore 3* Bernstein omits the first loud bar and has the second grow softly out of the last G major chord of the duet. He also, controversially, omits the dialogue between the dungeon quartet and 'O namenlose Freude'. A distinguished effort none the less.

A curiously abridged, two-sided selection has Anja Silja as a fascinating, flawed Leonore; in moments of stress she forces, but the tension of the recitative of 'Abscheulicher' and the rapt atmosphere of the slow part of the aria show the strength of her Leonore at its best. Arturo Sergi is a strong-voiced Florestan; Peter Lagger and Leonardo Wolovsky competent as Rocco and Pizarro; Matacic conducts.

Apart from the two great arias, neither recording companies nor singers have been greatly drawn to the opera. The *Fidelio* overture was occasionally recorded before 1939 (I have failed to locate the performance conducted by Zemlinsky, Schoenberg's teacher and first brother-in-law) and figures in many LP collections of Beethoven overtures, but for all its aptness in context, isolated it is not particularly revealing of either performer or opera.

The opening duet of Marzelline and Jacquino has attracted attention only once – Grete Forst and Arthur Preuss recorded it about 1909 (044 129). A fast tempo does not hide neat, attractive singing by each participant. Forst on another black pre-dog of 1908-9 (043124) is also responsible for the earliest version of Marzelline's aria: full, fresh, vigorous, enjoyable singing. The point about these two recordings is that the singers belonged to Mahler's ensemble in Vienna; though nothing about the actual performance can be deduced from such early recordings, we can at least tell something of the singers' individual characteristics. Mahler, according to Erwin Stein (*Opera*, April 1953), omitted Rocco's aria (so, by the way, did Böhm at the reopening of the Vienna Opera in 1956), but Wilhelm Hesch, who sang Rocco for Mahler, none the less recorded it twice in 1905 and 1907, perhaps to show how he would have done it had he been allowed to (3-42303 and 3-42733)! A less rewarding Mahler souvenir comes from a piano-accompanied, 1905 performance by Friedrich Weidemann of Pizarro's entry aria (3-42187), which reveals him as the possessor of a strong, wiry voice and considerable attack.

Elisabeth Schumann sang Marzelline's aria in a slapdash manner for Edison about 1915 (reissued on IRCC 3125); it is also one of the few gramophone souvenirs of the scintillating Adele Kern (Poly. 66946; LV 57). Schwarzkopf (LX 1410) recorded on excellent performance, and Ingeborg Stein sang it capably for Schallplatten-Volksverband. There are recent German performances, one lively by Anneliese Rothenberger (HMV ASD 1757), one stodgy by Erika Köth, and one wholly admirable by Pilar Lorengar (SXL 6525).

Beethoven flies in the face of operatic practice by depicting four conflicting emotions in canon, but the quartet is a miracle of musical beauty. Its first appearance in the catalogue is on a 1906 G&T with singers from Breslau (Widhalm, Neisch, Reichel, Beeg) but I have neither heard it nor gleaned information about its gallant performers. The former comment goes too for the interesting combinations of Nast, Eibenschütz, Rüiger, Rains (Dresden 1908) and Forst, Elizza, Preuss, Mayr. A justly famous performance was that in which Erna Berger and Henriette Gottlieb were joined in quixotic but successful casting by the dramatic tenor Marcel Wittrisch and baritone Willi Domgraf-Fassbaender (DB 4417; LV120). No less good is what I take to be a pre-war (radio?) recording on East Berlin's Eterna label with Marta Fuchs, Trude Eipperle, Peter Anders and Georg Hann. A later attempt at the sublime music comes in the Friends of Covent Garden album where Gwyneth Jones, Elizabeth Robson, John Dobson and David Kelly, excellently recorded, give a beautiful performance under the baton of Solti (SET 383).

However characteristic in context, Rocco's aria on records strikes me as a bore. A certain Robert Biberti attempted it on a seven-inch Zonophone in 1903, and Knüpfer, Vollmer, Aschner, Rains and Bender as well as Hesch followed his example before 1914. Richard Mayr (Mahler's Don Fernando but a year or two later Weingartner's Rocco), sang it without too much conviction in 1922; and subsequent performances have been by Bohnen, Norman Allin (in English), Georg Hann, that most solid of Viennese basses Ludwig Weber (LB 87), Franz Crass, the Hungarian Mihaly Szekely, and the Dutchman Arnold van Mill. Apart from Weidemann, only Alexander Haydter (Od. 38374) who noticed Pizarro's 'Ha, welch'ein Augenblick' in acoustic days, but Bohnen and Schorr recorded it before 1939. Schorr's beautiful singing is to my mind ruined by the excessive speed dictated by a 1927 twelve-inch disc (D 2112; HQM 1243) as witness the quite exceptional authority he shows at a slower tempo in the 1938 Metropolitan broadcast. There is also an acoustic version by Schorr (Poly. 62393; LV 241), just as hurried and with less presence. Geraint Evans brings intensity rather than weight (SXL 6262) and Otto Edelmann's version, recorded about 1951 when his bass-baritone singing was at its most powerful, reveals some unusually fluent singing (LXT 2672). Tom Krause gives a fine performance (GOSC 668).

Leonore's scene, 'Abscheulicher', is one of the great test pieces of the dramatic soprano's repertory and most have recorded it. Some are no more than souvenirs: by Schwarzkopf (33CX 1266) – a superb Marzelline with ideas temporarily about her station?; Rose Pauly (Covent Garden 1938); Christel Goltz; Martha Mödl; Helena Braun; and Hilde Konetzni; even Gré Brouwenstijn, one of the finest of post-1945 protagonists, whose 1966 recording (5C 053-24324) constitutes a less than adequate memorial. Gwyneth Jones was the first British soprano to record it (SXL 6249) but made a greater impression in the theatre. Leontyne Price (SER 5621) shows versatility by invading territory unfamiliar to her in the opera house and sings fluently, the gleam at the top of the voice partly compensating for some hoarseness lower down. Perhaps a less than true top B natural diminished Marilyn Horne's meticulously musical performance in my ears, but she is the only singer on disc to add a flourish before the final cadence (SET 309-10). Inge Borkh's rather light-voiced performance has considerable scale (DB 11544), as has the version of Birgit Nilsson, whose prodigious vocalism still seems to reach less than to the heart of the matter (SAX 2184). I heard Varnay sing the role in Munich as late as 1965, and her Rimington LP is a formidable sample of her considerable art. Even better perhaps is the opulent singing of Elisabeth Ohms, Leonore at La Scala with Toscanini in 1927 and at the Met with Bodanzky in 1930 (CA 8036; LV 159); placidity creeps in and is unfortunately underlined by a sluggish B natural at the end.

Elsa Bland sang just the Adagio for Odeon in 1906, with sumptuous, even tone and piano accompaniment (Od. 38379; CO 317). Lilli Lehmann recorded a tremendous performance in Berlin in 1907 (Od. 8006/7; CO 384/5). This version is *hors catégorie* as the French would say over a restaurant, appoggiaturas in place, the tone at the age of nearly 60 limpid, the technique amazingly flexible. Matzenauer's Edison, shorn of the concluding Allegro, contains weightily impressive singing, Melanie Kurt exhibits a fine voice and considerable bravura, Lilly Hafgren a lighter but still beautiful voice and true subtlety of phrasing (043357/8; LV 88), but the best of the acoustics may well be the performance by Helene Wildbrunn, recorded in 1922; the soft controlled singing of 'Komm, Hoffnung' is moving to hear and the voice rings out splendidly later (Poly. 72802/3; LV 70).

Finally, three extraordinary pieces of singing, all dating from before 1939. Even if the recitative is a little studio-bound, the slurring too frequent for my taste and the Philadelphia Orchestra in rotten form, there is no denying the urgent, even, clarion quality of Kirsten Flagstad's voice, nor the surge of confidence which hearing it inspires (DB 3439; VIC 1208). There is a Parlophone recording (R 20053; 1C 147-29116/7) by the most famous of twentieth-century exponents of the role, Lotte Lehmann, who sang it for ten years at Salzburg, culminating in Toscanini's performances of 1935-7. The invariably expressive colouring of tone and words, the glorious natural lyric sound of the voice itself and the unsurpassed sympathy she could engender for what she was doing combine to make this (even without recitative) a performance that is hard to surpass. Its main challenge is provided by Frida Leider (D 1497; 1C 147-30 785/6), whose voice is more ideally heroic, who can provide an equal sensitivity to word and colour, whose phrasing is nothing short of magisterial; her 1921 acoustic (Poly. 65743; LV 240) is just as well sung, less fully recorded. I should love to hear the music sung in the theatre as either of these two sings it.

The earliest discs of Florestan's aria come from the Bayreuth stalwart Heinrich Knote, Hans Tanzler, Hermann Jadlowker, Jacques Urlus and Karl Erb. Knote's fine voice and diction make for an impressive performance (042288; CO 355); Tanzler I have not heard; Jadlowker's uncut performance (Od. 76136/7; CO 312) shows off some fine, controlled singing; Erb's marvellous diction and bright, high voice (hardly changed when he came to make his Lieder records a dozen years later) do not compensate for a curiously disinterested performance (Od. 76341; 1C 147-30771/2). Urlus was Toscanini's Tristan at the Metropolitan from 1912 onwards and, with other conductors, the regular Florestan in the same period. His performance, recorded for Edison about 1915, omits orchestral introduction and the concluding Allegro, but the singing, from the soft attack on 'Gott!' to the end of the aria proper, is so perfectly articulated and so full of atmosphere that one almost forgets it is also a piece of immaculate vocalism. It was reissued on Club 99.21 and is strongly recommended. Earlier, in 1911, Urlus recorded just 'In des Lebens', omitting the recitative and final section (4-42501; CO 350 and GV 67). Fritz Krauss omits the recitative (Vox) but shows a beautiful voice and brilliant technique in the aria.

Few electrically recorded versions can hold a candle to Urlus's. I have not located a performance by August Seider; but Fritz Soot and Eyvind Laholm are no more than competent, and the same can be said for four post-war versions, by Frans Vroons, the burly-voiced James King, the tight-throated Rudolf Schock, and the cautious Nicolali Gedda. More interesting is the careful, clear singing of the veteran Johannes Sembach (Schallplatten-Volksverband ND 9619/20). René Maison's thick voice and clumsy singing do not hide his exemplary involvement in the music (Am. Col. 74140D). The exact converse is true of Piccaver's well-vocalized performance; he sang Florestan at Salzburg in 1927 with Schalk (Poly. 95482). Considerably more committed is Franz Völker (Salzburg 1931-4, under Clemens Krauss and Richard Strauss), who produces much lovely singing as well as real drive and artistry (LY 6113; LV 78). Set Svanholm (Victor 49-3206; VIC 1455) sings with high musicality, and, although it starts loudly, I very much liked the convincing performance of Peter Anders, made a year or two before his untimely death (DB 11543; 1C 147-29142/3), better by far than the well-voiced but lifeless singing of Ernst Kozub.

In the final analysis, there are two outstanding record of the scene as a whole (both of Urlus's are cut). The earlier is by Helge Roswaenge, who sang Florestan at Salzburg before the war with Toscanini and at Covent Garden with Beecham. His is strongly voiced indeed but the singing is always imaginative, the words well projected, and the stifled tone at the start of the quick section heralds some truly inspired singing (DB 4522; 1C 147-29240/1). Better still is the recording by Julius Patzak – no one on disc (nor, I suspect, in the theatre) has enunciated the words with such meaning and pathos, no one has so sharply pointed the contrast between the desperation of the recitative and the resigned nobility of the aria proper, no one has reached such a frenzy of delirium in the fast section of the scene (Decca X 489; ECS 812).

The remainder of the great prison scene has attracted few recording singers. 'Euch werde Lohn' was early represented in the German catalogues, excellently done by Melanie Kurt, Urlus and Knüpfer (reissued on IRCC 91). Not even his own complete set has the agony in the initial string attack which I remember from Furtwängler's performance in the opera house, and the only electrical recording of this trio is no exception. It is sung in Czech and features moreover that fine soprano Ludmila Dvořaková. Beno Blachut's line is strong but perhaps a little bland, but Rudolf Asmus (famous for Boris and the Forester in the *Vixen*) is an appropriate Rocco. The same singers with the addition of the hard-working Přemysl Koči have recorded the quartet and the duet, 'O namenlose Freude', and Dvořaková's singing is in its own way as exultant as Rysanek's.

Three records remain. Sembach and a good soprano called Ammermann rejoice appropriately in 'O namenlose Freude' on the reverse side of the tenor's *scena*. The prison quartet gets a thoroughly representative performance (DB 4417; LV 120) with Gottlieb, Walter Ludwig, Domgraf-Fassbaender and Walter Grossman, and the opening section of the finale, 'Heil sei dem Tag', an honest and unexceptionable one from the Chorus and Orchestra of the Berlin State Opera (Poly. 90083).

In the end, it is on the complete sets that *Fidelio* recordings will be judged, and the choice here is wide. I should hate to have to choose between Furtwängler's and Klemperer's, towering performances each, with Bernstein's not so far behind. Fricsay's on four sides represents quality as well as economy.

FIDELIO

F Florestan; *L* Leonore; *P* Pizarro; *R* Rocco; *M* Marzelline; *J* Jacquino; *Fer* Fernando

1943 (live performance) Ralf *F*; H. Konetzni *L*; Schöffler *P*; Alsen *R*; Seefried *M*; Klein *J*; Neralič *Fer*/Vienna State Opera Chorus and Orch./Böhm
Artia ℗ ALPS 504; Acanta ⓜ DE 23116-7

1944 (broadcast performance) Peerce *F*; Bampton *L*; Janssen *P*; Belarsky *R*; Steber *M*; Laderoute *J*; Moscona *Fer*/Chorus; NBC SO/Toscanini
RCA (UK) ⓜ VCM 9/1–4; (US) ⓜ LM 6025

1950 (in Russian) Kozlovsky *F*; Antonova *L*; Kruglikova *M*

1950 Sauerbaum *F*; Bäumer *L*; Hübner *P*; Savelkouls *R*; Engert *M*; Kuhnert *J*; Horand *Fer*/Leipzig Radio Chorus and Orch./Pfluger
Nixa ⓜ OLP 7301/1-3; Olympic © 9301

1953 Windgassen *F*; Mödl *L*; Edelmann *P*; Frick *R*; Jurinac *M*; Schock *J*; Poell *Fer*/Vienna State Opera Chorus, VPO/Furtwängler
HMV ⓜ RLS; Seraphim ⓜ IC 6022

1957 Haefliger *F*; Rysanek *L*; Fischer-Dieskau *P*; Frick *R*; Seefried *M*; Lenz *J*; Engen *Fer*/Bavarian State Opera Chorus and Orch./Fricsay
DG 2705 037

1960c (in Russian) Nelepp *F*; Vishnevskaya *L*; Ivanov *P*; Cekolov *R*: Maslennikova *M*; Tchevin *J*; Nekipalo *Fer*/Bolshoi Theatre Chorus and Orch./Melik-Pashaev
MK ⓜ DO 4518-23

1961 Peerce *F*; Jurinac *L*; Neidlinger *P*; Ernster *R*; Stader *M*; M. Dickie *J*; Guthrie *Fer*/Bavarian State Opera Chorus and Orch./Knappertsbusch
World Records SOC 104-6; Westminster S1003

1961 Vickers *F*; Ludwig *L*; Berry *P*; Frick *R*; Hallstein *M*; Unger *J*; Crass *Fer*/Chorus; Philharmonia/Klemperer
HMV SLS 5006 ④TC-SLS 5006; Angel SCL 3625

1964 McCracken *F*; Nilsson *L*; Krause *P*; Böhme *R*; Sciutti *M*; Grobe *J*; Prey *Fer*/Vienna State Opera Chorus, VPO/Maazel
Decca SET 272-3; London OSA 1259

1965 Patzak *F*; Kuchta *L*; Rehfuss *P*;
Kümmel *R*; Muszely *M*;
Kretschmar *J*; Wenk *Fer*/North
German Radio Chorus and
Orch./ Bamberger
Nonesuch HB 73005

1969 King *F*; G. Jones *L*; Adam *P*;
Crass *R*; Mathis *M*; Schreier *J*;
Talvela *Fer*/Dresden State Opera
Chorus and Orch./ Böhm
DG 2721 136 ④3378 054

1970 Vickers *F*; Dernesch *L*;
Kelemen *P*; Ridderbusch *R*;
Donath *M*; Laubenthal *J*; van
Dam *Fer*/German Opera Chorus,
Berlin PO/Karajan
HMV SLS 954; Angel SCL 3773

1977 Leonora (Original version)
Cassilly *F*; Moser *L*; Adam *P*;
Ridderbusch *R*; Donath *M*;

Buchner *J*; Polster *Fer*/Leipzig
Radio Chorus, Dresden State
Opera Orch. Blom stedt

1978 Kollo *F*; Janowitz *L*; Sotin *P*;
Jungwirth *R*; Popp *M*;
Dallapozza *J*; Fischer-Dieskau
Fer/Vienna State Opera Chorus,
VPO/Bernstein
DG 2709 082 ④3371 039

Excerpts

1950 (abridged) Soloists, Leipzig
Opera Chorus and Orch./Rubahn
Allegro ⑩ ALG 2066-7

1964 Sergi *F*; Silja *L*; Wolovsky *P*;
Bass *R*; Stahlman *M*; Wolinski
J; Lagger *Fer*/ State Opera
Chorus and Orch.
Frankfurt/Matačić
Ariola-Eurodisc K87625R

Der Freischütz

ALAN BLYTH

I wonder how many of the players who were in the first complete set of *Freischütz* recorded in Dresden under Rudolf Kempe around 1950 were in the Staatskapelle when Carlos Kleiber went to the city to make his performance some twenty-three years later. Certainly the timbre of the orchestra, warm and yielding, remained the same, even if the sound of the earlier set hardly flattered the orchestra.

Kempe was the first conductor whom I heard conduct the work. That was in 1957 at the Prinzregententheater at Munich with Elisabeth Lindermeier, then his wife, as Agathe, Hans Hopf as Max. Something of the authenticity of his reading from that occasion can be discerned through the dim recording of the Acanta set. It can be heard immediately in the hushed, almost spiritual handling of the overture's introduction, a passage not surpassed in any of the later performances, again in the placing of the chords at the start of 'Schweig, schweig', and in the dramatically coordinated interpretation of the whole Wolf's Glen scene, subsidiary ideas given their due, the final Presto a Toscanini-like crack of doom. Elsewhere, tempi, so often misjudged in other accounts, always seem perfectly chosen.

Sad to say, Kempe was given, with one most notable exception, an inadequate cast. Elfriede Trötschel is a hangdog Agathe, Irma Beilke (by then) an unsteady Aennchen. Bernd Aldenhoff an uningratiating, strained Max in the worst *Heldentenor* tradition, and the small parts indifferently taken. The exception is Kurt Böhme's *nonpareil* of a Caspar. In fresher voice than for Jochum, he has precisely the black, treacly sound needed for the part; also the pertinent enunciation of the text, the daemonic flair in its delivery. His speaking of the dialogue, or what little is left of it, is exemplary.

The 1951 Otto Ackermann set includes only a few phrases of dialogue (not a word about the funeral wreath). Ackermann's laboured account of the overture is unfortunately a harbinger of the performance ahead. Klemperer might have conducted the work at these speeds, but he would have justified them by his interpretation. Maud Cunitz is a deplorable Agathe, wobbly and dispirited. As the old *Record Guide* averred: 'In vain does she proclaim "All' meine Pulse schlagen!": the listeners' pulses are unstirred.' Hans Hopf, as in the theatre, was a clumsy Max, but one capable of the occasional inspiring phrase. Emmy Loose's lively Aennchen (her ariette delightfully done) puts her friend to shame. The veteran Marjan Rus, a rusty Caspar, rises to his part in the Wolf's Glen scene, undoubtedly the most effective section of this set, with a frightening Samiel. The Vienna Chorus, as in so many early Decca LPs, seems as if it had yet to recover from wartime depredations.

At the end of the 1950s EMI entered the lists with the first stereo version of the work – and very acceptable it still sounds. Dialogue was included (regrettably, spoken by actors) in the original issue, not in the HQS reissue, and space was found for the first scene of Act 3, which is only speech: Josef Keilberth's view of the score, in the Kempe tradition, was forceful, with mainly fast speeds – the chorus in 15 really seem like hungry huntsmen. The atmosphere of the Wolf's Glen has never been better conveyed (and without extraneous noises) with a clipped, dictatorial Samiel: this is properly spine-chilling.

The cast is headed by Elisabeth Grümmer's youthful, eager, natural Agathe, unsurpassed in complete sets or extracts. In her big scene you experience all her emotions with her, and the Cavatine in Act 3 is ideally fresh and poised. She contrasts aptly with Lisa Otto's lively Aennchen, the personification of *keck*. She is marvellously responsive to words, obedient to note-values, and makes much of that wonderful passage beginning 'Du zürnest mir?', where Aennchen expresses her tender sympathy for her friend (how much the interpretation of the recitative is crucial to the deeper meaning of the whole piece!). Rudolf Schock, happily half-way between lyric and heroic tenor, is a compelling Max, always ardent, always anxious. Karl Kohn's bass-baritone Caspar is more than adequate, but not particularly individual in utterance. Gottlob Frick delivers the Hermit's E minor, Sarastro-like dictums with unrivalled humanity and authority; the young Hermann Prey is a vivid Ottokar.

Eugen Jochum's powerful, rhythmically vital and large-scale interpretation surpasses even Kempe's and Keilberth's. Listen to the string articulation and placing of the trombone incursions in the overture, to the foreboding chord before 'Doch mich' in 3, the menace of 'Schweig, schweig', the mystery of the Mendelssohnian string semiquavers before the bullet casting, the exuberance of the huntsmen's chorus. This is the reading of someone brought up in the right tradition. Jochum is superbly supported by the Bavarian Radio Orchestra and Chorus and by a lifelike recording. The *entre-act* and first scene of Act 3 are left out.

His cast is more variable. Böhme trumps his own performance for Kempe with an even more formidable Caspar. The laugh in the dialogue before 'In Teufels Namen' is frightening indeed; so is his whole contribution to a splendid Wolf's Glen (no 'production'). He, like the rest of the cast, has the clearest enunciation on any set. Irmgard Seefried, in spite of some signs of wear around the break, is an appealing Agathe, full of girlish eagerness tinged with foreboding. Rita Streich sings her ariette with keenly conceived phrasing, makes little of the 'Kettenhund' story, but recovers for a most tender 'Du zürnest mir?' and aria. Her tone might have been conceived for the part.

Richard Holm, though overparted, is always an expressively intelligent, lyrical Max. Wächter is even better than Prey as Ottokar, Walter Kreppel a weak Hermit, but as an entity this performance is to my mind the most truthful and idiomatic set yet to appear.

The two versions from the later 1960s suffer from stodgy conducting and unsatisfactory casts. Lovro von Matačič's performance, once available in Britain on World Records, is a thing of threads and patches. It has lots of 'production', with wind machines and imitations of animal noises in the Wolf's Glen in an attempt to match Weber's stage instructions, but the effect, with a stagey Samiel, tends to be too melodramatic. The Act 3 first scene is included; the dialogue, pretty full, is spoken by the singers. Speeds are staid.

Claire Watson is a most musical Agathe, but the voice is shallow with a suspicion of unsteadiness that makes uncomfortable listening. 12 is carefully but stiffly phrased. Lotte Schädle is an ordinary Aennchen, strained above the stave. Schock, now a mature Max, is appropriately intense, anguished. Frick, now in the service of the devil rather than the church, is a bumpy Caspar, inclined to *Sprechgesang*, while Böhme, who has made the opposite change, sounds as if he has spent a good many years in his retreat as the Hermit: he is authoritative but the vibrato has loosened a good deal. All choruses enjoy their work in *Freischütz*, and the West Berliners are no exception.

The then 82-year-old Robert Heger is predictably weighty and deliberate (not much *grazioso* in 6). His approach bears fruit in a magisterial moulding of the third-act finale, where he shows his vast experience in a place in which some of his rivals fail, and the Bavarian State Opera forces show throughout that they have the music in their bones.

Perhaps this set has never been issued in Britain because it does no good to Birgit Nilsson's reputation: her singing is consistently ill-tuned and laboured (see below for her happier efforts) – an unfortunate performance. Erika Köth is a thin-voiced, twittery Aennchen, Nicolai Gedda a too strenuous and oddly unidiomatic Max, Walter Berry a lightweight but accurate Caspar (excellent in his dialogue). Franz Crass adds to the merits of the finale with his grave, urgent Hermit. The foreshortened dialogue has been rewritten, omitting Act 3, scene 1.

The much-admired Carlos Kleiber set does not wear well. What at first appeared as revelations become irritants on fuller acquaintance. Kleiber's insistence on dotting every 'i' and crossing every 't' tends to give his reading an inbred, sophisticated character foreign to Weber and emphasized by the almost clinical recording, while Kleiber's speeds veering from the over-fast (opening chorus and Caspar's drinking song, marked *Allegro feroce ma non troppo presto*) to the sleepy (start of Agathe's scene) suggest the unfortunate influence of Karajan (who has not recorded this work) on his younger colleague. However, Kleiber's sensitive delineation of detail (for example, the onstage string effect right at the end of Act 1, scene 1, and in the Wolf's Glen that illustrative figure as Max imagines Agathe leaping to her death) should be noted in his favour.

The production, with far too self-conscious actors speaking the dialogue, is unconvincing, because the voices sound so different, and the crowd effects are ineffective. The cast has been much praised, but I found, returning to the singers, with the knowledge of the best in other sets and on discs of individual items, that they were far from ideal. Gundula Janowitz's singing is certainly pure and secure, but she hardly suggests Agathe's predicament in her anonymous, streamlined, objective approach (no sense of expectancy as she awaits Max). Edith Mathis, on the other hand, seems to be trying too hard to make Aennchen characterful and ends up by sounding forced in her intepretation. Schreier's attempts at the troubled soul lead him into over-emphasis of what is already there in words and music. Theo Adam seems to be petulant rather than devilish, and his tone lacks the requisite bite.

Actors speaking for singers also mar the performance of the work by Carlos's father, Erich Kleiber, as their voices simply do not match. This is a live, 1955 account of the work, but recorded in the studio for a broadcast, not taken from the threatre. The interpretation is similar to his son's – dramatic and searching – but without so much highlighting of detail.

Erich Kleiber chooses to cut Aennchen's third-act romance and aria. The more's the pity because Streich, as for Jochum, presents one's near-ideal of an Aennchen, a fresh, full-throated idiomatically enunciated portrayal that proves an apt partner for Grümmer's lovely Agathe. Hopf is again something of a trial as Max, but in the studio he is at least more attentive to note-values. Max Proebstl, who was Caspar in the 1957 Munich performance under Kempe described earlier, is not as characterful as I recall him on stage but is never less than adequate. Böhme again wobbles as the Hermit. Poell is an imposing Ottokar.

Strange to say the two attenuated sets on 78s, for all their primitive recording, often convey as much of the work's essence as the LP performances. The Weigert 'potting' has an effective Wolf's Glen, complete with most realistic effects, an interesting Agathe in Elfriede Marherr, a dry Max in the veteran Fritz Soot.

Heger, on his wartime extracts (most numbers foreshortened), obviously took a more dramatic view of the score in his younger days. Carla Spletter is a smiling Aennchen, Georg Hann a menacing Caspar, August Seider a sympathetic Max, but the compelling performance here comes from Maria Müller as Agathe, allowed her scene in full. The vocal security, sad inflexions (on words such as 'Kummer'), and the classical phrasing are in the very best German tradition, and I suggest a model for sopranos today – if they would just stop and listen.

The Philips disc (overture 1 [in part], 3, 4, 5, 7, 8, 12, 13) is prosaically conducted by Heinrich Hollreiser, Gré Brouwenstijn (Agathe) is tremulous and non-committal in both her pieces (much better on a recital; see below), Rosl Schwaiger an average Aennchen, Berry (Caspar) much as in the Heger set. The reason for hearing this disc is for Waldemar Kmentt's exemplary account of Max's scene. His voice is a fair compromise between the lyrical and heroic, his accents, especially in the louring recitative, suggestive of Max's fear and loneliness.

A DG disc of similar vintage (DGM 19013) brings together various separate and distinguished performance. Fritz Lehmann gives a particularly sensitive account of the overture with the Berlin Philharmonic. Wolfgang Windgassen, though variable in pitch, is a thoughtful Max in 3, Streich an exceptionally spontaneous Aennchen in both her pieces, Anny Schlemm appreciable in both *Szene* and *Cavatine* and – not to be missed if you can find the disc – Hermann Uhde terrifyingly articulate and baleful as Caspar, giving 'Schweig, schweig' with a Pizarro-like attack of virulent animosity.

From the earliest days of recording, the hero's and heroine's main scenes have been frequently recorded. Take Max's 'Nein, länger trag' ich nicht die Qualen . . . Durch die Wälder'. I have found about thirty versions of this scene and aria in which Max has to establish his past happiness, then show how the powers of darkness have disrupted it. Vocally speaking, tenors have to find the right balance between the lyrical and heroic aspects of the part. Some of the earliest interpreter's are most successful in achieving this. Heinrich Knote (042213/4), with his personal mode of expression and dramatic declamation aided by appoggiaturas, is admirable when his wayward intonation allows. Karl Jörn (4-42479/80; CO 354), more delicate than Knote, catches the melancholy of the aria, has the heroic ring for the end. Richard Schubert (Polyphon 50126; LV 252) is superior to both, his articulation lending point to his involving interpretation – tender thoughts about his loved one (beautiful lyric singing here), concern at heaven's desertion, final despair. Johannes Sembach (Am. Col. A 5842) with his gentle line and keen vibrato, might have achieved Schubert's distinction had his version not been brutally cut. Fritz Vogelstrom (Parlo. P 523) and Wilhelm Grüning (3-42431) are lesser lights of the same school, Jacques Urlus (Edison 83628) a greater one, singing the first half of the scene deliberately and with high eloquence.

The more forceful, heavier exponents of the part from the start of the century are represented by Karl Burrian (4-42475/6, later version on Czech HMV AN 254), whose timbre is uncomfortable and phrasing often wooden. Aloys Burgstaller, obviously tired by *Heldentenor* over-exertions at Bayreuth, shows a voice in tatters on an old cylinder version. Hermann

Jadlowker (Od. 64353/4) begins disappointingly, but comes into his own in the later sections when one begins to warm to that peculiar timbre and vital declamation, anguish personified at the end. The oratorio singer Dan Beddoe (Victor 74244), a cut version, sings finely in English but the expression belongs more to *Elijah* than to *Freischütz*. Tudor Davies (D 932), also cut and in English, is his usual honest self, singing of his Agnes and adding appoggiaturas.

Next we encounter the flurry of great inter-war interpreters, any one of whom would sing present-day Weber tenors off the stage. The most lyrical, and in some ways most likeable, reading comes from the young Peter Anders (Telef. E 2277; A J6 42232) a forlorn, boyish Max, ready prey for Caspar's wiles. The fresh tone and consistently well-knitted phrases are most attractive. Helge Roswaenge. (DA 4418) is a much more extrovert forester with a smile in his voice and a healthy bloom on his juicy tone, though sometimes he emits it too bumpily. Franz Völker (Poly. 19683; LV 206) is an honest, straightforward, vibrant forester – a central version of great merit. Rudolf Laubenthal (EJ 565; LV 213) does not always tune his gleaming heroic tenor very finely, but with Coates's assistance, finds the right fevered touch for the final section. Fritz Krauss (Od. 0-6703; LV 158) trumpets his love for Agathe with metallic brilliance (no voice like this today) in a rhythmically free version, but hardly sounds perturbed by his predicament. The Berlin-based Jaro Dvorsky (any relation to the present tenor of that name?) is a fellow who obviously enjoys the open-air life and declaims with a Widdop-like confidence in an attractive though unsubtle rendering (EW 10).

Most recommendable of this group are two tenors who recorded their performances during or just after the war. Horst Taubmann (Poly. 67798) has nearly every virtue a Max needs: graceful line in the aria proper, a feeling for the drama in the recitatives (where Weber always exposes the heart of his characters), urgency in the last section, and his timbre, half-lyrical, half-dramatic, is ideal. Richard Tauber's performance, recorded in 1946 just two years before his untimely death (Parlo. RO 20551); is the one I was brought up with, and I remain faithful to his ardour, his enthusiastic accents (listen to 'nur dem Laub'), his individual yet highly appropriate timbre. He, like most German-trained tenors of the era, sings an unjustified but effective high A flat on the first syllable of the final 'foltert'. René Verdière (Od. 188621, in French) is at once arresting and elegiac, with a typically French vibrato.

Post-war contenders on LP need not detain us. Ernst Gruber (LPV 403), Franz Vroons (Philips NBR 6027), Walter Geisler (Falcon L-ST 7084), Ernst Kozub (Philips 837038 GY), James McCracken (SXL 6201) and the more commendable James King (SXL 6326) and Kenneth Neate (Rococo 5387), an almost forgotten name from early post-war days at Covent Garden, give dispiriting evidence of the decline in singing of this kind of music in recent years.

No.4, Caspar's 'Hier im ird'schen Jammerthal', finds Theodor Lattermann (Od. 99336/7) and Arnold Van Mill (Philips GL 5651) in rough form; both add 5, 'Schweig, schweig'. So does Michael Bohnen (Ultraphon F 738); he delivers his imprecations with resplendent attack, vivid enunciation and his own slight variations on Weber, Adam Didur, the Polish bass who became famous in both Italy and America, recorded both items twice. The earlier performances, though with piano (Fono. 39487/8; CO 360), are preferable. They reveal his Mephisto-like interpretation, sung in Italian. In 5 he uses the Faccio recitative in place of the dialogue, an interesting historical point. What confidence here! Wilhelm Hesch (3-42976; CO 300) displays an exemplary black bass and roisters almost as effectively as Alexander Kipnis (EW 91; LV 91) and Ludwig Weber (Col. LB 87), who adds a sinister 'Schweig, schweig' (LX 1310). Josef Hermann, a bass-baritone rather than bass (DB 7645; LV 49), reminds me of Berry, similarly relishing the text. Wilhelm Strienz (EG 3549) is no more than adequate. In 5 only the Czech bass-baritone Ladislav Mrasz, who died too young (Supra. SUA 10539), makes his mark, but the Czech text is odd.

Nos. 7 and 17, Aennchen's two pieces, may be taken together. Early versions by the Viennese Grete Forst (43618), by the Russian Maria Michaelova (2-423133, in Russian) and the Italian Ines-Maria Ferraris (Fono. 39450/1, in Italian) are uninteresting. Much more of the girl's *keck* quality comes out in Irene Eisinger's fresh, pointed ariette (EG 1821; LV 197) and in Erika Köth's bright singing of the same (Electrola 70502). Superior even to these is Elisabeth Schumann who recorded them with marvellous freshness at the start of her career on Edisons (82082/92; RLS 743). The Hungarian Aurelie Revy (Od. 64449) must have been a lively artist to judge from her 11, and more stylish than the garish Erna Sack (Telef. A 1771) or the *schmalzy* Ursula Farr (SXL 6557). Hilde Gueden (Poly. 68066) is superior to all these, indeed to almost all other Aennchens, in her spirited evocation of the story of the imagined ghost and sunny account of the invigorating six-eight aria in E flat. Early exponents of this, Hermine Bosetti (Od. AA 79016) and Elise Elizza (43791), sound ordinary and characterless after you have heard Gueden.

Elizza (2-23147, 2-43273) is much more interesting in 8, Agathe's great scene: 'Wie nahte mir der Schlummer', of which I have located some forty versions. What I would term third-division performances, often unidiomatic and no more than souvenirs of the sopranos concerned, are those by Michaelova, Marcella Roseler, Erna Denera and, in the modern era, Lois Marshall, Traute Richter, Teresa Stich-Randall (too insipid, but finely sung), and Leontyne Price. With standards so high in the best versions several distinguished singers only reach division two. Elisabeth van Endert (043206/7) is steady but also untroubled, altogether too majestic a lady. The much-admired Sigrid Arnoldson is more expressive, with her broad phrasing and commendable appoggiaturas – too often omitted by her successors – but she, like van Endert, remains too placid. Emmy Destinn, on her full American Columbia version, inclines to sentimentality through a too liberal use of portamento. Perceval Allen (03137, in English) provides fresh, forward tone, but makes unacceptable cuts. Singing the first half only, Gertrud Kappel (Favorite 1-16205; LV 117), always a warm artist, remains unaccountably uninvolved, as does Elizabeth Rethberg (Brunswick 50154).

Of more recent interpreters, Joan Hammond (C 3510, in English) betrays the fact that she did not sing the part on stage by approaching it in oratorio fashion, as does the impressive but impersonal Eileen Farrell (Philips ABE 10275). Maria Jeritza (DB 982; VIC 1455) is surprisingly off-hand. Polyna Stoska (Am. Col. C 72513), who created a stir at the Metropolitan in the late 1940s, is a buxom Agathe, who gets ecstatic in a Silja manner towards the end. Pilar Lorengar (Electrola 70503) lacks imagination and variety of expression but is immeasurably improved in her Decca version (SXL 6525). Brouwenstijn (Philips SBR 6206) and Nilsson (SAX 2284, SXL 6077) are both more involved and secure than in their complete or highlights renderings, but Nilsson is still miscast. Janowitz (DG 136546) sounds much more natural and unsophisticated than on the Kleiber set.

And so to the first division, the great ones. Lucie Weidt (43521), Mahler's soprano, uses words and tone, back in 1904 (with piano), to fill every phrase down to 'Engelschaaren' (where she ends) with meaning. A little later, Claire Dux in her second version (043291, 'Leise, leise' only) exhibits all the glorious certainty of the old school, portamento and all. This is classic singing *qua* singing but has little or none of the feeling for Agathe's situation shown by her immediate successors, such as the incomparable Lotte Lehmann, whose wonderfully fresh, forward 1918 performance (76482/356) spans the sixty years since it was made with its sense of eager anticipation at 'Er ist's', of wholehearted gratitude at 'Himmel, nimm des Dankes Zähren'; altogether the kind of spontaneous performance the LP era cannot reproduce. Her 1929 remake (Od. 0-8741; PMA 1057), much better known, keeps the impulsiveness, is more long-breathed, but is inevitably the out-pouring of a more mature woman.

Lehmann was a Sieglinde. So was Delia Reinhardt, and her version (Poly. 66949; LV 142) has the same amplitude of expression and a wonderful security and joyfulness in lifting the big tune. Meta Seinemeyer (Parlo. E 10484) catches the romantic ecstasy of 'O süsse Hoffnung' to perfection and the vocal emission is as smooth as a soft cushion, very tender and intimate. Hilde Konetzni (Telef. SK 2160) is sometimes careless with her words, but displays idiomatic inflexions, keenly supported by Schmidt-Isserstedt. Emmy Bettendorf (Poly. 0943059/60), is pure piety incarnate and phrases exquisitely. Ljuba Welitsch (LX 1090; SH 289) sings in her usual easy way, but misses the spirit by taking 'Leise, leise' too fast and generally sounding matter of fact.

Tiana Lemnitz, for some people *the* Agathe, recorded 8 three times. To me the 1934 Polydor version (CA 8233; LV 101) reveals a too-patient and pious girl (first part only). The 1938 performance (DB 5549; SHB 47) is much more positive, with a more lively realization of the text in a more forward voice production, but still lacking in the ultimate interpretative insight. For that one needs to turn to Elisabeth Schwarzkopf (SAX 2300). As John Steane has put it in *The Grand Tradition*: 'Nothing in the score has gone unheeded and, much more than that, the absolute fidelity combines with an imaginative grasp so that one feels that the scene has never been so completely realized before.' The poise and loveliness of this singer in her prime are beyond praise.

At the same time, Schwarzkopf recorded 12, the *Cavatine*, 'Und ob die Wolke'. This, too, is a lovely performance, the very essence of *Innigkeit*, the A flats even more ideally floated than in Lemnitz's famous 1934 version (numbers as above), which is also a mite fast for the Adagio mark. That is more surely obeyed on the 1948 re-make (DA 1881; SHB 47), where as in the 'Leise, leise' of the same session (DB 6802), there are signs of threads in the pristine tone. A more straightforward approach is also permissible. It is adopted by Janowitz (DG 136546) in her even, unaffected performance, and by Lehmann (Gram. 76988; LV 180), whose easy, natural singing is vitiated by the fast speed. Only Destinn, steady and unfussed, Dux, as in 8, and Felicie Huni-Mihacsek, shaping the phrases with delicacy, approach the standard of those already mentioned. Versions by Antionette Ries (punctuated by small coughs!), Lily Hafgren, Hammond, Reinhardt, Trude Eipperle, Margarete Teschemacher, Joan Sutherland (nearly wordless), Krilovici (vibrant, but miscast), Nancy Tatum (too off-hand) are little more than souvenirs of the artists concerned.

That leaves us with the Hermit's pronouncement and the odd ensemble disc. The bass-baritone Hermits, Leopold Demuth (42896, made in 1902) and Friedrich Schorr (E 586), singing with his own peculiar authority, find difficulties with the low notes. Two basses of the same generation, Paul Bender (4-42261; CO 311) and Richard Mayr (4-42176; LV 1) both sound warm and fatherly, but the contemporaneous Wilhelm Hesch (G&T 3-42498) proves even more authoritative and sonorous a Sarastro *redivivus*.

No.9, the trio for Agathe, Aennchen and Max, was partially recorded, 'Doch hast du . . . verdacht', by a trio including Leo Slezak as a forthright ranger (44241) made in 1902, and more fully and amenably by Käthe Heidersbach, Irene Eisinger with the veteran tenor Erik Wirl, an attractive little disc (EG 1822), presumably commemorating a 1932 Berlin ensemble. No. 6, 'Schelm, halt fest!' is sturdily sung by Hafgren and Bosetti (Od. 57886; LV 88).

My ideal cast would be Lehmann or Grümmer as Agathe, Streich as Aennchen, Kmentt or Tauber as Max, Waechter as Ottokar, Böhme or Uhde as Caspar, Frick as the Hermit, conductor Jochum. In fact, three of the singers (Grümmer, Streich, Böhme) turn up in the records of Furtwängler's 1954 live performance, but all are, at times, stretched by the conductor's inordinately slow tempi. However, Grümmer and Furtwängler between them give a reading of the *Cavatine* at a real Adagio which comes near to perfection in its poise and flow. Its sound is variable. Lehmann and Tauber, when only in their mid twenties, appeared together in the opera at Zoppot Waldoper in 1914.

DER FREISCHUTZ

Ag Agathe; *An* Aennchen; *M* Max; *C* Caspar; *O* Ottokar; *Kü* Küno; *Kil* Kilian; *H* Hermit

1950 Paludan *Ag*; Löser *An*; Wehofschütz *M*; Tuttner *O*; Duffek *Kü*; /Austrian State Chorus and Orch./Doehrer Remington ⓜ 199/100

1950 Trötschel *Ag*; Beilke *An*; Aldenhoff *M*; Böhme *C*; K. Paul *O*; Faulhaber *Kü*; Kramer *H*/Saxon State Opera Chorus and Orch./Kempe Acanta ⓜ DE 29268

1951 Cunitz *Ag*; Loose *An*; Hopf *M*; Rus *C*; Poell *O*; Bierbach *Kü*; Dönch *Kil*; Edelmann *H*/Vienna State Opera Chorus, VPO/Ackermann Decca ⓜ LXT2597-9

1954 (Salzburg Festival, live performance) Grümmer *Ag*; Streich *An*; Hopf *M*; Böhme *C*; Poell *O*; Czerwenka *Kü*; Dönch *Kil*; Edelmann *H*/Vienna State Opera Chorus, VPO/Furtwängler Cetra ⓜ L021/3

1955 (broadcast performance) Grümmer *Ag*; Streich *An*; Hopf *M*; Proebstl *C*; Poell *O*; Horn *Kü*; Marschner *Kil*; Böhm *H*/Cologne Radio Chorus and Orch./E. Kleiber Cetra ⓜ L042/3

1959 Grümmer *Ag*; Otto *An*; Schock *M*; Kohn *C*; Prey *O*; Wiemann *Kü*; Dicks *Kil*; Frick *H*/German Opera Chorus, Berlin PO/Keilberth EMI 1C 183 30171-3; Seraphim SIB 6010

1960 Seefried *Ag*; Streich *An*; Holm *M*; Böhme *C*; Wächter *O*; Peter *Kü*; Kuen *Kil*; Kreppel *H*/Bavarian Radio Chorus and Orch./Jochum DG 2726 061

1967 Watson *Ag*; Schädle *An*; Schock *M*; Frick *C*; C. Nicolai *O*; Ollendorf *Kü*; Lang *Kil*; Böhme *H*/German Opera Chorus and Orch./Matačić Ariola-Eurodisc XG 75607R; Everest S463

1968 Nilsson *Ag*; Köth *An*; Gedda *M*; Berry *C*; Anheisser *O*; Weller *Kü*; Crass *Kil*; Forster *H*/Bavarian State Opera Chorus and Orch./Heger EMI 1C 065 28351-3; Angel SCL 3748

1973 Janowitz *Ag*; Mathis *An*; Schreier *M*; Adam *C*; Weikl *O*; Vogel *Kü*; Leib *Kil*; Crass *H*/Leipzig Radio Chor./Dresden Staatskapelle/ C. Kleiber DG 2720 071

Excerpts

1929 Marherr *Ag*; T. de Garmo *An*; Soot *M*; Kandl *C*; Weitner *O*; Ernster *Kü*; Watzke *H*/Berlin State Opera Chor. & Orch./Weigert D-Pol. CA 8132–5

1947 Müller *Ag*; Spletter *An*; Seider *M*; Hanna *C*; Grossmann *C*; Domgraf-Fassbaender *O*; Greindl *H*/Berlin State Opera Chor./Berlin Municipal Orch./Heger

Sieens 68074–81; Am Decca X112

1950c Schlemm *Ag*; Schönen *An*; Frei *C*/Berlin Comic Opera Orch./von Zallinger
Supraphon ⑩ SUA 20295

1952–4 Schlemm *Ag*; Streich *An*; Wingassen *M*; Uhde *C*/Berlin PO, Munich PO, Bamberg SO/Lehmann, Leitner, Röther

DG ⑩ LPEM 19013

1957 Brouwenstijn *Ag*; Schwaiger *An*; Kmentt *M*; Berry *C*/Vienna State Opera Chor./VSO/Moralt
Ph. GL 5669

1964 Cloos *Ag*; Schöner *An*; Wilhelm *M*; Roth-Ehrang *K*; Günther Arndt Choir, German Opera Orch./Lange
Ariola-Eurodisc Z 75869R

Il barbiere di Siviglia

RICHARD OSBORNE

'Genuine humour on the operatic stage has become as rare as fine gray caviar', wrote Joseph Wechsberg from Vienna in 1960, a view unhappily confirmed down the years by the scarcity of genuinely memorable accounts of so seemingly indestructible a piece as *Il Barbiere*. But, then, the Rossini style is a rare concoction. *Il Barbiere*, like one of Rossini's famous *tournedos* steaks, will always have about it a semblance of interest; but how often it is bland on the palate or leaden to the digestion. How often the true, the enlivening piquancy is missing. The opera, as is well known, was dashed off in a mere thirteen days, and performed (at the second attempt) to much acclaim, facts which reveal a quite special operatic ambience. For the singer, Rossini's music is often exceptionally difficult. Rossini, who had inherited a great vocal style in decline, elaborated it into newness. Yet *Il Barbiere* was written before opera became big business, before the operatic empire-builders moved in. (When Rossini saw that looming he moved out.) At the time of the creation of *Il Barbiere* in 1816 opera was still, in essence, local and personal, buoyed along by special, private exuberances.

And so we have in *Il Barbiere* a peculiar blend of difficulty and innocence; an opera in which individual performances, whatever the virtuoso demands made on them, need to merge effortlessly into a finely honed ensemble, where characters even in the midst of the most fearsome solo pieces need to retain a certain nonchalance. A perfectly stylish *Barbiere*, so it seems, needs ease without superficiality, gaiety without loss of artistic seriousness, and at all times a perfect sense of balance. Rossini was, after all, one of the last of the great classical composers of his age. Buffoonery, of the kind which ruined the opera's ill-starred première, has no place in this finely poised comedy from the French; buffoonery, though, is what many a production of *Il Barbiere* has often descended to in the past.

The first electrical recording was made in La Scala, Milan, in 1929 under the direction of Lorenzo Molajoli and, like the opera's own first night, is a near-disaster. All vestiges of a Rossini style seem to have vanished. A piano accompanies the recitatives, note-values are freely abused, and none of the principals stays in the saddle long once Rossini launches him or her into a round of more or less difficult *fioritura*. The Rosina, Mercedes Capsir, is deft and silly, the Count is undistinguished, the bass dull. Nor does Riccardo Stracciari, then in the twilight of his career, greatly distinguish himself. No longer able to cope with Rossini's virtuoso writing for Figaro, he indulges in vocal skips, intrusive cackles and frequent changes of pace to the point where the reading finally parodies itself.

After this unpropitious start, nothing emerged from Italy until the Cetra set of 1950. Though a considerable advance on the 1929 La Scala set, this was by no means a complete solution. Again a piano accompanies the recitatives, again the Almaviva, Luigi Infantino, is caught by the *fioritura* like a fly in a web. On the other hand, Giulietta Simionato, a mezzo Rosina in the authentic style, is positively present, even if she sounds at times too like Azucena, a Spanish lady of quite another kidney. Her divisions in her second aria flash vividly by, but elsewhere the tone is often unaccountably cloudy. The Basilio of Cassinelli is rhythmically uneven, and the Bartolo is geriatric; Giuseppe Taddei, though, is a success as Figaro. Solecisms there are (such as a lugubriously taken high G at the end of the cavatina), but this is an agile and inventive reading. The voice is a big one, but Taddei brings many *mezza voce* effects to bear on the music. He is conscious of the fact that the role contains a good deal of musical thistledown, and he often carries Simionato and Infantino with him in the duets. The orchestral playing, a few imaginative touches from Fernando Previtali notwithstanding, is poor.

None the less, the 1950s did produce two outstanding sets: the HMV/Serafin in 1952 and the Columbia/Galliera in 1957. (I pass over the two non-Italian versions and the undistinguished Erede set in which Simionato again sings Rosina.) In spite of uneven orchestral playing and a tendency on Serafin's part freely to indulge *stringendo* effects, his 1952 version is genuinely stylish and, Bechi apart, finely sung. Nicola Monti, despite a certain severity of manner, is an elegant and expert *tenore di grazia*, perhaps the best of the post-war Almavivas, and the young Victoria de los Angeles, in her first complete recording of the role, is an entrancing Rosina. Svelte, feline, and a trifle lazy (rhythmically los Angeles has not the acerbic splendour of Supervia), this is a beautifully sung account of the role, less touched with pathos than her later Glyndebourne impersonation, gracious and yet full of character. For the rest, the ensemble in the Act 1 finale is stunning, ineffable and fierce by turns, Serafin at his most expert. Bechi, though, is a formidable stumbling block. In his cavatina he sounds like Scarpia in Barber's garb. When he is hatching the 'drunken' escapade with Almaviva he sounds like Iago gulling Cassio. 'A continual outrage on our artistic sensibilities', was the *Record Guide*'s view at the time. They were not wide of the mark.

Some were also outraged by Maria Callas's assumption of the role of

Rosina at La Scala in February 1956 (of which there is a Cetra live recording), an occasion on which, according to one observer, she reaped radishes rather than roses from a hostile gallery. 'In no way was Maria suited to this role', opined Elvira de Hidalgo, Callas's one-time teacher whose own 1909 recording of 'Una voce poco fa' (Fono. 92300/1; XIG 8009) – raw in intonation, full of conscious striving after vocal colour, with a laboured pulse and restricted top – makes her criticisms, at best, ungenerous. But whatever happened at La Scala under Giulini, the recording, produced by Walter Legge and conducted by Alceo Galliera, is superb. Here is a true mezzo Rosina – the voice smokey in the middle, agile at the top – full of wit and guile. 'A cunning pattern of excelling nature' was one critic's reaction to the 17-year-old Maria Malibran's performance, and one feels much the same about Callas's Rosina: threatening or insinuating, in love or out of love – who knows? Gobbi may not be as fresh-voiced here as he is in his 1948 account of the 'Largo al factotum' (see below), but the word-pointing is superb and, with Galliera an idiomatic conductor of Rossini's score, the ubiquitous Alva, and Nicola Zaccaria as Basilio, the set is a decided success, rich in closely observed dramatic detailing and full of beautifully articulated singing of Rossini's lithe yet difficult vocal lines.

All the Columbia set lacks is sweet, insinuating ease. For that we must turn to HMV's 1962 Glyndebourne set, a near-perfect *ensemble* performance redolent of warm Sussex summer evenings and fragrant Moselles, piquant and honey-deep. Gui conducts, paying out the rhythms with perfect poise. His is a gently smiling performance for a gently smiling Rosina. Does los Angeles now and again affect too strong a strain of romantic pathos? Perhaps, but hers is again an entrancing performance, and Alva is as sweet-toned as he has ever been in the role on record. Bruscantini, that most mellow and mercurial of Figaros, is in excellent voice, always allowing the comedy to well up from within the music. (How often Figaros impose themselves on to Rossini's score!) Ian Wallace's beautifully sung and immensely engaging Dr Bartolo, ripe and benign as Fielding's Mr Allworthy, is equally memorable. In spite of some small cuts in two (dramatically crucial) recitatives, this is, perhaps, the best *Barbiere* we have yet had on record, Gui, his singers, and Beecham's incomparable RPO conjuring a sense of style – musically harmonious and dramatically deft – which I am sure Rossini would have recognized and approved.

Another excellent set of the period is conducted *con brio e con amore* by Bruno Bartoletti for DG. The Almaviva is Monti, no longer as fresh-toned as on the earlier Serafin set, but most acceptable, and there is a blithe, flirtatious Rosina from Gianna d'Angelo, a soprano who throws off her roulades with such warmth, delicacy and charm that we can forgive her the un-Rosina-like lie of her voice. Capecchi is the Figaro in what is altogether a most engaging (if occasionally annoyingly foreshortened) *Barbiere*. Capecchi and Monti reappear on a Ricordi set of the early 1960s, this time with Rolando Panerai as Figaro and Graziella Sciutti as Rosina. Promising on paper, the set has never been easy to obtain outside Italy. A second DG set of that decade, conducted by Arturo Basile, has Maria Casula as Rosina: big-voiced, adventurous, often humourless and frequently strident. Marco Stecchi is a dangerous Figaro in the Bechi style. This set is savagely cut.

Absolutely complete and splendidly conducted by Leinsdorf, RCA's recording, based on a series of successful stage performances at the Metropolitan Opera, New York, does not wear especially well. Roberta Peters is the pert, coloratura Rosina which admirers of los Angeles, Callas and 'Una voce' in a sonorous E major, instinctively dread. She is often charmless in the Pons style; and the side-splitting, eye-rolling comic exaggerations of Corena, Merrill and Co. are difficult to tolerate on repeated hearings. Cesare Valletti sings Almaviva's big end-of-opera aria well enough, but Ugo Benelli, on the 1965 Decca set conducted by Varviso, is preferable. By and large, that Decca set is a disappointment. In the Act 1 finale Silvio Varviso sends the Rossini train swaying nicely over the points, but Manuel Ausensi is a hearty Figaro, big, blustering, and lacking in style; and Teresa Berganza, very magnetic on the stage, is oddly dull on record. Her cavatina begins appealingly enough, but once the pulse quickens and the music starts to dance quickly by, it all seems too effortless and uncomplicated, a performance which would serve equally Rossini's Rosina and Rossini's Elisabetta, who uses some of the same music.

Berganza is generally better partnered in the best of the 1970s sets, conducted by Claudio Abbado. Enzo Dara, for instance, is a stylish Bartolo with a scintillating line in patter, Alva is sweet-toned and idiomatic, and Hermann Prey is a great improvement on Ausensi. Yet, when Figaro suggests a furtive letter and Rosina reveals that she has already written it, the performance remains obstinately grounded by comparison with the Callas/Gobbi version, about which one could write volumes, at this point; and though the d'Angelo/Capecchi set is comparatively lightweight, here it too is irresistibly alert and alive.

Textually, the DG set is interesting, with everything back in place except (oddly) Almaviva's final aria. The recording, and Alberto Zedda's picture-cleaning work on the orchestral text, give the set a special, at times almost electric, brilliance, Rossini's textures now Picasso-bright. And yet for all his brilliance, Abbado as yet lacks guile and a sense of humour, relying overmuch on speed and polish to generate comic tension, and trusting too little to a steady spin of the rhythms and genuinely pointed phrasing.

HMV's set with Beverly Sills as Rosina is, by and large, a set to be avoided. Super-complete to the point of pedantic irrelevance, it includes an extra aria from Rossini's *Sigismondo* which Joséphine Fodor-Mainvielle (London's first Rosina) insinuated into a Venetian production of *Barbiere* in 1819. Alva, singing his fourth Almaviva on record, is badly off form, and Sherrill Milnes's Figaro is brash: wolf-whistles in the 'Largo al factotum' and moments when he becomes morose in the Rigoletto style. Assuredly *Barbiere* is not an opera for indulging *les larmes dans la voix*.

Moving on from complete sets, we come to a famous recording, the abridged de Lucia set of 1918, made when the distinguished tenor was in his late fifties, and transferred to LP in 1973 (Rubini SJG 121). As the abridgement is exclusively concerned to reveal de Lucia's art the set is inevitably ill-balanced musically, with famous numbers omitted and yards of comparatively uninteresting recitative for the tenor included. In the Act 1 finale it is members of the orchestra, rather than Almaviva, who seem to be intoxicated, and the duet 'All idea' proves to be uneven in execution. On the other hand, a fine sense of comedy is often in evidence. The shaving sequence is splendidly high-spirited, the elopement is the richer for the elegance and eloquence of de Lucia's line, and even Giorgio Schottler's highly garrulous Dr Bartolo has his moments.

That de Lucia was an incomparable Almaviva – one is tempted to say the only Almaviva – is sufficiently attested to by the four recordings he made, between 1902 and 1907, of the Count's two Act 1 arias. Desmond Shawe-Taylor has called de Lucia 'the last singer of the Rococo age'. Certainly he was the last Almaviva properly to deploy a wholly individual style of ornamentation: ornamentation as effortless, as mysterious yet as ineluctably right, as the play of light in a summer glade. Can the words 'la bella aurora' in 'Ecco ridente' itself have ever been painted so exquisitely on the voice as they are in these two recordings (050278, 1904, and 052250, 1907, both sung in B major, incidentally)? Does any other Almaviva catch in such measure the mingled pain and splendour, the intensifying charge of 'rendi men crudo'? Unrequited love draws from de Lucia all that is finest in his art, and in the *stretto* the beautifully flexed runs help perfectly to assuage the grief. The tremulous quality of the voice is amply stressed in his two recordings of the A minor *canzone* (52427, 1902, with piano and 2–52667, 1907, with orchestra, both in G minor). This may not please all tastes, but the finely shaded trill is ravishing and the play of the rhythm infinitely haunting. How tentative the start, how taut the first intimation of his name, how fine the slow-spun fall of tone at the phrase 'your name is on my lips'. One is reminded of Velluti as Stendhal describes him to us. A recording of the Act 2 trio, 'Ah! qual colpo' (054083; Saga XIG 8009), with Josefina Huguet and Pini-Corsi is also extant.

But how elusive the Count's music is. Alessandro Bonci, product of the Rossini Conservatoire in Pesaro, badly loses pitch and rhythm in his 1906 recording of 'Se il mio nome' (Fono. 39687) and there is a bleat on several high notes. Yet the top of the voice can be brilliant and sure. The rhetorical, step-wise ascent, 'che fido . . . che sposa . . . che a nome', is superbly taken first time around, and there are some exquisitely wafted long appoggiaturas. Other great tenors are partially successful too. Giuseppe Anselmi (Fono. 62268; XIG 8009) has some excellent decoration for the latter half of 'Ecco ridente', and Ferruccio Tagliavini (Cetra LPC 50155) bathes the first half of the air in fine April colours. Yet Schipa (DA 874; GEMM 151) in his 1926 recordings is less bewitching than one might have hoped, and Heddle Nash (DX 18; HQM 1234) is frankly dull. David Devries, a tremulous, nasal parody of de Lucia (Od. 188524), has a most disturbing falsetto whistle in the voice. Indeed, when we come to some of the safer present-day *tenore di grazia* artists like Monti and Alva, there are few genuinely outstanding Almavivas. Finally, Dimitri Smirnoff's remarkable 1917 recording (052410; 1C–049–03005), eccentric as it is in some of its detail, is certainly worth having for its free, flexible coloratura. Also worth hearing is the great Hermann Jadlowker, whose 1908 recording of 'Ecco ridente', uncut, may not have de Lucia's flexibility, but is a brilliant and fearless piece of coloratura singing which quite commands the view (Od. 76027; CO 312).

One of the earliest recordings of Figaro's entrance aria, the famous 'Largo al factotum', is the 1903 Warsaw recording of Mattia Battistini (52671; Perennial 3001). It is amazing that a man who found Sir John Falstaff merely risible should have condescended to sing the lowly Figaro, yet he treats the 'Largo' with enormous panache, at a speed which is not necessarily a by-product of short 78 sides. Even at speed this is a beautifully observed reading, with Battistini's predilection for aristocratic roles wittingly or unwittingly lending his Figaro a splendidly aspiring quality. Details of the barber's trade are passed over with impatience – razors, combs, lancets and scissors are all tossed deftly aside – making room for suave and grandiloquent treatment of such phrases as 'colla donnetta' and 'col cavaliere'. The Stretto is reckless and full of mistakes. 'I am like lightning', says Figaro; and for once we believe him. But even at his most reckless Battistini's Figaro is still something of a miracle. Giuseppe Campanari is certainly mercurial (1226–1B) but his version is cut. Stracciari, in a recording made in 1910 (Fono. 74183; GV 501) has a thrilling vocal quality, with high Fs and Gs given glowingly out and elegantly worked *fioritura*. Ruffo's 1907 recording (DB 502; COLH 155) is naturally interesting, a breathtaking display of vocal and verbal virtuosity from the first *a piacere* marking onwards. For rhythmic drive, some fine, fast *sotto voce* singing, and a potent array of verbal inflexions, the Neapolitan baritone Pasquale Amato (DB 156) is also worth seeking out.

Moving on to a slightly later generation of baritones, we have Mariano Stabile (Col. D 14719), ever the virtuoso of verbal, as opposed to musical, control, and his antitype Carlo Galeffi (D 18012; LV 220) whose 1926 recording sacrifices the text to vocal virtuosity. Apollo Granforte (DB 834; LV 90) is powerful, yet he retains a style. Among German Figaros, Willi Domgraf-Fassbaender (Poly. 95242; LV 41) shows a wonderful turn of speed, Heinrich Schlusnus (042525) a most engaging presence (though he is let down by an inexpert accompanist). Peter Dawson (C 1400; HQM 1217) transforms the 'Largo' into a music-hall turn, and he is not helped by an appalling English translation – 'there are joys in the harbour when you're a barber'. Dennis Noble suffers likewise, the whole reading (C 3141; HLM 7009) lacking Latin elegance in spite of a sizzling accompaniment by the Sadler's Wells Orchestra under Warwick Braithwaite. Yet, that said, Noble's earlier recording (Col. 9556) is a great success, very funny, and a fine example of his art.

Dominating the recordings of the 1930s and 1940s as Battistini dominates the earliest years on record, are Lawrence Tibbett and Tito Gobbi, though a singer such as Ernest Blanc (Pathé-Marconi ASTX 125) proves to be both reliable and vivid. Tibbett's version, recorded in April 1930 (DB 1478; VIC 1340), is flecked with things which will annoy the fastidious, but the performance is a *tour de force*. And how wonderful Gobbi is in his 1948 HMV recording (DB 6626; HLM 7018). Here the voice has a silvery agility which it lacks in the later, complete set. The whole aria – beautifully coloured on the voice, beautifully pointed through the text – has a quicksilver beauty, a fire and a truly Latin sense of nonchalance which no other post-war baritone matches or surpasses.

Before leaving Figaro, it is worth mentioning some of the best records of his duets with the Count ('All' idea') and Rosina ('Dunque io son'). Mario Sammarco and John McCormack should certainly be heard (DB 608; GEMM 155–60) if only for McCormack's inquiry as to the whereabouts of Figaro's shop, a simple moment in near recitative but a moment of immeasurable charm. Bonci and Corradetti, an engaging and plausible Figaro, should also be heard, primarily for the brilliance of Bonci's divisions (Fono. 39336/7; XIG 8009), superior to those encountered on Stracciari's recording with Fernando Carpi (Fono. 74189/90; RLS 743), but yielding to the marbled beauty of de Lucia's singing in a version with Pini-Corsi (054080). Dennis Noble and Webster Booth, the former very stylishly inebriated, admirably accompanied (C 3398), are not to be overlooked. In the duet with Rosina, Ruffo and Galvany sweep the board among earlier recordings (DB 400; XIG 8009), but Stracciari and Barrientos (Am. Col. 49612) and Carosio and Tagliabue (DB 6387) are not without interest. Lily Pons, a singer I do not much admire, must be granted a special mention, though. In spite of some aspirated runs, hers is a deft and delectable performance, accompanied with immense brio by Wilfred Pelletier. And who inspires Pons to such heights? None other than Giuseppe de Luca, another great singer (for all that he strains at his final high G) and an incomparable comic presence (DB 5815; VIC 1395): he was then (1940) at the end of a glorious career.

And so we come to Rosina, and here one must say that though many sopranos may be called to the role, few merit the choosing. Few have the wit, the vibrance, the radiance and the technique that the role demands. It is a sign of the difficulties we nowadays encounter that

Frederica von Stade should be accounted a successful Rosina. On the evidence of her 'Una voce poco fa' on her 1977 recital record (Philips 9500 098) she has many engaging ideas, ideas which are often deftly, even memorably, executed. What she lacks is any overall sense of character or style. Her performance is, in sum, no more than a potpourri of brilliant effects. Compare this with Callas's recital disc (SLS 5104), conducted with sober insight by Tullio Serafin: there vocal colour, musical line, and human psychology are hypnotically aligned. (Incidentally, this masterly performance is in the proper mezzo key of E.) No version is more wheedlingly sinuous than Callas's; no Rosina projects her admonitory 'ma' with more deadly aim; above all, none controls the quickening pulse of the piece, nor its fascinatingly varied *fioritura*, with more dramatic acumen. Callas *is* Rosina, and in 1954 she was in excellent voice.

'Una voce' must be sung in its original key, E major, if it is to make its full effect. After E major, a key rich in promise, full of splendour but capable of conveying, too, an arcane suggestiveness, F major (the key of the soprano Rosinas) is altogether more innocuous, vapid and watery. Strangely, though Luisa Tetrazzini made a recording in the higher key in 1911 (DB 690), her 1908 recording (053416) is in E. Perhaps the low tessitura at the start does produce a strained, discoloured quality, but when the music begins to soar, the voice, and the personality behind it, seem limpid and sweet. The magical upward elision on 'e cento trapole', the lightening 'ma', the seductively limpid descent on the word 'amorosa' convey a sense of play, a silken inventiveness, which no other soprano quite matches, though the earlier of Galli-Curci's two recordings (DB 261; VIC 1518) is quite exceptional, over-decorated, but full of lovely singing and deft effects. Maria Barrientos, the Spanish *soprano leggiero* who made her London debut in 1903 as Rosina, has an easy manner and a bell-like voice (Fono. 39459/60, 1906) but there is in the last resort some want of magic. Marcella Sembrich, nearing retirement, made a recording of the cavatina (in F) in 1907/8 (Victor 88097). Though she disappoints in the latter part, she is undeniably brilliant in the opening. Irene Abendroth, a dramatic coloratura in the Mei-Figner style (43250, Dresden 1902) is also of historical interest.

Conchita Supervia, like Callas, comes close to the style of the great dramatic sopranos of Rossini's own day: Colbran, Malibran, Viardot. Spanish by birth and inclination (an advantage which Callas did not share), Supervia was similarly possessed of a fierce vocal beauty and a technique that brilliantly, pragmatically served it. She was, if I may borrow Verdi's useful phrase, a great artist 'in spite of everything'. The tremulous quality, the evident beat in the voice at the words 'io son docile' is worth hearing; if you can accept this, the rest is magnificent (PXO 1015). If anything, her account of the singing lesson (Rossini's own, not a substitute aria) is even finer (PXO 1020). All Supervia's Rossini recordings were later gathered onto a single Parlophone LP (PMA

1025): an indispensable record for an insight into the important Spanish school of Rossini interpretation, as well as a memento of a very great artist.

High, dazzling Rosinas are not much to my taste, nor were they to Rossini's either, though he might have stirred a little to hear the brilliant French soprano Ritter-Ciampi (Poly. 66842), the tone needle-keen, with some fine *fil de voce* effects. A famous Rosina of Clemens Krauss's days in Vienna was Toti dal Monte; but her 1925 HMV recording (DB 830), though brilliant, lacks substance and charm. Preferable to dal Monte are several German and Austrian sopranos, including Fritzi Jokl (P 2167; LV 138) and, better still, Schwarzkopf's teacher, Maria Ivogün (Poly. 85309; LV 87). Ivogün sings the cavatina with great sweetness and beauty, with smiling descents from the high Cs, perceptibly Viennese in style, *Fledermaus* just around the corner. From Ivogün to another pupil, the usually delectable Rita Streich, is a sad declension. 'At last, a really *blithe* Rosina', wrote an eminent opera buff about Streich's 1958 recording of 'Una voce' (DG EPL 30052). But to my ears it is slow in pulse, muddled in style and unsure in decoration. Queen of all the Viennese Rosinas, if it is possible to imagine Rosina so elevated (she later becomes a Countess, of course) is Selma Kurz. Her HMV record (DA 408; GEMM 121/2) has the first part of the cavatina only, but it is a richly satisfying account, every phrase shaped to convey a sense of the imminence of passion. What a great singer Kurz was, with a unique ability to convey emotion, a fine technique, and tone as fluid, as sweet, as golden as some great wine from d'Yquem.

Although Bartolo's aria has been recorded by, among others, that skilled *diseur* Salvatore Baccaloni (Am. Col. 71193D; Odyssey Y 31736), it remains only to discuss Don Basilio's great 'Calumny' aria. Recordings by Didur (Fono. 74119; XIG 8009), Pinza (Am. Col. 72528), Navarrini (Fono. 74033; GV 16) and Tancredi Pasero (0–8751) all merit a passing nod. But two basses stand out: Alexander Kipnis and Feodor Chaliapin. Kipnis (D 2088; SH 280) sings in German but the spun legato on the phrase 'still und weise ist sein Wehen' ravishes sense, compensating for the absence of original Italian words like 'sottile' and 'dolcemente'. Admittedly, this Basilio is no snake; but the beautifully deployed legato, the superb diction and the massive dignity make for an entirely memorable assumption of the role. Chaliapin recorded the piece many times. An HMV recording (DB 932; GEMM 152) is well pitched, but in other recordings the great man's compassionate feelings for the poor, downcast wretch makes him waver badly on 'e il meschino', and the pitch goes down like the Titanic. Earlier, the calumnious breeze, and the gentle zephyr, are evoked with a roughened beauty, exquisite tones set against some jagged ones. At the word 'sottile' we are reminded by Chaliapin of Falstaff; and, indeed, this amusing specimen of a music-master is, in Chaliapin's performance, quite the rogue, a man of criminal intent putting on airs. Traditionally the aria is sung in C, but it is worth noting that among modern basses in the complete sets Carlo Cava sings it in the original D (for Gui, but not for Bartoletti) with great sensitivity; as does Ruggero Raimondi, rather plainly on the Varviso set, and Paolo Montarsolo under Abbado.

The overture to *Barbiere*, which exists in literally dozens of different recordings, did yeoman service for Rossini. Indeed, there is a Ricordi edition in which it appears as the prelude to the early *opera buffo*, *L'equivoco stravagante*. Spurious as that edition may be, it none the less shows a lively musical intuition, for the overture certainly suits a *buffo* piece better than a serious one. 'The Overture to the *Barber* caused great amusement in Rome', wrote Stendhal. 'The audience heard – or, rather, thought they heard – a musical dialogue containing all the threats and blusterings of the old, jealous, and infatuated guardian, and the plaintive sighs of the pretty ward.' Among Italian versions, Giulini's recording of the overture has great strength and architectural splendour (SAX 2377) but it wants spirit, mordancy and wit. Alceo Galliera, conducting the same orchestra, the Philharmonia, on a 78 (DX 1690) and on the complete set, is far more expert, with a sweet, singing introduction and the famous minor-key Allegro vivo racily vivid, flecked with irony. His account is preferable to Gui's in the Glyndebourne set, which, like Giulini's, is strangely circumspect. Serafin's recording with the Florence Festival Orchestra (C 4136) and again with the Sinfonia of Milan on the complete HMV set is a model of style, the slow-pulsing *ostinati* used as springboards for mercurial woodwind detailing (the repeated-note effects beautifully judged). The whole performance has a festive, anticipatory air. Toscanini's NBC performance (DB 6344; AT 108) is let down by tentative horns but the control of the great crescendi is masterly and the reading has great urgency. It is Toscanini's earlier, New York Philharmonic Symphony performance (D 1835; CDN 1055), though, which perhaps sets ultimate standards: a reading which is steady, relaxed, and ripe. With what comic complacency the strings gurgle over their trills (shades of *Falstaff*) before the oboe dances graciously in; how rubicund the horns; how vivid the crescendi! This is certainly a record to treasure.

IL BARBIERE DI SIVIGLIA

R Rosina; *B* Berta; *A* Almaviva; *F* Figaro; *Bar* Bartolo; *Bas* Basilio

1918–20 (partly abridged) Resemba, Ottein *R*; Sabantano *B*; de Lucia *A*; Novelli, Franci *F*; Schottler *Bar*; S. Valentino, Muñoz *Bas*/San Carlo Opera Chorus and Orch./Sassano Rubini ⓜ SJG 121

1919 Pereira *R*; Mometti *B*; Taliani *A*; Badini *F*; Carnevali *Bar*; Di Lelio *Bas*/La Scala Chrous and Orch./Sabajno HMV S 5110–38

1929 Capsir *R*; Ferrari *B*; Borgioli *A*; Stracciari *F*; Baccaloni *Bar*;

Bettoni *Bas*/La Scala Chorus and Orch./Molajoli
EMI ⓜ 3C 153 00697–8;
CBS (US) ⓜ EL 1

1950 Simionato *R*; Broilo *B*; Infantino *A*; Taddei *F*; Badioli *Bar*; A. Cassinelli *Bas*/Milan Radio Chorus and Orch./Previtali
Cetra ⓒ LPS 3211 ④ MC 129–30

1950 (live performance, Metropolitan Opera, New York) Pons *R*; Roggero *B*; Di Stefano *A*; Valdengo *F*; Baccaloni *Bar*; Hines *Bas*/Metropolitan Opera Chorus and Orch./Erede
Cetra ⓜ LO 3/3

1952 de los Angeles *R*; Canali *B*; Monti *A*; Bechi *F*; Luise *Bar*; Rossi-Lemeni *Bas*/Chorus, Milan SO/Serafin
HMV ⓜ ALP 1022–4; RCA (US) ⓜ LM 6104

1953 (in Russian) Firsova *R*; Kozlovsky *A*; Burlak *F*; Malyshev *Bar*; Reizen *Bas*/Moscow Radio Chorus and Orch./Samosud
MK ⓜ DO 1550–5

1955 (in French) Berton *R*; Betti *B*; Giraudeau *A*; Dens *F*; Lovano *Bar*; Depraz *Bas*/Paris Opéra-Comique Chorus and Orch./Wolff
EMI ⓜ 2C 153 11010–2

1956 Simionato *R*; Cavallari *B*; Misciano *A*; Bastianini *F*; Corena *Bar*; Siepi *Bas*/Florence Festival Chorus and Orch./Erede
Decca D38D3; Richmond ⓜ RS 63011

1956 (arias and ensembles only) Gatta *R*; Betner *B*; Spina *A*; Pedani *F*; Pudis *Bar*; Gaetani *Bas*/La Fenice Chorus and Orch./M. Wolf-Ferrari
Record Society ⓜ RS 15–6

1956 (live performance, La Scala, Milan) Callas *R*; Carturan *B*; Alva *A*; Gobbi *F*; Luise *Bar*; Rossi-Lemeni *Bas*/La Scala Chorus and Orch./Giulini
Cetra ⓜ LO 34/3

1957 Callas *R*; Carturan *B*; Alva *A*;

Gobbi *F*; Ollendorf *Bar*; Zaccaria *Bas*/Chorus, Philharmonia/Galliera
HMV SLS 853; Angel SCL 3559

1959 Peters *R*; Roggero *B*; Valletti *A*; Merrill *F*; Corena *Bar*; Tozzi *Bas*/Metropolitan Opera Chorus and Orch./Leinsdorf
RCA (UK) VICS 6102/1–3; (US) LSC 6143

1960c Janchulescu *R*; Sandulescu *B*; Teodorian *A*; Herlea *F*; Gabor *Bar*; Laghin *Bas*/Romanian State Opera Chorus and Orch./Brediceanu
Electrocord ⓜ ECEO 68–7; Sélect ⓜ 150057–9

1960 D'Angelo *R*; Carturan *B*; Monti *A*; Capecchi *F*; Tadeo *Bar*; Cava *Bas*/Bavarian Chorus and Orch./Bartoletti
DG 2728 005

1962 de los Angeles *R*; Sarti *B*; Alva *A*; Bruscantini *F*; Wallace *Bar*; Cava *Bas*/Glyndebourne Festival Chorus, RPO/Gui
HMV SLS 5165 ④ TGSLS 5165; Angel SCL 3638

1964 Berganza *R*; Malagù *B*; Benelli *A*; Ausensi *F*; Corena *Bar*; Ghiaurov *Bas*/Rossini di Napoli Chorus and Orch./Varviso
Decca SET 285–7; London OSA 1381

1965 (in German) Pütz *R*; Burmeister *B*; Schreier *A*; Prey *F*; Ollendorf *Bar*; Crass *Bas*/Berlin Radio Soloistenvereinigung, Berlin State Orch./Suitner EMI 1C 153 28918–9

1968 Casula *R*; Rafanelli *B*; Alva *A*; Stecchi *F*; Mariotti *Bar*; Washington *Bas*/Teatro Verdi Chorus and Orch., Trieste/Basile
DG 135 074–5

1970 Guglielmi *R*; Schubert *B*; Cucuccio *A*; Cappuccilli *F*; Valdengo *Bar*; S. Pagliuca *Bas*/Czech Philharmonic Chorus, Prague CO/Zani
Supraphon 112 0921–3

1972 Berganza *R*; Malagù *B*; Alva *A*; Prey *F*; Dara *Bar*; Montarsolo *Bas*/Ambrosian Opera Chorus,

LSO/Abbado
DG 2720 053 ④ 3371 003;
(US) 2709 041 ④ 3371 003
1974 Sills *R*; Barbieri *B*; Gedda *A*;
Milnes *F*; Capecchi *Bar*;
Raimondi *Bas*/Alldis Choir,
LSO/Levine
HMV SLS 985; Angel SCLX
3761 (Q) ④ 4X3S–3761
1974 (in French) Mesplé *R*; Millet *B*;
Burles *A*; Manuguerra *F*; Benoît
Bar; Mars *Bas*/Paris Opéra
Chorus and Orch./Marty
EMI 2C 167 12884–6

Excerpts

1935 (in German) Meyen *R*; Scheele-
Müller *B*; Patzak *A*; Weltner *F*;
Kandl *Bar*; Abendroth
Bas/Berlin State Opera Chorus
and Orch./Weigert
Polydor 95282–5
1942 Reggiani *R*; Browning *B*; Landi
A; Ramirez *F*; Gurney *Bar*;
Alvary *Bas*/Victor Chorus and
Orch./Bamboschek
RCA (US) ⓜ LBC 1083
1944 (in German) Reichelt *R*; Maier
B; Fehenberger *A*; Schellenberg
F; Frick *Bar*; Böhme
Bas/Dresden State Opera Chorus
and Orch./Striegler
Acanta ⓜ BB 23103
1951 Chiericati *R*; Donati *A*; Forni
F/Florence Festival Orch./Ghiglia
Remington ⓜ 199–14
1954 (abridged) Meyer *R*; Duval *B*;
Conrad *A*; Gorin *F*/Chorus,
Netherlands PO/Krannhals
MMS ⓜ OP6

1954 Reggiani *R*; Landi *A*; Valentino
F; Baccaloni *Bar*/Orch./Walther
Royale ⓜ 1597
1954 (in French) Berton *R*; Voli *A*;
Le Hémonet *F*; Depraz *Bar*;
Noguera *Bas*/SO/Menet
Barclay ⓜ 89014
1955 (in French) Doria *R*; Baroni *A*;
Huberty *F*; Legros
Bas/Pasdeloup Orch./Allain
Vega ⓜ 16046
1959 (in German) Köth *R*; Holm *A*;
Prey *F*; Frick *Bas*/Berlin
SO/Schüchter
EMI 1C 047 28573
1960 Rizzoli *R*; Troy *A*; Monachesi
F; Onesti *Bas*/Hamburg Radio
SO/Annovazzi
Musica et Littera 8007
1963 (in German) Hallstein *R*;
Kmentt *A*; Wächter *F*; Kusche
Bar; Frick *Bas*/Bavarian State
Opera Orch./Löwling
Ariola-Eurodisc K86802R
1963 (in French) Doria *R*; Vanzo *A*;
Massard *F*; Legros *Bas*;
Giovannetti *Bar*/SO/Etcheverry
Vogue LDM 30134 ④
B.VOC112
1963 (Act 1, in Hungarian) László *R*;
Divéky *B*; Réti *A*; Melis *F*;
Katona *Bar*; Székely
Bas/Hungarian Radio Chorus
and Orch./Gardelli
Qualiton SLP X11547
1965 (in French) Louvai *R*;
Mallabrera *A*; Gui *F*; Savignol
Bas/Orch./Etcheverry
Vega ST 90005

Norma

ANDREW PORTER*

Bellini's Norma is one of the most demanding operatic roles ever written. It calls for power, grace in slow cantilena, pure, fluent coloratura, stamina, tones both tender and violent, force and intensity of verbal declamation, and a commanding stage presence. Only a soprano who has all these virtues can sustain the role. There have not been many such sopranos. Richard Bonynge introduces the recording with his wife, Joan Sutherland, in the title role by saying:

The singer who can be a complete Norma probably has never existed – maybe never *will* exist. The opera requires almost too much of one soprano – the greatest dramatic ability, superhuman emotional resources, the greatest *bel canto* technique, a voice of quality and size, and I dare say many more attributes as well.

The critics of the nineteenth century delighted to describe and compare the fine points of performances by Giuditta Pasta (for whom Bellini composed the role), Giulia Grisi (the first Adalgisa, and then a famous Norma), Maria Malibran, Adelaide Kemble, and, later, Lilli Lehmann. Jenny Lind's Norma also had champions; the Germans were charmed by the 'maidenly' interpretation – which, as Chorley remarked, was 'praise original, to say the least of it, when the well-known story is remembered'.

Any discussion of *Norma* on records is bound to centre on Norma herself. Since the gramophone enables us to listen to opera and assess singers' art with the long ears of history, I approach the modern recordings by way of the earlier interpretations. We can still hear Lilli Lehmann, who sang Clotilde in her early Prague seasons (1866–8), and then Adalgisa, but refused all invitations to the title role until, in 1884/85, only after having mastered Donna Anna, Leonore, and Isolde, she felt she was ready to tackle a part she deemed 'ten times as exacting as Leonore'. The style and sound of the singers for whom Bellini composed his opera

*This chapter incorporates some material that originally appeared in the pages of *Opera, Gramophone, High Fidelity* and the *New Yorker*; I am grateful to the editors of those magazines for permission to re-use and rework it. I am also grateful to Colin Shreve, who played to me his copies of Josefina Huguet's 'Casta diva' recordings and several other rare items.

we can only guess at, reconstructing them in the mind's ear from what was written about – and for – them. The attempt should be made, if we are to understand the composer's intentions. *Norma*, of course, is far, far more than just Norma herself. I will say something about that when we reach the complete recordings.

There is no critical edition of the score. The printed versions show many divergences, and the autograph (which has been published in facsimile) presents several puzzles – such as passages cancelled, reinstated, then cancelled again. (Norma's verse of 'Mira, o Norma', surprisingly, has been crossed out.) Such textual points as have a direct bearing on what we hear on the records discussed below are mentioned as they crop up. On the whole, the Boosey & Hawkes vocal score edited by Arthur Sullivan and J. Pittman is the most reliable text generally available, but in a few places readings of the Novello (edited by Natalia Macfarren) and Ricordi vocal scores and the Ricordi miniature score are to be preferred. In particular, the Ricordi vocal score gives the fullest representation of the elaborate vocal instructions – *con devota fierezza, con voce cupa e terribile, con tutta la tenerezza, canto vibrato*, etc. – in Bellini's carefully worked autograph. It is worth looking out for the earlier Boosey score edited by W. S. Rockstro, 'pupil of Dr Felix Mendelssohn Bartholdy', which contains an interesting preface, a careful text, and useful indications of nineteenth-century staging traditions for the opera.

Norma was composed for the La Scala debut, in December 1831, of Giuditta Pasta. She was already celebrated, and in a smaller Milanese theatre, the Carcano, she had recently won a triumph as the *ingénue* heroine of Bellini's previous opera, *La sonnambula*. Bellini told her, with justice, that in Norma she would find a role suited to her 'encyclopaedic character'. Felice Romani's libretto was drawn from a play, Alexandre Soumet's *Norma*, which had opened in Paris earlier that year. In the title role, Mlle Georges had – in the words of Soumet's preface to the printed text –

obtained a clamorous success. After having been in turn, in the first four acts, the Niobe of the Greeks, the Lady Macbeth of Shakespeare, the Valléda of M. de Chateaubriand [in his novel *Les Martyrs*], after having traversed the entire circle of passions that can be continued in the female heart, she rose, in the mad scene of the final act, to heights of inspiration which will perhaps never be scaled again.

That last act – in which Norma, having killed one of her children, hurls herself, together with the other, over a precipice – was omitted by Romani and Bellini; but plenty remains.

Pasta was by all accounts a faulty vocalist but a spellbinding musician and actress. She brought *Norma* to London eighteen months after its Scala première, and, according to J. E. Cox's *Music Recollections*:

So faulty was her intonation that in the celebrated duet 'Mira, o Norma', she had gradually got down a whole tone, to which the string players were cleverly accommodating themselves, while those who had to deal with the wind instruments gave up altogether as a hopeless affair. . . . Pasta's tone still continued to ebb and flow to the end of the opera. Yet, in spite of this deficiency, her acting covered it.

Chorley says much the same: 'She steadily began her evening's task half a tone too flat. Her acting was more striking and powerful than ever, if that could be.'

Grisi had a more beautiful voice and an excellent technique, and she was a beautiful woman. She modelled her interpretation on Pasta's. People disagreed on it. Bellini himself found Grisi tame, but Chorley declared that her performance

perhaps, in some points, was an improvement on the model, because there was more of animal passion in it; and this (as in the scene of the imperious and abrupt rage which closes the first act) could be driven to extremity without its becoming repulsive, owing to the absence of the slightest coarseness in her personal beauty. There was in it the wild ferocity of the tigress, but a certain frantic charm therewith which carried away the hearer – nay, which possibly belongs to the true character of the druid priestess, unfaithful to her vows.

The tenor, Domenico Donzelli, was, at 41, something of a veteran. Back in 1815, Rossini had composed *Torvilda e Dorliska* for him; in 1822, he turns up at one of Beethoven's 'Academies', singing in the trio, 'Tremate, empi, tremate'. When Donzelli learned that he had been engaged for opening of the 1831/32 Scala season, he wrote at once to Bellini (with whom he had never worked before) to provide

precise details of my style of singing, my range, and my character of voice; to direct your inspirations so that I can render them in a way that corresponds to the effect which you want, and that will contribute to the success of your music and of my art. . . . The range of my voice, then, is nearly two octaves, from low D to top C. Chest voice to G, and it is in this range that I can declaim with vigour and sustain all the force of the declamation. From G to high C I can use a falsetto that, employed with art and with power, provides a means of decoration. I have a fair amount of agility, but find descents much easier than ascents.

Bellini took note. He used the full two-octave range but stressed full-voice Gs, wrote only one 'decorative' high C, and in coloratura emphasized downward descents. The role is very different from the high-flying, elegant tenor parts – in *Bianca*, *Il pirata*, *La sonnambula*, and *I puritani* – he composed for Rubini.

The bass, Vincenzo Negrini, seems to have left a mainly negative mark on the opera. Because, it was reported, he suffered from a weak heart, Bellini abandoned his idea of including a vigorous denunciation of Norma by Oroveso in the finale. The great Oroveso of early performances was Luigi Lablache. In Chorley's words:

An organ more richly toned or suave than his voice was never given to mortal. Its real compass was about two octaves – from E to E. In the upper portion of the register four or five of his tones had a power which could make itself heard above orchestral thunders or in the midst of any chorus, however gigantic either might be. This remarkable force was not, as in the case of many singers, displayed on all occasions; but it was made to tell in the right places, such as in the part . . . of Oroveso, the Druid priest in *Norma*, with prodigious and resistless lustre, put forth as it was without stint or the slightest apparent difficulty.

It was for Lablache, when he was singing Oroveso at the Théâtre-Italien, that Richard Wagner composed his virtuoso alternative for 'Ah, del Tebro'.*

Clotilde and Flavio, the companions of Norma and Pollione, are secondary roles of almost no importance.

Against that background, let us consider *Norma* on records.

Plainly, the starting point should be Adelina Patti, the great prima donna of the late nineteenth century. On 9 February 1843, Caterina Barili Patti was singing Norma at the Madrid Opera; her husband, Salvatore Patti, was the Pollione. Toward the end of the performance, Mme Patti felt unwell and was carried to the green room. There and then, so legend has it – but on the afternoon of the next day, according to more sober authorities – Adelina Giovanna Maria Patti was born. Seven years later, after a well-spent infancy listening to Jenny Lind, Grisi, etc., in rehearsal, young Adelina was placed by parents on a table and asked to sing an aria. Perhaps inevitably, she chose 'Casta Diva' – after all, she had almost literally been born with it. She sang the aria from memory and without mistake; her astonished parents arranged a concert, and little Miss Patti (again standing on a table) made her debut in Tripler's Hall, New York.

Her career began with 'Casta Diva' in 1850. Fifty-six years later she gave her formal farewell, in London, and also in 1906 she recorded the aria. She is short of breath, takes a breath between 'Casta' and 'Diva', goes astray at the end of the first verse and seems to be improvising a close; but she sings the aria with great beauty and purity, adding wonderfully deft little mordents to the vocal line. The second verse, 'Tempra, o Diva', is done with adornments, and Patti manages the ornaments, including an elaborate cadence and trill, with extraordinary virtuosity. She declaims the words 'lo zelo audace' with considerable dramatic force. She was 63 at the time. She takes the aria down, I think, into E major. (In Bellini's autograph 'Casta Diva' is in G, the cabaletta in F. The downward transposition of the cavatina to F is of long standing. It is found in the Ricordi and Novello scores, but not the Boosey; Pasta herself is said to have practised it.)

*Sarah Caldwell, ever adventurous, included the aria in her 1971 production of *Norma*, in Boston. It can be heard, sung by Donald Gramm, on the fill-up side of the Penzance 'pirate' recording of *Das Liebesverbot*. Wagner admired *Norma*; the aria seems to provide a curious commentary on what he heard in it. In this chapter, I mention only the 'pirate' recordings that have achieved fairly wide circulation and only the tapes that can be heard by the public in such collections as that of the New York Public Library.

Patti never sang Norma on the stage. Nor, so far as I can trace, did
Marcella Sembrich, who recorded 'Casta Diva' in 1908. She treats it as
a concert piece, singing only one verse of the cavatina (with additional
adornment and a very long cadential trill) and embellishing the cabaletta,
'Ah! bello a me ritorna', with brilliantly struck coloratura, some of it
Bellini's and some of it her own. In the same year, that great Norma,
Lilli Lehmann, recorded 'Casta Diva' in Berlin and, with her niece
Hedwig Helbig as Adalgisa, the duet 'Ah! si fa core', in German (Od.
50358; CO 384–5). Lehmann's records are justly famous. She was 59. She
sings here with strong, sure tone, noble phrasing, and astounding
flexibility. All the runs and ornaments are accurate; she adds two
(perfectly formed) trills to the two sustained Cs of the second florid
melisma on 'senza vel'. Hanslick's review of her Vienna Norma still
applies:

Her Norma was characterized in the slow cantilenas by the most beautiful
portamento and the securest and finest intonation and swelling of the high notes,
and in the florid passages by a pure and fluent coloratura. The latter was never
a coquettish intrusion; it remained noble, serious, subordinate to the situation.

Helbig turns up in Lehmann's autobiography as 'my dear little companion';
as the accompanist of a shipboard concert; and, much later, singing
Mozart duets with Lehmann in Salzburg, in 1904. Otherwise, she seems
to survive only by these recorded duets with Lehmann. (Besides *Norma*,
there are *Figaro* and *Così* duets, and Faure's *Crucifix*.) She was obviously
a fine singer. The two sopranos close the first duet with Bellini's elaborate
cadenza made still more intricate by additional mordents. I have not
heard their unpublished 'Mira, o Norma', but am told that it is even
more remarkable; it starts at 'Ah, perchè, perchè'; Aunt Lilli has the first
word.

Lehmann spoils one for other famous Normas, even for Celestina
Boninsegna's. Boninsegna's second, double-sided, Columbia version of the
aria (1910) is wonderful in a way, but, heard after Lehmann's, it sounds
less shapely in phrasing; the enunciation of the words is not sharp, and
dramatic ritenutos and tenutos strike one as out of style. There is a real
sense in which Maria Callas, despite her faulty vocalization (far less faulty
than Pasta's, if those old critics were right), recalls the 'old' singers. In
Callas's phrasing there are a delicacy and imaginative power that set her
apart from the Verdi sopranos and verismo sopranos of the early years
of our century. Yet Boninsegna's steady stream of controlled tone is fine,
and there is an exciting mixture of dignity and emotion in her
interpretation. She just separates the repeated high As in the famous
climax of the cavatina, and then spills over passionately from the last one
to a ringing, emotional B flat.

Here we come upon a textual point. In the autograph, Bellini wrote
this passage differently in each verse – deliberately and carefully; first

time, repeated syncopated attacks; second time, a solid semibreve, crescendo. (Bellini's intention is confirmed by his second writing-out of the passage when, in an inspired afterthought, he added the chorus to the second verse.) The Ricordi score follows suit; Boosey and Novello both repeat the first-time figuration, and so do most sopranos. Lehmann joins the As crescendo, while making each separate one felt, and then attacks the B flat with a new, sweeter and softer timbre. Rosa Ponselle – also a beautiful effect – makes a crescendo on the first four As and for the fifth drops to a *subito piano*, joining it to the B flat. Callas in her first complete recording is ugly, sprawling up in a raucous crescendo to a very sharp B flat. Her second is more delicate. Gina Cigna yaps the As. Claudia Muzio sings them evenly, without crescendo, joining the last to the B flat. Italian tradition in the early years of the century was to 'define' each repeated A by attacking it from the note below, as if from a lower appoggiatura. That is how Manuel Garcia recommended such passages should be treated. Josefina Huguet provides an extreme example of the practice, Giannina Russ a more artistic one, and Joan Sutherland (with Bs, not As, since she sings 'Casta Diva' in G) a modern revival of it.

Of course, there were *Norma* recordings before Patti's, most of them made in Milan. The earliest I have traced are Ida Sambo's and Romilda Nelli's of 'Casta Diva', both Zonophones of 1900. The first G&Ts arrive in 1902–3, with (eventually) five sides by the general-purpose tenor Carlo Caffetto. 1903–4 brings a crop of 'Casta Divas': Huguet, Boninsegna (the piano-accompanied single-side version that reappeared in the HMV Archive Series; it is hardly more than a sketch for the 1910 Columbia), Teresa Arkel (twice) on G&T; Leonilda Paini on Columbia.

Between 1905 and 1907 G&T built up a group of two solos and several ensembles, with Ida Giacomelli as the heroine and, except where noted, Lina Mileri as Adalgisa, Gino Martinez-Patti as Pollione, and Cesare Preve as Oroveso. They are:

050297	Ite sul colle (with chorus)
054116	Sola, furtiva, al tempio (Maria Cappiello as Adalgisa)
54323	Oh, non tremare (with Amelia Codolini and Luigi Colazza)
054115	Oh! de qual sei tu vittima (with Cappiello and Colazza)
053102	Dormono entrambi
54290 054058	Mira, o Norma
054059	In mia man
054060	Qual cor tradisti
54274	Deh non volerli vittime

The singers are standard G&T artists. As early as 1907, one could buy 'Casta Diva' sung by one's favourite soprano, and tenor solos sung by Caffetto, and then fill in with the records listed above to acquire a pretty full representation of the opera. A more interesting series was made by

Fonotipia, with Russ as its heroine. In 1906, Russ recorded 'Casta Diva', piano-accompanied and later, with orchestra, 'Ah! bello a me'. There are also five sides of duets with Virginia Guerrini as Adalgisa. 'Casta Diva' (done with chorus) is delicate, ethereal, a little vague in its florid passages, slightly tentative. Russ sang her first Normas in Florence in 1908. 'Ah! bello a me!' (without chorus, but with the accompaniment to the choral bridge played) and the duets are done with beauty and rich authority, in a voice that sounds at once youthful and commanding. Guerrini (Verdi's first Meg, and the season before that La Scala's Adalgisa to Teresa Arkel's Norma) seems, surprisingly, to have made no other records. Her mezzo is rich and colourful. She sings 'Mira, o Norma' (Fono. 69063) as a passionate appeal, with almost a sob of emotion on the final 'pietà'. Russ replies with sorrowful serenity, self-contained in her grief, until at 'hai vinto' she suddenly drops restraint. It is a beautifully conceived reading. (Conchita Supervia once sang Adalgisa to Russ's Norma; that is a performance one would like to have heard.)

A few other acoustics deserve a note. Armida Parsi-Pettinella's 'Sgombra è la sacra selva' (starting thus, with Adalgisa's opening words, though regularly listed as 'Deh! proteggimi') reveals a most beautifully formed, firm, and shining mezzo. For 1907 this is exceptionally well recorded, on a long side (Fono. 92060; Saga XIG 8012) that runs almost into the label. Huguet, in her earlier recording of 'Casta Diva' (G&T Barcelona, 1903) with piano, sounds like a stupid woman with a glorious voice. She makes a break, a glottal stop, between 'Casta' and 'Diva' and between 'queste' and 'sacre', not because, like Patti, she is short of breath but evidently so that the repeated note that starts the second word may have a definite attack – because she likes it that way. Her later version (Milan, 1907) with orchestra is forward and brighter, with wonderful breath control and legato phrasing. 'Ah! bello a me' is thrown off in exuberant and triumphant style, with a glorious burst of tone at 'Ah! riedi ancora'. In both versions, Huguet drops the E that starts the next phrase, 'Qual eri allora', down an octave – a strange effect. As early as this, even in these ten-inch records with shortened cavatina and cabaletta, the concluding march, or at any rate some it, is included at the end. It appears in full to close Ines de Frate's disc of the cabaletta – a free expansive interpretation, almost too free for my taste, with some loose *gruppetti*, but with an even more glorious outburst of radiant tone than Huguet's and an excitingly rolled *r* at 'Ah! riedi ancora' (53553).

Emma Calvé's 'Casta Diva' (cavatina only) is a failure. Bertha Kiurina's (Poly., double-sided, about 1919) is famous. Sung in German ('Keusche Göttin'), it is elegant and pure. Like Dusolina Giannini (see below), she sings both verses of the cabaletta – no other sopranos do until we reach Joan Sutherland – and adds decorations in the reprise. Feodor Chaliapin recorded 'Ite sul colle', very roughly (DB 106; LV 53). Alma Gluck and Louise Homer sing 'Mira, o Norma' purely as a concert number, coupled with 'I waited for the Lord' (DB 478). It is rushed, not pointful – curious in that Gluck, the soprano, sings Adalgisa, taking Adalgisa's words to the top line of the music when the voices join. Homer does not attempt the florid anything-you-can-do imitations at 'Teco del fato all'onte'.

As a bridge to the electric *Norma* recordings, let me list all the 'Casta Divas', acoustic and electric, 78 (or thereabouts) and LP, commercially published, that I know or know of – over sixty. Many of the earlier versions have a cabaletta on another single-sided disc. Most of them are without chorus – and Bellini's simple bi-tonality always sounds slightly startling when it is rendered entirely by orchestra.

Wera Amerighi-Rutili (Od. 5588)
Giannina Arangi Lombardi (CQX 10735)
Teresa Arkel (53315 and 053061)
Wanda Bardone (S 5442)
Celestina Boninsegna (053050 and Col. A5197; CO 358)
Grace Bumbry (ASD 2591)
Eugenia Burzio (Col. 74722, Pathé)
Johanne Brun (83520 and 83634)
Montserrat Caballé (RCA GL 42372 DX and set)*
Maria Callas (Cetra CB 20482 and 3 sets)
Emma Calvé (Pathé 0277; GV 57)
Anita Cerquetti (LXT 5289)
Gina Cigna (LX 234 and set)
Ines Citti-Lippi (37045)
Toti dal Monte (DB 2125)
Ines de Frate (053191)
Maria de Macchi (Fono. 39495)
B. Dragoni (Od. 12479)
(Martha Eggert) (Parlo. R 2090)
Elise Elizza (43831)
Adalgisa Gabbi (Zono. 93008)
Dusolina Giannini (DB 1576; LV 8)
Frieda Hempel (Poly. 76417; CO 349)
Josefina Huguet (53268 and 53510)
L'Incognita
Bertha Kiurina (Poly.)
Lilli Lehmann (Od. 52698; CO 384/5)

Luisa Malagrida (Monarch LP MWL 303)
Zinka Milanov (DB 6877; VICS 6044)
Claudia Muzio (LCX 23; COLC 101)
Romilda Nelli (Zono. 411)
Iva Pacetti (Col. DQ 684)
Leonilda Paini (Col. 10125)
Adelina Patti (03082; RLS 711)
Maria Pedrini (Cetra CC 2214)
Rosa Ponselle (Am. Col. 49720; GVC 9 and DB 1280; RCA 2641 371AG)
Rosa Raisa (Vocalion 55001 and Pathé 60055; GV 59)
Frida Ricci de Paz – cabaletta only (Zono. 2790)
Giannina Russ (Fono. 39890; CO 381)
Ida Sambo (Zono. 210)
Silvia Sass (SXL 6921)
Marcella Sembrich (053174; CSLP 500)
Beverly Sills (set)
Giulietta Simionato (SXL 2281)
Ina Souez (DB 2720; Orion ORS 7293)
Elena Souliotis (set)
Antonietta Stella (DG LPEM 19290)
Ebe Stignani (Cetra BB 25097)
Joan Sutherland (SXL 2556 and set)
Helen Traubel (Victor LM 123)
Ninon Vallin (Parlo. RO 20133)
Galina Vishnevskaya (MK DO 14019)

*'Set' refers to complete versions – see discography.

One name surprisingly absent from this list is that of Esther Mazzoleni, a proment Italian Norma between 1910 and 1926. Her 'Dormano entrambi' and (with Giovanni Zenatello) 'In mia man' are on Fono. 92811/2; CO 347. In Mazzoleni's own view, 'Russ was a superb virtuoso but a little cold, Boninsegna's tone was utterly ravishing but a little too sweet', and she herself 'combined the *bel canto* art with much fire.'

I have not heard all the records tabled above. Martha Eggert's contribution (included only because it appears in the *Gramophone Shop Encyclopaedia*), is from the film, 'The Divine Spark': 'Casta Diva' becomes a Neapolitan song, 'Occhi puri che incantate', with mandolin and violin obbligato and new soupy harmonies; yet Romani's name still appears on the label along with Bellini's. Toti Dal Monte's version is light and pretty, conjuring up the vision of a charming little priestess. Vallin sings the aria fast, without a great deal of character, but elegantly and in her attractive, individual timbre. She is the *only* soprano who sticks to the written notes exactly, to the very end, where she comes down to the A. Souez gives a cool, mysterious, and beautiful account of the cavatina, leaving holes between the As but making an artful *tenuto* before each chromatic descent. Her cabaletta is taken at a spanking pace, with some loose coloratura. Malagrida, on a Monarch LP (a relic of her appearance, not as Norma, at one of the London Stoll seasons) is not to be too lightly dismissed; the singing is correct, if without much feeling and insecure in ornament. With Maria Mandalari, she also made a 'Mira, o Norma'. Giannini's 'Casta Diva' is well thought of by those who admire Giannini. It is not delicate nor beautiful in sound (I find the rapid vibration in her voice disconcerting), but it is splendidly vocalized, with terrific breath control in the cabaletta, and dramatic. Muzio's record (cavatina only) was made late in her career, and I find it slightly characterless and inexpressive – though this is not the general view. From the list above it is evident that singers who would never have tackled Norma on the stage longed to sing 'Casta Diva' – even Stignani, who must have stood by in the wings hundreds of times waiting for the *sacra selva* to be *sgombra*, and hearing just about every Norma of note for some thirty years or more. She sings the aria down in E flat. I have not heard the recordings by Simionato, another famous Adalgisa, or by Grace Bumbry, who (like Shirley Verrett) sings both roles in the theatre.

When Rosa Ponselle went to Gatti-Casazza in 1918, he set her 'Casta Diva' to prepare for her second Metropolitan audition (in the course of which she fainted); and in her early days at the Met he used to urge her to study the aria 'just for vocalize'. During those early days, in about 1921, she recorded 'Casta Diva', on an acoustic Columbia. This is an astonishing disc. It *is* 'just vocalize', with little interpretative feeling, but the voice has a fleetness and brilliance very different from the lustrous and more darkly burnished timbre that came later. I suspect that Ponselle knew Sembrich's record. She sings a shortened cavatina, with the regular high note toward the close (though, surprisingly, she comes down to the A at the end), and then one verse of the cabaletta. Unless we count a short burst from Giannini before the second verse of her cabaletta, this is the last record in which Bellini's vocal line is adorned beyond a rise to a final F in 'Casta Diva'. Pasta would decorate the aria in an extremely florid way; her embellishments have been preserved.

Gatti-Casazza was grooming his soprano for the great role. In 1925, Ponselle in *La Vestale* pointed the way, and then in 1927 *Norma* was heard at the Metropolitan for the first time since 1892, when it had been sung there by Lilli Lehmann. Ponselle's second 'Casta Diva', with the introductory recitative, was recorded in 1928, and the cabaletta in 1929, the year she made her Covent Garden début, as Norma. Ernest Newman wrote then that 'Mme Ponselle proves to us that the finest singing – given a good voice to begin with – comes from the constant play of a fine mind upon the inner meaning of the music.' Ponselle's second 'Casta Diva' is mysterious and lovely. The voice sounds slightly less well in the cabaletta, and there is a disappointing moment when Ponselle flips out the divisions on 'diede' in groups of two. But it is a record of what was evidently a great performance.

The other members of that 1927 Metropolitan production are also on record. Ponselle and Marion Telva recorded a very fine 'Mira, o Norma' (DB 1276; CDN 1066/7). Giacomo Lauri-Volpi's 'Meco all'altar' (a single ten-inch side, stopping short at the Gallic gong; DA 983) is the best version I know, taken at an easy pace, fine and free and heroic. Ezio Pinza recorded each of Oroveso's arias twice. By comparison with his first, acoustic 'Ah! del Tebro' (DA 566; GEMM 163), the later one (DA 1108; LV 27) is more overtly dramatic; he takes his cue from the direction *con ferocia* and is less noble and 'classical'. He throws in added high notes at 'più tremendo a divampar'. Both versions are magnificent, but I prefer the earlier one. There is less difference between his HMV 'Ite sul colle' (DB 1203; LV 27) made at the same time as DA 1108, and the later American Columbia recording (72826; Odyssey Y 31148).

'Ah! del Tebro' brings up another textual point. The 'Moonlight Sonata' string triplets that accompany it are played *pizzicato* on DA 566 (but not on DA 1108), in a recording of the aria by Nicola Rossi-Lemeni, in the second of the two Callas recordings (conducted by Tullio Serafin), and in the Caballé/Cillario recording, and they are indicated as *pizzicato* in the Novello vocal score and in the Ricordi miniature. Just about everywhere else they are legato. In Bellini's autograph, the legato slurs that were once there have carefully been cancelled, and the *pizzicato* is plainly indicated. There seems to be no doubt that *pizzicato* was the composer's choice and also that few conductors agree with him.

In about 1930, Fonotipia/Odeon began to issue what soon amounted

to an extensive selection from the opera, with Wera Amerighi-Rutili as
its heroine, Lina Lanza as Adalgisa, Gino Colombo as Pollione (except
in the finale, where Oldrati takes over), and Antonio Righetti as Oroveso.
These are tabulated below, with first the Fonotipia and then the Odeon
numbers:

Fono.	Od.		
120207	5590	F	Ite sul colle (2 sides)
168502	6076	M	Meco all'altar . . . Me protegge
120205	5588	F	Casta Diva . . . Ah! bello a me
17219	55651	F	Va, crudele . . . Vieni in Roma
172194	5650	F	Sola, furtiva . . . Ah! sì fa core
168838	3778	B	Ma dì; l'amato giovane . . . Trio
172127	6649	N	Mira, o Norma . . . Sì, fino all'ore
172128	6650	N	In mia man . . . Ah! crudele
120206	5589	F	Qual cor . . . Deh! non volerli

Amerighi-Rutili (a second-cast Vestale, after Arangi-Lombardi, at La
Scala in 1929), Colombo and Righetti were Fonotipia regulars. The
soprano gives over-emotional performances, throwing in little sobs during
her part of 'Mira, o Norma', adding an audible sob to the tenor's 'Ah!
troppo tardi', and mauling horribly the phrase in the finale 'Padre, o
padre'. Her florid singing tends to be all over the place. Yet she is not
quite pointless. Her voice streams out, bright and powerful, at climaxes,
and she delivers the phrase (to Pollione) 'Preghi alfine? Indegno! è tardi!'
with tremendous drama. Both Colombo and Oldrati are gusty tenors,
addicted to swells and exaggerated portamenti. Lina Lanza displays a
small, keen, clear voice, rather attractive and incisive, and soprano in
timbre.*

*Grisi, the first Adalgisa, was a soprano, but in a day when no hard-and-fast
distinction was made between soprano and mezzo-soprano. By the end of the century,
Adalgisa had become the province of mezzo-sopranos – except in Germany, where, as
noted, Lilli Lehmann sang both Adalgisa and Norma, and where Grete Forst (a Lakmé,
Lucia and Olimpia) recorded 'Mira, o Norma' with the Norma of Elise Elizza (1908),
and Gertrud Förstel (a Gilda and Susanna) recorded it with the Norma of Margarethe
Siems, the first Chrysothemis, Marschallin, and Zerbinetta (1906). In our day, at least
two mezzo-soprano Adalgisas, Shirley Verrett and Grace Bumbry, have made the ascent
to Norma. The distinction between the two roles is one less of pitch than of weight,
timbre and character. Adalgisa should sound younger than Norma; a ripe, rich mezzo is
apt to sound older. (At Covent Garden in 1952, it was awkward to see Callas address
the veteran Stignani as 'o giovinetta', but on a record looks are unimportant.) When
Adalgisa is a mezzo, as today she nearly always is, the Act 2 duet, 'Deh! con te . . .
Mira, o Norma', is usually transposed a tone, from C and F to B flat and E flat. (Some
exceptions are noted below.) The transposition, effected during the preceding recitative at
the words 'nel Romano campo', is of long standing: a method of achieving it, different
from the one commonly used today, is already sketched (not in Bellini's hand) on a
blank stave of the autograph. At Covent Garden in 1978, Caballé and Bumbry fell out
because the former wanted the duet in the familiar lower keys while the latter (already
prepared to sing Norma herself, as she did in the last few performances) wanted the
original keys. But when Bumbry sang Norma, she, too, chose the lower keys for 'Casta
Diva' and the duet.

These eighteen sides were the nearest thing to a complete *Norma* until the arrival of the 1937 Cetra set on thirty-six sides, with Gina Cigna, Stignani, Giovanni Brevario and Tancredi Pasero. Neither the soprano nor the tenor is up to the music, and the set is notable only for Pasero's noble Oroveso, Vittorio Gui's fine conducting, and the young Stignani. (The duet is in the original keys.) Cigna is squally but she has temperament. Also from 1937, there is a pirate Metropolitan *Norma* with Cigna, Bruna Castagna, Martinelli, and Pinza, conducted by Ettore Panizza. After Ponselle's retirement, Cigna was perhaps the nearest approach to a Norma until, in 1943, the opera was revived at the Metropolitan for Zinka Milanov. Milanov's 'Casta Diva' (single-sided, with recitative, 1945) is not very individual, but it offers a beautiful voice and a kind of generalized grandeur of style. Bruna Castagna was the Adalgisa, and later Jennie Tourel, but Margaret Harshaw rehearsed the role, and with Milanov she recorded a beautiful double-sided 'Mira, o Norma' (Victor 11–8924; VIC 6044). Before her accession to Wagnerian heroics, Harshaw had an opulent mezzo. The performance of the duet is somewhat self-consciously artful, but it is rich, warm in emotion, glowing in sound, and admirably vocalized. Two 1944 Metropolitan performances with Milanov – one with Castagna, Frederick Jagel and Virgilio Lazzari, the other with Tourel, Jagel and Norman Cordon – both conducted by Cesare Sodero, have been issued on private labels.

Few of the post-war recordings of isolated numbers need special note. Most of the singers active in the opera have also appeared in one or other of the complete recordings. Anita Cerquetti's 'Casta Diva' is no more than promising, done with feeling but not with finish. The same promise and power mark her Rome pirate performance of 1958, with Miriam Pirazzini, Corelli and Giulio Neri. Boris Christoff's 'Ite sul colle' (SLS 5090) is noble. Gino Penno's and Mario del Monaco's versions of 'Meco all'altar' are brash.

Maria Callas sang her first Norma in Florence in 1948, and she reigned in the role until she sang her last Norma, in 1965. So far as the gramophone is concerned, she continues to reign supreme. There are sopranos who achieve beautiful effects of sound that Callas could not manage, but only Lilli Lehmann, in the short sections of the opera she recorded, is so convincingly and completely Bellini's Norma. Callas's performances of Norma are well documented. There are two commercial recordings from EMI, both made at La Scala, one in 1954 and one in 1960, both conducted by Tullio Serafin. In addition, a Mexico City performance of 1950, her Covent Garden début in 1952, a RAI studio performance of 1955 and a La Scala performance of 1955 have been issued on pirate sets; the La Scala performance has lately achieved something more than pirate status by its inclusion in Cetra's Live Opera series. Moreover, tapes circulate of a Trieste performance in 1953, of the unfinished Rome performance in 1958, of much of the final Paris performances, and of various concert performances of 'Casta Diva'. The details are given in John Ardoin's *The Callas Legacy*. The Mexico City version presents a young Simionato as Adalgisa. The Covent Garden has Joan Sutherland as Clotilde. The Trieste has Boris Christoff as Oroveso. In fact, most of these versions have points of interest besides the overriding one of observing – and thrilling to – the prima donna in her greatest role. Even in the final Paris Normas, when a voice never totally secure has become not at all reliable, there are *some* phrases more eloquently, excitingly and beautifully uttered than ever before. But for the general collector it is perhaps enough to concentrate on the two EMI issues, which sum up all that Callas learned about the role during her first six years of singing it, and then the further refinements and insights acquired during the next six years.

Moreover, these two *Normas* conducted by Serafin are more nearly 'complete' performances than any others – not in the sense that all the notes are there (they are not; the usual 'theatre cuts' are made), but because the soprano and the conductor approach the work in the spirit that Lilli Lehmann prescribes in her autobiography:

When I think back to that beautiful time [her first Normas in Vienna], and then consider with what lack of knowledge and affection this great opera has subsequently been treated, I must pity the artists who permit such great and rewarding tasks to escape them, as well as the public that thereby loses the lofty enjoyment of a work so rich in melody, the passionate action of which has more human grandeur than many a bungled modern composition that receives great applause. *Norma*, which bears so much love within it, may not be treated indifferently or just polished off. It should be sung and acted with fanatical consecration, rendered by the chorus and the orchestra, especially, with artistic reverence, led with authority by the conductor; and to every single quaver should be given the musical tribute that is its due.

The autograph of *Norma* reveals how carefully Bellini planned and revised and re-revised his opera, in large matters of formal balance and in small details of orchestral figuration and timbre. There is a penetrating study of all this in a chapter of Charlotte Greenspan's *The Operas of Vincenzo Bellini*, a Berkeley dissertation obtainable from University Microfilms. And, as Miss Greenspan puts it, 'In *Norma* Bellini takes a decisive step away from the use of the aria as the essential musical unit; the emphasis is on solo scenas without set numbers, and on ensembles'. Norma and Pollione have only one formal aria apiece, each of them in Act 1. Adalgisa has none. Oroveso shares his two numbers with the chorus; the second is headed 'Core e scena'. The chorus joins in every aria. Lilli Lehmann was right; and these two performances show it. To the names of Callas and Serafin should be joined that of Walter Legge, who produced both sets.

In 1949, Callas recorded for Cetra the mad scene of *I puritani*, Isolde's

Liebestod, and 'Casta Diva'. The cavatina is admirable, delicate, in its way as beautiful a performance of it as any she put on record, though less subtle than some of the later versions; the cabaletta is less eloquent than it soon became. The two complete recordings are complementary. In 1954, the voice above the staff is fuller, more solid, and more certain; in 1960, the middle timbres are more beautiful and more expressive, and an interpretation that was always magnificent has deepened in finesse, flexibility, and dramatic poignancy. True, her voice lets her down even as she essays some of her most beautiful details. The F that should crown a heart-rending 'Oh rimembranza' wobbles. The G wobbles in an exquisitely conceived 'Son io' (the moment when Norma removes her wreath and proclaims her own guilt) – and yet, how much more moving it is than the simpler, if steadier, *messa di voce* of the earlier set. Reaction to, and assessment of, Callas have always been personal. My reaction is that, on both sets, Callas gives an interpretation of Norma which Sutherland, Caballé and Sills, the heroines of later issues, do not begin to approach. Her vocal faults are easy to discern. The beauty, force and affecting power of her enunciation, timbres, timing and moulding of line are more easily experienced than described.

In 1954, the Adalgisa is Stignani, secure, accomplished, but mature in timbre. 1960 has Christa Ludwig, a clever choice, for she has a glamorous, full-toned, lustrous voice that reminds one of the shining Parsi-Pettinella or the colourful Guerrini. Given a mezzo, we are in both sets given a good one who blends well yet contrasts with Callas. Ludwig's downward scales, it must be admitted, are as ill-defined as her colleague's, whereas Stignani's are cleaner; however, she is no veteran Adalgisa but youthful and impetuous. There is just one serious blot: the phrases after 'Mira, o Norma' which change Norma's mind ('Renderti i dritti tuoi', etc.) are attacked badly sharp. The 1954 Pollione is Mario Filippeschi, who is crude. Franco Corelli, in 1960, is better. He bellows a bit in 'Meco all'altar', but as soon as he meets Norma one senses a striving for style. The voice is big and handsome. Nicola Zaccaria (1960) is a nobler, firmer, and smoother Oroveso than Nicola Rossi-Lemeni (1954). His two *scenas* carry their proper weight in this carefully proportioned score and make a great effect; they are not merely interludes to give the diva a rest. On both sets, the choral singing and orchestral playing are very fine. Serafin's conducting is spacious, eloquent, unhurried, yet never slack. Everything moves naturally, and the huge double climax of the finale proves overwhelming.

Textual points: 'Casta Diva' in F, 'Deh! con te' in B flat, 'Mira, o Norma' in E flat, in both sets. (At Covent Garden in 1953, Callas and Simionato sang the duet at the higher, written pitches, C and F.) The beautiful, quiet *maggiore* coda to the 'Guerra' chorus, reminiscent of the Pastoral Symphony, and found in Boosey but not in Novello or Ricordi, is both times restored, but Callas does not float through it the slow-rising arpeggio that should close it in much the way that 'La vergine degli angeli' (in *La forza del destino*) is closed. In the Act 2 prelude, Bellini sounded the *con dolore* melody twice, first with all the cellos, then with solo cello, clarinet and flute in octaves. In the autograph the second statement is cancelled, and Serafin cuts it.

Sutherland's complete recording, like Callas's, was preceded by a separate version of the aria (in the Decca album entitled 'The Art of the Prima Donna', 1960). It is sung in G and is a silvery, accomplished performance. The repeated, syncopated Bs are attacked from below, in the old manner. The complete recording (RCA, later Decca) shows that Sutherland and Bonynge had thought long and hard about their interpretation of Norma: about the characterization, and its portrayal in terms of timbre and phrasing. But what resulted was a performance very much in the *manner* of Callas – not a 'copy', but one in a similar vein – rather than the clear, bright, clean-cut, heroic reading one might have expected. There is much adoption of dark, cloudy, 'meaningful' tone and phrasing *con intenzione*. One can praise Sutherland's application to detail, her power and her brilliance; fault her in respect of Italian dramatic declamation (the intention is there but the utterance of the words is not forceful) and, often, clarity of tone. Sutherland's clouded *mezza voce* is not as beautiful as Callas's; on the other hand, there are none of the strident, curdled Callas notes from which one flinches.

Marilyn Horne, the Adalgisa, makes a tentative start with her entrance recitative and arioso. The idea is presumably to portray a shy, timorous priestess, but the music does carry indications like *con forza appassionata* which suggest more full-blooded singing, such as Parsi-Pettinella provides. Later, Horne becomes ringing and resolute – almost too much so; now one begins to long for a touch of poetry to infuse her determined brilliance and force. John Alexander is a forthright, capable Pollione – not much character but plenty of vigour, no coarseness, and all the notes securely there. The same can be said of Richard Cross's Oroveso. Bonynge shows considerable feeling for the delicacy and deftness of Bellini's orchestration, but in the matter of large shaping he is not the equal of Serafin.

Textual points: 'Casta Diva' and the duets at the original high pitches. The *con dolore* melody only once, but given to solo cello. Coda to the 'Guerra!' chorus done, but the *arpeggio* taken by the choral sopranos. A very successful version of the Act 1 trio finale (where establishing Bellini's text is particularly difficult). A repeat of Norma's 'Ah! riedi ancora' cut. There is a tape of a 1970 Metropolitan performance with Sutherland, Horne, Carlo Bergonzi and Cesare Siepi, conductor Bonynge, in the New York Public Library.

The abridged recording with Elena Souliotis as its heroine (Decca, 1967) is fitted on to four sides, as against the usual six. The largest cut is of 8, the principal chorus of the work and the ensuing recitative and aria ('Ah! del Tebro') for Oroveso. Since Carlo Cava is an unsteady Oroveso – though he sounds suitably grave and wise – this is not too regrettable. Among other cuts are: in 1 ('Ite sul colle'), thirty-two bars of the orchestral introduction, the twelve bars for chorus which start the Allegro, a fifteen-bar repeat, and sixteen bars of the coda. In 6 (the first-act finale) the third verse of the duet, 'Ah, sì fa core', Adalgisa's verse of the trio (two cuts that are often made; in fact the passages are missing in the Ricordi score), and about three pages of the *stretto*. Souliotis displays an exciting voice. She has the power, ferocity, and energy for the role, but not the delicacy. On some notes the timbre sounds uncannily like that of Callas (especially at 'Fine al rito', after 'Casta Diva', and at 'Lo compi . . . e parti', in the first finale, marked *riprimendo il furore*). There are some striking phrases, and she negotiates 'Casta Diva' (in F) with unexpected success. But there is a lack of variety, and insistence – which sometimes amounts to vulgarity – on making effects by power rather than subtlety.

Mario del Monaco, the Pollione, is also monotonous, though some of his ringing bugle tones provide a thrill. In the duet with Adalgisa, 'Vieni in Roma', where his first phrase is marked *con tutta la tenerezza*, it is almost comical to hear Fiorenza Cossotto, as she takes up the melody, give him a lesson in the supple phrasing of music he has just sung so brashly. His divisions are sketchy. Cossotto is a little heavy but her tone is always full and beautiful. She declines Bellini's invitation to deliver the sustained high A flat at 'Io l'obbliai' *con messa di voce assai lungo*, and makes it merely long and loud. 'Deh! con te' is in B flat, 'Mira' in E flat. Silvio Varviso is pleasantly spirited, but the playing of the Santa Cecilia Orchestra is not always polished. Cossotto is the only performer here with a real command of rhythm, of drawing a flexible, expressive line without losing impetus. Neither Souliotis nor del Monaco has this command of a slow tempo. Varviso spoils the twin climaxes of the finale by hurrying the approach to them and then broadening so much at the *ff* that the basic pulse is lost. No one has equalled Serafin's handling of the passage.

The sets with Montserrat Caballé (RCA, 1973) and with Beverly Sills (EMI/ABC, 1973) as their heroines both sound like 'assembly line' opera recordings. Caballé's was made as one assignment in a summer that also included recordings of Liù for Decca, and Mathilde (in *Guillaume Tell*) and Verdi's *Giovanna d'Arco* for EMI, along with Violettas at Covent Garden and a Caterina Cornaro in the Festival Hall. How can any soprano working to such a schedule put on record her finest, subtlest, more refined thoughts about each aspect of the tremendous role? And why should she, or we, be content with anything less? There are admirable passages to show the kind of Norma that Caballé should more consistently have been. All the dialogue before the duet and trio that close Act 1 is feelingly uttered, and the phrase 'Nol fossi!' is particularly fine. Then, the long, elaborate melisma in the final scene at 'un prego ancor' is achieved with a beauty, fullness, and smoothness of tone which both Callas and Sutherland might envy. But there are other phrases – Norma's wistful asides during Adalgisa's narration, the simple, terrible 'Sì, Norma', 'Io stessa' – which go for next to nothing, and which should be some of the most affecting moments in the opera. Of Pasta, of Malibran, and of Patti it was said that with two, three or four notes the soprano could stir an audience to the depths of its being. (Chorley said it of Pasta at Anna Bolena's 'Sorgi!', in the duet with Jane Seymour; Bellini said it of Malibran at Amina's 'Ah! m'abbraccia', at which point she 'gave such delight and expressed the phrase with such truth' that he was moved to a 'positively volcanic transport'; Verdi said it of Patti at Gilda's 'Io l'amo', which produced 'a sublime effect that no words can describe'.) The same can be – and has been – said of Callas. But it does not apply to Caballé in this performance. She commands what Hanslick discerned in Lehmann: 'In slow cantilenas the most beautiful portamento and the securest intonation and swelling (also magical floating and fining down) of the high notes'. There is plenty of power, which only occasionally turns to harshness. But some of the chromatic runs are slithers rather than 'pure and fluent coloratura', and some of the *fioriture* in 'Casta Diva' are skimped and hurried rather than lovingly, dreamily savoured and fully sounded. The turn in 'In mia man' is a half-hearted flick rather than an eloquent expression of feeling.

Caballé had the vocal equipment to become a great Norma. Her voice in 1973 was healthy, flexible, and splendid; none could surpass her in ease, amplitude, and tonal beauty; and her musical instincts were right. But in the recording there is a lack of variety and of imaginative energy, and apparently of the will to polish tricky passages until every note falls perfectly into place.

On pirate discs there is an RAI performance of 1971. There are tapes of two later Metropolitan performances (1973, with Cossotto and Cossutta; 1976, with Shirley Verrett and John Alexander) in the New York Public Library; also a La Scala performance of 1977 (with Tatyana Troyanos and Giorgio Casellato-Lamberti). They all tell much the same story – great achievement, but greater promise unfulfilled.

Cossotto is much as on the Souliotis set, but heavier, louder. Where Callas and Stignani, Callas and Ludwig, and, for that matter, Sutherland and Horne, can make one catch one's breath in delighted admiration for the supple, flexible phrasing, the delicious give and take between the voices, and neat 'returns' in the 'Senta/senta/sul tuo cor/sul tuo cor' episode (like a centre-court rally), Caballé and Cossotto suggest two big healthy girls jogging along in full, splendid cry – thrilling in its way, but unsubtle.

Placido Domingo slipped his Pollione into a busy schedule. There was published an account of a helicopter standing by outside the Walthamstow recording hall waiting to whisk him off to Heathrow airport, since 'he had to appear on stage within hours in some distant opera house'. What a way to record one of the most demanding works of the earlier nineteenth century! Nevertheless, he turns out to be on the whole the most satisfactory of all the Polliones on record. The aria needs further study; the duet with Adalgisa lacks romance and tenderness; but in all the scenes with Norma he sings nobly and well. And of all the Orovesos, Ruggero Raimondi comes closest to the 'prodigious and resistless lustre' that Chorley praised in Lablache. Carlo Felice Cillario, conducting, provides moments of vivid excitement and some good colours from the LPO, but he is apt to be indulgent, and at times he seems not to have made up his mind about the basic tempo at which a piece should flow. The 'Ah, riedi ancora' episode missing in the Sutherland set is included. The *maggiore* close to 'Guerra!' is omitted. The *con dolore* melody is played once, by all the cellos. The duet is down.

In 1971, Beverly Sills sang some Normas in Boston, for Sarah Caldwell, which were well received. In her autobiography, *Bubbles*, Miss Sills declares that 'I felt at the time, and still do, that Norma is not a very difficult role', and that 'there are some lines in *Norma* that always make me want to giggle'. Her recorded Norma is not flippant, but it is not grand either. There is simply not enough voice for the role. Shirley Verrett, a vivid Adalgisa, sounds more like a Norma. Enrico di Giuseppe and Paul Plishka, Pollione and Oroveso, are workaday. James Levine's conducting is energized, with crashing chords to punctuate the recitatives and inflexible treatment of the accompaniment figures. 'Casta Diva' and the duet are up at the original pitch. The *maggiore* coda to 'Guerra!' is omitted.

NORMA

N Norma; *A* Adalgisa; *P* Pollione; *O* Oroveso

1937 Cigna *N*; Stignani *A*; Breviario *P*; Pasero *O*/Turin Radio Chorus and Orch./Gui
Cetra © LPS 3204

1954 Callas *N*; Stignani *A*; Filippeschi *P*; Rossi-Lemeni *O*/La Scala Chorus and Orch./Serafin
· HMV © SLS 5115 ④
TC–SLS5115
Seraphim ⓜ IC6037

1955 (live performance) Callas *N*; Simionato *A*; del Monaco *P*; Zaccaria *O*/La Scala Chorus and Orch./Votto
Cetra ⓜ LO 31/3

1960 Callas *N*; Ludwig *A*; Corelli *P*;
Zaccaria *O*/La Scala Chorus and Orch./Serafin
EMI 3C 163 00535–7
Angel SCL 3615

1964 Sutherland *N*; Horne *A*; Alexander *P*; Cross *O*/Chorus, LSO/Bonynge
Decca SET 424–6 ④ K21K32
London OSA 1394

1967 (abridged) Souliotis *N*; Cossotto *A*; del Monaco *P*; Cava *O*/Santa Cecilia Academy Chorus and Orch./Varviso
Decca SET 368–9
London OSA 1272

1973 Caballé *N*; Cossotto *A*; Domingo

P; Raimondi *O*/Ambrosian
Opera Chorus, LPO/Cillario
RCA (UK) SER 5658–60
(US) LSC 6202
1973 Sills *N*; Verrett *A*; di Giuseppe

P; Plishka *O*/Alldis Choir, New
Philharmonia/Levine
Ariola Eurodisc XF 25437R
ABC ATS 20017 ④
5109–20017S

L'elisir d'amore

HAROLD ROSENTHAL

Nearly a third of Donizetti's seventy-odd works for the stage are comedies, variously described on their title pages by the Italian terms, *opera buffa, farsa, opera comica* or *melodrama burlesca*. Some, like *Don Pasquale*, are full-length works in three acts; others like *L'elisir d'amore*, are in two, and not a few, like *Il campanello* are short one-act romps. What they all have in common, however, are tuneful scores and absurdly funny situations. *L'elisir d'amore* has something else in addition; a libretto by Felice Romani, which is why I rate the piece higher than *Don Pasquale*.

L'elisir was not the only Donizetti opera for which Romani provided the libretto, but the others were mostly for the composer's serious works like *Anna Bolena* and *Lucrezia Borgia*. Because of the speed with which Donizetti had to compose *L'elisir* – the management of the Teatro Cadobbiana in Milan had been let down by one of their composers and asked Donizetti to give them a new work in a fortnight! – Romani and the composer decided on the plot *Le Philtre*, which the French librettist Scribe had written for Auber the previous year. A note written by Romani in the first edition of *L'elisir* states: 'The subject is imitated from Scribe's *Philtre*. It is a jest – he uses the word *scherzo* – and as such is presented to the gentle readers.' But as Andrew Porter has pointed out, *L'elisir* is not just a jest, or indeed a brilliant comedy; it is something more – a brilliant comedy about real country people which mirrors their emotions, behaviour and way of life brilliantly.

In performance then, remembering that Romani's libretto needs to be savoured by both audience and singers; that the heroine Adina is more than a clever minx; that Nemorino is more than a country bumpkin; Dulcamara more than just a stock *buffo* character; and that Belcore, despite his peacock posturing, is a soldier with a heart, we want singers not only equipped vocally to cope with Donizetti's *bel canto* music, but also able to do full justice to Romani's text and create flesh-and-blood characters.

The first two complete sets (HMV and Cetra) were both recorded in 1952; and though the Cetra was not available in England until much later it has the claim to being the first *L'elisir* on disc, for the pre-war

Columbia set, on 78s, was no more than a selection. Alda Noni (Cetra) is a charming and vivacious Adina, but Margherita Carosio has the edge on her, singing in a piquant and pointed manner, and displaying much charm and wit, especially in her big duet with Nemorino, in which Nicola Monti (HMV) sings with more charm than does Cesare Valletti, though the latter evokes memories of Schipa on occasions. Afro Poli (Cetra) is a dry-voiced Belcore. Although Tito Gobbi is apt to rant and sounds too close to the microphone at times, he and Carosio, who often sang in this work together at La Scala and elsewhere, react to each other with perfect timing. Sesto Bruscantini (Cetra) is a lightweight but none the less an amusing and musical Dulcamara. Melchiorre Luise, while not having the unctuousness of a Baccaloni or the vocal gifts of a Tajo, none the less gives a musical and unexaggerated performance. Gavazzeni (Cetra), who has made a special study of Donizetti, is a better musicologist than he is a conductor.

Gabriele Santini's reading of the score is full-blooded rather than subtle, and he keeps it moving. However, he sanctions the then-traditional cuts, especially in Act 2, where some twenty pages of the score, including the quartet for Adina, Nemorino, Giannetta and Dulcamara, go by the board.

The 1955 Decca set includes nearly all the portions that were cut in the 1953 HMV set, but not the quartet. However, because the conductor, Francesco Molinari-Pradelli, adopts more deliberate and broader tempi than Santini, the performance does not exactly sparkle. Hilde Gueden's Adina is not over-coy, but neither is it particularly Italianate, though it is well sung. Giuseppe di Stefano was a famous Nemorino, but he indulges in Gigli-like bad habits, sobs, intrusive 'h's and all. Renato Capecchi's Belcore is lightweight, lacking swagger; Fernando Corena as Dulcamara, although he sings well, does not display the true *buffo* style.

The last of the 1950s sets (EMI) was generally disappointing. Rosanna Carteri, who chose marriage and domesticity rather than a long stage career, was, in the flesh, an attractive performer, but here she displays faulty intonation and a surprising lack of charm. Neither she nor her colleagues is helped by the staid conducting of the veteran Tullio Serafin. Luigi Alva's Nemorino is not full-blooded enough in sound; and Rolando Panerai is apt to bluster as Belcore. Although Giuseppe Taddei is more a bass-baritone than a bass, his Dulcamara is very good indeed – especially his diction.

In 1966 EMI gave us its third complete set, not a successful one. It steadfastly refuses to come to life. Molinari-Pradelli, conducting his second *L'elisir* on disc, remains a stolid interpreter of Donizetti, and the Rome Opera Orchestra has rough moments. Mirella Freni, who in the theatre was an adorable Adina, fails to produce a really melting *mezza voce* (nearly always a fault with this soprano), and her singing is not incisive. Nicolai Gedda is a cool, uncharming and too sophisticated Nemorino. Mario Sereni's Belcore might just as well be any Donizetti baritone character. It is left to Capecchi to create a real-life character with his Dulcamara, which is well sung and marvellously articulated.

The first of the 1970s sets, the 1971 Sutherland–Bonynge performance, has a lot to recommend it, not least its musical completeness, the hallmark of nearly all Bonynge's performances. However, Bonynge, instead of including Adina's final Allegro (cabaletta), 'Il mio rigor domentica', replaced it with a waltz, 'Nel dolce incanto de tal momento', which, although written with Donizetti's acquiesence for Malibran, by her husband Beriot, sounds more like Arditi than Donizetti! None the less this is a delightful set as far as Sutherland and Pavarotti are concerned. The soprano, a more serious Adina than is usual, is in excellent voice. Pavarotti is almost on his best behaviour as Nemorino. 'Quanto è bella' could have been sung a little more intimately, but the famous 'Una furtiva lagrima' would melt a stone. Dominic Cossa's Belcore is adequate, but Spiro Malas turns Dulcamara into a dull dog; his Italian is poor and his performance self-conscious. The contribution of the English Chamber Orchestra under Bonynge is good, but not outstanding; the ECO may not be partial to Donizetti!

The most recent recording, that on the CBS label, is based on an actual opera-house production – that at the Royal Opera House, Covent Garden, in December/January 1976/77. Superbly conducted by John Pritchard, the recording captures the delightful atmosphere of the stage performance with the orchestra and chorus of the Royal Opera House on their toes, and the whole bubbling and sparkling like vintage champagne.

Ileana Cotrubas's effervescent and scheming Adina is a performance to treasure. Her clear, forward diction and impish sense of humour, in addition to her own characteristic voice, make her the best Adina on disc, surpassing even Carosio. Placido Domingo is the only member of the cast who did not sing his role at Covent Garden – there it was José Carreras. I miss the fresh, unsophisticated approach the latter brought to the role in the theatre, though Domingo's performance has much to commend it. For a budding Tristan and an established Radames and Otello to be able to sing Nemorino's music with such ease says much for Domingo's technique; and if his 'Una furtiva lagrima' is not as winning as it might have been a few years before, he is a believable Nemorino. The Swedish baritone, Ingvar Wixell, successfully captures the bombastic and ridiculous side of Belcore's character, and Geraint Evans's larger-than-life Dulcamara, if a trifle self-indulgent, is another classic performance.

Two more complete performances should be mentioned: that made in Prague in 1967 and issued on the Supraphon label, and one sung in German on Ariola-Eurodisc, made in 1962. The latter, obviously made for German domestic consumption, with an ageing Nemorino in Rudolf Schock, a pallid heroine in Stina Britta Melander and unidiomatic performances from the Belcore and Dulcamara need not concern us. The

Czech recording features the most famous Nemorino of the 1940s and 1950s, Ferruccio Tagliavini; by 1967 he had lost the lovely lyric quality his voice formally possessed, and because he had been taking a much heavier repertory, his Nemorino is sung in the worst *verismo* style, without charm. The same can be said of the Adina of Fulvia Ciano, in which her hard and brittle voice gives little or no pleasure. Gianni Maffeo is an adequate Belcore, Giuseppe Valdengo a baritone rather than a bass Dulcamara, and an unsubtle one at that. Ino Savini and the Prague Chamber Orchestra seem to be involved with a different composer.

Before turning to the 78s and extracts that can be found on LP recitals, mention should be made of the abridged version made by Italian Columbia in the early 1930s by the same artists, with one exception, who participated in that company's abridged *Don Pasquale*. They are Ines Alfani-Tellini, Cristy Solari, Lorenzo Conati (all these three in the *Pasquale*), and the *buffo*, Edoardo Faticanti, more baritone than bass. Faticanti, who sang under Toscanini at La Scala, appeared as Dulcamara, in the Verona Arena of all places, in 1936 (it was quite a cast, incidentally, with Carosio and Schipa, Serafin conducting). He is a better Dulcamara than many more famous interpreters of the role. Solari who, according to Riemens, recorded popular music under the name of Franco Lary, is a small-scale but elegant Nemorino.

L'elisir is not, at first glance, an opera that contains many extractable numbers yet surprisingly some fourteen different pieces have been recorded; what is even more surprising is that except for the much-repeated 'Una furtiva lagrima', the majority of the extracts date from acoustic days.

Nemorino has to sing his tenor aria, 'Quanto è bella', within minutes of the rise of the curtain; and even if it does not make such demands on the voice as does Radames's 'Celeste Aida' at a similar juncture in *Aida,* it requires a singer well-schooled in the art of *bel canto*. Strangely enough the performances by the two tenors whom we identify with this style of singing. Fernando de Lucia and Alessandro Bonci, hardly represent these artists at their best. De Lucia's recording (Phonotype C 2347) dates from *c.*1918 when the singer was in his late fifties. His voice does not appeal to all listeners, and I have never been enamoured of it. Bonci recorded the aria three times: in 1906 (Fono. 62123), the following year for the same label (92100), and in 1912/13 in New York (Col. A 1408). None of these performances shows Bonci at his best. Head and shoulders above all other recordings is that of Gigli, made in London in 1949 with chorus and orchestra conducted by Stanford Robinson (DB 21138; RLS 732); despite the singer being nearly 60, he captured all Nemorino's youthful charm and innocence: this is, by far, a better performance than his earlier one made in New York in 1915 (DA 797). There is a nice performance by Tagliavini (Cetra BB 25219) and a small-scale but none the less beautifully sung performance by Luigi Fort (Col.

DC 190). Others who have recorded this aria include Aristodemo Giorgini (2-52564), Emilio Perea (2-52419), Hippolito Lazaro (GQX 10146), Constantino Gero (Tima 7041), Cecil Sherwood (otherwise Lionello Cecil) (C 41908) and Fritz Wunderlich (E 80769).

Like Norina in *Don Pasquale,* Adina is discovered reading a book – in her case the story of Tristan and Isolde! Her opening *scena* (it can hardly be called an aria) has been recorded by Emilia Corsi (53472), Fernanda Rapisardi (Zono. 1726) and Elvira de Hidalgo (Fono. 92354), who was Callas's teacher.

Belcore's entrance scene 'Come Paride vezzoso' is more a piece of declamation than a full-fledged aria; in it he preens himself like a peacock in order to impress Adina. There are two excellent recordings, one by Antonio Scotti made in 1905 (Victor 85068; CO 363) and the other by Tito Gobbi in 1964 (ASD 606-7). Both these baritones were singing actors rather than mere vocalists; neither possessed great voices as such, but both were skilled vocalists, and both performances capture the swaggering self-confidence of Belcore. Giuseppe Valdengo (SUA 50617) certainly has self-confidence, but unfortunately he was in vocal decline when he recorded his performance. A recording by Francesco Federici (2-52702) I have not heard. Nor have I been able to listen to the Nemorino–Adina duet, which begins with the words 'Una parola Adina', recorded by de Lucia and de Angelis, the soprano, not the bass, of that name (Phonotype M 2223). There is a good performance of the main part of this duet by the Spanish soprano Marisa Galvany and Aristodemo Giorgini (054110), and a charmless one by Gigli and his daughter Rina (QALP 10352).

We now move on to the second most-recorded extract of the opera: the quack doctor Dulcamara's entrance aria, 'Udite, o rustici', with its quick patter section, 'Ei move i paralitici'. It is interesting to note that in acoustic days baritones rather than basses were favoured in the role of Dulcamara. Antonio Pini-Corsi, whom Verdi chose to create Ford in *Falstaff* and who was Covent Garden's first Lescaut (Puccini) also sang Tonio in *Pagliacci* there, as well as several *buffo* roles, including Dulcamara in the 1902 season in a cast that included Caruso and Scotti; he recorded 'Udite, o rustici' four times (052130, Pathé 84538, Od. 37183, and HMV 2-52703). Of these the best is the Pathé 1906 version. Another baritone, and also a prolific recorder, who committed this aria to disc was Ferruccio Corradetti, who offers a traditional Italian *buffo* performance, savouring the words (Fono. 39888-9). Another famous Toscanini artist, the baritone Ernesto Badini, who sang both Malatesta and Pasquale, Belcore and Dulcamara, continued the baritone *buffo* tradition (Od. 6647N).

Gaetano Azzolini, who also started his career in baritone roles, was considered with Pini-Corsi one of the great *buffo* basses of the past 100 years. He was another regular Toscanini artist at La Scala in the 1920s and he died in his early fifties during a series of performances of *L'elisir* at the Teatro Costanzi, Rome in 1928. His 1927 recording of 'Udite' (Od. 6567N) exhibits some of the bad *buffo* habits in which lesser Italian comic basses are still inclined to indulge. No one can call the great Salvatore Baccaloni, who inherited Azzolini's mantle, a lesser Italian bass; yet he was always inclined to exaggerate or, as the Italians say, 'overdo' when on stage. His earlier recording (CQX 16451) shows him naturally in fuller and younger voice than his 'overdone' performance on American Columbia (7138D; Odyssey Y 31736) in which at times he almost resorts to the Italian equivalent of *Sprechgesang*!

Luciano Neroni, never either a true *buffo* or a major singer, recorded the Dulcamara scene shortly after the war (Parlo. R 30019). So did Fernando Corena early on in his carrer, before he too had begun to indulge in mannerisms; he has given us a particularly well-sung account of it (Decca LX 3109). There are also performances by Arcangelo Rossi, Antonio Gelli, and Juliano Giulliani.

The Nemorino–Dulcamata duet, 'Obbligato, obbligato', after the quack doctor has sold the lovelorn Nemorino a bottle of the elixir, most surprisingly has not been recorded often. There is a performance by the stylish tenor Salvatore Salvatti and one F. Canali, who seems to have vanished without a trace (Od. 9306R), and one by de Lucia and Badini (54357), both dating from pre-1914 days. This latter version is highly thought of by many collectors. Desmond Shawe-Taylor notes the tenor's absolutely even singing in thirds and the long rubato and diminuendo as the two voices, poised on G and E fine the tone away with perfect unanimity to the merest thread. This, he points out, is the traditional *opera buffa* style at its most musical. That is all very well so long as the artists restrain themselves from taking too many liberties; and, of course, de Lucia and Badini always remain artists. The danger of the *buffo* style degenerating into a free-for-all, with singers thinking more of themselves than the composer, has been all too often evident in stage performances especially by provincial Italian touring companies, as will be remembered from the 1950s.

The Nemorino–Dulcamara scene is followed by one between the now tipsy Nemorino and Adina, the only performance of this I could trace was the 1905 one by Emilio Perea, a white-voiced tenor, and Emma Trentini, who displays a nice line in sauciness (5-4253).

The last extract from Act 1 is Nemorino's 'Adina credimi', which Schipa sings most winningly (DA 1016; LV 185) and Nino Ederle plaintively (Col. DQ 246). Salvatti recorded the extract; his disc (54459) also includes the Adina and Belcore parts

Act 2 opens with the hilarious pre-wedding party scene in Adina's farmhouse. The bride-to-be and Dulcamara join together in singing the latest new barcarolle from Venice – for two voices – 'Io son ricco'. This is a scene that calls out for recording, yet again, except for two very old versions, the first (1907) by Corradetti and Elisa Petri (Fono. 39890) and the other (1906) by Pini-Corsi and Maria Passeri (54281-2), nothing exists. Passeri, incidentally was also a Carmen!

The duet, 'Venti scudi', in which Nemorino signs on in the army in order to get the twenty scudi to buy another bottle of the elixir, survives in the classic performance of Caruso and de Luca (DM 107; ORL 316), made in 1919. Even at that late stage in his career Caruso's voice was still remarkably flexible and de Luca's Belcore is a model of its kind. Salvatti and Canali's performance does not bear comparison (054311-2).

Donizetti nearly always lets his *comprimarii* have a scene for themselves, and the village girl, Giannetta, is no exception. She has a scene with her friends in which she tells them that she has heard that Nemorino's uncle has died and left him a considerable inheritance; 'Sara possibile'. This was recorded by Ester Ferrabini and a small chorus in 1906 (53438).

Adina's second scene with Dulcamara is one of the most delightful in the opera – 'Quanto amore, ed io spietata'. The recording by Baccaloni and Aurora Rettore (DQ 244) shows the bass at his best, Rettore, who sang Musetta and Nannetta at Covent Garden in the 1920s, is a somewhat shrill Adina, but nowhere near as squally as the Argentinian soprano, Adelaide Saraceni, who was the hard-voiced Norina in the HMV plum-label *Pasquale*. She joins Afro Poli (another baritone Dulcamara) for a performance of the same scene (HMV HN 770). A much older recording by Elda Gonzaga and Corradetti is on Fono. 62008-9.

We now come to one of the most frequently recorded tenor arias in all opera, Nemorino's 'Una furtiva lagrima'. Obviously, to listen to all the recordings I have been able to trace, let alone all those others that must exist, would mean hours and hours of listening. My list, which is far too long to reproduce in full, numbers more than seventy performances, and I would hazard a guess that it covers only half the total. So I have decided to take the most representative performances, dividing them among the acoustic, the inter-war years, and those from the LP era.

Giuseppe Anselmi	Fono. 622172; CO 359
Alessandro Bonci	Fono. 39083 and Edison 83006
Jussi Björling	DB 6714 (recorded 1947); 1C 147 00947/8; and SER 5704 (recorded 1957)
Dino Borgioli	Col. D 16379 and D 18029
Enrico Caruso	Zono. X 1552 and 52346 (both 1902); HMV 52065 and 052073 (complete on the two discs, 1904); DB 126 (1911). All are reissued on Olympus
Giulio Crimi	Vocalion 54016
Richard Crooks	EW 76 (German) and Victor 15135; VIC 1464
Florencio Constantino	Pathé 10121; Victor 74065; Am. Col. 30227
Fernando de Lucia	Phonotype C 2347 and M1754
Anton Dermota	Telef. E 3755 (German)
Placido Domingo	SER 5613
Beniamino Gigli	Victor 7194 and HMV DB 1901; and RLS 729
Aristodemo Giorgini	052208
Charles Hackett	Am. Col. 49895 and M 9034

Arne Hendriksen	HMV ALPC 1
Hermann Jadlowker	052428; GV 62
Giacomo Lauri-Volpi	Fono. 74913; GV 516
John McCormack	DB 324; CO 382
Giovanni Malipiero	Parlo. DPX 24
Walter Midgley	DB 21501
Julius Patzak	Poly. 25001
Aureliano Pertile	DB 1502
Alfred Piccaver	Od. 76964 (1914), Vox 03018 (1921), Poly. 76543 (1923)
Tito Schipa	DB 1387; GEMM 151
Léopold Simoneau	DG 30451
Dimitri Smirnov	052373
Ferruccio Tagliavini	Cetra BB 25058 and HMV DB 6856
Cesare Valletti	Cetra BB 2589
Koloman von Pataky	Radiola SP 8015 and Poly. 66519
Fritz Wunderlich	Electrola E 80769

Other versions include those by Peter Anders (German), Mario Chamlee, Charles Craig, André D'Arkor (French), Roberto D'Alessio, Nino Ederle, Tano Ferendinos, Nicolai Gedda, Orville Harrold, Luigi Infantino, Sandor Konya, Hippolito Lazaro, Mario Lanza, Otto Marak, Giovanni Manurita, Heddle Nash (two, both in English), Emilio Perea, Brychan Powell, Alberto Remedios, Josef Schmidt, Rudolf Schock, Gino Sinimberghi, Alfredo Tedeschi and Emilio Venturini; there are also such oddities as one in Czech by O. Kovář and one in Swedish by F. Anderson.

If, like Michelin I were awarding rosettes for outstanding performances, three rosettes would go to Caruso's 1904 version; two to McCormack, Smirnov, Schipa, Tagliavini and Hendriksen; and a single one to Crooks, Jadlowker, Lauri-Volpi, Piccaver and Simoneau. I was pleased to find that John Steane in his invaluable and perceptive *The Grand Tradition* agrees with some of my choices, though as usual, he does not seem to like Gigli and swoons over de Lucia.

All critics agree that Caruso's 1904 version is not only the finest version of the aria on disc, but also one of the greatest, if not the greatest, of all Caruso's recordings. As Steane points out, it probably comes nearest to Caruso's La Scala performance of 1901, when there were twelve performances of the opera conducted by Toscanini who, as Steane says, probably would not have allowed the tenor to 'expand' so much with something of the free style of de Lucia. This is a beautifully characterized performance, with wonderful phrasing, a perfectly judged climax on 'Io vo'm'ama', with a meltingly lovely diminuendo. Then, in the second part, is a consummate display of *mezza voce* singing and aural proof of the tenor's vocal technique in the cadenza. By 1911, we hear that although Caruso can still sing sweetly and lyrically and also retain that remarkable agility in the cadenza, his performance is far less 'old-fashioned' – perhaps, as Steane suggests, because such 'refinements' as he displayed in the 1904 version were already out of keeping with the style of the day.

McCormack's performance, although not equalling that of Caruso – one feels it is more carefully studied – is none the less a fine example of the tenor's work and his *bel canto* style. Smirnov (for me) spoils his wonderful performance by adding an extra loud note at the end (I am a purist in these matters). The Russian tenor's breath control is phenomenal, the sound lovely.

Schipa's performance displays that tenor's elegance, purity of tone and marvellously forward diction. Gigli's second version, dating from 1929, was judged by Compton Mackenzie in *The Gramophone* as one of the loveliest vocal records he ever had heard. It was certainly one of the first Gigli records that I purchased in my early days as a collector. His honeyed tone and seamless legato coupled with most beautiful *mezza voce* singing makes this performance, for me, almost the equal of Caruso's. One had to wait until Tagliavini's wartime first recording of the aria (it was the second disc he ever made) to find as winning a performance. Lord Harewood ranked this as the best version available 'with the possible exception of that by Schipa', which obviously means that when he wrote that review (May 1949) he ranked Schipa's more classical performance above Gigli's more extrovert one.

Arne Hendriksen, my other contender for a two-rosette award, is a Norwegian tenor, who made his debut in 1940 as Nemorino in Oslo and then went to the Stockholm Opera where he was very successful during the 1950s and early 1960s. He never made an international career, yet his performance of 'Una furtiva' reveals a warm, Italianate voice and style, and a most winning way with Nemorino. I rank this as the best performer of the aria on disc of the past twenty-five years, eclipsing those by Gedda, Domingo and Björling. It is almost equalled by Simoneau's performance, which Steane ranks higher than I do, calling it the 'most even and finely poised modern recording'. Perhaps he has not heard Hendriksen's version.

Richard Crooks, the American tenor, recorded the aria twice – once in 1927, in German, a performance I have not heard, and again two years later in Italian. His performance is surprisingly nearer Caruso's than McCormack's in style and thrust. Lauri-Volpi's performance dates from 1920, when his career was barely a year old; despite one or two intrusive 'h's and a tendency to slide up to some notes, it is a characteristic performance. Piccaver's voice may not appeal to all tastes – there is always a nasal quality about it – but his command of legato is phenomenal, and the sound often described as 'silver' rather than 'golden' is instantly recognizable.

Jadlower has been described as a Wagnerian coloratura tenor, his vocal flexibility often making his the equal of de Lucia, but his voice has not the whiteness of his Italian counterpart, being more like Caruso's in its sensuousness and warmth. His account of Nemorino's aria is one of the best by a non-Italian of that period.

A few words about some of the non-'starred' versions that I have found enjoyable. Borgioli was a tenor much more admired in England than in his native Italy where his reticence and 'good taste' were not to the liking of many Italians. His 'Una furtiva', especially his second version, is sung with an open and at times nasal tone, but with Schipa-like elegance. Giovanni Malipiero was the same kind of singer, though his voice exhibited more warmth. Walter Midgley, a British tenor who might have made an international career had there been the same kind of opportunities existing in the immediate post-war period there are today, gives a sweet-voiced and appealing account of the aria, though it is somewhat lacking in true Italian style. Valletti, who often has been compared to Schipa, gives an uncharacteristically bad performance; and Patzak, although as musical as ever, seems far from happy in this Italian milieu, both vocally and verbally.

The last extract is Adina's Bellini-like 'Prendi per me', of which I have been able to trace four recordings though doubtless there may be more. Lina Pagliughi (Parlo. DPX 26) shows this soprano at her classic best; the voice is pure, the legato perfect, but the characterization almost nil. Carosio (DB 6867) also shows the singer at her very best; her singing is beautifully judged and her diction, as always, perfect. Callas's performance (33CX 1923), is one of the soprano's few failures; one simply cannot imagine her as Adina, and she never sang the role on stage. Her teacher, Elvira de Hidalgo, did, however, and her performance (Fono. 92355) shows just why she was so highly regarded as a *bel canto* singer, and even more importantly, why Callas was able to learn so much from her, though not as Adina.

L' ELISIR D'AMORE

A Adina; *N* Nemorino; *B* Belcore; *D* Dulcamara

1952 Carosio *A*; Monti *N*; Gobbi *B*;
Luise *D*/Rome Opera Chorus
and Orch./Santini
World Records ⓜ OC 226-7;
Victor ⓜ LM 6024

1952 Noni *A*; Valletti *N*; Poli *B*;
Bruscantini *D*/Rome Radio
Chorus and Orch./Gavazzeni
Cetra ⓒ LPS 3235 ④ MC 180-1

1955 Gueden *A*; di Stefano *N*;
Capecchi *B*; Corena *D*/Florence
Festival Chorus and
Orch./Molinari-Pradelli
Decca GOS 566-7; Richmond
RS 63524

1959 Carteri *A*; Alva *N*; Panerai *B*;
Taddei *D*/La Scala Chorus and
Orch./Serafin

EMI 3C 163 00863-4; Seraphim
SIB 6001

1962 (in German) Melander *A*;
Schock *N*; Ostenburg *B*; Welter
D/Berlin Chamber Choir, Berlin
SO/Märzendorfer
Ariola-Eurodisc S70011XR

1966 Freni *A*; Gedda *N*; Sereni *B*;
Capecchi *D*/Rome Opera Chorus
and Orch./Molinari-Pradelli
HMV SLS; Angel SB 3701

1967 Ciano *A*; Tagliavini *N*; Maffeo
B; Valdengo *D*/Czech
Philharmonic Chorus, Prague
CO/Savini
Supraphon 112 0621-3

1972 Sutherland *A*; Pavarotti *N*;
Cossa *B*; Malas *D*/Ambrosian

Opera Chorus, ECO/Bonynge
Decca SET 503-5 ④ K154K32;
London OSA 13101 ④ 5-13101
1977 Cotrubas *A*; Domingo *N*; Wixell
B; Evans *D*/Covent Garden
Opera Chorus and
Orch./Pritchard

CBS (UK) 79210; (US) M3-34585

Excerpts

1932 Tellini *A*; Solari *N*; Conati *B*;
Faticanti *D*/La Scala Chorus and
Orch./Molajoli
EMI Ⓜ CQX 10093-8;
CBS Ⓜ ML 4408

Lucia di Lammermoor

CHARLES OSBORNE

At first, all did not go well with *Lucia di Lammermoor*. In Donizetti's new contract with the Society of the Neapolitan Royal Theatres the management had undertaken to give him the approved libretto at least four months before the production of the opera. On 29 May 1835, Donizetti, writing a second time to the management, complained that any delay in the production of the new opera would be attributable to them, and confirmed that he had accepted the choice of Cammarano as librettist. Yet, in spite of these delays, the finished work was delivered on 6 July 1835, which means that it was written and completely orchestrated in forty days. But because of a run of operatic failures the direction of the Royal Theatres was now plunged into a financial crisis, and by the end of July it seemed that the society would fail. The situation was saved only by the personal intervention of the king. After a week's vacation at the beginning of August, all was ready by the 20th to begin the copying of the parts and rehearsals. However, on 5 September Donizetti wrote to Giovanni Ricordi that the society was again in trouble and that Tacchinardi Persiani, the Lucia, had not been paid and was refusing to rehearse; but on 16 September, writing to Jacopo Ferretti, he laconically remarks: 'On 28, Lucia.' Actually, the opera was given at the San Carlo on 26 September 1835. Besides Persiani, the cast included the famous French tenor Gilbert Duprez (Edgardo), the baritone Domenico Cosselli and the bass Carlo Porto. The work was an immediate success, a success that was repeated in Vienna on 13 April 1837, and in Paris on 12 December 1837, for four performances at the Théâtre des Italiens, where Persiani was again Lucia, with Rubini and Tamburini (tenor and bass). Astolfe, Marquis de Custine, praising Persiani, reports to Donizetti that Rubini was outstanding in the second-act finale, and Tamburini very fine in his first aria ('Cruda funesta smania') and in the Act 3 duet ('O sole più ratto') with Rubini. *Lucia* reached Her Majesty's Theatre, London, on 5 April 1838. Famous exponents have since included Verdi's Giuseppina Strepponi (for whom Donizetti wrote *Adelia*, produced at the Apollo Theatre, Rome, 1841), Piccolimini, Jenny Lind and Christine Nilsson and, nearer our own time, Adelina Patti, Marcella Sembrich, Etelka Gerster,

Nellie Melba, Luisa Tetrazzini, Frieda Hempel, Maria Barrientos, Amelita Galli-Curci, Toti dal Monte, Maria Callas, Renata Scotto, Joan Sutherland, Beverley Sills and Montserrat Caballé.

There are a great many complete recordings on LP, some more 'complete' than others, for most contain minor cuts, especially in the marriage scene and the mad scene, and one or two delete Act 2, scene 1, in its entirety. The earliest two are LP reissues of 78s, the first of the Columbia thirteen-disc set of the early 1930s whose Lucia is Mercedes Capsir, a singer for whom most critics usually apologize. Indeed, though she possesses an admirable skill and sureness in coloratura ornamentation, she is not an interesting interpreter and there is frequently the suggestion of an unfeeling, mechanical nightingale. Enzo di Muro Lomanto has a rich voice but makes little attempt at vocal acting. Armando Borgioli is an impressive Enrico. It should be remembered that the Raimondo, Salvatore Baccaloni, was famed as a *buffo* rather than a *basso cantante*.

In the Cetra reissue of Parlophone's wartime recording, Lina Pagliughi is dramatically lightweight but musically exciting. Her coloratura is freely and accurately produced, and though she is a touching heroine her addition of mordents and other embellishments to the vocal line gives the character a youthful gaiety which is unusual. Giovanni Malipiero sings Edgardo's difficult tessitura easily and suavely. His light voice has a cutting edge which can make its presence felt even in the most crowded ensemble. Luciano Neroni is outstanding in the end of the sextet at Raimondo's phrase 'Rispettate o voi, di Dio'; and in his 'Dalle stanze' he brings a tragic nobility to his narration of Lucia's madness. Unfortunately, Giuseppe Manacchini is merely adequate in the baritone role, and the two *comprimario* tenors are rarely even that. The recording of the orchestra under Ugo Tansini's direction certainly shows its age, but this set will remain valuable for the dazzling vocal quality of Pagliughi, here at the peak of her powers.

Of the two recordings featuring Lily Pons, the Metropolitan Opera's Lucia for at least twenty-five years from 1931, one is a private recording of a live performance at the Met probably in the very early 1950s, with Frederick Jagel and John Brownlee. It has souvenir status only. The other is distinguished by the extremely stylish singing of Richard Tucker as Edgardo. Though based on Metropolitan performances, this 1953 recording was made in the studio. Pons is still a dashing Lucia, but her coloratura is laboured and frequently slovenly. The rest of the cast, including Frank Guarrera (Enrico) and Norman Scott (Raimondo), is adequate only, but it is interesting to note that the tiny role of Normanno is sung by the not-so-tiny tenor, James McCracken, then at the outset of his career. (A better souvenir of Pons's Lucia is her mad scene on DB 1504, recorded in 1935.)

In 1953, Nixa recorded on three LPs an absolutely complete performance. Dolores Wilson, a pupil of Toti dal Monte, cannot compare with Pagliughi

or Pons for sheer vocal authority or experience, though she somewhat
resembles them both. Gianni Poggi (Edgardo) is not a subtle interpreter
or singer. Anselmo Colzani sings Enrico in a forthright manner, which
is at least telling in the sextet but elsewhere is out of style. The Raimondo
is poor, but the performance of the chorus and orchestra under Capuana
is particularly well recorded.

We come now, chronologically, to the first of the Callas Lucias. I have
always found Callas's vocal failings a great stumbling block, especially in
the *bel canto* operas which, in the earlier part of her career, she liked
to sing. Her 1953 Lucia is certainly more secure vocally than her later
recordings; I shall have more to say about her shortly. Di Stefano, in
fine voice, is particularly effective in the sextet, and phrases the long final
scene smoothly and movingly. Tito Gobbi is a splendid Enrico, but
Raffaele Arié a weak Raimondo. Tullio Serafin conducts with charm,
vigour and authority.

I have not been able to hear Perlea's 1957 recording with Renata
Ongaro and Giacinto Prandelli nor the 1958 Orpheus listed in the
discography. The performance with Roberta Peters is spoilt for me by
the rushed, insensitive conducting of Erich Leinsdorf. I remember hearing
this *Lucia* for the first time in 1959, a few months after experiencing Joan
Sutherland's first assumption of the role at Covent Garden. I thought
(and still think) Sutherland's dramatic coloratura the right kind of voice
for Lucia. I probably dismissed Roberta Peters too quickly as being in
the Lily Pons tradition. Listening to her again now, I find her highly
attractive when not being rushed along by her conductor. Jan Peerce is
a stylish and highly satisfactory Edgardo, but the other singers are
unexciting.

Ettore Bastianini's mellifluous Enrico was the only gripping performance
in DG's 1959 recording. Renata Scotto's Lucia lacked nothing in agility,
but I would have preferred to hear her later in the role. Then she was
dramatically a cipher. As Edgardo, Di Stefano was well past his best, and
Sanzogno is a dull conductor. In the same year, Callas's second studio
recording appeared, conducted again by Serafin with an eloquent warmth.
Callas's voice is, to my taste, far too dark for the role of Lucia, and is
in even less secure condition than in the earlier recording. Ferruccio
Tagliavini (Edgardo) was nearing the end of his career, but is at least
stylistically closer to the composer, and no one else is very good. For
a worthy account of what Callas was like in the theatre as Lucia, one
has to turn to her exciting performance conducted by Karajan at the
Berlin Städtische Oper on 29 September 1955. There are the usual cuts,
including the Wolf's Crag scene, but the opera is conducted with a
masterly intensity by Karajan and the excitement of Callas's performance
in the opera house comes across very strongly. Callas was convincing in
the theatre, in roles which the gramophone often tended cruelly to expose
her; on disc she is vocally inadequate or, at times, excruciating. If one

listens to this *Lucia*, however, as a theatrical performance and not as a document for all time, the experience can be thrilling. The sextet is repeated.

For the best *recorded* performance I think one must turn to one of Joan Sutherland's two Decca recordings: not the 1961 version tepidly conducted by John Pritchard, though it is virtually complete and even includes a bonus aria, often substituted in nineteenth-century performances for 'Regnava nel silenzio', and though Merrill and Siepi are fine. My preference is for the 1971 performance conducted by Richard Bonynge with dramatic flair, and with the soprano in superb form, fuller of voice than ten years earlier but still with that amazing flexibility and accuracy, and portraying a warm and convincing Lucia. The top notes, including a stunning E flat, are both secure and beautiful in quality. Again the score is given complete. Pavarotti makes a big, beefy sound, and Milnes is a superb Enrico once he gets past his first-act aria. The small parts are cast from strength, and Ghiaurov is by far the finest Raimondo on record.

The Beverly Sills Lucia on HMV (complete) is like Hamlet without the prince. Schippers conducts sensitively and gives us Donizetti's glass harmonica in the mad scene, sometimes instead of flute, sometimes doubling with it. Carlo Bergonzi sings gloriously and perfectly in style as Edgardo, and Piero Cappuccilli is equally impressive as Enrico. But Sills is hard, brittle, sometimes wobbly, very occasionally sweet-toned, though she has no difficulty with the coloratura.

Anna Moffo recorded the role twice: in 1966 for RCA, and more recently for Eurodisc (though this latter is the sound-track of a TV film, and is nowhere near complete). The Eurodisc, conducted ploddingly by Carlo Felice Cillario, is roughly sung, and the recorded sound is cavernous. The RCA is better, and complete, though Georges Prêtre is less than completely sympathetic. Bergonzi is in superb voice, but gives a better performance in the Sills-Schippers set than he does for Prêtre, and Moffo is no more than an efficient Lucia. The 1974 Supraphon set offers the attractive Lucia of Margherita Guglielmi and the respectably sung Enrico of Cappuccilli, but is let down by Flaviano Labò, the Edgardo.

One more complete performance remains to be mentioned, and that is the most recent. Montserrat Caballé's Lucia was presented as 'authentic', with the implication that earlier assumptions of the role were somehow inauthentic. This is a plain, largely undecorated Lucia, occasionally in higher keys than we usually hear, and with no interpolated high notes; but it is, alas, far too plainly characterized to be a serious rival to the best of the earlier versions. I should like to have heard the Edgardo of José Carreras in another context, and Vicento Sardiniero is a convincing Enrico, though without the vocal personality of Gobbi or Bastianini.

Recordings of arias and ensembles abound on 78s. The sextet was a favourite. There is a magnificent recording (DQ 102; GEMM 170), backed by an equally fine *Rigoletto* quartet, with Gigli, Galli-Curci, Homer, de Luca, Pinza and Bada, apparently a traditional coupling. Caruso appears with Journet in no fewer than three acoustic recordings of the sextet, with different Lucias: Tetrazzini, Sembrich and Galli-Curci and a fine assortment of supporting artists. Tetrazzini, Jacoby, Amato and Bada are with them on a single-side disc, the backing left off because of a false entry by Caruso in the *Rigoletto* quartet. Galli-Curci, Egener, de Luca and Bada on DQ 100, and Sembrich, Severina, Scotti and Daddi on DQ 101, are in both cases coupled with the *Rigoletto* quartet by the appropriate artists from the sextet. Considering the limitations of recording technique of that period, all are well recorded. My preference is for Tetrazzini's later disc. The earliest recording is DQ 101, made in 1908 when Sembrich, although still brilliant, was past her prime. These merits and faults are also evident in her 1906 recording of the first part of the mad scene.

Acoustic recordings of solo passages from the tomb scene have been made by John McCormack, Bonci, Schipa, Anselmi and Martinelli, and electric ones by Pertile, Cesare Valletti, Giacinto Prandelli and others. Made for G&T in 1908 when he was 58, the solos by the famous Verdian tenor Franceso Marconi (05221/234) are authoritative in style and reach back almost to the age of Donizetti himself. Gigli recorded several variants of the tomb scene, including 'Tombe degl'avi miei' (DB 122 or DB 2235) and the 'Tombe' (DB 870) without chorus and the finale 'Tu che a Dio'. There is little to choose between these discs reissued on GEMM 146. Gigli's voice is attractive in this music, his style less so.

Most 78s of the mad scene treat it as a soprano solo, omitting all other parts and chorus. They begin either with the recitative 'Il dolce suono' or 'Ardon gl'incensi', and the second part begins at 'Spargi d'amaro pianto'. Galli-Curci, an outstanding Lucia of her period, recorded acoustically 'Il dolce suono' (DB 260; the second part on DA 214; CDN 1024). Galli-Curci also recorded the duet, 'Veranno a te', with Tito Schipa, a most stylish performance by both (DB 811; CDN 1024). She is thus well represented on disc as Lucia whom, with her characteristic pearly vocal timbre, she makes a most sympathetic heroine.

Melba chose Lucia for her Covent Garden debut in 1888, but made so little impression that it was only through the persuasion of the eminent society leader Lady de Grey that she was re-engaged for the following year, whence her unassailed reign at the Royal Opera began. Her recordings from *Lucia* are slight but repetitive: fragments of the first part of the mad scene made at three different periods, the earliest in the brilliant London 1904 G&T series when she was already 47 (03020; RLS 719). Of her repetitions of this selection made in the United States, the 1907 recording is dim and the 1910, while more brightly recorded, finds Melba just that much older. Neither is worth seeking out. In addition to the sextet, Tetrazzini recorded not only the opening section of the mad scene twice, but also Lucia's Act 1 cavatina complete in two parts (DB 528; COLH 136), a vivid example of her brilliant vocalization.

Barrientos first recorded the love duet with Zenatello in 1906 when she was just over twenty (Fono. 39825; GV 27). Later, she recorded for American Columbia the duet with Hackett (49766), the mad scene (48627), 'Regnava nel silenzio' (48628), and the sextet (49768), when the limpidity of the young girl is replaced by a much more mature voice. Toti dal Monte was the most celebrated Lucia between the wars (at any rate in Europe). In that voice which embodied girlish charm with absolute security in *fioritura*, she recorded the first part of 'Regnava nel silenzio' (DB 1040) and a full version of the mad scene (DB 1015). The records of the German artists Maria Ivogün and Frieda Hempel on Odeon and of the French artists Jourfier, Brothier and Solange Delmas should not be overlooked. The question of language intrudes in the various selections made by Viennese singers, including Selma Kurz and Elisa Elizza which are for native consumption only, and the German Margarethe Siems, creator of the Marschallin, whose mad scene is remarkable more for her stunning vocalization than for her interpretative ability.

Among distinguished baritones who recorded the opening aria, 'Cruda funesta smania' in the 78 era, Battistini is outstanding. He sings with his typical noble, smooth legato coloured by that peculiar hint of a snarl, which is here excellently in character (052363). Stracciari (Col. CQ 693) is not far behind him in artistry. The aria was also recorded by, among others, Sammarco, Magini-Coletti and Franci. Of historical interest is the early 1906 Black G&T of the Wolf's Crag duet by Giuseppe Acerbi and Renzo Minolfi. Lucette Korsoff, a pupil of Saint-Saëns, recorded the alternative aria mentioned earlier, but in French as 'Que n'avons-nous des ailes', a rare and beautiful disc.

Those are simply the most important artists who recorded excerpts from *Lucia* on 78s. The LP age has not produced a great many items in solo recital discs which are likely to become collectors' pieces in the years to come, but I should mentioned Scotto's mad scene recorded in 1959 well before her complete recording, interpretatively bland but stunningly sung (33CX 1638); Sutherland's similarly pre-complete recording mad scene and 'Regnava nel silenzio' (LXT 5531), a magnificent souvenir of her 1959 debut in the role at Covent Garden, though she is recorded with the Paris Conservatoire Orchestra; well-sung accounts of 'Fra poco a me ricovero' by Pavarotti (SXL 6377) and Domingo (SXL 6451), and first-rate versions of that aria by Gedda and 'Verrano a te' by Gedda and Freni on their duet disc (ASD 2473).

LUCIA DI LAMMERMOOR

L Lucia; *Ed* Edgardo; *En* Enrico; *R* Raimondo

1933 Capsir *L*; de Muro Lomanto
Ed; Molinari *En*; Baccaloni *R*/La
Scala Chorus and Orch./Molajoli
OASI ⓜ OASI 1510

1942 Pagliughi *L*; Malipiero *Ed*;
Manachinni *En*; Neroni *R*/Turin
Radio Chorus and Orch./Tansini
Cetra ⓜ LPC 1205

1953 Wilson *L*; Poggi *Ed*; Colzani
En; Maionica *R*/'Milan' Chorus
and Orch./Capuana
Nixa ⓜ ULP 9231/1-3; Urania
ⓔ US 5232/3

1954 Pons *L*; Tucker *Ed*; Guarrera
En; Scott *R*/Metropolitan Opera
Chorus and Orch./Cleva
CBS (UK) ⓜ 78242; (US) ⓜ
Y2 32361

1954 Callas *L*; di Stefano *Ed*; Gobbi
En; Arié *R*/Florence Festival
Chorus and Orch./Serafin
HMV ⓔ SLS 5056 ④ TC-SLS
5056; Seraphim ⓜ IB 6032

1955 (live performance) Callas *L*; di
Stefano *Ed*; Panerai *En*;
Zaccaria *R*/La Scala Chorus,
Berlin RIAS Orch./Karajan
Cetra ⓜ LO 18/3; Turnabout
ⓜ THS 65144-5

1957 Ongaro *L*; Prandelli *Ed*; Maero
En/La Fenice Chorus and Orch.
Venice/Perlea
Remington ⓜ 199-200/3

1958 Peters *L*; Peerce *Ed*; Maero *En*;
Tozzi *R*/Rome Opera Chorus
and Orch./Leinsdorf
RCA VICS 6101

1958 Rinaldi *L*; Tei *Ed*; Pica *En*;
Tatone *R*/Rome Opera Chorus
and Orch./Pacletti
Orpheus SMS 2158

1959 Scotto *L*; di Stefano *Ed*;
Bastianini *En*; Vinco *R*/La Scala
Chorus and Orch./Sanzogno
DG 2705 009; Everest S 439/2

1959 Callas *L*; Tagliavini *Ed*;
Cappuccilli *En*; Ladysz
R/Chorus, Philharmonia/Serafin
HMV SLS 5166 ④ TC-SLS
5166; Angel SB 3601

1961 Sutherland *L*; Cioni *Ed*; Merrill
En; Siepi *R*/Santa Cecilia
Academy Chorus and
Orch./Pritchard
Decca GOS 663-5; London OSA
1327

1966 Moffo *L*; Bergonzi *Ed*; Sereni
En; Flagello *R*/RCA Italiana
Chorus and Orch./Prêtre
RCA SER 5550-2; (US) LSC
6170

1968 Guglielmi *L*; Labò *Ed*;
Cappuccilli *En*; S. Pagliuca
R/Czech Singers Chorus, Prague
CO/Ziino
Supraphon 112 1381-2

1970 Sills *L*; Bergonzi *Ed*; Cappuccilli
En; Diaz *R*/Ambrosian Chorus,
LSO/Schippers
HMV SLS 797; ABC ATS
20006 ④ 5109-20006S

1971 Sutherland *L*; Pavarotti *Ed*;
Milnes *En*; Ghiaurov *R*/Royal
Opera Chorus and
Orch./Bonynge
Decca SET 528-30; London
OSA 13103 ④5-13103

1972 Moffo *L*; Kozma *Ed*; Fioravanti
En; Washington *R*/Rome Radio
Choris and Orch./Cillario
Ariola-Eurodisc XF 85917R

1976 Caballé *L*; Carreras *Ed*;
Sardiniero *En;* Ramey
R/Ambrosian Singers, New
Philharmonia/Cobos
Philips 6703 080 ④ 7699 056

Excerpts

1949/51 Munsel *L*; Peerce *Ed*; Merrill
En; Pinza *R*/Chorus and RCA
Victor Orch./Cellini
Victor ⓜ LM 1710

1952 Rossi *L*; Valletti *Ed*; Mercangeli
En/La Scala Chorus and
Orch./Questa
Royale ⓜ ROY 1211

1954 Reggiani *L*; Landi *Ed*; Valentino
En/orch/Walther
Royale ⓜ ROY 1617

1956 (Live performance) Callas

L/Metropolitan Opera Chorus
and Orch./Cleva
Cetra ⓜ LO 18/3

1960 Mesplé *L*; Vanzo *Ed*; Massard
En; Serkoyan *R*/Chorus and
Orch./Sebastien

Barclay ⓜ 89009

1965 Agay *L*; Simándy *Ed*; Jámbor
En/Hungarian State Opera
Chorus and Orch./Kórody
Qualiton SLPX 11648

Don Pasquale

HAROLD ROSENTHAL

Although *Don Pasquale* is generally considered, with *Il barbiere di Siviglia, Figaro, Falstaff* and *Die Meistersinger* as one of the classic comic operas, it has never achieved the popularity of those works – that is, in the major opera houses of the world where it has had fewer performances than its four rivals. None the less, it has always held an attraction for singers, no doubt because Donizetti wrote it for four of the greatest artists of the day: Grisi, Mario, Tamburini and Lablache. So every attractive soprano, romantic tenor, elegant baritone, and *buffo* bass has seen themselves duplicating the success of the opera's creators.

Possibly the most famous revival of *Pasquale* this century was that at La Scala, Milan, in the 1904 season, when no less than twenty performances were given under Cleofonte Campanini with Rosina Storchio as Norina, Leonid Sobinov (later Aristodemo Giorgini) as Ernesto, Giuseppe de Luca as Malatesta and Antonio Pini-Corsi as Pasquale; all those artists recorded extracts from the opera. The performances at the Metropolitan, New York, early this century nearly all had Marcella Sembrich as Norina and Antonio Scotti as Malatesta, and they too have left recorded mementos of these performances. In Italy and at Glyndebourne before the second world war, *Pasquale* is remembered for the performances of Mariano Stabile as Malatesta and Salvatore Baccaloni in the title role. Unfortunately they never recorded together, but are none the less represented on disc, as are also Margherita Carosio and Tito Schipa, the most frequent interpreters of Norina and Ernesto on the Italian stages during the 1930s and 1940s.

Pasquale has translated well into German, and it enjoyed a great deal of popularity in Berlin in the inter-war years, with such singers as Maria Ivogün, Lotte Schöne and Willi Domgraf-Fassbaender. It was also heard at Salzburg under Bruno Walter in 1925 and 1930 with Ivogün and Karl Erb; again, most of the famous German artists who took part in performances in Berlin, Vienna, Salzburg and elsewhere, recorded extracts from the work.

To date there have been nine complete recordings of *Pasquale* – ten if one includes the pirated 'off-the-air' set of Metropolitan Opera performance in 1940 with Bidu Sayão, Nino Martini, Francesco Valentino, Salvatore Baccaloni and Alessio de Paolis, conductor Gennaro Papi, and one abridged version which I have not heard.

The 1933 HMV plum-label set which was transferred to LP in 1956 has Ernesto Badini in the title role. He was Toscanini's favourite Ford and had been the Malatesta of Covent Garden's 1920 revival (and also the first London Schicchi). He gives an outstanding performance, relishing the words and offering an authentic *buffo* performance without over-vulgarizing the part. He is ably partnered by Afro Poli as Malatesta; and although Adelaide Saraceni's Norina may lack charm and at times may sound a little acid, she sings with spirit. Tito Schipa's Ernesto is still unbeatable; and the orchestra and chorus, under the veteran Carlo Sabajno, were well recorded; the transfer to LP has been successfully accomplished.

The off-the-air set immortalizes Baccaloni's Pasquale: but already by December 1940, only eighteen months after his famous Glyndebourne performances under Busch, and without the watchful eye of Carl Ebert, Baccaloni was exaggerating and playing for laughs. Sayão, who should have made many more commercial discs than she did, is a charming Norina; Valentino (Glyndebourne's Macbeth) is a surprisingly good Malatesta, and Martini a lightweight and ineffectual Ernesto.

In the Urania set, of which I have only heard extracts, Dora Gatta is a shrill, steam-whistle Norina; Corena, then on the threshold of his career, a somewhat youthful Pasquale; Agostino Lazzari an adequate Ernesto; and Poli, for the second time on discs, a distinguished Malatesta. The Nixa set is hardly worth investigating further; only Melchiorre Luise's performance of the title role, which is both musical and full of humour, even though the voice lacks fruitiness, is worth preserving. Far more worthwhile is the Cetra 1954 set, with Bruscantini as a lightweight but stylish Pasquale, Alda Noni a delicious Norina, and Mario Borriello a suave Malatesta. Cesare Valletti, then early in his career, sang a most mellifluous Ernesto, and Mario Rossi conducts a stylish performance.

I have not heard either the 1952 Royale or Westminster sets; but certainly on paper they do not look particularly attractive. I did not find the Philips 1956 set much to my liking, though there is much to admire in Renato Capecchi's musical and beautifully articulated Pasquale.

Decca's 1965 recording found both Sciutti and Oncina in poor voice; Corena, on the other hand, sings excellently as Pasquale and gives a performance remarkably free from the mannerisms that have characterized some of his theatre and recorded performances; Tom Krause is a serious Malatesta and, like Kertesz, who conducts, seems distant from the Italian *buffo* tradition.

DG's 1965 recording under Ettore Gracis is a more authentic performance than the Decca set but there are vocal weaknesses all round, so a really satisfactory complete *Pasquale* is still awaited; the recent version, conducted by Sarah Caldwell, is unlikely to do that.

In addition to the above complete sets, Italian Columbia made an abridged version in the 1930s with Ines Alfani-Tellini, Cristy Solari, Lorenzo Conati and Attilio Giuliani, conducted, as were so many of the Columbia recordings in the years between the wars, by Lorenzo Molajoli. As with a number of the complete sets, there is little in this to interest the collector. There are however two selections in German, one on DG with Rita Streich, Kurt Wehofschitz, Karl Schmitt-Walter and Joseph Greindl, conductor Fritz Lehmann, which I have not heard; the other which I strongly recommend, has Anneliese Rothernberger as a charming Norina, Peter Schreier as an almost Mozartian Ernesto, and Günther Leib and Reiner Süss as a Malatesta and Pasquale well above the average; conductor, Siegfried Kurz with the Dresden State Opera Orchestra.

The Metropolitan Opera's production of the 1950s is not very worthily represented in the highlights disc with Dolores Wilson, a pupil of Toti dal Monte, as a shrill Norina, Charles Anthony as a prosaic Ernesto, and Baccaloni, a shadow of his former self, as Pasquale. Only Frank Guarrera as Malatesta displays the necessary style.

Before embarking on the 78s as a whole, I propose to deal with two groups of recordings totalling some thirty odd discs, that were published by G&T in 1906/7, and by Fonotipia between 1905 and 1908. These were a direct result of the success of the 1904 La Scala revival with Storchio, Giorgini, de Luca and Pini-Corsi. Obviously, because of contractual difficulties, it was not possible to get all four La Scala principals into one studio at the same time; and so G&T's La Scala Pasquale, Pini-Corsi, is partnered by Ernesto Badini, Giovanni Polese or Augusto Scipioni as Malatesta, and either Emilia Pini-Corsi (his cousin in fact), Josefina Huguet or Linda Brambilla as Norina. The Scala's Malatesta, Giuseppe de Luca, features on the Fonotipia discs with Ferruccio Corradetti as Pasquale, Aida Gonzaga as Norina and Carlo Dani as Ernesto.

I will deal first with the Fonotipia releases. Storchio recorded Norina's aria on two single-sided discs (39400 and 39401) in 1906, two years after the Scala revival. Not a coloratura soprano (she was of course the first Cio-Cio-San, Zazà and Lodoletta), she none the less displays a nicely sustained trill. Although there is an edge to her top notes, she makes Norina into a very positive and vivacious character. De Luca's elegant and beautifully pointed performance of Malatesta's 'Bella siccome un angelo' (39939) likewise dates from 1906; notice how he holds on to his top note in the phrase 'che v'innamora' to give effect to the point he is making, and to his almost Verdi-like style at the end of the aria; Pasquale's interjections are sensibly included. He also made an earlier version (52444) in 1903. He then joins Gonzaga for the famous 'rehearsal' duet on two discs (62010 and 62011); the soprano is quite adequate, but she displays a typical white Italian light-soubrettish voice. We next meet Corradetti and Dani in the exchanges between Ernesto and Pasquale, beginning with Ernesto's words 'Prender moglie' and leading to Ernesto's first aria, 'Sogno soave a casto' (39989 and 39990). The tenor is no Bonci or Schipa, but is acceptable enough, and the bass, a bit rough, but well-schooled in the Italian *buffo* style. Dani also recorded 'Cercherò lontana terra' (39965).

De Luca, Gonzaga and Corradetti recorded the first part of the scene in which Malatesta introduces his 'sister' to Pasquale, beginning with the old man's words 'Alcun viene'; the disc is usually labelled 'Via, da brava', which are Malatesta's words a few bars further on (74023). We then move to Act 3 with the scene between Pasquale and Norina, 'Signorina, in tanta fretta', leading to the slap on the face and Pasquale's 'E duretta la lezione' with Gonzaga and Corradetti (62006 and 62007).

The atmosphere of the theatre is very much present, with de Luca and Corradetti throwing in the odd aside both in the Act 2 scene mentioned above, and in the famous Pasquale-Malatesta patter duet, 'Cheti, cheti . . . Aspetta, aspetta, cara sposina' (39975 and 39976). This is a jewel of a performance and has been transferred on to several LP reissues. The last of these Fonotipia discs is Dani's stylish performance of 'Come'è gentil' (39966).

The common factors of the G&Ts are Pini-Corsi as Pasquale and Badini as Malatesta. Strangely enough, Pini-Corsi himself also recorded Malatesta's 'Bella siccome un angelo' on a black Columbia (10265) in 1904. The first of the selection is on 054091; this is the very beginning of the opera, with Pasquale awaiting Malatesta's arrival, 'Son nov'ore' (054091), followed by Pasquale's joyful outburst, 'Un foco insolito', in which the old man already feels rejuvenated and faces the prospect of at least half a dozen children (54301). Pini-Corsi here clearly demonstrates why his Pasquale was so generally regarded as being the finest since Lablache's. Next come Badini and Emilia Corsi in the Malatesta-Norina scene and, as on the Fonotipia, it is the Malatesta rather than the Norina who seems to be the *raison d'être* of the recording (054093 and 5430415). Badini recorded the scene to far better effect with Huguet the following year (054166 and 54348). Norina, in the person of Brambilla, is introduced to Pasquale by another Malatesta, Scipioni 'Via da brava' (054125). We then jump to the end of the act, where Norina begins to display her true colours; by this time Ernesto has joined the other three soloists – in this case he is another of the Corsi family, the tenor Gaetano who, with Brambilla, Antonio Pini-Corsi and Scipioni, begin the recording (54329) with Norina's words 'E rimasto là'; then, unaccountably for the finale of the act, beginning with Pasquale's 'Son tradito, beffeggiato', there is a change of Norinas (Huguet), and Badini reappears as Malatesta (54351).

The Act 3 extracts in this batch of G&Ts open with the Pasquale-Norina scene, 'Signorina in tanta fretta', which leads into Norina's 'waltz' – 'Via, cara sposina' (054094 and 54299). Once again there is the handicap of a white-voiced and shrillish Norina in Emilia Corsi, though her uncle, Antonio, is again heard to advantage. The first part of the patter duet is recorded by Pini-Corsi with Scipioni (54330), and, for no apparent reason, the second with Polese (54280). Giorgini sings a charming 'Come'è gentil' (052149) – he also recorded Ernesto's two earlier arias (2-52421 and 52197) accompanied on the piano by Carlo Sabajno, who later conducted many complete operas for HMV. He is joined by the nimble-voiced Maria Galvany for the 'Tornami a dir' duet (154111). The final moral, 'Bravo, bravo', is sung by Badini, Emilia Corsi and a small chorus (54305).

Act 1

From the fifteen or more recordings of 'Bella siccome un angelo', in addition to those already discussed, there is a version by Scotti (52061) which I do not find as elegant as de Luca's. More to my liking is Heinrich Schlusnus's performance in German (Poly. 62559; LV 110), beginning 'Ach wie ein Engel Himmlisch schön'; he sings it faster than most Italians would, but the rich voice and lovely legato he displays make it a well-worthwhile performance. According to Vivian Liff, Yale University possesses a version by Friedrich Schorr, which sounds a fascinating prospect. Other unheard versions include those by Taurino Parvis, Carmelo Maugeri, Rodolfo Angelini-Fornari, Giuseppe La Pluma and Carl Rittmann.

Fernando Corena and Geraint Evans both give effective voice to Pasquale's 'Un foco insolito'; the first on LXT 3109, the latter on SXL 6262; but this is not really an aria to record on its own. From the many performances of Ernesto's first aria, 'Sogno soave e casto', I have greatly enjoyed Giuseppe Anselmi's as much for his lovely voice as for his style (Fono. 62183), and Schipa's for his unfailing elegance (DA 885). I have never been a great admirer of Dino Borgioli's rather whining way with this kind of music (Col. DQ 1107), nor of de Lucia's very white and open style of singing (Phonotype C2344). Bonci, on the other hand, in his 1908 recording (Fono. 92328), which enlists Corradetti's help, gives us the whole of the scene between Pasquale and his nephew leading up to the aria – indeed the first section (92328) contains better singing from Bonci than the aria proper (92329), which opens to a rather shaky start. There are also versions by Fernando Carpi, Enzo de Muro Lomanto, Cecil Sherwood *alias* Lionello Cecil, Nino Ederle, Giuseppe Acerbi, Constantino Gero and Ferruccio Tagliavini.

Norina's two-part aria is not easy; the singer must show us her charm and her sprightly nature; also that she can be something of a minx and, of course, that she has a pure vocal technique. From among the older singers, I divide the palm equally between Maria Ivogün and Graziella Pareto. Ivogün made two versions, one in German (Od. 76972), the other in Italian (Poly. 85302), in which her very beautiful voice and quite amazing technique, coupled with her complete identification with the character, make hers an outstanding performance. Pareto (DB 567) is a more restrained Norina; but again, the voice is beautiful and limpid, and the style assured. Galli-Curci (DB 259) displays a very lovely legato and is also well in character; Toti dal Monte (DB 5396), on the other hand, only seems to come to life towards the end, and the voice inclines to whiteness. Lucrezia Bori (Edison 82003) I found rather disappointing – she is too subdued, though the voice is lovely and she phrases well.

More recent interpreters of the part have included Margherita Carosio, who makes Norina into a sexy young lady and produces a melting and often beautiful tone (DB 6858); Graziella Sciutti, who is very like Carosio in her approach (Philips N00765 and SXL 2271); and above all the charming Ileana Cotrubas (CBS 76521), whose Norina is a teasing minx with a sparkle in her eye and who sings with panache. Rita Streich (DGM 19137) and Roberta Peters (RCA RB 16018) are lightweight and soubrettish, but both are charming. Vina Bovy, who sang the role successfully in Paris both during and after the war, recorded this aria as well as the 'waltz', the finale, and the duet with Ernesto, sung with the operetta tenor Luis Mariano; all these titles were made in 1944 and have been transferred to a Belgian HMV LP (2C 051-23272). While not denying Bovy's fine technique and dramatic instinct, I find her voice too brittle and not intrinsically beautiful.

Other versions of Norina's aria have been made by Selma Kurz, Consuela Escobar de Castro, Hermine Bosetti, Olympia Boronat, Elvira de Hidalgo, Lucette Korsoff, Fritzi Jokl, Maria Gentile, Alice Nielsen, Licia Albanese, Elda Ribetti, Lina Pagliughi, Lyana Grani, Marie Tauberova (in Czech), Renata Scotto, Teresa Stich-Randall, Pierette Alarie, Maria del Pozzo, Renate Holm, Erna Berger, Erna Sack, Sylvia Geszty, Ruth-Margret-Pütz and Ninon Vallin, who sings only the first part of the aria in her fascinating autobiographical LP, 'Quarante ans de carrière lyrique', made in 1956 when she was 70 (Vega C 30X341).

There are three excellent versions of the 'rehearsal' duet in which Malatesta coaches Norina in the role she is to play. The most famous is probably that made by Sembrich and Scotti in 1906 (Victor 89002; GEMM 164); it only begins half-way through with Malatesta's words 'Brava, brava, bricconcella', which Scotti delivers with a wonderfully mischievous chuckle, and then proceeds to show us just why his Malatesta was so well thought of in New York. Sembrich, nearly 50 when this disc was made, displays her usual artistry. The Bori-de Luca disc (DK 102) was recorded in 1921, and is a far fuller version, beginning with Norina's 'Pronto io son'. Bori is far more inside the part here than in the aria mentioned above, and her coloratura technique and charm are both well exhibited; there are a few cuts in the second section and the end of the duet finds Bori's tone hardening; de Luca, however, is superb throughout. The best version is that by Schöne and Willi Domgraf-Fassbaender (DB 1546 in Italian, and 1563 in German). Perhaps the baritone's Italian is less than idiomatic, but his mercurial performance of Malatesta's role, and the soprano's equally brilliant portrayal of Norina, have yet to be equalled.

Act 2

There are several versions of Ernesto's aria which opens the act, generally known as 'Cerchero lontana terra', though some of the performances open with Ernesto's recitative 'Povero Ernesto'. Of the older versions, that by Leonid Sobinov sung in Russian (G&T 02202), reveals a most. beautiful voice; and even if this Ernesto sounds more akin to Lensky than most it is well worth hearing. Bonci's early record (Fono. 39685) is one of the tenor's best, full of character and a wonderful display of *mezza voce*; his later disc with orchestra (92101) displays some strained singing. de Lucia (Phonotype C2370) is again not for me; but Schipa's 1921 Pathé (54045; GVC 10) shows the tenor at his most elegant.

More recent performances include those by Nicolai Gedda on a Bellini and Donizetti disc, with Mirella Freni (ASD 2473), which is stylish, but a trifle laboured; and Cesare Valletti (Cetra BB 25290) who is almost as fine as Schipa. Other versions include those by Narcisco del Ry, Giovanni Manurita, Cristy Solari, Giacinto Prandelli, Gianni Raimondi, Barry Morell, Giuseppe Acerbi and Carlo Dani. Benvenuto Finelli (Bennet Fynn) essays the cabaletta 'E se fia' (Delta TQD 3038) but the sound is hardly pleasant.

Act 3

The famous *buffo* patter duet has remarkably few versions. Those by de Luca and Corradetti and Pini-Corsi and Polese/Scipioni have already been referred to. The great Baccaloni recorded the scene for Italian Columbia (DQ 663) with Emilio Ghirardini, who is no more than a passable Malatesta. In fact, I found this performance disappointingly dull. The Cambridge Theatre performances of 1945-6 with Stabile and Martin Lawrence are vividly brought to life, however, on LX 1094. I have not heard the versions by Fregosi and Azzolini or Autori and Montemezzi; nor the one in Russian by Georg Ots and O. Raukas, which Vivian Liff calls 'excellent'.

From the many versions of Ernesto's 'Come'è gentil', I have no hesitation in giving pride of place to Caruso's (DB 159; ORL 303), recorded in 1905: a superb example of the tenor's artistry and voice of this period; the sustained use of *mezza voce* and the impeccable turns are something to treasure. Dino Borgioli, if you like that kind of voice, shows a nice sense of style (Col. D 9963) and there is a fascinating and unexpected Martinelli version (DA 326), in which the heroic tenor has a shot at singing a languishing young romantic lover; he is vocally miscast. Piccaver, with a funny piano accompaniment (Od. 76805), sounds as if he is singing through clenched teeth, though the voice itself is more liquid that in some of his later recordings. The German tenor, Josef Traxel, gives a very nice performance (Electrola 7PW552) as does Valletti (Cetra BB 25290). The very light *tenorino* Luigi Fort (Col. DC 192) who sang the role at Glyndebourne in 1939 gives a rather 'pretty' performance. Luciano Pavarotti sings it far too loudly (SXL 6489); by the time he recorded it in 1971 he was already essaying more dramatic roles and seemingly had lost his honeyed *mezza voce*. Unheard versions include those by Gero, Gino Sinimberghi, Roberto d'Alessio and Mario Chamlee.

The last extract widely represented on disc is the Ernesto-Norina duet, 'Tornami dir'. Bonci and the Polish soprano, Regina Pinkert, give a classic performance (Fono. 39341) – a superb example of artists listening to each other while they sing. Schipa recorded the duet three times (four if one includes the complete opera): twice with Galli-Curci and once with dal Monte. The first with Galli-Curci (DA 646; CDN 1024) is superior to the electric recording (DA 1161), which dates from 1933, by which time the soprano's pure limpid voice, and even her agility, were not what they had been ten years earlier. Dal Monte partners Schipa admirably (DA 1351) as she did often on the stage in this opera. Other versions in Italian include those by Aurora Rettore and Dino Borgioli, Surinach and Borgioli, Joan Sutherland and Richard Conrad, Freni and Gedda, Emma Trentini and Acerbi, and Eva Tetrazzini and Acerbi.

Three performances in German have given me great pleasure: Erna Berger and Gino Sinimberghi (Poly. 67536), Ivogün and Erb (Od. 76998), and Erika Köth and Traxel (Electrola 7PW553), of which the best is undoubtedly that by Ivogün and Erb whose vocal partnership remains one of the classic ones in recorded history.

DON PASQUALE

N Norina; *E* Ernesto; *M* Malatesta; *P* Pasquale

1932 Saraceni *N*; Schipa *E*; Poli *M*; Badini *P*/La Scala Chorus and Orch./Sabajno
EMI ⓜ 3C 153 00680-2; Seraphim ⓜ IC 6084

1951 Gatta *N*; Lazzari *E*; Poli *M*; Corena *P*/La Scala Chorus and Orch./La Rosa Parodi
Urania © 5228/2

1952 Aimaro *N*; Oncina *E*; Colombo *M*; Luise *P*/Vienna Chamber Choir, Vienna State Opera Orch./Quadri
Westminster ⓜ WLP 6206/1-2

1952 (abridged) Tuccari *N*; Valletti *E*; Conti *M*; Neroni *P*/Rome Opera Chorus and Orch./Questa Royale ⓜ ROY 1205

1952 Noni *N*; Valletti *E*; Borriello *M*; Bruscantini *P*/Turin Radio Chorus and Orch./Rossi

Cetra © LPS 3242

1954 Guido *N*; Pirino *E*; Monachesi *M*; Mongelli *P*/Rome Opera Chorus and Orch./Ricci
Plymouth ⓜ 45 (3)

1956 Rizzoli *N*; Munteanu *E*; Valdengo *M*; Capecchi *P*/San Carlo Opera Chorus and Orch./Molinari-Pradelli
Philips ⓜ ABL 3140-1; Epic ⓜ 4SC-6016

1956 (live performance) Peters *N*; Valletti *E*; Guarrera *M*; Corena *P*/Metropolitan Opera Chorus and Orch./Schippers
Cetra ⓜ LO 23/2

1964 Maccianti *N*; Benelli *E*; Basiolca Jr *M*; Mariotti *P*/Florence Festival Chorus and Orch./Gracis
DG 2705 039

1965 Sciutti *N*; Oncina *E*; Krause *M*;

Corena *P*/Vienna State Opera
Chorus and Orch./Kertesz
Decca SET 280-1; London OSA
1260
1978 Sills *N*; Kraus *E*; Titus *M*;
Gramm *P*/Ambrosian Opera
Chorus, LSO/Caldwell
Angel SBLX 3871

Excerpts

1933 Tellini *N*; Solari *E*; Conati *M*;
Guiliani *P*/La Scala Chorus and
Orch./Molajoli
Columbia CQX 10100-5
1953 (in German) Streich *N*;

Wehofschütz *E*; Schmitt-Walter
M; Greindl *P*/Bavarian Radio
Chorus and Orch./Lehmann
DG ⓜ DG 17053
1957 (in German) Köth *N*; Traxel *E*;
Cordes *M*; Strienz *P*/German
Opera Chorus, Berlin
SO/Schmidt-Boelcke
EMI ⓜ 1C 047 28578M
1970 (in German) Rothenberger *N*;
Schreier *E*; Leib *M*; Suss
P/Leipzig Radio Choir, Dresden
Staatskapelle/Kurz
EMI 1C 063 29055

Macbeth

HAROLD ROSENTHAL

Verdi's *Macbeth* has never enjoyed universal popularity. Its vicissitudes and the differences between the composer's two versions (1847 and 1865) are admirably discussed by Julian Budden in the chapter devoted to the opera in his excellent *The Operas of Verdi,* volume 1 (London, 1973). Promised productions in London in 1861 and 1879 never materialized, but it was given in Dublin in 1869 with Pauline Viardot as Lady Macbeth. It was not heard in England, however, until the famous 1938 production at Glyndebourne under Fritz Busch, with Vera Schwarz as Lady Macbeth (not Margherita Grandi, that was the following year) and Francesco Valentino, with Carl Ebert producing, and sets and costumes by Caspar Neher. It was with *Macbeth* that the Verdi revival in Germany really got under way at Dresden in April 1928, when Robert Burg sang the title role, Eugenie Burkhardt that of Lady Macbeth, and Ivar Andrésen that of Banquo. The German version by George Göhler was soon heard in other German houses.

The first complete recording of the opera is the Urania set, based on the 1943 Vienna State Opera production under Karl Böhm, which was part of a Verdi cycle that Böhm organized that year to commemorate the 130th anniversary of Verdi's birth. Vienna heard three singers as Macbeth at that time, Paul Schöffler, Hans Hotter (which must have been a wonderful experience), and Mathieu Ahlersmeyer, who is the Macbeth of the recording (a radio broadcast); the rest of the cast remained virtually unchanged during the two seasons before the State Opera closed down. Elisabeth Höngen, whom Böhm called in his diary 'the greatest tragedian in the world', was certainly one of the great singing-actresses of her day but despite what Böhm wrote about her, I find her Lady Macbeth less impressive dramatically than I had hoped – the trouble is that she sings the role too beautifully, and her voice sounds too soft-grained, at least in this performance. Ahlersmeyer was, like Höngen, a highly regarded artist in Germany and Austria. He had been a member of the Klemperer ensemble at the Kroll Opera in 1930; he then went to Hamburg where he sang his first Macbeth under the young Böhm. I find his performance, despite its being in German, convincing, idiomatic, and beautifully sung. Highlights of this performance can be heard on the two-album set devoted to Ahlersmeyer on the Acanta label; it includes the Act 1 Macbeth-Lady Macbeth duet after Duncan's murder and Macbeth's Act 4 aria.

The RCA recording is, like the Urania set, based on a famous stage production, this one at the Metropolitan, New York, in February 1959, its first performance in the house. The production should have had Callas as Lady Macbeth, but she refused to sing that role followed by Violetta as Bing wanted her to (she did not mind doing it the other way round), and made her famous statement, 'My voice is not an elevator.' She was replaced by Leonie Rysanek, making her Metropolitan debut, with Erich Leinsdorf, replacing at very short notice Mitropoulos, who had been rehearsing the production but suffered a heart attack two weeks before the first night. Rysanek's Lady Macbeth is beautifully vocalized and yet at the same time highly dramatic. Warren, after a less than impressive opening scene, due more to the recording that his singing, gives one of his greatest and most impressive performances. His final aria, 'Pietà, rispetto, amore', is Verdi singing at its best, although it includes an unwritten final A flat. Macbeth's death scene from the 1847 version is also included. Bergonzi is a lyrical Macduff and Jerome Hines a noble Banquo. There is plenty of drive in Leinsdorf's conducting.

The first of Decca's two recordings is excitingly conducted by Schippers with a real Verdian sweep. Birgit Nilsson first sang Lady Macbeth in Stockholm in October 1947 under Busch, and although nearly twenty years later she had developed into the world's leading Wagner soprano, her amazing voice still had little or no difficulty with Lady Macbeth's music, although there is some fudging in the coloratura of the 'Brindisi' and her diction is not all one wants in the sleepwalking scene; nor does she succeed in creating a complete character. Giuseppe Taddei's solid voice, fine musicianship and gift for characterization make him a Macbeth to be reckoned with. Giovanni Foiani sings Banquo with generous tone, and Bruno Prevedi's Macduff, while not as mellifluously sung as Bergonzi's, has much to commend it. There are a number of cuts, some of which, as in the scene of Duncan's arrival, are neither logical nor forgivable.

Decca's second recording should have had Tito Gobbi in the title-role, but he fell ill and was replaced by Fischer-Dieskau in one of his self-conscious moods, dotting every musical 'i' and crossing every dramatic 't'; but still, he treats us to some wonderful singing, especially in the scene with the apparitions and in his last-act aria. Pavarotti is a rousing Macduff, Ghiaurov an admirable Banquo, and Lamberto Gardelli, at that time better in the recording studio than in the opera house, gives a fiery and impassioned account of the score, which is given complete, and so includes what Andrew Porter has called 'the best ballet music Verdi ever wrote'. And Lady Macbeth? Elena Souliotis goes to pieces in her opening scene, and rarely recovers.

Then in 1976, came *two* complete performances; one from DG under Claudio Abbado, based on La Scala's production (by Giorgio Strehler) that had opened the 1975/76 season there; the second under Riccardo Muti made in London during the summer of 1976. Both are strongly cast, but the palm must go to the DG set for, being based on one of the Scala's best productions (despite a few cast changes that include the luxury of having Domingo as Macduff), it has more than the whiff of the opera house about it.

Shirley Verrett on DG is outstanding as Lady Macbeth, far more subtle in her singing than Fiorenza Cossotto on HMV – and, after all, Lady Macbeth was by her nature a subtle schemer; Verrett is, except for Callas, the finest Lady Macbeth on disc. Piero Cappuccilli, inspired by both Abbado and his 'Lady', is in superb voice and gives us a lyrically sung but at the same time a virile and at times introvert Macbeth. Sherrill Milnes, despite his superb voice is, as so often, a self-conscious singer here, and his performance lacks spontaneity. José Carreras (HMV) has the edge over Domingo as Macduff, and Raimondi (also HMV) is a warmer and more human Banquo than Ghiaurov. Muti's reading is more elemental and at times more exciting than Abbado's, but the latter sees the work as a whole and, because he does not drive his forces as vehemently as does Muti, the moments of tension are more effective.

The Abbado recording includes all the ballet music and Macbeth's short arioso before his death. The Muti set has, on its sixth side, Lady Macbeth's original 'Trionfai' in Act 2, which was replaced in 1965 by 'La luce langue'; the original finale to Act 3; and Macbeth's death scene 'Mal per me che m'affidai'.

The Scala 1952 *Macbeth* was broadcast on 7 December 1952 and the tapes preserved by Radio Italiana; this forms the basis of the Cetra-Live issue. Callas sounds, as expected and remembered, in a word – superb; and one regrets that she never later recorded the role complete. Enzo Mascherini is what the Italians would describe as a 'correct' Macbeth; but he was dull, and in the theatre Callas certainly deserved a more worthy partner. De Sabata's conducting is fiery and exciting.

There is an amazing highlights disc on an American label, called Royale, LP 1409, with a fictitious cast, conductor and orchestra (Inge Camphausen, Herta Schenk, Horst Wilhelm, Gerhard Ramms, Berlin Symphony Orchestra, conductor Gerd Rubahn) – in reality these are Dorothy Dow, Marko Rothmüller, James Johnston, Frederick Dalberg, and the Royal Philharmonic Orchestra under Gui at Glyndebourne in 1952. Dow was an underrated singer, and although her Lady Macbeth may lack evil, it is extremely well sung; Rothmüller's familiar nasal tone is instantly recognizable, but what a good artist he was; and Dalberg's Banquo was solidly sung.

There are comparatively few recordings of individual arias from the opera. Lady Macbeth's three great scenes and Macbeth's final aria being the most recorded numbers from the opera.

Act 1

Lady Macbeth's extended *scena*, beginning with the reading of the letter from Macbeth, 'Nel di della vittoria', is followed by the entry of the messenger with the news that Duncan is expected, and this leads into the exciting cabaletta, 'Or tutti sorgete', Callas's 1959 recording (33CX 1628; SAX 2293) is without doubt the finest performance of this scene that exists, and one of the greatest things Callas ever committed to disc; every other Lady Macbeth pales beside her. Nilsson's 1963 version (SXL 6033) of the scene is more exciting than her performance in the complete set in which she later participated. Souliotis likewise recorded the scene (SXL 6306) before she made her complete recording of the opera – in her case some four years earlier. In the first part of the *scena* she is rather too deliberate, and throughout there is an over-use of her chest voice, but the cabaletta is most impressive. Gwyneth Jones (SXL 6376) displays a forward, bright voice, and there is much dramatic thrust in her performance. Grace Bumbry (DG LPM 13987) is cool and calculating, and although she sings well enough, she never sweeps you off your feet. By contrast Sylvia Sass (SXL 6921) shakes the listener out of his complacency, not by any subtle means, but because she exaggerates the situation by over-dramatizing it and making abrupt contrasts from one moment to the next. There are also versions by Inge Borkh (Decca CEP 645), Margaret Tynes (LPX 1074) and a private one by Leyla Gencer, in her day a fiery Lady Macbeth. The Act 1 duet of the Macbeths has been recorded by two Dutch singers – Christina Deutekom and Jan Derksen (5C 055 24966).

Act 2

Lady Macbeth's 'La luce langue', which has often been regarded as an early and shorter kind of 'Tu che la vanità', receives performances from Callas, Nilsson and Bumbry on the same discs as listed above (the Callas is also on SLS 5104); again it is Callas who walks away with the honours. Margherita Grandi (DB 6740) gives us a memory of her Glyndebourne performances and sings with great authority and sweep; Martha Mödl, who sang Lady Macbeth in Berlin soon after the war, follows the German tradition of casting a mezzo-soprano in the role (Sigrid Onegin, the most famous, unfortunately did not record anything from this opera). Despite the German text I find Mödl's performance (Telef. 3891) riveting. Inge Borkh sang the role in Germany and America in the 1950s, and she sings the aria (Decca LW 5335) in a cool, clear voice displaying a real sense of drama. Sass (SXL 6921) exhibits all her vocal weaknesses, breaking phrases, screaching out her top notes and making sudden changes of register; it is if she is trying to caricature Callas. The Czech soprano, Kniplova, gives a performance that is clumsy and not really worth considering. (Two other East European singers have recorded the *scena*; Sigrid Kehl and Raisa Babreva.)

Also from Act 2 is Banquo's 'Come dal ciel precipita', a typical Verdian bass aria, and an underrated one. One would have thought that it might have attracted more basses as an item to record than it has. To make its full effect, however, one needs to hear the preceding chorus of murderers, like 'Zitti, zitti' in *Rigoletto,* and Banquo's final words should, as indicated in the score, 'be heard in the distance' and sung out at the same level as the aria. Not even Ghiaurov's excellent performance on his Verdi recital disc (SXL 6643), which gives the scene in its entirety and has the advantage of the LSO under Claudio Abbado, follows that instruction. Ivar Andrésen, the excellent Norwegian bass, long a member of the Dresden and Berlin State Operas, and well-known at pre-war Bayreuth and Covent Garden, sings the aria in a rich firm and solid tone with a touch of Russian quality in the voice (DWX 1610; LV 45). Italo Tajo sang Banquo in the first post-war Glyndebourne *Macbeth* at the Edinburgh Festival and also in the 1952 Scala production; he recorded the aria during the war, with the Scala orchestra conducted by Alberto Erede (Telef. GX 61019); the voice is young-sounding and the performance is hurried. Theo Adam, better known for his Wagner performances, sings the aria in German and gives a most sensitive performance of it, displaying a rich and beautiful tone (Telef. SAT 22504). I have not heard the version by Luigi Nicoletti-Korman or those by Norman Treigle, Bonaldo Giaoitti and Ian Wallace.

Strangely enough, except for a Callas 'off-the-air' disc, there are no recordings of the 'Brindisi', which one would have thought a 'must' for Verdi sopranos.

Act 4

The lovely chorus of exiles has all but been neglected in favour of those from *Nabucco, Lombardi* and other works; there were one or two German versions and one in Italian conducted by Basile (VIC 1741).

Macduff's aria, 'Ah, la paterno mano', has attracted several tenors. The most famous was Caruso (DB 118; ORL 314), who sings it in a peerless fashion, displaying his usual wonderful phrasing and giving the words all the weight and emotion they deserve. By comparison, Bergonzi's performance (Philips 6599 923), beautifully sung though it is, pales; del Monaco (LXT 5127) sounds loud and coarse, and Pavarotti (SXL 6377) is dramatic and lachrymose, though he displays good breath control especially in the last phrase. Other versions include those by Ernst Kozub, Franciso Lazaro, Jess Thomas, Rudolf Shock and Ludovic Spiess.

Lady Macbeth's sleepwalking scene has been widely recorded. Gertrud Rünger, the German mezzo-soprano who developed into a Wagnerian dramatic soprano in the mid 1930s, was the Lady Macbeth of Krauss's 1933/34 *Macbeth* production in Vienna, and her performance of a somewhat truncated sleepwalking scene (Decca LY 6114) reveals her exceptional dramatic gifts and vocal extension. Grandi gives us the scene in full on three 78 sides (DB 6739-40) with Vera Terry as the Lady-in-Waiting and Ernest Frank as the Doctor, and there is added interest in that Sir Thomas Beecham conducts the Royal Philharmonic Orchestra. This is a highly dramatic performance despite one or two moments of vocal uncertainty from Grandi. Two other German dramatic mezzos can be heard in the same scene: Höngen (Poly. 18047), moving and beautiful, and Mödl (Telef. E 3891), more dramatic and in curdled voice.

Callas completes her three Lady Macbeth excerpts with a rather tentative exit, but there are no problems there as far as Nilsson and Grace Bumbry are concerned. There follow three sopranos who, as far as I know, have never sung the role on the stage: Régine Crespin, Leontyne Price, and Montserrat Caballé. Crespin (ALP 2275), a warm feminine singer if ever there was one, is not by temperament a Lady Macbeth, and ducks the final D flat – nor does Prêtre's insensitive conducting help matters. Price (SB 6742) likewise seems out of her depth as far as the character is concerned and the scene just does not come off. Caballé (ASD 2787) gives a good performance indeed, but her later (1977) recording (SXLR 6825) does not begin to convince. The Greek mezzo-soprano, Elena Nikolaidi (Col. 72884D), approaches the high D flat at the end (no octave drop after it) much as Calvé did (not in *Macbeth*, of course) with a kind of closed-mouth effect. Despite the dramatic performance, her voice often has a hollow sound and the vibrato is disturbing. Sylvia Sass (SXL 6841) is exciting. There are also performances by Margaret Tynes and Elena Stoickovac.

Macbeth's beautiful aria, 'Pietá, rispetto, amore', could well serve as a touchstone for Verdi baritones, much in the same way that Alvaro's 'O tu che in seno agli angeli' in *La forza del destino* does for tenors. It would almost seem to go without saying therefore that Battistini's account of the aria (DB 199) is hard to equal. Two other baritones of that period recorded the aria; Francesco Maria Bonini (Fono. 39672), whose career lasted from 1896 until 1927; and the Spanish baritone Ramon Blanchart (419 2124), who sang from 1885 until 1920 and was a great standby of the Boston Opera Company. Alexander Sved, the Macbeth in the 1938 Scala and 1939 Teatro Colón performances, sings with authority and a beautiful, if at times gruff, tone (DB 5366). Leonard Warren recorded the aria before his stage appearances in the role (VIC LM 2543) and sings in his usual generous manner. Giampiero Malaspina (Parlo. RO 30066) is clumsy and unmusical, and I have not heard Ivan Petrov (Rem. 199-93) with piano accompaniment or the versions by Jan Derksen and Nevin Miller. The most recent performance is that by Sherrill Milnes (RCA ARLI 0851) who not only sings the aria, but also returns after the battle to die, but not before he has sung 'Mal per me ch m'affidai', which can hardly be called an aria as it is so short. Julian Budden points out that although the scene is impressive, to include it when performing the 1865 version is to go against Verdi's own wishes; the composer wrote to Escudier, 'I too am of the opinion that we should change the death of Macbeth, but I can't think of anything better than a final hymn.' Perhaps Verdi was not lucky enough to have heard the aria and death scene sung as impressively and lovingly as they are by Milnes.

MACBETH

LM Lady Macbeth; *M* Macbeth; *Mac* Macduff; *B* Banquo

1943 (abridged in German) Höngen *LM*; Ahlersmeyer *M*; Witt *Mac*; Alsen *B*/Vienna State Opera Chorus, VPO/Böhm
Urania ⓜ URLP 220

1952 (live performance) Callas *LM*; Mascherini *M*; Penno *Mac;* Tajo *B*/La Scala Chorus and Orch./De Sabata
Cetra ⓜ LO 10/3;
Turnabout ⓜ THS 65131–3

1959 Rysanek *LM*; Warren *M*; Bergonzi *Mac*; Hines *B*/Metropolitan Opera Chorus and Orch./Leinsdorf
RCA VICS 6121/3–1

1964 Nilsson *LM*; Taddei *M*; Prevedi *Mac*; Fioani *B*/Santa Cecilia Academy Chorus and Orch./Schippers

Decca SET 282–4;
London OSA 1380

1970 Souliotis *LM*; Fischer-Dieskau *M*; Pavarotti *Mac*; Ghiaurov *B*/Ambrosian Singers, LPO/Gardelli
Decca SET 510–2;
London OSA 13102

1976 Verrett *LM*; Cappuccilli *M*; Domingo *Mac*; Ghiaurov *B*/La Scala Chorus and Orch./Abbado
DG 2709 062 ④ 3371 022

1976 Cossotto *LM*; Milnes *M*; Carreras *Mac*; Raimondi *B*/Ambrosian Opera Chorus, New Philharmonia/Muti
HMV SLS 992 ④ TC–SLS 992;
Angel SCLX 3833(Q) ④ 4X3S–3833

Rigoletto

RICHARD OSBORNE

Though two complete acoustical recordings of *Rigoletto* were made during the first world war, bold ventures whose existence serves to underline the opera's enormous popularity, it was not until 1927 and Sabjano's electrical HMV set that the opera took a serious foothold in the gramophone repertory. Complete on fifteen 78 records, that set still has a distinctly solid feel to it, a feeling which is reinforced by Sabjano's generally stately tempi and a Rigoletto, the baritone Piazza, who, though he is superb in his great outburst to the courtiers, is generally no more than reliable: strong-voiced but with a tendency to lapse into Scarpia-like emphases and *can belto* thrusts. The Spanish tenor, Tino Folger, is a sensitive, stylish Duke, almost effeminate, with a certain Schipa-like quality in 'Parmi veder'. Lina Pagliughi, who subsequently gave us a celebrated account of the role of Gilda on the Cetra label, is here raw.

Three years later the Columbia company moved into La Scala and under the somewhat more invigorating direction of Lorenzo Molajoli recorded a complete set with Mercedes Capsir as Gilda, Dino Borgioli as the Duke, and the veteran Riccardo Stracciari in the title role. Though he lacks the necessary legato for the long drawn-out final movement of 'Cortigiani', Stracciari is elsewhere wonderfully incisive, etching out Verdi's lines with an exemplary clarity, making it difficult for us not to thrill to the voice's remarkable focus and oaken power. The tenor is also appealing, and though he and Capsir – a hard-voiced though not necessarily hard-faced Gilda – are not exemplary stylists, they do well. The set, which is recorded with admirable clarity and presence, lacks pathos and misses many of the score's half-lights, but the kernel of the drama is here.

The 1944 Berlin set has a starry but not always apt cast, and the performance is in German. Heinrich Schlusnus's Rigoletto is the principal interest, for his fine high baritone and naturally humane way with Verdi's vocal lines make their mark, even in German and with Schlusnus in his fifty-sixth year. By contrast, Helge Roswaenge is fearfully Teutonic, tying Piave's text up into awkward knots of sound. 'Teurer Name' is appealingly sung by Erna Berger, but many will find her Lolita-like tones too girlish by half. Robert Heger conducts with character but, affecting as the performance is at times, it never really convinces us that it is anything other than *ersatz*. Berger appears again, with Leonard Warren as Rigoletto and Jan Peerce as the Duke, in what was to be the first fully-fledged LP set, made in America under the lively direction of Renato Cellini in 1949. Here Berger, now singing in Italian, gives a more mature, assured – and touching – performance. Warren is an imposing, sympathetic Rigoletto; 'Deh non parlare' is lovingly projected and spun, making his use of the once-familiar cut in the difficult first full statement of 'Ah! veglia o donna' especially frustrating. Peerce is a tight-voiced, unappealing Duke.

Ferruccio Tagliavini in the Cetra set is, by contrast, marvellously appealing, 'Questa, o quella' is liquid-toned and light as thistledown, helped by a typically expert accompaniment from Angelo Questa and the Turin Radio Orchestra. Later, 'Parmi veder' is equally intoxicating, equally lovely after a particularly brilliant recitative, the Duke's anger showing vividly through. Giuseppe Taddei's Rigoletto is also the real thing. His 'Pari siamo' may not be, in all respects, the equal of Gobbi's (see below) and he occasionally aspirates divisions, but he effects with skill the shifts between the lovingly sung duets with his daughter ('Ah, veglia, o donna' not cut this time) and the rages of 'Cortigiani'. On the face of it, Pagliughi is no less of a soubrette than Berger, and her breath control was not always faultless at this stage in her career, but she has the gift of dropping in phrases magically, confirming, among other things, Hegel's contention that the Italian language was made for Italian throats as surely as satins and silks were made for women of fashion and *pâté de foie gras* for the throats of gourmets. 'Caro nome' is down a semitone, but the coloratura is beautifully judged and the manner is never less than fresh and appealing. With sensitive conducting that goes some way beyond mere accompaniment, this remains one of the best of all complete *Rigoletto* recordings. I have not heard the 1949 set in Russian nor the 1951 Remington or the 1952 Cetra Live, with Callas: she is well represented below.

The 1954 set with Aldo Protti, Mario del Monaco and Hilde Gueden need not detain us. The 1955 Callas recording, though, requires detailed consideration. With Tito Gobbi as Rigoletto and Callas as Gilda it is the kind of set to which one instinctively turns; and, certainly, it is a memorable performance, though hearing it again I can see why, over the years, certain caveats have been entered about it. The miracle is Callas's Gilda, a performance which so rivets attention that one wishes she had a finer stylist than Giuseppe di Stefano as the man for whom she gives her life. There is in Callas's assumption of Gilda, a taut, virginal beauty, an inner radiance born of innocence, love and fear, which compels the respect. In a recording which is sometimes oddly opaque for the period, and against voices sometimes less sure of focus, she stands out movingly.

The characteristically masked tone is nowhere to be heard, for only colourings that are radically pure will serve Callas's Gilda. 'Caro nome', which sounds a trifle strange, out of context, on a recital disc (33CX 1681), is here unforgettable, with a fading, vanishing close as compelling as anything Callas, or Verdi, did in the somnambulistic line. Generally, Tullio Serafin is not at his urgent best. He conducts a performance notable for its care and for a certain burgeoning urgency at nodal points (the discovery of Gilda's abduction, for example) than for anything approaching early Verdian fire.

As for Gobbi, in the quieter, more confiding moments of his duets with Gilda I find him disappointing, the voice unable to support the effects at which he is aiming; a certain amount of vocal manipulation, the husbanding and covering of tones, is evident. This leads to self-consciousness in the singing. Yet in the other colloquies he is incomparable – I think of his exchanges with the courtiers in Act 3, all waspish irony, strange bemusement and fear; and the tense little scene with Gilda at the start of the final act. His 'Pari siamo' is not, at all points, the vocal equal of his exemplary earlier 78 version (DB 21227; HLM 7018) but it is none the less, memorable. This is, in sum, an important *Rigoletto*, and one to have, but it is not perhaps the potent, vibrant thing that might have been or that recollection makes it.

The 1957 RCA set has Jussi Björling as the Duke, cool and formal; and although those inimitable tones carry their own special thrill, his refusal to sing quietly is worrying. Robert Merrill seems more alive to the nuances of the role of Rigoletto here than in his later recording under Solti, but the vocal quality itself is less pleasing. Roberta Peters sings with a blanched, virginal quality, vibrant and thin *in alt*, with boyish tones that are not at all pleasing. Jonel Perlea conducts with a Toscanini-like impetus (and also sings in 'La donna è mobile') but rarely secures Toscanini's precision in Verdi or his singing cantabile line. By and large, it is not a set to remember and it was soon eclipsed by Francesco Molinari-Pradelli's Philips recording. Neither Richard Tucker, as the Duke, nor Renato Capecchi, as Rigoletto, sings his role as to the manner born, but the set has a most winning Gilda in the person of Gianna d'Angelo.

By the early 1960s, though, *Rigoletto* was going into a decline, increasingly the despair of reviewers looking for a good stereo alternative to the Cetra set. Gianandrea Gavazzeni's 1960 HMV set answered few prayers, though it has the merit of a generally Italianate style, the better of Renata Scotto's two Gildas, a preview of Alfredo Kraus's mettlesome Duke (he is to be heard again under Solti) and Ettore Bastianini's black-browed Rigoletto, a performance geared, more or less exclusively, to Rigoletto's grander moments. The conducting is competent, but Gavazzeni leaves no special mark on the score.

The first, and less successful, of Joan Sutherland's two sets appeared in 1962. In her recital record 'The Art of the Prima Donna' (SXL 2257)

Sutherland had given us a lovely 'Caro nome', not settled in every detail, but touched with some magical utterances. In the 1962 recording, though, everything is drift and dream – potentially light, bright tone heard through a nebula of half-formed words. (By contrast, the 1972 recording is both rapt and articulate.) It is true that Sutherland, as so often, draws from her colleagues lovely *bel canto* singing, but to my ears Cornell MacNeil's Rigoletto, lyrically affecting as it undoubtedly is, ends up not as a vital dramatic portrait but as a singing lesson.

And, in the DG set, a singing lesson is what many will see Dietrich Fischer-Dieskau's Rigoletto as being. Admittedly, after long hours spent with Italian baritones of middling musicianship, it is a joy to hear so wide a tonal palette being drawn upon, to hear the harmonic subtleties of Verdi's music being so magically attended to. Yet, as with this singer's Macbeth, the authority and potential malevolence of the character is sacrificed. There is also much self-conscious rhythmic pointing and tricks of accentuation. What's more, in the duets this obviously *bel canto* Rigoletto is poorly served by a Gilda, Scotto, who is edgy and out of sorts. ('Caro nome' is true-toned – until the cadenza – but slow to the point of distraction.) Here Rafael Kubelik is too subservient to his, on paper, distinguished cast. His reading lacks fire, a fact which compromises the performance of the tenor, Carlo Bergonzi, who needs more characterful accompaniments than these if his stylish impersonation of the Duke is to gather about it any real dramatic credibility. Notwithstanding many passing beauties, this is an oddly static and uninvolving *Rigoletto*.

Ironically, it appeared in the same month as one of the fieriest of modern performances: Solti's. It was a cruel juxtaposition, for both sets tended to suffer by their proximity. Heard at a safe distance, the Solti set has a great deal to command it. There is Kraus's fiery Duke, and Merrill's second Rigoletto, warmly human without ever being lachrymose, handling the lyrical elements in the role more successfully than on the earlier Perlea set. Anna Moffo is a touching Gilda. She may at times lack the technical capacity to convey love-lorn inwardness, but her evident femininity is matched with an obvious ingenuousness. Helped by Solti's accompaniments, which often point the music forward to the subtly orchestrated worlds of *Aida* and *Otello,* Moffo leaves her mark. Elsewhere Solti often drives the score very hard, and there is also a bright, artificial-sounding acoustic and a wide stereo spread to cope with. At times it is possible to think the conducting, and some of the singing (Merrill's 'Cortigiani', for instance) externalized; yet Moffo's hauntingly unpredictable Gilda and the sensitivity and sheer motoric impulse of Solti's conducting are things one does not easily forget.

HMV's later, 1967, set, conducted by Molinari-Pradelli, is well produced, but Reri Grist is pert and cool in the Peters style, and MacNeil is a gruffer and much less vocally assured Rigoletto than in the earlier Sutherland set. Nicolai Gedda has his moments as the Duke and the young Ruggero Raimondi puts in an appearance as Monterone, but as a whole this is a faithful *Rigoletto*, consistent without being at any point memorable.

The 1970s have produced only two complete recordings – a Dresden recording on Acanta, with an Italian cast and Rolando Panerai, that most lovable of baritones, once again proving himself unsuited to the role of Rigoletto (note his oddly explosive singing on a Columbia highlights record of the mid 1950s – 33CX 1305 – with the often excellent Mattiwilda Dobbs) and a second complete recording with Sutherland in the role of Gilda.

By and large, this second Sutherland set is magnificent. Throughout it is both splendidly recorded and well conducted. Occasionally in the past I have regretted Richard Bonynge's inability to generate tension as opposed to speed, but his conducting here is marvellously taut and idiomatic. Sutherland's Gilda is lovingly sung, lovingly phrased and much better acted than before. Only occasional discolouring of vowels in slower music (especially in 'Tutte le feste') could possibly be said to detract from the effectiveness of what is – along with the Callas and the Pagliughi – the best of all Gildas to date.

The great attraction of the set, though, is its all-round excellence. In the *comprimario* roles there is a stunning array of voices: Martti Talvela as Sparafucile, Huguette Tourangeau as Maddalena and singers like Ricardo Cassinelli, Christian du Plessis and Kiri Te Kanawa in even smaller roles. Milnes is a leonine Rigoletto. 'Pari siamo' is with him a powerful *cri de coeur*. Were he to rein the voice more, holding back its full weight for those moments when Verdi writes *con tutta forza*, and were he to deploy his affecting *mezza voce* more often, this would be an outstanding assumption. Perhaps the part lies a shade high for him at times – there are opaque tones in 'Deh non parlare' – but once again Sutherland and Bonynge seem to draw from their Rigoletto sensitive, literate singing of considerable *bel canto* refinement. As for Luciano Pavarotti, he is effortlessly stylish, full of elegance and insouciance. His rendering of 'E il sol dell'anima', a classic account aquiver with sexual ardour, is wonderfully free in tone and beautifully attuned to the letter and the spirit of Verdi's text. He also commands a thrilling high D. After the comparative blankness of the late 1950s and the 1960s this fine set came as a blessed relief.

Two records of extracts deserve special mention. First a record of highlights recorded in English by the Sadler's Wells company in 1962. The selection begins with 'Questa o quella', moves to 'E il sol dell'anima' ('Pari siamo' and the first Rigoletto-Gilda duet are omitted) and then on through highlights which more or less select themselves. The record establishes Donald Smith as an exceptional interpreter of the Duke, a role which has eluded better-known international names. Elisabeth Harwood's 'Caro nome' suffers from being taken at dictation speed, but there are many beautiful effects and a lovely final cadence. Peter Glossop's 'Cortigiani' is now murderously angry, now heart-rending in its pleas for news of Gilda, big and melodramatic. The record which is conducted by James Lockhart, says a lot for the musical standards of Sadler's Wells in the early 1960s. The quartet is especially successful.

And then there is Toscanini: only the final act, alas, but a wholly compelling experience with a fine cast which includes Warren, Zinka Milanov and, as a most impressive Maddalena, Nan Merriman. The death of Gilda, from the intensely singing orchestral cantabile beneath Rigoletto's 'Non morir mio tesoro', through to the *Aida*-like textures of 'Lassù in cielo' – exquisitely placed by Milanov within the line of Toscanini's great reading – is as fine as any on record. This is a performance to set beside, say, Toscanini's recording of *Un ballo in maschera*, from the first intimations of darkness on the strings at the very start of the act, through the wonderfully conducted 'La donna è mobile' – Peerce is the singer, but it is Toscanini who sets the music winging irresistibly along – and on through to the elementally vivid account of the storm trio. Everywhere one is aware of a beautifully controlled rhythmic flow, of vibrance, beauty and line. Notice how compellingly Toscanini leads us into the famous D flat Andante section of the quartet, and how lyrically he conducts it once there. (He refuses Milanov the option of a high D flat at the end, bringing out instead the hauntingly quiet crescendo beneath the voices.) The conspiratorial music which follows is shown to be possessed of uniquely evocative colourings, colours which Toscanini shows us are available on Verdi's orchestral palette as early as 1850, for all that they recur in their most tellingly atmospheric form at the close of the first scene of Act 3 of *Falstaff*.

With the exception of the great Rigoletto solos, the solo and duet items (and, of course, the quartet) tend to underline the fact that *Rigoletto* is, among other things a test of vocal personality. Listen to 'Caro nome' a score of times or spin your way relentlessly through an eternity of 'Questa o quella's' and you will be none the wiser about Gilda or the Duke, whose musical personalities remain fixed; beautiful, brilliant surfaces in which images of great singers can be clearly described. In this sense *Rigoletto* is a singers' piece and the quartet its apotheosis. And yet the score as a whole demonstrates a remarkable sleight of hand on Verdi's part: *bel canto* lyricism made the purveyor (in the music of Gilda and the Duke) of feelings which *seem* real, actual, psychologically germane. One character, though, goes beyond this seeming truth, beyond predetermined limits of character. And that is Rigoletto himself, a role in which Verdi challenges the actor, and teases the baritone voice, with mordent unconcern, in and out of the supplest lyricism and the darkest bravura. 'Read Shakespeare. He is never afraid of compromising his character', wrote Pushkin. This brilliant observation could equally well be applied to Verdi and to the role of Rigoletto, though in arriving at so rounded and

Shakespearian a portrayal Verdi frequently goes near to compromising his singer as well.

If we begin near the beginning we encounter at once one of the most leonine of Rigolettos, Titta Ruffo. He recorded substantial extracts from the role, which have since been gathered together on a single LP side (COLH 155 or ORL 217). They are 'Pari siamo' (DB 502), the duet with Gilda in Act 2 (DB 175; DA 564), the exchanges leading up to 'Cortigiani' (slightly cut) and 'Cortigiani' itself in two sections, ending at 'Difende l'honor' and resuming for the D flat major epilogue. (DB 175, DA 165). Then there is 'Piangi, piangi, fanciulla' (DB 177), its cabaletta (DA 564) and the final scene (DB 176). This final scene is with Graziella Pareto, and it is most successful. Unfortunately the other duets are to some extent compromised by the shrill-sounding Giuseppina Finli-Magrina and Maria Galvany; but only to some extent, for Ruffo himself is in majestic voice. Ruffo's Rigoletto has about it a massive authority. It is powerful, black-browed and intensely compelling, an assumption of the role in which fierce emotions are shaped by a wonderfully sure vocal technique and an ability to control emotion without distorting it. Twice in 'Pari siamo' and once towards the end of 'Cortigiani', emotion threatens to break palpably through. Yet the reading is never lachrymose. Histrionic and vocal elements are held in a tremulous balance, gloriously so. Significantly, nothing is wasted. Even the voice's by-products – its moments of quick vibrato, for instance – are put to creative use, so consummate is Ruffo's art. For a baritone who has at his disposal so ringing and majestic a high G – a baritone who can sing *tutta forza* with ease – the restraint and, at crucial moments, the deeply inward nature of the singing are remarkable. Thus the concluding cry, 'Ah, no è follia!', and its inward preface, 'Mi cogliera sventura', sit in the most affecting juxtaposition. Ruffo's is, in all respects, an exemplary 'Pari siamo', with the smallest details (the aping of the Duke's voice, the smooth descent on 'altr'uomo qui mi cangio') perfectly graded, contributing to the larger impression.

Only one baritone has, in my experience, matched Ruffo – provided, in fact, the perfect complement, sweeter and more humane – and that is Tito Gobbi. It would be foolish even to attempt to detail the many beauties and subtleties in Gobbi's 1950 recording of 'Pari siamo' (DB 21227; HLM 7018); as vain and foolish an endeavour as trying to capture in words the vocal and interpretative beauties of Sir John Gielgud's more or less contemporaneous recording of Hamlet. If the word 'Shakespearian' means, more or less, compendious – catching in the finest balance the many-faceted mystery of human personality – then Gobbi's recreation of Rigoletto's great soliloquy is certainly Shakespearian. Here anger sits side by side with regret, the power to mock is transformed in a moment to the sweetest kind of vulnerability, scorn turns to despair, self-pity to the noblest rousings. Gobbi's Rigoletto, on the evidence of this great record, is the interpretative equal of Ruffo's yet more humane. It is for me the epitome of all that the opera is, and if I could have no other representation of the score on record this would be it.

Although the artists cannot match Ruffo's achievement, records by two baritones from the early years of recording will be of interest to collectors. Francesco Maria Bonini's 'Cortigiani' (Fono. 39071. Milan 1904) is a good representative example of his art, and there are half a dozen records of items from *Rigoletto* recorded by Antonio Magini-Coletti for Zonophone ('Pari siamo' on 1509) and Fonotipia, including a further 'Pari siamo' (39434), a 'Cortigiani' (39441) and duet records with Giannina Russ and Oreste Luppi (the latter a dull record, 39415, of the duet with Sparafucile, with Luppi as the blackguardly assassin). Again, 'Cortigiani' is a good representative example of the work of a baritone whose principal attraction lies in the voice itself. Mario Sammarco ('Pari siamo', 52372) must also be mentioned, though his singing is often laboured; his recordings again seeming to fall short of the stage legend. With Riccardo Stracciari one again exclaims (of a 1919 recording of 'Pari siamo' on Col. 4019M; GV 501) 'what a voice!', acknowledging that for all the vocal extroversion there is here none the less something of the spirit of the suffering jester. Yet, when all is said and done, none of these singers comes close to Ruffo or Gobbi. To find some kind of comparability it is necessary to go not, surprisingly enough, to Giuseppe de Luca – marvellous in 'Piangi, fanciulla' with Galli-Curci (DA 1028) yet curiously lightweight in 'Pari siamo' (Fono. 39947) – but to Pasquale Amato. Here there are several recordings from which to choose. The 1910 Fonotipias (74137/8) do not show the great baritone at his best, nor do some later, 1924, Homocord discs; but the 'Cortigiani' of 1911 (DB 158; CO 346) is absolutely magnificent, gloriously produced on the voice and phrased with great dynamic beauty. Neither of Giovanni Inghilleri's accounts of 'Pari siamo' is in the Amato class, in spite of a fine voice and strikingly good diction, though the later of the two versions (D 1823) is distinguished. By and large, the heavier Amonasro-type voice is not ideally suited to the role of Rigoletto. Though there have been some distinguished Rigolettos in this tradition, there is often an unwelcome broadening of the character, not to mention a good deal of hectoring vocalization. Apollo Granforte's Rigoletto, on the evidence of 'Pari siamo' and 'Cortigiani' (DB 1450 and 1475; QALP 5338), is all brute force and strength. Finding a middle course between vocal beauty and dramatic strength is often difficult – however effortlessly Ruffo and Gobbi appear to manage it – and leads many a Rigoletto into a no-man's-land of interpretative compromise; as we can hear if we turn to Giuseppe Valdengo's 'Pari siamo' (Decca X 304; LX 3005) – or Ingvar Wixell's no more than reliable recent 'Cortigiani' (Philips 6580 171). Valdengo's Rigoletto certainly lacks the rounded authority of his Iago and his Falstaff in the famous Toscanini sets.

There were, between the wars, a number of distinguished non-Italian Rigolettos. 'Pari siamo' in Polish may not be everyone's idea of interpretative authenticity, yet I find Mossakowski's 'Pari siamo' fascinating (Muza XL 0012), supple and elusively beautiful. From England there is Dennis Noble. 'Yon assassin!' (C 3520) reveals exemplary diction and a fine sense of drama. Of the German baritone Gerhard Hüsch I had high expectations, for a lieder singer can bring quiet illumination to this role. Yet his 'Pari siamo' (Parlo. E 11034) is fierce and aquiline, the assonance and alliterative sweetness of Piave's text lost in a German translation which Hüsch brandishes at us with a fierce insistence. After this, Marko Rothmuller, though lacking weight in 'Cortigiani' (C 3738), is balm to the ear, his 'Pari siamo' (C 3689) touched with real calm and a Gobbiesque inwardness. Willi Domgraf-Fassbaender (Poly. 95029; LV 131) is reliable, but his 'Cortigiani' becomes lachrymose. Joseph Schwarz is also a shade tearful in the appeal to the courtiers (042507; LV 14) but in duet with Claire Dux, 'Deh non parlare' sung in German as 'Sprich nie mit einen Armen' (044314; LV 14) is ravishing, showing Schwarz to be possessed of the ideal voice for those who would have Rigoletto sung by a great lyric baritone. (And on the evidence of these records Schwarz was both those things.)

Quite outstanding, too, and equally necessary listening, are the records of 'Pari siamo' and 'Cortigiani', made by the Hungarian-born baritone, Alexander Sved (CA 8234). Sved studied with both Sammaroo and Ruffo, from whom he clearly learned much. The voice is dark, gloriously so, but this does not preclude great vocal resourcefulness. Could his singing of the last two pages of 'Cortigiani' not benefit from a shade more restraint, given a performance which tabulates, so completely, Rigoletto's suffering? Perhaps so, but these performances (which are superbly accompanied by Clemens Krauss) are none the less memorable.

I have already mentioned some of the more celebrated duet records. In addition it is worth noting that Domgraf-Fassbaender emerges more positively in duets with Hedwig von Debitzka; humane, dramatic performances in which he communicates an intense, even at times possessive, love for his daughter. Sved is less good in duet with Pagliughi (R 30042; SW 824/5), but Hempel and Amato (Victor 89082) should not be missed, and Granforte can also be heard with Nunu Sanchioni (DA 1128; LV 90). Carosio (on DB 6387) is very lovely, but Carlo Tagliabue is a dull Rigoletto. By contrast Gino Bechi is almost Gobbi-like with the dull Lyana Grani (DA 11334). Finally among the duets there is an interesting rarity: Sir Hamilton Harty conducting the Rigoletto-Sparafucile duet at the start of Act 2 with Cesare Formichi (a very reliable Rigoletto of the inter-war period) and Fernando Autori, a grand inquisitorial bass who makes a most impressive Sparafucile (Col. D 1488).

Apart from her contributions to the duets with Rigoletto and the Duke and the famous quartet, Gilda's role centres on two pieces: 'Caro nome' and 'Tutte le feste'. Of 'Caro nome' Verdi wrote:

> As for the cavatina in the first act, I don't see where agility comes into it. Perhaps you haven't understood the tempo which ought to be *Allegretto molto lento*. At a moderate pace and sung *sotto voce* it shouldn't give the slightest difficulty.

It is a delicate, introspective piece and it demands from the soprano discriminating vocalization channelled through a pure and dedicated sensibility.

Let us begin with Melba (03025; RLS 719), a recording made in 1904 and rich in promise of velvet-white tone, immaculate divisions and sure intonation. Alas, she takes the whole thing swiftly – and the first note by storm. No, this is not the touchstone of excellence one might have hoped, exquisite as much of it undoubtedly is. And Tetrazzini (DB 536; ORL 210)? Here is a most magical version and a most winning personality, in spite of everything – and everything includes no rests in the opening phrases, fudged low Es and F sharps and a bird-like brilliance in the cadenza. Yet with what heart-easing innocence the voice can soar: one goes back to the record for that alone. Later, in 1917, Amelita Galli-Curci was to produce another famous, more-or-less successful account of the aria (DB 257; CDN 1004). The bright beauty of the voice is a great joy, even though Galli-Curci begins on the sharp side of the note and avoids turning the private meditation into a public statement only by a hair's breadth.

Returning to the beginning of the century, I find myself fascinated by the less-well publicized versions of singers such as the young Frieda Hempel – a lovely early, German version (Od. 99219; CO 302) recorded in 1909; and by Marcella Sembrich (053078). There are also Regina Pacini (Fono. 39235), whose finely spun legato is especially memorable to the context of a reading well tuned to the aria's intrinsic *melodia staccata* character; Olympia Boronat, colouring and shading both 'Caro nome' (53348) and 'Tutte le feste' (053186) with a sweet and limpid quality and an exquisite sense of related vocal and dramatic values; Selma Kurz (53431; GEMM 121/2), whose 1906 Vienna recording, laden as ever with beautiful things, P. G. Hurst once hazarded it to be as good as any; and a most fetching version by that most engaging of all *leggiero* sopranos of the period, Maria Barrientos (Am. Col. 48649; GV 515). The coda is fluttery, but the main body of the aria is brightly, luminously done. Her 'Tutte le feste' (49611; GV 515) is also worth hearing.

Moving forward in time, we come across a caressively charming later Galli-Curci (DB 641), marred only by virtuoso display in the coda and a tendency to stand back from the bigger vocal jumps. And there is Toti dal Monte (DB 830; LV 184), a performance not entirely to my taste, though its technical accuracy and the freshness of the voice have been commended elsewhere. I find it a little thin, and would never prefer it to, say, the beautifully meditative Ivogün version (Poly. 85309; LV 69).

For innocence married with consummate charm (vocal sex-appeal of the purest kind, a Desdemona-like ravishment) one must go to Eidé Norena (Parlo. R 20162) or to a version by the great Russian-born, Italian-trained, singer Eugenia Bronskaya (Am. Col. A 5193) whose 'Caro nome' meets most of the piece's requirements with glowing assurance. 'Tutte le feste' is easily over-shadowed by the more famous cavatina, but let me add at this point mention of a fine recording of it: Pagliughi's Parlophone recording (DPX 26), a touchstone of excellence, inward and simple yet full of quiet anguish.

After the war in 'Caro nome' we have Carosio (QALP 5342), sweet-toned, and several recital versions (Callas's, for instance) merely duplicating what we hear in an increasingly regular succession of complete sets. There are two natural Gildas, though, who have not as yet committed the complete role to disc. Caballé (SXLR 6690) has a voice of fabulous pedigree, wonderfully well suited to Gilda's role. And yet her 'Caro nome' is a considerable disappointment – that is , until the exquisitely drawn coda. Earlier, the exaggerated *staccati* and strangely prolonged pauses put the aria badly out of shape; and Caballé's trills have a curiously flattened contour. Ileane Cotrubas, on the other hand, is fascinating, (CBS 76521). Here the postlude is the principal disappointment, the voice ill-served by the close, bright CBS recording. Elsewhere, though, there is a lot of intensity, a lot of character, and considerable vocal accomplishment.

The Duke's cavatina tosses convention brilliantly off, for 'Questa o quella' is a dancing *ballata* to be sung *con eleganza*. Like Shakespeare, Verdi knew a good deal about the importance of first impressions; deft and aerial as 'Questa o quella' superficially is, it none the less points the Duke's character – dashing, irresponsible, fatally engaging – with telling accuracy. Like the still better known 'La donna è mobile', the piece fits the Duke's character like a glove, provided it is sung with ease and elegance and not given out with the hectoring coarseness of a cockney pub-song. Between these two numbers there is the gentle 'Parmi veder le lagrime' and its fierce recitative 'Ella mi fu rapita!'. Here the tenor can generously deploy both his *bel canto* and his histrionic gifts. Should the Duke be allowed such exquisite music? Julian Budden, in *The Operas of Verdi*, provides the answer: 'Mozart . . . in *Così fan tutte* demonstrated once and for all that people who deceive themselves require a musical expression as intense and serious as those whose sentiments are pure, noble and self-aware'.

Again it is necessary to be selective, for few tenors have omitted to record one or all of the Duke's airs. In 1903 Alessandro Bonci gave us light readings of the two outlying arias, fine essays in *bel canto* singing (Fono. 39081) and preferable by a small margin to the 1904 recordings (39239). 'Ella mi fu rapita!' (Fono. 92098/9; BC 214) is ragged by comparison and less recommendable. De Lucia's best recording of the role is probably his Phonotype recording (M 1761) of 'Questa o quella', which is full of magical transitions and elisions, coloratura skills which few tenors could contemplate, let alone match. There is also a 'Donna' (G&T Milan, 1903, 52411) as well as a disappointing account of the Act 2 aria which sounds more like the effusions of a singing teacher than the outpourings of a lover. (C 1795; ORL 216). The many Caruso versions are necessary listening from the 1902/03 Zonophones onwards ('La donna è mobile' on 1555). His 1902 Red G&T 'Questa o quella' (52344; HLM 7030) is wonderfully elegant, very *agréable* (not quite the same thing as the English agreeable). There are Victor G&Ts from 1904 (2–52480 and 52062 respectively; ORL 303). A 1908 'Questa o quella' with orchestra (DA 102; RL 11749) has more or less everything: a cool, dispassionate elegance, a fine sense of style and a most compelling urgency; though 'La donna è mobile' from the same session (DA 561; RL 11749) is perceptibly heavy in rhythm. Other Caruso recordings include 'Parmi veder' (DB 126; ORL 312).

Nowhere in 'La donna è mobile' is Caruso's singing as mannered or as heavily nuanced as John McCormack's (Od. 575081; GEMM 155). But in the cavatina, recorded in 1913 (DA 498; CO 382), McCormack is excellent, a philandering Irishman singing with wonderfully easy articulation and finely spinning rhythm. Tito Schipa's recordings are strangely variable. A Pathé 'La donna è mobile' (A 5544; GEMM 164) is slow in pulse and exaggerated in phrasing and dynamics. On the other hand, there is a fine verbal sense and a certain wit in an HMV 'Questa o quella' (DA 885). Rather more interesting are his recordings of the Act 2 scene. His Italian account (252144/3) is airy and expressive, the Duke very much a man of sensibility. DB 1372 (GEMM 151), though, seems less affected, more mature, a model performance of its kind. In addition to the arias, there is also a fine, flexibly paced duet with Galli-Curci (DA 1161).

Lauri-Volpi (DA 1384; QALP 5057) gives a well-balanced account of 'Parmi veder'. Although there are liberties taken both with the phrasing and the musical text in 'La donna è mobile' (DA 5413) the suave and lively manner, and the naturally beautiful timbres of the voice, make their mark. Heddle Nash sings a nicely scaled 'La donna è mobile' (DB 932; HQM 1089) in English and is also excellent in 'Parmi veder' (Col. 4986). Joseph Hislop by comparison, is a shade over-careful (Pathé 90587; GV 43) and is unidiomatic in a duet with Lotte Schöne (DA 1127). Alfred Piccaver (Od. 99930; 99933/4; LV 26) is in especially good voice in 'Questa o quella', lyricism and a certain natural *slancio* nicely matched. There are few mannerisms and no intrusive laughs. 'La donna è mobile' is less successful, for here the insinuating manner occasionally gets the better of the rhythms. For a wildly exaggerated reading of the Duke's music go to Smirnov (DA 461; GV 74), the very reverse of Antonio Cortis (DA 1153), who shapes the music with an unerring sense of style.

There were several distinguished Dukes during the 1920s and 1930s.

Gigli's 'La donna è mobile' (DA 1372) offers near-perfect characterization, very suave, what the Italians call *molto signore,* yet fierce and insinuating too. Björling, working near the start of his career, has already an unmistakable timbre, but his 1936 performance (DA 1548; RLS 715) is not especially well integrated in terms of the idiomatic shaping of rhythm and phrase. (He is heard to better effect in a wartime recording of his duet with Gilda, on DB 6119, though the Gilda is poor.) Aureliano Pertile, one of Toscanini's favourite singers, is exceptionally successful in all three items (Fono. 120081). Martinelli, by contrast, made various unsuccessful attempts on the two well-known pieces (DA 285; DA 325, DA 842; ORL 224) where he is not so much out of his depth as out of the Duke's shallows.

The Duke's arias go well into French (a happy chance for the opera derives from Hugo's *Le roi s'amuse),* and Georges Thill's 'Comme une plume au vent' has both a measured beauty and a showpiece coda (Col. LF 148; LV 224). Miguel Villabella takes 'La donna è mobile' slowly (Od. 188806) but his duet with Eidé Norena is memorable (Od. 123010). Julius Patzak, singing in German, is generally out of sympathy with the style of the music, though his 'La donna è mobile' is acceptable. In the duet, singing with Berger, he is so gentle he might be Gilda's father (Poly. 67535). Among Austro-German singers, Richard Tauber is a more natural Duke, and his two 1927 recordings (Od. 0–4950; GEMM 153) have charm and character. Ferruccio Tagliavini ravishes sense in 'Parmi veder', an outrageously beautiful version, too effete perhaps, and tending to be lachrymose (Cetra BB 25058).

Among more or less contemporary artists Franco Corelli (Cetra LPV 450206) has his seven league boots on for the popular arias; Placido Domingo singing 'Questa o quella' and 'La donna è mobile' (RCA ARLI 0048 and SER 5613 respectively) deploys exaggerated *staccati* in the former and lacks real gaiety in the latter. He is more impressive in Act 2 (ARLI 0122) but the conducting is very poor (it is by Sherrill Milnes, a gimmicky idea). The much missed Fritz Wunderlich gives a good deal of pleasure in the Tauber style in the two popular pieces (1C 063-28123); but the most stylish of modern Dukes, apart from Pavarotti on the later Sutherland set, is Bergonzi, though drab conducting by Nello Santi takes some of the character out of his performance (Philips 6599 924).

Recordings of the quartet are legion, a reflection not only on the one-time popularity of the piece and its suitability to the single 78 side but of the willingness of singers in days gone by to make solo showpiece records together. Nowadays versions of the quartet are never forthcoming except in complete recordings of the opera. Among the most celebrated recordings of the quartet there are those featuring Enrico Caruso. The late, 1917, recording, with its richly nuanced opening statement and eloquently moulded lines of tone, is perhaps as fine as any (DQ 100; ORL 316). Galli-Curci, Perini and de Luca are also to be heard on this famous disc. For those who prefer the more youthful Caruso there is the 1907 recording (DO 100; ORL 304), where Caruso is partnered by Abbott, Homer and Scotti. Midway, there is a memorably seductive account made in 1912 with Tetrazzini, Amato and Jacoby (Victor Heritage 15–1019; ORL 310). Admirers of Sembrich, however, may wish to combine her artistry with that of Caruso, Severina and Scotti (DQ 101; ORL 215), though this is not a performance to set alongside those already mentioned. Further back, we have Bonci in a quartet which also includes Magini-Coletti (Fono. 69019, 1904), and Melba's celebrated version made in July 1906 (DM 118; RLS 719). It is said that this recording was made in the wake of a blistering row between Melba and her producer, Fred Gaisberg. It is certainly a performance that strangely blends fierceness and formality, with John McCormack leading off the quartet in a manner that will suggest exemplary musical taste to some collectors and excessive decorum to others. The recorded balance tends obviously to favour the Maddalena – the remarkable Edna Thornton – at the expense of the prima donna. And yet it is Melba who has the last word with a soaring, unimpeachably accurate high D flat. McCormack is heard to better advantage in a more relaxed account made with Bori, Jacoby and Werrenrath (DM 104; GEMM 155).

Apart from the Carusos, the obviously outstanding recording of the quartet is the 1927 version (DQ 102; GEMM 170) made by Galli-Curci, Homer and de Luca with Beniamino Gigli. The opening phrases alone proclaim Gigli an ideal Duke. The catalogues of the early years are full of dazzling permutations of great names, singing in Italian (Barrientos, Hackett and Stracciari, Col. 49782; GV 515); in English (Licette, Nash, Noble, Brunskill, DX 302); in French (an especially eloquent version by César Vezzani, with Brothier, Gallard and Morturier on DB 4869), and Norena and Villabella (Od. 123010) – superb soprano and tenor (who sing the duet on the reverse); and in German – a version led by Roswaenge on Telefunken (SK 1162; 6.42084 AJ) which is subtler and verbally sweeter on the ear than Roswaenge's account in the complete recording with Heger. And so one could go on with versions featuring Pertile (R 20027; LV 245), and Peerce, sounding like Pertile, on American Army V-disc conducted by Toscanini. But go to Toscanini's recording of Act 4 (ALP 1453) for the quartet finely sung, in context, prefaced by its scintillating introduction, and shorn of the spurious final high D flat beloved of many of the sopranos named above.

The death of Gilda, though better heard in context, has occasionally been recorded. Moscisca and Battistini (DB 204) and dal Monte and Luigi Montesanto (DB 2124) are cases in point – with both Battistini and Montesanto proving themselves, albeit briefly, to be nobly and sympathetically attuned both to the role of Rigoletto and to the opera's tragic close. You will go a long way, though, before you find a more exquisite Gilda or a more compelling Rigoletto in this final scene than on a disc already mentioned: Graziella Pareto, here (DB 176; ORL 217) in sweet voice, and the incomparable Ruffo.

RIGOLETTO

G Gilda *M* Maddalena; *D* Duke; *R* Rigoletto; *S* Sparafucile

1912 (in French) Vallandri *G*: Lapeyrette *M*; Lassalle *D*; Noté *R*; Dupré *S*/Paris Opéra-Comique Chorus and Orch./Ruhlmann Pathé 1536–70

1916 Ferraris *G*; Ciani *M*; Taccani *D*; Formichi *R*; Bettoni *S*/La Scala Chorus and Orch./Molajoli Columbia D 11732–42

1917 Borghi-Zerna *G*; Garrone *M*; Broccardi *D*; Danise *R*; Bettoni *S*/La Scala Chorus and Orch./Sabajno HMV 7–254023–34; 2–0252004–5; 2–0254014–28; 2–0254511

1918 De Angelis *G*: de Lucia *D*/Chorus and orchestra Phonotype F 1777/2299

1927 Pagliughi *G*; de Cristoff *M*: Folgar *D*; Piazza *R*; Baccaloni *S*/La Scala Chorus and Orch./Sabajno Bongiovanni ⓜ GB 1001–2

1930 Capsir *G*; Bassi *M*; D. Borgioli *D*; Stracciari *R*; Dominici *S*/La Scala Chorus and Orch./Molajoli EMI ⓜ 3C 153 17081–2; CBS (US) ⓜ EL 2

1944 (in German) Berger *G*; Klöse *M*; Roswaenge *D*; Schlusnus *R*; Greindl *S*/Berlin State Opera Chorus and Orch./Heger DG ⓜ 2700 702

1949 (in Russian) Maslennikova *G*; Borisenko *M*; Kozlovsky *D*; Ivanov *R*; Gavrischov *S*/USSR State SO and Chorus/Samosud MK ⓜ DO 11323–6

1950 Berger *G*; Merriman *M*; Peerce *D*; Warren *R*; Tajo *S*/Shaw Chorale, RCA Orch./Cellini HMV ⓜ ALP 1004–6; RCA (US) ⓜ AVM 2 0698

1951 Orlandini *G*; Melani *M*; Sarri *D*; Petrov *R*; Frosini *S*/Florence Festival Chorus and Orch./Ghiglia Remington ⓜ 199/58–60

1952 (live performance, Palacio de Bellas Artes, Mexico) Callas *G*; Garcia *M*; di Stefano *D*; Campolonghi *R*; Ruffino *S*/Palacio de Bellas Artes Chorus and Orch./Mugnaie Cetra ⓜ LO 37/3

1954 Pagliughi *G*; Colasanti *M*; Tagliavini *D*; Taddei *R*; Neri *S*/Turin Radio Chorus and Orch./Questa Cetra ⒸLPS 3247 ④ MC 92–3

1954 Gueden *G*; Simionato *M*; del Monaco *D*; Protti *R*; Siepi *S*/Santa Cecilia Academy Chorus and Orch./Erede Decca ⓜ GOM 519–21; Richmond ⓜ RS 63005

1955 Callas *G*; Lazzarini *M*; di Stefano *D*; Gobbi *R*; Zaccaria *S*/La Scala Chorus and Orch./Serafin EMI Ⓒ SLS 5018 ④ TC–SLS 5018; Angel ⓜ 353 CL

1957 Peters *G*; Rota *M*; Björling *D*; Merrill *R*; Tozzi *S*/Rome Opera Chorus and Orch./Perlea RCA ⓜ VIC 6041

1959 D'Angelo *G*; Pirazzini *M*; Tucker *D*; Capecchi *R*; Sardi *S*/San Carlo Opera Chorus and Orch./Molinari-Pradelli Phillips ④ 7699 063

1960 (in German) Coertse *G*; Wien *M*; Terkal *D*; Ruzdiak *R*/Hamburg Radio Chorus and Orch./Martin Musica & Lettera 8002-3

1960 (in French) Doria *G*; Scharley *M*; Vanzo *D*; Massard *R*; Legros *S*/chorus and orch./Etcheverry IPG 115 025–6

Four Great Sopranos

Above left: Elisabeth Grümmer as
Agathe (Harold Rosenthal Collection)
Top right: Astrid Varnay as Brünnhilde
(Decca)
Left: Meta Seinemeyer as Leonora
(*Forza*) (Harold Rosenthal Collection)
Above: Eva Turner as Turandot (Harold
Rosenthal Collection)

Left: Nellie Melba as Violetta (Harold Rosenthal Collection)

Right: Giovanni Martinelli as Otello (Harold Rosenthal Collection)

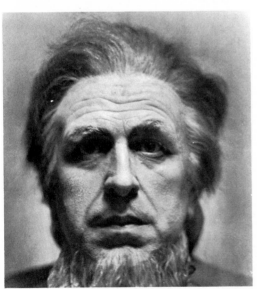

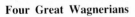

Four Great Wagnerians

Top left: Frida Leider as Isolde (Harold Rosenthal Collection)

Top right: Hermann Uhde as The Dutchman (Decca)

Above: Hans Hotter as Gurnemanz (Harold Rosenthal Collection)

Right: Max Lorenz as Siegfried (Harold Rosenthal Collection)

1960 Scotto *G*; Cossotto *M*; Kraus *D*;
Bastianini *R*; Vinco *S*/Florence
Festival Chorus and
Orch./Gavezzeni
Ricordi OCL 16003–5

1961 Sutherland *G*; Malagù *M*; Cioni
D; MacNeil *R*; Siepi *S*/Santa
Cecilia Academy Chorus and
Orch./Sanzogno
Decca GOS 655–7; London OSA
1322

1962 Benvenuti *G*; Pirazzini *M*;
Rocchi *D*; Monachesi *R*;
Gambelli *S*/San Carlo Opera
Chorus and Orch./F, Patané
Fabbri-Bastei Band 17–20

1963 (in German) Paller *G*; Gust *M*;
Curzi *D*; Gutstein *R*; Horne
S/Bavarian State Opera Chorus
and Orch./Galliera
EMI 1C 197 30708–9

1963 Ratti *G*; Freschi *M*; Brevi *D*;
Concone *R*; Botta *S*/Patagonia
Festival Chorus and Orch./de
Cross
Period TE 1112

1963 Scotto *G*; Cossotto *M*; Bergonzi
D; Fisher-Dieskau *R*; Testi *S*/La
Scala Chorus and Orch./Kubelik
DG 2709 014 ④ 3371 001

1963 Moffo *G*; Elias *M*; Kraus *D*;
Merrill *R*; Ward *S*//RCA Italiana
Chorus and Orch./Solti
RCA (UK) SER 5516–7
RCA (US) LSC 7027

1963 Ianculescu *G*; Palade *M*; Buzea
D; Herlea *R*; Rafael *S*/Bucharest
National Opera Chorus and
Orch./Bobescu
Fontana H71 AM 330

1964 Maccianti *G*; Casei *M*; Molese
D; Montefusco *R*; Davia
S/Vienna State Opera Chorus
and Orch./Rivoli
Orpheus

1965 (in Hungarian) Lászlo *G*; Barlay
M; Ilosfalvy *D*; Melis *R*; Bódy
S/Hungarian State Opera Chorus
and Orch./Gardelli
Qualiton SLPX 1231–3

1967 Grist *G*; di Stasio *M*; Gedda *D*;
MacNeil *R*; Ferrin *S*/Rome
Opera Chorus and
Orch./Molinari-Pradelli

EMI SAN 204-6; Angel SCLX
3718

1972 Sutherland *G*; Tourangeau *M*;
Pavarotti *D*; Milnes *R*; Talvela
S/Ambrosian Opera Chorus,
LSO/Bonynge
Decca SET 542–4 ④ K 2A3;
London OSA 13105 ④ 5–13105

1977 Rinaldi *G*; Cortez *M*; Bonisolli
D; Panerai *R*; Rundgren
S/Dresden State Opera Chorus,
Dresden State Orch./Molinari-
Pradelli
Acanta HA 21472

1978 Sills *G*; Dunn *M*; Kraus *D*;
Milnes *R*; Ramey *S*/Ambrosian
Opera Chorus, Philharmonia
Orch./Rudel
EMI; Angel – awaiting release

Excerpts

1940 Dickenson *G*; Browning *M*;
Tokatyan *D*; Warren
R/Publishers Service SO/Pelletier
RCA (US) ⓜ CAL 226

1944 (Act 4) Milanov *G*; Merriman
M; Peerce *D*; Warren *R*;
Moscona *S*/chorus, NBC
SO/Toscanini
RCA (UK) ⓜ VCM 10; (US)
ⓔ VICS 1314

1953 (in German) Streich *G*;
Munteanu *D*; Uhde *R*; Böhme
S/Orchs
DG ⓜ LPE 17011

1953 (in French) Doria *G*; Scharley
M; Fouché *D*; Blanc *R*/Chorus
and Orch./Etcheverry
Concert Artists ⓜ LPA 1090

1954 Reggiani *G*; Landi *D*; Valentino
R/Rome Eliseo Theatre Chorus
and Orch./Manrico
Royale ⓜ 1619

1954 Heusser *G*; Lorie *M*; Conrad *D*;
Gorin *R*; Smith *S*/Chorus;
Netherlands PO/Goehr
Musical Masterpieces Society
ⓜ OP 9

1957 (in German) Köth *G*; Wagner
M; Schock *D*; Metternich *R*;
Frick *S*/German Opera Chorus
and Orch./Schüchter
EMI 1C 047 28567

1959 (in German) Hollweg *G*;

Malaniuk *M*; Kónya *D*; Wächter
R/Orch.
DG SLPHM 237152

1959   (in French) Robin *G*; Michel *M*;
Blondel *D*; Dens *R*; Depraz
S/Paris Opéra Orch./Dervaux
EMI 2C 061 12128

1961   (in French) Micheau *G*; Blanc
R/Paris Opéra Orch./Prêtre
EMI ASTX 135

1962   (in French) Tavernier *G*; Kahn
M; Poncet *D*; Bianco *R*;
Haidinger *S*/Chorus and
Orch./Wagner
Philips 6747 186

1962   (in English) Harwood *G*; Guy
M; D. Smith *D*; Glossop *R*;
McIntyre *S*/Sadler's Wells Opera
Orch./Lockhart
EMI CSD 1466; Capitol SP 8606

1963   (in French) Mesplé *G*; Arrauzau
M; Lance *D*; Bacquier *R*;
Serkoyan *S*/chorus and
orch./Hartemann
Ades 16018 ④ C 8006

1964   (in German) Coertse *G*; Sobota
M; Kmentt *D*; Berry *R*/Vienna
Volksoper Orch./Quadri
Ariola-Eurodisc Z8004R

1964   (in German) Vivarelli *G*;
Rütgers *M*; Kozub *D*; Fischer-
Dieskau *R*; Lauhofer *S*/German
Opera Chorus, Berlin PO/Stein
DG 2535 276 ④ 3335 276

1971   (in German) Rothenberger *G*;
Burmeister *M*; Ilosfalvy *D*;
Wixell *R*; Vogel *S*/Leipzig Radio
Choir, Dresden State Orch./Kurz
EMI 1C 063 29056

Il trovatore

JOHN HIGGINS AND ALAN BLYTH

Few operas provide a happier or a richer hunting ground for collectors of vocal 78s than Verdi's *Il Trovatore*. From the earliest days of recording it attracted singers. Italian and non-Italian, mighty and mediocre. The baritones inevitably went for the Count of Luna's 'Il balen del suo sorriso', a hymn to Leonora's beauty almost as passionate as Romeo's first sight of Juliet – 'O! she doth teach the torches to burn bright'. Some Lunas were more concerned with the tempest in the Count's heart than Verdi's more serene description of the object of his love and vocally they were generally the losers.

Sopranos tackled Leonora's 'Tacea la notte' but tended to keep clear of the far more taxing cabaletta that follows. Tenors too were apt to prefer the silky Bellinian line of Manrico's 'Ah, si ben mio' to the pyrotechnics – the word may be used in its most literal sense – of 'Di quella pira'. The final duet of the opera, 'Ai nostri monti', was such a musical pillar of the Victorian and Edwardian drawing rooms that inevitably it too came out of the horn of the gramophone with regularity.

As the best of the 78s, as well as some of the less meritorious ones, have found their way to LP assemblies, *Trovatore* has stood its ground. It is there in collections of tenors reaching for high Cs or joining sopranos in famous love duets from opera; only in selections of drinking songs does *Trovatore* regularly get overlooked for the practical reason that the sole liquid provided by Cammarano for Verdi to set to music was poison.

I leave it to the editor, Alan Blyth, to act as a guide through the tangle of *Trovatore* extracts (see page 231); I will deal only with complete, or moderately complete, versions of the opera. The earliest shot was in 1912 on eighteen Pathé discs complete with chorus and orchestra, but the fact that it was sung in French, presumably at the instigation of the recording company, rules it out of consideration. *Trovatore* then re-emerged on the gramophone in 1930 in two versions, both in Italian, both using the backing of the Scala chorus and orchestra.

The names of the cast conducted by Lorenzo Molajoli faded fairly rapidly with the years, with the exception of the Manrico, Francesco Merli, who made a few Covent Garden appearances in the late 1920s and is represented decently among the *Trovatore* extracts. The second version is a different matter. EMI reissued it in Italy as part of the 'Stasera all'Opera' series in a type of electronic stereo. The *Professori*, as they are quaintly but often labelled, of the Scala orchestra do not benefit greatly from the reprocessing of the sound, which cannot conceal that Sabajno conducts them with a plodding deliberation which adds up to downright dullness. There is little attempt at dramatic balance : Manrico and Leonora sing the 'Miserere' as though they were standing side by side, which they probably were, rather than separated by several feet of prison wall. But the recording does capture the interpretations of two major artists, Aureliano Pertile and Apollo Granforte.

Pertile, because he tackled roles such as Andrea Chenier and Lohengrin, acquired the reputation of being a beefy singer, and there is certainly plenty of muscle in his rendering of 'Di quella pira'. But this overlooks the fact that the tenor whom Toscanini for long prized above all others was expert in the Bellini and Donizetti repertory. Manrico needs delicacy as well as brawn; Pertile supplies both in a performance which is far ahead of its time in its use of the gramophone for dramatic shading. In the final act Pertile is solicitousness itself as he tends and cherishes Azucena (a very adequate performance from Irene Minghini-Cattaneo). Pertile moulds and shapes his singing in a way many of his contemporary rivals disdained to do.

Granforte tends at times to live up to his surname, but he turns Luna into a worthy rival for Leonora's hand. The only problem is that in the shape of Maria Carena she is scarcely a woman deserving a tussle, let alone a fight. She manages to begin by making Leonora sound like an *ingénue* Gilda in 'Tacesa la notte' instead of a noble lady at the court of Aragon and ends by turning her into a Neopolitan fishwife. But despite this major blot the set is a valuable example of how *Trovatore* was tackled almost fifty years ago.

A couple of decades passed before the next important recording. *Trovatore*, for all its apparent popularity, goes into eclipse from time to time: Covent Garden ignored it throughout the 1930s until the final season before the outbreak of war when Jussi Björling arrived to sing Manrico. In 1951 Cetra took up *Trovatore* using the RAI orchestra and choir under Previtali and, in the title role, the tenor whom many considered Pertile's natural successor, Giacomo Lauri-Volpi.

Lauri-Volpi is one of those artists who is credited with being better than I suspect he actually was. The clarion tones are there, notably in Act 3, but the stridency of the voice becomes wearying; Lauri-Volpi, who was nearing the end of his career when the recording was made, indulges in too much playing to the gallery – or to whatever Italian Radio's equivalent of the gallery was. He had recorded 'Di quella pira' previously and with a good deal of panache, but on Cetra the final cry of 'All'armi' is all but swallowed.

Perhaps some of the blame should be placed on Cetra's engineers who did a poor job, which was little improved when this *Trovatore* was reissued via World Record Club. Lauri-Volpi's partners sang with more decorum, particularly Carlo Tagliabue, who must be one of the least villainous Counts on record. Catarina Mancini always has the measure of him during their Act 4 encounter, 'Mira, di acerbe lagrime', although she too is subdued and cautious during the opening scenes of the opera. Miriam Pirazzini the Azucena, provides some of the most delicate singing, although it is worth noting the presence of Graziella Sciutti in the tiny role of Inez. The *confidantes* of Leonora often step into the shoes of the ladies on whom they attend: in the highlights of *Trovatore* issued by Sadler's Wells some ten years later, of which more in a minute, Rita Hunter turns up in the very same part. But this Cetra *Trovatore* did little to invest the creations of Verdi and Cammarano with any character; these were people in a studio, not men and women in conflict on a stage.

As if to make up for time and opportunities lost, the following year, 1952, provided three more *Trovatores*. Only one had any chance of staying in the catalogue: that conducted by Renato Cellini with a quartet of singers who might have been encountered in those days on a particularly glossy evening at the Metropolitan – Zinka Milanov, Fedora Barbieri, Björling and Leonard Warren. The mezzo and baritone were to record their roles again, the tenor and soprano were not.

The issue was acclaimed, not least in Britain because it pointed out all too directly how much London had been missing because of the war. Neither Björling nor Milanov had been heard at Covent Garden since 1939; Warren had never appeared there and never would; Barbieri was an up-and-coming Italian mezzo, who had been seen only briefly when La Scala brought *Falstaff* to the British capital. Perhaps it was thirst for a top-class cast which caused the praise to be so lavish; it was supported by the over-quotation of Caruso's dictum that *Trovatore* requires the four best singers in the world.

The adulation overlooked the fact that the set has a number of cuts and is contained on four sides, where most *Trovatore*s run to three records. Renato Cellini was not the most inspiring Verdi conductor of his time, and the RCA Victor Orchestra contained a quantity of session musicians, all very competent but not able to produce the dramatic *frisson* of a group regularly playing theatre music. Nor am I convinced by the contribution of the Robert Shaw Chorale performing under its titular head.

There remains the contributions of those four world stars. Milanov has described this *Trovatore* as her finest achievement for the gramophone and her glowing, sumptuous Leonora effortlessly eclipses her earlier rivals in the part. She suggests, as Mancini never did, a woman worth fighting for and over; she puts some flesh on a character who too easily becomes a vehicle for an ample and agile voice, charting the change from the remote lady waiting expectantly in the castle gardens to the tragic heroine of the last act.

After such a distinguished contribution Milanov must have been a little peeved when EMI reissued this *Trovatore* on the death of Björling, putting the tenor's name in a type size triple that of the rest of the cast and billing it as a 'Memorial Edition'. Björling's Manrico is elegant, graceful and gracious but it lacks robustness. There is all the sweetness of tone for the expression of love both uxorious and 'maternal', but little suggestion of the outlaw who is as at home in the gypsy encampment as he is serenading the high-born. Warren is equally well-mannered as Luna, and his voice is more resplendent here than it was to be in 1959 when he re-recorded the opera with Leontyne Price. Barbieri's Azucena is full of vigour – too much vigour, for the timbre is too young-sounding for the witch who is tired of a sadly mismanaged life.

The other weakness of the set is that in reaching for the starriest available cast, RCA neglected to balance the singers according to the demands of the story. The hero and heroine are a little too old, the mother much too young, and the villain – if Luna is a villain, a debatable point, – unvillainous.

Barbieri made her Azucena much tougher – a muddling old woman quite capable of keeping a beady eye on revenge despite her excursions into a personal dreamland – when she came to record the role for Walter Legge and Columbia four years later. The Leonora by her side was Maria Callas, who put more bite into this part than any other soprano on record before or since. When Callas made her Covent Garden appearance as Leonora, only her second role there, in the Coronation Season of 1953, she provided much fine singing but, if memory serves rightly, only a minimum of acting. In the intervening years, Legge and the conductor of the recording, Herbert von Karajan, changed all that.

Callas in 1956 from the start of the opera suggested much of Leonora's desperation. There for the first time was the woman who feels herself trapped between two warring forces and their leaders, Manrico and the Count of Luna. At last one feels the gramophone getting to the heart of Verdi's opera, a dark centre which is illumined by a pale moon or by the flickering fire that brings warmth to some and death to others. The earlier recordings, or at least the best of them, had rejoiced in the melodies and militarism of the work but had stopped short at probing it to see what else it had to reveal. There are faults in Callas's singing, particularly at the top, of the vocal line; but hers is a Leonora to set the standard for others.

Giuseppe di Stefano's Manrico has nothing like this insight, but Callas's regular recording partner does a generally sound job. The weakness is Rolando Panerai who lacks the necessary weight for Luna and is forced to substitute likeability for aggression. Similarly, Nicola Zaccaria is a routine Ferrando. All too often this role is undercast: Ferrando has to open the opera by pinning back the ears of the assembled soldiery and he must be capable of doing the same to the audience.

Karajan's own contribution to the set with the Scala orchestra and chorus is infinitely distinguished. He has always been a champion of this particular Verdi opera, whether in Milan, Berlin, Salzburg or Vienna. He was not to surpass his 1956 version when he came to record *Trovatore* again twenty years later with the Berlin Philharmonic.

In the mid 1950s anything Columbia planned for Callas and di Stefano was likely to be scheduled by Decca for Tebaldi and del Monaco; naturally enough, the reverse too was the case. So in the same year as the Karajan *Trovatore* the Decca version arrived with the regular house team, although Tebaldi had not tackled the role of Leonora on stage. It was not helped by a boomy, reverberant acoustic nor was it aided by the routine conducting of Alberto Erede, who ironically had been in the pit, none too effectively, for that first Callas Leonora at Covent Garden.

Del Monaco, it took no soothsayer to predict, would give of his all and of his best in 'Di quella pira'. And he did. But the rest of his Manrico was monotonous, much in the way that Lauri-Volpi's was for Cetra; like the older tenor he also had an anonymous Luna, this time Ugo Savarese. On the other hand Decca cannot be criticized for underplaying Ferrando: Giorgio Tozzi does admirably as Verdi's story-teller.

It was no surprise when RCA cast him in the same part when they came to *Trovatore* in 1959. The set is chiefly important for being the first of the three so far made by Leontyne Price. Characterization has never been Price's strength and this distinctly faceless Leonora hardly contradicts that general impression, but there is no gainsaying the freshness and beauty of the voice. Here Price dispatches with ease the runs and trills that later were to cause her more trouble.

Richard Tucker, elegant and musicianly in everything he did, was a most accomplished Manrico, if a little staid. It was not a role associated with him and he was never opera's greatest actor. The rest of the contributions were mediocre: Basile and the Rome orchestra were no more lively in Verdi's score than had been Erede and his players from Geneva on Decca; Warren's Luna fell short of his performance for Cellini; and Rosalind Elias's Azucena offered no new insights into the role which Verdi himself had found the hardest of all to cast.

Nothing over the next decade was to challenge the supremacy of Karajan and Callas, although there were *Trovatore*s with highly recommendable parts. DG used the veteran Tullio Serafin and the La Scala forces. Carlo Bergonzi, probably the most sought-after Verdi tenor of the 1960s recorded his one and only Manrico on this set and performed with his customary refinement. His partners lacked glamour although none of them deserved much censure: Antonietta Stella, who rose and fell *come una stella*, as Leonora; Fiorenza Cossotto who was to be a better Azucena under Mehta in 1969; and Ettore Bastianini as a bland Luna.

EMI offered an unevenly cast issue in 1964, personified by Franco Corelli's Manrico which mingled thrilling notes with other sounds that never should have been allowed outside the studio doors. Gabriella Tucci is not my idea of a Leonora and, although Simionato had plenty to say about Azucena, she was nearing the end of her career at the time of this recording. It was left to Robert Merrill as Luna to provide the most distinguished singing and to Thomas Schippers and the Rome Opera to serve up undistinguished accompaniment.

A Roman-cast *Trovatore* (1965), sung in a sort of Italian on the Electrocord label is best passed over in the interests of preventing international incidents. The highlights disc based on the Sadler's Wells production at least avoids the Bucharest swimming-bath sound, but it will surely be cherished only for the sake of nostalgia and for displaying Rita Hunter, as already noted, as Inez and Donald McIntyre as Ferrando, even though Charles Craig makes a passable Manrico.

The first real challenge to Karajan came in 1969 when RCA brought out a new *Trovatore* with safe casting on the female side (Price and Cossotto) but taking a chance for Manrico and Luna on two young singers climbing up the ladder. Their names were Placido Domingo and Sherrill Milnes. Domingo's Manrico remains unsurpassed: it is a model of freshness, charm, purity of tone and impeccable musicianship. It has youth and buoyancy, two characteristics missing in so many Manricos tackled by tenors late in their career. The fervour of Domingo's troubadour, who has a young man's impetuousness and passion, is matched by Milnes's equally virile Luna. These two discover, almost effortlessly, the energy of the piece and its unashamed cruelty. Fire, the single most dominant element of Cammarano's libretto, is here throughout in the singing.

Zubin Mehta, who had too long been an underrated opera conductor, watches over the New Philharmonia and the score. While his singers fan the flames, Mehta reveals the darker side of Verdi – the shadows and the terrors which are never far out of sight in northern Spain. In this he is abetted by Price, who gives the unhappy Leonora a far more hooded tone than in her earlier recording.

This 1969 *Trovatore*, grudgingly received in some quarters when it first appeared, became my first choice and has remained so. Decca's version made in 1975 with Sutherland sat for two years awaiting release and did nothing to topple RCA. Richard Bonynge decided to include all the ballet music and place it in the middle of the action instead of as an optional extra at the end of the opera. The result was to make a laborious piece of conducting seem even more laborious. Leonora is simply not Sutherland's part, nor was Marilyn Horne well cast as Azucena. Luciano Pavarotti alone of the principals provided the style of singing needed to give Decca any chance of competing.

The most recent of the *Trovatore*s, based on Salzburg's Easter Festival performances, looked more promising in view of the involvement of Karajan and the Berlin Philharmonic. But while Decca was half-saved by their tenor, EMI has been scuppered by the selection of Franco Bonisolli who gives a coarse and blustering account of Manrico throughout. Elena Obraztsova makes a rousing Azucena and Piero Cappuccilli is the most dignified of Lunas, but Price sounds past her peak as the object of all the fighting. A disappointing set, then, offering fewer insights than Karajan's previous account of the opera.

TROVATORE ON 78
ALAN BLYTH

If you look at the score of *Trovatore,* there is no doubt that Verdi had in mind voices that were as much lyrical as dramatic: it is full of demands for trills, grace-notes and difficult cadenzas that would have come easily to contemporary interpreters of Bellini or Donizetti but are much harder to execute for singers schooled in later Verdi and *verismo.* On the other hand there is no doubt that the new vein discovered by contemporary critics in the work calls for a more heroic method, a style exemplified in the Italian term *spinto.* This dichotomy more than anything is responsible for the extraordinary freedom in the execution of *Trovatore* to be found on older records, in which many of Verdi's demands were ignored. As a generalization, it is the German school of singers in the inter-war period which significantly remained most faithful to Verdi, possibly because the artists' voices, as compared with their Italian confreres, were, as a rule, lighter while not lacking focus and power.

There are no Germans that I could find who had recorded Ferrando's opening narration. As John Higgins states above, its importance has not always been recognized on LP, so it is a pleasure to hear two great Italian basses of the inter-war years giving it the benefit of their rolling tone and incisive declamation. They are Ezio Pinza (Victor 8231; GEMM 163) and Tancredi Pasero (Od. 0–8751; LV 34). Pinza, with chorus, offers more of the music and is the more authoritative retainer; indeed he is unsurpassed in this as in so much of the Verdi he recorded.

With Leonora's 'Tacea la notte' (1) and her fourth-act aria (2), which need to be taken together, we come across the dichotomy already mentioned as well as the differences between the German and Italian schools. Both Luisa Tetrazzini (DB 540) and Amelita Galli-Curci (DB 813, DB 1474) demonstrate the advantages of lighter, flexible voices in the execution of this music, but both lack rounded characterization: the words mean little to them, although Galli-Curci's later, electric version have a curiously affecting, haunting sense to it. In German, their equivalent is Claire Dux (Gram. 76452; LV 84) in 2 only. Frieda Hempel (0423276; CO 349), offering two verses of the cabaletta of 1 sung with the utmost brilliance, adds little insight; her contemporary Margarethe Siems (043069) is little more communicative in 2, but the accuracy of her forward, steady tone and the clarity of her top D flat are admirable. These German versions are trumped by another of 2 in the same language by Luise Perard-Petzl (Gram. 65540; DJA 100), made in 1917. This Hamburg soprano, much acclaimed in German roles at pre-1914 Covent Garden, manages the accuracy of the aforementioned artists, trills in place a float *dolce* A flat, perfectly judged rubato, but makes all these technical virtues the engineers of an elegiac, musing interpretation which in my experience has not been surpassed. Needless to say, in its original form, this rare record is virtually unobtainable. More accessible is the well-known contemporaneous account of the same piece by Emmy Destinn (DB 646; VIC 1395) who, though not herself Italian, represents the best of that school at that time. Her account is on a grander, more heroic scale but it is also more marmoreal and, though she boasts a gleaming D flat, she is in other respects careless, singing over rests in the first bars, for instance. Celestina Boninsegna in 1 (053063; Saga 7013) gives us broadly arched phrases but not much involvement. In 1904 (VA 10) her version of 2 with piano is matter-of-fact; by 1910 (Col. 30351; 7013), she still exhibits wilfulness but also some of that well-defined *spinto* excitement for which she was famed, as does Félia Litvinne, singing in French (Od. 55221) in 1.

Edging into the next generation of sopranos, we find Rosa Ponselle as something of a model in 2 (Am. Col. 49559; GVC 9), where feeling and technique are happily in accord. Claudio Muzio in both pieces is to be preferred in her earlier Edison (82223; OASI 571) rather than in her Columbia of 1 only (LC 21; COLC 101) recorded in 1935. In her first 'Tacea' the tone is attractive and girlish, the technique sound; in the second the effort to do the same things shows. Her 2 is free but has fine trills. A few years later Hina Spani tried her hand, or rather her voice, at both. Her 1 (DB 1045; LV 147) has the recitative and aria sculpted in broad, classical phrases, with the touch of *con enttusiasmo* when Verdi asks for it, and the close sung, for once, as written without added frills (and how much better it sounds that way). Her 2 (DB 1503; LV 147) is scarcely less recommendable but, inspite of a strong D flat, is just a little laboured, which Eva Turner (L 2156; HQM 1209) is certainly not, although she spoils her Italianate strength with one smudged run. Maria Nemeth, Barbara Kemp, Vera Schwarz (all in German and in both arias), and Xenia Belmas in 1 are appreciable but do not require special comment.

Three other sopranos, two of them not associated particularly with this music, certainly do call for attention. Tiana Lemnitz (DB 7656; LV 160) sings with more beauty and as great an accuracy as Perard-Petzl; indeed she fulfils Verdi's markings throughout both arias, suggests the right expressive 'face', and knows as much as any so-called Golden-Age soprano about trills and graces. She sings the cadenza of 2 as written and again makes Verdi's case for him. Frida Leider, with an even surer tone, is no less commendable; she passes the D flat test and a dozen others with her colours untarnished. These Red Polydor rarities, sung in German, are on Rococo 5241 where, to add to one's pleasure, she sings an exciting account of the first-act trio with Robert Hutt and Heinrich Schlusnus, at his early best, and partners the baritone in an account of 'Mira d'acerbe' that would be hard to beat for attention to situation, character, strong tone and musical accuracy. Above all, Leider shows a woman of warmth and conflicting passions. So does Joan Hammond (C 3419), whose vocal attributes and Verdian style have been too easily overlooked. You would go far today to hear both arias sung so honestly and well. She sings in English. Giannina Arangi-Lombardi (Col. D 18028) is among the best of her generation in Italy, as she demonstrates in an expansive, vibrant account of 1.

In the following scene we meet Azucena, whose music can dominate the opera. All my selected mezzos, out of very many, would have done that, beginning with Armida Parsi-Pettinella (b. 1868), who makes the hair stand on end in her 'Condotta' (Fono. 92549; CO 372). She shows no less feeling or sense of style in 'Giorni poveri', partnered by that most vibrant of baritones, Pasquale Amato, as Luna (Fono. 92569/70; CO 372). Ebe Stignani shows as much dramatic sense (LX 1049; 3C 065-17659) as in the Cetra-Live set (see below) and her 'Stride la vampa' (R 30018; LV 237), though not so vital, is a model of strong, personal singing. Of others heard, Gerville-Réche (Victor 87065) has a big attack but hoots, and Eleanor de Cisneros (Nicole 15633; 7013) is inhibited by the dim 1904 recording. Again it is German-based and -singing mezzos who carry the day in revealing insights. Maria Olszewska (Poly. 70655) is not only steady but has a fine sense of rhythm in 'Stride la vampa'. Margarete Klose (DB 4502; LV 18) in both pieces gives marvellous detail to her assumption and is very properly terrified by her own *Racconto*. Even better than these notable ladies is the great Swedish mezzo Karin Branzell whose trills and dotted rhythm in 'Stride la vampa' (Poly. 62533; LV 182), albeit sung in German, explains the dramatic purpose of such detail. Her 'Condotta' (Parlo. E 10719; LV 182), in Italian, has the same precision, the same slight reticence. Barbieri in both pieces (DB 21261) displays real *brio*.

There are two classic accounts of 'Mal reggendo', both with Louise Homer as Azucena. With the incomparable Caruso (DM 112; ORL 306), she is in stronger voice than later with Martinelli (DB 1215), a version notable for that incisive tenor's bold, warrior-like attack. Elsa Bruno and Giovanni Zenatello (Fono. 92880; Saga 7013) are hardly less excellent, Margarete Arndt-Ober and Hermann Jadlowker uphold the best German

Verdian tradition in their restrained but involved singing (Od. 99358/9;
CO 305). The mezzo was later to be heard in a live account of part
of the passage from the Berlin State Opera in 1928 partnered by the
vigorous but unruly Tino Pattiera (EJ 287; LV 16).

The Count's 'Il balen' has, as John Higgins said, attracted famous and
infamous baritones; let us concentrate on the former. Here the Italians
excite much more attention and acquire better reports, not least Riccardo
Stracciari, especially in his earlier version (Fono. 92622; Saga 7013). Who
could resist the breadth, warmth, ease and keen vibrancy of this ideal
Verdian baritone? His later version (Col. 7354; LV 136) is only slightly less
admirable. Similarly Giuseppe de Lucas smaller means are put to even finer
artistic purpose on his earlier, 1906 Fonotipia version (39943; Saga 7005),
the tone having a cello-like timbre. The singer is free with
note-values and he, interestingly, takes the alternative, undecorated version
of the first 'la tempesta'. His electric remake (Victor 1591; CDN 1012),
to which he added 'Per me ora fatale' (DA 1169; CDN 1012), is still
an impressive piece of singing but less particular in its virtues. Surpassing
even these estimable gentlemen is the scandalously underrated Berlin
baritone Joseph Schwarz (042497; LV 14) who, in 1916, gave an object
lesson in *bel canto* in his warm, subtly decorated version, sung as if it
was a true love-song. He gives us the cadenza as written (though he then
adds a top E!), and how easy it sounds. By his side Titta Ruffo
(2–52528/9) seems a rougher would-be seducer, but his tone is as
resplendent as ever. A few others deserve mention, and they are not the
expected names: Heinrich Rekhemper (Polydor) in German, for his long
phrasing and correct cadenza, Willi Domgraf-Fassbaender (Artiphon
12041; LV 131) in German, for his individual timbre, catch in the voice
and easy high G; the Belgian baritone Armand Crabbe (DB 4824; 4C
051 23273) in French, for his forward tone and supple phrasing – a very
plausible Luna; and Dennis Noble (Col. 9556), in English, for his almost
de Luca-like lightness and his correct cadenza. A curiosity is Lauritz
Melchior's 1913 performance in Danish, but it remains little more than
a curiosity.

In what amounts to the aria's cabaletta, 'Per me fatale', Apollo
Granforte, in a different version from the complete set (DB 1220; LV
90), displays greater resources and more fire than the excellent Benvenuto
Franci (DB 1262). Schlusnus, in German (DE 7005; LV 110) is a smooth
and almost too likable Luna: his 'Il balen' (Poly. 6678; LV 110) is also
an appreciable performance.

The next excerpts belong to Manrico. The versions of 'Ah si, ben mio'
are legion. Martinelli tells us how he had it from Toscanini that the
interpolated B flat was as allowable as the top C in 'Di quella pira'; the
former is certainly preferable to the latter, as Martinelli himself shows
(DB 333; CDN 1030) with his pencil-fine line, but it is a pity he, and
virtually no other Italian Manrico, gives us the trills. Certainly not Caruso

(DB 112; ORL 305), but who could deny the glowing ardour of this account? He is almost matched by Björling in his classic 1939 performance (DA 1701; RLS 715), which is capped by his ardent C major 'Di quella pira'; Caruso, always shy on top Cs, sings it in B (DA 113; ORL 304). Lauri-Volpi, in better voice than in his LP set is a finely virile and lyrical Manrico in both pieces (Scala 830). Trumping all these, in both pieces, is the lyrical yet fiery young Pertile (Fono. 74946/7; GV 505).

Again, 'Ah si, ben mio' has many of its best interpreters from non-Italians, as well as Björling. Among the earliest on disc is the Dutch Jacques Urlus. Always a fastidious tenor, he here sings the music as an intimate address to his lady, just right (4–42502; CO 350) – and he really trills. So does Hermann Jadlowker (042482), who sounds more heroic than Urlus but is not such a refined singer. Leo Slezak (3–42732; CO 332) is predictably exciting, predictably unsteady when exerting pressure on his voice. Preferable is Tino Pattiera (Od. R00 80801; LV 16); indeed, quite thrilling. These versions are all in German. Charles Dalmores from the same generation (Victor 85123; Club-99) is the most fastidious, accurate tenor of all; his line and perfectly focused tone are to be admired and come down the years as fresh as ever. Léon Escalais (Fono. 39564) was half the artist but had perhaps twice the voice; his brilliant 'Di quella pira' (39577) is startling – and it might startle the neighbours. Mario Gilion (Fono. 39653/4; 1C 049–03005) would equally awake the sleeping but, once *compos mentis*, they might be shocked by his lack of any musical sense.

Germans dominate the next generation, with Franz Völker (Poly. 95186; LV 78) as ever dependable and straightforward, Richard Tauber (0–8233), more passionate, less in style and adding a 'Di quella pira', two verses, in B. Rudolf Laubenthal (Parl. 1060; LV 213) is as metallic as Martinelli but more strained. Helge Roswaenge is too forceful, Piccaver too lazy. Arthur Jordan (Col. 9180) and James Johnston (DX 1539) hold up the British flag with attractive accounts, but both are inclined to hurry their ardent message.

In 'Di quella pira', Tamagno (DR 102; ORL 211) goes slowly but manages the *gruppetti* with accuracy. His virile voice also releases the serenade, 'Deserta sulla terra' (DR 105; ORL 211), with a kind of authoritative insistence. Bernardo de Muro tranposes 'Di quella pira' to B (2–052121; LV 135) where he is excitingly forthright as is Hippolito Lazaro in the original key. Gigli apparently recorded the piece at a lower speed (DA 5398; RLS 729) so that at 78 it would sound in C! Martinelli eschewed all such gimmicks and gave us the thrust and bite the piece demands in the two verses of his acoustic version (7–52077; CDN 5105), which must have been recorded not long after he had fifty rehearsals in the part under Toscanini in 1914. The electric re-make, one verse only, is preceded by the recitative that comes before 'Ah, si ben mio', which is then cut, but in that passage he displays, as the old *Record Guide* averred, 'some of the finest tenor singing in the heroic manner ever recorded'. Völker's full-voiced German version (Poly. 24193; LV 206) is in B.

Martinelli is again to the fore in the 'Miserere' whether in the acoustic version with Destinn (DB 333; CDN 5105), again recorded in 1914 at the time of the Met performances and later with Ponselle (DB 1199), the disc that introduced me to his restrained yet intense art. Destinn was partnered by the plaintive Zenatello in a later version (Col. A 5399). Caruso and Alda's fiery singing (DK 119; ORL 306) is surpasssed by their own 'unpublished' disc made without the chorus when they were much less inhibited. Caruso's voice comes off the groove with unbelievable fidelity; happily this is also included in ORL 306. Miriam Licette and Heddle Nash (DX 302), in English, work up to a similar fervour with lesser means. In German, the unique Meta Seinemeyer, with John Gläser (Parlo. P 9815; LV 112), is comparably involved.

In 'Mira d'acerbe', we happily can meet again two superb baritones. Amato's subtle schemer of a Luna is worthily partnered by Johann Gadski's big-scale Leonora (Victor 8060; VIC 1395). His rolled 'r's and her attack at 'Io giuro' are dramatically apt. Joseph Schwarz recorded the two halves with different sopranos. His velvety, seductive tone and scrupulous musicianship is matched by that of Elisabeth van Endert and Claire Dux (044282 and 3–44157; LV 86 and 14). Stracciari and Ponselle sing a cut, one-sided version (Am. Col. 49922). The singing, however, is superb. Hardly less worth looking for are Boninsegna with Franceso Cigada (54264 and 54266), Emma Eames with Emilio de Gogorza (Victor 89022) and Rosa Raisa with Giacomo Rimini (Vocalion A–0221; GV 59). More powerful but less subtle than any of these are the versions by Tina Pola-Randaccio with Giovanni Inghilleri (Parlo. R 20110) and Arangi-Lombardi with Galeffi (L 2157; LV 220). Domgraf-Fassbaender's inspiriting art lends character to his German version with Margarete Teschemacher (DA 4403; LV 103).

'Ai nostri monti' seems to bring out the best in mezzos and tenors. I have hardly heard a poor version, but perhaps Martinelli, singing the phrase starting 'Riposa o madre' in one breath, again deserves to be at the top, and he and Homer sing the end in the right dreamy manner (DB 1215). Before them Parsi-Pettinella and Zenatello (Fono. 39819; GV 27) were also wistful obeying that injunction of Verdi's *addorment andosi a poco a poco*. Homer and Caruso are almost as reflective (DM 112; ORL 306) and, of course, the voices themselves have matchless beauty. Sigrid Onegin and Mario Chamlee (Bruns. 15093) are disappointing if you think of their reputations. Tauber is well up to his with Sabine Kalter (Od. 0–8224). Zenatello's rendering, this time with his wife Maria Gay (D 16328), has much atmosphere; so has that by Gigli and that underrated mezzo Cloe Elmo (DB 5385; RLS 129). Not to be despised are Edna Thornton and Walter Hyde, in English (D 120).

None of these studio performances is as rewarding as two from the Metropolitan in extracts from live performances there on private issues. The plaintive Björling partnered by the haunted Bruna Castagna in 1941 show just how much more feeling can be expressed in the theatre. As both are precise interpreters this Act 4, Scene 2, is tremendous, at least until the undistinguished soprano enters. Earlier Björling is no less impressive, although in the opera house he transfers 'Di quella pira' down a tone. This last scene is equalled only by that recorded five years earlier in the same venue when Elisabeth Rethberg, Katherine Meisle, Martinelli and Richard Bonelli were in the cast. They achieve a distinction of phrase and accent not repeated elsewhere in my experience. Gennaro Papi deserves to be acknowledged as the conductor. Verdi's masterpiece here comes into its own. A more recent live performance is the one issued by Cetra, a 1953 La Scala staging, mainly notable for recording the whole of Stignani's Azucena: she makes an arresting effect. Callas is good but less subtle than in her later EMI set. Gino Penno makes a fiery but sometimes uncertain Manrico. Carlo Tagliabue is a tired Luna.

Assembling my ideal cast would depend on my mood. If I wanted the most faithful to Verdi, I would call on Lemnitz or Parsi-Pettinella, Branzell, Urlus and de Luca or Schwarz. Were I minded to something almost as scrupulous but a little more characterful I would ask for Callas, Stignani, Martinelli and Stracciari. Pinza would be my constant Ferrando, and I would have Björling in the wings on both occasions in case either tenor fell ill.

IL TROVATORE

L Leonora; *A* Azucena; *M* Manrico; *C* Conte di Luna; *F* Ferrando

1912 (in French) Morlet *L*; Lapeyrette *A*; Fontaine *M*; Note *C*; Marvini *F*/Chorus and Orch./Ruhlmann
Pathé 1603–21

1930 Scacciati *L*; Zinetti *A*; Merli *M*; Molinari *C*; Zambelli *F*;/La Scala Chorus and Orch./Molajoli
EMI ⓜ 3C 153 03024–5
CBS ⓜ SL 120

1930 Carena *L*; Minghini-Cattaneo *A*; Pertile *M*; Granforte *C*; Carmassi *F*/La Scala Chorus and Orch./Sabajno
EMI ⓜ 3C 153 17083–5

1951 Mancini *L*; Pirazzini *A*; Lauri-Volpi *M*; Tagliabue *C*; Colella *F*/Rome Radio Chorus and Orch./Previtali
Cetra ⓜ LPS 3226 ④ MC 1323;

Turnabout ⓜ THS 65037–9

1951 (live performance, San Carlo, Naples) Callas *L*; Elmo *A*; Lauri-Volpi *M*; Silveri *C*; Tajo *F*/San Carlo Opera Chorus and Orch./Serafin
Cetra ⓜ L 029/2

1952 Milanov *L*; Barbieri *A*; Björling *M*; Warren *C*; Moscona *F*/Shaw Chorale, RCA Orch./Cellini
HMV ⓜ ALP 1832–3
RCA (US) ⓜ AVM 2–0699

1952 Anon. *L*; Petrova *A*; Nicolai *M*; Petrova *C*; Anon. *F*/Florence Festival Chorus and Orch./Tieri
ACE ⓜ 1011

1952 Roman *L*; Sawyer *A*; Sarri *M*; Manca-Serra *C*; Tatozzi *F*/Rome Opera Chorus and Orch./Ricci
Capitol (US) ⓜ PBR 8180

1953 (live performance, La Scala,
Milan) Callas *L*; Stignani *A*;
Penno *M*; Tagliabue *C*; Modesti
F/La Scala Chorus and
Orch./Votto
Cetra ⓜ LO 35/3
Turnabout ⓜ THS 65140–2

1956 Tebaldi *L*; Simionato *A*; del
Monaco *M*; Savarese *C*; Tozzi
F/Florence Festival Chorus,
Grand Theatre Orch.
Geneva/Erede
Decca GOS 614–6;
London OSA 1304

1956 Callas *L*; Barbieri *A*; di Stefano
M; Panerai *C*; Zaccaria *F*/La
Scala Chorus and Orch./Karajan
EMI SLS 879 ④ TC–SLS 869;
Angel ⓜ 3554CL

1959 L. Price *L*; Elias *A*; Tucker *M*;
Warren *C*; Tozzi *F*/Rome Opera
Chorus and Orch./Basile
RCA (US) LSC 6150

1962 Stella *L*; Cossotto *A*; Bergonzi
M; Bastianini *C*; Vinco *F*/La
Scala Chorus and Orch./Serafin
DG 2728 008

1964 Tucci *L*; Simionato *A*; Corelli
M; Merrill *C*; Mazzoli *F*/Rome
Opera Chorus and
Orch./Schippers
EMI SLS 916;
Angel SCL 3653

1965 Dima-Toriman *L*; Palli *A*; Stavru
M; Enigarescu *C*; Dimitrescu
F/Bucharest National Opera
Chorus and Orch./Massini
Electrocord ECE

1969 L. Price *L*; Cossotto *A*;
Domingo *M*; Milnes *C*; Giaiotti
F/Ambrosian Opera Chorus,
New Philharmonia/Mehta
RCA (UK) SER 5586–8 ④ RK
40002;
(US) LSC 6194

1971 Vajna *L*; Allegri *A*; Bardini *M*;
F. Pagliazzi *C*; Micalopoulos
F/Czech Philharmonic Chorus,
Prague CO/Savini
Supraphon 112 0501–3

1975 Sutherland *L*; Horne *A*;
Pavarotti *M*; Wixell *C*; Ghiaurov
F/London Opera Chorus,
National PO/Bonynge

Decca D82D3 ④ K82K3
London OSA 13124 ④ 5–13124

1975 Kabaivanska *L*; Cortez *A*;
Bonisolli *M*; Zancanaro *C*;
Luccardi *F*/Berlin Sate State
Opera Chorus, Berlin State Op
Orch./Gardelli
Ariola-Eurodisc 28169 XFR

1977 L. Price *L*; Obraztsova *A*;
Bonisolli *M*; Cappuccilli *C*;
Raimondi *F*/German Opera
Chorus, Berlin PO/Karajan
EMI SLS 119 ④ TC–SLS 5119;
Angel SCLX 3855Q

Excerpts

1935 (in German) Toros *L*; Dörwald
A; Völker *M*; Weltner *C*;/Berlin
State Opera Chorus and
Orch./Weigert
Polydor 15277–80

1935 (in German) Malkin *L*; Jung *A*;
Pattiera *M*; Schöffler *C*/Chorus
and Orch.
Parlophone E 11048–50

1944 (in German) Scheppan *L*; Schilp
A; Roswaenge *M*; Schmitt-
Walther *C*; Lang *F*/German
Opera Chorus and Orch./Rother
Acanta ⓜ BB 21449

1954 Ruggeri *L*; da Costa *M*;
Valentino *C*/Chorus and
Orch./Walther
Royale ⓜ 1601

1958 (in German) Muszely *L*; Wagner
A; Schock *M*; Metternich *C*;
Schmidt *F*/German Opera
Chorus, Berlin SO/Zanotelli,
Schüchter
EMI 1C 063 28998

1962 (in German) Davy *L*; Ahlin Z
A; Kónya *M*; Wolansky *C*;
Betram *F*/Württemburg State
Opera Chorus and Orch./Kulka
DG SLPEM 136405

1962 (in French) Le Bris *L*; Kahn *A*;
Poncet *M*; Quilico *C*;
Gontcharenko *F*/Lamoureux
Orch./Fournet
Philips 837 469

1962 (in English) Fretwell *L*; Johnson
A; Craig *M*; Glossop *C*;
McIntyre *F*/Sadler's Wells
Chorus and Orch./Moores

EMI ESD 7027 ④ TC–ESD 7027;
Capitol (US) SP8609
1965 (in German) Schreyer *L*; Draksler *A*; Kmentt *M*;

Wächter *C*; Welter *F*/Vienna Volksoper Chorus and Orch./Bauer-Theussel
Ariola-Eurodisc Z80003R

La traviata

ALAN JEFFERSON

Verdi's eighteenth opera, based on *La Dame aux camélias* by Alexandre Dumas *fils*, was first heard in Venice in 1853. It failed to appeal immediately because it was in contemporary dress – an unheard-of thing for an opera. In England the subject was considered to be thoroughly indelicate by some people and by the church, but out of these initial objections *La traviata* has risen triumphantly to become the most frequently performed and the most substantially recorded of all Verdi's operas. Indeed, no other single opera by any composer has appeared more often on record.

There are three stages in its recorded history: the multifarious acoustics; the fewer, generally excellent, electrical recordings on 78; and the LPs. The bulk of the acoustics are now exceedingly difficult to find. Quite often, too, the effort in searching is scarcely worthwhile. The earliest of them all was made in 1899.

This was a 'De' miei bollenti spiriti' by Ferruccio Giannini (whose daughter Dusolina is better known than he). It is on Berliner No. 1921. One of the first recorded Violettas was Bice Adami on a ten-inch Odeon (37210) with the baritone Ferretti, singing 'Dite alla giovine' with piano. His voice is acceptable enough although his interpretation verges on the comical. The coupling of this record is, curiously enough, the same duet with another soprano, dell'Agli.

The great Gemma Bellincioni, creator of Santuzza and of Fedora, made 'Ah fors'è lui' (053019) in 1904, later transferred to VB 11 in the HMV Archive series. Her interpretation was advanced for its time: she *thought* about what she was singing. The *scena* for Violetta at the end of Act 1 is properly in four distinct sections: 'E strano!', 'Ah fors'è lui', 'Follie! Follie!' and 'Sempre libera'. It was unusual for all four to be included on two sides in the early days, but this was possible so long as there were no repeats.

Geraldine Farrar recorded the *scena* on two single-sided G&T's in Berlin at the beginning of the century. These two (53344 and 53469) were made in 1905 and 1906 when she was in prime voice and in her middle twenties. Twenty years later, after she had retired, she gave a radio talk during a Metropolitan performance of *Traviata*. She sang the predictable soprano passages by way of illustrating Violetta's character, but added 'Di Provenza', the baritone aria from Act 2! It is a most interesting document and has been captured as a fill-up side to the pirated Ponselle *Traviata*.

There is a memorable Violetta-Germont duet from Maria Galvany and Titta Ruffo who sing 'Dite alla giovine' (DB 176), made at Milan in 1907. Galvany has a good, strong voice, full of character, but there is no question of remorse: she has made her decision and will stand by it – to start with. Then she stumbles, mentally, and is overcome by grief when Ruffo's voice enters. It is a marvellous, round baritone, used very intelligently and the diction is clear as a bell. He emerges as a bluffer Germont than Mattia Battistini.

Battistini, one of the greatest Italian baritones, recorded 'Di Provenza' in 1911, beginning, 'Mio figlio! Oh quanto soffrir!' On those first beats of the six bars, he sings the acciaccaturas perfectly, as few baritones do. It is a model version (DB 201).

Giovanni Zenatello was one of the outstanding acoustic Alfredos. The original records are hard to come by but some have been transferred to LP (Rococo 12, others on Olympus). There is 'Un di felice' (without a Violetta) dated 1903, and in 1905 he made two Fonotipias – 'De' miei bollenti' and the Scena della Borsa beginning 'Questa donna cognoscete'. In 'Un di', Zenatello finds a very attractive catch in the voice as if he is pent up with emotion as well as delight; and he shows a number of individual and graceful vocal attributes, such as a delicate little turn in the middle of the word 'del-izia'. His Act 2 aria is sung complete, with piano accompaniment, and he sounds very immediate.

Zenatello's senior, the honey-voiced Alessandro Bonci, recorded 'De' miei bollenti' (Fono. 62130) in 1907. It was later dubbed on to Olympus. He sings most beautifully, caressing the words with fond passion, and gives coloratura treatment to the last 'qu-asi'.

The great Fernando de Lucia recorded 'Un di felice', beginning at 'Ah, si da un anno' in 1904 (52080; VA 15). The smile that must have been on his face as he sang is reflected in the voice: there is no ornamentation and no cadenza, but there are a number of pauses, all for reasonable effect and in keeping with the words. He also recorded 'Parigi o cara' with the Spanish soprano Josefina Huguet in 1906 (054081; Rubini DEL 101).

Among the weightier sopranos, Lilli Lehmann recorded Violetta's Act 1 *scena* beginning 'Ah fors'è lui' on two single-sided Odeons (50353–4; GV 66) in 1907. They show a really big voice, utterly true in pitch, noble and firmly controlled. Luisa Tetrazzini's Act 1 *scena* was recorded in London in 1908 (DB 531; COLH 136).

In 1914, two outstanding duets appeared: Lucrezia Bori and John McCormack in 'Parigi o cara'; Alma Gluck and Caruso in the Brindisi with chorus. This is inexplicably the only record of *Traviata* which Caruso made, a justly famous one (DJ 100; many reissues). Gluck has an ideal voice for the duet while Caruso sounds suave and gentlemanly. They both ride the climaxes effortlessly. Bori and McCormack sing together most gracefully too. While the Irish tenor can never disguise his brogue (and divides 'Parigi' sharply from 'o cara' which no Italian tenor ever does) the voices match well (DM 104; GEMM 155). Bori also recorded the first part of *scena* (DB 1606) in 1928 and the 'Addio del passato' (DA 130). She has a pure and youthful voice and sings with meaning and pathos. McCormack's 'De' miei bollenti' (DB 631; GEMM 155) was first recorded in 1910. He gets a good ringing quality on the first 'vivo' which he holds strongly, as he does on the last-time 'memorie' and manages a skilful cadenza at the end. It is an excellent version.

This leaves one major and early protagonist undiscussed: Nellie Melba. Some say she was the greatest Violetta, others. . . . Every different 'take' of the same aria shows her producing *exactly* the same interpretation, the same technical resources, the same breaths, the same everything. It speaks volumes for her technique though less, surely, for her artistry. She made 'Ah! fors'è lui' on one side of DB 346, and another take of it on a lilac HMV 03026 of 1904. On 03017 she again recorded it, and followed with 'Sempre libera' which was subsequently blocked out of the issued record. Her 'Dite alla giovine' with her compatriot John Brownlee appeared in 1926 (DB 987). All these are transferred to LP on 'Nellie Melba: the London recordings' (RLS 719).

A distinguished little group of 78s was made by Amelita Galli-Curci, Tito Schipa and Giuseppe de Luca. Alone, or in combinations of soprano–tenor and soprano–baritone, they provided many people with the vocal ideal in the days before LP. 'Un dì' and 'Parigi o cara' came first acoustically on DA 711, then electrically (DA 1133; LV 219). 'Addio del passato' with the 'Sempre libera' was on DA 216, and in 1919 Galli-Curci made a fuller, though still incomplete version of the *scena* (DB 257). Schipa made Alfredo's Act 2 *scena* on Pathé (A. 5544; Ember GVC 10). Galli-Curci's and de Luca's 'Dite alla giovine' (a celebrated account) appeared in 1918 on 2–054099 and 2–054089, then on DB 174. It was remade electrically in 1927 on DB 1165. De Luca's 1929 'Di Provenza' is a masterly account (DB 1340; DN 1012).

Perhaps the finest, most ebullient version of Alfredo's *scena* is by Gigli (DB 1222), an exemplary piece of singing and characterization. He also made 'Un dì' and 'Parigi' with Maria Caniglia (DB 3811) in 1939, showing himself to be the perfect *vocal* Alfredo of the time.

Claudia Muzio's letter-scene and 'Addio del passato' date from June 1935 (LX 655; COLC 101). This was not long before her own death and is probably the most poignant version of the scene to exist. She begins by reading the letter from Germont in such a way that we know *she* knows every word by heart. She uses her chest register for speaking, clearly and solemnly. In the aria her last high A, starting with *un fil di voce* (a thread of sound, as Verdi requests) grows in volume until she breaks off with what we know is a stab of pain.

Among the many foreign-language 78s of *La Traviata* Margarethe Siems's first two sections of the *scena* (43533; Rococo 4) should be heard. The top notes ring out so accurately, purely and finely that they sound disembodied. Frieda Hempel, silver-voiced prima donna of the Berlin Opera, made 'Un di' and 'Parigi' with Hermann Jadlowker; the Act 2 duet with Pasquale Amato and most of the Act 1 *scena* (DB 294 and 272). Helge Roswaenge made three versions of the Act 2 *scena*, first on Electrola EG 814, and always followed it with 'O mio rimorso' – seldom recorded in those days and usually cut in performance. He is beefy and lacking in charm. His duets 'Un di' and 'Parigi' with the Greek-born Margherita Perras (DB 4458; LV 73) are, of course, in German. In the last war, a performance (presumably studio) of highlights from *Traviata* was recorded by Roswaenge, Maria Cebotari and Heinrich Schlusnus. It is interesting mainly for Cebotari's contribution.

There are three pairs of French *Traviata* singers, of which Georges Thill and the Belgian soprano Vina Bovy are the best – a gay Brindisi (LF 94) and 'Un di' (LFX 472). Bovy's complete *scena* is nicely phrased (DB 5004). Thill's *scena* (L 1964; LV 224) is good, and their 'Parigi' is on LF 149.

Of the 78 sets, the Molajoli has the ordinary Mercedes Capsir as Violetta, and the neighing Australian tenor 'Lionello Cecil' (Cecil Sherwood) as Alfredo. It was Columbia's only offering until after the last war. It possesses the advantage of Salvatore Baccaloni as the Doctor. Columbia's second version is favoured, with Paolo Silveri's young-sounding and well-executed Germont *père*; it was made in 1946 in Italy. Columbia's third set ran up against casting difficulties. We had hoped for Callas, but Antonietta Stella proved a poor substitute. Di Stefano's voice had declined in quality and Tito Gobbi was going through a bad patch. Only Tullio Serafin and the orchestra produced ravishing sounds.

HMV's first electrical set, 'Voce del Padrone', came out two years later than Columbia's first in competition with it. This was a pruned version, taking four sides less than its rival, though it turned out to be more serviceable. It lasted until after the war and was later transferred to LP. There was not another HMV *Traviata* until 1956, in which Leonard Warren was a memorable Germont but Pierre Monteux seemed utterly miscast if his slow tempi are anything to go by.

Victoria de los Angeles sings with distinction on the Serafin set providing one overlooks the fact that her constant vocal purity prevents her from belonging to the *demi-monde* of which she is supposed to be queen. The Alfredo, Germont and Rome Orchestra are all average. HMV's last *Traviata* has Beverly Sills as an unsubtle and un-Italian (especially un-French) sounding Violetta, unable to see and interpret all

the many facets to the character. Nicolai Gedda is a somewhat coarse
Alfredo; and Rolando Panerai is a hard, pushing Germont. In addition,
Aldo Ceccato handles the score as though he is afraid of soiling his
hands.

In the days when Victor was associated with HMV, Toscanini's *Traviata*
was all the rage. It proved to be totally acceptable in spite of the
conductor whose tempi seemed too fast and explosive for the nature of
the music after the first party scene. It introduced Robert Merrill, who
was later to sing Germont in two more recordings, deepening and
broadening his fine characterization as he went along. Jan Peerce's Alfredo
is all bounce and shout – very short on delicacy.

RCA's next set was very successful, with Anna Moffo as Violetta,
Richard Tucker as Alfredo and Robert Merrill again. Moffo is excellent:
bright and gay in Act 1, sympathy-catching in Act 2, pathetic and touching
in Act 3 where she reads the letter in a whisper – a telling stroke.
Merrill's performance is more perceptive than before and he has the right
bite to his words. Tucker has too cumbersome a voice though he possesses
a clean line. RCA's more recent *Traviata* is a superb one. Montserrat
Caballé at last fulfils most of the requirements for a rounded portrait of
Violetta, especially as her coloratura encompasses the Act 1 *scena* without
difficulty. Carlo Bergonzi is the ideal interpreter in his generation of
Alfredos, and Sherrill Milnes is a fine Germont, singing every note
accurately. Prêtre might have given a more positive lead here and there,
but this set is a powerful one.

In the first Decca version, made in 1954, their reigning soprano and
baritone – Tebaldi and Protti – were assisted by Gianni Poggi as Alfredo.
Tebaldi has to transpose down the second verse of 'Sempre libera' but
she improves all the time. Poggi is so-so and Protti is no more than
adequate.

Up to 1963 every *Traviata* had been made with cuts in the score. Then
Decca issued the definitive recording of the complete score, revealing, for
the first time, Verdi's architecture instead of mis-arrangements by
generations of impertinent conductors and singers. Sutherland is the
musically first-class Violetta, (although she might be singing in Patagonian);
Bergonzi and Merrill are the excellent son and father. John Pritchard
conducts with fine musical feeling. Decca's next set was abridged and
came out on two discs in 1969. The singing is distinguished, with Fischer-
Dieskau as Germont, but the loss of music is grievous (an odd *volte-face*
for Decca).

The first DG *Traviata*, issued in 1963, had Renata Scotto as a plausible
Violetta and Gianni Raimondi as a thoroughly acceptable Alfredo, but
Bastianini is a detached and uncommitted Germont. All the voices in this
recording came between orchestra and loudspeakers, thus reversing the
effect of an opera-house auditorium, Votto gets a move on. DG's latest
Traviata is the most up-to-date studio recording to reach us. Ileana

Cotrubas makes a winning Violetta, with her own tragic facial expression carried through to the voice in a well-conceived interpretation, beautifully sung. Placido Domingo is about all one could wish for as Alfredo and, likewise, Sherrill Milnes sings a superb Germont. The only criticism of this version is in the false economy of trying to get such good material on to four sides. Apart from some actual constriction and pre-echo, there have to be cuts in repeats; Cotrubas suffered worst from them. Carlos Kleiber is forced to drive the tempi too hard to push the music into four sides.

The version under Lamberto Gardelli is the best of the three short-measure *Traviatas*. Mirella Freni turns out one of the most beautiful pieces of singing and characterization to be recorded, exquisitely frail and loving. Franco Bonisolli is a little stiff as Alfredo, but thoroughly acceptable. Bruscantini emerges as a younger *père* than usual, less sure of himself and not as dark or demanding as others have been.

It has taken too long to reach the soprano who was probably regarded as the most exciting Violetta of her age in the opera house: Maria Callas. In 1952 Callas was in fine voice but her Alfredo and Germont were far below what she deserved in support. It is a glorious interpretation on her part with the vocal flaws making her singing sound all the more human. In 1955 a Callas *Traviata* was taken from a performance at La Scala. It is an immensely powerful interpretation and production (Visconti-Giulini) and has Giuseppe di Stefano as a good Alfredo. Bastianini is a less successful Germont. There are the 'usual cuts' and the sound is acceptable until the last two scenes. Nevertheless, it is the nearest to that 1955 Callas–di Stefano–Gobbi *Traviata* which never happened, with a live audience to give it a tingle of immediacy, Giulini at the helm and Callas acting for all she is worth.

This now leaves the smaller companies and their *Traviatas*. The two slightly dubious Remington recordings are unknown and unheard. The 1960 Musica et Litera recording made in Hamburg has Virginia Zeani as a robust, passionate Violetta with a very 'open' voice; she gives an intelligent performance. Giuseppe Savio and Paolo Gorin support her. (There was once a highlights disc on World Record Club in the UK from this set).

Orpheus produced a Viennese *Traviata* on two discs which had drastic cuts in the most unexpected places. Elena Tedeschi makes an impulsive Violetta who seems not to have the full measure of the character, while Augusto Vicentini is an average Alfredo. Renato Cesari turns out a respectable and noble Germont *père*.

There is one elusive recording of *Traviata*, unheard, made at the Patagonian Festival of 1961 on a USA Period release. It is mentioned briefly here for the sake of completeness.

There are three foreign-language performances of *La Traviata*, the oldest of which comes from the USSR and is sung in Russian. In many respects it takes the listener back to pre-Toscanini, pre-revolution times. The conductor, Aleksandr Orlov, was a White Russian prince who survived everything and continued as a conductor until the late 1950s. The soprano, Eliszaveta Sumskaya, is a cut above the usual, fluttering Russian diva who (Vishnevskaya in her prime apart) we have been hearing on USSR records for years. There is little trace of vibrato, and she gives the impression of living the character whole-heartedly. Given this zest, her performance is generally very good, but with one idiosyncracy: the 'Amami Alfredo' is dwelt on and pulled about too much. Her voice is well-balanced in duets with both the sublime Ivan Kozlovsky and with Pavel Lisitsian. Kozlovsky sounds incredibly young – he was nearly 54 when the recording was finished, at the end of more than fifteen months. His 'De' miei bollenti' has an accompaniment of *pizzicato* strings, not bowed as in the West (though two far more recent recordings have gone back to Verdi's marking). The Germont is dark and gruff, well sung, but not revealing of character. Cuts are usual, though Kozlovsky does sing 'O mio rimorso'.

In 1963 Gardelli, directed a performance in Hungarian at the Budapest Opera. The voices at his disposal, as well as the orchestral resources, were not altogether up to his fine requirements. Gabrielle Déry's Violetta and Lászlo Palócz's Germont are both sung with push and over-emphasis and miss the very subtleties which are the key to both characters. On the other hand. Robert Ilosfalvy's Alfredo is that of an international singer. The Hungarian language, more than Russian, seems a long way from either Paris or Busseto.

Zeani's Romanian *Traviata* is a performance on the grand scale, which works to a certain extent, though she has a job to control the over-athletic Ion Buzea, whose Alfredo is grand in the wrong way. Nicolae Herlea's conventionally portrayed Germont is nobly sung. Jean Bobescu is in complete charge of this performance which is otherwise well cast and well played.

Lastly, one of the most extraordinary of all versions. It is an 'off-the-air' performance from the Metropolitan in 1935 and has Rosa Ponselle as a hyper-exciting and vibrant Violetta who fairly pops out of the record. From the moment she takes her verse of the Brindisi more slowly than her Alfredo – Frederick Jagel – has done (and metaphorically wags a reproving finger at the conductor, Ettore Panizza) we know that her performance is going to be scaled to a nicety. Her *scena* at the end of Act 1 is embellished by an unrestrained and vulgar laugh between the end of 'Follie!' and the 'Sempre libera'. This is sung between clenched teeth. At the repeat of the 'Follie!' there is no laugh. Touches like that speak highly for the interpretative care and preparation. Jagel's artistic Alfredo is most effective in Act 2 when he is so clearly *thinking* about what he is singing. Tibbett's Germont sounds angry at his first encounter with Violetta, but Ponselle's gorgeous voice and fascinating presence soon set up a dramatic *rapprochement*, both telling and moving. 'Amami, Alfredo' is heart-rending, and Tibbett's 'Di Provenza' is a model of how the old war-horse of an aria should be rendered. In the last act, Ponselle's letter-reading is absolutely convincing; she sings 'Addio del passato' fairly straight, while her death brings tears to the eyes of even the hardiest *Traviata*-fancier. It is a pity that this shattering performance, enlivened by commentary on the artists as they appear before the curtain, cannot be given wider currency.

There are a few highlights discs dissociated from complete recordings, some of which are not sung in Italian. One of the most interesting of these is from a wartime studio performance, and has Maria Cebotari as a lovely Violetta, Helge Roswaenge as an Alfredo who has declined in charm (but not in volume) since his 78 days, and Heinrich Schlusnus as an excellent Germont. These excerpts are often longer in content than the general custom, and also include some unexpected additions. H. Steinkopf conducts the Berlin State Opera capably. Another German disc has Maria Stader as Violetta and Ernst Haefliger as a suave Alfredo. Stader has the equipment but her characterization seems wrong even in a German context. Hermann Winter is the Germont and Hans Schmidt-Isserstedt conducts the NWDR Orchestra. A much better version of German highlights had Hilde Gueden, Fritz Wunderlich and Fischer-Dieskau with the Bavarian State Opera Orchestra under Bruno Bartoletti. They all managed to give it an Italian feeling in spite of the language barrier. The British highlights record of 1963 (CSD 1556) is from a Sadler's Wells production. It would probably be far better done by the ENO today.

A number of singers who made complete *Traviatas* also recorded separate arias – Callas, Moffo, Sutherland; Bergonzi, del Monaco, Domingo; Fischer-Dieskau, Gobbi, Merrill. Among these must be singled out Tito Gobbi's magnificent 'Di Provenza' (DB 21227; HLM 7018). He makes telling use of the microphone by singing *mezza voce* in a real legato and with the greatest emotion, never overdone. Then there are duets in which the singers have not appeared together in the complete opera, such as Sutherland and Pavarotti. They give us the Brindisi, 'Un dï felice' and 'Parigi o cara' (SXL 6828), under Richard Bonynge with the National Philharmonic in a worthwhile and – who knows? – even a prophetic manner!

LA TRAVIATA

V Violetta; *A* Alfredo Germont; *G* Giorgio Germont

1912 (in French) Morlet *V*; Trosselli *A*; Albers *G*/Chorus and Orch./Archainbaud
Pathé 1587–1602

1918 Bevignani *V*; Tumminello *A*; Badini *G*/La Scala Chorus and Orch./Sabajno
HMV S 5620–41

1928 Capsir *V*; Cecil *A*; Galeffi *G*/La
Scala Chorus and Orch./Molajoli
EMI ⓜ 3C 165 18029–30
1930 Rosza *V*; Ziliani *A*; Borgonovo
G/La Scala Chorus and
Orch./Sabajno
HMV C 2214–26
Camden ⓜ CAL 287–9
1946 Albanese *V*; Peerce *A*; Merrill
G/Chorus, NBC SO/Toscanini
RCA (UK) ⓜ AT 202; (US)
ⓜ LM 6003
1946 Guerrini *V*; Infantino *A*; Silveri
G/Rome Opera Chorus and
Orch./Bellezza
EMI ⓜ 3C 153 17079–80; CBS
(US) ⓜ SL 103
1952 Noli *V*; Campora *A*; Tagliabue
G/Rome Opera Chorus and
Orch./Berrettoni
Remington ⓜ 199–77
1952 Schimenti *V*; Pola *A*; Monachesi
G/Rome Opera Chorus and
Orch./Ricci
Remington ⓜ 199–98
1953 Callas *V*; Albanese *A*; Savarese
G/Turin Radio Chorus and
Orch./Santini
Ember ⓜ GVC 2345 ④ ZCEB
2345; Turnabout ⓜ THS
65047–8
1954 Tebaldi *V*; Poggi *A*; Protti
G/Santa Cecilia Academy Chorus
and Orch./Molinari-Pradelli
Decca ⓜ GOM 522–4;
Richmond ⓜ RS 63021
1954 (in Russian) Shumskaya *V*;
Kozlovsky *A*; Lisitsian *G*/Bolshoi
Theatre Chorus and Orch./Orlov
MK ⓜ DO 6271–6
1955 (live performance, La Scala,
Milan) Callas *V*; di Stefano *A*;
Bastianini *G*/La Scala Chorus
and Orch./Giulini
Cetra ⓜ LO 28/2
1956 Carteri *V*; Valletti *A*; Warren
G/Rome Opera Chorus and
Orch./Monteux
RCA ⓜ VIC 6004
1956 Stella *V*; di Stefano *A*; Gobbi
G/La Scala Chorus and
Orch./Serafin
Columbia ⓜ 33 CX 1370–1;
Angel ⓜ 3545BL

1959 De Los Angeles *V*; del Monte
A; Sereni *G*/Rome Opera
Chorus and Orch./Serafin
EMI SLS 5097 ④ TC–SLS
5097; Angel SCL 3628
1960 Zeani *V*; Savio *A*; Gorin
G/Hamburg State Opera Chorus
and Orch./Annovazzi
Musica & Litera 7006–7
1960 Moffo *V*; Tucker *A*; Merrill
G/Rome Opera Chorus and
Orch./Previtali
RCA (UK) VICS 6111; (US)
LSC 6154 ④ ARK 3 2538
1961 Tedeschi *V*; Vicentini *A*; Cesari
G/Patagonia Festival Chorus and
Orch./Rivoli
Period TE 1092
1962 Scotto *V*; Raimondi *A*;
Bastianini *G*/La Scala Chorus
and Orch./Votto
DG 2726 049 ④ 3371 004
1962 Sutherland *V*; Bergonzi *A*;
Merrill *G*/Florence Festival
Chorus and Orch./Pritchard
Decca SET 249–41 ④ K19K32;
London OSA 1366 ④ 5–1366
1963 (in Hungarian) Déry *V*; Ilosfalvy
A; Palócz *G*/Budapest State
Opera Chorus and
Orch./Gardelli
Qualiton SLPX 1128–30
1967 Caballé *V*; Bergonzi *A*; Milnes
G/RCA Italiana Chorus and
Orch./Prêtre
RCA (UK) SER 5564–6; (US)
LSC 6180
1968 (in Romanian) Zeani *V*; Buzea
A; Herlea *G*/Bucharest Opera
Chorus and Orch./Bobescu
Electrocord ECE 0374–6
1968 Lorengar *V*; Aragall *A*; Fischer-
Dieskau *G*/German Opera
Chorus and Orch./Maazel
Decca SET 401–2; London OSA
1279 ④ 5–1279
1971 Sills *V*; Gedda *A*; Panerai
G/Alldis Choir, RPO/Ceccato
HMV SLS 960; Angel SCLX
3780 ④ 4X3S 3780
1973 Freni *V*; Bonisolli *A*; Bruscantini
G/Berlin State Opera Chorus,
Berlin State Orch./Gardelli
Acanta JB 21644

1977 Cotrubas V; Domingo A; Milnes
G/Bavarian State Opera Chorus
and Orch./C. Kleiber
DG 2707 103 ④ 370 024

Excerpts

1940 Steber V; Tokatyan A; Warren
G/Chorus, Publisher's Service
SO/Pelletier
RCA (US) ⓜ CAL 227

1944 (in German) Cebotari V;
Roswaenge A; Schlusnus
G/Berlin State Opera Chorus
and Orch./Steinkopf
Acanta ⓜ BB 21498

1950 Albanese V; Peerce A; Merrill
G Chorus, RCA Orch./Trucco
RCA ⓜ LM 1115

1954 Opawsky V; Larsen A; Driessen
G/Chorus, Netherlands
PO/Goehr
Musical Masterpieces Society
ⓜ MMS 2011

1954 Morales V; Simoneau
A/Lamoureux Orch./Dervaux
Philips ⓜ N00639R

1954 Hardy V; Schultz A; Sebaroli
G/Chorus and Orch./Peluso
Opa ⓜ 1001–2

1957 (in German) Müszely V; Schock
A; Metternich G/Berlin State
Opera Chorus and
Orch./Schüchter
EMI ⓜ 1C 037 28996

1958 (in German) Stader V; Haefliger
A; Winter G/Hamburg Radio
Orch./Schmidt-Isserstedt

DG SLPEM 136 005

1959 (in French) Robin V; Finel A;
Dens G/Paris Opéra
Orch./Dervaux
EMI 2C 061 12106

1960 (in French) Le Bris V; Chauvet
A; Bianco G/Orch./Amati
Véga 16048

1961 (in French) Doria V; Vanzo A;
Massard G/Orch./Etchéverry
Vogue LDM 30135 ④ B.VOC
411

1961 (in French) Micheau V; Blanc
G/Paris Opéra Orch./Prêtre
EMI ASTX 135

1961 (in German) Streich V; Kozub
A; Günter G/Chorus and
Orch./Wagner
Philips 6593 007

1961 (in German) Gueden V;
Wunderlich A; Fischer-Dieskau
G/Bavarian Radio Chorus and
Orch./Bartoletti
DG 2537 022

1963 (in English) June V; Wakefield
A; Easton G/Sadler's Wells
Opera Chorus and
Orch./Matheson
EMI CSD 1556; Capitol SP 8616

1965 (in German) Melander V;
Wilhelm A; Kloose G/German
Opera Chorus and Orch./Peters
Ariola-Eurodisc Z76305R

1970 (in German) Rothenberger V;
Ridder A; Anheisser G/German
Opera Chorus and Orch./Patanè
EMI 1C 063 29054

Simon Boccanegra

LORD HAREWOOD

When *Simon Boccanegra* was first performed at the Metropolitan Opera, New York, W.J. Henderson of the *New York Sun* wrote:

This is Verdi in his era of enormous political plots, conspiracies and crimes, feudal despotism grandiloquently voiced in pompous measures; dark passions delineated in sombre melodic phrases and gloomy instrumental utterances.

Verdi's subjects were chosen in a period of high romanticism, in the Italy of the Risorgimento, and they provided him with what he most wanted: situation – a collision of opposites, with clash of motive and an opportunity for the people of the drama to strike sparks off each other. This obsession with situation led occasionally to a neglect of narrative – the information that would once have been conveyed in dry recitative – and only gradually and with the operas of his maturity did Verdi find the balance that he had been half-consciously seeking all his career.

Simon Boccanegra was far from successful when first performed in 1857. The composer himself described the opera as monotonous and cold; however greatly recent audiences may have revised this opinion, the story remains essentially gloomy. Added to that is the apparent obscurity of detail: the difficulty the audience has in discovering exactly why this character or the other is in that particular place under a pseudonym, which of the other characters knows the truth about who he or she is and why he or she is there – for this Verdi's preoccupation with situation is largely responsible.

The subject is an important one – nothing less than an attempt at putting the quality of statesmanship on to the operatic stage, something which Mozart tried in *La clemenza di Tito*, and which Verdi himself was to glance at in *Un ballo in mashera* and to tackle squarely in *Don Carlos*. It is perhaps this emphasis on the political clash between the rival parties of Plebeians and Patricians that gives the opera its unusual interest for us. Although the opera failed in Venice in 1857 and two years later at La Scala, the composer had a special affection for it and, as in the comparable case of *Macbeth* (which he also thought underrated), many years after the première he set about revising it. The season at La Scala early in 1881 in a curious way provided a watershed in Verdi's career and marked the start of the final period. Not only was the revised *Boccanegra* his first attempt at collaboration with Boito, but two members of the outstanding cast (Anna D'Angeri, Francesco Tamagno, Victor Maurel and Edouard de Reszke, who two months earlier had sung *Ernani* together in the same theatre) were to lead the cast for *Otello* six years later.

Apart from a general tidying-up of dialogue, Boito wrote the masterly Council Chamber scene of Act 1, and Verdi's musical revision was even more thorough. Details of orchestration, of vocal line and of harmony are altered all over the place. Whole sections were recomposed, others made more effective, usually through the new understatement shown in the composer's later manner as compared with the insistent full-throatedness of the middle period. The outstanding features of the opera are to be found in Verdi's expressed affection for Genoa and its sea coast; the political clash, most explicit in the rivalry of Boccanegra and Fiesco; and the extraordinary characterization of the central figure. All through one cannot help but be impressed by the amazing consistency of the protagonist's music in spite of the discrepancy between the two periods in which Verdi worked on the opera. This is a mature, puissant figure, to the Italian baritone perhaps what Hans Sachs is to the German: long, exacting and immensely rewarding.

Since the war four complete recordings have been publicly available, while many opera enthusiasts have begged, borrowed or (the minority) bought one of the two private recordings made with the celebrated cast of the Metropolitan revival of the 1930s. Neither Cetra's set, nor HMV's, made respectively in 1951 and 1957, is ideal, but the presence of Tito Gobbi in the HMV cast is a strong asset. It is Gobbi's best performance on disc (and perhaps in the theatre as well) and nowhere else is his command of a role as a whole backed up by such immaculate detail, with every phrase contributing its just weight, every word its inflexion, to the grand picture. The voice itself lacks something of sensuous quality, but this detracts little from a performance that is ideal in concept, hardly less so in execution.

Paolo Silveri, for Cetra, with his youthful phrasing, by comparison with Gobbi struts rather than strides his way through the role. On HMV, Boris Christoff's Fiesco makes a fine foil to Gobbi's protagonist, and his singing is splendid throughout; Victoria de los Angeles's unique beauty of tone and phrasing does much to compensate for a small-scale performance, but Giuseppe Campora is none too secure as Adorno. Walter Monachesi, Paolo in each of these sets, sings much better for Cetra, for whom Mario Petri portrays Fiesco forcefully and with intelligence. For Cetra, Bergonzi, in his first year as a tenor, even if not yet the polished artist of later years, is far above average, and Antonietta

Stella, for all her lack of experience at the time of the recording, makes a strong Amelia. Cetra has only superannuated recording to set against the smooth technique of HMV – regrettable, as Francesco Molinari-Pradelli's dramatic conducting is preferable to the more prosaic reading of Gabriele Santini.

In 1973 and 1977 came new recordings from RCA and DG. RCA's has much to recommend it, with a strong performance of the title role from Piero Cappuccilli; fresh, rich singing from Katia Ricciarelli; a vivid Fiesco from Ruggero Raimondi; and in Domingo the finest Adorno on record – he demonstrates vocal splendour, positive phrasing and an old-fashioned firmness in the middle of the voice, once the *sine qua non* of the Verdi tenor. Gianandrea Gavazzeni is the expert, if slightly extrovert, conductor – and here lies the major difference between the sets.

Claudio Abbado for DG is the architect of a performance which combines nobility with an intensity hard to parallel among modern Verdi conductors, and most of his cast had been polished by him and Giorgio Strehler over five seasons at La Scala. A spacious recording allows for unusual expectancy in the prologue with its *sotto voce* markings, for electrifying attack at Fiesco's entry before his aria or the start of the first of the great confrontations between him and Boccanegra, and for beautiful detail throughout. Never have I heard the postlude to 'Il lacerato spirito' sound more compassionate, the prelude to Amelia's aria more beautiful, or the recognition duet more affecting. Cappuccilli, inspired by the urging of his Scala mentor, sings superbly with a legato worthy of Battistini and the expressiveness and response to words of a Fischer-Dieskau; he is here much finer than in the earlier set. The admirable Mirella Freni, a touching figure in the theatre, and José Carreras are lighter of voice than their RCA counterparts, but that is turned to advantage as youthful vulnerability. Nicolai Ghiaurov is nothing less than magnificent, and José van Dam very fine as Paolo. I cannot imagine this set will be quickly rivalled – it seems to me incomparable – but even its individual and collective excellence would not tempt me to part with Gobbi.

How does all this compare with the 'off-the-air' discs of the Metropolitan? As recordings, of course, they cannot compete technically, and imagination amounting to forbearance must be exercised. But at this point apology ceases. Ettore Panizza conducts with great authority both in the 1935 version (which originally lacked the prologue, since found and added) and that made in 1939, and the atmosphere of performance extends to sharp, short applause after the big numbers. Elisabeth Rethberg is the least Italianate of the cast, but her suave phrasing is supported by purity and intensity of style, and in 1935 her voice was close to its best. Giovanni Martinelli from his first offstage phrases demonstrates security, authority, and breadth of phrasing that are hard to equal today, and the voice moreover still had, in 1935, the sound of the commercial *Trovatore* discs made some eight years before. This was Ezio Pinza's greatest vocal period, with the voice at its most mature, fuller and more bass than in his early electrical recordings, freer than in those he made later. The performance is, however, likely to be best remembered because Lawrence Tibbett scored his greatest success in the title role, and, with the *Otello* recordings with Martinelli, it is his most satisfactory recorded performance. If at first it is the sheer brilliance of the all-round singing that we notice as we listen to these performances, we later realize that few of us since the war have heard more than a handful of Verdi performances to compare at any point.

Boccanegra is hardly an opera of excerpts to catch the fancy of the arbiters of the gramophone. Only the great bass aria, 'Il lacerato spirito', is to be found on acoustic records. Even after the start of the Verdi revival in Germany in the 1920s, few single excerpts were recorded, and has changed little today. The three members of La Scala's cast of 1881 who recorded for the gramophone chose nothing from *Boccanegra*, and even Mattia Battistini, who sang the title role there in 1890 and again in 1920 (in the latter year with Serafin as conductor), regrettably put nothing on to disc.

Early in the opera comes Fiesco's 'Il lacerato spirito', the one aria known out of context. I listened to some thirty recordings – more sides than all the other single excerpts from the opera put together! – in my quest for the best version. The finest souvenir from the past came from Francesco Navarrini (Fono. 62025; GV 14), whose firm line and exalted style explain why he was leading bass of La Scala from the late 1880s for some twenty years. By comparison José Mardones is unsubtle, and neither Vittorio Arimondi nor Giovanni Gravina sounds as though he took the gramophone seriously, though I was sorry to find no copy of the recording left by that fine singer Oreste Luppi.

From the 1920s there are enjoyable performances from Virgilio Lazzari (Vocalion), vivid, well-paced, impressive of voice; Norman Allin, splendidly weighty but perhaps lacking incisiveness; and from Pinza, who displays a glorious vocal quality and whose disc (DB 699; GEMM 163) includes some of the beautiful postlude. I was not too impressed by recordings from Michail Gitowsky, Augusto Beuf, Raffaele Ariè, Kim Borg and Norman Treigle, but there is something to be said for Neroni's strong, full-voiced performance (Cetra BB 25144), though the replacement of chorus by organ makes a bizarre effect. Italo Tajo's curiously idiosyncratic singing (Telef. SKB 3710) is in its own way effective. Giulio Neri's enormous voice is fully apparent, and Cesare Siepi (LXT 5096) will please his admirers. Howell Glynne's clean-cut singing with good English diction gains from the inclusion of some of the important postlude (C 3824) and no non-Italian performance gave me so much pleasure except, perhaps, that by Wilhelm Strienz (EH 1051; 1C 047-28557), whose voice may be lightweight but whose singing in German is outstandingly smooth and beautiful. Nikola Ghiuselev's fine voice and honest singing are alike impressive on Balkanton, but the surprise of the bunch came from Bernard

Ladysz (33 CX 1678). His performance is not perhaps truly idiomatic, chorus and postlude are omitted, but the sound of the voice is phenomenally full and powerful.

Though deprived of chorus and postlude, Giorgio Tozzi sounds very well (RB 16089) and Ghiaurov, unshorn, is responsive and sonorous (SXL 6443). Christoff's spacious performance (ALP 1585), with orchestra and chorus conducted by Vittorio Gui, is an improvement on that in the complete recording, besides containing the postlude in full, rare even on LP discs. Few singers have the Verdi line more naturally in the voice than Pinza and he was the outstanding stylist amongst Italian basses of his generation. He has chorus but no postlude in his Columbia recording (71975D) of the 1940s and also in the later one put out by RCA (RB 16040), which I slightly prefer – rich, stylish, authoritative singing. All the same, if I had to take one of these recordings to a desert island, it would unquestionably be that by Alexander Kipnis (D 2088; SH 280) where the beautiful poise of the recitative is followed by sensitive, generous singing, full of colour and contrast, and also a model of scrupulous phrasing. I doubt if Kipnis ever did anything better on record.

All through his operas, from *Oberto* to *Falstaff*, Verdi used extended duets as a main means of expressing drama. The two confrontations of Fiesco and Boccanegra provide massive pillars from which the structure of the opera is suspended, and that in the prologue is cut from the musical stuff of *Don Carlos* – of the duets between Philip and Posa, even Philip and the Grand Inquisitor – although ten years separate the two scores. Christoff and Gobbi sing it splendidly on the HMV set, Cappuccilli and Ghiaurov differently but no less well for DG, but nobody has thought it worthwhile tackling separately.

Amelia's aria at the start of Act 1, preceded by an extended, expressionistic prelude (the aria dates from 1857, the prelude from 1881), is full of atmospheric writing for the wind. Astrid Varnay, who successfully sang the role at the Metropolitan, turns in an interesting, stylish performance, even if the voice does not entirely lose its Wagnerian overtones (Remington 199.45). Leyla Gencer's beautiful singing on a private issue is dimly recorded, Leontyne Price (SER 5589) is unusually bumpy, but Anna Moffo, even without prelude, is in fine form (SB 6664). Maria Chiara's stylish phrasing and lovely voice bloom on her version (SXL 6605) and the grateful music receives an almost exemplary performance from her. The duet between Amelia and Gabriele Adorno fares badly in an unattractive recording and poor performance from Eileen Farrell and Richard Tucker, but there are two excellent examples of the splendid scene in which Boccanegra realizes that in Amelia Grimaldi he has found his daughter. In spite of a boxy recording, Tibbett has left a remarkable souvenir of his physical aptitude to the title role; the *dolcissimo* phrases lie within his vocal scope, and he sings the final sustained high F sharp with full tone as well as the softness and sweetness

Verdian pairs at Covent Garden

Above: Gré Brouwenstijn as Desdemona,
Ramon Viney as Otello (Houston
Rogers)

Above right: Montserrat Caballé as Aida,
Placido Domingo as Radames (Reg
Wilson)

Right: Regina Resnik as Mistress
Quickly, Sir Geraint Evans as Falstaff
(Harold Rosenthal Collection)

Maria Callas as Norma (EMI)

Joan Sutherland as Lucia (Donald Southern

Four memorable Covent Garden portrayals

Top left: Elisabeth Schwarzkopf as The Marschallin (Houston Rogers)
Top right: Elisabeth Söderström as Mélisande (Zoe Dominic)
Left: Birgit Nilsson as Elektra (Donald Southerr
Above: Hildegard Behrens as Salome (Reg Wilson)

required by the composer (DB 3950; COLH 127). On their single-sided recording, Tibbett and Bampton sing only what is technically the *stretta* of the duet, but Warren and Varnay in the middle 1950s recorded the scene in full. Varnay takes more happily to disc than Rose Bampton, but the same cannot be said of Leonard Warren, who arguably had finer vocal equipment than Tibbett but saw less penetratingly into the character's make-up than his compatriot. All the same, I would prize Warren's performance for his warmth at 'Ah, se la speme', the dawning of recognition (Victor LM 2453).

The Council Chamber scene in its present form dates from 1881, the material, apart from a rewriting of Amelia's narrative in the middle, being entirely new. We hear the cut-and-thrust of debate in Council; then after the story of the attempt to abduct Amelia, fraticidal bloodshed is prevented only by Boccanegra's intervention and his great plea for peace: 'Piango su voi'. The scene ends with the terrible business of the guilty Paolo being required by the Doge to join with him in cursing the culprit.

The HMV highlights disc (ALP 2067) taken from the complete recording contains the entire scene, and no mere excerpt can replace this. All the same, the plea for peace and the cursing of the criminal is admirably recorded in English (C 3825) by the principals of the famous production of 1948 at Sadler's Wells, the first time the opera was heard in England. Arnold Matters in the title role is vocally slighter than Gobbi, but his is a mature, resourceful performance. Tibbett, with Bampton, Martinelli and with Leonard Warren as Paolo, sings 'Piango su voi' (DB 3950; CSLP 503) with poise and authority and the recording has for many years been the best-known example of the opera on records, apart of course from the bass aria. Heinrich Schlusnus's performance of the heart of this scene (Poly. 67150, LV 110) shows him as vocally perhaps the most opulent of those who have recorded Boccanegra's music, but lacking in the sheer musical authority the role demands (the label mentions only Erna Berger among the supporting singers). Hans Reinmar, also in German, sings with less voice, more artistry on (Telef. F 1160; GMA 57), and Gobbi (ASD 606) in the early 1960s is just as secure as in the complete set and only less effective because out of context.

Adorno's exciting aria was first recorded by James Johnston (DX 1506) soon after the Sadler's Wells opening. The impetus of his performance is exemplary, and this is one of the best souvenirs of a singer to whom post-war British opera owed a great deal – much admired incidentally, particularly by Italians, when I played the record at a Verdi congress in Chicago some years ago. In Gino Penno's recording (LW 5111), sheer weight of voice and musical feeling are apparent, even if they do not quite generate the excitement I remember from an *Ernani* with him in Rome in 1951. Franco Corelli's vehement, lachrymose performance of some years ago lacks finesse and is hardly a souvenir the singer would be proud of nowadays. Bergonzi sings with fine attack and smooth line

(Philips 6580 150), Domingo (SB 6795) with perhaps less authority than in the RCA set, and Tucker, albeit with more attack than vocal bloom, to good effect (MS 6668).

Although it is perfectly suited to gramophone records in length, content and character, only the Sadler's Wells performance (C 3824) has left behind it a recording of the trio which follows Gabriele Adorno's recognition of Amelia as Boccanegra's daughter. Johnston is particularly effective, and Joyce Gartside and Matters give him excellent support.

The last act of the opera starts with the Patrician insurrection crushed, Paolo on his way to the scaffold, and the Doge dying of slow poisoning. The scene where the Doge contemplates the sea is one of the most beautiful in the opera, but only Paul Schöffler, who made a name for himself in the title role immediately after the war, has recorded it separately in that dark bass-baritone with the easily floated Fs we knew best in Wagner and Strauss (Amadeo AVRS 6022).

To what degree has Verdi succeeded in reconciling the two vintages which have gone to make the blend that we now know as *Simon Boccanegra*? It is curious how little the spirit of *Les Vepres Siciliennes* (or, as we might even say, *Trovatore*) conflicts with that of *Otello*, as can be seen in the Council Chamber scene, where Amelia's narration, considerably rewritten it is true, was transplanted from the first version to this very mature scene. Again, in the prologue, the fluent, suggestive understatement of the orchestral writing of the 1881 revision never seems to clash with Paolo's arioso, which was taken over (transposed) from the 1857 score. The balance of head and heart may have altered over the years, but in *Simon Boccanegra* may be seen how two creative periods twenty-four years apart can be reconciled, partly because of the master's sheer skill and craftsmanship, partly because the conception of the title role is of such power as to impose its own form of consistency, partly because in Verdi the gradual change added up to a difference of degree, never one of kind.

SIMON BOCCANEGRA

SB Simon Boccanegra; *F* Fiesco; *P* Paolo; *A* Amelia; *G* Gabriele

1951 Silveri *SB*; Petri *F*; Monachesi *P*; Stella *A*; Bergonzi *G*/Rome Radio Chorus and Orch./Molinari-Pradelli Cetra © LPS 3231; Everest – Cetra © S–434/3

1957 Gobbi *SB*; Christoff *F*; Monachesi *P*; los Angeles *A*; Campora *G*/Rome Opera Chorus and Orch./Santini

HMV © SLS 5090 ④ TC–SLS 5090
Angel ⓜ 3617 CL

1973 Cappuccilli *SB*; Raimondi *F*; Mastromei *P*; Ricciarelli *A*; Domingo *G*/RCA Italiana Chorus and Orch./Gavazzeni RCA (UK) SER 5696–8; (US) ARL 3 0564

1977 Cappuccilli *SB*; Ghiaurov *F*;

van Dam *P*; Freni *A*; Carreras
G/La Scala Chorus and
Orch./Abbado
DG 2709 071 ④ 3371 032

Excerpts

1948 (in English) Matters *SB*; Glynne
F; Sharp *P*; Gartside *A*;
Johnston *G*/Sadler's Wells
Chorus and Orch./Royal Opera
Orch./Mudie
HMV ⑩ RLS 707

Un ballo in maschera

LORD HAREWOOD

Un ballo in maschera was able to triumph over early vicissitudes of
censorship and casting so that D'Annunzio, fifty years after its première
and in no spirit of tongue-in-cheek, could call it the most operatic of
operas. More than half a century later still, and by now moving from
popular to highbrow acceptance, it strikes me after intensive playing of
dozens of records as little short of flawless, among the operas of this
period of Verdi's output better shaped than *La forza del destino*, more
exuberant than *Simon Boccanegra*, more Italian and less discursive than the
even greater *Don Carlos*.

Above all, the modern listener will admire the delicate balance between
the romantic and tragic elements of the music and its strongly ironic
characteristics, evidenced not only in what Oscar and the conspirators sing
but most of all in the rounded musical picture of the tenor hero, ranging
from the unreserved romanticism of the haunting 'La rivedrà', the love
duet and the last-act aria, through the exuberance of his lead of the
stretta to the first scene and the finale of Act 1, to his amused, even
witty, rejection of the portentous in his reaction to Oscar's plea for
Ulrica, above all in 'E scherzo od è follia'. Out of all this, Verdi fashions
an atmosphere which is unique among his operas, a subtler, more
believable portrayal by far of a closed community than that of *Rigoletto*,
as evocative of a court cultivated and liberal-minded (in Stockholm, until
the censor objected), about which most of us have read little, as is *Don
Carlos*'s music of one with which we are tolerably familiar.

The opera is well served with complete recordings, and the earliest I
have been able to hear a private set of a Metropolitan performance of
December 1940, with Jussi Björling, Zinka Milanov and Alexander Sved
and conducted by Ettore Panizza, is musically one of the best. It has the
perfect hero in Björling, twenty-nine years old and at his vocal peak;
moreover, in the only complete presentation of one of his best roles,
itself crying out for just such youthful brilliance, freshness, attack and
clear articulation as he brings to it. His urgency helps the otherwise
under-involved but always beautiful-voiced, smooth-phrasing Milanov give
one of her most beguiling recorded performances, but I care less for the

unsteady, bloated sounds of Sved's Renato – I imagine sheer vocal size counted for much in the theatre. Panizza has authority, although he is prepared to indulge his singers far more than is good for some of the score and he follows the Metropolitan's practice of omitting 'Ma se m'è forza perderti'.* The recording is inadequate but whatever effort of imagination is needed is amply repaid.

Just over a year later (February 1942), in another 'off-the-air' recording, Panizza had clearly decided to make a virtue out of necessity and follow his singers to the very end which, with the veteran Martinelli heading the Met's revival, is anything but bitter. This is a typical Met cast of the 1940s, with Bruna Castagna and Josephine Antoine good in the subsidiary roles of Ulrica and Oscar and Richard Bonelli excellent as Renato. Stella Roman as Amelia shows a lovely voice at the service of a gusty technique but makes an interesting partner for Martinelli, who had sung the role at Covent Garden immediately before and after the First World War, at the Metropolitan in 1916, and in San Francisco in 1931 and 1937. He was almost exactly double Björling's age when he succeeded him in the role, so that vocal colour is lacking, but he sings in great, broad, sweeping phrases and with splendid impact – the attack on A natural at 'Astro di queste tenebre' in the love duet is nothing short of tremendous. Poor recording but singing unusual enough to compensate.

Gigli, Gino Bechi and Maria Caniglia took part in a revival at La Scala in 1941 (Gigli in 1937 too), and they were in Rome in 1943 for the opera's first complete commercial recording, with Serafin conducting instead of Marinuzzi. Serafin's customary musical authority is not invariably in evidence, and this is very much a singers' performance, with interest concentrated on Gigli, his voice at 53 in 'third-period' state but, given that, in fine condition. The enthusiastic attack and the honeyed sound of many of the phrases compels sufficient admiration to make one forget some unstylish gulping and a slightly extrovert approach to this role. Caniglia's once first-rate material has deteriorated to such an extent that every recitative explodes – to sing above the stave is to sing flat – and hardly a phrase emerges as I feel she means it to. There's the tragedy: authority and knowledge are vitiated by early decay of vocal means. Bechi is characteristically hard and sinister from the outset, snarls his way through 'Eri tu', a stage villain rather than a man caught up in tragedy. Fedora Barbieri, early in her career, exhibits most of her well-known qualities as Ulrica, and Tancredi Pasero and Ugo Novelli are outstanding

---

*Inquiries from the Met's archive department and reference to the memories of other singers discloses a curious sequence. Björling sang the aria initially in San Francisco under Gennaro Papi in September 1940 on his first assumption of the role, but cut it at later performances when he found it a strain. Taking the role up three months later, he easily acquiesced in what is described as the Met's invariable practice in cutting it, an attitude quite unacceptable to Martinelli fourteen months later, when he not only sang the aria very well but instituted a precedent for subsequent Met tenors to follow.

as the conspirators. In spite of a poor quality transfer, the set is rewarding, and well represents aspects of Italian opera at a particular period.

Several recordings appeared in early LP days. I have not managed to hear the French performance conducted by Leibowitz, nor another 'off-the-air' Metropolitan performance of 1949 with Jan Peerce, Daniza Ilitsch, Margaret Harshaw and Leonard Warren. Cetra's moderate set (1954) has Ferruccio Tagliavini in stiff voice as Riccardo, Pia Tassinari improbably but not unsuccessfully cast as Ulrica, and Mary Curtis-Verna and Giuseppe Valdengo in only intermittently successful performances as Amelia and Renato.

Two notable private recordings exist from this period. The earlier is of Glyndebourne's production for the 1949 Edinburgh Festival, conducted with irresistible musicianship, knowledge and *brio* by Vittorio Gui, who gets, I venture to think, better performances out of each of his principals than they contrive elsewhere, who conjures up atmosphere with the first chord, the first exactly set tempo of every new scene. He is greatly assisted by the exceptional musicianship and detailed characterization of Mirto Picchi, a joy to hear throughout, most of all perhaps in his unsurpassed 'E scherzo od è follia', the best poised, rhythmically most alert I have heard from anyone. All the sadder that Gui cuts 'Ma se m'è forza perderti'. The pure, clear, silvery sound of the great Ljuba Welitsch may seem a little light in colour (though not in vocal weight) but her characterization is positive so that throughout one feels – almost uniquely on records – Amelia's vulnerability to the risks she is taking, and her line is as controlled and firm as the first violin's in a string quartet. Involvement on the part of all singers is this set's great virtue and Paolo Silveri sings better here than on commercial discs. Jean Watson is stronger than many another Ulrica, and I have the happiest memories of Alda Noni's witty, elegant, beautifully sung Oscar, which this set does not disappoint. Several small cuts, all to be deplored, do not spoil enjoyment of a vibrant, inspired performance.

Fritz Busch played a big part in the German side of the Verdi revival in the 1920s – *Ballo* under him in Berlin in 1932 was impressively cast with Maria Nemeth, Erna Berger, Sigrid Onegin, Koloman von Pataky and Hans Reinmar in Ebert's production – and in 1951 he conducted the opera again for the Cologne Radio, uncut and with the authority of a master who can still afford his singers plenty of time to sing. This is worthwhile since they include Dietrich Fischer-Dieskau, early in his career but as dynamic in approach and detailed in characterization as later; his Renato is more the highly-strung young man than any other baritone's but he provides a stirring account of the great penultimate scene, over which he strides like the colossus he (and at this point Renato) is. Lorenz Fehenberger is fluent and capable as Riccardo, and Walburga Wegner, though hardly living up to a splendidly floated top line in the opening trio, not less than adequate as Amelia. Martha Mödl's impassioned Ulrica and Anny Schlemm's unusually weighty but neat Oscar complete the cast of a highly satisfactory souvenir of a great man.

In January 1954, only weeks before he retired, Toscanini conducted an opera for the last time and chose *Ballo* for the occasion. He had done it at La Scala in 1903 (with Micucci-Betti, Silvestri, Parsi-Pettinella, Zenatello, Magini-Coletti), at the Met in 1913 and 1914 (with Destinn, Hempel, Caruso, Amato) and again at La Scala in 1926 (with Carena, Ferraris, Anitua, Pertile, Galeffi), and my only regret about this set concerns the poor quality of some of the singing – occasional little instrumental blemishes can be forgiven. Otherwise it is masterly, perhaps the most perfectly realized of all Toscanini's operatic recordings. Right at the outset in the prelude you hear how the maestro achieves passion in the melody of 'La rivedrà' without the conventional 'give' of lesser mortals. His is a performance in primary colours, woodwind strands standing out of the texture not as detail but as an essential, and very much a Verdian, ingredient of the total sound picture, the whole buoyed up on a firmly rhythmical bass. Clear articulation, fidelity to the markings and their implications (but refusal to take literally the *ppp*s of dynamic markings) – these are consistent aspects of Toscanini's reading, emerging most obviously at such moments as the unique bite of the strings' *staccato* underpinning 'Ah qual soave brivido', the attack at Amelia's first entrance and at the introduction to 'Eri tu', which in the latter case does not preclude a real tenderness at the end of the aria.

Jan Peerce, with his accuracy and strong expressive legato, nobly (at the age of 50) aids and abets his chief and, apart from a disappointingly stressful last-act aria, sings splendidly, as does Robert Merrill, a born singer able, moreover, to profit from Toscanini's direction. Virginia Haskins as Oscar has true brilliance in the voice, but neither of the other two principals lives up to score or conductor: Claramae Turner lacks vocal weight and penetration; Herva Nelli shows herself a slight, unimposing singer, and, apart from rhythmic accuracy, exhibits none of the qualities required of a Verdi soprano – solidity in middle and bottom registers, brilliance and reliability at top, the ability to sing long legato lines together with an aptitude for attack and a vocal size able to dominate orchestra and ensemble alike.

In much better sound than most 'off-the-air' sets, Cetra have preserved Mitropoulos's conducting of *Ballo* with the Metropolitan in January 1955, complete with stage noises and applause at entrances, as so often at the Met on Italian nights. Precision, clarity of line and detail, and urgency are characteristics of Mitropoulos's Verdi, and here he secures a fine performance from a cast without an Italian, though it is full of Metropolitan Italian specialists. Richard Tucker tops the bill, aged 42, at the height of his career and able with his clear, confident line and ringing top to match Mitropoulos's demands. Only a certain staidness in his approach to the essentially exuberant central role detracts from a fine performance, his best I think in a recorded Verdi opera on disc. Zinka Milanov, fourteen years after her first 'off-the-air' recording of Amelia, is a little less at ease than in 1940; some moments of uncertainty apart (notably a snatched C in the gallows aria and a sour B flat in the love duet), the opulent voice and generous phrasing give a lot of pleasure. A curiosity is that she omits the cadenza to 'Morrò, ma prima in grazia', as she had in 1940, as Roman did at the Met in 1942, and she herself was to on ALP 1476 – a Met quirk or what? Roberta Peters, full and strong of sound and with an easy *staccato*, makes a first-class Oscar, Jean Madeira a rich-sounding Ulrica, and only Josef Metternich, so careful and stodgy a Renato as to sound miscast, mars a roster well-matched throughout; James McCracken is easily recognizable in the tiny role of the Judge. Historically interesting as one of the few Met broadcasts officially issued on record and valuable for Mitropoulos's positive conducting, this set is none the less not quite on the level of the same conductor's *Forza*.

Antonino Votto's conducting of the opera for La Scala forces, recorded in September 1956, is a lesser affair, raised in stature by the great Amelia of Maria Callas, who here shows her customary but almost unique ability to fill phrases with musical, spiritual, dramatic content. There is magic in the big phrase of the trio, she is in her finest voice in the great span of the Act 2 aria and duet, and the veiled, tragic quality of sound in 'Morrò ma prima in grazia' is peculiarly apt and typical of her ability almost to recreate the colour and characteristics of the voice for each new role. If you want an example, compare her declaration of love with that of other prima donnas (notably the soft, dreamy attack on F natural at 'Ah! deh soccori tu') and hear the difference for yourself. Giuseppe di Stefano was at the top of his career at the time, and there is confidence, vocal ring, clear articulation in the singing, as well as an often too open production and less than the desirable elegance. Gobbi was perhaps not a true Verdi baritone, but the singing and characterization are so involved as to disarm criticism. Ulrica was always one of Fedora Barbieri's best roles, but Eugenia Ratti makes a rigid Oscar, with a certain neatness but little vocal characterization. The orchestral playing is good, Votto's conducting notable for balance and tact rather than the more positive virtues of shape and drive. There is a short but customary cut in the ballroom scene.

A live Scala performance from 7 December 1957 (I saw that on 10 December) has been issued by Cetra with a cast similar to EMI's or, where changed, better, all with good reason vociferously applauded. The sound is well below studio standard, the conducting brittle rather than brilliant in effect, but the element of actuality in the performance tells in favour of both Callas and di Stefano, bringing a certain bounce and effervescence to the latter's impersonation, a spaciousness and punch to the former. In the love duet ('Ah! deh soccori tu' apart) they surpass what they achieved under Votto, and Callas sings the third-act aria with wonderful conviction, as well as producing during the evening three of her best top Cs on record. Bastianini's lively musical imagination and the rounded, refulgent sound he makes together put him high among recorded Renatos, and no one sings the second part of Ulrica's *scena* like Simionato. No substitute therefore for EMI's 1956 studio recording, but a splendid gloss on it for admirers of Callas and di Stefano, and something of unique value to the historian of La Scala in a great period.

Four years after Votto, Gianandrea Gavazzeni also recorded *Ballo* with La Scala's forces and substantially the 1960 revival cast. In contrast to the live performance of 1957, his conducting is sane and balanced rather than urgent, but unfortunately neither the golden-voiced but wooden-phrasing Gianni Poggi, nor the overparted Adriana Lazzarini and Giuliana Tavolaccini (Ulrica and Oscar), nor the uncontrolled Antonietta Stella, in spite of the remains of a basically fine voice, makes a positive contribution. It is left to Ettore Bastianini to provide what impresses me as the finest performance of Renato on records. On his day, he was the best of post-war Italian baritones, with that burnished, brilliant tone, consistently aristocratic phrasing and fire in the belly; but that cannot save what is otherwise the least desirable of recent sets.

Georg Solti conducted an uncut and well recorded performance for Decca in 1961, full of energy, much excellent orchestral detail, fine overall shape, and some excellent singing. Carlo Bergonzi, if without the thrust of a Caruso or Martinelli, has the smooth tone and elegance the role requires and there is enough power to make him perhaps the most satisfactory Riccardo on any set apart from Björling. Birgit Nilsson, to my mind the great *vocal* phenomenon of the post-war age, is mostly splendid as Amelia; she may blur the turns at the entry, there may be a trace of bleakness in the attack on an occasional top note, but the line is consistently true, the tone almost unfailingly beautiful, a moving account of 'Ma dall' arido stelo divulsa' rises to a superb top C at the climax, and she effectively contradicts any critic who finds her singing cold. Sylvia Stahlman as Oscar is neat, sweet-voiced, and her C in 'E scherzo' floats more beguilingly than any other recorded since Frieda Hempel's, and Giulietta Simionato as Ulrica makes up in intensity what she lacks in depth for the lowest lying of all Verdi's mezzo roles. Cornell MacNeil, in one of his best recorded performances, is a little less than committed, but the solid, beautiful voice fits the role well.

Erich Leinsdorf's American-Italian set is excellently recorded; his conducting, more relaxed than Solti's, demonstrates his sheer skill and experience as an operatic practitioner. Bergonzi, stylish and in full free voice, makes a nearly ideal hero, lacking only the last degree of sparkle and brilliance that I have found on disc only in Björling (scheduled once, by the way, for Solti's set). Leontyne Price demonstrates truly Verdian poise at her entry, has her breathless moments in the great second-act aria, but compensates with some ringing sound and sizable phrasing in a role whose heaviest passages none the less tax her to the limit. Merrill is a tower of vocal strength and dramatic conviction, Shirley Verrett demonstrates her customary musical flair and Reri Grist is the youngest-sounding, most brilliant Oscar on any set.

In 1970 Decca, with Santa Cecilia of Rome, this time under Bruno Bartoletti, attempted to 'cap' Solti's recording, but without success. At this stage of their distinguished careers, neither Renata Tebaldi nor Regina Resnik should have been asked to record *Ballo*; Sherrill Milnes, big of voice but short of energy, makes less impact I found than in the theatre; Luciano Pavarotti, however, has the brilliance and youth which the music needs, turns in a fine *ballata* and love duet, but articulates 'E scherzo od è follia' with less accuracy than one could wish.

Riccardo Muti's HMV recording (1975) has no vocal weakness and much conducting strength. Fiorenza Cossotto is uniquely endowed for Ulrica, Piero Cappuccilli the most reliable if not always the most lively of Verdi baritones (he is, I find, more interesting when playing senior citizens – Boccanegra and Foscari rather than Luna and Renato), Grist is still a charming Oscar, Gwynne Howell and Richard Van Allan probably the best conspirators on records. Martina Arroyo gives one of her most considerable recorded performances, a little cool maybe and not too flexible in quicker music, but always confident and with the required solid tone. Placido Domingo's contribution is somehow harder to place. Stress in lighter passages and less than ideally buoyant tone are to be weighed against the grand moments so overwhelmingly voiced and the romantic so splendidly sung that it seems almost masochistic not to award him the palm, particularly when these qualities are combined with Muti's powerful, thrusting control of the performance as a whole.

In 1978, Colin Davis recorded the opera with Covent Garden forces in, as it were, the lower echelons, stars on top and never an Italian in sight. Subdued in comparison with conductors of other recordings, Davis still takes a generally vigorous view of the score, apart from some exaggerated slowing down in the love duet and at the start of Amelia's third-act aria. His cast is not the strongest on record, Caballé, in spite of some beautiful moments, seeming not ideally suited to Amelia – a big contrast with Elisabeth nine years earlier – though making some amends with a superior third-act aria after coming perilously close to defeat in the second-act *scena*. There are signs of stress from the ardent José Carreras, the first finale is not articulated with ideal clarity, and his performance, like those of Sona Ghazarian (Oscar) and Ingvar Wixell (Renato), lacks poise and individuality. Patricia Payne, a contralto of real weight, is short of Italiante 'bite' (and indeed occasionally on Italian enunciation) as Ulrica.

Toscanini's recording, however great the reservations about the singing, still seems to me the most exciting, but there is much to be said too for Solti's, Leinsdorf's and Muti's. In the end, a choice from these three, based on personal preference for one or other of the leading singers – Bergonzi with Nilsson; Price, Merrill, Bergonzi and Verrett; Domingo, Cappuccilli, Arroyo and Cossotto – will secure the enthusiast a fine recording of *Ballo*.

If you want a representative but not a complete set, you may go towards one of the double-sided collections of excerpts; if an opera composer's two greatest problems concern shape on the one hand and invention on the other, at least the latter will come through to you. Immediately after he had conducted the opera at the Met in January 1955, Mitropoulos recorded highlights interestingly if without the natural brilliance of Toscanini a year before. Milanov's grand manner (an excellent 'Morrò') and Peerce's incisiveness lead to a fine love duet; Marian Anderson, not too secure at top or bottom, is heard in the complete *scena* in what is a unique souvenir of her only operatic role (why did Victor economize by not engaging a chorus?); Leonard Warren impresses by sheer confident breadth of style and phrasing, and works up to a fine if not immaculate 'Eri tu'. 1943 excerpts by a Berlin cast are more notable for the confident, long-phrasing, youthful approach of Hilde Scheppan than for Helge Roswaenge's generally tough, semi-heroic approach to Verdi, although the love duet has ardour in plenty and the King's last-act aria is well-sustained. Karl Schmitt-Walter, Ingeborg Reichelt and Schilp give no more than adequate support.

Moderately satisfactory only is a selection of arias and duets (including the one from the ballroom scene) with the Dutch singers Gré Brouwenstijn and Frans Vroons singing in unidiomatic Italian. I value this disc as a souvenir of one of the leading Verdi sopranos of the post-war period, but it is pointless to pretend that the valiant Vroons makes much of an effect as a Verdi tenor. Another Dutchman, Theo Baylé, figures in a German selection, also conducted by Loibner, and featuring the Yugoslav Carla Martinis in gusty voice, and Roswaenge, forthright but inelegant as so often in Italian opera. Scottish Opera's selection sounds hastily done, with rushed tempi, slovenly intonation and inaccurate note-values, the more regrettable as the selection judiciously emphasizes scenes rather than arias sliced from them, and Charles Craig (the King) – with Patricia Hay (Oscar) the best of the soloists – is not well represented on records.

Ballo is rare among Verdi's operas in providing a longer, richer more rewarding part for tenor than for baritone. Though the subtleties of the role offer scope for maximum artistry, the music's high spirits also seem to me to call for vocal youth and brilliance; hence my predilection for Björling, Bergonzi and (with reservations) Pavarotti in complete sets. Three famous recording tenors have tackled four excerpts apiece. Caruso sang it at the Metropolitan from his second season, and recorded the two ensembles after the Toscanini revival in 1914. At 41 he has, as one would expect, tremendous authority, musical as well as vocal, exemplary rhythmic bounce and vitality, so that 'La rivedrà' is a lyrical delight, and irresistible power and intensity, as in the phrasing of 'E scherzo od à follia' (both on DM 103; ORL 312). 'Di tu se fedele', (DA 102; ORL 309), recorded a couple of years earlier, is very dark in sound if played at the proper speed, as is the last-act aria (DB 137; ORL 309) which receives, a few stressful sounds at the top apart, a purposeful, clear, expansive performance from the great tenor. Alessandro Bonci in 1926, 56 when he recorded the first three of these excerpts together with the duet of Act 2 (L 1960 and CQX 10223), could hardly bring ideally youthful sound to the role. All the same, consistently distinguished, elegant phrasing gives these early electrical recordings a value that is far more than historical (what about a reissue on LP including the rumoured but perhaps mythical 'Forse la soglia attinse')? Bonci's 'E scherzo od è follia' is the most famous version of the quintet, not only because he was the first to insert a cascade of laughs to fill in the rests (in Florence in 1898), but because he was able twenty-eight years later to demonstrate on disc the rare grace and dexterity with which he articulated his invention (reissued on GEMM 164).

In 1903, Toscanini revived the opera at La Scala with Giovanni Zenatello. As was his custom he refused encores, but on 14 April such was the public demand after 'E scherzo od è follia' that the conductor not only left the rostrum in the middle of the opera but abandoned his contract with the theatre for the following season, not reappearing there for over four years! Zenatello (who was Riccardo at Covent Garden in 1905 with Boninsegna and Sammarco), perhaps out of sudden diffidence, did not record this excerpt but there are four selections from him, recorded over more than twenty years. His Fonotipias (92332/3; ORL 209) of 1907 ('La rivedrà') and 1909 ('Di tu se fedele') reveal less sophistication than later, but a stronger, firmer line; two almost complete love duets, first with Eugenia Burzio in 1906 (Fono. 39665/6; ORL 209) and then in 1910 with Ester Mazzoleni (Fono. 92613/4) show extraordinary vocal splendour and fine style, which latter puts his partner in the later recording very much in the shade. In 1929 the veteran tenor, still only 54, again tackled two excerpts in the recording studio, a firm, ringing *ballata* and a moving death scene (AGSB 20; Club 99-25).

Mario del Monaco and Richard Tucker have essayed three excerpts each, the former hard and unsympathetic, the latter vocally fine but over-accentuated to the point of jerkiness in both *ballata* (ML 5062) and love duet (SBRG 72036), where the opulent-voiced Eileen Farrell makes a slightly disappointing partner, much better in the Act 3 aria (ML 4750), all CBS records.

Many tenors have recorded two excerpts, the earliest perhaps the massive-voiced, almost invariably communicative Leo Slezak (his *ballata* and 'La rivedrà' of 1907 are on CO 332). Julius Patzak sings the *ballata* with skill and verve (Poly. 90062), the Act 3 aria with a true perception of the recitative's heart-break and in the aria an exquisite sensitivity. If the style is as close to Schubert as to Verdi, this is nevertheless a disc to linger over if you can find it (Poly. 95267). As recorded, Roswaenge seems to produce little smoothness either of tone or phrasing, but he was probably much more impressive in the theatre than in the *ballata* (DB 4445; 1C 147-29240/1) or Act 3 aria (Poly. 67211). Others to tackle the *ballata* in German include the distinguished Josef Mann (Odeon), the hefty-voiced Eyvind Laholm, and the stressful, clumsy Ernst Kozub, whose fine voice shows better in the last-act aria.

Alfred Piccaver was frequently heard in the role in Vienna from 1922 onwards and must have found in it one of his most congenial impersonations, judging from his discs, that of the Act 3 aria (Poly. 76535; LV 106) containing one of his most appreciable pieces of singing, which catches the melancholy of the situation while exhibiting extraordinary breath control and power. The Spanish Antonio Cortis is an excellent, straightforward singer (Parlo. E 10205; OASI 531); the Hungarian Robert Ilosfalvy has the ideal voice for the role but does not make too much of either of these arias (SME 81032), a stricture which could not be applied to the equally suitable, though quite differently gifted, Nicolai Gedda (1C 036-02703). Bergonzi's finest performances come in his Philips album of Verdi arias (6580 150), where the careful observation of dynamic and other markings together with his controlled musicianship lead to ideal performances of the *ballata* and the Act 3 monologue.

To complete tenor 'doubles' that I have been able to hear is a disc by Aureliano Pertile, who sang the role in four different revivals at La Scala between 1926 and 1943, but whose disc of 'La rivedrà' and 'E scherzo' with his 1926 colleagues shows more musical fervour than vocal polish and, in the quintet, something not far from clumsiness (R 20007; GV 505).

Augusto Scampini, the tenor of La Scala's 1910 revival of *Simon Boccanegra*, exhibits his fine, open type of singing in 'La rivedrà', one of the earliest versions I have heard (2–52615; ORE 213). Among early recordings of the six-eight *ballata*, Mario Gilion (Fono. 92246; Club 99–72) has good top notes and Nicola Zerola a virile voice but little style; Carlo Albani combines distinction with cultivated singing (Victor 64082; Rococo 5224). Martinelli's 1915 record (DA 523; CDN 5105) reveals lyrical elegance and a much lighter timbre than his electrics, or of course than Caruso, with whom he shared the role at Covent Garden in 1914 (Caruso had sung it here in revivals of 1904, 1905, 1907). Jaroslav Gleich sings strongly in Czech and I enjoyed the ringing sound of Costa Milona (Parlo. E 10802), the thoroughly masculine performance of Tino Pattiera (Parlo. R 1216; LV 16), and, because of the unique sweetness of sound, Björling's 1944 disc (DA 1837; 1C 147-00947).

'E scherzo od è follia' has attracted few single discs. Caruso's and Bonci's are by far the best. Arthur Cavara recorded it quite neatly in German in Berlin with Erna Berger and Elsa Ruziczka among his colleagues (CA 8168), and he is among the minority that excludes Bonci's *risata* from performance; only Björling with Panizza at the Met in 1940, Fehenberger with Busch at Cologne in 1954 and Domingo and Carreras in their complete recording otherwise omit it.

In contrast, the splendid recitative and aria of Act 3, 'Forse la soglia attinse', and 'Ma se m'è forza perderti' have many recorded interpreters, few of those that remain to be discussed are rivals to the best already mentioned, namely Caruso, Piccaver, Martinelli, Bergonzi, Tucker and Patzak. Peerce shows fine intensity in various Victor recordings (from Victor 11–9295 to RB 16089), Josef Schmidt's German performance exhibits his beautiful voice and smooth style (Telef. E 978; TW 30066) but Gianni Poggi, recorded when other Italian singers were referring to him as a potential successor to Gigli, shows an unusual blend of the frenzied and the perfunctory. The heroic Romanian tenor Garbis Zobian sings with more vehemence than pathos (SUEC 868); the effectiveness of Donald Smith's splendid voice is partly nullified by faulty Italian and an over-resonant recording characteristic (OASD 7584); but there is a sympathetic performance from Rudolf Schock in German (1C 147 29140/1). As leaders among the young Italianate tenors, neither Pavarotti nor Domingo gives quite the performance one might hope for, the one then unready for the role, the other sounding a little remote, but José Carreras turns in a fine, urgent performance (Philips 9500 203). Francesco Vignas, a Spaniard well known for his Wagner at La Scala from 1889 to 1904, sang the part at Covent Garden in autumn 1904, and his 1906 disc contains some fine singing (Fono. 62083).

The role of Amelia is, with Aida, the heaviest Verdi ever wrote for soprano, and the great recitative and aria of Act 2 as taxing as almost anything in operatic literature – so I have always believed, and so Eva Turner once confirmed to me (why incidentally was there no recording, apart from Fear's feeble 'Eri tu', to recall the Covent Garden revival of 1935–7 with her, Dino Borgioli, Fear and Brownlee?). The *scena* takes singing on the biggest scale. Montserrat Caballé's forthright recitative and consistent drama on a private disc will surprise those who (like me) tend to think of her as not by nature a Verdian, but on SER 3598 there are definite signs of strain. Régine Crespin's powerful vocalism (ASD 2275) is perfectly apt to the role, particularly when, as here, the high C arrives (not without some effort) – unlike the only time when I heard her otherwise splendid singing of the role in Paris, when it did not come at all. A more appropriately Verdian voice is that of Meta Seinemeyer, who died in 1929 hardly out of her twenties and who recorded this *scena* memorably, but in German (E 11300; LV 115), with piercingly beautiful top notes and a style which demonstrates a great voice in full, majestic, tragic flight (a curiosity: she misses out the second 'Miserere' just before the end). Nobody combines the grand manner with expressive detail better than Maria Callas in her 1964 performance (ASD 2971), which would approach the definitive, but for a sad climactic, high C.

Elena Souliotis turns in a fine performance (on the fourth side of the complete *Cavalleria*; SET 343–4), well articulated, very correct in note-values and intonation – if only her hefty chest voice did not evoke Prince Orlofsky rather than a Verdian heroine. Milanov (ALP 1456 and VICS 1336) with suavity and Brouwenstijn (Philips NBR 6023) with greater drama but poor Italian have left fine souvenirs, as has Astrid Varnay (Remington 199.53) of her majestic, intense approach to the composer. Brouwenstijn on 5C 053-24324, recorded in 1966, five years before retirement, is solid and careful, less incandescent than one remembers her in the theatre. Vera Schwarz omits the prelude but is in excellent form on Parlo. R 1466, and even better on an acoustic dating from 1921 (Od. RXX 76207; LV 24), but Carla Martinis, Furtwängler's Desdemona at Salzburg in 1951, negates her fine vocal qualities with some explosive singing. Tebaldi (SXL 6152) in the early 1960s is far better than in the complete recording, with sweeter sound and a purer line.

Many recordings of the aria omit prelude and recitative, and of these outstanding are Elisabeth Rethberg (DB 1461) for overall distinction of style and musicianship and the purest tone; Hina Spani in spite of a cut in the middle of the aria, for individuality, intensity, and a stunning quality of sound (DB 1045; LV 147); Maria Nemeth (Poly. 66624; LV 214) for the nervous energy and the brilliant overtones of the voice itself; Gina Cigna for the drama she gets with her big, truly dramatic soprano (LX 235 and R 5251); Arangi-Lombardi (GQX 10704; QCX 7379) for distinguished, vibrant singing, an object lesson to most other Italians. I enjoyed Welitsch, who leaves a fine souvenir of one of the truly great post-war voices (ECS 811). Hilde Scheppan gives a sympathetic performance in German (Poly. 68307), a contrast with the coarse phrasing of Caniglia, the jerky, underpowered singing of Joan Hammond, and a disappointing performance in German from the usually reliable Margarete Tesche-macher. Among acoustic recordings my own preference is for the expansive style and vocal splendour of Helena Wildbrunn (Poly. 72807; LV 70), on disc undoubtedly a great singer, and the forthright, full-blooded performance of Boninsegna (Victor 15–1006; CO 358). Johanna Gadski provides typically firm, confident singing (DB 661; CO 362), Burzio (Fono. 39513/4) sings vibrantly with piano, and Emmy Bettendorf is characteristically fluent. Muzio's Edison and Tina Poli-Randacio's HMV (DA 173) are emotional and personal, but Muzio has the edge with her rare beauty of sound.

Amelia's other aria, early in Act 3, makes different demands on the singer, not on the scale of the *scena* and with the accent on intensity rather than drama. Much the same adjectives as I have used over their performance of the *scena* would apply to recordings by Rethberg, Wildbrunn, Nemeth, Gadski, Burzio, Welitsch, Brouwenstijn, Milanov, Arangi-Lombardi, Tebaldi, Caniglia and Hammond (all on discs already listed), but those by Souliotis and Crespin are perhaps even better than their other performances, Crespin's ability to weight the voice so as to push a phrase ahead, to lighten it so as to colour, giving the singing a quite unusual warmth (SXL 6075). Caballé (SXL 6690) too is more at home here than in the *scena*, and her phrasing would melt sterner hearts than most Renatos possess. Both Tebaldi and Callas recorded the aria in 1964, the former in perhaps her finest Verdian performance (SXL 6152), the latter, in spite of some vile distortion, a less than perfect B flat (but a splendid C flat), with that typical search for the heart of the matter which always distinguished her from other mortals (ASD 3535). Neither Cigna nor Boninsegna (in any of three different versions) seemed so good as in the *scena*, but Teschemacher's expansive style (DB 5635; LV 103) suits this better than the earlier aria. From the Balkans, Daniza Ilitsch exhibits scrupulous phrasing, Pauline Takacz (in German) an opulent voice reminiscent of her compatriot Maria Nemeth. Even if Anna Moffo's search for expression can lead to distortion of the line, this is one of her most appreciable discs (SB 6664), Amy Shuard was always at her best in this aria (SXLP 20046), and Gabriella Gatti, perhaps limited in scale by the naturally lyrical quality of the voice, is most distinguished and sensitive (Cetra BB 25142). Elsa Bland (43919; CO 317) is authoritative and full-voiced, Eugenia Burzio (Pathé, 1913) predictably more emotional, and from the Golden Age – I wish I had heard Maria Labia's 1909/10 Odeons – there remains the great Emmy Destinn, Amelia at the Met before and at Covent Garden just after the first world war, a supremely commanding singer but somehow singing this music with less emotional impact than the best of her rivals (DB 222).

Renato presents the reviewer of *Ballo* records with the greatest problems. His opening aria, 'Alla vita che t'arride', more of a muscle-flexer than a big statement and peculiar in that its fine recitative is given to the tenor and not to the baritone at all, has attracted a number of single discs, mostly by baritones who have also recorded the greatly taxing, greatly rewarding 'Eri tu'. Few fail in it, and I heard very good versions by Scotti (Victor 81070), Battistini (DB 198; ORL 121), Amato (1924 Homocord, three years after leaving the Met), Joseph Schwarz (042505; LV 86), Benvenuto Franci (DA 1093), Titta Ruffo (DA 358), Theodor Scheidl (Poly. 66672), adequate souvenirs from Blanchart, Cesare Formichi, Henrich Schlusnus, Gerhard Hüsch, Willi Domgraf-Fassbaender and less appreciable performances from Giacomo Rimini, Sved and Georg Oeggl. Warren is disappointingly sticky and Fischer-Dieskau demonstrates that this kind of simple tune can produce from him an un-Italian over-emphasis. If I had to award a prize, it would go to the authoritative Riccardo Stracciari (acoustic Fono. 69155, electric Col. GQ 1705).

'Eri tu' is another story. With its dramatic recitative it amounts to a true *scena*, requiring scarcely less dramatic intensity than Iago's 'Credo' in the first half of the aria proper (and a taxing low A), lyricism worthy of Papa Germont in the concluding section, and throughout making supreme demands on the sustaining qualities of a baritone voice as well as on its power. The aria is difficult to sing well, and many of the more than seventy different versions I have listened to seemed little more than reasonably acceptable souvenirs of the singers concerned – Lestelly, Hüsch, Redvers Llewellyn (in English, too late in his career), Blanc, Dens, Hiölski, Schlusnus, Sved, Harold Williams, Domgraf-Fassbaender, Ruzdjak, Arthur Fear, Urbano, Inghilleri (D 1823 and, twenty years later B 9712), Bonelli, Mihail Arnautu, Jordachescu, Tipton, Wixell, even Giuseppe de Luca, who cannot have been suited to the part either physically or vocally, Gino Bechi, whose snarl suits the recitative better than his graceless style does the aria, Apollo Granforte, whose perfect recording voice was once heard as Amfortas at La Scala, or even Carlo Galeffi, who sang with Toscanini at La Scala in 1926 and whose greatness was legendary but not apparent on GQX 10151. John Charles Thomas on an early Brunswick (reissued OASI 527) reveals some self-consciously beautiful singing but sounds uncommitted, in contrast to the virile Lawrence Tibbett (DB 1478), whose imperturbable singing gives pleasure in the same way as that of Silveri (DX 1367), but less perhaps than either the underrated Robert Weede (CTL 7080) or the colossus Hugo Hasslo (Z 308), than whom many a singer has sung the aria with more subtlety, few with more voice. Mathieu Ahlersmeyer had an important German career and recorded 'Eri tu' (Acanta DE 21488) when he was 44, powerfully and musically, if without the smoother vocalism of the splendid Czech baritone Zdenek Otava (Esta N 5141), whose control, energy and ringing top notes make a fine impression. Russians come out well from comparative listening, whether Oscar Kamionsky, with his smooth, even singing, or the more powerful George Baklanov (DB 584) before 1914; Pavel Lisitsian, whom I heard sing in the early 1960s at La Scala in *War and Peace* with all the authority but not perhaps the brilliant top shown in this record (Melodiya M–10 359048), which must have been made earlier; or the heavier-handed but authoritative George Ots. The American Arthur Endrèze with his exquisite diction is, paradoxically, far the best of the French singers (Pathé X 90066), and the German Heinrich Rehkemper demonstrates a lovely singing line as well as a very positive approach (Poly. 65702; Scala 809).

   This is the sort of music on which the singer of the Golden Age must have thrived. Do acoustic recordings support this hypothesis? Not, in spite of legato style, Léon Melchissédec's fabulously rare, truncated performance, recorded when he was very old, nor perhaps Mario Sammarco's (Fono. 39270; CO 348); firm and confident though it sounds, he is a lesser voice and vocalist surely than many of his contemporaries. Lesser than Giuseppe Pacini, who sounds truly great on a 1904 Fonotipia (39004) or the fabulous Ruffo, by whose gruff style I own to have been greatly disappointed (DB 398). Neither the smooth, cultivated Antonio Scotti (Covent Garden's Renato, 1904/5) nor the scrupulous Emilio de

Gogorza commands vocal riches of this sort, and suspicion remains that the latters recording is a supreme example of the triumph of mind over matter. Joseph Schwarz (042496; LV 14) and Ernst Fischer, the latter sounding like Friedrich Schorr, show that Germans – and Eric Marshall that English – can rival Italians in *bel canto*, an art exemplified by the great, smooth voice of Mario Ancona pouring out in controlled if dispassionately disposed streams of tone (Victor 15–10002; Rococo 5213) and on a later Pathé. Much more committed is Riccardo Stracciari, either in his splendid 1910 disc (Fon. 92621), or the much later electrical (L 2131), recorded when he was over 50 (it plays at around 76 rpm).

Choice of the sort I have been indulging in involves great personal preference and I hope to be forgiven if I suggest that Battistini sometimes, for all his incomparably controlled vocalism, strikes me as muttering 'Hark at me!' in impeccable *bel canto* during the singing of 'Eri tu' recorded at about 50 (DB 200; ORL 221); though he shirks, in common with several others, the awkward low A, the sense of shape which sweeps the music along is as much to be admired as the strong legato which controls it – both qualities, remarkably, hardly less in evidence on DB 738, cut in 1921 when at 64 the voice was as miraculously preserved as the singing was fluent. All the same, I preferred one version to either of Battistini's, namely, Amato's (DB 157, or his Fonotipia, reissued as PXO 81, little behind it). Some, though not all, of the meticulous style may be put down to the fact that he sang it with Toscanini at the Met in 1913/14, but this same perfect blend of the forceful and the suave, of ease in high-lying passages and power at each end of the scale, is to be observed in both the 1909 Fonotipia and the 1913 Victor (he shirks the low A in the earlier, takes it in the later). I personally could not want for a better practical definition of *bel canto*.

Among electrical recordings Giuseppe Danise's cultivated performance (Brunswick 50006; LV 238) exemplifies a finer tradition than that followed by Benvenuto Franci (DB 1320; LV 171), whose energy and over-vibrant method is all too typical of the singers favoured by Toscanini at La Scala in the 1920s but who compensates with some passages of smoothly expansive singing. One cannot ignore either of the top, early post-war American baritones, Leonard Warren, whose not wholly satisfactory versions on Victor all exhibit the exemplary thrust of the huge voice, but also some sound which is thick as well as rich; or Robert Merrill (SXL 6083) whose great voice remained after a generation at the Met even throughout its range, his technique undaunted by the aria's difficulties, but who does not invariably match fine expression to physical means. Fine too is Leonard Warren's successor, Sherrill Milnes (ARLI 0851), whose impressively scaled performance does not match Gobbi's poised, meaningful singing on a late 78 (DB 21606; RLS 738). If it came down to it, I should choose among modern versions between Bastianini's (SLPM 135032) and Fischer-Dieskau's (ASD 402): the one so wonderfully full and free of voice, so beautifully compact of tone, so patently when at his best (in which condition England seldom heard him) a thoroughbred Italian performer; the other the most involved, most sensitive of singers, who gives here a truly tremendous performance, the beauty of whose last section has haunted me since hearing it, so that it must stand in my mind as the major alternative to the versions of Amato and Battistini, similar in aim, different in means, no less beautiful.

Oscar is the gadfly of the score, the dispenser of musical spice and, logically in view of the historical Gustavus III's known predilections, the catalyst to bring out the most buoyant side of the hero's character. Oscar has three arias, 'Volta la terra' in Act 1 which establishes the character, 'Ah! di che fulgor' in the first scene of Act 3 (which turns into a quintet), and 'Saper vorreste' in the third, which precipitates the tragic denouement. Fritzi Jokl (Parlo. P 2001; LV 138, in German), Aurora Rettore (Col. D 1643), Alda Noni (DA 1954) and Rita Streich (DGM 19137) have recorded versions of the first and third arias which might best be described as neat but not gaudy, a description which could also apply to Emma Trentini's (Covent Garden 1904/3) on a seven-inch G&T of 'Volta la terra' (53155). Lotte Schöne exhibits charm rather than accuracy in German versions of both (EW 70; GV 16). The great Frieda Hempel achieves exemplary style and verve in a performance of the first aria made in 1916 after she had sung it with Toscanini (DA 248).

Even more interesting is Tetrazzini's 1912 singing of 'Saper vorreste', exhibiting her perfect *staccato* and strong legato and living up to the score's *brillantissimo* marking (DB 539). Minnie Nast (2–43284) starts with a cadenza, in which the rare beauty of her voice is more in evidence than in the aria itself – I have not managed to find her recording of the quintet in which she is joined by Elizza, Weidemann, Mayr and Stehmann. The classic performance of Vienna – of the world for that matter – is that of Selma Kurz, who sang the role everywhere, including at Covent Garden, between 1904 and 1907. Her discs preserve not only the individual, limpid sound, the incomparable trill (and for once the word is true: no one else's *has* compared), but also all those cadenzas and top notes with which she decorated music and situation alike; her trilling and waltzing around the stage caused her to fall foul of the conductor Mancinelli at Covent Garden in 1904 but succeeded Bonci's *risata* as a public attraction at the start of the century. The embellishments vary only slightly in her several different recordings, but the trill on DB 498 (reissue TQD 3020) is the best and longest of the lot and I suspect it is the most representative of her performance. As a matter of history, Maria Gerhart succeeded her in the role in Vienna in 1923/24, and her 1924 disc (reissue LV 75) shows some lovely sound, very neat singing, and decorations entirely in the Selma Kurz tradition, as is Elizabeth Gerö (Parlo. E 11111), with less voice but neat decoration. Will no conductor nowadays have the courage to cast a real coloratura in the role and give it back its one-time significance, decorations and all? Adele Kern, could, delectably, on the evidence of what is I think her finest recording (Poly. 62690; LV 195); the singing is strong, flourishes and decorations abound, and the pacing shows every sign of the hand of a major conductor – perhaps Clemens Krauss's, though I can find no evidence that she prepared or sang it with him in either Berlin or Munich from 1934, when she first sang it, until the war.

If Oscar is one of Verdi's least conventional roles, Ulrica remains a typical mezzo-soprano, albeit lower-lying than most in Verdi's canon. The second scene of Act 1 begins with her two-section *scena*, finely done by Irene Minghini-Cattaneo (DB 1402; LV 66), a Scala singer of great intensity who was Ulrica there in 1929; by the Czech Vera Soukupová (SUA 50589); by Marian Anderson. The splendid Dresden singer, Ottilie Metzger, recorded both sections (Od. 51849, 64896; CO 310), cutting the orchestral introduction, as did Jeanne Gordon, an impressive Canadian who sang at the Met, Margarete Klose (DB 4461; LV 18) in German and with cuts to fit a single-sided disc, and Grace Bumbry (SLPEM 138826), the latter with fine intensity but little contralto quality. The best recordings of Part 1 include those of Sigrid Onegin (Poly. 70619; DG 30194), a superb singer of amazing fluency and intensity; Ebe Stignani, virtually her equal in every department (R 30023; LV 237); Fanny Anitua, the opulent-voiced Mexican who finished her sixteen-year career at La Scala by singing the role with Toscanini in 1926, and who was at the Colón, Buenos Aires, for over twenty-five years (Col. DB 2912); the Romanian, Zenaida Pally, and Karin Branzell, whose great voice seems to toll the knell of doom (Poly. 62633; LV 47). The Canadian Jean Watson has left a fine souvenir of her work at Covent Garden and Glyndebourne (Col. 2912). Some of the best singing of all is by Armida Parsi-Pettinella, who recorded 'Re dell' abisso' in 1910 (Fono. 92581).

But, you will say, what about *Ballo's* fine duets and ensembles – the finales, the ballroom scene and so on ? I have only two excuses. First, the recording companies not me, are to blame, that single discs of, for instance, the poignant farewell duet (the mazurka) and the last scene have not been made, that even 'E scherzo od è follia' or 'La rivedrà' have lacked recorded interpreters, presumably because of the expense of collecting, in one case five, and in the other four, singers round a horn or microphone. Secondly, I have already mentioned the love duet, the greatest Verdi wrote before *Otello*, and the tenors who have figured in it. But there are other versions, often truncated, like the one in German by the full-voiced Margarete Teschemacher, always impressive on records, and the younger and very adequate Walter Ludwig (EH 909; LV 63); or simply a section, usually beginning 'Non sai tu', like the excellent performance, also in German, of Hermann Jadlowker and Maria Labia made in 1909, when she was 25 (Od. 50634; CO 312). Less interesting is the second half of the duet by Boninsegna and Luigi Bolis. The duet has recently been done several times in full, rather well by Caballé and Bernabe Marti, the former sometimes at her irresistible best, sometimes taxed to the very limit (ASD 2723); and, despite considerable intensity, in a slightly rough-and-ready performance by Katia Ricciarelli and Domingo (SER 5672). I had thought the best complete love duets outside the sets to be by Milanov and Peerce (ALP 1476) with Mitropoulos, followed by Zenatello and Burzio (Fono. 39665/6; ORL 209) among acoustics. But the performance by Price and Domingo (ARLI 0840) is a remarkable blend of physical excitement controlled by superb instinct and intelligence – glorious soft singing from the soprano, rare tenderness from Domingo alternating with incomparable breadth at climaxes, and splendidly conducted by Nello Santi – and I think it would be my final choice.

The other ensemble scene to have caught the gramophone's fancy is the finale of Act 2, one of Verdi's most fascinating scenes, foreshadowing *Forza* and *Falstaff*. Outstanding for the fine singing it contains is the early electrical version by Arangi-Lombardi, Molinari, Baccaloni, Bordonali and chorus (Col. D 14591), better because of the atmosphere it creates than those led by Frida Leider and Heinrich Schlusnus (Poly. 72961; LV 155), ideal Verdi voices each, or by Mafalda Salvatini and Scheidl, also in German. A rare curiosity is the 1913 performance with Battistini and E. Barbieri, each of whom is in fine dramatic form (05339).

UN BALLO IN MASCHERA

A Amelia; *O* Oscar; *U* Ulrica; *R* Riccardo; *Ren* Renato; *S* Samuel *T* Tom

1943 Caniglia *A*; Ribetti *O*; Barbieri *U*; Gigli *R*; Bechi *Ren*; Pasero *S*; Novelli *T*/Rome Opera Chorus and Orch./Serafin
World Records ⓜ SH 131–2
Seraphim ⓜ IB 6026

1951 Semser *A*; Valdarini *O*; Cahn *U*; Kérol *R*; Borthayre *Ren*; Mans *S*; Linsolas *T*/French Radio Chorus and Orch./Leibowitz
Period ⓜ 1082

1953 (live performance, Metropolitan, New York) Ilitsch *A*; Harshaw *U*; Peerce *R*; Warren *Ren*/Metropolitan Opera Chorus and Orch./Antonicelli
Classic Edition ⓜ 5001

1954 (broadcast performance) Nelli *A*; Haskins *O*; Turner *U*; Peerce *R*; Merrill *Ren*; Moscona *S*; Scott *T*/Shaw Chorale, NBC SO/Toscanini

RCA (UK) ⓜ AT 300;
(US) ⓜ LM 6112

1954 Curtis Verna *A*; Erato *O*; Tassinari *U*; Tagliavini *R*; Valdengo *Ren*; Stefanoni *S*; Susca *T*/Turin Radio Chorus and Orch./Questa
Cetra ⓒ LPS 3250

1954 Dezi *A*; Guido *O*; Sawyer *U*; Bardi *R*; Mazzini *Ren*/Rome Eliseo Theatre Chorus and Orch./Marini
Plymouth ⓜ 101

1955 (live performance, Metropolitan, New York) Milanov *A*; Peters *O*; Madeira *U*; Tucker *R*; Metternich *Ren*/Metropolitan Opera Chorus and Orch./Mitropoulos
Cetra ⓜ LO 4/3

1956 Callas *A*; Ratti *O*; Barbieri *U*; di Stefano *R*; Gobbi *Ren*;

Maionica *S*; Zaccaria *T*/La Scala
Chorus and Orch./Votto
EMI ⓜ RLS 736 ④TC–RLS
736
Seraphim ⓜ IC 6087

1957 (live performance, La Scala,
Milan) Callas *A*; Ratti *O*;
Simionato *U*: di Stefano *R*;
Bastianini *Ren*; Cassinelli *S*;
Stefanoni *T*/La Scala Chorus and
Orch./Gavazzeni
Cetra ⓜ LO 55/3

1960 Stella *A*; Tavolaccini *O*;
Lazzarini *U*; Poggi *R*; Bastianini
Ren; Cassinelli; *S*; Maionica
T/La Scala Chorus and
Orch./Gavazzeni
DG 138680–2

1961 Nilsson *A*; Stahlman *O*;
Simionato *U*; Bergonzi *R*;
MacNeil *Ren*; Corena *S*; Arbace
T/Santa Cecilia Academy Chorus
and Orch./Solti
Decca SET 215–7;
London OSA 1328

1966 L. Price *A*; Grist *O*; Verrett *U*;
Bergonzi *R;* Merrill *Ren*;
Flagello *S*; Mazzoli *T*/RCA
Italiana Chorus and
Orch./Leinsdorf
RCA (UK) SER 5710–2
(US) LSC 6179

1970 Tebaldi *A*; Donath *O*; Resnik
U; Pavarotti *R*; Milnes *Ren*;
Monreale *S*; Christou *T*/Santa
Cecilia Academy Chorus and
Orch./Bartoletti
Decca SET 484–6
London OSA 1398

1975 Arroyo *A*; Grist *O*; Cossotto *U*;
Domingo *R*; Cappuccilli *Ren*;
Howell *S*; van Allan *T*/Royal
Opera Chorus, New
Philharmonia Orch./Muti
EMI SLS 984 ④TC–SLS 984;
Angel SCLX 3762 (Q)

1979 Caballé *A*; Ghazarian *O*; Payne
U; Carreras *R*; Wixell *Ren*/Royal
Opera Chorus and Orch./C.
Davis
Philips – 6769 020

Excerpts

1944 (in German) Scheppan *A*;
Reichelt *O*; Schilp *U*;
Roswaenge *R*; Schmitt-Walter
Ren; Lang *S*; Schirp *T*/German
Opera Chorus, Berlin Radio
SO/Röther
Acanta ⓜ BB 22124

1953 (in German) Martinis *A*;
Roswaenge *R*; Baylé *Ren*/Vienna
Volksoper Chorus and
Orch./Loibner
Decca ⓜ LX 3126;
London ⓜ LPS 861

1953 Brouwenstijn *A*; Vroons
R/Vienna Volksoper Chorus,
Vienna SO/Loibner
Philips ⓜ NBR 6023

1954 Milanov *A*; Peters *O*; Anderson
U; Peerce *R*; Warren
Ren/Metropolitan Opera Chorus
and Orch./Mitropoulos
HMV ⓜ ALP 1476;
RCA (US) ⓜ LM 1911

1959 (in German) Siemeling *A*; Otto
O; Siewert *U*; Schock *R*; Cordes
Ren/German Opera Chorus,
Orch./Stein
EMI STC 80265

1964 (in German) Hillebrecht *A*; Otto
O; Töpper *U*; Schock *R*;
Wächter *Ren*; Sardi *S*; Rohol
T/German Opera Chorus and
Orch./Hollreiser
Ariola-Eurodisc K86612R

1965 (in German) Borkh *A*; Lear *O*;
Wagner *U*; Thomas *R*; Fischer-
Dieskau *Ren*/German Opera
Chorus and Orch./Patanè
DG 136420

1966 (in Hungarian) Takács *A*; Tiszay
U; Ilosfalvy *R*; Radnai
Ren/Hungarian Radio Chorus,
Hungarian State Opera
Orch./Gardelli
Qualiton SLPX 11665

1976 Deutekom *A*; Hay *O*; Craig *R*;
Derksen *Ren*; McCue *S*; Van
der Berg *T*/Scottish Opera
Chorus, Scottish National
Orch./Gibson
Classics for Pleasure CFP 40252

La Forza del destino

LORD HAREWOOD

Not as penetrating or as architecturally ambitious as any version of *Don Carlos*, not so direct or suggestive in story as *Un ballo in maschera* or *Simon Boccanegra*, none the less *La forza del destino* was from the 1920s to the 1950s the most popular of the half-dozen of Verdi's operas written in the eighteen years between *La traviata* and *Aida*.

That the records of the great set-pieces are numerous is not hard to explain, but why the popularity of the opera as a whole? The story is a jumble and disguise is the order of the day (the baritone even makes his entrance *incognito*); destiny is often indistinguishable from coincidence, motives are seldom clear, and Don Carlo invokes honour while behaving with what seems to us the finesse of the Mafia. The answer is simple: Verdi wanted situation and stage conflict, and this the story provided in plenty. Thus apparent inconsequence inspired a score in which the tunes are splendid and inexhaustible; the major roles are not only excellent but include in Melitone the composer's most ambitious (and successful) comic character to date; and even the once despised popular music (choruses of soldiers and *vivandières*, Preziosilla's solos, the Tarantella, above all the 'Rataplan' finale) provides a contrast which increasingly finds favour today – odd that the Metropolitan in the early years of the Bing administration omitted altogether the first scene of Act 2 (the Inn, with 'Son Pereda')!

There are eight important 'complete' recordings, all of particular historical interest in that they amount to much more than an assemblage of international stars; they represent, in fact, the style of performance and singing you would have expected to find in a particular place at a particular period.

The earliest is Cetra's, made in the summer of 1941, once partly available here on some haphazard 78s and also reissued on LP (three discs) varyingly engineered. It has those cuts traditionally made in Italy at the time – 'Sleale! il segreto fu dunque violato' the worst of them. The cast is typical of what might have been heard in Rome or Milan in the period following Toscanini's departure from La Scala, which was dominated among conductors by de Sabata, Guarnieri and Marinuzzi, the last-named of whom conducts this recording. It is an exciting performance which evokes theatre, not studio; dramatic impact is what the singers seem to be aiming at, not an exercise in immaculate phrasing. Typical is Galliano Masini (Alvaro), whose strength is a beautiful voice rather than a sense of style and who exemplifies the full-blooded, top-note-conscious tenor, with singing which is so buoyant and full of the Italian's instinctive feeling for the shape of a tune as partially (but not wholly) to disarm criticism. Much of his partner Maria Caniglia's singing as Leonora is beautiful, in spite of occasional flatness at the top of the range; she is intense, rhythmically accurate rather than smooth, and the performance is on a grand scale. Carlo Tagliabue (Carlo) was then in his best vocal period (some will remember a fine Rigoletto at Covent Garden for the San Carlo in 1946). Ebe Stignani (Preziosilla) is admirably supple, Tancredi Pasero a monumental Father Superior – perhaps the best on disc anywhere – and Saturno Meletti one of the most amusingly characterized of recorded Melitones.

EMI's 1954 set was newly engineered in 1978 to a semblance of stereo recording – it sounds very acceptable to me – and room has been found for the soup kitchen scene of Act 4, missing from the original issue. Now we lose a verse each in two of Preziosilla's solos, part of the baritone's cabaletta and, more unfortunately, the scene between Melitone and the Father Superior in Act 4. It was originally billed as from La Scala, and is in many ways representative of performances there in the middle 1950s, apart, that is, from Tullio Serafin's conducting (he was not heard there after 1947), which is here in the highest degree reliable and nothing short of brilliant in the genre and battle scenes. Richard Tucker's singing is musical and athletic, though I regret the intrusive sobbing, some tenor tricks of over-emphasis and clipped diction. Maria Callas's sometimes over-brilliant, not always steady high notes and her ambitiously weighted climactic phrases produce the stress on which her detractors like to fasten. Against that, her admirers can urge an unparalleled musical sensibility and imagination, subtle changes of tonal weight through the wonderfully shaped set-pieces, and a grasp of the musico-dramatic picture which is unique. Renato Capecchi was then already as brilliant a Melitone as much later in San Francisco, but there is little pleasure to be got from what is left of Tagliabue's burly voice, certainly far less than in his Cetra performance. Elena Nicolai is reliable, as is Nicola Rossi-Lemeni, then at the height of his career but still inclined to phrase with more weight than subtlety. Apart from its cuts and its poor Don Carlo, a fine set, which demonstrates the high musical demands La Scala could make on its artists at the time.

In 1978 Cetra issued a recording of a performance at the 1953 Maggio Musicale in Florence produced by Pabst. There is no compromise about Dimitri Mitropoulos's meticulously rehearsed performance, from the strong, positive attack on the overture to the very slow tempo he chooses for Leonora's dying utterances, and it is not hard to feel the contrast between this approach, insisting throughout first and foremost on musical values, and that of Serafin or Marinuzzi, who seem to compromise to accommodate tradition ('Tradition ist Schlamperei' said Mahler), which owes much, though not all, to the demands of the singers over the years. Here already is the clarity and rhythmic vitality of Giulini, of Abbado and Muti – inherited, one senses, from Toscanini – combined none the less with scrupulous care for the needs of the singers, which has always been central to Italian performing custom. Mitropoulos's cast was then young and he inspires them to such a degree that I doubt – a big claim I know – if any other recording reveals them with such vocal freshness or such musicality. If you did not know that Renata Tebaldi never became a central Verdi singer, you would predict otherwise on the evidence of this performance as Leonora, which took place when the lovely quality of her lyric soprano, at that period a glory of the Italian stage, was still undiminished. She confronts the music's difficulties boldly, her singing has more flow to it than in the later Decca recording and she can float the sound more evenly, whether in 'La Vergine' or at the soft B flat in 'Pace, pace' and stun the audience with her power in the full-throated climactic B flat at the end of the same aria. Listening to this set, the mind runs, not to the Tebaldi of later years, but to Milanov at her prime or even the recorded Ponselle. Mario del Monaco stood in the 1950s for an Italian ideal of vocal *machismo*, an ideal (happily) eroded by the advent of Bergonzi and later of such as Domingo, Pavarotti and Carreras, but here, whether because Mitropoulos brought out depths previously (and unfortunately later) hidden or because the tenor was in younger and more confident voice than we became used to, he sings powerfully as Alvaro but also very beautifully, and a moment of doubtful intonation apart, this is a major achievement. There is a sturdy, not very imaginative Don Carlo from Aldo Protti, a firm Padre Guardiano from Cesare Siepi (in top form a few months before his first splendidly voiced Don Giovanni), a substantial Preziosilla from Fedora Barbieri, and good support from Capecchi and de Palma. Unfortunately the big scene, 'Sleale! il segreto fu dunque violato', is cut, and a couple of other snippets disappear too. An oddity is the transplanting of the short choral 'Ronda' from the second part of Act 3 to its start. Though the sound is better than sometimes in live performances, but boxy compared with the studio, this is a set which I shall treasure not only because of its historical value and for the peaks its singers reach but also because it is one of the finest performances of the score I have ever heard.

Decca's 1955 performance is also representative of a period of Italian performance – at La Scala perhaps, on a night when Tebaldi rather than Callas was singing. The role of Leonora, with its big-scale lyricism and emphasis on sustained high *piano* singing, suits Tebaldi, a few violent top Bs apart, well, though many will regret not having the more searching

musicianship of Callas and others, the Tebaldi of two years before. Del
Monaco's vocal plenitude and splendour, apparent two years earlier in the
theatre, turns to unremitting loudness in the studio, unredeemed by musical
nuance but characterized some of the time by a firm line. Siepi, Giulietta
Simionato (Preziosilla) and Fernando Corena (Melitone) give appreciable
performances, but the finest singing in the set comes from Ettore Bastianini,
the rounded beauty of whose voice sits magnificently on Don Carlo's music
– to my mind the best performance of the role to be found on disc.
Francesco Molinari-Pradelli conducts well and the score is complete apart
from a page of 'Egli è salvo'.

The other four performances, although two are recorded in Italy, two
in England, are to a greater or lesser degree representative of Metropolitan
casts ranging over nearly twenty years. The first, from RCA (1959),
unfortunately has three of the principals in less than first-rate form, and
only Giorgio Tozzi compares well with his rivals. Admirers of Zinka
Milanov, one of the greatest of all Leonoras, should treasure her earlier
grouping of the solos and duets on ALP 1371, where she is on top form.
Hints of artistry from the leading singers are not enough to redeem a
disappointing set.

The remaining three recordings, all complete, are on a high level and
choice between them rests on personal preference among the leading
singers, all of whom are in representative form. For RCA (1964),
Schippers secures alert playing from the orchestra and straight, musical
singing from his cast, and the recording is good. Tucker is better than
in the Scala recording of ten years before, with fewer mannerisms, more
artistry and a fine line throughout. Robert Merrill's singing is ideally firm,
and the voice of vintage quality. Tozzi is again smooth and noble; Shirley
Verrett (Preziosilla) as painstaking as if she were singing Eboli; Ezio
Flagello a vocally rotund Melitone; and Giovanni Foiani an ideal Marquis.
There remains Leontyne Price in her first essay of the role of Leonora.
Her words are not always distinct, but the singing is beautifully fresh and
youthful, and the floating of her top notes hard to beat. If she is not the
most lyrical of Leonoras, she is perhaps on disc the most fluent.

HMV's recording (1969), conducted with no very personal stamp by
Lamberto Gardelli, is mostly sung by European artists though their
Metropolitan imprint remains. Carlo Bergonzi turns in a typically stylish,
finely judged performance as Alvaro, with a beautifully gauged recitative
and aria in the third act. Piero Cappuccilli (Carlo) is strong and direct
without the special distinction of Bastianini, Biancamaria Casoni's
Preziosilla lively if not endowed with a major voice, and Ruggero
Raimondi, though rather a 'slim' bass and not as strong on records as
in real life, is by no means without distinction as the Father Superior.
The resourceful Geraint Evans avoids exaggeration as Melitone, but it
is no disrespect to him to say that the best British Melitone of the
generation, Derek Hammond-Stroud, is also in the cast but in a minor

role. Martina Arroyo has not perhaps the strongest vocal personality, but the recorded voice is exceptional, and she is a fluent and soaring Leonora. In the end, a shortage of individual personality goes against this capable, well-organized recording.

The latest set from RCA (1976), recorded in Europe but again with a Metropolitan bias, is conducted by James Levine, urgently and with an authority that is often compelling in a way one begins to find typical of the Metropolitan under his direction. If the temperature sometimes drops when Placido Domingo is not singing, that is perhaps because there are drawbacks to the remainder of the cast. Leontyne Price, recording Leonora again after fourteen years, turns in a performance full of contrast and attack, and containing some singing of the greatest beauty, but the bottom of the voice is so cloudy as to sound positively hoarse; not to mention this would amount to dishonesty. Sherrill Milnes makes a sturdy Don Carlo, without much nuance. As Preziosilla, Fiorenza Cossotto's voice is still in splendid form after twenty years at the top of her profession, Michel Sénéchal sings Trabuco with extraordinary subtlety, and Gabriel Bacquier is a fine Melitone – the only one who bothers to sound sleepy when woken by Leonora at five o'clock in the morning! Bonaldo Giaiotti (Father Superior) sings powerfully, but the sound is not ingratiating, whereas Kurt Moll is an extraordinarily resonant Marquis. There remains the unfailingly musical Domingo, the only other tenor I know on record with Caruso's gift of stirring the listener to visceral excitement throughout the performance. He is not at his best in the aria, but no other recorded tenor makes one feel later in Act 3 the urgency and agony of Alvaro's plight. There is much to be said for this set and no one says it more persuasively than this great tenor.

Forza in complete form, therefore, exemplifies the style of immediately pre-war Italy, and of Florence and La Scala around the mid 1950s; also the vocal characteristics and, to a lesser degree, the performing style of the Metropolitan over the following twenty years.

The opera is too packed with memorable music to lend itself well to the 'selection' on double-sided LP, but equally too rewarding for singers to avoid the temptation to pare it to this form. Of the six double-sided selections I know, four are in German and of special value because of the singers interestingly deployed in them. The finest of all is the earliest issued, originally by Victor but later by HMV. Zinka Milanov at her grandest stands apart as a representative of Leonora and her great numbers are superbly represented in the set. Jan Peerce, Leonard Warren and Nicola Moscona give such support that their versions of solos, duets and trios compare favourably with almost any other on disc and are mentioned separately below. The record is a classic of its kind. The earliest of the German discs comes from a 1942 Berlin broadcast, with Helge Roswaenge and Heinrich Schlusnus as its stars, the former prodigal of tone on top notes, which is probably why the record exists at all, short (as I tend to find him in Italian opera) on line and style; the latter, with an ideal Verdi voice, exhibiting exemplary firmness and fervour in the aria as well as two duets. The sweet-voiced Hilde Scheppan makes a sympathetic heroine, and the great resonance of Ludwig Hofmann's voice – here he is a true bass, before and after the war he sang Wotan too – reveals in him a Germanic Giulio Neri.

From 1965 comes a brilliant, far from heavyweight selection conducted by Hans Löwlein. Fischer-Dieskau's Don Carlo is a main point of interest. From the buoyant, almost boyish 'Son Pereda', through 'Solenne in quest' 'ora' to a subtle account of the great Act 3 aria, this is an unusual and fascinating study, notable for its respect of Verdi's frequent *cantabile* markings. Jess Thomas, rare in Italian opera, sings most impressively and the voice rings out splendidly in Alvaro's aria, perhaps the best (with Lorenz's) of any in German. Stefania Woytowicz, delicate rather than dominant, sings the scene with Padre Guardiano with artistry – Georg Stern substantial here. Cvetka Ahlin is delightfully fluent as Preziosilla and the disc is recommended. Eurodisc's oddly arranged compendium – it finishes with Act 2's finale – dates from the same period. The music is allowed to speak through honest singing, with Rudolf Schock knowledgeable and experienced as Don Alvaro and still offering much sweetness of tone, Hildegard Hillebrecht (Leonora) wholly adequate in the little she is given to sing, and Thomas Tipton a Don Carlo in the Warren mould. Brigitte Fassbaender sounds more like a soprano than a mezzo in 'Rataplan'; Gottlob Frick is very impressive in his Act 2, scene 2 solo.

Electrola's selection, from the mid 1970s I would guess, has Helga Dernesch ('Rataplan') not too impressive in her only recorded mezzo role, and Grace Bumbry in her earliest unquestionably soprano recording; genuine excitement too in the Act 2 aria, 'La vergine', 'Pace, pace' and the finale. Hermann Prey's light, elegant singing of the *Ballata* and precise articulation of the Act 3 cabaletta compensate for some un-Italian lack of weight, but Nicolai Gedda is, chameleon-like, very much at home singing Don Alvaro in German, with youthful brilliance and real passion in the Act 3 aria and duet. Frick, not so fresh of voice as on Eurodisc, makes a fine contribution to the finale. Finally, a Hungarian cast singing in Italian: more interesting as an example of Budapest 'national' style than as an evocation of Verdi's opera, even though they sensibly opt for long stretches of Acts 2 and 3 rather than snippets. Eva Marton in the great scene of Act 2 sounds breathless and uncontrolled, in spite of the undoubted brilliance of the 'upper fourth' of the voice, singled out for praise in the sleeve note. Kolos Kováts is a noble Padre Guardiano, comparing well with those in complete sets. Inadequacies in the other singers make this an unrepresentative set.

The overture, arguably Verdi's best and certainly his most popular, receives a performance of headlong *élan* from Toscanini and the NBC

Orchestra, which obliterates other versions, apart from that by the Philharmonia under Giulini. Here, measured tempi are used to fill the music with detail (*à la* Furtwängler or Klemperer), and the drama is restrained to bring compassion to the score. Toscanini achieves continuity by a series of transitions as brilliant as his tempi, Giulini by a subtlety of phrasing so calculated that climaxes are proportioned exclusively in the interests of the total picture.

In Act 1, only Leonora's aria and her duet with Alvaro are recorded separately. Of 'Me pellegrina ed orfana' there exist a respectable version in German by Felicie Hüni-Mihacsek (CA 8211; LV 93), a powerful one by Gina Cigna (Col. D 14621; LV 137), and an impassioned performance by Eugenia Burzio (Pathé) made in 1913, an interesting souvenir of singing during Toscanini's first period at La Scala. Far the best is Zinka Milanov's on ALP 1371. Margarete Teschemacher and Walther Ludwig sing 'Ah, per sempre' in a cut but competent version, in German, like Schlusnus's recording of 'Son Pereda' from Act 2, one of the most attractive examples of his ringing baritone (LV 110). Also in German is the reliable Josef Herrmann (DA 4498; LV 49), recorded in 1942.

The second half of the act amounts perhaps to the outstanding scene of the opera: Leonora's aria 'Son giunta' and 'Madre, pietosa vergine', the *scena* between her and the Father Superior – a remarkable example of Verdi's habit of carrying forward the drama in extended duets – and a finale for them both with chorus. Short, single-sided versions usually begin the aria at 'Madre, pietosa vergine' and are often internally cut. I should mention the full sound and grand style of Celestina Boninsegna (053067, 053089 or her later Columbia), the affecting and musical singing of Göta Ljungberg (D 1352), an unattractive performance by Burzio (Fono. 62416), and an idiomatic if hardly imaginative version by Giannina Arangi-Lombardi (L 1833). Austral in English (0798) is hampered by trying to get too much on a single side but displays beautiful phrasing and a glorious voice in full flood. Maria Luisa Fanelli is tremulous (DB 1748); Cigna (Col. D 14621; LV 137) has a voice of true Verdian calibre; but the most interesting souvenir comes from Maria Nemeth (HMS 13; LV 248), whose imperfect Italian detracts little from the wonderfully brilliant sound of the voice. Amongst complete versions, I cannot unconditionally recommend Gré Brouwenstijn, singing with intensity but less than her best voice, or Joan Hammond, who makes a matter-of-fact impression. The great central phrases tax Maria Chiara's technical resources, though her voice sounds as beautiful as elsewhere (SXL 6606), there is impact and excitement from Floriana Cavalli (HMV 45 RES 4293), and Birgit Nilsson allies tragic vocal colouring to grandeur of scale (SXL 6033). My own preferences are for the strongly musical qualities of Dusolina Giannini (DB 1217; LV 8); for the noble and beautiful singing of Zinka Milanov (ALP 1247 and 1371); and for the rare control, the doomed, tragic sound, the great span of Meta Seinemeyer's performance (E 10605; LV 111). These last three compare well with the delicacy and drama of Callas in her sets.

The duet of Leonora and the Father Superior is in a number of contrasted sections, each pointing the psychological development of the scene. Teschemacher and Schwebs have done the scene rather fast in German (Col. LWX 376; LV 103), but otherwise I know only the celebrated and highly prized 'Chi può legger' (in German) of Seinemeyer and Ivar Andrésen (E 11115; LV 12) and the section beginning 'Sull'alba al pie' (Acanta KB 22179) – I wish I had heard Giannina Russ and Oreste Luppi in 'Chi può legger' in 1905 (Fono. 39055/64).

The finale of the act is in two parts: 'Il santo nome di Dio' for the bass and 'La vergine degli angeli' for the soprano. Of the first, Clabassi, Montarsolo and Vichegonov have recorded good, straightforward versions, Andrésen, in German, (E 10709; LV 45) and Rossi-Lemeni rather better. Boris Christoff's is a positive and beautifully gauged piece of dramatic singing (SLS 5090), but unrivalled for sheer quality of sound among Italian basses between the wars was Ezio Pinza, and his combination of velvety sound and taut phrasing puts him beyond competition (DB 1203). 'La vergine degli' angeli' has long been a favourite recording solo, and Boninsegna (53416), Russ (054024), Ruszkowska – a remarkable Polish soprano – and Ponselle soon after her Metropolitan debut (Am. Col. 49558; GVC 9) have all made individual and beautiful acoustic versions. Arangi-Lombardi (L 1833; QCX 10210) sings it strongly, as does Teschemacher (DB 5635; LV 103), and there is an 'off-the-air' curiosity of dubious artistic value in the 1939 American performance by Ebe Stignani and Norman Cordon. Less satisfactory are the jerky singing of Hammond, the well-balanced but undistinguished performance by Mala-grida, and the disappointing version of Cavalli.

Giannini's serene singing (DB 1228) is perhaps not as appreciable as the opulent and expressive performances by Milanov and Montserrat Caballé (ASD 2787), which in their turn yield place to the version by the great Seinemeyer (E 10709; LV 112); the matrix numbers suggest more of this scene was recorded with her and Andrésen; could the whole thing not be reissued on LP? Outstanding is Rosa Ponselle's 1928 recording (DB 1199; CDN 1006–7) – one feels nobody ever floated this tune quite as she did, and, with Pinza's cello-like bottom line fittingly introducing and then supporting her, the performance is beyond praise.

The third act divides itself into two main parts, the first containing the tenor's aria, the battle, 'Solenne in quest'ora' and 'Urna fatale' with its cabaletta; the second beginning with a fine duet for Alvaro and Carlo, then changing character with solos for Preziosilla and Trabuco, the Tarantella, Melitone's punning sermon and the final Rataplan. The first scene, sung virtually complete by the huge voices of Franco Corelli and Gian-Giacomo Guelfi (Cetra LPC 55017) emerges as a performance where vehemence is the keynote, size the criterion as each singer tries to outdo the other (and, as the Irishman would judge, usually succeeds). The disc represents an aspect of Italian singing of the 1950s/1960s and, though very loud, each of the arias is excitingly sung; done like this 'Solenne in quest'ora', however, emerges dangerously near to caricature.

'O tu che in seno agli angeli' is one of Verdi's major inspirations. The thinly accompanied opening phrases hover between F minor and A flat major, and the leaps of major and minor sixths and octaves most acutely convey the neurosis of Don Alvaro – who has deserted the woman he loves after having inadvertently killed her father, and who alternately proclaims the shame of his mixed blood and prison birth, and the glory of his noble ancestry. The aria appears not to have been in favour in acoustic days, but Giovanni Zenatello's 1909 version (Fono. 92610) shows purposeful phrasing and an imaginative approach, and Caruso's performance is as usual notable for the incomparable sound and the extraordinarily natural phrasing (DB 112; ORL 306). Beautifully voiced if a little melancholy is the 1928 version of Alfred Piccaver, the tenor of the first Viennese performance in 1926 (Poly. 66771), more apt vocally to the music than his Viennese successor in the role, the Hungarian Koloman von Pataky (Poly. 66558; LV 194, recorded in 1927), who sounds overparted. Other Germanic performances include Helge Roswaenge (Poly. 67211), smoother than in later recordings of Italian music but even then singing as though the musical directions *cantabile* and *dolce* were not in his vocabulary. More interesting is a fluent, finely voiced performance in German by the young Max Lorenz (EH 287; 1C 147 29154/5). Ernst Kozub, full of voice though laboured of manner, is no match for some of the post-1945 singers who attempt the aria in German in double-sided sections. Manuel Salazar turns in an appreciable 1929 performance (Am. Col. 4022X) vocally brilliant and with the nasal quality which typifies his singing. There is much to enjoy in the honest and musical qualities of Aureliano Pertile (DB 1208; LV 46) – is any worthwhile tenor remoter from the ideals of *bel canto*?; and the not wholly Verdian (because rhythmically imprecise) singing of Beniamino Gigli (1941) – the opening of the aria is perfectly poised and the flesh throughout beautiful, but the bone is sometimes hidden (DA 5410); and even more so is the recording of the tenor of Toscanini's 1928 revival at La Scala, Francesco Merli – a full-blooded account of the recitative and such beautiful shaping of the aria that I am convinced from his success he must have been recorded within easy reach of those performances (Col. D 1608).

Though del Monaco never gives the impression that the character he portrays has time to think amidst all the stress and energy he displays, there is something to admire in his singing of the aria some years before his complete recording (LXT 2845); but more in the artistry of Jan Peerce (ALP 1371) and in the powerful conviction of that Met stalwart Kurt Baum (Remington 19963), who has little nuance but lots of voice; and much too in that of Richard Tucker (MS 6668), whose phrasing is broad and whose voice rings out splendidly, apart from that cantor mannerism of a catch in the throat round the G to A flat break. Bruno Prevedi (SXL 6114), recorded in the early 1960s, starts well but runs into intonation problems later, in contrast to the frenetic but involved James McCracken (SXL 6201), whose mighty voice is painstakingly subdued to meet the music's demands. In spite of uncomfortable Italian, there is some evocative singing from Donald Smith (OASD 7584). The beautiful voice of José Carreras (Philips 9500 203) adorns a performance whose exceptional exuberance might be considered at variance with the introspection of the music. I particularly admired the fresh voice and well-controlled, musical singing of Carlo Bergonzi (Decca SPA 535), and there is just as much to be said for the poised, athletic, alert singing he provides in his much later Philips collection of Verdi arias (Philips 6570 045). Even though Bergonzi was a specialist in the role, to my mind the best version, notwithstanding that half the recitative is cut, is that by Giovanni Martinelli. This is the perfection of Verdian phrasing by one who is truly a composer's singer, with the sound and, above all, the breath control of an athlete, and the phrasing of a consummate artist. It is rare to find such perfection of detail allied to a performance whose vigour sweeps one off one's feet (DB 1089; CDN 1016).

Some of the records of 'Solenne in quest'ora' are little more than souvenirs: Martin and Rodrigo for instance, Garbin and Sammarco (Fono. 69015), Gilion and Bonini (Fono. 39811), Marconi and della Torre, Burian and Plaschke (044075; CO 306) – all fine voices; even Lauri-Volpi and Bechi, the former by then obviously short of breath, the latter in the firm vigour of his prime (DB 5449). Unexceptionable and individually impressive are Jadlowker and Josef Schwarz (2–054065; LV 86), in Italian; Tauber and Ziegler (Od. 0–8612), Pattiera and Bohnen (Poly. 78548; LV 61), Groh and Hüsch (R 1757), all in German; Mario Chamlee and John Charles Thomas (a 1924 rarity), Merli and Molinari (Pathé 0301; Cl.99.37), Titterton and Roy Henderson (K 506), the last-named sedately English. Both Kullman and Grossmann (DX 822) and Islandi and Skjaer (DB 5268) sing very well, the former pair in German, the Icelandic–Danish combination in good Italian, with Egisto Tango conducting (the conductor from whom Erich Kleiber used to say he learned Italian opera!). The versions of Chamlee and Bonelli and von Pataky and Schlusnus (Poly. 73090; LV 194) display remarkable voices, and that of Hislop and Granforte (DB 939; LV 90) the considerable artistry of the tenor as well. You could with impunity choose Björling and Merrill (RB 6585) or Peerce and Warren (Victor 11–9767), the latter distinguished by an impeccable vocal line by both singers; or, of more recent recordings, that by Domingo and Milnes (SET 5593). Because of the tenor's frequent indulgence in a form of hysteria, I cannot enthuse as I should like over Gigli's opulence and de Luca's immaculate control in what has become a famous version (DB 1050) – better than the slightly older, until recently unissued disc of Gigli and Ruffo. The classic performance is that by Caruso and Scotti (DM 105; ORL 304), an unusual example of expression obtained through smooth, unbroken, silky phrasing – it is hard to find more immaculately beautiful singing on record.

Roughly equivalent to 'Eri tu' in *Un ballo in maschera* is 'Urna fatale'. Ruffo's hurried performance is not amongst his best; Cesare Formichi is impressive in an acoustic of the 1920s; Stabile, in an early electric reissued on Tima 13, distinguished for intensity rather than vocal qualities. Giuseppe Danise (Brunswick 15045; LV 138) shows classic control, but Benvenuto Franci is pedestrian for a member of Toscanini's Scala cast (DB 1262; LV 171), Paolo Silveri lacks the poise of the great baritones, and the magnificently endowed Gian-Giacomo Guelfi turns in a reading whose sound and fury is frankly a bit larger than life. (Neither Formichi nor Stabile has the cabaletta.) Schlusnus is, with Josef Schwarz, the finest of Italianate German baritones on record, and his 1928 performance (Poly. 66763; LV 110) is very spirited indeed, providing too much competition for Josef Metternich (1C 047 28598), for all his powerful singing. Ingvar Wixell (Philips 6580 171) is a strong performer, Robert Merrill (SXL 6083), after exaggeration in the recitative, exhibits thoroughbred singing in the aria itself, and Sherrill Milnes (LSC 3076) turns in a scrupulously serious, big-scale performance, rather better, in that the voice sounds slimmer and better focused, than that in the complete recording. No one could fail to admire the extraordinary exhibition of vocal technique and sheer polish in Battistini's disc (listen to those immaculate turns!) and few present-day baritones have approached the subtlety of Fischer-Dieskau in this music. All the same, I find it hard to choose between the delicate, impassioned performance by the Tito Gobbi of the early 1950s (DB 21071), and the impressive (and more complete) version by Leonard Warren, displaying the full resources of his unique vocal riches (DB 21297; RCA 2641 372 AG).

The other half of the act does not yield so rich a recorded crop. Outstanding is the performance of the duet for Alvaro and Don Carlo (labelled, rather oddly, 'Sleale! il segreto fu dunque violato') by Caruso and de Luca, who sang the opera together in the Metropolitan première of 1918 (DM 107; ORL 316). Seldom has Caruso's line been more steady, buoyant, purposeful than here, in what I have always felt, partly because of this disc known from childhood, to be a particularly satisfactory scene (included in more than one of the German two-sided selections). Later on comes Melitone's punning sermon ('Toh, toh, poffare il mondo'), of which Edoardo Faticanti and Emilio Ghirardini (Col. D 16434) have recorded individual performances which are less good than the outstanding versions by Meletti and Capecchi in complete sets (Faticanti sang with Toscanini at La Scala in 1928). Gianna Pederzini is no match in the Rataplan – a brilliant piece, unique in Verdi's output – for Stignani in the old Cetra set, but there is a remarkable performance by Genia

Guszalewicz in German, full of elan and rhythmic energy and including an extra cadenza before the end (Poly. 66543).

Act 4 consists of a scene for Melitone and a duet for him and the Father Superior, the splendid duet between Alvaro and Carlo, Leonora's 'Pace, pace', and the final scene. Melitone's abuse of his clients in the soup kitchen is excellently done by Meletti (Cetra), rather less so by Faticanti (E 11380) or by Ghirardini (Col. D 16434), who is joined by Salvatore Baccaloni in one of his few serious roles (he was later a famous Melitone at the Metropolitan).

The extended scene in which Don Carlo runs Alvaro to earth, challenges him to a duel, fails to goad him from his priestly vows but finally taunts him into a noble frenzy, is one of the most impressive of the whole work. Ruffo and Ischierdo (the former fine) sing only half the duet (054102; CO 321); the other notable acoustic performance, by Caruso and Amato, contains magnificent singing on the first side but deteriorates later when the music is rushed in an effort to fit the disc (DM 106; ORL 309). Giuseppe Taccani and Amato (Fono. 92495) are positive in the second half of the duet, where Merli and Molinari exhibit no special virtues. Bechi is at the top of his form in this scene with Lauri-Volpi (DB 5448). Pertile and Franci are unsubtle (DB 1219; LV 171) but put the scene across in what one quickly comes to accept as fine style if one does not know the intelligently musical, fiery performance of Peerce and Warren (ALP 371). It is easy to understand why Lauri-Volpi wrote of Guelfi: 'He is one of the vocal phenomena of our era', but the overwhelming sound he and Corelli provide in this scene ends by becoming monotonous; though excitement runs high, I doubt whether Corelli's scooping, disturbing on disc, would be much more tolerable in the greater spaces of the opera house. The best performance of the lot is that by Martinelli and de Luca (DB 1172; CDN 1012), who were together in the opera at the Metropolitan and whose singing is remarkable for poise and dexterity and a vigour which always stops short of stress. Even Domingo and Milnes (SER 5593) cannot provide real competition.

'Pace, pace' is a favourite of sopranos, and decent souvenirs exist of Boninsegna, Burzio, Raisa (Vocalion), Hüni-Mihacsek, Steber, Muzio (recorded late and lacking in fluency), Teschemacher, Ilitsch, Bolechowska, Milashkina, Hammond, Nordmo-Lövberg, Cavalli and Ricciarelli; less attractive examples of Caniglia, even Ileana Cotrubas, whose poignancy is hard to reconcile with music of this dramatic import. Brouwenstijn is once again not at her best, either on Philips or a later EMI; Rysanek rich of sound but dragging of phrase, but Nemeth (HMV ES 571), in spite of a tendency to attack from below, provides rich, idiosyncratic singing. Ljüngberg is appreciable (D 1352; LV 178), and Gertrud Kappel (Poly. 66100; LV 117), another famous Wagnerian, sings the piece beautifully, contributing an interesting cadenza at the end in which she touches a soft top C. Cool in manner but exemplary in attack is Tetrazzini

(DB 538), the voice wonderfully even over the range and the performance (recorded in 1914) including a cadenza in the middle. Taking a deliberate tempo, Birgit Nilsson (33CX 1522) brings her usual vocal splendour to bear on the problem, but there is less dramatic awareness here than in her Wagner. Perhaps the scramble of the orchestral opening puts the usually so imaginative Giannini (DB 1288) off her stride, as it takes her a page or more before she reaches the level of her 'Madre, pietosa vergine'.

Anita Cerquetti (LXT 5289) starts less than smoothly, but the voice is splendid; this dramatic and emotionally persuasive performance makes one regret her very short career. In the same context regret at unrealised potential is re-emphasized by Elean Souliotis (SET 343–4) because of the clarity of her singing and the bloom on her B flats. I do not much care for the unidiomatic accompaniment to Vishnevskaya's beautiful, musicianly singing (ALP 157), but this is the performance of a fine artist. Gwyneth Jones (LXT 6249) is firmly confident, Grace Bumbry (1C 063–02055) a little more marmoreal in Italian with Ceccato than with Patanè in German, and Montserrat Caballé (ASD 2787) shows off her golden voice with self-conscious phrasing.

The basically dark but constantly varying tonal quality of Meta Seinemeyer (Od. 0–7648; LV 111), together with her controlled swelling and diminishing sustained high notes, highlight her supremacy amongst German artists in Italian roles. Zinka Milanov, with her glorious fullness of tone, is hard to beat, but owners of her immediately post-war 78 (Victor 11–8927; VICS 6044) will notice that there is more excitement if less smoothness than in ALP 1371. Again it is the Ponselle performance which stands out above all rivals, full of drama, persuasively phrased in a voice of velvet, the whole thing executed with supreme poise (DB 1275; RCA 2641 371 AG).

The finale is a product of Verdi's 1865 revision for the Italian première (Joachim Herz's Komische Oper production in Berlin of the 1970s used the original!). As the duel between Alvaro and Don Carlo ends, Don Carlo's cries for help are heard by none other than Leonora in her hermitage. The lovers' recognition, Leonora's realization that it is her brother whom Alvaro has mortally wounded, Alvaro's repentance, Carlo's vengeance on Leonora, and finally her death, supported by her lover and the Father Superior, gave Verdi the opportunity for one of his most expressive finales. Scacciati, Merli and Pasero, Toscanini's 1928 team (GQX 10206; LV 222), make all the points, but less persuasively and mellifluously than Milanov, Peerce and Moscona (ALP 1371). At the risk of sounding persuaded in advance, I must again give the palm to the version by Ponselle, Martinelli and Pinza (DB 1202; DN 1006–7) – here is the drama and the beauty of voice, the phrasing and the sheer élan which not only prove them three superbly equipped singers of Verdi but also point to just those qualities which all revivals of La forza del destino hope to harness.

LA FORZA DEL DESTINO

L Leonora; *P* Preziosilla; *A* Alvaro; *C* Carlo; *PG* Padre Guardiano; *M*
Melitone

1941 Caniglia *L*; Stignani *P*; Masini
     A; Tagliabue *C*; Pasero *PG*;
     Meletti *M*/Turin Radio Chorus
     and Orch./Marinuzzi
     Cetra ⓔ LPS 3236
1952 Guerrini *L*; Pirazzini *P*;
     Campora *A*; Colzani *C*; Modesti
     PG; Corena *M*/La Scala Chorus
     and Orch./La Rosa Parodi
     Urania ⓜ URLP 226
1953 (live performance, Florence
     Festival) Tebaldi *L*; Barbieri *P*;
     del Monaco *A*; Protti *C*; Siepi
     PG/Florence Festival Chorus and
     Orch./Mitropoulos
     Cetra ⓜ LO 17/3
     Turnabout ⓜ THS 65117–9
1954 Callas *L*; Nicolai *P*; Tucker *A*;
     Tagliabue *C*; Rossi-Lemeni *PG*;
     Capecchi *M*/La Scala Chorus and
     Orch./Serafin
     EMI ⓔ SLS 5120
     ④ TC–SLS 5120
     Seraphim ⓔ SIC 6088
1955 Tebaldi *L*; Simionato *P*; del
     Monaco *A*; Bastianini *C*; Siepi
     PG; Corena *M*/Santa Cecilia
     Academy Chorus and
     Orch./Molinari-Pradelli
     Decca GOS 598–9
     London OSA 1405
1959 Milanov *L*; Elias *P*; di Stefano
     A; Warren *C*; Tozzi *PG*;
     Mantovani *M*/Santa Cecilia
     Academy Chorus and
     Orch./Previtali
     Decca GOS 660–2; London OSA
     13122
1964 L. Price *L*; Verrett *P*; Tucker
     A; Merrill *C*; Tozzi *PG*; Flagello
     M/RCA Italiana Chorus and
     Orch./Schippers
     RCA (UK) SER 5527–30; (US)
     LSC 6413
1969 Arroyo *L*; Casoni *P*; Bergonzi
     A; Cappuccilli *C*; Raimondi *PG*;
     Evans *M*/Ambrosian Opera

Chorus, RPO/Gardelli EMI SLS
948; Angel SDL 3765 ④ 4X3S
3765
1970 Renzi *L*; Sylva *P*; A. Mori *A*;
     Maffeo *C*; S. Pagliuca *PG*; O.
     Mori *M*/Opera Stabile del Viotti
     Chorus and Orch./Savini
     Supraphon 112 1221–3
1976 L. Price *L*; Cossotto *P*;
     Domingo *A*; Milnes *C*; Giaiotti
     PG; Bacquier *M*/Alldis Choir,
     LSO/Levine
     RCA (UK) RLO 1864; (US)
     ARL 4 1864 ④ ARK 3 2543

Excerpts

1942 (in German) Scheppan *L*;
     Roswaenge *A*; Schlusnus *C*;
     Hofmann *PG*/Berlin Radio
     Chorus and Orch./Röther
     Acanta ⓜ BB 22026
1950 Milanov *L*; Peerce *A*; Warren
     C; Moscona *PG*/Shaw Chorale,
     RCA Orch./Cellini; RCA (US)
     ⓜ LM 1916; HMV
     ⓜ ALP 1371
1953 Corelli *A*; Guelfi *C*/Turin Radio
     SO/Basile
     Cetra ⓜ LPC 55017
1965 (in German) Hillebrecht *L*;
     Fassbaender *P*; Schock *A*;
     Tipton *C*; Frick *PG*; Röhrl
     M/German Opera Chorus and
     Orch./Schüchter
     Ariola-Eurodisc K87628R
1965 (in German) Woytowicz *L*;
     Ahlin *P*; Thomas *A*; Fischer-
     Dieskau *C*; Stern *PG*/Berlin
     RIAS Chamber Choir, Berlin
     Radio SO/Löwlein; DG 136416
1969 Marton *L*; Ercse *P*; Karizs *A*;
     Miller *C*; Kováts *PG*/Hungarian
     Radio Chorus, Budapest
     PO/Koródy
     Qualiton SLPX 11609
1975 (in German) Bumbry *L*;
     Dernesch *P*; Gedda *A*; Prey *C*;

Frick *PG*; Teschler *M*/Dresden   State Orch./Patanè
State Opera Chorus, Dresden   EMI 1C 063 28168

Don Carlos

LORD HAREWOOD

Don Carlos is a French opera, commissioned from Verdi for Paris and performed there in French, already with what now seem quite severe cuts, in 1867 (version *A*). It was revised by the composer for La Scala in 1884, shorn of its first act (already Italianized in 1867) and altered in order not only to quicken the action but also to turn what was a five-act grand opera with ballet for Paris into a four-act Italian opera without ballet for Milan (version *B*). In 1886 a further Italian five-act edition appeared (version *C*), containing in effect the first act of the published *A* joined to the four of *B*, presumably with the composer's sanction but put together by another hand. Starting in 1972, attempts have increasingly been made to promote performing editions of *A*, often without ballet but reinstating some of the passages cut in 1867 before the score was printed (version *AA*).

The restored cuts contain music that is beautiful as well as dramatic, and the long opera which results is not only consistent with the essentially French convention within which Verdi was writing; it is also appropriate to its huge historical subject and intricate human situations – nothing less than crises of political intrigue, of conscience, of emotion, involving no fewer than six major figures, and the dramatic resolution of the clashes which inevitably follow.

Working on this vast canvas has stimulated one of the finest and most richly textured of all the composer's scores, the culmination of a historico-political line working up from *I due Foscari* through *Les Vêpres Siciliennes* and *Simon Boccanegra* to this mighty climax. Perhaps Verdi, so private and enclosed himself, found peculiarly sympathetic the task of portraying in music the motivation of these hermetic, tortured figures – whether the self-limiting, self-questioning, suffering King Philip II, the serene and high-minded Elisabeth, or the unstable Don Carlos himself, with his vacillation between heroics and despair and his consequent hysterical ascents into the upper register. A supreme work.

There has been no attempt to record either of the French versions (*A* or *AA*),* and so the record companies cannot yet be said to have done

---

*An 'off-the-air' recording offers *AA* from a 1978 La Scala performance, conducted by Abbado, but in Italian.

full justice to *Don Carlos*. Two Italian recordings of *B* appeared in the 1950s, of which Cetra's (1951) leaned heavily on Serafin's famous 1950 Florence revival (of *C*), which I was lucky enough to see (the recording substituted Nicola Rossi-Lemeni and Fernando Previtali for the performances of Christoff and Serafin). Maria Caniglia here tackled Elisabeth for the gramophone late in her career; raw top notes and strident climaxes alternate with phrases of real artistry. Ebe Stignani, too, is no longer in first vocal youth, but Eboli is one of her grandest roles. She exhibits a brilliant flexibility out of reach of her competitors, and 'O don fatale' is splendid. Mirto Picchi's musical intensity overcomes a plangent quality of sound, but Paolo Silveri's vocal solidity cannot compensate for his four-square delivery of the music. Rossi-Lemeni's Philip is a noble concept built on the grandest scale, and it is regrettable that he allows himself occasional lachrymose moments and, in pursuit of expression in the great monologue, departures from pitch and bulges in the line. Giulio Neri is the grandest of Inquisitors, partly because of what seems like (and in the theatre was) unparalleled vocal power, partly because repetition had brought him unique understanding of the role's possibilities. I like very much Previtali's careful pacing of the score, less his omission of the invasion of the prison by the mob, the loss of a repeat, and three cuts in the last act.

In a way it was hard on Cetra that their pioneering effort of 1951 should have been capped by HMV's better engineered performance of three years later. Gabriele Santini, capable but perhaps less imposing than Previtali, is more severe with his cuts, removing Don Carlos's swoon in the middle of the love duet* Act 2, scene 2; two sections of the scene in the Queen's garden Act 3, scene 1; a couple of pages in Act 4, scene 1; the *marziale* section from the final duet. As if to make amends, this recording includes the mob scene at the end of Act 4, scene 2. Antonietta Stella in 1954 could float a tone more beautifully than seven years later, Mario Filippeschi is equal to the considerable physical demands of the title role, and Elena Nicolai, if without the authority of Stignani, is never less than competent. A moment or two of bleakness at the top of the voice apart, Tito Gobbi gives a performance of such dedication and tenderness as to disarm criticism, and his duet with Boris Christoff is a superb example of operatic logic on the part of both artists. Christoff, vocally less ample than Rossi-Lemeni, has a rare intensity and focus, and re-hearing this set convinces me that his full, fervent phrasing and ability to use the text bring him nearer than anyone else in their generation to rivalling the operatic *completeness* of Maria Callas – two foreigners on the Italian scene! His soft singing is perhaps the most expressive weapon in his vocal armoury, but in King Philip restraint and understatement count for much. Neri again is incomparable, Plinio Clabassi a fine Friar.

*Act descriptions for the four-act sets are referred to as if they were for the five-act versions.

In 1961, Santini for Deutsche Grammophon was responsible for the first recording of version C. His cast is strong, with Flaviano Labò a sympathetic Don Carlos, Fiorenza Cossotto – in those days singing softly when the music demanded – responsible for a powerful Eboli, and Christoff's thoroughbred performance no less good than in the earlier recording. The performance takes wing at Ettore Bastianini's first entrance as Posa, with his vocal brilliance and ability to suggest youthfulness, and the silky vocal line in the death scene is memorable. Only Stella sounds a little matter-of-fact, short of 'flow' and vocal beauty. What to my mind disqualifies the set is the ill-justified frequency of the cuts – in each of the three duets for the lovers; in Posa's Act 2, scene 2 *romanza*; the *auto-da-fé* scene; the trio of Act 3, scene 1; and in the scene between Philip and Elisabeth (some illogical compensation in the use of the beautiful soft ending properly belonging to *A*).

In 1965 came the first complete version *C*, conducted by Solti with Covent Garden backing and a fine cast. Throughout, Solti's tremendous energy is much in evidence, sometimes more so than is good for the music; the attack at the openings of Act 1 and Act 2, scene 2, for instance, would suit the youthful *Ernani* better then the mature *Don Carlos*. If a little more *gravitas* could sometimes be wished for, this is none the less a major account of the great work. The singers serve Solti well. Renata Tebaldi sings beautifully in all but the higher and more exposed passages of the role, Grace Bumbry is extraordinarily fluent as Eboli, and Carlo Bergonzi, the most consistently stylish of post-war Verdi tenors, is full of lyrical tenderness and beautiful phrasing – his floating of the Act 3, scene 1 trio hard to beat anywhere. If Dietrich Fischer-Dieskau is inclined to pounce on significant words and notes, he contributes a beautifully expansive death scene. Nicolai Ghiaurov's is the noblest voice of any Philip in a complete recording, and only a certain inner quality – the apartness of the absolute ruler? – eludes him so that the emotional spring seems coiled less tightly inside him than it is with Christoff. All the same, the clash with the Grand Inquisitor – Martti Talvela, early in his career – makes for a truly thrilling encounter of two great voices.

In 1970 appeared the other complete version of *C*, again with Covent Garden's orchestra (playing superbly) but this time with Giulini conducting, just as he did at the famous revival in 1958. Tempi throughout are set with supreme confidence, and I have never heard anyone better suggest the hieratic atmosphere of this grandest of all Verdi's operas. Like Solti's, his is a cast of a high order, and I cannot easily imagine a performance of the title role better than Placido Domingo's, whose voice has true heroic weight, whose phrasing is invariably expansive and ardent, and who conveys a constant sense of doom. Montserrat Caballé has one of those voices which captivate by sheer beauty of sound, and here the attack is exemplary and her contribution throughout, notably in the last-act aria, of the highest order. Admirable is the nervous involvement of Shirley Verrett, and Sherrill Milnes provides one of his most imaginative characterizations on disc. Ruggero Raimondi has not the vocal personality nor even the bass quality of the other singers of Philip, but his is none the less a noble performance. In the end, though, it is Giulini's magisterial conducting which makes me prefer this set to all others, even though only the two Spanish singers eclipse their rivals on the Decca recording.

For twenty years, *Don Carlos* has been a feature of Karajan's enterprises at Salzburg, and his 1978 recording is billed as a 'recording of the Salzburg Festival production' (Version *B* uncut). From the start with the sonorous Berlin horns and the orchestral swell below the monks' singing line, the Berlin Philharmonic's qualities can be felt, and the performance is full of telling orchestral detail, whether the brilliant clarity of the wind in the refrain to the 'Canzone del velo' or the strings *spiccato* at the start of the garden scene. This is a convinced and mature performance of the score, slightly marred for me by the conductor's constant tendency to over-react and so lose impetus in big lyrical moments, often when they are contrasted with others and whether marked *rit* or not; instances are the tenor-baritone duet which is short of tension, the second verse of Rodrigo's *romanza*, the middle section of the first Elisabeth-Don Carlos duet where Verdi's adjurations of *a tempo* after a bar's *rit* are ignored, the soloists' joining of the Flemish Deputies' petition in the *auto da fé* scene, or the slowing down of Elisabeth's Act 4 plea to Philip (marked *più animato*!).

The cast is without a weak link, and it is led by the beautiful lyrical singing of Mirella Freni and José Carreras, the former wonderfully fresh and even throughout as Elisabeth, the latter ideally ardent as Carlos. Piero Cappuccilli (Posa) sounds unusually youthful and there is evidence of his majestic breath control in the unbroken line at the start of 'Io morrò'. Agnes Baltsa is new on record to a Verdi role of this size, and makes a beguiling, almost vulnerable Eboli, not without steel when that is needed. A dozen years after the recording with Solti, Ghiaurov's major abilities are always in evidence, and Raimondi, less than ideally menacing at his entry and a little short of weight throughout, sings the Inquisitor with real beauty of tone. José van Dam contrives to sound at the same time firm and old as the monk. This recording perpetuates one of Karajan's longest-lasting operatic achievements, even though it would not displace either of the five-act recordings in my collection.

Of Don Carlos's unspectacular but expressive aria there are two recordings of *C* (the five-act Italian version), sung about 1910 with intensity by Carlo Albani, and some sixty years later by Carlo Bergonzi (Philips 6580 150), whose voice caresses the music to perfection and rings out perhaps more powerfully than in the Decca set. Of the 1884 revision (transposed down, simplified and with a new dramatic recitative – 'Io l'ho perduta' – to fit the changed dramatic situation), Bernardo de Muro in

1914 has left a full-blooded if unsubtle performance, (052429; LV 135) Jon Vickers in 1964 (SB 6577) a perfect example of his clean, powerful, committed singing. Jussi Björling (SER 5704) takes the aria briskly, but his glowing tone and the fervour of the singing make this into much more than just a souvenir of Bing's opening night at the Met (of whose sterling quality an 'off-the-air' recording provides ample evidence).

In B the aria is followed by the duet for Don Carlos and Posa, 'Dio che nell'alma infondere', which is to serve as a friendship motif for the rest of the opera. Domingo and Milnes sing it without special distinction (SER 5593); a strongly sung 1941 performance in German by Helge Roswaenge and Heinrich Schlusnus (Acanta DE 21487); Björling and Merrill (SER 5704) give a good if hurried account of it, but not so good as to eclipse memories of the involved and marvellous 1921 performance by Martinelli and de Luca (DK 127; RLS 743), as masterly an exhibition of Verdian style as of sheer singing and better even than the enjoyable Caruso–Scotti version (DM 111; ORL 310).

There was once a received critical notion that Verdi could not provide good music for social occasions, a charge to which the lie direct is given in the scene outside the Convent of San Juste (Act 2, scene 2), with its decorative *Canzone del velo* and evocative conversational music for Elisabeth, Eboli and Posa, constructed on a musical basis not unlike that of the last scene of *Ballo*. The most brilliant version of Eboli's taxing song is by Cossotto in the DG set. It is attractively sung too by Blanche Thebom, whose record (DB 21494) suffers only because it omits the page's part in the refrain. Margarethe Arndt-Ober (043251; CO 305) takes it fast and simplifies the flourishes which climax each verse; was this German practice then? Posa's romance, 'Carlo ch'è sol il nostro amore', has been recorded with ideal poise and polish by the great Giuseppe Kaschmann; a rarity in its original form (052031), it has been reissued on HRS 3004, but must be played faster than $33^{1}/_{3}$ if it is to sound, as it surely must, in the original key.

The emotional heart of Act 2, scene 2 comes with the great duet for Elisabeth and Carlos, 'Io vengo a domandar', inadequately served by Eileen Farrell and Richard Tucker in CBS's boxy recording, much better in the complete sets. As a pendant hangs Elisabeth's touching aria of consolation to the dismissed lady-in-waiting, 'Non pianger, mia compagna', sung with authority but some loss of control in high passages by Callas (SAX 2550); attractively by the then immature Katia Ricciarelli (SB 6863); and with considerable suavity and expressiveness by Felicia Weathers (SXL 6299). Only Ricciarelli includes chorus.

Act 2, scene 2 ends with the sombre, impressive encounter of Philip and Posa, with its clash of personality, its subtleties of feeling. It has been recorded separately in German by Frederick Dalberg and Horand (my disappointment at finding no copy increased by knowing the excellence of Dalberg's monologue), and again in German, rather unidiomatically, by Mathieu Ahlersmayer and Georg Hann, taken by Acanta from a 1944 Berlin broadcast.

Act 4 in version *A* contains the ballet music obligatory for a Paris production (sixteen minutes of it) and recorded by the Cleveland Orchestra under Lorin Maazel (SXL 6726), and by the Monte Carlo Opera under Antonio de Almeida (SXL 6377). In the first scene occurs the fine trio for Carlos and Eboli, later Posa, which was performed for an American broadcast in 1938 by Stignani, Dino Borgioli and Richard Bonelli and issued on OASI 540 in a performance that contains much beautiful singing.

The whole of Act 4, scene 1 (bar a short bit of the prelude) is on Acanta BB 22318 from a 1943 German broadcast, chiefly notable for Tiana Lemnitz's exquisite sensitivity which, in the scene where Elisabeth regains consciousness, rivals that of Caballé. Margarete Klose makes a fine Eboli until the live broadcast of 'O don fatale' finds her in some trouble. Georg Hann is coarse-fibred as Philip but provides a powerful bottom line in the quartet, Ahlersmayer is a strong Posa, but Walter Grossmann uninteresting as the Grand Inquisitor. The same scene has been recorded, also in German, by Hilde Konetzni, Elisabeth Höngen, Georg Oeggl, Alois Pernerstorfer and Alexander Welitsch. It may not be wholly Italianate Verdi, but it shows two of the finest post-war Viennese artists at their warmest and most womanly. Höngen's 'O don fatale' is a tremendous performance, full of insight and, incidentally, an object lesson in how translation can be made to sound as convincing as the original. The complete scene (with a cut in the prelude) has been done too by Hildegard Hillebrecht, Hertha Töpper, Marcel Cordes, Gottlob Frick and Kurt Böhme – admirably, with a particularly fine performance from Frick, a rarity in Italian music. He and Böhme make splendid adversaries, and the disc provides a memento of a number of good German singers of the day. Much more fragmentary, this time *only* a souvenir, are the privately issued excerpts, some of them quite long, from a Viennese performance of 1936 conducted by Bruno Walter. Alexander Kipnis is in glorious form (sounding like his E 555), but it is for the glimpse it affords of, on this evidence, Alfred Jerger's rightly famous Inquisitor (unfortunately not the complete scene) that I prize the disc – for that and a snatch of Franz Völker's beautiful singing of the last-act duet.

On records, far the most popular section of the opera is Philip's great monologue at the start of Act 4, scene 1, to the bass what 'Casta diva' is to the soprano; its simultaneous evocation of loneliness, dignity and despair as much a test of artistry as are its musical difficulties of vocal equipment and technique. Among pre-1914 acoustics, Plançon (1907), in spite of cuts, is outstanding (Victor 85116; ORL 218). He sings in French, with a fullness and beauty of sound, a nobility of style, a smoothness of execution that have to be heard to be believed. Behind the elegance of address – and that alone would be Verdi seen in terms of Gounod – the drama is present in all its intensity, hard and structural. Chaliapin (052292; ORL 220) does beautiful things but his expressive means basically did not include an Italian singing line. Leon Rothier is rotund and dull, Paul Knüpfer (D 811) vocally fine and musically slipshod, but Francesco Navarrini, the 1884 Inquisitor, with some splendid singing triumphs over piano accompaniment and ancient recording (Fono. 74034; GV 14). Marcel Journet sings, oddly enough, in Italian at a fast tempo (DK 127), but his expressive, muscular singing makes this, among early recordings, perhaps the most enjoyable after Plançon's.

The earlier acoustics are all single-sided, begin at the voice part and make small cuts. Most of the electricals (and post-1920 acoustics) are either complete (X) or else omit part of the orchestral prelude (Y). Among 'also-ran' versions of the great scene figure a number of recordings by Slav or Central European basses, all singing in Italian but in another tradition. Ivan Petrov's (X) is perhaps the best, the voice itself of more splendour than his rivals' (X, Melodiya). I particularly like the expansive singing of the Bulgarian Nicolai Ghiuselev (X), though his voice wavers under pressure (Balkanton). The Poles Bernard Ladysz and Kossowski (Y) sing respectably on 33 CX1678 and SLPM 136014, as does the Czech Vilem Zitek (Y), known at La Scala (1928–31) for Wagner and Mozart (Parlo. P 9601). Mihaly Szekely did it in Hungarian, with a less than top-rate recording but on an enviably big scale. There is less to be said for the rather lightweight Kim Borg, for Gitowsky (single-sided) or for Ivan Rebroff (Y); or, for that matter, for the frequently *parlando* performance by Norman Treigle (X), an American. Yevgeny Nesterenko (Y) magnificent of voice, gives a performance that seems a little short of nuance when compared with the best (Melodiya).

Germanic basses have recorded it repeatedly, some in Italian, but Schirp (no prelude), Strienz (X and Y), Greindl (X) and Ridderbusch reveal qualities better suited to Wagner or Lortzing than to Verdi. Paul Schöffler (Acanta DE 22694, in Italian) is unidiomatic (Y) but the vocal personality is great, Frick (Y) has considerable intensity in a careful, vocally impressive performance (1C 18730 150/1), but Franz Crass (1C 063–29 0731) in a resonant, well-sung performance (in Italian, X) exhibits much less individuality. I very much like Jerger in a 1921 double-sided acoustic (Y), reissued on LV 92, a truly beautiful expression of sad resignation, including (uniquely) a cadenza before the end! Kipnis's voice is a superb instrument and he recorded the scene twice in German, once in Italian. His third effort (E 555; SH 280, in German) expresses bitterness rather than resignation but occasionally he distorts the line in pursuit of drama (Y). Dalberg, who sang at Covent Garden for some years after the war, avoids any temptation of this sort and sings with great understanding and distinction (Y), to my ears perhaps the best of the German versions (Od. 0–3654), because even more appropriate to the mood of the scene than Kipnis's.

French performances have been recorded by Louis Morturier (Y), for many years a stalwart of the Opéra-Comique and singing beautifully here (Disque P 811) to demonstrate how much healthier French singing was between the wars than it is now supposed to have been; and Joseph Rouleau (X), stronger musically than vocally (SXL 6637).

Turning to singers who, whatever the nationality of their passports, may be thought a part of the central Italian tradition, I did not care too much for Italo Tajo's disjointed singing on Victor (X), nor for the heavyweight melodramatics of Nazzareno de Angelis (Y). Raffaele Arié (X) sings beautifully even if tension diminishes before the end (Decca X 442), but on both Cesare Siepi's records (X) there is more evidence of good vocalism than of strong character (Parlo. R 30016). Tancredi Pasero's voice is full and resonant, the phrasing musical and eloquent (E 11367; LV 34), and only a feeling that this was a splendid bass singer rather than Philip looking into the gloomy recesses of his heart keeps me from adding it to the short list.

In the end I would choose four singers to join Plançon and Journet, the most enjoyable of the acoustics. Pinza first recorded the music in 1927 (DB 1087; GEMM 162), starting at 'Dormiro sol' and exhibiting a richness of sound unique among electrically recorded basses. To quality of voice add a smooth technique and a sense of musical purpose which are exceptional in themselves and you get an irresistible performance. He repeated the scene on an American Army V-Disc about 1944 (Y), and again in 1946 for Columbia (Odyssey Y 31148) and in 1951 for Victor. Sadly, with a decline in vocal means, this fine singer starts to hurry difficult phrases until the performance loses touch with drama. But DB 1087 is pure gold. Nicolai Ghiaurov's glorious voice (SXL 6038) is particularly splendid at full throttle, but in the end, in spite of meticulous singing, it is the voicing that is more impressive than the music itself. Boris Christoff creates a superb Philip in the two sets he graces, a true psychological study of an intelligent tyrant in his turn in the grip of a greater tyranny than he controls. In an early recording of the monologue (DB 21007; RLS 735), (Y) the atmosphere of isolation is suggested through meticulous phrasing and imaginative vocal colouring, but there are some intrusive (if relatively discreet) sobs in the later part of the scene, an effect happily absent from a subsequent recording (ASD 2559), made about 1963, which demonstrates how the singer's absolute control over the vocal line increased rather than diminished with maturity, so that his poised singing of this music adds up to one of the wonders of post-war opera. There remains the great French singer Vanni Marcoux – singing Basilio and Don Giovanni, Colline and Golaud, Mephistophélès and Iago, was he bass or baritone? His recording (DB 4823; FJLP 5035) at first seems unspectacular but in a peculiarly satisfactory way generates drama through pure, cultivated singing. He sings in French, the voice is lighter than would be an Italian bass's, but the result is most beautiful and moving, and his record seems to me the nearest rival to Christoff's.

The scene between Philip and the Inquisitor, a clash of old and young conservative, extraordinarily enough has never attracted the attention of the companies, but 'O don fatale' is justly famous in and out of context. Written in A flat, the tessitura is frighteningly high for any mezzo (which only serves to remind one that Verdi wrote it for a French soprano). Of those who put it down from A flat to F, Kirkby Lunn (2–053000; HLM 7145) in glorious voice records an aria, not an operatic excerpt; Bruno Castagna (Am. Col. 71276 D) exhibits opulence but chops up the phrases; and Maartje Offers (DB 1158) sings with smooth, pure tone, albeit a trifle dully. In spite of cuts, weak top notes and an undramatic approach, Clara Butt is always interesting, especially for the rich, even sound in the section beginning 'O mia Regina'. Much the same applies to Marian Anderson (C 2065), whose great voice and solid singing compensate for interpretation which may not be theatrical but is never dull. Sigrid Onegin (DB 1292), if played at about 80, seems to put it down a semitone, and her brilliant vocalism conveys a curiously superficial, almost flippant view of Eboli at this moment of crisis. Margarethe Arndt-Ober (043252; CO 305), a fluent and brilliant singer, also transposes to G, changes the notes and then adds a striking top B natural at the end. Zara Dolukhanova's performance, again down a semitone, is very much of the concert hall.

The rest stick to the original key. Eleonora de Cisneros demonstrates a fine voice and an old-fashioned style; Olive Fremstad performs to suprisingly dull effect; Gertrud Rünger (in the Vienna revival of 1931) in German (LY 6114) shows a convincing *cantabile* line; the pre-war Klose (DB 4461; LV 18), in German, is big of scale and uncommonly convincing. Nini Giani, Irene Dalis, Blanche Thebom and Oralia Dominguez are perhaps of no more than souvenir value, but Martha Mödl (Telef. BLE 14 504) in German and Regina Resnik (LXT 5668) are highly dramatic. Appreciable in their different ways are the fluent if remote Birgit Nilsson (LXT 6033), Régine Crespin's often beautiful, sometimes stressful singing (ASD 2275), Callas's uniquely urgent perform-ance marred only by disaffecting top notes (SAX 2550), Bumbry's strong singing, better perhaps than in the complete recording (LPM 18826).

There remain Simionato, capable and satisfying in every way (LXT 5458); the powerful and very convincing Elena Obraztsova (ASD 3459); Rita Gorr's splendid voice and involved singing (ASD 456); and the irresistible Stignani (R 30010; LV 237), who sings the aria as if it had no difficulties whatsoever. Her shining C flat is rare enough in itself, but the voice has power throughout its compass, the phrasing is noble, and the performance altogether one of puissant authority. I thought her record unrivalled until I heard Frida Leider's (Poly. 72998; LV 172) which shows such understanding of Eboli's situation that what can out of context sound like melodrama becomes true tragedy.

Posa's death scene divides into two parts: (1) 'Per me giunto è il di supremo' and (2) 'O Carlo ascolta'. Among relatively modern recordings, few have combined the two parts so successfully as Gobbi in his wartime disc (DB 5447; HLM 7018 and RLS 738), or Fischer-Dieskau in his 1959 performance (ALP 544), full of detail and beautifully sung. Sherrill Milnes's is the only recording in French (SXL 6609), his fine singing showing how gracefully the original words fit the line. Hans Reinmar does the scene capably enough in German, Ingvar Wixell (Phillips 6580 171) is admirably smooth if a little lacking in individuality, and Robert Merrill (SXC 6083), without Gobbi's identification with music and role, sings with ideal firmness and glorious tone. Battistini exhibits his customary ease of production, but the characterization is stronger than usual, the smooth 'Per me giunto' contrasting vividly with a dramatic 'O Carlo ascolta', full of colour, *parlando* sentences and some exquisitely musical portamenti towards the end (DB 148; COLH 116). My own preference among acoustic recordings is for the pair by Giuseppe de Luca, emotionally as unforced as vocally, the line as firm and expressive as La Scala's cellos, the singing full of exquisite detail, like the touching effect of the alternative E flat at the end of 'Carlo mio, a me porgi *la* man' (Victor 6078).

Eugenio Giraldoni, the original Scarpia, has done 1 unremarkably, apart from a startlingly articulated trill (52404); Ruffo's is altogether too strenuously sung (DB 178); but Antonio Scotti's elegant 1905 version (Victor 85067) has impeccable line and refinement. Heinrich Schlusnus gets shortened versions of both arias on to one side (Poly. 67107), but the beautiful voice is offset by less than musical singing. In 1 Håkan Hagegård (Caprice) produces ideally poised, lyrical singing of real distinction, and the heroic high baritone of John Charles Thomas on a private issue is enviably free and confident. There are singles of 2: an acoustic by Arnold Gabor in German, electricals by Thomas Tipton and Ion Jordachescu of no special distinction. Paolo Silveri's is efficient; Baylé's long on singing, short on characterization; Gino Bechi's (DB 11322) made when his voice was at its best. A 1901 Zonophone by Lelio Casini, the teacher of Ruffo, gave me great pleasure. Renato Bruson's version (ANC 25003) comes from a public performance in 1977 at Verona. It is smoothly sung and scrupulously phrased if ultimately short of excitement.

Act 5 begins with Elisabeth's extended aria, 'Tu che le vanità', which has recently become something of a recording favourite but was virtually ignored in acoustic days, except by Giannina Russ, who sang Elisabeth at La Scala in 1912 with de Muro, Galeffi and de Angelis but whose version (Fono. 92747/8) is too hurried to allow for subtleties. With so high a standard, I cannot recommend Zdenka Ziková's truncated recording, Julia Wiener's involved but slightly unsteady singing, Eleanor Steber's fluent but cruelly abbreviated version, nor even Joan Hammond's clear, accurate singing. Ellabelle Davis, Deutekom, Nordmo-Lövberg, Bumbry, Tebaldi, Milashkina and Weathers in varying degrees provide worthwhile souvenirs, Gwyneth Jones something more positive (SXL 6376). Crespin with some beautiful soft singing (ASD 2275), Leontyne Price with a pure floated line (SER 5621), and Margherita Grandi, with big-scale phrasing and pulsating tone (DB 6631), sing the music thrillingly.

Nevertheless, three are outstanding, relying on *pianissimi* as much as on full-throated power, so that each has penetrated deep inside the character to reveal the pathos of Elisabeth's situation – the French princess in hostile, intractable Spain and married to the father of the man she loves. Gré Brouwenstijn, Elisabeth in the famous 1958 Visconti–Giulini revival at Covent Garden, sounds as committed as many of us remember from the theatre, more youthful and fresh on Philips in the 1950s than on EMI ten years later, but in each a sovereign interpreter of the role. Callas sang it only at La Scala in 1954, but her performance (SXLP 30166) is of the utmost delicacy and beauty, and she is paradoxically at the same time the most vulnerable as well as the most authoritative of queens. Technically there can be no comparison between her stereo and Meta Seinemeyer's 1928 vintage recording (Od. 0–7650; LV 112) – Seinemeyer died in 1929, still in the early stages of her career – but there is a uniquely tragic quality about Seinemeyer's singing, and such sensitive phrasing and caressing, lovely tone should be more generally known. I doubt if, after the orchestra's statement of the love theme, even Callas gets more heart-break into the single word 'Francia', with its overtones of half-forgotten happiness. Seinemeyer's humanity in this music touches the right note on which to leave the recordings of *Don Carlos*. Verdi in his music, whether the great issues are national, religious or political, never loses sight of the predicaments of a group of human beings whose private lives are overlaid by the public considerations in which they are so desperately involved.

DON CARLOS

El Elisabeth; *Eb* Eboli; *DC* Don Carlos; *R* Rodrigo; *P* Philip; *GI* Grand Inquisitor

1951 Caniglia *El*; Stignani *Eb*; Picchi
DC; Silveri *R*; Rossi–Lemeni *P*;
Neri *GI*/Rome Radio Chorus
and Orch./Previtali
Cetra ⓜ LPC 3234
Turnabout ⓜ THS 65054–6

1954 Stella *El*; Nicolai *Eb*; Filippeschi
DC; Gobbi *R*; Christoff *P*; Neri
GI/Rome Opera Chorus and
Orch./Santini
HMV ⓜ ALP 1289–2

Seraphim ⓜ IC 6004

1961 Stella *El*; Cossotto *Eb*; Labò
DC; Bastianini *R*; Christoff *P*;
Vinco *GI*/La Scala Chorus and
Orch./Santini
DG 2711 003

1965 Tebaldi *El*; Bumbry *Eb*;
Bergonzi *DC*; Fischer-Dieskau
R; Ghiaurov *P*; Talvela
GI/Royal Opera Chorus and
Orch./Solti

Decca SET 305–8 ④ K128K43;
London OSA 1432

1970 Caballé *El*; Verrett *Eb*;
Domingo *DC*; Milnes *R*;
Raimondi *P*; Fioani
Gl/Ambrosian Opera Chorus,
Royal Opera Orch./Giulini
HMV SLS 956; Angel SDL 3774

1979 Freni *El*; Baltsa *Eb*; Carreras
DC; Cappuccilli *R*; Ghiaurov *P*;
Raimondi *Gl*/German Opera
Chorus, Berlin PO/Karajan
EMI SLS 5154 ④ TC–SLS 5154

Excerpts

1943 (in German) Lemnitz *El*; Klose
Eb; Roswaenge *DC*; Hann *P*/
Berlin Radio SO/Rother
Acanta ⑩ BB 22318

1950 Thebom *Eb*; Björling *DC*;
Merrill *R*; Tajo *P*/Chorus and
Orch./Braithwaite, Cellini, Morel

RCA (US) ⑩ LM 1128

1950 (Act 3, scene 1) H. Konetzni
El; Höngen *Eb*; Oeggl *R*;
Pernerstorfer *P*; A. Welitsch
Gl/Vienna State Opera
Orch./Baltzer
Capitol (US) ⑩ P 8144

1969 Sudlik *El*; Ercse *Eb*; Albert *DC*;
Nagy *R*; Kovats *P*; Begányi
Gl/Budapest PO/Koródy
Qualiton SLPX 11608

1972 (in German) Moser *El*;
Fassbaender *Eb*; Gedda *DC*;
Fischer-Dieskau *R*; Moll *P*/Berlin
Radio SO/Patanè
EMI IC 063 28960Q ④1C 263
28960

1972 (Act 3, complete) Hillebrecht *El*;
Töpper *Eb*; Mercker *DC*;
Cordes *R*; Frick *P*; Böhme
Gl/Berlin SO/Stein
Ariola-Eurodisc K86811R

Aida

JOHN STEANE

Aida brings out the epicurean. At the prospect of a good performance, one feels like the character in Shakespeare who rubs his hands in anticipation, perceiving, as he says, that 'four feasts are toward'. The four feasts here are of music and drama, singing and spectacle, and each is of exceptional quality. All but the last can very well be enjoyed on records, and even that, elusive of presentation by sound alone, can nowadays be effectively suggested by an imaginative studio producer and resourceful engineers. Spectacle, we know, is the most primitive element in the opera, and the least valuable if not the least expensive. All the same, the ear should give to the mind's eye a picture of the great spaces of city, court and temple; the crowds should be a vivid presence; and the distant chanting of the priests should be set among the evocative sounds of the warm Egyptian night. There needs also to be a distinct separation of sound levels as the lovers sing from the tomb their farewell to earth while, above, the daughter of the Pharaohs prays for peace. All of this presents challenges and opportunities, so that it is not surprising that *Aida* has been as attractive to the record companies as to the public.

The most recent recording assembles just the kind of cast that conjures up a box-office queue which will curl half-way round the opera house. With Montserrat Caballé as Aida, Placido Domingo there to hymn her celestial virtues at the start and see her into the grave at the end, and with Fiorenza Cossotto, Piero Cappuccilli and Nicolai Ghiaurov in support, there may be many listeners who will feel that the vocal feast is richness enough, irrespective of the conductor. But he is Riccardo Muti, and not to be ignored. His brisk tempo moves the triumphal scene along at a pace which at some points impairs its breadth and nobility, and there is little imagination or feeling of tenderness in his conducting of the final duet. But these are exceptionable passages in a reading of the score that is both passionate and sympathetic, with fully responsive playing by the Covent Garden Orchestra.

Caballé's Aida often comes close to the ideal. Her voice, unmistakably Latin in quality, has also the softness and gentleness which, especially on high notes, are rarely to be found among her kind. Aida's first solo, ending with the exposed high notes on the word 'pavento', can often be taken as supplying a taste of things to come, and as Caballé sings it there is the promise of rare distinction. Thus the great aria, 'O patria mia' in Act 3, boasts a top C which is sung *dolce* as marked in the score, and it has its place in a broad phrase, to be followed by the most lovely floating of the perilous octave sighed forth at the very end of the solo. Nor is there any question of this being merely a pleasure to the ears: this is an Aida whose every phrase is in character and lives within a dramatic context, nothing shallow about it at all. There is an effective vocal contrast, too, with the harder-voiced Amneris of Cossotto, mercilessly penetrating in tone as she turns upon Aida in their duet, and growing in nobility to produce a towering impression (as she has so triumphantly done in the opera house) in Act 4. Compared with the women, who have a kind of inspiration in their performances, the men sing with fine voices and unmemorable style. Domingo is best in the Nile duet; Cappuccilli misses many opportunities in the role of Amonasro. It is still a fine recording, and – it must be said – infinitely preferable to its immediate predecessor.

This is the most dispensable of all the major complete sets, its unacceptability being largely due to its conductor, Erich Leinsdorf. The cast looks impressive enough, headed by Leontyne Price, who at her best, was the finest Aida of her generation. But she had sung better and acted just as well in an earlier recording under Solti, her voice, now less of a unity, having become cloudy in the lower registers and her style gusty in the more strenuous passages. Grace Bumbry, an opulent but unsubtle Amneris, can be heard to better advantage in the Mehta recording, and Domingo, Radames in the superior Muti set, gives a similar performance in this. Probably the sole recommendation, in fact, for this set is Sherrill Milnes's Amonasro, freshly felt and thought-out, with many a fine and unusual touch. Leinsdorf's conducting, however, is resolutely unidiomatic, the rare and mostly ill-judged modifications of its rigidity only momentarily driving endurance towards invective. Issued in 1970, the recording was intended to mark the centenary of the opera's first performance at Cairo.

Better, though still not in the front rank, is the version made three years earlier in Rome under Zubin Mehta. This also suffers from a certain lack of poetry and imagination – for example, that magical opening of the third act is quite without mystery or atmosphere, and one feels little sense of occasion in the great concerted passages. The last act is probably best, with Bumbry putting not only her magnificent voice but her soul into phrases like 'ministri di morti'. The Aida is Birgit Nilsson, and of course there is an interest in hearing what she will do with Verdi's music, so closely associated with singers of a different background. The silver ring of her voice, the power in ensemble, the effectiveness of some well-controlled, quiet singing – these are all welcome. Yet, despite the feeling she puts into the role, it is not, finally, an attractive performance.

Franco Corelli's Radames, on the other hand, is something to hear and hear again. The thrill of his voice (and it was a most exciting one) is captured better in an earlier recording on Cetra, but the style he commands here deserves more respect than it had at the time. His duets with Bumbry and Nilsson in the fourth act are fine pieces of singing and provide at least one good reason for valuing this set.

Better, on balance, than all of these, and certainly a recording that always rewards returning to, is the one under Solti dating from 1961. Some listeners may find the orchestra too much in the foreground (it is sometimes like having a seat in the front row next to the trombones); but the fineness of orchestral detail is itself a revelation, for everything here is fully cared for, and there is marvellous intensity in the performance, a sense of vision in its preparation. The solo singing also catches fire. Price at that time was at the height of her powers, and the role might have been written for her. With an utterly convincing absorption in the drama, she sings with much beauty of tone, her 'O patria mia' crowning this lovely and memorable performance. Her Radames is Jon Vickers, also in his best period as a singer, communicating that rare sense of devotion to the music, sometimes imprinting his individuality so that it is hard to hear phrases like 'sovra una terra estrania' in another voice, so beautifully haunted is it, half painfully, half entranced. The Amonasro is Robert Merrill and the Amneris Rita Gorr. The Belgian mezzo-soprano was then as fine an artist as any the post-war age is likely to have heard in the role. She was underemployed by the recording companies, but this sensitive and powerful portrayal shows her quality, and it is another great merit of the set that it serves as a memorial to one of the best singers of her time.

Turning from Solti to Karajan, one comes to a much more controversial reading. The speeds are slow, sometimes very slow, and the recorded sound, designed (as its producer John Culshaw says in the booklet) to capture the full perspective, runs disconcertingly to extremes. But there is always something to be newly appreciated here; there is no moment of dullness. The recording also preserves the Aida of Renata Tebaldi and the Amneris of Giulietta Simionato, the two most eminent Italian exponents of the roles in their time, though not the most characterful on record. Arnold van Mill deserves a special word of praise for his rich, suave singing of Ramphis. And Carlo Bergonzi – whose physical appearance limited the effectiveness of his Radames on stage – is first-class on record. His beautifully defined, very Italian voice is most gratefully heard; and one must recognize too the care given to detail (such as the rarely observed *dolce* marking over the high B flat on 'amori' in the Nile duet). As a whole, the recording remains one of the most distinguished, yet, despite the 'standard' nature of the casting, it has a place somewhat to the side, off-centre, among its fellows.

Serafin's conducting has the opposite quality – so reliably sound, understanding and sympathetic, yet rarely marked by a special insight or passion. He nevertheless conducts one of the most exciting of all the recordings. Here the focus of attention is upon the soloists, with Callas in their midst. If anyone doubts that genius is the word, they should put down the stylus at any point in this *Aida* (though preferably not at the climax of 'O patria mia'). The character is there in the very sound of the voice as well as in that special way of going to the heart of a phrase and making old things new. But it would be wrong to represent this as a prima donna's recording; it is in fact a triumphant piece of team-work. Fedora Barbieri's Amneris rises to the challenge of her great partner; Richard Tucker sings with fine ringing tone and his customary energetic rhythmic sense. Tito Gobbi is the incomparable Amonasro, giving with Callas a classic account of the Nile duet. The recording, coming from 1955, is still vivid, though not opulent. If reduced to just one recording of *Aida*, many of us would, I fancy, be found clinging to this.

High in the affections of the connoisseurs, however, is a recording made about the same time, in Rome instead of Milan, with the famous soprano of the Metropolitan Opera, Zinka Milanov, as the protagonist. Milanov's voice has something in common with Caballé's, excelling in the soft, high notes which at best were pure velvet. In other, more turbulent passages, she could be less pleasing, losing focus and displaying a beat. Some most lovely singing by her and Jussi Björling in duet, however, should be preserved if ever a really adequate archive comes into existence. 'La tra foreste vergine' (Björling also observing that rare *dolce* marking) and 'O terra addio' haunt the memory long afterwards with their loveliness. This set, too, is probably the most striking of all in the way it opens (once the curtain is up): Björling is in his best, fullest voice, but the first voice of all that we hear is Boris Christoff's, so impressive that it bids fair to refocus the whole opera on the High Priest.

With one exception, the other complete recordings on LP are of little account – though it should be noted that the Amonasro of the Russian set on MK is Pavel Lisitsian, who sounds on records (all too little-known over here) as though he may well have been the best Verdi baritone of the post-war years. The other important LP recording is the Toscanini, taken from two broadcasts in 1949. This has had less than its critical due, possibly because of the casting. Herva Nelli is no more than a competent Aida, and Eva Gustavson brings a good voice but not much character to the part of Amneris. On the other hand, Tucker is an excellent Radames, his young voice free and resonant, his style both careful and ardent. There is a rich-toned Amonasro in Giuseppe Valdengo (Toscanini's Iago and Falstaff), and the tantalising pleasure of hearing from offstage a High Priestess who ought to be singing Aida – her name, Teresa Stich-Randall. Still, the performance is Toscanini's. And what a lot of lessons it contains! The first is the value of a true singing tone in the strings – that is clear right from the first phrases. Then there is the precision, obtaining clarity and point without over-emphasis. Rubato is always finely judged; there is unostentatious majesty, disciplined passion; everything is justly proportioned – a classic reading.

In the three electrical recordings on 78s the soloists have much to offer. The one made in 1946 offers Gigli as Radames and Ebe Stignani as Amneris, which, with Serafin conducting, is sufficient recommendation for a start. Gigli sang the heroic role quite frequently in the later years of his career, but it cannot be said that he sounds well suited. He was 56 at the time of this recording and though the voice is still beautiful, it is not what it was, and it never was a Radames voice. Declamatory passages tempt him away from the note, and while there is feeling in his characterization there is not much nobility. Stignani, heard better here than in the later set with Tebaldi under Erede, displays her rich voice impressively. Maria Caniglia is a severe Aida, in difficulties with *piano* high notes. There is a sonorous Ramphis in Tancredi Pasero and a commanding, distinctive Amonasro is Gino Bechi.

Pasero also sang, sixteen years earlier, in the old Columbia recording, which had a prima donna of La Scala, now almost forgotten, Giannina Arangi-Lombardi, in the title role. She was a considerable artist, and there are many phrases (the repeated 'mai più' of 'O patria mia', the 'Numi pietà' of 'Ritorna vincitor') that lodge graciously in the memory. She has an Amneris, Maria Capuana, whose majestic tone and strong characterization are often equally imposing, and her command to tremble might well have intimidated Callas herself.

Then there is the HMV set which for many years held a proud place in the catalogue. Made in Milan, it presented in her only complete recorded role the remarkable Italo-American soprano Dusolina Giannini. She gives a curious performance, for there are legato phrases where one feels that this is just about the firmest and purest voice ever heard in this music, and more agitated passages where the focus and the beauty are quite lost. Oddly mixed, too, is the work of her Radames, the great Aureliano Pertile. Great he assuredly was, for a sufficient number of eminent musicians who knew his art well through his long years at La Scala are emphatic on the point. Yet he could force and quiver and disrupt like any disgrace to the name of tenor. Yet again – as in this set – he could sing with considerable refinement and with an unforgettable poetic imaginativeness: he does so in 'Celeste Aida' and again in 'O terra addio'. Amneris is Irene Minghini-Cattaneo, who also had a fine voice. Amonasro is Giovanni Inghilleri, a sturdy baritone with a great reputation in the 1930s. In fact it was a genuinely distinguished set in its day, bringing together, much as the most recent LP has done, the kind of cast that could be heard in a gala performance at one of the world's great opera houses. In the 1930 catalogue it occupied a special place, for most of the complete opera sets at that time drew upon the ranks of less celebrated artists. If one wanted to hear really great singing in those days, it was necessary to be content with single excerpts; but of these, in *Aida*, as in the other popular operas, the choice would often be complicated by an embarrassment of riches.

Not surprisingly (but it might have been just possible) we hear nothing from the principals in the original cast of 1871. Nor was Aida one of the rôles that Adelina Patti cared to recall at Craig-y-Nos in 1906, though it was in her repertory. And the great Tamagno did not include among his astonishing recordings anything from the music of Radames, whose aria, it is said, he liked to sing transposed a semitone *up*. But most of the other famous singers with whom these roles were closely associated have left behind them something through which their portrayals might be remembered; and of these artists I would like to choose four for detailed comment before moving on to a more general survey of excerpts.

Most beloved and least well recorded, probably, was Emmy Destinn. Opera-goers with long memories will still speak of her as the heroine of their young days, and it was not all that long ago that one was likely, during the intervals of any notable *Aida* at Covent Garden, to catch on the staircase or along the corridors a light sigh and part of a sentence running, 'Ah, but do you remember how Destinn would *float* the end of that aria?' Her 'floating' was not easy for the early recording processes to capture. 'Ritorna vincitor' she recorded twice in German (Od. 50027/8 and HMV 2–43090/1; CO 307) and twice in Italian (Col. A 5387 and HMV 2–053054). It is immediately clear that this is a true Aida voice; and there is, right in the earliest of these (from 1905), both urgency and poignancy in the interpretation. In the final section, the prayer, 'Numi, pietà', we hear something of the delicacy, the famous 'floating' tone, and also a good deal of the broad portamento style which is probably less pleasing to modern listeners. In the aria from the Nile scene, 'O patria mia', her greatness is more apparent, though one curses even more the limitations of recording. An early German recording (043095) and one made in Italian for the Victor company in 1914 (88469) both convey a vivid sense of longing, but neither gives a happy account of the climactic phrases or of the quiet end of the aria. Better is a Columbia recording from 1912 (30973), where one comes nearest to being able to hear this most famous Aida of her generation as in the opera house. What a chance was missed, one feels, in not bringing her into the studios to sing the Nile duet with Caruso as they sang it together at the Metropolitan. But at least there are two duets in which we can hear more of Destinn's Aida: a part of the scene with Amneris, sung by round-toned Kirkby Lunn (2–054023; Cantilena 6202), and 'O terra addio' with Giovanni Zenatello (Col. A 5399), but this is a performance of no special merit. Destinn's Aida lives most convincingly in the Columbia 'O patria mia'.

One great recording of that aria is also the most valuable testimonial to Destinn's successor, Elisabeth Rethberg. Her first Brunswick recording (50043; RLS 743) shows the radiant quality of her voice at its freshest

and loveliest. Moreover, when it comes to the climax, the high C is sung
dolce as marked and the whole phrase taken broadly and easily on a
single breath. In later versions, following tradition in the Metropolitan
Company which Rethberg had now joined, she sang the C with full voice;
the recordings (Brunswick 50084 and HMV D 1451; LV 29) are still fine
in the purity of legato and beautifully placed tone, but they are more
commonplace in style. In 'Ritorna vincitor' one feels the pressure of the
old recording studios, where all had to be completed within the four
minutes or so of a twelve-inch disc. Again the early Brunswick (50043)
is best, with more feeling for drama and nuance (and also more
portamento) than on the two later versions (both coupled with 'O patria
mia'). Recording conditions place some constraint upon the duets from
Act 3 which she sang with Giuseppe de Luca and Giacomo Lauri-Volpi,
and which nevertheless have their glories. The duet between father and
daughter (DB 1455) is not outstanding in its dramatic qualities, though
memory tends to underestimate them; where it is irreplaceable is in the
beauty of tone and purity of line. This is true too of the duets with Lauri-
Volpi (DB 1341, DB 1458; LV 36), Rethberg's 'Là tra forests vergine'
being most lovely in the sheer evenness and beauty of sound. Her voice
was essentially a delicate instrument, and though there was power at
command it is for purity rather than volume that her Aida remained for
two decades the classic performance of the age.

Her frequent partner in the United States, though not on records, was
Giovanni Martinelli, whose latter-day Radames survives complete in a
number of pirated recordings and the 1943 Cetra-Live set. A note on these
and other 'off-the-air' recordings is added at the end, but for the moment
I will discuss only the separate excerpts recorded earlier in the tenor's
career.

As always with Martinelli, the records affect listeners differently. In a
letter to *Gramophone* in its first years a correspondent asked advice over
'Celeste Aida' as he did not like his Martinelli. That was the acoustic
version (2–052100). A very rare recording had come out previously in
1912 on Edison 82069. Though there are fine touches in the recitative
and in the lyrical opening of the aria in the HMV version, it is easy to
sympathize with the plaintiff, especially if he was playing it at 78 where
it comes out a semitone high and is pinched in tone. The electrical
version (DB 979; LV 230) has immense authority and the characteristic
incisiveness; and there is also a very personal excitement in the attack
at the word 'ergerti' on the high B flat. Even so, he can do better than
this, and does it on an Edison electrical (82351; OASI 596), where the
phrasing is broader, and on a film track from 1926 (reproduced in a
special Memorial Album) where its breadth is indeed something of a
miracle; but there is nearly always a special way in which a record of
Martinelli remains vivid in the memory. In the temple scene there are
others who sing with richer or more ringing tone, but it is still Martinelli's

voice that haunts the memory (DB 1214; GEMM 162). He had also in that recording an incomparable partner in Ezio Pinza, as in the other duets he had Rosa Ponselle. The duets from the tomb scene were best-sellers for many years, and with Ponselle's beauty of tone and Martinelli's classic line it is no wonder (DA 809/810; CDN 5105). They also recorded most of the Nile duet; this remained unpublished until added to the Archive series after the second world war (HMV VB 73; CDN 1006–7). It is again one of those performances that becomes irreplaceable in one's mind: it is hard to imagine that such lovely tone as Ponselle's has ever been heard in 'Là tra foreste vergine', and Martinelli's fervour and utterly personal style and timbre are intensely memorable.

His great predecessor, of course, was Caruso. Five versions by him of 'Celeste Aida' are published, and he sings magnificently in the duets from the last act. With Louise Homer as Amneris, he gives a patrician account of Radames's role: the nobility of tone matches the dignity of spirit (DK 115, DM 111; VIC 1623). Then in the tomb scene, with the exceptionally sensitive Wagnerian soprano Johanna Gadski as Aida, he shows his ability to lighten the voice, though one would wish for more imaginative shaping of the phrases in 'O terra addio' (DM 114; VIC 1623). In 'Celeste Aida', the last recording, made in 1911 (DK 115; VIC 1623), is best. This is expansive, Caruso giving full space and unusual stateliness to the recitative, and phrasing the aria itself with greater breadth and security than he had done before. Going back, we have probably the least pleasing, made in 1908 (DB 114; ORL 305), where everything passes by too quickly and where the legato is less satisfying than usual. In 1904 (052074; VIC 1430, VIC 1395) he sang with a most lovely lyric quality and yet opened out with heroic fullness in the loud passages. That did not include the final note at that time, he still took it as softly as he could (it comes out at something like a *mezzo-forte*). Earlier still he had ventured a *pianissimo* on that high B flat, as written. In the second matrix of his 1902 recording (DA 549; ORL 302) he omits the last phrases altogether, but in the earlier matrix (issued on the same catalogue number but only for a few months and never doubled) he sings a well-placed falsetto note at the end of a beautifully dreamy, poetic performance (ORL 301).

There, then, are four singers in whose careers this opera played a major role and whose recordings are of special interest. Caruso's 'Celeste Aida' and particularly his treatment of that last note can lead us now into a survey of the wider field.

When Verdi wrote his direction to sing that high B flat softly, one wonders what hopes he entertained of having the instructions obeyed. He himself did suggest an alternative, where the note is sung loudly if need be and is followed by a descent to the lower B flat and a quiet repetition of the words 'vicino al sol'. This is what Tucker sings in the complete recording under Toscanini, and many years earlier it had been the arrangement used by the sonorous French heroic tenor Paul Franz

(032238). But there are a few tenors who have successfully sung the soft note as written. Perhaps Webster Booth is hardly in fair competition, for his voice was a very light one and the *mezza voce* is the next thing to falsetto; all the same it is a pleasure to hear and concludes a clean, musical performance in which the dynamics are all finely proportioned (C 3379; HLM 7109). The Hungarian, Koloman von Pataky, shows more convincingly perhaps how the aria benefits from having the kind of ending its composer intended (Poly. 66651; LV 54). In recent times the outstanding example has been set by Carlo Bergonzi who in his monumental Verdi album (an aria from each opera from *Oberto* to *Falstaff*) takes the note quietly, without preparatory breath and not in falsetto, and even manages a *diminuendo* (Philips 6580 150).

Quite apart from this single feature, there are numerous fine recordings Giuseppe Anselmi (Fono. 62561) and Giovanni Zenatello (Fono. 39507) sing in the style that might be expected of them; Alessandro Bonci (Fono. 39695) brings a fine legato to the aria but also some irregular vibrato, while Fernando de Lucia (Phonotype M 1763) lacks impulses and breadth of phrasing. John McCormack, surprisingly perhaps, recorded the aria (Fono. 84236; GEMM 155) and it is good to hear the precise definition and the ability to make this essentially lyric voice ring out. His fellow-countryman John O'Sullivan (L 1828; Club 99–6) rings on high notes too but is otherwise abominable. Only slightly better is Josef Mann (Od. LXX 80915; LV 74) who sings plaintively and with a slavonic wobble (and who was to die on stage during a performance of *Aida* in Berlin).

The Spaniards, Francesco Vignas and Miguel Fleta, are good in part: Vignas (1905 on Fono. 39136; GV 86) has exciting high notes that are too disparate from the rest of the voice, and Fleta mingles poetry and wobble in characteristic fashion (DB 1053). Leo Slezak's eleven recordings (from G&T 42900 in 1902 to Poly. 65771 in 1921) deserve mention for statistical rather than other distinctions (though I cannot claim to have heard them all). An interesting recording in German was made by the American, Richard Crooks (EJ 346) resonant, warm, varied, but a little nasal and rather fast. Best of all in the later 78 period is certainly Jussi Björling. His famous recording of 1936 (DB 3049, RLS 715) provided for many a listener an introduction to the most exciting new tenor voice for years, and listening to it again now one can take joy in the legato, the ring, the youthfulness and maturity of that sound. In recent years the young Placido Domingo made a comparably striking impression (SXL 6451) with a richer, rounder tone and with considerable dignity in his enunciation. It is doubtful whether either of these tenors improved on his earliest recordings.

Aida's first solo, 'Ritorna vincitor', was also a favourite in the early days, though it presented problems, being too long to fit on to a single side. A famous contemporary of Destinn's was Celestina Boninsegna whose voice made a great impression on the early gramophones. The full-bodied yet brilliant tone, with its magnificent chest voice and lovely *mezza voce*, is well heard on HMV 053253 (CO 358), though she made several other recordings of the aria on a variety of labels. Still more imaginative is Salomea Krusceniski, the Polish soprano who sang with great distinction at La Scala in the early years of the century. On Fono. 92086/7 she is allowed sufficient space to do the whole solo justice: 'e l'amor mio' has the intensity of a Callas and to the last section she brings the pathos of a Muzio. Impressive too is Giannina Russ (Fono. 39354/5); and less so, Felia Litvinne (Fono 39217; HMB 10), whose uninteresting phrasing is not counteracted by the unvibrant though powerful tone. Less expected among early sopranos is Margaretha Siems – she of the runs and trills (Pathé 55633) – ending with a highly regrettable climb to a top A flat. Luisa Tetrazzini (2–053064) is another unlikely Aida who might have been more successful with 'O patria mia'. In the latter inter-war generation of sopranos came Elisabeth Rethberg, mentioned earlier, and her great colleague at the Metropolitan, Rosa Ponselle (DB 1606), who gives a dramatic though hurried account, best in the lyrical passages and most beautiful towards the end. Very fine also are two German singers, Frida Leider and the tragically short-lived Meta Seinemeyer. Both sing in German, Leider (Poly. 65641) with glorious command and lovely softening of the big voice, and Seinemeyer (Parl. P.7646; LV 111) giving possibly the best performance of all, scrupulous in note-values and touchingly sincere in feeling. Our own Dame Eva Turner (L 2150; HQM 1209), with a very different kind of voice – invincible in sheet penetration for one thing – was also able to take two sides over the aria, and makes of it one of the best of her all too few recordings. And with a warmer timbre there is the ever-reliable musicianship of Florence Austral (D 695 and E 474). The Hungarian, Maria Nemeth, gives a very personal account in odd Italian (Poly. 66625; LV 214), contrasting with Tiana Lemnitz who is nevertheless far from being at her best in her post-war recording (DB 6608; WRC SHB 47).

On LP, several of the sopranos who were to record the role complete made separate recordings of the arias. In the first Tebaldi (SET 440) is vocally just (but only just) past her prime: still remarkably specific is interpretation and lovely in the final prayer. Leontyne Price (RCA LM 2506) shows herself near to the ideal. Nilsson (33 CX1522) is sensitive to the changes of mood but none too steady in tone. Caballé (ASD 2787) is less vivid and urgent than in the complete recording (Guadagno's uninspired conducting playing its part) but there is some fine phrasing. Neither Amy Shuard (SXLP 20046) nor Gwyneth Jones (SXL 6376) is a great pleasure to the ear though both have power and imagination. A highly intelligent, responsive account comes from Régine Crespin (ASD 2275); there is a proper sense of soliloquy in Leonie Rynsanek's recording (RB 16148); a freshness of approach makes one wish to hear more of the Bolshoi's Tamara Milashkina (ASD 2408); and the anxiety and tonal variety in Sylvia Sass's interpretation (SXL 6841) suggest that here is an interesting Aida for the future.

Aida's second aria, 'O patria mia' in the third act, finds many of the same artists exhibiting similar qualities. Boninsegna made three recordings (053049, Pathé 84523, 053232; CO 358) full of voice and feeling though not delicate or 'inner'. She, like most early sopranos, takes the high C loudly and with preparatory breaths – as does Gadski, though she also gives a hauntingly individual and nostalgic performance (Victor 88042; CO 362). Three who do not are Gertrud Kappel in a recording from 1911 (Favorite 1–16210; LV 117), Siems on Pathé and Leider (Poly. 65641); it is a pity these could not have had time and space to be taken more slowly for otherwise they are most lovely performances. Other early recordings are made by the Russian soprano Ermelenko-Jushina (opulent but unreflective on a rare record included in the Rubini album (GV 63)), Claudia Muzio (some fine phrases, others less so, Pathé 025106) and Ponselle (rich-toned but not fulfilling the highest expectations, DB 854). Among the electrical 78s, Eva Turner is again outstanding (L 2156 being the best and well reproduced; HQM 1209), with Tiana Lemnitz giving one of the loveliest of all performances with a beautifully quiet, broadly spanned climax and the kind of floated top A that (for a generation that did not hear Destinn) can well serve as the ideal (DB 6603; WRC SHB 47). On LP, Tebaldi, Price, Nilsson and Caballé record the aria in their recitals, all comparable to their versions in the complete sets. And one other who deserves note is the Turkish soprano Leyla Gencer whose under-recorded art is well sampled in this aria from 1956, remarkable for some finely sustained soft singing and much feeling (Cetra LPL 69001).

The duets for Aida and Radames have called forth some glamorous partnerships in addition to the ones already mentioned. In the 1920s at Dresden, evenings when Seinemeyer sang with Tino Pattiera were occasions looked forward to almost as eagerly as Melba-Caruso nights at Covent Garden. They sing the Nile duet (Parlo. E 10905; LV 16) a good deal faster, one imagines, than 'in the flesh', and Pattiera is square in his phrasing, but the soprano preserves fine tone and legato. A rare and early version by Jushina and her tenor husband Jushin (GV 63) is insensitive in expression, but Leider sings beautifully with Carl Gunther (Poly. 65691; LV 177). Another German recording, by Margarete Teschemacher and Marcel Wittrisch, is spoilt by the soprano's squally style, while Joan Hammond and Charles Craig (ESD 7033) are musicianly enough but lack temperament. The final scene brings the unexpected appearance of McCormack in the tomb, lyrical but lightweight, tender but unsentimental, singing with the fresh-voiced and accomplished American Lucy Marsh (DB 579; GEMM 155). Zenatello (whose undistinguished recording with Destinn has been mentioned) made further undistinguished recordings with Marie Rappold (Edison 83035 and 83066) and Ester

Mazzoleni (Fono. 92809; GV 27). Ponselle also did another recording apart from the famous one with Martinelli, this time with Charles Hackett, but it lacks style (Col. 49734; Ember GVC 9). The Austral-Fleta combination was a famous one in its time (DB 580): plenty of temperament here. And a fine version is one by Teschemacher (much better in this) and Wittrisch, who sings his solos meltingly (DB 4409).

Of the other characters, Amneris and Amonasro, we hear much less on single records. There were some early recordings of Amneris's part in the last act: Sigrid Onegin (043326) is outstanding for the elegiac tone and perverse rallentandi; and Rosa Olitzka (Col. 43741; RLS 724) has superbly rich contralto depth. Margarethe Ober sings with appealing pathos and a magnificent partner in Lauritz Melchior (Poly. 72936; LV 11). A still more surprising Radames stands up to the blandishments of Sabine Kalter (very hard to resist too) – Richard Tauber, resonant, fervent and lyrical (Od. 0–8225; HQM 1111). And a more recent but much less dignified recording was made by Sandra Warfield and James McCracken.

Amneris's other duet, from Act 2 with Aida, brings forth the sumptuous Louise Homer, confronting Gadski in a performance that triumphs marvellously over the old recording conditions (DB 666; VIC 1623). No less impressive is Edna Thornton, regal and dominant over Austral (D 776). The shrill but imaginative Tina Poli-Randaccio gives a memorable account of Aida's music, while the once famous Dutch contralto, Maartje Offers, reminds us what a fine artist she could be (DB 728). On electrical 78s a fine version was made in German by Emmy Bettendorf and Karin Branzell (E 10906), who again had that real contralto tone we rarely hear today – certainly not from Shirley Verrett in a none the less magnificent recording of the scene with Caballé (SER 5590).

Amonasro's short solo in the triumphal scene attracted some early baritones, Antonio Scotti (Victor 81042; CO 363) being stylish in the lyrical passages but less impressive than the young Riccardo Stracciari (Fono. 39160; GV 501), superbly even and healthy in resonance, and singing with a keen feeling for the rhythms. He would have been well worth hearing in the Nile duet; as it is, the most impressive baritone here is Pasquale Amato. Imaginative in his colouring and almost frighteningly vivid in declamation, he partners Gadski (DK 126; VIC 1623) and Mafalda Salvatini (Homocord 2–8494). Xenia Belmas finds a fit father in Willi Domgraf-Fassbaender – both having metal and vibrancy in their voices (Poly. 66849; LV 41). Seinemeyer, unluckily, has a ponderously Germanic baritone in Robert Burg, but she herself gives a heartfelt performance (Parlo. P. 9876; LV 114). And for her sake (as well as the spaciousness of the sound), it is well worth hearing the 1927 recording of the triumphal scene (P. 9171/2; LV 112), where that tense and hauntingly lovely voice soars clearly above the dense mass of the ensemble.

That recording was unusual in its time for the feeling it gave of being in an opera house rather than a box, so that one could hear the singers' voices in stage-perspective. There is often something exciting and instructive about hearing a stage performance, even at second remove, and for this reason certain live recordings require, at very least, a brief mention by way of postscript. A series of these, many of them enabling us to hear (or, as it were, *over*hear) occasions in the opera house from pre-war years, came out on the American EJS label. For instance, we can hear Rethberg's voice rising above the rest at Covent Garden as Seinemeyer's did at Dresden – not by exceptional power but by concentration of tone. She is heard in part of Act 2 from Covent Garden in 1936 on stage with Lauri-Volpi, Pinza and John Brownlee, all very vividly and excitingly caught. Martinelli's Radames has been recorded live from the Metropolitan in at least three complete performances. By 1943 his voice had dried out too much for enjoyment, though it is notable that, as he sings with Zinka Milanov, his older voice is distinctly firmer and better defined. On 22 March 1941, with Stella Roman, Bruna Castagna and Leonard Warren among the principals, Martinelli is his fervent, incisive self. And on 6 February, 1937, he sings the Nile scene like one inspired, while the sound of his voice in opera-house perspective makes an interesting comparison with the commercial recording of the tomb scene made some ten years earlier. This was also the occasion of Gina Cigna's American debut and, whatever the critics had to say about it, it is clear that she made a tremendous impression on the audience. Nearer to our own time, there is Callas's Aida as heard in Mexico City in 1950 and 1951 complete with high E flat in the finale of Act 2 and a strong feeling of competitiveness all round. And right back in the beginning of the gramophone's history there is a cylinder, where through all the hiss and crackle can be heard an echo from January 1903. On stage for Act 1 at the Metropolitan were Gadski, Homer, De Marchi and Journet. One would hardly know without being told; the gramophone has come a long way since the days of the Mapleson cylinders. We still have the privilege of looking – through a glass darkly – at another age; the experience may not be entirely musical, but it is a moving one, and it renews our sense of indebtedness to the gramophone.

AIDA

A Aida; *Am* Amneris; *R* Radames; *Amon* Amonasro; *Ra* Ramphis; *K* King

1906–7 Chelotti, Magliulo *A*;
    Colombati *Am*; Cosentino *R*;
    Novelli *Amon*; Brondi *Ra*/Chorus
    and Orch.
    Zonophone 12664–78, 24017,
    24019–25
1920 Bartolomasi *A*; Pagini *Am*;
    Trentini *R*; Pacini *Amon*;

Fernandez *Ra*/La Scala Chorus
and Orch./Sabajno
HMV S5150–80
1928 Giannini *A*; Minghini–Cattaneo
    Am; Pertile *R*; Inghilleri *Amon*;
    Manfrini *Ra*; Masini *K*/La Scala
    Chorus and Orch./Sabajno
    EMI Ⓜ 3C 153 01616–8M;

Discophilia ⓜ KS7–9

1930 Arangi–Lombardi *A*; Capuana
Am; Lindi *R*; A. Borgioli
Amon; Pasero *Ra*; Baccaloni
K/La Scala Chorus and
Orch./Molajoli
Columbia 9726–43; CBS (US)
ⓜ EL 3

1943 (live performance, Metropolitan,
New York) Milanov *A*; Castagna
Am; Martinelli *R*; Bonelli
Amon; Hatfield *Ra*/Metropolitan
Opera Chorus and
Orch./Pelletier; Cetra ⓜ LO
26/3

1949 and 1954 Nelli *A*; Gustavson
Am; Tucker *R*; Valdengo *Amon*;
Scott *Ra*; Harbour *K*/NBC SO
and Chorus/Toscanini
RCA (UK) ⓜ AT 302; (US)
ⓔ VIC S6113

1951 Mancini *A*; Simionato *Am*;
Filippeschi *R*; Panerai *Amon*;
Neri *Ra*; Massaria /Rome Radio
Chorus and Orch./Gui
Cetra ⓜ LPC 1228

1951 (live performance, Palacio de
Bellas Artes, Mexico City)
Callas *A*; Dominguez *Am*; del
Monaco *R*; Taddei *Amon*; Silva
Ra; Ruffino *K*/Palacio de Bellas
Artes Chorus and Orch./Fabritiis
Cetra ⓜ LO 40/3

1952 Tebaldi *A*; Stignani *Am*; del
Monaco *R*; Protti *Amon*; Caselli
Ra; Corena *K*/Santa Cecilia
Academy Chorus and
Orch./Erede
Decca ⓜ D47D3; Richmond
ⓜ RS 63002

1952 Roman *A*; Sawyer *Am*; Sarri *R*;
Manca Serra *Amon*; Tatozzi *Ra*;
Pugliese *K*/Rome Opera Chorus
and Orch./Paoletti
Capitol ⓜ PCR 8179

1954 (in Russia) Sokolova *A*;
Davidova *Am*; Nelepp *R*;
Lisitsian *Amon*; Petrov
Ra/Bolshoi Theatre Chorus and
Orch./ Melik–Pashaev
MK ⓜ DO 1576–82

1955 Milanov *A*; Barbieri *Am*;
Björling *R*; Warren *Amon*;
Christoff *Ra*; Clabassi *K*/Rome

Opera Chorus and Orch./Perlea
RCA (Europe) ⓜ 26.35004EA
(US) ⓜ VIC 6119

1955 Curtis Verna *A*; Dominguez *Am*;
Borsò *R*; Bastianini *Amon*; Scott
Ra/Fenice Theatre Chorus and
Orch./Capuana
Remington ⓜ 199–178

1955 Callas *A*; Barbieri *Am*; Tucker
R; Gobbi *Amon*; Zaccaria *Ra*;
Modesti *K*/La Scala Chorus and
Orch./Serafin
EMI ⓒ SLS 5108
④ TC–SLS 5108; Angel
ⓜ 3525CL

1956 Curtis Verna *A*; Pirazzini *Am*;
Corelli *R*; Guelfi *Amon*; Neri
Ra; Zerbini *K*/Turin Radio
Chorus and Orch./Questa
Cetra ⓒ LPS 3262 ④ MC
124–5

1959 Tebaldi *A*; Simionato *Am*;
Bergonzi *R*; MacNeil *Amon*;
Van Mill *Ra*; Corena *K*/Vienna
Singverein, VPO/Karajan
Decca SXL 2167–9 ④ K2A20
London OSA 1313 ④ 5–1313

1961 L. Price *A*; Gorr *Am*; Vickers
R; Merrill *Amon*; Tozzi *Ra*;
Clabassi *K*/Rome Opera Chorus
and Orch./Solti
Decca SET 427–9 ④ K64K32;
London OSA 1393 ④ 5–1393

1966 Nilsson *A*; Bumbry *Am*; Corelli
R; Sereni *Amon*; Giaiotti *Ra*;
Mazzoli *K*/Rome Opera Chorus
and Orch./Mehta
EMI SLS 929; Angel SCL 3716

1970 L. Price *A*; Bumbry *Am*;
Domingo *R*; Milnes *Amon*;
Raimondi *Ra*; Sotin *K*/Alldis
Choir, LSO/Leinsdorf
RCA (UK) SER 5609–11; (US)
LSC 6198 ④ ARK 3 2544

1971 Viner-Chenisheva *A*; Milcheva-
Nonova *Am*; Nikolov *R*;
Smochevski *Amon*; Ghiuslev *Ra*;
Tsiganchev *K*/Sofia National
Opera Chorus and
Orch./Marinov
Harmonia Mundi HMU 3470

1974 Caballé *A*; Cossotto *Am*;
Domingo *R*; Cappuccilli *Amon*;
Ghiaurov *Ra*; Roni *K*/Royal

Opera Chorus, New
Philharmonia Orch./Muti
EMI SLS 977 ④ TC–SLS 977;
Angel SCLX 3815 ④ 4X3S
3815

1975 Cruz-Romo A; Bumbry Am;
Gougalov R; Wixell Amon;
Ferrin Ra; Roni K/Turin Lyric
Theatre Chorus and
Orch./Schippers
Levon ML 1005–7

Excerpts

1938 (in German) Teschemacher A;
Karen Am; Roswaenge R;
Holzlin Amon; Weber Ra/
Stuttgart Reichssenders Chorus
and Orch./Keilberth
Acanta ⓜ DE 23057

1940 Bampton A; Summers Am;
Carron R; Warren Amon;
Cordon Ra; Alvary K/Chorus,
Publishers Service SO/Pelletier
RCA (US) ⓜ CAL 225

1943 (in German) Scheppan A; Klose
Am; Roswaenge R; Hotter
Amon; Lang Ra/Berlin State
Opera and Chorus/Rother
Acanta ⓜ BB 22025

1950 Williams A; Ibarrando Am; Gari
R; Winters Amon;/New York
City Opera Orch./Halasz
MGM ⓜ E3023

1952 Prada A; Braschi R; Nava
Amon/Florence Festival Chorus
and Orch./Ghiglia
Saga ⓜ XID 5263

1952 (abridged) Petrova A; Wysor
Am; Sari R/Florence Festival
Chorus and Orch./Tieri
Ace ⓜ 1009

1953 Moll A; Ruggeri Am; Da Costa
R; Valentino
Amon/Orch./Walther
Royale ⓜ 1583

1955 (in German) Rysanek A;
Wagner Am; Schock R;
Metternich Amon; Roth-Ehrang
Ra/German Opera Chorus,
Berlin SO/Schüchter
EMI ⓜ 1C 047 28581M

1961 (in German) Davy A; Ahlin
Am; Kónya R; Hotter Amon;
Schöffler Ra/Vienna State Opera
Chorus, Vienna SO/Quadri
DG 136402

1962 (in Hungarian) Déry A;
Komlóssy Am; Kónya R; Jámbor
Amon/Hungarian State Opera
Chorus and Orch./Koródy
Qualiton SLPX 1220

1962 (in German) Zadek A; Litz Am;
Kozub R; Crass Amon/Chorus
and Orch./Wagner
Philips 6593 013

1962 (in French) Jaumillot A; Kahn
Am; Poncet R; Borthayre
Amon; Karbel Ra/fanfare
trumpets, Chorus and
Orch./Wagner
Philips 6747 186

1962 Nilsson A; Hoffmann Am;
Ottolini R; Quilico Amon/Royal
Opera Orch./Pritchard
Decca SXL 6068; London OS
25798

1973 (in German) Bjöner A; Schröter
Am; Spiess R; Vogel Aman;
Stryczek Ra/Leipzig Radio
Chorus, Dresden State
Orch./Patané
EMI 1C 063 29090Q

Otello

ALAN BLYTH

'Esultate' exclaims Otello as he returns triumphant to Cyprus, in thirteen bars of the most taxing music for the tenor voice. When Giovanni Zenatello sang his first Otello anywhere at Covent Garden in 1908 he is said to have given the passage with such force that he seriously impaired his voice for the rest of the performance. However that may be, when he recorded the 'Esultate' in the 1920s (DB 1007; GV 85), he gave the most exciting account of it on disc. Zenatello had almost the ideal Otello voice and manner – heroic, trumpet-like timbre, incisive declamation, musical intelligence, pathos, nobility. The only other tenors to match him have been Tamagno (the creator), Giovanni Martinelli, and, in some respects, Jon Vickers.

Few tenors have recorded the 'Esultate'. The Zenatello version with its superbly held high A on 'L'armi' and perfectly managed *acciaccatura* B to A on the first syllable of 'l'urgano' is a model of how the music should go. Tamagno (DR 100; ORL 211) has the same classical declamation, but the voice is surely not quite what it was at the work's première in 1887. Antonio Paoli (052172; RLS 724) is as grand and powerful as Tamagno but less disciplined: he was a famous early interpreter of the part, however. John O'Sullivan, James Joyce's favourite tenor, shows a resplendent general (Col. D 9414; RLS 743). Of post-war versions, the del Monaco (DB 11337; 1C 147–18 226/27) gives promise of his later prowess in the role; that by Franco Corelli (Cetra 30/1123) is frankly careless. More interesting is an off-the-air performance by Gigli (Eterna 732), which is rich and amazingly powerful from a basically lyric voice. Zurab Andzhaparidzye, a Russian tenor, recorded this and other extracts (Melodiya C 04679/80) in a bull-like way. Nikola Nikolov, a Bulgarian (Balkanton 1051), who also added further pieces, shows tremendous commitment but little sense of style. Hans Kaart is massive in a McCracken-like way (5C 047 11646).

In 'Ora e per sempre', the pathos of the warrior's farewell to arms is what matters; we must sense that the Moor's whole world is disintegrating around him. Again, on separate records, Zenatello best suggests Otello's despair. His electrical record (DB 953, VB 17; GV 85) is one of several extracts made when the tenor returned to Covent Garden in 1926 and begins earlier with Iago's 'Non pensateci più' (Iago is the no-more-than-average Giuseppe Noto). The excitement of that live performance can be felt more than fifty years on. Zenatello's acoustic version (Fono. 92608) is fresher-voiced but less involved. Tamagno (DR 105; ORL 211) takes the excerpt more slowly than the score implies; the effect is measured and grand. Caruso (DA 561; ORL 307) never sang the part on stage, but his version of this extract, amply phrased, shows how overwhelming his interpretation might have become. Leo Slezak (Od. 50900; Eterna 747) and Francisco Vignas (Fono. 92350), two famous early, non-Italian Otellos, both reach to the heart of the matter. Nino Piccaluga (Fono. 168191; Club 99/33) declaims powerfully with a true *squillante* sound; so do a one-time Covent Garden Otello, Nicola Zerola (OASI 582), and Albert Alvarez, one of Tamagno's immediate and distinguished successors (Pathé 1639; RLS 724). Del Monaco (DB 11337; 1C 147–18 226/27) goes at it with force but no subtlety. Hans Kaart (5C 047 11646) has a certain power and pathos.

With the monologue we come to what I might term the 'A flat test'. The whole of the vocal part in the first section is written on that note, except where it three times falls to E flat. Otello is deceptively resigned, calm; all the poignancy of his situation is expressed in the gradually rising, yearning phrases in the orchestra. Verdi's pointed effect is almost wholly destroyed if his interpreter starts to use false histrionics and strays from the written notes. Martinelli, who also cuts off the semiquavers and quavers exactly and observes Verdi's injunction for a *voce suffocata*, is here the model in his Victor extracts discussed below. Zenatello, both in 1909 (Fono. 74104), live in 1926 (HMB 17; GV 85) and in 1929 (DB 1362), is almost as moving and over a twenty-year span. Bernard de Muro, who never sang the part on stage but recorded all the solos, is at his most convincing in 'Dio! mio potevi' (HMV 2–052120; LV 135) a *lirico-spinto* rather than a *robusto* tenor, singing with restraint, line and accuracy. LV 135 also has his 'Esultate' (broad and brilliant), 'Ora e per sempre addio' (fine attack) and death (where the pitch is variable).

Renato Zanelli is a fair representative of the more baritonal interpreters. He was also a superb actor to judge from his Covent Garden success in the part in 1928 and 1930. Zanelli's 'Esultate' (DB 1439), so similar to Ramon Vinay's, is awkwardly sung, but his 'Ora e per sempre' monologue (DB 1439) and death (DB 1173) are undeniably moving, in spite of superfluous histrionics. DB 1173 exists in two versions, the second conducted by Barbirolli being a great rarity, but that conducted by Sabajno actually has the better performances. Lauritz Melchior, another distinguished inter-war interpreter, is more creditably represented by his monologue and death recorded in German in 1927 (D 2307; 1C 147–01 259/60) than by his later Italian versions on American Columbia: in German his words mean something, in Italian they are vague. He easily passes the A flat test; so does the Costa Rican tenor Manuel Salazar, a notable Otello (L 2365). Gigli, Lauri-Volpi, Pertile, O'Sullivan, Merli, del Monaco, di Stefano all overplay their hand; but Lauri–Volpi (DB 5415; QBLP 5057) redeems himself through his true tone and keen enunciation. Carlo Bergonzi's very accurate modern version is worth hearing (Philips 6580 150), but he would probably be overparted on stage.

In the death scene, the ultra-lachrymose rule themselves out of court. Zenatello's live version (VB 8; GV 85) is, as *The Record Year* once stated: 'wonderfully sung with an overwhelming sense of pity and emptiness'. Tamagno (DR 100 and unpubl.; RLS 724) is again slow, but how noble. The quick vibrato and 'pellucid diction' (Michael Scott) are remarkable indeed. His near-contemporary Giuseppe Borgatti (Pathé 0312; Rococo 5323) has similar qualities but a lighter voice. Salazar suggests a great soldier struck down by tragedy (L 2365). Hermann Jadlowker (042514) displays Otello's sense of loss and despair; his voice is the epitome of tragic pathos; Jacques Urlus, the great Dutch tenor of that generation, singing in German, has even greater intensity of feeling (042312; CO 353). What breadth of phrasing is here! Franz Völker, also singing in German (Poly. 95436; LV 78), is restrained yet impassioned. Versions by De Negri, Piccaluga, Zerola, Merli, Kaart, Ludovic Spiess, Ernst Kozub and James McCracken are fair souvenirs of the singers concerned.

Of the 'German' Otellos, Jadlowker and Völker have already been mentioned. Leo Slezak (Od. 80077) suggests the power of his stage presence. Carl Martin Oehman, Björling's teacher, sings with inward feeling in the death, accenting the German text with eloquence (Telef. HT 46). Torsten Ralf, another Scandinavian, has similar qualities of restraint and tenderness in the monologue and death (DB 5630; LV 102). Helge Roswaenge (SK 1427; 6 42084 A3) is typically vivid, extrovert. Of French interpreters, I prefer José Luccioni with Charles Cambon as Iago, who together recorded the last part of Act 2 (DB 11193 and 11204; 2C 053 10643) to either Lèon Escalais (whose voice was correctly described in the Fonotipia catalogue as '*stupenda, estesa, vibrante e robusta*') or Thill; Thill recorded extensive extracts with Jeanne Segala, an excellent Desdemona, and José Beckmans as Iago (LFX 653–8; 2C 153–16211/4). After these worlds of 'Taschentuche' and 'mouchoirs', why not a 'kerchief' or two? Frank Mullings was apparently an astonishing Otello on stage. On record, in spite of technical shortcomings, he sounds virile, forceful and, in the monologue, pitiable, but the old light-blue Columbia records are poorly recorded (L 1334). Charles Stuart, a contemporary critic, said the phrases of the monologue were 'loaded with a tormented sigh'; so they sound here.

Mullings's 'Si pel ciel' – or, rather, 'Witness yonder marble heaven' – with Harold Williams (L 1604) has a rock-like steadiness. Most versions of this culmination of all Verdi's tenor–baritone duets are preceded by the passage in which Iago provides the supposedly clinching evidence of Desdemona's infidelity, the handkerchief just mentioned. It contains the line 'E il fazzoletto ch'io le diedi, pegno primo d'amor'. This sudden pang of remembrance on Otello's part, of happiness past and gone forever, is expressed with ineffable sadness by Martinelli in the excerpts already referred to. In fact his and Tibbett's handling of the whole passage from 'Oh! mostruosa colpa' is a model of how to execute Verdi's intentions. Caruso and Titta Ruffo (DK 114; ORL 312) run them close. Other versions that are justly renowned and usually recall stage partnerships are those of Zenatello–Amato (Fono. 92759; XIG 8015), Pertile–Franci (DB 1402; LV 46), Zenatello–Granforte (DB 1007), Zenatello–Noto (HMB 17, from the 1926 performance; GV 85) – but Zenatello's voice fails in the final phrase – and Björling–Merrill (RB 6585). Two German versions are notable for accuracy and comparative subtlety: Tino Pattiera–Michael Bohnen (Poly. 78546; LV 16) and Ralf–Hermann (DB 5620; LV 102). Another by the two Pauls – Kotter and Schöffler (Ultraphon E 361; HT 46)–is notable for the Viennese baritone's Italianate tone. Lauri-Volpi–Basiola and Wittrisch–Reinmar have eluded me.

Mention of Schöffler and Hermann moves us on to Iago's solos. Schöffler later recorded the Credo and Dream ('Era la notte') in Italian (K 1644): surely studied performances eclipsed by those he gave in the Furtwängler complete performance (see below). Hermann, in German (DB 7700 and 5647; LV 49) proves himself a vivid interpreter with keen enunciation and forward tone in both Brindisi and Credo in which Heinrich Schlusnus, also in German, is firm in tone, credible in characterization (Poly. 66852 and 65590; LV 110 and 187).

At least a dozen interpreters since the first, Victor Maurel, would grace any cast. You could choose from Pasquale Amato (DK 110; CO 346) – always an arresting artist – Giovanni Inghilleri (D 1698 or R 20075) and Mariano Stabile (L. 1969; Tima 13) – what panache, what diction – or perhaps the even more aristocratic Antonio Scotti (DA 377) for the Brindisi. In the Credo, you might prefer four strong, characterful, evil-sounding interpreters: Mario Ancona (052080) – dark-hued and sinister; Eugenio Giraldoni (Fono. 39446; HMB 9); Amato (DB 1465; CO 346); and Titta Ruffo (DK 114). The blander Mario Sammarco (Fono. 92174; XIG 8015), Giuseppe Pacini (Fono. 39024) and Antonio Magini–Coletti (Fono. 92216; Eterna 747) all have presence, and all take liberties. From the next generation. Granforte (DB 835; QALP 5338) is more telling in his complete set. Stabile (Fono. 74921; Tima 13) and Gino Bechi (DB 6506; QALP 10087) do not sound as menacing as the fierce Benvenuto Franci (DB 1154). Of the post-war generation, Gobbi finds more colours and variations (DB 21071; HLM 7018) than some of his predecessors and all his successors, but perhaps Giuseppe Taddei is a more plausible and therefore more dangerous Ancient (Cetra LPC 55006), a different reading from that on the Cetra set. Dennis Noble (in English), Robert Merrill,

Georg Ots, George London, Ettore Bastianini, Ernest Blanc, Norman Treigle, Jan Derksen, and Ingvar Wixell are all competent but not compelling. However, Michel Dens (Pathé DTX 30106), in French, is to be encountered, a profile of a sinister schemer.

In the Dream we have Maurel's 'creator' records; I do not know the rare G&T, only the later Fonotipia version (39042; ORE 202): it is smooth and reasonable. He substitutes ascending *acciaccaturas* (crushed notes) for the written, descending ones. Battistini (DB 212), also follows that practice; so does Sammarco in his ingratiating version (Fono. 92175). I wonder what is the authority (if any) for this variant. Battistini is much the most convincing of the three. Ancona (52129), Ruffo (DB 404), Stracciari (CQ 704;), Franci (DB 1154) and Bechi (DB 6506), all dramatically effective, use too much voice. Stabile (DQ 702; Tima 13) plays marvellously on the meaning of the text and so on Otello's nerve ends – but also takes liberties with the tempo. Hans Hotter (Poly. 68298), is persuasively buoyant, although hampered by the clumsy German text, as is Gerhard Hüsch (Parlo. R 979) in his beautiful, subtle rendition. The most accurate and convincing versions are those by Tibbett (VIC 1185) and Gobbi (DB 6626; RLS 738). Both maintain Verdi's required *mezza voce* throughout, start the section 'seguia più vago l'incubo blando' really *pianissimo* (marked with seven *p*s in the vocal score!), sing the high F on the second syllable of 'quasi' *pp*, observe accentuations and manipulate the text with supreme artistry.

For all these fascinating individual discs, *Otello* deserves, more than any other Verdi work, to be heard as a whole; then Boito's masterly condensation of Shakespeare and Verdi's equally masterly setting of it – his fusion of voice and orchestra, recitative and aria, and dramatic declamation into continuous music-drama – can be properly appreciated, and nowhere to such an extent as in Toscanini's 1947 performance. Its intense vitality and concentration have never been equalled on record. Such vocal deficiencies as there are pale into insignificance before Toscanini's achievement. Apart from a fiery yet sympathetic interpretation which allows time for the detail to be pointedly etched in, there is the old man's faithfulness to Verdi's tempo and dynamic markings. Put on your metronome where you will and you will find Toscanini playing fair by the composer while allowing his singers just sufficient leeway, by means of an almost imperceptible rubato, to phrase naturally, Ramon Vinay, so like Zanelli in timbre, is not my ideal Otello where voice is concerned, but his innate musicianship and his deep-rooted understanding of the role are so self-evident that the spirit scores over the physical limitations. As Iago, Valdengo gives the performance of his life (and I do not forget his Falstaff): sinister yet credible, incisive yet ingratiating, and he is extraordinarily observant of Verdi's dynamic and vocal injunctions. Herva Nelli, though no Ponselle or Rethberg, produces her not inconsiderable best for Toscanini – for instance, the vital phrase, 'guarda le prime lagrime', in her third-act appeal to Otello has just the urgency demanded by the *animando* marking.

A pirated version from the Metropolitan conducted by Fritz Busch a year or so after the Toscanini version has Vinay giving a more elemental, less detailed performance, Leonard Warren as an above-average Iago, Licia Albanese as a lachrymose but, in Act 4, touching Desdemona. Busch takes a Toscanini-like view of the piece without quite the master's total command.

Furtwängler is at the opposite extreme (you can safely ignore the intervening Urania set, a vigorous, Italian-provincial account of the work); it has a grandeur and elasticity that impart a greater tragic force to the opera than is to be found in any other performance. Speeds, as for the Brindisi, 'Era la notte' and the Cassio–Iago scene in Act 3, are very slow, but the cantabile line is never broken because of Furtwängler's horizontal approach. A sense of timelessness inhabits the love duet; of deep despair the monologue; of depraved evil the Dream, and these derive from the conductor's almost psychological approach to the orchestral parts. You may say that Verdi is here almost turned into Wagner, but at the time of hearing Furtwängler is mesmerizing.

He draws from Vinay his most subtle, introvert reading on disc, a performance much as I remember it at Covent Garden in 1956. Schöffler has difficulties with the Italian text and with pitch, but offers a plausible, interesting Iago. Carla Martinis sings many wonderfully imaginative phrases, others that are plain vulgar. Similarly the voice can sound sweet and true but at other times rough. One can hear just why she had such a success with the public; also just why her career was so brief. Anton Dermota is a lyrically ardent Cassio.

The Cetra set is worth investigating only for Taddei's appreciable Iago, a wholly credible assumption, as it was at Covent Garden. Similarly the old 78 set finds its justification in Apollo Granforte's magnificently sung Iago. Nicola Fusati is a clumsy, over-vibrant Otello, Maria Carbone an ordinary Desdemona.

The Erede version is quite superseded by the first of Karajan's (1) performances, with the same cast. The superb playing of the Vienna Philharmonic, the spacious recording, del Monaco's ringing and by then moving Otello, Tebaldi's central Desdemona – a most poetic 'Ave Maria' – are Karajan 1's undoubted assets, but Karajan's reading, for all its strength and poetry, misses the passion and drive of Toscanini's performance – and Aldo Protti's Iago is a distinct liability. Karajan here included the superfluous ballet, which comes as a shock in Act 3 if you are not expecting it, completely destroying the cumulative tension of the act. Serafin also included it in his set, which arrived on the scene shortly after Karajan 1. How sad he did not record it with Zenatello, Ruffo and Muzio, a cast he recalled in the original booklet. His understanding of the score, in particular its harmonic implications, is always evident; so is his quiet authority. Perhaps he is too retiring for such a tempestuous score, but his interpretation wears well. Leonie Rysanek is an affecting Desdemona in the Seinemeyer tradition, without that artist's vocal control. Vickers is a conscientious, restrained Otello here. So it is left to Gobbi to instil dramatic life into the recording – his pointed asides as he describes Cassio approaching Desdemona are a case in point, and his finely chiselled line is as ever a pleasure to hear, even if the actual tone is not always ingratiating.

The Barbirolli version is not satisfactory. His love of Verdi (his father and grandfather played in the work's première) leads him to slow speeds and too relaxed an approach without Furtwängler's compensating insights. The love duet and Willow Song are simply too drawn out, although they allow Gwyneth Jones as Desdemona to give one of her loveliest performances on disc. James McCracken's Otello, so impassioned and tormented on stage, emerges as mannered on disc (listen to the start of the monologue, delivered in a ludicrous *parlando*) and lacking in roundness or firmness of tone. Dietrich Fischer–Dieskau's Iago exudes intelligence, but the reading sounds in the end contrived.

Karajan's second recording is even more self-consciously expressive than Karajan 1 with a consequent flabbiness of rhythm except at forceful moments when he goes to the other extreme – the opening storm and end of Act 2 are examples of that. This quirkiness is emphasized by the corresponding quirks in the recorded sound, which is manipulated to a degree. In the set's favour is Vickers's tortured, psychotically unhinged study of the Moor, a portrait very much in the modern manner but often sung with an old-style trumpet-like tone. He also triumphantly passes that A flat test and thereby proves how much more effective is the monologue when sung with accuracy. Mirella Freni is an appealing, straightforward Desdemona, never very revealing in her verbal or musical phraseology but always stylistically sound. Glossop, too, is a musical Iago and often an intelligent one, but the voice is ordinary and not well focused.

Solti's version is the most dramatic since Toscanini's, but in places too emphatic, an emphasis accentuated by the Decca penchant for reverber-ation. Solti keeps the drama firmly moving, does not neglect significant detail (here he is helped by the VPO in top form) and shapes each act as a whole. Carlo Cossutta sings the music as well as anyone but seldom digs deep into Otello's character; perhaps that makes his gulling by Iago all the more reasonable, particularly as he is matched with Bacquier's quick-witted, insinuating Ancient. Bacquier is happier in the *parlando* passages than in the set-pieces, where his tone betrays rough edges and poor centring on key notes. Margaret Price's Desdemona is precisely, sensitively and surely sung, not always forward in emotional response but not by any means cold. I doubt if there is a more intelligently phrased interpretation in any other set and for more individuality one must go back beyond the LP era or the Scotto (see below).

This version was quickly challenged by the appearance of the RCA/ Levine set, which came even closer to Solti's in attempting to achieve Toscanini's sweep and drive. It largely succeeded, without finding the particular cohesion available to Toscanini through the recording of a live occasion. Levine and the National Philharmonic, a specifically recording orchestra, are helped by a close acoustic in bringing out relevant detail and in giving the score greater instrumental clarity than even Solti manages. Altogether Levine presents a compelling view of the work which matches the score's vibrancy although it may miss some of the tragic grandeur infused by Solti.

Domingo sings a superbly musical Otello (except when he fails the A flat test in the monologue, a serious fall from grace), also one with a more firmly controlled vibrato than Cossutta and a ringing edge to his tone. He suggests a broadly passionate and commanding general, whose ensuing downfall is all the sadder. Reservations are concerned only with his articulation of the text, which has not the clarity or individuality of Zenatello, let alone Martinelli. Domingo's Otello sounds very much like his José or his Chénier. A similar stricture applies to Sherrill Milnes's Iago, an intelligently sung portrayal, but one formed on fairly conventionally villainous lines and without the subtle inflectuons of Valdengo, Gobbi or Bacquier.

No, the great performance here comes from Renata Scotto, who surpasses all her modern predecessors in vivid rendering of Desdemona's various emotional states. The 'mi guarda' section of her Act 3 encounter with Otello, so tenderly inflected and keenly sung, puts her in the Callas class, and her Act 4 solos combine intensity of utterance with the most sensitive vocalization. I prefer Solti's opera-house orchestra and chorus to Levine's *ad hoc* groups, and Decca also has the better supporting cast, but by a hair's-breadth I would say this is the most successful recording of the masterpiece since Toscanini's. It is unlikely to be bettered for years to come.

Of one-disc highlights, that from Philips has a high reputation which I find unjustified. Vinay is less inspired than under more famous conductors than Cleva, Eleanor Steber is a heavy Desdemona, Guarrera an adequate but not outstanding Iago. In the German excerpts, Windgassen is a taxed but moving Moor, Fischer-Dieskau an unidiomatic Iago, Stratas a girlish Desdemona. A wartime broadcast in German yields up some treasure. Roswaenge, as ever, is an exciting singer: a superbly projected 'Esultate', a keyed-up contribution to 'Si pel ciel', and a surprisingly restrained death prompt the thought that Italians might never sing Wagner so well. Maria Reining is a fresh, natural and sexually aware Desdemona, and together with Roswaenge makes a poetic, *pianissimo* end to the love duet. Hans Reinmar is an athletic, thrusting Iago, but too emphatic in 'Era la notte'. Elmendorff conducts with a keen awareness of Verdian style (his training under Toscanini?).

More attention needs to be paid to the excerpts with Martinelli already mentioned. Stylistically he is almost in a class of his own but you have to accept his peculiar timbre, not to everyone's liking (it is to mine). He takes 'se dopo l'ira immensa' at the start of the love duet from low D flat to high G flat in one long breath and with an unfaltering line, the marking *dolce* implicit in his plangent tone. Indeed his legato throughout is unrivalled in my experience. Helen Jepson, his Desdemona, is a disappointment; so is the conductor, the dull Wilfrid Pelletier, but Tibbett's Iago, so firm in tone, so alive in utterance, is a fit partner for his Otello. As it happens the two sang the role together in the late 1930s at the Metropolitan under Panizza's whizzing baton and with Elisabeth Rethberg as a warm, impeccably stylish Desdemona. Some of these performances have been preserved in 'off-the-air' recordings. Here Martinelli, in fresher voice than for Victor, is almost unbearably eloquent in accent and tone – and all is achieved through a scrupulous observation of what Verdi demands so exactingly in his score. Tibbett is just as faithful to his composer and to his Otello (in the musical sense). These records are worth seeking for anyone who wants to discover the truest line of Verdian interpretation. Tamagno and Maurel could hardly have been better.

Poor Desdemona has received scant attention so far: anyone faced with almost countless 'Salces' and 'Ave Marias' might be daunted by listening to the far from short passages over and over again, yet one's admiration for this opening of Act 4 is only enhanced at each fresh hearing: nowhere else was Verdi so in command of his art. The LP era has yielded up many fine performances, none marked with more care and beauty than Maria Chiara's (SXL 6605), yet it is still to 78s that one turns for the nearest to perfection – to Melba (Victor 88148–9; XIG 8015) for exquisite purity of technique and tone, Frances Alda (Victor Heritage 15–1000) for warmth and conviction, Ponselle (DB 807) for vivid, moving characterization and rich, firm sound. Ponselle's veiled tone at 'prega per noi', her steady, floated A flat at the close of 'Ave Maria' are truly memorable. The only modern version to come near rivalling that is los Angeles's (SLS 5012), finely vocalized, intensely felt; note the catch in the voice on the second 'tanto' of the phrase 'son mesta tanto, tanto'. It is regrettable that she never sang this part at Covent Garden – where Melba made her 'farwell' records in 1926 including an amazingly fresh 'Salce' and 'Ave Maria' (RLS 719).

Most Desdemonas fall into one of two categories: the soft-grained German-lyric school, of which Meta Seinemeyer singing the 'Salce' (Parlo. E 10506), is the epitome and Lemnitz a worthy copy (DB 4595; SHB 47). Both sing the *dolce* phrase 'io per amar' with a perfectly judged rise to F sharp; Lemnitz's 'Ave Maria' is lovely too. Lehmann is predictably more spirited, also more gusty in her Willow Song (RO 20248; HQM 1121); her clear enunciation of the German only makes one long for the

Italian text. Delia Reinhardt (Poly. 72784; LV 142) sings beautifully but the performance is again hampered by the German words. Eidé Norena (DB 4852, DB 4861; LV 193), in French, catches the unsettled mood of the Willow Song, the resigned serenity of the 'Ave Maria'; in English Joan Cross (C 2932) is affecting.

Of 78s in the original, Rethberg (DB 1517; CDN 1018) is justly renowned, and deserves a place by Ponselle. Just after the war Gabriella Gatti recorded the scene complete with an Emilia, Nancy Evans (DB 6712–3), a rewarding performance full of thought and relevant detail. Dusolina Giannini, typical of the second category, the vibrant inter-war Italian style (DB 1791), presents a mettlesome, open-hearted creature; she has to hurry to get the 'Ave Maria' on side two, but once there sings with more thought and ease. Rosa Raisa is laboured.

In the LP era nearly every notable soprano of the day has seen fit to give us her version. Albanese, Sutherland, Crespin (twice), Zeani (rather moving), Leontyne Price, Stella, Anna Moffo, Felicia Weathers, Brouwenstijn, Ilitsch, Kabaiwanska all run true to their reputations, and need little comment. Not so several superior interpreters. Elisabeth Schwarzkopf is perhaps more faithful than any other soprano to the written note and dynamic mark (1C 181–52 291/2), although the voice itself may not have been intended for the part. Zinka Milanov (VICS 1198), right at the end of her career, when the tone was no longer as supple as of yore, gave a piercingly sad account of 'Salce' and a poised one of 'Ave Maria'. Renata Scotto (CBS 76426) is also heartrending by dint of her use of vibrato and a catch in the tone. Maybe there is too much artifice here, a modern fault, but there is art as well. For a diametrically opposed view, simple, clear and unfettered, I would recommend hearing Marthe Angelici, singing in French (FALP 567): her 'Chanson de saule' has a welcome lack of sophistication; more positively it reaches the heart; and the forward, clearly focused tone embraces the 'Ave Maria' gently, calmly. Finally there is Callas (SAX 2550), as usual *hors concours*, though here not for the best of reasons: no amount of thoughtful interpretation makes up for the often worn, hollow tone.

It may seem quixotic to have left the love duet to the end of this chapter but, after all, it is the recollection of Otello's 'Un bacio, ancora un bacio' that occurs at the very end of the opera both in voice and orchestra – 'Nessun maggior dolore' and all that; and it is the overwhelming nature of Otello's and his wife's passion for each other that makes subsequent events so tragic. Back in 1910, Zenatello and Lina Pasini-Vitale (Fono. 74157–8; Saga 8015) set a high standard in both the ardour and vitality of their singing, which still comes freshly off the old records. Unfortunately their version ends at 'ancora un bacio'. Maddeningly, Zenatello's later version with Hina Spani, the great Argentinian soprano, begins only at Desdemona's 'Quando narravi' (DB 1006; GV 86); it is another arresting performance. I find Sheridan's and Zanelli's admired performance (DB 1395) disappointingly laboured. Merli, with Muzio (LX 550; LV 222), is too tearful, but she, in spite of shortness of breath, is memorable; they are perhaps better suited to the recriminations of the third-act encounter, where they are to be preferred to Pertile and Gina Cigna (SKB 3303; HT 20). HT 20 also contains other extracts from a 1942 La Scala revival; sadly Pertile seems to have left his assumption of the part until too late. Lauri-Volpi's Otello is perhaps to be most worthily remembered by his version of the love duet with Maria Caniglia (DB 5417; QBLP 5052), the pungency of his declamation and the ardour of his delivery compensating for broken-up phrasing.

There are several excellent non-Italian versions. Tino Pattiera and Meta Seinemeyer (E 10816; LV 113), singing in the original, are both impassioned, making much of the ecstatic passages, but hurrying in-between. Ralf and Lemnitz (DB 4668; SHB 47), in German, are most poetic: how wonderful to hear the closing phrases for once sung *pianissimo* as written. In English, Licette and Mullings are appreciable (L 1562; RLS 743).

On LP, another excellent German version is to the fore – that by Sena Jurinac and Peter Anders (Electrola E 83380), chiefly valuable for Jurinac, who in the early 1950s had an ideal Desdemona voice and does justice to it in her interpretation. Eileen Farrell and Richard Tucker sound too mature (Philips BRE 72026). Rosanna Carteri and di Stefano (33CX 1598) phrase overtly but tenderly. Joan Sutherland and Luciano Pavarotti (SXL 6828) tell us what a fine Desdemona she once was at Covent Garden, what an interesting Otello he may become. Pavarotti sounds even better with Katia Ricciarelli (Ars Nova ANC 25001), while she is fresh and vulnerable with Domingo (SER 5672), who commands finer shades than with the lethargic Leontyne Price (ARL1 0840). Franco Bonisolli and Freni (BASF KBC 22007) recall a Hamburg partnership in their leisurely, long-phrased, tender version, one of the best. At Rudolf Bing's Met farewell Franco Corelli and Teresa Zylis-Gara, heavily prompted, are big-scale interpreters. Sandra Warfield and McCracken need not detain us.

The cast of my dreams would be Martinelli, Tibbett and Ponselle with Toscanini in the pit.

OTELLO

D Desdemona; *E* Emilia; *O* Otello; *I* Iago; *C* Cassio; *L* Lodovico; *M* Montano; *R* Roderigo

1931 Carbone *D*; Beltacchi *E*; Fusati *O*; Granforte *I*; Girardi *C*; Zambelli *L*; Spada *M*; Palai *R*/La Scala Chorus and Orch./Sabajno
EMI ℗ 3C 153 17076–8

1947 (broadcast performances) Nelli *D*; Merriman *E*; Vinay *O*; Valdengo *I*; Assandri *C*; Moscona *L*; Newman *M*; Chabay *R*/NBC Chorus and SO/Toscanini

RCA (UK) ⓜ AT 303; (US)
ⓜ LM 6107

1951 Lo Pollo *D*; Landi *E*; Sarri *O*;
Manca Serra *I*; Cesarini *C*;
Platania *L*; Stocco *M*; Russo
R/Rome Opera Chorus and
Orch./Paoletti
Urania ⓜ URL P216

1951 (live performance, Salzburg
Festival) Martinis *D*; S. Wagner
E; Vinay *O*; Schöffler *I*;
Dermota *C*; Greindl *L*; Monthy
M; Jaresch *R*/Vienna State
Opera Chorus, VPO/Furtwängler
Cetra ⓜ LO 6/3; Turnabout
ⓜ THS 65120–2

1954 Broggini *D*; Corsi *E*; Guichandut
O; Taddei *I*; Mercuriali *C*;
Stefanoni *L*; Albertini *M*; Soley
R/Turin Radio Chorus and
Orch./Capuana
Cetra ⓔ LPS 3252 ④ MC
145–6

1954 Tebaldi *D*; Ribachi *E*; del Monaco
O; Protti *I*; de Palma
C; Corena *L*; Latinucci *M*;
Mercuriali *R*/Santa Cecilia
Academy Chorus and
Orch./Erede
Decca ECS 732–4; Richmond
ⓜ RS 63004

1960 Rysanek *D*; Pirazzini *E*; Vickers
O; Gobbi *I*; Andreolli *C*;
Mazzoli *L*; Calabrese *M*; Carlin
R/Rome Opera Chorus and
Orch./Serafin
RCA (UK) SER 5646–8; (US)
AGL 3–1969

1960 Tebaldi *D*; Satre *E*; del Monaco
O; Protti *I*; Romanato *C*;
Corena *L*; Arbace *M*; Cesarini
R/Vienna State Opera Chorus,
VPO/Karajan
Decca D55D3 ④ K55K32;
London OSA 1324

1968 G. Jones *D*; Stasio *E*;
McCracken *O*; Fischer-Dieskau
I; de Palma *C*; Giacomotti *L*;
Monreale *M*; Andreolli
R/Ambrosian Chorus, New
Philharmonia Orch./Barbirolli
HMV SLS 940; Angel SCL 3742
④ 4X3S–3742

1974 Freni *D*; Malagù *E*; Vickers *O*;
Glossop *I*; Bottion *C*; van Dam
L; Mach *M*; Sénéchal *R*/German
Opera Chorus, Berlin
PO/Karajan
EMI SLS 975 ④ TC–SLS 975;
Angel SCLX 3809

1977 M. Price *D*; Berbié *E*; Cossutta
O; Bacquier *I*; Dvorský *C*; Moll
L; Dean *M*; Equiluz *R*/Vienna
State Opera Chorus, VPO/Solti
Decca D102D3 ④ K102K3;
London OSA 13130 ④ 5–13130

1978 Scotto *D*; Kraft *E*; Domingo *O*;
Milnes *I*; Little *C*; Plishka *L*;
King *M*; Crook *R*/Ambrosian
Opera Chorus, National
PO/Levine
RCA (UK) RLO 2951; (US)
CRL 3–2951 ④ CRK 3–2951

Excerpts

1939 Jepson *D*; Martinelli *O*; Tibbett
I; Massue *C*/Metropolitan Opera
Chorus and Orch./Pelletier
RCA (UK) ⓜ VIC 1185; (US)
ⓜ VIC 1365

1943 (in German) Reining *D*;
Waldenau *E*; Roswaenge *O*;
Reinmar *I*; Rödin *C*; Hüsch
L/Berlin State Opera Chorus
and Orch./Elmendorff
Acanta ⓜ BB 21360

1943 (in French) Segala *D*; Sibille *E*;
Thill *O*; Beckmans *I*/Paris Opéra
Orch./Ruhlmann
EMI ⓜ 2C 153 16211–4

1951 Steber *D*; Vinay *O*; Guarrera
I/Metropolitan Opera
Orch./Cleva
Philips ⓜ ABL 3005; CBS (US)
ⓜ ML 4499

1955 Moll *D*; da Costa *O*; Valentino
I/Chorus, Hamburg Philharmonia
Orch./Walther
Allegro-Royale ⓜ 1626

1965 (in German) Stratas *D*;
Windgassen *O*; Fischer–Dieskau
I; Lenz *C*; Ernest *L*/Bavarian
State Opera Chorus and
Orch./Gerdes
DG 2537 017

Falstaff

HAROLD ROSENTHAL

One finds interesting sidelights of operatic history in looking through *Falstaff* recordings and opera house casts. Thus, Salvatore Baccaloni, the Pistol of the complete 1932 recording, later became a famous Falstaff in Buenos Aires and San Francisco; Giuseppe Valdengo, Toscanini's 1950 recorded Falstaff, was singing Ford the previous year at the Metropolitan (many Fords graduate to Falstaff, Antonio Pini-Corsi, Mariano Stabile himself, Leonard Warren and Tito Gobbi among them); Regina Resnik, the famous Quickly, was, in her soprano days, an Alice Ford; while Gino del Signore, a pre-war Salzburg Fenton, is the Dr Caius on the Cetra 1951 recording.

There have been six complete recordings; nine if one includes the Cetra-Live performances, now available commercially, previously issued on various private labels, and the Preiser issue, deriving from a radio performance. The Cetra-Live gives us a complete *Falstaff* with Mariano Stabile in the title role, conducted by Victor de Sabata. It is aural evidence not so much of the baritone's declining vocal powers in 1951 – he was then 63 years old – but of the classic Falstaff of this century. To have heard Stabile simply speak the text would have been enough to show just why Toscanini and then de Sabata preferred him above all others. De Sabata and the Scala Orchestra give us a Toscanini-like performance; Silveri is a youthful but dramatic Ford, and Tebaldi a ravishing Alice. Cloe Elmo sings her famous Quickly, but Alda Noni is miscast as Nannetta.

The 1930 Columbia set, which was transferred to LP in Italy in 1955, has much to commend it, not least the outstanding Falstaff of Giacomo Rimini, the youthful and spirited Alice of Pia Tassinari, and the excellent small-part singers. The whole is welded together, with remarkable authority for the days of 78s, by Lorenzo Molajoli. Rimini was the nearest rival to Stabile as Falstaff in the inter-war years; he possessed a fruitier, rounder voice than Stabile ever had – more a bass-baritone than a baritone. Tassinari, who later was to marry Ferruccio Tagliavini, is certainly the best Alice on records; Ines Alfani-Tellini is a sprightly Nannetta, and Emilio Ghirardini a more than adequate Ford. The set's chief weaknesses are the unsteady and plummy Quickly of the Spanish mezzo-soprano Aurora Buades and the charmless Fenton of her husband, Roberto d'Alessio – they seem to have had package deals even in those days!

I would not exchange the Toscanini version for all the modern sets in existence. It is still one of the most glorious and splendid operatic performances ever to have been recorded. Toscanini is the genius who recreates the miracle that is *Falstaff*. The cast may not be ideal, but it includes the classic Mistress Quickly of Cloe Elmo, and the delightful Nannetta of Teresa Stich-Randall. Valdengo is not a natural Falstaff – at times he sounds more like Iago – but his scene with Alice, in Act 2, is delightfully done. Herva Nelli, the Alice, is ordinary. Frank Guarrera's Ford is excellent.

The 1937 Cetra Live recording, in poor sound, proves beyond doubt that Toscanini was anything but a martinet. Here he is working with the unique Stabile, and he is indulgent to the great baritones detailed, rounded characterization. Stabile returns the compliment by scrupulously observing note values with which he is elsewhere more cavalier. The vivacious Alice was the American soprano Marion Bruce Clark who made a successful Italian career as Franca Somigli and was especially famous for her Salome. Augusta Oltrabella is a mature Nannetta; and although Angelica Cravenco was Toscanini's chosen Mistress Quickly at that time she could not equal the famous and fruity Elvira Casazza of his Scala days. Piero Biasini, who eventually sang such Stabile roles as Iago and Scarpia at the Scala, reveals a large voice and an unsubtle way of using it. The cast also includes Giuseppe Nessi's classic Bardolph which he sang in virtually every Scala *Falstaff* for more than 30 years.

The other Cetra set was made like so many of that company's Verdi operas, in collaboration with Radio Italiana, as part of the 1951 Verdi celebrations. Giuseppe Taddei, like Rimini, has a really fat Falstaff voice, and his performance is a fruity one, wonderfully sung and vocally acted. Rosanna Carteri, who sang Nannetta more often than Alice, is too girlish-sounding for Mistress Ford, but her daughter Nannetta, Lina Pagliughi, who was probably twice the age of her stage mother when the performance was recorded, is delightful. Amalia Pini is a poor Quickly, Emilio Renzi an undistinguished Fenton, Saturno Meletti only a routine Ford. Mario Rossi's conducting is devised of magic.

The Karajan set, excellent from the technical point of view is over-polished and lacks heart. The conductor's meticulous approach has distilled the humanity out of the work. Tito Gobbi's Falstaff is a brilliant creation, which reaches its peak in the first scene in the last act. It is a joy to hear him mouth the words 'Mondo ladro, mondo rubaldo'. Rolando Panerai's voice is too much like Gobbi's in timbre, but he gives a fine performance of Ford's monologue. Elisabeth Schwarzkopf is more Frau Fluth than Alice Ford, though she sings in a refined, aristocratic style, and bubbles over with good humour. Fedora Barbieri, a large-voiced Quickly, not the equal of Elmo, is first-rate none the less; Anna Moffo, a magical-sounding Nannetta, sings the last-act aria with ethereal beauty; she is ably partnered by Luigi Alva, whose light and polished singing as Fenton has much to commend it.

The Solti performance, like Karajan's, is marvellously engineered, and displays all those things we expect from a Solti performance in the theatre: it is loud, brilliant, sparkling but in the last resort lacks inner warmth. Geraint Evans's Falstaff became, like Stabile's in the inter-war years, the classic one of his generation; and like Stabile, he knew how to play with words, and his sense of timing is superb. But here he is sometimes inclined to exaggerate, to clown. Still, he is one of the few artists who is able completely to project his personality on to disc. He is ably partnered by Ilva Ligabue, whose high spirits are well captured. Giulietta Simionato is a shade too subdued as Quickly, Mirella Freni is off-form as Nannetta. Robert Merrill sings well as Ford, but is not entirely under the skin of the part. Alfredo Kraus's Fenton, on the other hand, is wholly convincing

The Bernstein set is a considerable achievement. It may ultimately be short in spontaneity so that at times one is conscious of the art that fails to conceal art, but the infectious energy of the performance in the end proves irresistible. Dietrich Fischer-Dieskau is another baritone not cut out by nature for Falstaff. His voice is too youthful in sound, and he suggests a young, cultured knight. Ligabue is again one of the best of Alices. Regina Resnik's Quickly is a worthy memento of a great performance. By the time this set was made, Graziella Sciutti and Juan Oncina could no longer do full justice to Nannetta's and Fenton's music, but Panerai remained a first-class Ford.

Admirers of Hans Hotter will certainly want to hear the German Radio performance of 1939 in which the most famous post-war Wotan shows how good a Verdi baritone he was in the early days of his career. Admittedly such phrases as 'Die Ehre! Gauner!' ('L'onore! Ladri') and 'Ja, schon als Page' ('Quand'ero paggio') fall strangely on the ear; but this is valuable and rare as a glimpse of Hotter in Italian opera. The performance was broadcast from Radio Leipzig and conducted by Hans Weisbach (remembered by some as a Bach conductor).

On the Decca highlights disc, we hear the Honour monologue; the Alice-Meg-Nannetta scene from Act 1, scene 2; the whole of the first scene of Act 2; and the second scene from the beginning to the end of 'Quand'ero paggio'; Falstaff's monologue at the beginning of Act 3, and the Fenton and Nannetta arias from scene 2. Corena is in excellent form and is a very funny Falstaff; Renato Capecchi's Ford is outstanding it is a pity he did not record it complete; Ligabue, as usual, is an effervescent Alice, and Resnik, in first-rate voice, an incomparable Quickly. Alva and Lydia Marimpietri make an attractive pair of young lovers; Fernanda Cadoni is a most accomplished Meg; and the English *buffo* pair is first-class. Edward Downes takes it all at a cracking pace.

There is also in existence a private edition of the whole of Act 1, recorded at Salzburg in 1936, conducted by Toscanini, with Stabile. Piero Biasini, Franca Somigli, Augusta Oltrabella, Cravenco, Mita Vasari, Dino Borgioli, Nessi, Virgilio Lazzari, and Alfredo Tedeschi. The sound is remarkable, if played on a good modern machine, and shows us again Stabile in actual performance and in excellent voice.

Stabile can also be heard in most of the first scene of the opera from the moment just after he has told Bardolph to empty his purse and see how much money there is in it, beginning with the words 'So che se andiam', right up to the line before the Honour monologue (Col. DQ 696; Rococo 5277), with Romeo Bosacci as Bardolph and Aristide Baracchi as Pistol. One can follow this with Stabile's first recording of 'L'onore! Ladri' (Od. RO 20011, originally an acoustic Fonotipia 152027). The voice was wonderfully steady and beautiful at that stage of his career.

Other versions by Stabile of 'L'onore! Ladri' are on L 1970 and LX 1081. This latter disc was made in London in 1948 when Stabile was at the Cambridge Theatre; his voice was no longer as steady as it had been – the vibrato is more pronounced – but the diction, timing and phrasing are still a sheer joy. The conductor is Alberto Erede, who conducts more excerpts from this opera than anyone else, including the invaluable Telefunken set (SKB 3277–9; HT 1920). This issue, a memento of a wartime Scala production, includes, besides the two Falstaff monologues, virtually the whole of the first scene of Act 2, with Vittoria Palombini as Quickly, Afro Poli as Ford, the ubiquitous Nessi as Bardolph and Luciano Donaggio as Pistol.

Other Honour monologues include those by Scotti (DB 424; CSLP 500), beautifully articulated; Titta Ruffo, which I have not heard (DB 402); Gino Bechi (DB 11353); Lawrence Tibbett (Royale 1627); Giuseppe Taddei (Cetra LPC 55006); Giampiero Malaspina (CQX 11150), blustery and unsubtle; Geraint Evans (SXL 6262) in a recital conducted by Bryan Balkwill; Fischer-Dieskau in his Verdi recital conducted by Erede (ASD 407); Georg Hann, in German (Poly. 68396) and Arthur Fear, in English (C 1822).

From Act 2, scene 1, as well as the Stabile-Palombini-Poli set, there are the very old Fonotipias (39435–6) by the excellent Antonio Magini-Coletti with Elisa Petri, a fine mezzo, as Quickly; they are well worth hearing. The Ford-Falstaff encounter was recorded in German by Fischer-Dieskau, in his early days, with Josef Metternich as a good Falstaff if you do not mind 'Brav, alter Hans!' The short scene before Falstaff's exit to dress up, beginning with the words, 'Prima di tutto, senza complimenti', and ending with 'Te lo cornifico netto! Netto!' is on the reverse side of Stabile's Odeon Honour monologue (RO 20011). Ford's few words are recorded by a tenor, one Beretin! This is Stabile at his most superb.

There are a dozen or more recordings of Ford's Jealousy monologue. One of the best is that by the American baritone, Robert Weede, in his Verdi recital (Capitol CTL 7080), which reveals a fine dramatic-baritone voice; Leonard Warren also recorded this aria in the early 1940s (Victor 18923), but the voice is almost too bland. It was as Ford that Tibbett became famous overnight in New York, in 1925, and although he went on to sing Falstaff his was more a Ford voice, as his performance of the aria on the reverse of the Honour monologue shows (Royale 1627). Ford seems to have appealed to American baritones, and there are also versions by Frank Guarrera (Am. Col. MM 914) and Canadian-born George London (Am. Col. ML 4999). Other versions exist by Ghirardini, Afro Poli, Alexander Sved and György Melis. The excellent Swedish baritone, Ingvar Wixell, one of the few present-day singers with a true 'Verdi baritone' voice, includes it in his Verdi recital (6580 171). An interesting curiosity exists on a Vocalion record (K 05205) on which the British baritone Roy Henderson sings Falstaff, Bardolph and Ford, beginning with the words 'She's mine – She's mine!' and ending with Ford's monologue! There is also a first-rate performance, in English, by Redvers Llewellyn, who sang the part often at Sadler's Wells (C 3883), with Warwick Braithwaite conducting the Covent Garden Orchestra.

The second scene of Act 2 includes that gem, 'Quand'ero paggio', which really ought never to be snatched out of its context. However, when the creator of the role, Victor Maurel, recorded it (Fono. 62016), he was applauded by the little studio audience, and immediately sang it twice more! Coletti includes the short scene with Alice that precedes 'Quand'ero paggio' (Fono. 39436). The Alice is the famous Finzi-Magrini. Tibbett emulates Maurel and sings the little aria twice (TAP T314). The great Giuseppe de Luca, who never sang Falstaff in the opera house, included this piece in his farewell recital at Town Hall, New York, on 7 November 1947 (CRS 55A). Gobbi included it in his two-disc set, 'The Art of Tito Gobbi', conducted by Erede (ASD 606); Stabile made two 78 recordings of it – one with Guerrieri, which begins earlier in the scene at the entrance of Sir John, on the words 'Alfin t'ho colto' (Fono. 74916). More familiar, and sung with perfect timing, is his later version with Natalia de Santis (L 1970). There are also versions by Scotti (DA 668). Ruffo (DB 396) and Fear, in English (B 3123).

The third act opens with Falstaff's second great monologue, 'Mondo ladro! mondo rubaldo'. Stabile recorded it three times; once in the early 1920s (Fono. 74917); twice with Erede conducting – on the Telefunken set already referred to in 1942, and in London in 1948 on the reverse of the Honour monologue (LX 1081). Erede also conducts Fischer-Dieskau's self-conscious performance of it (ASD 407). There are also versions by Giampiero Malaspina, clumsy and blustery, and (in German) by Otto Edelmann who sounds more like Nicolai's than Verdi's Sir John. finally Evans gives a fine, rounded performance of it in the Covent Garden Album (SET 393).

Fenton's aria, 'Dal labbro il canto', from the beginning of the last scene was superbly recorded by Ferruccio Tagliavini early in his career; I doubt whether I have ever heard it so beautifully sung (Cetra CC 2233; LPC 50155) even by Schipa (Pathé 0334; GVC 10), Giuseppe Campora's performance lacks magic (LW 5230), I have not been able to hear Piero Paoli's performance or that by Richard van Vrooman.

There are several versions of Nannetta's fairy song, some with and some without chorus. The most magical is that by Frances Alda, which is exquisitely sung (Victor 88243; GEMM 104). This New Zealand-born soprano was a Marchesi pupil and much admired by Toscanini and Gatti-Casazza, whom she married. Toti dal Monte floats the soft top notes of the aria most beautifully (DB 1317). Mirella Freni's performance, unfortunately without chorus, is quite enchanting (WRC CM 19). Lina Pagliughi (Parlo. R 30004) recorded the aria long before her complete performance, and it is not one of her best efforts; nor is that by Hilde Gueden (LW 5178). The performances by Joan Hammond (ALP 1407), Onelia Fineschi (Parlo. BB 25196), Rina Gigli (DB 11315), Maria Minazzi (Cetra PE 169), and Margherita Benetti (Cetra SPO 1024) have little to commend them. Better is Marcella Pobbe's effort (Cetra LPV 45026). I have not heard the version by the Polish soprano, Stefania Woytowicz (SLPEM 06299).

FALSTAFF

F Falstaff; *A*; Alice; *N* Nannetta; *M* Meg; *Q* Quickly; *Fen* Fenton; *For* Ford

1930 Rimini *F*; Tassinari *A*; Alfani-Tellini *N*; Monticone *M*; Buades *Q*; D'Alessio *Fen*; Ghirardini *For*/La Scala Chorus and Orch./Molajoli
EMI ⓜ 3C 153 00695–6;
CBS (US) ⓜ EL 8

1939 (In German – broadcast performance) Hotter *F*; Neumann-Knapp *A*; Wulf *N*; Tegetthoff *M*; Fichtmüller *Q*; Rasp *Fen*; Schellenberg *For*/Leipzig Radio Chorus and Orch./Weisbach
Preiser ⓜ 012 046–7

1950 (broadcast performance) Valdengo *F*; Nelli *A;* Stich-Randall *N*; Merriman *M*; Elmo *Q*; Madasi *Fen*; Guarrera *For*/Shaw Chorale, NBC

SO/Toscanini
RCA (UK) ⓜ AT 301;
(US) ⓜ LM 6 111

1951 Taddei *F*; Carteri *A*; Pagliughi *N*; Canali *M*; Pini *Q*; Renzi *Fen*; Meletti *For*/Turin Radio Chorus and Orch./Rossi
Cetra ⓒ LPS 3207;
Everest-Cetra ⓒ S–416/3

1951 (live performance) Stabile *F*; Tebaldi *A*; Noni *N*; Anon *M*; Elmo *Q*; Valletti *Fen*; Silveri *For*/La Scala Chorus and Orch./De Sabata
Cetra ⓜ LO 14/3
Turnabout ⓜ THS 65114–5

1956 Gobbi *F*; Schwarzkopf *A*; Moffo *N*; Merriman *M*; Barbieri *Q*; Alva *Fen*; Panerai *For*/Philharmonia Chorus and

Orch./Karajan
HMV SLS 5037 ④TC–SLS 5037
Angel SCL 3552
1963 Evans *F*; Ligabue *A*; Freni *N*;
Elias *M*; Simionato *Q*; Kraus
Fen; Merrill *For*/RCA Italiana
Chorus and Orch./Solti
Decca 2BB104–6 ④ 110K3;
London OSA 1395
1965 Fischer-Dieskau *F*; Ligabue *A*;
Sciutti *N*; Rössl-Majdan *M*;
Resnik *Q*; Oncina *Fen*; Panerai

For/Vienna State Opera Chorus,
VPO/Bernstein
CBS (UK) 77392;
(US) D3S–750

Excerpts

1962 Corena *F*; Ligabue *A*;
Marimpietri *N*; Cadoni *M*;
Resnik *Q*; Alva *Fen*; Capecchi
For/New SO/Downes
Decca SDD 429;
London OSA 1164

Der fliegende Holländer

WILLIAM MANN

Before 1939 it was possible to own complete operas on record, but the perfect Wagnerite had to be nourished, from the recorded viewpoint, on substantial extracts from *Tristan, Meistersinger*, and from *The Ring*, for the rest only excerpts. There were enough of them from *Der fliegende Holländer* to keep any discographer busy. LP recording made complete sets a regular occurrence.

The earliest was issued in the USA by Mercury; highlights were later made available (Acanta DE 22017). The set was taken from a German wartime broadcast and is, in most respects, a great account of Wagner's first operatic masterpiece (I would say his finest achievement before *Die Walküre*, but that is a prejudice). In it Clemens Krauss, possibly the most rounded operatic musician of this century, gives a completely saturated account of the score, literally so in the first and last acts, which should splash a turbulent, hostile sea into our very faces, even without the ministrations of stage staff or record producer. Krauss cares always for pulse, balance and phrasing, and for the precision and attack of the cast, including the chorus, which is greatly superior to anything expected then and for some time later. Georg Hann was, in timbre and pointfulness, and as a character, just about the Daland of one's dreams, an incisive dark bass with a wide range of colour and expression, combining the qualities of, say, Frick and Talvela with something extra in sheer personality (all lovers of fine singing should know Hann's records). Hans Hotter was then at the height of his powers, a real baritone with a full, dark quality, already a cogent master of music drama in terms of tone and word; in the 1950s he achieved international greatness at the expense of some euphonious virtues heard here. The drawback of this set is the intelligent but ugly Senta of Viorica Ursuleac, but Franz Klarwein's Steersman is robust, and Luise Willer's Mary enjoyably disciplinarian.

Hotter again sang the title role in a performance at the Metropolitan, on 30 December 1950, which has been issued privately. It was the sixth performance of a new production which gave Hotter and the bass Sven Nilsson their local debuts. Hotter's voice had thickened and become more weighty (at the time of the earlier set he was still singing high Verdi baritone roles). In the Dutchman's first monologue he rants, but he excels in the first-act duet with Daland and in 'Wie aus der Ferne' which he begins in a magical *sotto voce* and, together with Astrid Varnay, brings to a magnificent climax. Her voice, possibly too grandiose for such a young, simple heroine, sounds firmer and more flexible than in the Decca set of five years later. The Ballad, taken steadily, goes well until the middle of the third verse when there is a sudden cut (tape disaster?) to Erik's entrance, so that we miss the Ballad's exultant coda, the climax of any performance.

Set Svanholm was the Erik, as likeable as any on disc, manly and quite unsentimental, a delight always (as few are in this tiresome part). Nilsson, swamped in the first-act duet, sounds lightweight and baritonal, though his low tones are cleanly focused. He excels as Senta's loving father. Fritz Reiner conducts decently, in the face of a barely adequate chorus (much praised after the first night, a month earlier). There is some fine orchestral playing, some less so. A pause is made after Act 2, not after the first act.

In 1955 Deutsche Grammophon made a studio version splendidly conducted by Ferenc Fricsay (the slow parts tend to somnolence), with a sensitive but vocally unsteady Senta in Annelies Kupper, and a sympathetic Dutchman from Josef Metternich (though his lower tones are weak, as with many pure baritones). Josef Greindl makes heavy weather of Daland, Wolfgang Windgassen's Erik gives unusual pleasure (many of the best tenors fail in the part). The opera is given in three acts, like the Mercury, but with less careful side breaks. In the same year Decca recorded a set at the Bayreuth Festival. It was given, as Wagner always wanted, in one act without pauses. The liveness of the event is accentuated by extra-musical noises before and during the performance; the music itself is dully conducted by Josef Keilberth, a Bayreuth favourite of those days and a millstone round the necks of ardent young Wagner students. The performance is redeemed by the collaboration of Hermann Uhde as the Dutchman and Ludwig Weber as Daland, a great partnership which can hardly be over-praised. Josef Traxel was delightful as the Steersman, Rudolf Lustig a run-of-the-mill Erik. Varnay's voice had matured further and grown bigger since 1950, so that she sounds even less like the romantic young girl; she phrases eloquently, it is true, but the timbre sounds somewhat sour, and high–lying music finds her tone imperfectly supported. The Bayreuth Festival Chorus lives up to its reputation, and the early stereo recording has a real flavour of the Festspielhaus's glorious acoustic.

On the first night of that year's Festival the opera was conducted by Hans Knappertsbusch, and that performance has also been issued on disc by Cetra, in mono only. It is a more deliberate, intense and searching interpretation than Keilberth's and finds the principals in even more splendid voice, Varnay included; Wolfgang Windgassen was the Erik on that night, a positive, vocally eloquent account.

HMV produced the next set in 1960, performed again in one act, vividly conducted by Franz Konwitschny, and with a superb Dutchman in Dietrich Fischer-Dieskau, whose rhythm, attention to words, and range of timbres leave no doubt of his admiration for Hotter and his special interest in Lieder. There is a glorious, characteristic Daland from Gottlob Frick, fine choral singing and magnificent orchestral playing by the forces of the (East) Berlin State Opera. But Marianne Schech sounds rusty and unlovable as Senta most of the time, and Rudolf Schock is a potato-voiced Erik.

Two further sets were made in 1961. From RCA came a one-act studio recording conducted, with curiously pernickety effect, by Antal Dorati, who only attains best form in the blustering maritime music. Covent Garden provided the lively but fallible chorus and orchestra. Leonie Rysanek as Senta offers lovely soft singing and a good, even scale, as well as fine feeling; but her vocal technique was not at its happiest in the part. George London, a distinguished Dutchman in the theatre, had trouble with intonation and focus, nor does he reveal much of Vanderdecken's inner character. Giorgio Tozzi was the cardboard Daland, lighter in timbre than London, Karl Liebl an expressive and mellifluous Erik, Richard Lewis a winning Steersman.

The Philips set is much more attractive. Though recorded at the 1961 Bayreuth Festival it perpetuates the famous Wieland Wagner production of 1960 when Franz Crass stepped out of the chorus to substitute for the indisposed George London, and disclosed a born Dutchman voice and a rare understanding of the character's significance. There was also the discovery of Anja Silja, who had hitherto never sung anything heavier than the Queen of Night, and whose Senta sounded eminently girlish yet marvellously dynamic. Res Fischer's imposing Mary (the part seldom makes much effect) and Josef Griendl's famous, by then slightly wobbly, Daland, the glorious Bayreuth chorus and orchestra, all added to the merits of the performance, but its special quality was the thrilling, anti-romantic, fresh and breezy interpretation directed by Wolfgang Sawallisch in three acts, the second beginning controversially at the Spinning Chorus. Erik and the Steersman are liabilities (they might beneficially have been replaced at this first revival), and the dry, noisy recorded quality may disturb some, but it is a gripping experience.

A statutory, even if uncalculated, *Frist* of seven years intervened before Otto Klemperer took the Dutchman and his crew to EMI's No. 1 Abbey Road studio in London and there conducted the recording of *Der fliegende Holländer*, which is generally reckoned *hors concours* for tonal splendour and tragic grandeur of expression. The interpretation is elemental, not fire, but water and air in mighty turmoil, with solid ground as contrast, the human characters moulded by those elements in joy, but more often and profoundly in sorrow. Klemperer's reading is essentially symphonic, conceived in one piece (though split into three separate acts) all of whose musical ideas connect with one another, and it is gloriously played for him by the New Philharmonia. But, because this is Wagner, and the conductor is Klemperer with sixty years' work in the theatre behind him, the reading is equally dramatic, concerned with melodic line and the human singing voice, the interplay of characters and the topography of situation. The set is carefully produced for realistic effect, in the placing of voices and instruments and provision for suitable periods of reverberation, and in the addition of necessary stage effects (breaking waves, howling winds, creaking ropes, etc.). Klemperer, doubtless seeking the rough texture of the contents, chose to conduct the Dresden version of the score, with blunt D major chords at the end of the overture and last act, rather than the *Tristan*-like redemptory cadence added later by Wagner, and with the brassy first version of Vanderdecken's solo, in the final scene, about his wretched destiny. Such a reading prescribes a larger-than-life Dutchman: Theo Adam, not always steady of voice, contrives by artistry, intelligence, and vocal power to convey the ageless sorrow, defiance, and longing of the doomed seaman. Beside him Silja's (second recorded) Senta is heard as a lesser creature transfigured by idealism, Martti Talvela's Daland as a bluff and burly business-man, eminently likeable and gregarious, perhaps a less greedy gold-digger than Erik suggests (Wagner insisted that Daland must never behave like a villain, nor a clown). Ernst Kozub sings a pompous but forthright Erik, Annelies Burmeister a strong, dependable Mary. Gerhard Unger exaggerates the fervour of the Steersman's ditty, but the characterizations through the opera are established with unusual acumen, down to each of the choruses. The set is not perfect (the voices often too closely recorded for natural balance, for instance) but it delves more deeply into Wagner's youthful masterpiece than any other.

Only three years later DG moved into Bayreuth to record August Everding's new production, as conducted by Karl Böhm with immense zest and urgency. Apart from the Bayreuth chorus, always at its best in this opera, the star of the show is Daland, lucidly and grandly sung by Karl Ridderbusch, alas more than a match for Thomas Stewart's dry, unresonant Dutchman (so much more eloquent in the DG highlights record discussed below). The Senta of Gwyneth Jones is touching, exquisite in soft music, raw and bumpy under emotional pressure. Erik and the Steersman, as often on record, give little pleasure, but Sieglinde Wagner is a telling Mary. The performance, given in one act, has plenty of atmosphere.

Decca's 1976 set, recorded in the Medinah Temple, Chicago, under Georg Solti, gives the work without breaks between the acts. The reading is vital, with radiant orchestral playing and a reverberant acoustic, the choruses lusty but tonally homespun (with German to match). Decca's deliberately untheatrical recorded production does the opera and its cast something of a disservice. Norman Bailey, on stage a Vanderdecken of high quality, hardly suggests a hero of tragic stature, though the nobility of voice and attention to words are appreciable ('Wie aus der Ferne' begins most unsteadily alas). Janis Martin's Senta sounds youthful, tender in soft music, a nice, healthy girl in *forte*, though with some beat and whine under pressure; the Ballad is taken uncomfortably fast. Talvela is never dull, but less striking than for Klemperer. René Kollo sings a powerful but uningratiating Erik, Werner Krenn a pleasing Steersman. As a whole, and on repeated hearing, the set disappoints reasonable expectation.

Among those discs of highlights not taken from complete recordings the most important is the DG/Löwlein, listed below and much hacked about; but the Senta, Evelyn Lear, is so eloquent that one could wish her in a complete set (most of whose Sentas she far excels); attentive to words, musicianly in phrasing, lovely and resourceful in tone quality. Kim Borg is the pleasing Daland, Thomas Stewart an intelligent Vanderdecken, vocally in stronger form than on his complete recording. James King is heard in Erik's first aria, a brief memento of the voice in the bloom of youth. A Urania disc of highlights in Czech (519OH) with Premysl Koci as the Dutchman and with Karel Kalas as Daland, has long tantalized me. Leonie Rysanek and Sigurd Björling together made a disc comprising 'Die Frist ist um', the Ballad, and the second-act duet (33C 1035), neither singer in riveting form.

To turn to individual items, the overture has been recorded scores of times, notably by Karl Muck, Richard Strauss, Erich Kleiber, Furtwängler, Beecham, Boult and Bruno Walter, to mention some personal favourites. The Steersman's 'Mit Gewitter und Sturm' was often recorded in pre–LP days, variously adapted *à la* Procrustes to fit on one side, usually omitting the orchestral interludes during the second verse and repeating the full refrain of the first verse. One such by Marcel Wittrisch (HMV EG 2542) ends with a choral refrain and orchestral coda as at the end of the act. Peter Cornelius (042199) sings in Danish and ends, winningly, with a lubricous chuckle. There was an English performance, with a comic translation about 'my lassie', recorded by Francis Russell (Col. 9246) in an agreeable light tenor but with less line than verbal clarity, despite a lisp. A superior version is that of Franz Völker (Poly. 95233). Lauritz Melchior did not include the opera in his mature repertory, regarding his voice as too heavy for Erik, but he used to sing 'Mit Gewitter' at concerts, and he recorded it (Victor 17725) with chorus and orchestra, so adapted as to include two verses of the Act 3 chorus 'Steuermann, lass die Wacht', one after each verse of the Act 1 solo which, it must be admitted, he sings to admiration. Among modern individual versions that by Kollo (CBS 77283) is performed gratifyingly *au pied de la lettre*, without cuts or alterations, and attractively sung too; he first came to attention, as Steersman, at Bayreuth in 1969.

Vanderdecken's first monologue 'Die Frist ist um' was superbly recorded by Friedrich Schorr (D 1813; LV 241): his low notes were fluffy, and his attention to enunciation spoiled his legato, but there is a splendour, a divine frenzy even, which no Wagnerite would be without. There is also an acoustic version (Poly. 65598). Joel Berglund's version (DB 6378) is marvellous in the bass register (the quality may recall David Ward whose noble Dutchman was never recorded alas) but the top is light and the interpretation unsubtle. Arthur Endrèze, a French Vanderdecken (Pathé PDT 267), has a colourful, lightish, nicely poised and spinning bass-baritone, a shade woolly, but scrupulous with the French text. Anton van Rooy recorded the last section, from 'Nur eine Hoffnung'; his raw timbre, quick vibrato and, at the end, fallible intonation, do no credit to the memory of a celebrated interpretation (undated Edison cylinder). Theodor Scheidl's 1930 recording (Poly. 95428; DG 2721 110) is quite full, with a short cut at the end of the first side, before 'Dich frage ich', and rousing orchestral accompaniment; Scheidl had a laudable legato technique, and a vibrant, sympathetic voice applied with nobility to the music, let down by some clumsy intonation and poor focus between baritone and bass registers (many Dutchmen have the same trouble). Fischer-Dieskau has re-recorded the solo (ASD 3499), here and there with new intensity, as a whole not more eloquently than in his complete set. Of the Daland-Dutchman duet in Act 1, there is a version by Schorr and Otto Helgers (Poly 65632; RLS 743), the bass a hearty yet sensitive Daland, vibrant of voice, Schorr his usual sterling self.

There were various 78 versions of the Spinning Chorus which begins the second act, notably two which united it with Senta's Ballad. Of these, the one conducted by Bruno Seidler-Winkler (DB 5595) had a vibrant, attractive Mary in Friedl Beckmann but a careless choir, and a Ballad sung by Marta Fuchs in a dark, chesty voice, only intermittently as fine as the singer's reputation; there are cuts. Much superior was (surprise?) an English version by Covent Garden forces under John Barbirolli with Nellie Walker as a confident Mary, and Florence Austral a sensitive, but not regularly legato Senta (D 1517; CLSP 502).

The Ballad itself was oft recorded, usually with one verse omitted to fit one side. Elisabeth Rethberg sang all three verses (DA 1115; CDN 1018) though she did without choir, but sang so neatly and with such lustre that one minded less. Frida Leider (Poly. 72978; LV 172) pitched unreliably but had splendid *gruppetti*, good attack and a lovely high register in her armoury. Maria Jeritza (DB 1811; LV 122), started each verse (not the second, omitted) staccato, rather comical, and did not end phrases neatly, though the singing is vivacious, and the hushed 'Johoho' touching. Emmy Destinn, vocally ideal for the aspiring purity of the part, recorded it twice for Odeon in 1906 (50166) and in 1908 (76916; CO 307) and once for Grammophon in 1908 (043064; DG 2721 115), where she omits verse two and substitutes her verse-one refrain for the chorus in verse three, is careless about words but most attentive to legato and vocal colouring. But I have also heard a version with a cut in verse three, less legato, more words; it must be one of the Odeon records. There is a problem here. An early, cut version by Melanie Kurt (Parlo. P 251; CO 345) is poised and sure. Verbal colouring is a feature of the beautiful version by Elisabeth Ohms, a vibrant, pearly voice careful about words, untidy in the coda (Poly. 66928; DG 2721 110). Emmy Bettendorf, a German soprano whose vocal allure rendered strong men weak at the knees, spread her exquisite and dignified account over two sides (Parlo. E 10706; LV 156), wonderful legato but a painful cut to fit the sides' length. There is a modern version by Birgit Nilsson (Philips 6500 294), complete though with a fake ending, of course, sung with remarkable fining-down of the massive voice so as to sound like the young Senta, possibly the ideal exponent of the role, greatly touching in word and nuance, though her torn is not exact; the John Alldis Choir contributes most sensitively to the performance. The same record is also worth investigation for desirable excerpts from *Die Feen* and *Rienzi*, to go no further. Erik's scene with Senta, 'Bleib, Senta', was recorded by Kurt with Ernst Kraus. His top register is rough, his chest register more impressive. The soprano's contribution is admirable as usual.

'Mögst du, mein Kind', Daland's gracious arioso when he presents his daughter to his guest, was recorded in 1915, by Paul Knüpfer (4–42601; DG 2721 109 or 115), slightly abbreviated, the note values imprecise, the manner diffident, the voice richly oleaginous and attractive. Another famous Ochs, Richard Mayr, also recorded it (4–42177) but, as in some other early records, sounds strangely lightweight for the music. Later versions by Hann (Poly. 67942) and Wilhelm Schirp (Telef. E3130) are worth hearing.

The great duet for Senta and the Dutchman, 'Wie aus der Ferne' (or parts of it), had some important individual recordings. Walter Soomer made the earliest of them, singing only the beginning (042425; DG 2721 109 or 115) and that not steadily or vividly. Quite different is that recorded by Melanie Kurt and Schorr (Poly. 65621; LV 241) memorable not only for his distinction in nuance, phrasing and appreciation of words, but for her purity and charm of voice (breath control and intonation may raise doubts). Schorr later recorded his opening solo separately (D 1355). Bettendorf and Werner Engel (E 10182) cut the difficult cadenza and another bit before 'Ach, könntest du', and they had one horrid lapse of ensemble, yet the singing is wonderfully pure and expressive. A shorter version by Ohms and Scheidl (Decca CA 8150; LV 159) has exquisite portamento and vibrant, exciting singing from her, some strong, grainy tone from him (and questionable intonation too, as in his monologue mentioned above). Nilsson and Hotter made a fine record of the duet in 1957 (SAX 2296), both in fine voice.

In the third act only Erik's cavatina has been selected at all significantly for individual representation, and the best of the versions that I have heard are those by the ever dependable Völker (Poly. 90051; LV 78) and by Peter Anders (Telef. E 3056; 6.48 012) and, more recently, by Kollo (CBS 77283). Old records of the choruses rouse only thankfulness for LP and the ensuing concentration on complete sets.

DER FLIEGENDE HOLLÄNDER

S Senta; *M* Mary; *E* Erik; *St* Steersman; *H* Holländer; *D* Daland

1944 (broadcast performance) Ursuleac *S*; Willer *M*; Ostertag *E*; Klarwein *St*; Hotter *H*; Hann *D*/Bavarian State Opera Chorus and Orch./Kraus
Mercury ⓜ MGL2

1955 Kupper *S*; S. Wagner *M*; Windgassen *E*; Haefliger *St*; Metternich *H*; Greindl *D*/Berlin RIAS Chorus, Berlin Radio SO/Fricsay
DG ⓜ LPM 18063–5

1955 (live performance, Bayreuth Festival) Varnay *S*; Schärtel *M*; Windgassen *E*; Traxel *St*; Uhde *H*; Weber *D*/1955 Bayreuth Festival Chorus and Orch./Knappertsbusch
Cetra ⓜ LO 51/3

1955 (live performance, Bayreuth Festival) Varnay *S*; Schärtel *M*; Lustig *E*; Traxel *St*; Uhde *H*; Weber *D*/1955 Bayreuth Festival Chorus and Orch./Keilberth
Decca D97D3
Richmond SRS 63519

1959 Schech *S*; S. Wagner *M*; Schock *E*; Wunderlich *St*; Fischer-Dieskau *H*; Frick *D*/Berlin State Opera Chorus and Orch./Konwitschnny
EMI 1C 157 00104–6; Angel SCL 3616

1961 Rysanek *S*; Elias *M*; Liebl *E*; R. Lewis *St*; London *H*; Tozzi *D*/Royal Opera Chorus and Orch./Dorati
Decca 2BB109–111; London OSA 1399

1961 (live performance, Bayreuth Festival) Silja *S*; Fischer *M*; Uhl *E*; Paskuda *St*; Crass *H*; Greindl *D*/1961 Bayreuth Festival Chorus and Orch./Sawallisch
Philips 6747 248

1968 Silja *S*; Burmeister *M*; Kozub *E*; Unger *St*; Adam *H*; Talvela *D*/BBC Chorus, New Philharmonia Orch./Klemperer
HMV SLS 934; Angel SCL 3730

1971 (live performance, Bayreuth Festival) G. Jones *S*; S. Wagner *M*; Esser *E*; Ek *St*; Stewart *H*; Ridderbusch *D*/1971 Bayreuth Festival Chorus and Orch./Böhm
DG 2709 040 ④3371 17

1976 Martin *S*; I. Jones *M*; Kollo *E*; Krenn *St*; Bailey *H*; Talvela *D*/Chicago SO and Chorus/Solti
Decca D24D3 ④K24K3;
London OSA 13119 ④5–13119

Excerpts

1964 Lear *S*; Emde *M*; King *E*; Elteste *St*; Thomas *H*; Borg *D*/German Opera Chorus, Bamberg SO/Löwlein
DG 136 425

1964 (in French) Sarroca *S*; Finel *E*; Blanc *H*/Saint Paul Choir, Bamberg SO/Löwlein
DG 136 466

Tannhäuser

JOHN STEANE

Tannhäuser has come upon hard times. Its golden age was around the turn of the century, when from 1890 to 1910 there was only one year in which it could not be seen at Covent Garden. Nowadays, in England at all events, it must be just about the most least-seen famous opera, having recently taken over the title from Gounod's *Faust*. The world shortage of heroic tenors cannot alone account for it. Tastes change, and whereas the Edwardians possibly enjoyed and saw an immediate relevance in the duality represented by seductive Venus and saintly Elisabeth, we find it difficult to take either very seriously. Musically, too, its appeal has probably waned. The idiom is not fresh: it has a certain slow-footed piety, a want of spring in the step, of vigour in the counterpoint, of something more bracing in the harmonies. Nor is there the intricacy of thematic cross-reference that enriches the later scores of Wagner. It has its own strongly creative life which no doubt will ensure its survival; but in the meantime it cannot be said to flourish as it did formerly, and the records reflect this.

Aptly enough in these circumstances, the one recording to deserve strong recommendation is not of the opera as it was heard during the golden years at Covent Garden, but of the revised version that Wagner made for a production at Paris in 1861. Solti and the Vienna Philharmonic give a magnificent account of the score, both in the more sophisticated, impassioned pages which are additional, and in the main body of the opera which remains untouched. This is indeed one of Solti's finest achievements on disc. From the very start one is aware of a special quality: the clarity, sonority, subtlety and passion are all present in a degree that immediately distinguishes this from the other sets. The greatly extended Paris version of the overture, carrying over with ballet music into the Venusberg scene, has huge swirling crescendos, with trumpets aflame over the whole glowing mass of sound, and the flame is unequivocally erotic. This intensity is maintained, so that the prelude to Act 3, which can often seem lugubrious, gains not only in meaning but excitement. All of the ensemble work is finely controlled, the great climaxes of Act 2 (and is it blasphemous to say that the best of them sounds to me like Bellini?) having a wonderful lyrical warmth. Many incidental touches in this recording are delightful in themselves – the use of the Vienna Boys Choir, the vivid creation of atmosphere with the bells from field and steeple, the distancing horns. It is a triumphant piece of record production as well as musicianship.

And what of the solo singing? So often the question has to be put with trepidation, and in certain of Solti's other Wagnerian recordings (*Der fliegende Holländer* and *Die Meistersinger* notably) there would be nought for your comfort in anything I could conscientiously say on the matter. Here the general report is distinctly reassuring. Christa Ludwig is in her finest voice, starting 'Geliebter, komm' with ravishingly soft tone, gorgeous in its full-bodied richness at climaxes. The Elisabeth is Helga Dernesch, always beautiful in the middle of her voice where most of the role lies. Then there is, for these days, an exceptional Wolfram in Victor Braun: he sings it very much as did his predecessors, Janssen, Hüsch and Schlusnus, with beautiful tone and fine lyrical evenness, more Italian than German in style and voice production. Hans Sotin (whose magnificent voice rarely sounds like its true self on records) is an impressive Landgrave, sonorous, firm and unforced. The Tannhäuser is René Kollo – which means that the first solo ('Dir töne Lob') will involve a series of shamelessly intrusive aspirates, and that at declamatory climactic points through the opera there will be resort to a throaty, guttural kind of production for emphasis. This is sad, for Kollo's voice at best resounds with a pure, well-projected tone that is like silver of great price. As it is, his faults do not ruin the set, but they do constitute its single major weakness.

Three other modern recordings have merit, though none to compete with this. One of them, conducted by Wolfgang Sawallisch and taken live from the Bayreuth Festival of 1962, mixes the Paris and original Dresden versions in a way which Wagner authorized (the intention being to gain the ballet music and avoid a clash of styles between the Tannhäuser-Venus duet and what follows). Strangely, at something less than the white-heat of Solti's performance, the music can have a sort of noisy emptiness, and that is how I found it here. There is also a lot of coughing and clomping about on the stage, which certainly does not help to transport one in spirit to the Mount of Venus. Grace Bumbry, in what was a sensational appearance at the Festival, does much to help, with her opulent tone and authoritative style (thrilling, too, in her return at the end of the opera). The rest of the solo singing is less pleasing. Anja Silja, the Elisabeth, was always better seen than heard; her solos are shallow-toned and unsteady. Eberhard Wächter as Wolfram lacks sweetness and (though he softens for the Evening Star) is too inclined to introduce a Germanic emphasis into phrases that call for a proper legato. Josef Greindl is an unspeakably bad Landgrave as recorded – though I am told he was an impressive artist 'in the flesh' – and Gerhard Stolze's mauling of Walther's song can hardly be spoken of temperately either. And again there is the problem of Tannhäuser himself. Here he is Wolfgang Windgassen, the best of Wagnerian tenors in the post-war period; but he too resorts to aspirates and a kind of gutteral emphasis. He is not on best form.

Certainly he was no worse some years later (towards the end of his career) when he recorded the role again, this time with the Berlin Opera Orchestra under Otto Gerdes. He seems to tire slightly near the end of Act 1, but generally one is grateful for his singing and his sincerity. The women in his life – 'how happy could I be with either were t'other dear charmer away' – are one, namely Birgit Nilsson, who consequently is never 'away' for very long. As a *tour de force* in the theatre it might be something to write home about, and of course her appearance could be disguised by make-up. On records, the doubling seems pointless, especially as her voice is not well suited to either role (not gentle enough for Elisabeth, not seductive enough for Venus). Theo Adam's Landgrave is appreciably younger than Greindl's but no less uneven in voice production (hear his first phrase, 'Dich treff'ich hier', for instance, in Act 2, and, if in the masochistic mood for it, hear how bad becomes worse before the act closes). Gerdes conducts a businesslike, faithful performance. Distinction enters only with Fischer-Dieskau's Wolfram. The school of singing represented by the baritones mentioned earlier is, to me, far preferable; but as an individual artist Fischer-Dieskau is in a class apart. Every phrase in this role has its special character newly apprehended; the singing of 'Blick'ich umher' in the second act is in itself an example of unequalled mastery.

A younger Fischer-Dieskau, more emphatic but still acutely observant, sings Wolfram in the other major modern recording. This is under Franz Konwitschny, and has a fine Elisabeth in Elisabeth Grümmer and the best of Landgraves in Gottlob Frick. Consequently, a lovely passage in this set, and one that deserves preservation after the performance as a whole has passed into oblivion, is the third scene of Act 2, where Frick's dark, noble tones are beautifully modulated and Grümmer is always a warm, womanly presence. Later in the 'trial' scene, incidentally, we also hear the best of Walthers – in Fritz Wunderlich. The Tannhäuser is Hans Hopf, whose voice was a remarkable one, weightily baritonal, and whose feeling for the role is often touchingly evident despite the stylistic faults of his singing and the effortful production of the higher notes. The other weakness in the casting is Marianne Schech as Venus; she produces a shallow, tremulous sound. She and Hopf together in the Venusberg scene are a telling argument for monasticism: it says a great deal for the rest of the cast that the performance recovers and goes on, in Act 2 especially, to give considerable pleasure.

As one thinks of the embarrassment of riches that can face a prospective purchaser of so many operas in modern recordings, it is clear that

Tannhäuser has not been well served. Each of the other three sets has its merits, but they hardly justify the whole recording, and essentially there is a choice of one – Solti's performance of the Paris version.

Two other and earlier recordings deserve mention. The earliest LP set still survives well. This is under Kurt Schröder and has Heinrich Schlusnus as Wolfram. The recorded sound, like the orchestral playing, lacks sharp definition, but it is warm and lifelike. The cast as a whole hardly distinguishes itself – Günther Treptow is another rather baritonal, sincere but limited Tannhäuser, Trude Eipperle a gentle but uneven Elisabeth, Aga Joesten an unlovely Venus. But in Otto von Rohr there is an admirable Landgrave, whose last solo ('Ein furchtbares Verbrechen') is excellent in legato, tone and authority. And from Schlusnus – then in his early sixties – we hear, at last, some perfect singing. His voice, never exceptional in power, is recorded close to microphone, the low notes are weak and the phrasing lacks breadth. But the texture of the voice is flawless, as in his singing of the first solo, 'Als du in kühnem Sange'. If Fischer-Dieskau's 'Blick'ich umher' serves as a master class in its own right, it should be followed by Schlusnus's record of this solo in Act 1: the art is less complex, but the lesson for singers is harder and even more important.

It is a lesson that at some early stage must have been learnt by Herbert Janssen, whose Wolfram is heard in the remaining set, a pre-war one made during the Bayreuth Festival of 1930. He makes an immediate impression through the sheer beauty of sound, and goes on to confirm it in the first solo. His 'Abendstern' aria in Act 3 is surely a classic, sensitive in mood yet without underlining. Unfortunately the general standard of the singing is no higher than in the more modern sets, with Sigismund Pilinsky's big voice spreading under pressure, Ivar Andrésen's deep bass sounding too stolid, and Maria Müller's Elisabeth registering as pleasant but somewhat characterless. The Venus is a singer new to me, called Ruth Jost-Arden, who attracts by the brightness and freshness of her tone – qualities also present in the Shepherd Boy, a very young Erna Berger. The recording is not complete (much of the Landgrave's solos, and some ensemble work are cut from Act 2, and in the last act Wolfram's Evening Star solo is followed immediately by Tannhäuser's Narration). But, interestingly, the text is the Paris version, and, under Karl Elmendorff, the company catches the spirit of the music well; the recording followed on performances under Toscanini, and his presence can still be felt.

That recording held its place unchallenged in the record catalogues of inter-war years, but it is not true to say that before then *Tannhäuser* was represented only by 'bleeding chunks'. In 1909, on twenty single-sided discs, there was a complete recording of Act 2 (recently issued CO 340), an astonishing fact but again testifying to the great popularity of the opera in those days. The job is well done, with none but the cuts that were customary in stage performances. Fritz Vogelstrom is a remarkably clear-voiced, attractive Tannhäuser, singing to the Elisabeth of Annie Krull, who earlier that year at Dresden had created the title role in *Elektra*. She makes an unusually commanding Elisabeth, though gentle and eloquent in the Adagio solo later on. Hermann Weil is a strong-voiced Wolfram, and New York-born Léon Rains a dignified, deep-voiced Landgrave. If you consider the conditions of recording (like making music in a sardine tin, as I think Roland Gellatt put it) the ensemble is wonderfully successful, and the conductor, Eduard Kunneke (unnamed, I see, in Bauer's *Historic Records*), deserves a small niche in gramophone history.

Whatever the shortcomings of the complete sets, either in quantity or quality, there has been no lack of selection in recordings of the most famous solos. Each of the three main characters has at least two arias that have been favourites from the earliest years of the gramophone. Tannhäuser's 'Song to Venus' even manages to catch the original Parsifal, Hermann Winkelmann (3–42370; 1C 181–30 671), though it finds him, at the age of 56, strained and unsteady, phrasing poorly and hitting hard. Another dreadful souvenir from early years is the 1904 record made by the Hungarian Desidor Matray (2–42924; 1C 181–30 671). Better, more resonant and precise, is Heinrich Knote (4–42360); far more imaginative is Leo Slezak (42082 and 42758, Od. 8029); and more exciting is Ivan Erschoff from St Petersburg (35472) and the Spaniard Francesco Vignas (Fono. 92897; GV 86). Franz Völker was among the inter-war tenors who recorded it, with vigour and pleasing tone (Poly. 24240; LV 78). And there is a recording, from 1940, by Lauritz Melchior, in which the vitality, ring and firmness all belie the singer's fifty years (Victor 17726; VIC 1500).

Melchior merits a paragraph to himself, for his records are still unequalled. Perhaps, however, it should first be said that the records themselves are not all equal. Several live performances have been issued on private labels. One from 1936, with Flagstad and Tibbett also in the cast, has not come my way, but that from the Metropolitan in December 1942 (Georg Szell conducting his first *Tannhäuser* there and using the Paris version of the opening) shows clearly Melchior's besetting sin of hurrying ahead of the beat. It must have been hellish for everybody in concerted passages and maddening throughout to the conductor. Yet it seems to have been a habit that grew in the later years of his career, and even then there is little of it in studio recordings. In this particular performance, incidentally, by far the finest singing comes from Janssen in the last act, although Helen Traubel sings out powerfully as Elisabeth, and Alexander Kipnis should be an ideal Landgrave (I say 'should be' because his voice has loosened by this time and it is badly affected by the wrong pitching, often a semitone low, of the recording). Melchior is still incomparable at best, but varies too unreliably to be satisfying.

Instead, one must return to is glorious solo recordings: to the 1940 recording of the complete Rome Narration (Victor 11–8677; VIC 1500), where there is such marvellous sensitivity as well as magnificence of tone, or even better to the recording made some ten or twelve years earlier (D 1675; 1C 147 01259) in which out of the strong came an additional sweetness. We could even go back one stage further, to 1924 (Poly. 72863 and 66439; DG 2721 115) and hear how the voice rings out while the orchestra is practically inaudible. Even at this time he was 'inward' in his feeling for the music. Melchior is sometimes still spoken of as though he were all voice and bulk and stamina. He was in fact – as his *Tannhäuser* records amply testify – an artist of unusually creative sensibility.

In recordings of the Rome Narration ('Inbrunst im Herzen'), Melchior has no shortage of competitors. Best of his predecessors, probably, was Jacques Urlus (Pathé 30215/6). Slezak (042257/6) is best when singing quietly; Hermann Jadlowker (Od. 99376/7; CO 312) produces his voice very evenly but is inexpressive; Heinrich Knote (042183/4 and 0–6766) is more lyrical in his earlier recording but still in impressively fine voice at the age of sixty. Völker (Poly. 95483; LV 78) is warm of voice, but not much more than conventional in feeling. Max Lorenz (EH 136; LV 121), singing feelingly at first, leaves a final impression of dullness. Windgassen in 1953 was clearly Melchior's successor in the role, his fine tone matched by an expressive style (DG 2721 111).

Elisabeth's greeting ('Dich teure Halle') and prayer ('Allmächt'ge Jungfrau') can be discussed together as so many sopranos sing both. The ideal, or next thing to it, is surely Tiana Lemnitz (CA 8243; LV 101). Her voice embodied that kind of warm, pure maidenliness that Elisabeth must represent, and she sings both solos to perfection, just a shade less youthful in her post-war, more expansive recording of the prayer (DB 6809; World Records SHB 47). More recently, Leonie Rysanek (DG 2721 115) has something of the Lemnitz quality in her soft singing, but is too often unsteady. Lovely performances come from Gré Brouwenstijn (ABL 3130), less lovely ones from Nilsson (33CX 1522), and surprising ones (in Italian) from Tebaldi in second-best voice (SET 439). Flagstad is exciting, though boxed up in unresonant recordings (Victor 8859, DB 2748, DB 6795; VIC 1517), while Traubel has trouble scaling down for the prayer (Victor 17268; VIC 228). For the rest, some greet and others pray. I hope that when Victoria de los Angeles greeted the hall of song (DB 21095; SLS 5012) somebody went along to say thank you, for it is as glorious a piece of song as the hall is likely to have heard. Rethberg (D 1420; LV 29), Germaine Lubin (Od. 123613; LV 225), and Frida Leider (Poly. 65627) also deserve applause. Destinn (043133), attacks excitingly; Sophie Sedlmair (043025) swoops alarmingly and from Olive Fremstad (Col. 30635) comes a precious memento of a great career. Among the prayers, Geraldine Farrar's record (Victor 88053; CO 368) reminds us that Elisabeth was considered one of her finest roles. From the 1920s Lotte

Lehmann (Odeon 0–4813; LV 94) sings with fine tone but disturbingly audible breathing, and Maria Jeritza (DB 1092; LV 2) sings with her customary lack of distinction on records. Worth hearing, if a chance arises, is the American contralto Edyth Walker (043094), rich of timbre, finely controlled and instrumental in style.

An 'instrumental' style, or the ability to turn the voice into a cello, used to be regarded as a great asset to any baritone who wanted to sing the most famous of *Tannhäuser* solos, Wolfram's 'O du mein holder Abendstern' or 'O star of eve'. Thus Maurice Renaud in 1902 (2–2702; GV 52), in French, or Giuseppe de Luca (Fono. 39987) in Italian, both with a characteristically national flavour, are alike in the fineness of their legato. A dreadful exception among early singers was the Spaniard, Francisco d'Andrade, who is dry, coarse, unsteady and sentimental. Then comes that marvellous profusion of baritones singing in Germany between the two wars. Friedrich Schorr (Poly. 65671 and D 1355; DG 2721 109 and HQM 1243) blesses the ears, especially in the earlier recording (in the later one it is clear that the tessitura is high). Karl Hammes (HMV AN 471; 1C 181–30 674) sings with a fine smooth line and interesting variety; Gerhard Hüsch (DB 4099) is firmly defined, if a little less affectionate than some; Karl Schmitt-Walter (Telef. E 2271) has warmth and an exemplary ease of production; Willi Domgraf-Fassbänder (EH 724; LV 131) is beautifully gentle and phrases broadly. Best, probably, is Janssen, his singing in the old Columbia set being a degree more lovely in tone than an American recording made some ten years later (LX 948). Interesting too are records by Lawrence Tibbett (DB 2262), slightly tired-sounding, and Kipnis (Col. 7280; LV 37) whose deep tones have fine effect in the opening 'Todesahnung' and are magically lightened later. And, it should be added, one could do much worse than listen to old Peter Dawson (C 1267; HQM 1217), but beware of the cello.

In 'Blick'ich umher', the solo from Act 2, several of the same singers are heard to much the same effect. A particularly well-sung and poetically conceived version is that by Hans Reinmar (Od. 0–6569; 1C 181–30 674). Gerhard Hüsch is marginally more imaginative in his Parlophone recording (E 11046) than on the later HMV (DB 4049). The famous Anton van Rooy sings Wolfram's solos in very early recordings, this one (042165) having great dignity and depth but considerable freedom with note values. Wolfram's solos also attract Italian lyric baritones – Battistini, Mario Ancona and Stracciari among them: Stracciari, for instance, is superbly resonant and also musical in his singing of 'Als du in kühnem Sange' (Fono. 39167; Club 99–29), making one so grateful to the Italian vocal tradition after the conscientious but dry-toned singing of Karl Scheidematel (3–42822; RLS724), the weighty unattractiveness of Robert Burg and so many more.

There are indeed many more recordings of this kind which I do not propose to list, and others that have proved elusive (the Rome Narration as sung by Borgatti, for instance, or Wolfram's solos by that giant pillar of old Bayreuth, Walter Soomer). We might take leave of the opera with two pleasant sounds in our ears: one, the little song for the Shepherd Boy as sung on an early recording by the glorious Rosa Olitzka (Col. 30849; Club 99–86), and the other, the Pilgrims' Chorus recorded by the Bayreuth Chorus at its finest in 1958 (DG 2721 111). It is as well these pilgrims did not enter the Tournament of Song: they might have defeated most of the soloists.

TANNHÄUSER

T Tannhäuser; *E* Elisabeth; *V* Venus; *W* Wolfram; *L* Landgrave

1930 (live performance, Bayreuth Festival) Pilinsky *T*; Müller *E*; Jost-Arden *V*; Janssen *W*; Andrésen *L*/1930 Bayreuth Festival Chorus and Orch./Elmendorff
EMI ⓜ 1C 137 03130–2

1949 Treptow *T*; Eipperle *E*; Joesten *V*; Schlusnus *W*; von Rohr *L*/Hessian Radio Chorus and Orch./Schröder
DG ⓜ 89633–7

1955 Seider *T*; Schech *E*; Bäumer *V*; Paul *W*; von Rohr *L*/Munich Radio Chorus and Orch./Heger
Nixa ⓜ ULP 9211/1–4; Vox ⓜ OPX 143

1961 Hopf *T*; Grümmer *E*; Schech *V*; Fischer-Dieskau *W*; Frick *L*/German Opera Chorus and Orch./Konwitschny
EMI 1C 153 30683–6; Angel SDL 3620

1962 (live performance, Bayreuth Festival) Windgassen *T*; Silja *E*; Bumbry *V*; Wächter *W*; Greindl *L*/1962 Bayreuth Festival Chorus and Orch./Sawallisch
Philips 6723 011

1969 Windgassen *T*; Nilsson *E*; *V*; Fischer-Dieskau *W*; Adam *L*/German Opera Chorus and Orch./Gerdes
DG 2740 142

1971 Kollo *T*; Dernesch *E*; Ludwig *V*; Braun *W*; Sotin *L*/Vienna State Opera Chorus, VPO/Solti
Decca SET 506–9 80K43; London OSA 1438

Exerpts

1909 (Act 2) Vogelstrom *T*; Krull *E*; Well *W*; Rains *H*/Orch.
Odeon 50699–710; 76125–6; 80046–8; 80051–3
CO 340

1943 Lorenz *T*; Reining *E*; Bäumer *V*; Schmitt-Walter *W*; Hofmann *L*/German Opera Chorus, Berlin Radio Orch/Röther
Acanta ⓜ DE 22119

1940 Carron *T*; Bampton *V*; Hober or Senderowna *V*; Harrell *W*/Publishers Service SO/Steinberg
RCA (US) ⓜ CAL 249

1954–5 Windgassen *T*; Rysanek *E*; Wächter *W*; Greindl *H*/Bavarian Radio Chorus/Orch.
DG ⓜ LPEM 19069

Lohengrin

CHARLES OSBORNE

Distance by no means always lends enchantment, but I do not think I am indulging in mere nostalgia when I say that the most moving portrayal of Lohengrin I have ever seen was also my very first: Ronald Dowd at the Princess Theatre, Melbourne, about thirty years ago. Orchestrally inadequate and scenically outlandish, most of the production has mercifully faded from my memory, but my aural remembrance of Dowd's performance remains fresh. He conveyed with consummate ease the spirituality of the role, and he sang with great delicacy and sensitivity – qualities notoriously absent from the majority of Lohengrins. He also sang in tune, which is even rarer. To my great regret he neither appeared in the role during his London years nor committed any of it to disc.

The earliest complete recording of *Lohengrin* is that which appeared in 1952, conducted by Rudolf Kempe; but an earlier, incomplete 'pirate' recording of 1943 deserves a mention, if only because it offers us the Lohengrin of Lauritz Melchior, somewhat past his prime, and the Elsa of the then 25-year-old Astrid Varnay. Varnay's huge voice had not yet settled down, and her Elsa is occasionally tremulous, but Melchior is in good voice, though his characterization is excessively bland. Kerstin Thorborg and Alexander Sved make a vivid pair of villains, Thorborg's Ortrud is especially exciting, and the opera is briskly conducted by Erich Leinsdorf. The recording, reasonably clear of its kind, emanates from a Metropolitan broadcast. I have not heard the 1947 Busch set.

Of the complete recordings commercially issued, one (again conducted by Leinsdorf) is 'completer than complete', for it includes a passage of fifty-six bars immediately after the end of Lohengrin's narration – 'Sein Ritter ich, bin Lohengrin genannt' – which Wagner himself asked Liszt to suppress when the first performance was being prepared. 'I have many times performed the whole work to myself', wrote Wagner, 'and I am now convinced that this second section of the Narration can only have a chilling effect. The passage must also be omitted from the libretto.' The cut was dutifully, and I think rightly, made, only to be restored by Leinsdorf in 1966. The other versions remain faithful to the composer's intention and explicit instruction. The first of them to appear, the Kempe set, seemed acceptable at the time, but in retrospect turns out to be the least successful of all to date. Kempe brings the often ponderous score to energetic life, but is defeated by the kind of cast which, in the post-war Wagner doldrums, we tended to grumble about less than we should have done. A Wagnerian slow wobble afflicts most of the singers, especially Marianne Schech as Elsa, though this *Haussopran* whom I associate with dull performances in Munich in the 1950s was then on the right side of 40. The Lohengrin, George Vincent, displays an unwieldy voice and an ox-like temperament, and the experienced Margarete Klose, though she has her moments as Ortrud, is heard to better advantage in a later recording. Kurt Böhme's Heinrich has great presence and, though he too displays a far from ideally steady emission of tone, this does not sound so distressing in a bass! Andreas Böhm's Telramund is ineffective. The recording is clear, though it has not the spaciousness of most later studio recordings or the immediacy and atmosphere of the live recording from Bayreuth.

The Keilberth Bayreuth performance and a studio recording conducted by Wilhelm Schüchter were released within the space of a few months in 1953. At the time, I thought the Bayreuth-based set an outright winner. I still prefer it, but rehearing Schüchter's version I find myself liking it more than I did, despite a huge cut in Act 3 made presumably to ease the work on to four discs instead of the usual five. Schüchter's Lohengrin is Rudolf Schock, an estimable tenor who was first presented to us as the successor of Richard Tauber, an artist whom he in no way resembled (though when I last heard Schock, it was in *Land of Smiles* at the Volksoper in Vienna). Schock sings attractively, though somewhat throatily, as Lohengrin, emphasizing the romantic at the expense of the spiritual content of the role, and he is surrounded by an excellent cast. Klose makes considerably more of Ortrud here than in the Acanta set, though she is past her prime, and Josef Metternich, surely the finest Wagner baritone of his time, is a superb Telramund. Gottlob Frick's Heinrich is almost as good as Böhme's, and the only real disappointments are the uninteresting Elsa of Maud Cunitz and the only intermittently gripping performance by Schüchter and his orchestra.

The 1953 Bayreuth recording brought to the gramophone something of the intensity and hypnotic grip of a performance of *Lohengrin* in the theatre. The individual, almost palpable Bayreuth acoustic is virtually the star of the recording: the star of the performance is Wolfgang Windgassen in the title role. In the theatre, Windgassen was frequently irritating, for he would too obviously save himself for the climactic moments of a role in order to preserve his voice and his stamina. But his Lohengrin on these discs is superb: tender and lyrical in the exchanges with Elsa, firm and commanding in the public scenes. He is ideally partnered by the Elsa of Eleanor Steber, strongly characterized and radiantly sung. The

Metropolitan's Elsa of ten years earlier, Astrid Varnay, contributes a thrilling Ortrud and that great actor-singer Hermann Uhde could hardly be bettered as Telramund. Josef Greindl humanizes King Heinrich interestingly. Joseph Keilberth, in charge of the superb Bayreuth orchestra, shapes and controls the performance magnificently. Wilhelm Pitz's chorus deserves more than a word of commendation.

A later Bayreuth live recording, conducted by Sawallisch, was less successful. The Bayreuth atmosphere is still there, and Sawallisch is a more than competent conductor; but Jess Thomas's Lohengrin leaves much to be desired and, despite her evident commitment to the role, Anja Silja's Elsa leaves even more. Varnay's Ortrud is less firm of tone than it was earlier, and the ex-tenor Ramon Vinay has a struggle with Telramund. I have also sampled a recording on four discs, presumably made in the 1960s, conducted by Hans Swarowsky. Well conducted and cleanly recorded, this set is vitiated by the dull Lohengrin of Herbert Schachtschneider, the tremulous Elsa of Leonore Kirschstein and the over-ripe Ortrud of Ruth Hesse. There are excellent contributions from the Vienna Opera Chorus and the South German Philharmonic Orchestra. A worthier undertaking is the set conducted by Jochum, but this too suffers from the casting of the two principal roles: Lorenz Fehenberger (Lohengrin) and Annelies Kupper (Elsa).

Deutsche Grammophon's second attempt at *Lohengrin* was more successful, principally because of the fine playing of the Bavarian Radio Orchestra under Rafael Kubelik, but, with the exception of Karl Ridderbusch as Heinrich, I find myself failing to respond to most of the cast. James King makes a dull stick of Lohengrin, Gwyneth Jones's Ortrud is a pain in the ears. Thomas Stewart's Telramund is lightweight. About the Elsa of Gundula Janowitz I have two opinions, and I offer them both: (a) she sings divinely, with fine, pure, somewhat steely tone; (b) she fails, in the slightest, to sound interested in what she is supposed to be singing *about*.

The Leinsdorf version, with Wagner's Act 3 cut restored, is a curious affair. I am no enemy to Leinsdorfian briskness, but the poetic baby appears to have been thrown out with the ponderous bath-water, and all one is left with, orchestrally and chorally, is healthy but intrinsically meaningless sound. The set's one real asset is the Lohengrin of Sandor Konya: a voice full of character, and retaining alongside its strength a lyrical sweetness. The ladies are disastrous, Lucine Amara completely at sea as Elsa and vocally in almost as much difficulty as Rita Gorr's Ortrud. William Dooley is simply not up to Telramund, Jerome Hines makes nothing of Heinrich, and the only other singer to make any effect, apart from Konya, is Calvin Marsh as the Herald.

There remain two complete recordings to be discussed: one an oddity for which I feel a curious affection, the other which is the finest of all *Lohengrin* recordings. The oddity is a four-disc set issued by Preiser of

Vienna with virtually no documentation other than the names of the principal participants. It is a live performance by the forces of the Berlin Staatsoper under Robert Heger, with Franz Völker (Lohengrin) Maria Müller (Elsa) and other regulars of the Berlin Staatsoper in the 1930s and 1940s. Most of these singers tactfully retired in 1945: from the condition of their voices on this recording, I would say the performance took place during the war years, probably just before the closure of the theatres. Evidence from elsewhere suggests 1941 as the probable year. The only cut used to be traditional in the theatre – 167 bars in Act 3, from Elsa's swoon after 'In fernem Land' to the chorus's cries of 'Der Schwan! Der Schwan!' (The 1943 Met live recording also makes this cut, but not, of course, the Bayreuth performances.) The time saved is not much more than four minutes, and one loses a splendid ensemble in Wagner's earlier, Italian manner.

What attracts me to this Berlin performance is its period flavour, the strong sense of audience presence and of stage action – the big scenes of assembly have an immediacy and excitement hard to catch in the studio, for which one has to pay by accepting a certain imprecision of ensemble, to put it politely, and a frequent lack of regard for note values on the part of the principals. None of the solo voices sounds young; in fact most are more frayed than they should be, considering that the majority of the singers were only in their forties. The exhaustion of the war years, perhaps. Ludwig Hofmann, the Heinrich, was in his prime a superb singer and artist; his vocalization here is occasionally wild, but there is no doubting his presence and authority. Margarete Klose offers the earliest of her three recorded Ortruds. She has a habit of anticipating the beat, but gives a performance which positively leaps forth from the speakers. Maria Müller sounds a matronly Elsa but makes much of the text. She, together with most of her colleagues from this performance, can be heard in fresher vocal state in excerpts from the 1936 Bayreuth *Lohengrin* with Völker a pleasantly unstrenuous hero (Telef. GMA 50). It is interesting to compare Völker with Melchior in the roughly contemporary live performance from the Metropolitan. Admittedly, Völker was nearly ten years younger than his rival; vocally, both are perfectly acceptable, but Völker was clearly the superior artist, phrasing with greater imagination and always keen to project the meaning of the words he sang. There is no trace of routine in his performance.

I come now to a really outstanding performance, Kempe's for HMV, recorded in the early 1960s with the Vienna State Opera Chorus, Vienna Philharmonic Orchestra, and a cast which is well-nigh perfect. Based on Vienna Staatsoper performances of the time, it was recorded in the studio but with great atmosphere and a sense of space. My only reservations concern the Lohengrin of Jess Thomas. He is much better here than in his Bayreuth recording, fresher of voice and with surer intonation, but he remains oddly earthbound. You will seek in vain for the spirit of the

Grail in this voice, or for a touch of poetry. But his is certainly an excellent performance by all but the most exacting standards.

The kind of feeling I miss in Thomas's Lohengrin is to be found in abundance in the Elsa of Elisabeth Grümmer, who projects the character's purity most beautifully. From her first words, 'Mein armer Bruder', she affects me in the way that opera-goers only a few years older than I used to be affected by Lotte Lehmann. Christa Ludwig manages magically to convey the evil of Ortrud in a voice of rich and sensuous beauty, and she is worthily partnered by Fischer-Dieskau's compelling portrayal of Telramund. Gottlob Frick is an even more effective Heinrich than he was ten years earlier for Schüchter. Rudolf Kempe was one of the finest Wagner conductors of the post-war years, and his reading goes right to the mystical heart of the work, without ignoring its theatrical extrovert side. This is a magnificent performance and recording.

I have not heard the Russian set nor the Polydor excerpts with Fritz Wolff. The LP conducted by Richard Kraus contains the expected excerpts, though often truncated: the major solos, the bridal scene and duet, Heinrich's Prayer, and the Procession to the Minster in Act 2. The singers, however, are no more than adequate. Maud Cunitz (Elsa) is pale of voice and effect; Walter Geisler is hardly more memorable as Lohengrin. This is an unsatisfactory and inartistic presentation.

Leafing through the score, the first piece one finds being recorded out of context is Heinrich's greeting to the men of Brabant, 'Gott grüss' euch'. The black bass of Ivar Andrésen makes much of this (Parlo. E 10670; LV 45), the disc beginning with the Herald (Eduard Habich) announcing him. The backing is Heinrich's prayer. Andrésen also recorded Heinrich's Act 3 address (E 10693; LV 97). His is a beautiful voice, which took kindly to recording. Several excellent recordings of the prayer exist, by Michael Bohnen, Emanuel List, Richard Mayr and Marcel Journet, amongst others. I especially like Ludwig Hofmann (Poly. 62684; LV 51) caught in his prime, a good fifteen years or so before that wartime Lohengrin, and Alexander Kipnis (Col. 7280; LV 37), richly impressive. Otto Edelmann sings both prayer and address (33CX 1568) but is dull in comparison with any of those pre-war basses.

I do not want to give the impression that I think the art of singing Wagner has declined. Indeed, I think it has improved, as all who have ears to hear can now discover easily, with so much from the distant past dredged up on to LP. The writer's space and the reader's patience preclude the possibility of dutifully describing Elsa's arias as recorded by even such excellent artists as Jeritza, Teschemacher, Destinn, Margaret Sheridan, Eva van der Osten (recorded in 1911), Rethberg, Fremstad, Vallin (in French), Melba (in Italian), Nemeth and so on. My own particular favourites include Elisa Stünzner (Poly. 95015; LV 149) for her purity of tone and ethereal quality in 'Euch Lüften'; Maria Schreker's impulsive freshness in both arias (issued, apparently for the first time, on

LV 217); the unique timbre of Delia Reinhardt (both arias, Poly. 66876; LV 142); the sympathetic Grete Stückgold (the Ileana Cotrubas of her day!) in 'Einsam in trüben Tagen' (Vox 02116; LV 788); Gertrude Rennyson, sensitive in the same aria (Am. Col. A5427; 1C 181-3--672) and, of course, Lotte Lehmann, whose ardent warmth was perhaps not ideally suited to the easily misled virginity of Elsa, but who sweeps all objections aside with the sheer beauty of her voice in 1924-5, her generosity of temperament and the intelligence and mastery of her projection of the text (Od. O-9518 and Lxx 80979; LV 94) Tiana Lemnitz also recorded the arias exquisitely in 1937 (CA 8243; LV 101) and, in 1948, the Elsa–Ortrud scene with Klose. Lemnitz retains her youthful, virginal quality, so right for Elsa, while Klose's familiar Ortrud enlivens the scene (unissued on 78: SHB 47).

There is a very early disc of the twenty-eight-year-old Lotte Lehmann in part of this scene, from 'Du Aermste kannst wohl nie ermessen' to the end of the scene, with Ortrud's part omitted. Lehmann's voice already has its own individual character, and the performance has all the maturity of her style of ten and twenty years later. This Elsa actually sounds friendly at 'Kehr bei mir ein!'.

In more recent times, there have been worthy recordings of Elsa's arias by Helen Traubel, Flagstad, Varnay, Joan Hammond, Gré Brouwenstijn, Birgit Nilsson, Régine Crespin and others, and memorable performances of both arias by Elisabeth Schwarzkopf (1C 181–52 291). The entire Ortrud–Elsa scene is 'included' on Schwarzkopf's disc, with Christa Ludwig a predictably thrilling Ortrud. The best of the pre-war recordings of this scene, to my mind, are those of Emmy Bettendorf and Karin Branzell (Parlo. E 10852; LV 182), and Yvonne Brothier and Marjorie Lawrence in French, mainly for Lawrence as Ortrud (DB 4890-1; LV 133). Lawrence and Martial Singher are a strong pair of evildoers in 'Erhebe dich, Genossin meiner Schmach' (DB 4900; LV 133), sung in French, and even better are Maria Olszewska and Emil Schipper (Poly. 72989-90). Modern Elsas who deserve a mention are Gundula Janowitz, though she is not to my taste (both arias, SLPEM 136546), the young and beautiful voice of Victoria de los Angeles in the Act 1 aria (DB 21095; SLS 5012) and the unidiomatic but easy-to-listen-to Tebaldi, in Italian, in the same aria (SET 439–440).

Lohengrin's arrival, 'Nun sei bedankt, mein lieber Schwan' has attracted the attention of tenors, and there are a number of pleasing recordings in a variety of languages by Pertile, Widdop, Sobinov and even Gigli though I do not know that he ever sang the role in the theatre. De Lucia's 'Merce, cigno gentile (52650 with piano recorded in 1902) is not as great an oddity as it is said to be, for he sounds a perfectly feasible Lohengrin, and he addresses the swan with an infinite tenderness and regret. Leo Slezak, a celebrated Lohengrin, is very much the assured Wagnerian *Heldentenor* in this excerpt (3–42809; CO 332) which he continues, omitting the chorus part, until just before Heinrich's 'Hab' Dank'. He also sings the Act 3 'Mein lieber Schwan' most beautifully and sensitively, with firm vocal control. I like, too, the firmness and intensity of Joseph Rogatchewsky, singing in French (Col. 12526).

The great Narration, 'In fernem Land', exists in a number of first-rate versions from, among others, Alfred Piccaver, Karl Erb, Max Hirzel (a busy member of the Dresden company in the 1920s and 1930s), Fritz Krauss (a penetrating, Remedios-like sound on HMV EJ140; LV 158), the lyrical Charles Kullmann (LX 729) the intense Marcel Wittrisch (EH 842; 1C 181–30 675), the splendid Georges Thill (Col. LFX 159) though the Farewell tends to bring out the prima donna in him (LFX 159). Richard Schubert's ringing top A is one of his greatest assets (Poly. 65670; LV 168), Björn Talén's steely account of the Narration is firmly accompanied by the Berlin Staatsoper Orchestra under Szell (Od. 06576), and I have a soft spot for Helge Roswaenge whose Narration and Farewell, with the Vienna Philharmonic under Moralt, were recorded in 1942 (DB 5698; LV 43). Performances of great character these, and real fervour (with splendidly clear diction, which I am sometimes tempted into thinking is the same thing.)

The two Richards, Crooks and Tauber, in many ways dissimilar, were boyhood favourites of mine; and I heard them both in recital in the late 1930s. Lotte Lehmann spoke highly of Crooks who once sang Cavaradossi to her Tosca: his voice was not large, and I do not know that he ever attempted Lohengrin in the theatre, but his 'In fernem Land' (DB 1598; VIC 1464) is gently floated, exquisitely sung, and the Farewell is most movingly interpreted (DB 3670; VIC 1464). Tauber was not one of nature's Lohengrins, but he could sing anything, and his 1937 version of the Narration taken from a broadcast, is scrupulously delivered in those irresistible Tauber tones (unissued on 78; Historia H 679).

Apart from his participation in recordings already mentioned, Völker left impressive versions of solo sections from the Lohengrin–Elsa duet (Poly. 90051 and 19711; LV 206), the latter backing 'In fernem Land', and the Farewell (19731; LV 206). Sigismund Pilinsky's Farewell (Parlo. E 10782; LV 202) has an attractive plaintive quality, and Max Lorenz has his admirers, though I find his voice production a shade relentless. He couples 'Atmest du nicht' from the duet, with the Farewell (EH 288; LV 121). Fritz Wolff's 'Atmest du nicht' has both sweetness and strength (CA 8023), and Charles Dalmorès in the same music is agreeably lyrical (DA 157). There are several Melchior versions of most of Lohengrin's solo passages, and in general the earlier they are recorded the better they are. 'Höchstes Vertrauen' (D 1505) is fine, and so is the comparatively late (1939) 'In fernem Land' (DB 3936; VIC 1500). Even later, but still excellent, is Lohengrin's arrival, beginning at 'Nun sei bedankt' and continuing to 'Elsa, ich liebe dich', with Varnay as Elsa, Herbert Janssen as Heinrich, the Columbia Symphony Orchestra under Leinsdorf, and the chorus missing!

The Swedish Wagnerian, Carl Martin Oehmann, sings both Narration and Farewell most sensitively (Parlo. E 10692; LV 181) and so too does his pupil, Nicolai Gedda (ASD 2364). Gedda wisely rations his stage Lohengrins, but on the recorded evidence he must be one of the most mellifluous as well as one of the most musical of interpreters of this difficult role. The rapt *sostenuto* of Gedda's 'In fernem Land' makes it the most successful of modern versions, but there are excellent performances by Windgassen (EPL 30085), Konya (SLPEM 136214) and Kollo (CBS 77283), and less good ones by Jess Thomas and James King.

Among the most attractive versions of the duet, 'Das süsse Lied verhallt', are those by Melchior and Emmy Bettendorf, though the tenor's intonation is not always exact (E 10515, 10527, 10540; 1C 147 01259–60); Melchior and a radiant-voiced Flagstad (ALP 1276); Torsten Ralf and Tiana Lemnitz (DB 4667; SHB 47); and the Viennese team of Margit Angerer and Alfred Piccaver (Poly. 66833). Melchior and Bettendorf make several cuts, and the latter two performances do not attempt the entire scene. Ralf and Lemnitz end with the tenor's ' . . . in schwerer Schuld Verdacht', while Angerer and Piccaver only get as far as ' . . . die nur Gott verleiht'. Walter Widdop and Göta Ljungberg are also impressive, the tenor, especially (D 2020), and Fritz Vogelstrom and Lilly Hafgren are sweetly tuned (Od. 969660; 1C 181–30 672).

I have space to mention just two more 78s, of the finales of Act 1 (Parlo. E 10933) and Act 3 (P 9837), with Seinemeyer, Pilinsky, Helene Jung, Robert Burg and Fritz Düttbernd, which are splendidly flavoursome and well recorded (1928), and give a vivid picture of Berlin Wagner style in the 1920s (both reissued on LV 114).

LOHENGRIN

L Lohengrin; *E* Elsa; *O* Ortrud; *T* Telramund; *H* Heinrich; *Her* Herald

1941 Völker *L*; Müller *E*; Klose *O*; Prohaska *T*; Hofmann *H*; Grossman *Her*/Berlin State Opera Chorus and Orch./Heger Preiser ⓜ LOH 2B

1947 (live performance, Metropolitan, New York) Melchior *L*; Traubel *E*; Harshaw *O*; Ernster *T*; Hawkins *H*/Metropolitan Opera Chorus and Orch./Busch Cetra ⓜ LO 24/4

1949 (in Russian) Kozlovsky *L*; Smolenskaya *E*; Stumskar *O*; Troytesci *T*; Galkin *H*; Bogdanov *Her*/Samosud

MK ⓜ D04734–41

1952 Vincent *L*; Schech *E*; Klose *O*; A. Böhm *T*; Böhme *H*; Wolff *Her*/Munich State Opera Chorus and Orch./Kempe Acanta ⓜ HB 22326

1953 Schock *L*; Cunitz *E*; Klose *O*; Metternich *T*; Frick *H*; Gunther *Her*/Cologne Radio Chorus, Hamburg Radio Chorus and SO/Schüchter HMV ⓜ ALP 1095–8; RCA (US) ⓜ LHMV 1095–8

1953 (live performance, Bayreuth Festival) Windgassen *L*; Steber

E; Varnay *O*; Uhde *T*; Greindl *H*; Braun *Her*/1953 Bayreuth Festival Chorus and Orch./Keilberth
Decca ⓜ D12D5; Richmond ⓜ RS65003

1953 Fehenberger *L*; Kupper *E*; H. Braun *O*; Frantz *T*; von Rohr *H*; Braun *Her*/Bavarian Radio Chorus and Orch./Jochum
DG ⓜ 2703 001

1962 (live performance, Bayreuth Festival) Thomas *L*; Silja *E*; Varnay *O*; Vinay *T*; Crass *H*; Krause *Her*/1962 Bayreuth Festival Chorus and Orch./Sawallisch
Philips 6747 241

1962–3 Thomas *L*; Grümmer *E*; Ludwig *O*; Fischer-Dieskau *T*; Frick *H*; Wiener *Her*/Vienna State Opera Chorus, VPO/Kempe
HMV SLS 5071 ④ TC–SLS 5071
Angel SEL 3641

1966 Kónya *L*; Amara *E*; Gorr *O*; Dooley *T*; Hines *H*; Marsh *Her*/Boston Pro Musica Choir, Boston SO/Leinsdorf
RCA PVL5 9046; (US) LSC 6710

1971 King *L*; Janowitz *E*; G. Jones *O*; Stewart *T*; Ridderbusch *H*; Nienstedt *Her*/Bavarian Radio Chorus and Orch./Kubelik
DG 2720 036

1973 Schachtschneider *L*; Kirschstein *E*; Hesse *O*; Imdahl *T*; Kreppel *H*; Helm *Her*/Vienna State Opera Chorus, South German Opera Orch./Swarowsky
Westminster WGSO 8285/4

Excerpts

1933 Wolff *L*; Malkin *E*; Gottlieb *O*; Watzke *T*; Helgers *H*; Weltner *Her*/Berlin State Opera Chorus and Orch./Weigert
Polydor 27395–8

1940 Carron *L*; Bampton *E*; Summers *O*; Harrell *T*; Cordon *H*/Chorus, Publishers Services SO/Steinberg
RCA (US) ⓜ CAL 223

1955 Liebl *L*; Graf *E*; Schlosshauser *O*; Kunz *T*; Wolovsky *H*/Frankfurt Opera Chorus and Orch/Bamberger
Musical Masterpieces Society ⓜ MMS 2029

1958 (in Hungarian) Soloists/Hungarian State Opera Chorus and Orch./Lukács
Qualiton ⓜ LPX 1052

1963 Geisler *L*; Cunitz *E*; Oelke *O*; Gritzka *T*; Roth-Ehrang *H*/Berlin Municipal Chorus and Orch./Kraus
Ariola-Eurodisc Z77039R

Tristan und Isolde

ROBIN HOLLOWAY

The first attempt at anything like a complete *Tristan* is the Bayreuth set of 1928 under Karl Elmendorff. The sound of the LP transfer is splendidly direct; with no knobs to twiddle and mikes to adjust, the voices and orchestra come straight out with a simplicity lost in many more sophisticated recordings. The Act 1 selection covers the prelude up to the end of the Sailor's second song; Kurwenal's song up to Isolde's 'Tod uns beiden!'; Brangäne's comfort; Tristan's entry, to the end. Nanny Larsen-Todsen is excellent in passionate anger or bitterness; in emotion – 'Seines Elendes jammerte mich' and later the deep 'ungeminnt' – an edge of whining gets into the voice. Tristan is dependable if rather wooden. Retrospectively this works well because both lovers are audibly transformed by the potion – very good to have got the internal chemistry into the voices like that. When the music gets going (pretty fast) they begin bemused and incredulous; later, when they are galvanized, he outpowers her.

Act 2 has only two small cuts. The hunting horns at the start make heavy weather and Isolde's 'Frau Minne' invocation is unremarkable. The difficult pages after Tristan's arrival, which can sometimes seem redundant, come off here very well indeed, with Gunnar Graarud, in particular, at his best. I am not sure that the reclamation of this passage is not this set's most valuable feature. The duet proper, 'O sink' hernieder', is less rapt and contemplative; its voluptuousness suffuses Brangäne also – she is not left out in the cold alone. The music is in perpetual ebb and flow, with absolutely echt *ritenuti* and pauses, shaped by an extremely experienced hand. Tristan remains good and Isolde comes into her own, making this one of the best love-duets, and the most overtly erotic. Ivar Andrésen gives his noble rather one-dimensional King Mark – all grief, no anguish or reproach.

Act 3 is allotted one side only (as against two for Act 1, three for Act 2). The choice of items makes an interesting comparison with a fuller but still mutilated third act from the late 1920s (D 1413/7). The emphasis – to us, misrepresentation – is upon mood (prelude) and the story of events with their external causes (how Tristan arrived in Kareol; first and second ships, etc.). The central madness is avoided and Tristan's *internal* voyage curtailed; the story returns from psychology to romance. The best conducting on any of these early discs comes from Albert Coates with his masterly fluctuations of speed after Isolde's arrival and Tristan's death, and the best singing from Andrésen's wonderfully eloquent Mark in the non-Bayreuth version. Widdop is constrained – not exactly cold, for he is very touching; rather tender, chivalrous, gentlemanly – more of a Lohengrin. Of the four Kurwenals, Herbert Fry is positively Jeeves-like, Eduard Habich the best. Guszalewicz's Brangäne is more interesting than her mistress Göta Ljungberg.

This is the best place to consider the incomplete CBS Act 3 (now cut rather than mutilated) under various conductors, dating from 1942–3. The point here is Melchior, who in some respects effaces all competition, while seeming oblivious of the music's complexity of expression. At first he is like a big animal who can only with difficulty assume a broken human speech: *Mei – ner . . . Vä – ter . . . mei – ner . . . Her – de:* a St Bernard with big warm eyes full of uncouth love. This animal quality is extraordinarily compelling; but in the later stages of Tristan's sickness he is so wrong – not *feeling* his inner torment, just *uttering* it as a beast who cannot understand what goads him. Janssen's Kurwenal is too expressive for a burly henchman, but his over-sobbing voice shows just how un-inward his master is. Roused by a *trumpet* as the shepherd's joyful pipe. Melchior is terrific for the diatonic pages following; 'but 'O diese Sonne' becomes too much of a rave. I have not heard the Metropolitan set, from the 1940s.

1950 produced two complete sets. One, with Marguerite Bäumer and Ludwig Suthaus under Fritz Konwitschny, I have not been able to hear. The pirated version under Hans Knappertsbusch is one of the great performances. No other 'live' version achieves the powerful narrative drive that impels this from first page to last; something that the studio cannot hope to emulate. The prelude begins very slow and fully moulded, then becomes more urgent and impulsive towards the climax – a different effect from the usual broadening-all-the-way. This complete control of weight and flexibility is ubiquitous. Some examples: the change of movement that accompanies Isolde's shift from present anger to past unhappiness; Tristan's entry, monumental in its power, and the tension electric between the lovers when at last they confront each other; the convulsions of the potion, which are extraordinarily intense; and correspondingly so the subsequent release of motion and emotion. Every phrase and every comma are dramatic. Helene Braun's Isolde is very fine, particularly her rage and Bs and withering scorn for Tristan's 'Herr und Ohm'. Günther Treptow first faces this vibrant creature with understandable timidity. He begins to come out at 'war Morold dir so wert', is soon effaced by 'des Schweigen's Herrin', comes out again for 'Tristans Ehre', and finally forthcomes fully in a superb 'O Wonne voller Tücke!'

Act 2, while still extremely distinguished, is less remarkable. Klose is characteristically emphatic and passionate, which makes a telling Isolde–Brangäne relationship in the early pages. Later she is simply too strong. Braun gives a good little incredulous laugh when warned to beware of Melot (who is excellent in his brief appearances – he really registers as a character, for once). Guided by Knappertsbusch's supple power she rises, after a wayward start, to a true Invocation to 'Frau Minne', and the cry for night to descend generates passionate heat. The 'problem-passage' from Tristan's arrival to 'O sink' is magnificent. Tenor and conductor in particular give an account that finally convinces me of the indispensability of these pages. After this the duet itself is not special; less relaxed, a day-lit rather than 'Nacht und Träume' performance, terrifyingly interrupted by the last belling of the hunting horns as the true quarry is run to earth. Treptow's invitation to the land of darkness is irresistible – who would hesitate for a moment? Braun's reply is less secret and pressing; he has sung only to her, but she grandly addresses the courtiers and their (unmemorable) king (Ferdinand Frantz) rather than her lover alone. Tristan rouses himself and is very fine denouncing Melot.

The orchestra, as well as its direction, is superb in Act 3. Treptow is rhythmically erratic here and there but can be readily forgiven, for the first section of delirium is quite magnificent, especially 'Isolde kommt' and his thanks to Paul Schöffler's Kurwenal (also excellent). The second delirium is less certain but still good, with a beautiful Vision, faster than usual, as is this performance's general tendency. The subsequent excitement is, by contrast, not fast; clear, emphatic, and all the more gripping, vertiginous in the mixture of triple and duple bars. The joyful piping this time is a *corno francese!* The pages from Isolde's gasp as Tristan dies up to the resumption of action with the arrival of the second ship are given the best performance I have heard. In a very slow tempo Braun is intensely passionate – as beautiful as Flagstad, and more utterly charged by the emotion – she has arrived too late to save her lover; he has died in her arms – no one conveys the truth of the situation so intensely. All the action music is outstandingly good too; the sense of drama, much aided by clashing swords, etc., is tremendous. The 'last appearances' of Kurwenal, Mark and Brangäne are incomparably good.

Actually the other great K's performance, also live (from Bayreuth 1952) makes a close comparison inevitable. Though Karajan has some excellent points he cannot match Knappertsbusch's combination of infallible authority, suppleness, and intensity. There are also accidental disadvantages – an indifferent recording, hair-raising side-turns, obtrusive audience and cues for Tristan. The prelude is magnificent and the sailor really *feurig* as requested. Ramon Vinay is similarly clear, direct, and a bit free with bar-lines – less successful when there is a rhythmic accompaniment to contend with. Brangäne is untidy too. The glory of this first act is Martha

Mödl. She has, here, the widest expressive range of any Isolde, from the intensity of her first talk of Tristan (the ambiguity of bitter and tender feeling toward him beautifully balanced), through fury, scorn, reckless wildness (though *vocally* quite secure!), sternness, accusation, sarcasm, imperious dignity – all melting at a touch into the underlying bitter tenderness. Again and again she is so right – a wonderful 'wie lenk'er sicher den Kiel', a wonderful 'Ungeminnt'. She can be vulnerable, even frightened – 'Tristan, was hast du mir zu sagen?' Karajan encourages and supports her every change. The finest feature of his control is the way that the potion-taking transports us so completely back to the prelude as to make the intervening pages seem like a troubled dream. The end of the act is full of electricity despite bad choral entries, frightful stage trumpets, and other natural disasters.

Act 2 is altogether less interesting – dry and dim, with a short-breathed Brangäne and Mödl, forgivable mistakes apart, less successful with this simpler Isolde than with the variety of the first act. Mark is strong but careless, and horrible in agony ('meiner Ehren Ende erreiche'). Vinay comes forth *al'italiana* for 'das Land' and is best when denouncing Melot. The difficult last two pages are more convincing under Karajan than any other. And the early part of Act 3 is also special, with an intense, fine-drawn prelude, an outstanding cor anglais, and perhaps the most touching assumption of Kurwenal on disc. Hotter had been fine and manly in Act 1; now in 3 he adds noble melancholy and radiant joy – really beautiful singing, so attentive to markings as to excuse the little liberty as, much later, he dies. But the main body of the act is hit-or-miss. The first delirium has good moments but is too hectic; more seriously, 'Die alte Weise' is matter-of-fact. Both soloist and orchestra are so external; hurried yet oddly devitalized, it all goes for nothing. Then 'Ha diese Sonne!' is *very* fast, driving superbly into Isolde's arrival. The crisis is over in a moment, then the actual death very slow. Mödl's squawk of anguish and disappointment has all her characteristic animal magnetism (in which she is comparable only to Melchior): but she does not produce the full expression of the subsequent pages that surely lay within her power. The *Liebestod*, however, is marvellous, especially the opening with its perfect rise to the A flat so crucial to success here, throughout, and finally as G sharp. Karajan arches a broad span, with a voluptuous orchestral sonority. This was the last *Liebestod* I heard out of so many; and was grateful still to be able to be so transported by it.

Yet another live recording from this period – La Scala, December 1951 – offers remarkable artistic experiences not duplicated elsewhere. The outstanding feature is the orchestra under Victor de Sabata; it is string-orientated throughout from the passionate heat of the prelude, to the dull warmth of the divided viola and cello writing early in Act 1, to a climax of silky smoothness in the second-act duet, and of high-charged intensity early in Act 3. Brangäne's first solo in the love duet gives a glimpse of another quality – a complex texture of delicacy and precision yet deep voluptuousness that recalls this conductor's famous record of Debussy's *Jeux*. Elsewhere de Sabata is direct, *a l'Italiana*, at once fierce and *cantabile*, rising to extraordinary emphasis for Tristan's entry in Act 1. He can excite an orchestra even more than Böhm. The early stages of Act 2 can take this, and he achieves a unique effect early in Act 3 with the almost violent surge of animal rejoicing as Tristan surfaces from his coma; but the end of Act 1 is merely wild. The advantages and disadvantages are neatly summarized in Brangäne's two comfort-sessions earlier on: the first is lost in scurry, the second is the most seductively lilting I have ever heard.

The singing is patchy. Max Lorenz is past his best, good only in moody vehemence, with a moment of fine anguish at the end of Act 2. Gertrud Grob-Prandl is splendid in the first act, another cross between Flagstad's warmth and Nilsson's brilliance; her scorching sarcasm is second to none, so that she and de Sabata can together shape the Narration into something powerful. The sound is, however, too poor and the cuts too numerous for permanent enjoyment. Not much of King Mark survives and Tristan's delirium is torn to shreds – the first half becomes virtually a monologue for man rather than master.

1952 also produced the first complete studio rendering, with Flagstad and Suthaus under Furtwängler. It remains one of the gramophone's proudest monuments and is still a standard around which other performances have to orient themselves. Which is not to say that it is the only way, or even that it is perfect of its kind. Simple imperfections can be quickly disposed of – the pale Brangäne, the vinegary Mark. More difficult to define is the hesitation over Flagstad's Isolde. The voice is of a beauty without peer in all these recordings, the range of expression is broader and simpler. After a Braun and a Mödl, her Act 1 is decidedly unvariegated. In the single-minded lyricism of 2 and 3 her incomparable warmth and beauty of tone can flower unperturbed by more complex demands. The voice is maternal rather than amorous, and while this gives credibility to the Oedipal view of the story favoured by Wieland Wagner, it does make it difficult to see Isolde as a *femme fatale*. She is Womanhood itself, rather than an individual woman pursued by a man's erotic ardour. This is of course rather an attempt at definition than a reservation.

Suthaus does not require any defence. He may lack Melchior-magnetism and the special urgency of some aspects of Treptow; and it is easy to find moments of deeper illumination or greater beauty in many other of these singers. But this is the completest assumption, rising in Act 3 to great heights of intensity without straining or eccentricity or cheapening. Furtwängler is at his greatest here too, and indeed this act is clearly the best suited to studio care rather than opera-house agitation. In the first two I feel he might have been very different live, and hanker for something of the electrical drama of Knappertsbusch's 1 and the more explicit eroticism of Elmendorff's 2. This performance none the less remains the most comprehensive and fully realized of any; it is hard to imagine its being surpassed.

The next two can be taken together; Decca's star-studded sonic-stager of 1960 with the VPO under Solti, and a three-record selection from 1962 vilely recorded with unknown singers and the Innsbruck Symphony Orchestra under Robert Wagner. Solti's *Tristan* is quite the worst of his Wagner recordings. It clearly shows both his deficient rhythmical sense (with its paradoxical combination of brutal rigidity and sloppiness) and the astonishing crudity of ear that can countenance the coarse noise he achieves in climaxes. A typical instance is Act 1 from potion-taking to the end; the included rehearsal record shows that Solti actually *wants* what he gets, evidently mistaking this garbled incoherence for excitement. What is true in small is true of the whole – he has no sense of paragraph, flow, structure. Thus Act 2 is all bumps and lumps; the duet seems to be a conscientious opposite to his usual punchiness – it is all too slow and careful with ebb and flow imposed upon, rather than breathing with it; while Act 3 is simply uncomprehended. Brangäne is feeble, Kurwenal (and his chorus) percussive, Mark dry and businesslike. The lovers are a spider pair – a powerless male and a devouring female. Poor Fritz Uhl has some nice phrases but they plainly exhaust him and in the duet he is pathetic. Birgit Nilsson is clad in stainless steel and seems completely incapable of tenderness. She attempts it but with no success. The Bs in Act 1 are terrific, but everything that should thrill with its ardour chills with its inhuman coldness. Why on earth does she want to extinguish that torch?

By contrast the Vox performance has a modicum of guts and feeling. Isolde and Brangäne strain away expressively enough with full-bosomed if third-rate voices. Tristan is rather better – a bit of a bawler but not without eloquence. It is necessary to hear a repertory performance like this in order to avoid becoming *blasé*. Though obviously mediocre, it is far from bad; if there were no other, enormous pleasure could be gained from it, and it serves to indicate just how high the standards are. The Solti is equally mediocre, and its faults are altogether more culpable; but the glossy presentation pretends something very different.

Böhm's live recording from the 1966 Bayreuth Festival does not give much joy, but there is no question that we are again in the presence of a first-class musician (listen to *his* rehearsal record!). Indeed this is what Solti would be like if, to all his talents as a disciplinarian, musical flexibility were added; externalized, but, when done like this, a legitimate approach to the work. Böhm has a quality of dry brilliance quite unlike the normal fat Wagner sound, and is interpretatively very direct. The prelude is as good an example as any, with its Strauss-y surging and dangerously headstrong horns. From the moment that the 'opera proper' starts (after the sailor's song) there is a brisk swing in the motion, refreshing after all those heavyweights. It has its dangers – the end of the act, after the goblet is (noisily) thrown away, quickly becomes incoherent – more excusable in a live performance when different criteria apply.

And Nilsson is transformed. From the start, and especially after the sailor's second song, she is *involved*. Her mockery bites, her passion is almost ugly, her cries of vengeance savage. Those meaninglessly magnificent Bs in the Solti are now used to convey something not very lovable but undeniably felt. Her imperiousness is such that one would fear to disobey. Christa Ludwig's Brängane is a perfect foil – there is dramatic insight in the relationship of the very different voices. Her insinuating 'Kennst du der Mutter Künste nicht?' is especially good. This is different from the sense of story so strong in Knappertsbusch's live recording. It is more verbal, and can surely be attributed to Wieland Wagner's sedulous concern with words. Ludwig is particularly attentive to meaning – a marvellously graphic warning early in Act 2 about Melot and the night hunt. Nilsson here is careless, and returns to her steely driving norm. Perhaps only anger, jealousy, scorn, can ever *touch* this extraordinary voice? So the orchestra alone, alas, is superb in the apostrophe to 'Frau Minne'. No other version except de Sabata's pursues this ebullient frothing; no other conductor could guide it so effortlessly to the climax of day-extinction. And after Tristan's arrival the Straussiness continues, with a kaleidoscopically rapid turnover of colour, almost too much of a rush to the head but just about contained, and finely relaxing into the duet and its beautifully precise articulation of the string throbbing. In Brangäne's Watch Böhm reads back into this original the sonority and emotional quality of the passages in Strauss and early Schoenberg that it inspired. Ludwig (as recorded) is much too loud – this is no disembodied virginal voice! Later in the duet I catch a shaft of warmth from Nilsson, round about that sweet little word 'und'. But she remains 'ungeminnt', whether erotically or maternally or plain vocally. Wolfgang Windgassen is excellent throughout but curiously unaffecting and unmemorable, except at one point, in the oppressive force of his self-hating death-wish just before he sets upon Melot. Martti Talvela is, of course, enormous, and so unlike the usual as to give the part a different meaning. There is no melancholy; here is a vigorous man in his prime, something to be reckoned with before one makes off with his wife. Then suddenly in the heaven-hell passage he completely crumples. The most beautiful vocal quality in this act comes from the woodwind solos (especially the clarinet) as Tristan defiantly embraces the strong–man's bride.

Both tenor and conductor are extrovert in Act 3. This is not necessarily due to a deficiency of feeling, for it can be a positive aesthetic ideal to avoid turgid inwardness and unnecessary soul-searching. But it is very incomplete; sometimes agonizings are called for, nowhere more than here. Tristan's delirium is superficial; Windgassen is careless, the cuivrë horns nasty; as tension mounts he tends to yell and the horns to bellow. The performers distinguish themselves in music better suited to them, for instance the radiant extravagance of gratitude to Kurwenal. But when Windgassen tells his vassal 'was ich leide, das kannst du nicht leiden,' we are not convinced. The visionary ship scuds unsteadily over shallow waters. The true ship (heralded now by the splendid Bayreuth *tromba di Cosima*) arrives in a frenzy of speed, and the subsequent pages are messy. With the fighting, extroversion is at last needed. The best singing in the act is Ludwig's explaining uselessly that all has been explained. Nilsson's *Liebestod* is athletic; she is no woman . . . but quite something as a Valkyrie. Böhm's special Wagnerian quality is shown here in small. His flow and surge are completely captivating for a *Liebestod*; but over the whole work the cost is a certain superficiality, and in the end a certain coldness.

This is preferable, though, to the glacial chill emanating from the most recent set, Karajan's studio recording of 1972. I think much less well of this than when I first reviewed it – not least in the light of his own performance twenty years before. Of course, the control is masterly (but what horribly prominent horns!); not so the knob-controlling, which seems to phase in and out whole planes of sound. Dernesch is touching but neutral; Ludwig has lost altogether the distinction of her previous version; and the main vocal pleasure is given by Karl Ridderbusch's Mark and Walter Berry's Kurwenal. And emphatically not by Vickers, who none the less is the oustanding feature of this set and (for all except Karajan-freaks) its *raison d'être*. For urgency and intensity his third act is without rival. It is absolutely authentic and extremely painful – the ravings of a stricken beast, what Melchior would be if he were not so irrepressibly cheerful. There is no doubt whatsoever about the stature of this *tour de force*, but it remains an extreme – something unique as if the story were, just this once, literally true. I can pay no higher tribute; but I never want to hear it again.

Extracts from *Tristan* date back to 1904. For purposes of comparison I shall deal with them chronologically through the story, rather than by date of recording.

ACT 1

A longish stretch early in the act dates from 1942. This (Acanta HB22 863–0) is not good but rather original. Whereas Paula Büchner's Isolde is uncharacterized, Klose presents Brangäne as a fierce vengeful fury – a reversal of their usual relationship. Max Lorenz's sulky, explosive Tristan, with the uncouth Kurwenal and the raucous sailors produce a unique air of primitiveness. Of three versions of Isolde's Narration and Curse, Flagstad's (DB 6748–9; HQM 1138) adds nothing to her complete recording; Helen Traubel (CBS 54036) is charged with steely warmth –

a cross between Flagstad and Nilsson (quite a combination!) – with prodigious powers of universal scorn – for Tristan (p. 98) Marke (102) for her fate (117); while Frida Leider (D 1667; IC 147–30 785) is simply magnificent.

ACT 2

First an ancient version of 'Dein Werk' by Pelagie Greef-Andriessen (043007; 1C 181–30 672) with an almost 'pre-Wagnerian' notion of expression that could well be a link with the authentic original. Of the two love duets the Flagstad–Svanholm (DB 21112–4) again does not extend what is already known; but the combination of Melchior and Leider (D 1723–4) is revelatory. In spite of wounding cuts (without even allowing time as healer) and tearing hurry, the result is incandescent. The clarity of interweaving phrase and answer between the two voices, both early on and in the Liebestod passage before the interruption, makes more musical sense than any other performance I know, though Florence Easton and Arthur Carron (IRCC 3004) have something of the same effect without anything like the same quality. In comparison Christel Goltz and Max Lorenz (DG 70231–2) are poor, he past his best, she not of the best, and the direction pedestrian and perfunctory under Ferdinard Leitner.

There are four worthwhile versions of Brangäne's Watch as a solo. Despite her fruity voice Emmy Leisner (Poly. 66737; DG 2721 109) is good because not overblown. Kerstin Thorborg (VIC 17223; LV 209) is richer still; in context this would detract from the lovers, as a self-contained *Lied* it is lovely. Klose's two versions are, like her complete performance, totally committed but almost over-expressive (first on Acanta HB 22 863–0, second on DG 2721 109–10). The version that best reaches (perhaps accidentally) the rapt disembodied quality needed here is the earliest, Margarete Arndt-Ober in 1913 (043230; CO 305).

The solo records of Mark's monologue only cover its first stage. Paul Knüpfer (042489–60; 1C 181–30 672) is uniformly cello-like – a younger king than usual, less weary but too undifferentiated. Andrésen (E 10829; LV 45) is infinitely sad – 'Leid' ohne Ende', heartbroken but no sobbing, all contained in the voice. The final extract is Tristan's Answer ('O König, das kann ich dir nicht sagen') with the first verse of 'Dem Land, das Tristan meint'. The earliest I have heard comes from Richard Schubert in 1920 (Poly. 65643; LV 252). He tends to be a 'tenor' in the bad sense, though the voice is attractive in itself and the line is well-sustained. He is a little narcissistic and too noble, as if giving a melancholy address. Of Melchior's two recordings, the first (D 1837; LV 124) is wonderfully chalorous, with an unforgettably beautiful 'das sag ihm nun, Isolde'! The second (Am. Col. 71388D; Odyssey 54036) is not so good, and the emphasis has changed towards greater gravity. Treptow in 1944 (Acanta

DE 23 104/5) is also lovely, his confident, baritonal quality fits the ardent lover much better than the pure fool in his contemporaneous excerpts as Parsifal. The other versions vary from middling (Lorenz) to awful (Martinelli *aetat* 65, and Fritz Soot, with no such excuse).

ACT 3

An undelightful record from a miserable year gives us Ernst Kraus's sour, wooden out-of-tune Tristan and Eduard Habich's too uniformly noble Kurwenal (044311; 1C 181–30672). Treptow (Acanta DE 23 104/5) gives a long extract from Tristan's delirium (Eulenberg pp 816–55), whose excessive speed pushes the voice into *Sprechgesang* at climaxes. There is a powerful sense of physical torment – the writhing discomfort of the accursed light and heat has not often been so graphically rendered – but of mental anguish rather less. Two versions of Tristan's Vision are as contrasted as possible. Heinrich Knote is agonizing (042253; CO 355): Melchior agonizingly beautiful (D 1839; 1C 181–30677). A third, Treptow (number as above), is strained and more baritonal than ever (it dates from 1947); his 'süsse Ruh', however, is most affecting.

And now for the Liebestod. The gradually changing interpretation of the work, both its performance-style and in what it is conceived to mean, are clearly shown in the procession of interpretations from 1910 to the present. Early versions are much faster (due in part, obviously, to the exigencies of 78 sides); and lighter, purer, cleaner. As voices become richer and more voluminous the orchestra swells and tempi broaden to support them. We are so accustomed now to hymn-like solemnity that a return to the earliest versions is disconcerting.

First comes Emmy Destinn in 1910 (043157; 1C 181–30672), powerful and shrill, with passionate soaring and dipping, and a ravishing last note. Melanie Kurt in 1911 (Parlo. P 1335; CO 345) is so fine as to be almost invisible in the gnat-wailings and bat-flutterings of the orchestra. Her seraphic purity is altogether abandoned in later ideas of what is right for Isolde. These two are at the opposite aesthetic and emotional pole from Flagstad.

For Helene Wildbrunn in 1919 (043311; LV70), the tempo has noticeably broadened; her voice is beautifully true and the expression calm and stately from beginning to end. Elisabeth Ohms in 1929 (Poly. 66928; DG 2721 110) is also halfway between two ideals. Again the tempo is broader and the voice fuller than in the pre-first world war versions, but the view of the character is still basically maidenly. Johanna Gadski (DB 660), also transitional, is less impressive; not so inward with the character, nor attentive to the strange and ecstatic things Isolde is saying; impatient, and with a touch of feverishness towards the climax. Lotte Lehmann (R 20122; PMA 1057) is different again; a paradoxical performance, at once intimate, addressing only him, yet impersonal, almost unmoved. The paradox remains unresolved; the result is certainly beautiful. Jeritza in 1928 (DA 1021; LV 122) is in a dimension of her own; for all the Italianate swooping, rock-hard, determinedly breasting the waves and compelling the disjointed phrases into a single line.

Leider has two versions. The earlier Red Polydor is rather a gasp – the voice tremendous, but seemingly out of humour with the music. (This performance shows clearest what a curious non-line the soprano has, especially at the climax, alternately drowning, and submerged by the orchestra.) Her second, dating from 1931 (DB 1545; 1C 147–30 785), is one of the greatest, imperiously commanding everyone nearby to burn with her in her supreme consumption. Inevitably such grandeur overshadows the contemporary version by Meta Seinemeyer (Parlo. E 10829; LV 112) which, though rushed, is memorable for a gentle warmth and a touchingly domestic quality in its ardour. Flagstad's early version (DB 2746; VIC 1455) is superb. Already (1935) the voice is in full bloom; its effortless amplitude gives, better than her later versions and better than any other Liebestod, an effect of almost religious certainty.

1942 brings apparently the only version in English (IRCC 3004); the elderly Florence Easton renders her own translation, at first staidly, but mounting to rapture upon rapture with convincing sincerity. Traubel's version in the 1942–3 abridgement discussed earlier is by comparison nothing special. Callas (Ember GVC 16) is different from all German and other Nordic singers, and would no doubt remain so even if she were not singing in Italian. She is *vulnerable,* pleading with her lover in little weeping phrases, for him to stay, to see her, to be alive, to see all these people, to smell these scents and hear this music. A *sospirando* ending, not glowing with fulfilment but quavering into extinction – original and moving, a human being, not Superwoman. Rita Gorr (ASD 456) is very good and also original – the Liebestod as blissful as sinking into a fleecy sofa. Varnay (DE 19192 – an otherwise dull LP of extracts), gives one of the best. In the very first phrase the intensity of the address to the 'Freunde' all around is special, and the vital A flat/G sharp is of superb quality – first and best on 'leuchtet', suitably enough. Her decorative turns are more confident than anyone's, and the gradually slower and slower tempo is completely sustained.

The changes in the Liebestod-ideal show Isolde developing from the lovelorn maiden of romance into an almost abstract idea of woman as ocean and as air-we-breathe. The shift in character is from erotic to maternal – the death-chant becomes a *Wiegenlied*; she croons over the loss of her man-son, and confidently accomplishes his rising again. Tristan has made a similar progress from romantic hero to psychological study; and the opera's centre of gravity is now usually seen as the Act 3 monologue rather than the Act 2 duet. The secondary (but still principal) roles of Kurwenal, Brangäne, and King Mark, have less opportunity to change, and can be completely realized in performance; but the lovers themselves are so various that it is not possible to imagine a single artist who could contain every aspect of the part. So in making my visionary cast, I have changed hero and heroine for every act. And also conductor; for he is the absolutely indispensable centre of every performance – and indeed the most rapturous warmth and finesse of phrasing I have ever heard in this music comes from the old 'symphonic syntheses' under Stokowski; they are without voices, and the loss is never for a moment regretted. No one in any of the recordings under notice can rival him either for fire or for precision.

Here then is a scheme for the perfect synthetic *Tristan*. Brangäne: Christa Ludwig (with a fond look at Klose). Kurwenal: Hans Hotter. King Mark: Ivar Andrésen. Tristan and Isolde are in Act 1 Gunther Treptow and Martha Mödl; in Act 2 Lauritz Melchior and (with an agonized pang of longing for Leider) Kirsten Flagstad; in Act 3 Ludwig Suthaus and Helene Braun. The conductors are Knappertsbusch for the first act; for the second, Stokowski; and the third, Furtwängler. Perhaps by the end of the century electronic techniques will have so advanced as to be able to bring this monster into being!

TRISTAN UND ISOLDE

I Isolde; *B* Brangäne; *T* Tristan; *M* Melot; *K* Kurwenal; *KM* King Mark

1941 (live performance, Metropolitan, New York) Flagstad *I*; Thorborg *B*; Melchior *T*; Darcy *M*; Hühn *K*; Kipnis *KM*/Metropolitan Opera Chorus and Orch./Leinsdorf Metropolitan Opera Fund ⓜ MET3(4)

1950 Bäumer *I*; Westenberger *B*; Suthaus *T*; Harand *M*; Wolfram *K*; Frick *KM*/Chorus, Leipzig Gewandhaus Orch./Konwitschny Urania ⓜ URLP 211

1951 (live performance, La Scala, Milan) Grob-Prandl *I*; Calvelti *B*; Lorenz *T*; del Signore *M*; S. Björling *K*; S. Nilsson *KM*/La Scala Chorus and Orch./De Sabata Cetra ⓜ LO 68/3

1952 Flagstad *I*; Thebom *B*; Suthaus *T*; E. Evans *M*; Fischer-Dieskau *K*; Greindl *KM*/Royal Opera Chorus, Philharmonia Orch./Furtwängler HMV ⓜ RLS 684; Angel ⓜ 3588EL

1952 (live performance, Bayreuth Festival) Mödl *I*; Malaniuk *B*; Vinay *T*; Stolze *M*; Hotter *K*; Weber *KM*/1952 Bayreuth Festival Chorus and Orch./Karajan Cetra ⓜ LO 47/5

1960 Nilsson *I*; Resnik *B*; Uhl *T*; Kozub *M*; Krause *K*; van Mill *KM*/Vienna Singverein, VPO/Solti Decca D41D5 ④K41K53; London OSA 1502

1966 (live performance, Bayreuth Festival) Nilsson *I*; Ludwig *B*; Windgassen *T*; Heater *M*; Wächter *K*; Talvela *KM*/1966 Bayreuth Festival Chorus and Orch./Böhm DG 2713 001 ④3378 069

1972 Dernesch *I*; Ludwig *B*; Vickers *T*; Schreier *M*; Berry *K*; Ridderbusch *KM*/German Opera Chorus, Berlin PO/Karajan HMV SLS 963; Angel SEL 3777

Excerpts

1926–8 (Act 3 – abridged) Ljungberg
I; Guszalewicz *B*; Widdop *T*;
Fry, Habich, Victor *K*;
Andrésen *KM*/LSO/Coates;
Berlin State Opera Orch./Blech;
orch./Collingwood
HMV D1413–7

1928 (abridged) Larsen-Todsen *I*;
Helm *B*; Graarud *T*;
Bockelmann *K*; Andrésen
KM/1928 Bayreuth Festival
Chorus and Orch./Elmendorff
EMI ⓜ 1C 181 03131–3M; CBS
ⓜ EL 11

1940 Bampton *I*; Summers *B*; Carron
T/Publishers Service SO/Steinberg
RCA (US) ⓜ CAL 224

1942–3 Traubel *I*; Melchior *T*; Janssen
K/Columbia Opera
Orch/Leinsdorf; Colon Theatre
Opera Orch./Kinsky
CBS (UK) ⓜ 61090; (US)
AAAXXX

1943 Buchner *I*; Klose *B*; Lorenz *T*;
Zimmerman *M*; Hoffmann *K*;
Prohaska *KM*/Berlin State Opera
Chorus and Orch./Heger
Acanta ⓜ DE 22316

1953 Mödl *I*; Blätter *B*; Windgassen
T/Berlin State Opera
Orch./Röther
Telefunken ⓜ DF6 48020

1955 Varnay *I*; Klose *B*; Windgassen
T; Borg *KM*/Württemburg State
Opera Orch./Leitner
DG ⓜ LPEM 19018; Decca
(US) ⓜ DL 9897

1959 Varnay *I*; Töpper *B*; Windgassen
T/Bamberg SO/Leitner
DG 136030

1962 (abridged) Bolotine *I*; Moreira
B; Fehenberger *T*; Leigemann
K/Chorus, Innsbruck SO/Wagner
Vox STOPBX 50123/1–3

Die Meistersinger von Nürnberg

RICHARD LAW

Die Meistersinger is one of those operas in a sense 'made' for LP, in that
a complete performance on 78s seemed far out of reach before the
second world war, even to those of us who dived with joy for the
complete Act 3 made in Dresden under Karl Böhm. It has fared well,
too, in that none of the LP sets is without merits even if one needs an
indulgent ear always to discern them. Four of the sets were in fact
recorded live in the theatre, including two of the three finest from a
purely musical point of view. My own preference is, in general, for studio
recordings, especially in a work as elaborate as this, partly because they
tend to be more accurate and partly because the difficult problems of
balance are more easily solved.

These comments are exemplified in the recently issued recording of a
Bayreuth performance conducted in 1943 by Furtwängler, which in fact
is not quite complete. Missing are the exchanges between Walther and
Eva in church (Act 1), and the climax of the Act 3 scene in Sachs's
house, including the quintet. This is a pity with so fine an Eva as Maria
Müller, one of the best on records, which is saying a lot, but presumably
no tapes were available from other performances to mend the gaps. Nor
is the sound good, even for the date. It is much inferior, for example,
to the 1930 Columbia *Tannhäuser*. The woodwind is backward and the
balance capricious, but nothing can diminish the warmth and grandeur
of Furtwängler's interpretation. One notices at once in the overture how
marvellous Wagner's part-writing sounds in his hands, founded on a rock-
like bass and propelled with passion. The combination of Furtwängler and
Müller, despite the occasional hardening of the latter's tone, raises the
emotional temperature at 'O Sachs, mein Freund', for example, to white
heat. I defy anyone to put the stylus down here and listen dry-eyed.

No doubt casting in 1943 presented problems, and most of the rest of
the singing is not on this level. Erich Zimmermann, a famous Mime, is
a spry but elderly David; the years in Nibelheim had taken audible toll.
Max Lorenz, too, sounds well past singing Walther: he is flat, effortful

and inaccurate. Nor is Eugen Fuchs's Beckmesser much better; his celebrity in the part is more understandable from the pre-war Böhm set of Act 3, but here his approximations to the text are hard to take. Josef Greindl, the Pogner, sings in an unremitting *forte* and often none too steadily; nerves is the charitable explanation, since it was his debut at Bayreuth and he was a mere 31. For Jaro Prohaska, the Sachs, I have a soft spot despite his unlovely tendency to bark. He is charming and skilful in the conversational passages, for example his enumeration of his materials to take dictation (' . . . hier ist Tinte, Feder, Papier'); and he is rare in giving full value to Sachs's flights of irony. With all that said there can be no doubt that Furtwängler put the whole together into a great performance, so that one is constrained again and again to listen with refreshed delight to the familiar notes.

That remarkable musician Rudolf Kempe made two recordings of the opera. The first had a short catalogue life complete, but a highlights disc (T 295) was available for a time on World Records. It originated in a wartime broadcast from Dresden. Scarcely better recorded than the Furtwängler set, it suffers from an even worse Stolzing. However it is worth having for the dulcet Eva of Tiana Lemnitz and for Ferdinand Frantz, a favourite singer of Kempe's, in fresher voice than in Kempe's 1957 Berlin set.

The latter seems to me the most generally satisfying of all complete sets, and certainly Kempe's best memorial. As often with him it is not easy to exemplify particular virtues, though there are countless subtleties of phrasing and rubato by the way: for example, the marvellous playing of the flowery, chromatic string writing where Sachs is putting Walther into the mood to tell his dream. But there is a total inevitability, a sort of splendid rightness, that is striking. The lead-in, for example, from the prelude to the opening chorus is achieved with a naturalness not managed by anyone else, and the whole scene sweeps forward to David's entrance as though in one breath, perfectly poised and balanced. The cast too was a fine one: Gerhard Unger had few equals as David; Gottlob Frick brings to Pogner his characteristic clarity, nobility, and command of legato, though there is little variety of tenderness in the voice; Rudolf Schock is a lightish and on the whole inoffensive Stolzing (high praise in this part!); Benno Kusche a splendid Beckmesser, clear and full of bile; Elisabeth Grümmer, another of Kempe's favourites – very understandably – is an enchanting Ev'chen with her silvery yet womanly tone and deep musicality. The Sachs is again Frantz, more bass than baritone and sounding gravelly by this date; but he makes a commanding figure, is admirably clear, and catches the man's humour perhaps better than any other recorded Sachs except Paul Schöffler. Balance inclines towards the singers, but the recording was good in its day, and the Berlin Philharmonic play like men possessed.

The only other conductor to have (so far) recorded the piece twice is

Karajan. The live 1951 Bayreuth performance embodies a notorious mistake by the Sachs (Otto Edelmann), and the recording balance is unfavourable to the woodwind. The string playing however is marvellous, and the differences from Karajan's 1971 Dresden recording are less marked than one might expect: greater flexibility of tempo (in 1951) and heavier accents are the most noticeable ones. Unger is again admirable as David but sounds less comfortable than under Kempe. The Stolzing is Hans Hopf, monochromatic and strenuous in Act 3, but bringing a genuinely heroic ring to 'Am stillen Herd'. Frederick Dalberg, the Pogner, will be remembered as having sung a good deal at Covent Garden in the 1950s. He comes across here as a pleasant singer of some sensitivity but vocally overparted; occasionally reminiscent of Hotter, he has that singer's faults without his virtues.

Another great name is recalled, to my ears at least, by Edelmann whose timbre is at times reminiscent of Schorr, though the comparison must stop there for he is a wooden and uninteresting Sachs with a forbidding relentlessness, despite the fine voice. Erich Kunz is none too accurate as Beckmesser, but the beautiful voice and his unhurried naturalness make him one of the best on records. As for Schwarzkopf's Eva, it seems to me incomparable, the best thing done on records by that remarkable but often over-artful singer: all the spontaneity and humour, as well as the coquetry, are managed to perfection.

By 1971 Karajan favoured a much more restrained, less massive orchestral sound, and gets lovely velvety playing from the Dresden Staatskapelle. A certain blandness is the price that has to be paid: the Act 3 prelude brings us a Sachs more courtier than cobbler, and this is reflected in the charming Sachs of Theo Adam. He is an artist more satisfying on stage than on records, where the grey patches in his voice make a disproportionate effect. A price too is paid for the youthfulness of this set's lovers: René Kollo lyrical but often prosaic and over zealous, Helen Donath letting the ensemble down with a breathy 'Selig wie die Sonne' and girlish rather than womanly in her Act 2 interview with Sachs. Petulance also disfigures Peter Schreier's David, whose pique at the idea of Walther's becoming a master is particularly babyish. Geraint Evans's Beckmesser is sometimes bothered by Karajan's slow tempi; he has trouble sustaining 'Ein saures Amt' as he goes to the marker's booth, but on the whole it is the adroit performance familiar to British listeners. Best of all is the noble Pogner of Karl Ridderbusch, rhythmical, poetic, relaxed. His opening words to Beckmesser, 'Seid meiner Treue wohl verstehen' are perfectly inflected and the whole performance is sustained on this level; but at the end I am left feeling that Karajan has given us here a series of beautifully finished scenes rather than a great performance of Wagner's huge opera.

Knappertsbusch's Vienna studio recording was released on LP at about the same time as Karajan's Bayreuth performance. It was the first complete *Meistersinger* I bought myself and it has kept a place in my affections largely because of Schöffler's Sachs. Better than any he catches the humour of the part, but he is also magnificent at 'Euch macht ihr's leicht'. Musical and noble, rather than poetic or sensitive, are the right adjectives here. In this set Edelmann sings Pogner, a part to which he is better suited than Sachs, though he sounds young and solemn; so does Anton Dermota's David, whose recital of the modes, with the conductor's connivance, is excessively leisurely; but he comes into his own with a ravishing 'Am Jordan Sankt Johannes stand'. Günther Treptow had the properly heroic tones for Stolzing though he begins to sound elderly by the time he gets to the prize-song rehearsals; Gueden is a notably fresh-sounding Eva, charming in Act 1 but overtaxed by 'O Sachs, mein Freund'. If Kothner has received little mention so far it is because the part is seldom well sung, but an exception must be made for the delicious and polished study by Alfred Poell in this set. In general Knappertsbusch is the most relaxed of conductors: his apprentices are sedate, orchestral accents are heavy; and *poco rallentandi* tends to be *molto rallentandi*, many of them unmarked, or, like that at the first chorus entry, expressly forbidden by Wagner. But the beauties are many, for example the leisurely accompaniment, perfectly sustained, to Sachs's disclaimer of Beckmesser's Act 3 song ('das Lied fürwahr ist nicht von mir'), and in general the playing of the VPO is lovely. Balance as usual favours the singers, but the orchestra was, for the date, well recorded.

The durable Kusche pops up again as Beckmesser (I would agree, 'kein besser') in the Keilberth set, recorded live in Munich in 1963 at the opening of the rebuilt National Theatre; he is still excellent. There is a fine no-nonsense feel about the Bavarian State Opera orchestra and King David's march is truly *sehr gehalten* with splendidly punchy brass playing. In general the performance is rapid, sometimes deteriorating into choppiness, with a lack of thrust and firmness in the string playing. It sounds well rehearsed but lacks light and shade as though Keilberth were over-strenuously bent on penetrating the back of a huge theatre. The singing varies a lot: Hotter a 'woofy' but noble Pogner; an inadequate David and Magdalene; Claire Watson charming and womanly as Eva but unable to sustain the legato of the opening bars of the quintet; Jess Thomas competent and musical, but monochromatic; Josef Metternich a sturdy Kothner. Indeed the Sachs, Otto Wiener, sounds so dry and Alberich-like that one wishes he and Metternich could have changed places. I confess that the unlovely singing of the central part, whatever Wiener's on-stage merits, effaces the virtues of this set.

Yet another live performance, this time from the 1974 Bayreuth Festival has an unusually 'close' but very clear acoustic, so much so that the prompter is unwelcomely audible. Balance favours the brass, especially trombones, but perhaps Silvio Varviso is to blame for forgetting Strauss's wise advice ('Never look at the trombones; it only encourages them').

He lets pass some minor inaccuracies, and is not͂ always observant of
Wagner's tempo variations, free though he is in such matters, allowing
a good deal of rubato at what are basically fairly brisk speeds. The
playing is admirably vigorous and weighty, as with Keilberth, and often
surprisingly elegant, but without much light and shade. The weaknesses
of the cast are a David and Walther both dry of tone and thin above
the stave, though Jean Cox especially was a 'natural' in the part; there
is also a Kothner who is coarsely effective but clumsy: 'Kein Koloratur'
indeed, and as *The Record Guide* remembered of one of his predecessors,
a disgrace to the guild. As Pogner, Hans Sotin is in magnificent voice,
but relentless and unyielding, as though Hagen were suddenly on the
loose in bourgeois Nuremberg. Anna Reynolds is a beautifully bright-
voiced 'Lene, and Hannalore Bode, while not ideally steady in tone,
brings the womanliness to Eva that Donath lacks. Klaus Hirte is a
surprising and refreshing Beckmesser, lively, youthful, a town clerk whose
humour is tempered by obstinacy and ambition rather than vindictiveness.
As to Ridderbusch, one is reminded, as earlier with Edelmann, that Sachs
is a different matter from Pogner; in a word he is colourless. This is in
spite of much beautiful singing, though he begins to sound tired by 'Euch
macht ihr's leicht', so that the voice starts to glare at E flat above the
stave.

Bode and René Kollo reappear in Solti's Decca recording made in 1975
in the Sofiensaal in Vienna, the latter sounding a little raw at the top,
but more imaginative than in his earlier performance – note, for example,
the almost whispered entreaties to Eva. Bode remains a musical and
careful, though somehow anonymous, Eva; Adolf Dallapozza presents an
intelligent though plaintive, even old-maidish, David. Bernd Weikl, who
sang the Nighwatchman (at times flat) for Varviso, here gives us a full-
voiced, lively Beckmesser, full of juice and venom. Indeed Beckmesser
has fared even better than Eva on LP. Kurt Moll makes a vigorous
Pogner, like Sotin but without his harshness again unreflective. There is
no intimacy of feeling at 'Will einer Seltnes wagen', where the old man's
self-doubt should really engaged one's emotions.

As to Norman Bailey's Sachs I hope it is not chauvinism and familiarity
that accounts for my partiality. He excels at just those sides of Sachs
where his only equal on LP, Schöffler, falls short: sensibility and poetry.
It is in Act 2 he really gets going, sustaining many of Wagner's long
phrases superbly in one breath. As to the orchestra, the general impression
given by this performance is, surprising in view of this conductor's
reputation, only that of all-round competence. The acoustic of the
Sofiensaal gives the prelude a massive start, with sharp accents in the
apprentices' music and a marked *allargando* at the final entry of the
march theme. A little more light and shade in the acoustic would have
been good, but the super-saturated sound is up to the VPO's best
standards and the singers are well recessed into the orchestra. Special

mention should be made here of the unusually scholarly essay and synopsis by Deryck Cooke that accompanies these records.

Lastly, Jochum's set is a real curate's egg. Finely, passionately, imaginatively conducted, it cannot conceal that the orchestra is not the VPO or Dresden Staatskapelle. Yet Jochum produces in the prelude a unique combination of massive tone with tempi far from slow. His ideas on phrasing and part-writing are also idiosyncratic. Yet for me the whole is put out of court by a central performance that combines much that is right with too much more than is wrong. The truth is that, at this stage in his career, Fischer-Dieskau is vocally better suited to Beckmesser than to Sachs. Perhaps he always was. A fine legato in the *Fliedermonolog* does not compensate for the hectoring dialogue, for the barked *fortes*, in short for the wrong vocal personality. Catarina Ligendza is a disappointment: often unsteady, even if musical and capable, but – like Bode – leaving no very definite impression. Peter Lagger, a hollow-voiced Pogner, pleases by making 'Das schöne Fest' not a public avowal but a confidence shared with a few friends. Horst Laubenthal, the David, is accurate, often waspish, but the recording is not always kind to him and the part sometimes strains his resources.

Roland Hermann is an admirably full-voiced Beckmesser, not always accurate and not without affectation, but self-regard is one of Beckmesser's traits and I will not cavil at that. Christa Ludwig is, with Reynolds, the best 'Lene on records, while in Gerd Feldhoff the guild has at last found a Kothner who can read the *Tabulatur* convincingly. Finally I do not see how there can be anything controversial about the choice of Placido Domingo as a gay Lothario of a Walther, so prodigal and forthright in utterance, again – to my ears – the best on LP. His German is not as bad as all that, and who else can match the ease and poetry of his singing?

It is frustrating that Mathilde Mallinger, the first Eva, made no records although she was only 21 in the year of *Die Meistersinger*'s première (1868), and thus younger than several recorded singers. If there are no links with that occasion on record, the list even of early 78s is long, since of all Wagner's mature operas it is the easiest to divide into excerpts and the one that made the most steady progress in public favour. Even so, the whole is more than the sum of the parts, and my own love for the work – since I must begin somewhere – goes back to the first complete stage performances I heard, those conducted in London by Beecham in 1951. Nothing of these survives on disc, but Columbia recorded four sides at Covent Garden under Beecham in 1936 (LX 645–6; RLS 742). Two are choral, and the tremendous thrust of 'Wach' auf' reveals the master hand. The other interest is that the Ev'chen was Tiana Lemnitz, unmentioned on the original label, doubtless for contractual reasons, but unmistakably soaring over the opening chorus, the answer to those who doubt the amplitude of that velvet voice. And she caps Torsten Ralf's musical, if nasal,

Preislied with a delicious 'Keiner wie du . . .'.

Ralf is also the Walther in the pre-war Dresden set of Act 3 conducted by Karl Böhm (DB 4562–76), modest in style but free from wobble or bleat. Singing and playing are throughout competent, which is intentionally faint praise in view of the set's reputation. Fuchs's pungent Beckmesser helps one forget his already-mentioned fallibility under Furtwängler, but Margarete Teschemacher is no match for Lemnitz, and Hans Hermann Nissen's Sachs is solemn rather than reflective, even a little dull, despite the beautiful voice.

Nissen was Toscanini's replacement for Schorr, then past his best, for his celebrated Salzburg performances. A tantalizing private record with much of Act 3 on it survives from 1937. This confirms the quality of Nissen's voice as well as his tendency to bluff heartiness. There is also an intelligent and musical Stolzing in Henk Noort. Primitive recording makes Beckmesser's entry sound like a bassoon concerto, but the playing lends new meaning to the word 'staccato', and there is no mistaking the delicate touches of rubato (Toscanini rigid, indeed!).

Mention of Friedrich Schorr brings us, so far as this opera goes, to the greatest name on records. His first were made in 1921 when he was 32, and his prime fortunately coincided with the arrival of electrical recording. His studio recordings are a magnificent group; some are backward but none is less than good. The 1921 *Schusterlied* (65673; DG 2721 109) compares interestingly with the electric version (D 1866; COLH 137). Both are of course curtailed and lack the interjections of the other characters; the earlier notable for its rhythmical command of the right (slowish) tempo, the later speeded up by the lively conducting of Albert Coates, with a high F at the end not quite effortless even in 1929. The *Fliedermonolog* (D 1351; COLH 137), dimly recorded, is a model, slow and quiet and freely declaimed on the breath as though by a great Lieder singer; the *Wahnmonolog* (D 1734; COLH 137) delights with a *pianissimo* high E natural.

He was usually given good colleagues in ensembles. Göta Ljungberg's 'Gut'n Abend, Meister' (D 2001; COLH 137) is matronly despite the fine voice; and Rethberg brings to 'Sieh' Ev'chen' an even better voice but a discouraging Saxon phlegm (DB 1421). This last, American-made, disc is notable for the standard of recording (high) and orchestral accompaniment (low). 'Grüss' Gott, mein Junker' (D 1990; LV 213) is a souvenir of Rudolf Laubenthal, whose bright, steady voice makes a properly dreamy Walther, though Coates's furious conducting disturbs even Schorr's poise in the opening dialogue. But the pick of the group is 'Aha, da streicht die Lene' (D 2002; COLH 137), in which Coates again sets a hot pace, followed by the quintet. Elisabeth Schumann's 'Selig, wie die Sonne' remains the standard by which others are judged – did she ever need to breathe?

By comparison 'Euch macht ihr's leicht' (D 2000; COLH 137) is a slight let-down, but Collingwood who here conducts was not the equal of Blech or Coates. In 'Abendlich glühend' (D 2000; COLH 137) the focus is on Melchior, but 'Verachtet mir die Meister nicht' (D 1354; COLH 137), once more with Blech and more remotely recorded than the English discs, is excellent again. Finally, there is an interesting set (EJ 277–286) made live in Berlin in 1928 under Leo Blech with a good cast. Unfortunately there is not very much of Leo Schutzendorf's legendary Beckmesser, honeyed and splenetic by turns, but Karl Jöken is a charming David, and Robert Hutt a fresh-sounding Walther (he was 50). Emanuel List's Pogner is unsteadily though intelligently sung, and he really captures the elderly father's affectionate concern. He is helped by Blech's celebrated skill at piloting his singers: note the nicely judged relaxation at the Act 2 entry of Eva and Pogner. There is more fluctuation of tempo than Blech and Schorr allowed themselves in the studio, and Schorr reveals a humour not there in evidence but which confirms his reputation as a complete Sachs: for example, his gentle mockery of Beckmesser as he repeats in Act 2 his criticisms of his shoes, or the sly humour of 'War das euer Lied?' The recording projects fine playing by the State Opera orchestra through a recording of naturally shallow perspective and poor differentiation.

Robert Hutt also recorded the standard excerpts separately. 'Am stillen Herd' (Od. Rxx 76581) produces a genuine lyric tenor, well-schooled, well-sustained singing; 'Fanget an' (042422) again the same qualities, a little dull here perhaps, but his long phrasing brings his *Preislied* (Rxx 76582) back into a high class.

Turning to earlier records, I find that it needs the ear of faith to account for the reputations of many singers, especially of Stolzing's music, so seldom satisfactorily sung in any circumstances. Act 1 is really written for a heroic, Act 3 for a lyric tenor. This challenge is sharply confronted by the many tenors who coupled 'Am stillen Herd' or 'Fanget an' with the *Preislied*. Ernst Kraus's 1901 'Am stillen Herd' (42432) is so laboured it nearly conceals the big style, but a primitive Pathé of van Dyck (60605) is worse. Hermann Winkelmann, the first Parsifal, is another great name whose bumpy record of Walther (42014–5; Rococo 5239), made in 1902 when he was 53, belies his fame. More to my taste is Giuseppe Borgatti, recorded in Italian in 1905 to a piano accompaniment (Fono. 39408; Rococo 5323), a leisurely performance of some distinction, if a bit prosaic. Karl Oestvig (Poly.; LV 28) is better in the trial song than here, where he is wobbly and not always in tune, but the singing is enlivened by plenty of character and a warm voice.

The 1906 G&Ts (3–42570; CO 355) of Heinrich Knote, the Munich tenor, show his satin diction despite the tendency of the voice to retreat, and – for a wonder – in the trial song (1909) the F on the word 'Fanget an' is sung diminuendo as suggested by the orchestral markings. The electric Odeons of 1930 are even better (0–6692; Discophilia KG-K–1), especially the prize song where he sings the whole phrase '. . . der Erde lieblichstes Bild' to 'so heilig ernst', with its high A, in one breath; a marvellous feat and chivalry personified. He was 60 at the time and retired the following year. Heaven knows why!

Richard Schubert (Poly. 65670 and 65611; LV 168), a great name in Vienna and Hamburg in the 1920s, has a sympathetic personality, not a common attribute of Stolzings, and exhibits a ringing top and a fearless attack, though not a voice of the highest quality. Carl Martin Oehmann (E 10552; LV 181), in the conventional coupling, reveals, in a way, the reverse qualities; an imposing – if throaty – voice but a prosaic view of the music. Passing over plodding versions by Paul Kötter, Set Svanholm and Joachim Sattler we come to Richard Tauber (Od. 123506) whose charm and delicious lyric style cannot conceal that he has the wrong voice. At least he does not (Poly. 95351), treat the music as a vocal rather than a theatrical episode, like Alfred Piccaver, clear though it is why they made their opera-house reputations in other music. The same applies to Patzak whose 'Am stillen Herd' (Poly. 90181), though made in 1931, sounds middle aged even then, though intensely musical; it is especially well accompanied by the Berlin State Opera orchestra under Alois Melichar. Karl Erb's version (Od. 98016; 1C 147–30771), with its characteristic plangent timbre, is also that of a lightweight, but not that of Helge Roswaenge (Telef. SK 1297; 6.42084 AJ) recorded in 1932 with prodigal attack and voice; just right here.

Altogether the 1930s have left us a rich legacy. Max Lorenz, the Bayreuth Stolzing of the day, is better recalled by his 78 (C 2153; LV 121), a fresh and poetic disc with a real feeling for the shy young man carried away, than by his 1943 recording with Furtwängler. As to Lauritz Melchior, *stat magni nominis umbra*! He was identified more with the *Ring* than this music and his 'Am stillen Herd' (DA 1227) is not Walther, with its brassy *fortissimi* above about F sharp, but none the less the vitality and sense of limitless resources are exhilarating. Franz Völker, also a genuine *Heldentenor*, sings well in a backward recording (Poly. 67102; LV 206), and the prize song is yet better with its ample phrasing and effortless high notes. Equally musical, and better recorded, is the poetic 1929 reading of Fritz Wolff (CA 8023; DG 2721 110), finely accompanied by Manfred Gurlitt. Wolff, a Bavarian and a famous Loge, won high praise in the 1930s for his London appearances, but like Laubenthal, Ralf, Lorenz and others he had to stand in Melchior's shadow.

Of more recent tenors Sandor Konya is outstanding (LPEM 1912); to a youthfully impulsive 'Am stillen Herd' he adds a lyrical *Preislied*, clear and uninflated, and he is excellently accompanied by the Berlin Philharmonic under Richard Kraus, son of Ernst.

The trial song, a less seductive 'number' than 'Am stillen Herd', was more seldom recorded in versions separate from the couplings already mentioned. An acoustic Parlophon (P 375) offers the intensely lyrical

Fritz Vogelstrom, light-voiced, rapid, bright-toned. Alois Hadwiger's vehement singing (042378), recorded in 1913 when he was 34, betrays a voice already muscle-bound. Erik Schmedes, a greater name than either, recorded in 1905 (042086; CO 301), shows a certain responsiveness to the text, but it is vitiated by a tightly produced voice and choppy phrasing. Völker's record (Poly. 95038; LV 206) is properly urgent but he fails to react to the rasps of Beckmesser's slate; such insouciance is uncalled for here.

In the *Preislied* the same names inevitably come up again. Leo Slezak's discography alone lists eleven attempts, and I have counted at least fifty-six versions. Among the earliest, and worst, is that of Werner Alberti, laboured and often sharp, but the big voice and style are reminiscent of Slezak. Little better is Heinrich Hensel (Od. 76302; CO 339). He was Covent Garden's first Parsifal in 1914, defying Cosima's wrath and the Bayreuth veto. The voice is bright and well produced but he is a Loge rather than a Walther, and the singing dull. More to my taste is Karl Jörn (042153; CO 354), a Latvian and a good artist with a nice airy style of much elegance. He ends with a fine crescendo on the last high A at the word 'Parnass'. What is a surprise for 1907 is that though the piece is cruelly curtailed (and no Eva), the chorus parts are complete. But the outstanding early version is that of Johannes Sembach (Col. A 5889), whose American admirers likened him to Jean de Reszke; and one can well believe that this beautiful, touching, yet passionate singing is our best hope of tasting the style of that legendary figure.

Now for 'foreign language' versions. In English Joseph Cheetham (Zono. Z–042042) is musical but retiring, but the field is generally dominated by the set of excerpts recorded acoustically under Albert Coates (D 745–758). Alas, the standard is modest, despite Coates's habitually hectic conducting, but the depressing translation might well have lowered the spirits of fierier singers than Tudor Davies, Florence Austral and Robert Radford, who doubles Sachs and Pogner. Davies re-recorded the prize song (D 1021) electrically under Goossens, and here the beauty of the voice does come through, punctuated by booms from the ubiquitous Radford, unnamed on the label. Francis Russell, though he sang Stolzing and Calaf for the BNOC, sounds on record more like a David (Col. 9924). Frank Mullings (L 1228) reveals a fine voice with a close, rapid vibrato but a lugubrious style.

McCormack in English (DB 329; GEMM 160) is something of a curiosity: rapid, effortless, and without any sense of gathering climax; but that this singer's gifts lay elsewhere will be news to none. The more commanding style of Joseph Hislop (DB 681 and DB 1351) is more to the point. Hislop never tackled the part in the theatre and his singing has every virtue except sheer power.

There can be no doubts about Walter Widdop's power (D 2053; HMQ 1164), or the security of his method, but the style is self-effacing. The tingle that is missing in McCormack and Widdop is supplied by James Johnston (DX 1506) despite a certain shallowness of tone, and he is backed by fine orchestral playing conducted by Michael Mudie. None of these sung the role on stage, I think.

The virtues of Giuseppe Borgatti (already mentioned) are also those of Fiorello Giraud (52048): broad phrasing, a leisurely tempo, a marked but acceptable vibrato. He was the first Canio, and the 1904 recording makes him sound a little like de Lucia. The reminiscence is also apt in considering Francisco Vignas (Fono. 74020), who was the first London Turiddu (at the Shaftesbury Theatre in 1891), in which part he was later favourably compared to de Lucia. A Spaniard, Vignas had a real heroic tenor; his Prize Song (in Italian) is hurried and the voice 'glares', but the singing is easy, natural and fluent.

I have been unluckier with French tenors, except for the admirable Georges Thill. Paul Franz, despite the splendid voice, and Charles Rousselière are just dull. Thill's performance (LX 424; 2C 061–12153), one of uncomplicated excellence, is backed by a passionate performance, abetted by the fiery Germaine Martinelli, of 'Ja, ihr seid es' from Act 2 (or rather, 'Oui, c'est vous'). It is well but anonymously accompanied and the whole hard to better in any language.

I return to the German mainstream via a number of other foreigners. Franz Pacal (Favorite 1–25053), a pupil of Gustav Walter, is baritonal and smooth, but dishonours his great teacher by being effortful and often flat. Of all those eleven Slezaks I have heard Col. A 5395, a backward recording made in 1912, through which the singer's high spirits and trumpet tones, but also some of his coarseness, emerge uninhibitedly. The *Preislied* of Hermann Jadlowker gives us his typical even and silvery timbre, beautiful singing, backed by chorus (Od. 64344). Only a little less attractive is Björn Talèn, a Norwegian trained in Italy, whose career ran mainly in Berlin. He has a fine Zenatello-type voice, but adopts a hectic tempo which is eccentric in that there is plenty of spare room on the disc (E 11177).

The American Richard Crooks was trained in Germany, but although his record (DB 1598; VIC 1464) nicely combines lyricism and *élan* it is not without some sense of strain; it is no surprise that the Metropolitan kept him mainly for parts like Des Grieux and Alfredo. On the other hand, his near contemporary, Charles Kullmann, also American, was a consistently successful Stolzing, and his version (LX 729; LV 144) is cool but charmingly poised. The young Melchior (Poly. 72870) takes the piece slower than on his later electric made with Barbirolli (DB 1858; LV 124), but I have already touched on his strengths and weaknesses; few singers on record or on stage have been more reliable in both media.

Returning to Germany we find a dullish Karl Erb (Od. 98000; 1C 147–30 771), and a plummy Walter Kirchhoff (042468) whose aristocratic style does not compensate for a soporific manner.

All the prize songs so far have, of course, been in the so-called 'concert version', shortened to fit a single side, except the Ralf/Lemnitz/Beecham Columbia. One of the only other tenors to make a double-sized version was Sigismund Pilinsky, a Bayreuth Tannhäuser in 1930–1 with a clear and steady, if plaintive, voice. His Ev'chen, though, is the magnificent Meta Seinemeyer (E 10947; LV 202), fifteen seconds of whom here kill all memory of the tenor's effortful eight minutes.

The more recent generation is done poor justice by James King (Electrola 1C 063–01850) whose singing is clean and honest but lethargic and middle-aged. A more interesting disc (Acanta HB 22863–0) featuring Ludwig Suthaus takes us from the *Preislied* to the end of the opera. Suthaus's limitations are known to all who have the Furtwängler *Tristan*: he is often casual over words, and on stage, as the *Record Guide* put it, he reminded one of Jeeves. But he is a sensitive and musical Stolzing; I like for example the regret – rather than irritation – with which he sings 'will ohne Meister selig sein', more in sorrow than in anger. Heger conducts with urgency, though he fails to make up for a prosaic Eva (Müller) and a rasping Sachs (Prohaska). We do, however, get a glimpse of Ludwig Hofmann's majestic Pogner. This comes from a wartime broadcast.

Hofmann, unlike Schorr, sang both Sachs and Pogner, and his name serves to bring us back to the central, though not the most recorded, character of the opera! Schorr's qualities make it easy to overlook both the relative shortness of his career and the excellence of such contemporaries as Hofmann and Michael Bohnen. The latter, who was a few months older than Schorr, recorded 'Grüss Gott, mein Junker' in 1914 (Poly. 65272; LV 192) and sang Sachs on stage as late as 1951. Though a Rhinelander by birth he is irrevocably associated with Berlin where for a short time after the last war he was director of the Städtischer Oper. A good singer and better actor, he was a bass rather than baritone Sachs, but that 1914 duet, with Ernst Kraus, confirms the quality of the voice. Kraus also recorded the passage in 1908 with Herman Bachmann (044086; CO 361), whose fine voice and legato are also apparent, though the whole thing is too hurried to make it easy to assess Kraus; he sounds affected despite the undeniably grand manner.

On the early records Sachs fares hardly better than Walther. Friedrich Weidemann's 1905 Odeons, for example, with a slapdash piano accompaniment, betray many lapses of intonation, late entries, and a generally cavalier attitude. Yet he was a famous Sachs and a protégé of Mahler. Hermann Weil's *Fliedermonolog* (042325) is charming but unremarkable. Leopold Demuth's record (042205; CO 303) like his *Wahnmonolog* (4–42283/4) is notable for his extrovert good humour, fine voice and overpowering Moravian accent but not for imagination or nuance. Others that rate a bare mention are Franz Kronen (light and good), Fritz Feinhals (nasal tone and poor legato), Murray Davey, Conny Molin (muffled and, furthermore, in Swedish), Theodor Scheidl (sensitive and lugubrious), Franz Crass (workmanlike but stodgy), Donald McIntyre (unsteady and poorly accompanied), George London (gritty and over-emphatic), Arthur Fear (sensitive but over-modest). The last-listed singers all couple the *Flieder* and *Wahn* monologues.

Of more attraction is Marcel Journet (DA 951) complete with some odd hammertaps. The voice is splendidly free at the top and the reflective declamation of the French text is a constant pleasure. The baritonal timbre of the voice (a plus in this listener's view) is even more marked in *Wahn* (VA 71). A fascinating English version by Lawrence Tibbett substantiates the belief that his career may have been shortened by singing parts too high for him. Sachs's self-doubts are outside his range but one must admire the ease and power of the singing voice. Josef von Manowarda, a great name at Bayreuth, though not as Sachs, made an acoustic Polydor (65651; LV 175) which highlights his wide vibrato but also the artist's sensibility and clarity: he makes a total success of the tricky passage 'dem Vogel der heute sang . . .' Manowarda was more bass than baritone, but the reverse was true of Rudolf Bockelmann, whose records make his popularity in London easy to understand. His 'Jerum' *(Schusterlied)* is too straight and unvaried, but 'Verachtet mir die Meister nicht' (C 2255; LV 9) gives us some lovely free singing, thoroughly baritonal and easy at the top. The *Fliedermonolog* (SK 1325) is even better, with beautiful soft singing and complete control. Bockelmann does not give the sense of being a moral force like Schorr or Hotter, but Sachs can seldom have been better sung.

Alfred Jerger, famous as the original Mandryka, was a conductor before he became a singer. His *Fliedermonolog* (Poly. 65649; LV 92) is early and charms by his Czech accent, but youth turns it into a mere concert piece. Emmy Bettendorf joins him on the other side in 'Gut'n Abend, Meister' and sounds attractive but sleepy. Josef Herrmann's record (DB 5623; LV 44) is not in this class, but Ludwig Hofmann (Classic MD 9643/4; LV 51) reveals a majestic grasp of the part. None the less, his timbre is a bit insistent for Sachs, and he was no doubt better as Pogner and better still as Gurnemanz.

This brings us to Paul Schöffler's 78 (K 1731), different from but similar to his LP performance. The playing of the orchestra of the Zurich Tonhalle under Knappertsbusch is expressive and typically leisurely. The other great post-war Sachs, Hans Hotter, recorded the two monologues twice during the war, once in the studio (Poly. 67855), then for the radio (Acanta 22017–6) when he was at his best. One remarks the steady tone and effortless high notes, as well as the eloquent recollection of emotion in tranquillity. Hotter brings off to perfection the effects unsuccessfully aimed at by singers such as Fischer-Dieskau. Wonderful records, these.

In 'Gut'n Abend, Meister', also made in Zurich, Schöffler is joined by Maria Reining (Decca X 312). He is in good form, she intelligent but monochrome. Those seeking more excitement will turn to Lotte Lehmann and Bohnen recorded in 1916 (Poly. 76357; RLS 743). Bohnen is recorded very forward: this is a big performance softened by much delicacy, for example where he is evidently at pains for Eva's sake to temper his criticisms of Walther's trial song. When Lehmann recorded her 'O Sachs, mein Freund', she was 28 and never sounded better (Poly. 76364; LV 94). Delia Reinhardt's record (Poly. 66783; LV 142) is not up to Lehmann's, though she too was clearly a great 'communicator'.

David is even less recorded than Eva. Hans Bechstein, a Dresden tenor, recorded part of the recital of the modes and David's little Act 3 song to Sachs (Parlo. P 693), but I note it as a curiosity, since the singing is featureless, the shallow tone that of a Mime rather than a David.

To come back to Sachs's Act 2 music. Early 'set piece' recordings of the *Schusterlied* include versions by Anton van Rooy (Col. 30098), recorded in 1906, which is majestic if a bit jerky, and by Theodor Latterman (P 361) is equally firm in tone and altogether more varied. The *Wahnmonolog* in Act 3 brings us to a singer not yet mentioned, Wilhelm Rode (CA 8157; LV 17), who made a success at Covent Garden in 1928 but was never re-engaged. He afterwards became Intendant of the Deutches Opernhaus (Charlottenburg), Berlin. Despite his unusual care for Wagner's markings, this record is, alas, humdrum. Whitehill (DB 442) has little to offer. Herbert Janssen's recording (LX 947), late in his career, is hollow-voiced and somehow wrong in spite of his musicianship: Sachs as aristocrat rather than shoemaker. Schöffler's record (K 1573) is predictably good, but unpredictably accompanied by Karl Rankl and the National Symphony Orchestra.

'Aha, da streicht die Lene schon ins Haus' is more than the lead-in to the great quintet. Walter Soomer's version (042426) pleases with the smooth tone production typical of the best pre-1914 singers, but he pulls the words and tempo about as though he were Weidemann himself. As for the quintet, inevitably dominated by the Eva, one of the earliest versions (044144) is also one of the best. The soprano is Grete Forst whose control and legato are near perfect; she is backed by, among others, Slezak and Demuth. Another version (044078) has an Eva wholly different but equally fine in Gadski with her majestic phrasing and attack, rock steady and plumb in tune. Later on the Sachs, Journet, enters half a bar early and sticks to his error thereby giving us a few hilarious moments more like Stravinsky than the Master. Happy days, and no nonsense about retakes! Emmy Bettendorf's acoustic version (P 1504; LV 156) is backward but good in the Schumann/Forst manner, and she finishes with a finely managed trill. Later she made an electric (E 10544) with Bohnen, Oehmann, Gombert and Lüders, this time more vividly recorded; but the orchestra conducted by Weissmann is like suet and the recording becomes too congested to give pleasure.

An all-star Polydor (78543) with Lily Hafgren, Fritz Soot, Manowarda, Maria Olczewska and Henke is disappointingly sleepy. Roswaenge and Hans Reinmar feature on a Telefunken disc (SK 1162; 6.42084 AJ) dominated by the delicious singing of the Eva, named as P. Yoder (who was she?). Yoder has the sensuality missing in the girlish tones of Erna Berger (Poly. 35006) for all the latter's competence. Berger's colleagues include Max Hirzel and – as Sachs – Karl August Neumann, long a stalwart of the Polydor list and admired at Covent Garden in 1936 as Faninal and Beckmesser. In 1938 with that enigmatic figure Hans Weisbach he made what is the only record I have found of Beckmesser's prize song, 'Morgen ich leuchte' (Acanta HB 22863–0), and very good it is too: musical and full of character.

Janssen in his autumn also recorded the quintet with a group of his Metropolitan colleagues (Col. 72518–D). It is kept moving nicely by the conducting of Max Rudolf, and Ralf is a tower of strength as Walther. Polyna Stoska, the Eva, nearly spoils it by singing flat, but her ample phrasing and warm personality explain her reputation. Hilde Konetzni's record with Schöffler (Telef. TE 1008) is put out of court by her habit of attacking everything from below.

Annelies Kupper on a Heliodor LP (478126) with Herrmann, Herta Töpper, Windgassen and Richard Holm is, like Konetzni, outclassed on record by the competition, but the rest is worth having for Windgassen's clean and musical singing of 'Fanget an' and the *Preislied*. The disc is transcribed from separate discs, so the latter lacks Eva's accolade, but it is one of the best on records despite the singer's unyielding vocal personality. There is a certain extravagance about Herrmann's contribution as though to compensate for a voice not really of the requisite weight.

The best remaining Sachs not yet to have received his due is the Austrian Hans Reinmar. He made a reputation at Bayreuth just before the war as Amfortas and Gunther; his 'Euch macht ihr's leicht' (Telef. E 1609) is, as one would expect, more satisfactory than the more testing 'Verachtet mir die Meister nicht' (E 1610). The latter imposes some strain on a lightish voice, while the former is enjoyable for his spacious, intense manner and intelligent declamation. Josef Lindlar and Scheidl are eminently forgettable, but Emil Schipper's majestic singing (LV 503) is undeniably imposing despite a certain fierceness: Sachs as Führer rather than poet.

Alexander Kipnis seemed incapable of singing badly, and he makes Sachs's closing address grave and beautiful (EJ 46; LV 165), without destroying the conviction that Pogner was his part. His 'Das schöne Fest' (DB 1543; SH 280) is justly famous; the hurried tempo escapes notice in one's fascination at the magisterial tone and at the strong Russian accent in which he declaims the text with a matchless combination of sensibility and authority. Leon Rains (042154) is steady but self-effacing; while back in the top class with Kipnis (and Ridderbusch) is the superb

Wilhelm Hesch (042133; CO 300) with his extrovert manner and splendidly trained voice – no trouble here with F above the stave – and the recording is excellent for 1906. I end on a note both more and less cheerful: Ivar Andrésen (Col. L 2341; LV 45) has a voice hardly inferior to that of Kipnis or Hesch, a real black bass, but neither their technique nor sensibility, so that Pogner's little flourishes, for example, go for nothing with him. None the less, all his records are a legacy of a remarkable if flawed singer and it is a depressing fact that he died in Stockholm in 1940 in degrading poverty. He was 44 years old.

To sum up: as omnipotent Intendant, what ideal cast would I choose? For Sachs, that's easy: Friedrich Schorr, and I would want him understudied by Hotter or Bailey. Pogner has to be Ridderbusch, painful though it would be to pass over Hesch and Kipnis. Beckmesser must go to Kusche, with Klaus Hirte waiting in the wings, though if one could persuade Erich Kunz to polish it up a bit and drop the Viennese charm . . .? To round out the principal masters the Kothner would have to be either Alfred Poell for character or Gerd Feldhoff for sheer singing. Only for David is there an automatic first choice: Gerhard Unger. As for Walther, ideally Heinrich Knote in heroic vein for Act 1 and Sembach for the rest, and if that is felt to be cheating I choose Placido Domingo for the lot. For Magdalene, Christa Ludwig. Eva is the most difficult of all because of the *embarras de richesse*. I pass over Lehmann, Seinemeyer and Schumann only because they recorded so little from the opera, though the quality of what they did and their reputations make it probably a mistake to look further. First offer would go to Elisabeth Grümmer, but I should half hope she would cancel so that I could send for Schwarzkopf (first choice) or Lemnitz.

Finally, I would have the performance prepared by Karajan and conducted by Furtwängler or Kempe, with the Berlin Philharmonic in the pit and the Bayreuth chorus on stage.

DIE MEISTERSINGER VON NÜRNBERG

S Sachs; W Walther; B Beckmesser; P Pogner; K Kothner; D David; N Nightwatchman; E Eva; M Magdalene

1943 (live performance, Bayreuth Festival) Prohaska S; Lorenz W; Fuchs B; Greindl P; F. Krenn K; E. Zimmermann D; Pina N; Müller E; Kallab M; 1943 Bayreuth Festival Chorus and Orch./Furtwängler EMI ⓜ 1C 181 01797–801

1950 Schöffler S; Treptow W; Dönch B; Edelmann P; Poell K; Dermota D; Pröglhöf N; Gueden E; Schüroff M/Vienna State Opera Chorus, VPO/Knappertsbusch Decca ⓜ GOM 535–9; Richmond ⓜ RS 65002

1951 Frantz S; Aldenhoff W; Pflanzl B; Böhme P; Paul K; Unger D; Faulhaber N; Lemnitz E; E. Walther-Sacks M/Dresden State Opera Chorus, Saxon State Orch./Kempe

VOX ⓜ OPBX 142
1951 (live performance, Bayreuth
Festival) Edelmann *S*; Hopf *W*;
Kunz *B*; Dalberg *P*; Pflanzl *K*;
Unger *D*; Faulhaber *N*;
Schwarzkopf *E*; Malaniuk
M/1951 Bayreuth Festival Chorus
and Orch./Karajan
Seraphim ⓜ IE 6030; EMI
ⓜ C90275–9
1956 Frantz *S*; Schock *W*; Kusche *B*;
Frick *P*; Neidlinger *K*; Unger *D*;
Prey *N*; Grümmer *E*; Höffgen
M/Berlin State Opera Chorus,
Berlin Municipal Opera Chorus,
St Hedwig's Cathedral Choir,
Berlin PO/Kempe
EMI ⓜ RLS 740 ④ TC–RLS
740; Angel ⓜ 3572EL
1963 (live performance, Bavarian State
Opera House, Munich) Wiener
S; Thomas *W*; Kusche *B*; Hotter
P; Metternich *K*; Lenz *D*; Ernst
N; Watson *E*; Benningsen
M/Bavarian State Opera Chorus
and Orch./Keilberth
Ariola-Eurodisc XI 70851R
1970 Adam *S*; Kollo *W*; Evans *B*;
Ridderbusch *P*; Kélémen *K*;
Schreier *D*; Moll *N*; Donath *E*;
Hesse *M*/Dresden State Opera
Chorus, Leipzig Radio Chorus,
Dresden State Orch./Karajan
EMI SLS 957; Angel SEL 3776
1974 (live performance, Bayreuth
Festival) Ridderbusch *S*; Cox *W*;
Hirte *B*; Sotin *P*; Nienstedt *K*;
Stricker *D*; Weikl *N*; Bode *E*;
Reynolds *M*/1974 Bayreuth
Festival Chorus and
Orch./Varviso
Philips 6747 167
1975–6 Bailey *S*; Kollo *W*; Weikl *B*;
Moll *P*; Nienstedt *K*; Dallapozza
D; 'Klumlikboldt' *N*; Bode *E*;
Hamari *M*/Gumpoldskirchner
Spatzen/Vienna State Opera
Chorus, VPO/Solti
Decca D13D5 ④ K13K54;

London OSA 1514 ④5–1512
1976 Fischer-Dieskau *S*; Domingo *W*;
R. Herrmann *B*; Lagger *P*;
Feldhoff *K*; Laubenthal *D*; Von
Halem *N*; Ligendza *E*; C.
Ludwig *M*/German Opera
Chorus and Orch./Jochum
DG 2740 149 ④3378 068

Excerpts

1923–4 Radford *S*, *P*; Davies *W*;
Michael *B*; Halland *K*; Austral
E; Walker, Lemon *M*/Chorus
and Orch./Coates
HMV D745–58
1928 Schorr *S*; Hutt *W*; Schutzendorf
B; List *P*; Joken *D*; Marherr
E/Berlin State Opera Chorus
and Orch./Blech
IGI ⓜ IGI 298
1928 Schorr *S*; Melchior, Laubenthal
W; B. Williams *D*; Schumann,
Ljungberg *E*; Parr
M/Orchs./Barbirolli, Coates,
Blech
EMI ⓜ COLH 137; Angel
ⓜ COLH 137
1936 (Act 3) Nissen *S*; Ralf *W*; Fuchs
B; S. Nilsson *P*; Schellenberg *K*;
Kremer *D*; Teschemacher *E*;
Jung *M*/Dresden State Opera
Orch. Saxon State Orch./Böhm
HMV DB 4562–76; RCA (US)
ⓜ LCT 6002
1950 Grossmann *S*; Hansen *W*; Von
Kovatsky *E*/Prague Opera
Chorus and Orch./Wentzel
Allegro ⓜ 3061–2
1951 Ramms *S*; Nachtigall *W*;
Camphausen *E*/Dresden State
Opera Chorus and
Orch./Schreiber
Royale ⓜ 1429
1951–3 J. Herrmann *S*; Windgassen
W; Holm *D*; Kupper *E*; Töpper
M/Bavarian Radio Chorus and
Orch./Leitner
DB ⓜ LPEM 19047

Der Ring des Nibelungen

ALAN BLYTH

Who would have guessed in 1958, when Decca with much trepidation began its recording of a complete cycle with *Das Rheingold* that by now there would have been eight versions of the cycle, even more if you include the briefly available 1953 Keilberth and 1968 Swarowsky sets. Of course, three of the performances (the two Furtwänglers, and the Knappertsbusch) predate the Solti, but they have only been issued to the general public in recent years.

There is a marked division in these complete sets between those that are a record, in the strictest sense of the word, of performances in the opera house and in one case, Furtwängler's Rome version, of a concert *Ring* for the radio, and those made in the studio. Nobody has put the advantages of live recordings more succinctly and accurately than that eminent Wagnerian, the late Deryck Cooke, writing in *Gramophone*: 'It means that we have a spontaneous, living, public performance from beginning to end, instead of a skilful amalgamation of the best bits of several attempts, a passage at a time, made in the laboratory of the recording studio.' I should add, in fairness to Mr Cooke's memory, that he did not overlook the disadvantages of recording in the theatre – mainly the inability to correct mistakes that may become tiresome on repetition – but in the cases under consideration here, they dwindle into insignificance before the greater reality. It is noteworthy that it is in the Wagnerian field, far more than any other, that live recordings have been favoured. There are three reasons for that phenomenon. Bayreuth is an excellent opera house in which to make records and its performances have a unique aura about them; Furtwängler and Knappertsbusch (probably the two greatest Wagner interpreters of the past fifty years) worked far more successfully in the theatre than out of it; and in the 1970s – another unique occurrence – the English-language, Goodall *Ring* at the Coliseum, through the generosity of the Peter Moores Foundation, was recorded at various performances for posterity.

That recording was spread over five years, but it still has a unity about it not achieved in the Solti set, which was also recorded over a longish period (eight years) during which Solti seemed to alter his view considerably. I propose to discuss these studio sets before turning to those recorded live (I do not intend to waste space on the Swarowsky account, inferior in almost every respect).

As Wolfram Schwinger, the German critic has commented, Karajan's reading (*K*) 'fascinates by virtue of its radiant clarity, its virtuosity of sound, its highly effective contrasts, its *cantabile* quality, and its noble vocal and instrumental beauty', that in comparison with the 'ecstatic dynamism' of Solti (*S*). Both performances were made specifically with the gramophone in mind (although Karajan uses casts that had been assembled for performances at the Salzburg Easter Festival). Karajan uses the resources of the studio, as always, to entrance the ear and fascinate the mind with sensuous sound, bringing forward detail too often lost in the theatre. In *Rheingold* and *Götterdämmerung*, the most successful performances, the requisite Wagnerian energy and epic quality are also there; in the two middle operas, Karajan's chamber-music approach sometimes detracts from the sweep and strength of Wagner's vision, and the sheerly beautiful sound is often bought at the expense of the elemental force that must and does pervade the greatest interpretations. Still, as in *Siegfried*, the hero reaches the mountain-top and awakes Brünnhilde, the glory of Karajan's unrivalled Berlin Philharmonic is almost seductive enough to set aside other considerations.

Solti never neglects the work's grander aspects, and throughout the cycle he makes the *Ring* exciting as a story. Aided by that more-than-lifelike recording technique of John Culshaw's team, with stage details made manifest in the home and movement to match, this is undoubtedly an exciting experience in the home. It is surely the set by which a whole generation of Wagner-lovers will have got to know the work. Those who have enjoyed it – and the immediate thrills are apparent enough – may wonder why other conductors in the theatre or on record approach the vast work with less emphasis on the excitements of the moment or why in other sets the orchestra plays less potently. In other words, Solti and Decca between them have realized the cycle brilliantly on one plane, but others are left unexplored. This is, as Decca once called it, 'Sonicstage' *par excellence*.

Solti's other merits lie in his cast, in spite of the changes that were for one reason or another needed during the course of the cycle's recording (incidentally it was not recorded in sequence, as a glance at the discography will show). Karajan's singers were carefully chosen but they are on the whole less consistent in approach. In *Rheingold*, Solti's team has a definitely veteran feeling about it, except for George London's youthful-sounding Wotan. Set Svanholm's straightforward Loge and Kirsten Flagstad's staid but grandly sung Fricka have by now something of a historic importance to them. Gustav Neidlinger as Alberich is at the height of his powers for Solti: a menacing, confident performance that has set standards not yet equalled, let alone surpassed. He fulfils the view of Alberich as Wotan's alter ego better than any. Karajan has an exaggerated but brilliant Loge in Gerhard Stolze, a good second to Neidlinger in Zoltan Kelemen as Alberich, a Wotan in Fischer-Dieskau who matches his conductor in intelligence and subtlety but lacks vocal heft, a characterful Fricka in Josephine Veasey, the best of Fasolts in Martti Talvela (so moving in his farewell to Freia) and a winning, firm trio of Rhinemaidens.

In *Walküre*, Solti again fields a much more experienced team than Karajan, and this time it is an undoubted advantage. Régine Crespin's Brünnhilde (*K*) has marvellous moments – 'Zu lieben was du liebst' is just one, so heartfelt – but she is no match for Birgit Nilsson (*S*), who encompasses the characters expression of sympathy, grief, passion and finally humility – not with ideal individuality or warmth but with unfailing response to Wagner's vocal demands. Her Wotan is the incomparable Hans Hotter, no more in his late 50s the Titan he was for Knappertsbusch (see below) but still showing an unrivalled authority and subtlety. To passage after passage he brings a Lieder-singer's attention to meaning and detail. The depth of the god's anguish, misery, bitterness, love is expressed throughout this great portrayal, a command that Thomas Stewart (*K*), for all his intelligence, cannot match. Christa Ludwig (*S*) is an admirable Fricka and with Hotter the Wotan–Fricka scene goes magnificently – 'Deine ew'gen Gattin' rolls off her tongue in dignified fashion – but she does not, in this part, sing with the assurance of Veasey (*K*).

For Solti, Crespin has reverted to Sieglinde, not as personal in expression as some and too careful in the love duet but rising finely to 'O hehrstes Wunder'. She is partnered by James King, virile of voice, pedestrian in interpretation. Jon Vickers's Siegmund (*K*) is as intense and committed as one might expect but also too artificial in some of his effects. Gundula Janowitz, his Sieglinde, is unexpectedly rapturous, nowhere more so than in the phrases 'Doch nein! Ich hörte sie neulich'. Karajan's reading, for all its restraint, has many moments such as these of vocal revelation. No wonder singers adore him so. Gottlob Frick's Hunding (*S*) is dark and dour, Talvela's (*K*) hardly less so.

The Solti *Siegfried* is again more obviously histrionic, big-scaled. In the title role, Wolfgang Windgassen, as we know now a late replacement for Ernst Kozub, gives one of the performances of his life: his tone may tend to dryness, but his deeply felt, thoughtful assumption showing disgust with Mime, impetuosity when sword-forging, eloquence in the forest, loneliness (wonderful passage) after killing Mime and in 'Selige Öde' are nowhere matched by Jess Thomas (*K*); for all his clear enunciation and clean tone, his singing is anything but heroic. In the final scene he is no match for Helga Dernesch's radiant Brünnhilde. At 'wild wütende Weib' she sounds just like that. 'Ewig war ich' is intimate and sensitive. Nilsson (*S*) is just as impressive, taking 'Heil dir, Sonne' in one breath in goddess-like voice, and melting into womanly vulnerability at 'Dort seh' ich Grane'.

Hotter (S) wobbles in Act 1, but a single phrase 'und dass doch das liebeste ihm lebt?', so expressive, so authoritative, makes one forgive the apparent vocal decline. Stewart does not equal him here, or in the world-weariness of his final appearance. Stolze's more natural, less exaggerated Mime (K) is much preferable to his other, cackling self (S). There is not much to choose between the adequate but, Neidlinger's Alberich apart, not extraordinary interpreters of the smaller parts.

In *Götterdämmerung*, Dernesch as Brünnhilde (K) – obviously over-stretched by the role but often singing with noble beauty – is surpassed by Nilsson, but for all her heroic stature there is more in the role than she finds (see below). Windgassen is again appreciable but here he is not a match for his younger self in other sets. Helge Brilioth (K) is a scrupulous musician with the right voice but only in Act 3 do his interpretative gifts show themselves. As Waltraute, Ludwig is too much the tragedy queen in both sets, but especially for Solti. The vocal competence is never in question. Frick's assurance as Hagen (S) is vitiated only by melodramatic touches, but he certainly chills the marrow more than the almost world-weary Karl Ridderbusch (K). Fischer-Dieskau's Gunther (S) would surely have outwitted the most wily gnome's son. More conventional vacillation and craven weakness is to be heard from Stewart (K). Claire Watson is a febrile Gutrune (S), Janowitz too cool. Adequate Norns in both sets, superb Rhinemaidens in Karajan's.

Before considering the most searching albeit very different interpretations, I will deal with the Karl Böhm/Bayreuth performance, not to dismiss it but to place it perhaps one or two rungs lower than those discussed below. It must be listened to, 'viewed' is perhaps the *mot juste*, in relation to the Wieland Wagner production of the time, his second attempt at staging the great work of his grandfather. With the help of the copious illustrations in the accompanying booklet in its most recent manifestation, it is possible to transport oneself back to Bayreuth, 1966–7, when the recordings were made.

Böhm's interpretation, as can be confirmed in the 1969 Bayreuth listings of various conductors' times, is on the fast side (though not as fast as Boulez more recently). That can come as a relief after too many slow performances (for example Goodall's), and the quicker tempi, particularly in the context of a live recordings, make for a more direct, dramatic reading. Certain passages that can seem portentous, even dull, in the wrong hands at a slower pace, are gathered together here into the sweep of a convincing interpretation – the 'colourful, pulsating, *al fresco* style', as Schwinger put it. Wotan's Narration in *Walküre*, the opening of *Siegfried*, Act 2, the end of that act, the Norns' and transformation scenes in *Götterdämmerung* are instances of his dynamic approach, while the surge of the *Walküre* love music or the different ardour of the *Siegfried* finale find in Böhm an admirably inspiriting conductor.

By and large he is extraordinarily faithful to the composer's markings.

So often other conductors ignore Wagner's injunction for movement, 'sehr belebt', or else make a *rallentando* before it is required. Böhm is always scrupulous in their observation. If all that suggests something of the *Kapellmeister* approach, it would be right. In certain grave passages, as the introduction to the *Todesverkündigung*, where rests are liberally asked for by Wagner, Böhm ignores them, and at his pace the Funeral March is not the noble tragedy it should be. Still, the interpretation is, on the whole, valid in its own right and an often welcome antidote to more ponderous ones. The Bayreuth orchestra, here a wonderful instrument, finds an honest, natural relationship with the singers not evident, or sought, on the studio-made sets.

Böhm's cast is not uniformly excellent, but Nilsson's tireless Brünnhilde, not surprisingly more involved than for Solti and showing a keen understanding of the character's development, together with Windgassen's Siegfried, unfailingly musical and miraculously fresh, except at the end of *Siegfried*, are the summation of these two artists' Wagnerian work (their Bayreuth *Tristan* excepted). James King's Siegmund, heard to greater advantage than for Solti, is possibly his best performance in any part on record: he benefits greatly from Böhm's speeds. So does Theo Adam as Wotan, taking many passages in a single breath that Wagner surely intended to be sung that way but which become impossible to manage thus at a slower pace. Adam's interpretation is at times prosaic, not sufficiently inward or anguished, yet he is a straightforward singer in sympathy with Böhm's approach.

Several other Bayreuth stalwarts of the 1960s are represented here. Leonie Rysanek, not in best voice, is still an appreciable Sieglinde, expressive and, above the stave, thrillingly intense. Neidlinger's Alberich is as strongly sung and characterized as ever. The three veteran basses, Kurt Böhme (a sinister, lugubrious Dragon), Josef Greindl (though now hard-pressed as Hagen), and Gerd Nienstedt are a formidable trio in their various incarnations. The young Talvela is a moving Fasolt once again.

Rheingold is weakened by Windgassen's underplayed Loge, but has Erwin Wohlfahrt's exemplary Mime, also an asset in *Siegfried*. The weaker ladies of the cycle are well represented by Anja Silja and Ludmila Dvorakova. Vera Soukupová's fruity Erda, Anneliese Burmeister's blustery Fricka are less admirable, Martha Mödl, once a great Brünnhilde (see below), gives a Waltraute full of vocal insights but requires indulgence for tonal unevenness. Among the Valkyries, nobody could miss the potential (since fulfilled) of Dernesch or Danica Mastilovic but others sound overdue for retirement from hunting duties.

The Knappertsbusch *Ring* of a decade earlier, at last available, is at the opposite end of interpretation from Böhm, grand and conceptual where Böhm's is lyrical and impulsive. To me it is a magisterial and central achievement, delivered in long, lucid paragraphs, a feeling not always evident in encountering individual episodes. Although by Bayreuth timings, Knappertsbusch's are slow, they are considerably faster than Goodall's, because Knappertsbusch, unlike his English disciple, knew just when not to dally. Then passages such as Siegfried's Rhine Journey have a joyous energy not found in the English conductor's reading. Knappertsbusch also knew better than any how to conjure up a sonorous glow from the Bayreuth acoustic. That, and so much else, makes his reading a deeply spiritual journey almost on a par with his *Parsifal*. Knappertsbusch eschews obvious beauty of detail or momentary revelations, but I believe that what is sacrificed in that respect is amply compensated for by the profundity of the whole.

The singers are those most closely associated with Bayreuth in the 1950s, one of its greatest eras. The cast is headed by Hotter's again authoritative, introspective Wotan, offering unforgettable and influential insights not equalled by his often imitative successors. At times, during the first part of *Walküre*, Act 3, and in the Siegfried colloquy with Erda, the voice becomes unsteady and 'woofy' in that peculiarly Hotter manner, but for the rest the reading has a potent inevitability of utterance. Here Hotter is caught in his prime for future generations to wonder at (I hope). Nowhere is that more so than in the dialogue with Fricka, the movingly sustained monologue and, of course, in the tender, paternal farewell. In *Rheingold* and in the second act of *Siegfried*, his encounters with Neidlinger's Alberich, here at the peak of his vocal powers, are the epitome of intelligent Wagnerian interpretation, subtly supported by the conductor.

Varnay's interesting Brünnhilde is also here preserved as a whole for posterity. The vocal mechanism is, as always with this singer, not faultless, but the sense of a total being involved is matched only by her contemporary, Mödl, for Furtwängler, and her singing is not technically at ease either. Perhaps a lack of perfection in tonal production induces greater thought about verbal meaning. Listen to how Varnay unforgettably inflects 'Siegfried kennt mich nicht' in Act 2 of *Götterdämmerung*, the phrase and enunciation compounded of distress, anger and shock, or the incredulity of 'Bist du von Sinnen?' in the conversation with sister Waltraute. The finale of *Siegfried*, though impressive, does not have Nilsson's gleam. Nilsson herself is here engaged as Sieglinde, eager, youthful but not ideally warm. Almost needless to say, she is magnificent in 'O hehrstes Wunder'. Her Siegmund is the highly intelligent Ramon Vinay, not very lyrical, but intense and articulate in declamatory passages.

In *Rheingold*, we meet the veteran Ludwig Suthaus (successively Siegmund and Siegfried for Furtwängler – see below) as a musically free, occasionally unsteady and consistently vivid Loge, Paul Kuen as a keen-edged, occasionally exaggerating Mime (still more detailed in *Siegfried*), Elisabeth Grümmer's ideally life-giving Freia, Josef Traxel's beautifully sung Froh, Arnold van Mill's lucid, eloquent Fasolt. Greindl, here as

Fafner, even more as Hunding and Hagen, uses his dark-hued, sinister bass to telling effect. Georgine von Milinkovic is a conventional Fricka. Maria von Ilosvay (Covent Garden's Fricka in the 1950s) is a moderate Erda, an unaffected, urgent Waltraute. She is also a grave Norn; so is Nilsson – casting from strength indeed. Hermann Uhde's Gunther is an unsurpassed study of weakness, sung in that paradoxically commanding way of his.

What of the hero? Bernd Aldenhoff, then near the end of his career, stepped in at short notice (for an indisposed Windgassen) for Siegfried. He still produces authentic *Heldentenor* sounds, and suggests more intelligence than he was given credit for. Some intrusive vibrato and the occasional inaccurate bray can be excused in a portrayal that produces the youthful brashness of the character, but he displays little of the poetry of Windgassen, who returns for *Götterdämmerung* to display his freshest singing in any cycle. One oddity: Knappertsbusch cuts the first verse of the second forging song in the first act of *Siegfried*.

Furtwängler must wait in the wings no longer. Legends when closely investigated do not always live up to their repute; not so with Furtwängler's performances of the *Ring* at La Scala in March and April 1950. It is emphatically not for the hi-fi enthusiast, nor even for those who may just about accept Knappertsbusch's very adequate mono sound, nor for those who require technical perfection in musical matters. Here we are offered an unvarnished look at the truth. There are audience coughs to contend with (the Italians sometimes seem unforgivably inattentive to the aural feast laid out before them), tape joins are abrupt, recorded levels alter, prompts are audible, side changes are rudely done, entries are sometimes muffed. If you can overcome and forget these human and mechanical fallibilities, you will be rewarded by a reading of a lifetime from a great conductor at the peak of his power. The perfectly adequate Rome concert-hall performance is surpassed in almost every way by this incandescent account, which holds one in thrall right from the announcement of the gold motif in the opening scene of *Rheingold* through to the transfiguring nobility of the Immolation. That incandesence, and Furtwängler's command of Wagner's *unendliche Melodie*, is heard at its most obvious and potent throughout the first act and final scene of *Walküre*. They are enhanced by the refulgent sound he could draw from any orchestra. The La Scala players, much more accomplished than their Rome brethren, enable Furtwängler to knit together scenes with unerring breadth at quicker speeds than those in either his Rome performance or his 1936 Bayreuth *Ring*.

His approach, at once romantic and tragic, elemental and profound was characterized thus by Deryck Cooke in discussing the Rome records: 'His ability to make the music surge, or seethe, or melt, so that one has left the world of semiquavers altogether' – though no one was in fact more adept than this conductor at making Wagner's semiquavers sound – 'and

is swept up in a great spiritual experience.' I quote Cooke lest you think
I am too glowing in my praise. Here is another witness, Alec Roberstson,
actually writing about the 1953 studio *Walküre*: 'He carries all Wagner's
directions in his head and visualizes each scene in the composer's terms.'

What is true on those sets is even more so in this opera-house recording.
You can hear it in the upsurge of glowing sound after Freia is saved,
in the 'sehr ausdrucksvoll' passage which is just that before the Wälsungs
arrive in Act 2 of *Walküre*, in the whole of the Waltraute scene in
Götterdämmerung, and of course in the Funeral March and Immolation
that crown the whole edifice magnificently, solemnly. Wagner's immense
peroration has never been at once so spaciously, so thrillingly realized.
In this the conductor inspires Flagstad to her greatest achievement. In
any case this set at last preserves her complete Brünnhilde for posterity.
Mödl and Varnay may extract more intense responses from the text and
so convey more of Brünnhilde's anguish and ecstasy, but neither they nor
even Nilsson could equal the vocal amplitude and lyrical beauty of
Flagstad's singing enshrined here. It is exemplified in the passage 'Der
diese Wonne' in the last scene of *Walküre* and 'O, Siegfried! Dein war
ich von je' in the Siegfried love duet. On this and other evidence.
Furtwängler was able to draw from Flagstad a readier response to words,
a more subtly expressive manner of phrasing than others.

Most of the other roles are here taken by German-speaking singers,
which leads to the inestimable advantage of clear, idiomatic enunciation.
But there is more to it than that. Most of the artists were admired by
the conductor, who obviously admired singers who relished their words
and particularly their consonants. In *Rheingold*, for instance, the veteran
Joachim Sattler, whose career stretched back well before the war, has not
the most ingratiating voice, but his intelligent, accurate delivery precisely
fits the description of the character as the *Ring*'s sole intellectual. Those
used to Neidlinger's dominating Alberich may be disconcerted by
Pernerstorfer's less powerful portrayal, but again he sings the notes as
written without anything of the Bayreuth bark to his delivery. Elisabeth
Höngen, not the steadiest of Frickas, is a model of clear utterance,
moving too at 'Wotan Gemahl'. Ludwig Weber is another singer who
cossets his words and colours his tone in presenting a sympathetic Fasolt.
Ferdinand Frantz's Wotan, prosaic on the Rome set, is here enlivened
by being heard, as it were, in the theatre. In a sense the whole cast
support what is happening in the orchestra; the piercing semiquavers as
the gold is stolen, the significant solemnity of the horns, English and
French, as love is abjured, the bleak thundering of the Giants' motif, the
strings' expansion in Loge's pictorial narration, the sheer evil energy of
Alberich's exultation in the third scene.

In *Walküre*, Günther Treptow is almost the Siegmund of one's dreams,
a really lyrical *Heldentenor* who also possesses an intelligent mind and
an inspired soul so that he is forgiven one or two fluffs as he gets carried

away by the excitement of the moment. Hilde Konetzni, in much surer form than three years later, is an eager partner for this Siegmund. The heightened responses to the last scene of Act 1 could not possibly be kindled in the studio. Act 2 is less remarkable (Wotan's narration also has a sizeable cut), a moving *Todesverkündigung* from two great singers apart, but in Act 3 a whizzing Ride leads into a splendid final scene, furious Wotan being turned to love by Flagstad's eloquence – and who would not be?

Siegfried was not supposed to be Furtwängler's opera, but here he does marvels with all the voices-of-nature music and with the driving energy of the forging music. The recollection of the Wälsungs' woe in Act 1 could hardly be more moving, the closing duet more ecstatic. The Siegfried is the youthful-sounding, heroic Set Svanholm, so poetic in the Forest Murmurs. Inevitably he tires somewhat towards the end of the long role. Peter Markworth is not such an accurate or precise Mime as Julius Patzak, who sings in the Rome set, but his deft characterization avoids Stolze's exaggerations. Josef Herrmann, a *Heldenbariton* I much admire (see below), is impressive not only for his authentic, unforced tone but also for his legato and superb diction. Höngen's Erda is a considerable achievement, but her best performance in the cycle comes as Waltraute in *Götterdämmerung*, remarkable for its urgency and grave tones.

This final opera is distinguished by Max Lorenz's eager, young-sounding (remarkable when you consider he was almost fifty at the time) Siegfried. There are pages when he is too free with his music, but the touch of wonder in his third-act narrative is not be found elsewhere in the complete sets. Weber's plausible, but roughly sung Hagen, Herrmann's virile Gunther (is he too good for the part?), Konetzni's comely Gutrune and more-than-adequate Norns second Flagstad's glorious Brünnhilde. The men of the Scala Chorus suggest raw energy without resorting to coarseness.

The Rome reading is a lesser achievement only when set beside the Scala one; in essence all the positive Furtwängler qualities are to be heard without the full intensity of the opera-house experience, but again there is no doubt that one of the world's great epics is being unfolded before us in a broad yet vigorous performance. Many of the cast are the same as in the Scala-Furtwängler or in other versions, but there are some notable assumptions not yet mentioned or yet encountered, not least Sena Jurinac's lovely Woglinde, and Gutrune and Third Norn, Suthaus's vivid and fine-sounding Siegfried, Rita Streich's ideal Woodbird. Patzak's Mime, as I have already implied, is the work of a scrupulously musical artist – for once sung as Wagner wrote it and the effect is arresting. Alfred Poell is, like Herrmann, an upright Gunther. Margarete Klose, another favourite of this conductor, is a worried Waltraute partnered by Martha Mödl's Brünnhilde, whose committed interpretation, warm, womanly portrayal and uncanny way of judging the precise colouring of words and tone – try 'Ruhe du Gott' – are singular to her.

She connects us with the 1953 Keilberth recording, where she is perhaps even more searching. I do not propose discussing this set in detail; it has never had more than a very limited circulation (one of the singers forced Allegro to withdraw it) and, in any case, it is surpassed in different respects by one or other of the remaining issues. However, I should note Erich Witte's pointed Loge, Uhde's doubling of Donner and Gunther (one artist sang both parts in the first-ever cycle), Hotter's Wotan in splendid form (and here partnered for the only time on disc by Mödl in *Walküre*, a rewarding combination), and Keilberth's generally straight-forward, convincing interpretation. Windgassen's Siegfried is not as full of character as it was to become.

No, if you cannot tolerate the bad sound in Furtwängler's Scala performance or the indifferent acoustic (and poor playing of the orchestra) in the Rome set, you may want to turn to the Goodall/ENO set. Here, as I have suggested, we have the ensemble performance incarnate under the direction of a true Wagnerian. No matter that he adds some ten minutes to the timing of each act as compared with the slowest Bayreuth conductor; he justifies the breadth of his approach, particularly in the closing work of the tetralogy, by the tragic grandeur and long-drawn phraseology, a total view of the drama that does not exclude care for the *Hauptstimmen* and for instrumental detail. The growth is organic and natural, its effect cumulative. It does not carry you forward irresistibly, inevitably, as does Furtwängler's, but at the end of the journey there is no doubt that the experience has been worthy of the concept.

His singers, as is generally known, have studied their roles in the most meticulous and arduous manner with Goodall, thus enabling them to phrase in the broad way he requires and at the same time encompassing Andrew Porter's lucid translation, so faithfully wedded to Wagner's notes and, where possible, to the verbal emphasis of the German. His cast is headed by Rita Hunter's gleaming yet expressive Brünnhilde sung with unflagging consistency of tone and sensitivity, down to the exact execution of the *gruppetti* in the prologue to *Twilight of the Gods*, as it should be called in this context. Indeed it is in that opera that the heroic proportions of her reading can best be heard: in the two preceding operas she seems just marginally less individual and assured in her portrayal.

In the last two operas she is partnered as ever by Alberto Remedios's ever-fresh, eager Siegfried. Others have made individual episodes more memorable, produced a more full-blooded tone (Melchior certainly, see below), but Remedios's achievement, above all his innate musicality, assure him of a place among the great ones. Norman Bailey's Wotan shows a similar consistency and understanding, only some grittiness in his tone and an occasional reserve of emotion detracting from whole-hearted enjoyment of an articulate assumption. Derek Hammond-Stroud's biting, keenly enunciated Alberich, Emile Belcourt's subtle, witty Loge, Katherine

Pring's able Fricka adorn *Rhinegold*. The *Valkyrie* sees Remedios as a lyrical Siegmund and Margaret Curphey as an involved Sieglinde, but here, as in the first act of *Siegfried* (where Gregory Dempsey's Mime conveys character without caricature), there is want of energy, a forward-moving pulse that is inclined to vitiate the physical energy and fire Wagner surely wanted. The bass roles are all well taken, but it would be idle to deny, and chauvinistic to suggest, that for all its welcome ensemble quality, these performances are at all points the answer to a Wagnerian's dream that they have been considered in some quarters. In a highly competitive field, and with the overwhelmingly great records of individual scenes still to be discussed, its merits fall into perspective. They *are* remarkable but not unique.

DAS RHEINGOLD

There are no 'official', separate recordings of *Rheingold*. Of pirated records, I have heard only the 1937 Met 'off-the-air' performance. This is labelled 'April 3'. It seems there was no *Rheingold* in New York that afternoon; but there was a matinée performance in Boston. The sound is as good as one can expect from this source. The set preserves for us Friedrich Schorr's complete *Rheingold* Wotan, no longer what it was a few years earlier (the upper register has become hollow), but definitive enough in all conscience, full of interesting detail and still sung in that firm, authoritative manner well-known from his 'commercial' discs. There is also a subtle, well-articulated Loge from René Maison, when he remembers to come in on time. Eduard Habich's Alberich is past its best, but Norman Cordon's Fasolt is a memorable performance. Another veteran, Emanuel List, is a surly Fafner. Karin Branzell's Fricka is surprisingly uninteresting, and Doris Doe as Erda is not in fresh voice, but dispenses her words of wisdom with considerable force. The conductor is the veteran Artur Bodansky.

Apart from Stokowski's various 'pottings', which I have chosen to ignore, the only substantial LP highlights come from no lesser a baton than that of Rudolf Kempe, sadly the sole part of his *Ring* in existence. It graphically confirms all that his admirers say about his performance, its unforced lyricism and unwavering line. Here we have the whole of the first scene following the Prelude with excellent Rhinemaidens (Otto, Muszely, S. Wagner) and Benno Kusche's lustful, powerful Alberich, frightening in Alberich's Curse on side two. Ruth Siewert's Erda (similar to that of Anne Collins in Goodall's set) and Frantz's Wotan do not differ from their performances for Böhm and Furtwängler respectively. Helmut Melchert gives us a brief reminder of his clear Loge. There is a spacious recording to match the interpretation.

In the 78 era, Wagnerites had really to go to the opera house to gain any idea of the continuity of the work. One acoustic record (D 677) has

Robert Radford as Alberich stealing the gold, then briefly impersonating Wotan before his departure to Nibelheim (with Edith Furmedge as his Fricka), before reappearing briefly as Alberich. The bars included are listed by Vivian Liff in the ENO's booklet discography of records of the *Ring* in English (the translation is quaint). Albert Coates conducted as he did in the much more vivid electric record of similar passages (D 1546) with Arthur Fear now as Alberich; Trenton, Suddaby and Nellie Walker are the Rhinemaidens. Walter Widdop turns up briefly as Loge on side two.

Specific passages on 78s tell us, as usual, much about the style and character of certain revered singers of the past although, except in the case of several Erdas and of Schorr as Wotan, modern singers do not have a great deal to fear from the comparisons. None of the Rhinemaiden trios seems to me, for instance, to surpass those on the Karajan set and dim recording does not help to distinguish the voices. That by Elise von Catopol, Else Knepel and Grete Manke (Parlo. E 10432), however, contains some lovely and steady singing, and Josefine von Artner, Maria Knüpfer and Ottilie Metzger (44406; 1C 181–30669) do give us the flavour of an early generation of Wagner singers, as it was recorded in 1902.

In 'Wotan's Awakening', the Berlin singer Hermann Bachmann (4–42020; 1C 181–30669), who was Wotan at Bayreuth in 1896, displays a firm, resonant *Heldenbariton*. I have not heard versions by Theodor Bertram or Anton Van Rooy, but I have encountered them in 'Abendlich strahlt' (see below). Paul Knüpfer (excellent) and Fritz Koerfer (poor) bring the Giants on to the scene on an ancient Monarch disc (044244). Loge's so-called Narration has several notable exponents, of whom Richard Schubert (Poly. 65615; LV 168) is the best. His fresh, sweet tone is a constant pleasure and his diction is immaculate. A famous Siegfried too, he is described by Prawy in his Vienna Opera book as 'a heroic tenor with beautiful legs'! The voice evidently matched them. Erik Schmedes, another Siegfried 'slumming it' as Loge, is also keen and characterful (3–42945) but lacks Schubert's lyrical quality at 'so weit Leben und Weben'. A modern Siegfried assuming Loge's garb is Jess Thomas (SLPEM 136387), prosaically, I regret to say. Erich Zimmermann, heard at Bayreuth during the last war (Acanta 22 863–0), is expressive, but can no longer sustain a legato.

The Berlin tenor Walter Kirchhoff recorded the 'chunk' twice, backing it on the first occasion, with 'Über Stock und Stein', describing the Gods' decline when they lack Freia's apples, but without their contributions. He brings a good deal of variety to his declamation, broadening out where Wagner asks for that and turning nasty at mention of Alberich. His acoustic Polydor (15849) is less effortful than the Pathé electric (X 7197), recorded in Paris in 1929 at the time of the *Ring* performances there under Van Hoesslin, who conducts on this record. The Rhinemaidens of those performances are heard on the reverse; they are a poor trio. Karl

Erb shows why he went on to become such a great Lieder singer on his version (Od. 76519). His is a chilling, mercurial Loge, and he demonstrates just how Wagner always finds the right note values for the expression of character and concept.

Those noted Wagnerian tenors Karl Jörn (0424767; CO 354) and Heinrich Hensel (042259/60; CO 339), both adding 'Über Stock und Stein', bring ingratiatingly clear tone to their unexaggerated versions. They, like Schubert, indicate the high standard of enunciation prevalent in the first decades of the century. So does the Bayreuth Loge Otto Briesemeister (Od. 64787/8). Fritz Soot (not issued on 78; LV 123), recorded in 1922, is just as intelligent in delivery but vocally less pleasing.

Early versions of Alberich's Curse include those by Max Dawison (Bayreuth, 1904), Robert von Scheidt (who also did the earlier passage 'Die in linde Lüfte weh'n', both in 1904), Alexander Haydter, and Desider Zador, who sang the part at Covent Garden in 1905 (4–42213) – he has a high old time with intrusive cackles and so on, daemonic in its melodramatic way. Otto Goritz (Victor 64203) who sang Wagner roles at the Met for many years before 1914, is articulate and menacing, and refrains from barking.

Erda's warning, 'Weiche, Wotan, weiche' has, naturally, attracted rich-voiced contraltos since the dawn of recording. The list is headed by Ernestine Schumann-Heink, that most formidable of singers. On her 1907 G&T (043090; VIC 1409), she displays to perfection one school of singing the passage. Here is the dominating earth-mother to the life. Urgency is conveyed by the crisp consonants and rock-like chest register, a richness of tone carried right up to the top of her compass. Unlike most Erdas in this passage, she has a Wotan to partner her: the mellow Herbert Witherspoon. Margarete Arndt-Ober also has a Wotan in one of her two versions (Victor 74396) but I have heard only the other (043230; CO 305). She represents a different, more subtle type of Erda, a distant, nebulous creature of any and no time. The text is less pointedly uttered, but the smooth, marvellously unfettered flow of tone seems to me near-ideal for the part; so is the steadiness, seldom encountered nowadays. The singer was a notable Verdian as well as a great Wagnerian. Ottilie Metzger (Od. 51627; CO 310), Bayreuth's Erda before the first world war, and London's second Clytemnestra and first Herodias in 1910, is another singer of uncompromising steadiness and real tone. Her life ended tragically at Auschwitz in 1942, as did those of many of her Jewish colleagues.

A little less authoritative but more caressing with her effortless stream of plush tone is Margarethe Matzenauer (043128). I much prefer her to her Metropolitan colleague, the hooty Edyth Walker (043093), although the latter's grand style is to be admired. All these singers are generous with their portamento; so is my favourite Erda, Sigrid Onegin (Poly. 72692; DG 2721 109), who is the withdrawn, dignified earth-goddess to the life. The voice is sumptuous, round and warm; the movement from note to note impeccable. Fruitier and weightier in the same generation is Emmi Leisner (Poly. 66737); a more lyrical (and quicker) Erda of the 1930s is the Swedish mezzo Karin Branzell (Poly. 66853; LV 47), a Bayreuth Waltraute and Fricka in the early 1930s. Maria Olszewska is by these standards a little awkward in her vocalization and her consonants are indifferent. She prolongs the extract beyond Wotan's second entry (Poly. 72785).

Kerstin Thorborg, preferable as Fricka, sounds too worldly, too beseeching for Erda, but the confidence of her singing is not to be denied (Victor 17221; LV 209). Similar remarks apply to Blanche Thebom, who is none the less steady and impressive (Victor 11–9795). Any of the ladies so far mentioned would grace a performance today when their particular type of voice seems in abeyance. Neither of their successors, the central European mezzos Erzsébet Komlóssy (with András Faragó as Wotan (Qualiton SLPX 11329) or Vera Soukupová (Supra. SUA ST 50644), who also sings Erda for Böhm, is in the same class.

A fascinating old disc (044215–6) has what is called 'Ruf des Donner', roughly sung by Koerfer; it closes with a more attractive contribution from the Froh of Kurt Sommer. On the reverse he and Koerfer turn into Wotan and Loge for what is called 'Schlussgesang der Rheintöchter'. The good trio of Rhinemaidens on this 1910 Berlin disc are Adelaide Adrejewa, Ida von Scheele-Müller and Arndt-Ober. Hans Breuer, who was Bayreuth's only Mime from 1896 to 1914, recorded the passage 'Wer hälfe mir' in 1904 with piano (2–42922; 1C 181–30669). This is an interesting historical document, but his singing is lachrymose and hardly accurate.

And so to 'Abendlich strahlt', Wotan's greeting to his new abode. That was grist to the mill of any Wagnerian bass-baritone in the days of 78s. van Rooy recorded it twice. The cello-like, grainy quality of his tone can be heard on both the ten-inch (2–2701) and twelve-inch (042168) of 1902 and 1908 respectively. Oddly enough the earlier recording is somewhat better; less remarkably it shows van Rooy in fuller, richer voice but the later version with the top F perfectly taken is not to be dismissed and it is certainly easier to come by. Theodor Bertram, who alternated as Wotan with van Rooy in the 1901–2 Bayreuth Festivals, is inclined to bark (2–42917; CO 316), but his huge voice, more bass than baritone, has a certain old-fashioned richness and glory. His career ended tragically and prematurely when he took to the bottle after the death of his wife. Fritz Feinhals's tone is much lighter with little resonance to it, and his version (4–42469) lacks steadiness. Michael Bohnen's version (Poly. 65567; LV 12) is notable for the singer's incredible breath control – 'In des Morgens ... herrenlos' taken without a break – and its long, effortless line, while Alfred Jerger (Parlo. 9139; LV 92) concentrates, almost to a fault, on individual words in his detailed, too drawn-out rendering. Wilhelm Rode (Poly. 66782) slides about horribly and is rightly described by John Steane in *The Grand Tradition* as 'lugubrious and effortful'. Marcel Journet draws a fine line but sounds uninvolved; he was a famous French Wagnerian. David Ward, in the Covent Garden Anniversary Album (SET 393), is as warm-voiced as ever, but slack in phrasing.

Four versions stand out as exceptional. Hermann Bachmann (4–42021), full, smooth tone and easy delivery; Rudolf Bockelmann (Telef. SK 1342) for his pure lyricism and his upright *Heldenbariton* sound; Hans Hermann Nissen, though forced to hurry on his ten-inch disc (DA 4460; LV 58), for his lovely, rounded tone and authoritative manner; and, of course Friedrich Schorr (D 1319). To quote Steane again: 'He ... performs that peculiar kind of disservice of which all great artists are guilty, for no one who carries in his head Schorr's singing of "Abendlich strahlt" ... is likely to hear another performance without some yearning to get back to the gramophone and listen again to Schorr.' His singing is remarkable for its majesty, inevitability and command. The other side of that disc takes us to the end of the opera under Leo Blech's splendid baton and with Waldemar Henke as Loge and Genia Guszalewicz as Fricka (their names do not appear on the record, but they have been thus identified). I have not heard the 1902 Leopold Demuth (42888), Clarence Whitehill's admired version (042197), but Josef von Manowarda, from the next generation (Poly. 62345; LV 175), famous at Vienna and Bayreuth, suggests a sympathetic presence though not a very steady voice.

Finally, an oddity: two Danish 78s (DB 5206–7), sung in Danish with piano, and including a spoken introduction, presumably announcing the singers, and telling us that these were the artists of the first Danish production. The discs were made in 1936–7 and include the Rhinemaidens' trio, Alberich's Curse, the Giants' entrance from Freia's contribution. The singing is very moderate indeed.

DIE WALKÜRE

Of the two complete recordings issued commercially, the one conducted by Furtwängler preserves his interpretation in more amenable sound, and the Vienna Philharmonic provides orchestral playing far superior to anything heard on the Scala or Rome performances. Here you can hear, more than anywhere else, how his peculiar magic in Wagner emanates from his consistent treatment of the cellos and basses, which seem to take the great work almost imperceptibly forward from beginning to end. Nowhere is the slow unfolding of the various Sieglinde–Siegmund motives and their awakening passion so deeply, timelessly expressed as by Furtwängler and the Vienna Philharmonic. Rysanek and Suthaus begin the first act poorly, end it superbly. Rysanek's intrusive unsteadiness clears in time for 'Du bist der Lenz'; from then on she is the inspired artist she so often seems to be on stage. In Act 3 her voice opens out powerfully at the top of its range. Suthaus hardly sounds the exhausted warrior when he first enters, but as the first act progresses one begins to admire more and more his authentic treatment of the text, his true *Heldentenor* voice. His 'Winterstürme' is even more poetic than Vickers's, and his 'Zauberfest' more touching than any other in complete sets; but his commitment to the part sometimes leads him to be careless of note values. His interpretation, like those of so many singers brought up, vocally speaking, before the war, is as much dominated by a feeling for the text as for the music, and these touches of individuality are most welcome in a stereotyped age.

Frantz is as ever a reliable Wotan and his clear diction is always an asset; but he seldom sounds moved by what he is singing, and he turns down Wagner's frequent request for a muffled – *gedämpft* – voice in the narration. Nor is there anything of Hotter's sense of shock at 'Das Schwert' in the scene with Fricka, here sung by Margarete Klose with immense authority but declining vocal strength. Nobody understood the requirements of a Brünnhilde better than Mödl, but here her effortful vocal production and broken line is more troublesome than in the Rome performance. Both she and Frantz rise to the heights, however, in the final scene, aided by Furtwängler's magisterial direction.

The Leinsdorf recording has been underrated. His Wagnerian experience goes back to Toscanini's Salzburg *Meistersinger* and to performances in the late 1930s at the Metropolitan (see below) where he 'under-studied' Bodanzky. He paces the work firmly, though he finds it difficult to relax. Compared with, say, Karajan, this is the grand, epic, traditional reading as against an introverted, scaled-down modern one. There is tremendous excitement in Leinsdorf's treatment of the departure of Wotan after he has given Brünnhilde her marching orders in Act 2, in the fight at the end of the act, in the Valkyries' ride; passion, too, in his reading, as in the eloquent orchestral passage following Wotan's farewell. The recording is at times over-resonant, and the wind machine in Act 1 is unnecessary. The British Valkyries are a fine brood, and the LSO play well, though they do not come into the Berlin or Vienna Philharmonic class.

Vickers's ardent Siegmund and Gré Brouwenstijn's eloquent Sieglinde help to make Act 1 the outstanding part of this performance. Brouwenstijn handles 'Der Männer Sippe' more imaginatively than any soprano on record in a complete recording, other than Lotte Lehmann, and if her tone – particularly in Acts 2 and 3 – is not as fresh-sounding as one might ideally wish, one is consoled by her superb diction. Ward's voice is too soft-grained for Hunding, and Rita Gorr is rough and characterless as Fricka. London is a powerful, but unsubtle Wotan, so that 'So nimm meinen Segen' comes off splendidly but the earlier part of the long narration sounds matter-of-fact lacking Hotter's insight and verbal mastery, but London's direct, no-nonsense approach to the role accords well with Leinsdorf's.

Nilsson's Brünnhilde is inferior to her later performances. The extraordinary increase in her understanding of the part by the time she recorded it for Solti and Böhm is most noticeable in the *Todesverkündigung* and in the passage at the beginning of Act 3 where Brünnhilde hurriedly explains her situation – and Sieglinde's – to her fellow Valkyries ('Hört mich in Eile', etc.).

Leinsdorf is also to be heard in a pirated performance from the Metropolitan. It enshrines one of the first really complete performances at the Met (30 March 1940) after all the infamous Bodansky cuts had been restored by Leinsdorf; it therefore contains Friedrich Schorr's only complete Wotan. Unfortunately the great baritone was vocally well past his best – his register reduced at both ends – but his authority, tenderness and above all understanding of the role are, of course, undiminished, although like all veteran Wotans he tends towards the sentimental in the farewell. Lehmann and Melchior sing with their usual involvement and intensity, though Lehmann sounds maturer than in the Walter recording (see below). Thorborg's Fricka is regal and authoritative. Marjorie Lawrence is a youthful, womanly Brünnhilde with a bright top register but she does not seem to have a full understanding of such inward sections as the *Todesverkündigung*. Leinsdorf conducts with the inner strength and forward pulse that characterizes his commercial version. The sound is good, all things considered.

On an earlier 'off-the-air' Met performance (30 Nov. 1936) of Act 2 only, Schorr already seems to be having difficulty with his high notes. His first top F sharp is a croak. Fritz Reiner makes the old cuts so that Schorr's contribution here is not so important as on the Leinsdorf discs. Lehmann is superb in her brief, distracted utterances, Melchior most moving in 'Zauberfest', but the real reason for acquiring this single disc, if you can possibly obtain it, is for Flagstad's Brünnhilde, here heard in its pristine glory. Quite apart from her unique vocal quality, she seems here to act much more with her voice than in some of her later recordings and to move the listener with her noble yet affecting vocalization. An oddity is the ending of this disc: an announcer takes us gently away from the performance, declaring the curtain to be falling even before Wotan has dispatched Hunding!

Between the HMV/Furtwängler *Walküre* of 1954 and the RCA/Leinsdorf set of 1961, came the Decca recordings of Acts 1 and 3 with Flagstad as Sieglinde and Brünnhilde, and Knappertsbusch and Solti as the respective conductors. John Culshaw has described in detail how these came about, and how the Act 3 became the 'pilot' for Decca's complete *Ring*. Although Culshaw considers that Knappertsbusch was a failure in the recording studio, his slow unfolding of the Act 1 drama, his refusal in any way to pander to the modern way of doing things has much to commend it as in his complete Cetra-Live set – for instance, he is the only conductor on record not to speed up the orchestral coda of the act. Flagstad was a matronly, staid Sieglinde by 1957, and the set is more worth hearing for the conducting and for Svanholm's Siegmund. His singing was idiosyncratic, he was inclined to reach notes from below, and his upper register was undoubtedly dry, but the eloquence of his phrasing and the intensity of his peculiar timbre are something none of his successors has equalled. Van Mill is a stiff Hunding.

The fourth side of the Act 3 set is devoted to the *Todesverkündigung* with Flagstad and Svanholm. Both singers show some vocal decline as compared with their 1949 recording under Böhm (HQM 1138), who also paces the scene more naturally than Solti could manage at that early stage of his Wagnerian career. In Act 3 Solti is exciting – this is a youthful reading – and Decca was well on the way to the recording standard of their complete *Ring*. Flagstad's Brünnhilde is nearly as radiant as in her early career. Otto Edelmann, the Wotan, produces plenty of warm, rounded tone, but misses much of the inner soul of the great part. Marianne Schech is a lumpy Sieglinde, but the Valkyries – Decca was adept at choosing them – are another fine team.

Klemperer's records of Act 1 and Wotan's Farewell are as expected weighty and slow, stretching the singers to the utmost, but the reading is grandly proportioned and wonderful in detail. Momentary lapses of ensemble are a small price to pay for such a resolutely architectural approach, although some may wish for a greater rush of blood to the head in the love music than the veteran conductor could manage. In the work's finale, Klemperer is frankly plodding. Dernesch's Sieglinde is warm and sensitively phrased but not exactly impassioned. William Cochran expands after a stodgy start. Hans Sotin's Hunding is black and louring, not a fellow to meet alone on a dark night. Bailey manages, with prodigious breath control, to cope with his conductor's slow pace.

Another veteran, Karl Elmendorff, is to be heard in precisely the same music on a 1944 broadcast, recently resuscitated in Austria. Elmendorff's tempi are just as deliberate as Klemperer's, and are as well sustained by the Dresden Staatskapelle as by the Philharmonia. The cast is interesting and typical of the pre-war German school, with tone and words much more forwardly and immediately produced than singers seem willingly to try today. Margarete Teschemacher is a Sieglinde with true wonder in her voice. She is partnered by Max Lorenz, here at his most ardent and winning, even if he is as free as ever with note values. The young Kurt Böhme is simply the most menacing, formidable Hunding I have heard in this whole survey. The recording is amazingly wide-ranging and well-balanced for its time. On the fourth side, Elmendorff is much more convincing than Klemperer in showing the exaltation and eloquence of this music, and the much underrated Josef Herrmann gives one of his several recorded accounts of the Farewell, in all of which he displays an unforced, firm, sympathetic way of singing the music. Altogether an admirable pair of discs.

From a similar time, sung in a similar style, comes the Wotan/Brünnhilde scene and a complete Act 3, conducted by Wolfgang Brückner, and deriving from a 1938 broadcast on Reichssender Königsberg. Wilhelm Rode, a famous Wotan, interprets the monologue almost like *Sprechgesang*, words given here almost too much importance. He often sings out of tune, but his authority is undeniable. Gertrud Rünger, a well-known German dramatic soprano of the time, who left few records and no others of her Wagner, is heard here as a good but not particularly enlightening Brünnhilde. The conducting is not much more than adequate (LV 153/4). Part of this performance appears again on Acanta DE 23–114/5, which also includes considerable excerpts of Act 1, from 1938. It is a valuable memorial of Fritz Krauss's vital Siegmund and Maria Reining's radiant Sieglinde.

Much more exciting is the 1951 Bayreuth Act 3, conducted by Karajan at his young, forceful and inspiring best. The orchestral playing throughout is on the highest level of achievement. Varnay, as for Knappertsbusch six years later, inflects Brünnhilde's music subtly but effortfully, very much in the post-war psychological manner. Sigurd Björling's typically Scandinavian heroic baritone, brassy in timbre, is just right for the part, but his understanding of the role is limited. Rysanek is at her exciting best, the voice opening up thrillingly at 'O hehrstes Wunder'.

Another Act 3 set was made with the New York Philharmonic in 1945. Artur Rodzinski is the adequate conductor, Helen Traubel an extrovert Brünnhilde, Herbert Janssen an underpowered, but highly intelligent, Wotan. Goodish orchestral playing, poor recording. This set was originally made to complete the recording of the whole work begun before the war with the famous Bruno Walter set of Act 1, made in Vienna in 1935. Walter's poetic, lightweight direction corresponds closely with Kempe's in more recent times. The glory of this set is Lehmann's Sieglinde, which is no less enthralling than those who heard her in person would have us believe: the declamation of the text instilled with vitality and urgency, the tone full of rapture. One is really carried away as much by the eager inquisitiveness of her first entry and the extraordinary vividness of the narration ('Der Männer Sippe') as by her ecstasy in the love music. Melchior's Siegmund has many of the same qualities and is extremely faithful to Wagner's markings, especially 'zögernd' (hesitatingly), though not always so respectful of his note values. Emanuel List, the Hunding, treats words most imaginatively, but his voice is not ideally steady.

This set was followed a couple of years later by Act 2, which for political reasons was partly made in Berlin with Bruno Seidler-Winkler as a competent, but not particularly inspired, conductor, partly in Vienna – the Sieglinde scenes – with Walter again at the helm. There are cuts in the Wotan-Fricka scene and in Wotan's Narration. The recording is exceptionally clear and natural-sounding, and I have a great affection for this old issue. Klose, here in her prime, is a marvellous Fricka and another instance of the ability of pre-war singers to bring a greater meaning and individuality to the text than present-day artists (though not the 1950s Bayreuth school) find possible or necessary. Listen to how she relishes the words 'Lugte lüstern der Blick'. Hotter, at the beginning of his career, is the Wotan, not as psychologically perceptive as later, but still mightily impressive and, in fresh, steady voice. Marta Fuchs's Brünnhilde is much like Varnay's, womanly ('Brünnhilde bittet' is tenderly inflected) and involved, Lehmann and Melchior are again superb. Alfred Jerger sings Wotan's few phrases on the last side – and sounds not the least like Hotter!

This brings me to the fun John Culshaw had at the expense of the pre-war way of recording Wagner, more especially the changing of conductor and singers in the first-ever attempt at a 'complete' set of *Walküre* (D 1320–33). Issued in one of those beloved old red albums, it was called 'A representative series of selected passages from the Music Drama'. The conducting is shared between Albert Coates – a great Wagnerian – and Leo Blech, who conduct respectively the LSO and the Berlin Philharmonic. Frida Leider is the Brünnhilde, a magnificent bright-toned one, in all scenes but the *Todesverkündigung*, in which she is replaced by the less sensitive but rich-voiced Florence Austral. Apart from their short entries at the very end of Act 2, when they were replaced by Howard Fry and Louise Trenton, Schorr and Göta Ljungberg are the Wotan and Sieglinde. Schorr at this stage of his career had the ideal Wotan voice, heroic, firm and warm, and his portrayal is at once authoritative, tender, and classically refined. Ljungberg is a passionate, lyrical Sieglinde. Walter Widdop, the Siegmund throughout, shows true *Heldentenor* quality and his line never falters. He can be touching when he tries as in the 'Zauberfest' passage, one of the best on record. In Act 1 he tends to be a little unyielding. The cuts are heavy and too complicated to describe in detail here. The recorded sound, if you can get hold of a fresh-looking set, is remarkable for its date of recording – around 1927. By the way, Leider is the only Brünnhilde in these sets who commands a real trill. Much of her contribution has been reissued on 1C 147–30 785.

Two companion discs to supplement this set were issued around the same time, containing the Fricka–Wotan scene with Schorr and Leisner (DB 1720–1; LV 125). Schorr is as faithful to the score as ever and Leisner, a very contralto-sounding Fricka as opposed to our modern mezzos, is excellent too. These discs, not easy to obtain in the original form, are well worth acquiring on the reissue.

The 1951 DG Act 1 finds Maria Müller past her best but still touching as Sieglinde. Windgassen, as for Furtwängler in Rome, is a stolid Siegmund. Ferdinard Leitner is an adequate conductor.

There are a number of discs including complete scenes. The most important of these is the Toscanini 1941 recording of Act 1, scene 3 (part of VCM 4) to which I have referred already. Taken at a fair old lick, this is immensely exciting. Melchior, near the end of his career, is inspired to give of his very best after a cloudy and breathless start. Traubel is a good Sieglinde. However, it is the incandesence, the Italian lyricism of the conducting – try the moment when Siegmund draws out the sword – that is irresistible. Maria Reining and Lorenz, with Arthur Rother as conductor, have also recorded the whole of this scene. Reining is a clear-voiced Sieglinde, as she was in the 1938 extracts; Lorenz here phrases carelessly but once more displays the true *Heldentenor* timbre so rarely come by nowadays. Speeds are impossibly fast and the whole venture reduces Wagner to something like superior operetta (Acanta DE 221–22). I have not heard a 78 version of this whole scene by Elisabeth Friedrich and Carl Hartmann (Parlo. R 1703–4).

As I have suggested, the Svanholm-Flagstad *Todesverkündigung* with Böhm conducting is preferable to the singers' later version, with Flagstad singing most beautifully and tenderly at 'So wenig achtest du'. Another interesting recording of this scene comes on two old Parlophone 78s (E 11257–8; LV 198). Margarete Bäumer is the sympathetic Brünnhilde, Gotthelf Pistor – an underrated artist – the eloquent Siegmund. A version of this scene is another precious memento of Varnay's Brünnhilde (DG DGM 19063), also a recollection of Windgassen's attractively youthful Siegmund. The conductor is Leopold Ludwig, who was also in charge of the final scene of the whole opera with Hotter and Nilsson on a 1957 Columbia LP (SAX 2296). Neither singer rises to the inspired level each managed in complete sets. The orchestral playing is adequate, no more.

There is a pirated recording of the whole of the last act of a 1937 performance at Covent Garden conducted by Furtwängler. The pre-war Royal Opera Orchestra was in effect Beecham's LPO. The strings indulge in much portamento. The conductor manages to inspire them to give a thrilling account of the score. Flagstad again excels herself for Furtwängler. Rudolf Bockelmann is a sound Wotan, but hardly a rival to his great contemporary, Schorr. All the notes are there, truly sung, but the expression is stiff. The Valkyries are a squally lot, though Edith Coates's Siegrune is to be noted. Maria Müller was the Sieglinde. The farewell is included in the Acanta Wagner box (HB 22 863–0).

Act 1

Extracts from Act 1 must begin with the discs made around 1908 beginning at 'Müd am Herd fand ich den Mann' in the second scene going on to 'Wunder und wilde Märe' to 'Künde nun, Gast' with the Bayreuth singers Maria Knüpfer-Egli as Sieglinde, Ernst Kraus as Siegmund and Paul Knüpfer as Hunding (044168; 044170/1). The music is sung intelligently but without with any particular vocal distinction. There are not many versions of 'Friedmund darf ich!' Jacques Urlus (042275; CO 350) gives a clear, poetic reading of Siegmund's desperate narration. Melchior's 1924 version (Poly. 72867; DG 2721 109) finds the young tenor in marvellous form; every word is savoured and sung with feeling, with ideally full, well-focused tone.

There is no such paucity of versions of 'Ein Schwert verhiess mir der Vater'. Roughly in historical order, I begin with Erik Schmedes, the Danish tenor who was stationed in Vienna. Like many Siegmunds who began as baritones, his timbre is thick, but he is a true *Heldentenor* with just one or two signs of strain. His version (3–42980–1; CO 301) is moving, though just a trifle sentimental at times. From this generation (pre-first world war), I prefer Urlus (042274; CO 350) whose superb diction and varied tone bring Siegmund's mixed, imaginative thoughts vividly before us. There is a small cut in this single-sided 1909 version as Urlus sings the extract at the right pace, rather than hurrying it, as others do, to accommodate the needs of a 78. In 1924 he recorded it again, this time complete (Od. 0–8583; 1C 181 30–669). From the same generation comes Heinrich Knote (042297; CO 355) revealing similar qualities of light, immediate, vibrant singing. He really makes you believe Siegmund is helpless in his enemy's hands. Richard Schubert's 1920 version (Poly. 65615; LV 168) suggests a less poetic, more heroic Siegmund; the cries of 'Wälse' have a feeling of defiance as well as desperation. The enunciation is vivid indeed.

The inter-war years saw a plethora of fine, upstanding Siegmunds. As an alternative to Melchior, you could hear Lorenz, Franz Völker, Gotthelf Pistor, not to mention the French and British interpreters. Lorenz's bright, easily produced voice here gives an object-lesson in phrasing and observation of dynamics in both his versions (EG 860 or DB 4547, various re-issues). Völker's richer tone shows an equal sensitivity (Poly. 67142, earlier version 27291); listen to the expression he puts into 'Ist es der Blick', etc. Melchior himself is in fresh voice on D 2022, sounding marvellously eager and youthful. He also recorded it on Polydor 72869 (reissue DG 2721 176) and German HMV EJ 300 (reissue 1C 147 01259/60). Both the HMVs have Leo Blech as conductor of the Berlin State Opera. Pistor, the German tenor, takes two sides of a 78 (E 10720; LV 198), and sings with beauty and deliberation, a lovely, dreamy reading.

René Verdière (Od. 123683), in French, is delicate but too lightweight. Georges Thill (LX 468; 2C 061–12153) is more idiomatic, though he, unlike his compatriot, never seems to have sung the part on stage. Thill is always a winning performer and his pure, natural delivery manages here even to make sense of the French translation. In the immediate post-1945 era, Set Svanholm dominated the scene. His expressive version, in those peculiarly individual accents, can be heard on DB 21116. His 'Wälse' cries are strained. Incidentally, it is interesting to note that singers like Lorenz and Völker, or those of the earlier generation, do not show off their high notes at this point for nearly as long as Siegmunds are inclined to do these days. Ticho Parly's voice (DG 135022) is similar in timbre to Svanholm's, but his singing is not so distinguished or clean. I prefer Jess Thomas on another DG disc (SLPEM 136387). Though the tone is tightly produced, he uses it intelligently, and when he made this disc, he had not yet developed a wobble. There are no more than adequate modern versions by Jean Cox and Rene Kolló, and del Monaco (SXL 6140) is quite at sea. I have not heard César Vezzani (DB 4857), Charles Rousselière (Poly. 516606), but Isadoro Fagoaga, in Italian (GQX 10269), is remarkably in character.

Sieglindes divide themselves into the lyrical sopranos and the *Hochdramatische* – the latter those who are typically cast as Brünnhilde. The earliest version of 'Der Männer Sippe' is by the Mahlerian soprano, Lucie Weidt, a famous Kundry. Her stately, true account (043142) gives some idea of how Wagner was sung in the early years of the century; so does the steady, unemotional Melanie Kurt recorded in 1911 (043190; CO 345). Delia Reinhardt (Poly. 66868; LV 142), from the next generation, represents the lyrical school *par excellence*. She gives the impression of really telling a story through her clear, meaningful diction and her careful delivery. 'Dort haftet schweigend das Schwert' comes across especially vividly. Astrid Varnay (Remington 19945) was perhaps more a Sieglinde than a Brünnhilde when she made this record (her Met debut was in this part); at any rate, she sings with her usual immense intelligence and individual enunciation. Flagstad (SDD 212) sounds much too grand and matronly. Crespin, starting at 'Eine Waffe' (on WRC ST 983), is less imaginative than on the Decca set but in more radiant voice. Ludmila Dvořaková (Supraphon SUA ST 50799) is too mezzoish and handles the text heavily, as though she did not relish its meaning. Perhaps this poor impression was the result of hearing her version immediately after Nilsson's (SXL 6077). This Brünnhilde certainly understands her relative's language. Not only does Nilsson sing with her familiarly glorious, glowing tone but she puts much feeling into the text, and manages the marvellous modulation at 'Herein' with proper significance and rises superbly to the climax at 'O fänd ich ihn heute'. The French Wagnerian soprano, Germaine Lubin, singing in her native tongue (Od. 123684; LV 225), in 1930, wholly justifies her reputation with her impassioned performance, gloriously sung.

Musicians often discuss whether or not 'Winterstürme' is a good tune. Well, after listening to some three dozen versions, my opinion is that it depends on the singer. Van Dyck, my earliest Siegmund, singing in French in 1901, does little for it on a Pathé hill-and-dale, reissued on IRCC 5007, by his unvaried singing, though he apparently was a moving interpreter. The Czech tenor, Karl Burrian, the creator of Strauss's Herod, is also effortful and throaty in a 1911 recording (4–42473; CO 306). His later version (Parlo. P 286) is better. Of the pre-first world war singers I much prefer Heinrich Hensel (4–42453; CO 339), the first London Parsifal, who had a much fresher, steadier voice and consequently brings an appropriate ardour and youthfulness to Siegmund's outpouring. Paul Althouse (Victor

54076), clumsy and unsteady, need not detain us; nor need Karl Oestvig (Poly. 72829; LV 28), who makes heavy weather of the lovely music. Of the same generation, Schubert has a sweeter voice and more poetry (Poly. 65643; LV 28) and Knote (Odeon 2908) is more heroic and steadier. Johannes Sembach, an early Bayreuth Siegmund (Vox 3015), is another poetic yet heroic interpreter. Versions that rate only as souvenirs of the singers concerned come from, among others, Wilhelm Grüning, Ernst Kraus, Alfred von Bary, Peter Cornelius, Karl Jörn, Fritz Vogelstrom, Rudolf Berger (who was earlier a *Heldenbariton*, see below), and Walter Kirchoff, with Cornelius's Danish version (082034; 1C 181–30 669), one of three, notable for some finely lyrical phrasing; he sang the part in Richter's Covent Garden *Ring* in 1907.

Britain's representatives of about this time hold their own. Tudor Davies, starting from 'Dich selige Frau' on D 679, sounds youthful and romantic. Hyde (D 598; HQM 1228), already mentioned, has good legato, a quick vibrato, and gives a stylish though not very thrilling performance. Both use the Jameson translation. Giuseppe Borgatti (Italian Columbia D 6073; Rococo 5323), Heddle Nash's teacher, is light, lyrical and unidiomatic in Italian.

In the late 1920s and the 1930s we find an abundance of talent, Lorenz is here virtually unbeatable (EG 861, various reissues) with his sense of spontaneity, immaculate phrasing, ardent delivery. Völker (Poly. 67142) keeps a fine balance between the lyrical and heroic as well, spinning a warm legato. His timbre is not dissimilar from Tauber's, who recorded 'Winterstürme' with his own inimitable fervour (Od. 0–8230) early in his career, though he takes the music at a very steady pace. Gunnar Graarud (Od. 25321; LV 504) is a little monotonous, but the tone has that bright Scandinavian ring to it. Paul Kötter (Telef. FB 1019; 642 332A) is acceptable in a straightforward way.

Melchior seems to have recorded the piece seven times, if you include the complete Walter and Toscanini sets; he is remarkably consistent. The early, Danish version (Phon. 3–82086; Asco 121) is, not surprisingly, baritonal in timbre, as Melchior had only just turned tenor in 1920. The Brunswick (73057) is a little four-square in phrasing. The 1931 HMV (DA 1227) is preferable, a youthful, glowing performance. On the 1938 Philadelphia record (DA 1664; RB 16198), the voice is not as fresh-sounding, though still preferable to almost anything we hear today.

There are also souvenirs of such excellent tenors as Torsten Ralf, Fritz Krauss, Rudolf Ritter, Marcel Wittrisch and Günther Treptow, all in German, of course. Of French versions those by Georges Jouatte, Rene Verdière and Charles Rousselière are unidiomatic. Thill, on the other hand (Col. D 1610; 2C 061 12153), with his eager, rounded tone and sympathetic reading, is invaluable. I have not heard the Met tenor, René Maison. The British are here represented by Frank Titterton (Decca K 516), singing too phlegmatically as was his wont, in anglicized German.

Gigli is Gigli-ish in Italian and inaccurate to boot.

Post-war performances seem few and far between, Svanholm, starting from 'Keiner ging' on DB 21116, is his usual individual self. Parly and Hans Hopf are hard and stiff. For different reasons del Monaco and Martinelli, recorded too late in life, are best passed over in silence.

There are surprisingly few versions of 'Du bist der Lenz'. Olive Fremstad is very much a Brünnhilde–Sieglinde; so is Lilli Lehmann (PO 63; CO 384/5), but we must remember that she was around 60 when she made her recording. Katharina Fleischer-Edel, who sang Sieglinde at Bayreuth in 1906 and 1908, is magnificently forward and fresh (Od. 50423; 1C 181–30669). Jeritza is joyful (Victor 1037), Reinhardt lethargic (Poly. 66783; LV 142). Lehmann (R 20122) is in fresher voice but less ecstatic than on the Walter set. Varnay is again a paragon where diction is concerned (Am. Col. 17354), and with Leinsdorf conducting, she makes the outburst seductive and exciting. Flagstad's 78 (DA 1623) is much to be preferred to her later Decca version (SDD 212). Aase Nordmö-Lövberg (33CX 1651) sings decently enough but without any great involvement. Not so Nilsson (SXL 6077) who again displays her vocal accomplishment and her complete identification – all the more amazing in one not associated with the role.

'Siegmund heiss' ich' calls for more of the *Heldentenor* than the Spring Song. Knote (042186; CO 355) has this, and a fine, fiery manner but he is inclined to sing flat. Schubert is occasionally strained, but finds the right touch of exalted virility (Poly. 50101; LV 168). Early versions by Erik Schmedes and Alfred von Bary are not recommended. Melchior shows tremendous drive and attack in his two versions (D 2022 and EJ 300; 1C 147–01259/60, LV 124); his third version with Leider is discussed below. Fritz Krauss (EJ 142) is also admirable in this music, fiery and elevated. Paul Kötter (Telef. E 654), who has an unnamed Sieglinde to accompany him, unlike those above, offers strong, clean singing. So does Thill (LFX 220; 2C 061 12153), in French, but he is also typically energetic and forthright; his Sieglinde is Germaine Martinelli. Verdière, with Lubin (Od. 123683), has to simulate the heroic flavour. Tudor Davies (D 679), in English, sings with an attractive blush on his tone, and here del Monaco's virile attack (SXL 6140) makes its effect.

Finally, in Act 1, there are various versions of the duet. Early ones by Lily Hafgren-Dinkela, who also recorded a 'Du bist der Lenz', with Fritz Vogelstrom (Od. 79118/9) and Bertha Morena with Ernst Kraus, from 'Du bist der Lenz' (044191/2) are more recommendable for the sopranos than the tenors – indeed Morena makes a thrilling Sieglinde. We then come to three interpretations of this music of the utmost significance, for they provide, in their different ways, object-lessons in singing this music. Beginning at 'Du bist der Lenz', Leider and Melchior give it with classical certainty of tone and breadth of phrasing, allied to unforced intensity of expression, a model for aspiring singers in this field

(Poly. 72934, 72867; DG 2721 109). This recording dates from 1924, just too early for the electric process to add lustre to the accompaniments. In 1936, at Bayreuth (though not live), Maria Müller and Franz Völker recorded the finale, but starting here with Völker's ardent 'Winterstürme' (SKB 2047/8; DG 2721 110). This pair are more overtly expressive, more obviously in love, their phrasing more intimate and lyrical (after all, these singers did not go on to become Brünnhilde and Siegfried, as did Leider and Melchior), and the vocal and interpretative skill is just as true. Heinz Tietjen and the Bayreuth Orchestra provide worthy support. Finally in this exhaustive and exhausting survey of Act 1, the unique Meta Seinemeyer begins at 'Der Männer Sippe' and tells her story in those peculiarly warm, vibrant tones of hers, every word made to tell – listen to the thrill of 'dem sollte der Stahl geziemen' and then on to an enraptured climax. Any Siegmund would be in thrall to such a marvellous Sieglinde. Curt Taucher responds with properly infatuated tones, even if they are none too ingratiating. He was a notable Met Siegmund and Siegfried in the 1920s. Then Seinemeyer bursts forth with an ecstatic 'Du bist der Lenz', which has no peer except Lehmann's, and Seinemeyer had the better voice. Sadly the impassioned duet, thrillingly inflected by both singers, ends abruptly at Siegmund's '. . . Wälse genannt' (Od. 7565/6; LV 115).

Act 2

Act 2 is, naturally enough, less well represented: the extracts are much more difficult to make. There is much singing on an epic scale from several early Brünnhildes in 'Ho-jo-to-ho', particularly from Ellen Gulbranson, regular Brünnhilde at Bayreuth from 1896 to 1914 (Pathé 90288; 1C 181–30669). Matzenauer (43938) is exciting but strained. Felia Litvinne is a little squally and overparted in her 1903 recording (33163; Rococo 38). Fremstad gives a hint of what a great Brünnhilde she must have been in her frisky cries (A 1451). Edyth Walker (43999) is marvellously steady, Gadski (Victor 87002) classically poised and paying more attention to note values than many. Her diction, especially at 'Die armen Tiere', is at once crisp and meaningful. De Cisneros, an 'upped' mezzo, rushes her fences and sounds too detached. Jeritza (DB 1459), who did in fact sing this role as well as Sieglinde on stage, sounds a little over-parted and makes a womanly rather than goddess-like impression. The appropriately named Helene Wildbrunn (2–43530; LV 70), a Berlin and Vienna singer of the 1920s, is a certain, rich-voiced singer. The young Flagstad (DA 1460) is similarly endowed; so is Kappel (not issued on 78; RLS 743). Austral with Robert Radford, stalwarts of the British National Opera Company in the 1920s, sing from 'Nun zäume dein Ross' to the end of 'Ho-jo-to-ho', and then from 'O heilige Schmach' to before Wotan's monologue, and finally from 'Fahre denn hin' to Wotan's exit (D 680).

Radford must have been an impressive Wotan. Austral is her usually strong, clear-voiced self.

Fricka without Wotan makes a literally one-sided effect. Kerstin Thorborg in Fricka's three major contributions to their dialogue (Victor 17221; LV 209) is right inside the part, and sings with authority and care. Blanche Thebom (Victor 11–8928) is not in the same class, and her German is tinged with an American accent. Regina Resnik (SXL 6805), sings a little more of the part; she is unsteady but has intensity. From an earlier generation Arndt-Ober (043231; CO 305) is, contrariwise, steady but uninvolved; her 1913 recording is another useful link with a past style of interpretation.

Melanie Kurt and Urlus sing only the first part of the *Todesverkündigung* (044107; CO 345), the tenor inward in expression yet classically poised. Minnie Salztmann-Stevens and Cornelius start at 'Wer bist du, sag'. The soprano shrieks, the tenor is a dramatic Siegmund. Austral and Davies (D 681) sing a snatch of the music with feeling. Leider is at her most lyrically persuasive in her 1925 acoustic version with the honourable but dry-voiced Soot (Poly. 72986/7; LV 155).

Siegmund's 'Zauberfest' passage just before the fight, as he leans over his sleeping beloved, was recorded with results true to the three tenors' form by Urlus, Kraus and Soot.

Act 3

Here we start with an oddity, or rather two. Matzenauer sings both Brünnhilde's and Sieglinde's part from 'Fort denn eile', opening up excitingly at 'O hehrstes Wunder' (Victor 87102). Gadski does the same, magnificently (Victor 87281). Wotan's 'Zorn' (Anger), as it was known in the early years of recording – beginning at 'Nicht straf' ich dich erst' was superbly delivered in ideal *Heldenbariton* voice by Walter Soomer (042415; 1C 181–30 669), excluding Brünnhilde's two lines, this carries on to '. . . bist du verbannt'. Soomer was Bayreuth's Wotan from 1908 to 1914.

In 'War es so schmählich', Salomea Kruscenzski (Fono. 92938; Rococo 5211), the Polish soprano who saw *Butterfly* through from failure to success, matches a perfect technique to a lovely voice intelligently used, but she sings in Italian. Jeritza (DB 1459), using her words carefully, is all tenderness at 'der diese Liebe'. She and Martha Fuchs (DB 4555; LV 44) add this section of the Wotan-Brünnhilde encounter. Fuchs sings a little clumsily but with plenty of commitment. Matzenauer begins at 'Nicht weise bin ich' (043129), a little matter-of-fact but as steady as all early Brünnhildes. Gadski (Victor 88183) is again heard to thrilling effect: she must have been a superb Brünnhilde. Frida Leider (Poly. 72978; DG 2721 110) is much as in the HMV excerpts.

And so to the many Farewells. They divide clearly into heroic baritones and basses. The great Anton van Rooy (2–2685; 1C 181–30 669) in 1902 surely has the right voice – a noble *Heldenbariton*, nobly used; he produces a splendid *messa di voce* on the word 'freie'. He sings only 'Leb wohl', not 'Der Augen leuchtendes Paar' (hereinafter called 'Der Augen'). David Bispham, the American baritone, can hardly be heard as recorded by Mapleson's horn at the Met, transferred to an IRCC record. His contemporary, the Russian, Vladimir Kastorsky sings only 'Der Augen' (3–22871; GV 2) in a rich, resonant bass, without much understanding of the part as far as one can tell.

Leopold Demuth (042036 and 4–42124/5; CO 303) gives us a good idea of the slow, sentimental style that some Wotans seem to have adopted around the turn of the century – plenty of rubato and portamento, sympathetic interpretation. He sings both parts of the Farewell, as does his Viennese contemporary Friedrich Weidemann (3–42963 and 4–42102; CO 308). Weidemann seems the more stylish exponent of the part while managing to be just as expressive. Michael Bohnen (Od. 76570/1) is a dull interpreter with resonant low notes.

Versions by Bertram (42803), Bachmann (4–42046), Soomer (4–42349), and Rudolf Berger (Od. 34479) – the first two in 'Der Augen' only – confirm the high standards prevailing at Bayreuth and elsewhere in Germany before 1914. From the immediately following generation Heinrich Schlusnus is steady but dull (Poly. 62362 and 'Loge, hör' on 65574; LV 187). Alfred Jerger's version (Poly. 62384) is smooth, his timbre sympathetic, but he seems to lack some of the authority the role needs. Rode (Poly. 66871–2) is here splendidly steady and exhibits marvellous diction. His disc is marred only by moments of doubtful intonation and by one or two unfortunate slides. Rudolf Bockelmann gets his version on to two sides (C 2179; 1C 181–30 75) by comic cuts in the orchestral parts. Without in the least sentimentalizing 'Der Augen' he manages to be moving, and his voice has power and security too.

As with Siegmunds there was also an almost embarrassing number of fine Wotans in this era. In addition to Rode, Bockelmann and Schorr, who also recorded a version in the acoustic era, there was the underrated Hans Reinmar, whose version (Ultraphon FP 707–8) displays a lighter voice than we associate with the role but, like all his contemporaries, his forward production precludes a wobble and encourages clarity of diction, smoothness of line. He occasionally mauls the music and makes the traditional but unwarranted *rallentando* towards the end of 'Der Augen'. This is an appealing performance. Kipnis (D 1225; Club 99/55) is an example of a bass Wotan – and a superb one. His opulent voice encompasses the notes magnificently and without the least sign of strain that even some baritones show at the calling of Loge. Lawrence Tibbett (DB 2471/3) with Stokowski conducting, draws a fine line but hardly has the authority of a true Wotan. Hermann (DB 7675–6; LV 49), whose career was marred by the war, is certainly that, and his version is among the best. So is that by the Munich-based Hans Hermann Nissen (Homocord

4–8803/4; LV 178) whose rich, commanding, warm singing demands attention. Manowarda (Poly. 62386; LV 175) has authority and legato, but wobbles.

Neither Etienne Billot nor André Pernet, in French, are impressive but André Gresse is moving (032049/50). The only English version I have heard is Norman Allin's omitting 'Der Augen', on L 1390 – dry but firm singing. Harty is the conductor. Unfortunately I have not heard Clarence Whitehill's various Wotan discs (DB 439–42).

Hotter's first version, recorded in 1942 (Poly. 67972; DG 2721 111), gratifyingly steady, is already phrased with emotional intensity. Heger conducts. In the post-war period, Paul Schöffler recorded the Farewell three times (K 1597–8, LXT 2644, Amadeo AVRS 6022). All present a fatherly, sympathetic Wotan rather than a god-like one. The second Decca version is the one to have. Moralt conducts confidently and the singer seems inspired to give of his considerable best. Edelmann (33CX 1568) does not do as well as in the complete Decca Act 3. London (SDD 143) is powerful and unsubtle. Mark Reizen, in Russian on Melodiya, is hardly idiomatic, but one can hardly fail to succumb to such a wonderfully rich and sympathetic sound. Fischer-Dieskau (ASD 3499), without quite the tonal strength, is tender and yet God-like, with Kubelik as his superb conductor. Donald McIntyre's version on a New Zealand record was made too early in his career to be representative of his mature reading of the role.

SIEGFRIED

The first attempts to record any large chunks of *Siegfried* date back to acoustic days. Indeed HMV D 700–2 must create the all-time record for 'potting' an opera: *Siegfried* (in English) squeezed on to six 78 sides, snippets from all three acts. On the first side Tudor Davies forges the Sword with great aplomb, ably supported by Albert Coates. Side 2 has Austral heard briefly as the Woodbird(!) and Sidney Russell as a terrible Mime. By side 3, we are at the end of Act 2, with a different Woodbird and Davies again in fine voice. Sides 4, 5 and 6 have chunks of the final duet (side 4: 'Heil dir, Sonne'; side 5, 'Ewig war ich'; side 6: closing section). Austral is a womanly Brünnhilde.

HMV's next attempt at *Siegfried* was rather more substantial. On D 1530–5, there is a little more of each act in a performance that one longs to hear complete. Rudolf Laubenthal is the Siegfried, a role he sang at Covent Garden with success in 1927–8 and in 1930. His true, lyrical yet strong tenor is just what we need today. His interpretation is not as vivid as that of Melchior, who was of course London's chief pre-war Siegfried, but Laubenthal is a very good second to him. I particularly like his lovely *mezza voce* in Forest Murmurs and his brilliance in the (cut) final scene where his Brünnhilde is Leider at her most resplendent. Even on the scratchiest of 78s (which these are) the quality of this performance, grandly supported by the Berlin State Opera Orchestra and Leo Blech, is unmistakable. Karl Alwin and the Vienna State Opera Orchestra accompany a sturdy Maria Olszewska, and a rough Emil Schipper – wife and husband suitably enough – in the Erda-Wanderer scene. This is a set all Wagnerians should have and it should be reissued in LP form.

Next the Gramophone Company became more ambitious with four sets recorded not long after each other (D 1690–4, D 1836–7, DB 1578–83, DB 1710–3, later coupled together with D 1533–4 on DB 7252–70, then reissued, minus five sides, on Electrola 80774–5). There is no consistency here of orchestras, conductors or singers – except that Melchior is the Siegfried throughout, and what a Siegfried! I am well aware of his sometimes faulty sense of rhythm and vagueness over note values, but what are these set against his unsurpassed fullness of tone, his ability to convey the part's many moods (in particular its youthful ardour) and his peculiar vividness of articulation? All prospective Siegfrieds should be locked up with his Sword and Forging songs ('Nothung' and 'Schmiede, mein Hammer') until they can manage them both with Melchior's control and perception. He is just as exemplary in the peace of the Forest Murmurs, and the worry and sadness of 'Selige Öde', once available separately on the HMV German list as EJ 485, almost my first acquaintance with the singer along with 'Nothung' from this set (backed by a matchless Prize Song, DB 1858).

The rest of the cast, all from Covent Garden, is more variable. Heinrich Tessmer's truly sung Mime turns into Albert Reiss's caricature by the end of Act 1. Eduard Habich is a menacing Alberich. Schorr's Wanderer, subtle and often poetic in Act 1, is succeeded by Bockelmann's more prosaic but not inconsiderable portrayal in Act 3 (Schipper is, of course, heard in Act 2). Nora Gruhn holds up British interests with a perky Woodbird. Florence Easton, London's 1932 Brünnhilde and one of New York's regular interpreters of the role from 1924, presents a human, vulnerable goddess (a contradiction in terms I know). Her bell-like tone and superfine diction, much admired at the Metropolitan, are much in evidence here. Heger and Coates, both expert Wagnerians, share the conducting.

Act 1

And so to individual items and scenes. One of the earliest records I have encountered also happens to cover Mime's first utterances. The singer is also one of the oldest in this chapter – Julius Lieban, a famous Berlin Mime from the mid 1880s until 1933 (when he was 75). On 4–42532–3 we can hear how he colours and varies his tone without ever debasing it; all is grounded on good articulation, not on exaggeration. On the second side, beginning 'Das ist nun der Liebe, schlimmer Lohn!', Lieban's singing is more legato than we hear from today's Mimes. This record is part of a series involving Lieban and Kraus. On 044218/9, they sing from 'Vieles lehrtest du, Mime' to 'Wer Vater und Mutter mir sei'. Again one admires Lieban's line and diction. Kraus is an unappealing Siegfried but the voice is a real heroic tenor, white in tone, intense in expression even when his phrasing inclines to stiffness. 'Zwangvolle Plage!' has also been recorded by Albert Reiss and Hans Bechstein, neither of whom I have heard. An early Bayreuth Mime Hans Breuer recorded 'Als zullendes Kind' in whining tones (2–42923; 1C 180–30 670).

The first major 'bleeding chunk' is the Wanderer's 'Auf wolkigen Höh'n', his final reply to Mime's interrogations. Fritz Feinhals (4–42470; CO 314) begins uncertainly but recovers to give a noble, baritonal account of the passage. Friedrich Weidemann (3–42182 and 4–42135; CO 3080), one of Mahler's Wotans in Vienna, is a better representative of that era with his richer tone and more authoritative interpretation. Rudolf Berger (Od. 79067; CO 336) is dry and wooden, but his Bayreuth contemporary, Theodor Bertram (Favorite 1–15403; CO 316), displays a vast voice, but also an unsteady one. The next generation of Bayreuth singers is represented by Theodor Scheidl (Poly. 62354) a warm, wise Wanderer. Schipper also recorded the extract (Poly. 72967). Hans Hermann Nissen's firmly articulated version, is perhaps a little lightweight (DA 4460; LV 58).

I have located some thirty or so versions of the passage beginning 'Nothung, Nothung', variously known as the *Schmelzlied* or *Schwertlied*, Melting or Sword Song, many of them backed by the *Schmiedelied*, or Forging Song. Erik Schmedes, a famous Bayreuth Siegfried at the turn of the century is free with the tempo, basically a measured one. He is so effective that one wonders if today's usual speed is not too fast (4–42034; CO 301). Leo Slezak (42854) is too effortful and jerky. Schubert, the Vienna *Heldentenor* of the 1920s, recorded both extracts in 1921 (Poly. 65603; LV 168) with a thrillingly vibrant tone, plenty of spirit and with the right *rit* at 'Was musstest du zerspringen', declaimed with real meaning. Still more exciting, with his attractive, quick vibrato, is Schubert's contemporary, Johannes Sembach (the first Aeghistus, incidentally), much admired at the Metropolitan. He does only 'Nothung'. José Palet (HMV 7–52103), singing in Italian, sounds, naturally enough, bright and Italianate.

Melchior dominates the next generation of Siegfrieds. In addition to his 'complete' versions, he recorded both 'songs' acoustically (Poly. 72857; DG 2721 110) in 1924 and sounds predictably youthful; indeed this is probably the best reading of either that I have heard. The later versions – 'Nothung' (DA 1664; VIC 1500) and 'Schmiede' (Victor 17725; VIC 1500) – are still glowingly dispatched, although the timbre is noticeably darker. Max Lorenz, who recorded both pieces twice (SKB 2054; GMA 50 and DB 4470; LV 121), has a lighter, more lyrical tone than Melchior. As always his singing is vital and likeable. In both versions, which are similar, the Forging song is taken slowly. The Bayreuth (SKB) version of this is to be preferred because it gives us a glimpse of Erich Zimmermann's crafty Mime. Lorenz here throws off the line 'kalt lachtest du da' challengingly, freshly. Joachim Sattler (both, Poly. 67923) is a bouncy, lightweight Siegfried – he sang Melot and Froh at Bayreuth – but he sounds attractively youthful. Pistor, who sang Siegfried in the late 1920s at Bayreuth, is another boyish Siegfried, careless in phrasing and over note values (both extracts, Parlo. E 10708; LV 198). Soot (both, Poly. 65805) shows little relish for the work in hand in 'Nothung' but recovers for a crisply efficient 'Schmiede'. Knote, who belongs really to a slightly earlier generation (he sang Siegfried at Covent Garden as early as 1900) but went on singing until the 1930s, is marvellously steady in both extracts (4–42375/6; CO 355), heroic too. Fritz Vogelstrom, the Dresden tenor, is lyrical and steady in 'Nothung' on Beka-Meister 1194 M. In 'Nothung' only, the French tenors Verdière (Od. 123020; ORX 149) and Rousselière (Poly. 50611) – the latter suitably once a smith in Algiers – need not detain us, although Verdière's effort is lively enough. Frank Mullings (both, L 1399), in English, is much more inspiriting with his exciting, powerful, if unpolished singing. This is certainly one of Mullings's most worthwhile discs. Cornelius, displays his huge voice and eager interpretation of both pieces (02159), singing in impeccable English: he was Richter's Siegfried in the first English *Ring*.

The modern generation is modestly represented on LP. Hans Hopf, whom I heard at Bayreuth in 1960 as Siegfried, is just as I remembered him, thick-voiced and ungainly. He sings the whole scene from 'Nothung' with Herold Kraus as Mime (Eurodisc 71188). I particularly dislike his aspirated 'bla-ha-ha-se balg'. Ticho Parly is little better (DG 135022) with his throaty tone and effortful phrasing. Even Windgassen's early recording of both songs (DG 2721 111) cannot be commended; the tone is fresh enough but the interpretation is stiff compared with what it was to become. The Mime is unnamed on the label, but I believe he is Walter Carnuth. Further versions include those by Jörn (4–42504/5), Taucher (Polydor 70668), Kraus (3–42670/1), Urlus (Pathé Hill & Dale 15756), Otto Briesemeister (Od. 79274), Paul Franz (French Pathé H&D 0266), Rudolf Ritter (Vox 03468), and Ivan Erschov (022034; OASI 620), a great rarity in its original form. It should be heard on the reissue, for Erschov, singing in Russian at St Petersburg in 1903 displays one of the century's most bright and exciting dramatic tenors.

Act 2

The beginning of the second scene was once recorded by Kraus and Waldemar Henke, a famous German character-tenor. There are several interesting *Waldweben* (Forest Murmurs). Pride of place goes to Heinrich Hensel (Od. Rxx 105), a pure, lyrical, eloquent account of these beautiful pages. He was London's 1911 Siegfried. Knote's disc (042294/5) is nearly as attractive. Lorenz (SKB 2055; DG 2721 110) is once again most expressive in his 1936 Bayreuth disc, with the text given almost a spiritual accent; his sad half-tones are undoubtedly moving, although not more so than Melchior's on the 'complete' set (I have not heard Melchior's Parlophone E 10042 disc; LV 226). Pistor (E 10658; LV 198) is a little uncertain vocally and the extract is foreshortened. Rousselière, on a disc that plays at about 75 r.p.m. (Poly. 566043), also sings with deep emotion – this passage, not surprisingly brings out the best in tenors, as witness Parly's eloquent account (DG 35022). Franz Lechleitner, whom I recall as a bullish Radames, is poetic (Decca LX 3034): 'Warum aber starb sie da?', in a tender half-voice is only one of this version's telling points. Versions exist by Kraus (042194/5), Soot (Od. 80096/7), Otto Wolf (Poly. 95696), Urlus (Pathé 15759–60). An oddity is the version recorded about 1960 by Zoltán von Zavodsky (Qualiton HLP MK 1527), a tenor described by Knappertsbusch as the greatest Parsifal he had ever known, but who never had much of a career outside Budapest. He was near 70 when the above record was made – in Hungarian. It reveals a tenor of sweet, plangent quality, and the reading matches it.

For the rest of Act 2 there are one or two odd bits. Kraus and Lieban recorded Siegfried's and Mime's final encounter (044288/9) from 'Er sinnt und erwägt' up to just after Siegfried's summary execution of the dwarf. Again Lieban characterizes Mime without exaggeration, and the two artists adopt an almost conversational style throughout. This is a remarkably clear and enjoyable old disc, which ends with Lieban adding Alberich's mocking laughter. There are various versions of Siegfried with the Woodbird, some longer than others. Kraus (3–44133/4) is led on by the wonderfully pure sound of Käte Herwig's Woodbird. Knote offers the epitome of loneliness (so marvellously depicted by Wagner) and is then re-directed by a forthright bird in the vocal chords of Marie Dietrich, a pupil of Viardot and a Bayreuth Woodbird in the 1890s. There's vocal history on disc for you (042298, 044182; CO 355). Pistor is his usually ardent, slightly over-parted self (E 10658; LV 198) with a bright, steady Woodbird – M. Pfahl-Wallerstein. Heinz Kraayvanger (Poly. 67922) displays a somewhat Scandinavian timbre with a Roswaenge-like ring to it; but he is uncertain in rhythm. Coba Wackers is the indifferent Woodbird. In 1904, Emilie Feuge, Bayreuth's Woodbird from 1897 to 1906 recorded 'Hei! Siegfried' (43575; 1C 180–30 670) with admirable clarity.

Act 3

Clarence Whitehill's Wotan in 'Wache! Wala!' (DB 441; 1C 180–30 670) reminds me very much of Norman Bailey's. The reverse side described as 'Siegfried's Ascent to the Valkyrie Rock' begins at 'Blick nach der Höh' (or rather, 'Look up on high'); Davies is again an outstandingly sure Siegfried, Coates the exciting conductor. Richard Mayr (4–42433; LV

42), more usually a Hagen and Pogner, sings the passage in a warm, lyrical manner but it lies high for him. Wilhelm Rode (Poly. 66782), on the other hand, revels in the high-lying phrases, but he indulges in his usual habit of sliding up to them. His peculiarly vivid enunciation must account for his good reputation. Josef von Manowarda (Poly. 62385; DG 2720 110), who sang mainly the bass roles at Bayreuth, offers a flowing, urgent account of the passage.

In an extraordinary but fascinating 1908 disc with piano, the great Ottilie Metzger (Od. 64931, 64524; LV 310 or 1C 181–30 6670) recorded all of Erda's music in her scene with the Wanderer except the final four lines. She inflects the grave, nebulous statements with firm contralto tones.

'Selige Öde', Siegfried's arrival at the mountain-top, is most sensitively, purely done by Hensel (042292/3) and by Svanholm on an LP (Victor LM 2761), recorded in 1949, a disc which begins here and goes on to the end of the opera. Erich Leinsdorf is the impressive conductor. Svanholm is in much fresher voice than in his recording with Flagstad (see below). Eileen Farrell, his Brünnhilde, has a powerful voice which she uses artistically but the total effect is of a concert performance. With stage experience she might have become a splendid interpreter of the part.

The opening section of the duet was recorded by Hensel with Elsa Hensel-Schweitzer (044165; CO 339), a singer unknown to me but possessing a gloriously bright, fresh voice; in no later performance will you find such steadiness and purity. Hensel is again a fine Siegfried. The 'potted' version of Leider and Soot (Poly. 72985; LV 172) is another interesting souvenir of the soprano at the beginning of her Brünnhilde career, radiant as ever. Soot's tone is hard, but he never falters against the strong opposition.

Practically every version of 'Ewig war ich' has something to commend it. Weidt (043143) offers a typically Italianate sound, steady, free with portamento, and a perfect trill on 'heiter' but I sense little understanding of what Brünnhilde is saying. Gadski (Victor 88186) is more temperamental and has a richer voice, but here the portamento is altogether too much for me. Pelagie Greef-Andriessen (43839), a famous German *Hochdramatische* soprano (who began as a mezzo) of the 1890s, has the usual steadiness of the era, but she pulls the music about unmercifully. Of the next generation the underrated Helene Wildbrunn (043317; LV 70), Leider's equal on recorded evidence, sings with unmatched opulence, long-breathed phrasing, yet delicacy – listen to the way she just touches the A flat on 'Herrlicher' and to her perfectly attacked high C on 'leuchtende'. Leider's version (Poly. 72977; LV 172), not so cleanly vocalized, has more subtlety of expression, particularly evident in her use of rubato. I would not be without either version on a desert island. Germaine Lubin (Od. 123684; LV 225), singing in French, is womanly but her account is marred by uncomfortable slidings from note to note. Nanny Larsén-Todsen (Od. 0–7643), the Swedish soprano, is similar to her recent compatriot, Berit Lindholm, clear and intense with a good trill. Ludmila Dvořáková (Supra. ST 50799) is too occluded in tone, words unclear.

Margarete Bäumer and Reimer Minten recorded an abridged version of the whole duet – it excludes the section where Brünnhilde has her doubts, restarting at 'Ewig war ich' (E 11117–8; LV 216). Bäumer is a tender, responsive Brünnhilde, especially eloquent at 'Deine Mutter kehrt dir nicht weider'. Minten is a stolid, serviceable Siegfried. Minnie Saltzmann-Stevens and Cornelius bring memories of the pre-first world war Richter *Ring* in a much abridged version (044111). On LP, Varnay and Windgassen recorded a most desirable reading of the whole duet (Heliodor 478127). Varnay sings with her accustomed understanding and peculiarly personal utterance and is unsurpassed in the passage beginning 'Du wonniges Kind'. She also brings womanly *Innigkeit* to 'Ewig war ich'. Her vibrato borders on a wobble but admirers of this great artist learn to overlook this vocal handicap. Windgassen is reliability itself. Flagstad, with Svanholm (HQM 1138), is in almost her warmest and most magnificent voice, fining it down to touchingly tender accents in 'Du wonniges Kind' and 'Ewig war ich'. Svanholm, as I have already suggested, is in indifferent form, but shows all his innate understanding of Siegfried's role. Sebastian is the phlegmatic conductor.

Of private discs I have so far heard only the fragments of a Vienna performance in (?) 1937 with Hotter singing part of the Wanderer-Mime (unknown singer) scene (he is in youthful and sure voice) and another fragment with Lorenz and an unknown Woodbird (Margherita Perras?): interesting snippets. There also exists a final scene with Traubel and Svanholm, con. Stiedry, Met, 1951, a final scene with Flagstad and Carl Hartmann, con. Bodanzky, Met, 1938, extracts from a 1937 performance under Bodanzky with Flagstad, Melchior and Schorr, and bits of the final duet with Flagstad and Melchior. A distant echo of Lilian Nordica can be heard on a reissue of the Mapleson cylinder (IRCC 154) in the final duet and of Jean de Reszke, even harder to hear, on another Mapleson.

GÖTTERDÄMMERUNG

Before the days of LP, there were desultory efforts to record substantial chunks, bleeding or otherwise, of the opera. The first of these, still in the acoustic era, was the set of four discs added on to the ones from *Siegfried*, sung in English. These 78s (D 703–6) include the dawn duet (Austral and Davies in their usual forthright form), Radford in Hagen's Watch and Call (good, solid work) and a cut version of the Immolation with Austral. The conductors are Coates, Percy Pitt and Eugene Goossens. As soon as electric recording came in, Fred Gaisberg of HMV was keen to record more Wagner. As he wrote: 'In 1925 Coates, who was recognised as England's greatest conductor of Wagner, joined with me in the endeavour to satisfy the eager appetite for Wagner's music, which had been denied throughout the war ...' I have already commented on his *Walküre* and *Siegfried* excerpts, with other conductors also concerned. The *Götterdämmerung* set, two volumes of eight 78s (D 1572–87), were made partly in London with Coates, partly in Berlin with Leo Blech and Karl Muck.

These records are fascinating for various reasons. In the first place there is Muck's rich, authoritative account of the Rhine Journey and Funeral March with the then superb Berlin State Opera Orchestra, discs that are also a tribute to the spacious sound being achieved as early as 1927. The vocal records start with an only moderate Prelude and Norns' Scene (Noel Eadie, Evelyn Arden, Gladys Palmer). Then come Austral and Widdop in a rousing Dawn duet (transferred to COLH 147), taken at an almost incredibly fast pace. (All Coates's Wagner is speedy, but this is ridiculous.) After the Rhine Journey, Gunther and Gutrune welcome Siegfried. 'Siegfried Drinks the Potion' in the inimitable words on the old record. An unremarkable disc, with Göta Ljungberg (Gutrune), Frederic Collier (Gunther) and Arthur Fear (Hagen) joining Widdop until the tenor reaches 'Vergäss' ich alles', which he phrases more tenderly, more accurately than any other tenor except Windgassen.

Andrésen, in both Hagen's Watch, and later in Hagen's Call, sings with the kind of firm, black tone simply not encountered today, a truly menacing figure. He is accompanied by Blech in Berlin. Back to London and another sterling artist, Maartje Offers, for Waltraute's Narration. The Dutch contralto, who was Erda and Fricka during Toscanini's regime at La Scala in the 1920s, sings with the expression kept within the musical bounds, a typical attribute of an age when the perfection of tonal delivery during the 'Golden Age' had not been forgotten but feeling had entered into singers' consideration. After the scene with the vassals done in Berlin, back to London for Siegfried's oath, Widdop clear but uninvolved, Austral as honest and womanly as ever. She is joined by an indifferent Collier and Fear for the second act's final trio.

In Act 3 we encounter truly great Wagner singing. The Rhinemaidens (listed as Tilly de Garmo, Lydia Kindermann and Marker, but who are apparently de Garmo, Kindermann and Elfriede Marherr) are nothing special, but Laubenthal's Siegfried, which I admired in *Siegfried*, is not far short of ideal in this scene, the Narration (reissued on LV 213) and Death. He can be most aptly and briefly characterized as being a Wagnerian Martinelli, with the same taut, pencil-edged tone, the same clear enunciation, and something of the same piercing intensity of declamation in his bright, incisive delivery of Siegfried's previous exploits. This is also one of the most clearly balanced 78s I have ever heard. Blech is the conductor here up to the Funeral March, then back to Austral and

Coates and his urgency for the Immolation (also on COLH 147), where I again admire Austral's unaffected, unforced delivery – not an individual performance but a lovable one. There is a small cut before 'Ruhe, du Gott'.

Although most of Melchior's discs are dealt with below. I ought to include here the scene starting 'Hast du Gunther ein Weib?' through to just before Hagen's Watch, as it was obviously meant to fill in one of the gaps in the above set (D 1700; LV 124). Melchior's Siegfried has the one quality missing in Laubenthal's, a kind of youthful exuberance, perfectly suited to this scene of oath-taking with the Gunther of no less a singer than Schorr. Their refined management of the phrase 'hold wir tranken' is worth hearing on its own. The Berlin and Bayreuth singer Rudolf Watzke, the Hagen, is yet another black bass of distinction. Liselotte Topas (though unnamed on the original disc) contributes Gutrune's few phrases.

About the same time Pathé, in France, issued a 'potted' version of the opera (7209–15) including the Prelude and Rhine Journey, Hagen's Watch and Call, the Rhinemaidens' scene, Siegfried's Death and a cut Immolation. This was made in Paris under von Hoesslin, who conducted at the Opéra. The cast boasts Ludwig Hofmann's appreciable Hagen, soft-grained, Greindl-like. Walter Kirchhoff, the Siegfried, is a typically throaty *Heldentenor* of the German school, with a clear, intense delivery. Henriette Gottlieb, the Brünnhilde, has a generous but unsubtle style. The conducting is good, but the orchestra does not play as well as its HMV counterparts of the time.

Eleven years later, Toscanini made one of his two contributions to the opera's discography, in a recording of a 1941 concert with Traubel and Melchior (RB 16274). Here we have Daybreak, 'Zu neuen Taten', and the Rhine Journey (unfortunately given a vulgar concert ending). Traubel sounds uninvolved, Melchior misses one entry, and is more lethargic than as Siegmund on the other side of the disc, but the incandescence of Toscanini's Wagner is conveyed; so is his care for detail, even to the point where the NBC Symphony's brass become blatant. I wish we had something more substantial of his *Ring*.

At the opposite pole of Wagnerian interpretation comes Goodall. As a foretaste of his complete *Twilight of the Gods*, we had the admirable Unicorn two-record set (UNS 245–6) of Act 3 from Siegfried's Narration to the end. The full flavour of his long-spanned conducting and the singers' long-breathed phrasing is caught here; so is the extraordinarily tragic power of his Funeral March. Remedios's lyrical, lucid Siegfried, Bailey's craven Gunther and Hunter's deeply expressive Brünnhilde (though the voice is recorded as if in a different acoustic from the rest in the Immolation) are all well-known to English readers. The records also preserve something of Clifford Grant's Hagen, a role that he has now relinquished – to our loss. I should add that the complete Fjelstad set of 1955 (see discography) can be safely ignored.

As ever one is surprised and delighted at how many varied and enjoyable versions of bits of the *Ring*, so unkindly dubbed 'bleeding chunks', were recorded in the early days of the gramophone. In the case of *Götterdämmerung* we have souvenirs of practically every famous interpreter from the earliest years of the century, and as time goes by, almost needless to say, they became more and more valuable as historical documents (and, as collectors will know, the 78 originals go up correspondingly in price).

Prologue

We begin appropriately enough with one of the oldest records (1908), a grave performance by Hermine Kittel, the Viennese contralto, of the First Norn's 'An der Weltesche' backed by part of Waltraute's Narration (2–43310; CO 319). It appears to be the only separate disc of any Norn. 'Zu neuen Taten' is better represented. One of the earliest (044143) has Weidt in resplendent voice, steady, radiant, unflustered in partnership with the laboured Erik Schmedes of whom John Steane in *The Grand Tradition* comments: 'His records were numerous and nasty'. The disc ends at 'Brünnhildes zu gedenken'. About the same time Perceval Allen and Cornelius (04029) recorded a heavily cut, single-sided version that I have not heard. Leider, in the first of her *Götterdämmerung* discs, is her usual confident self but in her only record of this duet is again partnered by the stiff, dry-voiced Fritz Soot (Poly. 72984; LV 155).

Bäumer, a warm, womanly Brünnhilde, is partnered by the throaty Kirchhoff (Parlo. R 1523–4). The last side has the oath scene from Act 2. Flagstad, in fresh voice, is matched by Melchior in matter-of-fact, yet wonderfully secure form and with Edwin McArthur as an insensitive, hurrying conductor (Victor 17729; RB 6604) for their 1939 disc. I have not heard Kurt and Jörn (044269–70) or Larsén-Todsen and Erik Enderlein (not issued on 78; 1C 181–30 676).

In the LP era there have been surprisingly few versions. Astrid Varnay and Wolfgang Windgassen, conducted by Hermann Weigert (then the soprano's husband), are sluggish (DG 2721 111); they are heard to greater advantage on the complete Knappertsbusch set. Eileen Farrell sounds past her best, Jess Thomas too effortful though always musical on a 'private' recording under Bernstein, which also includes the only separate recording of the final scene of Act 1, and Thomas is laboured in the Narration and Death. Hunter and Remedios, with Mackerras (CFP 40008) are their usual sound selves, although singing unidiomatic German. What a pity Leider and Melchior did not record the duet together in their prime.

Act 1

Schmedes and Demuth make heavy weather of the 'Blühendes Leben', blood-brotherhood scene (3–44064; CO 301). The Dresden pair Carl

Burrian and Friedrich Plaschke (2–44319; CO 331) are much steadier, more solid artists who sing without any vibrato. I have not heard Kraus and Bachmann, recorded in 1907 (044109–10), whose version starts at 'Vergäss ich alles'.

Hagen's Watch fitted neatly on to one side of a 78 record, and was thus frequently recorded. The Pauls, Knüpfer (042546; CO 304) and Bender (3–42908; CO 311), are both powerful, sturdy basses, stolid in delivery. Richard Mayr (4–42434; DG 2721 115), an early Bayreuth Hagen, although a bit lugubrious, is more imaginative and displays a rich, juicy tone. These pre-first world war singers are bettered by inter-war versions. List is fluent and articulate (Parlo. E 11359; LV 28). Andrésen (as in the HMV excerpts) is deeply expressive (Col. L 2341). His faster speed allows him to take the phrase starting 'Die eigene Braut' in one breath. Norman Allin, singing in English (L 1488), is sturdy and steady, but does not sound dangerous, more a comfortable family man than a killer. Ludwig Weber was caught 'live' at Covent Garden in 1936 in this scene and Hagen's Call to the vassals, with Herbert Janssen excellent in what is known as Gunther's Address and Beecham conducting. Weber has not the black tone of some Hagens but is characterful and imaginative (LX 636–7; SHB 100). I have not heard Marcel Journet or Theodor Lattermann. Post-war basses are represented by Greindl (2721 111) who is the same as on various complete records, Böhme (Acanta DE 22 028–1, recorded 1946), whom I have not heard, and Frick (ASD 363), who is less exaggerated than in the Solti recording, in stronger voice and magnificently evil here and in the Call.

Waltraute's Narration, fitting nicely on to two 78 sides, was not unnaturally a favourite for recording. Practically all the well-known mezzos (or contraltos as they were then known and proved the fact with their voluminous chest registers) of the first half of the century attempted it. Among the first (1910) and most glorious was Metzger. Her reading (043167–8; CO 310) has the classical qualities of grave, steady tone, rock-like technique and urgency in delivery of the text. She, unlike her contemporary and Bayreuth colleague Margarethe Matzenauer (043126–7; CO 313), does not hurry herself. Matzenauer, in spite of her lovely voice, sounds more superficial in consequence.

Of the immediately following generation, Sigrid Onegin (Poly. 72739; LV 82, DG 2721 115), with a voice of 'deep port-wine' (Steane), begins in steady, restrained, almost placid manner but gradually shapes the scene with a superb sense of line, given a generous portamento that does not appeal to all ears. At 'noch einmal ..., zum letzten Mal' she becomes truly eloquent, the word 'dein' tenderly breathed. Karin Branzell (Poly. 65631; LV 182) is even more free with her portamento and sings with similar security, but just a little less feeling than Onegin. Similar attributes but used with marginally less artistry are found in Maria Olszewska's performance (Poly. 72982; LV 25), also in Rosette Anday's (Poly. 66778;

LV 15), which has ringing G flats and is altogether vocalized with a fitting urgency. Helene Jung (Vox 02125) is less remarkable only in comparison with those already mentioned.

Of Metropolitan interpreters at about the same time Schumann-Heink was the touchstone of greatness. She was 68 when she recorded an abbreviated version of the Narration (HMV AGSB 1; VIC 1455) in 1929. The authority and tenderness exhibited console us for some sense of strain. Kerstin Thorborg (Victor 17222; LV 209) sounds hearty enough to have slain her quota of heroes; her interpretation is appreciable, without striking real depths of feeling. Blanche Thebom (Victor 11–9296) is by comparison pedestrian and uninteresting. Elisabeth Höngen (Preiser 1111 165) surpasses even her performance on Furtwängler's 1950 set with her intelligent, keenly shaped and dramatic singing, although some may find her vibrato bordering on a wobble.

Act 2

Hagen's Call finds an early taker (1908) in the American bass Allen C. Hinckley (3–42994; 1C 181–30 670), who sang frequently at Bayreuth. The recording is too primitive, the chorus too comical for one to make much judgement on his prowess. Allin (L 1488) is too jovial, Greindl, in various versions (DGM 19042, a 'variable micrograde' 78 and DG 136006), is effective but less subtle than he was later to become. Frick (ASD 363) firmly grips his consonants and relishes such phrases as 'Ein freisliches Weib', but he, like most Hagens, lacks a trill. List (E 10904; LV 59) is powerful but short-breathed.

So we come to that famous private disc which catches the third scene to the end of the act at Covent Garden in 1938 with Furtwängler showing the same sense of urgency and grandeur as in his complete sets. Leider is even more involved than on her commercial discs, so much so that she seems to be pushing her conductor to ever more speed. Her cries of 'Betrug!' are majestic and tragic. Melchior and Janssen (Gunther) are in marvellous voice, and Wilhelm Schirp an imposing, forceful Hagen with an appropriate Rhineland accent. It was reissued on Acanta HB 22863–0. Other extracts from this act include 'Helle Wehr, heilige Waffe' with Larsén-Todsen and Enderlein (Acanta KB 22179–2) and 'Welches Unholds List' with Larsén-Todsen, Janssen and Andrésen (unpubl.; LV 174), surely marking a Bayreuth performance. The soprano is indeterminate and dull, but Janssen is a properly troubled Gunther, Andrésen again a Hagen with presence and vocal bite – his diction is impeccable, his tone ideal. Gadski contributed Brünnhilde's part of these scenes (AGSA 36; Cantilena 6205) with splendid attack and security of declamation, 'Intensity and grandeur' are Steane's words for her. Cornelis Bronsgeest recorded Gunther's Address (Od. 50565).

Act 3

There are various uninteresting early bits of the Rhinemaidens and a longer extract that, however, completely omits Siegfried's part, with Elisabeth Kühnlein, Alfhild Petzel, and Paula Lindberg conducted by Max von Schillings (Parlo. E 10987–8). Lorenz was caught in his prime (1944) with a strongly cast trio of Rhinemaidens: Hilde Scheppan, Ingrid Langhammer and Margarete Klose (Acanta DE 22–22120/2), authoritatively conducted by Robert Heger. Lorenz, as is his wont, is free with the music but he shows such life and spirit, sings with such a smile in his tone, that one forgives him much. On the same disc he offers Siegfried's Death with tragic feeling.

And so to numerous versions of Siegfried's Narration. None matches what Conrad L. Osborne once called the 'festive brilliance and exuberant masculinity' of Melchior (D 1838–9; 1C 147–01259). The breadth of phrasing, placing of the voice and legato ('Ein wonniges Weib') are exemplary. Otto Helgers is the Hagen, Heger the conductor (again excellent) and the two 78s carry through to the Death, where Melchior clouds over his tone in a subtle and valid fashion.

Some earlier versions almost match this standard. Taucher, the first Menelaus (*Aegyptische Helena*), sings with a bright, ringing tone and growing excitement as Siegfried recalls his exploits (Poly. 72831). Urlus (0423523; Rococo 5238), whom Steane rightly calls 'one of the best singers the century has known', is the most scrupulous, articulate, poetic of all, but lacks some of Melchior's energy. Schubert (Poly. 65598; LV 168) almost matches Urlus in sensitivity, an accurate, youthful and forward account of the part, worlds away from the heavy-voiced Schmedes (4–42025; 1C 181–30 670), who offers only the first half of the narrative, while Soot (unpubl.; LV 143) sings only the second half, sounding like a German Parry Jones – uningratiating tone redeemed by his intelligence. Burrian (042352; CO 306) is four-square but has a heroic ring. He makes a number of mistakes. Lorenz, on another of those long-playing 78s that DG brought out about 1950 (72032 B), is joined by Georg Hann. It finds the tenor in querulous voice. This is side 4 of a two-disc set of the *Tristan* love duet, sung with Goltz. A pleasing oddity is the performance in Italian (Col. D 14728) of Isadoro Fagoaga, the Spanish tenor who was a famous Scala Siegfried, singing the Narration in Italian, a predictably lyrical and attractive performance with much illuminating detail. Salvatore Baccaloni is the unlikely Hagen.

I have not heard Sattler (Teleton 500), nor Kraus with Habich (044224), but Kraus in Siegfried's Death (044265; DG 2720 1078) as always lacks expression and is consequently insensitive. Knote is more sensitive in the Death scene. Good as he was in his acoustic version (042296; CO 355) with his gleaming tone and quick vibrato, his more restrained 1930 performance, when he was 60, is to be preferred (E. 11162; Discophilia

KG–K–1), an inward, expressive performance of dignity. Soot, (unpubl.; LV 143) is adequate; Schmedes (4–42337) better than usual. Lorenz is described above. Windgassen (DG 27221 111, recorded in 1953) is less involved than he later became. Parly (DG 135022) is uningratiating, Hopf (Eurodisc 71188 KR) wobbly and lumpy, Kollo (CBS 77283) sensitive but lightweight.

The history of Immolation recordings begins with the glimpse of Lillian Nordica caught on a Mapleson cylinder (IRCC 154). She sounds as brilliant and exciting as witnesses tell us she was. Gadski (Victor 88185; Cantilena 6205) is as always marvellously assured, but in order to get the end of the scene from 'Fliegt heim ihr Raben!' on a single side she has to hurry unduly. Saltzmann-Stevens (03135) sings bits of the scene in English with a good, honest attack. From 1909 we jump to 1924 and Helene Wildbrunn (Od. Rxx 80872–3; LV 70). Again I can do no better than quote Steane: 'no whisking or wobbling, no lapse from lyrical standards, even in the most strenuous passages ...' By her side her contemporary Kappel (Poly. 66099–100: LV 117) is underpowered, but the bright, warm tone is consistently attractive if the reading is a bit matter-of-fact. Larsén-Todsen (E 10756; LV 174) has a heavy, cloying tone and is often flat, but finds eloquence in the passage beginning 'Wisst ihr wie das ward', a point where Leider (D 2025–6; 1C 147–30 786) lacks inner feeling. In every other respect her performance is wonderful, the voice heroic yet human and moving. She begins at 'Schweigt eures Jammers' with Elfriede Marherr-Wagner as Gutrune.

Anni Konetzni (Telef. F 1362), who sang pre- and post-war at Covent Garden, is unsteady but enunciates the text with meaning. Elsa Alsen (E 10253), beginning at 'Grane, mein Ross', has a rich voice, but only a precarious hold on the music.

'Grane, mein Ross' becomes 'Grane, ami' in French and such phrases as 'Anneau maudit' and 'Seule chérie' bring one up short. Germaine Lubin (Od. 12324/5; LV 225), sings them in bright, Hunter-like tones, but is excessive with her portamento. Marjorie Lawrence, singing if the record books are correct when she was but 24 (DB 4914–5; LV 133), is simply amazing. On this evidence, she must have been one of the most exciting artists of her generation. For once, a Brünnhilde really sounds as if she had been a woman totally consumed with love for Siegfried. The youthful high spirts of this 1933 version are confirmed by Irving Kolodin's 'The Metropolitan Opera'. When she made her debut a couple of years later he says she 'climaxed a strong Brünnhilde by swinging herself to the back of Grane at the end of the Immolation and riding briskly off stage'. The lack of caution is there in the singing, and Piero Coppola admirably seconds it in his fiery conducting.

After that her Met colleague of the time, Flagstad, seems tame, but she, of course, had other attributes. Her earliest performance with McArthur and the San Francisco Opera Orchestra (DB 6008, DB 6011) show the voice in pristine condition, but it lacks the greater dramatic authority and penetration of the text she brought to the two performances with the Philharmonia under Furtwängler. The first recorded in 1948 (DB 6792–4) is the most inspired and finds the singer in lustrous voice, the second in 1952 (ALP 1016) is backed with the conductor's superb accounts of the Rhine Journey and Funeral March. These seem to disprove Culshaw's statement that she had an unhappy recording career before going to Decca. Flagstad's most involved, incandescent performance of all comes in the Scala-Furtwängler complete set. A final performance (WRC T 366), taken from the singer's Carnegie Hall Farewell on 22 March 1955 shows, as does the almost contemporaneous Norwegian complete set, only a small falling off in vocal opulence as a quick switch from 1937 to 1955 illustrated.

Of her contemporaries Helen Traubel is most impressive, helped no doubt by Toscanini's conducting (Victor 11–8664/6; VIC 1369). The marvellously ringing tone in the final section supported by the most exact orchestral semiquavers heard in this passage. The slow, grand pace of the whole reading allow one to forget the execrable recording. Neither of Eileen Farrell's recordings (VIC 1191, with Münch; CBS MS–6353, with Bernstein) is so impressive. Both are sensitive and well vocalized but need the greater insights that come from stage performances. Bernstein, although too excitable, provides more eloquent support than Münch. Neither Varnay (DG 2721 111), recorded in 1954, nor Mödl (Telef. LGX 66036) equals her performance in the complete sets; indeed both sound more effortful, with the voices close to the microphone. Christa Ludwig (Eurodisc S 71395) is predictably human, and the 'Alles, alles' section benefits from her rich low notes. Throughout, her performance is newly imagined and surprisingly effortless.

Dvořákova (Supra. SUA ST 50799), so much admired in London a few years ago, is choppy at the start, with words ill-defined. Her tone becomes freer, richer as she addresses Grane. Nadeshda Kniplova (SUA ST 1120785) sings queer German and phrases in ungainly manner as in the complete Westminster set. Hunter (CFP 40008) is less impressive than in her English version, but as always makes a glorious and incisive sound, lacking only in variety of timbre. I have not heard Tatiana Makushina's Edison Bell discs, sung in English, nor versions by Sigrid Kehl and Margaret Harshaw. The versions by Konetzni, Larsén-Todsen and Wildbrunn do not include the final, most taxing section.

Culshaw mentions, *en passant*, that Decca recorded the whole of the *Ring* (in *stereo*!) in 1955. Presumably this was with Varnay and Hotter (at that time committed to another company). If these tapes still exist surely it is Decca's historical duty to issue them one day, for that partnership in *Walküre* was one of the greatest in post-war operatic history and both singers were then at the height of their powers.

Pressed to choose an ideal cast for the main roles, I would have the following: Karajan's Rhinemaidens, Neidlinger as Alberich, Belcourt as Loge, Wohlfahrt as Mime, Talvela as Fasolt, Frick as Fafner, Klose or Thorborg as Fricka, Metzger as Erda, Grümmer as Freia, Hotter or Schorr as Wotan, Seinemeyer as Sieglinde, Melchior as Siegmund, Böhme as Hunding, Leider as Brünnhilde, Melchior or Knote as Siegfried (with Lorenz as reserve), Jurinac as Gutrune, Höngen as Waltraute, Uhde as Gunther and Andrésen as Hagen, conductor Furtwängler.

DAS RHEINGOLD

W Wotan; *D* Donner; *F* Froh; *L* Loge; *A* Alberich; *M* Mime; *Fas* Fasolt; *Faf* Fafner; *Fr* Fricka; *E* Erda

1950 (live performance, La Scala, Milan) Frantz *W*; Mattiello *D*; Treptow *F*; Sattler *L*; Pernerstorfer *A*; Markworth *M*; Weber *Fas*; Emmerich *Faf*; Höngen *Fr*; Weth-Falke *E*/La Scala Orch./Furtwängler Murray Hill ⓜ 940 477; Everest ⓒ 473/2

1953 (live performance, Bayreuth Festival) Hotter *W*; Uhde *D*; Stolze *F*; Witte *L*; Neidlinger *A*; Kuen *M*; Weber *Fas*; Greindl *Faf*; Malaniuk *Fr*; von Ilosvay *E*/Bayreuth Festival Orch./Keilberth Allegro-Elite ⓜ 3125–7

1953 (broadcast performance) Frantz *W*; Poell *D*; Fehenberger *F*; Windgassen *L*; Neidlinger *A*; Patzak *M*; Greindl *Fas*; Frick *Faf*; Malaniuk *Fr*; Siewert *E*/Rome Radio Orch./Furtwängler EMI ⓜ RLS 706; Seraphim ⓜ IC 3076

1957 (live performance, Bayreuth Festival) Hotter *W*; Blankenheim *D*; Traxel *F*; Suthaus *L*; Neidlinger *A*; Kuen *M*; van Mill *Fas*; Greindl *Faf*; von Milinkovic *Fr*; von Ilosvay *E*/Bayreuth Festival Orch./Knappertsbusch Cetra ⓜ LO 50/3

1958 London *W*; Wächter *D*; Kmentt *F*; Svanholm *L*; Neidlinger *A*; Kuen *M*; Kreppel *Fas*; Böhme *Faf*; Flagstad *Fr*; Madeira *E*/VPO/Solti

Decca SET 382–4 ④ K; D100D19; London OSA 1309 ④ 5–1309

1966 (live performance, Bayreuth Festival) Adam *W*; Nienstedt *D*; Esser *F*; Windgassen *L*; Neidlinger *A*; Wohlfahrt *M*; Talvela *Fas*; Böhme *Faf*; Burmeister *Fr*; Soukoupová *E*/Bayreuth Festival Orch./Böhm Philips 6747 037

1967 Fischer-Dieskau *W*; Kerns *D*; Grobe *F*; Stolze *L*; Kélémen *A*; Wohlfahrt *M*; Talvela *Fas*; Riddersbusch *Faf*; Veasey *Fr*; Dominguez *E*/Berlin PO/Karajan DG 2740 145 ④ 3378 048/9

1968 Polke *W*; Knoll *D*; Doussant *F*; Uhl *L*; Kühne *A*; H. Kraus *M*; Von Rohr *Fas*; Okamura *Faf*; Hesse *Fr*; Boese *E*/South German PO/Swarowsky Westminster WGSO 8175/3

1974 (in English – live performance, Coliseum, London) Bailey *W*; Welsby *D*; Ferguson *F*; Belcourt *L*; Hammond Stroud *A*; Dempsey *M*; Lloyd *Fas*; Grant *Faf*; Pring *Fr*; Collins *E*/English National Opera Orch./Goodall HMV SLS 5032 ④ TC–SLS 5032, SLS 5146 ④ TC–SLS 5146; Angel SDL 3825Q

Excerpts

1959 Frantz *W*; Metternich *D*; Schock *F*; Melchert *L*; Blatter *F*; Siewert *E*/Berlin PO/Kempe Classics for Pleasure CFP 109

DIE WALKÜRE

W Wotan; *S* Siegmund; *Si* Sieglinde; *H* Hunding; *F* Fricka; *B* Brünnhilde

1950 (live performance, La Scala,
Milan) Frantz *W*; Treptow *S*; H.
Konetzni *Si*; Weber *H*; Höngen
F; Flagstad *B*/La Scala
Orch./Furtwängler
Murray Hill ⓜ 940 477; Everest
ⓔ 474/3

1953 (live performance, Bayreuth
Festival) Hotter *W*; Vinay *S*;
Resnik *Si*; Greindl *H*; Malaniuk
F; Mödl *B*/Bayreuth Festival
Orch./Keilberth
Allegro-Elite ⓜ 3128–32

1953 (broadcast performance) Frantz
W; Windgassen *S*; H. Konetzni
Si; Frick *H*; Cavelti *F*; Mödl
B/Rome Radio
Orch./Furtwängler
EMI ⓜ RLS 702; Seraphim
ⓜ IE 6077

1954 Frantz *W*; Suthaus *S*; Rysanek
Si; Frick *H*; Klöse *F*; Mödl
B/VPO/Furtwängler
EMI ⓜ HQM 1019–23;
Seraphim ⓜ IE 6012

1957 (live performance, Bayreuth
Festival) Hotter *W*; Vinay *S*;
Nilsson *Si*; Greindl *H*; von
Milinkovic *F*; Varnay
B/Bayreuth Festival
Orch./Knappertsbusch
Cetra ⓜ LO 59/5

1961 London *W*; Vickers *S*;
Brouwenstjin *Si*; Ward *H*; Gorr
F; Nilsson *B*/LSO/Leinsdorf
Decca 7BB 125–9; London OSA
1511

1966 Hotter *W*; King *S*; Crespin *Si*;
Frick *H*; Ludwig *F*; Nilsson
B/VPO/Solti
Decca SET 312–6 ④ K3W30,
D100D19; London OSA 1509
④ 5–1509

1966 Stewart *W*; Vickers *S*; Janowitz
Si; Talvela *H*; Veasey *H*;
Crespin *B*/Berlin PO/Karajan
DG 2740 146 ④ 3378 048/9

1967 (live performance, Bayreuth
Festival) Adam *W*; King *S*;

Rysanek *Si*; Nienstedt *H*;
Burmeister *F*; Nilsson
B/Bayreuth Festival Orch./Böhm
Philips 6747 037

1968 Polke *W*; McKee *S*; Sommer *Si*;
von Rohr *H*; Hesse *F*;
Kniplová *B*/South German
PO/Swarowsky
Westminster WGSO 8176/5

1973 (in English – live performance,
Coliseum, London) Bailey *W*;
Remedios *S*; Curphey *Si*; Grant
H; Howard *F*; Hunter *B*/English
National Opera Orch./Goodall
HMV SLS 5063 ④ TC–SLS
5063, SLS 5146 ④ TC–SLS
5146; Angel SELX 3826 (Q)

Excerpts

1935 (Act 1) Melchior *S*; Lehmann
Si; List *H*/VPO/Walter
Electrola 1C 049–03 23

1944 (Act 1, Act 3) Hermann *W*;
Lorenz *S*; Teschemacher *Si*;
Böhme *H*/Saxon State
Orch./Elmendorff
Preiser ⓜ LV 153–4

1951 (Act 1) Windgassen *S*; Müller
Si; Greindl *H*/Württemberg State
Opera Orch./Leitner
DG ⓜ 2548 735

1957 (Act 1) Svanholm *S*; Flagstad *Si*;
Van Mill *H*/VPO/Knappertsbusch
Decca GOS 581–2; London OSA
1204

1971–2 (Act 1; Act 3, Wotan's
Farewell only) Bailey *W*;
Cochran *S*; Dernesch *Si*; Sotin
H/New Philharmonia
Orch./Klemperer
EMI SLS 968; Angel SBLX
3797

1937–8 (Act 2) Jerger, Hotter *W*;
Melchior *S*; Lehmann *Si*; List
H; Flesch, Fuchs *B*/VPO/
Walter, Berlin State Opera
Orch./Seidler-Winkler
EMI ⓜ

1945 (Act 3) Janssen *W*; Jessner *Si*;

Traubel *B*/Chorus/New York
PO/Rodzinski
CBS (UK) ⓜ 61452; (US)
ⓒ 32260018E
1951 (Act 3 live performance, Bayreuth
Festival) S. Björling *W*; Rysanek
Si; Varnay *B*/Bayreuth Festival
Orch./Karajan
EMI ⓜ 1C 181 03035–6M; CBS
(US) ⓜ SL 116

1957 (Act 3; Act 2) Edelmann *W*;
Schech *Si*; Flagstad *B*/VPO/Solti
Decca GOS 477–8; London OSA
1203
1938 (excerpts) Rode *W*; F. Krauss *S*;
Reining *Si*; von Manowarda *H*;
Rünger *B*/Stuttgart Senders
Orch./Leonhart; Königsberg
Opera Orch./Brückner
Acanta ⓜ DE 23114–5

SIEGFRIED

S Siegfried; *M* Mime; *W* Wanderer; *A* Alberich; *F* Fafner; *E* Erda; *B*
Brünnhilde; *W* Woodbird

1950 (live performance, La Scala,
Milan) Svanholm *S*; Markworth
M; Herrmann *W*; Pernerstorfer
A; Weber *F*; Höngen *E*;
Flagstad *B*; Moor *W*/La Scala
Orch./Furtwängler
Murray Hill ⓜ 940 477; Everest
ⓒ 475/3
1953 (live performance, Bayreuth
Festival) Windgassen *S*; Kuen
M; Hotter *S*; Neidlinger *A*;
Greindl *F*; von Ilosvay *E*; Mödl
B; Streich *W*/Bayreuth Festival
Orch./Keilberth
Allegro-Elite ⓜ 3133–7
1953 (broadcast performance) Suthaus
S; Patzak *M*; Frantz *W*;
Pernerstorfer *A*; Greindl *F*;
Klöse *E*; Mödl *B*; Streich
W/Rome Radio
Orch./Furtwängler
EMI ⓜ RLS 702; Seraphim
ⓜ IE 6078
1957 (live performance, Bayreuth
Festival) Aldenhoff *S*; Kuen *M*;
Hotter *W*; Neidlinger *A*; Greindl
F; von Ilosvay *E*; Varnay *B*;
Hollweg *W*/Bayreuth Festival
Orch./Knappertsbusch
Cetra ⓜ LO 60/5
1962 Windgassen *S*; Stolze *M*; Hotter
W; Neidlinger *A*; Böhme *F*;
Höffgen *E*; Nilsson *B*;
Sutherland *W*/VPO/Solti
Decca SET 242–6 ④ K,
D100D19; London OSA 1508
④ 5–1508

1966 (live performance, Bayreuth
Festival) Windgassen *S*;
Wohlfahrt *M*; Adam *W*;
Neidlinger *A*; Böhme *F*;
Soukoupová *E*; Nilsson *B*; Köth
W/Bayreuth Festival Orch./Böhm
Philips 6747 037
1968 McKee *S*; H. Kraus *M*; Polke
W; Kühne *A*; Okamura *F*;
Boese *E*; Kniplová *B*; Jasper
W/South German PO/Swarowsky
Westminster WGSO 8177/5
1968–9 Thomas *S*; Stolze *M*; Stewart
W; Kélémen *A*; Riddersbusch *F*;
Dominguez *E*; Dernesch *B*;
Gayer *W*/Berlin PO/Karajan
DG 2740 147 ④ 3378 048/9
1973 (in English – live performance,
Coliseum, London) Remedios *S*;
Dempsey *M*; Bailey *W*;
Hammond Stroud *A*; Grant *F*;
Collins *E*; Hunter *B*; M.
London *W*/Sadler's Wells Opera
Orch./Goodall
HMV SLS 875 ④ TC–SLS 875,
SLS 5146 ④ TC–SLS 5146

Excerpts

1928–33 Laubenthal, Melchior *S*;
Reiss, Tessmer *M*; Schipper,
Bockelmann, Schorr *W*; Habich
A; Olszewska *E*; Leider, Easton
B; Gruhn *W*/Berlin State Opera
Orch./Blech; VPO/Alwin; LSO/
Coates; LSO/Heger; Royal
Opera Orch./Heger
EMI ⓜ E 80744–5

GÖTTERDÄMMERUNG

B Brünnhilde; *S* Siegfried; *G* Gunther; *A* Alberich; *H* Hagen; *Gut* Gutrune

1950 (live performance, La Scala, Milan) Flagstad *B*; Lorenz *S*; Herrmann *G*; Pernerstorfer *A*; Weber *H*; H. Konetzni *Gut*/La Scala Orch./Furtwängler Murray Hill Ⓜ 940 477; Everest ⓒ 476/3

1953 (live performance, Bayreuth Festival) Mödl *B*; Windgassen *S*; Udhe *G*; Neidlinger *A*; Greindl *H*; Hinsch-Gröndal *Gut*/Bayreuth Festival Chorus and Orch./Keilberth Allegro-Elite Ⓜ 3138–42

1953 (broadcast performance) Mödl *B*; Suthaus *S*; Poell *G*; Pernerstorfer *A*; Greindl *H*; Jurinac *Gut*/Rome Radio Chorus and Orch./Furtwängler EMI Ⓜ RLS 702; Seraphim Ⓜ IE 6079

1955 Flagstad *B*; Svanholm *S*; Johnsen *G*; Gronneberg *A*; Nordsjö *H*; Björner *Gut*/Oslo Opera Chorus, Norwegian Radio Chorus, Oslo PO/Fjelstad Decca Ⓜ LXT 5205–10; London Ⓜ OSA 52438

1957 (live performance, Bayreuth Festival) Varnay *B*; Windgassen *S*; Uhde *G*; Neidlinger *A*; Greindl *H*; Grümmer *Gut*/Bayreuth Festival Chorus and Orch./Knappertsbusch Cetra Ⓜ LO 61/5

1964 Nilsson *B*; Windgassen *S*; Fischer-Dieskau *G*; Neidlinger *A*; Frick *H*; Watson *Gut*/Vienna State Opera Chorus, VPO/Solti Decca SET 292–7 ④ K; D100D19; London OSA 1604 ④ 5–1604

1967 (live performance, Bayreuth Festival) Nilsson *B*; Windgassen *S*; Stewart *G*; Neidlinger *A*; Greindl *H*; Dvořáková *Gut*/Bayreuth Festival Chorus and Orch./Böhm Philips 6747 037

1968 Kniplová *B*; McKee *S*; Knoll *G*; Kühne *A*; van Rohr *H*; Sommer *Gut*/Vienna State Opera Chorus, South German PO/Swarowsky Westminster WGSO 8178/6

1969–70 Dernesch *B*; Brilioth *S*; Stewart *G*; Kélémen *A*; Ridderbusch *H*; Janowitz *Gut*/German Opera Chorus, Berlin PO/Karajan DG 2740 148 ④ 3378 048/9

1977 (in English – live performance, Coliseum, London) Hunter *B*; Remedios *S*; Welsby *G*; Hammond Stroud *A*; Haugland *H*; Curphey *Gut*/English National Opera Chorus and Orch./Goodall HMV SLS 5118 ④ TC–SLS 5118; SLS 5146 ④ TC–SLS 5146

Excerpts

1920s Austral *B*; Widdop, Laubenthal *S*; Fear *G*; List, Andrésen, Collier, Zador *H*; Ljungberg *Gut*/LSO/Coates, LSO/ Collingwood, Berlin State Opera Orch./Blech and Muck HMV D1572–87

1950 Kovatsky *B*; Hansen *S*; Ramus *H*/Prague Opera Chorus and Orch./Wentzel Allegro Ⓜ 3065

1972 (in English – Act 3, scenes 2 and 3) Hunter *B*; Remedios *S*; Bailey *G*; Grant *H*; Curphey *Gut*/Sadler's Wells Opera Chorus and Orch./Goodall Unicorn UNS 245–6 ④ZCUND 245

Parsifal

ROBIN HOLLOWAY

Recordings of sizeable sections of *Parsifal* get off to a start which still remains without parallel, Karl Muck's 1928 version of most of Act 3. This is a revelation for its lightness of sonority and ease of movement. Nothing is allowed to impede the flow – thus the Coronation is grand but ungrandiose, with the four pause bars at the climax perfectly judged; thus there is no voluptuous lingering in the Good Friday meadows. No lumps – everything is held together in seamless momentum that can accommodate the most refined detail and grow naturally into the starkness of the transformation-music and the vehement accusation of the chorus. The soloists' Lieder-like delicacy is in complete accord with the orchestra's almost vocal phrasing. Words are exceptionally clear without undue emphasis; the uniformity of utterance leaves them to speak for themselves.

Ludwig Hofmann's Gurnemanz is nobility personified; Gotthelf Pistor's Parsifal a touching embodiment of troubled adolescence; while Cornelis Bronsgeest's Amfortas is almost *too* light and mellifluous in addressing his dead father, though finely agitated later. The exaltation of the closing pages, as the inevitable outcome of a long, deftly guided journey, is not surpassed in any later version. It is a different ideal of the sublime from the more customary weightiness, and for me it realizes better than any other Wagner performance the idea of 'endless melody'.

Though the cast is mouth-watering, it is difficult to enjoy much in a 'pirated' set broadcast from the Metropolitan in 1938. The recording is so vile that little can be distinguished – anyone coming to the work for the first time would find these discs incomprehensible, and even familiarity finds itself at sea. The noise and distortion and frightful little accidental omissions – a few bars here, the top of a climax there, and now and again two or three whole pages – are nightmarish.

Nonetheless there are valuable qualities. Klingsor (Arnold Gabor) is convincingly fierce and accurate and the good, strong Gurnemanz (Emanuel List) moves along Act 1 with lively naturalness and is grandly authoritative rebuking Parsifal (Lauritz Melchior) for wearing armour on Good Friday in Act 3. Friedrich Schorr is very fast in Amfortas's first monologue, which causes a certain loss of inwardness; but the hectic quality is not inexpressive, and his cries of 'Ebarmen!' reveal human anguish rather than, as so often, mere whale-sized endurance. In Act 3 he addresses his father 'den einst die Engel sich neigten' most beautifully, and the subsequent excitation is superb.

The performance's chief glory is also the greatest loss of these horrible discs. For against expectation Flagstad is clearly a real Kundry, and not only where one might expect her characteristic qualities to tell – the first thrilling sound of the hero's name, the pages of riddling over what it means, and later her comfort after his first access of grief. She is convincing also in aspects that are not so obviously suited to her – Kundry the devil-woman, half-reluctantly half-eagerly involved in Klingsor's evil spells. So the early stages of Act 2 are gripping, and her 'Gelobter Held' is the most appealing account of this 'above-the-belt' seduction I have heard. Her vanity is *stung* by Parsifal's dismissal; the passage about mocking the Crucifixion emerges as natural female defence rather than expressionist set-piece, and she still vibrates with indignation afterwards, which bursts forth in a fine 'So war es mein Kuss'. No more than any other Kundry does she capture the combination of nyphomaniac desperation and repelling defiance, though her scorn for the hero who fell and her cursing of the hero who withstands are good. Melchior seems to feel the complexities of 'Liebe-als-Qual' better in this music than in Tristan's delirium. The great moments here have the intensity of a stage performance, but for vocal quality one has to hear his contemporary records of excerpts. In Act 2 he is only heard to advantage as he wields the spear and razes the castle. But something of the Act 3 narration comes over, not least the lovely baptism of Kundry.

The live, radio recording of 1950 under Vittorio Gui, a private issue, takes us decisively out of the German mainstream, sung as it is in Italian by artists not usually associated with Wagner – the young Callas as Kundry, the young Rolando Panerai as Amfortas, the young Christoff as Gurnemanz. Callas is none too convincing in Act 1, though the low notes of her weary self-recrimination are good, but later she fascinates: even the two timorous groans and the two sung words in Act 3 have a quality all their own, while the core of the role in Act 2, from the really *musical* screams as Klingsor first conjures her up, to the superb inflammation of her angry bafflement at Parsifal's resistance, is remarkable. Here is no Nordic *Hausfrau*, but a devil-woman; wild, then suddenly cowed, waif-like, pitiably vulnerable in her appeal, before summing up vehement reserves of malignity towards the end of the act.

The focus of her attentions, Africo Beldelli's Parsifal, is exciting too, volatile and hot blooded in this outcry and moving with a psychological sureness, unsurpassed in any other performance of the part, from horrified attraction towards Kundry's blandishments to stern, self-enforced dismissal. In Act 1 he is occasionally off the note, but I admit to finding that less important in Wagner than a good voice, musicality and generous identification, with the role, all shown by Beldelli together with the real *sine qua non* (lacking in many German singers), rhythmic certainty. In Act 3 he is at first finely weary and restores faith more with sensibility than a brazen display of strength – another welcome change.

Christoff's Gurnemanz is no exception to the roll of tender, noble assumptions; he sings with particular beauty early in Act 3. Panerai's Amfortas is puzzling. Perhaps it is because one has become so habituated, without actually liking it, to explicitly rendered anguish that his almost disengaged restraint does not at first seem to get the measure of the part; yet it behoves one to understand a new way – and has the part ever been so beautifully *sung*? Occasionally he reaches a height of eloquence (Eulenburg, pp. 254–7) all the more moving for not wearing the wound, so to speak, on the sleeve. In Act 3, like Parsifal, Amfortas is exhausted (artistically, I mean), and even the strenuous section of this monologue is given in a light, muted way – further orginality.

In spite of the great value of the remarkable singing, the chief interest in these records lies in the orchestra. Gui was clearly a disciplinarian; the accuracy, especially in rhythm, and care for phrasing and voicing are unsurpassed by any other conductor. They put Boulez's precision and Solti's dictatorship into perspective because accompanied by complete musicality. His passion for accuracy and his elaborate calculation of transitions are directly in the service of a passion for what he is expressing. The result is always spontaneous and pleasingly Italian in its solicitous orientation towards the voices. Yet no other reading offers such clarity of detail. It is the opposite of Bayreuth in being a wind rather than string-based sonority; this enables strings to follow wood, instead of the usual drowning of wood by strings. That, together with Gui's attention to voicing, produces spectaculary beautiful *Harmonie* in both Grail scenes.

In Act 1 the grand and steady march-movement of the transformation still underlies the choruses with its crisp, springing bass until the masterly turning-point (pp. 232–3). The whole enormous passage seems to focus on pp. 239–40, winds wonderfully fade into silence (242) out of which Titurel's voice is heard, the line-drawing of the Communion is fine, and the choruses afterwards rock-steady, with just as firm inner and bass lines from the orchestra. In Act 2, he ranges from the biting sharpness of Parsifal's fight to the ravishing tonal sonority of Parsifal's description of Kundry's wiles and the electricity of the final destruction. In Act 3, the glorious flow of the Good Friday music (voice not to the fore here!) ends uniquely in a noon-day haze of complete immobility through which the bells steal in as if across a distance of time and space. Yet in the transformation that follows they will dominate the orchestra, all but drowning even the trombones, preparing us for a strangely *sotto voce* funeral chorus all the more menacing in its depleted accusation.

So, all in all, Gui is the only successor to Muck in a view of *Parsifal* as predominantly lyrical and flowing. Against that must be set the numerous cuts, some of them hefty, and in Acts 1 and 3 involving the loss of important narration, but – sometimes – one feels the need of cuts, and many a complete performance offers a distinctly less integral artistic experience than this excised one.

The core of *Parsifal* recordings is still the two Bayreuth sets, from 1951 and 1962, under Knappertsbusch. Granted the essential similarity, they show a notable difference of emphasis. A sense of special occasion permeates the earlier, which rises to greatness in set-pieces like the transformations and choruses in the outer acts, but can elsewhere be sectional and even (at a high level) pedestrian. The later performance is less solemn and devotional – more *present* both in musical detail and in its dramatic pacing; a music-drama rather than a 'stage-consecrating festival play'.

The difference can be heard at once in the 1962 prelude with its fleecy rapture, so much freer and more radiant than in 1951. This greater fluidity gets into the total shaping of Act 1; it moves more naturally and coheres better. The 1951 recording is memorable for detail, for instance the marvellous first appearance of Klingsor's motif, the first reference a moment later to the spear, and the gentle glow of the choral prophecy of the pure fool just before the real thing lurches on to the stage. 1951 produces a wonderful Act 3 prelude, but again the act as a whole does not flow. The baptism-music is stodgy; the bad comma just before the Good Friday music incorporates the 'Dresden Amen' is symptomatic. Whereas 1962 achieves a complement to Muck, Knappertsbusch retains his own heavy grandeur and builds it into rolling architectural masses. One example of this magnificent long-range shaping is the way he conveys the feeling that the long-drawn-out cadence as Parsifal at last stands revealed is the act's first real downbeat. Gurnemanz's baptizing music, so held back in 1951, now flows nobly forth. Its solemnity culminates in a grandly powerful but not portentous Coronation; its sweetness in a Good Friday scene as voluptuous in its way as the wicked flowers of Act 2. The momentum is weightier than Muck and just as irresistible.

Oddly enough the wicked flowers are more delectable in 1951. Though the scene begins dimly the main waltz section has such a lilt as to make one wish for Parsifal not to get beyond this stage in his education. That would, however, be a pity because the magical pages after his name is called and the girls dismissed – extraordinary music that seems to hold out welcoming arms to Debussy, Scriabin, Szymanowski, early Schoenberg, Berg, Delius – are more entrancing here than in any other recording (the 'Du . . . Thor' is really marvellous). In 1962 all this is not nearly so suggestive – which is more the fault of the singers than of the conductor. Wolfgang Windgassen as Parsifal is careless and a bit perfunctory in Act 1, but with the girls he comes to life and when his mother-lover calls his name he is galvanized into commitment. Martha Mödl is wonderful in this act. She covers more than any other Kundry the wide range, from

cringing abasement to voluptuous abandon. Her every utterance in Act
1 had been memorable – the malevolent snarl of 'Sind die Thiere hier
nicht heilig?'; the sulky dejection of 'Ich . . . helfe nie'; the urgency and
(if it does not sound insulting) naturalness of her animal noises. And at
this point in Act 2 we still feel the tingle of her terrifying screams,
laughter and groaning *chez* Klingsor. Now in the duet she comes fully
into her own (though she cannot keep 'Ich sah das Kind' steady as a
cradle song but has to push and pressure it). The main body of the act
is *understood* by both participants as in no other performance, and their
confrontation instead of being an exchange of challenges and slogans
becomes something that compels and involves us in both of them as
closely as we are involved with the lovers in *Siegfried*, Act 3, or *Tristan*
Act 2. And Mödl's laughter really rings down the centuries like no other
Kundry's.

The 1962 pair are altogether less interesting. Jess Thomas's strained
voice only conscientiously flirts with the girls, and when Kundry calls his
name he is dull and dry, entirely missing the note of wonderment. Irene
Dalis phrases lumpily and articulates blotchily (her own fault in 'Ich sah
das Kind', for she has pushed the conductor faster than he wants to go);
her account of Herzeleide's death sounds like a lesson in diction. But,
here and later, she is at least *trying* to reach something deep and difficult
in the part, whereas Thomas is inadequate in his outburst of pain and
illumination, lacking the vocal and artistic reserves to persuade us that
he suffers anything more than a pain in his side.

Earlier in the work Dalis is a sort of Mödl-parody, with the same range
of noises, done in a hard and artificial manner. Thomas, however, is at
his best here, serious and nicely boyish, touching in the interrogation with
Gurnemanz that reveals his pure foolery, and unlike Windgassen always
alert and in time. But he gets lost in Parsifal's third-act wanderings and
'Nur eine waffe' shows his resources strained to their limit. None of the
smaller roles are memorable except for Gustav Neidlinger's Klingsor in
1962 – a little careless but very much in the part – yet no match for
1951's superb Hermann Uhde. George London sings Amfortas in both
recordings. In 1951 he is already big and emphatic; not deep in the part
but with a certain massive straightforwardness that in the second
monologue tends towards stolidity. By 1962 the emphasis is insupportable,
though the power of the voice as such is impressive. He seems incapable
of singing softly or of shaping the direction of thought and emotion. Both
monologues are a big, black bawl, with no sense of physical wound and
spiritual exasperation. Only once for a brief phrase in the second ('Erlöser,
gieb meinem Sohne Ruh!') does the voice relent, abate its volume, and
melt into pliable *espressivo*.

The vocal glory of both these sets, as indeed of almost every other,
comes in the part of Gurnemanz. Ludwig Weber is warm and generous;
were it not for the comparison with Hans Hotter his performance would

stand high. But Hotter is all-surpassing and makes every other Gurnemanz seem generalized. His norm is simple tenderness, from which he rises to whatever kind of eloquence is needed, whether stern, sad, or celebratory. Phrase after phrase in both words and music is considered and valued as if for the first time; there are endless felicities of detail that no other singer has bothered with, like the touch of colour on 'Arabia' when Amfortas enquires the origin of Kundry's strangely fashioned vial.

Hotter is at his greatest early in Act 3 with singing of sustained tender nobility that culminates in easily the best account of the unrewarding vocal line in the unfolding benediction of the Good Friday meadows. In Act 1 his power of narration exactly fits Knappertsbusch's unsurpassed feeling (shown also in his complete *Tristan*) for *story*. Together these two artists shape Gurnemanz's long exposition into a dramatic and poignant history. This performance completely vindicates Wagner's bold idea of hanging the first hour or so of music upon a recitative, and his absolute sureness in timing and placing the apparent sidetracks which all, in fact, serve to further the progress of knowledge until at the last and biggest interruption, when narration has told everything it can, action is initiated.

So just for this benevolent presence presiding over the outer acts I have to prefer 1962 to 1951; with many a lingering backward glance at the earlier Flowermaidens, their *madame*, and the hero who is too foolish to stay and enjoy himself with either. Other advantages of the later recording, apart from the generally easier flow already mentioned, include the superb singing of the chorus, and a much higher level of accuracy; for in 1951 there is so much habitual sloppiness in rhythm from some of the singers (Windgassen, Weber, and the boys' chorus are the chief culprits) as to give the performance as a whole a feeling of impressionistic fuzziness.

The next complete set also comes from Bayreuth; the 1970 performance under Boulez. The cast is mixed. Franz Crass, a decent Gurnemanz, seems pedestrian with Weber, Frick, and especially Hotter in mind. More seriously disappointing is James King's Parsifal. He is accurate, especially in rhythm, but unlikeable. Thomas with inferior vocal equipment is more affecting in the no answers and quaint little questions – 'Wer ist gut?' 'Wer ist der Gral?' – of Act 1. King is charmless with the Flowermaids, hard almost to ugliness in self-recrimination over his mother's death, dry and fierce almost to shouting in his outburst after the kiss. He does not learn ruth; he remains right to the end the uncouth lout who shoots swans. So in the third act he rings out the climax of his narration, and 'Nur eine Waffe', effectively; but never gives vocal pleasure nor appears inward with the part.

Gwyneth Jones, by contrast, knows what Act 2 is about. Her first act is not interesting, but from the moment she is within Klingsor's clutches she convinces, especially in the whirlwind contradictions of mood late in the duet. Donald McIntrye's Klingsor is good, and since Boulez seems to share Debussy's preference for the castrated enchanter over the 'shop-girl whinings' of his principal victim, the opening scene of Act 2 is remarkably powerful. The prelude is febrile, which is not nice but makes psychological sense, and the *outré* sonorities of the demonic pair and the obsessive rhythms of Klingsor's description of Parsifal's battle suit him extremely well. Here is something this conductor seems to understand and feel; he brings it to life like no one else.

But, for the rest, he sounds simply bored. The palpitating section of the Flowermaidens is rushed in a way that denies rather than reveals its sense; their waltz · is charmless, colourless, carelessly phrased, and the magical pages of Kundry's and Parsifal's first encounter are deadpan. More serious for the work as a whole is Boulez's professed distaste for what can for convenience be called its Christian aspects (though it is surely obtuse of him to reduce this amazing web of ideas-in-music to 'conventional imagery of holiness and purity'). Hence the bouncily tripping choruses in Act 1 and the dreadful account, through speed and determined deflation, of the early part of Act 3. Elsewhere he sounds committed but surprisingly crude, as in both transformations, the edgy but sweeping Good Friday music, and the good if brassy end (balance of heavy brass is bad throughout). He skims a little insouciantly over the surface of the music, so that predictably enough it yields few of its treasures. He makes the work restless and rootless; the final effect is of a diminution of meaning. Yet having said this I must admit that I can think of few moments in all these records so sonorously beautiful as the start of Act 1 under Boulez, with its light silvery clarity and the perfect blend of the different layers of sound.

Only Solti's 1972 set (with all the advantages of a studio recording for greater accuracy and clarity of detail) is comparable; and here also, great sonorous beauty accompanies a distinct deficiency in architectural grasp and interpretative depth. But this *Parsifal* is none the less an admirable achievement – as admirable as his *Tristan* is deplorable. They are closely related, for he seems in *Parsifal* to be consciously rectifying his old faults, curbing and refining the tendency to brashness. The result can be curiously dead, as if his approach depended on excess to be vital at all. A predominantly slow score exposes his wooden sense of rhythm (something he shares with Boulez, who simply cannot sustain anything slow) both in the small, where notes are rushed and swallowed with awkward unevenness, and in the large, in the absence of any effect of cumulation whether grand as in Knappertsbusch or light as in Muck. Yet there are long passages where his sense of the sheer beauty of the music overcomes his respectful awe at its elevation; notably in the pages in Act 3 where Gurnemanz recognizes Parsifal, and the remarkably warm and unfebrile 'Nur eine Waffe'.

His cast is distinguished. Hotter having been the most beautiful Gurnemanz now makes the best Titurel, and is replaced by Gottlob Frick

Norman Bailey as Hans
Sachs (Anthony
Crickmay)

Janet Baker as Vitellia
La clemenza di Tito
(Reg Wilson)

Leonore and Florestan

Kirsten Flagstad and Julius Patzak at Salzburg (Harold Rosenthal Collection)

Helga Dernesch and Jon Vickers at Covent Garden (Donald Southern)

Singers and Conductors

Below: Victoria de los Angeles, Nicolai Gedda with Beecham (Carmen) (EMI)
Right: Elisabeth Schwarzkopf with Karajan (EMI)

Left: Martha Mödl with Furtwängler (EMI)
Above: Maria Callas and Christa Ludwig with Serafin (EMI)

in a role that seems to produce only their best from whomever takes it on. Zoltan Kélémen is a most convincing Klingsor, René Kollo is an under-defined but more than adequate hero. Christa Ludwig is an interesting Kundry, and Fischer-Dieskau a too-inward, too-thoughtful Amfortas – the great, wooden *noise* of London seems more appropriate, in the context of the forces pitted against it, than this sensitive Lieder style. Thomas Stewart in the Boulez set balances the two successfully, and is superb in the later stages of his second outcry.

The set's greatest vocal joy (as well as its warmest orchestral pleasures) come from the Flowermaidens – and reading their names one sees why! Here Solti has transcended his limitations. The fluttery section trembles with incipient delight, while the waltz, slower than usual, moves from charming blandishments through ever-rich colouring into an intoxication of sensuous delight that provides a carnal complement in sonorous perfection to Boulez's account of the Act 1 prelude. This Flowermaid scene is the best Wagner performance by Solti that I have heard.

There is not a great wealth of recorded extracts from *Parsifal*, but standards are high, and in a few cases the singing surpasses what can be heard in the complete sets. I shall go through the work by character rather than by chronology.

The impression of mannerism that Fischer-Dieskau's Amfortas gives in his complete performance is dispelled by his later record (ASD 3400) of the two monologues. This is a wonderful assumption; his long mastery of Lieder is now no longer an inhibition, but is used, in its total inwardness and precise articulation of deeply understood and deeply felt words, to convey an extraordinarily complete view of the complex character. He alone has the key to the weird paradox of Amfortas, that for all his longing for death he is kept alive by what should kill him – that therefore he loves his wound even while it tortures him. And he alone knows how to turn the succession of contradictory states into a coherent emotional and artistic utterance. Rafael Kubelik's contribution is distinguished, especially in the Act 3 monologue, by a slowness and attention to every detail that achieves an ideal virtually impossible in the opera house. It is difficult to imagine an Amfortas to surpass this. I have heard two other versions of the Act 1 outcry – Percy Heming, in 1925, in English and cut (D 1028; HLM 9009), very fast and not good; much better, Hans Hermann Nissen in 1928 (Homocord 4–8931; LV 58) – and one other of the Act 3 piece, an unremarkable account from 1943 by Hans Reinmar (Acanta HB 22 863–0).

The role of Gurnemanz is obviously by its nature not well suited to extracts. Act 1 provides only two, a very beautiful 'Titurel, der fromme Held' from Ivar Andrésen in 1927 (HMV EJ151; LV 45); and an unmemorable 'Nun achte wohl' from Joseph von Manowarda in 1938 (HB

22 863–0). There is one notable version of the meadow episode in Act 3, recorded under Siegfried Wagner in 1927 (L 2013/4; 1C 181–30 669/78) Kipnis is grand (and Fritz Wolff, his Parsifal, tender) in a broad tempo with masterly control of paragraph, and a sense of underlying slow-motion waltz-movement that subliminally establishes the connexion of the good flowers to the evil flowers of Act 2 as Wagner *père* surely intends. An earlier version (DB 497) has Paul Knüpfer's lovely Gurnemanz (with Hermann Jadlowker his wooden Parsifal); while Josef Greindl in 1952 is *un*lovely, with such a dash of vinegar in his voice 'on this holiest day of all'.

Turning to Parsifal and Kundry essentially means concentration upon Act 2. For forepleasures there is Günther Treptow flirting with the girls in 1950 (Decca LX 3036); promising but not enough in itself to tell how he would cope with a more demanding situation. Moving on to the serious stuff, I have encountered seven versions of Kundry's 'Ich sah das Kind' and five of Parsifal's 'Amfortas! die Wunde!'. The first two versions of 'Ich sah' come from Melanie Kurt in 1914 (043256; CO 345) and Lili Hafgren in 1921 (Poly. 65676; DG 2721 109) – the first is quaint and thin, the second not even so memorable as that. The part becomes interesting with the two versions by Leider. In 1925 (Poly. 72977; LV 155) she is warm but her idea of the music's character, and therefore of its shape, is far from complete. In 1931 (DB 1545; 1C 147–30 786) she is better; there is a clear idea of what the music means, and she is much more inward for Herzeleide's death. Kersten Thorborg in 1940 (Victor 17223; LV 209) with her full bloom of rich voice is almost as good as can be, done straightforwardly. While Flagstad at the end of her career (SDD 212) is the perfection of straightforwardness; vocally outstanding of course, and for once no hurry or fretting towards the climax (the conductor is Knappertsbusch). But it is *so* straightforward! Seductive wiles and undercurrents of psychological danger are simply absent. Only with Crespin's 1963 record (World Records ST 983) does sexiness prevail over maternality – a welcome change, but still not the whole way. There should be more Latin and fewer Nordic attempts on Kundry!

The earliest version of Parsifal's outcry, by Karl Jörn in 1913 (042431; CO 354) is too remote to have much impact, though there is a good sob at 'rette mich'; the orchestra is painfully hilarious in this of all places. Gotthelf Pistor (Parl. E 10771; LV 198) dates from the same time as his Act 3 under Muck and is, as there, light and prevailingly lyrical with no loss of gravity. Melchior recorded the passage three times. In 1925 (Parlo. E 10298; LV 226), the interpretation is unformed. In 1938 (DB 3781; Victor 1455) it begins ridiculously fast with the words a gabble. It improves later and becomes similar to the superior version of the next year (DG 2721 109), recorded from a broadcast. This is the best memento of Melchior's Parsifal. He brings all his characteristic animal intensity, making the music more physical than any other singer. We are made to *feel* the wound burning in the side, as later the beguiling motions of Kundry's hair, arms, mouth. There is physical immediacy also in his vehement dismissal of her; but it is not really inward. What does that pain really *mean*? The conductor is Nicolai Malko. Günther Treptow takes side burning in his stride (Acanta 22 104/5), his powerful voice cutting through dangers, musical and psychological that ought to daunt him more.

Some further excerpts involving the hero and heroine (if they can be so called) are of interest. The first, dating from the late 1920s, runs from 'Ich sah' through to Parsifal's outburst, then resumes at Kundry's account of her endless wait for salvation (D 1025–31). Walter Widdop makes a gentle, musicianly Parsifal, but the records are memorable chiefly for the range and intensity of Göta Ljungberg as Kundry, from the ravishing 'War dir fremd noch der Schmerz' to the wild raving of the later passage. Melanie Kurt's record of this later passage (Eulenburg score, pp. 589–92) should be included as a curiosity (043256/7; CO 345). This was a bold choice in 1914 when the music must still have been very advanced. The result, however, is a trifle absurd with tuba and trombones on the lower string parts, and little to be learnt from the voice. Another 1914 recording, with Rudolf Berger's hero and a few notes from Eduard Habich's Klingsor, runs from 'Auf Ewigkeit' to the end of the act (044261/2; CO 336). The performance is fierily dramatic and made memorable by Erna Denera's light-voiced demoness of a Kundry (a sort of Wagnerian Queen of Night), and the rise of Berger (a Verdi baritone-turned-*Heldentenor*) into vocal magnificence for demolishing the *Zauberschloss*.

There are two versions of the complete duet. The first, from 'Dies alles hab'ich nun geträumt' to the end of the act, is one of the work's classic recordings (RCA RB 6604) with Flagstad and Melchior in top form. Flagstad's 'Ich sah das Kibd' is so warm, lovely, gorgeous that one wonders what is missing. Maybe the passage describing Herzeleide's grief at the loss of the boy (Eulenburg, p. 530ff.) can tell us: with all her abundance, she is so imperturbable and emotion is so generalized as to be smoothed out altogether. Yet soon afterwards her exhortation to Parsifal to acknowledge his guilt and learn love (541ff.) is so ravishing that complaint seems churlish. Then, again, much later one feels that the torment and urgency of the character are simply not intense enough.

Melchior produces a vibrant 'Amfortas! die Wunde', and the pages of mingled wailing and exaltation, culminating in the half-demented vision of Christ's voice, produce the most inward singing that I have heard from this artist. The duet is well-shaped by Edwin MacArthur (apart from the accidental curtailment of a very beautiful passage, pp. 464–5), who provides sympathetic support for two magnificent voice-animals, relishing their vocal exercise in the prime of their health and bloom. Their company is exhilarating; but a dimension is lacking, and it is certainly not supplied in the other complete duet (from the girls' stabbing 'Thor!'), dating from 1975 (Philips 6500 661). Helge Brilioth is a decent Parsifal, doing his best,

and sincere in anguish and exaltation. Nilsson begins badly, trying against
the grain to be inward with the part but remaining hard and external, with
rhythmic inaccuracy unforgivable in a studio recording. Later she improves.
The vigorous music suits her better, though she makes it Brünnhilde-like,
and the 'Ich sah . . . Ihn' suggests a real feeling for at least one aspect of the
multifarious character. The orchestral direction is undistinguished.

And so to the apotheosis, Parsifal's *Liebestod* (as it were), 'Nur eine
Waffe', the penultimate stage of Act 3. Heinrich Hensel in 1912 (Od.
76302; CO 339) is light and bright, reedy, too thin-spun, unlike his
magnificent photograph. Karl Jörn the year after (042431; CO 354) is
unremarkable, while Fritz Soot in 1924 (Poly. 66728) is positively bad.
Heinrich Knote recorded Parsifal's apotheosis in 1930 at the age of 60
(Parl. E 11162); he is dry and clear, penetrating without hardness, and
only a little tight. The heroic ring, less commanding than Melchior, is
splendid in itself, and the *parlando* quality provides an interesting link
with an earlier Wagnerian style.

The memorable feature of Max Lorenz's 1933 version (Acanta HB 22
863–0) is Strauss's conducting; he goes right on (without chorus) to the
end of the act with a lazy spaciousness that works rather well. Georges
Thill in French (Col. D 15121; 2C 061–12153) projects a strong visual
image – one can see Parsifal standing in the scene, a male Joan of Arc,
frank, clean, exalted. But he has only this one dimension; this cut-out
Parsifal has no sense of the deep psychological thrill in returning the
spear to the cup. Melchior in 1938 (DB 3664; VIC 1500) is hearty and
none too clear. It is impossible to mistake the note of triumph in the
voice, but again one misses the inward exultation at the completion of
the progress. Treptow in the early 1940s (Acanta DE 22 104/5) is
comparable. The deep, confident voice certainly suits the hero's apotheosis
better than his moment of exhaustion (Eulenburg, pp. 708/9–722/3, also
included in this set with Greindl's Gurnemanz); and unlike Melchior,
Treptow articulates clearly, though thereby losing the line somewhat. But
these two grand voices are better constituted for razing Klingsor's castle
than for restoring the wholeness of the community, the body, the psyche.

Parsifal on the whole has been lucky on record, both in the complete
recordings and in the amplification and fuller realization of individual
moments given by some of the excerpts; but the ultimate luck of
something absolutely definitive has eluded it. There is more in the two
principal roles than any singer on record has yet reached. Parsifal is
hardly a straightforward part – I suppose what is needed is a combination
of Lohengrin and Tamino crossed with the delirious hero of *Tristan* Act
3; something at once virile and Italianate but bowed down with much
experience of suffering. While Kundry is required to embrace extremes
that are on the face of it positively contradictory – a combination of
Carmen and Elektra and Lulu with Nurse and Mother. The most complete
Parsifal I have heard is Vickers, the most inspired conductor of it,

Goodall (so there is a great opportunity lost). But a Kundry who has *everything*? . . . 'das ist ein And'res'. Still, after nearly a hundred years (a mere fraction of *her* life-span of course) this most extraordinary of all operatic parts has not been fully expressed.

PARSIFAL

P Parsifal; *Am* Amfortas; *T* Titurel; *G* Gurnemanz; *Kl* Klingsor; *Kun* Kundry

1950 (live performance, Bayreuth Festival) Windgassen *P*; London *Am*; van Mill *T*; Weber *G*; Uhde *Kl*; Mödl *Kun*/1951 Bayreuth Festival Chorus and Orch./Knappertsbusch Decca ⓜ GOM 504–8; Richmond ⓜ RS6 5001

1962 (live performance, Bayreuth Festival) Thomas *P*; London *Am*; Talvela *T*; Hotter *G*; Neidlinger *Kl*; Dalis *Kun*/1962 Bayreuth Festival Chorus and Orch./Knappertsbusch Philips 6746 250

1970 (live performance, Bayreuth Festival) King *P*; Stewart *Am*; Riddersbusch *T*; Crass *G*; McIntyre *Kl*; G. Jones *Kun*/1970 Bayreuth Festival Chorus and Orch./Boulez DG 2713 004

1972 Kollo *P*; Fischer-Dieskau *Am*; Hotter *T*; Frick *G*; Kélémen *Kl*; Ludwig *Kun*/Vienna Boys' Choir, Vienna State Opera Chorus, VPO/Solti Decca SET 550–4 ④ K113K54; London OSA 1510

Excerpts

1924 (in English) Widdop *P*; Heming *Am*; Radford *G*; Baker *Kl*; Ljungberg *Kun*/Chorus and Orch./A. Coates HMV D1025–31, DB 862

1928 (Act 3) Pistor *P*; Bronsgeest *Am*; Hofmann *G*/Berlin State Opera Chorus and Orch./Muck HMV D1537–44

1942–3 (Prelude; Act 3) Hartman *P*; Reinmar *Am*; Weber *G*; Larcen *Kun*/German Opera Chorus and Orch./Knappertsbusch Acanta ⓜ DE 23036

1950*c* Neumeyer *P*; Meesen *K*; Ramms *G*/Dresden State Opera Orch./Schreiber Allegro ⓜ ALL 3095

Faust

KENNETH FURIE

To anyone who loves *Faust*, the history of its recordings is discouraging. It is not merely that there has been no adequate complete set (and that the more recent efforts have strayed progrssively farther from the mark), but that the recordings of excerpts have shed all too little additional light, tending to reinforce the misconception of the piece as a sequence of display numbers. Although nearly every recording of this music has something to tell the confirmed enthusiast, if only by negative example, there is not much to make the uninitiated understand why some of us persist in regarding the opera as a masterpiece.

Gounod was no innovator, but he knew how to take advantage of the resources available to him, which means above all a supply of wide-ranging, attractive, limber, forceful voices. The current view of *Faust* (and of Gounod's *Roméo et Juliette* for that matter) as a musty relic has much to do with the fact that such singers have become, in all voice categories, an endangered species. The writing for Marguérite, Faust, and Valentin in particular has a nasty way of exhibiting what singers of the last two or three decades have been unable to do; as a result, our star singers – unlike those of the late nineteenth and early twentieth centuries – generally steer clear of these roles, which go instead to people whose qualifications are: the ability to get through them, albeit barely, and a willingness to sacrifice their larynxes so that the show can go. In other words, lambs to slaughter.

The role of Faust, for example, requires declamatory power and articulateness for the opening scene; purity, sweetness and breath control for the cavatina, 'Salut, demeure', and the garden scene duet; clarity and force, especially above the break, where few contemporary tenors have either, for the duel trio. The aria is excrutiatingly difficult, not so much for the notes – which, except for the high C (an important exception, since this C cannot be fudged), should be in the arsenal of every professional tenor – but for the absolute ease with which Gounod expects them to be uttered, bound together, controlled, and shaped. The writing is so exposed that it will spotlight mercilessly any defect in the singer's technique; the tenor who cannot spin a long legato line, who cannot rise effortlessly from chest into head register at soft as well as loud dynamics, has little chance of making any emotional statement, unless you count the expression of acute vocal discomfort as such.

Any soprano tackling Marguérite must start by working out how she will get through the Jewel Song, which leaves little leisure for such niceties as portraying the yearning melancholy of the 'Roi de Thulé' or wrenching the heart with her garden scene recollection of her poor little sister. Casting Valentin involves a different sort of complication: if we had a suitable high baritone, one whose upper range extends to a free, ringing G why would he waste his time with such a relatively minor role?

These casting problems are compounded by the failure of the French to maintain the vocal standards that once kept the world's operatic stages so well stocked – and of course produced such works as *Faust*. The voices Gounod knew were of types particular to France, and the language he set with such lyrical eloquence and declamatory force is one that uniquely combines these qualities: French. From its earliest years, *Faust* attracted the best singers on the international circuit, but in the French repertory their standards were set by that splendid native crop. One could still speak of a French school in the 1930s, even if its ranks were thinned; the decline since then has been precipitous, to the point that the appearance today of a French singer of international calibre, even by our depressed standards, would be cause for wonder and celebration.

Signs of the times: the best Méphistophélès of the last forty-five years were Italians, Ezio Pinza and Cesare Siepi; and the best Fausts since the war have been a Swede, Jussi Björling, and an Italian, the young Giuseppe di Stefano. (Unfortunately only Siepi recorded his role commercially – and that quite early in his career – although di Stefano's Faust can be heard in the 1949 Metropolitan Opera broadcast performance issued in Cetra's Live Opera series.) And while EMI did choose to make its latest *Faust* in Paris with Opéra forces, the principals are an Italian soprano, a Spanish tenor, a Bulgarian bass and a British baritone.

This business of style is elusive, and French style especially so. There is a widespread view that 'authentic French style' consists of feeble nasal piping, a notion that is not only aesthetically repugnant but historically unfounded, as can be heard by reference to HMV's early electric *Faust*, which contains two of the more distinguished performances to be founded in a recording of the complete opera: the Faust of César Vezzani and Méphistophélès of Marcel Journet, the last of the great French basses.

The Corsican Vezzani is a noble representative of that vanished breed, the French *spinto* tenor; it is a pleasure to have this reminder that voices of such juice and ring once existed and were put at Gounod's service. Unforced lyricism was not Vezzani's greatest strength – in that regard he yielded to his more famous junior (by eleven years), Georges Thill – but he was the image of poetic grace compared to most of what we have had to endure since. And where ringing excitement is called for, as in the climactic passages of the duel trio, his only equals are Caruso and, more recently, Franco Corelli. The contrast between Vezzani's Faust and that of Thill, another great French *spinto* (whose Faust is well documented in excerpt form), affords a fascinating demonstration of the range embraced by 'authentic French style'.

Journet was 62 at the time of his complete Méhistophélès and the voice is unmistakably more spread and extended than it was in the *Faust* excerpts he made in his late thirties and forties – notably the 1909–10 Victor series with Geraldine Farrar and Caruso. But the Journet of 1931 remained an authoritative and aristocratic singer, his interpretative instincts buttressed by an additional two decades' accumulated wisdom. Although he exercises considerable rhythmic freedom, his devil is happily not of the coarse, leering sort so often encountered. Although HMV's other singers are ordinary, they know what they are about, and the subtle responsiveness of Henri Busser's conducting minmizes their inequalities.

The only other complete *Faust* on this level comes from a source that on its face promises a performance wildly outside the 'authentic' tradition: the 1947 Soviet recording. There is no denying that *Faust* sounds somewhat odd in Russian, and that the voices heard here are of specifically Russian rather than French types. At the time time, the Soviet Union may be the only place where the tradition of full-scale grand opera survived into the 1950s and 1960s (indeed it is still not quite extinct), and the work of the *Faust* soloists, chorus, orchestra and conductor is marked by a degree of active belief rarely to be found these days in the West. Thus it is only partly the size of her voice that makes Elizabeta Shumskaya possibly the best Marguérite on records. Her robust *spinto* soprano is certainly agreeable to hear, but the distinction of her performance lies in the emotional commitment with which she deploys those vocal resources – she can be rapt in the garden scene and harrowing in the church scene.

Ivan Kozlovsky, the Faust, represents a link to another lost operatic tradition: voices of lyric weight capable of projecting with proper force. In the West, Björling was the last lyric tenor to do this with consistency (di Stefano could do it too, but he was not content to remain a lyric tenor); and as a result a whole cluster of roles, including Faust, that ought to belong to lyric tenors seem now to call for bigger voices. But to hear one of Björling's Metropolitan 'off-the-air' performances of the *Faust* love duet is to realize that what is required is not volume of sound for focused intensity. Kozlovsky's somewhat acid tone may not be very sensuous, but the voice was manged with a mastery of technique and phrasing which seems quite astonishing today; since the other distinguished Fausts – Caruso, Vezzani, Thill, Corelli – are all of larger voice types, there is a case to be made for Kozlovsky's as the most 'idiomatic' on commercial records.

There are no qualifications, language aside, to be made about the Valentin of Pavel Lisitsian – it is simply a great piece of singing under impeccable artistic guidance. The voice sails through the aria and the sword chorale; if there is any surprise, it is that his sunny, sympathetic timbre adapts so effectively to Valentin's savagery in the death scene – but then, Lisitsian also sang the finest Amonasro on records.

Without denying the attractions of the Melodiya recording, we cannot pretend that it solves the *Faust* problem. It is in the wrong language and heavily cut; its sound is dated; and it has a Méphistophélès, Alexander Pirogov, who performs expertly but tiresomely in the hammy, post-Chaliapin tradition.

The search for signs of life among the other complete recordings turns up only a few individual contributions. Sir Thomas Beecham certainly had the right idea, but the cast of his French-language recording, although stylistically sound, is at best workmanlike. His earlier, English-language recording is one of the more bizarre footnotes in the history of the phonograph. Even the one vocally able member of the cast, Heddle Nash, is so stuffily polite that one cannot imagine this Faust and Marguérite getting beyond a cool handshake.

André Cluytens too was a dependable *Faust* conductor, but both his recordings smack too much of going through the motions. In both cases the most interesting principal is the Valentin: the knowing, refined Jean Borthayre in the mono set; the vocally brilliant Ernest Blanc in the stereo set. The other principals are heard in both. Boris Christoff's tedious Méphistophélès (another Chaliapin imposture) is marginally more bearable, vocally and interpretatively, in the earlier version; with Victoria de los Angeles and Nicolai Gedda we face an uninspiring choice between relative vocal freshness and slight interpretative deepening. The later version's early stereo sound and relative completeness earn it a queasy recommendation among the modern recordings, but do not be deceived – it is no better than a least offensive alternative.

The Decca set has two important attractions: the most complete textual presentation possible while Gounod's autograph materials remain sequestered by his heirs (producer Ray Minshull's extensive annotations are themselves indispensable for *Faust* lovers) and Corelli's Faust. The role hardly figured in his career, and so one is all the more struck by the emotional intensity, the refusal to settle for either pretty sound or surface gesture – we have heard nothing comparable in the role since Björling and di Stefano, and the heft of Corelli's instrument makes possible some thrilling climaxes accessible only to a full-fledged *tenore di forza*. French did not come easily to him (the unstressed 'e' gives him particular difficulties) but in every phrase you hear an effort at verbal communication in a different imaginative league from the 'correct' diction of a Gedda.

Joan Sutherland makes predictably lovely and fluent sounds, but the last thing Marguérite needs is an extra overlay of languishment. At the time of his first Méphistophélès, Nicolai Ghiaurov was still in his sonorous vocal prime, but here his legato is so aggressively overweighted as to challenge Christoff's fragmentation for obnoxiousness. The rest of the cast is nondescript, and Richard Bonynge's skittish conducting makes the score sound even less substantial than usual.

Erato's recording is nearly as complete as Decca's (it lacks only Siebel's second song and some connective scraps absent from standard published scores), but the performance is still less satisfactory. Giacomo Aragall and Paul Plishka have fine voices of ideal calibre for Faust and Méphistophélès, but neither make any contact with his role. Montserrat Caballé, at her droopiest, makes Sutherland sound almost animated, and the supporting cast is feeble. For anyone who recalls Alain Lombard's trim, coherently proportioned Metropolitan *Faust*s, it is hard to believe that he presided over this sleepy affair.

The more one scavenges among the LP recordings, the more attractive CBS's old Metropolitan recording starts to sound. The superiority of Siepi's Méphistophélès over the post-war competition is evident even in this rather bland form, and Eleanor Steber's Marguérite is firm, conscientious, and vocally agreeable. Eugene Conley may not be Björling (the Met's premier Faust at the time the recording was made), but he holds his own against most of the competition. If Fausto Cleva's conducting is neither poetic nor galvanic, it does move; with a sufficient effort of will and imagination, you can close your eyes and almost hear something resembling *Faust*.

As noted above, the Decca set contains more music than any other. It was in fact the first recording to offer the usually omitted Marguérite-Siebel scene with which Gounod opened Act 4; Erato subsequently included Marguérite's spinning song ('Il ne revient pas') and the duet, but not Siebel's later-added 'Si le bonheur', for which the best source in any case is Karin Branzell's recording (Brunswick 15190; LV 47).

The other problematic scene is the *Nuit de Walpurgis* (including the ballet music sometimes credited to Delibes), which should open Act 5. It can be heard complete in the second Cluytens/HMV, the Decca and the Erato sets, and in part in the Busser/HMV set and in the 1937 Stuttgart broadcast performance issued by Preiser; the complete ballet music is given as an appendix to the Soviet recording (although the synopsis in the most recent issue of it would have us believe that the ballet is actually performed after the death of Marguérite!). The omission of the *Nuit de Walpurgis* from the CBS set is regrettable; Siepi was particularly effective in this scene.

No other scene is handled as rudely as these two, but the older recordings do make various internal cuts. Ideally the opera should be given in as complete an edition as possible – there is not a bar in the score that does not contribute something to the whole – but, as should be clear by now, *Faust* conditions are far from ideal; I would gladly settle for a performance that makes aesthetic sense of what it does include.

The two most important groups of excerpts have already been noted.

What makes the 1909–10 Victor series built around Caruso, Farrar, and Journet so important is its extensive representation of the ensembles: the end of the Faust-Méphistophélès scene (from 'O merveille', 89039); from the Kermesse, the Méphistophélès-Valentin scene leading into the sword chorale (with Amato, 89055); the garden scene quartet (with Gabrielle Gilibert as Marthe, 95204–5) and duet (89031–2) plus Marguérite's window apostrophe (with Méphisto but without Faust, 89090); the Marguérite-Méphistophélès church scene (89035, 89037); the duel trio (with Scotti, 95205; from the prison scene, the duet (89033–4) and final trio (95203). It is easy to understand why this music has been recorded far less often than the big solo numbers: why bother with it unless you have singers capable of bringing the characters to life? If you do, and if they happen to be of this vocal calibre, you may begin to discover what *Faust* is all about.

Now we need a careful LP transfer of the lot, with the same principals' more or less contemporaneous solo recordings inserted in place: Caruso's 'Salut, demeure' (88003); Farrar's 'Roi de Thulé' (88229) and Jewel Song (88147); Journet's 'Veau d'or' (64036), Invocation (64119), and Serenade (64137); Scotti's 'Avant de quitter' 81022 and 9920) and death (88282), both in Italian. Fortunately Thill's Columbia *Faust* excerpts – the opening scene (LFX 143 and, with Fred Bordon, LFX 150), the aria (LF 17), the garden scene duet (with Bordon and Marthe Nespoulos, LFX 182–3), and the final trio (with Bordon and Marise Beaujon, D 15180) – *have* been gathered on LP (2C 061 12073).

We might designate a third *Faust* 'group': the Chaliapin recordings. My earlier comments on the doleful influence of Chaliapin's Méphistophélès should not be taken as a blanket condemnation of the model, which may have been 'wrong' but must have been a whale of a performance, the product of a theatrical imagination pretty much unique in this century. Each of the innumerable performances (in Russian and French) of the three set-pieces is in its own way inimitable and wonderful. Most readily accessible are the 1928 Covent Garden live recordings first published in the EMI set (RLS 710), but the strongest sense of Chaliapin's dramatic presence emerges from the church scene with Michailova (DB 899).

This is the sort of indestructibly dramatic excerpt that may seduce even those who think themselves *Faust*-proof, and some mention should be made of two other performances, also (by coincidence?) in the wrong language: Nazzareno de Angelis with Gina Cigna, in Italian (LX 233); and one by Meta Seinemeyer and Emmanul List, in German (Parlo. E 10835; LV 114). Another such scene is Valentin's death, of which there is an especially distinguished account by Schlusnus (Poly. 73085; LV 108).

The Schlusnus recording is of course in German, and is part of a surprisingly vital German *Faust* discography – co-existing with the crude barking one expects from such sources – dating back to the interesting 1908 more-or-less 'complete' set with Destinn, Jörn, and Knüpfer and running through excerpts LPs of the 1950s (DG's, with solid work by Maria Stader and Heinz Hoppe and a most impressive unhysterical 'Veau d'or' and Serenade by Kim Borg – one wishes he had more to do) and 1960s (Eurodisc's, with Hilde Gueden's lovely Marguérite), certainly more communicative than the excerpt LPs that have come out of France in that time. (In French but not from France are the Concert Hall excerpts made in Vienna, noteworthy for Heinz Rehfuss's Méphisto – similar to and as impressive as Borg's – and for some solid singing by Léopold Simoneau in the title role.) Alas, the German *Faust* tradition seems to be another casualty of the 1970s, at least judging by Electrola's *Querschnitten* disc, which, not withstanding its starry cast and its considerable refinements of the ghastly long-standard German translation, is dreadful.

Otherwise, there are of course myriad recordings of *Faust*'s hit tunes, and among them there is much agreeable vocalism (and a lot more that is not so agreeable). There is not, however, much to tell us why we should care about these people, and nothing will kill the opera more surely than severing the connection between its opportunities for vocal display and its emotional content. Yes, Gounod knew how to show off a great voice, but he expected his singers to use those opportunities to flesh out his character sketches. The text tells us what we need to know about Marguérite's feelings of abandonment and isolation, and the resulting sense of romantic longing; now we need a soprano to use Gounod's richly expressive music to fill out the picture, to tell us what sort of person she is and why her situation matters.

Vocal display is by no means incompatable with Gounod's dramatic intention. On the contrary, the right kind of vocal display is a *sine qua non*. Valentin's aria is nothing if not a showpiece; the more freely the voice rings out, the better the baritone's chance of communicating the core of egocentric insensitivity lying beneath that bluff, hearty exterior – for a demonstration, try Tibbett (DB 2262), crummy French and all.

The vocal resources have to be there, but they are just the raw materials for *Faust*. Pinza's commercial recordings of the Méphistophélès excerpts are in varying degrees well sung, but they hardly prepare the listener for the eloquence of his 1940 Met broadcast performance. The forty-eight-year-old singer can be heard husbanding his resources shrewdly, tailoring them precisely and hypnotically to the music; the performance works because it grows as directly out of Pinza's personality as Chaliapin's had grown out of his, and it manages too to project more fully than any *Faust* performance I have heard, what Conrad L. Osborne has called the 'dignity and grace' of Gounod's writing.

For the reasons suggested earlier, few tenors relish tackling Faust's man-eating aria, another of those display pieces. But on those rare occasions when a singer can not only get out the notes but command them, and do so with real poetic impulse, the result can be indescribable. It does not matter that McCormack's famous 1920 version (Victor 88230;

Pearl GEMM 155/60) is in Italian, or that Björling – whose 1939 'Salut, demeure' (DB 3887; RLS 715) is his only commercial *Faust* recording – always inclined to dot Gounod's rhythms a bit; their artistry unleashes the expressive power lying dormant in music that our sophisticated taste-makers write off as hopelessly, even laughably tepid and old-fashioned.

They are wrong. '*Faust* is not great literature, profound thought, or subtle music drama,' Osborne has written. I happen to love the piece. I even think it has real musical and theatrical stature. I am not sure, though, that a very effective case can be made for it on paper, except at truly analytical length. Its case resides in the theatre, in performances of transcendent beauty or gut impact that have nothing to do with analysis or argument. Fortunately we have at least a handful of recordings to help argue the case.

FAUST

M Marguérite; *S* Siebel; *Mar* Martha; *F* Faust; *V* Valentin; *Méph* Méphistophélès

1908 (in German) Destinn *M*; Götze *S*; von Scheele-Müller *Mar*; Jörn *F*; Zador *V*; Knüpfer *Méph*/Chorus and Orch./Seidler-Winkler
Discophilia ⓜ KS 4–6

1912 Camredon *M*; D'Elty *S*; Goulancourt *Mar*; Beyle *F*; Noté *V*; Gresse *Méph*/Chorus and Orch./Ruhlmann
Pathé 1622–49

1920 (in Italian) Bosini *M*; Timitz *S*; Garrone *Mar*; Romagnoli *F*; Pacini *V*; Autori *Méph*/La Scala Chorus and Orch./Sabajno
HMV S5260–98

1929–30 (in English) Licette *M*; Vane *S*; Brunskill *Mar*; Nash *F*; Williams *V*; Easton *Méph*/BBC Choir, SO/Beecham
Columbia DX 88–103

1931 Berthon *M*; Cozette *S*; Coiffiers *Mar*; Vezzani *F*; Musy *V*; Journet *Méph*/Paris Opéra Chorus and Orch./Büsser
HMV C2122–41; Club 99 ⓜ OP 1000

1937 (in German: broadcast performance) Teschemacher *M*; Spletter *S*; Waldenau *Mar*; Roswaenge *F*; Nissen *V*; Hann *Méph*/Stuttgart Radio Chorus and Orch./Keilberth
Preiser ⓜ FST3

1947–8 Boué *M*; Saint-Arnaud *S*; Bannerman *Mar*; Noré *F*; Bourdin *V*; Rico *Méph*/Chorus, RPO Beecham
HMV DB 9422–37; RCA ⓜ LCT 6100

1949 (live performance, Metropolitan Opera, New York) Kirsten *M*; Mansky *S*; Turner *Mar*; Di Stefano *F*; Warren *V*; Tajo *Méph*/Metropolitan Opera Chorus and Orch./Pelletier
Cetra ⓜ LO 1 (3)

1949 (in Russian) Shumskaya *M*; Gribova *S*; Ostrumova *Mar*; Kozlovsky *F*; Lisitsian *V*; Piriogov *Méph*/Bolshoi Theatre Chorus and Orch./Nebolsin
MK ⓜ DO 5776–83

1951 Steber *M*; Roggero *S*; Votkipa *Mar*; Conley *F*; Guarrera *V*. Siepi *Méph*/Metropolitan Opera Chorus and Orch./Cleva
CBS (UK) ⓜ 77360; (US) ⓜ Y3–32103

1954 Angeles *M*; Angelici *S*; Michel *Mar*; Gedda *F*; Borthayre *V*; Christoff *Méph*/Paris Opéra Chorus and Orch./Cluytens
HMV ⓜ ALP 1162-5;

RCA (US) ⓜ LM 6400

1958 Angeles *M*; Berton *S*; Gorr
Mar; Gedda *F*; Blanc *V*;
Christoff *Méph*/Paris Opéra
Chorus and Orch./Cluytens
HMV SLS 819; Angel SDL 3622

1966 Sutherland *M*; Elkins *S*; M.
Sinclair *Mar;* Corelli *F*; Massard
V; Ghiaurov *Méph*/Ambrosian
Singers, LSO/Bonynge
Decca SET 327–30; London
OSA 1433

1977 Caballé *M*; Terzian *S*; Tallion
Mar; Aragall *F*; Huttenlocher *V*;
Plishka *Méph*/Rhine Opéra
Chorus, Strasbourg PO/Lombard
RCA Erato STU 71031–4;
RCA (US) FRL 4-2493

1979 Freni *M*; Command *S*; Tallion
Mar; Domingo *F*; Allen *V*;
Ghaiurov *Méph*/Paris Opéra
Chorus, and Orch./Prêtre
HMV SLS 5170 ④ TC–SLS
5170; Angel SDLX – awaiting
release

Excerpts

1934 G. Martinelli *M*; Lapelletrie *F*;
Cambon *V*; Beckmans
Méph/Chorus, Lamoureux
Orch./Wolff
Polydor 566070–4

1933/5 Nespoulos, Beaujon *M*; Thill
F; Bourdon *Méph*/chorus and
orch./Bigot, Gaubert
EMI ⓜ 2C 061 12073

1935 (in German) von Debicka *M*;
Roswaenge *F*; Schlusnus *V*;
Kandl *Méph*/Berlin State Opera
Chorus and Orch./Weigert
Polydor 27377–81

1936 (Act 1, in Italian) Melandri *F*;
de Angelis *Méph*/La Scala
Chorus and Orch./Molajoli
Columbia D 14586–8

1940 Steber *M*; Tokatyan/Jobin *F*;
Cehanovsky *V*; Cordon
Méph/Chorus, Publishers' Service
SO/Pelletier
RCA ⓜ CAL 221

1943 (in German) Eipperle *M*;
Waldenau *S*; Roswaenge *F*;
Wocke *V*; Hann *Méph*/Berlin
State Opera Chorus and
Orch./Rother

Acanta ⓜ BB 22138

1953 Marques *M*; Curtsinger *F*; Lore
V; Wilcox *Méph*/Chorus and
Orch./Peluso
Opa ⓜ 1003-4

1954 Yeend *M*; Petrak *F*; Scott
Méph/New York City Opera
Orch./Halasz
MGM ⓜ E3023

1955 Stader *M*; Naaff *S*; Hoppe *F*;
Wächter *V*; Borg
Méph/Bavarian Radio Chorus,
Orch./Various Conductors
DG ⓜ 89651

1955 Bonelli *M*; da Costa *F*; Sgarro
Méph/Orch./Walther
Royale ⓜ 1616

1956 (abridged) Graf *M*; Graar *S*;
Larsen *F*; van de Ven *V*; Gorin
Méph/Netherlands PO/Goehr
Musical Masterpieces Society
ⓜ M127

1957 Alarie *M*; Berton *S*; Léal *Mar*;
Simoneau *F*; Bicos *V*; Rehfuss
Méph/Vienna State Opera
Chorus, Vienna Festival
Orch./Rivoli
Concert Hall SMS 2374

1960 Guiot *M*; Silvy *S*; Botieux *F*;
Bianco *V*; Dépraz *Méph*/chorus
and orch./Etcheverry
Vogue LDM 30128 ④ VOC
417

1961 Jaumillot *M*; Broudeur *S*; Poncet
F; Bianco *Méph*/Karlsruhe
Opera Orch./Couraud
Philips 837023 GY

1965 (in German) Gueden *M*;
Schirrmacher *S*; Schock *F*;
Beresford *V*; Frick
Méph/German Opera Chorus and
Orch./Schuchter
Ariola-Eurodisc K86813R

1973 (in German) Moser *M*;
Groenewold *S*; Gedda *F*;
Fischer-Dieskau *V*; Moll
Méph/Berlin RIAS Chorus,
Berlin Radio SO/Patanè
EMI 1C 063 28961 (Q)

1975 Sass *M*; Kalmár *S*; Korondy *F*;
Miller *V*; Kováts *Méph*/choruses,
Hungarian State Opera
Orch./Lukács
Qualiton SLPX 11712

Carmen

RODNEY MILNES

Carmen is one of those operas in which creative genius of the highest order has, after an uncertain rather than (as generally supposed) a disastrous première, been answered by lasting popularity, the popularity reflected in a steady flow of records from the turn of the century onwards. I have by no means been able to hear them all.

To allow shorthand assessments later, it is necessary to establish certain points at the outset. After the uncertain première at the Opéra-Comique in 1875, *Carmen*'s eventual popularity was founded on successful performances in Vienna later the same year; thence it travelled all over Europe, the success finally confirmed by the Paris revival of 1883. Thus there is an almost definable German-language *Carmen* tradition which persists to this day, a tradition emphasized by the fact that in Vienna and virtually everywhere (save at the Opéra-Comique) until twenty years ago, the dialogue was replaced by Guiraud's recitatives. Thus on the one hand we have a swift-moving, quintessentially French *opéra-comique*, its detachment underlined by mercurial changes of mood from light comedy to tragedy, and on the other a ponderous, through-composed, heavy-breathing melodrama – one that influenced the Italian *verismo* school and, as far as Italian performance style is concerned, was swallowed up by it: you still hear Italian Josés singing like Canio, and Italian Carmens who sound like Santuzza in bangles.

The way the Frenchness of the work has evaporated may be judged from the fact that of eleven stereo recordings, in only one are Carmen and José sung by French singers. Another startling fact is that in no two of these eleven, nor indeed in any of the complete recordings I have heard, is the text the same. For an opera written in 1675 that would be understandable, but for one written just over one hundred years ago...? A modern edition of *Carmen* has always been needed, and it is tragic that when it came (from Fritz Oeser, Alkor Edition, 1964) it should have been, in the words of Winton Dean (*Bizet*, Dent, 1975), 'perhaps the most corrupt score of any major masterpiece published in modern times' (for Mr Dean's detailed demolition see *Musical Times*, November 1965). This would be relatively unimportant were it not that for obvious practical reasons this edition, usually with the worst howlers expunged, has been used for all modern recordings. Some hold that it is all a matter of mere textual details, but can serious misreadings of the first meeting of Carmen and José, the climax of the third act and the moment of the murder be considered mere details? I fear not.

At least Oeser made the spoken dialogue and *mélodrame* easily available: thus far his edition is a blessing. The reasons for preferring the dialogue, apart from the fact that this is how Bizet set the work, are obvious: first, dialogue tells you more about the characters in less time than recitative – for instance, we should be told at the beginning that José is repressed and given to violence; second, the suppression of the dialogue also suppresses one vital facet of Carmen's character – her humour – and on record only one singer of the Guiraud version, Victoria de los Angeles, has succeeded by purely vocal means in putting it back; third, the incidence and length of the passages of dialogue are all part of the work's classically perfect structure; fourth, Guiraud's recitatives are dreadful.

Carmen is an opera, like *Così fan tutte*, in which the passing of time has affected audience reaction. Until comparatively recently the protagonist would have been considered a sluttish *femme fatale* who destroyed a decent, upright soldier; today, perhaps, we might regard her as an honest ('Jamais je n'ai menti', and she's telling the truth, as always) and liberated woman murdered by a maternally dominated psychopath. There are many shades of emphasis between these two extremes to be investigated by resourceful singers. Micaela's is perhaps the most misunderstood role. She is emphatically no milksop: she must suggest her role as mother-substitute while showing peasant wit in the first act and peasant strength in the third. There are few sopranos who can manage all three. To his fatuity, all too often funked by baritones, Escamillo must add the Toreador's cruelty if he is allowed the whole of the third-act duet (few are) and an element of glossily packaged, supermarket sex-appeal. A final word on the text. Meilhac's and Halévy's libretto strikes me as no less masterly than Bizet's score, and it is ideally interpreted by French artists. Only a Frenchwoman can deliver a line like Carmen's 'Mon pauvre coeur, très consolable' and get all there is out of it. It is one of the sad facts of life that few non-French singers can sing the language perfectly – certainly not Italians, and hardly any Spaniards, Germans or Anglo-Saxons. The very Frenchness of *Carmen* (and remember, as Noël Coward did in verse, that '*Carmen* by Bizet/is no more Spanish than the Champs-Élysées') both literally and aesthetically means that recordings from France have a head start.

The Gallic/non-Gallic, Guiraud-versus-dialogue conflict is demonstrated by the three most recent complete versions. Claudio Abbado's reading is all Mediterranean fire, sparkling, clear, fleet, perhaps flashy rather than elegant, but he conveys his enjoyment of the purely musical values most vividly. Teresa Berganza's views on the title role, expressed in an open letter to Peter Diamand, then director of the Edinburgh Festival where she first sang Carmen, are reprinted in the booklet; she regards the Carmen of tradition as a slight on Spanish womanhood. Her interpretation is thus on the light side, full of humour, of self-mockery even, in the Habanera. It is bewitchingly sung, with great attention to musical detail; she makes more of the *marcati* in the Séguedille than any other mezzo I have heard. All that prevents her being *the* Carmen is a lack of allure, of engagement in her relationship with José, too close a placing *vis-à-vis* the microphone and a corresponding lack of dynamic variety, and by the highest standards a lack of tragic stature in the finale. Her card song, however, is one of the best on record – absolutely *égal* and wonderfully dark in timbre. The supporting cast is not strong, with Ileana Cotrubas a wilting (though admittedly appealing) Micaela, Sherrill Milnes a dull Toreador, and only average smugglers and gypsies.

There is much in common with the Solti recording: Placido Domingo, an acceptable José by today's standards but not in the context of seventy years of recordings (too little vocal finesse, too little variety in characterization); dialogue, though there is more on the Solti and it is better delivered; and the opening of cuts made by Bizet in rehearsal. The full version of the cigarette chorus is nice but not essential; the few bars of Carmen's sarcasm after 'Au quartier' is spine-tingling and absolutely essential; Solti gives the full version of the duel duet in the third act, and makes it work, Abbado does neither. Abbado sanctions two nasty bits of Oeserie, whereas Solti made a careful study of the score and achieves perhaps the most satisfying version of the text on record – the reasons are given in his persuasive essay in the booklet. Solti has an idiomatic Escamillo (José van Dam) and in Kiri Te Kanawa an heroic, attentive Micaela short only on wit in the first act. To find a livelier pair of smugglers than Michel Sénéchal and Michel Roux you have to delve back thirty years and to the Opéra-Comique, and Norma Burrowes and Jane Berbié are fine gypsies. In both recordings the choruses miss the spirit of those in earlier, French-based versions. Which leaves Decca's Carmen, Tatiana Troyanos. She is what Italian critics would call 'correct' – accurate, musical, somewhat lacking in 'face', although her dialogue is first rate. Solti is commendably faithful to the markings and enjoins his singers (Domingo excepted) to show similar respect, but his is a European rather than a specifically French reading, on the heavy side, serious certainly, most compelling in the dramatic passages, but without Abbado's *élan*. Yet as a performance, Solti's works.

Alain Lombard's recording used the Guiraud recitatives – this at a time when all others were investigating the dialogue, typical of France's cavalier attitude to one of her dramatic masterpieces – and sits, like the city of Strasbourg whence it hails, on the international fence. It has the advantage of an entirely French cast (with the exception of Jeannette Pilou, though

no one would know it from her delivery) and freedom from any sense
of routine. Nevertheless, his reading is on the *ernst* side and notable for
slow tempi. Although it might be thought that a mezzo role could suit
a soprano no longer in the first flush of youth, this is not altogether the
case. From the top of the stave upwards, Régine Crespin is unsteady and
unable to control dynamic shading. But what pleasure it is to hear,
uniquely in stereo recordings, a Frenchwoman launching into the Habanera:
the way she lingers momentarily on the very first labial of 'L'amour'
promises an authentic delivery of the text. Her Carmen is free of vocal
hip-swinging, restrained, perhaps too ladylike; she commands the style,
the 'class' essential to the role, but not the animal magnetism. Her José,
Gilbert Py, is well towards the top of the list: he gets more out of the
words than any modern interpreter, his voice has body towards the
bottom of the range (the first José was an ex-baritone), and he has the
technical control for the *pianissimo* passages in the first act – it is thus
doubly sad that he should bellow the final B flat of the flower song. The
only drawback is his occasionally unsteady tone. But the way he *lives* the
role makes him virtually unique amongst post-war interpreters. The rest
of the cast is good: if only they had been allowed to speak the dialogue....

The version conducted by Rafael Frühbeck de Burgos is ruined by one
bêtise: actors are used to speak the dialogue, and lots of it, but the voices
do not match, the singers' French pronunciation is barely acceptable, and
any sense of a dramatic performance is lost. The musical performance
is strangely undistinguished from what on paper is a distinguished cast.
Grace Bumbry is dull, of all things. Jon Vickers is worthy in intention,
less so in execution; at the time (ten years ago) his attack on notes
tended to be that of a sapper, approaching from underneath, and while
this may work in Wagner it certainly does not in Bizet. His praiseworthy
attempt at the flower song, *pianissimo* B flat and all, is spoiled by his
and Frühbeck's pulling the tempo around too much, making it sound
melodramatic. (An earlier 'private' recording by Vickers of this number
in English is just as accurate dynamically, cleaner in attack, and altogether
marvellous.) What makes the Frühbeck *Carmen* of more than passing
interest is that it uses the text as printed in the 1875 vocal score. Thus
only here do we get the 'Pantomime' for Morales and the chorus at the
beginning of the first act, a poor piece which holds up the action and
was rightly cut by Bizet during the first run.

The remaining modern dialogue versions are quickly disposable. The
Bernstein, based on the Metropolitan production by Göran Gentele
(realized by Bodo Igesz), is too eccentrically, not to say archly and self-
consciously, conducted for serious consideration: it sounds nothing like
Bizet, which is not altogether surprising as it is also full of Oeser. All
this is a pity, as under happier circumstances Marilyn Horne could be
a formidable Carmen. As it is, the performance is infinitely preferable
to her brash singing on the Decca Phase-4 highlights disc. Lorin Maazel's

recording, the first in stereo with the dialogue (though so drastically cut as to render it meaningless), also uses Oeser, and is the only one to play his ludicrous misreading of the end of the third act. Add to all this Anna Moffo's quavery crooning, Franco Corelli's second-rate *verismo* José (much of it sounding tracked and with an anonymous actor helping out with the dialogue), Piero Cappuccilli's unimaginatively bawled Escamillo, and Maazel's fidgety pointing of the music, and you have a version which vies with Bernstein's as the worst *Carmen* ever committed to disc.

Georges Prêtre's recording was advertised at the time as 'The Callas *Carmen*', which is just what it is; it is hardly Bizet's. As with everything the diva did, her Carmen is a wholly committed and commanding interpretation, but her gypsy is devoid of any charm and, like Mérimée's as opposed to Meilhac's and Halévy's, on the cruel side. Carmen as tigress, no more. As to a lesser extent with Crespin's version, Callas shows this is no role for a fading soprano: there are similar problems with dynamics. Her French is individual. Prêtre's reading is swift and Gallic, without much dramatic weight. Nicolai Gedda turns in one of his two excellent recorded performances as José. His flower song is here perfectly realized in vocal terms, every nuance, every marking as the composer intended. He is similarly delicate in the first act, but throughout there is little hint in his smooth vocalization of the darker side of the character, and a certain lack of metal in the later acts. But he is one of the few post-war tenors with the technique for the role. Andrea Guiot is similarly one of the few wholly successful modern Micaelas: lively, accurate, intense when need be. She is not in her best voice here. Robert Massard is only a fair Escamillo (*forte* throughout); the supporting roles are well taken. Ironically in the event, it is Callas who prevents this being a seriously considerable recording. The Karajan version of the same year is a fine example of the Viennese view of the opera. It starts promisingly, with Leontyne Price balancing her sexy voice with a lightly humorous approach. But as the set progresses, 'seriousness' takes over and the Gallic qualities of the score are swamped by high melodramatics, and by Karajan worrying the music: in trying to get the most out of it by way of expression, he ends up with the least. Franco Corelli, a Canio out of his depth if ever there was one, is no help. Mirella Freni is a placid, dull Micaela heard next to Guiot, and Robert Merrill a poor Escamillo. Chorus and orchestra are, to paraphrase Sir Noël, no more French than the Ringstrasse.

The Thomas Schippers recording has a busy, only occasionally over-obtrusive production by John Culshaw, and notably lively chorus and orchestra. Schippers keeps the opera on the move. All that is missing is soloists. Regina Resnik, a formidable performer on stage, does not come across on record – the voice lacks distinction. Mario del Monaco is a Turiddu out of his depth, and his French has to be heard to be believed. Joan Sutherland is an impossibly droopy Micaela. Horst Stein's version for German EMI, sung in German, is interesting for Christa Ludwig's

Carmen. Her characterization has a cool, detached quality which I find convincing in the early acts, and she darkens her tone to fine effect later on. In all a considerable reading by a fine singer despite the language barrier, and marred only by some vulgar shouting in the last scene. Rudolf Schock is a Danilo out of his depth. Hermann Prey's accurate Escamillo has charm in abundance and more edge to the voice than we hear from him nowadays. The live performance from the Bolshoi with Irina Arkhipova is a curiosity. Del Monaco sings either in Italian or bad French as the mood takes him, and there are two prompters with good, penetrating delivery. Luckily the best of Arkhipova is preserved elsewhere.

The first *Carmen* of the stereo era is still one of the best, certainly the best of the Guiraud recordings. Sir Thomas Beecham's conducting is elegant, witty, charming and full of love, and to these qualities he adds (but only where needed) the passion and pain found in few of the French performances and to excess in so many others. In a word, he strikes just the right balance between ironic detachment and whole-hearted involvement. Victoria de los Angeles is a Carmen in, almost literally, a thousand. The humour of her first act is wholly bewitching, and her delivery of the spoken line about the *épinglette* at the first meeting (found in isolation in so many Guiraud versions and missing, strangely enough, in most of those with dialogue) certainly justifies its inclusion. The Séguedille is perfectly judged, the rage in the second act on a human rather than an elemental (or Callas) scale. The sense of seductiveness after the flower song, of calm acceptance in the card scene, and the dignity, pride and heroic stature of the finale – all are overwhelming. As with Beecham, all facets of the role find expression in this classic interpretation. Gedda counters with a more involved though marginally less accurate José than in the later Prêtre recording – an outstanding performance. Janine Micheau is a stylish Micaela, but too maternal at the expense of the humour and resourcefulness of the character. Ernest Blanc is a good Escamillo, violent rather than fatuous. This set is a milestone in the history of *Carmen* on record.

Briefly, Karajan's Cetra-Live version (La Scala, 1955) is one of those in which momentary doubts about individual contributions are swept away by the dramatic power of the performance as a whole. The conducting is infinitely less mannered than in the later RCA set. A mixture of Guiraud and dialogue is used, and the French is variable. Giuseppe di Stefano and Giulietta Simionato, both at the height of their powers, may frequently step beyond the bounds of the French idiom, and indeed throw notes and everything to the winds in the last scene, but the way they bring the characters alive makes this an exciting theatrical experience if far from a classic reading of Bizet's opera.

The Record Guide found Risë Stevens's Carmen the best since Supervia's, and although there was precious little competition, one sees what the authors meant. Yet her virtues are mainly negative: she overdoes nothing, but never does enough. This is a careful, musical, accurate, faceless reading. The main point of interest in this set (the sound, incidentally, remarkably vivid for its age) is Fritz Reiner's conducting, which is always faithful to the composer and shares with Beecham's an adroit mixture of detachment and commitment, as well as an ability to shade expression within a basic tempo – a subtlety of approach that wholly escapes conductors of the Karajan and Bernstein school. Jan Peerce is a musical and involved José, though his French is poor. Merrill is once more a thunderously dull Escamillo. Licia Albanese's heroic-scaled singing of Micaela's aria is outstanding in its response to the words: she manages to sound both brave and scared out of her wits at one and the same time. She is less effective in the first act. There is a big surprise on side six: 'A deux cuartos' is changed to 'Tournez, dansez' and followed by the gipsy dance from *La Jolie fille de Perth* and the Farandole from *L'Arlésienne*. Such was the respect shown for the dramatic shape of Bizet's masterpiece in earlier days. But on Reiner's account alone this set is well worth hearing.

The Albert Wolff recording is interesting only in that it features what must be the dullest performance of the title role on record: Suzanne Juyol's metallic, unyielding tone is as charmless as her noctambulistic handling of the words. The Swiss tenor Libero de Luca has a good José voice, and might have made more impact with a less bored conductor – the standard of ensemble is throughout unacceptable. Micheau is in marginally fresher voice than for Beecham eight years later. That this sloppy performance should have emerged from the same stable – the Opéra Comique – as the same year's Columbia version passes all belief, since the latter is another milestone in the saga of *Carmen* on record: hearing it has made me rethink my whole attitude to the work and to all other complete recordings. The dialogue is used – it was to be twenty years before anyone else risked it – and delivered with exhilarating panache by the singers. There is too little of it in the first act, much more later on. At first, I found André Cluytens's breakneck speeds simply grotesque, but as the piece progresses one sees what he is up to: his is the ultimate in detached – one might almost say alienated – readings. Yet the Habanera, after all, is a simple, teasingly articulated statement of fact, not an earth-shaking philosophical credo on the scale of the *Communist Manifesto*, and that is how it sounds here. Solange Michel throws it away almost with a shrug. Throughout she stresses the humour of Carmen and her normality, especially in the brilliant handling of the dialogue. Her baiting of Zuniga is hilarious, her almost *parlando* Séguedille ('très consolable' sung with indescribable innuendo) utterly functional, her mocking of José positively wounding in its sarcasm, her 'Bel officier' making one laugh out loud. The touchstone of her interpretation is the card song, the recitative betraying momentary panic (normality again), the singing, *piano* and *égal*, suggesting calm acceptance of the inevitable, the whole capped by forceful orchestral playing of the string turns and those stomach-emptying bassoon phrases. This thoroughly convincing reading is followed straight away by the broad comedy of the ensuing dialogue. This, surely, is what *opéra-comique* is all about – the sort of effect that no Guiraud version can ever achieve. The gripping finales of both third and fourth acts have an ideally conversational, indeed un-operatic quality: they sound like realistic dramatic exchanges that happen, only incidentally, to be sung; in no other recording is the fluency, the endless subtlety of Bizet's word-setting so vividly demonstrated.

The supporting cast fits into the style set by conductor and protagonist. Raoul Jobin's inattention to the markings and his occasionally graceless singing pale into insignificance beside his total involvement in the role; the same is true of Marthe Angelici's Micaela. Michel Dens is an ideally suave Escamillo, and one who gives full vent to the needling cruelty of his baiting of José in the third act. The gypsy girls are vocally uningratiating but full of spirit; the smugglers sound like actors rather than singers, and all the better for it. The disadvantage of Cluytens's speeds is that it is virtually impossible for the singers to obey all Bizet's instructions as to dynamic – they are simply too busy getting the notes out; but the advantage is in dramatic urgency – the performance builds steadily via quicksilver changes of mood to an incandescent climax. This is living theatre caught on record. The sound is forward and clear, spoiled only by occasional tape joins. For all its imperfections, this is an extraordinary, nay unique recording, and its recent reissue in France is to be welcomed.

I have heard one other complete post-war version. It derives from a concert performance of 1949 with Ebe Stignani and Beniamino Gigli. It demonstrates all too clearly the Italian way with the piece; when singers see a note above the stave they hang on to it for dear life and *fortissimo* into the bargain, never mind the havoc this wreaks with what Bizet wrote. Gigli's José, full of gulps and sobs, may be magnificently sung but it has nothing to do with the case. Stignani's mature and maternal Carmen sounds no more alluring than a mother superior, but she has her moments in the finale.

I have only been able to hear excerpts from two inter-war sets. The Columbia version of 1933, from La Scala and in Italian, is well conducted by Lorenzo Molajoli. Aurora Buades is a metallic, unyielding Carmen, and Aureliano Pertile a virile but, as so often with Italian tenors, melodramatic and cringing José – the finale is full of sobs, gulps and unpitched shouts. Benevuto Franci is a dull Escamillo, and Inez Tellini an attractively bright-voiced and musical Micaela. The Disque set of 1930 is much more interesting, using Opéra Comique forces but the Guiraud text. Lucy Perelli is a classically cool, French Carmen, but one with full, well rounded tone and excellent diction. José de Trevi's Don José commands great variety of delivery, the Micaela duet as delicate (and accurate) as any I have heard, and the third-act finale stentorian and involved, so much so that he forgets to dot the opening lines of 'Dût-il m'en coûter la vie'. Yvonne Brothier is an acid, unyielding Micaela, and Louis Musy a relentlessly loud and dull Escamillo. The chorus is ideally lively, and the whole – or rather the extracts I have heard – has an exciting theatrical feel to it thanks to the expert conducting of Piero Coppola.

The complete recording of 1908 with Emmy Destinn wings across the decades, its impact undimmed, and affords a fascinating glimpse of how *Carmen* was played thirty years after the première. It is presumably nearer the Viennese than the French tradition, being sung in German and in the Guiraud version (also with the *épinglette* dialogue) and strongly dramatic in atmosphere rather than detached. Destinn's performance is amazingly vivid, though sung in curiously accented (presumably Czech) German. I imagine that the sort of allure we take for granted today would have been thought highly indecent then, and her characterization is a mixture of the hoydenish and the witchlike, half hockey-stick, half broom-stick. In the Habanera she sounds like an unruly schoolgirl, in the Séguedille like a witch (here and elsewhere she takes soprano alternatives), and she follows the reprise of the Habanera at the end of the act with a fearsome cackle ('Donnerwetter' exclaims Zuniga, and with reason). The second-act dance is *frech* rather than seductive. But from 'Au quartier' onwards her performance gains in weight and depth; the card song is darksome and dramatic, the finale tough and unyielding. Karl Jörn's José tends towards the lachrymose, but he is heavily involved in the role and gives a vivid impression of mental breakdown in the two finales. Like Destinn, he throws in top Cs at the slightest provocation. Minnie Nast, the first Sophie, is a pure-toned and touching Micaela and Hermann Bachmann, a noted Wotan, is a swaggery, inky-voiced Escamillo. The anonymous conductor does not get much of a look in – the singers decide the tempi, usually several within each one of Bizet's. The orchestration is drastically modified.

With complete performances, the criterion is whether or not they work as a dramatic whole, but with excerpts and more especially single items the niceties of vocal art assume greater importance. The most famous excerpts are those by Conchita Supervia (and beware, incidentally, of the recent, wretchedly transferred reissue on CBS). The Spanish mezzo's interpretations were for years the yardstick by which all other Carmens were judged, wrongly to my mind. She has also been hugely influential on succeeding interpreters – in particular los Angeles, Callas and Berganza, who have variously imitated (and improved upon) her extravagant portamenti in the Habanera and her generous use of chest register. I find her singing too self-consciously prima-donna-ish and her characteristic tight vibrato curiously unsettling. But her musicianship and temperament are undeniable. The Habanera is vividly delivered, but the Séguedille is so uncompromisingly tigerish that any sensible José would run a mile. (Her José is the Corsican Gaston Micheletti, and very fine too.) The Chanson Bohème comes complete with unwritten castanets and 'Olé's' at the end. In the second-act scene with José the frequent resort to chest register and generally carpet-chewing approach are hard to take. The card song is the best of the excerpts; in the finale, for my money, she is upstaged completely by Micheletti. Supervia was so positive and forceful an artist that reactions to her, as to Callas, must be highly subjective, and many will not agree with mine.

The extracts (so generous as almost to count as a complete recording) with Georges Thill, first issued on 78s in 1929, are deeply satisfying purely for the tenor – Marthe Nespoulos is a fair Micaela, Louis Guénot a bland Escamillo, and Raymonde Visconti a dull Carmen until the finale, when her matter-of-fact approach starts to pay dividends. Thill's open-toned and contained singing needs no recommendation from me: here is a *locus classicus* of French vocal art. He encompasses the delicacy of the duet with Micaela with little resort to the head (save on the A at the end, which is ravishing), and gives a most musical and thought-through account of the flower song (the B flat, alas, very loud). The finale of the third act is extraordinarily gripping, the tone darker, more baritonal, and the stentorian delivery of 'Dût-il m'en coûter la vie' reminding one that he had a successful career in Wagner. His searing singing in the fourth act (every note precise in pitch) has the sound of an Otello. The technical and emotional range of this great artist are seldom matched, or even approached, by post-war tenors.

The excerpts with Geraldine Farrar and Giovanni Martinelli were made in 1914, with Farrar's 1908 account of Micaela's aria added to the Camden reissue. The soprano's teasing Habanera is lovingly shaded, the portamenti perfectly judged. The Séguedille (without tenor) has that element of self-parody we also find with Berganza: the laugh at 'mon amoureux' for once does not sound forced, 'très consolable' is sung as to the manner born, and the pause before 'je l'aimerai' is used for a suggestive sigh. This is wholly bewitching. The second-act scene goes well, with Farrar extremely musical in the dance and just fierce enough in the outburst of temper; Martinelli tends to be lachrymose in the rejoinders. He takes the flower song too slowly, but he uses the words (his French is good) and obeys the markings; the B flat is open rather than *pianissimo* and swells – this is so sensitively managed that it is acceptable. 'Non! Tu ne m'aimes pas' is taken (as a solo) slowly and the tempo pulled about; there are thus precedents for, respectively, Bernstein and Supervia. Farrar sings the card song a semitone up and very accurately; possibly the despair at the end is over-articulated, but the total effect is alive. In the Micaela aria her voice is wonderfully fresh and pure, the expression faultless. A dubious climactic B would be cause for a re-take today. The finale starts with a snatch of 'Les voici', continues with the Escamillo duet (bawled by

Pasquale Amato) and has cuts in the exchanges between Carmen and José. Farrar's characterization is spot-on: calm and patient at first, the growing resolution and pride carefully orchestrated. Martinelli, like so many Italians, cringes too much at the beginning, but finds thrilling metal for the second part. All the notes are sung. If I had to find a touchstone for the *Carmen* style, it would be these excerpts rather than those with Supervia: they are unfailingly stylish and dramatically vivid.

Post-war highlights need not detain us long. On the first of the three Philips discs, Risë Stevens gives altogether livelier accounts of the main numbers than on the complete Reiner set, but Jobin only strikes form in the finale. Robert Weede is an above-average Toreador. The Philips (later CBS) record is notable only for Andrea Guiot's Micaela: to both the aria and the third-act finale she brings the urgency and sure sense of style we heard on the Prêtre set, but she is in far warmer voice here. On the third Philips disc she is marginally less at ease. Jane Rhodes shows that she has a fine, fruity Carmen voice but does nothing with it. There is little distinction on the DG record, save for Ferenc Fricsay's alert conducting and Maria Stader's fair stab at Micaela. The Vox excerpts with Jean Madeira conducted by Pierre Dervaux did not make me want to hear the complete set. The Sadler's Wells record is remarkable for loyal attention to the markings, but Colin Davis's speeds are so deliberate that the music lacks the excitement it ought to generate even in highlights form. The last extract, incidentally, is the Micaela aria: neither finale is included. Patricia Johnson is a tigerish, over-characterized Carmen; the best item is a graceful version of the José–Micaela duet by Elizabeth Robson and Donald Smith. All the singers enunciate the poor translation with the utmost clarity: 'I lift my glass to soldiers gay and bold' sings poor Raimund Herincx as Escamillo.

And so to single numbers. I incline towards the Habanera as a statement, charmingly articulated, rather than as a challenge to the world, and to light and laughing rather than plummy or dramatic delivery. Emma Calvé recorded it four times. Her earliest version, 1902, with piano (3281) is notable for its false start; that of 1907 (DB 160; CSLP 500) is with orchestra and is the most satisfactory from the point of view of sound; her 1916 recording (Victor 88085; RLS 724) is with piano again and extremely fast – too fast for words and notes; and on that from 1919 (Pathé 0273) with orchestra, she sounds a long way from the microphone – or whatever it was she had to sing into – and liberties are taken with the tempo. On all four versions, however, her interpretation strikes an ideal balance between humour and allure; her singing is always musical, her tone-colour most intelligently used and her expression vivid yet never overstated. Jeanne Gerville-Réache (Victor 88278; Victor Heritage 15–1008) sounds plummy and her portamenti – even when not required by the composer – and chest voice give too vampish an effect. The Spanish mezzo Maria Gay (Col. A 5279) has a good, vibrant Carmen voice but pulls the tempo about and goes in for some odd emphases. Her portamenti on 'Je t'aime' obviously influenced Supervia. Not a great singer, but bags of character. Zélie de Lussan (Victor 64004; Belcantodisc BC 205), with piano, is full of temperament and her turns are exceptionally neat, but the basic rhythm is so pulled about as to be virtually indecipherable. Germaine Cernay (Od. 188575) has a bright, vibrant voice with plenty of body. Her portamentos are as musical as they are suggestive and her expression is forceful without being blatant – a classic version. Jennie Tourel (CBS Odyssey Y2 32880) starts *piano* – all too few do – and strikes an ideal balance between verbal expression, musical delivery and quietly humorous understatement: a most distinguished version from a wonderful singer.

Mezzos singing the Habanera in German start with a disadvantage. Karin Branzell (Poly. 62634; LV 47) has plummy tone and her account is full of little *tenuti* within about four different tempi – a restless version. Kerstin Thorborg (Od. 0–11935; LV 209) is on the respectable side but musical, *piano*, and alive to the words; she sounds a steely, warning note on the last phrase. Thorborg was a famous Orpheus and sounds like it. Margarete Klose (Poly. 67789) follows the skittish, hockey-stick tradition, but her vocalization is too heavy for her to bring it off. The light, accurate version by Elisabeth Höngen (Preiser 1111 165) is compromised by unsteady tone and the conductor's strong, military rhythm. Martha Mödl, too, has to contend with strict-tempo accompaniment at a march-like clip (Telef. BLE 14 504) and for all her good intentions this is a laboured account. Edith Coates (B 9766), *the* English post-war Carmen, is firm, loud, no-nonsense, a bit schoolmistressy, and has to contend with a ponderous conductor; she makes much (too much) of the indescribable English translation.

The earliest Séguedille I have heard comes from Marie Gutheil-Schoder (43175; GV 72) with piano accompaniment, in German, made in 1902. This is a perky, *staccato*, rather than seductive, account in the hoydenish or Destinn tradition. The *marcati* are good, the flat B less so. Sigrid Arndoldson (33609; Rhapsody 6018) is even more playful: fast, accurate, with lots of tone colour. She follows 'mon amoureux' with a hearty 'Wheeeee!' The accompanying piano is incredibly ill-tuned. On neither of these is there a tenor. There is one, albeit anonymous, with Alice Raveau (Pathé X 90025); the words are lively, the notes accurate, the whole full of insinuation – a distinguished account, well conducted. So is Suzanne Brohly's without tenor (33732) recorded in 1908; her turns are clean and her phrasing as neat and attractive as her bright tone. Ninon Vallin (Od. 188541) sings *forte* throughout. Coates does without tenor (B 9766; RLS 707), starts softly, but again sounds too respectable; the atmosphere is that of the *thé dansant*. Tourel (Odyssey Y2 32880) is as musical and attentive to the text as ever but gets nowhere near the *pianissimo* as marked – a sad disappointment after her marvellous

Habanera. Irina Arkhipova, singing in Russian (ASD 2408), is quite wonderful: light, playful yet forceful – there is no doubt that she will get what she wants – and gloriously musical in her treatment of the portamenti at 'Qui veut mon âme?' This is a splendid version, winningly conducted by Alexander Melik-Pashayev, but with a stentorian José in Zurab Andzhaparidze.

The Micaela–José duet is difficult to bring off. Non-French, and especially German, singers and conductors over-sentimentalize it. This is certainly true of Frieda Hempel and Hermann Jadlowker (Od. 98069/70; Club 99–42) in a version firmly in the German tradition. She is sweet-toned, a little too given to sickly portamento, but attentive to the markings; his voice is ideally baritonal in quality yet free and flexible at the top. Richard Tauber and Elisabeth Rethberg also have to contend with glutinous accompaniment (Od. 0–8054; several reissues); she sounds motherly and concerned and he manages some beautiful things in the G major section, but in general the piece is pulled about too much. Giovanni Zenatello and Ersilde Cervi-Caroli (Fono. 62004/5; ORL 209) are comically accompanied by an out-of-tune and accident-prone piano. She is quavery and uninteresting; he sings the *piano* phrases in the G major section *di petto* yet softly – a magical effect. To my taste John McCormack and Lucy Isabelle Marsh (Victor 74345; GEMM 156) are far too sentimental and inattentive to the markings. Charles Friant and Jane Rolland (Od. 123807; CBS 78314) are among the very best though the reissue is not good in sound. She is a sweet, delicate and musical singer; he has no trouble at the top even though he does not care to sing softly as often as Bizet requires him to. But there is wonderful ardour to his delivery. Giuseppe di Stefano and Rosanna Carteri (3C 053–17658) make the duet sound like Lehár.

The Chanson Bohème has little point in excerpt, and I have heard only few versions. Lise Charny (Od. ORX 501) has a steely voice, is full of temperament, and attacks the turns and runs with exhilarating accuracy. There is little dynamic variety, however, and even less in Bruna Castagna's account. Charny's 'Là-bas, là-bas' (Pathé 0299) is similarly vibrant, and her way with the words almost makes sense of this bleeding chunk.

The whole point of the Toreador's song it seems to me is the diminuendo on the C leading to the *piano* chorus and a *pianissimo* end to it: therein lies the *fatuité* of the number. Most bass-baritones simply belt the number *fortissimo* throughout and they will not be listed here. One of the most accurate and characterful is Arthur Endrèze (Parlo. E 11215; CBS 78314): his firm, incisive voice is always a joy. Heinrich Schlusnus (Poly. 65578; LV 187) is also accurate and his voice is rounder. He sings in German. So does Hans Hotter (Poly. 67854; Heliodor 88003); he gives one verse only, takes it slowly, and the markings are faithfully observed. He hardly sounds the sort of chap to inspire frenzy in the bull ring, however. Amato sings in Italian (DB 157) and suggests rather than makes the diminuendo, but his delivery of the chorus is so deliciously fatuous and his second verse so funny that he more than merits inclusion.

Similarly, one of the points of the flower song is the *pianissimo* B flat at the end of the penultimate phrase; the words suggest a gentle reproach, not a furious accusation. But to reject every singer who bellows that note would result in a very small entry here, and there are after all other qualities demanded – musicianship, and living a narration rather than just singing an aria. But I must confess to growing frustration as tenor after tenor does everything right and then botches that phrase. Lucien Muratore (Od. 3983; Rococo 5327) is accompanied by piano and is wayward as to note-values – the song depends to a large extent on natural forward motion – and his B flat is pleasantly open rather than *forte*. (His 'Dût-il m'en coûter la vie' on Od. 3984 is similarly pulled about but exciting.) Charles Dalmorès (Victor 85122; Club 99–8) has a lovely, open, sweet voice and brings an astonishingly wide range of colour and dynamic to his 1907 version. In the past one has often felt the need to make allowances for uniformly loud and monochrome singing on acoustic records, but not after hearing Dalmorès. His response to the words is always vivid and his B flat, although loud, is at least not yelled. I must mention here his account with Calvé of the following year of the ensuing passage, 'Là-bas, là-bas' (Victor 89019; Club 99–8); she is nicely smoky in delivery but pulls the tempo around to excess and opts for soprano alternatives: at the end she goes up to a top B (or thereabouts) for 'La liberté', and it seems only right and proper that Dalmorès's next words should be a *sotto-voce* 'Mon Dieu!'

Enrico Caruso's flower song of 1909 (DB 130; ORL 308) is also pulled about, but he is duly attentive to expression until a *fortissimo* B flat. His French is good. John McCormack (DB 343; GEMM 156) sings in Italian and although he conveys the emotions of the piece strongly, the singing as such is not distinguished. David Devriès's account (Od. 123548; Club 99–39) is one to set next to, if not above, Dalmorès. He also has a clean, open delivery, sings off the words, and even suggests (few others do) the diminuendos on the last page of the piece ('Car tu n'avais qu'à paraître' *et seq.*). The phrase ascending to the B flat is taken slowly, broken, and ends with an exquisite *pianissimo* note: this, you feel, is exactly how the sentence should sound, since it conveys the necessary emotion to perfection and is truly the climax of the aria. A classic rendering. Jacques Urlus (042347; Rococo 5238) has appropriately virile tone and is musical if uninvolved; his penultimate phrase is taken in the same way as Devriès's and is almost as winning.

Unlike most Josés, Richard Tauber (Od. 0–8226) starts dully – too slow, getting slower, so that the mild *stringendo* comes as a relief – but the last phrase, in this acoustic version, in German, is meltingly taken as written, and without so intrusive a break as Devriès. Gaston Micheletti (Parlo. E 10999) gets top marks for musicianship (the very first phrase is a gift which not every tenor accepts as gratefully as Micheletti), uses the words and puts in plenty of light and shade without destroying the basic tempo. The B flat is loud, but not aggressively so. The vocal quality of Fernand Ansseau (DB 482; LV 116) is wonderfully pure and with an expressive vibrato; he, of course, makes much of the words but there is little variety of dynamic. The B flat is loud, but there is a magical swell and diminuendo on the penultimate C of the aria. Julius Patzak (Poly. 90183) gets alpha-plus for musical values and words (in German), but perhaps his tone is too consistently mellifluous for all the emotion to come through. The B flat starts *mezzo-forte* and swells to *fortissimo*, which seems a pity. Giacomo Lauri-Volpi (DB 1514; GV 516) sings loudly and in fair French, but the expression is his, not Bizet's; the B flat is bellowed. Franz Völker (Poly. 95037; LV 78) is musical, and I respond to his honeyed yet full tone. His is a gentle, yet likable version, sung in German. Charles Friant (Od. 171028; CBS 78314) is well up in the top five, even though the voice is unremarkable and there is too little variation in dynamic; but no one else sings off the words so vividly or conveys the meaning of the aria with such gripping intensity. As with Devriès, the penultimate line is taken slowly, broken, and capped with a meltingly soft B flat. Jussi Björling (DB 3603; Da Capo 1C147–00947) is predictably musical but bland as to expression. Helge Roswaenge (Decca K 2313) is duly impassioned, but wayward as to tempo. Marcel Wittrisch (DB 4408; LV 98) is by far the best of the tenors singing in German; his tone is wonderfully honeyed, though not without edge and metal in the second part of the aria, and there is a good dramatic shape to his singing. His penultimate phrase is beautifully soft and sung without the break in the line that his French colleagues of the previous generation introduced. This is a lovely record.

Of three tenors singing in English, Heddle Nash (C 3405) is the most satisfying: his gorgeously honeyed tone is allied to vivid treatment of the (dreadful) words. He manages the diminuendos at 'Car tu n'avais' and starts the B flat loudly, then fades it away to nothing: an acceptable alternative. Tudor Davies (D 739) has a magnificent voice, but his dynamic ranges only from *forte* to *fortissimo*. James Johnston (DX 1539) is not helped by the translation; his clean, musical singing lacks subtlety and, just to keep us on our toes, he starts the B flat softly and swells to *fortissimo*.

The card song really sings itself: Bizet has done all the work and all the mezzo has to do is observe the marking *égal* and the dynamic instructions. If only it were that easy. Gerville-Réache (Victor 87039) is properly attentive and the piece suits her better than the Habanera. Mary Garden thinks she knows better, and although I never thought the day would come that I actively disliked a record by this outstanding artist, here it is (Victor 1539; CSLP 502). She tampers with the note-values – dotting, if you please – and sings in peculiarly Scottish French. Calvé

(Pathé 0273) takes it slowly and not too *également* and, as on her Habanera on the other side, she sounds too distant. She produces dark chest notes for a dramatic end to the aria. Raveau (Pathé X 90025) is as fine here as in her Séguedille – her round, fascinatingly colourful tone is consistently lovely, and her account is one of infinite sadness rather than fearful or fatalistic. Branzell (Poly. 62634; LV 209) is less than *égal* and plummy in tone. Gay (Col. A 5279) is neither *égal* nor *pianissimo*, and throws in assorted gulps. Thorborg (Od. 0–11935; LV 209) strikes a clever balance between absolute *égalité* (which would be boring) and subtle light and shade, and suggests momentary panic most effectively. Tourel (CBS Odyssey Y2 32880) is as always responsive to musical and textual values but sings *mezzo-forte* throughout. This number, like the Chanson Bohème, is admittedly hard to bring off outside its dramatic context.

Micaela's aria is another where if you follow the composer's markings meticulously you cannot go far wrong. Luisa Tetrazzini (2–053060) sings in an indeterminate language which eventually emerges as Italian and uses a lot of her own markings which are not, by and large, as interesting as Bizet's; like many sopranos she hangs on to the first G at the top of the stave ('Mais j'ai beau faire') which destroys the flow, and she shows off by tying notes where Bizet marks a rest. Her *liants*, however, are lovely. She ends the aria with an interpolated high E flat – a total outrage. Claudia Muzio (Edison 82324) is impulsive and dramatic, hurling out the B and B flat to fine effect; she sounds about as frightened as Attila the Hun, but never mind – this is thrilling singing. Luise Helletsgruber (Parlo. E 11358; LV 57) also sounds as if she could give Carmen as good as she gets; the German words do not help the line, but she responds to them, and the coda is exquisitely sung. Of Eidé Norena's two versions, the earlier (Od. 188631; LV 193) is tonally steadier and fuller but lacking in impulsiveness compared to the two ladies above; the later recording (DB 4922) starts dully and unsteadily, but the *da capo* and coda are nicely moulded. Solange Delmas (Od. 123698; CBS 78314) has a white, metallic voice which no one could describe as beautiful, but her response to the meaning of the words and to Bizet's markings are deeply satisfying.

'Je suis Escamillo', the José-Escamillo duet in the third act, may seem an odd single item since it is never performed in full, but in the conversational opening it gives many opportunities to both singers. In the version by Dalmorès and Marcel Journet (Victor 85114; Club 99–8) the tenor's musical and dramatic range is simply astounding; the baritone does not get a look in. Journet also partners Ansseau (DB 1098) in an account lacking the necessary tension from the orchestra, though Journet sounds splendidly complacent. Friant and Roger Bourdin (Od. 171013; CBS 78314) turn in a thrilling performance: Bourdin's cruel teasing of the unfortunate José could only come from a bullfighter, and Friant's reactions are spine-tingling – the first 'Carmen' shouted, the second *parlando* and barely audible, and 'coups de navaja' barked in a truly alarming fashion. Here is a man goaded way beyond the end of his tether. Friant must have been amazing on stage. Léon Campagnola shows a similar sympathy with José's plight in his vivid version with Joachim Cerdan, an accurate and smooth Opéra bass (Disque Y 13).

And so to the finale, a confrontation which, for acuteness of psychological observation and unhaltable dramatic momentum, has yet to be surpassed in opera. It starts with Carmen calmly trying to use reason with a man whose grasp on it is growing steadily less sure; it is important that whatever other emotions she brings to her lines – pride, resolution, impatience even – she should not lose her temper until Bizet tells her to, at 'Eh bien, frappe moi donc'. Similarly, José tries desperately to retain control; it is at that twisting trombone phrase after the first 'Tu ne m'aimes donc plus?' that he starts irrevocably to lose it. The inexorable progress to murder is mapped step by step with the utmost precision. And it is wise, on the whole, to sing the notes rather than resort to shouting. Giovanni Zenatello and his wife Maria Gay (VB 43) go at the scene hammer and tongs in Italian and in a very Italianate manner; he gets too weepy too soon and she is too cruel, shrieking with laughter at his 'Mais moi, Carmen, je t'aime encore'. He then lapses into the full sob-stuff (at no stage, surely, should José lose his dignity) and both shout the *allegro fuocoso* passage. The end is sheer Mascagni. It is certainly exciting, but nothing to do with Bizet. Barbara Kemp and Tino Pattiera sing in German (Parlo. E 11013) and start accurately and steadily; the tempi are pulled about in the second part, she takes soprano alternatives, and both start to shout. The best thing is her blood-curdling scream at the end.

Ansseau is partnered by Helen Sadoven, who sounds like a bad Supervia (DB 784). His start is properly low-key yet insufficiently differentiated as to dynamic – always his besetting sin; the basic voice, though, is ideally clean, even and bright. He builds to a hair-raising climax, always using the words and sometimes more than the words, making what was presumably a traditional insertion at 'entre ses bras – ha, ha! – rire de moi'. His 'démon' is terrifying, and it is a pity he immediately resorts to shouting 'veux-tu me suivre?' Yet this is a thoroughly idiomatic and exciting account of the scene. Friant and Vallin are both superb (Od. 171024; GV 511). She starts quietly, acquires metal as the scene progresses, finally loses control at 'frappe moi donc', and sings the final 'Tiens' yet at the same time making it sound unmistakably *avec rage*. He suggests the tension underneath his equally calm opening and orchestrates the character's growing dottiness with great subtlety, culminating in a searing 'Nous nous aimions naguère'. He also throws the 'ha, ha!' into 'entre ses bras'. As with the third-act duet, he always suggests a stunning stage performer.

Campagnola and Suzanne Brohly (Disque W 672), noted French

interpreters, both have ideal vocal equipment, he baritonal in quality, she warm, even and smooth in timbre; the first part of the scene has, rightly in my view, a classical purity about it. But with his gulp at 'Tu ne m'aimes donc plus' the duet starts to get overheated; he sharpens and sobs, and goes one better than Friant and Ansseau with 'Entre ses bras – ha, ha, *ha*! – rire de moi'. But despite some unmusical shouting towards the end, there is a theatrical quality to this recording which I find utterly compelling. Perhaps the most surprising account of the finale comes from Margarete Klose and Marcel Wittrisch (DB 4418) singing in German. Klose's other excerpts had not prepared me for her straight, contained and attentive singing, marred only occasionally by attack from beneath the note. The record starts, incidentally, with a snatch of the chorus and the Escamillo duet, nicely phrased by the mezzo. Wittrisch is nothing short of excellent, the markings all faithfully observed in the first part, and the odd lapses of pitch in the *fuocoso* passage and shouting later all stemming from thoroughly involved singing from both artists. Wittrisch's last phrases are as moving as those of any tenor on record: his dignity is intact. The scene is extremely well conducted by Fritz Zweig of the Berlin Staatsoper.

An ideal cast? Los Angeles, Farrar, perhaps Michel on stage; Devriès, Dalmorès, Thill, Micheletti – *embarras de richesse* – but definitely Friant on stage; Guiot if on form, with Te Kanawa covering; Bourdin or Endrèze. And it would have to be conducted by Beecham, with a French chorus and, it goes without saying, *all* the dialogue.

CARMEN

C Carmen; *M* Micaela; *J* José; *E* Escamillo

1908 (in German) Destinn *C*; Nast *M*; Jörn *J*; Bachmann *E*/Chorus and Orch./
G&T 2–40829/044506

1912 Mérentié *C*; Vallandri *M*; Affre *J*; Albers *E*/Paris Opéra-Comique Chorus, Orch./Ruhlmann
Pathé 1650–76

1920 (in Italian) Anitua *C*; Ferraris *M*; Bolis *J*; Formichi *E*/Chorus and Orch./uncredited
Columbia D4620–43

1928 Visconti *C*; M Nespoulos *M*; Thill *J*; Guénot *E*/Paris Opéra-Comique Chorus and Orch./Cohen and Gaubet
Columbia 9527–41; CBS (US) 67544–58D

1930 Perelli *C*; Brothier *M*; Trévi *J*; Musy *E*/Paris Opéra-Comique

Chorus and Orch./Coppola
EMI L695–711; RCA (US) ⓜ CCL 100

1931 (in Italian) G. Besanzoni *C*; Carbone *M*; Pauli *J*; E. Besanzoni *E*/La Scala Chorus and Orch./Sabajno
HMV C2310–28; RCA (US) 11849–57

1933 (in Italian) Buades *C*; Tellini *M*; Pertile *J*; Franci *E*/La Scala Chorus and Orch./Molajoli
EMI ⓜ 3C 153 17071–3

1949 (in Italian – film soundtrack) Stignani *C*; R. Gigli *M*; Gigli *J*; Bechi *E*;/Rome Opera Chorus and Orch./Bellezza
EMI ⓜ 3C 153 18255–7

1950 Michel *C*; Angelici *M*; Jobin *J*; Dens *E*/Paris Opéra-Comique Chorus and Orch./Cluytens

Spaniards in the Studio
Above: Teresa
Berganza recording
Cosi fan Tutte (Decca)
Right: José Carreras
recording for
Phonogram
(Phonogram
International)

Recording duos
Above: Ruggero
Raimondi and Carlo
Bergonzi (Phonogram
International)
Right: Montserrat
Caballé and Luciano
Pavarotti recording
Turandot (Decca)

Opposite top: Mirella
Freni and Jessye
Norman recording
Figaro (Phonogram
International)
Opposite below: Jon
Vickers and Colin
Davis recording *Peter
Grimes* (Phonogram
International)

Prima donnas of today

Below: Galina Vishnevskaya making up as Tatyana (Harold Rosenthal Collection)
Right: Renata Scotto (Clive Barda/CBS)
Bottom left: Frederica von Stade (Clive Barda/CBS)
Bottom right: Ileana Cotrubas (Clive Barda/CBS)

EMI ℗ TRI 33308–10; Angel

1950 Juyol C; Micheau M; de Luca
J; Giovannetti E/Paris Opéra-
Comique Chorus, Orch./Wolff
HMV ⓜ ALP 1115–7; RCA
(US) ⓜ AVM3 0670

1952c (in Russian) Borisenko C;
Shumskaya M; Nelepp J; Ivanov
E/Bolshoi Theatre Chorus and
Orch./Nebolsin
MK ⓜ DO 1508–15

1955 (live performance, La Scala,
Milan) Simionato C; Carteri M;
di Stefano J; Roux E/La Scala
Chorus and Orch./Karajan
Cetra ⓜ LO 22/3

1956 Madeira C; Vivalda M;
Filacuridi J; Roux E/Paris
Conservatoire Chorus, Pasdeloup
Orch./Dervaux
Vox ⓜ OPBX 159

1957 (live performance, Metropolitan,
New York) Stevens C; Amara
M; del Monaco J; Guerrera
E/Metropolitan Opera Chorus
and Orch./Mitropoulos
Cetra ⓜ LO 48/3

1959 Rubio C; Alarie M; Simoneau J;
Rehfuss E/Paris Conservatoire
Chorus and Orch./Le Comte
Concert Hall SMS 2184

1958–9 Los Angeles C; Micheau M;
Gedda J; Blanc E/French
National Radio Chorus and
Orch./Beecham
HMV SLS 5021
④TC–SLS 5021; Angel SCL
3613

1959 (in Russian and Italian)
Arkhipova C; Maslennikova M;
del Monaco J; Lisitian
E/Bolshoi Theatre Chorus and
Orch./Melik-Pashaev
MK DO 29833–9

1960 (in German) Cervena C;
Croonen M; Apreck J; Lauhöfer
E/Leipzig Radio Chorus and
Orch./Kegel
DG 2701 008

1961 (in German) C. Ludwig C;
Muszely M; Schock J; Prey
E/Berlin Municipal Chorus and
Orch./Stein

EMI 1C 183 30209–11

1962 Resnik C; Sutherland M; Del
Monaco J; Krause E/Grand
Theatre Chorus, Geneva; Suisse
Romande Orch./Schippers
Decca SET 256–8; London OSA
1368

1963 L. Price C; Freni M; Corelli J;
Merrill E/Vienna State Opera
Chorus, VPO/Karajan
RCA (UK) SER 5600–2
④ RK 40004; (US) LSC 6199
④ ARK 3–2542

1964 Callas C; Guiot M; Gedda M;
Massard E/Rene Duclos Choir,
Paris Opéra Orch./Prêtre
HMV SLS 913; Angel SCLX
3650 ④4X3S–3650

1960s Miltcheva C; Vassileva M;
Nikolov J; Ghiuselev
E/Romanian State Opera Chorus
and Orch./Marinov
Electrecord/Sélect CC 15083–5

1970 Bumbry C; Freni M; Vickers J;
Paskalis E/Paris Opéra Chorus
and Orch./Frühbeck de Burgos
HMV SLS 952; Angel SCLX
3767

1971 Moffo C; Donath M; Corelli J;
Cappuccilli E/German Opera
Chorus and Orch., Berlin/Maazel
Cetra LPS 3276; Ariola-Eurodisc
XG 80489R

1972 Horne C; Maliponte M;
McCracken J; Krause
E/Manhattan Opera Chorus,
Metropolitan Opera Orch./
Bernstein
DG 2740 101 ④3371 006

1974 Crespin C; Pilou M; Py J; van
Dam E/Rhine Opera Chorus,
Strasbourg PO/Lombard
RCA Erato (US and UK) STU
70900–2

1975 Troyanos C; Kanawa M;
Domingo J; van Dam E/Alldis
Choir, LPO and National
PO/Solti
Decca D11D3 11K33; London
OSA 13115 ④ 5–13115

1977 Berganza C; Cotrubas M;
Domingo J; Milnes E/Ambrosian
Singers, LSO/Abbado
DG 2709 083 ④3371 040

Excerpts

1908–14 Farrar *C*; Martinelli *J*; Amato
E/Metropolitan Opera Chorus
and Orch./Setti
RCA (UK) ⓜ CDN 1014

1927–30 Supervia *C*; Micheletti
J/Orch./Cloëz
Parlophone ⓜ PMA 1024;
Decca (US) ⓜ DL 9522

1937 (in German) Ruzicka *C*; Marherr
M; Roswaenge *J*; Schmitt-Walter
E/Berlin State Opera Chorus
and Orch./Weigert
Polydor 95337–41

1940 Peebles *C*; Jobin *J*; Warren
E/Chorus, Publishers Service
SO/Pelletier
RCA (US) ⓜ CAL 221

1940s (in German) Höngen *C*;
Trötschel *M*; Ralf *J*; Herrmann
E/Dresden State Opera Chorus
and Orch./Böhm
Acanta ⓜ BB 21362

1946 Stevens *C*; Connor *M*; Jobin *J*;
Weede *E*/Metropolitan Opera
Chorus and Orch./Sebastien
CBS (UK) ⓔ 30069; (US)
ⓔ Y–32102

1946 Swarthout *C*; Albanese *M*;
Vinay *J*; Merrill *E*/Shaw
Chorale, RCA Victor
Orch./Leinsdorf
RCA ⓜ LM 1007

1952 Wysor *C*; Utley *J*; Fortunato
E/Paris Opéra Orch./Allain
Remington ⓜ 199–15

1952 Alberts *C*; Stagliano *M*; Lloyd *J*;
Tibbetts *E*/Goldovsky
(narrator/piano)
Boston ⓜ 1000

1950s (abridged) Meyer *C*; Van
Beckum *M*; Larsen *J*; Holthaus *E*/
Chorus, Netherlands PO/Goehr
MMS ⓜ

1956 (in German) Wagner *C*;
Schlemm *M*; Schock *J*;
Metternich *E*/German Opera
Chorus and Orch./Schuchter
EMI 1C 047 50582

1956 (in Italian) Tassinari *C*; Benetti
M; Corelli *J*; Guelfi *E*/Turin
Radio Chorus and Orch./Basile
Cetra ⓜ LPC 55020

1958 Betti *C*; Guiot *M*; Neate *J*;
Bacquier *E*/Chorus and Orch.
Philips ⓜ 6556 010

1958 (in German) Sjöstedt *C*;
Draksler *M*; Niekerk *J*; Krause
E/Vienna Volksoper Chorus and
Orch./Quadri
Qualiton ⓜ BLP 11464; Ariola-
Eurodisc ⓜ Z77027R

1960 (in German) Dominguez *C*;
Stader *M*; Simandí *J*;
Metternich *E*/Bavarian State
Opera Chorus and Orch./Fricsay
DG 2535 297 ④3335 297

1960 Rhodes *C*; Guiot *M*; Lance *J*;
Massard *E*/Orch./Benzi
Philips 6500 206

1960 Scharley *C*; Doria *M*; Botiaux *J*;
Legros *E*/Chorus and
Orch./Etcheverry
Vogue LDM 30126 ④B.VOC
100

1961 (in English) Johnson *C*; E.
Robson *M*; D. Smith *J*; Herincx
E/Sadler's Wells Opera Chorus
and Orch./C. Davis
HMV CSD 1398; Capitol (US)
SP 8605

1961 (in German) Dalis *C*; Owen *M*;
Hoppe *J*; Schmitt-Walter
E/Arndt Chorus, Berlin
Municipal Opera Orch./Martin
Teldec AG6 41912

1963 Kahn *C*; Jaumillot *M*; Poncet *J*;
Borthayre *E*/Karlsruhe Opera
Chorus and Orch./Couraud
Philips 6747 187

1964 (in German) Litz *C*; Schwaiger
M; Kozub *J*; Crass *E*/Chorus
and Orch./Couraud
Philips 6593 006

1964 (in Hungarian) Komlóssy *C*;
László *M*; Szönyi *J*; Jámbor
E/Hungarian State Opera
Orch./Ferencsik
Qualiton SLPX 1269

1956 Boué *C*; Doria *M*; B. Marty *J*;
D. Marty *E*/SO/Menet
Barclay ⓜ 89011

1970 Horne *C*; Pellegrini *M*; Molese
J/Chorus, RPO/Lewis
Decca PFS 4204 ④ KPFC 4204;
London CS 21005

Manon

ALAN BLYTH

A single 78 disc (Od. 123529) of the 'duo de la lettre' by Emma Luart and Gaston Micheletti poses an ideal style for this work – a Manon who can suggest the character's frailty, pleasure-seeking and sensibility, a Des Grieux at once tender, ardent and vulnerable, both artists having the ideal voices for their parts and, perhaps above all, a feeling for the French language as set to music, which has become almost a thing of the past (and that from a Manon who hailed from Brussels, a Des Grieux who came from Corsica). There is still more to it than that: both these singers, helped by the conductor Gustav Cloez (ubiquitous in the inter-war period on the Odeon label), judge those almost imperceptible rubatos, so essential in this score, to perfection. I returned to that record time and again while compiling this chapter and on each occasion I was struck anew by its freshness and immediacy.

That passage, the letter duet, like so many others in the whole opera, exhibits Massenet's unerring skill in matching music to situation, after all an essential attribute in any operatic composer. What is more he makes that music of truly memorable and individual accent: any page is immediately identifiable as *Manon* and nothing else. Not without reason did Newman describe it in *Opera Nights* as 'undeniably a masterpiece in its own genre', and like all the greatest operas, it has stood up to the test of continuous repetition without one ever tiring of even that most oft-recorded piece, the Dream, of which I have heard upwards of sixty versions.

Roméo et Juliette has often been described as one long, interrupted love duet. The same can almost be said of *Manon*. The love-at-first-sight encounter of heroine and Des Grieux in Act 1, the brief moment of happiness in the rue Vivienne, St Sulpice, the exchanges at the Hôtel Transylvanie (with Des Grieux's marvellous outburst, 'Manon! Sphinx étonnant, véritable sirène'), and the last farewell on the road to Le Havre (this must have seemed even more true when the Cours-la-Reine scene was cut in American and Italian performances before the war, with the Gavotte inserted unhappily in the hotel scene). The rest, characters and events, are atmospheric incidentals, done with all Massenet's ability to capture character (Lescaut's extrovert 'Ne bronchez pas', Le Comte's sentimental 'Epouse quelque brave fille') and milieu (countless examples), but essentially extraneous to the main theme. Writing of the two principals themselves, Newman argued that the 'psychological centre of the Abbé Prévost's famous story is not really Manon but Des Grieux'. Massenet, rightly for operatic purposes, tilted the balance back towards the heroine, but it is still Des Grieux whose character bends and alters during the course of the work: Manon remains her own fickle, enchanting self from start to finish. It is a similar case to that of Carmen and José.

The opera came just too early for the original interpreters to have recorded any excerpts, but we do have the Fabliau, written specially for Bréjean-Silver, sung by her (see below) and also many items recorded by the many famous interpreters of the first years of this century. The next era of great interpreters, the 1920s and 1930s, is also well represented, but where are the great French interpreters today? They are hard to find. Oddly enough there are comparatively few complete recordings, considering the opera's place in the repertory. There have been only five 'official' ones as far as I know, and these include the Hill-and-Dale Pathé on forty eight sides (!), recorded in Paris in 1923. The struggle to reproduce these satisfactorily was well worthwhile, because they contain a performance of the title role, by Fanny Heldy, of great charm, sung in that typically forward, light, French manner here displayed in a well-nigh perfect technique. She was in fact Belgian, but was famous at the Opéra and Opéra-Comique in this part from 1917 to 1939. Her entrance aria suggests a flighty creature and has perfectly executed coloratura. Her 'Adieu, notre petite table' is sung with exemplarily controlled emotion and at just the right pace, not too slow, and the rest is of a piece. Jean Marny, who must have often partnered Heldy on stage, is an aristocratic Des Grieux with a fine-grained, clear, honest tenor, just a little monochrome in tone. He is throughout wonderfully true to Massenet's dynamic markings, as in the sweet *piano* at 'mon père' on his first appearance and he summons up unexpected reserves for the heroics of St Sulpice. Léon Ponzio is a light, neat Lescaut, full of character; Pierre Dupré, a low-baritone Count, sings with great feeling.

Henri Busser takes much of the score too fast, which may be the result of the exigencies of acoustic recording, or the 78 process as a whole, as Elie Cohen also moves too quickly on the otherwise superb Columbia set dating from the early 1930s. Germaine Féraldy must have been an adorable Manon, a 'natural' for the part. Here she moves easily from the girlishness and boredom of her first solos, through the first stirrings of love to the airy *élan* of the Gavotte to the desperation of St Sulpice and back to the hectic pleasure seeking of 'A nous les amours'. She mixes ideally the amoral and pathetic qualities of the character, the latter marvellously shown in the phrase 'On oublie' in that subtly written Cours-le-Reine encounter with Des Grieux *père*.

The Russian-born tenor, Joseph Rogatchewsky, who made his career in Belgium and France after the revolution in his own country, is a fit partner for such a Manon, with his plangent tone and ardent delivery that includes a not unattractive catch in the voice. He can be careless over note-values from time to time, but the heart of the matter is in him, as witness the *pianissimo* start to 'Ah fuyez, douce image' demanded by Massenet but ignored by many tenors. The supporting cast is strong, the whole performance thoroughly authentic in character.

Cohen makes the traditional theatre cuts, and also omits one or two short linking passages. The truncations in the first LP set, so far the only one from the Decca stable, are much more grievous. The charming snatches of dialogue over orchestral accompaniment are almost eliminated in favour of a French running commentary. For all that, it has its merits, in the competent but poker-voiced Manon of Janine Micheau (at best when on her last legs in Act 5), the eager Des Grieux of Libero de Luca (when he remains in tune), and a more than adequate Lescaut and Count. The ensembles come off very well under Albert Wolff's experienced, idiomatic direction.

But he is no match for Pierre Monteux on what is still the most desirable LP recording. Originally a viola player at the Opéra-Comique, later a conductor at the Opéra and the Metropolitan, Monteux had the music in his blood and here dispenses it with authority and spirit, and as much care for the pastiche music of Act 3 as for the 'purple' passages. He has in Victoria de los Angeles an enchanting and moving Manon, whose voice has enough personality on record for those of us who saw her on stage to recapture those live performances.

Manons divide into the light, effervescent kind (Heldy, Féraldy) and the more serious, of whom Ninon Vallin and los Angeles are the classic examples. Los Angeles is not at her most convincing to start with, sounding too coy with her brother and Des Grieux in Act 1 (although she is already vocally at her best). She comes into her own in the mixed mood of Act 2, indecisive about her relationship with Des Grieux, delivers a deeply felt 'Adieu' and a full-toned Gavotte (but a strained 'Je marche'), and like most Manons of her kind, is superb in the St Sulpice scene, the prayer and 'N'est-ce plus ma main' phrased with unerring distinction. She sounds totally committed in her declamation of 'Mon être tout entier, ma vie, et mon amour' in Act 4, projects the nervous excitement of 'A nous les amours', and suggests Manon's apparent transfiguration on the road to Le Havre at 'Ah! je sens une flamme' – a great performance. Henri Legay is a lightweight, but ardent Des Grieux, a little overparted but never inadequate. Jean Borthayre's experienced, authoritative Count and Michel Dens's lively Lescaut are further reasons for the set's success; so is the splendid contribution of the Opéra-Comique forces.

The sound of the Rudel set is too reverberant, even unnatural. Beverly Sills's tone seems glassy and too soubrettish, her girlishness too studied, her emotions too overtly and self-indulgently expressed. For all that, her complete achievement is greater than its individual components. Nicolai Gedda is an impassioned Des Grieux but also, beside earlier interpreters, too forceful at times. The rest of the cast, even Gérard Souzay's well-characterized Lescaut, leave something to be desired and that 'something' is, I fear, a tradition nearly lost. Julius Rudel, too, sounds heavy-handed after Monteux and Cohen.

The only 'complete' pirated set I have heard (EJS 149) stems from a matinée on 13 January 1940 at the Metropolitan with Grace Moore as a *spinto*-like Manon, a considerable performance in a generalized way, and Richard Crooks as a first-rate Des Grieux. John Brownlee is a good Lescaut, Pelletier a conductor in a hurry.

Even highlight discs are few and far between. Renée Doria is a piquant, bright but insubstantial Manon on a Philips disc, with all the usual pieces except the Gavotte. Alain Vanzo promises more than he delivers as Des Grieux, but is not unattractive. Anna Moffo in RCA's 'Portrait of Manon' (two discs, the other devoted to *Manon Lescaut*, sounds quick-witted, sparkling and eminently desirable; she also has (very nearly) the right manner, particularly in the Gavotte and death scene. Giuseppe di Stefano is much less happy in French, but as always his native ardour makes you forgive his stylistic *faux-pas*, although in the 'Dream' he goes too far, and has lost the sweet timbre shown in his earlier discs from the opera: St Sulpice here strains him to the limits. Robert Kerns misses the point of 'Ne bronchez pas'. René Leibowitz's conducting is wonderfully vivid. Di Stefano can also be heard in the Cetra Live series. He is in fresh voice with Mafalda Favero as an appealing but Italianate Manon.

An 'off-the-air' record (EJS 290) is of a broadcast in 1936 of extracts linked by Deems Taylor with added dialogue spoken in an exaggeratedly histrionic manner by actors. Lucrezia Bori is still a Manon to be reckoned with here (see below for more on her). Joseph Bentonelli (*né* Benton), who had a brief Met career, after walking into the theatre for an audition at a time when Crooks was ill and being immediately engaged for Des Grieux, sings with grace and fervour.

A much more exciting broadcast was the BBC 1939 *Manon*, in English, with Maggie Teyte and Heddle Nash, of which extracts have been issued privately, and more still recently revived on the radio. Teyte, who never sang the role on stage, is not surprisingly Manon to the life; frivolous, charming, romantic – her prayer in St Sulpice is the most tenderly pleaded I know – and her re-seduction of Des Grieux irresistible. Nash, who sang Des Grieux first in 1927 and again, at Covent Garden, in 1947, is in his element, able by vocal means, by that sweet, elegant tone and line alone, to suggest the passionate, volatile youth, the all-or-nothing lover. His attack at 'Enchanteresse' ('Vision entrancing', here) is unbeatable, so is much of his contribution to St Sulpice, where the singers and Stanford Robinson, an absolutely idiomatic conductor who keeps the score on the move, generate the sense of a live performance; no wonder listeners demanded repeats. Dennis Noble is a characterful Lescaut, Norman Walker a warm father.

Manon might have been written for the days of 78s since most of its solos and duets fit neatly either on to one or two sides of old shellac discs, so from the earliest days it was well represented in the catalogues. Manon introduces herself with her naive 'Je suis encore tout étourdie'; it establishes her flippant yet endearing personality and it needs light, airy treatment, just what it gets from Georgette Bréjean-Silver (Od. 56069) recorded in 1906. She sounds impetuous and child-like and enhances her reading with wonderful enunciation and with a top E. shirked by many others. In 'Voyons, Manon' (56040), she again gives full meaning to the text, invests it with almost too much melancholy, manages a perfect octave jump on 'chimères'. Massenet, as I have said, wrote the Fabliau for her; she gives it (56011) a hard, glittering performance, shading into something more sensitive in the pensive middle section. She sings the alternative coloratura. Earlier there is a fine *pianissimo* top A at 'encore'. It is worth recalling that she created Massenet's Cinderella in 1899.

Her contemporary Sigrid Arnoldson has an intrusive vibrato in her version of 'Voyons, Manon' (33797) but, despite the German text, manages a good deal of subtlety. Her 'Adieu, notre petite table' (33793) is too sentimental for my taste, but certainly her darker tone enables her to provide many shades of feeling, which she manages again in 'N'est-ce plus ma main' (33844). Frances Saville, Covent Garden's 1897 Manon, recorded 'Voyons, Manon' (43280) and the Gavotte (43224) five or so years after, and reveals a skittish, conversational manner, unhelped by the German text. Charlotte Agussol (Od. 33447) is laboured and too stately in 'Je suis' – Bauer lists her as a mezzo as well as a soprano, and one can hear why. Emma Carelli is much too cavalier in 'Je suis' (Fono. 39650) and 'Adieu' (053032), both sung in Italian.

Much preferable to any of these is their contemporary Lise Landouzy, star of the Opéra-Comique, who possessed a lovely, bell-like vocal quality and precise articulation of notes and words, as in 'Je suis' (Od. 56022), 'Adieu' (56067), and she sings a voluptuous 'A nous les amours' (56022). Perhaps her interpretation might seem a little stately and grand to us today. Aline Vallandri, a slightly younger singer at the same house, is just as admirable with her quick vibrato, sense of urgency and full, passionate tone in 'Adieu' (34197). Lucette Korsoff shows a typical 'Golden Age' vocal control and pin-point accuracy in 'Je marche sous les chemins', the Gavotte (33690/1) and 'N'est-ce plus ma main' (33687); she was another star of the Opéra-Comique before the first world war. What prodigality of talent!

The immediately succeeding generation had perhaps an even finer galaxy of Manons, headed by the ubiquitous (on record) Ninon Vallin. Her Manon is surely the touchstone of style in this role; what a pity she did not record it complete. 'Je suis' (Pathé X 7195), is very fresh – such wonderful delicacy on the word 'paradis', what clean coloratura – but it is perhaps surpassed by the light, airy, youthful Pathé Hill-and-Dale (X. 0109) and by the Odeon (188863), where there is even more attention to shades of meaning, as at 'Ah, mon cousin'. In 'Voyons, Manon' (188862 or X 7166), she changes timbre for the changes of mood. Her 'Adieu' (Pathé X 90052) is more deeply felt than on her Parlophone version (R 20203). In the Gavotte, she is more lady than demi-mondaine, and so better in the minor section. Pathé 90034 again shows more feeling and is better vocalized than R 20203, but the preceding 'Je marche' (X 90053) suggests the pleasure-loving girl all right. Of her 'A nous les amours' discs, X 7165 has still more élan and frivolity than X 90082.

If you could not get Vallin in the 1920s and 1930s there were always Heldy, Féraldy, Yvonne Gall and Emma Luart to call on. Besides her complete recording, Féraldy recorded several separate items. Her 'Adieu' (L 2227) has a palpable moment of emphasis on the word 'imaginable' and a fine morbidezza throughout. 'Je marche' (Col. D 13055) has Manon at her most extrovert. Most enjoyable of all, and one of those records whose discovery makes all the hard work worthwhile, is her Fabliau (L 2227) – lovely liquid tone, clear characterization, absolute fidelity to the score. Martha Angelici in 'Voyons, Manon' sounds very determined; hers is a likeable, honest, performance (FALP 567).

Luart has a voice able to encompass both sides of Manon's character. She can get a smile or tear into her voice, and does so on her versions of the various excerpts (Od. 18857, 188518, 188571, 188522, 188650), three containing ideal interpretations of 'Adieu', 'Je marche', Gavotte and 'A nous les amours'. What a seductive, tender singer! Heldy, who sang the part at Covent Garden in 1926, is more cavalier than in her complete set in 'Je suis' (DB 1409), 'Voyons, Manon' (DB 1512), and 'Adieu' (DA 1250), a clear, meaningful account. Gall is a musician's dream in her natural-sounding 'Je suis' (Pathé H&D 0211), grand 'Je marche' (0240) and long-breathed 'Adieu' (2040), keenly savouring 'comme il m'aimait'.

Bidu Sayão also did justice on disc to her individual, keenly thought-out interpretation that delighted Met audiences in the late 1930s and early 1940s. The first-act solos show off Manon's already coquettish side (Am. Col. 71769D, 72899D) but her 'Adieu', given just sufficient weight, and Gavotte (17301D), where the sound is rich yet bright, are versions to conjure with.

In 'Je suis', records by Solange Delmas, Hélène Baudry, Lucienne Jourfier, Geori-Boué, Joan Hammond and Mady Mesplé are no more than souvenirs of the artists concerned. Yvonne Prinvot, a Marseilles soprano (how well the French companies treated their native singers between the wars), offers a very French timbre, an exquisitely phrased account of 'Voyons, Manon (Disque W 419) and a vivid, tender 'Adieu' (P 439), backed by part 1 of St Sulpice with the fine Charles Friant.

Germaine Corney gives a considerable performance of the piece (Poly. 522561); the Belgian Clara Clairbert a classically shaped, pensive reading (Poly. 66917), as does Carmen Melis, a famous Italian interpreter. Delmas and Yolande Marculescu are less remarkable.

In 'Adieu', Geori-Boué gives a good account of herself, showing some eloquence (Od. 188944). Marcelle Ragon comes close to the best (Disque P 776); so does Lotte Schöne (EJ 669), a sensuous, *innig* performance in German, reissued in the HMS 78 series: this Manon is a very warm being. Teyte (EJS 478, recorded in 1946) does not linger and gets a not unpleasing urgency into what can become a sentimental piece. Callas, for instance, is surely just too doom-laden for this only half-serious, sentimental farewell (SLS 5104), but one capitulates to the colour and phrasing none the less. Los Angeles (DB 6994; SLS 5012) sings 'with emotion and simplicity' as Massenet commands and is up to speed (the marking is 'sans lenteur', after all). Of the Italian brigade, I surrender to Magda Olivero (Cetra LPC 55011), intimately persuasive, who shows up the various shortcomings of Dalla Rizza, Spani, Guerrini, Melis, Carosio, Fineschi (terrible), Tebaldi, and Freni (in French). The last-named, in comparison with Olivero, shows the decline in sheer character of interpretation since the war. Versions by Streich, Hammond, Corney, Danco, Kabaivanska are more-or-less satisfactory souvenirs of the singers concerned.

Yvonne Brothier, another notable Manon, gets real devil-may-care into her 'Je marche' (P 819). Geneviève Vix has panache in this and the Gavotte (HRS 105), but tends to wildness. Frances Alda, a famous Met interpreter, is as always irresistible. Geraldine Farrar's Gavotte (DA 510) is exact but lacks a top D; so do Xenia Belmas's versions (Poly 66749 and, in Italian, 66636), and she is careless over note-values. Ragon (P 776) is thoughtful and already remorseful. Bori (DA 1694) is bright and cheerful but hardly the queen of Cours-la-Reine. Galli-Curci (DA 611) is fragile and too bland. Kurz, in German (2–43381; Delta TQD 3020) is appropriately indolent and exhibits her usual perfection of scale. Dorothy Kirsten is estimable (DB 21184).

Of the Germans, Lotte Lehmann is, well, Lehmann, eager and attractive, but a Manon for outdoor rather than indoor pursuits, (RO 20248), Maria Ivogün (Brunswick 50081; LV 68) and Elizza (43963) are mistresses of coloratura, but their singing is under-vitalized for this part. Hedwig Francillo-Kaufmann is pure-sounding (2–4196). Schöne (EJ 669) caps them all with her charm and insouciance. Moderate versions by Duchesne, Streich, Dobbs, Tebaldi, Lorengar. Clairbert's Fabliau (Poly. 66917) is worth noting; so is Brothier's (P 819).

Des Grieuxs are even more numerous than Manons but they have only two (compared with five) solos in which to display their wares. There seem to have been as many, if not more, impressive tenors for this music in the early years of the century than soprano Manons. Edmond Clément, who sang at the 500th Opéra-Comique performance of *Manon* on 13 January 1905, deserves pride of place. His performance of 'Le Rêve' is a classic; that is the 1911 one (DB 166) with piano, so fresh, easy and imaginative, and taken at exactly the right speed. The 1916 account with orchestra, taken faster, is less impressive. Clément's tone was a trifle white for 'Ah, fuyez' but there is a patent honesty in the singing. Pathé H&D 0120 differs little from Od. 56001. Emile Scaremberg in 'Ah, fuyez' (Fono. 39174) places emphasis on the text, is more overtly emotional than Clément. That kind of division is marked in nearly all the performances.

A version of the Dream to rival Clément's is that by Louis Cazette (Disque W 487), mellifluous, unhurried, truly dream-like, faultless in legato with a fine *messa di voce* on the final high A. The twelve-inch format obviously helped Cazette to give such a subtle, broad reading, and he treats the St Sulpice scene similarly. His successful career at the Opéra-Comique was cut short by illness and early death. Léon Campagnola (Disque U 48), a tenor of La Monnaie and L'Opéra from just before the first world war, obviously had a voice of beauty and power, both of which give excellence to his versions of the Dream and 'Ah, fuyez'. In the former he is one of the few tenors to observe the 'hairpin' marking on the top A at 'faut', rather than the customary *forte* followed by a diminuendo, and his top B flats in the latter have real 'ping' to them. He foreshortens 'Ah, fuyez' as do most ten-inch recordings. His Pathé H&D (0291) of the Dream is just as delicate as the HMV needle-cut version.

When the Belgian tenor Fernand Ansseau sang Des Grieux to Heldy's Manon at Covent Garden in 1926, his *mezza voce* was described as 'one of the sweetest things imaginable', and one can hear why from his account of the Dream (DB 486), where his legato has an exemplary flow to it and where the phrasing is full of character without becoming self-indulgent. His French (and Opéra-Comique) contemporary Emile Marcelin displays a typically Gallic, light, floated nasal timbre, attractive but anonymous (Disque Y 57), backing it with a finely articulated 'Ah fuyez', unfortunately cut despite being a twelve-inch disc. His ten-inch Dream (Disque P 729) is disappointing.

Albert Vaguet, another Des Grieux of the turn of the century, sings the Dream sweetly but too quickly (H&D 0137). I prefer his contemporary, Léon Beyle, whose Dream, attractive though it is, is surpassed by his intense 'Ah, fuyez' (Zono. 82606; there are other versions).

In the 1920s and 1930s we come to a long list of Pathé and Odeon Opéra-Comique tenors, all of whom seemed to have set up in competition as purveyors of the Dream. Francis Banuls, Paul-Henri Vergnes, Enrico De Mazzei, José Janson, Jean Planel (always a pleasing artist) are of little more than local interest. David Devries (Od. 188505) calls for attention; he represents the cultivated French tenor style at its best, and his phrasing here, especially the lift from D to A at 'faut', is aristocratic and perfectly controlled. His contemporary, Charles Friant (188668), is still better, sincere, dreamy, youthful and well-varied in colouring despite the basically dry quality of his voice. His Pathé version is less desirable.

Of the lyric-dramatic tenors of this generation, Gaston Micheletti (188655), while not unimpressive, seems less at ease than usual, but his version is notable for its peculiarly appealing timbre and for having an unnamed Manon (Luart?) in attendance. I have not heard his 'Ah, fuyez' (188660), a piece that would surely suit his general style. Georges Thill (LFX 478; 2C 153–11660/1) surely adopts the ideal speed for it, not self-indulgent but spacious. Unfortunately his phrasing is a bit unimaginative, the tone in *piano* ill-focused. 'Ah, fuyez' on the reverse is more successful, but still not irreproachable, in spite of the ringing B flats, I prefer in this piece, Villabella (Od. 123550; there are other versions), ardent, clear, exciting. His Dreams (188806 or Pathé X 90083) both display a plangent tone, a mellifluous manner. Rogatchewsky recorded both extracts, apart from his performance on the complete set. In spite of a tendency to slide, his Dream is most affecting (Col. D 15011), with easy, liquid tone. His 'Ah, fuyez' offers dedicated, impassioned singing indeed, a little free with note-values.

The two Americans, Mario Chamlee and Richard Crooks, both make an impression, the former singing with his accustomed charm in the Dream (Brunswick 15040), to which Crooks (DB 2093; VIC 1464) brings more sophistication, less spontaneity. Crooks's 'Ah, fuyez (DB 3670; VIC 1464) is refined but under-characterized. James Melton, in both pieces, is flattered by the gramophone into sounding like McCormack (Victor 11–893-0). When he was at the Met, Beecham, dubbed him 'the gentleman jockey'. Theodor Ritch (Col. D 1590) displays a silvery tenor, a forward, free production in the Dream.

Once we leave the French language, we enter a very different world, mostly of sobbing Italian tenors, who seem determined to destroy Massenet's delicate plant with too much kindness. Indeed, as Desmond Shawe-Taylor pointed out in a radio talk. Italian tenors 'more or less adopted Massenet, and made him for the time being an honorary Italian, meaning it, of course, as a high compliment. They all interpolate turns, and some alter the vocal line to add intrusive high notes: I wonder who began this tradition. Both versions by Caruso avoid most of these excesses, although he includes the turn. The earlier G&T (52345; HLM 7030) is surpassed by the 1904 Victor (81031). His 'Ah, fuyez' is in French, and all the better for it (DB 130), a gorgeous 1911 performance; this Des Grieux really sounds convinced by his conversion from couch to church. Edoardo Garbin, Carlo Dani, de Lucia, Lauri-Volpi (much to offer) must all be passed over in favour of Giuseppe Anselmi (Fono. 62165), most graceful and sensitive of the early Italians, judging his vibrato to a nicety. Gigli, too, cannot be denied (DA 1216); who could resist that honeyed *mezza voce*? His 'Ah, fuyez' (DB 6346), heavily aspirated, is only for his fans. Dino Borgioli in the Dream (Col. D 14710), is as cultivated as ever, one of his best discs. Miguel Fleta (DB 986) has to be heard to be believed, a collector's piece of tenor licence. By comparison, even by absolute standards. Tito Schipa is a model of style and individuality, but his Pathé (86567) is preferable to his later, downward-transposed HMV version (DA 875; GEMM 151). His 'Ah, fuyez' is impassioned, but there are signs of strain (DB 2237). Antonio Cortis (DB 1363) is fine and heroic in the same aria. Of the Italian Irishmen, McCormack sings the Dream exquisitely, but I detect not an ounce of Des Grieux's feeling in his version, and Tom Burke (Col. 7204) apes many of the Italians' more unattractive mannerisms. The Russian Dimitri Smirnov (DB 583) is, as always, the great artist, even if he is inclined to show off.

In German Leo Slezak (3–42714/5) sounds cumbersome in both pieces. Helge Roswaenge is unkind to Massenet's marks of expression in the Dream (DB 4655), but his ardent, forward singing can prove an antidote to too many perfumed French voices. His early 'Flieh, o flieh' (Telef. E 2253; 6.42084J) is irresistible in its individual way. Julius Patzak's seamless legato and innate musicianship make his Dream (Poly. 90062; LV 191) among the most winning; his even more youthful 'Flieh, o flieh' (95267; LV 191) has the typical Patzak plangency; he also takes the first phrase in a single breath. Hermann Jadlowker's versions are too emphatic for my taste, but at least he is more involved than Alfred Piccaver, who strikes me as cool and uninterested. Wittrisch, at the opposite extreme (EH 1095), becomes lachrymose. Anton Dermota's versions are quite beautifully articulated (Tele. E 2910). Of more recent vintage is Peter Schreier (Teldec. 211156), who delivers a euphonious Dream, a slightly forced 'Flieh, o flieh'.

The small British contingent is headed by Heddle Nash's eloquent, intensely musical Dream (Col. DB 961; HLM 7004), although he far surpasses himself in his own exquisitely phrased version on the BBC extracts. Browning Mummery (B 3121), using a different translation, is also highly attractive with his clear, liquid tone. The young Richard Lewis sings in excellent French (K 2291) and with a pure, unforced, if characterless tone. Walter Midegly (DB 21358), who was los Angeles's Des Grieux at Covent Garden in the 1950s, has an open, light, free tone in both pieces, but blots his copy by vulgarly altering Massenet's vocal line at the end of 'Ah begone' as if to show off his own voice; even the Italians eschew that. His Dream was reissued on HQM 1228.

Some separate 'Ah, fuyez's: Lucien Muratore (Pathé H&D 63004) sings with great intensity in a Martinelli-like manner; the fact that he was a great actor emerges clearly from this performance. Sydney Rayner, who sang at the Opéra-Comique from 1930 to 1935 and at the Met from 1936 to 1938, uses his clear, untarnished tenor splendidly (Decca K 685), José de Trevi (W 867), César Vezzani (DB 4844), Armand Tokatyan should not be ignored. Joseph Schmidt gives a sad, very beautiful account

(Parlo. R 1443; 1C 047–28 558). Of various, cut, ten-inch, pre-first world war renderings, I like the legendary Léon David (Brown Od. 97178) for his broad phrasing and classical French elocution, and Adolphe Maréchal (3–32424) for his clear, manly, high tenor. The German version by Franz Naval of the same generation (Brown Od. 50430) is pure in style but not ardent in manner. Of the early Italians, Rocca (3–32829) is too emphatic, Edoardo Garbin bleats, Alessandro Bonci (Fono. 92221) ignores note-values to an intolerable extent but is forgiven because of his exquisitely etched line.

Just before we leave the legion of tenors, we must not forget the representatives of the post-war generation, of whom Jussi Björling in both pieces (DB 3603 and DB 6249; 1C 147–00947) is as always an exemplar in combining musicality with feeling. Léopold Simoneau, with his lighter, suaver style, is also commendable (DGM 19101). Placido Domingo in 'Ah fuyez' (SER 5613) is lachrymose, but the tone is always, rich and the phrasing generous. Of the Italians di Stefano's Dream (SDD 390) is not inconsiderable, his 'Ah, fuyez', made in his best days (DB 6868) is impassioned in the marvellous manner that thrilled everyone in the late 1940s. Tagliavini (DB 6854), in Italian, sings a honeyed Dream, Richard Tucker is tight and throaty in 'Ah, fuyez', Georges Liccioni vibrant but bleaty, Antonio Salvarezza poor.

And so we turn to the much less frequently recorded excerpts of the Lescauts and Counts. Lescaut establishes his extrovert, jolly, equivocal character by his 'Ne bronchez pas', words of advice on his first encounter with the still-innocent Manon in the first act. The most important point to note in the five singers I have heard in this piece is their light tone and flexibility of phrasing. Most debonair of all is Hector Dufranne (3–32766), who made his Opéra-Comique debut as Thoas in 1900 and created Golaud in 1902. His inflexion has marvellous variety; I particularly like his near-chuckle on the first syllable of 'bronchez' and the wealth of meaning he gives to 'parole'.

Paolo Ananian (Brown Od. 60236) has a heavier voice with an attractively quick vibrato, and there is a cynical note in his tones, he is inclined to be careless about the text. André Baugé, of the Opéra-Comique, (P 406) gives a classic account with rolled 'r's on 'bronchez', a cheeky accent to his delivery, and a certain, steady voice. Emile Roque (Od. 188791) is good but less interesting; Roger Bourdin (188508), a little nasal in tone, is full of character, with a smile in the voice.

Lescaut's other solo, at the Cours-la-Reine, shows him in good humour, first in the quick-fire 'A quoi bon l'économie', asking why he should economise at the gambling-table of L'hotel de Transylvanie round the corner and then apostrophizing his Rosalinde in sentimental fashion. Baugé, on the reverse of his other solo, is again master of this piece – master of rubato, and subtle treatment of the text. Dufranne marvellously differentiates between Lescaut's two moods, while Roque has some beautiful phrasing to offer. Bourdin is much as above.

We encounter some of the same singers in the Count's tender 'Epousez quelque brave fille', his advice to his son at the beginning of the St Sulpice scene, as the role appears to have been written for a high bass. Dufranne (Zono X 82745) is at once sympathetic and unaffected, and he obeys Massenet's injunction 'sans lenteur'. Alexis Boyer (H&D 0407) uses his full, fruity voice effectively. Ananian (Black Od. 73010) is much happier in this role than as Lescaut, his rich bass rolling out effortlessly. Etienne Billot (Od. 188527), another Opéra-Comique stalwart, suggests sad resignation in his lighter interpretation. André Pernet of the next generation again has that inevitable way with the French language now neglected (Od. 188716), but still better is the Chicago-born Arthur Endrèze (188864), a lovely, natural performance. Richard Mayr (4–42346), in German, has a line and voice not to be encountered today.

Indeed, none of the versions by recent singers is satisfactory. My notes say: Norman Treigle is too studied and melodramatic, Souzay is not authoritative or paternal enough, and Nicolai Ghiaurov is too declamatory and too generalized in manner. In the duet at the Cour-la-Reine for the Count and Manon, a favourite passage of mine, the strains of an antique minuet accompany her urgent inquiries about how her lover has taken her desertion. It begins 'Pardon! mais j'étais là'. The version by Vallandri and Dufranne (034021) is superb, a wonderful memento, surely, of pre-first world war performances at the Comique, especially in the expressive Andantino passage, where the Count explains that youth and love are bound to fade; Dufranne is here at his most eloquent and Vallandri in the words 'On oublie' makes us realize why she is to hurry off to remind Des Grieux of her charms. The vital Augusta Garcia is partnered by one of the noblest of French basses, Paul Payan (W 419), who sings, as asked, 'légèrement et cependant avec expression'. In a recording from a later period, Vallin and André Balbon (Pathé X 2621) take the passage more quickly, more intimately but just as sensitively.

But back to the beginning of the affair, and the 'Duo de la rencontre'. First we meet Marguerite Carré, one of the earliest recorded Manons, partnered by Beyle in the latter part of the duet from 'Nous vivrons'. She is a delightfully eager young girl, he an ardent Des Grieux (H&D 2534). Beyle is partnered by the charming Jeanne Daffetye with piano (34101 and 110) in a splendidly confident turn-of-the-century (1904) performance of the whole duet. Muratore recorded the duet twice. I have not heard the Favorite version with Laute-Brun, but that with a lesser Manon, Jeanne Leclerc, again shows what a winning Des Grieux he must have been. The lovely Vallandri is partnered by Albert Vaguet (H&D 2503). Brothier and Marcelin sound a little too sedate and cultivated (Disque Y 64); so do their 1920s contemporaries Marcelle Ragon and Peret, an Opéra-Comique heroine with an Opéra hero, a languid but none the less interesting performance on three ten-inch sides (P. 791–2) with Ragon's 'A nous les amours' on the fourth.

In a different class altogether is the version by Vallin and Villabella (X 7225), the exchanges eager and fresh from these two fine artists. The ever-ardent Thill is weakly partnered by Mary McCormic (Col. 12509; 2C 153–16212); they also recorded the St Sulpice Scene. Perhaps best of all from this period are Luart and Friant (Od. 123657), she wonderfully savouring 'à Paris', he whispering seductively 'viens', both employing immaculate diction. Jeanne Guyla, who sang one performance of Louise at Covent Garden in 1928 when Heldy was ill, is characterless beside the fervent Vezzani (DB 4846). More recently Pierrette Alarie is overparted but is soundly partnered by her husband, Léopold Simoneau (Ducretet DTL 93018). Carosio and Carlo Zampighi, in Italian (ALP 1353), go at it with a will but are miles from the right manner. A recent account by Mady Mesplé and Nicolai Gedda (2C 069–14010), slowly conducted by Pierre Dervaux, lacks conviction on the soprano's part. The tenor is again too forceful.

Eloped, the lovers set up at the rue Vivienne (in-joke as that was the address of the opera's publishers?). Here we have the lovely 'Duo de la lettre'. I began with a paean to the performance of Luart and Micheletti, and it remains supreme, but there are others in contention. Vallandri and Vaguet on the back of the aforementioned disc set a high standard of intimate colloquy, followed by the youthful Vallin with Beyle (H&D 2519), who also recorded it with the delightful Korsoff (34203). Both savour memorably 'au zéphir parfume qui passe'. A beautiful partnership is that of Berthe César and Léon Campagnola with their forward, attractive voices and keen exchanges (U 22). Farrar and Caruso (DM 110) are too familiar to call for much comment, a lovely performance.

Vallin, now partnered by Villabella (Pathé X 90034), sing in their usual impeccable style. Delmas and Friant (Od. 123706), like Luart and Micheletti, recorded the piece complete, that is until the interruption of Lescaut and de Brétigny. The characterful, ensuing quartet, with its many asides, was once done by Luart, Friant, Bourdin and Jean Vieuille (123581), a fascinating disc.

Landouzy, partnered by the splendid tenor Codou, a Monnaie singer, recorded the St Sulpice duet (Od. 56030/1), around 1906 with piano. They are undeniably wayward over note-values, but the big scale of their energetic performance comes across the years. Vallin and Marny (H&D 2553) are more accurate and just as effective, but both these early versions are eclipsed by that of César and Campagnola (034111/120), who give the sort of interpretation that suggests a live performance. Even from this distance in time, one relishes their impassioned singing, kept within the composer's bounds. By contrast, Heldy and Ansseau in their much-admired reading (DB 1410), sound less caught up in the situation, although Ansseau delivers some thrilling B flats. I prefer from that generation Jacqueline Roger, a most seductive Manon of whom I know nothing, with

Marcelin – an involved performance (W 697). Friant partners Luart (Od. 171029), so convincingly repentant, and re-seducing Des Grieux with a 'N'est-ce plus ma main' fulfilling Massenet's 'avec un grand charme et très caressant', but then I turn to Vallin with Villabella (X 90081) and find an equally definitive performance. Nor are Guyla and Vezzani (DB 4816) to be dismissed with their exciting, fevered build-up of the emotional pressure. A live, pirated version by Favero and Gigli in the late 1930s works up the piece to fever pitch. Recently Renata Scotto, with Domingo, reminded us what a convincing Manon she can be (CBS 76732).

On the road to Le Havre, we are left with few competitors. Luart, so sensuous, so touching in her management of the dialogue in these final exchanges, recalling, in musical terms, past happiness, and Friant, whose commitment must not be underestimated, here complete their superlative set of duets (Od. 123658); as do that other indomitable pair, Guyla and Vezzani (DB 4847). A Victor (87083) of the final moments of Act 4 has given me a brief hearing of Aristodemo Giorgini's impassioned Des Grieux; he also recorded the two solos.

My ideal would be Luart, Clément or Friant, Baugé, and Dufranne (as the Count), with Monteux conducting.

MANON

M Manon; *G* Des Grieux; *L* Lescaut; *C* Comte des Grieux

1923 Heldy *M*; Marny *G*; Ponzio *L*;
Dupré *C*/Chorus and
Orch./Büsser
Pathé 1718–41

1932 Féraldy *M*; Rogatchewsky *G*;
Villier *L*; Guénot *C*/Paris Opéra-
Comique Chorus and
Orch./Cohen
EMI ⓜ 2C 053 10746–8; CBS
ⓜ EL6

1951 Micheau *M*; L de Luca *G*;
Bourdin *L*; Giovannetti *C*/Paris
Opéra-Comique Chorus and
Orch./Wolff
Decca ⓜ LXT 2618–20; London
ⓜ A4305

1955 los Angeles *M*; Legay *G*; Dens
L; Borthayre *C*/Paris Opéra-
Comique Chorus and
Orch./Monteux
HMV ⓒ SLS 5119 ④ TC–SLS
5119; Seraphim
ⓜ ID 6057

1970 Sills *M*; Gedda *G*; Souzay *L*;
Bacquier *C*/Ambrosian Singers,
New Philharmonia/Rudel
HMV SLS 800; ABC ATS
20007 ④ 5109–20007S

Excerpts

1947 (in Italian – live performance)
Favero *M*; di Stefano *G*;
Borriello *L*/La Scala Chorus and
Orch./Guarnieri
Cetra ⓜ LO 11

1960 Doria *M*; Vanzo *G*; Legros
C/Chorus and Orch./Etchéverry
Philips ⓜ GL 5652

1962 Moffo *M*; di Stefano *G*; Kerns
C/RCA Italiana Chorus and
Orch./Leibowitz
RCA (UK) SER 5512; (US)
LSC 7028

Werther

LORD HAREWOOD

I heard Werther innumerable times, with all the most popular interpreters. Here and now, I affirm that the expression of feeling and the moves were entirely falsified and in no way fitted the style which Massenet asked of his performers. One too easily forgets that the work is made up entirely of emotions, intense but all coming from within, and there is invariably too much noise, too little feeling, not enough variety of nuance, not enough music.... I repeat that, performed as it is now at the Opéra-Comique, *Werther* has nothing whatsoever to do with what Massenet wanted.*

Werther is full of contradictions. For Charlotte, Massenet apparently had in mind the voice and personality of Rose Caron, a soprano, but in the event it was a young mezzo, Marie Delna, who created it in France, though a soprano had been the original Charlotte in Vienna a year earlier, one, moreover, who had once sung Manon. The tenor role is perhaps even more exacting. The original, Ernest van Dyck, was a Bayreuth stalwart; other Wagnerians have sung it frequently, and so have most French lyric tenors; and it was one of the favourite roles of Tito Schipa, who would not have described himself as a *Heldentenor*. So the list of recorded singers is amazingly varied.

Its admirers prize *Werther* above all for the delicacy, the precision and the musical nuance with which Massenet has reinterpreted Goethe's early novel – Ibos, the first French Werther, suggests as much above – but the gramophone, while by no means ignoring the conversational style flowering continually to arioso which is so attractive a feature of the music, has not unnaturally concentrated on the splendid soliloquies. Outside complete or abridged sets, I could find fewer than a dozen performances of the 'Clair de Lune' scene, one of the finest examples of the conversational style, but without much searching, some forty of Werther's opening Invocation, thirty of the 'Air des lettres', and getting on for one hundred of the 'Lied d'Ossian'. *Werther* nevertheless adds up to much more than the sum of its solos, for all their beauty, and it is therefore in the

*Guillaume Ibos, *Souvenirs*. Ibos was the creator of the title role in the first French performance.

complete recordings and, to a lesser extent, in the two-sided selections that one will find most satisfaction.

The earliest complete set, made in the mid 1930s, has Ninon Vallin and Georges Thill supported by Emile Rocque, Germaine Féraldy, and Armand Narçon, with the Opéra-Comique Orchestra conducted by Elie Cohen (fifteen 78s now well transferred to three LPs) and it is to my mind still the best performance. Cohen's conducting is 'classical', in the sense that passion mounts from within and that it is imbued with the supposedly French virtues of balance and elegance. I cannot imagine grander singing of the main roles than we get from Vallin and Thill; she a little cool at the start of her great third-act scene, but filling the prayer with abandoned intensity, he with glorious tone at all times and the poise and control of a truly great singer. A curiosity of the set is to have passed a 'bubble' in the second climactic A sharp in an otherwise immaculate 'Pourquoi me réveiller?' Féraldy is a mature Sophie, but Rocque is Albert to the life. The whole cast could give a lesson in French enunciation.

On an altogether lower level is the 1953 recording conducted in pedestrian style by Georges Sebastian. Charles Richard has a good voice but not much else; Suzanne Juyol was one of the finest Ortruds I ever heard but cannot find the colour or intimate manner for Charlotte. Far stronger competition for Vallin–Thill–Cohen is provided by the admirable 1968 HMV recording with Victoria de los Angeles, Nicolai Gedda, Mady Mesplé and Roger Soyer, under Georges Prêtre. There is no more convincing Charlotte than los Angeles, with a charm that never cloys, unfailing beauty of tone and a sense of detail that runs the gamut from the heart-break of her realization in the middle of the 'Clair de Lune' that she cannot be Werther's to the white but still live vocal sound she brings to the reading of the letters – one of the most appreciable performances of a rare and cherished artist. In spite of beautiful tone and much *élan*, the stylish Nicolai Gedda veers disconcertingly from very loud to very soft, which tends to mannerism and is perhaps the result of too much tape-splicing. The supporting cast is good, though there is something in the majestic voice of Soyer a little at variance with the domestic Albert. Recorded sound throughout is fine – better, I have to admit, than in the pre-war Columbia – and Prêtre keeps things moving along well, but falls too easily into the trap of over-reaction, not to say sentimentality, something of which Cohen is never guilty.

A little behind this HMV issue is one made for Mondiophonie in 1964, with Rita Gorr, Albert Lance, Mesplé and Gabriel Bacquier, ORTF Orchestra, conducted by Jésus Etchéverry, which is well recorded and admirably cast throughout. Gorr, with her rich mezzo-soprano, gives very much a theatrical performance, big in scale though not devoid of detail or feeling, but she does not efface memories of los Angeles. Lance, on the other hand, seems to me to have the ideal voice for Werther; he relies on beauty of tone and long-breathed phrasing rather than nuance for his effects, but he is never stretched by the music. He sang the opera often with Gorr, and only a certain monotony of sound – to oversimplify, *forte* and *piano* too much alike – put him perhaps below Thill and Kozlovsky among the complete performances. This set ranks high, though.

Three 'foreign' recordings must be mentioned, one in Russian, the others by Italians in French and Italian. Ferruccio Tagliavini and his wife Pia Tassinari sang the opera at La Scala and elsewhere after the second world war, and, if some of the French of this excellent performance (1953) is less than idiomatic, the singing of the principals, including the stylish Albert of Marcello Cortis, has that elusive quality of 'presence' – the opposite of anonymity. Tassinari makes a powerful assault on the great scenes of Act 3, and I find Tagliavini's concentrated, 'nutty' tone attractive; he has the same knack of creating atmosphere as had his great predecessor, Beniamino Gigli. A fine set, well conducted by Molinari-Pradelli, even if not a candidate for the definitive version. In Italian and in moderate sound is a Mexican performance (1949) with Giulietta Simionato and Giuseppe di Stefano. For all the tenor's tendency to turn everything into Italian opera, there is glorious freedom in his singing and he was then at the height of his form. Simionato is always stylish.

More interesting is the Russian performance with the veteran Ivan Kozlovsky, Maksakova, Sakharov, Svesdina and the Soviet Radio Orchestra, conducted by Bron. I should imagine it was made in the late 1940s. These Russians unerringly capture the elegance of the music as well as its fervour. An acid Sophie, a no more than honest Albert and Maksakova's straightforward Charlotte surround the outstanding Werther of Kozlovsky, who, I have no hesitation in saying, identifies himself more completely with the character than anyone apart from Charles Friant, singing the music clearly and accurately, phrasing in the grand manner, missing no opportunity for colour or expression, and above all treating Werther's music as something in which the listener, as a matter of course, would expect to hear that blend of splendid singing with subtle musicianship which I hope most of us mean by *bel canto*. His ardent phrasing in, for instance, the 'Clair de Lune' is that of a young man first in love, his grandiose, personalized performance of the 'Lied d'Ossian' is passionate as well as a quite unusual piece of virtuoso singing, culminating in a long (unwritten) diminuendo *pianissimo* A sharp. Not everyone to whom I played this recording likes it as much as I do, but I think it takes a hard heart to resist it. I could not.

Excerpts:

1 Invocation: 'Je ne sais si je veille/O nature pleine de grâce'
2 'Quelle prière de reconnaissance et d'amour'
3 Duo: 'Clair de Lune'
4 'Voici trois mois que nous sommes unis'
5 Désolation: 'Un autre est son époux!/J'aurais sur ma poitrine'
6 'Au bonheur, dont mon âme est pleine/Mais, comme après l'orage'

7   'Du gai soleil'
8   Duo: 'Ai-je dit vrai?/Ah! qu'il est loin'
9   'Lorsque l'enfant revient d'un voyage'
10   Air des lettres: 'Qui m'aurait dit/Ces lettres!'
11   Air des larmes: 'Va! laisse couler mes larmes'
12   Prière: 'Seigneur Dieu!'
13   Retour de Werther: 'Oui! c'est moi!'
14   Lied d'Ossian: 'Pourquoi me réveiller?'
15   Duo: 'N'achevez-pas'
16   Mort de Werther

I have found half a dozen selections of very different quality and interest. The oldest, a private recording, has a dimly recorded single side with Tito Schipa and Gianna Pederzini at La Scala in 1934; this was made at the time of the first of five revivals Schipa inspired there between 1934 and 1944. Included are only 1, 3, 14 and a bit of 16, but the tenor shows the same exquisite control as we know on his published records, if a more robust tone, and the gently caressing phrasing with which he fills the Invocation and the 'Clair de Lune' seems to me in its own way the height of romantic passion. This single side and some snatches from a San Francisco performance (bilingual, from all accounts) of the following year with Schipa, also a 'pirate' version, have their own value as documents of what was clearly a most compelling impersonation.

Perhaps it is convenient to talk here of Schipa's studio recordings, two of number 14, one (DA 870; GEMM 151) sung in less than idiomatic French, presumably for the American market, the other (DB 2237, recorded in 1934) in Italian and including some phrases of recitative – the aria on DB 2237 is transposed a semitone, as in the two stage performances. The voice is not robust, as we know from his other electric recordings, but an exquisite art informs every phrase and the passionate intensity with which he approaches the second stanza in each of these four different performances is exemplary; great singing if not great vocalism. The voice is more threadbare in the wartime Invocation (DA 5420) but the singing of the opening phrases is wonderfully sensitive and, in spite of some effortful top notes, this is still an evocative souvenir.

Much to be recommended is a single-sided selection with Irma Kolassi and Raoul Jobin (LXT 5034: 1, 9, 10, 12, 13, 14, 15). This was recorded late in the tenor's career, but his excellent diction and the strong attack and reserves of power are much in evidence. The Charlotte is a Greek mezzo-soprano who never appeared on the stage, but her sensitivity as a recitalist is evident here. Far less interesting is a double-sided selection (Philips GL 5667: 1, 3, 5, 7, 8, 9, 10, 11, 14, 15, 16) with Jean Brazzi, who sang Werther at Glyndebourne, and Andrée Gabriel. The recording characteristic is fierce, the singing (apart from the admirable Liliane Berton in a snatch of Sophie's music) coarse and beset with pitch problems.

I did not much enjoy the double-sided selection with the strong-voiced Bernabé Marti, direct and not very French as Werther, and Géori Boué as Charlotte. It is hard to recognize in this acid, matter-of-fact performance a soprano who was once so poetic (Vogue LDM 301.30; 1, 3, 5, 9, 10, 11, 12, 13, 14, 15). Better, but a badly chosen selection (half a side taken up with the complete death scene, and no programme notes), is an RCA recording dated 1962 (SB 6512; 1, 2, 3, 4, 5, 10, 11, 14, 16). Cesare Valletti, who made his American debut in 1953 as Werther in San Francisco, is up to a point a poetic Werther, with his scrupulous attention to dynamics and phrasing, but Rosalind Elias makes as little of the great Act 3 scene as can a mezzo with a good voice who is also an accurate musician. An interesting feature is the fine singing of Gérard Souzay, the Albert, in a romantic role (2,4).

If I had to choose a two-sided selection to demonstrate *Werther's* qualities, it would have to be either the Odeon compendium featuring Charles Friant, Germaine Cernay, Roger Bourdin and some others, or that in Italian from a performance of the mid 1960s with Magda Olivero and Agostino Lazzari. The Italian selection (2G.2KP 10083: 3, 8, 10, 11, 12, 13, 14, 15, 16) is not very well engineered but includes almost all of Charlotte's role. The tenor is positive in the four duets (3, 8, 13–15, 16) and sings with some of the grace of his famous Italian predecessor, Schipa. Olivero's smouldering passion would perhaps be hard to find in a French Charlotte, but her delicate singing of the letter scene, with incomparably expressive changes of vocal colour as well as her rare dramatic fervour, put her into a category of her own. Such imaginative singing is rare on records in any role, and I do not know who can match this penetrating intensity, controlled for all its naked emotion, except perhaps Callas herself. I find Olivero one of the most powerfully musical singers of our time and this recording has qualities that are nothing short of great.

Authenticity of the highest order is found on the two deleted Odeon LPs, taken from 78 originals, sung by dominating French singers of the late 1920s and early 1930s (ORX 118: 1, 3, 5, 6, 8, 9, 10, 12, 14, 16). The recorded quality is dry and the voices arguably not the greatest, but Cernay is rich-toned and a smooth, communicative singer. Charles Friant, from whom we get all but 5 and 14, conveys the impetuosity of the title role with so exact a gradation of tonal colour, such invariably constructive phrasing and so natural a use of language that one is tempted to label him unique. In his singing, Werther's sorrows are drawn reluctantly from him even in the heaviest passages of the score. It is recommendation enough that the considerable efforts of these two singers are backed up by the fresh-voiced Albert of Roger Bourdin, a performance of the 'Lied' in the grand manner by Nequeçaur, an impassioned 5 by that sterling artist René Verdière, to say nothing of numbers 10 and 12 from Ninon Vallin in younger voice than in the Columbia complete recording. Those who want to see what enthusiasts for French singing are talking about should do all they can to hear this recording. There are other Odeon discs from Friant (not in this collection), particularly 13, 14, 15, all with Cernay, again with every phrase appropriately weighted, every nuance captured in the wax. Numbers 3, 5, 9, 13 have now been reissued on GV 511, devoted to Friant's refined, involving art.

Van Dyck was Werther at the première in Vienna (1892), and both he and the French creator of the role, Guillaume Ibos (1893), have left us souvenirs of the 'Lied d'Ossian'. Van Dyck's is dry and cannot be representative (Fono. 39113; MCK. 500; in French, not the German of Vienna); but Ibos's recording is interesting, recorded fourteen years after the event in a virile voice, an interpretation full of rubato but honest and moving, and with a soft ending, contrary to the score's indications (AFG 9). The great Marie Delna, the original French Charlotte (aged eighteen), sang both 10 and 11 some fourteen years after the première, when she was still only 32 years old. The sound is wonderfully full and beautiful (Pathé 4879, 3512; MCK 500).

Many singers of a long-gone age have recorded short excerpts, and perhaps that by Medea Mei-Figner of 11, made in Russian in 1901, should take pride of place. If there is less than the instrumental-like control of Delna, Mei-Figner's voice is of a glory which is rare to find (23124; Rubini RS 301). Another voice of outstanding beauty is that of Geneviève Vix (also of 11), a versatile soprano whose singing is expressive and fluent (1907).

One of the curiosities of opera is that Massenet should himself have rewritten the title role to suit the great baritone Battistini, who recorded not only the 'Lied' beautifully and in free style, but also a most peculiar affair combining 5 and 6 in the wrong order (DB 149), which sounds as though the singer had realized half-way through that he had forgotten the tune! From the same generation comes the equally great, but here slightly uninvolved, Fernando de Lucia, in 14 (52435). From a little later come Alessandro Bonci (Fono. 39698; Rococo R42), in a full-blooded and finely phrased performance of 14, and Giuseppe Anselmi in 1, 6 and 14 on Fonotipia (62276/7; CO 359) with an alternatively limpid and brilliant sound, clean phrasing and true, old-fashioned grace. Emile Scaremberg (Fono. 39179; Rococo R18) is vigorous and controlled in the grand manner in the Désolation, better still in an unpublished version of the same aria with piano, and hardly less fine in 14 (Fono. 39186), Cornubert sang a strong, controlled 14 for Odéon (56046); the Russian David Yuzhin shows power in 1; the French Léon Cazauran recorded 14 in Milan in Italian on a 1904 Black G&T (52163), as did the Spaniard Florencio Constantino, in a beautifully individual voice, and the Russian Vladimir Rosing, aged about 20. Albert Vaguet sang 1 and 14 beautifully for Pathé some years after his premature retirement from the stage. Few have quite the poise and grace of that extraordinary French stylist, Edmond Clément, the Metropolitan's Werther at the 1910 revival, whose 1911 Victor seems virtually ideal until one has heard the even more sensitive 1916 Pathé. He is also responsible for an ideally graceful Invocation. Hard to beat among the old-timers are two Russians, Leonid Sobinov, who sings in Russian, a committed performance of wonderful poise and buoyancy (DB 891); and Dimitri Smirnov, who sings in French with majestic and grandiose phrasing (DA 618).

The rehabilitation of *Werther* in Paris is supposed to have come with the casting by Albert Carré in 1903 of Léon Beyle and Marie de l'Isle in the main roles. Beyle, a strong, manly tenor of declamatory style, recorded 1, 3, 5, 13, 14, 15 and 16, mainly with Suzanne Brohly (3, 10, 11, 13, 15, 16), a fine, Tosca-weight French soprano of the early years of the century, and an involved Charlotte, who also recorded 4 with Dupouy. De l'Isle recorded a section of the 'Clair de Lune', part of the letter scene and the 'Air des Larmes', but the voice comes over on records without much personal distinction. Tenors light and heavy tackled the title role over the years, and Charles Rousselière (1, 3, 5, 14) is an example of a Wagnerian. Lucien Muratore (5, 14) is plainly an artist of high calibre, but neither Emile Marcelin (1, 5, 9, 13, 14) nor René Lapelletrie (13 and 15 with Marie Charbonnel) have the strength or subtlety of Léon Campagnola (1, 3, 5, 9, 13, 14, 15, 16), who, judging by his records, was a most distinguished performer, and at his best in the Retour sequence, where his partner is the no less admirable Marie Lafargue (Y 36). Much lighter in tone but always notable is David Devriès (1, 5, 14); if the Lied is a little less notable than I had hoped, the Désolation, a heavy assignment for him when he recorded it in the 1920s for Odeon, is better on an earlier Pathé, recorded when he was apparently 26. The numbers of these discs, too many to list, will be found in Bauer or WERM or the HMV French Catalogue of 'Voices of the Past'.

To match this group of tenors from the earlier part of the century, it is hard to find a comparable list of Charlottes. Miral, in a truncated 10, is not very expressive (Homophone 8685); Marthe Chenal not much better in 11 (Pathé); Fanny Anitua (11) sounds as though she would rather be singing Verdi; Eva Gauthier (11) made many more interesting discs than this, but Marguerite Mérentié (11) exhibits a sumptuous voice on an early G&T (33654) as well as later on Pathé, for whom she also sang 10. There remains the peerless Gerville-Réache, unfortunately only in 11, but using that wonderful, purple-rich voice in a performance of classical weight as well as classical restraint (Victor 81091; Rococo 14).

The role of Werther belongs to the Latins and I can trace very few Germanic tenors who essayed it. The Czech Karel Burian (3-42565/6; CO 306: 5 and 14) in 1906 is exuberant if not wholly idiomatic, and his fellow countryman, Otto Marak (Supraphon reissue), sings cleanly. Hermine Kittel from Vienna (reissue CO 319) is short of breath in 11. I do not know if Alfred Piccaver sang the title role opposite Lotte Lehmann, but his records of 1 and 14 suggest his lovely soft tone must have been nearly ideal (Od. O-8099; LV 26: and Polydor fifteen years later, 95353). Much later but still Germanic is Julius Patzak with less voice but appealing musicianship in both 5 and 14 (the Lied, Poly. 30031, recorded by the way, seven years later than the Désolation, Poly. 35083).

The 1918–39 generation of sopranos and mezzos was much more prolific, foreigners as well as French. Lucy Perelli's 'Air des Lettres' is a sound performance, Ninon Vallin's fine Odeon discs (171022, 188517) I mentioned earlier, and Alice Raveau, like Vallin, recorded 10 and 11 on Pathé, revealing a seamless mezzo voice rather than a great interpreter. Lise Charny and Madeleine Sibille sang well on Pathé. Supervia (who was Charlotte in Chicago in 1915 opposite Muratore) may never have heard her 'Air des Larmes', which was unissued until recently but shows a much brighter quality of voice than we tend to associate with this drama-ridden music (OASI 560). Rose Pocidalo, an Opéra-Comique mezzo, again unusually bright in quality, has a strong vocal personality and her 10 (Parlo. 29514) is an excellent performance. Germaine Martinelli, a concert singer pure and simple, recorded both arias (Poly. 524117) with an opulence and grandeur of manner that is almost Wagnerian, but also with precise and expressive detail and an iron control over the pent-up emotion. To me she must take pride of place in her generation among the French singers of this music, even though there are good performances of 10 and 12 by Germaine Cernay (Od. 188647, 188607), and of 11 by Leila Megane, a French-trained Welsh girl with a beautiful voice, de Silvéra (D 12043), and Germaine Pape (LF 192).

The grandiose singing of 11 by Nadezhda Obukhova has been reissued in Russia, and shows a voice and interpreter of apparently limitless possibilities. Gianna Pederzini, Schipa's partner at La Scala, recorded 11 on a wartime disc in Italian (DA 5424), and if the rest of her singing of the role was on this level of response, it must have been fine indeed. Bruna Castagna, whose career was mainly American, sings 10 in splendid voice (Col. 71390), but to me the most emotionally charged of all the inter-war Charlottes is that of Lotte Lehmann (RO 20240; PMA 1057). Her letter scene is in German, but the intimacy and intensity of the singing is more truly that of a vulnerable young girl than on any other disc of the period I know.

Tenors were more prolific still, and you can choose, if you can find them, between the records left by light voices – Charles Friant, already discussed, takes pride of place – and those of Wagnerian calibre. Jean Marny (Pathé – 1 and 16) is as good a Werther as he was a Des Grieux in Pathé's *Manon*. Joseph Rogatchewsky (1, 9, 14, 16: reissued on LV 239) is a Russian who rightly became an examplar of French style (I last met him as Intendant in Brussels); Villabella (1, 5, 14) another foreigner whose career, like his style, was French – I like the contained Latin passion of his Désolation as much as the perfect blend of vocal ease and emotional involvement in the Lied (Od. 123784, 188816). Some of the best French tenors were Corsicans, and Gaston Micheletti (1, 5, 9, 14) is one of them, brilliant and vibrant of voice, turning in one of the most distraught of all versions of the Désolation (Od. 188510; ORX 504), and an admirably restrained 9 (Od. 188654). Enrico di Mazzei (1, 9, 14) was an Italian who sang mainly in France, and I greatly enjoyed his 'Lorsque l'enfant revient', far more than the pedestrian versions of his more famous countryman, Giuseppe Lugo, who chooses the same selections, sang with Vallin in the one-thousandth performance of the work at the Opéra-Comique in 1938, but whose main claim to notoriety is that on my copy of Poly. 566171 he sings *two* different versions of the Invocation, one on either side – a pressing error? José Luccioni (1, 5, 14) is strenuous and unsubtle (FJLP 5052) – Samson before the gates of Gaza rather than Goethe's poet. Sidney Rayner, an American active in both Paris and New York, is authoritative and brilliant of voice (1, 5), and José Janson, one of the lightest tenors to record Werther (he sang it at the Opéra-Comique in 1939), successfully negotiates one of the heaviest passages (9) and sings a strenuous 14 (Pathé PG 111). José de Trevi, of La Monnaie, produces refined, imaginative performances of 9 and 14 (Disque P 767).

Two outstanding tenors remain: Fernand Ansseau (1, 5, 13, 14, 15) and César Vezzani (3, 5, 9, 13, 14, 15, 16), the former a Belgian, the latter Corsican by birth, each with Wagnerian tendencies. Vezzani's *Werther* recordings show a sensitivity I had not suspected. He recorded 9 and 14 for Odeon about 1920 with the voice of a young Otello, but there is greater involvement some seven years later in 5 (Disque P 808) and 9 (P 844). A powerful version of the great scene of the return, the 'Lied d'Ossian' and succeeding duet (DB 4825) unfortunately has Lucy Perelli as a drab partner, and again there is singing in the grand manner in the complete death scene, still with the pallid Perelli (DB 4813–4), who however appears to better advantage in their 'Clair de Lune' (Disque W 1138).

Ansseau divides opinions; some think the voice too thick for pleasure, I find him one of the most communicative and masculine of French tenors. He sang Werther opposite Mary Garden in Chicago in 1924 and 1925. His earlier efforts (unlike Vezzani's) are among his best, and it is hard to find a more ideal blend of passion and classical restraint than his Lied (DA 427; Rococo R 26), made about 1920. He first recorded 1 and 5 in 1919 (DB 485), but in 1927 (DB 1085; LV 116) the great breadth of phrasing is just as sure, the lyrical impulse more in evidence, the abandonment in the Désolation even more heart-rending. DA 1122 (1930) has 1 and 5 in similar if perhaps slightly shorter-breathed performances. A sadness of gramophone history is that both DB 783 (1925) with Hélène Sadoven, and DB 1451 (1930) with Edith Orens have 13 and 15 without the all-important 14 in between. Ansseau here is nothing short of magnificent and Orens, not as far as I know a singer of particular fame, is ideally sensitive as his partner. A stunning disc!

Other inter-war tenors must be polished off briefly. Giovanni Martinelli (14) is more French than most Italians, certainly than Lauri-Volpi, who sings 14 in mannered if rather beautiful fashion, and 1 amazingly if unwisely at the age of 69 (H 1003). The Spaniard, Antonio Cortis, sings 1 (Parlo. 1634) and 14 (DA 1076) at full throttle, but the Portuguese, Tomaso Alcaide (LB 7), produces some lovely diminuendo top notes in a virtuoso performance of 14, and, in the same aria, the Russian Badridze, apparently of Tartar extraction, also exhibits beautiful soft top notes (reissue GV 54). Souvenirs of 14 come from the finely controlled Luigi Fort, the rich-voiced Costa Milona, the fresh-sounding Cristy Solari, the stentorian Nino Piccaluga, the fine voice of the Ukrainian K. Ognevoy, Raoul Girard, André d'Arkor, Richard Crooks; of 1 and 5 from Louis Morrisson and Perret, of 1 from the more graceful Giovanni Malipiero (DB 5405), and of 5 and 14 from the straightforward Mario Altery, who sang at the Opéra-Comique. To finish on an up-beat, Joseph Hislop's Lied (DB 944) exhibits an aristocratic style and brilliant top A sharps – a fine souvenir of a distinguished artist.

After 1945, the advent of the LP places more emphasis on the singers of Charlotte. Nevertheless, pride of place to the Russians, some of whom may admittedly be just pre-war. Certainly Kozlovsky's earliest 'Lied d'Ossian' must have been sung about 1930–1, and it is an outstanding version, as is a later performance, similar to his treatment of the aria in the complete recording. The soft tone combined with brilliant attack in 1 and 5 is so good that I doubly regret that he and Rozhdestvenskaya (USSR 9166/7) should have recorded only a single side's worth of 3 and 16, so well does Kozlovsky sing in each. Orfenov's name will be known through his *Cenerentola* set with Dolukhanova, and there is little wrong with his singing of 1 and much to be enjoyed in his performance with Rozhdestvenskaya of 12, 13 and 14 (and in her contribution too). Haabjarn, an Estonian, sings 14 powerfully. Lemeshev, whom I heard still singing well in Moscow in 1961, sounds uninvolved and the voice not in fresh condition, but his discs are with Galina Vishnevskaya, to me one of the major natural vocal talents of post-1945 years. Her singing of 10 is a fine sample of her talent and her contribution to 12, 13, 14, 15, is a source of maximum pleasure, every nuance in place and the voice ringing out boldly, confidently, beautifully. The lovely mezzo of another Russian, Dolukhanova, suits French music admirably and her recordings of 10 and 11 are full of style.

Charlotte brings out the best in the sopranos and mezzos, but a few recordings must be dealt with summarily, not because they are bad but because the competition is high. In 10 and 11, Fedora Barbieri (DA 11302, 11304) gives externalized performances, more a Laura than a Charlotte, and even Marilyn Horne sounds portentious in 10, though her firm line suits 11 well (SXL 6345). In 10, Ebe Stignani (QALP 10144) is matter-of-fact, Cloe Elmo too robust (BB 25009), the Yugoslav Breda Kalef hampered by poor French (STV 213323), and the powerful Lyne Dourian (Philips 835.791) lacking in temperament. I very much enjoyed in 10 the Bulgarian Micheva-Nonova (Balkanton), the Romanian Zenaida Pally, and Gladys Swarthout in a committed performance late in her career (Victor 12–1002; VIC 1490); also, in 11, the Romanian Elena Cernei (Electrecord ECE. 0378).

Of the top post-war performances, amazingly few are by French or Belgians. Régine Crespin (Véga) in 1961, when many of us found her a Marschallin of rare stature, recorded 10 with little feeling, only ten years later (SET 530) to set a standard of expression in this music that would be hard to beat. If the voice sounds a shade weighty for 11, and 12 turns out a bit heavy, the letter scene haunts the memory. Giulietta Simionato (LXT 5458) turns in a forceful, involved performance in French on the highest level, and Rita Gorr (ASD 141) is no less powerful and dramatic. My only complaint about Frederica von Stade's perfect blend of reticence and passion in 11 (in spite of a verbal slip in the first line) is that she did not record the whole scene (CBS 76522).

There remain two performances of the letter scene which seem close to perfection. Shirley Verrett (LSC 3045) skilfully lightens her voice to achieve wonders of subtlety, and has the gift of keeping the line silken-smooth and yet full of colour, light and shade. The same words could be used to describe Callas's incomparable singing (SLS 5057: and another, pirated version). Her reading seems an act of penitence, the comments forced from her against her will; she achieves the paradox of the voice remaining pulsatingly alive while the words themselves emerge deadened with misery. Every inflexion sounds spontaneous and only later does one realize it must be the product of infinite study, of the finest-tuned instinct. As always, she seems to invent a new voice for a new role, but she never sang Charlotte on the stage and one reminds oneself of the years of waste when this greatest of modern operatic artists could have given us a world of new roles.

Post-war tenors are less impressive. Albert Lance in 1 and 14 (FCX 678) reveals the same vocal splendour and aptitude as in his complete set; Alain Vanzo, the most underrated of top post-war French tenors, has sweetness in the voice, like the meat nearest the bone, and his 1 (Vega 16.020) and 14 (CMD 9487 Disques Mode) are uncommonly convincing. Appreciable are the more heroic Raoul Jobin, famous before the war but little recorded since; Nicolai Gedda (CX 1130 and FCX 906), the lyricism of whose earlier disc seems preferable but whose scrupulous musicianship makes either a good buy; Richard Tucker, who never sang the role but vocalizes it in 5 and 14 to perfection (MS 6831). Giacinto Prandelli sang it at La Scala, and 1 and 14 are honestly done, as are versions of the same arias by the more subtle Cesare Valletti (Cetra).

'Pourquoi me réveiller?' has been worked almost to death – with style remote from Massenet by the golden-voiced Gigli (DB 6346), by the 1959 di Stefano (LXT 5504), by Franco Corelli with stentorian top notes (LPC 53019), by del Monaco (DA 11333: IC 147–18226/7), by Tony Poncet, whose prodigious voice is out of place in this context. More to the point is a beautiful performance by Domingo in án RCA Gala (DPS 2004); two by Tagliavini, sung stylishly in Italian in 1948 (BB 25234) and later even better in French (DB 6854); manly efforts in French by Rudolf Schock (Eurodisc), Georges Noré (Pathé) and Ion Piso (ECE 0149); a pleasant version by Welsh Opera's star of twenty years ago, Tano Ferendinos (DX 1475), and another by Georges Liccioni (Polaris L 80.014). The Slovak Peter Dvorsky has recorded it in rotten French and with richly Italianate sound (Opus 9112 0544), but the best recent performance I have heard is by the Spanish Alfredo Kraus (Carillon CAL 13), with a tear in the voice worthy of Tito Schipa, not a little of whose fervour and musical elegance he inherits. He is to record the whole opera with Berganza. This, and versions with Obratzsova and Domingo and von Stade and Carreras, are awaited with interest.

The 'Clair de Lune' has fared less well in post-war years. Caballé and di Stefano sing it unidiomatically on Alhambra; Loretta di Lelio and Corelli truncated on SPO.1007; and only Tagliavini and Tassinari (BB 25233/4, three 78 sides) in Italian in 1948 make something of the lovely scene, although in this case it comes out as pure Italian opera.

As a postscript to this scene – its counterpart, you might say, when, after 'Pourquoi me réveiller?', Werther and Charlotte admit their love – stands the section beginning 'N'achevez pas!' Mostly it has been recorded in connection with 13 and 14, but the Czechs, Eva Zikmundová and Zdeněk Svehla, sing a good, routine performance on Panton 11.0321.

We are left with Sophie (7) and Albert (2). Dinh Gilly, Albert to Farrar's Charlotte at the Metropolitan in 1910, sings 2 – to my taste too grandly – on IRCC 7012; Dupouy sings the complete scene well, with Bakkers a charming Sophie (034088); André Gaudin and Roger Bourdin (Od. 188518) are fluent, Dupré a little less so on Odeon, but Robert Massard (Polaris: L 80.012) is ideal. Marthe Coiffier on Pathé sings 7 very prettily and on the reverse the scene between 10 and 11 – pointless this, without a Charlotte; and Germaine Cornay does 7 with even more spontaneity (Col. D 12048).

And what would Monsieur Ibos, with whose quotation I began this review, make of it all, if he had been listening to these discs? I think he would have liked Clément, Smirnov, Sobinov, Schipa, much of Kozlovsky and Tagliavini, some of Lance and nearly all of Thill and Vallin. He would have succumbed to los Angeles, and seen the point of Lehmann, Callas, Olivero and Verrett – and might he have found his ideal in Friant?

WERTHER

C Charlotte; *S* Sophie; *W* Werther; *A* Albert

1933 Vallin *C*; Féraldy *S*; Thill *W*;
Rocque *A*/Paris Opéra-Comique
Chorus and Orch./Cohen
EMI ⓜ 2C 053 10746–8

1949*c* (in Russian) Maksakova *C*;
Sakharova *S*; Kozlovsky *W*;
Svesdina *A*/Bolshoi Theatre
Chorus and Orch./Bron
MK ⓜ DO 1825–8

1949 (in Italian – live performance)
Simionato *C*; di Stefano
W/Mexican Philharmonic Union
Chorus and Orch./Cellini
Cetra ⓜ LO 30/3

1953 Juyol *C*; Léger *S*; Richard *W*;
Bourdin *A*/Paris Opéra-Comique
Chorus and Orch./Sebastian
Nixa ⓜ ULP 9233/1–3; Urania
ⓔ US 5223/3

1953 (in Italian) Tassinari *C*; Neviani
S; Tagliavini *W*; Cortis *A*/Turin
Radio Chorus and
Orch./Molinari-Pradelli
Cetra ⓜ LPS 3245

1964 Gorr *C*; Mesplé *S*; Lance *W*;
Bacquier *A*/Paris ORTF Chorus
and Orch./Etcheverry
Adès 7.025–7; Mondiophonie

SCAL 1–3

1968 los Angeles *C*; Mesplé *S*;
Gedda *W*; Soyer *A*/Paris ORTF
Chorus and Orch./Prêtre
HMV SLS 5105 ④ TC–SLS
5105; Angel SCL 3736

1979 Obraztsova *C*; Augér *S*;
Domingo *W*; Grundheber
A/Cologne Children's Choir,
Cologne Radio Chorus and
SO/Chailly
DG 2709 091 ④ 3371 048

Excerpts

1954 Kolassi *C*; Jobin
W/LSO/Fistoulari
Decca ⓜ LXT 5034

1960 Gabriel *C*; Berton *S*; Brazzi
W/Karlsruhe Opera
Orch./Couraud
Philips ⓜ GL 5667

1961 Boué *C*; Marti *W*/Orch./Fekete
Vogue LDM 301.30 ④B.VOC
415

1962 Elias *C*; Valletti *W*; Souzay
A/Rome Opera Orch./Leibowitz
RCA (UK) SB 6512; (US) VICS
1516

Boris Godunov

DAVID HAMILTON

Consideration of Mussorgsky's masterpiece on records is complicated, first by the fact that two distinct versions of it survive from the composer's own hand (the more concise 'initial' version of 1869 and the expanded 'definitive' form of 1872), and second by the long history of reworkings undertaken by other hands, most prominently by Nikolai Rimsky-Korsakov. Today, half a century after the publication of the full score of Mussorgsky's two versions – and three decades after the introduction of LP records – we have at last a complete recording of the opera in something like its original form, along with a handful of partial recordings and excerpts.

The bulk of the remaining recordings, including all the other 'complete' versions, present Rimsky-Korsakov's 1908 revision, which – and this cannot be too often emphasized – was much more than a simple re-orchestration. Mussorgsky's younger colleague went through the opera like a composition teacher 'correcting' the work of a student, to remove what he described as its 'impractical difficulties, fragmentary musical phrases, clumsy vocal writing, harsh harmonies and modulations, faulty counterpoint, poverty of instrumentation, and general weakness from a technical point of view'. Rimsky also deleted several important episodes and composed developments and transitions of his own. Since 1928, study and hearing of the original score has convinced most musicians that the features to which Rimsky objected are in fact often the valid, striking, even inspired evidences of Mussorgsky's genius.

That Rimsky's version, coupled with Chaliapin's interpretation of the title role, made a place for *Boris* in the international repertory cannot be gainsaid (though one may speculate that, in the absence of a Rimsky version, Chaliapin would still have been irresistibly attracted to the role and would have made the same impression with it). Rimsky made his own ultimate position clear: 'If the time comes when the original is considered better and of greater value than my revision, then my version will be discarded and *Boris* will be given according to the original score.' Inertia is a powerful force in the world of opera, but many important Western theatres have now mounted the original, and this trend is likely to continue, especially now that the performing materials are readily available, in David Lloyd-Jones's excellent new edition (Oxford University Press).

The recent Semkow recording, too, should play a role in dispelling prejudice about the supposed impracticability of the original. At the same time, one must add with regret that this essentially undramatic performance may help perpetuate the myth that without Rimsky's professional ministrations *Boris* is a dull work. That recording is a considerable disappointment. Semkow is evidently trying hard not to impose on the original the interpretative habits traditional to the Rimsky version, but his erratic and often sluggish tempi fail to maintain the continuity of important scenes; for example, Pimen's first narrative breaks down into a series of almost unrelated episodes, and the big choral scenes never get off the ground. Nor is Martti Talvela's Boris a vividly realized character; the Finnish bass seems satisfied with the mere emission of tone – an imposing sound, to be sure – but eschews singing in the fullest sense of that word. Some other members of the cast contribute good work (Mróz's solid Pimen, Hiolski's oily Rangoni, Gedda's reliable Dimitri) amidst the lacklustre surroundings; the Polish chorus and orchestra are competent, though registered with less than ideal clarity.

Welcome as this recording surely is, to help us clean our ears and memories of the sound of Rimsky's version, there is room for a better one, which might also well avoid the solecism of conflating Mussorgsky's two versions. (For a fuller discussion of the textual problem than is possible here, see Edward R. Reilly's admirable summary in *Musical Newsletter*, vol. 4, no. 4, autumn 1974, or Arthur Jacobs's briefer one in *Opera*, May 1971.) Mussorgsky clearly intended the Kromy Forest scene to supersede that before St Basil's Cathedral, and in this respect at least Rimsky kept faith with his intentions (though a 'Rimsky-style' orchestration of the St Basil scene, made in 1926 by Ippolitov-Ivanov, has allowed Rimsky-based recordings to indulge in the same reprehensible redundancy; in such recordings, the original order of the two final scenes is usually restored, so that Boris's death separates the two scenes ending identically with the idiot's lament). Granted that the St Basil scene is impressive and moving – its proper place is in a recording of the 1869 'initial' score, which would obviously be most welcome.

Before turning to recordings of the Rimsky *Boris*, let me mention the few partial ones that hew more closely to the original. In Matačič's German language excerpts (coronation, monologue, Pimen's tale, farewell and death, the end of Kromy Forest), the scoring has been marginally touched up by an unidentified hand, but Gottlob Frick's imposing Boris is worth hearing. For volume nine of HMV's 'History of Music in Sound', Lawrance Collingwood directed a good performance of the opera's opening pages. Raphael Arié's several recordings of excerpts used the original scoring; I have heard only the farewell and death, monochromatic in its restraint (Decca K 2229). Feodor's two songs from the second act were recorded in English by the boy soprano Derek Barsham (K 1601); with its public-school propriety, this is a funny record, and the tempi are far too slow. Ferdinand Frantz recorded the monologue in German (Electrola 1C–047–29127), a strongly sung, stolid reading.

For the Metropolitan Opera's 1953 revival (in an awkward English translation), Karol Rathaus made an edition of the opera, essentially a touching-up of Mussorgsky's scoring rather than a revision. The two-disc selection recorded by RCA is strongly conducted by Mitropoulos but weakly sung.

Shostakovich's new orchestration, on the other hand, was made from scratch, on the basis of the 1928 vocal score, a curiously naive procedure that, though faithful to Mussorgsky's harmonic and structural intentions, yielded a bland, anachronistic result. The Telefunken excerpts (coronation, monologue, clock scene, polonaise, fountain duet, Pimen's tale, farewell and death, part of Kromy Forest) are sung in German by a predominantly light-voiced cast. More important is the Kirov recording of Act 2 featuring Boris Shtokolov. For some reason, Shostakovich orchestrated all of the material for both the 'initial' and the 'definitive' versions, and this recording (though not so labelled in its American issue) actually represents the 'initial' version of Act 2, markedly more concise (and less dramatic) than the familiar form. The performance is a strong one, and gives us a glimpse, albeit slightly distorted, of this earlier stage of the work's development, not otherwise recorded.

A study of the numerous Rimsky-version recordings of *Boris* over more than half a century suggests the validity of some sort of generalized distinction between two approaches to the role of the Tsar: we might call them, roughly, the 'singing' and 'acting' approaches. This is not to be understood as a qualitative matter, and it surely does less than justice to interpreters on either side. A 'singing' Boris such as Mark Reizen can prove quite as dramatic and expressive as an 'acting' one, nor would I dream of suggesting that a Chaliapin or a Christoff is any less accomplished a singer than Reizen, although there are acting Borises to whom the other option does not seem to be very promising! Indubitably, the 'acting' Borises, however well they may sing, do sing *less*, electing a naturalism of declamation often considerably exceeding what is already incorporated into Mussorgsky's vocal line, itself naturalistic to a degree revolutionary for its time.

Conceivably this exaggeration of the opera's naturalism, concentrated in the person of the Tsar, was a necessary condition for success, especially before Western audiences, who for the most part could not be expected to understand the Russian words. Such a view would also tend to explain why Western Borises singing in their native languages on the whole have been less prone to exaggeration, and why the majority of Soviet exponents of the role fall clearly within the category of 'singing' Borises.

Without question, the avatar, and often the explicit model, for the 'acting' Borises is Feodor Chaliapin, and it seems appropriate, indeed inevitable, to begin consideration of Rimsky-version recordings with his. Though he did not take part in the revision's 1896 première at the St Petersburg Conservatory, Chaliapin was thereafter associated with its introduction into most of the major operatic centres: Moscow (1898 at Mamontov's Private Opera, and 1901 at the Bolshoi), St Petersburg (1904, Maryinsky), Paris (1908, Diaghilev's famous production, for which Rimsky made his final additions and revisions), Milan (1909, La Scala), and London (1913, Drury Lane). He continued to sing the part in the West until after 1930 (though not in the Soviet Union, which may bear on the relative weakness of his influence on modern performances there). Preserved on recordings and in the memories of singers and coaches, Chaliapin's Boris has continued to cast its spell, both positively and negatively, over performances ever since; consider the comment of Ezio Pinza, who sang Pimen to Chaliapin's Boris in 1927: 'He was a superb actor, so compelling that only my professional experience and a perfect knowledge of my role saved me time and again from missing my cue, so absorbed was I in watching him act.'

This influence should not be interpreted narrowly, in terms of mere mechanical imitation of Chaliapin's performance; rather, it involves a general acceptance of the naturalistic lines along which Chaliapin worked. 'Acting' Borises incline, especially in the second act and in the death scene, to *parlando* effects, to snarls, gasps, and vocal shudders, sometimes to just plain shouting. (A characteristic point is the snarling inflection on the line 'Aha! Shuisky knyaz!,' shortly after the monologue; although no recording survives to tell us how Chaliapin sang this line, the prevalence of this reading strongly suggests a common ancestor.) If indulged without restraint, such an interpretation can turn Boris from a guilt-ridden mortal into a carpet-chewing monster, and of course it sacrifices basic musical points asserted by the pitches and rhythms that Mussorgsky wrote.

The power of Chaliapin's interpretation is attested by his recordings: some eighteen 78 sides published between 1910 and 1931 (as well as six sides of excerpts from the roles of Pimen and Varlaam, the latter of which he occasionally sang in the theatre). Most memorable are the passages recorded by HMV during the Covent Garden performance of 4 July 1928. The monologue, clock scene, and farewell and death (DB 1181/2, 3464) are reissued on HMV RLS 710, along with Chaliapin's only published recording of the coronation scene; two further sides, from the beginning of the Duma scene, were also published on 78 (DB 1183), and it is a shame they were not included in the reissue, for they extend through the Tsar's entrance. (Tragically, the other masters recorded at this performance, among them the dialogue with Shuisky, were found technically unsatisfactory and were destroyed.)

What Chaliapin did at that performance would be unacceptable today, but the power of his one-man show is vividly transmitted, and still involving. In the dialogue with Feodor (Margherita Carosio, singing like everyone except Chaliapin in Italian) preceding the monologue, the conductor (Vincenzo Bellezza) is evidently hard put to predict where the next downbeat will come, and sometimes he guesses wrong. In the clock scene, the liberties are incredible: virtually a new vocal line, with inserted additional text from Pushkin's play. The tonal colouring of the farewell really suggests a dying man, who only later summons up reserves of power to assert his tsardom one last time and the prayer is spun out on an incredibly suave, apparently endless *fil da voce*.

From these discs, it is clear that Chaliapin liked to take his time playing before an audience, and most of the studio recordings have nothing like the same atmosphere. The 1931 version of the monologue is palpably rushed to fit the confines of a single 78 side, though the interpretation is otherwise remarkably consistent, as are the liberties in the clock scene recorded the same day (DB 1532; COLH 100). The pre-first-world-war recordings of the farewell and death, Pimen's two monologues, and Varlaam's song have been reissued on Scala 852. Of Chaliapin's late acoustics and early studio electricals DB 934 (Monologue and Death) and Victor 1237 (Varlaam's song) have been reissued on Gemm 152*.

Despite a variety of choral excerpts recorded on 78s, of which only those with the Riga Opera under Emil Cooper (Parlo. E 11290/1) were in the original language, it took the advent of complete recordings to make us aware of how much else there is in the opera besides Tsar Boris – that, as has often been said, the Russian people constitute a second protagonist. The first of the complete recordings was made in the Soviet Union and issued initially on twenty-two 78 discs, which were soon 'pirated' on several American labels (sometimes clumsily: the Colosseum editor, evidently unfamiliar with the practice of omitting the Idiot and the boys from Kromy Forest when St Basil is performed, slewed a repeat of that 78 side into the 'appropriate' place!). This recording represents the Bolshoi's new production of 1948 – still in use, incidentally when the company came to New York in 1975. The sound is dim and congested, but not so much as to obscure the powerful singing of the chorus and the committed playing of the orchestra.

Golovanov's is an extravagant reading, taking many high-handed but convincing liberties with the tempi and with the orchestration as well. Since some of these divergences from the published Rimsky score, such as a celesta doubling the violas in Boris's final prayer, survive into the Melik-Pashayev recording more than a decade later and are found in no Western recordings, some local tradition seems to be at work. Alexander Pirogov, with a big, black, gravelly voice, is a powerful presence, showing

---

*(for full details of Chaliapin's *Boris* recordings, see the admirable discography by Alan Kelly, in *Record Collector*, vol. 20, nos. 8–10 (August 1972).

some of the Chaliapin influence and also singing out of tune a good deal. The supporting cast has important strengths: Ivan Kozlovsky's poignant, truly sung Idiot, Bogdanov's proclamatory Shchelkalov, Mikhailov's firm Pimen, Maksakova's light and feminine Marina. 'Standard' cuts are made in the Pimen scene and the second act, only the second Polish scene is performed (with the Rangoni episode omitted), and St Basil is included.

In 1975, to celebrate the bicentenary of the Bolshoi, Melodiya reissued this recording – but with Mark Reizen as Boris (pirated in the US on Recital Records RR–440). The non-Boris scenes appear to be identical with the Pirogov recording (I have not been able to compare them directly), while some of Reizen's scenes are definitely the same as the separate recordings made around 1950 and issued on Parlophone (GB) and Monitor (US), which means that the St Basil scene, at least, is conducted by Vassili Nebolsin, not Golovanov. A hybrid this may be, and the sound (at least in the Recital Records version) anything but an improvement on earlier issues, but the result is remarkably satisfying. Reizen, with his big, smooth, rich voice, is the prototype of a 'singing' Boris, eloquent and loving in his enunciation of the words, expressive in his verbal and timbral colouring. There is no superficial excitement in this performance; the communication is essentially musical, and intense. (Reizen also recorded the scenes in Pimen's cell and the inn; these, too, are highly recommended.)

A second Bolshoi recording, in stereo, has also appeared in two versions. Melik-Pashayev's reading is more straightforward than Golovanov's, with a wonderful rhythmic firmness that shapes equally well the meditative monastery scene and the lively genre material. It is also much better recorded, if with insufficient presence for the chorus and orchestra, which, as before, constitute an incomparable strength. Petrov is another 'singing' Boris, not as firm as Reizen (the pitch is not always precise, and he tends to slide up into the higher notes) but none the less expressive and authoritative.

Irina Arkhipova's authoritatively sung, sharply characterized Marina makes the Polish scenes uncommonly absorbing (the first of them, happily, is restored for the recording, though Golovanov's other cuts remain). Mark Reshetin and Kibkalo are also exceptionally good, Gueleva a vigorous if conventional Varlaam, Ivanovsky an acceptable Dimitri. On the debit side, the Shuisky is no pleasure to hear, and the Mityukh is a disaster in the St Basil scene, which on this occasion falls short of its usually infallible effectiveness.

After George London became the first non-Russian to sing Boris at the Bolshoi in 1960, he was invited to record the role there; this took place in May 1963, at which time all of the Tsar's music (and Act 2 in its entirety) was freshly recorded, with Melik-Pashayev again conducting, and then slotted into the existing recording. By this time, London, the first Boris of the 1953 Metropolitan revival, was near the end of his career, and his tone lacks the steadiness of earlier days (monologue and clock scene, with Jean Morel conducting, Odyssey Y–32669 from about 1954); a longer selection, splashily conducted by Thomas Schippers, was recorded in the U.S. around 1960. Definitely in the Chaliapin tradition – though the written rhythms, if not the pitches, of the clock scene are adhered to – this is a weighty, serious interpretation, not as virtuoso in tone as that of Boris Christoff, London's leading contemporary Western rival in the part.

Christoff is the protagonist in two of the three Western recordings of the opera – indeed, more than simply the protagonist, for he undertakes the roles of Pimen and Varlaam as well, an indefensibly self-aggrandizing procedure. The confrontation this entails between himself and himself in the Duma scene forces Christoff to limit the tonal variety of Pimen's music to a destructive extent, though his soft singing is often very beautiful. The Varlaam doubling is less obviously a problem, but given Christoff's exceptionally distinctive sound one cannot help hearing Tsar Boris in this monk's clothing as well, denouncing himself in the Kromy Forest. Nobody reproduces Chaliapin's inflections and phrasings more literally that Christoff and, though I have come to find his interpretation excessively hysterical (at least on records), there is no denying its frequent effectiveness, especially in the earlier, vocally fresher version led by Issay Dobrowen. Some still earlier 78s, including Varlaam's song and Pimen's monologue, do not differ in any significant ways from the 1952 recording; Christoff's interpretation has remained remarkably consistent over the years. They have been reissued on RLS 733.

Of the two Christoff recordings, Dobrowen's is surely the more tautly conducted and the more strongly cast. The young Nicolai Gedda is the best imaginable pretender, Eugenia Zareska an admirable partner, and Kim Borg makes much of both Schelkalov and Rangoni with his warm, expressive tones. The White Russian chorus is enthusiastic but sometimes ragged in detail; in this respect the later version is superior, but the conducting of André Cluytens there is soft-edged and slack by comparison, and the supporting cast offers few comparable inducements (Dimiter Uzonov may be the worst-sounding Dimitri on records). As stereo 'remakes' go, this one strikes me as a failure; the mono predecessor is decidedly preferable. Cluytens presents Rimsky's 1908 version complete, while Dobrowen makes the standard cuts in the Pimen and fountain scenes; properly, both omit St Basil.

The sables-and-diamonds sound of Karajan's Salzburg 'Cinemascope Spectacular' is undeniably seductive, but in this stately, under-articulated tone poem it is not easy to hear much of Mussorgsky's drama; an exception is the Kromy Forest scene, where all the rehearsal time and technical expertise really does pay off. Ghiaurov stands at the opposite pole from his compatriot Christoff, for he is a 'singing' Boris – though not, I find, a vivid one, for all his beautiful sounds. Talvela sings a solid but dramatically inert Pimen – less crippling, this, than his Boris for Semkow. Alexei Maslennikov doubles Shuisky and the Idiot; a canny vocal actor, he makes much of both roles, but the self-confrontation this entails (in St Basil, which is included along with a complete Rimsky text) proves it another undesirable practice. Ludovic Spiess is a tolerable Dimitri, Vishnevskaya an intelligent Marina whose vocal layout is simply wrong for the part. For all its executive virtues, this is a performance that I think even Rimsky-Korsakov would have found essentially irrelevant.

Neither of the two East European sets has much to recommend it. Baranovich's Belgrade version is as drastically cut as Golovanov's (no St Basil, either), ponderously conducted, and vocally undistinguished except for Melanie Bugarinovich's rich-toned Marina (a limited asset, since her first scene is omitted entirely). Miro Changalovich, not a negligible singer, cannot do much in these surroundings. Experts tell me that the Western Slav accent of the singers is not at all authentic, and if one is going to learn one's Russian from a recording of *Boris*, one might as well learn the real thing!

From Sofia, Naidenov's uncut version (including St Basil) gives us Nicola Ghiuselev's partial emulation of Christoff: he doubles Pimen, but not Varlaam. His is a fairly tame interpretation. Naidenov's conducting, clumsy of transition and deficient in momentum, keeps this on the level of a provincial undertaking. (On an independent recording, Harmonia Mundi HMB 130, Ghiuselev can be heard in more vivid form, singing Boris's main scenes, Varlaam's song, and Pimen's two solos.)

Aside from Chaliapin, not many early Borises left recorded souvenirs, and fewer still have circulated on LP. Lev Sibiriakov recorded Pimen's tale and Boris's monologue (4–22128, 022289; GV 1): clean, singing performances, the words not strongly projected. I have not been able to hear the two sides recorded for Pathé by Adam Didur, the Boris of Toscanini's 1913 Metropolitan production in Italian (it used the Golovin-Benois sets, purchased from Diaghilev, and was one of the few early productions that did not star Chaliapin). Paul Althouse, the Dimitri of this cast, recorded part of the fountain duet (Victor 76031, dubbed flat on Rococo 6216) with Margarete Arndt–Ober, the alternate Marina: strong, bright singing, though Ober is often under the note. Toscanini conducted an orchestral version of the opening of this scene and the polonaise at a 1943 concert with amazing verve and textural clarity (ATS 1036). The Metropolitan Shuisky, Angelo Bada, can be heard briefly in the 1928 Chaliapin/Covent Garden excerpts. Smirnov, the Dimitri of London's first *Boris*, recorded most of the Pimen's cell scene with C.E. Kaidanov (DB 765) and part of the fountain duet (DB 753) with Davidova (who sang Feodor in those performances; the Polish scenes were omitted), but these have not come my way.

Several later Borises recorded substantial portions of the role: usually the coronation, monologue, clock scene, farewell and death, occasionally adding Varlaam's song and some choral excerpts. The first of these was

Alexander Kipnis, whose 1945 highlights set for RCA Victor catches him past his best, singing consistently too loudly and with exaggerated 'bogey-man' inflections in the dialogue with Shuisky (this was the first recording ever of that crucial episode). The chorus in these discs, trained by the young Robert Shaw, is most impressive. A better measure of Kipnis as Boris can be had in the 1943 Metropolitan broadcast (he in Russian, the rest in Italian), excerpts from which have circulated in the underground; even then, his breath control was failing, but there is more dynamic variety than in the studio version.

Nicola Rossi-Lemeni, who sang the part often in the early 1950s, made two sets of highlights. The first of these stems from his appearances with the San Francisco Opera in 1953; Leopold Stokowski was brought in to conduct the recording – and to exercise an editorial hand which had more to do with the 'synthesizing' of the excerpts (including such unusual choices of the offstage monks' chorus from the Pimen scene) than with rectifying Rimsky-Korsakov's rescorings. Rossi-Lemeni's rough, hollow sound impels him to a *reductio ad absurdum* of the 'acting' approach; his death scene is simply hysterical. The later, scantier Saga selection has even less to recommend it.

Before turning to *Boris* in translation, let me gather up a few loose ends. In the monologue, Boris Gmyria matches Reizen's gorgeous sound but not his imaginative treatment of the text (Melodiya 33D–033117/8). Sadoven and Nagachevsky recorded the fountain duet on 78s (HMV EK 94): idiomatic but not arresting. Dimitri's second aria from this scene (after the polonaise) is well sung by Nicolai Gedda (EMI 1C–063–28070), who did not get to sing it in the Dobrowen set because of a cut. The strong work of the Covent Garden chorus and orchestra under Edward Downes is the best thing about the coronation scene included in the house's twenty-first birthday album. Disappointing are Kim Borg's excerpts (monologue, Pimen's tale, farewell and death); though he enunciates beautifully, the advice to Feodor is hectoring in tone and the final pages are mostly shouted (DG 135090).

Recordings in languages other than Russian present a different picture. For one thing, Chaliapin's inflections were not easily copied in languages with other phonetic structures. And these singers came to the music with their own national vocal traditions. Thus Pinza, who as we have seen was much impressed by Chaliapin's performance, tempers that memory with his native feeling for a cantabile line and with his warmer, brighter sound. Like Kipnis, he is better heard in performance recordings (preferably the 1939 Met broadcast, conducted by Panizza) than in the studio highlights taken five years later, when the original smoothness and evenness of the voice was on the wane and the studio ambience evidently did not kindle his dramatic imagination. (A 1943 Met broadcast also circulates, firmly directed by Szell but showing Pinza already below his best level; here may be heard Baccaloni's licentious Varlaam, quite as grotesque as the excerpt on Odyssey Y–31736 suggests.) Pinza's final recordings from *Boris* were in Russian: the coronation and death scenes, made in conjunction with the film 'Tonight We Sing', in which Pinza played the role of Chaliapin (RCA Victor LM–7016; death scene only in LM–617); they are mainly of curiosity value. The best of all Italian-language *Boris* recordings is Pasero's of the monologue (QALP 10409), the Tsar's profound weariness implicit in the timbre and thus not impeding the music's progress.

Among the Germans, Leo Schützendorf (monologue and clock scene, Poly. 65816; LV 123) sounds as if he might have been effective in the theatre, with interestingly varied declamation, though the mushy tone, tending to flatness, is not very inviting on records. Robert Burg (coronation and monologue, Parlo. P–2172; LV 211), is simply dull, with a dead, grey tone. Theodor Scheidl (monologue and farewell, 66525; clock scene, Acanta MA 22177-6), though sensitive to the words, does not pitch too securely and is rushed by the time limitations; in the clock scene he sounds merely passive except for a brief and startling Hitlerian screech. After a perfunctory start, Wilhelm Strienz (farewell and death, DB 5594; 1C 047–28557 – a flat transfer, incidentally) movingly expresses Boris's resignation in the face of death. In the fountain duet, Helge Roswaenge's clarion tones dominate the not-quite-firm Marina of Freidel Beckmann (DB 5593; LV 43). Ludwig Weber, a famous German Boris, appears to have recorded only Varlaam's song (1C 177–00933/4), a performance so hectic that its non-release on 78s is understandable.

The two most prominent of the inter-war French Borises, Vanni Marcoux and André Pernet, recorded major selections from the role in French. Both are essentially fine-grained singers, which makes all the more effective their touches of violence in the clock scene. Marcoux recorded the coronation (DB 4950), the monologue and clock scenes (DB 1112), and the farewell and prayer (DB 1114), all dubbed too slowly on Club 99; there were also some earlier acoustics, including Varlaam's song, which I have not heard. Pernet's somewhat more powerful voice is heard in the monologue and clock scene (Od. 123723; ORX 146). A Martial Singher recording of the monologue is on IRCC L–7019, presumably from a concert later in his career; though the voice has an effective bite, its colour is thick and heavy. In English, there is Robert Radford's recording of the monologue, from 1918 (D 115; HLM 7054, another flat transfer); unfortunately, the rushed tempo forces him virtually to gabble large stretches of the text.

Complete recordings of Russian opera obviously present difficult challenges, and *Boris* especially so, with its long and difficult choral parts, its multitude of small roles. EMI found in 1962 that the White Russians of Paris, barely satisfactory ten years earlier, were now over the hill, and they had to import a chorus from Sofia (as did Karajan, too, though he used the Vienna State Opera Chorus as well). The Eastern European alternative has not yielded good results, whether in Crakow, Belgrade, or Sofia. So our best chance of new and better recordings would seem to be the Soviet Union – except that the Bolshoi still performs the Rimsky version, the Kirov (at last report) the Shostakovich. Should the directors of the Bolshoi take it into their heads to scrap their three-decade-old production in favour of a new 'original-version' staging, a recording would probably soon follow. Therein, I suspect, lies our best hope for an improvement in the recording situation. Or, if a big Western singing or conducting star should undertake to espouse the original (and the Russian text), there might also be salutary recorded consequences – though probably not from the enormously successful (but textually imperfect) Metropolitan Opera version, for as everyone knows opera recordings are impossibly expensive in New York.

BORIS GODUNOV

B Boris; *P* Pimen; *V* Vaarlam; *S* Shuisky; *D* Dimitri; *M* Marina; *N* Nurse; *Sh* Shchelkalov; *R* Rangoni

Rimsky-Korsakov versions

1949 Pirogov *B*; Mikhailov *P*; Yakuschenko *V*; Khanaev *S*; Nelepp *D*; Maksakova *M*; Verbitskaya *N*; Bogdanov *Sh*/Bolshoi Theatre Chorus and Orch./Golovanov
Ultraphone ⓜ 159-62; MK ⓜ DO 5836–43

1952 Christoff *B*; *P*; *V*; Bielecki *S*; Gedda *D*; Zareska *M*; Romanova *N*; Borg *Sh*/Russian Chorus of Paris, French National Radio Orch./Dobrowen
EMI ⓔ SLS 5072; Seraphim ⓜ ID 6101

1954 Changalovich *B*; Pivnichki *P*; Tzveych *V*; Andrashevich *S*; Branjnik *D*; Bugarinovich *M*; Miladinovich *N*; Popovich *Sh*/Belgrade National Opera Chorus and Orch./Baranovich
Decca ⓜ LXT 5054–6; London ⓜ

1962 Petrov *B*; Gueleva *V*; Reshetin *P*; Shulpin *S*; Ivanovsky *D*; Arkipova *M*; Verbitskaya *N*; Ivanov *Sh*; Kibkalo *R*/Bolshoi Theatre Chorus and Orch./Melik-Pashaev
Chant du Monde LDX 78315–8

1962 Christoff *B*; *P*; *V*; Lanigan *S*; Uzunov *D*; Lear *M*; Bugarinovich *N*; Mars *Sh*; Diakov *R*/Sofia Opera Chorus, Paris Conservatoire Orch./Cluytens
EMI SLS 90; Angel SDL 3633

1963 London *B*; Reshetin *P*; Gueleva *V*; Shulpin *S*; Ivanovsky *D*; Arkipova *M*; Verbitskaya *N*; Ivanov *Sh*; Kibkalo *R*/Bolshoi Theatre Chorus and Orch./Melik-Pashaev
CBS (US) 77393; (US) D4S–696

1970 Ghiaurov *B*; Talvela *P*; Diakov *V*; Maslennikov *S*; Spiess *D*; Vishnevskaya *M*; Cvejic *N*; Markov *Sh*; Kélémen *R*/Vienna State Opera Chorus, Vienna Boys' Choir, Sofia Radio Chorus, VPO/Karajan
Decca SET 514–7 ④K; London OSA 1439

1973 Ghiuslev *B*; *P*; Tchavdarov *V*; Bodourov *S*; Damianov *D*; Miltcheva-Nonova *M*; Bojkova *N*; Bakardjev *R*/Sofia National Opera Chorus and Orch./Naidenov
Harmonia Mundi HMU 4.4144

Original version

1944 (in Italian – Rimsky-Korsakov
version) Pinza *B*/Metropolitan
Opera Chorus and Orch./Cooper
CBS (US) ⓜ Y33129

1945 (Rimsky-Korsakov version)
Kipnis *B*; *V*; Tamarin *D*;
Sh/Chorus, Victor
Orch./Berezowsky
RCA ⓜ VIC 1221

1948 (Rimsky-Korsakov version)
Reizen *B*; *P*; *V*; Khanaev *S*;
Nelepp *D*/Bolshoi Theatre
Chorus and Orch./Golovanov
and Nebolsin
Parlophone ⓜ PMA 1047–8;
Monitor ⓜ 2016

1952 (Rimsky-Korsakov version) Orlov
B; Petrov *D*; Orlova *M*;
Gavrenko *Sh*/Marinsky Theatre
Chorus and Orch./Kabalevsky
Colosseum ⓜ CRLP 10170

1953 (Rimsky-Korsakov/Stokowski
version) Rossi-Lemeni *B*/San
Francisco Opera Chorus, Boys'
Choir, San Francisco
Orch./Stokowski
RCA ⓜ LM 1764

1956 (in English – Rimsky-Korsakov
version) Tozzi *B*; Scott *P*;

Kullmann *S*; Da Costa *D*;
Rankin *M*; Warfield *N*; Budney
Sh; Valentino *R*/Metropolitan
Opera Orch./Mitropoulos
RCA (US) ⓜ LM 6063

1961 (Rimsky-Korsakov version)
London *B*; Fried *S*/Chorus,
Columbia SO/Schippers
CBS (US) 32110012; (UK) 72071

1962 (Rimsky-Korsakov version)
Rossi-Lemeni *B*; *V*; Hamburg
Radio SO/Singer
Saga SAGA 5174; CMS/Summit
1020 ④ 41020

1965c (in German – basically
originally version) Frick *B*;
Krukowski *V*; Talvela *P*; Katona
S; Schock *D*; Klöse *N*/German
Opera Chorus and Orch./Matačić
Ariola-Eurodisc K86817R

1977 (in German – arr. Shostakovich)
Adam *B*; Vogel *P*; Hölzke *S*;
Ritzmann *D*; Kühse *M*; Schaal
R/Dresden Philharmonic
Children's Choir, Leipzig Radio
Choir, Dresden State
Orch./Kegel
Telefunken AS6 41290

Eugene Onegin

ALAN BLYTH

To be successful a performance of Tchaikovsky's most popular opera must convey the intimacy, longing and sadness of the work which themselves mirror the composer's state of mind when writing it. He had married against his better judgement; the union lasted three weeks, after which Tchaikovsky went to Italy and Switzerland to compose himself – and to compose. At the same time the other woman in his life, Nadeshda von Meck, gave him psychological and financial support.

These events may have altered the shape of the opera but Pushkin's work had already fired his imagination.

> How delightful to get away from all the commonplace pharaohs, Ethiopian princesses, poisoned chalices, and all the stories about puppet creatures. What poetry is to be found in *Onegin*! I am blind to its faults. I quite see that it doesn't give scope to full operatic treatment; but the richness of the poetry, the simple, human subject to be found in Pushkin's inspired verse, will compensate for whatever it lacks in other ways.

Tchaikovsky's music was to make up for 'what it lacks in other ways', and its realization, as I have suggested, depends on eschewing 'full operatic treatment'. That is understood in four of the five Bolshoi sets that must form the basis of any discussion of the opera on disc, and of those four, one is considerably superior to the other three.

The first of these Bolshoi versions, recorded in 1936 but virtually unknown in the West, came to light recently as a Soviet LP reissue. It sets the tone of all these Moscow-made sets: a feeling for ensemble, disciplined orchestral playing and choral singing, total conviction. From the soloists' point of view it is notable mainly for the refined, committed, eloquent Lensky of Sergei Lemeshev, then a youngish man. The supreme happiness shown in the first scene turns to sadness personified in the great aria. The voice itself is ideal for the role. Lavira Zhukovskaya, the Tatyana sounds appropriately impressionable and youthful, but the accents are not distinctive. The first of P. M. Nortsov's two complete Onegin's is adequate, no more. The Olga of Zlatogorova is wobbly but full of character. Pirogov is a fatherly Gremin. The support is estimable. Nebolsin proves almost as persuasive conductor as Khaikin (see below) and that is saying much. The recorded quality, as it came to me on a tape transfer, was dim, but fair enough for me to enjoy an appreciable interpretation.

The second Bolshoi set is correctly described in WERM as 'Almost complete' because 7, the closing number of Act 1, scene 1, is excluded and there are a few other very minor cuts. It has the benefit of Alexander Melik-Pashayev's authoritative conducting. He certainly understands that the piece needs – except at the St Petersburg Ball, the feeling of an intimate elegy – but he is also aware of the inner tensions of the three principal characters, all of whom surely have something of Tchaikovsky himself in them. As far as one can hear through the execrable sound quality on the Period LP transfers, the orchestra plays as well for him as for anyone and the chorus, particularly in the peasant pieces, has a fresh natural quality not exceeded on any of the other sets.

Elena Kruglikova is here a clear-voiced, girlish Tatyana, who marvellously catches the idea, so important in the letter scene, of an internal monologue, and avoids any suggestion of it being a showpiece. Similarly, in the scenes that precede and follow it, her exchanges with V. Makarova's excellent Nurse are done as intimate dialogues. Indeed the sense of a play set to music permeates all the scenes: nobody was better than Ivan Kozlovsky at this almost conversational way of rendering *parlando* passages. He and Nortsov in his second Onegin exhibit that style at its most effective in their exchanges at Larina's party.

Kozlovsky, who can be an aggravatingly mannered and self-indulgent singer (see below), is here for the most part one of a team, and his Lensky in this set is indeed almost a model for tenors in this part, although they may not want to take 'In your house', Lensky's launching of the finale of the ball at Larin's house, in such a leisurely manner, while the aria is phrased with such eloquence, such a feeling for Tchaikovsky's ideal matching of notes to words that a stone might be made to cry. Nortsov has a peculiar, lazy voice-production, but he too is a master of word painting. If you add to this recording's assets, the best Olga (Elena Antonova) and the most eloquent Gremin (Maxim Mikhailov, who doubles as a louring Zaretzky) in any of the Bolshoi sets, and a Triquet (S. M. Ostroumov) who has an almost Schipa-like delicacy, its merit is beyond doubt. One feels that the tradition of a great past still hovers over this and the 1936 performances. Three textual points: Tatyana takes the alternative E flat (following Tchaikosvky's vocal score) rather than a high A flat in the letter scene, Nortsov sing an unauthorized high F at the end of his aria (as do his two successors, but not Mazurok) and, again as his two successors, Ostroumov sings one verse of his couplets in French, another in Russian. These alternatives were also observed in 1936.

The Orlov set calls for less comment. He is a slack conductor who allows Kozlovsky undue licence, which he uses to turn Lensky into a star turn; he is also in noticeably less good voice, although the inimitably smiling tone is still there. Kruglikova has become less steady, less fresh, but she rises in impassioned manner to the last scene, perhaps because Andrei Ivanov is such a pressing Onegin, suggesting all the agony of his new-found love: their account of the 'Happiness was so near' duo is wonderful, with tone colouring used to the utmost effect. Like all his rivals, Ivanov has that superbly resonant high register peculiar to Russian baritones. The Olga is another mezzo with a lively sense of her personality. Mark Reizen's authority as Gremin is vitiated by thinnish tone. The Larina and Triquet are above average. Both these versions need to be played at about 31 rpm.

The next set is to my mind the most successful by far to date. Admittedly the Bolshoi Orchestra sports, as in all the company's sets, watery horns, but its conductor here, Boris Khaikin, brings into ideal balance the dramatic and yearning aspects of the score and, with his definite beat, characterizes those many passages of deep-seated feeling that must surely be exposed for the opera to make its most telling effect. He may have been inspired by Galina Vishnevskaya's marvellously spontaneous account of Tatyana, in which every passage receives the thought and the vocalization it calls for. Her – and Khaikin's – account of 8 (the scene with Filipyevna) adumbrates the fine qualities of this version. Khaikin sets the scene most beautifully. Eugenia Verbitskaya's Nurse sounds the right earthy note. Vishnevskaya is at first anxious, unsettled; then at the Andante con moto, her confession of love is sudden, impulsive. In the letter scene that follows, the Adagio where she decides she cannot subdue her passion is wonderfully articulated; then the expression of the letter seems to move forward with a sure inevitability, the outpouring of a warm-hearted girl. The way Vishnevskaya carries over the F in one breath before the *meno* marking, gradually fading the tone, is magical. Again in the passage of questions, each one is perfectly graded and weighted in tone, which even the horns' vibrato cannot spoil. Great singing and interpretation indeed. In the second scene with Filipyevna, it is the repetition of 'Onegin's house' with its touch of eager impatience and its sudden crescendo, that so aptly encompasses the music's needs.

Eugene Belov is not in this class as an interpreter, but he too sings with meaning and, with Vishnevskaya, makes the last scene as desperate and highly charged as it should be. He sings the unauthorized high F at the end of his aria. He also bares his teeth with vigour when accused by Lensky of being a seducer. The whole of the Larina dance, starting with a chorus of vigour and character, is well realized. Lensky's growing jealousy is again depicted with true pathos by the great Lemeshev, whose plangent tone has already been noted in his fine-grained account of his arioso. Like Kozlovsky he indulges in prolonged holds, but somehow makes them less obvious. The aria is given with inner sadness, and the following little duet with Belov is, as in all these Bolshoi sets, done *pianissimo* and with a knowledge of the futility of the duel. Ivan Petrov depicts a Gremin with a good legato, but isn't he too solemn? The Olga, Larisa Avdeyeva, is edgy but characterful. By now Triquet is singing his couplets wholly in Russian and Andrei Sokolov is altogether too powerful a tenor for this cameo role. For its central, and now historic, performances this set deserves to be reissued.

It certainly is not equalled by the 1970 Bolshoi effort, made at the time of the company's visit to Paris. Rostropovich proved an eccentric conductor, adopting tempi that are inordinately slow and adding to the portentousness of his reading by unmarked *rallentandi* within those slow speeds. He may be said to kill the score with too much kindness. His direction is at its most debilitating in the conversational passages, which seem to die on the lips of the singers who, in any case, seem to have lost the art of their predecessors of 'speaking' the lines. Vishnevskaya (who now takes the high A flat in the letter scene) sounds mature besides her younger self, and also less steady, but her phrasing is as ideal as ever and she makes good use of her husband's leisurely speeds, even if 'Are you an angel?' in the letter scene is impossibly dragged.

Yuri Mazurok possesses a bright, clean voice, but his reading is an external one which fails to capture the bored, supercilious side of Onegin – which Ivanov does so well – and only catches some of Vishnevskaya's fire in the last scene. Vladimir Atlantov, similarly, makes a beautiful sound, but in the modern way it is an impersonal one: he might as well be the Duke of Mantua or Cavaradossi as Lensky; one longs for Kozlovsky with all his eccentricities. The support, except for Tamara Sinyavskaya's delightful Olga and Mikail Shkaptsov's superbly vibrant Zaretsky, is uninteresting. The recording is unconscionably recessed, the chorus, too large, sounding as if it was in a bull ring. Triquet sings the couplets in Russian. Mazurok restores the authentic end to his aria. Incidentally no Onegin, apart from Ivanov, offers Onegin's line just as Tatyana departs. I wonder why.

This line is also left out of the first stereo version, the Belgrade performance conducted by Danon. This is a lovable performance, my second preference. It again exudes the sense of a company working together, as do the Bolshoi sets and, as in the first four of those, the intimate Chekovian atmosphere of the opening scenes is keenly felt with the voices well balanced as a team; especial praise is due to Biserka Cvejic's lively Olga, lighter in tone than any of the Bolshoi mezzos, and nicely contrasted with the more edgy (vocally and emotionally) Tatyana of Valerie Heybalova. She and Danon make much of the letter scene without achieving the ultimate in individuality or distinction. Dushan Popovich is a more forceful Onegin than some; his reading suggests the character's contrasts of mood, also what Tchaikovsky intended as a 'cold dandy penetrated to the marrow with worldly *bon ton*'; his delivery sometimes has an unwanted forcefulness. Drago Startz, lacking a voice with much colour, shows himself a committed Lensky wedded to the right style if not to Olga. His contribution to the Larina party show his calibre. Miro Changalovich, a lugubrious Gremin, spoils his line with excessive vibrato. As a whole, then, this set is likeable but not greatly distinguished in detail. The choral singing and orchestral playing is no more than adequate.

The second set from the Decca stable is strong just where the other is weak and vice versa. The chorus (John Alldis) and orchestra (Covent Garden's) sing and play with splendid accuracy and ardour for Solti, and the recording is among the company's most spacious and realistic, but the cast suffers from 'international-itis', never sounding like a homogeneous team. A Polish Tatyana, Hungarian Olga, Viennese Onegin, Welsh Lensky, Bulgarian Gremin, French Triquet (excellent!), English Larina and Filipyevna, do not all sound at home in Russian. In consequence about the whole performance there is a lack of the spontaneity and truth that you find in the other recordings, whatever their individual faults. The voices are mostly beautiful, the readings careful, and the results lifeless. Still, it would be unfair not to point out that for musical accuracy this is the most notable set, and for that reason some may warm to it more than I do.

The work does eventually come to life in the final scene. Teresa Kubiak, who fails to touch the heart earlier, here expresses all Tatyana's new-found emotional maturity and Bernd Weikl, till then a correct rather than committed Onegin (but he shows a nice touch of irony when speaking of his second before the duel), becomes appropriately passionate. Stuart Burrows sings elegantly and plangently as Lensky but the very clarity of his diction shows up the unidiomatic sound of his Russian. Still his stage experience in the role often allows him to make significant points. Nicolai Ghiaurov, of course, has no difficulty with the text. His delivery is gravelly at times, where it should be warm and even, but he does exude the right kind of complacent happiness. Anna Reynolds is an admirably forthright Larina.

Solti's beat is flexible and and deft in its handling of Tchaikovsky's bold and beautiful orchestration, but he often fails to pierce to the work's emotional core. No. 8, the conversation with the Nurse before the letter scene, is a case in point. You never feel, as with the best of the Russian performances, the pangs of love entering Tatyana's poetic soul in those yearning string phrases. There is also little anticipatory excitement as the letter scene itself begins, and the *forte* chords a little later are actually sluggish. Here and elsewhere one almost longs for Rostropovich's exaggerations: at least they were the expression of a commitment to the music here seemingly absent.

The various discs of highlights sung in German reveal a similar change of style to the Russian records. In the excerpts under Fritz Lehmann, all four singers show a care for words not exhibited in the later records. Elfride Trötschel, in spite of a faulty technique, suggests a wilful, excited girl by the force of her diction. Walther Ludwig, though hardly youthful, is also attentive to the text. Greindl is a gruff Gremin, but also a sympathetic one. Josef Metternich is uninteresting as Onegin. Each has his or her aria; the makeweight is the dances.

The EMI record has only one side devoted to *Onegin*. Therein Fritz Wunderlich sings a sad, finely vocalized account of Lensky's aria (he is even better on the DG record). There follows the canon-duet with Hermann Prey's self-conscious Onegin. Gottlob Frick breaks his line in Gremin's aria. After a cut we hear Onegin's ballroom arioso. Finally comes the last scene complete with Melitta Muszely as a second-rate Tatyana, Prey a fulsome Onegin. Evelyn Lear, DG's Tatyana, has more to say about the part in a kind of Lotte Lehmann way, impulsive in the letter scene, dignified in the finale. Fischer-Dieskau is bumpy and mannered in his aria, much more impressive in the finale. Gremin's thoughts flow easily from Martti Talvela's throat in a well-groomed line, but without much individuality. Otto Gerdes overheats the score. The disc conducted by Kegel can be safely ignored.

Tatyana's letter scene has not often been recorded separately, but its heartfelt sentiments have brought the best out of most sopranos who have tackled it. The accounts by Russian sopranos confirm that. Tamara Milashkina (Melodiya CM 02625/6) is much in the Vishnevskaya mould but without the older singer's specific insights. She sings without wobble, without fuss, and with a great deal of vibrant tone. She is vividly accompanied by Mark Ermler and the Bolshoi orchestra. She sings the alternate E flat. So does Oda Slobodskaya on her very different recording (unpublished; LXT 5663), thus indicating that this is a long-standing Russian tradition. The great lady was at least fifty when she made her version in 1945; in consequence she hardly sounds girlish or fresh in tone, but her performance is notable not only for its authority and authenticity but also for its feeling and for the singer's savouring of the text.

Leontyne Price (SER 5621) is a placid Tatyana. One listens to the glorious voice and the innate musicality, but nothing of the music's passionate character is conveyed. Elisabeth Söderström is at the opposite pole in her 1973 recording (4E 061–34788). The thoughts of the idealistic girl seem to be pouring out of her involuntarily and with eager anticipation of Onegin's favourable reply. Söderström sings with her usual scrupulous musicianship and well-integrated tone. I miss only something of inwardness. She was a notable Glyndebourne Tatyana. Amy Shuard had one of her first successes at Sadler's Wells in the role. She was my first Tatyana, and I looked forward to hearing her version, gamely sung in Russian (XLP 20442). It proved a sad disappointment, and the unflattering adjectives are best left unwritten; so are comments on Licia Albanese (BLP 1078) with Stokowski.

Tatyana *als deutsche Mädel* (in Philip Hope-Wallace's pictorial phrase) is a frequent phenomenon. Lotte Lehmann recorded half the scene, from the D flat section, in 1917 when she was 29 (Poly. 76369; LV 180). From the old recording shines out an impulsive whole-hearted creature, ready for new experience. By her side Tiana Lemnitz in her 1943 Berlin radio performance, which includes the preceding scene with Filipyevna (Acanta 22 2211–5), sounds staid and calculated. This is a woman too mature and knowing to fall so instantly in love, but Lemnitz's familiar intelligence and Arthur Rother's fervent conducting make the performance far from negligible. Elisabeth Lindermeier (Electrola E 80027) has an attractive vibrato, clear diction and apt phrasing, but never suggests the pointedly Russian character of the music. She is greatly aided by the accompaniment of Rudolf Kempe, then her husband, and the Berlin Philharmonic, while Elisabeth Schwarzkopf is positively hindered by the slack, uninterested direction of Alceo Galliera (1C 181–05292) in a version made in 1967, too late for her to suggest the girlish impulsiveness so vital to the scene. We are consoled for some archness in the diction by the thought and care that has gone into the phrasing and by the *Innigkeit* she brings to the D flat section. Claudio Muzio, who sang Tatyana at the Metropolitan in 1920, recorded the last part of the letter scene about then in Italian with thrilling commitment and clear tone (Edison 82224).

Ljuba Welitsch in a sense spans the Russian and German approach, for she has the right Slavonic accents and timbre but sings in German (LX 1108/9; WRC SHB 289). She was at the peak of her all-too-short career when she recorded the piece in 1947 and brings just that youthful impetuosity and quickening of the pulse so much of the music requires. This is an unfettered confession of first love expressed in natural, crystal-clear tone, finely controlled. Welitsch has less difficulty with her high notes than any of the other sopranos; they shine like fiery beacons. Walter Susskind and the Philharmonia provide superb support, with Dennis Brain's horn-playing of particular flair.

Both of Joan Hammond's versions (DX 1134/5 and CFP 154), separated by about ten years, both sung in English, are close to Welitsch and Vishnevskaya in distinction. This still underrated soprano shows herself aware of Tatyana's subjective emotions and projects them with an even, fresh tone that is most appealing, and her diction is exemplary. She is well partnered on the LP disc by Sargent and the BBC Symphony. She confirms her understanding of the part on another record (SXLP 30205) where with Susskind and the Philharmonia she sings the beginning of the final scene, also in English. Here one notes and admires the breadth of the phrasing, even if there is just a hint of the English schoolmistress about her reprimands. What a pity an Onegin was not engaged to complete the scene.

Any survey of Lensky's music must begin with those three great Russian tenors from the two opening decades of the century: Andrei Labinsky, Leonid Sobinov and Dimitri Smirnov. I have not heard all their versions of the character's music, but sufficient to judge their qualities. Labinsky's versions (2–22761, 2–22766) of the aria (17) and arioso (6) made in 1906 display his typically Russian timbre, white, clean and smiling. Smirnov in either his 1921 (DB 581) or 1928 (Parlo. 53401; GV 75) discs of 17 and his 1912 'In your house' (022299–COLH 129) is more individual in accent. He always phrases with imagination and skill, but his long fermatas and sudden *diminuendi* strike me as self-conscious and mannered. Both records of 17 omit the reprise to get the aria on to a single side of a 78 record. Sobinov makes the same excision in his version (DB 889; COLH 129), which also has 6 on it. (Incidentally COLH 129, 'Singers of Imperial Russia', a long-deleted HMV reissue, scrupulously prepared by Desmond Shawe-Taylor, ought to appear again.) Sobinov's account of this music seems to me to establish standards by which all later versions need to be judged. The voice is fuller, more vibrant, less monochrome than Smirnov's catching the smiling, relaxed quality of the arioso, the plangent melancholy of the aria, and in his case rubato and *ritenuti* are used in the cause of the music and the character. Not having heard Sobinov's account of the aria for some time, I returned to it after listening to the many others discussed below and was suddenly aware that this was precisely how Tchaikovsky must have wanted the music to sound.

A modern account in Russian that comes closest to Sobinov's 1910 record is that recorded by Nicolai Gedda in 1954 (33CX 1130), and this, of course, has the advantage of being complete; indeed Gedda's *pianissimo* handling of the reprise is as delicate as could be wished. His reading suggests an inner monologue, tender and unexaggerated, and is in its way as moving as Kozlovsky and Lemeshev in the sets. Two modern Russian tenors, on Melodiya – Virgilius Noreika and Nikolai Ogenric – both of whom sing 6 and 17 – are idiomatic but uninteresting in delivery. Denis Korolev, also on Melodiya, in the aria only, shows more sense of grief, more individuality. Better still is G. P. Vinogradov (USSR 12769/70), who sounds the vulnerable poet to the life. Among other East Europeans, I need mention only two. Wieslav Ochman (Muza XL 0465), who sang the part so well at Glyndebourne in the 1960s, but is disappointingly casual here, in spite of his refined singing. Beno Blachut on a 78 (Supraphon 048375/6), singing in Czech, hardly lives up to his reputation. The tone tends to be bleaty, the style lachrymose.

It is German tenors of the inter-war years and just after, singing in their native tongue, who come closest to Sobinov's ideal. Not perhaps Richard Tauber (O–8171; GVC 4) and Helge Roswaenge (DB 5580; LV 43), who are both too extrovert with their very personal styles and highly charged emotionalism, but certainly Peter Anders (Telef. E 1761; HT 2) Julius Patzak (Poly. 90060; LV 191) and Anton Dermota (LGX 66048), each of whom has something special to say about the aria. Anders's easy, natural style and unaffected delivery suggest a less complicated Lensky than Patzak, who pierces the heart with his cry to Olga that her bridegroom waits for her. The phrasing is perfectly adjusted to the music and his repeat of 'doch du' is hauntingly beautiful. Dermota also realizes the inner meaning of this piece, where Tchaikovsky is surely being almost autobiographical, and he, like Patzak, uses words and an individual timbre to telling effect. From an earlier generation The Czech Otto Marak gives both arioso and aria (cut version) on two G&Ts (272261/2) with plangent but tight tone. Hermann Jadlowker (Od.99361) sings with just as much feeling in that peculiarly steady, metallic tone of his and with a breadth and freedom of expression that place his version among the very best too. By its side Charles Kullmann sounds ordinary, Rudolf Laubenthal laboured, Walter von Stolzing on the wrong ground.

Aksel Schiotz (DB 10523; MOAK 19), in Danish, sings with his usual reliability and finds the elegiac accents of the aria. Jussi Björling (SER 5706), in Swedish, does that even more successfully in a performance of beauty and deep feeling, the voice at his final recording session in August 1960 as even and golden as ever. Walter Hyde (D 532), in English, has to hurry because of the exigencies of the 78 side, but his expression is from the heart. It has similarities, among them an unauthorised high F at the end, with Martinell's Italian version (Victor 74712; CDN 1034), both suggesting a more fiery temperament than is perhaps appropriate to Lensky. Caruso (DB 127; ORL 314) sings in French (!), cuts the recitative and goes too fast, but the tone as ever is thrilling in itself, the reading eloquent within its confines. Placido Domingo courageously tackles the Russian text (SB 6795). It does not help him to give any special character to his rendering, although it is, of course, beautiful singing as such.

Onegin's solos have not been recorded so frequently. Their study must begin at Warsaw in 1902, when that most elegant of baritones, Mattia Battistini, was a star there, and made his famous and rare series of records, among them one in Italian (52665; COLH 116) of Onegin's first-act aria (12). As is to be expected from this artist, it is an exercise in sweet, mellifluous singing, a certain legato style personified, ending with that high F perfectly placed and floating away into eternity. Eugenio Giraldoni (Fono. 39918) is almost as persuasive. So are Nicolai Shevelev (022267), a smooth, sophisticated Onegin on this evidence, the irreproachable Mikhail Kararesh, who displays a marvellous variety of tone, and Georges Baklanov (022339), all of whom have the advantage of the original language and use it to project Onegin's complacent advice with well-shaded tone. Baklanov's 1918 version of the arioso (DA 464) catches precisely Onegin's sudden access of feeling. His later performance (Am. Decca 20423) shows a sad decline in voice and style. From that generation, Goncharov (Col. E 701) displays mellow tone in 12, but the manner is matter of fact. More convincing is the de-Luca-like sound of N. Naidovich (Victor 4074), whose account of both pieces is finely shaped and convincingly interpreted. None of these versions of 12 includes the recitative. Nor does the suave, sonorous one in Swedish by John Forsell (Swedish HMV 82986; GV 65).

It is included, of course, in the LP versions. On Melodiya, Ladislav Konya, Yevgeny Kibkalo and Mazurok (the latter pair adding 21) maintain the tradition of warm, firm, sympathetic Russian baritones, but only Kibkalo, particularly in an inspired account of 21, gives much individuality to his music. All sing the top F at the end of the aria. So does Pavel Lisitsian who is anything but anonymous in his superbly sung version of both pieces – has there been a more exciting baritone voice in the past thirty years? These pieces, and much more of his repertory, have been reissued by Melodiya (MI0 35905–10), a set worth acquiring if you can find it. Andrzej Hiolzki (Muza XL 0185) displays a warm timbre but a casual style. The only German version I have located, a worthy one, is by Heinrich Schlusnus (Poly. 350161; LV 110), whose even tone and line, so much to be preferred to the method of his successor, Fischer-Dieskau, almost reconcile one to the German text. Max Maksakov (22270), in Onegin's second aria, displays all the character's excitement at that point.

Imagine being the lucky administrator able to choose for the upright Prince Gremin between two basses as rich-toned and eloquent as Lev Sibiriakov and Vladimir Kastorsky. Both were members of the company in the great days of the Marynsky Theatre in St Petersburg before the first world war. Both recorded Gremin's aria, albeit it in differently cut versions. Sibiriakov (022279; GV 1), who leaves out the reprise all excepting the final line, has the lower, richer, 'cello-like timbre, and he uses it to produce a seamless legato of suitably prince-like breadth. Kastorsky, who simply omits the whole middle section (3-22873; GV 2), is less sepulchral, but the phrasing is if anything more distinctive, more free, the expression alternately smiling and tender. These versions are matched in interpretative insights and vocal splendour by only two more recent ones. Unpublished; RLS 743 and Kipnis (Victor 11–9284) provides even greater imagination in his projection of the text: he is a very lively old general indeed, not as graceful as some but an admirable husband no doubt. Boris Christoff (DB 21626 – the last DB number of music ever issued; RLS 735) is perhaps more benign than any of these and he provides a refined half-voice at the thought of Tatyana as the angel sent to give him happiness. It is sad that he has a hurry a little to fit the whole piece on to one 78 side.

Not far behind them are two other versions. Mark Reizen (CCCP 162666/7), sensibly spreading his version over two sides of a ten-inch 78, is heard to far better advantage than on the Orlov set. This is a lighter interpretation than the ones so far considered, shaded with great artistry as Gremin ponders on the amorality of the world in the middle section, and the tone is firm and flexible. Bernard Ladysz (33CX 1678) is almost as excellent – a sound, unfussy, slightly bland reading, but one to live with. At the opposite extreme is the hammy, sometimes tearful expression of Adolf Katkins (HMV EL 1002), but there is no doubting the strength of his voluminous, vibrant voice; this must have been telling in the theatre. Alexander Pirogov (Melodiya 023231) was obviously past his best when he recorded his version with unsteady tone, but the remnants of an authentically accented performance are there, a grizzly veteran indeed. The Bulgarian Nicola Ghiuselev (Balkanton BOA 1464) sounds uncannily similar to his fellow-countryman Ghiaurov. He presents a dignified but not very characterful Gremin. Kim Borg (DG 135090) suggests a younger man with his supple bass-baritone; so does Raffaele Arie (LW 5061) in his estimable performance. Versions in German include those by Richard Mayr (4–42488; LV 42) who cuts the middle section, Franz Crass (1C 063–29 073), too much like a Pogner masquerading as a Gremin, and Frick (Electrola E 70504), who far surpasses his account on the highlights record already mentioned; here he is in wonderful voice and etches a firm line to second a more positive interpretation. Wilhelm Strienz (Electrola EH 1051; 1C 047–28557) is tender and persuasive in his flexible utterance.

Olga's aria (3) has been recorded, without any distinction, by the Czech mezzo S. Stepanova (in Czech). Max Titov's record of Triquet's couplets takes us back to pre-first world war St Petersburg (2–22762), and indicates that even then Russian character tenors were in the habit of singing one verse in French, one in Russian. To end at the end, there are three modern versions of the final scene, two of them with Mazurok. On one (Melodiya CM 02697/8), he is partnered by Maria Bieshu, who has a steady, refulgent voice and sings with considerable feeling, especially when she implores Onegin to leave her. Altogether the two singers make a powerful thing of the unhappy end, splendidly supported by Mark Ermler. The slow tempo set for several passages here and by the same conductor in Mazurok's disc with Milashkina (CM 02625/6) shows that Rostropovich is only following practice at the Bolshoi. Milashkina sings the Andantino solo with great eloquence and is altogether an impassioned but now maturer Tatyana than she was in the letter scene. On both these LPs, Mazurok evinces more commitment than in the complete set. Neither of these versions is a match, however, for that by Vishnevskaya and Georg Ots with Melik-Pashayev made in about 1960 – in other words between the soprano's complete sets. Here she still has the freshness of tone of the earlier set to which is added the greater interpretative judgement of the later one (ASD 2451). Ots takes liberties with the notes and his tone is inclined to be gravelly, but he is deeply involved in the part, inspired by Vishnevskaya's impassioned Tatyana. Indeed her confession on that high A flat that she still loves Onegin was one of the most gratifying moments in this whole survey. In a much earlier version with Karakesh (024080/1), Ekaterina Pipova, the Tatyana, displays a grand, pure-voiced manner appropriate to Russian imperialist days and a keen involvement. Karakesh is again a model Onegin.

My ideal cast would include Vishnevskaya as Tatyana (with Welitsch in reserve), Karakesh as Onegin, Sobinov (or in a more indulgent mood

Lemeshev) as Lensky, Kastorsky or Kipnis as Gremin, conductor Boris Khaikin.

EUGENE ONEGIN

EO Eugene Onegin; *T* Tatyana; *O* Olga; *L* Lensky; *G* Gremin; *La* Larina; *F* Filipyevna; *Tr* M. Triquet; *Z* Zaretsky

1948 Nortzov *EO*; Kruglikova *T*; Antonova *O*; Kozlovsky *L*; Mikhailov *G*; Rudintskaya *La*; Makarova *F*; Ostroumov *Tr*; Mikhailov *Z*/Bolshoi Theatre Chorus and Orch./Melik-Pashayev
Period SPLP 1003

1953 Ivanov *EO*; Kruglikova *T*; Maksakova *O*; Kozlovsky *L*; Reizen *G*; Ambrovskala *La*; Petrova *F*; Kovalenko *Tr*/Bolshoi Theatre Chorus and Orch./Orlov Chant du Monde
ⓜ LDX 8088–90; MK
ⓜ DO 9377–82

1955 Popovich *EO*; Heybalova *T*; Cvejvic *O*; Startz *L*; Changolovich *G*; Vershevich *La*; Bugarinovich *F*; Andrashevich *Tr*; Gligorievich *Z*/Belgrade National Opera Chorus and Orch./Danon
Decca GO S551–3; Richmond SRS 63509

1956 Belov *EO*; Vishnevskaya *T*; Avdeyeva *O*; Lemeshev *L*; Petrov *G*; Petrova *La*; Verbitskaya *F*; Sokolov *Tr*; I. Mikhailov *Z*/Bolshoi Theatre Chorus and Orch./Khaikin
Parlophone ⓜ PMA 1050–2; Bruno ⓜ BR 23001–3L

1970 Mazurok *EO*; Vishnevskaya *T*; Sinyavskaya *O*; Atlantov *L*; Ognivstev *G*; Tugarinova *La*; Avdeyeva *F*; Vlassov *Tr*; Shkaptsov *Z*/Bolshoi Theatre Chorus and Orch./Rostropovich
HMV SLS 951; Angel/Melodiya SRCL 4115

1974 Weikl *EO*; Kubiak *T*; Hamari *O*; Burrows *L*; Ghiaurov *G*; Reynolds *La*; Hartle *F*; Sénéchal *Tr*; Van Allan *Z*/Alldis Choir, Royal Opera Orch./Solti
Decca SET 596–8 ④ K57K32; London OSA 13112

Excerpts

1951 (in German) Metternich *EO*; Trötschel *T*; W. Ludwig *L*; Greindl *G*/Bamberg SO/Lehmann
DG ⓜ LPEM 19023

1953 (in German) Ramms; Camphausen; Horst/Dresden State Opera Chorus and Orch./Schreiber
Allegro ⓜ ALL 3098

1955 (in German) Cordes *EO*; Lindermeier *T*; Schock *L*; Frick *G*/Choruses and Orchs./Kempe, Schüchter, Schmidt-Boelcke
EMI ⓜ E80440

1961 (in German) Prey *EO*; Muszely *T*; Wunderlich *L*; Frick *G*/Bavarian State Opera Orch./Zallinger
HMV ASD 566; EMI 1C 063 29011

1965 (in German) Fischer-Dieskau *EO*; Lear *T*; Fassbaender *O*; Wunderlich *L*; Talvela *G*/Bavarian State Opera Chorus and Orch./Gerdes
DG 2537 005

1965 (in German) Leib *EO*; Croones *T*; Burmeister *O*; Hölzke *L*; Adam *G*/Berlin Radio Chorus, Berlin State Opera Orch./Kegel
Philips 6593 008

Die Fledermaus

ALAN BLYTH

My earliest operatic experience was hearing *Gay Rosalinda* (not a permissible title today!) at the Palace Theatre in 1943, a Korngold confection based on *Die Fledermaus*, conducted by Richard Tauber with Ruth Naylor as Rosalinda and Cyril Ritchard as Eisenstein. Irene Ambrus was the Adele, whose arias she recorded at the time (Col. DB 2187), with Tauber conducting. I recall, even at that tender age, being critical enough to wish that the great tenor had been on the stage rather than in the pit.

That reminiscence is relevant here only because it led to the train of thought that records of *Fledermaus*, more than those of any other work, have tended to stem from stage productions. A disc of the closing scene of Act 2, from Falke's 'Brüderlein' (C 2107), made in 1930, is a memento of the Covent Garden touring company of the time, with Barbirolli conducting (soloists include Marjorie Parry, Nora Gruhn, Gladys Parr, and Edward Leer). Heddle Nash and Dennis Noble delightfully planning their way to Orlofsky's party – 'Come with me; no risk you run' (DX 212) – were Eisenstein and Falke at Covent Garden in the short 1936/37 winter season. The abridged version of the work, of which more below, recorded in 1928, obviously represents what one might have heard at the Berlin State Opera at the time.

The theory can be extended much further back in time than that. Incredibly enough, the work was recorded virtually complete on twenty-one G&T sides (mixed ten-inch and twelve inch) back in 1907 at Berlin, with a Hofoper cast and Bruno Seidler-Winkler, that old stalwart of the German catalogue right up to the second world war, as conductor. This shows that performing traditions, such as unmarked vocal variants and tempo alterations, were prevalent at a fairly early stage in the work's history; but the Orlofsky is mercifully a mezzo, very good too, the Eisenstein a tenor, and what ballet is included, the Polka, is from the score. There is more dialogue than on many LP versions! It is spoken with a clarity of diction redolent of its age. Apart from the absolute steadiness of the voices, the singers do not have anything special to offer that we cannot match or surpass today, although Marie Dietrich, whom

I have praised elsewhere for her Woodbird, is a charming Adele, whose trill, even if used as a show-off, would put most of her successors to shame, and Emilie Herzog (born as long ago at 1859) has a soprano obviously used to more serious operatic tasks. In the second-act ensemble, the whole cast, no doubt crowded round the horn, seems to be enjoying itself hugely. Hermann Vantin is a dotty Frosch.

Perhaps the nearest we can get to the work's 1874 première (and how tantalizingly close we must have been to having it on disc) is to listen to the voice of Fritz Schrödter on a seven-inch G&T (42776) recorded in 1903 at Vienna, where he was a protégé of Strauss himself. Though a tenor, he sings (nicely) 'Brüderlein' to a piano accompaniment. Schrödter appeared at Covent Garden under Richer in 1884 as David, the Steersman and in other Wagner roles.

Elisabeth van Endert, a Dresden and Berlin soprano in the early years of this century, appears on several early discs of the operetta, none of them very remarkable, although she offers the earliest example of the amusing false dramatics in the trio, 'So muss allein' (2–944267/8), a performance that also puts to shame, with its innate high sirits, many recent, tamer readings on complete sets. Sophie Sedlmair, a Fidelio and Isolde in her day, shows on an ancient disc of Orlofsky's couplets that the part can be cast with a soprano and need not be guyed to make its effect.

That takes us to the abridged Polydor recording, already mentioned. Each of the ten 78 sides runs to more than five minutes of music, the longest in my experience. Although the music is of course foreshortened, something of all the main numbers is included, and a good deal of dialogue, which suggests the *Stimmung* of a live performance. Margret Pfahl, the Rosalinde, is perhaps the weakest member of the cast. Adele Kern is a model of an Adele, charming, full of fun, only in 'Spiel' ich die Unschuld' sometimes overstepping the bounds of genuine characterization. Henke is a veteran Eisenstein in the Patzak mould, but stemming from a German rather than an Austrian tradition. Willi Domgraf-Fassbaender's mellifluous Falke and Franz Völker's lyrically ardent Alfred suggest the opera-orientation of the cast, as does Else Ruziczka's aristocratic Orlofsky. Eduard Kandl shows that modern actors of Frosch have no monopoly in drunken-comedy effects.

We move from Berlin to Vienna for our next set and from the strict German beat of Hermann Weigert to the light, lilting Austrian hand of Clemens Krauss, who gives the score, as the old *Record Guide* declared, 'an almost incredible delicacy of nuance'. For exhilaration it has found its peer only in the recent Carlos Kleiber version, but even that set cannot boast the ravishing charm of Hilde Gueden and Julius Patzak, particularly in the 'Dieser Anstand' duet, and the lift and phrasing of Dermota's contribution as Alfred. All these three, and the veterans Alfred Poell and Kurt Preger, could give a lesson to their juniors in clear diction. Sieglinde Wagner sings Orlofsky's solo in its proper key. What a pity then that we have no dialogue here, and a waltz instead of the ballet music. This cast, obviously familiar with each other's ways, would have done the former so well.

Yet another stage performance stimulated the next recording, of the same age as Krauss's, but with almost nothing to recommend it. It recalls the successful Metropolitan revival with Ormandy as conductor, but on disc he drives too hard, and the cast, Welitsch apart, are oceans away from the idiom of the piece. They are hampered by the slangy, rewritten English dialogue. It may be as well to deal here with the RCA disc of highlights conducted (with more *brio*) by Fritz Reiner and with alternative members of the Metropolitan cast. The young Regina Resnik makes a delightfully dizzy Rosalinde, James Melton a lively Eisenstein, Patrice Munsel a spirited Adele. Robert Merrill makes much of 'Brüderlein', sorry, 'Brother dear'. Most of the main numbers are included, apart from the third-act trio, but there are inevitably cuts within them.

We travel back across the Atlantic to London for the next, Philharmonia-based performance, with the sure hand of Walter Legge to guide it. It is graced by Elisabeth Schwarzkopf's irresistible Rosalinde, nicely differentiating between Viennese and Hungarian accents and speaking the dialogue with more point than any rival. The young Nicolai Gedda is a wonderfully ardent, fresh Eisenstein. Rita Streich makes an appealing Adele, Erich Kunz a *gemütlich* Falke, Karl Dönch a model Frank (so endearing in this third-act drunken state), Helmut Krebs a pale but not uningratiating Alfred. Legge (presumably) edited and produced the dialogue so that the plot is clear and intimately spoken. His choice of a tenor Orlofsky is almost justified by Rudolf Christ's sensitive performance. There is no ballet, but Karajan includes that bit of the opening chorus to Act 2, with the servants, that is usually omitted (though Krauss's version also has it). I love Franz Boheim's Frosch. Karajan is much more successful than in his later recording in catching the work's *élan*.

EMI's stereo remake proved a sad disappointment. With Gerda Schreyer a poor replacement for Schwarzkopf and Otto Ackermann laying a heavy hand on the proceedings, there is little to enjoy save Walter Berry's wonderfully warm-hearted Falke. Kunz, the cheery Falke of the Karajan set, is demoted (promoted?) to Frosch, where he excels himself. Christa Ludwig suddenly reawakened my interest when she opens Act 2: here is a nonpareil among Orlofskys, aristocratic *ennui* personified.

Karajan's own remake, for Decca, has always been controversial. 'Production' abounds in that company's 1960-ish mode, which alienates the listener, although 'Omar Godknow', actually Christopher Raeburn, is funny as an English Lord, speaking in broken German. The cast, representing Vienna's best at the time, lacks individuality, although Giuseppe Zampieri, then Vienna's resident Italian tenor, suggests the fatuity of the breed perhaps too realistically while singing superbly. Resnik has to transpose Orlofsky's couplets down a third, and the dialogue turns her into an elderly man – quite wrong. Karajan is to be praised for including every note of the ballet music. Peter Klein is the best Blind on disc.

The original set included the famous and now surely historic 'Gala Performance'. My favourite contributions, apart from the oft-broadcast Simionato–Bastianini 'Anything you can do', are the young Berganza in a Spanish ditty, Nilsson's 'I could have danced all night' (and woe betide the partner who refuses her, one feels), and Björling's Swedish verse of 'Dein ist mein ganzes Herz', not forgetting the far-from-voiceless Welitsch's paean to Wien.

RCA made an attempt to rival Decca in its 1964 version, with Anneliese Rothenberger singing a nimble, graceful 'Frühlingsstimmen' at the party. Her Adele is one of the few bright contributions to this undistinguished version, conducted with a sluggish beat by Oskar Danon. Kunz, now as Frank, is amusing and authentic. Otherwise the cast make heavy weather of the score, George London to the extent of suddenly transposing 'Brüderlein' down a whole tone. When the rest of the ensemble joins in, the original key is restored – an extraordinary and unmusical procedure. At the start of Act 3, there is no Frosch, no song from Alfred's cell, and an attenuated *melodram* for Frank. London adopts the same methods on some highlights, recorded in English at the same time, and also conducted by Danon. Anna Moffo makes an attractive Rosalinde, singing an excellent Czardas, Jeanette Scovotti is a lively Adele.

The Ariola/Eurodisc version, issued here by World Records, must date from the mid 1960s. It has little to offer. Robert Stolz is the lethargic conductor. Rudolf Schock is a passable Eisenstein, Wilma Lipp a poor, wobbly Rosalinde, Renate Holm – in the first of three recordings – a fresh-voiced Adele. Otto Schenk is very funny as Frosch – I like his remark, 'Nicht die Oper, aber ein seriöses Lokal', at one point in his dialogue. Playing only the Polka again seems a good solution to the ballet problem.

The Boskovsky set is a good, middle-of-the-road version. The cast, as can be seen below, could hardly be stronger for its day, but there is something a little synthetic and sophisticated both in the production, in the speaking of the dialogue, and in the casting – a combination unlikely to be found in a theatre. Fischer-Dieskau, a predictably unconventional Falke, is given an extra aria in place of the ballet. Berry is now Frank, and splendidly vital. Gedda has become a strenuous Eisenstein. Adolf Dallapozza is an agreeable Alfred. Rothenberger is promoted successfully to Rosalinde. Brigitte Fassbaender, with a marvellously exuberant 'Ich lade gern', bids fair to match Ludwig in the part. Schenk is a quietly offbeat Frosch.

Karl Böhm, in his set, unfortunately opted for a tenor, the roué-like Wolfgang Windgassen, as Orlofsky. Predictably, Böhm offers an elegant, gracious but a rather slow account of the score, lovingly supported by his beloved Vienna Philharmonic. Eberhard Wächter, a baritone Eisenstein as he was *chez* Danon, chooses unauthorized lower alternatives. Kunz as Frank, also adapts his notes to suit his reduced vocal circumstances. Waldemar Kmentt, now a persuasive Alfred – he was Eisenstein for Karajan II – serenades the creamy, accurate but characterless Rosalinde of Gundula Janowitz. I have not heard the Russian nor the Hungarian and French sets, nor the Polydor conducted by Marszalek.

The choice of Orlofsky, the squeaky Rebroff, is a serious deterrent to admiration of the Kleiber set – but admire it we must for its superb *Schwung*, for its typically accurate observance of note-values by singers and orchestra. *Schlamperei* wholly banished, and for its wonderfully vivid cast of singers, including Varady's spirited Rosalinde (listen to her *Frischka*), Popp's straightforward yet bright-eyed Adele, Hermann Prey's idiomatic albeit baritone Eisenstein, who shirks no high notes.

Kleiber plays the Thunder and Lightning Waltz, regrettably, in place of the ballet music. The choice of dialogue is sensible. To discuss the variants in the speech on each set would be tedious. Similarly, a recital of events in the many highlights discs would be depressing. Wilhelm Schüchter's ten-inch LP has Schock presumably as Alfred and Eisenstein, a common procedure, and Sari Barabas singing the Czardas in her native Hungarian, as she did in the theatre. The 1959 Sadler's Wells excerpts are a reminder of another enjoyable stage production – on the company's first and abortive visit to the Coliseum – with Christopher Hassall's excellent translation of the lyrics keenly delivered by such company stalwarts of the time as Victoria Elliott, Alexander Young (an elegant Eisenstein), John Heddle Nash, and Anna Pollak, an aristocratic, unexaggerated Orlofsky.

A real collector's piece is a disc (Nixa NLP 18001) derived from the sound track of the film *Oh Rosalinda!*, which updated the story to a 1950s Iron Curtain setting. Most of the actors had singing 'doubles', but not Anthony Quayle, who growls his way through Orlofsky's couplets, and Redgrave has a shot at Eisenstein. 'Oh je, oh je' becomes 'Oh boy, oh boy, that hurts me so'. Alexander Young makes a stylish Alfred. Barabas and Rothenberger are the familiar Rosalinde and Adele. Berry (Falke) sings, in excellent English: 'Be my friend' ('Brüderlein').

Various Polydor issues of extracts under Marszalek's direction have appeared from time to time; they are inartistic pot-pourris. Hidden away among them are one or two notable assumptions, including Ingeborg Hallstein's ingratiating, warmly sung Rosalinde. The 1960 HMV disc listed below has Gueden, as always adept at the mock sadness of the first-act trio, and Rothenberger again as a winning Adele, but the men are poor. The Readers' Digest/RCA disc is very American. The translation has some ghastly lines such as 'Not a lipstick smear'. Rosalind Elias makes a pointed Orlofsky. Highlights on Concert Hall and Vox need not detain us, except that the former has Walter Goehr as conductor, Uta Graf as Rosalinde.

The earliest of the pot-pourris dates from the early 1930s, a quick run-through with Erna Berger, Anni Frind and Peter Anders briefly heard in assorted roles. It conveniently takes us back to the days of 78s, and a number of memorable performances, although by and large the LP era, as I have indicated, has done well by *Fledermaus* and has little to fear in comparison with past interpreters. 'Täubchen, das entflattert ist' is sung with almost Tauber-like charm as a solo by Herbert Ernest-Groh (Parlo. R 2168). Marcel Wittrisch is joined by Anni Frind (EG 3870) in a performance notable for airy tone and clear diction. Both are surpassed by the Danish tenor Marius Jacobsen on Danish HMV (X 4012), who adds on 'Trinke Liebchen' from later in the act. Singing in Danish with a typically Scandinavian timbre, he brings a freshness and spontaneity to the music that equals Dermota's (Paris's entrance from *La Belle Hélène* on the reverse is just as entrancing).

Nash and Noble, on the disc already mentioned, are the only takers for 'Ein Souper'. They make the most of the old Kalisch translation ('My sweetest mousekin', indeed), and sing it as through they really meant to have the time of their life at the ball. Koloman von Pataky, Glyndebourne's first Ottavio, sings 'Trinke Liebchen' as a solo with suave tone and a nice lift (R 2205), far surpassing the wobbly Max Lichtegg (K 2232). Volker (PO 5002), with his well-judged rubato, makes much more of the excerpt in the company of Elsa Kochhann. Fritz Wunderlich (Eurodisc EP 42365 CE) is his usual attractive self.

'Mein Herr, was dächten Sie von mir' is given as a solo by Lotte Lehmann (Parlo. RO 20171; PMA 1057) and by Lotte Schöne (D 1733; LV 6). The former uses the music more freely, ignoring the rests that give the piece its character, but does more with words, such as 'Pascha'. The latter, really an Adele, gives the music a wonderful lift: listen to the low A to high G jump at 'Im tête à tête'. What a lovely voice this is, the very epitome of the Viennese style at its best. As Adele, Schöne, who sang the part eighty five times, firstly under Weingartner in 1919, is incomparable (Od. 0–8116; Rococo 5290). She, like the best of her contemporaries, sings both solos (and I shall treat them together) with a forward delivery, the words 'speaking' so quickly and naturally, in a manner lost today. She takes few liberties, throws off the coloratura effortlessly, and only disappoints with no top D at the end of 'Spiel' ich die Unschuld'.

Maria Ivogün (Poly. 85312; LV 69) is almost Schöne's equal. The touch is even lighter and more gentle, the rubato free but delicate, the reading a little too ladylike. She adds a delightful cadenza. Elisabeth Schumann, in both numbers (E 545; 7ER 5108), a famous disc, has more weight and presence – you can 'see' her acting – but is a little too arch for my taste, and vocally not so fresh as the previous two. Erna Berger

(PO 5100), with her country-girl voice, accuracy, sweetness, and charm, fills every word with life, in both pieces, and holds back 'mit dem Talent' just sufficiently to make her point: a lovely record. Gwen Catley is almost in this class for 'Mein Herr Marquis' (B 9724), but on the LP remake, adding the second piece (DLP 1115), shows a distressing decline in vocal powers. Erna Sack (Telef. E 2571) sounds fun, but then adds those infamous notes *in alt* and ruins everything. Gertrud Runge (not to be confused with the Wagnerian Gertrud Rünger) in her 1906 'Mein Herr' (43775) is a good, straightforward singer: the power of her voice reminds us that she was also a Rosalinde, Fritzi Massary (043306) is surprisingly uninteresting, and lacks a trill. Miliza Korjus (Victor 11–8579; 7ER 5108) is too fast in 'Mein Herr', but has a Galli-Curci-like lightness.

There are unremarkable souvenirs of Sylvia Geszty (Telef. TS 3250), Elfie Mayerhofer (Decca LM 5048), Kiri Te Kanawa (Kiwi SLC 46), and June Bronhill, caught live at Sydney Opera House in 1975 in 'Mein Herr', and of Sona Ghazarian (Amadeo 14705) in 'Spiel'ich'. Ghazarian is more successful in the Czardas, to which she brings a heartfelt vigour. This showpiece has had many appreciable interpreters, the earliest of whom, Selma Kurz (DB 500), is far from the best – too hurried, and hard in tone. Elisabeth Rethberg (DB 1812; CDN 1018) gives a very grand reading, but is harassed in the *Frischka*. Is her version sung a semitone down, I wonder? Lehmann (RO 20171) sounds really moved by memories of her supposed homeland, but makes a huge cut and is also worried by the demands of the *Frischka*. Their Hungarian-born contemporary Maria Ivogün, in her 1932 record (DB 4412; 7ER 5116), is predictably more admirable; indeed until she fails at the last fence (the final run ignored), hers is the most accurate account of the piece I have heard, not excepting the very individual Ljuba Welitsch (CBS 61080) who gives, however, a much more characterful performance, even when she runs ahead of the beat as was her custom. Maria Reining (Telef. E 3055), as one might expect, is workmanlike, adequate. Cristina Deutekom (CFP 191) provides not inappropriately husky tone, but sings odd German and gargles through the *Frischka*. I have searched in vain through all my listening to hear sixteen bars of the Czardas that are printed in all editions including the recent Eulenberg *Revisionsbericht*.

In two Berlin ensemble versions of 'Brüderlein', famous tenors usurp the baritone territory of Falke. On the first it is Völker (Poly. 22173), the excerpt starting at 'Im Feuerstrom' and ending after 'Duidu'. Kochhann (Rosalinde), the delectable Irene Eisinger (Adele), and Henke (Eisenstein) are among the company. Tauber leads the other, even more distinguished gathering (R 20085). This starts at 'Herr Chevalier' and goes to the end of the act, excluding the ballet, of course. Having sung 'Brüderlein', Tauber switches to Eisenstein's part for the rest. Did he do this in performance? He certainly sings the paean to brotherhood with all his accustomed sincerity. Lehmann is the fun-loving Rosalinde, Karin Branzell, no less, the Orlofsky. Yet another Berlin version, from 'Brüderlein' (1C 147–29137), has Vera Schwarz as Rosalinde: it is otherwise unremarkable. I have already referred to the Covent Garden 1930 disc.

Last but very far from least, Tauber and Schwarz came together in a fast but marvellous 1928 account of 'Dieser Anstand' (177070 – issued in South America only; K 147–29137) in which the tenor is in his most seductive, juicy form. Just before the coda, Tauber comments, 'Das ist die Gräfin Kralowatsch' – that remark must have a history, and is again surely a memento of stage performance.

An immortal administrator might choose the following cast: Schwarzkopf as Rosalinde, Schöne as Adele, Dermota as Alfred, Patzak as Eisenstein, Berry as Falke, Kunz as Frank, Klein as Blind and Schenk as Frosch; conductor Krauss.

DIE FLEDERMAUS

E Eisenstein; *R* Rosalinde; *Al* Alfred; *Ad* Adele; *O* Orlofsky; *Fro* Frosch; *B* Blind; *F* Falke; *Fra* Frank; *I* Ida

1907 Phillip *E*; Herzog *R*; Lieban *Al*; *B*; Dietrich *Ad*; Schelle-Müller *O*; Arnold *Fra*; Begemann *F*; Vantin *Fro*/Chorus and Orch. G&T 044059–61; 44213–22; 44624; 40563; 41971–4; 043074; 42789

1950 Patzak *E*; Gueden *R*; Dermota *Al*; Lipp *Ad*; S. Wagner *O*; Preger *Fra*; Poell *F*; Jaresch *B*/Vienna State Opera Chorus, VPO/C. Krauss Decca ⓜ DPA 585–6; Richmond ⓜ RS 62006

1950 (in English) Kullman *E*; Welitsch *R*; Tucker *Al*; Pons *Ad*; Harvout *Fra*; Brownlee *F*; Lipton *O*; Franke *B*/Metropolitan Opera Chorus and Orch./Ormandy CBS (UK) ⓜ 78245; (US) ⓜ Y2–32666

1955 Gedda *E*; Schwarzkopf *R*; Krebs *Al*; Streich *Ad*; Christ *O*; Böheim *Fro*; Donch *Fra*; Kunz *F*; Majkut *B*; Martini *I*/Chorus/Philharmonia/Karajan EMI ⓜ RLS 728 ④TC–RLS 728; Angel ⓜ 3539BL

1955 (in Russian) Neverov *E*; Sakharova *R*; Shchavinsky *Al*; Rachevskaya *Ad*; Petrov *Fra*;

Zakharov *F*/Moscow Radio Chorus and Orch./Samosud MK ⓜ D0 1774–7

1959 Terkal *E*; Schreyer *R*; Dermota *Al*; Lipp *Ad*; Ludwig *O*; Kunz *Fro*; Berry *Fra*; Wächter *F*; Majkut *B*; Martini *I*/Philharmonia Chorus and Orch./Ackermann Columbia SAX 2336–7; Angel SBL 3581

1960 Kmentt *E*; Gueden *R*; Zampieri *Al*; Köth *Ad*; Wächter *Fra*; Berry *Fro*; Resnik *O*; Klein *B*; Kunz *F*; Schubert *I*/Vienna State Opera Chorus, VPO/Karajan Decca SET 201–3 (with Gala Ball scene); SXL 6015–6 ④ K58K22 London OSA 1319 (with Gala Ball scene); OSA 1249

1964 Wächter *E*; Leigh *R*; Kónya *Al*; Rothenberger *Ad*; Kunz *Fra*; London *F*; Stevens *O*; Majkut *E*/Vienna State Opera Chorus and Orch./Danon RCA (UK) SER 5514–5; (US) LSC 7029

1966 Schock *E*; Lipp *R*; Curzi *Al*; Holm *Ad*; Berry *Fra*; Nicolai *F*; Steiner *O*; Gruber *B*; Schenk *Fro*/Vienna State Opera Chorus,

Vienna SO/Stolz
Ariola-Eurodisc XD 88610E or
XF 71567

1967 (in Hungarian) Udvardy *E*; Agay
R; Korondy *Al*; Lássaló *Ad*;
Külkey *O*; Palócz *Fra*; Bende
F; Latabar *Fro*/Hungarian State
Radio Chorus and Orch./Lehel
Hungaraton SLPX 16558–60

1967 (in French) Mallabrera *E*;
Broissin *R*; Gruselle *Al*; Clément
Ad; Bodoin *O*; Depray *Fro*;
Linsolas *F*; Gya *B*; Tirmont
Fra/Paris ORTF/Chorus and
Orch./Harteman
Polydor 237905–6

1972 Gedda *E*; Rothenberger *R*;
Dallapozza *Al*; Holm *Ad*; Berry
Fra; Fischer-Dieskau *F*;
Fassbaender *O*; Foerster *B*;
Schenk *Fro*; Wengral *I*/Vienna
State Opera Chorus, Vienna
SO/Boskovsky
EMI SLS 964; Angel SBL 3790
④ 4X2S–3790

1974 Wächter *E*; Janowitz *R*; Kmentt
Al; Holm *Ad*; Kunz *Fra*;
Holeck *F*; Windgassen *O*;
Kuchar *B*; Luken *I*/Vienna State
Opera Chorus, VPO/Böhm
Decca SET 540–1; London OSA
1296

1976 Prey *E*; Varady *R*; Kollo *Al*;
Popp *Ad*; Kusche *Fra*; Weikl *F*;
Rebroff *O*; Gruber *B*;
Muxeneder *Fro*; List *I*/Bavarian
State Opera Chorus, Bavarian
State Orch./C. Kleiber
DG 2707 088 ④3370 009

Excerpts

1929 Pfahl *R*; Völker *Al*; A. Kern *A*;
Ružická *C*; Domgraf-Fassbaender
F; L. Kern *Fra*; Kandl
Fro/Berlin State Opera Chorus
and Orch./Weigert
Decca-Polydor CA 8118–22

1951 Anday; Oeggl; Meyer-Welfing;
Bosch; Funk/Vienna Volksoper
Chorus and Orch./Schonherr
Saga ⓜ SAGA 5363

1951 (in English) Melton *E*; Resnik
R; Peerce *Al*; Munsel *Ad*;
Stevens *O*; Merrill *F*;

Lechner/Shaw Chorale, RCA
Orch./Reiner
RCA (UK) ⓜ RB 16109

1953 Anders *E*; *Al*; Trötschel *R*;
Streich *Ad*; Hoffmann;
Schneider/Chorus and
Orch./Marszalek
Polydor ⓜ 478108

1954 (abridged) A. Kunz *E*; Graf *R*;
Bartsch *Al*; Heusser *Ad*;
Schmid/Zurich Radio Chorus and
Orch./Goehr
Musical Masterpieces Society
ⓜ 2002; Concert Hall ⓜ CM
2022

1959 (in English) Young *E*; Elliott *R*;
R. Jones *Al*; Studholme *Ad*;
Pollak *O*; J. H. Nash *F*; Sharp
Fra/Sadler's Wells Opera Chorus
and Orch./Tausky
HMV CSD 1266

1960 Equiluz *E*; Gueden *R*; Terkal
Al; Rothenberger *Ad*/Vienna
State Opera Chorus,
VPO/Hollreiser
Classics for Pleasure CFP 40251

1962 Grobe *E*; *Al*; Schöner *R*; *Ad*;
Ferenz *O*/Hamburg State Opera
Chorus and Orch./Müller-
Lampertz
Pye Marble Arch ⓜ MAL 561

1962 (in English) Nagy *E*; Scovotti *R*;
W. Lewis *Al*; Moffo *Ad*; Elias
O; Cass *Fra*; Chapman
F/Chorus and Orch./Engel
Reader's Digest RDS 9331

1964 (in French) Brumaire; Berton;
Forli; Fléta; Corazza; Benoît;
Roux; Pruvost/Paris
Conservatoire Orch./Pourcel
EMI 2C 051 12195

1964 (in English) R. Lewis *E*; Moffo
R; Franchi *Al*; Scovotti *Ad*;
Hauxvell *Fra*; London *F*/Vienna
State Opera Chorus and
Orch./Danon
RCA LSC 2788

1965 Hoppe *E*; Barabás *R*;
Wehofschitz *Al*; Schwaiger *Ad*;
Rootering *O*; Kreppel
F/Bavarian State Opera Chorus
and Orch./Michalski
Ariola-Eurodisc Z72333E

1965 (in French) C. Collins *E*;

Darclée *R*; *Ad*; Giannotti
Al/Vienna State Opera Chorus
and Orch./Reinold
Bellaphon CV 1013
1968 P. Alexander *E*; Hallstein *R*;
Hoppe *Al*; Popp *I*; Goulbach
Fra; Kusche *F*/Grand Operetta
Orch./Marazalek
Polydor 2430 264
1970 Lutze *E*; Janz *R*; Wocke *Al*;
Stilo *Ad*; Richter *O*; Liebling
F/Leipzig Radio Chorus and
Orch./Dobrindt
Philips 6592 001

Cavalleria Rusticana
Pagliacci

CHARLES OSBORNE

Cav and Pag, as they are affectionately known, did not burst upon the world already twinned. *Cav* was the 26-year-old Mascagni's first opera, which won a competition and was produced in Rome in 1890, bringing its composer instant fame both in Italy and abroad. Within months, Mahler had produced it in Budapest, and by the end of the following year there were few major operatic centres where it had not been performed. Leoncavallo, Mascagni's senior by five years, had already composed two unperformed operas when he wrote *Pagliacci*, which was produced in Milan in 1892 with enormous success.

The one-act *Cavalleria rusticana* is the longer of the two operas, playing for about an hour and a quarter. The two-act *Pagliacci* is a few minutes shorter. Neither being long enough to stand on its own, they were usually performed as part of a double bill. In its early days at the Metropolitan, New York, *Cavalleria rusticana* often found itself with full-length, *bel canto* bedfellows: Gluck's *Orfeo ed Euridice*, Donizetti's *Don Pasquale*, *L'elisir d'amore* or *La fille du régiment*; but, as early as 1893, the Met coupled *Cav* and *Pag*. It has proved a lasting marriage.

The two operas have frequently been coupled on LP recordings, taking up three discs between them. Separate performances usually run to two discs, with the extra side devoted to miscellaneous arias sung by one of the principals. Nowadays, it should not be difficult for recording companies to get *Pagliacci* on to one disc, and there is at least one recording which proves that the same can be done for *Cavalleria rusticana*.

CAVALLERIA RUSTICANA

The earliest recording of *Cav*, apart from an obscure acoustic set, was conducted by Aylmer Buesst in 1927, with members of the British National Opera Company. May Blyth, the conductor's wife, was an admired Santuzza with the company. Heddle Nash's Turiddu is not very Sicilian, and although Harold Williams's Alfio has vitality and excellent English enunciation, this English-language *Cav* has really only sentimental appeal today.

Carlo Sabajno's 1929 version, based on La Scala forces, is not strongly or individually cast. Lorenzo Molajoli's for Columbia is much better, with Arangi-Lombardi's accomplished Santuzza and the young Bruna Castagna making her mark as Lola. I have not heard the abridged French version conducted by Gustav Cloez. The most interesting of these pre-war recordings is surely that (later transferred to LP) conducted by the composer. This was made in 1940, shortly before Italy entered the war, and was part of *Cavalleria*'s fiftieth birthday celebrations. Mascagni's own tempi, somewhat deliberate, are presumably to be taken as authoritative. Lina Bruna Rasa makes an exciting, if not always musically accurate Santuzza, and Gigli is in his element as Turiddu, with Gino Bechi a virile Alfio. The young Giulietta Simionato sings not Lola but old Mamma Lucia.

When Simionato next recorded *Cavalleria*, she was the Santuzza (though officially a soprano role, it presents no difficulties to high mezzo voices). This was in Cetra's 1952 recording, in which the other roles are only passably well performed. Simionato is heard to better advantage, her individual timbre well caught, in Decca's 1960 *Cav*, conducted in somewhat stately fashion by Serafin, in which Mario del Monaco shouts his stentorian way through Turiddu's music, and Cornell McNeil deals efficiently with Alfio. Simionato is also the affecting Santuzza in Cetra's Live Opera recording of a performance from La Scala in 1955. This has all the immediacy of live performance, finds Giuseppe di Stefano on form as Turiddu, and is conducted never less than efficiently by Antonino Votto. (Occupying three sides, the recording is coupled to five sides of Mascagni's *Iris*.)

LPs of the 1950s and 1960s which I have not heard are the 1952 Remington, the 1958 Period, and the various German discs of excerpts with the exception of the German EMI which offers the sultry, smoky voice of Leonie Rysanek (Santuzza), a dramatic Alfio from Josef Metternich and Rudolf Schock's commanding Turiddu. Most of the other complete recordings have something to recommend them. RCA in 1953 had the highly individual if erratic Zinka Milanov as Santuzza. She is wobbly in the Easter Hymn, but sings beautifully in the duet with Turiddu, who is the suave (perhaps a trifle staid) Björling, also in superb voice. Renato Cellini conducts stylishly. In the same year, Franco Ghione conducted a routine performance for Decca, with the mezzo Elena Nicolai as a dramatic Santuzza and the relentlessly loud and boring del Monaco as Turiddu. There is little to recommend here, other than Aldo Protti who makes a convincing Alfio.

One of the most successful complete recordings is that in which Callas sings Santuzza. It is not a role she ever portrayed on the stage, but its violent emotions came easily to her, and she makes the character stand thrillingly alive before the listener, even if she is vocally as uneven as ever. Callas is well partnered by di Stefano. (What a world of difference there is between their duet here and those concert performances for which they later emerged from semi-retirement, pirated records of which reveal them barking at each other in the same music.) Rolando Panerai makes Alfio a sympathetic and believable character, and Serafin brings a certain welcome restraint to the proceedings.

There is less to be said for a 1954 recording, based on Metropolitan forces, though it gets the opera on to one disc, for Margaret Harshaw's voice and temperament are both dull; but Fausto Cleva conducts well, and Richard Tucker's Turiddu is certainly an asset, indeed one of the finest Turiddus on record. A pity that his exciting portrayal was not given a worthier partner. Better than this, though not a serious rival to Callas–di Stefano–Serafin, is the performance conducted for Decca by Alberto Erede. Superficially, Erede's account of the score may seem earthier than Serafin's, though it lacks the musical distinction brought to Mascagni by the older conductor. The soloists are first-rate. Björling's Turiddu is as restrained as it was five years earlier, but here he seems to bring a livelier imagination to the role. Tebaldi makes a glorious sound, and is effective and moving in 'Voi lo sapete'. I liked the richness and individuality of Ettore Bastianini's timbre as Alfio; an interesting set.

As an example of a routine, mid-season performance at the San Carlo, Naples, the Philips 1959 version is fine. Caterina Mancini, a kind of poorman's Caniglia, certainly gives a performance; Gianni Poggi is awful, and a tame San Carlo conductor, Ugo Rapalò, is inclined to let it all take its own course. To be taken more seriously is Gabriele Santini's careful approach for HMV in 1963. Victoria de los Angeles makes Santuzza's music sound more beautiful than any other singer has managed to do, though one could complain that it all ought to be coarser than this. As Alfio, Mario Sereni contrives to be both dramatic and mellifluous. For roughness there is the Turiddu of Franco Corelli.

The version conducted dully by Silvio Varviso has Elena Souliotis giving a lively, sub-Callas performance, del Monaco at his unsubtle best, and Tito Gobbi strongly characterizing Alfio. Far better, in my view the only real rival to Callas-Serafin, is the Karajan version. His ability to make the most hackneyed score sound fresh and new is well known, and he gives *Cavalleria rusticana* the 'whiter than white' treatment without robbing it of any of its earthiness. Fiorenza Cossotto, a mezzo Santuzza, sings superbly, and Bergonzi brings the stylistic distinction of a Björling to Turiddu while sounding more authentically Italian. In the only new recording of *Cav* since Karajan's, Luciano Pavarotti is an unvaryingly loud Turiddu, Julia Varady a convincing Santuzza, and Piero Cappuccilli a restrained Alfio. I like Gavazzeni's way with the score, precise yet not lacking in lyricism.

My account of individual numbers on disc from *Cavalleria rusticana* (and from *Pagliacci*) will, of necessity, be highly selective, for the sheer volume of material to choose from is impossibly daunting. The creators of the roles of Santuzza and Turiddu were the husband and wife team of Gemma Bellincioni and Roberto Stagno. Bellincioni's rich, firmly placed dramatic soprano, with its quick vibrato, must have made her a highly effective Santuzza. She recorded the opera's most popular aria, 'Voi lo sapete, o mamma' (053018; MCK 500) as did a number of other early interpreters of the role, among them Emma Eames, Calvé and Emmy Destinn. Since then, there has hardly been an Italian soprano (or mezzo) of any eminence who has not left her performance of the aria for posterity: Muzio, Boninsegna, Dusolina Giannini – an especially moving performance, this (DA 892; LV 8) – and, my own favourite performance from the distant past, Mafalda Salvatini (043361) recorded in 1916. Santuzza was said to be one of her best roles. Bianca Scacciati's account of the aria (Col. D 14712) has its admirers, but I find her too squally.

From other excellent performances of 'Voi lo sapete' by Stignani, Caniglia, Eva Turner, Rosina Buckman, Aulikki Rautawaara, Ponselle, Felicia Litvinne and others, I would single out two of the German-language versions: the beautiful voice of Helene Wildbrunn (043312; LV 70) and the characterful performance by Göta Ljungberg (D 2036; LV 176), Margarete Teschemacher (EH 1032; LV 103) also stands out. Among more recent (i.e. post-war) versions, I have enjoyed Gré Brouwenstijn, Simionato (conducted by Solti in Chicago), Milanov, Joan Hammond and Rysanek. More recent still, I would pick out Grace Bumbry for her dramatic attack (SLPM 138826), Amy Shuard for a reminder of her Covent Garden performances (XLP 20046), Tebaldi for sheer beauty of voice (SXL 6152), Victoria de los Angeles for the same reason, only more so (ASD 2274), but not the bland Caballé.

The much admired 1932 recording of the Santuzza–Turiddu duet by Giannini and Gigli (DB 1790; COLH 144) still sounds as gripping as when I first heard it as a child. I am also fond of a full-blooded account of the duet by Scuderi and Ferracuti, a tenor I used to hear in scratch performances by an Italian company in Australia (C 3769) and that of Shuard and James Johnston in English (DX 1748). Another excellent English version is that by Florence Austral and Tudor Davies (D 840; RLS 707) recorded in 1924: they were to sing in the opera at Sadler's Wells in 1938. Best of the German versions is Teschemacher with Marcel Wittrisch (DB 4459; LV 103). Some of these Santuzzas also participated in recordings of the Easter Hymn.

A few Alfios have recorded their entrance song, 'Il cavallo scalpita', but they make more of an effect in their scene with Santuzza ('Oh, il Signor vi manda'). Willi Domgraf-Fassbaender and the mysterious Xenia Belmas sing this superbly (Poly. 66848; LV 41).

As for tenors, after one has listened to one, two or all three of Turiddu's arias sung by Gigli, Björling, del Monaco, Tucker, di Stefano,

Poggi, Corelli, Caruso, Anselmi, de Lucia, Slezak, D'Arkor, Martinelli, McCormack, Patzak, Zenatello, Chamlee, Crooks, Herbert Ernst Groh, Völker, Pertile, Peerce, Wunderlich, Titterton, Hislop, Schipa, Pataky, Pattiera, Merli, Piccaver, Lanza, Donald Smith, Schmidt, Anders, Johnston, and a score or more others including Nicolai Figner (!), one's only surviving unnumbed feeling is one of immense gratitude to Richard Tauber and Nicolai Gedda for having resisted any impulse they may have felt to rush into the nearest studio and have a go. And I tactfully refrain from mentioning the majority of the German-language tenors who tend to sound like one another. Here are some brief notes on a few tenors in each aria:

First, the Siciliana. The young Caruso's famous 1902 recording (DA 545; HLM 7030) hardly needs my recommendation. Its directness and vigour are highly engaging, but I prefer the vocal elegance of Tito Schipa in his 1919 recording (Pathé 80846; GVC 10). The Hungarian tenor, Koloman von Pataky, singing in Italian, preserves a nice balance between *bel canto* and 'can belto' (Poly. 66651; LV 54) and an interesting oddity is the excellent version sung in French by Giuseppe Lugo, the Italian tenor most of whose career was spent in France and Belgium (Gram. 561088). A word of commendation, too, for Jaro Dvorsky (EJ 135), for Björling in superb voice (ALP 1841) and for the often underrated Jan Peerce (Philips GL 5853).

The Brindisi ('Viva il vino spumeggiante') seems to find most tenors at their best. Schipa makes it sound gentler in spirit than it is, for which I cannot find it in my heart to criticize him (252128; GV 29); the second of Piccaver's recordings (the first is too stately) is convincing and attractive (Poly. 74626); and I like the stentorian, though not unsuitably so, Mario Chamlee, with a touch of Martinelli-metal in his voice (Brunswick 15056; LV 228). Francesco Merli's is a typical *verismo* voice, vibrant with passion, and he is well supported by the Scala chorus under Molajoli (Col. GQX 10156; LV 162). Tino Pattiera gives a good imitation of an Italian performance (Parlo. R 1216; LV 16), and Lauri-Volpi would be perfect if he did not sound more than a trifle narcissistic (Brunswick 15085; GV 516). Among the German versions, I particularly like Josef Mann (Od. Lxx 80914; LV 74) for his musicianship and superb voice.

A German tenor who specialized in Italian roles was Carl Günther whose 'Mamma, quel vino è generoso' is sung in fine style (Poly. 65628; LV 177). Other recommended versions of Turiddu's farewell include Tucker (LX 5108), Björling (BLP 1055) and Domingo (SXL 6451). Honesty compels me to add that I imagine a Sicilian audience would go wild over Mario Lanza (DB 21523), and that, in this music, I can understand why.

PAGLIACCI

There have been even more complete recordings of *Pagliacci* than of *Cavalleria*. I have not heard the G&T discs or HMV's 1917 effort. The earliest version I know is the BNOC conducted by Eugene Goossens Snr with a strong English-singing cast. This is still less satisfactory than the BNOC's *Cav*. Miriam Licette was an excellent soprano, but she brings a touch of oratorio to Nedda; and, though Frank Mullings was no doubt electrifying in the theatre, he sings badly on these discs. One is left with the ever reliable Harold Williams as Tonio, Dennis Noble excellent as Silvio, and an elegant Beppe from Heddle Nash, all of them nearly defeated by a dreadful English translation.

That was in 1927. The Italian recordings roughly contemporary with Goossens and the BNOC are Columbia and HMV with their respective house conductors, Lorenzo Molajoli and Carlo Sabajno. Usually, in their rival versions, Molajoli had a starrier cast than Sabajno, but this time the honours are fairly even. Molajoli's Canio is Francesco Merli, whose temperament matched his full-bodied voice. With him are the excellent Rosetta Pampanini (Nedda), and Carlo Galeffi, whose beautiful baritone voice and intense, individual style are well suited to Tonio. This is roughly a La Scala line-up of the 1920s. Sabajno's Canio, Alessandro Valente, was a great favourite on records – especially his 'Nessun dorma' – though he did not have a distinguished stage career (unless you call singing in English variety theatres as Alex Vallo distinguished). I find him an impressive Canio, and wish I were not allergic to the voice of his Nedda, Adelaide Saraceni. Tonio is the superb Apollo Granforte, a dark, heavy baritone voice of great expressiveness.

In the early 1930s, HMV put out what seemed an even more richly cast *Pagliacci*, under the baton of Franco Ghione. Gigli is his lachrymose self as Canio, Iva Pacetti is average as Nedda, and it remains for Mario Basiola (Tonio) to save the day. A baritone of great presence with a steady, steely voice, Basiola was an intelligent artist, and a superb singer.

A 1936 Metropolitan performance with Queena Mario, Giovanni Martinelli and Richard Bonelli, conducted by Gennaro Papi, can be heard on two pirated discs (with, on the fourth side, a stunning Act 4, scene 2 of *Trovatore* (qv) with Martinelli, Rethberg, Bonelli and Katherine Meisle). Martinelli's Canio has a shattering intensity that one cannot fail to respond to, however unrelentingly steely one may find his vocalism, and the American soprano Queena Mario has an engaging charm.

I have not heard the wartime DG set, though Roswaenge's individual 78s not only of 'Hüll dich in Tand nur' ('Vesti la giubba') but also of the baritone Prologue suggest a Canio of unusual power and intensity. Of the post-war recordings, those I have not heard are the 1950 Cetra and the Russian and French versions. I have listened to the 1960 German EMI version, but not recently enough to make any other comment than that Schock must have been effective, for I still remember his hard-voiced account of 'Vesti la giubba'. The German 'Volksplatte' highlights disc is enjoyable if you want highlights in German!

The 1951 CBS Metropolitan recording gets the opera on to one disc, which ought to be standard practice, though it is only fair to add that CBS achieved it by observing the traditional cut made in performance in the Nedda–Silvio scene. This is a splendidly conducted performance (Fausto Cleva), and both Richard Tucker in one of his greatest roles as Canio and Giuseppe Valdengo as Tonio could hardly be bettered. Lucine Amara (Nedda), on the other hand, could easily be bettered.

Cetra's 1952 recording offers only two-thirds of the score, or at least it does in the Cetra-Everest repressing (7411) in which I possess it. All the 'plums' are there, though in a constricted, boxy recording. Carlo Tagliabue, whom I remember as an affecting Germont in the theatre, contributes a firm, confident Prologue, and Carla Gavazzi is a sympathetic Nedda. Bergonzi simply does not sound like the Bergonzi I know from the theatre and countless other recordings, but he offers a firm line and a not too exaggerated dramatic passion.

An oddity of Decca's first LP *Pagliacci* is that the Prologue is sung, not by the Tonio, Afro Poli, but by the Silvio, the much younger, less interesting Aldo Protti. I gather that, for the initial American issue of this set, the Canio sang the Prologue. He is the Italian answer to Frank Mullings, Mario del Monaco, and I suppose he does this kind of thing well if you can bear his loud, incessant bawling. Clara Petrella is somewhat heavy-going, and Erede seems out of sympathy with his singers and perhaps with the music – not one of my favourite performances of the opera.

On paper, the cast of HMV's 1954 recording promises well. But Victoria de los Angeles, though she sounds beautiful, lacks temperament, and Leonard Warren's virtues are also vocal rather than dramatic. Cellini conducts tamely, and it is left to the superb artistry of Björling to raise the musical and dramatic temperature with his moving and accurately sung Canio. Far superior to this is the recording issued in the same year by Columbia as a kind of rival, but later reissued on HMV after EMI's final suppression of its Columbia label. This is one of Tullio Serafin's finest performances. What a remarkable conductor he was, with a far wider range of musical sympathies than he was often thought to possess. Callas's Nedda is convincingly acted and sung. Di Stefano is disappointing, but Gobbi matches Callas in dramatic involvement, and the roles of Beppe (Monti) and Silvio (Panerai) are strongly cast.

The San Carlo version for Philips is no better than its companion *Cav* with the same conductor, chorus and orchestra, and two of the same singers. Protti, promoted to Tonio, is still dull, and neither Poggi (Canio) nor Aureliana Beltrami (Nedda) is at all impressive. I pass on quickly to an exciting performance under Molinari-Pradelli for Decca, vitiated less than one would expect by Mario del Monaco's Canio, for he did tend to improve in artistry as his vocal powers began to wane, and here he appears to have been caught just at the right moment. He gives a performance of great intensity, only a little over the top at the end of 'Vesti la giubba'. Gabriella Tucci is an excellent Nedda, despite vocal resources that are no more than adequate, and Cornell McNeil (Tonio) is in his best form.

Even better is Lovro von Matačič (Columbia), conducting a lively performance in which Franco Corelli reveals that he, too, can rise to the occasion. This is not the most imaginative of readings, but he manages his voice more easily than del Monaco, and though he is uneven his best moments are superb. Gobbi sings Tonio for the second time, and is again magnificent, though he sounds a little worn at the top, Lucine Amara is better than she was in the earlier Met recording, though she fails to bring her character to life as Gobbi and, intermittently, Corelli do theirs.

Karajan, with the Scala chorus and orchestra in 1965, is simply superb. The orchestra surpasses itself for him, and the music is made to sound quite beautiful without losing anything of its dramatic quality. The intended Nedda falling ill, Joan Carlyle stepped in at somewhere near the last moment: she contributes a cool, but well sung account of the role. The other principals are superb, Bergonzi now sounding like Bergonzi and giving the lie to all, well *some*, of my generalizations about Italian tenors, and Giuseppe Taddei enjoying himself hugely as Tonio. The smaller roles are excellently and strongly cast: Ugo Benelli (Beppe) and Rolando Panerai (Silvio). Given the strong competition from Serafin and Karajan, there is little point in lingering over Gardelli's *Pagliacci* for Decca. McCracken's Canio is vocally all over the place, Pilar Lorengar is an unsteady Nedda, and it is left to Robert Merrill (Tonio) to give some distinction to the performance. The RCA set is blandly conducted by Nello Santi. It has beautifully sung but curiously uninvolved, and thus uninvolving, performances from Montserrat Caballé, Placido Domingo and Sherrill Milnes. The most recent Decca version has Pavarotti as Canio, a role to which his forthright style is well suited. Mirella Freni's Nedda is strongly characterized, as is Ingvar Wixell's Tonío. Guiseppe Patanè conducts capably.

The first *Pagliacci* cast, under Toscanini in Milan, 1892, included two fine baritones, Victor Maurel (Tonio) and Mario Ancona (Silvio). It was at Maurel's suggestion that Leoncavallo composed the Prologue for him to sing. The younger Ancona later moved from Silvio to Tonio, which he sang in the London première of the opera with Melba and de Lucia. (These three were also in the Met's first *Pagliacci*.) Ancona recorded the Prologue, with piano, in 1907: a somewhat rasping voice, but a broad, dramatic style (Victor 88055). Like Scotti's Prologue (052107), which is interesting more as a souvenir of a great voice of the past than as an enjoyable performance, Ancona stops before the final recitative-like passage.

Other early interpreters who left recordings include de Lucia, whose 'No, Pagliaccio non son' and 'Vesti la giubba' are somewhat perfunctory; Caruso, whose 1904 'Vesti la giubba' (52066; VIC 1430), a performance of brooding intensity, is preferable to his 1902 version (there is also the 1907 version, DB 111, which probably sold more copies than any acoustic disc); the whitish sound, not unattractive, of Nicolai Figner ('Vesti la giubba': Melodiya D–026237–8); Emmy Destinn, a mature but flexible Nedda in 'Stridono lassù' (2–43092); and the Nedda–Tonio 'So ben che deforme', sung by Giuseppina Huguet and Francesco Cigada, conducted by Leoncavallo himself. Its value is largely historical, though the soprano's lively personality shines through, and the baritone is firm (054150).

Other historical recordings worth hearing include Mattia Battistini's patrician Prologue (DB 239), an exciting one from Lawrence Tibbett (DB 975) and a magisterial one from Titta Ruffo (DB 464; COLH 155). Claudia Muzio is affecting and arresting in 'Stridono lassù' (Pathé 10346), and Gigli (DB 3158) and Björling (the 1944 performance on DB 6163) are their attractive selves in 'Vesti la giubba'. Not only because I was for a time his pupil, I have a fondness for this aria sung in English by Browning Mummery (C 2662 sounds better and is a more confident performance than C 1330). He betrays his Australian origin only when he sings 'laugh Punch-uh-nello'. There are strong versions of 'No, Pagliaccio non son' and 'Vesti la giubba' by the metallic-voiced Martinelli (DB 1139; CDN 1016) and an interesting oddity is Gigli's Prologue, recorded in Berlin in 1943, his style less tearful than usual now that he is posing as a baritone!

Two years before his participation in the 1929 complete recording, Valente recorded an exciting, overwrought 'Vesti la giubba' (C 1387; LV 236). Aureliano Pertile, Toscanini's tenor, recorded both Canio's pieces with impressive ardour but bumpy phrasing (DB 1118; LV 245). Nicola Zerola, an admired Otello, has left curiously routine performances of Canio's music.

Here are a few more of the more attractive (or more unusual) versions of the most popular excerpts:

Prologue ('Si puo')

Galeffi in a way is typical of the excellent Italian baritone who can sing this kind of music in his sleep; but he is one of the best of his kind, and his version stays in the memory (GQ 7043; LV 220). The freely produced and much admired baritone of Riccardo Stracciari is equally memorable (Col. 7355; LV 136), and I also like Inghilleri for his dramatic presence (D 2051), and Pasquale Amato for his robust vocal quality (DB 156; CD

346). Renato Zanelli, who became a tenor and was a near ideal Otello in the 1920s and 1930s, began his career as a baritone and recorded the Prologue in 1919 (DA 398): a performance glowing with vocal splendour and fine musicianship, as well as a certain self-restraint, for he does not interpolate an unwanted high note as most baritones do.

Modern versions include perfectly acceptable performances by Leonard Warren, Merrill and Rolando Panerai, an interesting one from Geraint Evans (SXL 6262) and a superb one by Tito Gobbi in 1948 (DB 6822; HLM 7018). My own record library is overstocked with German-language singers from whom I will this time press upon the reader only the metallic voice but great presence of Josef Herrmann, a Berlin wartime recording (DB 7700; LV 49), Schlusnus, both mellifluous and dramatic, with perfect diction (recorded c.1921, reissued on Heliodor's 'Berlin damals', a two-disc LP album: 2700 708), and Hans Hotter (DG 67854). Georges Baklanoff, in Italian, should not be overlooked, for a beautifully sung, dramatic account of the Prologue (052424) recorded in 1913. Also worth mentioning are the current Swedish charmer, Håkan Hagegård (Caprice CAP 1062), and two stalwart performances in English by Dennis Noble (C 3141) and Peter Dawson (C 1259; HQM 1217).

'Un tal gioco'

Several of the tenors I mention below under 'Vesti la giubba' have also left noteworthy accounts of 'Un tal gioco', among them Vickers, Thill, Pattiera and Grosavescu. I am especially fond of Pattiera's lively, dramatic performance (Poly. 66627; LV 61).

Nedda's Ballatella, 'Stridono Lassu'

Xenia Belmas makes a strong impression (Poly. 67001), as she does too in the Nedda-Silvio scene with Willi Domgraf-Fassbaender (66847; LV 41). There are also: an attractive German version by Gitta Alpar (Homocord 4–9903), a dramatically improbable but stunningly musical performance from Joan Sutherland (SET 247), and a very well sung performance in Italian by Joan Hammond (C 3725). The Nedda–Silvio duet ('E allor perchè') is also winningly done by Hina Spani and Apollo Granforte (HMV DB 1046; LV 147), and there are versions not without interest by Salvatini-Schlusnus and Albanese-Merrill.

'Vesti la guibba'

This, of course, has been recorded by practically every tenor. Among those not yet mentioned but by no means to be dismissed are Lauri-Volpi, Piccaver, Melchior and Pataky. I was impressed by Michele Fleta's reflective, intelligent clown (DB 1034), and by Richard Tucker (LX 1545), as good as Caruso. I have listened, with varying degrees of pleasure, to Grosavescu, Carl Günther, Richard Schubert, Marcel Wittrisch, Melchior, Josef Mann (impressive, in Polish: Od. Lxx 80922; LV 74), Hislop, Rudolf Laubenthal, Josef Kalenberg, Franz Völker, Fritz Soot and Joseph Schwarz. I have a soft spot for Georges Thill in French, (Pauvre Paillasse' Col. D 1609; LV 224), for I saw him as Canio at the Opéra-Comique in 1953 and thought him superb (having heard him some years earlier sing off pitch the entire evening). Parry Jones, in English, is well worth hearing (WA 5711; RLS 707). He sang the aria, pseudonymously, as Roland Oliver!

Among more recent performers, I am tolerant of Mario Lanza (DA 1983), have enjoyed Björling's post-war 78 (DB 21602), Charles Craig (CLP 1271), Jan Peerce (SGL 5853) and Placido Domingo (SET 5613). I thought Harry Secombe (Philips PB 523) superior to James McCracken (SXL 6201), and consider Jon Vickers (SB 6577) as fine as any of the legendary stars of the past.

Two postscripts: among the recorded versions of Harlequin's Serenade, sung by Beppe in the opera, I must mention the classic Tito Schipa (DA 875), and Heddle Nash (in English, with Joan Hammond singing Nedda: C 3924; HQM 1089).

In the British film version of *Pagliacci* directed by Tauber (1936), which I saw at the National Film Theatre not long ago, the great tenor appropriated most of the other characters' music as well as Canio's, and I have a recording of the sound-track to prove it. Nedda, Silvio, Canio's Prologue (of course), Beppe, even the chorus, Tauber unashamedly gobbled up their music in the film and also recorded much of it for Parlophone at the time, in English. His English language 'On with the Motley', in fact, is moving. He had earlier made a German version of the Prologue, which is a characteristic piece of Tauber *chutzpah* (RO 20161).

CAVALLERIA RUSTICANA

S Santuzza; *L* Lola; *T* Turiddu; *A* Alfio; *Luc* Mamma Lucia

1916 Ermolli *S*; Rabelli *L*; *Luc*;
Tumminello *T*; Perna *A*/La Scala
Chorus and Orch./Sabajno
HMV S5092–5105

1927 (in English) Blyth *S*; Parry *L*;
Nash *T*; Williams *A*; Griffiths
Luc/British National Opera
Company Chorus and
Orch./Buesst
Columbia 5127–36

1929 Sanzio *S*; Pantaleoni *L*;
Breviario *T*; Biasini *A*; de
Franco *Luc*/La Scala Chorus and
Orch./Sabajno
HMV C1973–81; RCA (US) VM
98

1930 Arangi-Lombardi *S*; Castagna *L*;
Melandri *T*; Lulli *A*; Mannarini
Luc/La Scala Chorus and
Orch./Molajoli

Columbia D14623–32

1940 Bruna Rasa S; Marcucci L; Gigli
T; Bechi A; Simionato Luc/La
Scala Chorus and
Orch./Mascagni
HMV ⓜ ALP1610–2; Seraphim
ⓜ IB6008

1943 (in German) Scheppan S; Beilke
L; Hopf T; Hann A; Waldenau
Luc/German Opera Chorus,
Berlin Radio Orch./Rother
DG ⓜ LPEM 19247–9

1952 Simionato S; Cadoni L; Braschi
T; Tagliabue A; Pellegrino
Luc/Turin Radio Chorus and
Orch./Basile
Cetra ⓒ LPS 3238 ④MC 126

1952 Petrova S; Benucci L; Ruhl T;
Petrov A; Malani Luc/Florence
Festival Chorus and
Orch./Ghiglia
Remington ⓜ 199–74

1953 Milanov S; Smith L; Björling T;
Merrill A; Roggero Luc/Shaw
Chorale, RCA Victor
Orch./Cellini
RCA ⓒ VICS 6044

1953 Nicolai S; Didier L; del
Monaco T; Protti A; Anelli
Luc/Milan Chorus and
Orch./Ghione
Decca ⓜ ACL 199–201;
Richmond ⓜ RS 62008 or RS
63006

1953 Callas S; Canali L; di Stefano
T; Panerai A; Ticozzi Luc/La
Scala Chorus and Orch./Serafin
EMI ⓒ SLS 819 ④TC–SLS
819; Angel ⓜ 3528CL

1953 Harshaw S; Miller L; Tucker T;
Guerrera A; Votipka
Luc/Metropolitan Opera Chorus
and Orch./Cleva
CBS ⓜ 61640 ④40–61640; CBS
(US) ⓜ Y3–33122

1954 Apolai S; Geri L; Spruzzola T;
Campolonghi A; del Ol
Luc/Fenice Theatre Chorus and
Orch./Sebastien
Remington ⓜ 199–175

1955 (live performance, La Scala,
Milan) Simionato S; di Stefano
T; Guelfi A/La Scala Chorus
and Orch./Votto

Cetra ⓜ LO 15/2

1958 Tebaldi S; Danieli L; Björling
T; Bastianini A; Corsi
Luc/Florence Festival Chorus
and Orch./Erede
Decca GOS634–5; London OSA
12101

1958 Zanelli S; Castro L; Visetti T;
Campo A; Ferrari Luc/Chorus,
Lombard Promenade Orch./Falco
Period X–110

1959 Mancini S; Lazzarini L; Poggi T;
Protti A; Cattelani Luc/San
Carlo Chorus and Orch./Rapalò
Philips SFL 14002–3

1960 Simionato S; Satre L; del
Monaco T; MacNeil A; di
Stasio Luc/Santa Cecilia
Academy Chorus and
Orch./Serafin
Decca GOS558–9; London OSA
1213

1962 de los Angeles S; Lazzarini L;
Corelli T; Sereni A; Vozza
Luc/Rome Opera Chorus and
Orch./Santini
EMI SLS 903; Angel SBL 3632

1965 Cossotto S; Martino L; Bergonzi
T; Guelfi A; Allegri Luc/La
Scala Chorus and Orch./Karajan
DG 2709 020 ④3371 011

1966 (in German) Hillebrecht S;
Jasper L; Schock T; Wächter
A; Oelke Luc/German Opera
Chorus and Orch./Hollreiser
Ariola S72245XR

1967 Souliotis S; Malagù L; del
Monaco T; Gobbi A; di Stasio
Luc/Rome Opera Chorus and
Orch./Varviso
Decca SET 343–4; London OSA
1266

1967 (in Hungarian) Dunszt S; László
L; Simandy T; Radnai A;
Barlay Luc/Hungarian State
Opera Chorus and Orch./Lukács
Qualiton SLPX 1195–7

1976 Varady S; Gonzales L; Pavarotti
T; Cappuccilli A; Bormida
Luc/London Opera Chorus,
National PO/Gavazzeni
Decca D83D3 ④ K83K33;
London OSAD 13125

1978 Scotto S; I. Jones L; Domingo

T; Elvira A; Kraft
Luc/Ambrosian Opera Chorus,
National PO/Levine
RCA (awaiting release)

Excerpts

1933 (in French) Cernay S; Hena L;
Micheletti T; Endrèze A; Arty
Luc/Paris Opéra-Comique Chorus
and Orch./Cloëz
Odeon ⓜ ODX 120
1952 Schech S; Fehenberger T; Pease
A/Munich State Opera Chorus,
Wurttemberg State Opera
Chorus and Orch./Leitner
DG ⓜ LPEM 19011 (in
German); DG ⓜ LPE 17009 (in
Italian)
1954 Ruggieri S; Da Costa T;
Valentino A/Orch./Walther plus

Mascagni (pno)
Royale ⓜ 1581
1959 (in French) T'Hézan S; Delouret
L; Chauvet T; Bianco A; Notti
Luc/Orch./Etcheverry
Véga 16123
1960 (in German) Rysanek S; Schock
T; Metternich A/St Hedwig's
Cathedral Choir, German Opera
Chorus and Orch./Schüchter
EMI 1C 063 28999
1961 (in German) Davy S; Nagano L;
Kónya T; Berry A/German
Opera Chorus and Orch./Kulka
DG SLPEM 136413
1963 (in German) Wenglor S;
Siemeling L; Wunderlich T;
Niese A; Stroka Luc/Gunther
Arndt Choir, German Opera
Orch./R. Kraus
Ariola-Eurodisc Z75881R

I PAGLIACCI

N Nedda; C Canio; B Beppe; T Tonio; S Silvio

1907 Huguet N; Paoli; Barbaini C; G.
Pini-Corsi B; Cigada T; Badini
S/La Scala Chorus and
Orch./Sabajno
G&T 052164–5; 052168;
054153–6; 054158
HMV D319–23; DA 415; DB
469; E128, 135
1917 Conti N; Bolis C; Prat B;
Montanelli T; Badini S/La Scala
Chorus and Orch./Sabajno
HMV S10091–9
1927 (in English) Licette N; Mullings
C; Nash B; Williams T; Noble
S/British National Opera
Company Chorus and
Orch./Goossens Snr
Columbia 4347–58
1929 Saraceni N; Valente C; Palai B;
Granforte T; Basi S/La Scala
Chorus and Orch./Sabajno
HMV C1827–37
1930 Pampanini N; Merli C; Nessi B;
Galeffi T; Vanelli S/La Scala
Chorus and Orch./Molajoli
EMI ⓜ 3C 165 17998–9M
1934 Pacetti N; Gigli C; Nessi B;

Basiola T; Paci S/La Scala
Chorus and Orch./Ghione
World Records ⓜ OC215–6;
Seraphim ⓜ IB 6009
1943 (in German) Scheppan N;
Roswaenge C; Wessely B; Hann
T; Schmitt-Walter S/Berlin Radio
Chorus and SO/Rother
DG ⓜ LPEM 19247–9
1950 Malagrida N; Poggi C;
Castannoli B; Bersellini T;
Lamacchia S/Comunale Theatre
Chorus, Bologna; San Remo
PO/Gavarini
Cetra ⓜ LPC 1271
1951 Amara N; Tucker C; Hayward
B; Valdengo T; Harvout
S/Metropolitan Opera Chorus
and Orch./Cleva
CBS (UK) ⓜ 61658
④ 40–61658; (US) ⓜ Y3–33122
1952 Gavazzi N; Bergonzi C; di
Tommaso B; Tagliabue T; Rossi
S/Turin Radio Chorus and
Orch./Simonetto
Cetra ⓒ LPS 3227 ④ MC 131
1952 La Pollo N; Sarri C; Donato B;

Petrov T/Florence Festival
Chorus and Orch./Ghiglia
Royale ⓜ 1520–1
1953 Petrella N; del Monaco C; de
Palma B; Poli T; Protti S/Santa
Cecilia Academy Chorus and
Orch./Erede
(NB Protti sings the Prologue)
Decca ⓜ ACL201–2; Richmond
ⓜ RS 62009 or RS 63003
1954 de los Angeles N; Björling C;
Franke B; Warren T; Merrill
S/Shaw Chorale, RCA Victor
Orch./Cellini
HMV ⓜ ALP 1126–8
Seraphim ⓜ IB 6058
1954 Callas N; di Stefano C; Monti
B; Gobbi T; Panerai S/La Scala
Chorus and Orch./Serafin
HMV ⓒ SLS 819 ④TC–SLS
819; Angel ⓜ 3528CL
1960 (in German) Müszely N; Schock
C; Schmidt B; Metternich T;
Cordes S/German Opera Chorus
and Orch., Berlin/Stein
EMI STE 80501–2S
1960 Beltrami N; Poggi C; Nobile B;
Protti T; Monachesi S/San Carlo
Opera Chorus and Orch./Rapalò
Philips SFL 14002–4
1960 Tucci N; del Monaco C; de
Palma B; MacNeil T; Capecchi
S/Santa Cecilia Academy Chorus
and Orch./Molinari-Pradelli
Decca GOS 588–90; London
OSA 1212
1961 Amara N; Corelli C; Spina B;
Gobbi T; Zanasi S/La Scala
Chorus and Orch./Matačić
Columbia SAX 2399–2400; Angel
SBL 3618
1961 (in Russian) Iakovenka N;
Uzunov C; Pistkaev B;
Zachanov T; Lisitsian S/Moscow
Radio Chorus, Moscow
PO/Samosud
MK ⓜ DO 3090–3
1961 (in French) Castelli N; Finel C;
Corazza B; Dens T; Cales
S/Paris Opéra-Comique Chorus
and Orch./Dervaux
EMI ASTX 130527–8
1964 (in Hungarian) Orosz N;
Símandy C; Réti B; Radnai T;

Palócz S/Hungarian State Opera
Chorus and Orch./Komor
Qualiton SLPX 1195–7
1965 Carlyle N; Bergonzi C; Benelli
B; Taddei T; Panerai S/La Scala
Chorus and Orch./Karajan
DG 2709 020 ④3371 011
1967 Lorengar N; McCracken C;
Benelli B; Merrill T; Krause
S/Santa Cecilia Academy Chorus
and Orch./Gardelli
Decca SET 403–4; London OSA
1280
1972 Caballé N; Domingo C; Goeke
B; Milnes T; McDaniel S/Alldis
Choir, LSO/Santi
RCA (UK) SER 5635–6 ④RK
40003; (US) LSC 7090
1976 Freni N; Pavarotti C; Bello B;
Wixell T; Saccomani S/London
Voices, Finchley Children's
Music Group, National
PO/Patané
Decca D83D3 ④K83K33;
London OSAD 13125

Excerpts

1940 Steber N; Carron C; Bontempil
B; Warren T; Cehanovsky
S/Chorus, Publishers Service
SO/Pelletier
RCA (US) ⓜ CAL 226
1953 (in German) Schlemm N;
Anders C; Wächter T; Winters
S/Wurttemberg State Opera
Chorus and Orch./various
conductors
DG ⓜ LPEM 19199
1955 Bonelli N; Martinelli C; Leone
B; Valentino T/Orch./Walther
Royale ⓜ 1614
(NB *WERM*, vol. 3, states: 'said
to contain Martinelli's
unpublished 1929 recording of
Vesti la giubba and a 1955
recording of *Un tal gioco*'.)
1957 (in German) Rothenberger N;
Traxel C; Metternich T; Prey
S/German Opera Chorus, Berlin
SO/Schüchter
EMI 1C 047 28571
1961 (in German) Hollweg N; Kónya
C; Wächter T/Orch.
DG SLPHM 237150

1962 (in German) Schlemm *N*; Kónya
     C; Grobe *B*; Berry *T*;
     Winkenstern *S*/German Opera
     Chorus, Berlin Radio SO/Kulka
     DG SLPEM 136413
1963 (in French) Boué *N*; Poncet *C*;
     Giannotti *B*; Legros *T*; Gui
     S/SO/Etchéverry
     Philips 837 497 GY
1963 (in Russian and Italian)

Maslennikova *N*; del Monaco
C; Vespov *B*; Ivanov *T*/Bolshoi
Theatre Chorus and
Orch./Tiesovkini
Everest © 3190E
1965 (in German) Losch *N*; Kónya C;
     Vantin *B*; Brauer *T*; Niese
     S/German Opera Chorus and
     Orch./R. Kraus
     Ariola-Eurodisc Z75881R

Salome and Elektra

ALAN JEFFERSON

SALOME

Richard Strauss's *Salome*, like many works for the stage, loses a major part of its effect when it is heard without being seen. When you *have* seen it, and can make your own mental picture of an ideal décor and ideal cast, then a recorded performance can be most enjoyable. Some of the visual detail is difficult to bring off in the theatre: how are we to find Strauss's ideal Salome for a start? The composer has firmly described the essential requisite: a 'sixteen-year-old Princess with the voice of an Isolde', and Strauss admitted that he was asking the impossible. A soprano with the right size and quality of voice, yet a voice that must not sound too mature, used at one time to exist in fat old frumps. Today we would not tolerate them on the stage. Yet the casting of Salome herself matters most of all in whatever medium she is heard.

Under consideration are eight commercially issued complete sets (each of two records) and five private recordings. In addition to excerpt records from commercial sets, and another wrongly purporting to have been conducted by the composer, Salome's Dance has figured as a concert item with twenty-seven LP versions, nine of which were dubbings from 78s.

When we agree that *Salome* on record may give us pleasure, the rider has to be added: not in short fragments. Strauss's music flows expansively, and breaks are destructive. Consequently it is very much an LP opera. However, in the old days, even going back to 1907, the first year of any Strauss operatic recordings, no fewer than five singers recorded snippets on single-sided ten-inch 78s. They were Rudolf Berger (Od. 50321; 51176), Baptist Hoffmann (3–42712 & 42711) and Friedrich Brodersen (Beka 6877), all as Jokanaan. Emmy Destinn sang two brief and contradictory snatches (43874/5; Rococo 5217), remarkable for being with orchestral accompaniment and for the conductor, Bruno Seidler-Winkler, being named. In addition Ernst Kraus, the first Berlin Herod, sings two injunctions to Salome after the Dance (3–42709–10), clear and beautiful singing, though with piano accompaniment. Destinn is the only early Salome to have recorded, so she is worth noting in a little detail. Her first entry (fig. 91) on 'Jokanaan, ich bin verliebt in deinen Leib' is on an F sharp at the top of the stave that grows out through a huge orchestral chord. It is glorious, perfectly placed and glowing with expressive yearning. But her intonation goes off at the end, the last note being almost a semitone flat, the sound pinched. The other side starts (fig. 110) just before her words 'Dein Haar ist grässlich' and goes to the end of the solo passage. Here again the words are sometimes poorly enunciated, top notes are pinched, but the whole is alive with longing and a masterly range of vocal colours. Since Destinn was the Berlin creator of Salome, we must be grateful for an opportunity thus to know something of how the three principals sounded to the Kaiser and to his Kaiserin, who did her best to prevent the opera's production there. The sounds that come from them to us on these old records are the nearest we shall get to the première of the opera in Dresden a few months earlier.

In 1924, the Swedish soprano Göta Ljungberg sang Salome at Covent Garden and then made her first (tentative) version of the final scene with a whacking great cut at the turnover. This was one of three records from the opera which Albert Coates conducted for HMV (D 908–910). Five years later, Ljungberg again recorded a cut final scene, this time in Berlin under Leo Blech (D 1699; LV 176), which showed her to be in full command of the passages.

The last singer of a past age on 78s is Marjorie Lawrence who curiously sings an uncut final scene in French (DB 4933–4; LV 133). The translation necessitates considerable distortion of the vocal line but the erotic mumblings at the end go very well in French and Miss Lawrence sings superbly. There is no Herodias or Herod.

Final scenes have been dominated by Ljuba Welitsch ever since this glorious, red-headed, Bulgarian ball of fire sang the whole role in performance under Strauss's baton at his seventieth birthday celebrations. That was in 1944 in Vienna, when she was only 21. Five years later she recorded the final scene in the studio as a solo *tour de force*, with Fritz Reiner and the Metropolitan Opera Orchestra (LX 1241–2; CBS 61088) and it was long considered to be without parallel.

However, in 1972, HMV issued HLM 7006, a Welitsch recital, (now on WRC SH 289), and it included a hitherto unknown final scene, live from a concert performance in Vienna in the autumn of 1944. Lovro von Matačič and the Vienna Radio Orchestra accompany her. It gives a wonderful impression of Welitsch's youthfulness, strength and musicianship – perhaps the nearest any soprano has got to Strauss's impossible demand for the ideal Salome sound. Her voice sears and soars above the orchestra, tinged with not a little childish innocence to start with; but the way in which she fondles and cuddles the severed head dispels any possibility of innocence. She sings close to the microphone so that every breath and gasp is audible, guaranteed to produce a lively response from any listener even though he be a monk.

Yet another final scene (or most of it) turned up unexpectedly in 1978. This was the fabled, 'lost' recording made by Walter Legge, Karajan, the Vienna Philharmonic, Ljuba Welitsch and two other singers in November 1948. The sessions went well, everybody was delighted with the results, and an especially comfortable effect was achieved by spreading the scene over five 78 sides instead of the usual four. It was absolutely complete, including the voices of Herodias (Gertrud Schuster) and of Herod (Josef Witt). But on the flight back from Vienna to London, the master of side two was irreparably damaged. The remaining masters, including an orchestral side of the Descent into the Cistern, were put into storage and left there.

In the autumn of 1978, World Records wisely decided that this flawed masterpiece was too good to leave abandoned for ever, and they issued it (SH 286) in spite of its missing side. A moment's silence (as in reverence) is a small price to pay. (The cut is from four bars after fig. 324 to three before fig. 339.) What has been preserved and issued at last is a beautiful piece of singing and orchestral playing supported by a magnificent balance and cunning engineering. Yet it is a stiffer performance than the live one, perhaps it is almost too perfect, and it lacks to a marked degree the vivid eroticism of the 1944 performance.

Welitsch also appears as Salome in two pirated sets from the Metropolitan: the first in March 1949 with good voice, and with Herbert Janssen as Jokanaan. However, as issued this is not the complete stage performance, and chunks from elsewhere (mainly commercial recordings) have been 'patched in'. The second Met *Salome*, also conducted by Fritz Reiner, dates from January 1952 when Welitsch's voice was beginning to fray, but she has the support of Hans Hotter as an incomparable Jokanaan.

When the Vienna State Opera brought Welitsch to London for the first time in 1947, she shared the role of Salome on the stage with Maria Cebotari. Hers was a very different voice, much lighter; she also recorded the final scene in 1941 (Heliodor 88030). Cebotari's approach to the scene is thoroughly convincing and most musical, though less highly coloured and incandescent than Welitsch's. Arthur Rother must be held responsible for the weirdly un-Straussian orchestral ending.

The first commercial *Salome* on LP was recorded in 1950 and released at the end of that year. Joseph Keilberth conducted the Dresden State Orchestra and had Christel Goltz as Salome, Josef Herrmann as Jokanaan and Bernd Aldenhoff as Herod. Goltz was the reigning Salome after Welitsch. Her interpretation was crude, while her goings-on with the head had to be seen to be believed. She features in four sets of which one, from a 1953 Met performance under Mitropoulos is pirated.

Walburga Wegner with the Vienna Symphony Orchestra under Rudolf Moralt gives a creditable performance, recorded in 1952. Her voice is ardent and steady and some of her qualities recall Welitsch. Josef

Metternich as Jokanaan and Georgine von Milinkovič as a well-characterized Herodias are supported by ranking singers like Walter Berry as the First Soldier and Second Nazarene, Oskar Czerwenka as the Cappadocian and First Nazarene and Waldemar Kmentt as Narraboth.

Decca retaliated in 1954 with an excellent recording in the true Vienna style under Clemens Krauss with Goltz as Salome, Patzak as Herod (superbly characterized) and Anton Dermota as Narraboth. Again the smaller parts were taken by seasoned singers: Ludwig Weber as the First Nazarene, and Berry as the Second Soldier. This was issued at a time when the commercial recordings of *Salome* were restricted to only two for a period of eight years.

A private issue of 1955 brought a starry *Salome* cast from the Met to those lucky (or clever) enough to know how to get hold of such records when they were regarded with a good deal of suspicion. This time Goltz had Paul Schöffler as Jokanaan, Ramon Vinay as Herod and Blanche Thebom as Herodias. James McCracken (then little known) was the Second Jew and Nicola Moscona the First Nazarene. Nothing to complain about over casting, but like most recordings taken on the spot, it lacked definition, and the voices were not always in focus.

In the spring of 1962, Goltz faced her main opponent when Birgit Nilsson's recording for Decca was released. The 'Sonicstage' technique developed by Decca was used to great advantage by the producer, John Culshaw. There is a greater range of colour and separation in the stereo than before, while Nilsson's supporting artists are of high calibre. Eberhard Wächter sings Jokanaan, Waldemar Kmentt (again) Narraboth, and Gerhard Stolze and Grace Hoffman are the two odious parents.

The next two sets are less than satisfactory. The RCA has Montserrat Caballé as Salome, James King as Narraboth and the remainder of the cast recruited in London, among whom is Richard Lewis as a fine, frenetic Herod; but the whole concept of this production seems wrong. The supporting cast is in no way as impressive as others had been, Leinsdorf's direction is idiosyncratic, and Caballé's bell-like voice does not disguise the fact that she sounds the width of the Mediterranean away from the true character of a Middle-Eastern princess.

Then came the much vaunted DG production from 'takes' at the rehearsals and several performances in November 1970 at the Hamburg State Opera. As the first, commercial live, *Salome* it fails to take advantage of any audience excitement or tension and has to make do with inadequate microphone placings. Gwyneth Jones is a squally and ugly Salome; Fischer-Dieskau fails to find any point of contact with Jokanaan. Richard Cassilly puts across all the nastiness of Herod, but the real hero of this lost cause is the conductor, Karl Böhm, who gives a grand and magisterial reading of the complex score which he clarifies to the extent of allowing us to hear the Jews' quarrel scene perfectly in every detail.

Astrid Varnay used to sing Salome in the 1950s, in what seemed a staid manner after Welitsch and Goltz, but nevertheless with vocal distinction. She is the Salome in a 'private' issue from Munich in June 1953. Hans Hermann Nissen is a dark, serious Jokanaan, Patzak gives his stylish performance as Herod, and that fine mezzo Margarete Klose, sings Herodias. Hans Hopf's Narraboth is distinguished by its strength rather than its passion. The conductor is Varnay's husband, Hermann Weigert.

Another private performance exists of such splendour, imperfection, irritation and frustration that it must be mentioned. In March 1934, Arthur Bodansky conducted a cast at the Metropolitan which had Ljungberg as Salome, Friedrich Schorr as Jokanaan, Max Lorenz as Herod and Emanuel List as the First Nazarene. About every four minutes, ten seconds elapse while the acetate discs were being changed on the single recording machine owned, it is said, by a New York dentist. Those acetates suffered horribly before being transferred to LP, and the result is a mush of sound, often so thick as to obscure all music. Then suddenly, and for a few seconds only, like clouds moving away from the sun, all is clear and glorious, and one gets a flash of an idea what this performance must have been like. But in general it cannot be regarded as a cogent interpretation of Strauss's *Salome*.

The excellent Dresden Staatskapelle under Otmar Suitner accompanied a fine cast for *Salome* in 1963. Goltz sings her last Salome on record, with Ernst Gutstein as a noble Jokanaan, Helmut Melchert and Siw Eriksdotter as a magnificent Herod and Herodias, and Theo Adam as a stalwart First Nazarene.

In the most recent set, Karajan conducts the Vienna Philharmonic in a performance that differs considerably from the same orchestra's performance under Solti. The 'clean' Decca set still possesses considerable merit, and in many ways does not rival Karajan's. Here we have a less intense, more fateful interpretation in which disaster, presaged from the very start, sweeps through the four sides to its preordained conclusion. Hildegard Behrens is almost perfect as Salome: it is a stunning achievement, and the supporting cast is as excellent. José van Dam manages to extract more than C major sympathy from Jokanaan, Karl-Walter Böhm and Agnes Baltsa are a properly dreadful pair of decadents as Herod and Herodias. Wieslaw Ochman's Narraboth is a joy to hear as well as the perfect voice to open the opera. This set is spoilt only by the tentative First Nazarene of Jules Bastin.

Generally speaking, excerpt discs all produce the same selection of highlights: opening of the opera, part (at least) of the dialogue between Salome and Jokanaan, the Dance, Herod's ecstasy and the final scene. But in the case of single discs it boils down to the Dance and final scene always. Inge Borkh, who often sang Salome on the stage but never recorded it in full, made a final scene in 1956 for RCA (VICS 1392) with the Chicago Orchestra under Fritz Reiner. It is well done, well thought-out, but a little on the mature side. The British singer, Margaret Tynes, makes a straight-laced Salome with the Budapest Philharmonic under Pal Varga (Qualiton SLPX 1074).

In 1966, a single disc of Leontyne Price included the Dance (when one had to imagine her) and the final scene in which the Boston Symphony Orchestra under Erich Leinsdorf seemed to be playing down to her (SB 6639). She failed to get under the skin of the part.

Then in 1974 there appeared an extended final scene, beginning with the impatient girl waiting for the head to be cut and served. Anja Silja had a success on stage in Wieland Wagner's production of the opera in Stuttgart, but the recording yields little evidence of her ability (SXL 6657). Her voice sounds small and it lacks quality at the top. Youth is in it, to be sure, but in passages where Strauss advances into atonality, Miss Silja is adrift.

ELEKTRA

The gramophone companies have, in general, treated *Elektra* skimpily, compared with *Salome*, her elder sister and rival in horror. The two current commercial recordings in Britain and the USA date from 1960 and 1967 respectively, while the only other one, long since deleted in Britain, was from a performance in 1950.

The opera is so constructed that it has only two 'arias' – even if one can call them that – one for Elektra and the other for her sister, Chrysothemis. There is also the terrifying duet between Elektra and Clytemnestra, and the extended Recognition scene for Elektra and Orestes that can be lifted out of the whole from the point of view of separate items.

The programme of the first performance of the opera at Covent Garden in 1910 carries an advertisement by the Gramophone Company listing four single-sided twelve-inch records of scenes, sung by Miss Perceval Allen and Mr Frederic Austin. They both appeared in that 1910 Beecham season in London: she in other operas, and Frederic Austin in the last two performances as Orestes. But Perceval Allen never sang Elektra in Britain. The four records are 'Allein! Weh, ganz allein' (043118); 'Ich kann nicht sitzen', as Chrysothemis (043117; and 044112 and 043119) in the climax of the Recognition scene, the first side of which is with Austin. Allen's voice is full, perfectly pitched and controlled, and she expresses great feeling. Austin, a lightish baritone for Orestes, has an urgent, impulsive thrust behind his singing which is right.

Thila Plaichinger, the Berlin creator of Elektra in 1907, made two ten-inch records of part of the Recognition scene with Baptist Hoffmann as Orestes; one is a Hill-and-Dale Pathé (15729), the other an International Record Collectors' Club dubbing (IRCC 3032) with poor reproduction of an anonymous orchestra.

Between the wars, the Hungarian dramatic soprano, Rose Pauly, was the most successful Elektra. She sang at Salzburg in 1934 and 1937, in a concert performance of the opera at Carnegie Hall in 1937 and under Beecham at Covent Garden in 1938. The Carnegie Hall concert with the New York Philharmonic under Arthur Rodzinski on 16 March 1937 has alone been preserved, but its preservation is restricted to the Elektra scenes, fortunately. Pauly's voice is at its very best, and when she sang the role at Covent Gardent, it was said to be 'the performance of a lifetime' (Ernest Newman). Three sides of a pirated issue allow us to hear Pauly in blazing voice, fully substantiating Newman's opinion. The rest of the cast is less happy. Julius Huehn sings Orestes and Enid Szantho Clytemnestra. Frederick Jagel has his moment as Aegisthus. It is a most valuable document but, of course, with dated sound. The voices are clear enough but the orchestral parts need considerable filtering to give any warmth.

Towards the end of the 78 era, RCA Victor instructed their British colleagues, HMV, to record the final scene of *Elektra* which Sir Thomas Beecham was preparing for two BBC broadcasts in connection with his 1947 Richard Strauss Festival in London. Strauss was there, in the studio at Maida Vale, for both of them. HMV afterwards recorded separately the whole Recognition Scene and finale in their own Abbey Road studios (DB 9394–6; RCA RL 42821). This contains two cuts, but is in good sound and the voices are of exceptional quality: Erna Schlüter as Elektra, Walter Widdop as Aegisthus, Ljuba Welitsch as Chrysothemis, Elisabeth Höngen as Clytemnestra and Paul Schöffler as Orestes. The last three singers were borrowed from the visiting Vienna State Opera. The Royal Philharmonic Orchestra was conducted exclusively by Beecham, while his assistant conductor, Norman del Mar, stood beside him, conducting the singers. Beecham had no time to spend on them, and in any case expected them to know their roles and to follow him. This they were not altogether able to do with inadequate rehearsal, hence the two conductors!

Nevertheless, the broadcast performances (recently repeated from the archives) were recorded privately and 'complete' without the small cuts made at the commercial recording, but the sound is thick and muddy for its age although it has immense gusto. Another *Elektra* from a Carnegie Hall concert of 1949 has twice been issued privately. This has Astrid Varnay as Elektra, Herbert Janssen as Orestes and the conductor is Mitropoulos.

Two years later Varnay performed Elektra again, at the Metropolitan under Reiner, a great Strauss conductor. Although she struck one as cool and a faintly implausible Elektra on the stage, Varnay nevertheless got round the vocal side of this strenuous part without much difficulty, which is almost all that matters on records. Here she had Schöffler as Orestes, Höngen as Clytemnestra and Set Svanholm as an excellent Aegisthus.

A third private issue with Varnay comes from a Salzburg performance under Karajan in 1964 and shows her still well able to cope, though with some of the former brilliance a little diminished. Eberhard Wächter is Orestes, Martha Mödl is Clytemnestra and James King the Aegisthus; it is a truly festival performance and in far better sound than Varnay's other recordings. Although she performed Elektra over these years in New York, Salzburg and elsewhere, she never made a commercial recording of the opera.

In August 1957, Inge Borkh sang Elektra at Salzburg under Mitropoulos, with a strong cast; Kurt Böhme, Jean Madeira and Max Lorenz, with Lisa Della Casa as Chrysothemis, Kerstin Meyer and Marilyn Horne among the Maids. The sound on this pirated issue is pretty fair for its age and the voices come over extremely well. Böhm chose Borkh when he made the DG *Elektra* in 1960, for a while the only commercial version available. Fischer-Dieskau gives a most interesting portrayal of Orestes. Borkh is an impassioned Elektra, Madeira a marvellously vivid, accurate Clytemnestra, Marianne Schech an involved Chrysothemis. Böhm's cuts are distressing.

This *Elektra* was not, however, the first commercial set to be made. It had been preceded by Cetra's version in 1950 when they recorded a performance live from the Florence Festival of that year. Hilde Konetzni seems outparted as Elektra and in spite of the presence of Mödl (Clytemnestra) and Hans Braun (Orestes), it cannot be recommended. It has poor sound and little feeling.

In 1952, Georg Solti made one of those extended 78s, with Goltz (the reigning European Elektra and Salome) singing the first big scene, 'Allein', for DG, with the Bavarian State Opera Orchestra. It is excellent. In the following year Solti made an LP of the duet for Elektra and Clytemnestra with Goltz and Höngen, followed by the Recognition Scene with Goltz and Ferdinand Frantz. It stopped there, but is a well-planned and well-executed disc.

In 1968 *Elektra* and Solti came together in the Decca studios with the issue of the first truly complete recording of the opera. Nilsson represented one of a new generation of Elektras, and the supporting cast had been carefully chosen for experience and authenticity. Tom Krause is a noble and powerful Orestes, Regina Resnik a suitably raddled Clytemnestra, Marie Collier a highly nervous-sounding Chrysothemis and Gerhard Stolze a fear-crazed Aegisthus.

The most recent *Elektra* (with usual cuts) issued in 1978 on Acanta DE 23.073 turns out to be the oldest, predating Beecham's by four years. Like Beecham's it has the same Elektra in Erna Schlüter, with firmer voice and even greater control. Gusta Hammer is a superb Clytemnestra, Annelies Kupper a good Chrysothemis, Peter Markwort a well-cast Aegisthus. Gustav Neidlinger makes his mark in the tiny part of Orestes's Tutor; Maria von Ilosvay leads the Maids. Nearly all the other singers' names will be unfamiliar to gramophiles as they were residents of the wartime Hamburg Opera and did not manage to achieve international status afterwards through

LP. Hammer is the most remarkable of them all. Orestes himself is extremely well taken by Robert Hager and the performance, from 1943, is said to be conducted by Hans Schmidt-Isserstedt. Research has attributed it, however, to Eugen Jochum!

Every sung line comes over remarkably cleanly and crisply with the orchestra placed somewhat behind the singers so that there is never any question of 'Louder, louder! I can still hear the singers!' (as Beecham is reputed to have commanded in 1910). But rather than emerging as an encouraging performance from Hamburg in wartime (and with all the restrictions which that entailed), it is a magnificent achievement, well worthy in artistic terms to take its place beside contemporary commercial recordings. Only once or twice is there a noticeable falling-off in sound quality, and as this is mono it cannot help sounding a bit thin; but the compelling nature of the performance soon pushes this aspect to the background. This was not a live performance – there is no audience noise or applause – there are no slamming of stage doors and so on, but whips, yes. They are in the score. Hammer acts up best, but without overdoing anything. What a pity we cannot hear her in anything else.

A Kirsten Flagstad disc (Cetra LO 513) which includes her performance of Elektra's recognition of Orestes beginning and ending with the three cries of 'Orest!'. Georges Sebastian conducts the Berlin State Opera Orchestra; the occasion was a public concert in Berlin on 9 May 1952. Although it is surprising to hear Flagstad as Elektra, for she would never have tackled the whole role, her sunny and radiant voice is totally suited to this moment in the hectic score. It is thus both interesting as a curiosity and distinguished as a beautiful piece of singing.

SALOME

S Salome; *H* Herodias; *Her* Herod; *N* Narraboth; *J* Jokanaan

1950 Goltz *S*; Karen *H*; Aldenhoff
Her; Dittrich *N*; Herrmann
J/Dresden State Opera
Orch./Keilberth
Olympic ⓒ 9101/2

1952 Wegner *S*; Von Milinkovic *H*;
Szemere *Her*; Kmentt *N*;
Metternich *J*/Vienna SO/Moralt
Philips ⓜ ABL 3003–4; CBS
(US) ⓜ SL 126

1954 Goltz *S*; Kenney *H*; Patzak *Her*;
Dermota *N*; Braun *J*/VPO/C.
Krauss
Decca ⓜ GOM 549–50;
Richmond ⓜ RS 62007

1961 Nilsson *S*; Hoffman *H*; Stolze
Her; Kmentt *N*; Wächter
J/VPO/Solti
Decca SET228–9 ④ K111K22;
London OSA 1218

1963 Goltz *S*; Eriksdotter *H*; Melchert
Her; Hoppe *N*; Gutstein
J/Dresden State Orch./Suitner
EMI STE 91320–1

1968 Caballé *S*; Resnik *H*; R. Lewis
Her; King *N*; Milnes
J/LSO/Leinsdorf
RCA (UK) SER 5582–3; (US)
LSC 7053

1970 G. Jones *S*; Dunn *H*; Cassilly

Her; Ochmann *N*; Fischer-
Dieskau *J*/Hamburg State Opera
Orch./Böhm
DG
1977 Behrens *S*; Baltsa *H*; K–W
Böhme *Her*; Ochmann *N*; Van
Dam *J*/VPO/Karajan
HMV SLS 5139 ④ TC–SLS

5139; Angel SBLX 3848

Excerpts

1953*c* Von Kovatsky *S*; Schenck *H*;
Wilhelm *Her*; Ramms *J*/Leipzig
Opera Orch./Rubahn
Allegro ⓜ ALL 3057

ELEKTRA

E Elektra *E*; *Ch* Chrysothemis; *Cl* Clytemnestra; *A* Aegisthus; *O* Orestes

1943 Schluter *E*; Kupper *Ch*; Von
Ilosvay *Cl*; Markwort *A*;
Neidlinger *O*/Hamburg State
Opera Chorus and
Orch./Jochum
Acanta ⓜ DE 23073
1950 (live performance) A. Konetzni
E; Ilitsch *Ch*; Mödl *Cl*;
Klarwein *A*; Braun *O*/Florence
Festival Chorus and
Orch./Mitropoulos
Cetra ⓜ LPO 2010; Turnabout
ⓜ THS 65040–1
1960 Borkh *E*; Schech *Ch*; Madeira
Cl; Uhl *A*; Fischer-Dieskau
O/Dresden State Opera Chorus
and State Orch./Böhm
DG 2721 187
1966–67 Nilsson *E*; Collier *Ch*; Resnik
Cl; Stolze *A*; Krause *O*/Vienna

State Opera Chorus, VPO/Solti
Decca SET 354–5 ④ 124K22;
London OSA 1269

Excerpts

1947 (Closing scene) Schluter *E*;
Welitsch *Ch*; Widdop *A*;
Schöffler *O*/Chorus,
RPO/Beecham
RCA (UK) ⓜ RL 42821; (US)
ⓜ LCT1135
1952–3 Goltz *E*; Höngen *Cl*; Frantz
O/Bavarian State Opera
Orch./Solti
DG ⓜ LPEM 19038; Decca
(US) ⓜ DL 9723
1956 Borkh *E*; Yeend *Ch*; Schöffler
O/Chicago Lyric Opera Chorus,
Chicago SO/Reiner
RCA (US) ⓜ LM 6047

Der Rosenkavalier

ALAN JEFFERSON

One does not have to look far to see why *Der Rosenkavalier*, of all Strauss's operas, has been the most frequently recorded since 1911, the year of its première in Dresden. Sometimes described as 'the greatest high-comedy in all opera', it has offered immense possibilities in both the 78 and LP eras. At the present time only one of the major recording companies is without a *Rosenkavalier* in its lists, and of current performances available, the oldest was released in 1954, the latest in 1977.

The backbone of all *Rosenkavalier* collections on 78 was the famous set of HMV's 'Selected Passages' on 13 DBs (2060–72; SH 181–2). This recording was made in five days in September 1933 in Vienna with Lotte Lehmann as the Marschallin, Elisabeth Schumann as Sophie, Maria Olszewska as Octavian and Richard Mayr as Baron Ochs. The three sopranos are in their prime; Mayr is a little past his best and gives only a 'straight' account of the seedy aristocrat, marvellous even so, in the voice that Strauss wanted all along to sing at the première. The Vienna Philharmonic Orchestra and Vienna State Opera Chorus, not to mention all the other characters, respond wonderfully, and it is only Robert Heger, the conductor, who fails to project his intentions as sharply as the cast do.

The only other set of 78 records was a smaller one, unsung, but of great historical interest. Richard Strauss came to London in 1926 to conduct an enlarged pit orchestra at the Tivoli Cinema in the Strand for a film version of the *Rosenkavalier* which departs considerably from the operatic story. He recorded seven sides of this arrangement for HMV (D 1094–7) which are most interesting, not only because the composer is conducting but also because several points of issue in interpretation (even of notes) are clearly expressed. Although the music is largely what we know from the opera score, there are transpositions and condensations, as well as one additional march, the Presentation March for Octavian's arrival at Faninal's Palace, which Strauss had previously composed for a military occasion, only one of those which the film score contains. This set was among the first electrical discs recorded in London.

Yet these were by no means the earliest *Rosenkavalier* records to be made. Eight acoustics appeared soon after the Dresden première with the three creators of the major soprano roles. The German branch of HMV (Grammophon) and Odeon each made four. They duplicated the Octavian–Sophie duet 'Mit Ihren Augen' from Act 2, the trio and the final duet. Grammophon also made the Marschallin's monologue in Act 1, 'Kann mich auch', and Odeon's distinctive contribution was a shortened version of the Presentation scene starting at 'Mir ist die Ehre'. The actual sound from the Odeon record in the final duet is preferable to that of the Grammophon, though it is a much rarer record. In the Grammophon version the celesta seems to have been placed behind the strings so that its resonance is obliterated by them, making it sound lifeless, if not somewhat comical. Unfortunately this is the version which has twice been dubbed on to LP. The excerpts from Acts 1 and 3 are on Rococo. The trio and final duet have been transferred on Acanta KB 22–179.

In 1911–12, a number of telling moments in the score were recorded in Berlin: the tenor aria by Karl Jörn (4–42527); the finale of Act 2 by Paul Knüpfer, the first Berlin Ochs (044226; CO 352), with Therese Rothauser, the first Berlin Annina; and Knüpfer again, with Elisabeth van Endert as Octavian, in the first scene of Act 3 (044227). These are all representative of the spirit of the first Berlin performance and can be heard alongside the more staid Dresden discs.

As supplements to these more substantial extracts, there are a number of separate 78s commemorating significant interpreters. Meta Seinemeyer, a notable Marschallin, recorded (in 1928) the scene where she and Octavian (Elisa Stünzner) are dismayed at hearing a man's voice outside the door (Parlo. E 110864/5; LV 114). Ochs is sung by Emanuel List. These two discs make it possible for us to appreciate what a fine Marschallin Seinemeyer must have been.

Of fifteen versions of the Italian tenor's aria on 78, there are appreciable accounts by Peter Anders (Telef. A 2321; GMA 59), Koloman von Pataky (Poly. 62603; LV 194). Herbert Ernst Groh's version (Parlo. R 1674) is disarmingly well sung. More famous than these are the performances by Tauber (Od. 0–8230; RLS 743), although I find this disappointing, and the brilliant Helge Roswaenge, a Danish-born tenor, German-trained, aping an Italian (DA 4465; E 83382). On LP there are reasonable versions by di Stefano, Traxel, Gedda, Roswaenge again (and Mario Lanza – with piano accompaniment!).

After the record of the Marschallin's monologue by the Berlin creator, Frieda Hempel (DB 373), there are worthwhile ones by Elisabeth Ohms (CA 8108; LV 159), Emmy Bettendorf (E 10341; Rococo 5376), Barbara Kemp (D 1431; LV 13) – she adds various other solo fragments – and Hilde Konetzni, whose early version (Telef. SK 3732) is to be preferred to her later Columbia (LX 1135). Several of these monologues are backed by the Marschallin's part of her extended duologue with Octavian, usually starting at 'Die Zeit, die ist ein sonderbar Ding'. The second side of the

Ohms is divided into two parts by the omission of an Octavian; nevertheless Ohms gives a most moving account of the description of stopping the clocks, singing with deep sensitivity and secure technique.

The sprightly Spanish mezzo Conchita Supervia recorded the Presentation scene and final duet with the Italian soprano Ines-Maria Ferraris, in Italian (R 20078–9; LV 150). This is something of a curiosity, but the voices blend well enough. There are also versions of the Presentation by Emmy Loose and Elisabeth Höngen, perpetuating a Vienna partnership (Telef. E 3877) and, in French, by A. Talifert and Livine Mertens. Ester Rethy and Höngen recorded the little love duet of Act 2 (DB 5617); they sound charming and youthful. Mayr did a separate version (L 2340; LV 10) of the second act's finale, conducted by Bruno Walter. Anny Andrassy is the Annina. Mayr's voice has more bloom than in the HMV extracts, and the whole performance is intoxicating. Kipnis is vocally if not histrionically imposing with Elsa Ruziczka (DB 1543; SHB 280). In a French version (Pathé PDT 83) Albert Huberty, a real bass, acts well with his voice. Versions on LP include those by Theo Adam, Mihaly Szekely, Emanuel List and Georg Hann.

There are some excellent versions of the Act 3 trio. Seinemeyer, with Stünzner and Grete Merrem-Nikisch as Sophie (E 10865; LV 114) are warm and well integrated. Ohms, Adele Kern and Elfriede Marherr (CA 8021; LV 159) sing with exceptional skill, although Ohms inexplicably omits the words, 'In Gottes Namen'. The account by Viorica Ursuleac as the Marschallin, Lemnitz as Octavian, and Erna Berger as Sophie (CA 8238; Discophilia KG U1) is marred by Krauss's slow conducting, which seriously taxes his wife Ursuleac, but the voices blend successfully and the playing of the Berlin State Opera Orchestra is a model of refinement and understanding. There is a further 78 version by the trio Konetzni–Höngen–Loose.

In the final duet Kern and Marherr (CA 80218) are respectable. There is a fine version by Berger and Lemnitz (CA 8238).

The first *Rosenkavalier* record to emanate from a public performance of the opera appeared in the same year as the Supervia records, 1928. It was the final trio from an Oper Unter den Linden performance in Berlin, then recently restored and reopened with several galas, but because some of the artists were not under contract to HMV, the record (D 1629; LV 13) had to be labelled 'anonymous soloists and conductor'. These have since been established as Barbara Kemp (Marschallin), Marion Claire (Sophie) and Delia Reinhardt (Octavian) and the conductor is Richard Lert. For many years it was known that Barbara Kemp was singing, but it was thought that the Sophie was Hedwig von Debička. Many more sides from the performance were recorded at the time, but only these two were ever issued.

The last 78s that warrant consideration are three Columbias (LX 1225–7) the first three sides of which, recorded in 1947, have a long section of the Presentation scene and *tête-à-tête* from Act 2, with Elisabeth Schwarzkopf as Sophie (which she sang at Covent Garden) and Irmgard Seefried as Octavian (which she also sang there much later). The Vienna Philharmonic Orchestra is now known to have been conducted by Herbert von Karajan, although the labels did not say so. The three other sides (of 1949) have Ludwig Weber in his incomparable portrayal of Ochs in the finale to Act 2 with Dagmar Herrmann as Annina. Otto Ackermann is the conductor. These two excerpts from the opera are characteristic of the style of the late 1940s. They are now on LP (SHB 286).

The oldest commercial LP version of *Der Rosenkavalier* is on Vox, taken from a broadcast concert performance in Munich in April 1944. Clemens Krauss conducts the Bavarian State Opera Orchestra; his wife Viorica Ursuleac sings the Marschallin gustily and with little vocal beauty; Georgine von Milinkovič is an appealing Octavian, and Adele Kern a bright-voiced, brittle Sophie. Ludwig Weber sings Ochs. There is great authenticity and 'go' in this performance which, despite its age, is still worth hearing.

The first studio recording of the opera was made at Dresden as early as 1950. A young Saxon conductor showed sufficient promise to be given the direction of it. His name was Rudolf Kempe. Margarete Bäumer was the vocally faded Marschallin, although she had once been a very good singer; Tiana Lemnitz sings the Octavian, and this is the main joy of the recording, apart from Kempe's direction and the playing of the Saxon State Opera. The relatively young Kurt Böhme sings Ochs with relish, although it is, as yet, an incomplete study of the old rogue. Ursula Richter is a satisfactory Sophie and Emilia Walther-Sacks is a jovial Annina. Kempe, though, is the hero of this issue.

In June 1954, Decca set up a *Rosenkavalier* recording of the complete score, which has turned out to be the most durable of all. Maria Reining is the not altogether satisfactory Marschallin, though preferable to either Ursuleac or Bäumer; Sena Jurinac is an adorable Octavian; Hilde Gueden the bright and youthful Sophie, not so much the minx as elsewhere; and Ludwig Weber again the Ochs. Among other singers in this recording must be mentioned Walter Berry as the Police Commissar, Alfred Poell as a highly-nervous Faninal, Anton Dermota as a sweet-voiced Tenor Singer, and Peter Klein as an insinuating, slippery Valzacchi. Erich Kleiber conducts the Vienna Philharmonic. This version set the standard for recordings of the opera until Decca produced their next one, sixteen years later.

There were two more in between. In 1957 Columbia brought out a very good set, but with the usual stage cuts. It was conducted by Herbert von Karajan and produced by Walter Legge. The Philharmonia Orchestra was then the best in London and played superbly throughout the strongly cast opera. Schwarzkopf sings the Marschallin with distinction, more so after the levée scene than before it; Christa Ludwig is an excellent Octavian, but does not better Jurinač on Decca; Teresa Stich-Randall is a most successful Sophie: her white voice is ideal. Otto Edelmann sings Ochs, richly and lustily, and with an amusingly strong Viennese accent; Kerstin Meyer is the Annina and Ljuba Welitsch the Leitmetzerin. In the Presentation scene, Karajan flattens an exposed trumpet note, contrary to tradition, contrary even to what Strauss does in the same passage in his old set of 78s with the Tivoli Orchestra. Karajan's note invoked strong criticism until it was explained that Strauss had changed his mind. He always played it this way during the 1930s in Germany and Austria.

Next in chronological order of issue comes DG's version of the opera, again from Dresden and conducted with loving care by Karl Böhm. The 1960 cast was a strong one: Böhme has expanded and deepened his characterization of Ochs in the intervening ten years since he sang it with Kempe; Marianne Schech is an adequate, though not a scintillating Marschallin; Seefried is a lovely Octavian; but Rita Streich overdoes the vixenish aspect of Sophie's character. Fischer-Dieskau, surprisingly, takes the relatively small part of Herr von Faninal and makes a great success of it. Gerhard Unger and Sieglinde Wagner are a well-matched pair of plotters.

Then, in 1970, came the second Decca success. The most lavish programme book of all time accompanies the records, complete with colour reproductions of Roller's designs for sets and costumes. Georg Solti conducts the Vienna Philharmonic and the cast seems to have been hand-picked. Régine Crespin sings the Marschallin with that desirable touch of the French manner in Vienna; Yvonne Minton is the impetuous and aggressive Octavian; Helen Donath makes a lovely Sophie. Baron Ochs is taken by the then relatively unknown Viennese bass, Manfred Jungwirth, who had sung the role at Glyndebourne in 1965 after a long and varied career all over Europe. It was courageous of Decca to cast him in this important role, and it paid off handsomely. Alfred Jerger, the veteran bass-baritone (and creator of Mandryka in *Arabella*) sings the Notary with great aplomb; Luciano Pavarotti brings out the full Italian style in the Tenor's aria. Anton Dermota makes a welcome reappearance as the Innkeeper; and so does Emmy Loose as the Leitmetzerin. This quality and experience in the smaller roles lends a further touch of authenticity to the whole enterprise. The sound, in true stereo, is richer and subtler than any previous recording, and Decca again set new standards.

The Vienna Philharmonic Orchestra, Chorus, and Vienna itself were again involved in the next *Rosenkavalier* for CBS under Leonard Bernstein. He gave several gala performances at the Staatsoper in 1971 and subsequently recorded his *Rosenkavalier* with the same cast. This has Christa Ludwig as an assured Marschallin. Gwyneth Jones sings poorly as Octavian. Lucia Popp is a soubrettish Sophie and Walter Berry an inexperienced though endearing portrayer of Ochs. Placido Domingo,

unexpectedly, makes not nearly enough of the Tenor Song; Essentially
what seems to have caused this *Rosenkavalier* to have misfired is
Bernstein's whole approach: far too slow tempi at the start for the scene
between the Marschallin and Octavian, then too vulgar and 'schmalzy'
for too much of the time; but the orchestra loved him and they play
beautifully. It is also good to hear Murray Dickie again, as Valzacchi.
Bernstein's version embodies the usual stage cuts.

The latest complete recording of *Der Rosenkavalier* comes from Philips
and, like the two Deccas, is absolutely complete. It has the Rotterdam
Philharmonic conducted with great sensitivity by Edo de Waart, but
without the real substance of sound that, in particular, the Decca/Solti
possesses. The Philips recording's main attraction lies in its ensemble,
rather than in starry casting of principals. The American soprano, Evelyn
Lear, gives a well-controlled interpretation of the Marchaallin, warm and
womanly and her fellow countrywoman, Frederica von Stade, is an
excellent Octavian. Ruth Welting fails to imbue the part of Sophie with
any more than capable singing, but Derek Hammond-Stroud, well known
for his Faninal at Covent Garden, brings out all the dottiness of the
parvenu. Jules Bastin, the Belgian bass, makes a thoroughly acceptable
Baron Ochs, well sung and acted, well thought out and mercifully without
vulgarity. To complete this United Nations cast of principals, José
Carreras, a Spaniard, sings a melodious Tenor Song. Nearly everybody
else is Dutch.

One of the latest recordings of the opera is neither a commercial one
in the strict sense, nor does it qualify as a private recording, though really
it is. Subscribers of $100 and more to the Met Opera Fund receive a
complimentary copy of a *Der Rosenkavalier* on record from the Met
archive, with Lotte Lehmann, Risë Stevens and Emanuel List, but only
in fair sound. Even so it is a distinct improvement on a private recording
of a 1938 performance with Lehmann and List and Kerstin Thorborg and
Dorothée Manski as Octavian and Sophie. It has ten-second breaks every
four minutes or so, which makes for infuriating listening. Furthermore,
Lotte Lehmann produced it, emphasizing her own role by extensive cuts
in Ochs's, especially at the beginning of Act 3.

Emanuel List also appears in another private version emanating from
a performance in Buenos Aires under Erich Kleiber in 1947. Rose
Bampton is the Marschallin; Elsa Cavelti, the celebrated Swiss mezzo,
sings Octavian; the rest are local singers.

The Cetra performance, issued in 1978, was taken live at the 1949
Salzburg Festival. George Szell, who had the work in his repertory at the
Unter den Linden in the 1920s, is the conductor. Maria Reining, the
Marschallin, is here heard in the part four years before her Decca
recording. For the only time on disc we can hear two notable readings
– Jarmila Novotna's Octavian and Jaro Prohaska's Ochs.

The verdict is generally good. The only bad performance and it really is bad, comes unexpectedly from Roswaenge as the Italian Tenor. His strained and exaggerated singing is fit only to be forgotten. Reining is good, and one realizes the reason for her reputation and long reign at Vienna between 1937–55. There is considerable difference between her Marschallin here and that later under Kleiber; the *Sanduhr* had certainly been at work by the later recording.

Novotna is a musical Octavian though not an outstanding interpreter. Her voice is not as dark as one would wish to contrast with Reining's, and her performance is a little stiff. Hilde Gueden, who was almost 32 at the time, has great freshness as Sophie and an enviable sparkle. Her indignant prattling about Ochs to the Marschallin in Act 3 is a moment in point.

Prohaska makes a marvellous character of Ochs. His thick Viennese accent, broad humour and complete mastery of the role ensures a thoroughly endearing performance. Nobody else has put so much fun and then hypocrisy into the Act 1 line 'Ich liess ein solches Goldkind, meiner Seel', nicht unter das infame Lakaienvolk.' The voice is more baritone than bass and has not the bottom to it that can yield a comfortable E below the stave at the end of Act 2. Prohaska reaches down for it after obvious preparation, and just manages to sing the note although he has to cover up so as to sustain it. Nevertheless this is slight criticism against the advantages from his vocal and dramatic agility throughout.

George Szell's contribution to the recording is praiseworthy. His tempi are at times unexpected, though on reflection completely sensible: the swift opening prelude; the decelerando towards the end of Act 3 with an exceedingly fast few bars once Mahomet has snatched up the handkerchief and the curtain comes down. He also makes thoroughly meaningful pauses during that dramatically embarrassed section before the trio.

Technically there is a preponderance of timpani because of the placing of a microphone too close to them; a bad patch during the Police Commissar's scene produces split vocal tone, but otherwise the sound is acceptable. The usual stage cuts are embodied. A booklet comes with the set of four records. It contains fuzzy orange photographs from the production, no text or essay, and a cast list with quaint German spelling for some of the characters.

In the 1955 highlights disc, the Berlin Philharmonic is conducted by Wilhelm Schüchter. It presents a well-balanced account of the opera despite the first band. This is Josef Traxel singing the Tenor aria lustily. Next comes the Marschallin's monologue and return of Octavian. Then the Presentation Scene and Och's finale to Act 2, grimly sung by Gustav Neidlinger. The last band is from the trio to the end of the opera. The three ladies are Leonie Rysanek, a capable Marschallin; Elisabeth Grümmer, a satisfactory Octavian; and Erika Köth a bright, hard Sophie.

A curious disc from Decca in 1965 (SXL 6146) has the three sopranos only: Régine Crespin is as yet an unsettled Marschallin who indulges in French *schmalz* and many scoops; Elisabeth Söderström a magnificent, impeccable Octavian; and Hilde Gueden as Sophie – not as good as elsewhere. Silvio Varviso conducts the Vienna Philharmonic in far too relaxed a manner.

An even more unconventional disc arrived from Dresden three years later in which Lisa Della Casa and Annelies Rothenberger sing respectively the Marschallin and Octavian in Act 1 on side 1, and then Octavian and Sophie in Acts 2 and 3 on side 2. It is regrettable that there was never a complete recording of *Der Rosenkavalier* with Della Casa, and this Freudian effort scarcely compensates for that omission. Her singing is excellent, especially as Octavian, even at that late stage in her career. Rudolf Neuhas conducts the marvellous Dresden Orchestra (ASD 2335). The most recent highlights disc comes from Glasgow. Sir Alexander Gibson conducts the Scottish Opera Singers and Orchestra (CFP 40217) in a conventional selection. Helga Dernesch is the Marschallin, Anne Howells the Octavian and Teresa Cahill the Sophie. Michael Langdon gives the best individual performance as Ochs in the Act 2 finale with Claire Livingstone as Annina.

There are some 'off-the-air' curiosities. An Act 3 from the San Francisco Opera dated October 1945 has Lotte Lehmann in her old role and at the end of her career, Risë Stevens is the Octavian, Nadine Connor the Sophie and the Hungarian bass, Lorenzo Alvary the Ochs. George Sebastian conducts and the fact that it is a live performance helps to hold it together.

Some excerpts from Vienna in 1936–7 have Hilde Konetzni as the Marschallin, Jarmila Novotna as Octavian and Elisabeth Schumann as Sophie. They were conducted by Hans Knappertbusch in spite of the fact that the label says Richard Strauss and names the Marschallin as Lotte Lehmann.

Another excerpt disc from Vienna in 1933 has Clemens Krauss conducting his wife, Ursuleac as the Marschallin, Eva Hadrabova as Octavian, Adele Kern as Sophie, Koloman von Pataky as the Tenor Singer and Richard Mayr as Ochs. This is an interesting selection; it remained unreleased until 1977.

A worthwhile, commerical LP from DG, which came out in 1951 has Tiana Lemnitz now as the Marschallin and singing beautifully, Georgine von Milinkovič as Octavian and Elfriede Trötschel as Sophie. One side sweeps from the end of the *levée* to the end of Act 1, the other goes from the exit of Ochs in the Inn, to the end of the opera – a very sensible arrangement. The idiomatic conductor throughout is Ferdinand Leitner.

There are innumerable arrangements and suites of *Rosenkavalier* music, some of which are authentic in that they were made or authorized by Strauss himself, and they exist in almost every conceivable combination from piano to military band. Among the most curious piano arrangements is one by Percy Grainger called 'Ramble on Love', based on the final duet, on a Columbia 78, (DB 28). And one should not overlook the inclusion of the first phrase in the trio into the most significant melody of the film 'Close Encounters of the Third Kind', the tune which unites all people in whatever galaxy they live.

Possibly the greatest omission among all the *Rosenkavalier* recordings is a vocal example conducted by Strauss. The reasons for this, as I have suggested elsewhere, are probably twofold. Firstly, Strauss would never have wished to favour some singers at the expense of others, for if the neglected ones were piqued, performances – and his royalties – would consequently suffer. And secondly, a recorded interpretation by the composer might be taken by everyone else as the only authentic way to do it, and thereafter performances might tend to congeal. Strauss was always anxious to accommodate different singers in different ways, so as to bring out the best in them. He was wiser to let others interpret his most successful opera in their own manner for whatever they do with it, *Der Rosenkavalier*, like any masterpiece, remains indestructible.

DER ROSENKAVALIER

M Marschallin; *S* Sophie; *O* Octavian; *Oc* Ochs; *V* Valzacchi; *T* Italian Tenor; *A* Annina; *F* Faninal

1944 Ursuleac *M*; Kern *S*; von Milinkovic *O*; Weber *Oc*; Reger *V*; Klarwein *T*; Willer *A*; Hann *F*/Bavarian State Opera Chorus and Orch./C. Krauss
Vox ⓜ OPBX 140

1949 (live performance, Salzburg Festival) Reiner *M*; Gueden *S*; Novotna *O*; Prohaska *Oc*; Klein *V*; Roswaenge *T*; Hermann *A*; Hann *F*/Vienna State Opera Chorus, VPO/Szell
Cetra ⓜ LO 69/4

1950 Bäumer *M*; Richter *S*; Lemnitz *O*; Böhme *Oc*; Sautter *V*; Leibing *T*; Walther-Sachs *A*; Lobel *F*/Dresden State Opera Chorus, Saxon State Orch./Kempe
Acanta ⓜ JA 23039

1954 Reining *M*; Gueden *S*; Jurinac *O*; Weber *Oc*; Klein *V*; Dermota *T*; Rössl-Majdan *A*; Poell *F*/Vienna State Opera Chorus, VPO/E. Kleiber

Decca ⓜ 4BB 115-8; Richmond ⓜ RS 64001

1956 Schwarzkopf *M*; Stich-Randall *S*; Ludwig *O*; Edelmann *Oc*; Kuen *V*; Gedda *T*; Meyer *A*; Wächter *F*/Chorus, Philharmonia/Karajan
HMV SLS 810 ④ TC–SLS 810
Angel SDL 3563

1958 Schech *M*; Streich *S*; Seefried *O*; Böhme *Oc*; Unger *V*; Francl *T*; Wagner *A*; Fischer-Dieskau *F*/Dresden State Opera Chorus, Saxon State Orch./Böhm
DG 2721 162

1968–9 Crespin *M*; Donath *S*; Minton *O*; Jungwirth *Oc*; Dickie *V*; Pavarotti *T*; Howells *A*; Wiener *F*/Vienna State Opera Chorus, VPO/Solti
Decca SET 418–21 ④ K3N23;
London OSA 1435

1971 Ludwig *M*; Popp *S*; G. Jones *O*; Berry *Oc*; Dickie *V*; Domingo *T*; Lilowa *A*; Gutstein *F*/Vienna

State Opera Chorus,
VPO/Bernstein
CBS (UK) 77416, (US)
M4X–30652

1976 Lear *M*; Welting *S*; von Stade
O; Bastin *Oc*; Coppens *V*;
Carreras *T*; van Sante *A*;
Hammond-Stroud *F*/Helmond
Concert Choir, Netherlands
Opera Chorus, Rotterdam
PO/De Waart
Philips 6707 030 ④7699 045

Excerpts

1933 Lehmann *M*; Schumann *S*;
Olszewska *O*; Mayr *Oc*; Gallos
V; Paalen *A*; Madin *F*/Vienna
State Opera Chorus, VPO/Heger
World Records ⓜ SH 181–2;
Seraphim ⓜ 1C 6041

1951 Lemnitz *M*; Trötschel *S*; von
Milinkovic *O*/Wurttemburg State
Opera Orch/Leitner
DG ⓜ 478012

1951 Anonymous soloists, chorus and
orch./Rubahn
Royale ⓜ 1352

1955 Rysanek *M*; Köth *S*; Grümmer
O; Neidlinger *Oc*; Traxel *T*;
Wagner *A*/Chorus, Berlin
PO/Schüchter
HMV ⓜ CLP 1139; EMI ⓜ 1C
047 28566M

1964 Crespin *M*; Gueden *S*;
Söderström *O*; Holecek
F/Vienna State Opera Chorus,
VPO/Varviso
Decca SXL 6146; London OS
25905

1964 Hillebrecht *M*; Köth *S*; Ludwig
O; Berry *Oc*; Curzi *V*; Töpper
A/German Opera Chorus and
Orch./Hollreiser
Ariola-Eurodisc K8682OR

1975 Dernesch *M*; Cahill *S*; Howells
O; Langdon *Oc*/Scottish National
Orch./Gibson
EMI CFP 40217

La Bohème

EDWARD GREENFIELD

It is a paradox that an opera so central to the current Italian repertory
as *La Bohème,* a superb vehicle for great singing, should have thrived
in the recording studio – at least in the age of LP – at the hands of
conductors of the strongest personality. It is the only opera which both
Toscanini and Beecham recorded complete, and more recently both
Karajan and Solti have added their names to the long list of conductors
who have directed recordings.

If you look closer at *La Bohème*, this phenomenon is not so surprising.
Few four-act operas have a structure so directly linked to that of a
symphony, the outer acts each starting with a motif which Puccini
originally wrote for his early *Capriccio Sinfonico*. The short second act
clearly has the role of *scherzo* in the scheme, the third with its atmospheric
stillness at a grey dawn has elements of a slow movement. Add to that
the overall compactness, which has one wondering what it would be like
to see the work without intervals, and the devotion of great conductors
is perfectly understandable.

On record the Toscanini–Beecham comparison provides some fascinating
contrasts. Toscanini's set was taken from two broadcast performances on
3 and 10 February 1946, made in the notorious Studio 8H at Radio City,
New York. The soloists included Licia Albanese, who a decade earlier
was the Mimì in the complete 78 set with Gigli: these were concert
performances broadcast over the NBC network, the first of the series of
Italian opera performances Toscanini did for NBC, the others stretching
at irregular intervals until 1954. (Previously in 1944 he had given *Fidelio*
as his first NBC opera performance.)

Beecham's set was also made in America. Some enterprising executive
found that Sir Thomas was in the offing, comparatively free of
engagements. So was Victoria de los Angeles. That Jussi Björling, Robert
Merrill, Fernando Corena, Giorgio Tozzi and Lucine Amara were all
brought in at short notice is a splendid tribute to American organization.
Sir Thomas's optimism about what he intended to get through at recording
sessions was proverbial but with *Bohème* the whole project was somehow

finished on time – on the very last day before los Angeles had to fly off to Europe.

When the Toscanini set appeared there was, as usual, talk of the old man racing through the score without giving his singers proper breathing space. When the Beecham came out there was talk of his slow speeds and the leisureliness of this approach. There is truth in these accusations – Beecham is expansive over 'Che gelida manina', 'Si, mi chiamano Mimì' and 'O soave fanciulla', for example, and Toscanini ridiculously fast for his basic speed in 'Vecchia zimarra' – but detailed comparisons reveal a surprising number of instances where Beecham and Toscanini chose identical basic speeds for a passage. This is particularly noticeable in the opening scene of Act 1 between the four Bohemians where the speeds change frequently. Yet the general impression in the Toscanini is of haste – drive if you prefer it – and in the Beecham of relaxed humour. It is not simply a question of Toscanini ignoring speed variations. Often his *rallentandi* are extreme, but somehow they rarely give the normal feeling of relaxation. In part that is due to Toscanini's habit of producing a *rallentando* as it were in a geometrical progression of increasing slowness. Most *rallentandi* – certainly Beecham's – are not so constant but ease the phrase to its close. In other words, it is more a question of rubato which distinguishes Beecham from Toscanini. At fig. 10 in Act 1, for example, where the six-eight rhythm is resumed and the waiters enter to the astonished cries of 'Legna! Sigari! Bordò!', Toscanini and Beecham take virtually identical speeds; but while Toscanini sounds stiff and almost unidiomatic, Beecham provides a sprung rhythm which exactly catches the right feeling of sprightliness. Unhappily it is in just this passage where Beecham's Schaunard, John Reardon, gets badly left behind in the ensemble – a blemish which no doubt would have been corrected had there been more time for the recording. Reardon makes up for this with a superb Oxford pronunciation for his Englishman saying 'Incominciam!' (an English accent is expressly ordered in the score but I have never heard so convincing an attempt as here).

When Mimì first enters. Toscanini gives his singers (Licia Albanese and Jan Peerce) plenty of breathing space, it is true, but there is no relaxation and the flute trills and runs sound strangely matter-of-fact. Where at fig. 26, at the words 'Si sente meglio', the *andante moderato* should sound gentle, Toscanini is still unbending and much too exact in his measuring of the beat. There is nothing of the tentative feeling which Beecham so rightly finds in the music at this point. When at 'Oh! sventata, sventata!' the duet proper begins, Toscanini is much faster in the way one would expect, and though there is a fine sweep to the phrases this hardly makes up for the lack of delicacy.

In the two arias, 'Che gelida manina', and 'Si, mi chiamano Mimì', Beecham's speeds for the principal Grand Tunes are slower than Toscanini's – also than Erede's and Votto's – so that all Björling's and los Angeles's powers of breath control are needed for spanning over the phrases. It is in these two arias that the most surprising point of the Toscanini interpretation emerges. At the climax of each Toscanini suddenly lets himself go, not only with extraordinary groans (even more impressive than Casals's recorded examples) but in *stringendi* that one would normally associate with a flashy, give-it-all-you've-got interpretation. Beecham's comparative restraint in not running away with the speed is not so immediately exciting, but the result is not only more tasteful but emotionally richer and more telling.

But whatever the flaws no one could miss the unparalleled drive with which Toscanini makes the overall structure sound more tightly knit than usual. It would be interesting to know how the New York performances compared with those he gave earlier in his career – especially the unsuccessful première at Turin in 1896. Some interesting evidence has been given – notably by Robert Marsh in *Toscanini and the Art of Orchestral Performance* – that over the years Toscanini's performances got faster. Hard-driven as his New York *Bohème* sounds, there is evidence that this may not have happened here. Surprisingly, Erede on Decca, representing Italian tradition, has even faster speeds than Toscanini – at the opening of both Acts 1 and 2 for example – and there are remarkable parallels between the Toscanini performance and that of Molajoli on 78s. Molajoli was conducting a Scala cast towards the end of the Toscanini era at La Scala when his influence was obviously still great. There is the same frenetic lack of relaxation in the opening scene, and though Molajoli is gentler with Mimi when she enters, he has the same unashamed *stringendi* in the two big arias as Toscanini.

Erede's performance on Decca, apart from the fast speeds, is free from eccentricity. It is dimly recorded, but even allowing for that, it is less full-blooded than its rivals. It is a remarkable point about the Beecham that restrained as it is in many ways, it yet has more panache (for example in Act 2) than the others, and the climax of Act 4 is unbearably moving – helped by los Angeles. Votto's performance with Callas as Mimi is unashamedly full-blooded with swirling strings (entrance of Mimi in Act 4), superb crescendos, exciting brass (notably in the climax of the Act 3 quartet), and generally excellent discipline. But there is one interpretative blot. After the disappearance of Mimi and Rodolfo off-stage at the end of Act 3, the orchestra dims down to a long held soft chord on the horns, rounded off – by a stroke of genius – with the *fortissimo* dominant-tonic figure which punctuates the early part of the act. I have often thought that Puccini cribbed the idea of a *fortissimo* full-stop to a quiet coda from the Nightwatchman ending of Act 2 of *Meistersinger*, but Votto tries to improve on Puccini with the ugliest of swells on the horn chord before the final cadence. No doubt such a device can prevent an audience from clapping too soon, but it is unjustifiable on records.

The Callas–Tebaldi–los Angeles contrast presented in these three sets is equally instructive. It is not surprising to find that, although Tebaldi has the richest top register with a splendid opening-out for the climax of 'Si, mi chiamano Mimì', she rarely gives any fresh insight into the music. By contrast, both los Angeles and Callas live the part; Callas's interpretation is in effect not a portrait of the little woman, melting and submissive, whom we normally have as Mimì – such a scaling would have been too much for her – but still a character entirely believable and in one important way more convincing than the conventional interpretation. This Mimì at least, one imagines, could well be unfaithful to Rodolfo. Vocally this is one of Callas's finest recorded performances. Though there are some sour notes and flapping wobbles, the concentration of the singing triumphantly overrides such consideration. There are countless examples of the way Callas can take a phrase and make it seem entirely new. I think of the change of tone-colour for 'Ma quando vien lo sgelo', in 'Si, mi chiamano', quickly opening out for the climax; or again in the meeting with Marcello where the deliberate absence of vibrato underlines the pathos.

Callas is undoubtedly the more vibrant personality, but los Angeles in the Beecham set is the more completely compelling Mimì. She is more coquettish – unashamedly the little woman – but very much able to convey weight of feeling. Compare for example the interpretation of the climax 'Si rinasce' in Act 4. Vocally, again it is beauty of phrasing and tone-colour that marks this out as a fine performance. With los Angeles the ranges of tone-colour are different, from the golden 'Buon giorno, Marcello' in Act 4 – Callas by contrast makes this phrase almost skittish – to the leaden dullness of her entry in Act 3.

If there is one moment in los Angeles's interpretation which transcends other recorded performances, it is the passage towards the end of 'O soave fanciulla' where successively the dropping phrases 'Vi starò vicina', 'Obbedisco, signor' and 'Io t'amo' have a melting intensity. She gains from the slow speed Beecham sets, and from the freedom he allows within that speed. It is a pity that she does not sound completely comfortable on the high top C which ends the act half a dozen bars later. There is certainly no question of a fading *perdendosi* but then there are remarkably few recorded performances where any *perdendosi* is attempted to all.

In an early edition of *Bohème* dated 1898 it is interesting to find a variant suggested for the end of this duet, by which the final 'Amor!' up to the held top C could be omitted entirely so that the final cadence would be left to the orchestra alone. Certainly it would more subtly convey the effect of the lovers going off – and some day it might be tried by a soprano uncomfortable on top, but it would need courage. The disappointment of any Italian audience at so bare-faced a 'get out' is terrifying to imagine.

Earlier, in the days of 78 records, such a passage usually prevented a true fading away. A version in German of 'O soave fanciulla' by Meta Seinemeyer and Tino Pattiera (Parlo. E 10976; LV 111) is marred not only by an obviously unatmospheric ending but because the orchestral reference to 'Che gelida manina' has to be hurried shamelessly to fit a 78 side. Otherwise from Seinemeyer – a singer still under-appreciated – it is an enchanting performance with a beautifully poised 'Io t'amo', or rather 'Ich liebe dich'. Selma Kurz and Leo Slezak, in German also lack magic but Kurz, now in Italian, sings a vocally sure, interpretatively shy and fragile 'Mi chimano Minì!'. The best of her Mimì is recalled on Pearl GEMM 121.

A lack of atmosphere marred the relatively few complete recordings of *La Bohème* in the 78 era. The 1938 Gigli–Albanese, the Marini–Pampanini of 1930 and the Giorgini–Torri of 1928 are all disappointing for that and other reasons. Not surprisingly Albanese is fresher and younger-sounding than she is in the later Toscanini set, but there is already a tendency to shrillness, and the rest is respectable rather than exciting including the Marcello of Afro Poli and the Musetta of Tatiana Menotti. What makes the set cherishable none the less is the singing of Gigli as Rodolfo, far from perfect in detail but even his lapses have a way of being endearing – his cooing or pouting tones, his boyish sob – so that the character comes vividly to life. This of all tenor voices has a wonderful way of hinting at a chuckle. But alas in 'Che gelida manina' where at the end his famous 78 version (DB 1538) he brought a delightful portamento up a third, the complete set finds him uttering an outright, ugly, sob.

As for the earlier HMV set, Rosina Torri's Mimì is nervous-sounding, and in 'Si, mi chiamano Mimì' her line veers uncomfortably between sharp and flat. Aristodemo Giorgini sounds aged as Rodolfo, ready to be pensioned off perhaps as Emperor of China in *Turandot*, though his pinched tone suddenly leaves him for the climax of 'O soave fanciulla' to confirm that he should have recorded the role earlier. The Columbia, vocally secure for the greater part, has some obvious blemishes, notably an uncomfortably sharp top C from Rosetta Pampanini at the end of 'O soave fanciulla'. Elsewhere she sings beautifully, and her Farewell is delightful. Luigi Marini as Rodolfo may sound edgy next to Gigli, but with a tone colour in some ways akin to that of Pertile his firmness makes for a satisfying performance.

Among sets from the early days of LP certain individual performances are worth remembering. The 1951 Cetra recording had Rosanna Carteri's affecting Mimì, Ferruccio Tagliavini's sweet-voiced and personable Rodolfo, Giuseppe Taddei's bonhomous Marcello. The 1955 Russian version caught Sergei Lemeshev late in his career as Rodolfo, Lisitsian at the height of his as Marcello. Ivan Kozlovsky was recorded even later than Lemeshev in the 1961 Melodiya version. The long list of excerpt discs, mostly in German and French, were, and are, mostly for local consumption, but the 1930s extracts preserve the delightful art of Felicie Hüni-Mihacsek, the forthright Rodolfo of Helge Roswaenge, and the 1954 Electrola disc has a distinguished cast – but perhaps one for another opera.

The first complete recording to bring this opera into the stereo era – and that with most atmospheric sound and a convincing production – again featured Renata Tebaldi as Mimì, intensifying the performance she had given under Erede. This time her conductor was far more stylish, for Tullio Serafin gave one of his most dramatic opera performances on record, helped by an excellent cast which included Carlo Bergonzi, a keenly intelligent Rodolfo, Ettore Bastianini and Cesare Siepi both vocally rich as Marcello and Colline, and with even the small parts of Benoit and Alcindoro (as so often taken by a single artist) given the benefit of Fernando Corena's magnificent bass.

In the early 1960s came three more complete recordings. Deutsche Grammophon having recorded a version in German with a cast which sounds tempting – Pilar Lorengar, Sandor Konya, Rita Streich and Fischer-Dieskau – went on the following year at the Maggio Musicale, in Florence, to record the opera again with an Italian cast. For the Berlin recording in German DG copied Decca in choosing Erede to conduct and for its Florence recording it copied EMI in choosing Antonino Votto who had conducted for Callas.

Renata Scotto, then at the start of her career, made an affecting Mimì, and it was fascinating to have so positive a singer as Tito Gobbi singing the role of Marcello, but the contribution of Gianni Poggi as Rodolfo was little short of disastrous, in places almost comically coarse and grotesquely unlyrical. That disappointing DG set was quickly followed in 1962 by the one from RCA. The conductor was Erich Leinsdorf who directed crisply in what might broadly be described as the Toscanini tradition, though he achieved only intermittently the sort of driving intensity and cohesion that marked the older conductor's conception. As Rodolfo, Richard Tucker sang with intelligence, only occasionally disturbing his fine legato with the sort of lachrymose tricks which always afflicted him periodically. (An earlier Met performance from him, attractively youthful in the mid 1940s, has since appeared in the otherwise undistinguished CBS set). Robert Merrill made a magnificent Marcello, and in essence Anna Moffo's assumption of the role of Mimì was attractively sweet and tender, though already in 'Si mi chiamano Mimì' there were hints of the under-the-note attack which later in her career was to afflict her so seriously.

A recording of an altogether more consistent quality arrived early in 1964, with Rome Opera House forces conducted by the American Thomas Schippers and with Mirella Freni as Mimì opposite EMI's favourite all-repertory tenor, Nicolai Gedda, in the role of Rodolfo. At first the un-Italianate side of Gedda's performance was what seemed most striking, but quickly one could appreciate the acuteness of detailed interpretation of word meaning which made even the best-known passages sound new and fresh. In 'Che gelida manina' one actually registers what the poet is talking about instead of just revelling in the melodic line. Freni made an enchanting Mimì, as melting and tender as los Angeles and with more vivacity, while Schippers's vigorous direction, not at all forced and full of Italianate passion, reinforced her range of expression. It was a pity that the roles of Marcello and Musetta received performances of less imagination from Mario Sereni and Mariella Adani.

Amazingly with so popular an opera, *La Bohème* was then allowed by the record companies to remain fallow for a whole decade until in 1973 came a recording that set new standards in many directions. Like Beecham's set made in New York, the new one was recorded against an unusually tight schedule, but happily with a conductor and orchestra who can respond to such a challenge in work of the finest quality, Herbert von Karajan and the Berlin Philharmonic. A positive gain in communication – with Karajan less studied and self-conscious than he can be on record – came from the long 'takes' which the Decca engineers were required to use, even if occasionally there was a slight imprecision of ensemble of a kind rare in Karajan recordings. Such tiny blemishes are minimal compared with the enormous positive merits of a recording that not only features superb playing and magnificent singing from an outstanding cast but sets them against a warm, atmospheric acoustic.

It was significant that ten years after the Schippers set Freni was still first choice for the role of Mimì, and this time the spacious Decca recording allowed her voice to be given an extra bloom. Against Karajan's equally spacious tempi she is not always able to achieve the same vivacity as on the Schippers set, but hers remained a most tenderly appealing performance. As for Luciano Pavarotti's performance as Rodolfo it set new standards, for he combines in a totally engaging performance the vocal merit of an enormous range of tone from lyrical tenderness to heroic power, the musical merit of consistent imagination, and the dramatic merit of creating a fully rounded character, as detailed in expression as Gedda's portrait and as sparkling as Gigli's. In 'Che gelida manina' Pavarotti starts almost conversationally, yet the intensity of live communication is created at once, and the tension rises consistently up to the culminating top C at the end. The scale of the voice and the range of tone is enhanced by the fact that the voice is balanced a little more distantly than is common with celebrated tenors. It was a blot however that Karajan allowed him to take the top C alongside Freni at the end of Act 1. If Elizabeth Harwood provides little contrast of timbre as Musetta next to Freni as Mimì, hers is still a most sensitive performance, while Panerai as Marcello also gives a refreshingly intelligent performance, marring it only with a strange fit of near-crooning in the Rodolfo–Marcello duet in Act 4, 'Ah, Mimì tu più non torni'.

As for Karajan himself, his reading has a commitment and perception to translate the opera in the way that otherwise only Beecham and (more controversially) Toscanini do. Like Beecham, Karajan chooses spacious tempi and stands by them, and how subtly he varies his degree of spring in the skipping six-eight rhythms for the Bohemians, matching each mood. Most illuminating of all is Karajan's treatment of emotional climaxes, key passages in Puccini which require total thrust for their impact to be fully felt but which equally must not be allowed to degenerate into vulgarity. So Karajan, at the climactic moment in Act 2 when Musetta falls into Marcello's arms in reconciliation, meticulously observes Puccini's dynamic markings, limiting the full thrust of *fortissimo* with heavy brass to the three bars of triple *forte* as marked. The result has a tingling freshness which follows through into the delicate passage immediately following.

When a year after the Karajan set appeared, a rival version came from RCA with Georg Solti (normally a Decca conductor) in charge of the London Philharmonic Orchestra, it was fascinating to compare his reading not only with that of his direct rival, Karajan but with Toscanini, who many years earlier in Salzburg had been his mentor. If the very start with a fast tempo relentlessly pursued, suggested that Toscanini's example was setting the pace (outdoing the maestro in speed), that view was quickly modified. Particularly in accompanying the singer who takes the role of Mimì, Montserrat Caballé, Solti shows that he can be as flexible and sympathetic as any Puccinian today, though significantly it must be remembered that Solti when he made his recording had never actually conducted *La Bohème* in the opera house.

Wide as is the expressive range of Solti's reading, Caballé's singing provides the most distinctive point of the set. This singer who so often seems the opposite of gentle and wilting transforms herself into the perfect Puccinian 'little woman', in places actually outshining her compatriot los Angeles. So in the death scene of Act 4 her brief quotation from 'Che gelida manina' is sung not with the weight of death on her but with the lightness of a happy memory, a magic touch born of rethinking the role, and at the end of 'O soave fanciulla' she caps everything with the magic of her half-tone phrase: 'Tù sol comandi, amor!' Next to such imagination the singing of Placido Domingo seems relatively ordinary, and certainly he does not as a rule match his rival Pavarotti in detailed illumination. Particularly revealing is the comparison of the two interpretations of 'Che gelida manina', but the contrast is consistent. Judith Blegen is an attractive Musetta with a grainy voice which contrasts well with that of Caballé. Sherrill Milnes gives a strong, intelligent performance as Marcello, and Ruggero Raimondi is a formidable Colline who cunningly restrains his power until the very end of the Coat Song.

In the age of the LP the complete set has been paramount, and few if any of the recordings of individual arias or ensembles require detailed assessment, but the era of 78 recording from the earliest acoustic days onwards is different. Not that the earliest recordings were always impressive vocally. At times even the examples which have been transferred to modern LP are as dim musically as they are in recorded sound. As, for example, the recording of 'Si, mì chiamano Mimì' made in Milan in 1902 by Cesira Ferrani (53281). It was chosen to represent the role's creator in the first volume of EMI's, 'The Record of Singing' (RLS 724), and if anything Michael Scott's unenthusiastic comments in the accompanying book are too kind. Ferrani he says has 'little support left and not much legato', but then Melba, who recorded Mimì's Farewell for the first time four years later also with piano accompaniment produced unattractive tone, which in part may be blamed on the recording process (03071; RLS 719). But only in part, for Melba's contribution to the celebrated version with Caruso of 'O soave fanciulla' (054129; ORL 304) is variably attractive, not nearly a match for her partner except in the glorious ping of attack on exposed high notes. Caruso if anything was in finer voice still when in 1912 (AGSB 50; CO 368) with Geraldine Farrar he recorded the duet again, a version whose issue was at first vetoed by Caruso. If Farrar's placing of the voice is not always so crisp as Melba's her expressive range is far wider with phrasing consistently more sympathetic. And there are no strained Australian vowels. Another fine version of the period was that of Lucrezia Bori and McCormack with the tenor superb at the opening (DA 379; GEMM 156). Giovanni Martinelli and Frances Alda also recorded the duet (DK 100) in a most tenderly sensitive performance.

Farrar and Caruso had taken part in 1908 in a fine account of the quartet from Act 3 (DO 101; CO 368) in which it remains fascinating to observe the varying dominances of personality. Antonio Scotti is just as intense as Farrar at the start until Caruso's power of personality as well as voice finally brings the tenor forward. Farrar's attempt at a peal of laughter is not entirely happy, but here and even more strikingly in her account of the Act 3 duet with Scotti, recorded a year later in 1909 (DK 111; CO 368) the natural unforced expressiveness of her singing matches that of her partner, both singers projecting feeling and personality vividly despite the dimness of recording.

It was with Scotti that Caruso in 1907 recorded the most celebrated of early accounts of the duet 'Ah, Mimì tu più non torni' (DM 105; ORL 304), and once again the tenor dominated, though that is partly a question of recording balance. The partnership is more even in the famous Gigli–de Luca version (DB 1050; GEMM 146) with Gigli's tone at its most beautiful and de Luca wonderfully smooth, as it is in Gigli's lesser-known version with the huge-voiced Titta Ruffo (AGSB 56; HQM 1194). The characterization too is delightfully spontaneous-sounding in both. By comparison the McCormack–Sammarco version is disappointing, if only because of the discrepancy of tone between McCormack's finely pointed tenor and Sammarco's woolly-sounding production (DB 630; GEMM 156).

When it comes to Rodolfo's 'Che gelida manina', it is surprising that Caruso did not do more than one version. Even that is far from perfect – a good example of full-throated singing but with little detail (DB 113; ORL 304). Caruso transposes down a semitone, leaving himself with a top B at the end. There is a famous story that when auditioned by Puccini as a young man, he claimed not to be able to manage a top C. Puccini promptly excused him from it, suggesting that too many tenors saved themselves just for that, spoiling the rest.

Martinelli's record of the same aria (DB 979; ORL 224) is also disappointing, with exaggerated portamenti at 'riscaldar' and some tight tone. Of the rest, McCormack's (DB 343; GEMM 156) stands as one of the most satisfying alongside the famous Gigli version, already mentioned, which for many years was a best-seller in the 78 catalogue. Another favourite account in the 1930s was from Björling (DB 3049; RLS 715) and the vocal tone is recognizably younger and more rounded than that on the Beecham set of some twenty years later.

Both Bonci's Fonotipia versions recorded in 1905 and 1910 are recommendable. His third version, a 1912 Columbia, was used by the legendary Jean de Reszke in his lessons. Bonci made his Covent Garden debut (1900) in *Bohème* alongside Melba. On that occasion, *The Times* commented: 'So well did he sing that his extremely diminutive stature was forgotten and the repetition of his charming song in the first act was insisted on' – an interesting reflection on operatic habits. Versions of this aria abound. A recital of their merits or otherwise would be tedious. Those in Italian by Pertile, Lauri-Volpi, Tagliavini, Piccaver and Cortis are worthy of the respective tenor's reputation, similarly ones in German by Patzak, Roswaenge and Wittrisch, in English by Heddle Nash and James Johnston.

When it comes to the following aria for the heroine, 'Si, mi chiamano Mimì', it is the voice of Bori that from all the 78 versions comes to my mind first, not the electrical recording (DB 1644) but the more imaginative acoustic (DB 152; ORL 304). There is a lightness of tone that yet conveys depth of emotion, while the really magic touch comes just at the start of the great melody on 'Ma quando vien lo agelo'. Bori leads up to the word 'Ma' with a little portamento and without a breath, transferring the end of phrase to a note later.

At about the time as Bori recorded her acoustic version a young 21-year-old soprano was also recording the same aria: Claudia Muzio, a great singer who was poorly treated by the record companies. At the peak of her career in the late 1920s she was totally neglected for recording, and only in the last two years of her life in 1934 and 1935 did she return to the recording studio. She was already ill, but still managed to record searching performance of – among other arias – 'Si mi chiamano Mimì.' The contrast between the early Muzio version of 1912 (Edison 82234; OASI 571) and her 1935 Columbia (LX 583; COLC 101) is interesting, the one light and fresh even if the voice is already most characterful around the middle register, the 1935 performance much slower and more intense with greater weight and more confident portamenti. The sudden lightening on 'Vivo sola, soletta' gives a flash of revelation in the contrast of tone. Other versions not to be overlooked include those in Italian by Margherita Carosio (DB 6343) and Magda Olivero (Cetra BB 25053; LPC 55015) both famous Mimìs, in German by Maria Cebotari (DB 4415; 1C 147–29 118), and in English by Joan Cross, who claims attention with the greatest (C 2824).

Mimì's Farewell I have already mentioned in Melba's somewhat coarse version of 1904, but the one which in every way must command first attention is the extraordinary account recorded electrically on stage at Covent Garden during her own farewell performance (DB 943; RLS 719). It is amazing how well the voice was preserved, and the final 'Addio', sustained longer than ever one would expect, is superbly steady. There is sweetness too, which perhaps suggests that the acoustic recording process had been unkind to the bright, clear timbre of this singer. 'Lisa Perli' (see below) is estimable in this passage on the last side of Beecham's Act 4. Many of the sopranos already mentioned also recorded excellent 'Addio's'.

If one of the most satisfying accounts of Colline's Coat Song, 'Vecchia zimarra', comes predictably from Ezio Pinza (DA 908), the irony is that the most celebrated recording of that item was not recorded by a bass at all but by Caruso. It was put on disc immediately after an incident in Philadelphia when during a live performance the bass Segurola lost his voice on stage, and Caruso took over in a sort of ventriloquist's act with his back to the audience. The recording, kept in storage for many years, was finally issued on HMV DL 100 coupled with a spoken introduction from Frances Alda (who was also singing in the performance) and Wally Butterworth – a tasteful enough performance but not really so remarkable when that number reaches down only to the C sharp below middle C.

Musetta's Waltz Song has attracted a few interpreters, among them Bori (DA 981), Supervia (RO 20180; HQM 1220), Lotte Schöne (EW 70; LV 16) and Ljuba Welitsch (LB 82; SH 289), each individual in its own very different way.

If this survey started with Beecham's LP recording, it must end with a reference to his other recording of this opera. With a Covent Garden cast which included Dora Labbette (alias Lisa Perli) as an exquisite Mimì and with Heddle Nash and John Brownlee singing splendidly (if with clipped English vowels instead of open Italian ones), Beecham on 78 recorded Act 4 complete (LX 523–6; HQM 1234). Though the pre-war LPO plays with less vivacity than the post-war RCA Victor Orchestra, the remarkable point is Beecham's own consistency. But then, as he claimed himself, he had studied the score in detail with the composer when he came to London in 1920 for the first Covent Garden performance of *Trittico*. Even if one takes with a pinch of salt Beecham's claim that he sorted out all the problems in the score over speeds and unclear markings, it is interesting that thanks in part to his LP recording, it is Beecham's example, rather than that of Toscanini, Puccini's long-time associate and first interpreter of this opera, that has latterly had a most profound impact, influencing almost every performance on record since. Even Karajan, the most individual interpreter of this opera, since Beecham, seems to have taken note, and though plainly spacious tempi put extra demands on singers, there is every sign that latter-day sopranos and tenors – at least the most distinguished like Pavarotti for Karajan and Caballé for Solti – are willing to accept the challenge.

LA BOHÈME

M Mimì; *Mus* Musetta; *R* Rodolfo; *Mar* Marcello; *S* Schaunard; *C* Colline; *B* Benoit; *A* Alcindoro

1918 Bosini *M*; Giana *Mus*; Andreini *R*; Badini *Mar*; Barrachi *S*; Bettoni *C*; Ceccarelli *B*; *A*/La Scala Chorus and Orch./Sabajno HMV S5056–78

1928 Torri *M*; Vitulli *Mus*; Giorgini *R*; Badini *Mar*; Baracchi *S*; Manfrini *C*; Baccaloni *B*; *A*/La Scala Chorus and Orch./Sabajno HMV C1513–5

1930 Pampanini *M*; Mirella *Mus*; Marini *R*; Vanelli *Mar*; Baracchi *S*; Pasero *C*; Baccaloni *B; A*/La Scala Chorus and Orch./Molajoli Columbia 9846–58

1938 Albanese *M*; Menotti *Mus*; Gigli *R*; Poli *Mar*; Baracchi *S*; Baronti *C*; Scattola *B*; *A*/La Scala Chorus and Orch./Berrettoni Music for Pleasure ⓜ MFP 2076–8; Seraphim ⓜ IB 6038

1946 (broadcast performance) Albanese *M*; McKnight *Mus*; Peerce *R*; Valentino *Mar*; Cehanovsky *S*; Moscona *C*; Baccaloni *B*; *A*/NBC Chorus and Orch./Toscanini RCA (UK) ⓜ AT 203; (US) ⓔ VICS 6019

1947 Sayão *M*; Benzell *Mus*; Tucker *R*; Valentino *Mar*; Cehanovsky *S*; Moscona *C*; Baccaloni *B*;

A/Metropolitan Opera Chorus and Orch./Antonicelli CBS (UK) ⓜ 78243; (US) ⓜ Y32364

1950 Tebaldi *M*; Gueden *Mus*; Prandelli *R*; Inghilleri *Mar*; Corena *S*; Arié *C*; Luise *B*; *A*/Santa Cecilia Academy Chorus and Orch./Erede Decca ⓜ ACL 121–2; Richmond ⓜ RS 62001

1951 Ilitsch *M*; Bösch *Mus*; Delorco *R*; Baylé *Mar*; Oeggl *S*/Vienna State Opera Chorus, Austrian SO/Loibner Remington ⓜ 199–80

1951 Carteri *M*; Ramella *Mus*; Tagliavini *R*; Taddei *Mar*; Latinucci *S*; Siepi *C*; Zorgniotti *B*; *A*/Turin Radio Chorus and Orch./Santini Cetra ⓔ LPS 3237 ④ MC 96–7

1952 Schimenti *M*; Micheluzzi *Mus*; Lauri-Volpi *R*; Ciavola *Mar*; Titta *S*; Tatozzi *C*; Passarotti *B*; *A*/Rome Opera Chorus and Orch./Paoletti Remington ⓜ 199–99

1955 (in Russian) Maslennikova *M*; Sakharova *Mus*; Lemeshev *R*; Lisisian *Mar*; Sakharov *S*; Dobrin *C*/Moscow Radio Chorus and Orch./Samosud MK ⓜ DO 416–22

1955 Tyler *M*; Bjister *Mus*; Garen *R*;
Gorin *Mar*; Holthaus *S*;
Wolovsky *C*; Augenent *B*;
A/Netherlands Opera Chorus and
Orch./Bamberger
Musical Masterpieces Society
ⓜ MMS

1956 (in French) Angelici *M*; Castelli
Mus; Gardés *R*; Roux *Mar*;
Vieuille *S*; Depraz *C*; Hivert *B*;
Hérent *A*/Paris Opéra-Comique
Chorus and Orch./Tzipine
EMI ⓜ 2C 053 10902–3M

1956 Los Angeles *M*; Amara *Mus*;
Björling *R*; Merrill *Mar*;
Reardon *S*; Tozzi *C*; Corena *B;*
A/Columbus Boychoir, RCA
Victor Chorus and
Orch./Beecham
EMI ⓔ SLS 896 ④ TC–SLS
896; Seraphim ⓔ SIB 6099

1956 Callas *M*; Moffo *Mus*; Di
Stefano *R*; Panerai *Mar*;
Spatafora *S*; Zaccaria *C*; Badioli
B; *A*/La Scala Chorus and
Orch./Votto
EMI ⓔ SLS 5059 ④ TC–SLS
5059; Angel ⓜ 3560 BL

1957 Stella *M*; Rizzoli *Mus*; Poggi *R*;
Capecchi *Mar*; Mazzini *S*;
Modesti *C*; Luise *B*; Onesti
A/San Carlo Opera Chorus and
Orch./Molinari-Pradelli
Philips 6720 008

1958 Tebaldi *M*; D'Angelo *Mus*;
Bergonzi *R*; Bastianini *Mar*;
Cesari *S*; Siepi *C*; Corena *B*;
A/Santa Cecilia Academy Chorus
and Orch./Serafin
Decca D5D2 ④ K5K22;
London OSA 1208

1958 Beltrami *M*; Voltriani *Mus*;
Antonioli *R*; Testi *Mar*;
Oppicelli *S*; Ferrein *C*; Peruzzi
B; *A*/Bologna State Theatre
Chorus, Berlin Radio SO/Rigacci
Eterna 820168–9

1960 (in German) Lorengar *M*;
Streich *Mus*; Kónya *R*; Fischer-
Dieskau *Mar*; Gînter *S*; Bertram
C; Ollendorf *B*; F. Hoppe
A/Berlin State Opera Chorus
and Orch./Erede
DG 2726 059

1961 Scotto *M*; Meneguzzer *Mus*;
Poggi *R*; Gobbi *Mar*; Giorgetti
S; Modesti *C*; Carbonari *B*;
A/Florence Festival Chorus and
Orch./Votto
DG 2705 038

1961 (in Russian) Shumskaya *M*;
Yakovenko *Mus*; Kozlovsky *R*;
Burlak *Mar*; Tichonov *S*;
Koriolov *C*; Demianov *B*;
A/Chorus, Moscow PO/Samosud
MK DO 2554–9

1961 Moffo *M*; Costa *Mus*; Tucker *R*;
Merrill *Mar*; Maero *S*; Tozzi *C*;
Corena *B*; Onesti *A*/Rome
Opera Chorus and Orch./
Leinsdorf
RCA (UK) SER 5500–1; (US)
LSC 6095

1963 Freni *M*; Adani *Mus*; Gedda *R*;
Sereni *Mar*; Basiola Jr *S*;
Mazzoli *C*; Badioli *B*;
Montarsolo *A*/Rome Opera
Chorus and Orch./Schippers
EMI SLS 907 ④ TG SLS 907;
Angel SBL 3643 ④ 4X2S–3643

1973 Freni *M*; Harwood *Mus*;
Pavarotti *R*; Panerai *Mar*;
Maffeo *S*; Ghiaurov *C*; Sénéchal
B; *A*/German Opera Chorus,
Berlin PO/Karajan
Decca SET 565–6 ④ K2B5;
London OSA 1299 ④ 5–1299

1974 Caballé *M*; Blegen *Mus*;
Domingo *R*; Milnes *Mar*;
Sardinero *S*; Raimondi *C*;
Mangin *B*; Castel *A*/Alldis
Choir/LPO/Solti
RCA ARL2 0371; ARD2
0371(2) ④ ARK2 0371

1979 Riccarelli *M*; Putnam *Mus*;
Carreras *R*; Wixell *Mar*;
Hagegård *S*; Lloyd *C*; Van
Allan *B*; *A*/Royal Opera Chorus
and Orch./C. Davis
Philips: awaiting release

Excerpts

1936 (Act 4) Perli *M*; Andreva *Mus*;
Nash *R*; Brownlee *Mar*; R. Alva
S; Easton *C*/LPO/Beecham
HMV ⓜ HQM 1234

1936 (in French) Corney *M*; Sibille
Mus; Claudel *R*; Gaudin *Mar*;

Payan *S*; Beckmans *C*/Paris
Opéra-Comique Chorus and
Orch./Wolff
Polydor 566077–81

1936 (in German) Hüni-Mihacsek *M*;
Jungkurth *Mus*; Roswaenge *R*;
Weltner *Mar*; Heyer *S*; Kasenow
C; Hattemer *B*; Wenke *A*/Berlin
State Opera Chorus and
Orch./Weigert
Polydor 95362–6

1940 Steber *M*; Dickey *Mus*;
Tokatyan *R*; Cehanovsky *Mar*;
Kent *S*; Alvary
C/Chorus/Publishers Service
SO/Pelletier
RCA (US) ⓜ CAL 222

1944 (in German) Eipperle *M*;
Gueden *Mus*; Anders *R*;
Domgraf-Fassbaender *Mar*;
Windisch *C*/Berlin Radio Chorus
and SO/Steinkopf
Acanta ⓜ BB 21496

1951 Albanese *M*; Munsel *Mus*; Di
Stefano *R*; Warren *Mar*;
Cehanovsky *S*; Moscona *C*/RCA
Victor Orch./Cellini, Trucco
RCA (US) ⓜ LM 1709

1952 Miniguzza *M*; Hopkins *Mus*;
Gero *R*; Giorgetti *Mar*/Florence
Communale Theatre Chorus and
Orch./Ghiglia
Saga ⓜ SAGA 5261

1954 (in German) Berger *M*; Köth

Mus; Schock *R*; Fischer-Dieskau
Mar; Prey *S*; Frick *C*; Hauck
A/German Opera Chorus,
Orch./Schüchter
EMI ⓜ 1C 047 28572

1960 (in French) Doria *M*; Cumia
Mus; Vanzo *R*; Massard *Mar*;
Giovannetti *S*; Legros *C*/
SO/Ghiglia
Vogue LDM 30132 ④ B.VOC
413

1961 (in French) Jaumillot *M*; Poncet
R/orch./Etchverry
Philips 432614

1963 (in German) Rothenberger *M*;
Pütz *Mus*; Wunderlich *R*; Cordes
Mar; Völker *S*; Frick *C*; Clam
A/Berlin Komische Oper Chorus,
Berlin SO/Klobucar
EMI 1C 063 28529

1964 (in German) Eipperle *M*; Pütz
Mus; Wunderlich *R*; Koffmanne
Mar; Roth-Ehrang *C*/German
Opera Chorus and Orch./Kraus
Ariola-Eurodisc Z75871R

1966 (in German) Schreyer *M*; Holm
Mus; Kmentt *R*; Wächter *Mar*;
Welter *C*/Vienna Volksoper
Chorus and Orch./Bauer-Theussel
Ariola-Eurodisc Z80005R

1960s (in Hungarian) Házy *M*; László
Mus; Ilosfalvy *R*; Melis *Mar*;
C/Budapest PO/Erdély
Qualiton SLPX 11503

Tosca

EDWARD GREENFIELD

Whatever the truth of the suggestion that Puccini wrote his arias to fit ten-inch 78 sides (no evidence at all, as far as I know) *Tosca* might well have been written for the gramophone. Not only are 'Recondita armonia', 'E lucevan le stelle' (so convenient as a coupling) and 'Vissi d'arte' classic examples of the 'ten-inch aria', but the whole opera has carried on the same tradition of gramophone convenience in the age of LP. What other work has so consistently enforced a standard division of the three acts on to four very well-filled sides? Stereo itself might have been invented for *Tosca* with all the impressive effects in depth – the Te Deum, the cantata, the torture of Cavaradossi, the bells and the shepherd's song.

The 1963 recording with Leontyne Price as the heroine and Herbert von Karajan conducting provides an admirable instance of a new perspective that can be revealed by imaginative gramophone performance. Thanks largely to Karajan, but also to the engineers, the opening of the Te Deum scene has an impact rarely achieved even in the theatre. After the enunciation of the Scarpia theme the pivoting ostinato of the bells, B flat to low F, starts not only *pianissimo* but really from afar – 'come da lontano'. Against this the sinister muttering of Giuseppe Taddei as Scarpia, 'Tre sbirri . . . una carozza . . .' is the more tense. The main ominous theme with its relentless triplet rhythm enters extremely slowly. Karajan observes Puccini's *sostenuto molto* added to *largo religioso*, and – with an eerie reverberance that immediately takes one atmospherically into Sant' Andrea della Valle – the music sounds at once still and beautiful yet profoundly ominous for the future. Karajan's crescendo to the climax of the Te Deum is remarkable, the total impact the more powerful because of the slow speed and the bigger contrast of dynamic.

Such a passage shows of course that *Tosca* as well as being a soprano's opera (as Callas and others have shown), a tenor's opera (as Gigli has shown) or a baritone's opera (as Gobbi has shown) is a conductor's opera too. Karajan's set demonstrates the point in many places, as so much earlier did the 1953 set in which Victor de Sabata gives a sometimes mannered but always gripping and intensely musical account of the score to match the singing. In that same passage at the end of Act 1 de Sabata distinctively treats the coda after the choral unison with a marked *accelerando*, and more even than Karajan provides a sharp pay-off to the act. His is far from a conventional view of the opera, but its imagination has come to be recognized as parallel with that of Callas as the heroine and of Gobbi as the villain, two supreme performances.

Since de Sabata and Karajan a whole sequence of younger virtuoso conductors have recorded this opera, often with distinguished results. In some ways the most distinguished of all is Colin Davis who, with Covent Garden forces and splendidly refined recording, directed the opera with a cast including Montserrat Caballé as Tosca, José Carreras as Cavaradossi and Ingvar Wixell as Scarpia. In the first place he was an unexpected choice of conductor for this opera, but he proved an ideal advocate of Puccini in the role of operatic symphonist. In his set his scrupulous but unfussy observance of markings not only tautens the musical structure but heightens the impact of the drama. Helped by the finely textured recording, he also brings out the detailed subtleties of Puccini's orchestration just as much as Karajan does, though with less flamboyance. When he allows Caballé the slowest possible tempo for 'Vissi d'arte', it is disappointing to find him choosing a relatively fast tempo for the ominous pivotal music of the Scarpia aria already mentioned. Even so, in such a passage as that, such conductors as Zubin Mehta, who like Karajan recorded the opera with Price in the role of heroine and Lorin Maazel – who recorded it in Rome with the masterful Birgit Nilsson as Tosca – miss the monumental quality. Mehta can hardly be faulted for his tempi at any point. His is an intelligent, understanding interpretation, but it is one which has few touches to stay indelibly in the mind, and even with the strong cast of Placido Domingo and Sherrill Milnes alongside Price, the result is markedly less individual than several other sets of the 1970s. Maazel is oddly perverse, nudging and squeezing almost every phrase, seemingly determined to 'interpret' the music. But then when an initial phrase cries out for special pointing – for example at the beginning of the first-act love duet – Maazel then inconsistently runs straight over, letting the moment go for nothing.

One could never accuse Mstislav Rostropovich of letting the music go for nothing at any point in this opera. He recorded it in Paris after a stage production at the Paris Opéra with his wife, Galina Vishnevskaya, as the heroine, and the result, helped by the opulent Deutsche Grammophon recording, is individual in the extreme. It is fascinating to compare Rostropovich and Maazel at the very start of the opera with the broad chords of the great Scarpia theme quickly followed by the sliding chromatic writing which represents Angelotti's flight. Both of them take the Scarpia theme exceedingly slowly, and then rush off hell-for-leather on the flight theme, taking an extreme view of both; but where Maazel – who in other recordings, notably more recent ones for CBS, has shown himself a strongly architectural Puccinian – presents his extremes with little sense of logic, Rostropovich, helped no doubt by directing the same performers in the opera house, is clearly telling a dramatic story and the extremes are at once justified in a sense of spontaneity. He of all the conductors since Karajan presents the end of Act 1 with monumental expansiveness, helped by the baritone who among latter-day exponents comes closest to Tito Gobbi in his richness and range of tone, Matteo Manuguerra.

There you have a broad idea of the conducting styles involved, and almost inevitably my survey bases itself on these and other complete sets. On that framework I shall fit excursions into 78 territory for the four principal arias, both of Cavaradossi's, Tosca's 'Vissi d'arte' and Scarpia's Te Deum. I am sorry to leave out of discussion many famous records: Titta Ruffo's exciting account of the solo from Act 2 (DA 163) and the disappointing one from Antonio Scotti (DB 423); the opening night at San Franciso in 1932 with Claudia Muzio in Act 1, privately recorded; the Mapleson cylinder of Emilio De Marchi, creator of Cavaradossi, in a Metropolitan performance of 1903 (IRCC L–7004). These are fascinating fragments, but *Tosca* more than most operas has come into its own since the arrival of complete opera sets and of LPs.

My own *Tosca* training was on the old Decca set with Renata Tebaldi, and Alberto Erede conducting the Santa Cecilia Chorus and Orchestra. I still find it an honest, reliable performance with honest, reliable (if under characterized) singing from Giuseppe Campora as Cavaradossi and Enzo Mascherini (practically unknown otherwise on the gramophone) as a too young-sounding Scarpia. Tebaldi is at her forthright best. Her 'Vissi d'arte' is more extrovert and less beautiful than on the later Decca set (of which more later) but the top A flats at the beginning and the top B flat at the end are all more secure than in the later version.

It is not a performance that brings moments of special illumination but there are two exceptions to that. Tebaldi's singing of the off-stage cantata is enchanting, with the grace notes pointed exquisitely; and the closing of the window is managed splendidly, just a sharp cut-off that suddenly makes you appreciate the claustrophobic oppressiveness inside Scarpia's room with Cavaradossi imperilled. The Karajan set, instead of leaving Puccini's score to do the job of simulating the shutting of the window (a masterly stroke by any standards), has the clanging reproduction of a casement shutting.

The other moment of special magic in the Tebaldi set is the reunion of Cavaradossi and Tosca in Act 3. The force of the climax comes over more convincingly than in any other set. Erede achieves this by ignoring the second marking of *incalzando* when, after the swirling of strings, the 'mia gelosa' theme from Act 1 appears (just before Fig. 15) and climbs scale-wise a full twelve notes instead of the six in the original theme. It conveys extreme exhilaration – fulfilment after frustration, producing a moving moment – and Erede is right in treating it with the extra expansiveness possible when the *incalzando* is ignored on the first three of the climbing triplets and the *allargando* made pronounced on the final one.

In those early years of LP, *Tosca* provided the classic contrast between the rival arts of Tebaldi and Callas, with each at her most powerful and convincing. Now with much greater competition all round, one can appreciate their relative merits the more dispassionately. Tebaldi's account of the part (and this applies to her later Decca version, too, with Mario del Monaco and George London) for all its beauty and strength is not distinctive enough to remain irreplaceable in the catalogue in the way that Callas's always will be.

Even Callas's sternest critic could not doubt for a moment that here, in her first recording, is the most penetrating character study of Puccini's jealous heroine. Callas is Tosca. Or so she makes us believe, from the moment we hear that commanding call of 'Mario!' off-stage. Others tend to make that summons enticing merely: with Callas it commands already from afar.

Callas is so imaginative musically, as well as dramatically, even in the brief passages of rapid conversational recitative, as in the exchanges at the very end of the Act 1 love duet. Here her conveying of jealousy is so much more intense than that of her rivals. She uses a wonderful range of tonal colour, so that after the fire-eating jealousy of the opening passage there is a magical softening for 'Ah, Mario mio' and the strings' enunciation of the Tosca theme.

Then when Cavaradossi does not show enough interest in her plans Callas's change of expression in the voice, several times over in successive phrases, is a miracle of precision – 'Non sei contento?' . . . 'Tornalo a dir!' . . . 'Lo dice male'. Then, more obviously, in the climax following her recognition of the Marchesa Attavanti in the portrait of the Magdalene. Callas is unrivalled in the conviction behind her fury. It is a brave man who could ever have faced such a cry of 'Ah, la civetta! A me, a me!', with B flat and A flat firm and clear. Then passion spent, what meaning Callas gets into 'Ah, quegli occhi' before the salving lyricism of Cavaradossi's tribute to Tosca's own eyes.

If Tebaldi failed in her second recording to add anything significant to what she had communicated in the earlier Decca version. Callas, when she recorded the opera a second time, similarly repeated herself rather than extending or intensifying our knowledge of a unique assumption. It is no secret that, though Tosca was the role on which perhaps she most indelibly stamped her mark, she herself preferred singing a number of other roles in opera. True in her second recording even with Georges Prêtre, a conductor markedly less individual and imaginative than de Sabata, the reading is again magnificent. Though the voice had obviously deteriorated with the years, the tang of the Callas timbre remains irresistible and 'Vissi d'arte' still has great poise as well as dramatic intensity but there are few passages in this second recording where one could confidently say that Callas had improved on the first. One exception comes momentarily in Act 1 at the point where Scarpia shows the heroine the fan he has picked up and Tosca recognizes the crest. In the brief phrases leading up to the snarl of jealousy on 'E l'Attavanti!' Callas adds a new dimension even beyond what she had given before.

The other soprano who has recorded the role twice is Leontyne Price. She also failed in her second recording – with Mehta – to add significantly to what she had given in her first recording – with Karajan. Indeed in many ways the result sounds less spontaneous and so less involving. It is largely a question of timing pauses; where Karajan encouraged his *prima donna* to draw them out, Mehta – in most ways pacing the performance with great warmth and understanding – lets his heroine have her head, so that occasionally she jumps the gun. None the less it is a fine, richly satisfying performance, and at the point which Callas made her own – where in recounting the murder of Scarpia she has the chest-phrase 'rullavan i tamburi' – Price at her second attempt is even tougher and more involving, a match even for Callas herself; but to hear Price at her best in this role one has to go to the earlier Karajan set. Compared with Callas in the first-act love duet Price's expressions of jealousy may not be so biting, but the sheer opulence of tone is thrilling with the impression given of still more strength in reserve. The evenness of tone too is richly satisfying. Unlike Callas she sings the difficult arpeggio phrase in the 'casetta' section of the love duet ('le voce delle cose', five bars after fig. 29) without hardening the tone for the top B flat and A flat, although the attack is not so clean-cut.

Galina Vishnevskaya's view of the role is dramatic, and the commitment of her singing is never in doubt. This is a performance, matching the mercurial qualities of the conducting of her husband, Rostropovich. It suggests facial expression consistently in the pointing of words and shaping of phrase. But there are too many vocal flaws for comfort; some of the exposed notes are intolerably raw and not always steady.

Caballé in the Colin Davis set is in some ways at the opposite pole to Vishnevskaya, for she makes a point throughout of producing flawlessly beautiful tone. Some may find the assumption under characterized, but that hardly goes for her first appearance. Her off-stage cries of 'Mario!' have a petulance that suggests not the jealous lover so much as the nagging wife, and that, emotionally, starts her performance questionably. Even so, the poise and beauty of her singing make this a memorable Tosca, and nowhere more impressively than in 'Vissi d'arte'.

Puccini's own doubts about this aria as an intrusion, lyrical and essentially self-contained, into an otherwise taut and dramatically compressed act, have substance enough. But Caballé with her spacious tempo and purity of line – enhanced rather than disturbed by perfectly

controlled portamenti make the interlude welcome for its own sake, well
set in Colin Davis's clean-cut incisive reading. The most remarkable point
is that Caballé achieves, in spite of the slow speed, a feat that was earlier
achieved on record only by the Italian-American soprano Dusolina
Giannini (DA 892) and which rightly has earned her much praise. In the
culminating climax Caballé, like Giannini, takes all three top notes – B
flat, A flat and G flat – in a single breath, where others by long custom
take a breath after the B flat.

Giannini's is only one of many fine versions of 'Vissi d'arte' from the
78 era. Meta Seinemeyer (E 10851; LV 113), Hina Spani (DA 1060; LV
147), Eva Turner (L 2118; HQM 1209), Olive Fremstad (Col. 30644) all
recorded it memorably, and Melba's version (DB 702) was remarkable
for a stunningly clean leap up to the B flat. Another early version from
Geraldine Farrar (DB 246; CO 368) has purity and expansiveness
comparable on the face of it to Caballé's in our own time, but there is
no hint of portamento at the start, and instead – surprisingly with so pure
an approach – hints of sobbing attack on certain notes. The version of
Emmy Destinn (2–053053; CO 364) is another remarkable for its poise at
a slow tempo, and it is marred by no such idiosyncrasy as Farrar's little
sobs, while the combination of individuality and forthrightness is irresistibly
commanding, the final climax even more expansive than the rest. By
comparison the version recorded by Muzio at the very end of her life
(LB 40; COLC 101) is more intimate, and with consonants much clearer
(maybe thanks to the electrical recording) and a delectable shading-down
to *pianissimo*. This is singing full of inner expressiveness. At the opposite
extreme, comes a version as flawed as any ever put on record which yet
comes from one of the most celebrated Toscas of all times, the Tosca
prostrata who sang the aria lying full length on the stage, Maria Jeritza.
Hearing her record (DA 972; LV 2) has one almost disbelieving that her
reputation, or at least fame, could have been so great. By contrast Magda
Olivero (Cetra BB 25053; LPC 55015) confirms her fame with a compelling
account, sung with that peculiarly vibrant, affecting tone of hers – and,
incredibly she was still singing the part – and at the Metropolitan –
almost forty years later.

From the performances in the complete sets Callas's, in the first of her
recordings, naturally stands out, even more darkly intense than Muzio's
though not so inward-turning. The hairpin expression mark at 'fiori agli
altar' is finely exact, but it is disappointing that she does not carry the
diminuendo further in the climactic phrase down from the top B flat.
That is one of the points where Tebaldi in her later recording achieves
near-perfection, though as I have said Caballé has now set a new standard,
and without taking a breath. Callas's later recording in the Prêtre set has
many of the same qualities as her earlier performance, and with a more
inward manner, but there is some tendency, resisted before, for the voice
to sharpen, and though for the most part the vibrato is not intrusive, the

aria culminates in something not far short of flapping wobbles on the three top notes.

Leontyne Price's two versions in her complete sets make an interesting comparison, though she was finer still in the version she recorded first of all in an earlier recital disc (SB 6506). As John Steane has said of that separate account in an appendix to his survey of singing on record, *The Grand Tradition* (Duckworth, 1974): 'Here we have the grand sweep of the music, the Tosca whose soul is bold in extremity and even before God.' That is so again in her performance for Karajan, where every word conveys full meaning, but where the vibrato is not so fully under control. The performance with Mehta is straighter. There is less coloration in the voice, so that any accusations of suspect intonation disappear, and as the voice is recorded closer, not distanced as before, it sounds a degree richer and weightier. The simple point which makes it ultimately less satisfying, if still gloriously rich, is that there is less involvement, less 'face', less registration of word-meaning – a subtle contrast but a vital one. The Karajan performance, though questionable at points, is still one of the most vital of all, a powerful statement to have one registering the music afresh.

Zinka Milanov in the RCA version of the opera with Erich Leinsdorf conducting – a generally unconvincing set, curiously static – was disappointing, for in 1956 she was already well past the peak of her career, and the excessive vibrato and tendency to scoop outweigh the undoubted beauty of her natural tone. Maria Caniglia on the most striking of the complete sets of the 78 period may nowadays seem an odd choice for the heroine in an opera which revolves round her, but HMV in recording *Tosca* at that time was thinking less about the casting of the heroine than that of the tenor, for the recording was primarily designed as a vehicle for Beniamino Gigli, and his preferences were paramount. The singer first cast as Tosca was Iva Pacetti, but late in the day she had to withdraw. Caniglia was brought in as a substitute who may not have been the finest Tosca in the world at that time, but who delivered a performance with many felicities. Though her vibrato is occasionally obtrusive, her voice has plenty of bite, and in the first-act duet on the key words 'Ma falle gli occhi neri' ('But make her eyes black ones') she strikingly observes Puccini's marking *maliziosoamente*, where even Callas sings the phrase merely wistfully. And on the glorious line in Act 2 where Tosca comments on Scarpia after murdering him, 'E avanti a lui tremava tutta Roma', she delivers a sonorous and brilliantly effective *parlando* instead of the monotone usually adopted, a point where one would dearly have loved Callas to orate instead of singing.

That set with Caniglia, recorded in Rome in 1938 under Oliviero de Fabritiis, remains an important document, when Gigli as Cavaradossi gives a performance that has not been surpassed in characterfulness in more recent recordings. Anyone who thinks of Cavaradossi as an empty figure will be surprised what detail and point Gigli achieves.

With him Cavaradossi is not merely believable but acquires a distinctive and even a commanding character – easy-going where his lover is concerned, but volatile and with a great sense of humour. If anyone wants to sample in a single phrase what makes Gigli's Cavaradossi uniquely interesting let him find 'Davanti la madonna' at the end of the love duet. Tosca, to show that her jealousy has finally vanished, offers her cheek to be kissed. Cavaradossi, himself an unbeliever, teases his lover for forgetting her religious scruples. 'What, before the Madonna?' and Puccini marks the phrase *scherzoso,* which is exactly what Gigli achieves with the most infectious hint of a chuckle. So much of the lovers' relationship, their profound differences of belief as well as their love, is revealed in that one phrase.

Musically, Gigli is also delightful. The opening of 'Qual occhio al mondo' brings a half-tone of breathtaking beauty, and though later he indulges in too much *marcato* in phrases which are marked *legato*, there is always compensation in the feeling of clear confidence, the ability to compel interest in any phrase. Jussi Björling in the old RCA set may be more reliable, but there is nowhere near the same magic and Leinsdorf's heavy-handed treatment of this passage (characteristic of his handling throughout) puts any magic a long way off.

Giuseppe di Stefano is far from overshadowed by such distinguished rivals. He appears in both the Callas set of 1953 and the Price set of 1963. His earlier contribution is much the more reliable, with a glorious top B flat at the climax of the 'casetta' section (eleven bars after fig. 30) and some lovely phrasing-over (in the manner of Gigli) in 'Qual occhio al mondo'. The Karajan has many of the same qualities, although one realizes now and then what ravages time has wrought on the voice. I find the defects less rather than more troublesome on repetition; and, unlike Björling, di Stefano does give Cavaradossi a sense of humour.

Curiously in the Act 3 solo for Cavaradossi, 'O dolci mani', where he takes Tosca's hands in his, it is not Gigli who gives what I regard as the Gigli performance. One can so readily associate the phrases with Gigli's near-cooing half-tone that it comes as a surprise to find him singing the passage a little carelessly, and not as gently as one would like. It is di Stefano in the Columbia set with Callas who achieves that delicacy surprisingly well. I find it a beautiful performance; and though in the Karajan set (in what amounts to a self-imitation) di Stefano goes perilously close to the border of unsupported crooning, yet that is also a felicitous account. Later in the duet Gigli comes into his own – unrivalled, I think, in the quiet clarity of the *dolcissimo* of 'Amaro sol per te' (full-voice not half-tone) and in the forthright attack of the phrase leading up to the top B flat a few bars later.

Gigli's performance remains unique, and I have been specially fascinated by the contrast between his 'E lucevan le stelle' in the complete set and his 1934 version (DA 1372). In the 1934 version the tonal beauty of the phrases beginning 'O dolci baci' is ravishing, but the *legato* line is marred by far too many near-sobs. It is different in the complete set. The pace is slower, the mood more relaxed. Gigli's tone is not so heavenly, but the phrasing is marvellous and he takes the climactic phrase 'E non ho amato mai tanto la vita' all in one breath. That is something which, to give him credit, di Stefano does in both his sets, although the later version has nothing like the same power and the half-tone again comes too close to crooning.

Although half-a-dozen top tenors have recorded the role since di Stefano, none has overshadowed his engaging performance, let alone Gigli's. The nearest to doing so, the one who produces more character in his singing than the others, is the ever-intelligent Carlo Bergonzi on Callas's second set with Prêtre, but whether in his big arias or elsewhere he is not helped by the relative coarseness of the conducting. In any case next to others on the list his seems a small-scale performance, and that is not a question of recording balance. Placido Domingo for example in Price's second recording is placed at a distance (surprisingly far for a star performer), but the heroic size and colour of the voice are never for a moment in doubt. His is a commanding performance, not just in the arias, but it is also curiously unspecific in detail, as though Cavaradossi for him is not a particular person so much as just another hero with good tunes to sing.

José Carreras on Colin Davis's set combines many of the qualities of both Bergonzi and Domingo, for the voice, though not as rich as Domingo's, is finely heroic with a glorious cutting edge, and though the manner is forthright there is plenty of good detail. In the slow tempo which Davis sets for 'E lucevan le stelle', Carreras sustains the line superbly, and again like Domingo he is helped rather than belittled by the slight distancing of the voice. Carreras manages the potentially embarrassing sobs at the conclusion of that aria effectively, but Franco Bonisolli on the set conducted by Rostropovich bursts out in an old-fashioned histrionic style which may be fair enough on an Italian stage, but which sounds exaggerated and coarse on records. He is also self-indulgent in his phrasing, determined simply to exploit his beautiful tenor tone. In that style – self-indulgence allied to ripe tone – he is yet no match for Franco Corelli, who in the Maazel set matches the self-consciousness of the conductor. The tone may be glorious, but the result has little spontaneity, and the two arias fail to make the emotional points required. The 1956 Cetra set is notable only for Ferruccio Tagliavini's famous, honeyed Cavaradossi.

From the days of 78, gramophone evidence suggests that it took a surprisingly long time for tenors to realize the interpretative possibilities of 'E lucevan le stelle'. Early accounts tend to be straightforward, and Enrico Caruso's final version (DA 112; ORL 307) provides a natural illustration. Giovanni Martinelli's too is not specially distinguished (DA 842; ORL 224). One of the first to sing it with some attention to tonal subtlety and the use of head voice was Giacomo Lauri-Volpi (DA 983; LV 36). Miguel Fleta, despite his grotesque pulling-about of phrases and a sobbing climax, is wonderful tonally – his later version (DA 1087; LV 96) more exaggerated in its hysteria than the earlier one (DA 446).

Björling's 78 version (DA 1584; 1C 147 00947–8) was dignified rather than passionate. That approach ran with him through his career, and his account on the old RCA set is distinguished by his genuine, accurate singing of all the monotone phrases of the first stanza. The restraint does not prevent him from achieving a magnificent climax in the second stanza, though I should have liked him to phrase over 'E non ho amato mai tanto la vita' as Gigli and di Stefano do.

'Recondita armonia' also shows Björling (DA 1548) at his wonderful, forthright best. In the complete set, Leinsdorf wishes a slow speed on him, but (just as he did with Beecham's slow speeds for the arias in the New York recording of La Bohème) Björling copes without any flinching whatever, indeed seems to thrive on it. This kind of vigorous attack on the aria with little attention to characterization (not to mention Puccini's markings) seems traditional Caruso's tone is incomparably rich, with a stunning top B flat at the end, but that last climax is chopped about rather curiously, with the notes done in pairs rather than phrased-over legato. Martinelli, too, in his earlier version (DA 285), is pure and forthright rather than imaginative, with strong, steely tone.

With Martinelli there are no intrusive aspirates, which is more than one can say for Gigli. In the complete set an otherwise glorious and golden-toned account is marred by these occasional disturbances of smooth phrase-lines. The warmth of Gigli's voice, of course, is much more in keeping with the character than the other versions I have mentioned, but on the complete set it is di Stefano who makes the best attempt at obeying Puccini's marking of *piano* at the beginning of the aria – surely one of the most impossible markings ever. He shows clearly, however, how much more effective it is to have a comparatively quiet beginning and to reserve one's opening out for the phrase 'e te beltade ignota' with its shining top A. Di Stefano, alas, is not nearly so impressive in his later RCA set. Plainly it was not easy for him to cope with the top of the stave at less than full volume, but he still made an attempt at variation.

Two versions of the love duet deserve to be noted, one for its tenor, one for its soprano. With the average Florence Quartaro, Ramon Vinay proves himself an impassioned, stylish Cavaradossi (DB 6857; VIC 1395). With the adequate Richard Tucker, Ljuba Welitsch reminds us that her Tosca was finely sung and temperamentally volatile (CBS 61088). Her 'Vissi d'arte' on the same disc is also admirable.

Finally to Scarpia. Of 78 versions of the Te Deum, Lawrence Tibbett's is the classic (DB 1298) with its rich tone, dramatic intensity and long-breathed phrasing over. Pasquale Amato, with his dark, burnished tone (DB 637) has similar qualities, and also not to be overlooked from an earlier era are Mariano Stabile (L 1969; Ţima 13), who was still so impressive in the part at the Cambridge Theatre just after the war, Giovanni Inghilleri (D 1701; LV 169), who added on the same record, 'La povera mia cena' from Act 2. In many ways the most menacing of all is Riccardo Stracciari, either his later version of the Te Deum (L 2133); or his 1914 versions of the so-called Cantabile and of 'Gia, mi dicon venal' (Fono. 69157–8; CO 375). The Cantabile as also recorded in contrasting fashion by the elegant Scotti (DB 423) and the forceful Ruffo (DA 163). There is also a decent souvenir of that imposing early post-war baritone Marko Rothmuller with Franca Sacchi (also recalling a Cambridge Theatre performance) in 'Gia, mi dicon venal' (C 3689).

But just as completely as Callas in the part of Tosca, so Gobbi as Scarpia has tended to revolutionize our ideas about this unbelievably villainous villain. In fact Gobbi in his recording does not interpret the character in quite the way one expects. There are snarls enough, true, Gobbi would not be Gobbi without them, but dramatically what makes his assumption of the role so remarkable on the de Sabata discs is his restraint. In Gobbi's interpretation Scarpia does not show his hand nearly so obviously as usual. Where most baritones – and Giuseppe Taddei on the Karajan set is a good example – bring out the threatening, villainous side of the man from the start (so that one wonders why Tosca should for a moment believe anything he says), Gobbi is often almost heroic.

This restraint in Act 1 allows Gobbi to develop his part in Act 2 all the more effectively. When the mask is taken off, the result is all the more frightening and dramatic. The way that Gobbi shouts out the information that Tosca has given him of Angelotti's hiding place 'Nel pozzo del giardino' is so much more effective than usual. Yet even in Act 2, there is the subtlest gradation of effect. When at 'O che v'offenden, dolce signora' (fig. 75) Puccini marks Scarpia's part 'mellifluo': Gobbi is just that and does not indulge in the crude insinuations that one normally expects.

Gobbi, when he made his first recording, had the advantage of having his voice in glorious condition, and the complete sets show how the part requires first and foremost a completely focused voice with no woolliness or excessive vibrato. I prefer, for example, Enzo Mascherini's colourless account, which is nevertheless reliable vocally, to the ill-focused singing of George London in the later Decca set and the wobbly efforts of Leonard Warren in the old Leinsdorf version. Even Taddei on the Karajan set shows weaknesses in the voice. After a magnificent opening to the Te Deum which I have already mentioned, he plainly finds the opening-out too great a strain, and the wobble on the first top E flat is fearsome. It is a momentary lapse, happily.

When Gobbi made his second recording with Callas in 1965, his voice was still superb, and but for his performance twelve years earlier being even sharper-focused and more intense, it would naturally be regarded as a classic account. There are points of detail with so imaginative and spontaneous an artist, where the second version is valuable for its own sake, but there are few if any positive advantages. In the following year it was the world's most versatile baritone who essayed the part in Maazel's recording with Birgit Nilsson, Dietrich Fischer-Dieskau. Characteristically he found much to illuminate in the pointing of word meaning, but even at his finest he has something of the manner of a Gobbi-imitator and his failure to expand at the climax of the Te Deum indicates clearly enough why he falls short of that example. Quite apart from the un-Italianate tone, the voice at that point fails to ride the orchestra, and that is not just a question of recording balance.

Comparable in some ways to Fischer-Dieskau as Scarpia is another keenly intelligent singer from outside the Italian school, Ingvar Wixell who sings the role in Colin Davis's version. The tone often verges on the gritty, but detailed pointing is excellent, and one has a vivid picture of a keenly intelligent villain, younger and more virile than is common. Youth and virility are never in doubt either in the reading of Sherrill Milnes on the Mehta set with Leontyne Price, and there the tone is centrally satisfying from the singer who latterly has become the universal recording baritone in Italian (and other) opera. But like Domingo, the Cavaradossi in the same set, Milnes's fine singing with its rich tone-painting and musical intelligence fails ultimately to create a character specific enough. Scarpia's villainy becomes too generalized. It remained for a relatively little-known singer, Matteo Manuguerra, on Rostropovich's set, to give a performance that came closer than others in recent years to matching the achievement of Gobbi. As recorded by the Deutsche Grammophon engineers his is a voice of almost as many nuances of colour as that of Gobbi himself. In complete sympathy with the volatile Rostropovich, Manuguerra similarly creates a character which is three-dimensional, not merely an unbelievably villainous villain but an operatic figure as rich in dimension as Iago in Verdi's *Otello*, a figure who at least as much as the heroine herself transforms Puccini's opera into a work of dramatic art on a totally different plane form the original Sardou melodrama.

TOSCA

T Tosca; *C* Cavaradossi; *S* Scarpia

1920 Bartolomasi *T*; Salvaneschi *C*;
Pacini *S*/La Scala Chorus and
Orch./Sabajno
HMV S5701–24
1929 Melis *T*; Pauli *C*; Granforte

S/La Scala Chorus and
Orch./Sabajno
HMV C1902–15; Discophilia
ⓜ DIS 23
1930 Scacciati *T*; Granda *C*; Molinari

S/La Scala Chorus and
Orch./Molajoli
Columbia 9930–43; CBS Ⓜ EL
4

1938 Caniglia *T*; Gigli *C*; A. Borgioli
S/Rome Opera Chorus and
Orch./De Fabritiis
EMI Ⓜ 3C 153 0067–8;
Seraphim Ⓜ IB 6027

1951 Guerrini *T*; Poggi *C*; Silveri
S/Turin Radio Chorus and
Orch./Molinari-Pradelli
Cetra Ⓜ LPC 1230

1951 Dall' Argine *T*; Scattolini *C*;
Colombo *S*/Vienna Academy
Chorus, Vienna State Opera
Orch./Quadri
ABC Ⓜ WGM 08252–3; ABC-
Westminster Ⓜ XD 27677R

1951 Petrova *T*; Ruhl *C*; Campolonghi
S/Florence Festival Chorus and
Orch./Tieri
Remington Ⓜ 199–62

1951 Tebaldi *T*; Campora *C*;
Mascherini *S*/Santa Cecilia
Academy Chorus and
Orch./Erede
Decca Ⓜ ACL 154–5; Richmond
Ⓜ RS 62002

1952 (live performance, Palacio de
Bellas Artes, Mexico City)
Callas *T*; Di Stefano *C*;
Campolonghi *S*/Palacio de Bellas
Artes Chorus and Orch./Picco
Cetra Ⓜ L 041/2

1953 Callas *T*; Di Stefano *C*; Gobbi
S/La Scala Chorus and Orch./De
Sabata
EMI ⓔ SLS 824 ④ TC–SLS
825; Angel Ⓜ 3508 BL

1956 Milanov *T*; Björling *C*; Warren
S/Rome Opera Chorus and
Orch./Leinsdorf
RCA (UK) VICS 6000, (US)
VICS 6000 ④ V82–1022

1956 Frazzoni *T*; Tagliavini *C*; Guelfi
S/Turin Radio Chorus and
Orch./Basile
Cetra ⓔ LPS 3261 ④ MC 94–5

1957 Stella *T*; Poggi *C*; Taddei *S*/San
Carlo Opera Chorus and
Orch/Serafin
Philips 6720 007

1959 Tebaldi *T*; Del Monaco *C*;
London *S*/Santa Cecilia Academy
Chorus and Orch./Molinari-
Pradelli
Decca GOS 612–3; London OSA
1210 ④ 5–1210

1960 (in French) Rhodes *T*; Lance *C*;
Bacquier *S*/Paris Opéra Chorus
and Orch./Rosenthal
Véga 28017–9

1960 (in German) Woytowicz *T*;
Kónya *C*; Borg *S*/Berlin State
Opera Chorus, Berlin State
Orch./Stein
DG SLPM 138722–3

1963 L. Price *T*; Di Stefano *C*;
Taddei *S*/Vienna State Opera
Chorus, VPO/Karajan
Decca 5BB123–4; London OSA
1284

1964 Callas *T*; Bergonzi *C*; Gobbi
S/Paris Opéra Chorus, Paris
Conservatoire Orch./Prêtre
EMI SLS 917; Angel SCL 3655

1964 (in Russian) Milashkina *T*;
Andzaparidzye *C*; Klenov
S/Chorus, Moscow Radio
SO/Svetlanov
MK CM 02315–20

1966 Nilsson *T*; Corelli *C*; Fischer-
Dieskau *S*/Santa Cecilia
Academy Chorus and
Orch./Maazel
Decca SET 341–2; London OSA
1267

1973 L. Price *T*; Domingo *C*; Milnes
S/Alldis Choir, New
Philharmonia/Mehta
RCA (UK) ARL2 0105; (US)
ARL2 0105 ④ ARK2 0105

1976 Vishnevskaya *T*; Bonisolli *C*;
Manguerra *S*/French National
Chorus and Orch./Rostropovich
DG 2708 087 ④ 3370 008

1976 Caballé *T*; Carreras *C*; Wixell
S/Royal Opera Chorus and
Orch./C. Davis
Philips 6700 108 ④ 7699 034

1978 Freni *T*; Pavarotti *C*; Milnes
S/London Opera Chorus,
National PO/Rescigno
Decca D134D2 134K22; London
OSA 12113 ④ 5–12113

Excerpts

1932 (in French) Vallin *T*; Di Mazzei
    C; Endrèze *S*/Paris Opéra-
    Comique Chorus and Orch/Cloëz
    Odeon Ⓜ ODX 121
1943 (in German) Ranczak *T*;
    Roswaenge *C*; Hann *S*/Berlin
    Radio SO/Steinkopf
    Acanta Ⓜ BB 21497
1953 Malagrida *T*; Franzini *C*; Salzedo
    S/orch./Guarnieri
    Philips Ⓜ GBL 5537
1953 (in French) Sarroca *T*; Luccioni
    C; Blanc *S*/Paris Opéra-Comique
    Orch./Wolff
    London Ⓜ TW 91132
1959 (in German) Della Casa *T*;
    Schock *C*; Metternich *S*/German
    Opera Chorus, Berlin
    SO/Klobucar
    EMI 1C 063 28509
1960 (in French) Crespin *T*; Finel *C*;
    Blanco *S*/Paris Opéra

Orch./Prêtre
    EMI 2C 061 10608
1961 (in French) Jaumillot *T*; Poncet
    C/orch./Etchéverry
    Philips 432 614
1961 (in French) Sarroca *T*; Botiaux
    C; Legros *S*/orch./Amati
    Vogue LDM 30133 ④ B.VOC
    412
1964 (in French) Schreyer *T*; Kmentt
    C; Wächter *S*/Vienna Volksoper
    Chorus and Orch./Bauer-Theussel
    Ariola-Eurodisc Z77035R
1966 (in German) Silja *T*; King *C*;
    Fischer-Dieskau *S*/Santa Cecilia
    Academy Chorus and
    Orch./Maazel
    Decca AH6 41801
1968 (in Russian) Milashkina *T*;
    Atlantov *C*; Sokolov *S*/Bolshoi
    Theatre Orch./Ermler
    Ariola-Eurodisc K887804

Madama Butterfly

EDWARD GREENFIELD

The operas of Puccini from the earliest years after their composition have regularly inspired recordings of supreme quality, and since the advent of the LP the role of the conductor in the interpretation of Puccini has come to be appreciated as at least equal to that of the singers. As the other Puccini chapters in this book may indicate, the greatest conductors of the last half century have between them produced some of the finest Puccini opera recordings. Yet if a single Puccini opera set had to be chosen to represent the master in any archive of recording, not just for the quality of the conducting but of the singing too, then to my mind the answer would be plain. I would still feel a pang at not choosing the Beecham recording of *La Bohème*, a classic set if ever there was one, but the Puccini recording which establishes even higher claims is of *Madama Butterfly*, the set which Herbert von Karajan recorded with the Vienna Philharmonic in 1974 with Mirella Freni in the extraordinarily taxing role of the heroine and Luciano Pavarotti in the equivocal role of the hero.

Any latter-day survey of *Madama Butterfly* on record can conveniently be made to revolve round this surpassingly beautiful version, not because it is in any way a conventional or even centrally traditional reading, but because in almost every area it sets standards which the others rarely match. As in his recording of *La Bohème*, made for the same label in Berlin a couple of years earlier, Karajan takes an expansive view of the score, regularly bringing out the detailed refinement of orchestral texture (as in the night music of the first-act love duet which here has unexpected Bartokian parallels) and above all pinpointing precisely and accurately the great emotional body-blows of the work. As in *La Bohème*, but if anything with even greater subtlety, Karajan by scrupulously observing Puccini's carefully graded dynamic markings has the best of both worlds, simultaneously achieving power and refinement.

As always in Puccini scores, *fortissimo* markings are surprisingly rare, but by underlining them when they do occur instead of condoning generalized loudness, as is common, Karajan enormously reinforces the power of the climaxes. The climax in Act 2 for example when Butterfly has sighted Pinkerton's ship and realises that he has returned brings a passage marked for a brief six bars *tutta forza* and triple *forte*. That is exactly what Karajan insists on, neither more nor less, and the impact is shattering before Butterfly and Suzuki launch into their flower duet, here with Karajan taken much slower than usual so that the dotted rhythms in four–four never run the risk of sounding like ordinary compound time of twelve-eight as they normally do. And though Karajan puts his personal imprint on the recording in almost every bar, he proves the most benign and understanding of virtuoso conductors, when it comes to giving his principal singers their expressive freedom. True his often slow tempi put great strains on breath control, even with the finely equipped singers he has chosen, but he actually encourages them – where Puccini's writing assumes a *tenuto* as on a top note – to draw it out to the full. There is one point in Pinkerton's first-act duet with Sharpless (on 'furor' just before fig. 32) where Karajan actually extends an *allargando* longer than his tenor, for Pavarotti indicates clearly enough that he has had enough of his top B flat.

If that example suggests less than perfect accord, that is a false impression, for much of the greatness of this performance lies in the combination of detailed refinement and a grand overall sweep of surging spontaneity, of affectionate treatment for individual phrases and a rich appreciation of the long emotional view, with the broad expanse of the second act conveying Wagnerian concentration. It is not just the pointing of climaxes such as I have mentioned that achieves this, but the impression throughout that Karajan has considered each passage afresh and has drawn new insight from what the score tells him. I have already mentioned the distinctive manner of the opening of the flower duet, and the end of the same duet brings comparable individuality when the loving phrases in thirds for the two soloists (Christa Ludwig as Suzuki superbly matching Freni) are echoed by the orchestra to produce almost Viennese rapture, with hints of portamento on the violins – a daring touch perhaps but one superbly controlled in the hands of a Karajan.

In all this Freni's portrait of Butterfly has comparable concentration to that of the conductor, for it too is far from conventional. The quality in it which sets it apart – surprisingly when it is a quality which should immediately be associated with such a heroine – is the sense of vulnerability conveyed. Freni as prima donna may be in superb technical command – only rarely do Karajan's slow tempi tax her too far – but in emotional terms she is the vulnerable girl to the life. She underplays the skittishness in Act 1 – the showing of her treasures is restrained – but her sweet, girlish sound along with the character develops, not as so often in a sudden transformation, but gradually and believably. 'Un bel dì' typically slow, emerges fresh and communicative, starting with a *fil di voce* beautifully placed with the different sections of the narrative sharply contrasted. 'Chi sarà, chi sarà?' is quick and volatile to be followed by 'Chiamera Butterfly dalla lontana' dark with longing. When Freni was chosen for the role, hers might not have been thought a weighty enough voice, but paradoxically her placing at a distance on the sound stage actually increases the sense of power, and Freni's account of the final scene, emerging after Pinkerton has fled, sets the seal on the whole performance, detailed and gripping.

The Pinkerton of Luciano Pavarotti is also remarkable for its total conviction. In the first act clearly enough here is an open-faced, ball-playing Yankee whose feelings are genuine enough but whose sensibility is severely limited. His and Freni's singing ravishingly matches the sensuousness of the orchestral playing in the love duet. But on his return in the final scene one is forced to believe, without Pavarotti having to indulge in lachrymose histrionics, that the full horror of his actions has only just come upon him, and that he is overwhelmed with self-reproach when he sings 'Io son vil!' As always in such emotional music Pavarotti in every phrase seems to have an immediate, identifiable response, the voice doing the acting so that the facial expression is clear.

There is also the implied chuckle in the voice, a quality which has often seemed to link Pavarotti with a great compatriot of an earlier generation, Beniamino Gigli. But in fact Gigli's recording, made in 1939, presents a quite different portrait. What it has in common with Pavarotti's is that the hero is made not just a cad but understandable and even engaging; but the humour is far nearer the surface with Gigli, and even the way he speaks (not sings) the famous inquiry to Sharpless 'Milk punch or whisky?' presents us with a clear picture of a quizzical face and raised eyebrows. As for the following passage, 'Amore o grillo', it might have been written with Gigli's voice in mind, and the recording brings out both the chuckling and pouting tone which are so distinctive with this tenor. He is at his most individual too, when he talks of his 999 years' purchase, and conveys vivid conviction, when he assures Sharpless (the blank Mario Basiola) 'not to worry, my dear Consul'. His confidence (at a faster tempo than usual) is ominous.

The Butterfly in that 78 set is a soprano who inevitably divides opinion by the very timbre of her voice as recorded, Toti dal Monte. Her artistic merits in the part are not in doubt, and they have been eloquently rehearsed in the section on her singing in John Steane's *The Grand Tradition*. There he says: 'The child of fifteen whom dal Monte's pure and high-pitched voice makes so real is still physically present when the character has achieved a maturity to stand with such generous nobility before the woman to whom she has lost'. There, rightly, he pinpoints as a peak of intensity in her performance the letter duet with Sharpless in Act 2, and, like Freni, dal Monte never fails to convey the character's vulnerability. None the less the plaintive quality of the voice has to be heard with 'creative ears' if it is genuinely to suggest the child of 15. Heard fresh, it is more likely to convey something of the piping of middle or even old age. Even so, the set makes a treasurable document.

The conducting of Oliviero de Fabritiis, generally brisker than we are accustomed to today (maybe the effect of 78 recording techniques), is not one of the more treasurable elements. For fine conducting in *Butterfly* one has to turn to the LP sets. Karajan's earlier recording with La Scala forces has two principal soloists of outstanding insight and intelligence – Nicolai Gedda and Maria Callas. For 'Amore o grillo' Gedda uses at the start an attractively light head-voice, and to a remarkable degree he makes one forget the need for Italianate tone in this role, but it is for the absorbing, sharply defined characterization of the heroine by Callas that the set retains its fascination. So much so that Callas's contribution clearly outweighs that of Karajan himself. True, the refinement and spaciousness of the Karajan reading are already apparent, but nowhere so intensely as in the later Vienna set. Instead those qualities provide a fine frame for Callas's inspired scaling-down of voice and character to fit herself into the role of Puccinian 'little woman'. Already she had recorded a memorable Puccini recital which included 'Un bel dì' and the final 'Tù, tù, tù piccolo Iddio' (33CX 1204), both in fine intense performances, the latter reissued on SLS 5057. Exceptionally, the original recital presents a series of contrasted portraits of Puccini heroines, and Callas's *Butterfly* is distinct from her Mimì and her Manon, and in the complete set the characterization is developed further. The eyes may flash menacingly at times with a suspicion of the tigress, but here is a youthful charmer, one whose every word carries sharp, clear meaning.

If Karajan with Callas is relatively reticent, the conductor who in positive, detailed imagination and richness of emotional thrust comes closest to Karajan's later example is Sir John Barbirolli in the HMV set he recorded in Rome in 1966. This was surprisingly his first complete recording of a full-length opera, and his first recording project in Italy, where orchestras can be notoriously difficult with conductors unused to their strange ideas of discipline. Enough to say that Barbirolli – British by birth but Italian by extraction – charmed his players from the start, and the result is a ripely expressive reading in the broadest Italian tradition, rougher in detail than the Karajan performance, but comparable with it in the total thrust of emotion at the great climactic moments. One realizes from the start that Barbirolli is so much more in alliance with his singers and players than most opera conductors on record, so that he regularly displays that untranslatable Italian quality contained in the phrase 'con slancio', and his feeling for tempo rubato is lovingly rewarding – regularly witnessed by the groans from the conductor's lips which rival the singing of Toscanini as an expression of joy. Like Karajan, Barbirolli turns the atmospheric orchestral prelude to the final scene – musically one of the less cogent passages – into something compelling, and the first scene of Act 1 brings an account of the duet between Pinkerton and Sharpless that in sheer ardour has rarely if ever been matched. At the passage where Sharpless toasts distant families Karajan may secure a more ravishing sound from the first violins, but Barbirolli's expressiveness in the phrasing makes for an even bigger tug of emotion.

Barbirolli has as his Pinkerton the keenly intelligent Carlo Bergonzi, who had earlier recorded the role just as satisfyingly with the same concern for detail in the second of the Decca sets featuring Renata Tebaldi. In that first-act duet, however, he is enormously helped by having a comparably intelligent singer as Sharpless, Rolando Panerai – and here it might be said that the only blemish worth noting on the Karajan set is the relatively colourless Sharpless of Robert Kerns. Barbirolli's heroine is Renata Scotto. Although the microphone placing – closer than usual – is not kind to her timbre, and in particular the tendency of her voice to spread under pressure, she gives a most affecting performance, reflecting in weight of expressiveness the inner tensions of Barbirolli's reading. Her care for detail can be illustrated in her subtly contrasted treatment of the two appearances in the Act 1 love duet of the key phrase 'Rinnegata e felice'.

Just over ten years later, early in 1978, Scotto recorded the role of Butterfly again, once more with an unusually positive conductor, Lorin Maazel, who was setting out to be the first to put a complete Puccini opera cycle on record. With Scotto the development of ten years in almost every way had been an advantage. Nothing illustrates that development more clearly than a direct comparison of the most obvious passage, the aria 'Un bel dì'. In the Barbirolli version the first note is not securely placed, and though the legato is beautiful and the hairpin dynamic marks are meticulously observed, the portamenti are at times a little ungainly. Not so in the later Maazel version, where in addition the intensity of communication and the concern for word meaning are far more impressive, following on a pure and delicate *pianissimo*, finely poised, on the very first phrase. There is still a tendency for the voice to spread into a wobble at the climax, and there one must draw a parallel with Callas, whose fine performance is dotted with such moments of potential discomfort. One variation between the Scotto performances is that with Barbirolli she takes the high D flat option in her entry music, and it was not the sweetest of sounds, where for Maazel she wisely takes the lower melodic alternative.

In his conducting Maazel characteristically keeps a taut control of the musical structure. There is never any lack of weight at climaxes, but the result has not anything like the same sensuousness as the readings of Karajan or Barbirolli, and due in part to the CBS recording quality, the atmospheric warmth of Puccini's instrumentation is less apparent. It is strange too that Maazel countenanced a backward placing of the orchestra, although the voices are not so much in close-up as to coarsen the timbre. Placido Domingo sounds typically heroic, maybe too much so for such a character, and there is relatively little in his performance to distinguish it from his singing in a dozen and more other high-romantic operas. Still, his ringing tone is a joy to the ear, which is more than can be said for the somewhat gritty-toned Sharpless of Ingvar Wixell, intelligent as always but not totally sympathetic to the role.

One might compare the Pinkerton of Domingo with the assumption of another singer who in his time was comparably the universal recording tenor, Jussi Björling. His is an unsmiling Pinkerton. In the HMV set of 1960 made in Rome with Victoria de los Angeles as the heroine, he shines in the first scene opposite a dull Sharpless (Mario Sereni), but the performance is less remarkable for detailed characterization than for the headily beautiful tone-colours and a marvellously expansive account of the duet's final phrase on 'sposa americana'.

That leads immediately into the entry of the heroine, and one might say that los Angeles represents the Butterfly of a whole generation. What is too often forgotten is that los Angeles recorded the role twice in a matter of six years, once in 1954 in mono with Gianandrea Gavazzeni and then later in the Rome set with Gabriele Santini conducting. The range of tone-colour in the singer's voice made for a wonderfully complete and endearing portrait on both sets, and the consistency of her rendering makes it hard to distinguish between the performances, except to say that where the earlier one is outstanding for its expression of radiant joy in the first act (the phrase 'or son contenta' in the love duet unforgettably touching), the later one brings darker timbres that reinforce the tragic intensity of the later scenes. In particular 'Che tua madre' is agonizingly heartfelt. That is a relative contrast, and los Angeles has a way in both performances of conveying 'face' in the changes of expression which sounds totally spontaneous, to be contrasted there with the more calculating Callas.

Apart from the extra illumination which the earlier 1954 reading gives on los Angeles's assumption of the role of heroine, that set also contains two outstanding performances from the Pinkerton and the Sharpless, while the conducting of Gavazzeni has been consistently underestimated. Like his earlier compatriot, de Fabritiis, on the dal Monte/Gigli set, Gavazzeni chooses generally fast tempi, but in context they have a volatile quality, so that the exchanges of Act 1 in particular are given much more of a conversational quality than is common. That is also due to the singing of Giuseppe di Stefano as Pinkerton – sparkling in the first flush of his success – and of Tito Gobbi as Sharpless. Di Stefano in his first act solo about the 'Yankee vagabondo' uses the fast tempo to give more swagger, and the conversational tone is intensified, when Gobbi answers the prosaic question about more whisky in a way that really convinces. Gobbi has been criticized for presenting too weighty a portrait of the Consul, but in detail over and over again he puts himself in a class apart, so that his warnings to Pinkerton ('è un facile vangelo') are far more ominous than usual, the wise old head clearly shaking in premonition. And when di Stefano delivers an urgently ardent rendering of 'America for ever!', thoughtless as ever, Gobbi responds with the same phrase much slower and wiser, the distinction clearly established.

In los Angeles's later performance, Santini's conducting, like Sereni's rendering of the role of Sharpless, is flat and uninspired. None the less there is no question of the performance being valuable only for the contribution of the heroine, especially when Jussi Björling sings so attractively as Pinkerton. The phenomenon of a performance centring only on a fine Butterfly has been observed more totally with the recording made in Spain with los Angeles's compatriot, Montserrat Caballé as heroine. That link with los Angeles is clear and delightful. From first to last Caballé pours out a stream of ravishingly beautiful tone, and consistently, as in her portrait of Mimì in the Solti recording of *La Bohème*, she shows herself able to a remarkable degree to get inside the character of the Puccinian 'little woman'. The little-girl exchanges in Act 1 have a delicacy matched otherwise only by los Angeles, just avoiding the archness which with mature sopranos can be embarrassing. The opening of 'Un bel dì' with its narration is lightly touched in, but that allows even greater impact at the climax, and there is no lack of power when the child-bride emerges as a fully tragic character, though the suicide aria is too much on the heavy side. Interpretatively, there is some self-indulgence – the conductor Armando Gatto is so negative he allows her every freedom – and that is evident at Butterfly's first entry which practically comes to a halt at the end of each phrase, while in her pursuit of ever-gentler and sweeter tone-colours Caballé falls too readily into the mannerism of a downward portamenti, exquisitely effective the first time, less so with each repetition. Otherwise the set has little to commend it, with Bernabé Martí, Caballé's husband, as an expressive Pinkerton whose voice never expands enough.

It is remarkable that Renata Tebaldi – who recorded the role of Butterfly twice for Decca, both times with success – had never played it in the opera-house before she came to the studio. She had already recorded the two big arias in separate recital versions, and with her big, flawlessly rich tone, those had promised much. Few sopranos of the time could float a high *pianissimo* with such apparent ease, and when it came to her complete recordings the richness of her tone was all-enveloping. In both, the actual characterization was heavy-handed, and she was the very opposite of Caballé in failing to lighten her manner convincingly for the girlish first-act figure. In both sets the laughter is altogether too hearty to fit the character, not schoolgirl giggling at all, and the sudden darkness on 'Cosa sacre e mia' when Butterfly is asked about her father's sword goes for nothing. Erede's conducting in the earlier set is more robust and dramatic than Serafin's expansive view in the later stereo version, and that helps the character to develop convincingly, where for all the beauty of the voice, the later performance too often conveys anguished palpitating rather than deep emotion. Giuseppe Campora,

Tebaldi's Cavaradossi in her first *Tosca* recording, also sings Pinkerton in her mono *Butterfly* with sweet tone and unaffected manner. But Bergonzi in the stereo version gives an outstanding performance, just as detailed, appealing and intelligent as that on his later set with Barbirolli, and not surprisingly the voice is fresher.

The role of the American lieutenant has, of course, been sung by American tenors on record. Richard Tucker recorded it twice, once at the beginning of his career in 1948 in a recording for CBS featuring the Metropolitan Opera Company under Max Rudolf, and later to greater effect opposite Leontyne Price in the RCA version of 1962. The first time he had the formidable Eleanor Steber as Butterfly opposite him, a splendid singer who was yet not well suited to this role, too obviously purposeful to convey pathos. Price's portrait, though it has something of the conventional opera heroine about it, is altogether more sensitive, though the detail of the performance is often laid on too heavily, and the impression is certainly not of a Puccinian little woman. Most effective are the two big arias, 'Un bel dì' and 'Tù, tù piccolo iddió, done with glorious richness and range of tone.

More delicate is another portrait of Butterfly by an American soprano, also on the RCA label and also with Erich Leinsdorf conducting. That is with Anna Moffo, recorded four years before the Price set, and the portrait of the heroine is charming, fresh and young-sounding without any heavy coyness. In Act 1 she conveys admirably the element of wonder, the child bride almost overwhelmed, but the portrait is not consistently detailed. Despite his name, the tenor opposite her, Cesare Valletti, is American too, at times injecting meaning into words too effortfully but using his light, attractive voice well. I have not been able to hear the sets with Maria Chiara and Raina Kabaivanska as heroine: they look notable only for the singing of these two appreciable Puccini sopranos. Similarly the excerpts with Licia Albanese and Marie Collier (who was well-known as a Sadler's Wells exponent of the role) are worth hearing for their contributions. The many German contenders are not inspiring, but Fritz Wunderlich's golden tones make their mark as Pinkerton in the 1960 disc.

In the years of 78s before the dal Monte/Gigli set there were other complete recordings including the first of all, an acoustic set of 1922 recorded in English with Eugene Goossens Snr conducting and with a cast including Rosina Buckman as Butterfly and the redoubtable Tudor Davies as Pinkerton. Much more widely circulated was the 1929 Columbia set electrically recorded with a cast from La Scala conducted by Lorenzo Molajoli. Like other Puccini sets of the period from that source it featured the company's principal lyric soprano of the late 1920s and early 1930s, a great favourite in Milan and elsewhere, Rosetta Pampanini. It was a good performance but not one to set the listener afire as dal Monte's was later to do. Similarly Margaret Sheridan on the 1931 HMV set, also from

La Scala but with Carlo Sabajno conducting, was totally reliable but in the end unmemorable. The bright-toned Pinkerton was Lionello Cecil, the Italian pseudonym of one Cecil Sherwood. Excerpts are reissued on LV 201.

As with other Puccini operas in the days of 78s the really important recordings were of individual arias – the heroine's above all – sung by the greatest operatic stars of the day. In the years immediately following the first performance of Butterfly in 1904 the most notable series of recordings of excerpts – not recorded consistently but over a period – came from the quartet of singers who took the principal roles in the first production at the Metropolitan in New York in February 1907. Caruso was Pinkerton with Antonio Scotti as Sharpless, while Louise Homer sang Suzuki opposite the richly secure and satisfying Butterfly of Geraldine Farrar. Caruso – a little like Placido Domingo in our day – does not seem to have characterized the role sharply, but used it to produce the most gloriously satisfying stream of rich tenor tone, whether in 'Amore o grillo' with Scotti (DM 113) or the love duet with Farrar (DM 110) or above all in the pulsating version (again with Scotti on the reverse of DM 113) of Pinkerton's 'Addio fiorito asil!' Puccini feared that without such a passage no top tenor would agree to sing the role, and Caruso's relishing of the music makes one appreciate why.

Farrar and Homer went to the RCA Victor Studio in Camden, New Jersey, only nine days after the Metropolitan première to record the flower duet (DK 125) and to this day it remains a most refreshing document, urgent and resilient in the first part, but then expanding luxuriantly for the 'Viennese' passage in thirds in a way that artists on 78s often failed to achieve. In this and other passages from *Butterfly* which she recorded, Farrar's singing was centrally satisfying, whether in the Entry (DA 204), the love duet with Caruso, already mentioned, the letter duet of Act 2 with Scotti as Sharpless (DK 118) or above all the two big arias, 'Un bel di' (DB 246) and 'Tu, tu piccolo iddio' (DA 508), all sung with freshness of tone and purity of style. All these 78s were collected on one LP disc (VIC 1600).

Among early versions of those two big arias Emmy Destinn's are also remarkable, the more so when this was a singer who considering her impregnable reputation made generally disappointing records. 'Un bel di' (053171; CO 364) begins with a delightfully clear, pure opening phrase, but even more notable is her rendering of the death scene (53533), totally passionate and committed with thrilling fullness of tone. When considering the many versions of 'Un bel di' one finds surprisingly few impressive ones from Italian singers (even Galli-Curci's was disappointing), but a relatively formidable list of fine versions by German singers. Apart from Destinn (actually a Czech by birth) there were notable records in German by Lotte Lehmann (Od. 0–4834; LV 22) and from Lotte Schöne, best remembered for her exquisitely beautiful singing of the 'Liù' arias in

Turandot, who here coupled the big aria with the later second-act solo, 'Che tua madre' (EJ 422; LV6). Most memorable among German singers in this era was Meta Seinemeyer using Italian (Parlo. E 10805; LV 113). Recorded not long before the singer died in 1929, this is one of the richest and most vibrant versions ever put on disc, full-voiced as well as poised and with the most subtle shading. On the reverse Seinemeyer sings the entry charmingly (in German) and she also recorded the flower duet with Helené Jung (E 10883; LV 115). Maria Cebotori sounds ecstatic in her pre-war, German account of the love duet with the Tauber-like Herbert Ernst Groh (Od. 0–25627; 1C 147–29 119), less fresh and easy in tone in her Italian 'Un bel di' and death, recorded in Italian in 1948 (DB 6940; 1C 147–29 119).

Two British sopranos in 'Un bel di' must also be mentioned – Joan Cross and Joan Hammond, both in English. Cross's version (C 2824) is the more delicate – characteristically refined and sensitive but with telling dramatic power, a product of her early years with Sadler's Wells, while Hammond's (DX 1003) was for years a famous best-seller, revealing the voice at its most vibrant and expressive. Later in her career on an LP recital Hammond recorded the aria again, but it was less rich and less spontaneous sounding. Another famous recording in English of a passage from *Butterfly* featured two unexpected singers in the love duet, the soprano Isobel Baillie and the tenor, Francis Russell (Col. 9654). Although the translation gives the extract an unpromising title, 'Give me your darling hands' it was a delightful and refreshing performance, which in no way revealed the singers' lack of experience in this particular repertory.

The love duet prompted combinations of famous singers on several occasions, not just the aforementioned Caruso and Farrar. Most memorable perhaps were Frances Alda and Giovanni Martinelli (DK 100). A beautifully warm, cleanly rhythmic version in German came from Elisabeth Rethberg and Richard Tauber (Od. Rxx 80732–3; LV 170) who also recorded a tenderly phrased account, in German, of 'Addio fiorito asil' (Od. 0–8228). In the duet, Margaret Sheridan and Aureliano Pertile made a version (DB 1119; LV 245) noted for its unbridled passion, as did Pampanini with Francesco Merli (CQX 10229), Dusolina Giannini and Marcel Wittrisch (DB 1946; 1C 147 29 118–9).

Zenatello, the first Pinkerton, recorded the love duet with Lina Cannetti (Fono. 92815–6; Eterna 726), forward and ardent on his part. Sheridan (DB 1084) and Lehmann, in German (PO 157; HQM 1121), should also be noted, in addition to Seinemeyer, in Butterfly's entrance. In 'Addio fiorito asil' Lauri-Volpi (DA 1385) and Julius Patzak, in German (PO 5007) deserve mention for, in their different ways, stylistic strength and tender phrasing.

The Viennese quality of Patzak's voice brings one full circle round to the Vienna performance of Karajan with its sweetness and warmth and its imaginative touches of Viennese popular music. It is the genius of

Puccini in *Butterfly*, even beyond his achievement in other operas, regularly to skirt the cliff-edge of vulgarity – in his very choice of subject as well as the characterization and the musical inspiration – and Karajan more than anyone on record has been able to distil that improbable mixture and present *Madama Butterfly* as an unmistakable masterpiece.

MADAMA BUTTERFLY

C Cio-Cio San *P* Pinkerton; *Su* Suzuki; *Sh* Sharpless

1922 (in English) Buckmann *C*; Davies *P*; Walker *Su*; Ranalow *Sh*/chorus and orch./Goossens Snr
HMV D893–906

1928 Pampanini *C*; Granda *P*; Velasquez *Su*; Vanelli *Sh*/La Scala Chorus and Orch./Molajoli
Columbia 9784–97

1931 Sheridan *C*; Cecil *P*; Mannarini *Su*; Weiberg *Sh*/La Scala Chorus and Orch./Sabajno
HMV C1950–65; Club 99 ⓜ OP 1001

1939 dal Monte *C*; Gigli *P*; Palombini *Su*; Basiola *Sh*/Rome Opera Chorus and Orch./Fabritiis
EMI ⓜ 3C 153 00669–70; Seraphim ⓜ IB 6059

1940s (live performance, Metropolitan, New York) Albanese *C*; Melton *P*; Brownlee *Sh*/Metropolitan Opera Chorus and Orch./Cimara
Metropolitan Opera Fund ⓜ MET 2

1949 Steber *C*; Tucker *P*; Madeira *Su*; Valdengo *Sh*; Metropolitan Opera Chorus and Orch./Rudolf
CBS (US) ⓜ Y3–32107; (UK) ⓜ 78246

1950s (in Russian) Shumskaya *C*; Kozlovsky *P*; Gribova *Su*; Selivanov *Sh*/Bolshoi Opera Chorus and Orch./Bron
MK ⓜ DO 7923–8

1951 Ilitsch *C*; Delorco *P*; Rössl-Majdan *Su*; Jaresch *Sh*/Chorus, Austrian SO/Loibner
Remington ⓜ 199–81

1951 Tebaldi *C*; Campora *P*; Rankin *Su*; Inghilleri *Sh*/Santa Cecilia

Academy Chorus and Orch./Erede
Decca ⓜ ACL 59–61; Richmond ⓜ RS 63001

1953 Frati *C*; O. Taddei *P*; Bertolini *Su*; Giorgetta *Sh*/Florence Festival Chorus and Orch./Ghiglia
Allegro-Royale ⓜ 1495–7

1954 Petrella *C*; Tagliavini *P*; Masini *Su*; Taddei *Sh*/Turin Radio Chorus and Orch./Questa
Cetra ⓒ LPS 3248 ④ MC 98–9

1954 los Angeles *C*; di Stefano *P*; Canali *Su*; Gobbi *Sh*/Rome Opera Chorus and Orch./Gavazzeni
World Records ⓜ OC 161–3; Seraphim ⓜ IC 6090

1955 Callas *C*; Gedda *P*; Danieli *Su*; Boriello *Sh*/La Scala Chorus and Orch./Karajan
EMI ⓒ SLS 5015 ④ TC–SLS 5015; Angel ⓜ 3523CL

1956 (in French) Angelici *C*; Lance *P*; Collard *Su*; Giovannetti *Sh*/Paris Opéra-Comique Chorus and Orch./Wolff
EMI ⓜ 2C 153 12186–7

1958 Moffo *C*; Valletti *P*; Elias *Su*; Cesari *Sh*/Rome Opera Chorus and Orch./Leinsdorf
RCA VICS 6100

1958 Tebaldi *C*; Bergonzi *P*; Cossotto *Su*; Sordello *Sh*/Santa Cecilia Academy Chorus and Orch./Serafin
Decca D4D3; London OSA 1314

1960 (in German) Schlemm *C*; Kónya *P*; Plümacher *Su*; Borg *Sh*/Württemberg State Opera Chorus and Orch./Leitner

DG 138750–2

1960 los Angeles C; Björling P;
Pirazzini Su; Sereni Sh/Rome
Opera Chorus and Orch./Santini
EMI SLS 5128 ④ TC–SLS
5128; Angel SCL 3604 ④
4X3S–3604

1962 L. Price C; Tucker P; Elias Su;
Maero Sh/Rome Opera Chorus
and Orch./Leinsdorf
RCA (UK) SER 5504–6, (US)
LSC 6160 ④ ARK 3 2540

1966 Gordoni C; Molese P; Casei Su;
Meucci Sh/Vienna State Opera
Chorus and Orch./Santi
Orpheus SMS 2481

1966 Scotto C; Bergonzi P; Stasio Su;
Panerai Sh/Rome Opera Chorus
and Orch./Barbirolli
EMI SLS 927 ④ TC-SLS 927;
Angel SCLX 3702

1969 Kabaivanska C; Gino Taddei P;
Marcossi Su; Maffeo Sh/Naples
Academy Chorus, Naples
PO/Rapalo

1971 Chiara C; King P; Schmidt Su;
Prey Sh/Bavarian Radio Chorus
and Orch./Patané
Ariola-Eurodisc XG 68515R

1974 Freni C; Pavarotti P; Ludwig
Su; Kerns Sh/Vienna State
Opera Chorus, VPO/Karajan
Decca SET 584–6 ④ K2A1;
London OSA 13110 ④ 5–13110

1976 Caballé C; Martí P; Mazzieri
Su; Bordoni Sh/Barcelona Liceo
Theatre Chorus, Barcelona
SO/Gatto
Decca D68DR3; London OSA
13121 ④ 5–13121

1978 Scotto C; Domingo P; Knight
Su; Wixell Sh/Ambrosian Opera
Chorus, Philharmonia
Orch./Maazel
CBS (UK) 79313

Excerpts

1946 Albanese C; Melton P;
Browning Su/RCA
Orch./Weissmann
RCA (US) ⓜ LM 2

1951 Stader C; van Dijk P; Töpper
Su/Bavarian State Opera Chorus
and Orch./Hollreiser

DG ⓜ 478076

1953 (in German) Berger C; Schock
P; Wagner Su; Fischer-Dieskau
Sh/Berlin Opera Chorus and
Orch./Schüchter
EMI ⓜ 1C 047 28570

1955 (in French) Le Bris C; Luccioni
P; Berbié Su; Massard
Sh/Chorus and Orch./Hartemann
Vega ⓜ L 18011

1956 Albanese C; Peerce P; Rota Su;
Capecchi Sh/Rome Opera
Chorus and Orch./Bellezza
Victor ⓜ LM 2054

1957 (in French) Boué C;
D'Apparecida P; Cadiou Su;
Depraz Sh/SO/Menet
Barclay ⓜ 89015

1960 (in English) Collier C; Craig P;
Robson Su; Griffiths Sh/Sadler's
Wells Opera Chorus and
Orch./Balkwill
EMI ESD 7030 ④ TC–ESD
7030; Angel S35902

1960 (in Hungarian) Orosz C;
Ilosfalvy P; Komlóssy Su;
Jámbor Sh/Hungarian State
Opera Orch./Vaszy
Qualiton ⓜ LPX 1127

1960 (in German) Lorengar C;
Wunderlich P; Wagner Su; Prey
Sh/Berlin Komische Oper
Chorus, Berlin SO/Klobucar
EMI 1C 063 29000

1961 (in French) Monmart C;
Sénéchal P; Benoît Sh/Brasseur
Chorale, Orch./Leitner
DG 136 264

1962 Rizzoli C; Savio P; Tasso Su;
Monachesi Sh/Milan New
Theatre Chorus, Hamburg Radio
SO/Annovazzi
Saga ⓜ SAGA 5172

1963 (in German) Eipperle C;
Wunderlich P; Hilbert Su;
Zilliken Sh/German Opera
Chorus and Orch./Kraus
Ariola-Eurodisc Z75873R

1963 (in French) Cumia C; Vanzo P;
Hahn Su; Bianco Sh/Chorus and
Orch./Ghiglia
Vogue LDM30131 ④ B.VOC
414

1969 (in German) Rothenberger C;

Gedda *P*; Wagner *Su*; Prey
Sh/Berlin Radio Chamber Choir,

German Opera Orch./Patanè
EMI 1C 063 29006

Turandot

EDWARD GREENFIELD

The odd thing is that many of the most desirable recordings of *Turandot* have never been published. In its early years, at least, there seemed to be a jinx on the opera. EMI took its recording team to Milan in 1926, when after Toscanini's opening performance at La Scala (as Puccini left the score), Ettore Panizza conducted the remaining performances of the season with Alfano's ending. The jinx saw to it that the live recordings of Panizza made in the November were imperfect (stories are told at Hayes of the engineer failing to get his sound-box down on time and shouting: 'Start it again!') and later the test lacquers were accidentally destroyed. Only one record emerged from the project (D 1241) containing two choruses merely – 'Gravi, enormi' introducing scene two of Act 2 and an item called 'O divina' which was in fact the final chorus of Act 3 'Diecimila anni'.

According to the archives at Hayes two other choruses, recorded at the time, were prepared for issue and then shelved – 'Gira la cote' and 'Ecco laggiù in barlume' from Act 1. It may seem strange that none of the solo items emerged from the project (neither Rosa Raisa, the first Turandot, nor Miguel Fleta, the first Calaf, ever recorded a note of their parts commercially) but the live recording techniques were primitive and probably the chorus alone achieved the necessary volume. Strangely the label of D 1241 gives no clue that it was recorded at these historic live performances. About the rest we can only guess now that the original lacquers are destroyed.

The other instance is much more famous. EMI recorded selected extracts from two of the performances of *Turandot* given at Covent Garden in the Coronation season of 1937. The juxtaposition of Eva Turner as the Icy Princess and Giovanni Martinelli as Prince Calaf has always roused the keenest expectation, particularly when Barbirolli was conducting. The existence of this recording in the company's archives had long been talked about, but commercial issue on the HMV label was always held up by arguments over royalties and who exactly was playing in the London Philharmonic on each night. Copies somehow found their way out, and then in the 1960s came LP versions of both sets of extracts which, presumably, provide no royalties to anyone. One of these private issues covers one of the early performances of the season with Mafalda Favero as Liù. Another is specifically dated, the performance of 10 May 1937 with the young Licia Albanese as Liù. Some copies have Martinelli's two big arias ('Non piangere, Liù' and 'Nessun dorma') transferred a semitone high, making the voice harder than it should be, but the one I used for my comparison was different. Barbirolli's tempi were consistently slow – we heard the same phenomenon in his HMV *Butterfly* recorded in Rome nearly thirty years later – and in 'Non piangere, Liù' even Martinelli found it hard to spin out his breath. By 10 May there had obviously been backstage discussions and the tempi both for 'Non piangere, Liù' and Turandot's 'In questa reggia' were not just faster, but fast by any standards. If in the earlier version the pauses between phrases in both arias tended to make the music sag a little, it was on the whole preferable, allowing the voices fuller span, to the hint of perfunctoriness in the later performance. In both versions of 'In questa reggia' Barbirolli changed gear into an exceptionally fast speed for the culminating melody, though the score's marking is *largamente*. For the rest, Favero as Liù is hard-toned and not very interesting, Albanese much more sympathetic, with 'Signore, ascolta' pure and clean, spoilt marginally by a loud final phrase. The chorus was almost past belief in oratorio-trained Englishness in both performances, and the LPO strings were still in the habit of swooping.

While mentioning Turner's non-commercial recordings one must not forget the BBC studio performance she gave with Dino Borgioli as Calaf and Stanford Robinson conducting on 8 November 1937, a few months after the Covent Garden performances. Another private issue has 'In questa reggia' and the riddles to the end of Act 2 – not surprisingly very like the opera-house performances but with the voice a shade fresher, the vibrato less noticeable. But in all these live performances the magnificence of Turner's assumption of the role is never for a moment in doubt: top Cs in the Covent Garden performances that without any strain ride gloriously over the loudest ensemble. Formidable in characterization too, the grand manner coming naturally, with no falseness.

Inevitably the atmospheric tension is less in the commercial recordings of 'In questa reggia' in which Turner's Turandot is officially commemorated. Curiously both versions were recorded in 1928. The earlier of the two (Col. D 1619) has brilliant singing, but the acoustic is dry. The other version made in Westminster Central Hall with an orchestra conducted by Stanford Robinson is much better known (D 1631; HQM 1209). In Central Hall the voice has room to ring out. At the beginning there is not the same tenderness on such phrases as 'Principessa Lou-Ling' as in the Covent Garden performances (by 1937 Turner's Turandot spanning a wider range of emotion) but the increasing 'pull' of the phrasing is irresistible, first up to 'Ah, rinasce' and then through all three of the culminating phrases, Calaf's as well as Turandot's (different practice from D 1619). The top C on the last phrase is nothing less than triumphant, phrased over, as it should be down to the E flat. And who cares if the words in that last phrase are not all there?

When it comes to other Turandots on 78s the temperature inevitably gets lower. I shall leave considering the artists on the LP sets until the end, but it is surprising how few sopranos in the days of 78 even attempted to record any of Turandot's music. Those that did tended to come not from the Italian school at all but from farther north. Puccini held that Lotte Lehmann was his favourite Suor Angelica, and so she was asked to sing Turandot. It was in Vienna, and she knew at once that it was a mistake, a role that she was magnificently equipped to portray emotionally but which was too much of a strain on the voice. She was persuaded to record 'In questa reggia' (R 20014), but stopped before the final phrases (could there be a greater anti-climax?). In 'Dal primo pianto', Alfano's best passage, (R 20014), the word-meaning, the characterization is predictably compelling, a face you can see during the singing; an interpretation tough but sympathetic, vocally spoilt only by a scoop upwards at the climax.

Otherwise the first Arabella, Viorica Ursuleac, wife of Clemens Krauss, did a sensitive recording of 'In questa reggia' (CA 8227). The beat in her voice was too fruity for the music, the top Bs were uncomfortable and there was little Italianate expansion, but 'Principessa Lou-Ling' was exquisitely gentle, and the diminuendo on the 'caravane' phrase was beautifully controlled.

Of the others Maria Nemeth's version of 'In questa reggia' (CA 8190; LV 214) is the most remarkable. Here was a voice that could cope not only with Turandot's and Tosca's music, but with that of the Queen of Night and Donna Anna. The half-tone musing at the beginning of 'In questa reggia' is most beautiful, with real mystery on 'Principessa Lou-Ling'. The voice when pushed does not sound so happy, but the repeated low Fs on 'spense la sua fresca' are superb. Fine, well-projected top Bs but a disappointing top C. Anna Roselle, the Dresden Turandot of 1926 (CA 8180; LV 77), displays glorious tone-colour on top, but sounds miscast.

Joan Hammond (DA 1988; HQM 1186) phrases with Eva Turner's distinction if not with the vocal amplitude of her fellow DBE. Amy Shuard (MFP 2057), who not only was taught by Dame Eva but followed her in the role at Covent Garden a decade or so later, bids fair to rival her mentor. Eileen Farrell (SABL 177) begins more slowly than is customary, with more deliberate expressiveness and refined contrasts of tone, but hardness emerges at climaxes.

Liù's music in the days of 78 attracted more contestants than Turandot's (not surprisingly) and again the German school tended to predominate. Lotte Schöne's account of the two arias (E 503; LV 6) was the most famous and in some ways the most beautiful, for there was a lightness of tone and control of phrase (with beautiful portamenti) that is not so far distant from the art of Elisabeth Schumann. The final *codetta* of 'Signore, ascolta' is particularly beautiful, but, like others of this period, Schöne surprisingly failed to cope gracefully with the problem of the final rise to B flat. She takes an awkward extra breath just as she is going up from A flat to B flat. Vocally I prefer the version (sung in German) of Luise Helletsgrüber, with much more detail of characterization (Parlo. E 11358). The tempo is slow, but is beautifully sustained, and already she observes what one might call the 'echo-phrase' tradition in each stanza. The composer may not have marked the repeated phrases at the end of main melody to be sung in echo, but it is an obvious and effective gloss, which he might well have added had he lived to see the score published. Rosina Torri, with the same coupling, produces fresh bright singing but is not helped by a stiff conductor (B 2409). There is no *calore* and a big breath before the final E flat of 'Tù che di gel sei cinta'.

A number of sopranos coupled 'Tù che di gel sei cinta' not with 'Signore, ascolta' but with 'Tanto amore e segreto'. Fresh girlish singing, almost a Butterfly sound comes from the Norwegian Eidé Norena (DA 4832; LV 193) with a big, romantic *allargando* for the final phrase of 'Tù che di gel'. The same coupling is sung most memorably in German by Berta Kiurina (Parlo. P 9165; LV 91) – superb half-tones, lovely legato, but with moments of toughness in 'Tù che di gel'. There is a poor bottom E flat, but obviously fine control and fine artistry, although one finds that she must have been nearing 50 when she made the record around 1930. Of the others of the period, Rosetta Pampanini is disappointing, tremulous with over-emotional expressiveness. Others, too numerous to comment on, include Albanese, Rosanna Carteri and Magda Olivero. In recent times Maria Chiara (SXL 6548) has recorded a tender, poised 'Signore, ascolta'.

When one comes to the part of Calaf the dominance of Martinelli is almost equal to that of Turner as Turandot, but alas not on ordinary commercial records. Surprisingly, he did not sing the part until that Coronation season I have already noted. Puccini saw Martinelli in 1921 when the score was well-advanced, got him to sing 'Nessun dorma' at sight, demanded an encore in full voice and said he wanted him for his first Calaf. Toscanini, too, was eager – when, after Puccini's death, the opera was finally presented incomplete – to have Martinelli singing, but there was a problem with Gatti-Casazza and Martinelli's contract at the Metropolitan. In 1927 when the opera reached New York, Martinelli understandably refused Gatti-Casazza's offer for him to sing in the production. Lauri-Volpi did it instead. Apart from the Covent Garden records I have already mentioned, there is the ultimate in curiosities in an extract from the Seattle performance of 21 January 1967, when

Martinelli was 81. He took the role of the Emperor, and the power and projection are still formidable. Unfortunately the dubbing on a 'private' label brings a misguided gimmick. A studio record of the aged Martinelli singing Calaf's phrases in the riddles is set against his own Emperor. He is wildly flat in Calaf's music, and not surprisingly his versions of 'Non piangere, Liù' and 'Nessun dorma' made in 1950, when he was 65, are not fair to his reputation either.

The list of tenors who did those two arias on 78 contains some unexpected names. Richard Tauber (Od. 0–8401) does *echt*-Viennese versions in German, heavy, too sweet in their outpouring of golden tone. Unlike almost every other tenor, he sings the final phrase of 'Nessun dorma' as Puccini wrote it with the top B merely flicked at, not sustained. Alfred Piccaver (CA 8116) was another who poured forth a glorious stream of tone, but with careless rhythm particularly in 'Nessun dorma' the result is disappointing. Charles Kullmann (Col. DW 3068; LV 144) singing 'Nessun dorma' in German brings a light heady tone, expanding *con calore* and ringing final phrases which sound marvellous on record but which might not have rung so gloriously in the flesh. Tom Burke's version of 'Nessun dorma' (Col. D 1593) is another off the beaten track that I have enjoyed particularly: big pure tone, fine production, a fine build-up of imperfect Italian – 'Splendurrah'.

Excellent versions of both arias come from Antonio Cortis (DA 1075) with rich tone and a smooth line. Alessandro Valente's version (B 2458; LV 236) had the distinction of being reissued later at popular request on a more expensive label (DA). The tone is free and heady with no coarsening at climaxes; not much flow in 'Non piangere, Liù'. Gigli's version of 'Nessun dorma', recorded in London a few weeks before his sixtieth birthday, may not be the most stylish, but the projection of warmth is characteristic – the chorus coming in at the end with the music which Alfano put at the end of the opera (DB 21138; RLS 732).

Jussi Björling did a clean, straightforward version of 'Nessun dorma' during the war (DA 1841; RLS 715), but it is his interpretation of the whole part on LP in the RCA version conducted by Leinsdorf that deserves closer attention. Leinsdorf was at that period in the habit of setting unusually slow tempi for Björling. The RCA *Tosca* set provides an obvious example, and one which to my mind fails. With the part of Calaf the challenge succeeded, but I suspect that the legato would have been more seamless in the first part of 'Nessun dorma' had it been taken a little quicker. Then a marvellous 'pull' of momentum develops as the big tune starts on 'Ma il mio mistero'. There is a gentle start to the second stanza as marked – a rare thing.

Surprisingly there are one or two touches in 'Nessun dorma' missed by Björling that are brought out by Franco Corelli in the set conducted by Molinari-Pradelli: In 'Non piangere, Liù' he tackles 'portalo via con te' with imagination and provides a good sustaining link on 'Questo, questo'.

On the earlier Decca set Mario del Monaco is less coarse than usual but dull. This mid-1950s period found him producing an even flow of rich tone without too much straining, but interpretatively he has little to offer. Eugenio Fernandi, a minor Italian tenor, was a curious choice for the *Turandot* with Serafin conducting and Callas as the Princess – not a bad one as it turned out, for the voice is attractive with interesting tone, and the phrasing is well-managed if with the effect of too much careful study. He projects little personality.

That is just where Luciano Pavarotti scores in the later Decca set with Joan Sutherland as Turandot, Zubin Mehta conducting. Helped by the strong but flexible conducting of Mehta – his feeling for the natural ebb and flow of Puccinian writing has never been more convincingly demonstrated on record – Pavarotti's observance of the meticulous markings modifying the tempo sounds totally spontaneous, so that even an aria like 'Non piangere Liù' has an almost conversational quality, with the meaning of the words conveyed in detail. On the 1978 set made in Strasbourg with Alain Lombard conducting, José Carreras, an intelligent tenor with a fine even tone throughout his range, still gives dull performances of the big arias, thanks largely to the unimaginative, conducting.

If Pavarotti's ebb and flow of expression sounds spontaneous, that is not quite true of Elisabeth Schwarzkopf's equally scrupulous observance of markings – *ritenuto, poco ritenuto, a tempo* and so on – in her singing of the role of Liù in the Serafin mono set opposite Callas's Turandot. This is one of the most memorable portraits of the second heroine ever put on record, but where usually Schwarzkopf's care over detail makes for extra illumination, the two big arias at least sound a little too careful. There is glorious Strauss-like singing for the rising and falling octaves at the end of 'Signore ascolta' and a fine crescendo on the concluding B flat, if a less certain diminuendo. It is almost as though Schwarzkopf is attempting a Butterfly voice in both arias, and one notes links with the long-admired Lotte Schöne.

The idea of Liù as a first cousin of Butterfly tends to run through the portrayals by most of the other sopranos in the LP sets. Renata Scotto as Liù on the HMV/Molinari-Pradelli set provides no *mezza voce* on the echo phrases of 'Signore ascolta' and generally the performance is lacking a little in detail, but the tone is beautiful and the phrasing nicely flexible with a natural forward movement. Mirella Freni, who with Karajan has recorded surpassingly beautiful performances in the roles of Mimi and Butterfly, starts at a disadvantage as Liù in the Lombard performance on HMV, not just because of pedestrian conducting but because the recording is unflattering to the voice, giving a hint of flutter. Like Scotto at the end of 'Signore ascolta' she takes a breath before the final rising octave but much more obtrusively, using it to expand formidably on the final top B flat.

A comparable expansion comes in the first of Renata Tebaldi's two recorded performances of Liù, the Decca one with Alberto Erede conducting, but there she cuts the top note off too sharply. That version, with its exceptionally slow speed enhancing Tebaldi's most affectingly simple style with fine shading of echo phrases, is clearly differentiated from her performance of six years later with Leinsdorf on the RCA set. There that aria is altogether faster and lighter. There is more care over detail (on 'io l'ombra' for example) but some warmth is inevitably lost. In 'Tù che di gel sei cinta' the earlier version is more heavily expressive, but in the first appearance of 'prima di questa aurora' the delicate contrast of tone is more beautifully managed, and there is more urgency in the big opening out at the end.

But the singer who most clearly differentiates the character of Liù is Montserrat Caballé. She responded to the challenge of singing the role opposite so formidable a Turandot as Joan Sutherland not by turning it into a dramatic role (as both Scotto and Freni show signs of doing) but by producing her gentlest and sweetest tones whenever she can. In 'Signore ascolta' she deliberately lightens the voice at the very start, and ends the aria with the most breathtaking *pianissimi* on the rising octaves, allowing no crescendo on the final B flat (the vocal part does not have one marked) but spinning the note out in a hushed tone which only at the very end deteriorates, with a hint of unsteadiness as it reaches a whisper. With no breath on the last rising octave it is a masterly demonstration of technique as well as of expressive warmth.

In both arias Mehta's conducting (as for Pavarotti) allows a greater variation of tempo and expression than usual but with an underlying firmness. However, the culmination of Caballé's performance comes not so much in the aria, 'Tù che di gel sei cinta', but in the actual confrontation with the Icy Princess preceding that, when physically in Kingsway Hall at the recording sessions the two great sopranos actually confronted each other. I happened to be present to witness the tensions and felicities of the occasion, but even had I not been, I think I would have detected the sense of challenge which Caballé accepted to the full. There her singing is ecstatically beautiful, above all in the honeyed tones she produces for the key phrase 'del mio amore'. In some of the heavier passages Caballé's voice is not perfectly steady, but as a whole it is an outstandingly beautiful performance.

Caballé, when five years later she tackled the role of Turandot herself, used comparable imagination, but with less sympathetic treatment from the engineers, apart from the effects of time on the voice and of possibly a less appropriate role, the result has not the same command. It remains a keenly memorable portrayal. The voice as recorded for EMI may sound light in relation to Sutherland's on the Decca set, but her shading of *pianissimi* is so striking, it produces powerful results almost by a kind of musical ju-jitsu. On the climactic phrase of the first part of the aria 'In questa reggia', to the words 'quel grido e quella morte!', Caballé expands conventionally enough and most impressively up to the top B flat on 'grido', but then shades the phrase off to an unexpected *pianissimo* on 'morte', no longer vehement about the death of Princess Lou-Ling but profoundly saddened. The very gentleness with which earlier in the aria she mentions that name points towards the unexpectedly gentle treatment of the climax.

Of earlier complete performances the first of all in the days of 78 discs had Gina Cigna in the role of Turandot. It was issued in 1938 on sixteen discs. It was dim in sound with the EIAR Chorus and Orchestra of Turin under Franco Ghione providing comparably dim performances. Cigna, loud-voiced and edgy, was at least more successful as Turandot than she had been as Norma in Cetra's complete Bellini opera set of the previous year. Francesco Merli sang strongly in the dramatic music (he did separate versions of the two arias for Columbia), but it was Magda Olivero, later to become an almost legendary figure on both sides of the Atlantic, who was the most appealing principal, singing tenderly as Liù, though spoiling the end of 'Signore ascolta' with uncontrolled sobbing. Curiously the set omits 'Dal primo pianto' while providing an unnecessary filler in the Hymn to Rome on side 32.

As I have already suggested, the conducting of Mehta is outstanding in the later of the two Decca sets of the opera, but earlier Serafin was almost equally impressive in the set with Callas, Schwarzkopf and a cast from La Scala. True, the choral work is typically ill-disciplined in places (as it is in the other Italian-made sets, a pity when the chorus is at times the protagonist) but Serafin is particularly impressive in such a passage as the end of Act 1 in the surging coda leading up to Calaf's striking of the gong. It is questionable just how much *accelerando* is permissible how soon (the marking *incalzando* is left relatively late) but Serafin certainly builds up more tellingly than, say, Molinari-Pradelli, not to mention Leinsdorf, who may be the most literal in following the score – a slow steady tempo for the long crescendo and then fast final bars – but whose reading lacks tension. Erede has less momentum still. It is typical of Serafin that the 'casa in Honan' passage of the trio in Act 2 for Ping, Pang and Pong is delightfully affectionate and gentle. His rhythmic pointing is delicate too in other passages such as the interlude in Act 2 with its crisp ostinato rhythm bringing a vein of wit, though Mehta matches him and more, helped by superb playing from the LPO and brilliant stereo recording.

It is a pity that Birgit Nilsson, by voice quality an ideal choice for the role of Turandot, did not record the role with either Serafin or Mehta. Her two versions are both fine, but in each one suspects that a more challenging, more positive conductor would have drawn out not just the commanding vocal quality (as both Leinsdorf and Molinari-Pradelli certainly do) but keener and more detailed imagination both over words and musical phrasing. None the less the comparisons between the two are fascinating. Thanks in part to warmer recording quality, the HMV performance of 'In questa reggia' avoids the unpleasant plaintive timbre which mars the RCA performance in the opening passage. But against that at a slower speed Nilsson is more delicate in the RCA performance, shading the tone beautifully, and responding more to the words. Inge Borkh on the early Decca set also starts with curious timbre which with its rapid vibrato will not please all ears, but then the imagination of her singing expands with the ripeness of the voice as the aria progresses. On 'purezza' she adds a delightful Mozartian appoggiatura, though the tension stays low. There is much else to enjoy in her singing throughout the set, even if she rarely achieves the supreme penetration of tone and magnificence of command of Nilsson.

If Caballé on the one hand has delicacy of detail and Nilsson epic strength, the two sopranos who give performances on record which combine consistent thoughtfulness and imagination with commanding vocal qualities are Callas and Sutherland. In a way one might regard their interpretations as complementary, for where Callas in a way which characteristically illuminates every phrase has one visualizing the traditional flashing-eyed princess Sutherland makes her human and believable. It was only in the early years of her career that Callas felt able to sing this role on stage, but Walter Legge made an inspired decision when he decided to promote her recording with Serafin. The full voice is edgy but no more so than is fitting or desirable with a Turandot, and though the expansive first top B in 'In questa reggia' on 'grido' is not matched by an equally expansive B on 'Ah rinasce' and the beat is obtrusive, the command is irresistible, and the subtlety of her phrasing – as in the *tenuto* on 'L'orror di chi l'uccise' – is pure delight.

That Sutherland could record a performance of comparable musical imagination with comparable felicity in word meaning along with richer and more reliable vocalization might not have been predicted before her recording by any but her keenest admirers. That is what she achieved, adding a new dimension to the role by giving the Icy Princess an element of vulnerability from the start, setting seeds of warmth early on when by tradition singers make her merely implacable. Particularly when the Liù opposite her, Caballé, is a singer who already had qualities to make her a potential Turandot, the dramatic contrast between the two heroines becomes much subtler than usual, not just a question of black and white, cruelty against purity, power against gentleness. The corollary is that this approach makes the final transformation far more believable.

'In questa reggia' begins in an *espressivo* style that is also regal and commanding. The result is not immediately chilling, and as with Caballé there is an element of mystery. Towards the climax of the aria, 'Mai nessun m'avrà' shows the heroine proud rather than evil, and there is pride too in the immediate rivalry between soprano and tenor at the very end of the aria, culminating in a magnificent top C held superbly on the unison phrase, when both relish the display of power. In the spare-textured pages following the aria and before the riddles the distinctive point of Sutherland's interpretation is the element of femininity. Even here we are not presented with the predatory female, not one who inevitably conceals feelings behind a steely facade.

But it is the transformation in the final scene which sets the seal on this portrait of the heroine, giving Alfano's completion of the opera a sense of genuine culmination such as it has never had otherwise on record and rarely had in the opera house, with Mehta as conductor the obvious catalyst. Calaf's cries of 'Ti voglio mio' leading up to his first kiss bring a superb resolution, and by the time the hero sings 'Oh! Mio fiore mattutino' and women's voices offstage provide melismatic comment, the atmosphere of sensuousness is complete. The final pages intensify the exotic colours. The exchanges before Turandot's long solo, 'Dal primo pianto', show the Princess humbled but still proud, the responses very human because confused, not clearcut. In other words the vital transition emerges not as a sudden flash but with convincing preparation, until the final resolution of Turandot's phrase 'Il suo nome è Amor!' comes over with total conviction, not as a feebly symbolic statement.

Although the history of Turandot's composition and Puccini's failure to complete the final scene may suggest that the death of Liù brought a creative block, the transformation of the princess was in fact the key element which attracted the composer to Gozzi's fairy-story in the first place. He may have been in love with 'the little woman', but he wanted above all to solve the secret of the powerful Princess. Though Nilsson and Callas both in their ways have provided portraits of Turandot on record which reveal her at her most commanding, as Dame Eva Turner did in an earlier generation, the achievement of Sutherland is to have given us new dimensions, ones which the composer himself would have appreciated.

TURANDOT

T Turandot; *L* Liù; *C* Calaf; *Tim* Timur; *Ping*; *Pang*; *Pong*

1938 Cigna *T*; Olivero *L*; Merli *C*; Neroni *Tim*; Poli *Ping*; del Signore *Pang*; Zagonara *Pong*/Turin Radio Chorus and Orch./Ghione
Cetra ⓒ LPS 3206 ④ MC 184–5; Turnabout ⓜ THS 65049–50

1955 Borkh *T*; Tebaldi *L*; del Monaco *C*; Zaccaria *Tim*; Corena *Ping*; Ercolani *Pang*; Carlin *Pong*/Santa Cecilia Academy Chorus and Orch./Erede
Decca GOS 622–4; London OSA 1308

1953 Grob-Prandl *T*; Ongaro *L*; Zola *C*; Scott *Tim*; Mercuriali *Ping*; M. Caruso *Pang*; Rossi *Pong*/La Fenice Chorus and Orch./Capuana
Remington ⓜ 199–169

1957 Callas *T*; Schwarzkopf *L*;
Fernandi *C*; Zaccaria *Tim*;
Boriello *Ping*; Ercolani *Pang*;
de Palma *Pong*/La Scala Chorus
and Orch./Serafin
EMI ⓜ RLS 741 ④ TC–RLS
741; Angel ⓜ CL 3571

1960 Nilsson *T*; Tebaldi *L*; Björling
C; Tozzi *Tim*; Sereni *Ping*; de
Palma *Pang*; Frascati *Pong*/Rome
Opera Chorus and
Orch./Leinsdorf
RCA (UK) SER 5643–5; (US)
LSC 6149 ④ ARK 3–2537

1965 Nilsson *T*; Scotto *L*; Corelli *C*;
Giaiotti *Tim*; Mazzini *Ping*;
Riccardi *Pang*; De Palma *Pong*/
Rome Opera Chorus and
Orch./Molinari-Pradelli
HMV SLS 921; Angel SCL 3671

1973 Sutherland *T*; Caballé *L*;
Pavarotti *C*; Ghiaurov *Tim*;
Krause *Ping*; Poli *Pang*; de
Palma *Pong*/Alldis Choir,
Wandsworth School Boys' Choir,
LPO/Mehta
Decca SET 561–3 ④ K2A2;
London OSA 13108 ④ 5–13108

1977 Caballé *T*; Freni *L*; Carreras *C*;

Plishka *Tim*; Sardiniero *Ping*;
Cassinelli *Pang*; Corazza
Pong/Rhine Opera Chorus,
Strasbourg *PO*/Lombard
HMV SLS 5135 ④ TC–SLS
5135; Angel SCLX 3857

Excerpts

1952 Anonymous artists/Roselle
Remington ⓜ PL–2–149

1962 (in German) Ekkehard *T*;
Arnold *L*; Esser *C*/Berlin Radio
SO/Stein
Philips 6592 002

1962 (in Hungarian) Takács *T*; Orosz
L; Simándy *C*/Hungarian Radio
Chorus and State Opera
Orch./Lukács
Qualiton SLPX 11579

1972 (in German) Bjöner *T*;
Rothenberger *L*; Spiess *C*;
Vogel *Tim*; Anheisser *Ping*;
Neukirch *Pang*; Hiestermann
Pong/Leipzig Radio Chorus,
Dresden Philharmonic Children's
Choir, Dresden State
Orch./Patanè
EMI 1C 063 29092Q

Pelléas et Mélisande

FELIX APRAHAMIAN

Debussy's one and only completed opera is a spell-binder. And it casts its spell on those who conduct it as much as on those who listen to it. One who adored and venerated this score was the conductor of two of the six complete recordings, Ernest Ansermet. In December 1968 John Mordler (then with Decca) and I were the last to see him on the last day of his last visit to London. At lunch, he told us that he would conduct no more concerts, but that he looked forward to his final public appearance as a conductor – of a revival of *Pelléas* at the Grand Théâtre of Geneva in March 1969. He left no doubt that he wanted to record it again – for the third time. He was not spared, and the sixth complete recording proved to be one linked with the revival of the opera at Covent Garden under Pierre Boulez, Debussyite of a younger generation.

The first performance of *Pelléas* at the Paris Opéra-Comique on 30 April 1902 was just as much of a landmark in the history of opera as that of Debussy's *Prélude à l'après-midi d'un faune*, eight years earlier at the Société Nationale, was in the history of music generally. Despite their extraordinary sensitivity, both works were revolutionary in effect and profoundly affected what came after them. Any opera composed after *Pelléas* could only avoid its pervading influence deliberately, by rejecting it and, like Stravinsky's *The Rake's Progress*, for example, seeking earlier models. Yet *Pélléas* remains unique, not only in Debussy's *oeuvre*, but also in the operatic repertory. No opera has a more intimate appeal, and none loses less in a recording.

Debussy's avowed intention was to project the text as clearly as possible, with his music as its servant rather than obtrusive master. In *Pelléas* he carried out this aim to perfection. Maeterlinck's text, which depends little on stage action and makes a static opera, is always clearly audible. Over and above this clarity, in which two voices are heard singing together only at the very climax of the final love scene, what makes Debussy's masterpiece ideal armchair listening is the musically haunting manner in which he paints each scene. On the one hand there is absolute audibility of the text throughout, on the other, a tonal background which makes every scene a musical entity. Orchestrally, was there ever a more vividly depicted forest, age-old and mysterious, or sundown before storm at sea, grotto suddenly illumined by moonlight, mephitic subterranean vault, ascent to a windswept seashore with a view of sunlit terraces above with noonday bells a-ringing?

The score offers no variants or similar complications to cause textual differences among the six different recordings. The opera, although in five acts like the play, reduces Maeterlinck's nineteen scenes to fourteen: those omitted are mainly symbolical, like the very first, in which the serving women are seen washing the threshold of the sad castle where the pathetic romance of Pelléas and Mélisande unfolds. The only cut Debussy made after composing the score was one of fifteen bars towards the end of Act 3 when, in the scene between Golaud and his small son Yniold, there is mention of the word *lit*. No less an arbiter of French public morals than the Under-Secretary of State for Fine Arts would have vetoed the entire crucial scene had Debussy not agreed to this cut. It was observed in the full score and in the second edition of the vocal score, although the original (Froment) vocal score contains the offending reference to a bed. Debussy agreed to omit the fourth-act scene between Yniold and the unseen Shepherd for the first performance, after a barbarian dress-rehearsal audience had made fun of it, but he retained it in both the full score and second edition of the vocal score. The extended symphonic interlude linking the separate scenes of the first four acts are now an important integral part of the opera and, like the scene with Yniold and the Shepherd, are included as a matter of course in most performances and in the complete recordings.

The most recent version, from EMI, was recorded in Berlin, and the conductor is Herbert von Karajan, the hero of the set, in a better sense than the most obvious, for it represents, as I hear it, the culminating point of his long-standing love-affair with French music. Already, his versions of Debussy and Ravel orchestral works stand high in the lists, and now this *Pelléas* confirms an equally committed approach to the French score of scores. It is a curious fact that in so much classical music Karajan has given the impression of a super-Svengali manipulating the music marvellously, but at one remove, controlling it from outside, as it were. Here, the orchestral music, though played as immaculately as ever, seems to well up as a more deeply felt emotion, yet without the least, exaggeration or contradiction of Debussy's expressive markings. This applies not only to the symphonic interludes but to the warp and weft of a tapestry in which the singers supply a vocal thread, an important thread that is never less than perfectly clear, but not a kind of *appliqué* with the orchestra relegated to a dim, mysterious background. Debussy's own insistence that his score should be subservient to the text has in the past resulted, perhaps, in a more distant and etiolated accompaniment than is strictly necessary, achieving the kind of ensemble that led the wretched Camille Bellaigue to write: Orchestre 'grêle et pointu . . . Il fait peu de bruit, je l'accorde, mais un vilain petit bruit'. There is nothing at all *vilain* about the glowing colours of the Berlin Philharmonic Orchestra on these discs: they have the richness and intensity of jewels.

None of the other versions is more likely to ingratiate itself with those who love their Wagner. Does this dynamic up-grading of the orchestra destroy the mystery and the atmospheric distance? Not at all, thanks to an acoustic ambience which supplies this element: not only are the forest, grotto and castle-dungeons cavernous, but so, too, is the room in the castle in which Geneviève reads the letter to Arkel – cavernous, archaic, ancient. The general sound and balance, then, provide the most striking features of this new *Pelléas*; not, however, because of any deficiency in the cast, which is superlative. There is warmth and something of Jacques Jansen's youthful ardour in Richard Stilwell's Pelléas, as well as the role's ideal timbre and tessitura. The purity of Frederica von Stade's tone does not prevent her every reply to Golaud or Pelléas from illuminating the character of Mélisande. José van Dam is a glorious-voiced Golaud, as much a pawn in the drama as the young people, more a victim of jealousy, exciting sympathy, than a monster of cruelty. Ruggero Raimondi's Arkel sounds younger and less patriarchal than some, and not all his phrases, among the most beautiful in the opera, are endowed with memorable warmth and expressiveness. The Geneviève (Nadine Denise) is excellent, so are Yniold (Christine Barbanse) and, particularly the physician (Pascal Thomas), who, earlier, as the Shepherd, is almost inaudible as well as invisible, for in that symbolic scene, both he and little Yniold are made to sound tiny figures in a burgeoning musical landscape. If, strangely enough, the magical chords for *divisi* violas and cellos and held horn-note, which should support 'On a brisé la glace avec des fers rougis' are less well-nourished than the string harmonics at that point, this is a minor flaw, off-set by a thousand orchestral felicities.

The interesting CBS set was made in 1970 in which Pierre Boulez conducts the Covent Garden cast of the time, with George Shirley, a true tenor yet not lacking the baritone quality required in some of the wonderful melodic lines of the part of Pelléas; Elisabeth Söderström, vocally mature and assured as ever, yet perfectly capable of conveying the scared *naïveté* of a Mélisande escaped from Bluebeard's castle, as well as the depression she experiences as the still young second wife of the grey-haired Golaud, and no less convincingly the rapture of falling in love for the first time – with his younger half-brother, Pelléas. Donald McIntyre is in magnificent voice as Golaud; so is David Ward as Arkel, the near-blind King of Allemonde who has the most memorably beautiful music in the opera. The singing of McIntyre and Ward in the final scene around Mélisande's deathbed shows their curious similarity of vocal colour; they are by no means a strongly contrasted pair. Yvonne Minton, admirably sure as Geneviève; Dennis Wicks capably doubling the roles of Shepherd and Doctor; and a real boy, Anthony Britten, singing the part of Yniold (as at the first performance but not on any other recording) complete a strong cast. Their enunciation is uniformly good and their French, considering that not one member of the cast is French, quite remarkable.

Only one attribute is lacking in this version: a sense of mystery and remoteness. The introductory essay by Boulez (missing from the latest issues of the set) makes it clear that this is deliberate. Recognizing that the plot sets a common bourgeois situation in a vague, timeless context, Boulez is nevertheless anxious that there shall be no coyness in presenting it. Those who see Maeterlinck's text as a period piece, a shadowy symbolist drama, suggesting the situation rather than postulating it, paralleled exactly by Debussy's musical sensitivity, may find this new, clear, unflinchingly near version impeccable as a reading of the score, yet lacking the archaic distance and magic of less strongly illuminated interpretations.

Preceding this was the second Decca/Ansermet recording of 1964, on which that remarkable musician hoped to improve in a third. When he died in 1969 he was one of the few remaining guardians of the true Debussy tradition. His scientific and philosophical probings into the very nature of music made him more aware than most of his colleagues of the close links between the aural and the visual in the human mind, so that, from sunless forest to the winter sunlight that falls on the dying Mélisande, through Debussy's fourteen varied scenes, he proved a guide in a million to a miraculous score.

Turning to the cast of this version, I find the Pelléas, Camille Maurane, was vocally the best possible. Short of stature, he was never a stage Pelléas, but at the age of fifty-four, this recording showed him as an ideal *baryton-Martin* in not only beautiful but *youthful* voice. I imagine that Erna Spoorenberg's enchanting performance in Frank Martin's *Monsieur de Pourceaugnac*, the première of which Ansermet conducted in Geneva, was her passport to singing Mélisande in this important recording. And, incidentally, she was once again Ansermet's choice for the third recording he would have liked to make. Vocally and in expression, her performance is delightful: only a few vowel sounds betray the fact that she is not French. She proves herself equal to the singing of the little couplet Mélisande sings at the opening of the first tower scene, a passage which Mélisandes often find curiously taxing, and her understanding of the role is more complete than that of its other non-French post-war exponents – Belgian, Spanish and German – always excepting the unique Söderström.

George London is here the powerful, hectoring Golaud. The Arkel, Guus Hoekman (who sang the role at Glyndebourne in 1962, the Debussy centenary year) has a voice of fine timbre but intrinsically less weighty than that of any of his predecessors on record, and so he contributes a touch of frailty that is not out of place. The lesser parts are all well sung, with Josephine Veasey as a young but acceptable Geneviève (without impeccable French) and John Shirley-Quirk, who finds intelligent expression for the physician's few lines in the final act. Rosine Brédy is an outstanding Yniold, with a child-like voice apt to the role and the right heart-rending accents of terror at the climax of the second tower scene. Ansermet's Suisse Romande Orchestra sound at their best in this version, and the Decca engineers made sure that the castle vaults had extra resonance.

Ansermet's earlier version has Pierre Mollet's often admirable but generally unequal Pelléas and Suzanne Danco's crystalline Mélisande. Here, Heinz Rehfuss is the distinguished and vehement Golaud, and André Vessières the ideal Arkel whose noble bass voice has no difficulty in the higher tessitura and has, in the lower, that cavernous quality which gives him greater age, seniority and grandeur than Golaud. Then in her early fifties, Helène Bouvier had the right elderly timbre for Geneviève. With Flora Wend (Yniold) and Derrik Olson (Doctor), this set wears its years very well.

Between the two Ansermet versions came two other complete recordings of *Pelléas*. The Paris set conducted by André Cluytens with the magnificent Orchestre National of the time contained a mixture of elements, old and new – traditional and experimental. In France, ever since the première in 1902, there has been a kind of *famille Pelléas* in which individuals have maintained a performing tradition almost like an operatic laying-on-of-hands. A glance at the Opéra-Comique cast lists for the first twenty years of *Pelléas* will show that the family evolved gradually. In this 1957 recording, the small part of the physician is sung by Jean Vieuille – the nephew of Félix Vieuille, the original Golaud! Golaud is sung by a singer I took Ansermet to hear in a BBC studio ten years earlier as a potential Pelléas. Even with the possible *pointages*, the young Gérard Souzay lacked one essential note, otherwise he would have been engaged on the spot. A darkening and deepening voice eventually made him the Golaud heard here. Then, two members of the cast, Jacqueus Jansen (Pelléas) and Pierre Froumenty (Arkel) belonged to what is still remembered among Parisian *Pelléastres* as *la grande distribution* to be explained when we reach it. The Geneviève (Jeannine Collard) and Yniold (Françoise Ogéas) were also French, but the Mélisande came as a surprise – Victoria de los Angeles. As Alec Robertson suggested in his review at the time it was first issued, the role compelled her to 'subdue the native warmth of her voice'. Her artistry enabled her to do this, and she did not lack the voice beautiful, yet her Mélisande remained more real than fey.

The other complete version which appeared between the Ansermet versions of 1951 and 1964 was that conducted by Jean Fournet, with the Lamoureux Orchestra of Paris in 1953. The Pelléas was again Maurane, nearly a decade younger; Michel Roux, the splendid Golaud, with Xavier Depraz (Arkel), Rita Gorr (Geneviève) and Annik Simon (Yniold). But here, again, there was a less authentic Mélisande. Janine Micheau, a star soprano with a coloratura range, sounded far too sophisticated and un-fey a voice for the part. Of Fournet's devotion to and understanding of the score, there was no question: he was a frequent conductor of *Pelléas* at the Opéra-Comique in those years, and worked often with what I have already referred to as *la grande distribution*.

This was the wartime French cast which recorded *Pelléas* in Paris in 1942 under Roger Désormière for French HMV, and took the opera far and wide – Dublin in 1948 and London (Covent Garden) in 1949. The two unforgettable young principals were Irène Joachim (grand-daughter of *the* Joachim) and Jacques Jansen. Both later became professors at the Paris Conservatoire. The Golaud, Henri-Bertrand Etcheverry, was the greatest of all. The Arkel of the recording was Paul Cabanel, whose magnificent bass voice was not always reliable as to text. (His successors in the live performance of *Pelléas* given by the well-named *grande distribution* were Pierre Froumenty, whose stage Arkel towered physically even over Etcheverry's imposing Golaud; then Henri Médus and André Vessiéres.) The remarkably fine Geneviève was Germaine Cernay and the Yniold, Léila ben Sedeira. Despite their age, these 78s and their later LP transfer remain the classic recorded version of Debussy's opera.

The booklet which originally accompanied it was inscribed to the memory of Georges Truc, the conductor who was to have conducted this recording, but who died in 1941. He was, however, the conductor of one of the two previous recordings of selections from the opera. This was the Columbia set of six 78s made in 1928. It consists of the initial encounter of Golaud and Mélisande (Act 1, scene 1) – two sides; the letter scene (Act 1, scene 2) – two sides; Golaud's bedroom scene (Act 2, scene 2) – two sides; the tower scene between Pelléas and Mélisande (Act 3, scene 1) – three sides; and, on the final side, the orchestral interlude from Act 4. The unusual interest of this set is that its Golaud is Hector Dufranne, who sang in the 1902 première. The Mélisande is Marthe Nespoulos, and, opposite her, the 1914 Opéra-Comique Pelléas, Alfred Maguenat. The Geneviève is Claire Croiza, and the Arkel to whom she reads Golaud's letter to Pelléas is Armand Narçon, who sings the part of the physician in the Désormière set.

The other set of selections, on HMV, conducted by Piero Coppola, offers the voices of Yvonne Brothier (Mélisande), Charles Panzéra (Pelléas), Willy Tubiana (Golaud) and Vanni–Marcoux (Arkel). Vanni Marcoux, who first sang the role of Golaud at the Opéra-Comique in 1914 before the war, could still sing this role twenty years later. He was Covent Garden's first Arkel, in 1909, and was also the 1937 Covent Garden Golaud. He also recorded for HMV an extract from Act 2, scene 2: 'Ah! tout va bien', and one from Act 4, scene 2: 'Une grande innocence' (DA 902).

There remain the collectors' items of the voices of the first two Mélisandes, the Scot Mary Garden and the Anglo-Irish Maggie Teyte. For a Gramophone Shop set (GSC 21; RLS 716), Dame Maggie recorded, to Gerald Moore's piano accompaniment, Geneviève's letter scene and the first fountain scene, in which she sings not only Mélisande's part but also that of Pelléas in duet with herself! And in 1948, she was caught live at New York Town Hall singing various short scenes and taking the roles of Pelléas, Mélisande, Arkel, Geneviève, Yniold and the Shepherd (DESMAR GHP 4003). Finally, there is Mary Garden singing an Act 3 excerpt from the role she created, to the piano accompaniment of the composer himself, a reissue by the US International Record Collectors' Club (IRCC 106).

Dame Maggie Teyte, who died in 1975, was probably the last surviving member of the older *famille Pelléas*, though I remember Désormière telling me of an elderly taxi-driver who seemed amused to be asked to take him to the Opéra-Comique on one of the evenings he was conducting *Pelléas* there in the 1940s. Depositing him at the stage door, he revealed his identity – the boy Blondin, who had sung as *le petit Yniold* at the first performance!

PELLÉAS ET MÉLISANDE

M Mélisande *P* Pelléas; *G* Golaud; *A* Arkel; *Gen* Geneviève

1942 Joachim *M*; Jansen *P*;
Etcheverry *G*; Cabanel *A*;
Cernay *Gen*/Y. Gouverné Choir,
Paris Conservatoire
Orch./Désormière
EMI ⓜ 2C 153 12513–5; Victor
ⓜ LCT 6103

1951 Danco *M*; Mollet *P*; Rehfuss *G*;
Vessières *A*; Bouvier
Gen/Chorus, Suisse Romande
Orch./Ansermet
Decca ⓜ GOM546–8; Richmond
ⓜ R63013

1953 Micheau *M*; Mauranne *P*; Roux
G; Depraz *A*; Gorr *Gen*/E.
Brassuer Chorale, Lamoureux
Orch./Fournet
Philips ⓜ ABL 3076–8; Epic
ⓜ SC 6003

1957 los Angeles *M*; Jansen *P*;
Souzay *G*; Froumenty *A*;
Collard *Gen*/French National
Radio Chorus and
Orch./Cluytens
Word Records ⓜ OC 210–2

1963 (live performance) Grancher *M*;
Maurane *P*; Mars *G*; Vessières
A; Bellary *H*/ORTF Chorus and
Orch./Ingelbrecht
Barclay 995 014–6

1964 Spoorenberg *M*; Maurane *P*;
London *G*; Hoeckman *A*;
Veasey *Gen*/Chorus, Suisse
Romande Orch./Ansermet
Decca SET 277–9; London OSA
1379

1970 Söderström *M*; Shirley *P*;
McIntyre *G*; Ward *A*; Minton
Gen/Covent Garden, Chorus and
Orch./Boulez
CBS (UK) 77324; (US)
M3–30119

1978 Command *M*; Dormoy *P*;
Bacquier *G*; Soyer *A*; Taillon
Gen/Bourgogne Vocal Ensemble,
Lyon Orch./Baudo
Eurodisc 919034

1978 von Stade *M*; Stilwell *P*; van
Dam *G*; Raimondi *A*; Denize
Gen/German Opera Chorus,
Berlin PO/Karajan
EMI SLS 5172 ④ TC–SLS 5172

Excerpts

1924 Brothier *M*; Panzéra *P*; Tubiana
A; Vanni-Marcoux *G*/Pasdeloup
Orch./Coppola

French HMV P 520–2; DA 677;
W 614–7
1928 Nespoulos *M*; Maguenat *P*;
Dufranne *G*; Narcon *A*; Croiza
Gen/orch./Truc
Pearl Ⓜ GEMM 145; CBS

Ⓜ RL 3092
1932 Brothier *M*; Panzéra *P*; Tubiana
A; Vanni-Marcoux *G*/Pasdeloup
Orch./Coppola
HMV D2083–6; E603–5

Peter Grimes

ALAN BLYTH

Although it can no longer be considered precisely a new work, *Peter Grimes* is probably the only opera since *Wozzeck* to lay claim to a permanent place in the repertory, a place confirmed in 1979 when it was accorded the honour of a second complete recording, and one (from Colin Davis) which seems to place it even more centrally in the mainstream of operatic development than the composer's own set. Listening to Davis's powerful and theatrical conduct of the piece, the affinities that the work has with Verdi and Tchaikovsky, two composers much admired by Britten, become even clearer and other similarities, one even with the Elgar of the *Gerontius* Demons Chorus (at 'him who despises us, we'll destroy' in Act 3), are invoked. Yet, as with all the greatest operas, these influences are transmuted by the new composer's genius into something entirely his own, and that the impact of the piece is just as strong today as it apparently was on its first audiences some thirty-five years ago is a tribute to its lasting value: the message of an outsider, a stranger with unorthodox ideas, battling against the orthodoxies and prejudices of a puritanical and reactionary society, still has validity today – and self-evidently they have found a sympathetic response, not to say an empathetic one, in Davis and in his Peter Grimes, Jon Vickers.

Their interpretation is, strangely, more subjective, almost more involving than that of Britten and Peter Pears, perhaps because, as Davis himself has suggested, Britten was almost afraid of the energies and feelings unleashed in his own masterpiece. In Davis's and Vickers's hand and voice the opera goes to greater extremes; tempi are often substantially slower or faster than those marked by the composer, and the colours of the orchestration seem darker, more opaque. Grimes seems to be fighting against an even severer, more restricting society than that imagined by Britten. Vickers also makes Grimes into a rougher fisherman, a more tortured creature than does Pears, although paradoxically, since he seems almost deranged from the start, the unhinging of Grimes's mind in the last act becomes less moving.

That also has something to do with the contrast between the vocal approach of the two singers. Vickers paints with a broader brush, takes more liberties with the notes, and often attacks them from below. At first that may seem more affecting, as does his hushed, dreamy *mezza voce*, while the brilliance and power of his attack, earlier in the opera (something Pears cannot emulate), suggests the physical danger of this Grimes; but in the long run, and on repeated hearings, Pears's more exact, more naturally phrased and more musical singing pays the more heartfelt dividends. Perhaps his more middle-class accents do not agree precisely with the rude vigour Grimes should proclaim, but the beauty and clarity of his phrasing and often of his tone are more suggestive of Grimes's dreamy side, of his wish to marry Ellen and become a respectable member of society. And precisely that quality makes his mad scene that much more moving.

Vickers also spoils his performance by some unwanted (and unauthroized?) changes in the text. He alters the words at the start of his ticking-off of the boy John. He fails altogether later in that scene to utter the parenthetical asides, half-spoken, as Grimes recalls how his earlier apprentice died (chillingly articulated by Pears) and, perhaps because of Vickers's well-known moralistic attitude, he changes the word 'breast' to 'heart' in his mad scene. Still, both interpretations are valid in their own ways and they are complementary to each other.

Both sets employed supporting casts, chorus and orchestra from Covent Garden. In general, though not wholly, the 1978 team is stronger than the 1958. The chorus has more bite in the newer version; the orchestral playing is admirable in both. Of the soloists, I prefer James Pease's warmer, more mature Balstrode to the more youthful, less pointed Jonathan Summers. On the other hand, John Dobson as Boles makes more of his words and characterizes more sharply than Raymond Nilsson, good as he is. Thomas Allen's singing is firmer than Geraint Evans's as Ned Keene. Forbes Robinson is a more accurate Swallow than Owen Brannigan (who created the role), but both are characterful, as are the Mrs Sedleys. John Lanigan's younger self is preferable as the Rector to his more quavery reading for Davis. Richard van Allan has more voice as Hobson than his predecesor.

The recording method is very different in each version. Philips did not attempt any kind of dramatic production, and the sound tends to be too reverberative and all-engrossing. Erik Smith, the producer of the Decca version, tried with a good deal of success to simulate a stage performance. There is evident movement of characters and many sound effects, including the sobbing of Grimes's boy when he is chastised by Peter. On this version, the chorus righly process off, to a gradual *diminuendo*, as they go on their manhunt for Grimes. That is an essential factor and should also have happened on the Philips.

I have deliberately left discussion of Ellen Orford to last because in this case there is the added interest of substantial extracts from the classic reading of the part by Joan Cross, its creator, in EMI's 'Stars of the Old

Vic and Sadler's Wells' (RLS 707). Claire Watson sings the part on the Britten set, and takes great care to deliver it accurately and with feeling, but she does not exhibit the full understanding of Ellen's character found in Heather Harper's less evenly vocalized but more eloquently inflected account of the role for Davis: she is particularly good in her delivery of the key phrase 'We've failed' and in the sad, haunting Embroidery aria; but there she is quite surpassed by Cross, who seems actually to *be* Ellen Orford, more tender, more sympathetic; hardly surprising as the part was created for her.

What we have on RLS 707 is Act 2, scene 1, from fig 3. to one bar before fig. 18, the Embroidery aria, and also Act 3 from fig. 44 to fig. 53, thus encompassing the whole of the mad scene. These extracts were recorded in 1948 after the first performance of the work at Covent Garden, whose orchestra is here conducted by Reginald Goodall; he was in charge of the première. They were not issued, for some reason, in 1948, even though the composer supervised them, and they have since been deleted even in their LP form. That is a pity as they seem to me to represent the work at white heat, straight off the stage, in a way not equalled even by Davis. Goodall makes the score even more immediate than either Davis or the composer and obtains electric playing from the Royal Opera House Orchestra. Pears here, both in the crucial second-act encounter with Ellen (where Joan Cross is again incomparable) and in his final appearance, sings with an abandon and commitment not quite managed ten years later. His fearless attack and bright, shining tone here are truly remarkable. Indeed the mad scene leaves one overwhelmed with compassion for the tormented figure of Grimes. The flavour of that arresting 1945 première is surely caught here. The matrix numbers tend to suggest that more of the work was recorded in 1948; if so, it should all be issued as an important historical document.

As a footnote to the other recordings of the complete operas conducted by Britten, mention should be made of major excerpts from *The Rape of Lucretia* (C 3699–C 3706; MFP 2119), also conducted by Goodall, where – as in the case of *Grimes* – Pears, now as Male Chorus, is in freer voice than in the Decca set and where many of the original cast (though, sadly, not Kathleen Ferrier as Lucretia) give authoritative interpretations, with Margaret Ritchie's ethereal Lucia, Joan Cross's moving Female Chorus, and Frederick Sharp's keen-edged Tarquinius particularly remarkable. Their enunciation is superb. Nancy Evans, who was the alternative Lucretia at the time of the première in 1946 (the recording came a year later), makes much of her role, though does not match Janet Baker on the complete set.

It remains only to mention the brief memento of Forbes Robinson's excellent Claggart – the first-act monologue – in *Billy Budd* and the lover's awakening quartet, sung by Elizabeth Robson, Kenneth Macdonald and Anne Howells, from *A Midsummer Night's Dream*, on the 1968

Covent Garden anniversary album (SET 392–3). Both are also reminders of Solti's energetic work on behalf of the Britten operas during his regime at the Royal Opera. They make interesting alternatives to the performances in the complete versions.

THE OPERAS OF BRITTEN

PETER GRIMES

PG Peter Grimes; *EO* Ellen Orford; *B* Balstrode; *H* Hobson; *S* Swallow; *MS* Mrs Sedley; *A* Auntie; *N1* Niece; *N2* Niece 2; *BB* Bob Boles; *R* Rector; *NK* Ned Keene

1959 Pears *PG*; C. Watson *EO*; Pease *B*; Kelly *H*; Brannigan *S*; Elms *MS*; J. Watson *A*; Studholme *N1*; Kells *N2*; Nilsson *BB*; Lanigan *R*; G. Evans *NK*/Royal Opera Chorus and Orch./Britten Decca SXL 2150-2 ④ 4K71K33; London OSA 1305

1978 Vickers *PG*; Harper *EO*; Summers *B*; van Allan *H*; Robinson *S*; Payne *MS*; Bainbridge *A*; Cahill *N1*; Pashley *N2*; Dobson *BB*; Lanigan *R*; Allen *NK*/Royal Opera Chorus and Orch./C. Davis Philips 6769 014 ④ 7699 089

Excerpts

1948 Pears *PG*; Cross *EO*/Choirs, Royal Opera Orch./Goodall EMI ⓜ RLS 707

THE RAPE OF LUCRETIA

MC Male Chorus; *FC* Female Chorus; *C* Collatinus; *J* Junius; *T* Tarquinius; *L* Lucretia; *B* Bianca; *Luc* Lucia

1948 (abridged version) Pears *MC*; Cross *FC*; Lumsden *C*; Dowling *J*; Sharp *T*; Evans *L*; Nielsen *B*; Ritchie *Luc*/CO/Goodall Music for Pleasure ⓜ MFP 2119

1970 Pears *MC*; Harper *FC*; Shirley-Quirk *C*; B. Drake *J*; Luxon *T*; Baker *L*; Bainbridge *B*; Hill *Luc*/ECO/Britten Decca SET 492–3; London OSA 1288

ALBERT HERRING

1964 Fisher *Lady Billows*; Peters *Florence Pike*; Cantelo *Miss Wordsworth*; Noble *Vicar*; Evans *Mayor*; Brannigan *Superintendent*; J. Ward *Sid*; Pears *Albert Herring*; C. Wilson *Nancy*; Rex *Mrs Herring*; Amit *Emmie*; Pashley *Cis*; Terry *Harry*/ECO/Britten Decca SET 274–6; London OSA 1378

THE LITTLE SWEEP

S; Sam; *MB* Miss Baggott; *R* Rowan; *J* Juliet; *G* Gay; *Soph* Sophie; *Jo* John;
T Tina; *H* Hugh; *BB* Black Bob; *Tom*; *C* Clem; *A* Alfred

1955 Hemmings *S*; N. Thomas *MB*;
Vyvyan *R*; Cantelo *J*; Ingham
G; Fairhurst *Jo*; Soskin *H*;
Anthony *BB*; *T*; Pears *C*;
A/Chorus, English Opera
Group/Britten
Decca Ⓜ ECM 2166; London
Ⓜ

1978 Monck *S*; Begg *MB*; Wells *R*;
Benson *J*; Wills *T*; Lloyd *BB*;
Tom; Tear *C*; *A*/Finchley
Children's Music Group; King's
College Choral Scholars, Medici
Quartet, Constable, Greir/Ledger
EMI ASD 3608 ④ TC–ASD
3608

BILLY BUDD

1967 Glossop *Billy Budd*; Pears
Captain Vere; Langdon *Claggart*;
Shirley-Quirk *Redburn*; B. Drake
Flint; Kelly *Ratcliffe*; Dempsey
Red Whiskers; D. Bowman
Donald; Brannigan *Dansker*; R.

Bowman *Squeak*; D. Bryn-Jones
Bosun/Ambrosian Singers,
LSO/Britten
Decca SET 379–81; London
OSA 1390

THE TURN OF THE SCREW

1955 Pears *Prologue*; *Quint*; Vyvyan
Governess; Hemmings *Miles*;
Dyer *Flora*; Cross *Mrs Grose*;
Mandikian *Miss Jessel*/English

Opera Group./Britten
Decca Ⓜ GOM 560–1;
Richmond
Ⓜ RS 65021

NOYE'S FLUDDE

1961 (live performance, Aldeburgh
Festival) Anthony *Voice of God*;
Brannigan *Noye*; Rex *Mrs Noye*;
D. Pinto *Sem*; Angadi *Ham*;

Clack *Mrs Sem*; M.T. Pinto *Mrs
Ham*; O'Donovan *Mrs
Jaffett*/Choirs, ECO/del Mar
Argo (UK) ZK1; (US) ZNF1

A MIDSUMMER NIGHT'S DREAM

1966 Deller *Oberon*; Harwood *Titania*;
Pears *Lysander*; Hemsley
Demetrius; Veasey *Hermia*;
Harper *Helena*; Shirley-Quirk
Theseus; Watts *Hippolyta*;
Brannigan *Bottom*; Lumsden

Quince; Macdonald *Flute*; Kelly
Snug; Tear *Snout*/Ambrosian
Singers, LSO/Britten
Decca SET 338–40; London
OSA 1385

CURLEW RIVER

1965 Pears *Madwoman*; Blackburn
Abbot; Shirley-Quirk *Ferryman*;
B. Drake *Traveller*; Webb *Voice
of the Spirit*/Instrumental

Ens./Britten
Decca SET 301 *or* 1BB 101–3;
London OSA 1156

THE BURNING FIERY FURNACE

1967 Pears *Nebuchadnezar*; B. Drake   Group/Britten
      Astrologer; Shirley-Quirk   Decca SET 356 *or* 1BB 101–3;
      Shadrach; Tear *Meshach*;   London OSA 1163
      Dean *Abednego*/English Opera

THE PRODIGAL SON

1969 Pears *Tempter*; Shirley-Quirk   Group/Britten and Tunnard
      Father; B. Drake *Elder Son*;   Decca SET 438 *or* 1BB 101–3;
      Tear *Younger Son*/English Opera   London OSA 1164

OWEN WINGRAVE

1970 Pears *General*; Luxon *Owen*   *Wingrave*/Wandsworth Boys
      Wingrave; Vyvyan *Mrs Julian*;   Choir, ECO/Britten
      Baker *Kate*; Shirley-Quirke   Decca SET 501–2; London OSA
      Coyle; Harper *Mrs Coyle*;   1291
      Douglas *Lechmere*; Fisher *Miss*

DEATH IN VENICE

1974 Pears *Ashenbach*; Shirley-Quirk   Mackay *Girl Player*; Saunders
      Traveller, Fop, Gondolier, Hotel   *Strawberry Seller*/English Opera
      manager, Bacchus; Bowman   Group, ECO/Bedford
      Apollo; Bowen *Porter*; Leeming   Decca SET 581–3; London OSA
      Clerk; Williams *Boy Player*;   13109

Index

(select index of artists)

Abbado, C., 145, 151, 203, 205, 252, 462–3

Abendroth, I., 149

Ackermann, O., 131, 570

Ackland, E., 36

Adam, T., 97, 113, 123, 134, 205, 341, 348, 378, 397

Adami, B., 240

Adani, M., 56, 583

Agussol, C., 485

Ahlersmeyer, M., 201–2, 271, 297

Ahlin, C., 282

Alarie, P., 31, 50, 103, 493

Albanese, L., 324, 467, 577, 578, 581, 612, 619

Albani, C., 267, 295

Alberti, V., 385

Alcaide, T., 504

Alda, F., 236, 327, 336, 487, 585, 587, 614

Aldenhoff, B., 131, 399, 559

Alessio, R. d', 332

Alexander, J., 168

Alfani-Tellini, I., 176, 194, 331

Allan, R. van, 80, 98, 264, 638

Allen, Perceval, 138, 562

Allen, Thomas, 638

Allin, N., 253, 421, 431, 432

Almeida, A. de, 297

Alpar, G., 551

Alsen, E., 434

Althouse, P., 416, 515

Altmann, H., 119

Altmeyer, T., 18

Alva, L., 77, 81, 91, 93, 144, 145, 174, 333

Alvarez, A., 320

Alvary, L., 89, 574

Amara, L., 356, 548, 549, 577

Amato, P., 147, 215, 216, 221, 233, 236, 243, 270, 272, 288, 315, 322, 473–4, 550, 601

Ameling, E., 101

Amerighi-Rutili, W., 164

Ananian, P., 491, 492

Ancona, M., 272, 322, 323, 549–50

Anday, R., 431–2

Anders, P., 125, 128, 136, 345, 527, 568

Anderson, M., 265, 274, 300

Andrade, F. d', 352

Andrésen, I., 205, 284, 349, 358, 363, 364, 371, 391, 428, 431, 447

Andzhaparidzye, Z., 319, 473

Angeles, V. de los, 67, 143, 144, 243, 251, 327, 351, 359, 455, 462, 466, 469, 483, 487, 496, 544, 545, 548, 577, 579–80, 610–11, 633

Angelici, M., 328, 468, 486

Angelis, N. de, 299, 457

Angelo, G. d', 144, 210

Angerer, M., 361

Anitua, F., 36, 274, 501

Anselmi, G., 147, 196, 312, 489, 500

Ansermet, E., 629, 632–3

Ansseau, F., 38, 476, 477, 488, 493, 503–4

Anthony, C., 194

Antoine, J., 259

Aragall, G., 456

Arangi-Lombardi, G., 232, 236, 269, 275, 283, 284, 308, 543

Arié, R., 186, 253, 299, 509, 530

Arimondi, V., 253

Arkel, T., 159

Arkhipova, I., 466, 473, 513

Arndt-Ober, M., 233–4, 296, 300, 371, 405, 419, 515

Arnoldson, S., 137, 472, 485

Arroyo, M., 79, 80–1, 264, 281
Artôt de Padilla, L., 66, 72
Artner, J. von, 404
Asmus, R., 128
Ausensi, M., 145
Austin, F., 562
Austral, F., 283, 313, 315, 343, 412, 418–19, 421, 427, 428, 429, 545
Autori, G., 216
Ayars, A., 32
Azzolini, G., 177–8

Baccaloni, S., 66, 73, 150, 178, 179, 185, 192, 193, 194, 198, 243, 275, 288, 433, 516
Bachmann, H., 387, 404, 407, 420, 469
Bacquier, G., 63, 98, 281, 325
Badini, E., 177, 178, 193, 195
Badridze, 504
Bailey, N., 342, 380, 402, 410, 429
Baillie, I., 614
Baker, J., 23, 35, 52, 53, 98, 639
Bakker, M., 103, 104
Bakkers, M., 506
Baklanov, G., 271, 528, 551
Balbon, A., 493
Baltsa, A., 295, 561
Bampton, R., 121, 255
Baranovich, 515
Barbieri, F., 227, 228, 233, 259, 262, 275, 279, 307, 333, 504
Barbirolli, J., 325, 343, 608–9, 618–19
Barenboim, D., 63, 81
Barrientos, M., 148, 149, 189, 217, 221
Barsham, D., 510
Bartoletti, B., 144, 247, 264
Bary, A. von, 417
Basile, A., 145, 229
Bastianini, E., 186, 210, 244, 245, 263, 272–3, 280, 294, 544, 582
Bastin, J., 64, 97, 561, 572
Battistini, M., 66, 72, 147, 148, 189, 221, 241, 270, 272, 275, 287, 301, 323, 500, 528, 550
Battle, K., 114
Baugé, A., 491
Baum, K., 285
Baumann, P., 119
Baümer, M., 122, 413, 427, 430, 570
Baylé, T., 265, 301
Beattie, H., 22
Bechi, G., 143, 216, 259, 271, 286, 288, 301, 308, 322, 323, 334, 543
Bechstein, H., 389

Beckmann, F., 343
Beddoe, D., 136
Beecham, Sir T., 106, 107–8, 206, 381, 431, 455, 466, 563, 577–9, 587–8
Behrens, H., 561
Beilke, I., 131
Belcourt, E., 402
Beldelli, A., 441–2
Bellezza, V., 512
Bellincioni, G., 240, 545
Belmas, X., 232, 315, 487, 545, 551
Belov, E., 522
Bence, M., 20
Bender, P., 139, 431
Benelli, U., 145, 549
Benetti, M., 336
Bentonelli, J., 484
Berberian, C., 19, 21
Berbié, J., 63, 98, 463
Berganza, T., 35, 37, 51, 52, 63, 83, 98, 100, 145, 463, 469, 535
Berger, E., 32, 49, 64, 76, 99, 107, 125, 199, 208–09, 220, 537–8, 569
Berger, R., 420, 423, 449, 557
Berglund, J., 343
Bergonzi, C., 187, 202, 205, 211, 220, 229, 244, 251, 255–6, 263, 267, 280, 286, 294, 295, 306, 312, 321, 544, 548, 549, 582, 599, 609, 612
Bernstein, L., 124, 333, 464, 571–2
Berry, W., 57, 75, 78, 79, 82, 92, 94, 110, 113, 123, 133, 135, 370, 534, 535, 560, 570, 571
Berton, L., 30
Bertram, T., 406, 420, 423
Bettendorf, E., 76, 138, 269, 315, 344, 359, 361, 388, 389, 568
Beuf, A., 253
Beyle, L., 488, 492, 493, 501
Biasini, P., 332
Bieshu, M., 530
Billot, E., 492
Bise, J., 18
Bispham, D., 420
Björling, Jussi, 210, 220, 226, 227, 228, 235, 237, 258, 259fn, 267, 268, 286, 296, 307, 312, 322, 453, 454, 459, 474, 491, 528, 535, 543, 544, 547, 548, 550, 552, 577, 578–9, 586, 598, 600, 610, 611, 622
Björling, Sigurd, 342, 411
Blachut, B., 128, 527
Blanc, E., 148, 455, 466
Blanchart, R., 206

Bland, E., 126–7, 270
Blech, L., 383, 407, 412, 414, 422, 428, 558
Blegen, J., 63, 584
Blyth, M., 542
Bobescu, J., 246
Bockelmann, R., 388, 407, 413, 420, 422
Bodansky, A., 120, 403, 561
Bode, H., 380
Bogard, C., 22
Bordanov, 513
Böhm, Andreas, 355
Böhm, Karl, 45, 46, 47, 57, 60, 79, 82, 93–5, 106, 110, 111, 122, 123, 201, 341, 368–70, 382, 396–7, 413, 535–6, 560, 571
Böhme, Kurt, 110, 131, 132, 133, 134, 297, 355, 397, 410, 564, 570, 571
Bohnen, M., 137, 286, 322, 389, 406, 420
Bolis, L., 274
Bonci, A., 146, 148, 176, 196, 199, 218, 221, 241, 266, 312, 491, 500, 586
Bonelli, R., 237, 259, 286, 297, 547
Bonini, F. M., 206, 215, 286
Boninsegna, C., 158, 159, 162, 232, 236, 269, 270, 274, 283, 284, 312–13, 314
Bonisolli, F., 231, 245, 329, 599
Bonynge, R., 79, 154, 168, 175, 187, 212, 230, 247, 456
Booth, W., 148, 312
Borg, K., 109, 253, 298, 342, 458, 514, 516, 530
Borgatti, G., 321, 383, 416
Borgioli, Armando, 185
Borgioli, Dino, 182, 196, 198, 208, 297, 490, 619
Bori, L., 72, 99, 197, 221, 241–2, 484, 487, 585, 586, 587
Borkh, I., 126, 204, 561, 564, 626
Boronat, O., 217
Borriello, M., 88, 193
Borthayre, J., 455, 483
Bosetti, H., 137, 139
Boskovsky, W., 47, 50, 535
Boué, G., 487, 499
Boulez, P., 445–6, 631–2
Bourdin, R., 476, 491, 492, 499, 506
Bouvier, H., 633
Bovy, V., 197, 243
Bowman, J., 19
Boyer, A., 492
Braithwaite, W., 148

Brambilla, L., 194, 195
Branningan, O., 638
Branzell, K., 38–9, 233, 274, 315, 359, 403, 406, 431, 456, 472, 476, 538
Braun, Victor, 347
Braun, Helene, 364–5
Brazzi, J., 498
Brédy, R., 633
Bréjean-Silver, G., 485
Breuer, H., 406, 423
Brevario, G., 165
Briesemeister, O., 405
Brilioth, H., 396, 450
Britten, A., 631–2
Brohly, S., 472, 477–8, 501
Bronsgeest, C., 440
Bronskaya, E., 218
Brothier, Y., 34, 189, 221, 359, 469, 487, 492, 634
Brouwenstijn, G., 135, 137, 265, 269, 283, 288, 302, 351, 408
Brownlee, J., 73, 88, 242, 316, 484, 587
Bruck, C., 32
Bruckner, W., 411
Bruckner-Ruggeberg, F., 22
Bruno, E., 233
Bruscantini, S., 56, 57, 90, 144, 174, 193, 245
Bruson, R., 301
Buades, A., 332, 468
Buchner, P., 370
Buesst, A., 542
Bugarinovich, M., 515
Bumbry, G., 27, 37, 162, 164fn, 204, 206, 274, 282, 289, 295, 300, 305, 347, 464, 545
Burg, R., 315, 352, 361, 517
Burgstaller, A., 135
Burke, T., 490, 622
Burmeister, A., 60, 63, 97, 341, 397
Burrian, K., 135, 286, 415, 431, 433, 501
Burrowes, N., 463
Burrows, S., 48, 52, 80, 102, 112, 524
Burzio, E., 266, 269, 270, 275, 283
Busch, F., 42, 43–4, 46, 73, 87–8, 260, 324
Busser, H., 482
Butt, C., 39, 300
Buzea, I., 246

Caballé, M., 98, 163, 164fn, 169–70, 187, 206, 218, 244, 264, 268, 270, 275, 284, 289, 294, 304–5, 313, 456, 506,

549, 560, 584, 592, 595–6, 611, 624–5, 626
Cabanel, P., 634
Calabrese, F., 56, 57, 91
Callas, M., 38, 67, 143–4, 149, 158, 163, 165–8, 170, 182, 186, 202, 203, 204, 206, 209–10, 228, 237, 316, 328, 373, 441, 465, 469, 487, 505, 543–4, 548, 579–80, 594–5, 596–7, 608, 609, 623, 626
Calusio, F., 17
Calvé, E., 67, 160, 471, 474, 545
Campagnola, L., 477–8, 488, 493, 501
Campanari, G., 65, 147
Campora, G., 251, 336, 593, 611–12
Caniglia, M., 242, 259, 269, 278, 293, 308, 597
Cantelli, G., 91–2
Capecchi, R., 59, 144, 174, 175, 193, 210, 278, 279, 333
Cappiello, M., 159
Cappuccilli, P., 59, 187, 203, 231, 252, 264, 280, 295, 304, 305, 465
Capsir, M., 143, 185, 208, 243
Capuana, M., 308
Carbone, M., 324
Carelli, Emma, 485
Carelli, Gabor, 58
Carena, M., 226
Carlyle, J., 549
Carosio, M., 148, 174, 182, 192, 197, 216, 218, 493, 512, 587
Carré, M., 492
Carreras, J., 175, 203, 252, 264, 268, 286, 295, 572, 592, 599, 623
Carron, A., 371
Carteri, R., 174, 329, 332, 473, 581
Caruso, E., 179, 180, 198, 205, 219, 220–1, 233, 234–5, 236, 241–2, 265–6, 285, 287, 288, 296, 311, 320, 322, 457, 474, 489, 493, 528, 546, 550, 585–6, 587, 599, 613
Casapietra, C., 97
Casini, L., 301
Casoni, B., 280
Cassinelli, R., 143, 212
Castagna, B., 165, 237, 259, 300, 473, 502, 543
Casula, M., 51, 62, 145
Catley, G., 115, 538
Catopel, E. von, 404
Cava, C., 151, 169
Cavalli,, F., 283, 284
Cavara, A., 267

Cazauran, L., 500
Cazette, L., 488
Cebotari, M., 65, 68, 243, 247, 559, 587, 614
Ceccato, A., 244
Cellini, R., 209, 227, 543, 548
Cerdan, J., 477
Cernay, G., 472, 487, 499, 500, 506, 634
Cernei, E., 38, 505
Cerquetti, A., 165, 289
Cerri-Caroli, E., 473
César, B., 493
Cesari, R., 245
Chaliapin, F., 150, 160, 298, 455, 457, 508, 511–12
Chamlee, M., 236, 286, 489, 546
Charny, L., 473, 502
Cheetham, J., 385
Chiara, M., 254, 283, 327, 612, 621
Christ, R., 534
Christoff, B., 76, 165, 166, 251, 254, 284, 293, 294, 299, 307, 441, 442, 455, 514, 529
Ciano, F., 176
Cigada, F., 236, 550
Cigna, G., 159, 165, 269, 270, 283, 316, 457, 625
Cillario, C. F., 23, 163, 171, 187
Cisneros, E. de, 233, 300, 418
Clabassi, P., 284, 293
Clairbert, C., 487
Clark, M. B., 332
Clément, E., 487–8, 500–1
Cleva, F., 456, 544, 548
Cloez, G., 481
Cluytens, A., 455, 467–8, 514, 633
Coates, Albert, 364, 382, 385, 404, 412, 421, 422, 425, 427–8, 429, 558
Coates, Edith, 413, 472
Cochran, W., 410
Codolini, A., 159
Cohen, E., 482–3, 496
Coiffier, M., 506
Colazza, L., 159
Cold, U., 114
Collier, M., 564, 612
Collingwood, L., 101, 383, 509
Colombo, G., 164
Colzani, A., 186
Conati, L., 176, 194
Conley, E., 456
Constantino, F., 500
Cooper, E., 512
Coppola, P., 469, 634

Corboz, M., 18
Cordon, N., 284, 403
Corelli, F., 167, 220, 230, 255, 284, 288, 306, 319, 329, 455, 465, 507, 544, 549, 599, 622
Corena, F., 66, 75, 78, 103, 104, 145, 174, 178, 193, 196, 280, 333, 577, 582
Cornelius, P., 342, 419, 424, 427
Cornubert, 500
Corradetti, F., 148, 177, 194–5
Corsi, Emilia, 72, 194, 195
Corsi, Gaetano, 195
Cortis, Antonio, 219, 267, 490, 504, 622
Cortis, Marcello, 497
Cossa, D., 175
Cossotto, F., 59, 169, 170, 203, 229–30, 264, 281, 294, 304, 305, 544
Cossutta, C., 325
Cotrubas, I., 63, 68, 98, 117, 175, 197, 218, 245, 288, 463
Coudère, S., 38
Cox, J., 380, 415
Crabbe, A., 234
Craig, C., 230, 265, 314, 552
Crass, F., 78, 110, 111, 123, 133, 298, 340, 388, 445, 530
Cravenco, A., 332
Crespin, R., 206, 268, 269–70, 300, 302, 313, 395, 415, 448, 464, 505, 571, 574
Crooks, R., 180, 181, 312, 360, 386, 484, 489
Cross, Joan, 68, 101, 328, 587, 614, 638–9
Cross, Richard, 168
Cuénod, H., 23, 57
Cunitz, M., 43, 131–2, 355, 358
Curphey, M., 403
Curtis, A., 21–2, 23
Curtis-Verna, M., 260
Cvejic, B., 523

Dalberg, F., 203, 298, 378
Dalis, I., 444
Dallapozza, A., 44, 124, 380, 535
Dalmorès, C., 235, 360, 474, 476
Dam, J. van, 63, 83, 113, 252, 295, 463, 561, 631
Danco, S., 31, 56, 75, 101, 633
Dani, C., 194–5
Danise, G., 272, 287
Danon, O., 523–4, 535
Dara, E., 145
David, L., 491
Davies, Ryland, 45, 47, 98

Davies, Tudor, 115, 136, 385, 416, 417, 419, 421, 425, 427, 475, 545, 612
Davis, C., 44–5, 52, 61, 62, 80, 98, 264, 471, 592, 596, 637
Dawison, M., 405
Dawson, P., 148, 352, 551
Dean, S., 45, 81
Debitzka, H. von, 216
Della Casa, L., 33, 57, 58, 75, 94, 564, 574
Delmas, S., 189, 476, 493
Delna, M., 36, 495, 500
Dempsey, G., 403
Demuth, L., 139, 387, 420, 430
Denera, E., 449
Dens, M., 323, 468, 483
Dermota, A., 74, 75, 94, 102, 109, 324, 379, 490, 527, 533, 560, 570, 571
Dernesch, H., 124, 282, 347, 370, 395, 396, 397, 410, 574
Dervaux, P., 471, 493
Déry, G., 246
Désormière, R., 634
Destinn, E., 66, 67, 138, 139, 232, 236, 270, 309, 343, 351, 372, 457, 469, 545, 550, 557–8, 596, 613
Deutekom, C., 112, 539
Devries, D., 147, 474, 488, 501
Didur, A., 137, 150, 515
Dietrich, M., 425, 532–3
D'Indy, V., 17
Dobbs, M., 212
Dobrowen, I., 514
Dobson, J., 125, 638
Doe, D., 403
Dolukhanova, Z., 300, 504
Domgraf-Fassbaender, W., 73, 88, 108, 125, 129, 147, 192, 197, 216, 234, 236, 315, 352, 533, 545, 551
Domingo, P., 170–1, 175, 189, 203, 220, 230, 245, 252, 256, 264, 268, 275, 281, 286, 288, 294, 296, 304, 305, 312, 326, 329, 381, 463, 491, 506, 528, 546, 549, 552, 571–2, 584, 592, 599, 609–10
Donath, H., 21, 29, 81, 113, 123, 378, 571
Donzelli, D., 156
Dooley, W., 356
Dorati, A., 340
Doria, R., 484
Dourian, L., 38, 505
Dow, D., 203
Downes, E., 334
Dufranne, H., 491, 492, 634

Dünnwald, J., 89
Dupouy, M., 506
Dupré, P., 482
Düsing, D., 82
Düttbernd, F., 361
Dux, C., 68, 138, 139, 216, 232, 236
Dvořaková, L., 128–9, 397, 415, 427, 435
Dvorsky, J., 136, 546
Dyck, E. van, 415, 495, 500

Eames, E., 68, 236, 545
Easton, F., 371, 373, 422
Ebert, C., 42, 55
Edelmann, O., 121, 126, 336, 358, 378, 379, 410, 421, 571
Ederle, N., 178
Eggert, M., 162
Eipperle, T., 125, 139, 349
Eisinger, I., 72, 88, 137, 139
Elias, R., 58, 229, 499, 536
Eliasson, S.O., 21
Elizza, E., 137, 189, 487
Elmendorff, K., 326, 349, 363, 410–11
Elmo, C., 236, 331, 332, 505
Endert, E. van, 137, 236, 533, 568
Endrèze, A., 271, 343, 473, 492
Engel, W., 344
English, G., 20
Equiluz, K., 64
Erb, K., 50, 127, 192, 199, 360, 384, 386, 405
Erede, A., 205, 229, 334, 335, 544, 548, 579, 593–4, 611, 625
Ericson, E., 107, 114
Ermelenko-Jushina, N., 314
Ernster, D., 92
Erschoff, I., 350, 424
Escalais, L., 235, 321
Esswood, P., 21
Etcheverry, H.-B., 634
Evans, G., 62, 63, 81, 93, 126, 175, 196, 280, 333, 334, 336, 378, 551, 638
Ewerhart, R., 20, 22–3

Fabriitis, O. de, 597, 608
Fagoaga, I., 415, 433
Fanelli, M. L., 283
Farrar, G., 67, 240–1, 351–2, 457, 470–1, 487, 493, 585, 596, 613
Farrell, E., 138, 254, 266, 296, 329, 426, 430, 435, 620
Fassbaender, B., 51, 64, 95, 99, 103, 282, 535

Faticanti, E., 176, 287, 288
Favero, M., 484, 494, 619
Fear, A., 334, 335, 388, 404
Fehenberger, L., 260, 268, 356
Feinhals, F., 387, 406, 423
Feldhoff, G., 381
Féraldy, G., 31, 482, 486, 496
Fernandi, E., 623
Ferrabini, E., 179
Ferrani, C., 585
Ferraris, I.-M., 137, 569
Ferretti, C., 240
Ferrier, K., 31–2, 39
Feuge, E., 425
Figner, N., 550
Filippeschi, M., 167, 293
Finelli, B., 198
Fineschi, O., 336
Finli-Magrina, G., 214
Finnilä, B., 63
Fischer, Ernst, 272
Fischer, Res, 340
Fischer-Dieskau, D., 28, 33, 59, 60, 63, 67, 76, 78, 79, 95, 110, 111, 112, 122, 124, 202, 211, 244, 247, 260, 270, 272–3, 282, 294, 301, 325, 326, 333, 334, 340, 343, 348, 358, 381, 395, 396, 421, 447, 525, 535, 560, 571, 602
Flagello, E., 79, 96, 280
Flagstad, K., 37, 120, 127, 351, 361, 367, 370, 371, 373, 394, 400, 401, 409, 413, 415, 417, 418, 427, 430, 434–5, 441, 448, 449, 565
Fleischer-Edel, K., 417
Fleta, M., 312, 315, 490, 551, 600, 618
Foiani, G., 202, 280
Folger, T., 208
Formichi, C., 216, 287
Forrester, M., 28
Forsell, J., 528
Forst, G., 125, 137, 389
Fort, L., 176, 198–9
Fournet, J., 633–4
Franc, T., 51
Franceschi, E. de, 17
Franci, B., 234, 270, 272, 287, 288, 322, 323, 468
Francillo-Kaufmann, H., 487
Frank, E., 206
Frantz, F., 377, 400, 403, 408, 510, 564
Franz, P., 311–12, 386
Frate, I. de, 160
Fremstad, O., 300, 351, 417, 418, 596
Freni, M., 61, 78, 80, 174, 189, 198,

245, 252, 295, 325, 333, 336, 465, 549, 582, 605, 606–7, 623
Friant, C., 473, 474, 476–7, 486, 489, 493, 494, 499, 500, 502
Fricsay, F., 33, 59, 76, 107, 109–10, 122, 339, 471
Froment, L. de, 30
Frick, G., 64, 77, 110, 121, 122, 123, 132, 133, 282, 297, 298, 340, 348, 355, 358, 377, 395, 396, 431, 432, 446–7, 509, 525, 530
Frind, A., 537
Frühbeck de Burgos, R., 464
Fry, Herbert, 364
Fry, Howard, 412
Fryatt, J., 63
Fuchs, Eugen, 377, 382
Fuchs, Marta, 125, 343, 412, 419
Fürtwangler, W., 73, 106, 108–9, 121, 128, 140, 324, 367, 376–7, 399–402, 407–8, 413, 432, 435
Fusati, N., 324

Gabor, A., 440
Gabriel, A., 498
Gadski, J., 72, 236, 269, 311, 314, 316, 372, 389, 418, 419, 426, 432, 434
Gähwiller, S., 22
Galeffi, C., 147, 236, 271, 547, 550
Gall, Y., 486
Galli-Curci, A., 66, 149, 188, 197, 199, 215, 217, 219, 220, 221, 231, 242, 487
Galliera, A., 144, 151, 526
Galvany, M., 148, 177, 196, 214, 241
Ganzarolli, W., 61, 80, 98
Garbin, E., 286, 491
Garcia, A., 492
Gardelli, Elsa, 49, 50, 99, 101
Gardelli, Lamberto, 202, 245, 246, 280, 549
Garden, M., 475, 634–5
Gartside, J., 256
Gatta, D., 193
Gatti, G., 270, 328
Gaudin, A., 506
Gavazzeni, G., 174, 210, 252, 263, 544, 610
Gay, M., 36, 236, 471–2, 476, 477
Gedda, N., 30, 44, 48, 53, 75, 78, 98, 102, 110–11, 128, 133, 174, 189, 198, 211, 244, 267, 282, 361, 455, 464, 466, 484, 493, 496, 505, 509, 514, 516, 527, 534, 535, 582–3, 608
Geisler, W., 136, 358

Gencer, L., 204, 254, 314
Gerdes, O., 348, 525
Gerhart, M., 273
Gerö, E., 273
Gerville-Réache, J., 37, 233, 471, 475, 501
Geszty, S., 97, 113
Ghazarian, S., 264, 538
Ghiaurov, N., 79, 187, 202, 203, 205, 252, 255, 294, 295, 299, 304, 455–6, 492, 514, 524
Ghirardini, E., 198, 287, 288, 331
Ghiuselev, N., 253, 298, 515, 530
Giacomelli, I., 159
Giaiotti, B., 281
Giannini, Dusolina, 162, 163, 283, 284, 289, 308, 328, 545, 596, 614
Giannini, Ferruccio, 240
Gibson, B., 33
Giebel, A., 110
Gigli, Beniamino, 76–7, 176, 177, 180, 181, 188, 220, 221, 235, 236, 242, 259, 285, 286, 308, 319, 417, 468, 489, 494, 506, 543, 545, 547, 550, 581, 585, 597–9, 600, 607, 622
Gigli, Rina, 336
Gilion, M., 235, 267, 286
Gilly, D., 506
Ginster, R., 48, 49
Giorgini, A., 177, 192, 196, 494, 581
Giraldoni, E., 301, 322, 528
Giraud, F., 386
Gitowsky, M., 253, 298
Giuliani, A., 194
Giulini, C. M., 58, 77, 82, 151, 245, 283, 294–5
Giuseppe, E. de, 171
Gläser, J., 236
Gleich, J., 267
Glossop, P., 213, 325
Gluck, A., 160–1, 241–2
Glynne, H., 253
Gmyria, B., 516
Gobbi, T., 24, 66, 68, 74, 144, 148, 174, 177, 186, 209, 210, 214–15, 243, 247, 251, 255, 262, 272, 287, 293, 301, 307, 323, 325, 333, 544, 548, 549, 551, 582, 601–2, 610–11
Goehr, W., 22, 23, 103
Gogorza, E. de, 72, 236, 272
Golovanov, 512–13
Goltz, C., 371, 559–60, 561, 564
Goncharov, 528
Gonzaga, A., 194, 195

Goodall, R., 393, 402–3, 429, 639
Goossens, E., 547, 612
Gordon, C. van, 36
Gordon, J., 274
Gorin, P., 245
Goritz, O., 405
Gorr, R., 38, 300, 306, 356, 373, 408, 496, 505, 633
Gottlieb, H., 125, 129, 429
Graarud, G., 363, 416
Gracis, E., 193
Grandi, M., 204, 206, 302
Granforte, A., 147, 215, 216, 226, 234, 271, 286, 322, 547, 551
Grani, L., 216
Grant, C., 62, 63, 429
Gravina, G., 253
Greef-Andriessen, P., 371, 426
Greindl, J., 108, 110, 339, 340, 347, 356, 377, 397, 398–9, 431, 432, 448, 525
Gresse, A., 421
Grisi, G., 156, 164fn
Grist, R., 62, 79, 95, 211, 264
Grob-Prandl, G., 43, 108, 367
Grossman, W., 129, 286, 297
Gruber, E., 136
Gruberova, E., 113
Gruhn, N., 422
Grümmer, E., 64, 132, 134, 140, 348, 358, 377, 398, 573
Grüning, W., 135
Guadagni, G., 26, 37
Guarrera, F., 89, 99, 185, 194, 326, 332, 335
Gueden, H., 47, 50, 56, 60, 75, 110, 137, 174, 209, 247, 336, 379, 458, 533, 536, 570, 573, 574
Guelfi, G.-G., 284–5, 287, 288
Guénot, L., 470
Guerrini, V., 160
Guglielmi, M., 187
Gui, V., 57, 144, 151, 165, 203, 254, 260, 441, 442
Guiot, A., 465, 471
Gulbranson, E., 418
Günther, C., 546
Gustavson, E., 307
Guszalewicz, 288, 364
Gutheil-Schoder, M., 472
Guyla, J., 493, 494

Habich, E., 364, 372, 403, 422, 449
Hackett, C., 221, 315

Hadwiger, A., 385
Haefliger, E., 76, 78, 95, 108, 109, 122, 247
Hafgren, L., 127, 139, 361, 390, 417, 448
Hagegård, H., 103, 114, 301, 551
Hager, R., 565
Hahn, R., 101
Hallstein, I., 123, 536
Hammer, G., 564–5
Hammes, K., 352
Hammond, J., 138, 139, 233, 269, 283, 284, 301, 314, 336, 526, 551, 614, 620
Hammond-Stroud, D., 280, 402, 572
Handt, H., 44
Hann, G., 125, 134, 297, 334, 338, 344
Hannsmann, R., 19
Harnoncourt, N., 19, 20–2, 23
Harper, H., 63, 65, 81, 639
Harshaw, M., 165, 544
Härtel, F., 17
Harty, Sir H., 216
Harwood, E., 212–13, 583
Haskins, V., 261
Hassler, E., 89
Hasslo, H., 271
Hay, P., 265
Haydter, A., 126, 405
Hayes, S., 22
Heger, R., 133, 209, 357, 422, 567
Heidersbach, K., 139
Helbig, H., 68, 101, 158
Helbling, M., 22
Heldy, F., 482, 486, 493
Helgers, O., 343
Helletsgrüber, L., 73, 88, 476, 621
Heming, P., 447
Hempel, F., 115, 189, 216, 217, 232, 243, 273, 473, 568
Henderson, R., 286
Hendriksen, A., 180, 181
Henke, W., 424, 533
Hensel, H., 385, 405, 415, 424, 426, 450
Hensel-Schweitzer, E., 426
Herlea, N., 246
Hermann, R., 381
Herrman, J., 137, 283, 322, 388, 390, 401, 410, 420, 551, 559
Herwig, K., 425
Hesche, W., 65, 116, 125, 137, 139, 391
Hesse, R., 356
Heusser, 74
Hidalgo, E. de, 182
Hillebrecht, H., 282

Hines, J., 202, 356
Hinckley, A. C., 432
Hiolzki, A., 529
Hirzel, M., 360
Hislop, J., 219, 385, 504
Hoekman, G., 632
Höffgen, M., 110
Hofmann, Ludwig, 282, 357, 358, 387, 388, 429, 440
Hofmann, Peter, 113
Holecek, H., 65
Hollreiser, H., 135
Hollweg, W., 48, 63
Holm, Renate, 535
Holm, Richard, 133
Homer, L., 34–5, 160–1, 221, 233, 236, 311, 315, 316, 613
Höngen, E., 108, 201, 206, 297, 400, 401, 432, 473, 563, 564, 569
Hopf, Gertrude, 43
Hopf, Hans, 122, 131, 132, 134, 348, 378, 417, 424, 434
Hoppe, Heinz, 458
Hoppe, Karl, 89
Horne, M., 29, 35, 38, 52, 126, 168, 230, 464, 504–5
Hotter, H., 111, 323, 333, 338–9, 344, 366, 379, 388, 395, 396, 402, 408, 412, 413, 421, 444–5, 446, 473, 551, 559
Howell, G., 264
Huguet, J., 147, 159, 160, 194, 195, 241, 550
Hüni-Mihacsek, F., 101, 139, 283, 582
Hunter, R., 227, 230, 402, 429, 430, 435
Hüsch, G., 65, 76, 107, 115, 216, 286, 323, 352
Hutt, R., 233, 383
Huttenlocher, P., 97, 113
Hyde, W., 236, 416, 528

Ibos, G., 500
Ilitsch, D., 101, 270
Ilosfalvy, R., 246, 267
Ilosvay, M. van, 399, 564
Infantino, L., 143
Inghilleri, G., 215, 236, 308, 322, 550, 601
Ischierdo, E., 288
Isle, M. de l', 501
Ivanov, A., 522
Ivogün, M., 115, 150, 189, 192, 196, 199, 218, 487, 537, 538

Jacobsen, M., 537
Jacoby, D., 221
Jadlowker, H., 48, 101, 115, 127, 136, 147, 180, 181, 233–4, 235, 243, 274, 286, 321, 351, 386, 448, 473, 490, 528
Jagel, F., 246, 563
Janowitz, G., 28, 60–1, 95, 110, 124, 134, 138, 139, 356, 359, 395, 396, 536
Jansen, J., 633, 634
Janson, J., 503
Janssen, H., 120, 121, 349, 350, 352, 364, 389, 390, 411, 431, 432, 559, 563
Jedlicka, R., 65
Jepson, H., 327
Jerger, A., 108, 297, 298, 388, 406, 412, 420, 571
Jeritza, M., 138, 343, 352, 373, 417, 418, 419, 596
Joachim, I., 634
Jobin, R., 468, 471, 498, 505
Jochum, E., 95, 103, 132, 356, 381
Joesten, A., 349
Johnson, P., 61, 471
Johnston, J., 203, 235, 255, 256, 386, 475, 545
Jöken, K., 383
Jokl, F., 150, 273
Jones, Gwyneth, 123, 125, 126, 204, 289, 302, 313, 325, 341, 356, 445, 560, 571
Jones, Parry, 552
Jordan, A., 235
Jörn, K., 135, 385, 405, 448, 450, 457, 469, 568
Jost-Arden, R., 349
Journet, M., 298, 316, 388, 389, 407, 453, 454, 457, 476
Jung, H., 361, 432
Jungwirth, M., 124, 571
Jürgens, J., 19
Jurinac, S., 44, 55, 56, 57, 74, 76, 89, 109, 121, 122, 329, 401, 570
Jushin, D., 314, 500
Juyol, S., 467, 496

Kaart, H., 319, 320
Kalas, K., 342
Kalef, B., 505
Kalter, S., 236, 315
Kamionsky, O., 271
Kappel, G., 138, 288, 314, 418, 434
Karajan, H. von, 55, 56, 63, 64, 90, 106, 109, 124, 186, 228–9, 231, 295, 306, 324, 325, 333, 365–6, 370, 378,

395–6, 411, 465, 466, 514, 534–5, 544, 549, 559, 561, 570–1, 583–4, 588, 591, 595, 605–6, 608, 630–1
Karakesh, M., 528, 530
Kastorsky, V., 420, 529
Katanosaka, E., 19
Katkins, A., 529
Keilberth, J., 132, 339, 356, 379, 402, 559
Kelemen, Z., 64, 124, 395, 447
Kelly, D., 125
Kemp, B., 232, 477, 568, 569
Kempe, R., 131, 355, 357–8, 377, 403, 526, 570
Kern, A., 274, 533, 569, 570, 574
Kerns, R., 484, 609
Kertesz, I., 51, 64, 99, 193
Khaikin, B., 522
Kibkalo, Y., 529
King, J., 111, 123, 128, 136, 342, 356, 387, 395, 397, 445, 560, 564
Kipnis, A., 66, 76, 108, 116, 120, 137, 150, 254, 297, 298, 350, 352, 358, 390, 420, 448, 516, 529, 569
Kirchhoff, W., 386, 404, 429, 430
Kirchstein, L., 356
Kirkby-Lunn, L., 36, 52, 300, 309
Kirsten, D., 487
Kittel, H., 430, 501
Kiurina, B., 100, 160, 621
Klarwein, F., 43, 338
Kleiber, Carlos, 133–4, 245
Kleiber, Erich, 47, 56–7, 121, 134, 536, 570
Klein, P., 108, 109, 570
Klemperer, O., 62, 78, 92–3, 106, 110–11, 123, 340–1, 410
Klose, M., 32, 34, 36, 39, 233, 274, 297, 300, 355, 357, 359, 365, 370, 371, 401, 408, 411–12, 472, 478
Kmentt, W., 92, 135, 536, 560
Knappertsbusch, H., 122, 339, 364–5, 378–9, 388, 397–9, 409–10, 443–5, 448, 574
Knepel, E., 404
Kniplova, N., 204–5, 435
Knote, H., 127, 135, 350, 351, 372, 383–4, 414, 416, 417, 424, 425, 433, 450
Knüpfer, Paul, 128, 298, 344, 371, 404, 413, 431, 448, 457, 568
Knüpfer, Maria, 404, 413
Koch, H., 17
Koči, P., 128, 342

Koerfer, F., 404, 406
Kohn, K., 64, 76, 132
Kolassi, I., 498
Kollo, R., 124, 342, 345, 347, 361, 378, 380, 415, 434, 447
Komlóssy, E., 37, 406
Konetzni, Anni, 434
Konetzni, Hilde, 108, 122, 138, 390, 401, 564, 568, 574
Konwitschny, F., 340, 348
Konya, S., 356, 361, 384
Korolev, D., 527
Korsoff, L., 189, 485, 493
Kostlinger, J., 114
Köth, E., 33, 64, 96, 125, 133, 137, 199, 573
Kötter, P., 416, 417
Kováts, K., 282
Kozlovsky, I., 29–30, 39, 246, 454, 497, 504, 513, 521, 581
Kozma, L., 19
Kozub, E., 128, 136, 267, 285, 341
Kraayvanger, H., 425
Krásová, M., 39
Kraus, Alfredo, 94, 210, 211, 333, 506
Kraus, Ernst, 344, 372, 383, 387, 413, 423, 424, 425, 433, 557
Kraus, Richard, 358, 384
Krause, T., 63, 64, 98, 99, 103, 123, 126, 193, 564
Krauss, Clemens, 338, 533, 560, 569, 570, 574
Krauss, Fritz, 128, 136, 360, 411, 417
Krebs, H., 18, 534
Krenn, W., 51, 64, 102, 342
Kreppel, W., 133
Krilovici, M., 139
Krips, J., 75
Kronen, F., 387
Kruglikova, E., 521, 522
Krusceniski, S., 313, 419
Kubelik, R., 211, 447
Kubiak, T., 524
Kuchta, G., 122
Kuen, P., 398
Kullmann, C., 286, 360, 386, 528, 622
Kunneke, E., 350
Kunz, E., 55, 66, 73, 88, 94, 109, 378, 534, 535, 536
Kupper, A., 339, 356, 390, 564
Kurt, M., 127, 128, 344, 372, 415, 419, 448, 449
Kurz, Selma, 68, 115, 150, 189, 217, 273, 487, 538, 581

Kurz, Siegfried, 194
Kusche, B., 377, 379, 403

Labia, M., 274
Labinski, A., 526–7
Lablache, L., 156–7
Labo, F., 187, 294
Ladysz, B., 253–4, 298, 529
Laholm, E., 128, 267
Lagger, P., 61, 124, 381
Lammers, G., 17
Lance, A., 496–7, 505
Landouzy, L., 485, 493
Langdon, M., 63, 574
Lanigan, J., 638
Lanza, Lina, 164
Lanza, Mario, 546, 552
Larsen-Todsen, N., 363, 427, 432, 434
Laszlo, M., 23
Lattermann, T., 137, 389
Laubenthal, Horst, 124, 381
Laubenthal, Rudolf, 136, 235, 382, 421, 428, 528
Lauri-Volpi, G., 163, 180, 181, 219, 226, 235, 286, 288, 310, 316, 321, 329, 475, 546, 600, 614
Lawrence, Marjorie, 359, 409, 434, 558
Lawrence, Martin, 198
Lazaro, H., 235
Lazzari, Agostini, 193, 499
Lazzari, Virgilio, 253
Lazzarini, A., 263
Lear, E., 111, 342, 525, 572
Lechleitner, F., 425
Legay, H., 483
Legge, W., 58, 94, 166, 228, 534, 559
Legros, J., 26
Lehane, M., 20
Lehmann, Fritz, 135
Lehmann, Lilli, 67, 68, 72, 101, 127, 154, 158, 159, 163, 164fn, 166, 241, 327, 417
Lehmann, Lotte, 67, 68, 120, 127, 138, 139, 140, 352, 359, 372, 389, 409, 411, 412, 502, 525–6, 537, 538, 567, 572, 574, 613, 614, 620
Leib, G., 97, 113, 194
Leibowitz, R., 484
Leider, F., 72, 127, 233, 275, 300, 313, 314, 343, 351, 371, 373, 412, 417–18, 419, 421, 426, 430, 432, 448
Leinsdorf, E., 58, 77–8, 96, 99, 145, 186, 202, 263, 305, 354, 356, 408–9, 426, 560, 562, 582, 597, 622, 625

Leisner, E., 34, 38, 371, 406, 412
Leitner, F., 412, 574
Lemnitz, T., 36, 67, 107–8, 139, 232–3, 297, 313, 327, 329, 351, 359, 361, 377, 381, 526, 569, 570, 574
Lenz, F., 111
Lemeshev, S., 520, 522
Leppard, R., 23, 35
Lerer, N., 21
Levine, J., 171, 281, 326
Lewis, Henry, 38
Lewis, Richard, 23, 44, 88, 340, 490, 560
Liccioni, G., 491
Licette, M., 221, 236, 547
Lieban, J., 422–3, 425
Liebenberg, E., 38
Liebl, K., 110, 340
Ligabue, I., 333
Ligendza, C., 381
Lindermeier, E., 131, 526
Lipp, W., 108, 109, 110, 535
Lisitsian, P., 246, 271, 307, 454–5, 529, 581
List, E., 120, 383, 403, 411, 431, 440, 457, 561, 568, 572
Litvinne, F., 232, 313, 418
Ljungberg, G., 283, 288, 361, 364, 382, 412, 449, 545, 558, 561
Llewellyn, R., 335
Lloyd, David, 115
Lloyd, Robert, 52
Lockhart, J., 213
Lomanto, E. di Muro, 185
Lombard, A., 97, 113, 114, 456, 463–4, 623
London, G., 58, 103, 109, 335, 340, 388, 394, 408, 421, 444, 513–14, 535, 632
Loose, E., 93, 109, 132, 569, 571
Lorengar, P., 29, 33, 50, 57, 80, 98, 112, 125, 138, 549
Lorenz, M., 285, 351, 360, 367, 370, 371, 372, 376, 384, 401, 410, 413, 414, 416, 423–4, 425, 433, 450, 561, 564
Löwlein, H., 282
Luart, E., 481, 486, 493, 494
Lubin, G., 351, 415, 426–7, 434
Luca, Giuseppe de, 65, 66, 68, 148, 192, 194, 195, 197, 215, 220, 221, 234, 242, 271, 286, 287, 288, 296, 301, 310, 335, 352, 585
Luca, Libero de, 467, 483
Luccioni, J., 321, 503

Lucia, F. de, 146, 148, 176, 178, 179, 180, 196, 198, 218–19, 241, 312, 359, 500, 550
Ludwig, Christa, 57, 78–9, 93, 94, 110, 123, 167, 347, 358, 369–70, 381, 395, 396, 435, 447, 465–6, 534, 570–1, 606
Ludwig, Leopold, 413
Ludwig, Walther, 50, 101, 108, 129, 274, 283, 525
Lugo, G., 502, 546
Luise, M., 174, 193
Lund, G., 50
Luppi, O., 215, 284
Lussan, Z. de, 472
Lustig, R., 339

Maag, P., 35
Maazel, L., 82, 123, 297, 464–5, 592, 609
Macarthur, E., 449
McCormack, J., 73, 148, 180, 181, 219, 221, 241–2, 312, 314, 385, 458, 473, 474, 490, 585, 586
McCracken, J., 122, 136, 185, 262, 286, 315, 325, 549, 552, 560
McDaniel, B., 99
McIntyre, D., 230, 388, 421, 445, 631
Mackerras, C., 28
MacNeil, C., 211, 263, 543, 549
McNeil, D., 44
Macurdy, J., 82, 83
Madeira, J., 262, 471, 564
Maffeo, G., 176
Magini-Coletti, A., 215, 221, 322, 334
Maionica, S., 36
Maison, R., 120, 128, 403
Maksakov, M., 529
Maksakova, 497, 513
Malagrida, L., 162, 284
Malaniuk, I., 92
Malas, S., 175
Malaspina, G., 206, 334, 335
Malibran, M., 144, 170
Malapiero, G., 182, 185
Manacchini, G., 185
Mancini, C., 227, 544
Manke, G., 404
Mann, J., 267, 312, 546, 552
Manowarda, J. von, 388, 390, 407, 421, 426, 447
Manuguerra, M., 593, 602
Marak, O., 528
Marcelin, E., 488, 492, 501
Marc'Hadour, Y. le, 24

Marchi, E. de, 316, 593
Marconi, F., 188, 286
Marcoux, V., 299–30, 517, 634
Mardones, J., 253
Maréchal, A., 491
Marherr, E., 134, 569
Marimpieti, L., 333
Marini, L., 581
Marinuzzi, G., 277–8, 279
Mario, Q., 547
Markworth, P., 401, 564
Marny, J., 482, 493, 502
Marone, A., 17
Marsh, Calvin, 356
Marsh, Lucy, 314, 473
Marshall, L., 52
Marti, B., 275, 499, 611
Martin, J., 342
Martinelli, Germaine, 502
Martinelli, Giovanni, 165, 198, 220, 233, 234, 235–6, 237, 252, 255, 259, 267, 286, 288, 289, 296, 310, 316, 320, 322, 327, 372, 417, 470–1, 504, 528, 547, 550, 585, 586, 600, 614, 618–19, 621–2
Martinez-Patti, G., 159
Martini, N., 193
Martinis, C., 265, 269, 324
Marton, E., 282
Mascherini, E., 203, 593, 601
Masini, G., 278
Maslennikov, A., 515
Massard, R., 465, 506
Matačič, L. von, 124, 133, 549, 558
Mathis, E., 46, 60, 82, 123, 134
Matray, D., 350
Matters, A., 255, 256
Matzenauer, M., 405, 418, 419, 431
Maurane, C., 632, 633
Maurel, V., 72, 323, 327, 335
Mayr, R., 65, 66, 126, 139, 344, 425–6, 431, 530, 567, 569, 574
Mazurok, Y., 523, 530
Mazzei, E. di, 503
Mazzoleni, E., 162, 266
Mehta, Z., 230, 305, 592, 595, 623, 624, 625
Mei-Figner, M., 500
Meili, M., 17, 24
Meisle, K., 237
Melander, S. B., 175
Melba, N., 66, 67, 188, 217, 221, 242, 327, 585, 587, 596
Melchert, H., 403, 561

Melchior, L., 234, 315, 320, 342, 350–1, 354, 360, 361, 364, 371, 372, 384, 386, 409, 411, 412–13, 413–14, 416, 417, 422, 423, 425, 429, 430, 432, 433, 440, 441, 448–9, 450
Melchissédec, L., 271
Meletti, S., 278, 288, 332
Melik-Peshayev, A., 123, 473, 513, 521
Melis, G., 37
Melton, J., 489, 534
Menzel, G., 43
Merentié, M., 501
Merli, F., 225–6, 285, 286, 288, 289, 329, 546, 547, 614, 625
Merrill, R., 145, 187, 210, 211, 230, 244, 261, 264, 272, 280, 286, 287, 301, 306, 322, 333, 465, 467, 534, 549, 577, 582
Merriman, N., 33, 37, 90–1, 95, 213
Meplé, M., 36, 493
Metternich, J., 262, 287, 334, 339, 355, 379, 525, 543, 560
Metzger, O., 35, 274, 404, 405, 426, 431
Meyer, S., 48
Michaelova, M., 137
Micheau, J., 30, 49, 466, 467, 483, 633
Michel, S., 38, 467–8
Micheletti, G., 470, 474–5, 481, 489, 493, 503
Midgley, W., 182, 490
Mikhailov, V., 513
Milanov, Z., 165, 213, 227–8, 258, 262, 265, 269, 275, 280, 281, 283, 284, 289, 307, 328, 543, 597
Milashkina, T., 314, 525, 530
Milcheva-Nonova, A., 35, 505
Mildmay, A., 73
Mileri, L., 159
Milinkovic, G. von, 399, 560, 570, 574
Miljakovic, O., 65
Mill, A. van, 137, 306, 398, 410
Miller, M., 99
Milnes, S., 82, 96, 146, 187, 203, 206–7, 212, 220, 230, 244, 245, 264, 272, 281, 286, 287, 288, 295, 296, 301, 305, 326, 463, 549, 584, 592, 602
Milona, C., 267
Minazzi, M., 336
Minghini-Cattaneo, I., 226, 274, 308
Minten, R., 427
Minton, Y., 52, 62, 93, 99, 571, 631
Mitropoulos, D., 261–2, 265, 278–9, 510, 563
Mödl, M., 38, 121, 206, 260–1, 300,

366, 397, 400, 401, 402, 408, 435, 443–4, 472, 564
Moffo, A., 34, 58, 76, 99, 187, 211, 244, 254, 270, 333, 465, 484, 535, 582, 612
Molajoli, L., 142, 194, 208, 225, 331, 468, 543, 546, 547, 579, 612
Molinari, E., 275, 286, 288
Molinari-Pradelli, F., 174, 210, 211, 252, 280, 497, 548–9
Moll, K., 113, 281, 380
Mollet, P., 633
Monachesi, W., 251
Monaco, M. del, 165, 169, 205, 229, 266, 279, 280, 285, 319, 320, 415, 417, 465, 466, 506, 543, 544, 548, 549, 623
Montarsolo, P., 78, 151, 284
Monti, T. dal, 150, 162, 189, 197, 199, 217, 221, 336
Montesanto, L., 221
Monteux, P., 33, 243, 483
Monti, N., 143, 144, 174
Moore, G., 484
Moralt, R., 74, 92, 421, 559
Morel, J., 514
Morena, B., 417
Morturier, L., 221, 299
Moscona, N., 281, 289, 560
Moser, E., 28, 44, 45, 83, 113
Mossakowski, 216
Mrasz, L., 137
Muck, K., 428, 440
Müller, M., 134–5, 349, 357, 376, 387, 412, 413, 418
Mullings, F., 321, 385, 424, 547
Mummery, B., 550
Muratore, L., 474, 490, 492, 501
Muro, B. de, 235, 295–6, 320
Musy, L., 469
Muti, R., 203, 264
Muzio, C., 159, 162, 232, 242–3, 269, 314, 476, 526, 550, 586–7, 593, 596

Naidenov, 515
Naidovich, N., 528
Nash, H., 55, 77, 88, 102, 115, 147, 219, 221, 236, 455, 475, 484, 490, 532, 536, 537, 542, 547, 552, 587
Nast, M., 273, 469
Naval, F., 491
Navarrini, F., 150, 253, 298
Neate, K., 136
Nebolsin, V., 520–1
Nequeçaur, J., 499

Negrini, V., 156
Neidlinger, G., 394–5, 396, 397, 398, 444, 564, 573
Nelli, Herva, 261, 307, 323, 332
Nelli, Romilda, 159
Nemeth, M., 232, 269, 283, 288, 313, 620
Nentwig, K., 51, 89
Neri, G., 253, 293
Neroni, L., 178, 185, 253
Neshdanova, A., 115
Nespoulos, M., 470, 634
Nessi, G., 332
Nesterenko, Y., 298
Neumann, K. A., 390
Neumann, V., 27
Nienstedt, G., 397
Nikolai, E., 35, 278, 293, 543
Nikolaidi, E., 306
Nikolov, N., 319
Nilsson, Birgit, 44, 78, 79, 122–3, 126, 133, 138, 202, 204, 206, 263, 283, 289, 300, 305, 313, 344, 348, 351, 368, 369, 395, 397, 398, 399, 408–9, 413, 415, 417, 450, 535, 560, 564, 625–6
Nilsson, Raymond, 638
Nissen, H. H., 382, 407, 420–1, 423, 447, 561
Noble, D., 66, 115, 148, 216, 221, 234, 485, 532, 537, 547, 551
Noni, A., 56, 99, 174, 193, 260, 273, 331
Noort, H., 382
Nordica, L., 434
Nordin, B., 114
Nordmö-Lövberg, A., 417
Noreika, V., 527
Noréna, E., 116, 218, 220, 221, 328, 476, 621
Norman, J., 62
Nortsov, P. M., 520, 521
Novelli, U., 259
Novotna, J., 108, 572–3, 574

Ober, M., 315
Obraztsova, E., 231, 300
Obukhova, N., 502
Ochman, W., 46, 527, 561
Oehmann, C. M., 321, 361, 384
Oestvig, K., 383, 416
Offers, M., 300, 315, 428
Ogenric, N., 527
Ohms, E., 126, 344, 372, 568–9
Oldrati, 164

Olitzka, R., 315, 353
Olivero, M., 487, 499, 587, 596, 625
Ollendorf, F., 60
Olszewska, M., 233, 359, 390, 406, 422, 431, 567
Oltrabella, A., 332
Oncina, J., 193, 333
Onegin, S., 37, 204, 236, 274, 300, 315, 405–6, 431
Orfenov, 504
Orlov, A., 246, 521–2
O'Sullivan, J., 312, 319
Osvath, L., 108
Otava, Z., 271
Ots, G., 198, 530
Otto, L., 91, 132, 403
Ott-Penetto, M., 22

Pacal, F., 386
Pacini, Giuseppe, 271, 323
Pacini, Regina, 217
Pagliughi, L., 100, 182, 185, 208, 209, 216, 332, 336
Paini, L., 159
Palet, J., 423
Pally (Palij), Z., 37, 274, 505
Palócz, L., 246
Palombini, V., 17
Pampanini, R., 581, 612, 614, 621
Panerai, R., 56, 57, 91, 95, 145, 174, 212, 228, 244, 332, 333, 441, 442, 544, 549, 583, 609
Panizza, E., 165, 246, 252, 258, 259, 618
Paoli, A., 319
Papi, G., 237, 547
Pareto, G., 196, 214, 222
Parly, T., 414, 417, 424, 425, 434
Parsi-Pettinella, A., 160, 233, 236, 274
Pasero, T., 150, 165, 231, 259, 278, 289, 299, 308, 517
Pasini-Vitale, L., 328
Pasta, G., 154–5, 163, 170
Pataky, K. von, 101, 285, 286, 312, 537, 546, 568, 574
Patti, A., 67, 72, 157–8, 170
Pattiera, T., 234, 235, 267, 287, 314, 322, 329, 477, 546, 551, 581
Patzak, J., 77, 102, 115, 119, 122, 128, 182, 220, 266, 384, 401, 475, 490, 502, 527–8, 533, 560, 561, 614
Pavarotti, L., 175, 187, 189, 199, 202, 205, 212, 230, 247, 264, 268, 329, 544, 549, 571, 583, 605, 607, 623

Payan, P., 492
Payne, P., 264
Pears, P., 637, 638, 639
Pease, J., 638
Pederzini, G., 502
Peerce, J., 121, 122, 186, 209, 213, 221, 244, 261, 265, 268, 275, 281, 285, 286, 288, 289, 467, 546, 552, 578
Pelletier, W., 148, 327, 484
Pennefort, K. de, 38
Penno, G., 165, 237, 255
Perard-Petzl, L., 232
Perea, E., 178
Perelli, L., 468, 502, 503
Perlea, J., 210
Perli, L., 587
Pernerstorfer, A., 74, 400
Pernet, A., 492, 517
Perras, M., 76, 115, 243
Pertile, A., 220, 221, 226, 235, 267, 285, 288, 308, 322, 329, 468, 550, 614
Peters, R., 33, 58, 89, 111, 145, 186, 197, 210, 262
Petri, Elisa, 334
Petri, Mario, 56, 251
Petrov, I., 298, 513, 522–3
Piazza, L., 208
Piccaluga, N., 320
Piccaver, A., 128, 180, 181, 198, 219, 235, 267, 285, 360, 361, 384, 490, 502, 546, 622
Picchi, M., 260, 293
Pilinsky, S., 349, 360, 361, 387
Pilou, J., 463–4
Piltti, L., 49
Pini, A., 332
Pini-Corsi, A., 146, 148, 177, 192, 194, 195
Pinkert, R., 199
Pinza, E., 23, 65, 66, 73, 116, 150, 163, 165, 231, 252–3, 254, 284, 289, 299, 311, 316, 453, 458, 511, 516–17, 587
Pipova, E., 530
Pirazzini, M., 227
Pirogov, A., 455, 512, 520, 530
Pistor, G., 413, 414, 424, 425, 441, 448
Plaichinger, T., 562
Plançon, P., 116, 297–8
Plaschke, F., 286, 431
Plessis, C. du, 212
Plishka, P., 171, 456
Plümacher, H., 51, 89
Pobbe, M., 336
Pocidalo, R., 502

Poell, A., 56, 74, 134, 379, 401, 533, 570
Poggi, G., 186, 244, 263, 268, 544, 548, 582
Poli, A., 174, 179, 193, 548, 581
Poli-Randaccio, T., 236, 269, 315
Pons, L., 148, 185
Ponselle, R., 159, 162–3, 232, 236, 246–7, 284, 289, 311, 313, 314, 315, 327
Ponzio, L., 482
Popovich, D., 523
Popp, L., 51, 64, 93, 99, 110, 124, 536, 571
Pospiš, R., 35, 37
Prandelli, G., 505
Prêtre, G., 187, 206, 244, 465, 496
Preuss, A., 125
Preve, C., 159
Prevedi, B., 202, 286
Previtali, F., 56, 143, 226, 293
Prey, H., 33, 60, 95, 103, 104, 112, 132, 145, 282, 466, 525, 536
Price, Leontyne, 47, 78, 96, 126, 206, 229, 230, 231, 254, 263–4, 275, 280, 281, 302, 305, 306, 313, 329, 465, 562, 591, 592, 595, 597, 612
Price, Margaret, 49, 50, 52, 63, 67, 81, 93, 325
Pring, K., 403
Prinvot, Y., 486
Pritchard, J., 44, 48, 100, 175, 187, 244
Proebstl, M., 134
Prohaska, J., 377, 387, 572–3
Protti, A., 209, 244, 279, 324, 543, 548
Pütz, R. M., 27
Py, G., 464

Questa, A., 209

Radev, M., 37
Radford, R., 404, 418–19, 427, 517
Ragon, M., 487, 492–3
Raimondi, R., 83, 151, 171, 203, 212, 244, 280, 295, 584, 631
Rains, L., 350, 390
Raisa, R., 236, 328, 618
Ralf, T., 321, 322, 329, 361, 381–2
Rasa, L. B., 543
Raskin, J., 34, 96
Ratti, E., 78, 262
Raukas, O., 198
Raveau, A., 31, 472, 476, 502
Raybould, C., 101, 102

Rayner, S., 490, 503
Reardon, J., 578
Rebroff, I., 298
Rehfuss, H., 57, 458, 633
Reichelt, I., 265
Reiner, F., 74, 339, 409, 467, 534, 558, 561, 563
Reinhardt, D., 138, 139, 328, 359, 389, 415, 417, 569
Reining, M., 326, 388, 411, 413, 538, 570, 572–3
Reinmar, H., 72, 255, 301, 326, 352, 390, 420, 447
Reizen, M., 421, 510, 513, 522, 529
Rekhemper, H., 234, 271
Remedios, A., 402, 403, 429, 430
Renaud, M., 72, 352
Rennyson, G., 359
Renzi, E., 332
Resnik, R., 264, 300, 333, 419, 465, 534, 564
Rethberg, E., 65, 66, 67, 138, 237, 252, 269, 309–10, 313, 316, 327, 328, 343, 351, 382, 473, 538, 614
Reti, J., 102
Rettore, A., 179, 273
Revy, A., 137
Reynolds, A., 110, 380, 524
Rhodes, J., 471
Ricciarelli, K., 252, 275, 296, 329
Richard, C., 496
Richter, Karl, 27
Richter, Ursula, 570
Ridderbusch, K., 124, 341, 356, 370, 378, 380, 396
Riedner, G., 43
Riegel, K., 83
Ries, A., 139
Righetti, A., 164
Rimini, G., 236, 331
Rinaldi, M., 44
Ritch, T., 489
Ritter-Ciampi, G., 100, 150
Robinson, Forbes, 638, 639
Robinson, Stanford, 176, 484–5, 619
Robson, E., 125, 471
Rocca, L., 491
Rocque, E., 491, 496
Rode, W., 389, 406–7, 411, 420, 426
Rodzinski, A., 411, 563
Rogatchewsky, J., 34, 38, 483, 489, 502
Roger, J., 493–4
Rogers, N., 19
Rohr, O. von, 349

Rolland, J., 473
Roman, S., 259
Roni, L., 80
Rooy, A. van, 343, 352, 389, 406, 419–20
Rosbaud, H., 30, 57, 76
Roselle, A., 620
Rosing, V., 500
Rossi, M., 193, 332
Rossi-Lemeni, N., 163, 167, 278, 284, 293, 516
Rostropovich, M., 523, 592–3, 595
Roswaenge, H., 101, 107, 108, 128, 136, 208, 221, 235, 243, 247, 265, 267, 281–2, 285, 296, 321, 326, 360, 384, 390, 475, 490, 517, 527, 547, 568, 573, 582
Rothenberger, A., 27, 44, 60, 113, 125, 194, 535, 536, 574
Rother, A., 32, 413, 526, 559
Rothier, L., 298
Rothmuller, M., 104, 203, 216, 601
Rouleau, J., 299
Rousselière, C., 386, 424, 425, 501
Roux, M., 463, 633
Rudel, J., 483–4
Rudolf, M., 74
Ruffo, T., 147, 148, 214, 222, 234, 241, 270, 271, 287, 288, 301, 322, 323, 334, 335, 550, 585, 593, 601
Runge, G., 538
Rünger, G., 205–6, 300, 411
Rus, M., 132
Russ, G., 159, 160, 162, 215, 284, 301, 313
Russell, Francis, 342, 385, 614
Russell, Sidney, 421
Ruzskowska, 284
Ruziczka, E., 66, 533, 569
Rysanek, L., 122, 202, 288, 313, 325, 340, 342, 351, 397, 407-8, 411, 543, 573

Sabajno, C., 193, 196, 208, 225, 320, 543, 547
Sabata, V. de, 203, 331, 366–7, 591–2
Sack, E., 137, 538
Sadoven, H., 477
Salazar, E., 285, 321
Salvatini, M., 275, 545
Salvatti, S., 178
Salztmann-Stevens, M., 419, 427, 434
Sambo, I., 159

Sammarco, M., 66, 148, 215, 271, 286, 322, 323, 585
Samosud, 30
Sanchioni, N., 216
Santi, N., 275, 549
Santini, G., 174, 252, 293, 294, 544, 611
Santley, C., 66
Saraceni, A., 179, 193, 547
Sardi, I., 76
Sardiniero, V., 187
Sass, S., 50, 204, 206, 314
Sattler, J., 400, 424
Savarese, U., 229
Saville, F., 485
Savini, I., 176
Savio, G., 245
Sawallisch, W., 107, 112, 340, 347, 356
Sayão, B., 193, 486
Scacciati, B., 289, 545
Scampini, A., 267
Scaremberg, E., 488, 500
Schachtschneider, H., 356
Schädle, L., 133
Schech, M., 43, 340, 348, 355, 410, 564, 571
Scheidemantel, K., 352
Scheidl, T., 270, 275, 343, 344, 388, 423, 517
Scheidt, R. von, 405
Schenk, O., 535
Scheppan, H., 265, 269, 282
Schiötz, A., 77, 102, 115, 528
Schipa, T., 37, 147, 178, 180, 181, 188, 192, 193, 196, 198, 199, 219, 242, 336, 490, 495, 498, 546, 552
Schipper, E., 359, 390, 422, 423
Schippers, T., 187, 202, 230, 280, 465, 514, 582–3
Schirp, W., 344, 432
Schlemm, A., 32, 135, 261
Schlusnus, H., 67, 76, 147, 196, 208, 233, 234, 243, 247, 255, 275, 281–2, 283, 286, 287, 296, 301, 322, 349, 420, 457, 473, 529, 551
Schlüter, E., 563, 564
Schmedes, E., 385, 404, 414, 417, 423, 430, 433, 434
Schmidt, J., 268, 490
Schmidt-Isserstedt, H., 44, 47, 138
Schmitt-Walter, K., 103, 109, 265, 352
Schock, R., 128, 132, 133, 175, 268, 282, 340, 355, 377, 466, 506, 535, 536, 543
Schöffler, P., 57, 65, 93, 120, 122, 256, 298, 322, 324, 365, 379, 388, 421, 560, 563
Schöne, Lotte, 99, 116, 192, 197, 219, 273, 487, 537, 587, 613–14, 620–1
Schorr, F., 120, 126, 139, 196, 343, 344, 352, 382, 387, 403, 407, 409, 412, 422, 429, 440, 561
Schottler, G., 146
Schreier, P., 44, 45–6, 47, 48, 52, 79, 82, 95, 97, 113, 123, 134, 194, 378
Schreker, M., 358
Schröder, K., 349
Schrödter, F., 533
Schubert, R., 135, 360, 371, 384, 404, 414, 416, 417, 433
Schüchter, W., 355, 536, 573
Schumann, E., 66, 67, 68, 72, 125, 137, 382, 537, 567, 574
Schumann-Heink, E., 39, 52, 53, 405, 432
Schützendorff, L., 382, 517
Schwaiger, R., 135
Schwartz, M., 18
Schwarz, Joseph, 216, 234, 236, 270, 272, 286
Schwarz, Vera, 49, 99, 232, 269, 539
Schwarzkopf, E., 49, 55, 58, 59, 73, 77, 90, 91, 94, 110, 123, 125, 126, 139, 328, 332, 359, 378, 526, 534, 570, 623
Schymberg, H., 101
Scipioni, A., 194, 195
Sciutti, G., 56, 57, 75, 77, 91, 92, 99, 145, 193, 197, 227, 333
Scott, N., 185
Scotti, A., 67, 177, 192, 196, 197, 221, 270, 271, 287, 296, 301, 315, 322, 334, 335, 457, 549–50, 585, 593, 601, 613
Scotto, R., 186, 189, 210, 211, 244, 326, 328, 494, 582, 609, 623
Secombe, H., 552
Sedlmair, S., 351, 533
Seefried, I., 50, 56, 59, 68, 73, 96, 108, 109, 122, 132–3, 570, 571
Seider, A., 134
Seidler-Winkler, B., 411, 532, 557
Seinemeyer, M., 138, 236, 268, 283–4, 289, 302, 313, 314, 315, 327, 329, 361, 373, 387, 418, 457, 568, 569, 581, 596, 614
Sembach, J., 128, 129, 135, 385, 416, 423
Sembrich, M., 68, 149, 158, 188, 192, 197, 216, 221

Semkow, J., 509
Sénéchal, M., 281, 463
Senius, F., 101
Serafin, T., 149, 151, 163, 165–7, 174, 186, 210, 229, 243, 259, 278, 279, 306–7, 308, 324–5, 543, 544, 548, 582, 611, 625
Sereni, M., 175, 544, 583, 610, 611
Sergi, A., 124
Sgourda, A., 81
Shaw, R., 33
Sheridan, M., 612–13, 614
Sherwood, C., 613
Shevelev, N., 528
Shirley, G., 45, 48, 96, 631
Shirley-Quirk, J., 81, 632–3
Shuard, A., 270, 313, 525, 545, 620
Sibiriakov, L., 515, 529
Siems, M., 189, 232, 243, 313, 314
Siepi, C., 56, 75, 78, 187, 253, 279, 280, 299, 453, 456, 582
Siewert, R., 403
Silja, A., 124, 340, 341, 347, 356, 397, 562
Sills, B., 145, 169, 171, 187, 243, 488–9
Silveri, P., 243, 251, 260, 271, 287, 293, 331
Simionato, G., 143, 162, 166, 167, 230, 263, 280, 300, 306, 333, 466, 497, 505, 543
Simoneau, L., 30–1, 44, 48–9, 50, 52, 53, 75, 90, 102, 103, 110, 180, 191, 458, 491, 493
Simons, D., 50
Singher, M., 359
Sinimberghi, G., 199
Slezak, L., 101, 139, 235, 266, 312, 320, 321, 350, 351, 359–60, 386, 423, 490, 581
Slobodskaya, O., 525
Smirnov, D., 147, 180, 181, 219, 490, 501, 515, 526–7
Smith, Donald, 212, 268, 286, 471
Smith, Erik, 61
Sobinov, 192, 198, 501, 526–7
Sodero, C., 165
Söderström, E., 21, 62–3, 66, 525, 574, 631
Solari, C., 176, 194
Solti, G., 28–9, 38, 97, 107, 111–12, 126, 211, 263, 295, 306, 325, 333, 341, 346–7, 368, 393–6, 409–10, 446–7, 463, 524, 571, 584
Sommer, K., 406

Soomer, W., 344, 389, 419, 420
Soot, F., 128, 134, 372, 390, 405, 419, 424, 426, 430, 433, 434, 450
Sotin, H., 93, 124, 347, 380, 410
Souez, I., 73, 88, 101, 102, 162
Soukupová, V., 35, 36, 37, 274, 397, 406
Souliotis, E., 168–9, 202, 204, 269, 289, 544
Souzay, G., 24, 35, 37, 484, 492, 499, 633
Soyer, R., 81, 496
Spani, H., 232, 269, 328, 551, 596
Spletter, C., 134
Spoorenberg, E., 47, 632
Stabile, M., 66, 68, 74, 147, 192, 198, 287, 322, 323, 331, 332, 334–5, 601
Stade, F. von, 52, 53, 63, 66, 67, 97, 149, 505, 572, 631
Stader, M., 33, 47, 49, 59, 76, 110, 247, 458, 471
Stahlman, S., 263
Steber, E., 50, 89, 100, 301, 326, 355, 456, 612
Stecchi, M., 145
Stefano, G. di, 174, 186, 209, 228, 243, 262, 329, 453, 466, 473, 484, 491, 497, 506, 543, 544, 548, 598–9, 600, 610
Steffek, H., 28, 94
Stein, Horst, 33, 465–6
Stein, Ingeborg, 125
Steinkopf, H., 247
Stella, A., 229, 243, 252, 263, 293, 294
Stern, G., 282
Stevens, R., 33, 36–7, 57, 466–7, 471, 572, 574
Stewart, T., 341, 342, 356, 395, 396, 447
Stich-Randall, T., 28, 47, 49, 57, 75, 92, 100, 137, 307, 332, 571
Stiedry, F., 32, 89–90
Stignani, E., 37, 162, 165, 167, 233, 237, 274, 278, 284, 287, 293, 297, 300, 308, 468, 505
Stilwell, R., 631
Stokowski, L., 374, 516
Stolze, G., 347, 395, 396, 560, 564
Storchio, R., 192, 194
Stoska, P., 138, 390
Stracciari, R., 143, 147, 148, 189, 208, 215, 221, 234, 236, 270, 272, 315, 323, 352, 550, 601
Stratas, T., 97, 99, 326
Streich, R., 32, 33, 49, 57, 78, 99, 110, 133, 134, 135, 150, 197, 273, 401, 534

Striegler, K., 65
Strienz, W., 107, 137, 253, 517, 530
Stückgold, G., 358
Stünzner, E., 359
Suitner, O., 59–60, 96, 107, 113, 561
Summers, J., 638
Sumskaya, E., 246, 454
Supervia, C., 149, 160, 469–70, 502, 569, 587
Süss, R., 194
Suthaus, L., 367, 387, 398, 401, 407–8
Sutherland, J., 77, 80, 139, 159, 166, 175, 186, 187, 189, 210–11, 212, 230, 244, 247, 329, 455, 465, 551, 623, 626–7
Svanholm, S., 120, 128, 339, 371, 394, 401, 410, 413, 414, 417, 426, 427, 563
Sved, A., 206, 216, 258, 259, 354
Svehla, Z., 506
Swarowsky, H., 74, 356
Swarthout, G., 505
Sydney, L., 35, 38
Szantho, E., 36, 563
Szekely, M., 298
Szell, G., 572–3

Taccani, G., 288
Taddei, G., 58, 74, 77, 94, 143, 174, 202, 209, 322, 332, 334, 549, 581, 591, 601
Tagliabue, C., 148, 216, 227, 237, 278, 548
Tagliavini, F., 147, 178, 180, 181, 186, 209, 221, 260, 336, 491, 497, 506, 581, 599
Tajo, I., 56, 74, 103, 205, 253, 299
Takacz, P., 270
Talén, B., 360, 386
Talvela, M., 79, 111, 112, 123, 212, 294, 341, 342, 369, 395, 397, 509, 514, 525
Tamagno, F., 235, 319, 320, 321, 327
Tansini, U., 185
Tappy, E., 18
Tarr, E. H., 18
Tassinari, P., 260, 331, 497, 506
Tattermuschova, H., 35, 36
Tatum, N., 139
Tauber, R., 77, 115, 136, 140, 220, 235, 236, 286, 315, 360, 384, 416, 473, 474, 527, 538–9, 552, 568, 614, 622
Taubmann, H., 43, 136
Taucher, C., 418, 433
Tavolaccini, G., 263
Tear, R., 45, 62, 81

Tebaldi, R., 229, 244, 264, 269, 270, 279, 294, 306, 313, 324, 331, 351, 359, 544, 545, 579–80, 582, 593–4, 611, 624
Tedeschi, E., 245
Te Kanawa, K., 81, 83, 97, 113, 212, 463
Tellini, I., 468
Telva, M., 163
Terry, V., 206
Teschemacher, M., 139, 236, 269, 270, 274, 283, 284, 314, 315, 382, 410, 545
Tessmer, H., 108, 422
Tetrazzini, L., 72, 149, 188–9, 217, 221, 231, 241, 273, 288–9, 313, 476
Teyte, M., 484, 487, 634–5
Thebom, B., 88–9, 296, 406, 419, 433, 560
Thill, G., 220, 243, 321, 360, 386, 414, 416, 417, 450, 454, 457, 470, 489, 493, 496, 552
Thomas, Jess, 282, 356, 357–8, 379, 404, 415, 430, 444, 445
Thomas, J. C., 22, 271, 286, 301
Thorborg, K., 38, 354, 371, 406, 409, 419, 432, 448, 472, 476
Thornton, E., 39, 221, 236, 315
Tibbett, L., 148, 246–7, 253, 254–5, 271, 322, 323, 327, 334, 335, 352, 388, 420, 458, 550, 600
Tinsley, P., 45
Tipton, T., 282
Titterton, F., 286, 416
Tomasi, H., 31
Tomova-Sintov, A., 63, 82
Töpper, H., 59
Torri, R., 581, 621
Toscanini, A., 32–3, 37, 106, 108, 120, 127, 151, 213, 221, 261, 266, 282–3, 307–8, 323, 332, 349, 412–13, 429, 435, 515, 577–9
Tourangeau, H., 212
Tourel, J., 50, 472, 476
Tozzi, G., 58, 229, 254, 280, 340, 577
Traubel, H., 350, 351, 370, 373, 411, 413, 429, 435
Traxel, J., 102, 198, 199, 339, 398, 573
Treigle, N., 253, 298, 492
Trentini, E., 178, 273
Trenton, L., 412
Treptow, G., 349, 364–5, 371–2, 379, 400, 448, 449, 450
Trevi, J. de, 468–9, 503
Trötschel, E., 131, 524, 574
Troyanos, T., 60, 96, 463

Truc, G., 634
Tucci, G., 230, 549
Tucker, R., 89, 185, 210, 229, 244, 254, 256, 261, 266, 278, 280, 285–6, 296, 307, 329, 491, 505, 544, 546, 548, 551, 582, 612
Turner, Claramae, 261
Turner, Eva, 232, 313, 314, 596, 618, 619–20
Tynes, M., 561–2

Udovick, L., 44
Uhde, H., 108, 135, 339, 356, 399, 402, 444
Uhl, F., 368
Ulfung, R., 114
Unger, G., 122, 123, 341, 377, 378, 571
Urlus, J., 115, 127, 128, 135, 235, 321, 351, 413, 414, 419, 433, 474
Urrila, I., 114
Ursuleac, V., 338, 569, 570, 574, 620

Vaguet, A., 488, 493, 500
Valdengo, G., 176, 177, 215, 260, 307, 323, 332, 548
Valente, A., 547, 550, 622
Valentino, F., 193
Vallandri, A., 485, 492, 493
Valletti, C., 78, 145, 174, 182, 193, 198, 499, 505, 612
Vallin, N., 162, 197, 472, 485–6, 492, 493, 494, 496, 499, 502
Vanzo, A., 484, 505
Varady, J., 46, 536, 544
Varnay, A., 126, 254, 255, 269, 339, 354, 356, 373, 398, 400, 411, 413, 415, 417, 427, 430, 435, 560–1, 563–4
Varviso, S., 145, 151, 169, 379–80, 544, 574
Veasey, J., 110, 395, 632
Verdière, R., 136, 414, 417, 424, 499
Verrett, S., 34, 162, 164fn, 171, 203, 264, 280, 295, 315, 505
Vessières, A., 633
Vezzani, C., 221, 453–4, 493, 494, 503
Viardot, P., 26, 34, 149
Vicentini, A., 245
Vichegonov, 284
Vickers, J., 123, 124, 296, 306, 325, 370, 395, 408, 464, 552, 637–8
Vignas, F., 268, 312, 320, 350, 386
Villabella, M., 220, 221, 489, 493, 494, 502–3
Vinay, R., 323, 324, 326, 356, 365, 366,

398, 560, 600
Vincent, G., 355
Vinogradov, G. P., 527
Visconti, R., 470
Vishnevskaya, G., 123, 289, 504, 515, 522, 523, 530, 592, 595
Vivante, G., 17
Vix, G., 487, 500
Vogel, S., 113
Vogelstrom, F., 135, 350, 361, 385, 424
Völker, F., 128, 136, 235, 236, 297, 321, 342, 345, 350, 351, 357, 360, 384, 414, 416, 418, 475, 533, 537, 538
Votto, A., 262, 543, 579
Vroons, F., 128, 136, 265

Wächter, E., 58, 59, 77, 133, 347, 536, 560, 564
Wagner, Robert, 368
Wagner, Sieglinde, 108, 341, 403, 534, 571
Walker, Edyth, 352, 405, 418
Walker, Nellie, 343
Walker, Norman, 485
Wallace, I., 144
Wallberg, H., 65
Walter, B., 120, 411
Ward, D., 407, 408, 631
Warfield, S., 315
Warren, L., 202, 206, 209, 213, 227, 228, 229, 243, 255, 265, 270, 272, 281, 286, 287, 288, 324, 335, 548
Watson, Claire, 78, 133, 379, 396, 639
Watson, Jean, 36, 260, 274
Watson, Lillian, 62
Watzke, R., 429
Weathers, F., 296
Weber, L., 75, 109, 137, 339, 400, 401, 431, 444, 445, 517, 560, 570
Weede, R., 271, 335, 471
Wegner, W., 260, 559
Weidemann, F., 125, 387, 420, 423
Weidt, L., 138, 415, 426, 430
Weikenmaier, A., 51
Weikl, B., 380, 524
Weil, H., 350, 387
Weisbach, H., 333
Welitsch, L., 73, 74, 138, 260, 269, 526, 535, 538, 558–9, 563, 571, 587, 600
Wengler, I., 122
Wenzinger, A., 18, 24
Wernigk, W., 108
Whitehill, C., 425
Wicks, D., 631

Widdop, W., 361, 364, 385, 404, 412, 428, 449, 563
Wiener, Julia, 301
Wiener, Otto, 379
Wildbrunn, H., 127, 269, 372, 418, 426, 434, 545
Willer, L., 338
Williams, H., 542, 547
Wilson, D., 185–6, 194
Windgassen, W., 121, 135, 326, 339, 348, 351, 355, 361, 369–70, 390, 395, 396, 397, 402, 412, 413, 424, 427, 430, 434, 443, 445, 535
Winkelmann, H., 350, 383
Winter, H., 247
Wirl, E., 139
Witherspoon, H., 405
Witte, E., 402
Wittrisch, M., 115, 125, 314, 315, 342, 360, 475, 478, 490, 537, 545, 614
Wixell, I., 62, 80, 175, 215, 264, 287, 301, 335, 549, 592, 602, 610
Wohlfahrt, E., 397
Wolff, Albert, 467, 483
Wolff, Fritz, 360, 384, 448
Wolf-Ferrari, E., 43
Wollitz, E., 20
Wolovsky, L., 124
Woytowicz, S., 282

Wunderlich, F., 111, 220, 247, 348, 525, 537, 612

Yachmi, R., 65
Yoder, P., 390
Young, A., 44, 53, 536

Zaccaria, N., 144, 167, 228
Zadek, H., 50, 75
Zador, D., 405
Zampighi, C., 493
Zanelli, R., 320, 551
Zareska, E., 514
Zavodsky, Z. von, 425
Zeani, V., 245, 246
Zednik, H., 63
Zenatello, G., 233, 236, 241, 266, 275, 285, 309, 312, 314, 319–20, 321, 322, 328, 473, 477, 614
Zerola, N., 267, 320, 550
Zhukovskaya, L., 520
Zikmundova, E., 506
Zikova, Z., 301
Zimmermann, E., 376, 404, 424
Zinetti, G., 35
Zitek, V., 298
Zobian, G., 268
Zweig, F., 478
Zylis-Gara, T., 82, 329